WILLS, TRUSTS, AND ESTATES

Sixth Edition

WILLS, TRUSTS, AND ESTATES

Jesse Dukeminier

Maxwell Professor of Law
University of California, Los Angeles

Stanley M. Johanson

Fannie Coplin Regents Professor of Law
University of Texas

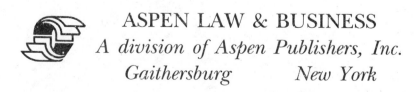

ASPEN LAW & BUSINESS
A division of Aspen Publishers, Inc.
Gaithersburg   New York

Permissions
Aspen Law & Business
1185 Avenue of the Americas
New York, NY 10036

Printed in the United States of America

1 2 3 4 5 6 7 8 9 0

Library of Congress Cataloging-in-Publication Data

Dukeminier, Jesse.
   Wills, trusts, and estates / Jesse Dukeminier, Stanley M. Johanson. — 6th ed.
      p.   cm.
   Includes index.
   ISBN 0-7355-0636-1 (hardcover)
    1. Wills—United States—Cases. 2. Estate planning—United States—Cases. 3. Future interests—United States—Cases. 4. Trusts and trustees—United States—Cases. I. Johanson, Stanley M., 1933–   . II. Title.
KF753.A7D8   2000
346.7305'2—dc21   99-23694
                                       CIP

About Aspen Law & Business, Legal Education Division

In 1996, Aspen Law & Business welcomed the Law School Division of Little, Brown and Company into its growing business — already established as a leading provider of practical information to legal practitioners.

Acquiring much more than a prestigious collection of educational publications by the country's foremost authors, Aspen Law & Business inherited the long-standing Little, Brown tradition of excellence — born over 150 years ago. As one of America's oldest and most venerable publishing houses, Little, Brown and Company commenced in a world of change and challenge, innovation and growth. Sharing that same spirit, Aspen Law & Business has dedicated itself to continuing and strengthening the integrity begun so many years ago.

ASPEN LAW & BUSINESS
A Division of Aspen Publishers, Inc.
A Wolters Kluwer Company
www.aspenpublishers.com

For our students,
who have taught us more than they know

SUMMARY OF CONTENTS

Contents   xi
List of Illustrations   xxxiii
Preface   xxxvii
Acknowledgments   xli

1. Introduction to Estate Planning   1
2. Intestacy: An Estate Plan by Default   71
3. Wills: Capacity and Contests   159
4. Wills: Formalities and Forms   223
5. Will Substitutes: Nonprobate Transfers   331
6. Construction of Wills   409
7. Restrictions on the Power of Disposition: Protection of the
   Spouse and Children   471
8. Trusts: Creation, Types, and Characteristics   553
9. Building Flexibility into Trusts: Powers of Appointment   665
10. Construction of Trusts: Future Interests   709
11. Duration of Trusts: The Rule against Perpetuities   787
12. Charitable Trusts   859
13. Trust Administration: The Fiduciary Obligation   903
14. Wealth Transfer Taxation: Tax Planning   977

Table of Cases   1081
Author Index   1089
Index   1095

CONTENTS

List of Illustrations   *xxxiii*
Preface   *xxxvii*
Acknowledgments   *xli*

Chapter 1.   Introduction to Estate Planning   **1**

   Section A.   The Power to Transmit Property at Death: Its
             Justification and Limitations   1
                       Jefferson's Works   1
                       Blackstone, Commentaries   1
                       Hodel v. Irving   *3*
                       Notes and Questions   10
                       Halbach, An Introduction to
                          Death, Taxes and Family
                          Property   13
                       Bentham, The Theory of
                          Legislation   14
                       Oliver, Shapiro & Press,
                          "Them That's Got Shall
                          Get"   14
                       Ascher, Curtailing Inherited
                          Wealth   16
                       Note: Inheritance in the
                          Erstwhile Soviet Union   18
                       Blum & Kalven, The Uneasy
                          Case for Progressive Taxation   18

                              Langbein, The Twentieth-
                                Century Revolution in
                                Family Wealth Transmission   20
                              Shapira v. Union National Bank   24
                              Notes, Questions, and
                                Problems   30
        Section B.   Transfer of the Decedent's Estate   34
                     1.   Probate and Nonprobate Property   34
                     2.   Administration of Probate Estates   35
                          a.   History and Terminology   35
                          b.   A Summary of Probate Procedure   39
                               (1)   Opening probate   39
                                     Question   42
                               (2)   Supervising the representative's
                                     actions   43
                               (3)   Closing the estate   43
                          c.   Is Probate Necessary?   44
                                     Problems   46
                          d.   Universal Succession   48
        Section C.   An Estate Planning Problem   49
                     1.   The Client's Letter and Its Enclosures 49
                     2.   Some Preliminary Questions Raised by
                          Brown's Letter   51
                                     Problems   51
                     3.   Additional Data on the Brown's Family
                          and Assets   52
                          a.   Family Data   52
                          b.   Assets   54
                          c.   Liabilities   57
                          d.   Assets and Liabilities: Summary   58
                     4.   Professional Responsibility   59
                                     Simpson v. Calivas   59
                                     Notes   64
                                     Hotz v. Minyard   66
                                     Notes   70

Chapter 2.   Intestacy: An Estate Plan by Default   71

        Section A.   The Basic Scheme   71
                     1.   Introduction   71
                                     Uniform Probate Code
                                     §§2-101, 2-102, 2-103,
                                     2-105   72
                                     Question   74

	2.	Share of Surviving Spouse			74
			Problems and Question		75
			Janus v. Tarasewicz		*78*
			Problems and Note		85
	3.	Shares of Descendants			86
			Problem		88
			Uniform Probate Code §2-106		88
			Note: Negative Disinheritance		90
	4.	Shares of Ancestors and Collaterals			90
			Table of Consanguinity		92
			Massachusetts General Laws		
			Annotated ch. 190, §3(6)		93
			Problems		96
			Note: Half-Bloods		96
			Problem		97
Section B.	Transfers to Children				97
	1.	Meaning of Children			97
		a.	Posthumous Children		97
		b.	Adopted Children		98
			Hall v. Vallandingham		*98*
			Uniform Probate Code		
			§§2-113, 2-114		101
			Notes, Problems, and		
			Questions		102
			O'Neal v. Wilkes		*108*
			Note, Problem, and Question		113
		c.	Nonmarital Children		115
			Question and Notes		116
			Hecht v. Superior Court		*117*
			Notes and Questions		126
	2.	Advancements			128
			Problems		129
			Uniform Probate Code §2-109		130
			Question		131
			Note: Transfer of an		
			Expectancy		131
	3.	Managing a Minor's Property			132
			Problem		134
			An Exercise in Lawyering		136
			Will of Howard Brown (with		
			Testamentary Trust)		137
Section C.	Bars to Succession				141
	1.	Homicide			141
			In re Estate of Mahoney		*141*
			Notes and Problems		145

2.   Disclaimer   148
                Problem   150
                Troy v. Hart   *151*
                Notes and Questions   156

Chapter 3.   Wills: Capacity and Contests   159

Section A.   Mental Capacity   159
         1.   Why Require Mental Capacity?   159
                In re Strittmater   *159*
         2.   Test of Mental Capacity   163
         3.   Insane Delusion   165
                In re Honigman   *166*
                Notes and Questions   171
                Langbein, Living Probate:
                   The Conservatorship Model   174
Section B.   Undue Influence   175
                Lipper v. Weslow   *177*
                Question and Notes   183
                Note: No-Contest Clauses   184
                Note: Bequests to Attorneys   185
                In re Will of Moses   *188*
                Questions   192
                Gray, The New "Older
                   Woman"   192
                In re Kaufmann's Will   193
                Question and Notes   196
                An Exercise in Lawyering:
                   Seward Johnson's Estate   197
                Notes and Questions   209
Section C.   Fraud   213
                Problem   215
                Latham v. Father Divine   *215*
                Notes   220
                Note: Tortious Interference
                   with Expectancy   221
                Problem   222

Chapter 4.   Wills: Formalities and Forms   223

Section A.   Execution of Wills   223
         1.   Attested Wills   223
                Gulliver & Tilson,
                   Classification of Gratuitous
                   Transfers   223

		Uniform Probate Code	
		§2-502	226
		In re Groffman	227
		Notes, Problems, and Questions	233
		Estate of Parsons	236
		Problems: Purging Statutes	241
		Recommended Method of Executing a Will	242
		Note: Safeguarding a Will	246
		In re Pavlinko's Estate	247
		Problem and Note	251
		Uniform Probate Code §2-503	252
		In re Will of Ranney	252
		Notes, Questions, and Problems	259
	2.	Holographic Wills	262
		The Jolly Testator Who Makes His Own Will	262
		Gulliver & Tilson, Classification of Gratuitous Transfers	264
		In re Estate of Johnson	264
		Notes and Problems	268
		Kimmel's Estate	271
		Notes	273
		Unusual Will Names Dancer	275
Section B.		Revocation of Wills	276
	1.	Revocation by Writing or Physical Act	276
		Uniform Probate Code §2-507	276
		Problems: Revocation by Inconsistency	277
		Harrison v. Bird	277
		Problems	279
		Note: Probate of Lost Wills	280
		Thompson v. Royall	280
		Questions and Problems	283
		Problem	285
	2.	Dependent Relative Revocation and Revival	286
		Carter v. First United Methodist Church of Albany	286
		Problems	290
		Note and Problem	291

	Estate of Alburn	*292*
	Note: Revival	296
	Uniform Probate Code	
	§2-509	297
	Problems	298
3.	Revocation by Operation of Law: Change in Family Circumstances	298
	Uniform Probate Code	
	§2-804	299
	Problem and Note	299
Section C.	Components of a Will	301
1.	Integration of Wills	301
2.	Republication by Codicil	302
3.	Incorporation by Reference	303
	Uniform Probate Code	
	§2-510	303
	Clark v. Greenhalge	*303*
	Simon v. Grayson	*309*
	Notes and Problems	309
	Uniform Probate Code	
	§2-513	311
	Johnson v. Johnson	*311*
	Problems and Note	317
4.	Acts of Independent Significance	318
	Uniform Probate Code	
	§2-512	318
	Problems	319
Section D.	Contracts Relating to Wills	319
1.	Contracts to Make a Will	320
	Problems	320
	Question	321
2.	Contracts Not to Revoke a Will	322
	Uniform Probate Code	
	§2-514	322
	Via v. Putnam	*323*
	Notes and Problems	328

Chapter 5. Will Substitutes: Nonprobate Transfers   331

Section A.	Contracts with Payable-on-Death Provisions	331
	Wilhoit v. Peoples Life Insurance Co.	*331*
	Note	336
	Estate of Hillowitz	*336*

		Uniform Probate Code	
		§6-101	337
		Questions	338
		Cook v. Equitable Life Assurance Society	*339*
		Notes and Questions	343
Section B.	Multiple-Party Bank Accounts		344
		Franklin v. Anna National Bank of Anna	*345*
		Notes and Problems	348
Section C.	Joint Tenancies		350
Section D.	Revocable Trusts		351
	1.	Introduction	351
		Farkas v. Williams	*352*
		Notes and Problem	358
		In re Estate and Trust of Pilafas	*361*
		Problems	367
		State Street Bank & Trust Co. v. Reiser	*368*
		Notes and Problems	371
	2.	Pour-over Wills	371
		Uniform Testamentary Additions to Trusts Act (UPC §2-511)	373
		Questions, Problem, and Note	374
		Clymer v. Mayo	*375*
		Notes and Problem	384
	3.	Use of Revocable Trusts in Estate Planning	386
		a. Introduction	386
		b. Consequences During Life of Settlor	387
		Question	389
		c. Consequences at Death of Settlor: Avoidance of Probate	389
		Note: Marketing of Living Trusts	395
Section E.	Planning for Incapacity		396
	1.	The Durable Power of Attorney	396
		Franzen v. Norwest Bank Colorado	*397*
		Problems and Notes	401
	2.	Directives Regarding Health-Care and Disposition of the Body	403
		a. Living Wills	403
		b. Durable Power of Attorney for Health Care	404
		c. Disposition of the Body	405

Chapter 6. Construction of Wills   **409**

  Section A. Admission of Extrinsic Evidence   409
       1. Interpretation of Wills   409
          Mahoney v. Grainger   *410*
          Notes and Problem   412
          Fleming v. Morrison   *414*
          Questions   417
          Estate of Russell   *417*
          Notes, Questions, and
           Problems   424
       2. Correcting Mistakes   427
          Erickson v. Erickson   *427*
          Question and Notes   436
          Restatement (Third) of
           Property, Donative
           Transfers, §12.1   438
  Section B. Death of Beneficiary Before Death of Testator   438
          Uniform Probate Code §2-605
           (1969)   441
          Allen v. Talley   *441*
          Problem and Notes   444
          Jackson v. Schultz   *446*
          Note and Problem   448
          Dawson v. Yucus   *449*
          Note   454
          In re Moss   *454*
          American Law of Property
           §22.13   457
  Section C. Changes in Property After Execution of Will:
        Specific and General Devises Compared   459
          Wasserman v. Cohen   *459*
          Notes and Problem   463
          Uniform Probate Code
           §2-606   465
          Problems and Note   466
          Note: More on Specific and
           General Devises   468

**Chapter 7. Restrictions on the Power of
            Disposition: Protection of the Spouse
            and Children**   **471**

  Section A. Rights of the Surviving Spouse   471
       1. Introduction to Marital Property Systems   471

2. Rights of Surviving Spouse to Support 473
    a. Social Security 473
    b. Private Pension Plans 475
        Problem 476
    c. Homestead 476
    d. Personal Property Set-Aside 477
    e. Family Allowance 477
    f. Dower 478
        Problems 479
3. Rights of Surviving Spouse to a Share of
    Decedent's Property 480
    a. The Elective Share and its Rationale 480
        Uniform Probate Code,
            Article II, Part 2, General
            Comment 481
        Note: The Marital Deduction
            and the Dependency of
            Women 484
        Note: Must the Surviving
            Spouse Accept a Life Estate? 487
        In re Estate of Cross 488
        Notes and Questions 490
        In re Estate of Cooper 492
        Notes 497
    b. Property Subject to the Elective
        Share 500
        (1) Judicial decisions 500
            Sullivan v. Burkin 500
            Notes and Problems 505
        (2) Uniform Probate Code 507
            Problems and Note 511
        (3) Other statutes 512
            In re Reynolds 513
            Problem and Note 517
    c. Waiver 517
        Uniform Probate Code §2-213 517
        In re Estate of Garbade 518
        In re Grieff 520
4. Rights of Surviving Spouse in Community
    Property 521
    a. Basic Information 521
    b. Putting the Survivor to an Election 524
5. Migrating Couples and Multistate Property
    Holdings 525

a.   Moving from Separate Property State
     to Community Property State   526
b.   Moving from Community Property
     State to Separate Property State   527
     Problem   529
6.   Spouse Omitted from Premarital Will   530
     Estate of Shannon   *530*
     Uniform Probate Code
     §2-301   534
     Questions and Notes   535
Section B.   Rights of Issue Omitted from the Will   536
             Azcunce v. Estate of Azcunce   *537*
             Espinosa v. Sparber, Shevin,
             *   Shapo, Rosen & Heilbronner*   *540*
             Notes and Problems   543
             Uniform Probate Code
             §2-302   545
             Notes, Problems, and
             Questions   546
             In re Estate of Laura   *548*
             Note: Testamentary Libel   550

Chapter 8.   Trusts: Creation, Types, and Characteristics   553

Section A.   Introduction   553
             1.   Background   553
             2.   The Parties to a Trust   557
                  a.   The Settlor   557
                       Problem   559
                  b.   The Trustee   559
                       Problem   561
                  c.   The Beneficiaries   561
             3.   A Trust Compared with a Legal Life
                  Estate   562
                       Question and Note   566
Section B.   Creation of a Trust   567
             1.   Intent to Create a Trust   567
                  Jimenez v. Lee   *568*
                  Notes   575
                  The Hebrew University
                  *   Association v. Nye (1961)*   *575*
                  The Hebrew University
                  *   Association v. Nye (1966)*   *578*
                  Notes   580

      2. Necessity of Trust Property   581
           Unthank v. Rippstein   *581*
           Question, Problem, and Note   583
           Note: Resulting and
               Constructive Trusts   584
           Scott, Trusts §§31.4, 31.5   585–586
           Brainard v. Commissioner   *586*
           Speelman v. Pascal   *589*
           Notes and Problems   593
           Note: Taxation of Grantor
               Trusts   594
      3. Necessity of Trust Beneficiaries   597
           Clark v. Campbell   *598*
           Note and Problem   600
           In re Searight's Estate   *602*
           Notes   605
           Note: Shaw's Alphabet
               Trusts   607
      4. Necessity of a Written Instrument   608
        a. Oral Inter Vivos Trusts of Land   608
           Evicted Couple Leave Pictures
               of Son Who Threw Them
               Out   609
           Hieble v. Hieble   *609*
            Notes and Question   613
        b. Oral Trusts for Disposition at Death 614
           Olliffe v. Wells   *614*
            Notes and Problems   616
Section C. Discretionary Trusts   617
           Marsman v. Nasca   *618*
           Notes, Problems, and
               Questions   627
           Note: New Forms of Trusts   630
Section D. Creditors' Rights: Spendthrift Trusts   631
           Shelley v. Shelley   *633*
           Notes and Questions   639
           Problem   642
           United States v. O'Shaughnessy *643*
           Question   647
           Note: Trusts for the State-
               Supported   648
           Problems   650
Section E. Modification and Termination of Trusts 651
           In re Trust of Stuchell   *652*
           Notes and Questions   654
           In re Estate of Brown   *657*

	Notes	660
	Note: Changing Trustees	661
	Kristof, An Heir of Confidence	662
	Uniform Trust Act §706	663
	Problem	664

Chapter 9. Building Flexibility Into Trusts: Powers of Appointment   665

Section A.	Introduction	665
	1. Types of Powers	665
	2. Does the Appointive Property Belong to the Donor or the Donee?	667
	Irwin Union Bank & Trust Co. v. Long	*668*
	Notes and Questions	671
	Note: Tax Reasons for Creating Powers	673
Section B.	Creation of a Power of Appointment	676
	1. Intent to Create a Power	676
	Problem	677
	2. Powers to Consume	677
	Sterner v. Nelson	*677*
	Notes and Questions	681
Section C.	Release of a Power of Appointment	682
	Seidel v. Werner	*683*
	Question	688
Section D.	Exercise of a Power of Appointment	688
	1. Exercise by Residuary Clause in Donee's Will	688
	Beals v. State Street Bank & Trust Co.	*688*
	Notes	693
	Uniform Probate Code §§2-608, 2-704	694
	Note and Problem	695
	2. Limitations on Exercise of a Special Power	696
	Problem	698
	3. Fraud on a Special Power	699
	4. Ineffective Exercise of a Power	699
	a. Allocation of Assets	700
	b. Capture	701
Section E.	Failure to Exercise a Power of Appointment	702
	Loring v. Marshall	*702*
	Problem and Note	706

Chapter 10. Construction of Trusts: Future Interests **709**

Section A. Introduction 709
Section B. Classification of Future Interests 710
  1. Types of Future Interests 710
  2. Future Interests in the Transferor 711
    a. Reversion 711
      Problem 711
    b. Possibility of Reverter; Right of Entry 712
  3. Future Interests in Transferees 712
    a. Remainders 713
      Problems 714
      Problems 715
    b. Executory Interests 716
      Problems and Note 717
Section C. Construction of Trust Instruments 718
  1. Preference for Vested Interests 718
    a. Acceleration into Possession 719
      In re Estate of Gilbert 720
      Notes 725
    b. Transferability and Taxation 726
      Problem and Notes 727
    c. Requiring Survival to Time of Possession 728
      First National Bank of Bar Harbor v. Anthony 729
      Note 732
      Security Trust Co. v. Irvine 733
      Notes 738
      Clobberie's Case 740
      Notes and Problem 741
      Note: Uniform Probate Code §2-707—A New System of Future Interests for Trusts 742
  2. Gifts to Classes 750
    a. Gifts of Income 750
      Dewire v. Haveles 750
      Problem and Note 754
    b. Gifts to Children or Issue 755
      (1) Per stirpes distributions 755
      (2) Adopted children 759
      Uniform Probate Code §2-705 760

		Minary v. Citizens Fidelity		
		Bank & Trust Co.		*760*
		Notes and Problems		763
		(3)	Nonmarital children	767
	c.	Gifts to Heirs		768
		Estate of Woodworth		*768*
		Notes		774
		Uniform Probate Code		
		§2-711		775
		Note: The Doctrine of		
		Worthier Title		775
		Note: The Rule in Shelley's		
		Case		776
	d.	Increase in Class Membership: The		
		Class-Closing Rule		777
		(1)	Introduction	777
		(2)	Immediate gifts	778
			Problems	779
		(3)	Postponed gifts	780
			Problems	780
			Lux v. Lux	*781*
		(4)	Gifts of specific sums	785

Chapter 11. Duration of Trusts: The Rule against
Perpetuities   **787**

Section A.	Introduction		787
	1.	Development of the Rule	787
	2.	Summary of the Rule	793
		a. Introduction	793
		(1) The rule and its policies	793
		(2) Why lives in being are used to	
		measure the period	794
		(3) The rule is a rule of proof	794
		Problems and Note	796
		b. When the Lives in Being Are	
		Ascertained	797
Section B.	The Requirement of No Possibility of Remote		
	Vesting		798
	1. The Fertile Octogenarian		798

De Bruxelles, Baby Conceived
After 60th Birthday
Celebration 799
Questions and Problems 800
2. The Unborn Widow 801
*Dickerson v. Union National
Bank of Little Rock* 801
Problems and Notes 805
3. The Slothful Executor 806
Section C. Application of the Rule to Class Gifts 807
1. The Basic Rule: All-or-Nothing 807
Question 808
Question 809
Ward v. Van der Loeff 809
Problems 812
2. Exceptions to the Class Gift Rule 813
a. Gifts to Subclasses 813
*American Security & Trust Co.
v. Cramer* 813
b. Specific Sum to Each Class Member 817
Section D. Application of the Rule to Powers of
Appointment 818
1. General Powers Presently Exercisable 818
a. Validity of Power 818
b. Validity of Exercise 819
Problem 819
2. General Testamentary Powers and Special
Powers 819
a. Validity of Power 820
b. Validity of Exercise 821
(1) Perpetuities period runs from
creation of power 821
(2) The second-look doctrine 821
*Second National Bank of New
Haven v. Harris Trust &
Savings Bank* 822
Questions and Note 826
Note: The "Delaware Tax
Trap" 827
Section E. Saving Clauses 829
Note: Attorney Liability for
Violating Rule 830
Section F. Perpetuities Reform 830
1. The Cy Pres or Reformation Doctrine 831
2. The Wait-and-See Doctrine 832
Question 833

a.   Wait-and-See for the Common Law
     Perpetuities Period   834
b.   The Uniform Statutory Rule Against
     Perpetuities   835
          Uniform Statutory Rule
          Against Perpetuities §§1, 2,
          3, 4, & 5   837
          In re Trust of Wold   *840*
          Notes and Questions   845
          Problems and Questions   849
          Note: The Dynasty Trust   849
3.   Abolition of the Rule against Perpetuities   852
Section G.   The Rule against Suspension of the Power of
             Alienation   856

Chapter 12.   Charitable Trusts   **859**

Section A.   Nature of Charitable Purposes   859
             Shenandoah Valley National Bank v.
                 Taylor   *859*
             Notes and Questions   865
Section B.   Modification of Charitable Trusts: Cy Pres   869
             In re Neher   *870*
             Posner, Economic Analysis of Law   872
             San Francisco Chronicle: The Buck
                 Trust   872
             Notes and Questions   877
             Philadelphia Story: The Barnes
                 Foundation   879
Section C.   Supervision of Charitable Trusts   883
             Carl J. Herzog Foundation, Inc. v.
                 University of Bridgeport   *883*
             Notes and Questions   892
             Posner, Economic Analysis of Law   895
             Hawaii Journal: The Bishop Estate   896
             Questions   900

Chapter 13.   Trust Administration: The Fiduciary
Obligation   **903**

Section A.   Duties of the Trustee   903
             1.   Duty of Loyalty   903
                       Hartman v. Hartle   *903*
                       Notes   904
                       In re Rothko   *906*
                       Notes   916

		Note: Co-Trustees	918
		Problems	918
		Restatement (Second) of Trusts §258	919
	2.	Duties Relating to Care of the Trust Property	919
		a. Duty to Collect and Protect Trust Property	919
		b. Duty to Earmark Trust Property	920
		Problems	920
		c. Duty Not to Mingle Trust Funds with the Trustee's Own	921
		Problem	921
	3.	Duty Not to Delegate	922
		Shriners Hospitals for Crippled Children v. Gardiner	922
		Note	926
		Restatement (Third) of Trusts §§171 & 227, Comment j	927
		Questions	928
	4.	Duty of Impartiality	929
		Dennis v. Rhode Island Hospital Trust Co.	929
		Note	936
		Restatement (Third) of Trusts §§240, 241	936
		Notes	937
	5.	Duty to Inform and Account to Beneficiaries	938
		Fletcher v. Fletcher	938
		Questions and Note	943
		National Academy of Sciences v. Cambridge Trust Co.	944
		Note and Question	948
Section B.	Powers of the Trustee		950
		Uniform Trustees' Powers Act §3	950
		Notes	952
		Uniform Trustees' Powers Act §7	953
		Problems	954
Section C.	Investment of Trust Funds		954
		Langbein & Posner, Market Funds and Trust Investment Law	954
		Estate of Collins	957
		Notes and Question	962

Uniform Prudent Investor Act §3,
Comment   963
Restatement (Third) of Trusts   965
Introduction and §227   965
Notes and Questions   969
Uniform Prudent Investor Act §2   970
Note: ERISA   973
Questions   974
Section D.   Liability of the Truestee to Third Parties   975
Uniform Probate Code §7-306   976

Chapter 14.   Wealth Transfer Taxation: Tax Planning   **977**

Section A.   Introduction   977
1.   A Brief History of Federal Wealth
Transfer Taxation   977
Note: Estate and Inheritance
Taxes Distinguished   980
2.   The Unified Federal Estate and Gift Taxes   981
Unified Transfer Tax Rate
Schedule   982
Question and Note   984
Section B.   The Federal Gift Tax   985
1.   The Nature of a Taxable Gift   985
Holtz's Estate v. Commissioner   986
Notes and Problems   989
Note: Income Tax Basis   990
Problem   990
2.   The Annual Exclusion   991
Internal Revenue Code §2503(c)   991
Problem   993
Estate of Cristofani v. Commissioner   994
Notes and Problem   1001
3.   Gifts Between Spouses and from One
Spouse to a Third Person   1003
Problems   1004
Section C.   The Federal Estate Tax   1005
1.   A Thumbnail Sketch of the Federal Estate
Tax   1005
2.   The Gross Estate: Property Passing by Will
or Intestacy   1007

a. Section 2033: Property Owned at
    Death   1007
        Problem   1008
b. Section 2034: Dower or Curtesy   1008

3. The Gross Estate: Nonprobate
    Property   1009
    a. Section 2040: Joint Tenancy   1009
        (1) Joint tenancy between persons
            other than husband and wife   1009
            (a) Gift tax   1009
            (b) Estate tax   1010
                Problem   1011
        (2) Joint tenancy and tenancy by the
            entirety between husband and wife   1011
            (a) Gift tax   1011
            (b) Estate tax   1012
    b. Section 2039: Employee Death
        Benefits   1012
    c. Section 2042: Life Insurance   1013
        Problems   1013

4. The Gross Estate: Lifetime Transfers   1014
    a. Section 2036: Transfers with Life
        Estate or Control of Beneficial Rights
        Retained   1014
            Problems   1015
            Estate of Maxwell v.
                Commissioner   *1016*
            Notes   1022
            Old Colony Trust Co. v. United
                States   *1022*
            Note and Question   1026
    b. Section 2038: Revocable Transfers   1027
            Problems   1028
    c. Section 2037: Transfers with
        Reversionary Interest Retained   1028
    d. Section 2035: Transfers within Three
        Years of Death   1029
            Problems   1031

5. The Gross Estate: Powers of Appointment
    (§2041)   1032
            Estate of Vissering v.
                Commissioner   *1035*
            Question and Note   1038
            Estate of Kurz v. Commissioner   *1038*

6. The Marital Deduction   1042
   a. Introduction   1042
      Problem   1043
   b. Interests that Qualify for the
      Deduction   1043
      (1) The nondeductible terminable
          interest rule   1043
          Problem   1045
      (2) Exceptions to the terminable
          interest rule   1045
          (a) Limited survivorship
              exception   1045
              Problem   1045
          (b) Life estate plus general
              power of appointment trust
              exception   1046
              Note   1046
          (c) Estate trust exception   1046
          (d) Qualified terminable
              interest property (QTIP)
              exception   1047
              Estate of Rapp v. Commissioner   *1049*
              Pond v. Pond   *1057*
              Note and Problems   1060
      (3) Noncitizen spouses: qualified
          domestic trusts   1061
   c. Tax Planning   1061
7. The Charitable Deduction   1063
   Problems   1064
Section D. The Generation-Skipping Transfer Tax   1065
1. The Nature of the Tax   1065
   Problem   1069
2. Rate and Base of Tax   1070
   Problem   1070
3. Exemption and Exclusions   1070
   Problem   1072
4. Definitions   1073
   a. Transferor   1073
   b. Skip Person; Ascertaining Generations   1074
      Problems   1074
   c. Interest   1075
5. Tax Strategies   1076
6. Consequences on Estate Planning of
   Generation-Skipping Transfer Tax   1077

Section E.   State Wealth Transfer Taxes   1078

Table of Cases   *1081*
Author Index   *1089*
Index   *1095*

LIST OF ILLUSTRATIONS

Chapter 1

Justice Sandra Day O'Connor (photograph)	4
Drawing by William Hamilton ("fine old name")	19
Judge Richard A. Posner (photograph)	31
Joe Jackson's signature on will	42

Chapter 2

Diagram of representation	86
Diagram of per stirpes distribution	87
Diagram of per stirpes distribution	88
Diagram of per capita at each generation distribution	89
Diagram of representation among collaterals	91
Table of consanguinity	92
Drawing by M. Stevens ("other mother")	106
Justice Leah Sears (photograph)	111
Deborah Hecht (photograph)	119

Chapter 3

Drawing by Frank Modell ("blew it all")	164
Lord Hannen (etching)	176
Drawing by Peter Arno (lawyer as will beneficiary)	186
Seward and Basia Johnson (photograph)	199
Seward Johnson's will signature	206
Father Divine (photograph)	217

Chapter 4
  Professor John Langbein (photograph)   261
  Will written on a chest of drawers   274
  Will written on a handbag   275
  Farm painting by Thomas Hinckley   305
  Cartoon by Marvin Tannenberg ("Hi there, Sidncy!")   321

Chapter 5
  Norman F. Dacey, How To Avoid Probate   360

Chapter 6
  Thelma Russell's property, 1999 (photograph)   419
  Drawing by Stevenson (pet as devisee)   423
  Judge Ellen A. Peters (photograph)   433
  London Daily Telegraph   455
  Aunt Fanny's snuff bottles   467

Chapter 7
  Drawing by Peter Arno ("disinherit everyone")   474
  Justice Herbert Wilkins (photograph)   501

Chapter 8
  Professor Austin Scott (photograph)   558
  Professor George G. Bogert (photograph)   571
  Marianne Speelman (Zaya Kingman) (photograph)   591
  The Rev. Eleazar M.P. Wells (photograph)   614

Chapter 10
  Surrogate Renee Roth (photograph)   721
  Diagram of Wilson family   735
  Diagram of per stirpes distribution   757
  Doris Duke and her butler (photograph)   766
  Doris Duke's will signature   766

Chapter 11
  Duke of Norfolk (painting)   790
  Lord Chancellor Nottingham (painting)   791
  Professor W. Barton Leach (photograph)   833
  Drawing by William Hamilton ("trust funds")   851

Chapter 12

Beryl H. Buck (photograph)   874
Barnes Foundation Gallery (photograph)   881
Nursing School, University of Bridgeport (photograph)   884

Chapter 13

Painting by Mark Rothko   907
Justice Stephen G. Breyer (photograph)   930
Providence, Rhode Island, downtown   932
Leonard Troland (photograph)   945

Chapter 14

Judge Frank H. Easterbrook (photograph)   1039
Judge Betty B. Fletcher (photograph)   1050

PREFACE

This book is designed for use in a course in decedents' estates and trusts, and as an introduction to estate planning. Our basic aim in this sixth edition remains as before: to produce not merely competent practitioners in the estates and trusts field, but lawyers who think critically about problems in family wealth transmission and compare alternative solutions. We seek to educate policy analysts as well as estate planners.

The first edition of this book appeared in 1972. Glancing at it, we are struck not by the similarities, of which there are, of course, many, but by the enormous changes that new developments in this field have dictated. Since the 1960s, the law of wills has been undergoing a thorough renovation. Initially, the change was brought on by a swelling public demand for cheaper and simpler ways of transferring property at death, avoiding expensive probate. Then imaginative scholars began to ventilate this ancient law of the dead hand, challenging assumptions and suggesting judicial and legislative innovation to simplify and rationalize it. New types of wealth, such as pension and tax-deferred savings, were created. Medical science complicated matters by creating varieties of parentage and death-deferring machines unheard of a generation ago. And legal malpractice in drawing wills and trusts arrived with a bang. The ensuing changes in both law and practice have been many, and they are far from over.

The use of trusts to transmit family wealth has become commonplace, not only for rich clients, but also for those of modest wealth. During the last quarter of a century lawyers have come to regard the trust as the best solution to all sorts of client problems. As a result, trusts have proliferated. We now have the living trust, the supplemental needs trust, the unitrust, the dynasty trust, and new variations on old forms. In expanding, the law of private trusts has annexed the law of future interests and powers of appointment, reducing these two subjects largely to problems in drafting and construing trust instruments. The fiduciary obligation—with its attendant duties to beneficiaries—has become the most useful and important principle in our society for managing resources of all types, public as well as private.

Taxation of donative transfers has changed dramatically. The unlimited marital deduction—which permits spouses to make unlimited tax-free gifts and bequests to each other—is now a central feature of estate planning. In 1986, Congress enacted the generation-skipping transfer tax, implementing a policy of taxing away about half of millionaires' wealth each generation. This new tax is having a profound effect on estate planning for the very rich and, like an invisible boomerang, is delivering potentially lethal blows to the Rule against Perpetuities.

Throughout the book we emphasize the basic theoretical structure and the general philosophy and purposes that unify the field of donative transfers. To this end we have pruned away mechanical matters (such as a step-by-step discussion of how to probate a will and settle an estate, which is essentially local law, easily learned from a local practice book). So too we have omitted old technical learning and disappearing distinctions of little contemporary importance. At the same time, we have sought historical roots of modern law. Understanding how the law became the way it is illuminates both the continuing growth of the law and the sometimes exasperating peculiarities of thought inherited from the past.

Although we organize the material in topical compartments rather precisely fit together, we have also sought a more penetrating view of the subject as a staggering tapestry of humanity struggling to merge dreams with reality. Every illustration included, every behind-the-scenes peek, every quirk of the parties' behavior has its place, as a piece of ornament fitting into the larger whole. Understanding the ambivalences of the human heart and the richness of human frailty, and realizing that even the best-constructed estate plans may, with the ever-whirling wheels of change, turn into sand castles, are essential to being a *counselor* at law, as opposed to being a mere attorney.

We said in the first edition of this book, in 1972,

> In this book we deal with people, the quick as well as the dead. There is nothing like the death of a moneyed member of the family to show persons as they really are, virtuous or conniving, generous or grasping. Many a family has been torn apart by a botched-up will. Each case is a drama in human relationships—and the lawyer, as counselor, draftsman, or ad-

vocate, is an important figure in the dramatis personae. This is one reason the estates practitioner enjoys his work, and why we enjoy ours.

This observation remains true for students preparing themselves to counsel clients in the twenty-first century. In a changing reality the human drama abides.

Our production manager, Margaret Kiever of the UCLA Law School, assembled the manuscript on her word processor with incomparable skill. Her patience with continual revisions of small (and large) matters has been boundless. "God is in the details," Mies van der Rohe said of architecture. We believe the same to be true of casebooks. We cannot imagine how we could have brought about the thorough, detailed renovation of the earlier edition without the assistance of Margaret Kiever, to whom we are greatly indebted.

We want to thank also our supervising editor at Aspen, Louise Bloomfield, who brought rich intelligence and sound judgment to the task and was a joy to work with.

Jesse Dukeminier
Stanley M. Johanson

August 1999

Editors' note: All citations to state statutes and the United States Code are to such statutes as they appear on Lexis on the date cited. Throughout the book, footnotes to the text and to opinions and other quoted materials are numbered consecutively from the beginning of each chapter. Some footnotes in opinions and secondary authorities are omitted. Editors' footnotes added to quoted materials are indicated by the abbreviation: — Eds.

ACKNOWLEDGMENTS

Books and Articles

American Law Institute, Restatement (Second) of Trusts (1959), Restatement (Third) of Trusts (1992). Copyright © 1959 & 1992 by the American Law Institute. Reprinted by permission of the American Law Institute.

Ascher, Mark L., Curtailing Inherited Wealth, 89 Mich. L. Rev. 69 (1990). Reprinted by permission of the author and the Michigan Law Review.

Blum, Walter, & Harry Kalven, The Uneasy Case for Progressive Taxation, 19 U. Chi. L. Rev. 417 (1952). Copyright © 1952 by The University of Chicago. Reprinted by permission of Professor Blum and the University of Chicago Law Review.

Buck, Estate of. California Superior Court Opinion, 21 U.S.F. L. Rev. 691 (1987). Reprinted by permission of the University of San Francisco Law Review.

Casner, Andrew James, Estate Planning, vol. 5 (5th ed. 1983). Copyright © 1983 by A. James Casner. Reprinted by permission of the author and Little, Brown and Co.

de Bruxelles, Simon, Baby Conceived After 60th Birthday Celebration, The (London) Times, Jan. 16, 1998. © Times Newspapers Limited, 1998. Reprinted by permission of News International Syndication.

Dukeminier, Jesse, The Uniform Statutory Rule Against Perpetuities: Ninety Years in Limbo, 34 UCLA L. Rev. 1023 (1987). Copyright © 1987 by the Regents of the University of California. Reprinted by permission.

Oliver, Melvin L., Thomas M. Shapiro & Julie E. Press, "Them That's Got Shall Get": Inheritance and Achievement in Wealth Accumulation, *in* The Politics of Wealth and Inequality 69 (Richard E. Ratcliff, Melvin L. Oliver & Thomas M. Shapiro eds. 1995).

Posner, Richard A., Economic Analysis of Law (5th ed. 1998). Copyright © 1998 by Richard A. Posner. Reprinted by permission of the author and Aspen Law & Business Publishers, Inc.

Scott, Austin W., The Law of Trusts, vol. 1 (William Fratcher 4th ed. 1987). Copyright © 1987 by the Estate of Austin Wakeman Scott. Reprinted by permission of Little, Brown and Co.

Illustrations

Barnes Foundation Gallery. © Copyright The Barnes Foundation. Photograph. Reproduced by permission of The Barnes Foundation.

Bogert, George G. Photograph. Reprinted by permission of the University of Chicago Library, Special Collections.

Breyer, Stephen G. Photograph. Reproduced by permission of Justice Breyer.

Buck, Beryl H. Photograph. Reproduced by permission of the Marin Community Foundation.

Devine, Father. Photograph by Otto Bettmann. Reproduced by permission.

Duke, Doris. Photograph of signature on her will. From Surrogate's Court, New York County, New York.

Duke, Doris, and her butler. Photograph by Marina Garnier. Reproduced by permission of Marina Garnier.

Easterbrook, Frank H. Photograph. Reproduced by permission of Judge Easterbrook.

Fletcher, Betty B. Photograph. Reproduced by permission of Judge Fletcher.

Hamilton, William. Drawing. From William Hamilton's Anti-Social Register. © 1974 by William Hamilton and used by permission of cartoonbank.com. All Rights Reserved.

Hannen, James. Etching. Reproduced by permission of the National Portrait Gallery.

Hecht, Deborah. Photograph. Reproduced by permission of the Los Angeles Times Syndicate.

Hinckley, Thomas. Oil painting. Reproduced by permission of Virginia M. Clark.

Jackson, Joe. Photograph of signature on will, by Bart Boatwright. Reproduced by permission of Bart Boatwright.

Johnson, Seward. Photograph of signature on will. From Surrogate's Court, New York County, New York.

Johnson, Seward and Basia. Photograph. Reproduced by permission of David Margolick.

Langbein, John H. Photograph. Reproduced by permission of Professor Langbein.

Leach, W. Barton. Photograph. Courtesy of Art & Visual Materials, Special Collections Department, Harvard Law School Library.

New Yorker, The. The New Yorker Magazine, Inc., holds copyrights in the following drawings: (1) drawing by Peter Arno, copyright © 1940, 1968, 1996; (2) drawing by Peter Arno, copyright © 1942, 1970, 1998. These drawings are reprinted by permission of The New Yorker Magazine, Inc. The New Yorker Magazine also holds copyrights in the following: (1) drawing by Wm. Hamilton, copyright © The New Yorker Collection 1977; (2) drawing by Frank Modell, copyright © The New Yorker Collection 1972; (3) drawing by Mick Stevens, copyright © The New Yorker Collection 1994; (4) drawing by Stevenson, copyright © The New Yorker Collection 1991. These drawings are reprinted by permission of the Cartoon Bank, a division of The New Yorker Magazine (cartoonbank.com). All rights reserved.

Norfolk, Duke of. Painting by Gerard Soest, 1677. Reproduced by permission of the Tate Gallery, London.

Nottingham, Lord Chancellor. Painting after Godfrey Kneller, 1680. Reproduced by permission of the National Portrait Gallery, London.

Nursing School, University of Bridgeport. Photograph. Reproduced by permission of Magnus Wahlstrom Library, University of Bridgeport.

O'Connor, Sandra Day. Photograph. Reproduced by permission of Justice O'Connor.

Peters, Ellen Ash. Photograph. Reproduced by permission of Justice Peters.

Posner, Richard A. Photograph. Reproduced by permission of Judge Posner.

Providence, Rhode Island. Photograph (1947). From Providence City Planning Commission, Downtown Providence 1970 (1961).

Roth, Renee. Photograph. Reproduced by permission of Surrogate Roth.

Rothko, Mark. Number 22. Oil on canvas, 9' 9" (h) × 8' 11⅛" (w). 1949. The Museum of Modern Art, New York. Gift of the artist. Photograph © 1999 The Museum of Modern Art, New York.

Russell, Thelma, property at 4122 Palm Ave., La Mesa, California. Photograph. Reproduced by permission of David Sanders.

Scott, Austin W. Photograph by Bachrach. Courtesy of Art & Visual Materials, Special Collections Department, Harvard Law School Library.

Sears, Leah. Photograph. Reproduced by permission of Justice Sears.

Snuff bottles. Photograph. Reproduced by permission of Jesse Dukeminier.

Speelman, Marianne. Photograph, provided by Joel S. Lee. Reproduced by permission of the New York Daily News.

Table of Consanguinity, *in* California Decedent Estate Administration, vol. 1, at 805 (1971). Copyright © 1971, 2000 by the Regents of the University of California. Reproduced by permission from the California Continuing Education of the Bar practice book California Decedent Estate Administration.

Tannenberg, Marvin. Cartoon. Copyright © 1966 by Playboy. Reproduced by special permission of PLAYBOY Magazine.

Troland, Leonard. Photograph. Reproduced by permission of the Harvard University Archives.

Wells, Eleazer M.P. Photograph. Reproduced from The Church Militant, April 1944, p.4, by permission of the Episcopal Diocese of Massachusetts.

Wilkins, Herbert. Photograph. Reproduced by permission of Justice Wilkins.

WILLS, TRUSTS, AND ESTATES

1

INTRODUCTION TO ESTATE PLANNING

SECTION A. THE POWER TO TRANSMIT PROPERTY AT DEATH: ITS JUSTIFICATION AND LIMITATIONS

THOMAS JEFFERSON, 7 JEFFERSON'S WORKS 454 (Monticello ed. 1904): "The earth belongs in usufruct to the living; the dead have neither powers nor rights over it. The portion occupied by any individual ceases to be his when he himself ceases to be, and reverts to society." (Letter to James Madison dated Sept. 6, 1789.)

2 William Blackstone, Commentaries
*10-13

The right of inheritance, or descent to the children and relations of the deceased, seems to have been allowed much earlier than the right of devising by testament. We are apt to conceive, at first view, that it has nature on its side; yet we often mistake for nature what we find established by long and inveterate custom. It is certainly a wise and effectual, but clearly a political, establishment; since the permanent right of property, vested in the ancestor himself, was no *natural*, but merely a *civil* right. . . . It is probable that [the right of inheritance arose] . . . from a plainer and more simple principle. A man's children or nearest relations are usually about him on his death-bed, and are

1

the earliest witnesses of his decease. They become, therefore, generally the next immediate occupants, till at length, in process of time, this frequent usage ripened into general law. And therefore, also, in the earliest ages, on failure of children, a man's servants, born under his roof, were allowed to be his heirs; being immediately on the spot when he died. For we find the old patriarch Abraham expressly declaring that "since God had given him no seed, his steward Eliezer, one born in his house, was his heir."[1]

While property continued only for life, testaments were useless and unknown: and, when it became inheritable, the inheritance was long indefeasible, and the children or heirs at law were incapable of exclusion by will; till at length it was found, that so strict a rule of inheritance made heirs disobedient and headstrong, defrauded creditors of their just debts, and prevented many provident fathers from dividing or charging their estates as the exigencies of their families required. This introduced pretty generally the right of disposing of one's property, or a part of it, by *testament;* that is, by written or oral instructions properly *witnessed* and authenticated, according to the *pleasure* of the deceased, which we, therefore, emphatically style his *will.* This was established in some countries much later than in others. With us in England, till modern times, a man could only dispose of one-third of his movables from his wife and children; and in general, no will was permitted of lands till the reign of Henry VIII; and then only of a certain portion: for it was not till after the Restoration that the power of devising real property became so universal as at present.

Wills, therefore, and testaments, rights of inheritance and successions, are all of them creatures of the civil or municipal laws, and accordingly are in all respects regulated by them; every distinct country having different ceremonies and requisites to make a testament completely valid; neither does anything vary more than the right of inheritance under different national establishments.

Until the 1980s, it was generally accepted that the right to pass property at death is not a constitutionally protected right. Even the

---

1. Genesis 15:3. [The words put in quotation marks are Blackstone's paraphrase of two verses of the Bible, which no one has yet translated from the original Hebrew to everyone's satisfaction. Blackstone's statement that servants took as heirs in the absence of children has been disputed by many scholars. "Israel does not know a general rule like this for regulating the inheritance." Gerhard Von Rad, Genesis 178 (John H. Marks trans. 1961). Cf. Richard H. Hiers, Transfer of Property by Inheritance and Bequest in Biblical Law and Tradition, 10 J.L. & Relig. 121, 127 (1994). Abraham's declaration was never put to the test for thereafter, when Abraham was 100 years old and his wife Sarah was 90, Sarah gave birth to a son, Isaac. Genesis 17:15. — Eds.]

Supreme Court itself said in Irving Trust Co. v. Day, 314 U.S. 556, 562 (1942):

> Rights of succession to property of a deceased, whether by will or by intestacy, are of statutory creation, and the dead hand rules succession only by sufferance. Nothing in the Federal Constitution forbids the legislature of a state to limit, condition, or even abolish the power of testamentary disposition over property within its jurisdiction.

But Hodel v. Irving, decided in the 1980s when the Court revived its interest in protecting private property through the Just Compensation Clause, changed all that.

Hodel v. Irving
Supreme Court of the United States, 1987
481 U.S. 704

O'CONNOR, J.   The question presented is whether the original version of the "escheat" provision of the Indian Land Consolidation Act of 1983, Pub. L. 97-459, Tit. II, 96 Stat. 2519, effected a "taking" of appellees' decedents' property without just compensation.

I

Towards the end of the 19th century, Congress enacted a series of land Acts which divided the communal reservations of Indian tribes into individual allotments for Indians and unallotted lands for non-Indian settlement. This legislation seems to have been in part animated by a desire to force Indians to abandon their nomadic ways in order to "speed the Indians' assimilation into American society," Solem v. Bartlett, 465 U.S. 463, 466 (1984), and in part a result of pressure to free new lands for further white settlement. Ibid. Two years after the enactment of the General Allotment Act of 1887, ch. 119, 24 Stat. 388, Congress adopted a specific statute authorizing the division of the Great Reservation of the Sioux Nation into separate reservations and the allotment of specific tracts of reservation land to individual Indians, conditioned on the consent of three-fourths of the adult male Sioux. Act of Mar. 2, 1889, ch. 405, 25 Stat. 888. Under the Act, each male Sioux head of household took 320 acres of land and most other individuals 160 acres. 25 Stat. 890. In order to protect the allottees from the improvident disposition of their lands to white

Justice Sandra Day O'Connor

settlers, the Sioux allotment statute provided that the allotted lands were to be held in trust by the United States. Id., at 891. Until 1910 the lands of deceased allottees passed to their heirs "according to the laws of the State or Territory" where the land was located, ibid., and after 1910, allottees were permitted to dispose of their interests by will in accordance with regulations promulgated by the Secretary of the Interior. 36 Stat. 856, 25 U.S.C. §373. Those regulations generally served to protect Indian ownership of the allotted lands.

The policy of allotment of Indian lands quickly proved disastrous for the Indians. Cash generated by land sales to whites was quickly dissipated and the Indians, rather than farm the land themselves, evolved into petty landlords, leasing their allotted lands to white ranchers and farmers and living off the meager rentals. . . . The failure of the allotment program became even clearer as successive generations came to hold the allotted lands. Thus 40-, 80-, and 160-acre parcels became splintered into multiple undivided interests in land, with some parcels having hundreds and many parcels having dozens of owners. Because the land was held in trust and often could not be alienated or partitioned the fractionation problem grew and grew over time.

A 1928 report commissioned by the Congress found the situation administratively unworkable and economically wasteful. L. Meriam, Institute for Government Research, The Problem of Indian Administration 40-41. Good, potentially productive, land was allowed to lie fallow, amidst great poverty, because of the difficulties of managing property held in this manner. . . . In discussing the Indian Reorganization Act of 1934, Representative Howard said:

> It is in the case of the inherited allotments, however, that the administrative costs become incredible. . . . On allotted reservations, numerous cases exist where the shares of each individual heir from lease money may be 1 cent a month. Or one heir may own minute fractional shares in 30 or 40 different allotments. The cost of leasing, bookkeeping, and distribut-

ing the proceeds in many cases far exceeds the total income. The Indians and the Indian Service personnel are thus trapped in a meaningless system of minute partition in which all thought of the possible use of land to satisfy human needs is lost in a mathematical haze of bookkeeping. 78 Cong. Rec. 11728 (1934) (remarks of Rep. Howard).

In 1934, in response to arguments such as these, the Congress acknowledged the failure of its policy and ended further allotment of Indian lands. Indian Reorganization Act of 1934, ch. 576, 48 Stat. 984, 25 U.S.C. §461 et seq.

But the end of future allotment by itself could not prevent the further compounding of the existing problem caused by the passage of time. Ownership continued to fragment as succeeding generations came to hold the property, since, in the order of things, each property owner was apt to have more than one heir. In 1960, both the House and the Senate undertook comprehensive studies of the problem. . . . These studies indicated that one-half of the approximately 12 million acres of allotted trust lands were held in fractionated ownership, with over 3 million acres held by more than six heirs to a parcel. Further hearings were held in 1966, but not until the Indian Land Consolidation Act of 1983 did the Congress take action to ameliorate the problem of fractionated ownership of Indian lands.

Section 207 of the Indian Land Consolidation Act — the escheat provision at issue in this case — provided:

> No undivided fractional interest in any tract of trust or restricted land within a tribe's reservation or otherwise subjected to a tribe's jurisdiction shall descendent [sic] by intestacy or devise but shall escheat to that tribe if such interest represents 2 per centum or less of the total acreage in such tract and has earned to its owner less than $100 in the preceding year before it is due to escheat. 96 Stat. 2519.

Congress made no provision for the payment of compensation to the owners of the interests covered by §207. The statute was signed into law on January 12, 1983, and became effective immediately.

The three appellees — Mary Irving, Patrick Pumpkin Seed, and Eileen Bissonette — are enrolled members of the Oglala Sioux Tribe. They are, or represent, heirs or devisees of members of the Tribe who died in March, April, and June 1983. Eileen Bissonette's decedent, Mary Poor Bear-Little Hoop Cross, purported to will all her property, including property subject to §207, to her five minor children in whose name Bissonette claims the property. Chester Irving, Charles Leroy Pumpkin Seed, and Edgar Pumpkin Seed all died intestate. At the time of their deaths, the four decedents owned 41 fractional interests subject to the provisions of §207. The Irving estate lost two interests whose value together was approximately $100; the Bureau of Indian Affairs placed total values of approximately $2,700 on the 26 escheatable interests in the Cross estate and $1,816 on the 13 escheatable interests in the Pumpkin Seed estates. But for §207, this property would have passed, in the ordinary course, to appellees or those they represent.

Appellees filed suit in the United States District Court for the District of South Dakota, claiming that §207 resulted in a taking of property without just compensation in violation of the Fifth Amendment. The District Court concluded that the statute was constitutional. It held that appellees had no vested interest in the property of the decedents prior to their deaths and that Congress had plenary authority to abolish the power of testamentary disposition of Indian property and to alter the rules of intestate succession.

The Court of Appeals for the Eighth Circuit reversed. Irving v. Clark, 758 F.2d 1260 (1985). Although it agreed that appellees had no vested rights in the decedents' property, it concluded that their decedents had a right, derived from the original Sioux allotment statute, to control disposition of their property at death. The Court of Appeals held that appellees had standing to invoke that right and that the taking of that right without compensation to decedents' estates violated the Fifth Amendment. . . .

II

The Court of Appeals concluded that appellees have standing to challenge §207. 758 F.2d, at 1267-1268. The Government does not contest this ruling. As the Court of Appeals recognized, however, the existence of a case or controversy is a jurisdictional prerequisite to a federal court's deliberations. Id., at 1267, n.12. We are satisfied that the necessary case or controversy exists in this case. Section 207 has deprived appellees of the fractional interests they otherwise would have inherited. This is sufficient injury-in-fact to satisfy Article III of the Constitution. See Singleton v. Wulff, 428 U.S. 106, 112 (1976).

III

The Congress, acting pursuant to its broad authority to regulate the descent and devise of Indian trust lands, Jefferson v. Fink, 247 U.S. 288, 294 (1918), enacted §207 as a means of ameliorating, over time, the problem of extreme fractionation of certain Indian lands. By forbidding the passing on at death of small, undivided interests in Indian lands, Congress hoped that future generations of Indians would be able to make more productive use of the Indians' ancestral lands. We agree with the Government that encouraging the consolidation of Indian lands is a public purpose of high order. The fractionation

problem on Indian reservations is extraordinary and may call for dramatic action to encourage consolidation. The Sisseton-Wahpeton
Sioux Tribe, appearing as amicus curiae in support of the Secretary
of the Interior, is a quintessential victim of fractionation. Forty-acre
tracts on the Sisseton-Wahpeton Lake Traverse Reservation, leasing
for about $1,000 annually, are commonly subdivided into hundreds
of undivided interests, many of which generate only pennies a year
in rent. The average tract has 196 owners and the average owner
undivided interests in 14 tracts. The administrative headache this represents can be fathomed by examining Tract 1305, dubbed "one of
the most fractionated parcels of land in the world." Lawson, Heirship:
The Indian Amoeba, reprinted in Hearing on S. 2480 and S. 2663
before the Senate Select Committee on Indian Affairs, 98th Cong.,
2d Sess., 85 (1984). Tract 1305 is 40 acres and produces $1,080 in
income annually. It is valued at $8,000. It has 439 owners, one-third
of whom receive less than $.05 in annual rent and two-thirds of whom
receive less than $1. The largest interest holder receives $82.85 annually. The common denominator used to compute fractional interests
in the property is 3,394,923,840,000. The smallest heir receives $.01
every 177 years. If the tract were sold (assuming the 439 owners could
agree) for its estimated $8,000 value, he would be entitled to
$.000418. The administrative costs of handling this tract are estimated
by the Bureau of Indian Affairs at $17,560 annually. Id., at 86, 87.
See also Comment, Too Little Land, Too Many Heirs — The Indian
Heirship Land Problem, 46 Wash. L. Rev. 709, 711-713 (1971).

This Court has held that the Government has considerable latitude
in regulating property rights in ways that may adversely affect the
owners. See Keystone Bituminous Coal Assn. v. DeBenedictis, 480 U.S.
470, 491-492 (1987); Penn Central Transportation Co. v. New York
City, 438 U.S. 104, 125-127 (1978); Goldblatt v. Hempstead, 369 U.S.
590, 592-593 (1962). The framework for examining the question of
whether a regulation of property amounts to a taking requiring just
compensation is firmly established and has been regularly and recently reaffirmed. See, e.g., Keystone Bituminous Coal Assn. v. De-
Benedictis, supra, at 485; Ruckelshaus v. Monsanto Co., 467 U.S. 986,
1004-1005 (1984); Hodel v. Virginia Surface Mining and Reclamation
Assn., Inc., 452 U.S. 264, 295 (1981); Agins v. Tiburon, 447 U.S. 255,
260-261 (1980); Kaiser Aetna v. United States, 444 U.S. 164, 174-175
(1979); Penn Central Transportation Co. v. New York City, supra, at
124. As The Chief Justice has written:

> [T]his Court has generally "been unable to develop any 'set formula' for
> determining when 'justice and fairness' require that economic injuries
> caused by public action be compensated by the government, rather than
> remain disproportionately concentrated on a few persons." [Penn Cen-

tral Transportation Co. v. New York City, 438 U.S.], at 124. Rather, it has
examined the "taking" question by engaging in essentially ad hoc, factual
inquiries that have identified several factors — such as the economic
impact of the regulation, its interference with reasonable investment
backed expectations, and the character of the governmental action —
that have particular significance. Ibid. Kaiser Aetna v. United States,
supra, at 175.

There is no question that the relative economic impact of §207
upon the owners of these property rights can be substantial. Section
207 provides for the escheat of small undivided property interests that
are unproductive during the year preceding the owner's death. Even
if we accept the Government's assertion that the income generated
by such parcels may be properly thought of as de minimis, their value
may not be. While the Irving estate lost two interests whose value
together was only approximately $100, the Bureau of Indian Affairs
placed total values of approximately $2,700 and $1,816 on the escheatable interests in the Cross and Pumpkin Seed estates. These are not
trivial sums. . . . Of course, the whole of appellees' decedents' property interests were not taken by §207. Appellees' decedents retained
full beneficial use of the property during their lifetimes as well as the
right to convey it inter vivos. There is no question, however, that
the right to pass on valuable property to one's heirs is itself a valuable right. Depending on the age of the owner, much or most of the
value of the parcel may inhere in this "remainder" interest. See 26
CFR §20.2031-7(f) (Table A) (1986) (value of remainder interest
when life tenant is age 65 is approximately 32% of the whole).

The extent to which any of appellees' decedents had "investment-
backed expectations" in passing on the property is dubious. Though
it is conceivable that some of these interests were purchased with the
expectation that the owners might pass on the remainder to their
heirs at death, the property has been held in trust for the Indians for
100 years and is overwhelmingly acquired by gift, descent, or devise.
Because of the highly fractionated ownership, the property is generally held for lease rather than improved and used by the owners.
None of the appellees here can point to any specific investment-
backed expectations beyond the fact that their ancestors agreed to
accept allotment only after ceding to the United States large parts of
the original Great Sioux Reservation.

Also weighing weakly in favor of the statute is the fact that there is
something of an "average reciprocity of advantage," Pennsylvania
Coal Co. v. Mahon, 260 U.S. 393, 415 (1922), to the extent that
owners of escheatable interests maintain a nexus to the Tribe. Consolidation of Indian lands in the Tribe benefits the members of the Tribe.
All members do not own escheatable interests, nor do all owners

belong to the Tribe. Nevertheless, there is substantial overlap between the two groups. The owners of escheatable interests often benefit from the escheat of others' fractional interests. Moreover, the whole benefit gained is greater than the sum of the burdens imposed since consolidated lands are more productive than fractionated lands.

If we were to stop our analysis at this point, we might well find §207 constitutional. But the character of the Government regulation here is extraordinary. In Kaiser Aetna v. United States, supra, at 176, we emphasized that the regulation destroyed "one of the most essential sticks in the bundle of rights that are commonly characterized as property — the right to exclude others." Similarly, the regulation here amounts to virtually the abrogation of the right to pass on a certain type of property — the small undivided interest — to one's heirs. In one form or another, the right to pass on property — to one's family in particular — has been part of the Anglo-American legal system since feudal times. See United States v. Perkins, 163 U.S. 625, 627-628 (1896). The fact that it may be possible for the owners of these interests to effectively control disposition upon death through complex inter vivos transactions such as revocable trusts, is simply not an adequate substitute for the rights taken, given the nature of the property. Even the United States concedes that total abrogation of the right to pass property is unprecedented and likely unconstitutional. Moreover, this statute effectively abolishes both descent and devise of these property interests even when the passing of the property to the heir might result in consolidation of property — as for instance when the heir already owns another undivided interest in the property. Cf. 25 U.S.C. §2206(b) (1982 ed., Supp. III). Since the escheatable interests are not, as the United States argues, necessarily de minimis, nor, as it also argues, does the availability of inter vivos transfer obviate the need for descent and devise, a *total* abrogation of these rights cannot be upheld. But cf. Andrus v. Allard, 444 U.S. 51 (1979) (upholding abrogation of the right to sell endangered eagles' parts as necessary to environmental protection regulatory scheme).

In holding that complete abolition of both the descent and devise of a particular class of property may be a taking, we reaffirm the continuing vitality of the long line of cases recognizing the States', and where appropriate, the United States', broad authority to adjust the rules governing the descent and devise of property without implicating the guarantees of the Just Compensation Clause. See, e.g., Irving Trust Co. v. Day, 314 U.S. 556, 562 (1942); Jefferson v. Fink, 247 U.S., at 294. The difference in this case is the fact that both descent and devise are completely abolished; indeed they are abolished even in circumstances when the governmental purpose sought to be advanced, consolidation of ownership of Indian lands, does not conflict with the further descent of the property.

There is little doubt that the extreme fractionation of Indian lands is a serious public problem. It may well be appropriate for the United States to ameliorate fractionation by means of regulating the descent and devise of Indian lands. Surely it is permissible for the United States to prevent the owners of such interests from further subdividing them among future heirs on pain of escheat. See Texaco, Inc. v. Short, 454 U.S. 516, 542 (1982) (Brennan, J., dissenting). It may be appropriate to minimize further compounding of the problem by abolishing the descent of such interests by rules of intestacy, thereby forcing the owners to formally designate an heir to prevent escheat to the Tribe. What is certainly not appropriate is to take the extraordinary step of abolishing both descent and devise of these property interests even when the passing of the property to the heir might result in consolidation of property. Accordingly, we find that this regulation, in the words of Justice Holmes, "goes too far." Pennsylvania Coal Co. v. Mahon, 260 U.S., at 415. The judgment of the Court of Appeals is
Affirmed.

NOTES AND QUESTIONS

1. Observe that almost all the controlling cases cited by Justice O'Connor involve governmental regulation of land use. Why should tests that were designed to determine when compensation should be given for land use regulation be used when inheritance is regulated? A fundamental issue in the former area is whether the government is "forcing some people alone to bear public burdens which, in all fairness and justice, should be borne by the public as a whole." Armstrong v. United States, 364 U.S. 40, 49 (1960). Is this relevant to regulation of inheritance? To §207 of the Indian Land Consolidation Act?

In Hodel v. Irving, the Court's opinion appears to rest on the assumption that the right to transmit property at death is a separate, identifiable stick in the bundle of rights called property, and, if this right is taken away, compensation must be paid. The Court does not look at the impact of the statute upon the value of the whole bundle of property rights, including lifetime use, but only at the impact of the statute upon the right to transmit the property at death. If the issue is the amount of economic loss suffered by the property owner as a consequence of the statute, as it is in regulatory taking cases, should the court consider the impact of the statute on the whole bundle of rights or only on one strand? Either one is extremely difficult to measure, particularly because inter vivos transfer of the fractional interest is not prohibited by the statute. The Court cites as evidence of the value of the right to pass property at death only the value of a remainder interest, which is the value of the *right to receive,* not the value of the *right to transmit.*

For comment on Hodel v. Irving, see Ronald Chester, Inheritance in American Legal Thought, in Inheritance and Wealth in America 23 (Robert K. Miller, Jr. & Stephen J. McNamee eds., 1998).

2.   If a legislature decides to abolish transmission of property by will or intestate succession, to be effective it is also necessary to abolish or severely limit donative transfers during life, which seems not feasible. (Think what a world would be like where persons could not give property away. How would a court police the difference between a permitted sale and a forbidden gift?) In the United States, several kinds of inter vivos transfers serve the same function as a will and are widely used: joint tenancy; gift of a remainder interest, reserving a life estate, often in a revocable trust; designating a death beneficiary on a contract, pension plan, or bank account. Indeed, in this country more property passes at death to survivors by way of these inter vivos arrangements than by way of will or intestacy. Property passing by will or intestacy "goes through probate," whereas property subject to these other arrangements does not, and, as we shall see, many people want to avoid probate because it is costly, public, and time-consuming.

In Hodel v. Irving, the court says, somewhat disingenuously, "The fact that it may be possible for the owners of these interests to effectively control disposition upon death through complex inter vivos transactions such as revocable trusts, is simply not an adequate substitute for the rights taken, given the nature of the property." Perhaps the court has in mind revocable trusts prepared for Rockefellers and the like, but in fact a revocable trust can be very simple. A signed writing providing, "I hereby declare that I hold my fractional interest in Sioux Tribal lands in a revocable trust, for my benefit for my life, and on my death the interest is to go to Patrick Pumpkin Seed," is a valid and sufficient revocable trust (see infra pages 351-361). The donor now holds the property in trust, and it will go to Patrick Pumpkin Seed on the donor's death, without probate, unless the donor revokes the trust. There is nothing inherently more complex about an inter vivos trust than about a will.

3.   In many societies wills are not permitted. With respect to Indian tribal lands, for example, wills were unknown until Congress forced individual allotments on the Indians. Even then, before 1910, Indian allottees were not permitted to devise their lands.

In some countries, on the continent of Europe for example, children cannot be disinherited. They are "forced heirs." In Anglo-American history, the right to devise property has always been in uneasy tension with forced succession. As Lawrence M. Friedman, The Law of the Living, The Law of the Dead: Property, Succession, and Society,

1966 Wis. L. Rev. 1, 14 (1966), observes, "Practically speaking, forced succession means succession within the family — to the wife, children and other dependents. Forced succession . . . converts private property at death to family property." In early feudal times, forced succession had the upper hand. Prior to 1540, when the Statute of Wills was enacted, a will of land was not permitted at law in England. The legal title to land owned at death passed to the eldest son, subject to the surviving spouse's dower or curtesy. In the United States, married women could not devise land without the consent of their husbands until the enactment of Married Women's Property Acts in the late nineteenth century. By the twentieth century, forced succession reappeared when statutes were enacted giving the surviving spouse a forced share of one-third or one-half of the decedent's estate, which the surviving spouse may not be deprived of by the decedent spouse's will. In Louisiana, where the civil law of France was introduced, minor and disabled children may not be disinherited. (On protection of spouse and children, see Chapter 7, infra.)

Although §207 of the Indian Land Consolidation Act speaks of "escheat" to the tribe, in effect the section makes the tribe the successor to, or heir of, the Indian owner of the affected fractioned land. Why is forced succession by a tribe not constitutionally permissible when forced succession by family members would be? If the Indians wanted tribal ownership restored, is there any way to change back to tribal ownership without paying individuals for their allotted lands? Is there any way to get the genie back in the bottle?

4. While Hodel v. Irving was being argued in the Eighth Circuit Court of Appeals, in October 1984, Congress amended §207 of the Indian Land Consolidation Act to provide: "Nothing in this section shall prohibit the devise of such an escheatable fractional interest to any other owner of an undivided fractional interest in such parcel or tract of trust or restricted land." 98 Stat. 3173, 25 U.S.C. §2206(b). The amendment was not retroactive and hence did not affect the operation of §207 on the property involved in the case.

The amended statute was held unconstitutional in Babbitt v. Youpee, 519 U.S. 234 (1997), on the ground that the statute permits devise only among a very limited group (other owners of the parcel), which is not likely to include a lineal descendant of the decedent, usually the primary object of the decedent's bounty.

5. For further reading on the changing institution of inheritance in this country, from its earliest days to the present, see Carole Shammas, Marylynn Salmon & Michel Dahlin, Inheritance in America from Colonial Times to the Present (1987); Marvin B. Sussman, Judith N. Cates & David T. Smith, The Family and Inheritance (1970).

For a fascinating study of the legal minefield of devising property to slaves in the antebellum South, see Adrienne D. Davis, The Private

Law of Race and Sex: An Antebellum Perspective, 51 Stan. L. Rev. 221 (1999). The fundamental challenge to courts was how to uphold testamentary freedom without disrupting racial hierarchies. Slaves were regarded as property, and the idea of property owning property was baffling. Professor Davis examines the wills of white men who devised property to their children by slave women, or to the women themselves, and the tensions and contradictions in legal doctrine these devises caused. (Thomas Jefferson, who is thought to have fathered at least one child by his slave Sally Hemings, left no property to Sally or her children.)

Edward C. Halbach, Jr., An Introduction to Death, Taxes and Family Property
Death, Taxes and Family Property 3, 5-7 (Edward C. Halbach, Jr., ed. 1977)*

What justifications are there for the private transmission of wealth from generation to generation? And how do we rationalize allowing only some individuals, selected by accident of birth, to enjoy significant comforts and power they have not earned?

Many arguments are offered in support of the institution of inheritance. One is simply that, in a society based on private property, it may be the least objectionable arrangement for dealing with property on the owner's death. Another is that inheritance is natural and proper as both an expression and a reinforcement of family ties, which in turn are important to a healthy society and a good life. After all, a society should be concerned with the total amount of happiness it can offer, and to many of its members it is a great comfort and satisfaction to know during life that, even after death, those whom one cares about can be provided for and may be able to enjoy better lives because of the inheritance that can be left to them. Furthermore, it is argued, giving and bequeathing not only express but beget affection, or at least responsibility. Thus, society is seen as offering a better and happier life by responding to the understandable desire of an individual to provide for his or her family after death.

Just as individuals may be rewarded through this desire, it can also be used by society, via inheritance rights, to serve as an incentive to bring forth creativity, hard work, initiative and ultimately productivity that benefits others, as well as encouraging individual responsibility — encouraging those who can to make provision that society would otherwise have to make for those who are or may be dependents. Of course, some doubt the need for such incentives, at least beyond modest levels of achievement and wealth accumulation, relying on the quest for power (or for recognition) and other motivations — not to mention habit. Long after these forces have taken over to stimulate the industry of such individuals, however, society may continue to find it important to offer property inducements to the irrepressibly productive to save rather than to consume, and to go on saving long after their own lifelong future needs are provided for. And what harm is there if individuals, through socially approved channels, pursue immortality and psychological satisfactions? The direct and indirect (e.g., through life insurance and through corporate accumulations) savings of individuals are vital to the economy's capital base and thus to its level of employment and to the productivity of other individuals.

Consequently, it is concluded, inheritance may grant wealth to *donees* without regard to their competence and performance, but the economic reasons for allowing inheritance are viewed in terms of proper rewards and socially valuable incentives to the *donor.* In fact, some philosophers would insist, these rewards are required by ideals of social justice as the fruits of one's labors. . . .

JEREMY BENTHAM, THE THEORY OF LEGISLATION 184 (C.K. Ogden ed. 1950): "[W]hen we recollect the infirmities of old age, we must be satisfied that it is necessary not to deprive it of this counterpoise of factitious attractions [prospects of inheritance by the younger giving care to the older]. In the rapid descent of life, every support on which man can lean should be left untouched, and it is well that interest serve as a monitor to duty."

Melvin L. Oliver, Thomas M. Shapiro & Julie E. Press, "Them That's Got Shall Get": Inheritance and Achievement in Wealth Accumulation
The Politics of Wealth and Inequality 69, 73-74
(Richard E. Ratcliff, Melvin L. Oliver & Thomas M. Shapiro eds. 1995)

The role and extent of inherited wealth is an important issue that occupies considerable attention among economists. However, their theoretically driven models of the importance of inherited wealth support a wide and quite contradictory range of findings. One end estimates that 80 percent of great wealth is inherited. The other end estimates that inherited wealth comprises only 20 percent of the wealthy's stockpile and 80 percent is earned the old fashioned way. In any event the amount and meaning of inherited wealth is considerable. For example, the wealthiest generation of elderly people in America's history is in the process of passing along its wealth.

Between 1987 and 2011 the baby boom generation stands to inherit an estimated 6.8 trillion dollars. Much of this wealth was built by their parents between the late 1940s and the late 1960s when real wages and savings rates were higher and housing costs were considerably lower. For the elderly middle class, the escalation of real estate prices over the last 20 years has meant a significant boon to their assets. Of course not all will benefit equally, or at all. The richest one percent will divide one-third of the worth of estates, each inheritance per estate receiving an average inheritance of $6 million; the next richest nine percent will divide another third for an average inheritance of about $396,000. Much of this wealth will be property. Philosopher Robert Nozick says that this "sticks out as a special kind of unearned benefit that produces unequal opportunities."

De Tocqueville warned the first new nation about the social and political dangers of inherited wealth becoming the basis of enduring privilege. He wrote: "What is the most important for democracy is not that great fortunes should not exist, but that great fortunes should not remain in the same hands. In that way there are rich men, but they do not form a class."

Forbes Magazine, in its 1998 annual report on the 400 richest people in America, listed 400 individuals from Bill Gates, with $58 billion, to several persons with $500 million, the minimum wealth to qualify for the list. It was impossible to say accurately what percentage of wealth was earned and what inherited, because many — like the Bass Brothers in Texas — inherited a few millions and parlayed them into vastly more through work. Forbes designated about one-third of the 400 richest as having inherited their wealth.

The most powerful argument against permitting transmission of wealth is that the transfer of great fortunes perpetuates wide disparities in the distribution of wealth, concentrates inherited economic power in the hands of a few, and denies equality of opportunity to the poorer. It also tends not to reward merit and productivity of the recipients but the chance of fortunate birth. See Ronald Chester, Inheritance, Wealth and Society (1982); Remi Clignet, Death, Deeds and Descendants: Inheritance in Modern America (1992); Inheritance and Wealth in America (Robert K. Miller, Jr. & Stephen J. McNamee eds. 1998); Edward N. Wolff, Top Heavy: A Study of the Increasing Inequality of Wealth in America (1995); William G. Gale and John Karl Scholz, Intergenerational Transfers and the Accumulation of Wealth, 8 J. Econ. Perspectives (No. 4) 145 (1994).

In the United States this argument has found a receptive ear in Congress, which, for most of the twentieth century, has imposed substantial estate and gift taxes on the rich. Under current law, these taxes are imposed on individuals transferring property worth $675,000 or more in the year 2000, with the tax exemption rising in gradual annual increases to $1 million in 2006. Rates start at 37 percent and increase to 55 percent on property in excess of $3,000,000. Federal estate, gift, and generation-skipping taxes are dealt with in Chapter 14 of this book.

Mark L. Ascher, Curtailing Inherited Wealth
89 Mich. L. Rev. 69, 72-76 (1990)

About $150 billion pass at death each year. Yet in 1988 the federal wealth transfer taxes raised less than $8 billion. Obviously, these taxes could raise much more. If, to take the extreme example, we allowed the government to confiscate all property at death, we could almost eliminate the deficit with one stroke of a Presidential pen. This nation, however, rarely has used taxes on the transfer of wealth to raise significant revenue. Our historical hesitancy in this regard strongly suggests that we as a nation are unwilling to abolish inheritance in order to raise revenue. Nonetheless, thinking about using the federal wealth transfer taxes to abolish inheritance may not be entirely futile. It may permit an entirely new type of analysis. Conventional attempts to reform the federal wealth transfer taxes inevitably bog down in the Anglo-American tradition of freedom of testation. As begrudged intruders upon a general rule, these taxes necessarily end up playing an inconsequential role. One willing, for purposes of analysis, to discard freedom of testation could start from the proposition that property rights should end at death. Inheritance then would be tolerated only as an exception to that general rule. This article does just that. I invite the reader to join me in speculating whether it might not make sense to use the federal wealth transfer taxes to curtail inheritance, thereby increasing equality of opportunity while raising revenue.

My proposal views inheritance as something we should tolerate only when necessary — not something we should always protect. My major premise is that all property owned at death, after payment of debts and administration expenses, should be sold and the proceeds paid to the United States government. There would be six exceptions. A marital exemption, potentially unlimited, would accrue over the life of a marriage. Thus, spouses could continue to provide for each other after death. Decedents would also be allowed to provide for dependent lineal descendants. The amount available to any given descendant would, however, depend on the descendant's age and would drop to zero at an age of presumed independence. A separate exemption would allow generous provision for disabled lineal descendants of any age. Inheritance by lineal ascendants (parents, grandparents, etc.) would be unlimited. A universal exemption would allow a moderate amount of property either to pass outside the exemptions or to augment amounts passing under them. Thus, every decedent would be able to leave something to persons of his or her choice, regardless whether another exemption was available. Up to a fixed fraction of an estate could pass to charity. In addition, to prevent circumvention by lifetime giving, the gift tax would increase substantially.

My proposal strikes directly at inheritance by healthy, adult children. And for good reason. We cannot control differences in native ability. Even worse, so long as we believe in the family, we can achieve only the most rudimentary successes in evening out many types of opportunities. And we certainly cannot control many types of luck. But we can — and ought to — curb one form of luck. Children lucky enough to have been raised, acculturated, and educated by wealthy parents need not be allowed the additional good fortune of inheriting their parents' property. In this respect, we can do much better than we ever have before at equalizing opportunity. This proposal would leave "widows and orphans" essentially untouched. The disabled, grandparents, and charity would probably fare better than ever before. But inheritance by healthy, adult children would cease immediately, except to the extent of the universal exemption.

This proposal sounds radical, perhaps even communistic. Inheritance does seem to occupy a special place in the hearts of many Americans, even those who cannot realistically expect to inherit anything of significance. For example, in 1982, sixty-four percent of the voters in a California initiative voted to repeal that state's inheritance tax. Michael Graetz, who, like me, finds this element of the American psyche puzzling, explains it as a product of "the optimism of the American people. In California, at least, sixty-four percent of the people must believe that they will be in the wealthiest five to ten percent when they die." This fascination with inheritance perhaps explains the minimal public debate about using the federal transfer taxes to raise substantial amounts of revenue. But curtailing inheritance is hardly radical. For years Americans have written seriously and thoughtfully on the subject. My proposal builds on that tradition and reaches the conclusion that substantial limitations on inheritance would contribute meaningfully to the equality of opportunity we offer our children. It also concludes that such limitations are fully consistent with our notions of private property. Neither conclusion is new. What is new is a $200 billion deficit. Now, as at few other times in this nation's history, our government needs new sources of revenue. Accordingly, I suggest changes in the federal wealth transfer taxes that would curtail inheritance and raise revenue. If we cannot, or will not, control the deficit, this generation's primary bequest to its children will be the obligation to pay their parents' debts.

NOTE: INHERITANCE IN THE ERSTWHILE SOVIET UNION

In 1918 the Soviet Bolsheviks, carrying out the teaching of Marx and Engels, abolished inheritance. The 1918 law, translated into English, read: "Inheritance, testate and intestate, is abolished. Upon the death of the owner his property (movable and immovable) becomes the property of the R.S.F.S.R." [1918] 1 Sob. Uzak., RSFSR, No. 34, item 456, Apr. 26, 1918. Within four years, however, inheritance was reestablished. The abolition of inheritance proved unpopular, and the Soviet rulers, on second thought, decided it was an institution encouraging savings and an incentive to work. Inheritance was also viewed as a method of providing for dependents of the deceased, relieving the state of this burden, and of furthering family unity and stability. Before the dissolution of the Soviet Union, the Soviet law of inheritance did not substantially differ from the civil law of inheritance found in western Europe. Similarly, the Chinese inheritance system differs little from those in effect in civil law countries. See Frances Foster, The Development of Inheritance Law in the Soviet Union and the People's Republic of China, 33 Am. J. Comp. Law 33 (1985); Comment, Soviet Inheritance Law: Ideological Consistency or a Retreat to the West?, 23 Gonz. L. Rev. 593 (1988).

Even though inequality may result from inherited wealth, inequality may also result from the creation of human capital in children. The following excerpt makes this point brilliantly and raises the following question: If economic inheritance were abolished, would it be even more difficult to break up an upper class?

Walter J. Blum & Harry Kalven, Jr., The Uneasy Case
for Progressive Taxation
19 U. Chi. L. Rev. 417, 501-504 (1952)

There is still another road leading to the problem of equality. Almost everybody professes to be in favor of one kind of equality — equality of opportunity. What remains to be investigated is the relationship between this kind of equality and economic equality. . . . In

"Having a fine old name really has been enough for me."

Drawing by Wm. Hamilton
Copyright © The New Yorker Collection 1977.
Reproduced by permission.

terms of the justice of rewards, the point is that no race can be fair unless the contestants start from the same mark. . . .

It might simplify matters somewhat to go directly to the heart of the problem — the children. . . . The important inequalities of opportunity are inequalities of environment, in its broadest sense, for the children. It is the inequalities in the worlds which the children inherit which count, and this inheritance is both economic and cultural.

. . . The critical economic inheritance consists of the day to day expenditures on the children; it is these expenditures which add up to money investments in the children's health, education and welfare which in the aggregate are, at least in our society, gravely disparate. No progressive inheritance tax, or combination of gift and inheritance taxes, can touch this source of economic inequalities among children. On the other hand a progressive income tax can, as one of its effects, help to minimize this form of unequal inheritance. It is income, not wealth, which is the important operative factor here, and by bringing incomes closer together the tax tends to bring money investments in children closer together.

But the gravest source of inequality of opportunity in our society is not economic but rather what is called cultural inheritance for lack of a better term. Under modern conditions the opportunities for formal education, healthful diet and medical attention to some extent can be equalized by economic means without too greatly disrupting

19

the family. However, it still remains true that even today much of the transmission of culture, in the narrow sense, occurs through the family, and no system of public education and training can completely neutralize this form of inheritance. Here it is the economic investment in the parents and the grandparents, irrevocably in the past, which produces differential opportunities for the children. Nor is this the end of the matter. It has long been recognized that the parents make the children in their own image, and modern psychology has served to underscore how early this process begins to operate and how decisive it may be. The more subtle and profound influences upon the child resulting from love, integrity and family morale form a kind of inheritance which cannot, at least for those above the minimum subsistence level, be significantly affected by economic measures, or possibly by any others. If these influences on the members of the next generation are to be equalized, nothing short of major changes in the institution of the family can possibly suffice. At a minimum such changes would include socializing decisions not only about how children are to be raised but who is to raise them. And this in turn would call into question the very having of children.

John H. Langbein, The Twentieth-Century Revolution
in Family Wealth Transmission
86 Mich. L. Rev. 722, 723-724, 729, 732-733,
736, 739-740, 743-745 (1988)

The main purpose of this article is to sound a pair of themes about the ways in which these great changes in the nature of wealth have become associated with changes of perhaps comparable magnitude in the timing and in the character of family wealth transmission. My first theme, developed in Part II, concerns human capital. Whereas of old, wealth transmission from parents to children tended to center upon major items of patrimony such as the family farm or the family firm, today for the broad middle classes, wealth transmission centers on a radically different kind of asset: the investment in skills. In consequence, intergenerational wealth transmission no longer occurs primarily upon the death of the parents, but rather, when the children are growing up, hence, during the parents' lifetimes.

My other main theme, developed in Part III, arises from the awesome demographic transformation of modern life. For reasons that I shall explore, those same parents who now make their main wealth transfer to their children inter vivos are also living much longer. The need to provide for the parents in their lengthy old age has put a huge new claim on family wealth, a claim that necessarily reduces the residuum that would otherwise have passed to survivors. A new institution has arisen to help channel the process of saving and dissaving for old age: the pension fund. The wealth of the private pension system consists almost entirely of financial assets. I shall emphasize a distinctive attribute of pension wealth, namely, the bias toward annuitization. When wealth is annuitized, virtually nothing is left for transfer on death. . . .

II.   WEALTH TRANSFERS THROUGH HUMAN CAPITAL

The same underlying technological and economic forces that caused the dissolution of family-based enterprise have also stripped the family of much of its role as an educational institution. This development, which is in a sense quite obvious to us all, has had enormous implications for family wealth transmission, implications that have not been adequately appreciated. . . .

My thesis is quite simple, and, I hope, quite intuitive. I believe that, in striking contrast to the patterns of last century and before, in modern times the business of educating children has become the main occasion for intergenerational wealth transfer. Of old, parents were mainly concerned to transmit the patrimony — prototypically the farm or the firm, but more generally, that "provision in life" that rescued children from the harsh fate of being a mere laborer. In today's economic order, it is education more than property, the new human capital rather than the old physical capital, that similarly advantages a child. . . .

From the proposition that the main parental wealth transfer to children now takes place inter vivos, there follows a corollary: Children of propertied parents are much less likely to expect an inheritance. Whereas of old, children did expect the transfer of the farm or firm, today's children expect help with educational expenses, but they do not depend upon parental wealth transfer at death. Lengthened life expectancies mean that the life-spans of the parents overlap the life-spans of their adult children for much longer than used to be. Parents now live to see their children reaching peak earnings potential, and those earnings often exceed what the parents were able to earn. Today, children are typically middle-aged when the survivor of their two parents dies, and middle-aged children are far less likely to be financially needy. It is still the common practice within middle- and upper-middle-class families for parents to leave to their children (or grandchildren) most or all of any property that happens to remain when the parents die, but there is no longer a widespread sense of parental responsibility to abstain from consumption in order to transmit an inheritance. . . .

III.   THE PENSION REVOLUTION

The other great chapter in the saga of fundamental change in family
wealth transmission being told in this article concerns the phenome-
non of retirement and the rise of the private pension system. . . .

As late as World War II, the private pension system was minuscule.
Today, the assets of nonfederal pension plans (that is, private plans
plus the pension funds of state and local government employees) total
approximately two trillion dollars. As of 1984, pension funds owned
22.8% of equity securities in the United States and about half of all
corporate debt. For many middle- and especially upper-middle-class
families, pension wealth is their largest asset. But pension wealth has
traits that mark it off sharply from traditional property, especially
when we look at it from the standpoint of family wealth transmission. . . .

In propertied families, today's elderly no longer expect much financial support from their children. The shared patrimony in farm or
firm that underlay that reverse transfer system in olden times has now
largely vanished. Instead, people of means are expected to foresee
the need for retirement income while they are still in the workforce,
and to conduct a program of saving for their retirement. Typically,
these people have already undertaken one great cycle of saving and
dissaving in their lives — that program by which they effected the
investment in human capital for their children. Just as that former
program of saving was oriented toward a distinctively modern form
of wealth, human capital, so this second program centers on the other
characteristic form of twentieth-century wealth, financial assets. . . .

From the standpoint of our interest in the patterns of family wealth
transmission, what is especially important about the pension system is
that it has been deliberately designed to promote lifetime exhaustion
of the accumulated capital. The same body of federal law that encourages pension saving also tries to ensure that pension wealth will be
consumed over the lives of the worker and his spouse. I do not mean
to say that the federal policy in favor of lifetime consumption of
retirement savings cannot be defeated for particular clients using appropriately designed plans; indeed, that is one of the major avenues
of tax and estate planning for the carriage trade that has arisen with
the pension system. My point is simply that, in the main, the federal
policy achieves its goal, and only a negligible fraction of pension
wealth finds its way into intergenerational transfer.

The mechanism by which pension wealth is consumed is annuitization. Just as life insurance is insurance against dying too soon, annuitization insures against living too long. Annuitization allows people to
consume their capital safely, that is, without fear of running out of
capital while still alive. Annuitization requires a large pool of lives,

which is achieved by various methods of aggregating the pension savings of many workers. Sometimes the employer runs the pool, sometimes an intermediary such as an insurance company or (for multiemployer plans) a labor union. Annuitization requires assets that can be liquidated predictably as distribution requires. That is a trait characteristic of financial assets. Annuitization is wonderfully effective in allowing a person to consume capital without fear of outliving his capital, but the corollary is also manifest: Accounts that have been annuitized disappear on the deaths of the annuitants. Not so much as a farthing remains for the heirs.

For stimulating further discussion of arguments for and against inheritance, see Stephen R. Munzer, A Theory of Property 380-418 (1990); Adam J. Hirsch & William K.S. Wang, A Qualitative Theory of the Dead Hand, 68 Ind. L.J. 1, 6-14 (1992). Both studies cite many earlier contributions to the literature.

During life, a person can use wealth to influence the conduct of another person. To what extent should a person be able to use wealth to influence behavior after death? Hobhouse wrote over 100 years ago, in condemning the "cold and numbing influence of the Dead Hand,"

> A clear, obvious, natural line is drawn for us between those persons and events which the Settlor knows and sees, and those which he cannot know and see. Within the former province we may push his natural affections and his capacity of judgment to make better dispositions than any external Law is likely to make for him. Within the latter, natural affection does not extend, and the wisest judgment is constantly baffled by the course of events. . . . What I consider to be not conjectural, but proved by experience in all human affairs, is, that people are the best judges of their own concerns; or if they are not, that it is better for them, on moral grounds, that they should manage their own concerns for themselves, and that it cannot be wrong continually to claim this liberty for every Generation of mortal men. [Arthur Hobhouse, The Dead Hand 188, 183-185 (1880).]

The following case introduces you to the power of the dead hand and its limitations. The limitations society places — or ought to place — on the dead hand will be a recurring theme in this book.

Shapira v. Union National Bank
Ohio Court of Common Pleas, Mahoning County, 1974
39 Ohio Misc. 28, 315 N.E.2d 825

HENDERSON, J.   This is an action for a declaratory judgment and
the construction of the will of David Shapira, M.D., who died April
13, 1973, a resident of this county. By agreement of the parties, the
case has been submitted upon the pleadings and the exhibit.

The portions of the will in controversy are as follows:

Item VIII. All the rest, residue and remainder of my estate, real and
personal, of every kind and description and wheresoever situated, which
I may own or have the right to dispose of at the time of my decease, I
give, devise and bequeath to my three (3) beloved children, to wit: Ruth
Shapira Aharoni, of Tel Aviv, Israel, or wherever she may reside at the
time of my death; to my son Daniel Jacob Shapira, and to my son Mark
Benjamin Simon Shapira in equal shares, with the following qualifications: . . .

(b) My son Daniel Jacob Shapira should receive his share of the bequest
only, if he is married at the time of my death to a Jewish girl whose both
parents were Jewish. In the event that at the time of my death he is not
married to a Jewish girl whose both parents were Jewish, then his share
of this bequest should be kept by my executor for a period of not longer
than seven (7) years and if my said son Daniel Jacob gets married within
the seven year period to a Jewish girl whose both parents were Jewish,
my executor is hereby instructed to turn over his share of my bequest to
him. In the event, however, that my said son Daniel Jacob is unmarried
within the seven (7) years after my death to a Jewish girl whose both
parents were Jewish, or if he is married to a non Jewish girl, then his
share of my estate, as provided in item 8 above should go to The State
of Israel, absolutely.

The provision for the testator's other son Mark, is conditioned
substantially similarly. Daniel Jacob Shapira, the plaintiff, alleges that
the condition upon his inheritance is unconstitutional, contrary to
public policy and unenforceable because of its unreasonableness, and
that he should be given his bequest free of the restriction. Daniel
is 21 years of age, unmarried and a student at Youngstown State
University.

CONSTITUTIONALITY

Plaintiff's argument that the condition in question violates constitutional safeguards is based upon the premise that the right to marry
is protected by the Fourteenth Amendment to the Constitution of the
United States. Meyer v. Nebraska (1923), 262 U.S. 390; Skinner v.

Oklahoma (1942), 316 U.S. 535; Loving v. Virginia (1967), 388 U.S. 1. . . . In Loving v. Virginia, the court held unconstitutional as violative of the Equal Protection and Due Process Clauses of the Fourteenth Amendment an antimiscegenation statute under which a black person and a white person were convicted for marrying. In its opinion the United States Supreme Court made the following statements, 388 U.S. at page 12.

> There can be no doubt that restricting the freedom to marry solely because of racial classifications violates the central meaning of the Equal Protection Clause.
> . . . The freedom to marry has long been recognized as one of the vital personal rights essential to the orderly pursuit of happiness by free men.
> Marriage is one of the "basic civil rights of man," fundamental to our very existence and survival. . . . The Fourteenth Amendment requires that the freedom of choice to marry not be restricted by invidious racial discriminations. Under our Constitution, the freedom to marry, or not marry, a person of another race resides with the individual and cannot be infringed by the State.

From the foregoing, it appears clear, as plaintiff contends, that the right to marry is constitutionally protected from restrictive state legislative action. Plaintiff submits, then, that under the doctrine of Shelley v. Kraemer (1948), 334 U.S. 1, the constitutional protection of the Fourteenth Amendment is extended from direct state legislative action to the enforcement by state judicial proceedings of private provisions restricting the right to marry. Plaintiff contends that a judgment of this court upholding the condition restricting marriage would, under Shelley v. Kraemer, constitute state action prohibited by the Fourteenth Amendment as much as a state statute.

In Shelley v. Kraemer the United States Supreme Court held that the action of the states to which the Fourteenth Amendment has reference includes action of state courts and state judicial officials. Prior to this decision the court had invalidated city ordinances which denied blacks the right to live in white neighborhoods. In Shelley v. Kraemer owners of neighboring properties sought to enjoin blacks from occupying properties which they had bought, but which were subjected to privately executed restrictions against use or occupation by any persons except those of the Caucasian race. Chief Justice Vinson noted, in the course of his opinion at page 13: "These are cases in which the purposes of the agreements were secured only by judicial enforcement by state courts of the restrictive terms of the agreements."

In the case at bar, this court is not being asked to enforce any restriction upon Daniel Jacob Shapira's constitutional right to marry. Rather, this court is being asked to enforce the testator's restriction upon his son's inheritance. If the facts and circumstances of this case were such that the aid of this court were sought to enjoin Daniel's marrying a non-Jewish girl, then the doctrine of Shelley v. Kraemer would be applicable, but not, it is believed, upon the facts as they are.

Counsel for plaintiff asserts, however, that his position with respect to the applicability of Shelley v. Kraemer to this case is fortified by two later decisions of the United States Supreme Court: Evans v. Newton (1966), 382 U.S. 296, and Pennsylvania v. Board of Directors of City Trusts of the City of Philadelphia (1957), 353 U.S. 230.

Evans v. Newton involved land willed in trust to the mayor and city council of Macon, Georgia, as a park for white people only, and to be controlled by a white board of managers. To avoid the city's having to enforce racial segregation in the park, the city officials resigned as trustees and private individuals were installed. The court held that such successor trustees, even though private individuals, became agencies or instrumentalities of the state and subject to the Fourteenth Amendment by reason of their exercising powers or carrying on functions governmental in nature. The following comment of Justice Douglas seems revealing: "If a testator wanted to leave a school or center for the use of one race only and in no way implicated the State in the supervision, control, or management of that facility, we assume arguendo that no constitutional difficulty would be encountered." 382 U.S. 300.

The case of Pennsylvania v. Board, as the full title, above, suggests, is a case in which money was left by will to the city of Philadelphia in trust for a college to admit poor white male orphans. The court held that the board which operated the college was an agency of the state of Pennsylvania, and that, therefore, its refusal to admit the plaintiffs because they were negroes was discrimination by the state forbidden by the Fourteenth Amendment.

So, in neither Evans v. Newton nor Pennsylvania v. Board was the doctrine of the earlier Shelley v. Kraemer applied or extended. Both of them involved restrictive actions by state governing agencies, in one case with respect to a park, in the other case with respect to a college. Although both the park and the college were founded upon testamentary gifts, the state action struck down by the court was not the judicial completion of the gifts, but rather the subsequent enforcement of the racial restrictions by the public management.

Basically, the right to receive property by will is a creature of the law, and is not a natural right or one guaranteed or protected by either the Ohio or the United States constitution. . . . It is a fundamental rule of law in Ohio that a testator may legally entirely disinherit his children. . . . This would seem to demonstrate that, from a constitutional standpoint, a testator may restrict a child's inheritance. The court concludes, therefore, that the upholding and enforcement of the provisions of Dr. Shapira's will conditioning the bequests to his sons upon their marrying Jewish girls does not offend the Constitution of Ohio or of the United States. United States National Bank of Portland v. Snodgrass (1954), 202 Or. 530, 275 P.2d 860, 50 A.L.R.2d 725; Gordon v. Gordon (1955), 332 Mass. 197, 124 N.E.2d 228; 54 Mich. L. Rev. 297 (1955); cf. 39 Minn. L. Rev. 809 (1955).

PUBLIC POLICY

The condition that Daniel's share should be "turned over to him if he should marry a Jewish girl whose both parents were Jewish" constitutes a partial restraint upon marriage. If the condition were that the beneficiary not marry anyone, the restraint would be general or total, and, at least in the case of a first marriage, would be held to be contrary to public policy and void. A partial restraint of marriage which imposes only reasonable restrictions is valid, and not contrary to public policy: . . . The great weight of authority in the United States is that gifts conditioned upon the beneficiary's marrying within a particular religious class or faith are reasonable. . . .

Plaintiff contends, however, that in Ohio a condition such as the one in this case is void as against the public policy of this state. . . . Plaintiff's position that the free choice of religious practice cannot be circumscribed or controlled by contract is substantiated by Hackett v. Hackett (C.A. Lucas 1958), 78 Ohio Law Abs. 485, 150 N.E.2d 431. This case held that a covenant in a separation agreement, incorporated in a divorce decree, that the mother would rear a daughter in the Roman Catholic faith was unenforceable. However, the controversial condition in the case at bar is a partial restraint upon marriage and not a covenant to restrain the freedom of religious practice; and, of course, this court is not being asked to hold the plaintiff in contempt for failing to marry a Jewish girl of Jewish parentage. . . .

It is noted, furthermore, in this connection, that the courts of Pennsylvania distinguish between testamentary gifts conditioned upon the religious faith of the beneficiary and those conditioned upon marriage to persons of a particular religious faith. In In re Clayton's Estate (1930), 13 Pa. D. & C. 413, the court upheld a gift of a life estate conditioned upon the beneficiary's not marrying a woman of the Catholic faith. In its opinion the court distinguishes the earlier case of Drace v. Klinedinst (1922), 275 Pa. 266, 118 A. 907, in which a life estate willed to grandchildren, provided they remained faithful to a particular religion, was held to violate the public policy of Pennsylvania.[2] In *Clayton's Estate,* the court said that the condition concerning marriage did not affect the faith of the beneficiary, and that the condition, operating only on the choice of a wife, was too remote to be regarded as coercive of religious faith. . . .

The only cases cited by plaintiff's counsel in accord with [plaintiff's contention] are some English cases and one American decision. In England the courts have held that partial restrictions upon marriage to persons not of the Jewish faith, or of Jewish parentage, were not contrary to public policy or invalid. Hodgson v. Halford (1879 Eng.) L.R. 11 Ch. Div. 959, 50 A.L.R.2d 742. Other cases in England, however, have invalidated forfeitures of similarly conditioned provisions for children upon the basis of uncertainty or indefiniteness. . . . Since the foregoing decisions, a later English case has upheld a condition precedent that a granddaughter-beneficiary marry a person of Jewish faith and the child of Jewish parents. The court . . . found . . . no difficulty with indefiniteness where the legatee married unquestionably outside the Jewish faith. Re Wolffe, [1953] 1 Week. L.R. 1211, [1953] 2 All Eng. 697, 50 A.L.R.2d 747.[3]

The American case cited by plaintiff is that of Maddox v. Maddox (1854), 52 Va. (11 Grattan's) 804. The testator in this case willed a remainder to his niece if she remain a member of the Society of Friends. When the niece arrived at a marriageable age there were but five or six unmarried men of the society in the neighborhood in which she lived. She married a non-member and thus lost her own membership. The court held the condition to be an unreasonable

2. In In re Estate of Laning, 462 Pa. 157, 339 A.2d 520 (1975), the court stated that the *Drace* case was correctly decided on the ground that the testator sought to require his grandchildren to "remain true" to the Catholic religion, and that the enforcement of a condition that they remain faithful Catholics would require the court to determine the doctrines of the Catholic church. "Such questions are clearly improper for a civil court to determine." The court went on to uphold a provision in Laning's will that the gift be distributed to certain relatives who held "membership in good standing" in the Presbyterian church; the court construed the provision to mean only a formal affiliation with the specified church, thus avoiding improper inquiry into church doctrine. — Eds.

3. In In re Tuck's Settlement Trusts, [1977] 2 W.L.R. 411, a trust was set up by the first Baron Tuck, a Jew, for the benefit of his successors in the baronetcy. Anxious to ensure that his successors be Jewish, he provided for payment of income to the baronet for the time being if and when and as long as he should be of the Jewish faith and married to a wife of Jewish blood and of the Jewish faith. The trust also provided that in case of any dispute the decision of the Chief Rabbi of London would be conclusive. The court held that the conditions were not void for uncertainty. Lord Denning was of the view that if there was any uncertainty, it was cured by the Chief Rabbi clause. The other two judges declined to reach that issue.

The question — who is a Jew — is not easy to answer, not even in Israel where it has provoked continuing controversy. See Meryl Hyman, Who is a Jew? (1998); Jack Wertheimer, A People Divided: Judaism in Contemporary America (1993); Comment, Israel's Law of Return: An Analysis of its Evolution and Present Application, 12 Dick. J. Intl. L. 95 (1993).

See generally Peter Butt, Testamentary Conditions in Restraint of Religion, 8 Sydney L. Rev. 400 (1977); Francis M. Nevins, Jr., Testamentary Conditions: The Principle of Uncertainty and Religion, 18 St. Louis U.L.J. 563 (1974). — Eds.

restraint upon marriage and void, and that there being no gift over upon breach of the condition, the condition was in terrorem, and did not avoid the bequest. It can be seen that while the court considered the testamentary condition to be a restraint upon marriage, it was primarily one in restraint of religious faith. The court said that with the small number of eligible bachelors in the area the condition would have operated as a virtual prohibition of the niece's marrying, and that she could not be expected to "go abroad" in search of a helpmate or to be subjected to the chance of being sought after by a stranger. . . . The other ground upon which the Virginia court rested its decision, that the condition was in terrorem because of the absence of a gift over, is clearly not applicable to the case at bar, even if it were in accord with Ohio law, because of the gift over to the State of Israel contained in the Shapira will.

In arguing for the applicability of the Maddox v. Maddox test of reasonableness to the case at bar, counsel for the plaintiff asserts that the number of eligible Jewish females in this county would be an extremely small minority of the total population especially as compared with the comparatively much greater number in New York, whence have come many of the cases comprising the weight of authority upholding the validity of such clauses. There are no census figures in evidence. While this court could probably take judicial notice of the fact that the Jewish community is a minor, though important segment of our total local population, nevertheless the court is by no means justified in judicial knowledge that there is an insufficient number of eligible young ladies of Jewish parentage in this area from which Daniel would have a reasonable latitude of choice.[4] And of course, Daniel is not at all confined in his choice to residents of this county, which is a very different circumstance in this day of travel by plane and freeway and communication by telephone, from the horse and buggy days of the 1854 Maddox v. Maddox decision. Consequently, the decision does not appear to be an appropriate yardstick of reasonableness under modern living conditions.

Plaintiff's counsel contends that the Shapira will falls within the principle of Fineman v. Central National Bank (1961), 87 Ohio Law Abs. 236, 175 N.E.2d 837, 18 O.O.2d 33, holding that the public policy of Ohio does not countenance a bequest or device conditioned on the beneficiary's obtaining a separation or divorce from his wife. Counsel argues that the Shapira condition would encourage the beneficiary to marry a qualified girl just to receive the bequest, and then to divorce her afterward. This possibility seems too remote to be a

4. The American Jewish Yearbook of 1976 estimates the Jewish population of Youngstown, Ohio, to be 5,400 in 1974. Taking into consideration other U.S. census data about the male to female ratio and the ages of the population in Youngstown, we estimate that about 540 Jewish females were in the 15-24 age group. If this estimate is correct, do you think this gives Daniel "a reasonable latitude of choice"? — Eds.

pertinent application of the policy against bequests conditioned upon divorce. . . . Indeed, in measuring the reasonableness of the condition in question, both the father and the court should be able to assume that the son's motive would be proper. And surely the son should not gain the advantage of the avoidance of the condition by the possibility of his own impropriety.

Finally, counsel urges that the Shapira condition tends to pressure Daniel, by the reward of money, to marry within seven years without opportunity for mature reflection, and jeopardizes his college education. It seems to the court, on the contrary, that the seven year time limit would be a most reasonable grace period, and one which would give the son ample opportunity for exhaustive reflection and fulfillment of the condition without constraint or oppression. Daniel is no more being "blackmailed into a marriage by immediate financial gain," as suggested by counsel, than would be the beneficiary of a living gift or conveyance upon consideration of a future marriage — an arrangement which has long been sanctioned by the courts of this state. Thompson v. Thompson (1867), 17 Ohio St. 649.

In the opinion of this court, the provision made by the testator for the benefit of the State of Israel upon breach or failure of the condition is most significant for two reasons. First, it distinguishes this case from the bare forfeitures in . . . Maddox v. Maddox (including the technical in terrorem objection), and, in a way, from the vagueness and indefiniteness doctrine of some of the English cases. Second, and of greater importance, it demonstrates the depth of the testator's conviction. His purpose was not merely a negative one designed to punish his son for not carrying out his wishes. His unmistakable testamentary plan was that his possessions be used to encourage the preservation of the Jewish faith and blood, hopefully through his sons, but, if not, then through the State of Israel. Whether this judgment was wise is not for this court to determine. But it is the duty of this court to honor the testator's intention within the limitations of law and of public policy. The prerogative granted to a testator by the laws of this state to dispose of his estate according to his conscience is entitled to as much judicial protection and enforcement as the prerogative of a beneficiary to receive an inheritance.

It is the conclusion of this court that public policy should not, and does not preclude the fulfillment of Dr. Shapira's purpose, and that in accordance with the weight of authority in this country, the conditions contained in his will are reasonable restrictions upon marriage, and valid.

NOTES, QUESTIONS, AND PROBLEMS

1. What social objectives are accomplished by honoring control of a beneficiary's behavior by the dead hand, a hand that does not

Judge Richard A. Posner

have a live mind controlling it and making a continuously informed, intelligent judgment as circumstances change, that can no longer be affected by the opinions of mankind, and that does not suffer the consequences? Compare Richard A. Posner, Economic Analysis of Law §18.6 (5th ed. 1998):

> Suppose a man leaves money to his son in trust, the trust to fail however if the son does not marry a woman of the Jewish faith by the time he is 25 years old. The judicial approach in such cases is to refuse to enforce the condition if it is unreasonable. In the case just put it might make a difference whether the son was 18 or 24 at the time of the bequest and how large the Jewish population was in the place where he lived.

This approach may seem wholly devoid of an economic foundation, and admittedly the criterion of reasonableness is here an unilluminating one. Consider, however, the possibilities for modification that would exist if the gift were inter vivos rather than testamentary. As the deadline approached, the son might come to his father and persuade him that a diligent search had revealed no marriageable Jewish girl who would accept him. The father might be persuaded to grant an extension or otherwise relax the condition. But if he is dead, this kind of "recontracting" is impossible, and the presumption that the condition is a reasonable one fails. This argues for applying the cy pres approach in private as well as charitable trust cases unless the testator expressly rejects a power of judicial modification.

You are Judge Posner. Daniel Shapira appears before you six-and-a-half years after his father's death and alleges that he has found no Jewish girl whom he desires who will accept him. What do you do?

In 1994 the editors asked the attorney who represented Daniel Shapira for information about the aftermath of the case. The attorney contacted Mr. Shapira, who declined to give any information. It was a bitter experience, he said, which he wanted to forget.

2. Restatement (Second) of Property, Donative Transfers §6.2 (1983), provides that a restraint to induce a person to marry within a religious faith is valid "if, and only if, under the circumstances, the restraint does not unreasonably limit the transferee's opportunity to marry." Comment a provides that, "the restraint unreasonably limits the transferee's opportunity to marry if a marriage permitted by the restraint is not likely to occur. The likelihood of marriage is a factual question, to be answered from the circumstances of the particular case." The motive or purpose of the testator is irrelevant. Suppose that Daniel Shapira were gay. Would the get-married provision in Dr. Shapira's will be enforceable?

3. A will or trust provision is ordinarily invalid if it is intended or tends to encourage disruption of a family relationship. Thus, provisions encouraging separation or divorce have usually been held invalid, unless the dominant motive of the testator is to provide support in the event of separation or divorce. See Restatement (Second) of Property, Donative Transfers §7.1 (1983); In re Estate of Donner, 263 N.J. Super. 539, 623 A.2d 307 (1993) (upholding father's trust denying daughter trust income or principal until age 65 unless her husband's death or a divorce should earlier occur, on ground that the decedent had a reasonable economic basis to withhold support unless daughter became breadwinner of family). Compare Hall v. Eaton, 259 Ill. App. 3d 319, 631 N.E.2d 805 (1994).

In Girard Trust Co. v. Schmitz, 129 N.J. Eq. 444, 20 A.2d 21 (1941), the court held invalid a condition that the testator's brothers and sisters must not communicate, either orally or in writing, with a brother and sister disliked by the testator. The court said it would not "lend its hand to help the testator use the power of his wealth to disrupt this family. . . . [S]ociety condemns all acts, be they contractual or testamentary, which tend to disturb the peace and harmony of families and to make inharmonious that which the state is interested in creating and preserving. 'As are families, so is society.' " Id. at 471, 20 A.2d at 37. Accord, Estate of Romero, 115 N.M. 85, 847 P.2d 319 (Ct. App. 1993) (voiding condition discouraging youthful children from living with their mother, testator's former wife).

4. Frederick Foagy has a daughter-in-law who goes by the name of Nicole Bates-Foagy, coupling her maiden name, Bates, with that of her husband, Arthur Foagy. Frederick, no feminist, doesn't cotton to women using double-barreled names. Frederick dies. His will leaves $100,000 to Nicole on condition that she legally change her name to Nicole Foagy and use only that name. Is this condition enforceable? See Restatement (Second) of Property, Donative Transfers, §7.2, Reporter's Notes 5 & 6 (1983).

5. *Destruction of property at death.* A fundamental justification of pri-

vate property is that society's total wealth will be maximized by permitting private individuals to decide what is the best use of their property. Each individual will, we assume, make rational choices to maximize her wealth, and the fact that economic loss from foolish or wrong decisions will fall on the individual acts as a deterrent to irrational decisions. A person can, if she wishes, destroy her property during life (unless it is subject to historic preservation or similar laws), but she suffers the economic consequences of her decision, plus or minus. Should a testator be permitted to order the destruction of property at death when the economic loss is not visited upon the testator but on others? Consider the following:

(a) The testator's will directs his executor to tear down the testator's house, as he does not want anyone else to live in it. Can the executor tear down the house? Should a court order the house destroyed? See Eyerman v. Mercantile Trust Co., 524 S.W.2d 210 (Mo. Ct. App. 1975) ("a well-ordered society cannot tolerate" waste); In re Estate of Pace, 93 Misc. 2d 969, 400 N.Y.S.2d 488 (Sur. Ct. 1977).

(b) Justice Hugo L. Black of the United States Supreme Court was of the view that private notes of the justices relating to Court conferences should not be published posthumously. Justice Black feared publication might inhibit free and vigorous discussion among the justices. Black was struck ill, destroyed his conference notes, resigned from the Court, and died a few weeks later. Suppose that Justice Black had died suddenly while on the bench and that his will had directed his executor to destroy his conference notes. Could the executor do this without a court order? Should a court order destruction of the notes, which might have enormous value to a Court historian? Who would have standing to object?

(c) Franz Kafka bequeathed his diaries, manuscripts, and letters to his friend Max Brod, directing him to burn everything. Brod declined to do so on the ground that Kafka's unpublished work was of great literary value. Should Brod have ordered a bonfire? See Max Brod, Postscript, *in* Franz Kafka, The Trial 326 (1925, Mod. Lib. ed. 1956), discussed in William R. Bishin & Christopher D. Stone, Law, Language, and Ethics 1-9 (1972). Suppose that Franz Schubert and Giacomo Puccini had ordered their unfinished works destroyed at death, thus depriving the world of Schubert's unfinished Symphony in B Minor and Puccini's unfinished opera Turandot. Should a court order destruction?

Professor John Orth of North Carolina calls to our attention that Virgil left instructions to destroy the Aeneid ("Arms and the man I sing"), which he left unfinished. The Emperor Augustus ordered the executors to disregard the order. See Moses Hadas, A History of Latin Literature 142 (1952). Orth asks: "The course of Western literature would be unimaginable without 'arms and the man'! Who would have guided Dante in Hell?''

6.   Restatement (Third) of Trusts §29(b) (T.D. No. 2, 1999) invalidates trusts "contrary to public policy." The comment and reporter's notes contain an extensive discussion of the issues raised above. Generally, the Restatement (Third) frowns on restraints on beneficiary behavior, including restraints on marriage or religious freedom, disrupting family relationships, and choice of careers, but calls for balancing of conflicting social values.

For a penetrating analysis of testamentary gifts conditioned upon specified conduct by the beneficiary, see Jeffrey G. Sherman, Posthumous Meddling: An Instrumentalist Theory of Testamentary Restraints on Conjugal and Religious Choices, 1999 U. Ill. L. Rev. _____. Professor Sherman rejects the balancing test of "contrary to public policy" and makes a principled analysis of why testation should be permitted and under what limitations. He concludes that testamentary conditions calculated to restrain legatees' personal conduct should not be enforced. The article is especially readable because laced with Sherman's delicious wit.

SECTION B.   TRANSFER OF THE DECEDENT'S ESTATE

1.   *Probate and Nonprobate Property*

All of the decedent's assets at death can be divided into probate and nonprobate property. Probate property is property that passes under the decedent's will or by intestacy. Nonprobate property is property passing under an instrument other than a will which became effective before death. Nonprobate property includes the following:

(a) *Joint tenancy property.* Under the theory of joint tenancy, the decedent's interest vanishes at death. The survivor has the whole property relieved of the decedent's participation. No interest passes to the survivor at the decedent's death. In order for the survivor to perfect title to real estate, all the survivor need do is file a death certificate of the decedent.

(b) *Life insurance.* Life insurance proceeds of a policy on the decedent's life are paid by the insurance company to the beneficiary named in the insurance contract. The company will pay upon receipt of a death certificate of the insured.

(c) *Contracts with payable-on-death provisions.* Decedent may have a contract with a bank, an employer, or some other person or corporation to distribute the property held under the contract at the decedent's death to a named beneficiary. Pension plans often provide survivor benefits. Tax-deferred investment plans (IRAs, Keoghs, and the like) often name a death beneficiary. In many states, it is possible to put a death beneficiary on stock custodian accounts held in a brokerage firm. To collect property held under a payable-on-death contract, all the beneficiary need do is file a death certificate with the custodian holding the property. See infra pages 331-344 for a full discussion of payable-on-death contracts, which are not valid in some states.

(d) *Interests in trust.* When property is transferred in trust, the trustee holds the property for the benefit of the named beneficiaries, who may have life estates or remainders or other types of interests. The property is distributed to the beneficiaries by the trustee in accordance with the terms of the trust instrument. The trust may have been created by the decedent during life or by some other person. If created by the decedent, the trust may be revocable or irrevocable. Revocable trusts are valid in all states. If the decedent has a testamentary power of appointment over assets in the trust, the decedent's will must be admitted to probate, but the trust assets are distributed directly by the trustee to the beneficiaries named in the will and do not go through probate.

As indicated above, distribution of nonprobate assets does not involve a court proceeding, but is made in accordance with the terms of a contract or trust or deed. Distribution of probate assets under a will or to intestate successors may require a court proceeding involving probate of a will or a finding of intestacy followed by appointment of a personal representative to settle the probate estate. See John H. Langbein, The Nonprobate Revolution and the Future of the Law of Succession, 97 Harv. L. Rev. 1108 (1984).

Nonprobate transfers are dealt with in Chapter 5 of this book.

2.   Administration of Probate Estates

a.   History and Terminology

When a person dies, and probate is necessary, the first step is the appointment of a *personal representative* to oversee the winding up of the decedent's affairs. The principal duties of the personal representative are (1) to inventory and collect the assets of the decedent, (2) to manage the assets during administration, (3) to receive and pay the claims of creditors and tax collectors, and (4) to distribute the remaining assets to those entitled. If the decedent dies testate and in the will names the person who is to execute (i.e., carry out the terms of) the will and administer the probate estate, such personal representative is called an *executor*. When the person in charge of administering the estate is not named in the will, the personal representative is called an *administrator*. Personal representatives are appointed by, under the control of, and accountable to a court, generally referred to as a probate court.

One of the advantages of writing a will is that the testator can designate who is to administer the estate.[5] If a person dies intestate or leaves a will that fails to name an executor who qualifies, the administrator is selected from a statutory list of persons who are to be given preference, typically in the following order: surviving spouse, children, parents, siblings, creditors.

The person appointed as administrator must give bond. In most states, if the will names an individual rather than a corporate fiduciary as executor, the executor also must give bond unless the will waives the bond requirement. Thus, another reason for writing a will is that the requirement and expense of a fiduciary bond can be eliminated if that appears desirable.

Historically, in England, three courts had jurisdiction over probate. The king's common law courts controlled succession to land, which was the base of power in the feudal system. The ecclesiastical courts controlled succession to personal property, which, before the time of the Tudors and the rise of England as a trading power, was of little value (cows, sheep, utensils, personal ornaments, and such made up the personal property of medieval life). During the course of the sixteenth century, after Henry VIII's break with Rome, the ecclesiastical courts declined drastically in power. When Parliament attempted to strengthen the ecclesiastical courts a hundred years later by enacting the Statute of Distributions (1670), it was too late. A basic shift in the public's attitude toward the proper role of the church in secular affairs had already occurred, and the common law courts and chancery continued to impede the clergy's control of administration of personal property. With its flexible procedure and its power to enforce personal duties, chancery gradually took over the administration of personal property. Ecclesiastical jurisdiction over decedents' estates was finally abolished in 1857, when a court of probate was established in chancery. However, the common law courts' jurisdiction

---

5. In a number of states, nonresident corporate fiduciaries cannot be appointed as executor, and in a few states this prohibition extends to nonresident individuals. These restrictions have been held constitutional. In re Estate of Greenberg, 390 So. 2d 40 (Fla. 1980), appeal dismissed, 450 U.S. 961 (1981).

over the succession to land continued. Not until 1925, with the Administration of Estates Act, was one English court given sole jurisdiction over succession to real and personal property.

Today, in this country, one court in each county has jurisdiction over administration of decedents' estates. The name of the court varies from state to state. It may be called the surrogate's court, the orphan's court, the probate division of the district court or chancery court, or something else. But all of these differently named courts are referred to collectively as probate courts. And "to go through probate" means to have an estate administered in one of these courts.

One needlessly complicating factor in this field is that we have two legal vocabularies — one applicable to real property, the other to personal property. It is often suggested that these parallel vocabularies are traceable to the historic fact that the English common law courts had jurisdiction over succession to real property whereas ecclesiastical courts controlled succession to personal property in England until the nineteenth century. But in most instances this is not provable. Take *last will and testament*. A common belief is that this phrase arose because a *will* disposed of real property and a *testament* disposed of personal property; therefore one instrument disposing of both was a will and testament. The belief that *testament* referred to personal property is based on its Latin origin (testamentum). It is assumed that the Latin-trained ecclesiastical courts introduced *testament* into the language to refer to an instrument disposing of property over which they had jurisdiction. It is then assumed that *will*, an old English word, was used by the common law courts and by a process of association came to relate to the type of property over which these courts had jurisdiction. The evidence does not support these assumptions. As far back as the records go, the words have been used interchangeably. To speak of a testament disposing of land, or of a will disposing of a cow, would not have sounded strange to the medieval ear. Professor Mellinkoff believes the phrase *last will and testament* is traceable to the law's habit of doubling Old English words with synonyms of Old French or Latin origin (e.g., had and received, mind and memory, free and clear), "helped along by a distinctive rhythm." David Mellinkoff, The Language of the Law 331 (1963). In any case, the myth that a will disposes of land and a testament disposes of chattels dies terribly, terribly slowly. Today, it is perfectly proper to use the single word will to refer to an instrument disposing of both real and personal property.

A person dying testate *devises* real property to *devisees* and *bequeaths* personal property to *legatees*. Using devise to refer to land and bequest to refer to personalty became a lawyerly custom little more than a hundred years ago,[6] although the distinction, like that between will and testament, is sometimes erroneously thought to have had more ancient roots in the different courts handling the decedent's property. Although these linguistic distinctions still have currency, there are signs that synonymous usage is returning in respectable circles. The Restatement of Property applies devise to both realty and personalty. In drafting wills, "I give" is an excellent substitute for "I devise," "I bequeath," and "I give, devise, and bequeath." "I give" will effectively transfer any kind of property, and no fly-specking lawyer can ever fault you for using the wrong verb.

When intestacy occurs we use different words to describe what happens to the intestate's real property and what happens to his personal property. We say real property *descends to heirs;* personal property is *distributed to next-of-kin.* At common law, heirs and next-of-kin were not necessarily the same. For example, when primogeniture, which applied only to land, was in effect, real property descended to the eldest son, but personal property was distributed equally among all the children. Today, in almost all states, a single *statute of descent and distribution* governs intestacy. The same persons are named as intestate successors to both real and personal property. Thus, today the word *heirs* usually means those persons designated by the applicable statute to take a decedent's intestate property real and personal. *Next-of-kin* usually means exactly the same thing.

At common law, a spouse was not an heir; he or she had only curtesy or dower rights. Today, in all states the statutes of descent and distribution name the spouse as a possible intestate successor, depending upon who else survives, and a spouse thus may be an heir.

In this book, we do not use the Latin suffix indicating feminine gender for women playing important roles in our cast: Testator, executor, and administrator. Although testatrix, executrix, and administratrix are still in current fashion, other -*trix* forms either have disappeared from use (e.g., donatrix, creditrix)[7] or would sound odd to the contemporary ear (e.g., public administratrix). And of course it does not matter whether the person in the given role is a man or a woman.[8] We have tried to avoid words that assign a role to one sex, but we dare not hope that we have succeeded in a field so long dominated by assumptions of male superiority in property management. We believe it was Bentham who observed, "Error is never so difficult to be destroyed as when it has its root in language."

---

6. Cf. William Shakespeare, King John, act I, scene 1, line 109: "Upon his deathbed he by will bequeath'd/His lands to me. . . ."

7. See -*trix* in Oxford English Dictionary (1989).

8. The Supreme Court has held unconstitutional a statute giving preference to a male to serve as executor or administrator. Reed v. Reed, 404 U.S. 71 (1971).

b. A Summary of Probate Procedure

(1) Opening probate

Though the general pattern of administering decedents' probate estates is quite similar in all jurisdictions, there are widespread variations in the procedural details. In each state, the procedure is governed by a collection of statutes and court rules giving meticulous instructions for each step in the process. Happily, this precludes our being concerned about specific rules and procedures and enables us to advise you that you can safely postpone any concern about the mechanics of probating a will and administering an estate until you can "learn by doing" when that first estate file comes across your desk. When that day comes, you will find that there are available in most jurisdictions excellent probate practice books, which will be of assistance. The purpose of the following description is to provide background information necessary for estate planning.

Probate performs three functions: (1) it provides evidence of transfer of title to the new owners by a probated will or decree of intestate succession; (2) it protects creditors by requiring payment of debts; and (3) it distributes the decedent's property to those intended after the creditors are paid. Probate procedures are designed with these functions in mind.

The will should first be probated, or letters of administration should first be sought, in the jurisdiction where the decedent was domiciled at the time of death. This is known as the *primary* or *domiciliary* jurisdiction. If real property is located in another jurisdiction, *ancillary administration* in the jurisdiction is required. The purpose of requiring ancillary administration is to prove title to real property in the situs state's recording system and to subject those assets to probate for the protection of local creditors. Ancillary administration may be costly because the state may require that a resident be appointed personal representative, with a local attorney. Executor's commissions and attorney's fees will be paid to them on the value of the ancillary assets; the domiciliary representative and attorney also are entitled to fees based on the ancillary assets.

Each state has a detailed statutory procedure for issuance of *letters testamentary* to an executor or *letters of administration* to an administrator authorizing the person to act on behalf of the estate. Several states, mainly east of the Mississippi, follow the procedure formerly used by the English ecclesiastical courts in distinguishing between contentious and noncontentious probate proceedings. Under the English system, the executor had a choice of probating a will *in common form* or *in solemn form.* Common form probate was an ex parte proceeding in which no notice or process was issued to any person. Due execution of the will was proved by the oath of the executor or such other witnesses as might be required. The will was admitted to probate at once, letters testamentary were granted, and the executor began administration of the estate. If no one raised any questions or objections, this procedure sufficed. However, within a period of years thereafter an interested party could file a caveat, compelling probate of the will in solemn form. Under probate in solemn form, notice to interested parties was given by citation, due execution of the will was proved by the testimony of the attesting witnesses, and administration of the estate involved greater court participation. Ex parte or common form procedure is recognized in many states, sometimes preserving the common form/solemn form terminology, but more often not.

The majority of states do not permit ex parte proceedings but require prior notice to interested parties before the appointment of a personal representative or probate of a will. In these states, the petition for letters must be accompanied by an affidavit stating that the statutory notice requirements have been met (personal service, mailing, or publishing). At the hearing, if a will is to be probated, it must be proved by the testimony or affidavits of the witnesses. The hearing may be before the probate judge or a clerk.

The Uniform Probate Code, originally promulgated in 1969 and revised in 1990, and adopted in a number of states, is representative of statutes regulating probate procedures. It provides for both ex parte probate and notice probate. The former is called *informal probate* (rather than common form probate), the latter *formal probate* (rather than solemn form probate). The person asking for letters can choose informal or formal probate; the theory is that one may be more useful in a particular estate than another and a choice should be available. Uniform Probate Code §3-301 sets forth the requirements for informal probate. Without giving notice to anyone, the representative petitions for appointment; the petition contains pertinent information about the decedent and the names and addresses of the spouse, the children or other heirs, and, if a will is involved, the devisees. If the petition is for probate of a will, the original will must accompany the petition; the executor swears that, to the best of his or her knowledge, the will was validly executed; proof by the witnesses is not required. A will that appears to have the required signatures and that contains an attestation clause showing that requirements of execution have been met is probated by the registrar without further proof. UPC §3-303. Within 30 days after appointment, the personal representative has the duty of mailing notice to every interested person, including heirs apparently disinherited by a will. UPC §3-705.

Formal probate under the Uniform Probate Code is a judicial determination *after notice* to interested parties. Any interested party can demand formal probate. A formal proceeding may be used to probate a will, to block an informal proceeding, or to secure a declaratory judgment of intestacy. Formal proceedings become final judgments if not appealed.

No proceeding, formal or informal, may be initiated more than three years from the date of death. UPC §3-108. If no will is probated within three years after death, the presumption of intestacy is conclusive. The three-year statute of limitations of the Uniform Probate Code changes the common law, which permits a will to be probated at any time, perhaps many years after the testator's death. See Annot., 2 A.L.R.4th 1315 (1980).

For a description of estate administration under the Uniform Probate Code, see Paul G. Haskell, Preface to Wills, Trusts and Administration 181-224 (2d ed. 1994).

Time for contest. The time for contesting probate of a will is dependent upon a statute in the particular jurisdiction. The period of limitations for filing a will contest is ordinarily jurisdictional and is not tolled by any fact not provided by statute. If the constitutional and statutory requirements for notice are complied with, when the period of limitation passes, the probate court no longer has jurisdiction to revoke probate. Probate of a will thereby becomes final. See Larkin v. Ruffin, 398 So. 2d 676 (Ala. 1981) (holding order admitting will to probate cannot be set aside three-and-a-half years later when evidence is discovered showing will had been revoked).

Barring creditors of the decedent. Every state has a statute requiring creditors to file claims within a specified time period; claims filed thereafter are barred. These are known as "nonclaim statutes." They come in two basic forms: either (1) they bar claims not filed within a relatively short period after probate proceedings are begun (generally two to six months), or (2), whether or not probate proceedings are commenced, they bar claims not filed within a longer period after the decedent's death (generally one to five years). Under short-term statutes, creditors usually are notified of the requirement to file claims only by publication in a newspaper after probate proceedings are opened. The Supreme Court has held, however, that the Due Process Clause requires that known or reasonably ascertainable creditors receive actual notice before they are barred by a short-term statute running from the commencement of probate proceedings. Tulsa Professional Collection Services, Inc. v. Pope, 485 U.S. 478 (1988) (statute barring known creditors two months after newspaper publication objectionable). A one-year statute of limitations running from the decedent's death, barring creditors filing claims thereafter, is believed to be constitutional even without notice to creditors. Most states have such a statute. See, for example, Uniform Probate Code §3-803. See also Sarajane Love, Estate Creditors, the Constitution, and the Uniform Probate Code, 30 U. Rich. L. Rev. 411 (1996); Mark Reut-

hereby nominate, constitute and apoint   my wife Katie Jacks

f this my last will and testament,

REOF, I have hereunto set my hand and seal this
f _March_ 1951.A.D.

_____ _JoeJacksn_ _____

, published and declared as and for his last will and
Joe Jaskson   in the presence of us, present at the
, at his request, in his presence and in the presence an
e of each other, have hereunto subscribed our names as
lay and year last above set forth.

Joe Jackson's will signature

linger, State Action, Due Process, and the New Nonclaim Statutes:
Can No Notice be Good Notice if Some Notice is Not?, 24 Real Prop.,
Prob., & Tr. J. 433 (1990).

QUESTION

The original of a probated will is filed in the courthouse and kept
there indefinitely. Contrast the recording of deeds, where the clerk
files away a Xerox or photographic copy and returns the original
deed to the buyer. Now here's the question:

Shoeless Joe Jackson, who, together with seven of his Chicago White
Sox teammates, was barred from baseball for throwing the 1919 World
Series, was almost illiterate and rarely signed his name (his wife signed
baseballs for him). In 1991, one of his signatures, ripped from a lease
he signed in 1936, was sold by Sotheby's, the New York auction house,
for $23,100. Shoeless Joe died in 1951 with a probated will bequeath-
ing his property to his wife. She died in 1959, bequeathing all her
property to two charities. When the charities learn of the auction sale,
they petition the probate court for permission to withdraw the original will and substitute a Xerox copy. If permission is granted, the
charities plan to sell the signature on the original will at auction.
Should the petition be granted? American Heart Assn. v. County of
Greenville, 331 S.C. 498, 489 S.E.2d 921 (1997).

(2)   Supervising the representative's actions

In many states the actions of the personal representative in administering the estate are supervised by the court. This supervision can be time-consuming and costly. The court must approve the inventory and appraisal, payment of debts, family allowance, granting options on real estate, sale of real estate, borrowing of funds and mortgaging of property, leasing of property, proration of federal estate tax, personal representative's commissions, attorney's fees, preliminary and final distributions, and discharge of the personal representative. The sale of real estate may require several trips to the courthouse to get an order to sell, to file notice of all offers received, to give notice that a previous low bidder has overbid the previous high bid, and, finally, to get approval of the terms of the sale to the highest bidder.

In some states, the practice is for the personal representative to handle all these matters informally without court order, provided the interested parties are adults and will approve the fiduciary's account and release the fiduciary from liability. If minors are involved, judicial supervision is necessary.

The Uniform Probate Code authorizes unsupervised administration as well as supervised administration. If any interested party demands supervised administration, the probate court supervises the personal representative. But if no party demands it, administration is independent of the court. Under independent administration, after appointment, the personal representative administers the estate without going back into court. The representative has the broad powers of a trustee in dealing with the estate property and may collect assets, sell property, invest in other assets, pay creditors, continue any business of the decedent, and distribute the estate — all without court approval. UPC §3-715. The estate may be closed by the personal representative filing a sworn statement that he has published notice to creditors, administered the estate, paid all claims, and sent a statement and accounting to all known distributees. UPC §3-1003. If at any time during independent administration an interested party is dissatisfied with the personal representative's actions, he may compel the representative to obtain court supervision. UPC §3-501.

(3)   Closing the estate

The personal representative of an estate is expected to complete the administration and distribute the assets as promptly as possible. Even if all the beneficiaries are amicable, several things that must be done may prolong administration. Creditors must be paid. Taxes must be paid and tax returns audited and accepted by the appropriate tax authorities. Real estate or a sole proprietorship may have to be sold.

Judicial approval of the personal representative's action is required to relieve the representative from liability, unless some statute of limitations runs upon a cause of action against the representative. The representative is not discharged from fiduciary duties until the court grants discharge.

c. Is Probate Necessary?

Much is heard nowadays about the excessive cost of probate — or, as some have put it, the high cost of dying. The administrative costs of probate are mainly probate court fees, the commission of the personal representative, the attorney's fee, and sometimes appraiser's and guardian ad litem's fees. In most states, the personal representative's commission is set by statute at a fixed percentage of the probate estate. The fee of the attorney for the personal representative is sometimes set by statute, but more often it is determined by the court by reference to a number of factors (including customary charges for probate work, complexity of the estate, and time and labor required). These fees are deductible for federal estate tax or income tax purposes. Federal estate taxes begin on estates of $675,000 in the year 2000 (with the exemption rising to $1 million in 2006) with graduated rates from 37 percent to 55 percent. Hence, the net cost of probate fees in large estates may be substantially less than appears. See Robert A. Stein & Ian G. Fierstein, The Role of the Attorney in Estate Administration, 68 Minn. L. Rev. 1107 (1984).

In most jurisdictions a lawyer who serves as executor is entitled to fees for serving in both offices. See Estate of Hackett, 51 Ill. App. 3d 474, 366 N.E.2d 1103 (1977); cf. In re Estate of Waldman, 172 Misc. 2d 130, 658 N.Y.S.2d 565 (Sur. Ct. 1997) (for an attorney-executor to receive both full statutory executor's commission and attorney's fee, testator must execute written acknowledgment that attorney has disclosed the double fees; without the acknowledgment, the attorney is entitled only to one-half the statutory executor's commission and a reasonable legal fee). In a minority of jurisdictions, the lawyer who receives an executor's commission is not entitled to an attorney's fee as well. This is viewed as prohibited self-dealing by a fiduciary. See Cal. Prob. Code §10804 (1998). See William M. McGovern, Jr., Sheldon F. Kurtz & Jan E. Rein, Wills, Trusts and Estates §14.5 at 631 (1988).

Comparison of Probate Fees

	Fee for Estate of Indicated Value		
State	*$100,000*	*$300,000*	*$600,000*
California	$3,150	$ 7,150	$13,150
Florida	2,000	7,500	18,000
Georgia	2,500	7,500	12,000
Illinois	5,000	10,000	16,000
Michigan	3,000	7,000	10,000
New York	5,000	13,000	22,000
Ohio	3,000	6,000	10,000
Pennsylvania	5,000	13,000	22,000
Texas	3,000	7,000	9,000
Virginia	3,000	7,000	9,000

The above table is based on a study by the California Law Revision Commission of probate fees. Cal. L. Revision Commn. Rep. No. L-1036/1055, at 7, Oct. 26, 1988. The table assumes probate of a relatively simple estate with a house and no major valuation issues or disputes between persons interested in the estate. The estimated fees will be higher if complexities arise during probate. The fees will be lower if no real property is involved. The fees are for the estate attorney only, and do not include the executor's commission, which will be roughly the same amount.

In view of the costs of probate and the attendant delays, the question is often asked: Can probate be avoided? The answer is Yes, provided the property owner during life transfers all his or her property into a joint tenancy or a revocable or irrevocable trust or, in many states, executes a contract providing for distribution of contract assets to named beneficiaries on the owner's death. As you will discover later, however, as you study these will substitutes, it is quite difficult for a rich person with a wide variety of assets to dispose of all property by nonprobate methods. Some property is not suitable for joint tenancy or trust; most property is not subject to disposition by contract. And, in any case, a will serves a back-up function to catch overlooked property or property acquired after inter vivos changes in ownership have been made. Hence, even though a large portion of a person's assets can be arranged so as to avoid probate, probate administration may be necessary for some assets that pass by will or intestacy.

Nonetheless, even with property transferred by will or intestacy, probate is not always necessary. As a practical matter, establishment of the transferee's title is not necessary for many items of personal property, such as furniture or personal effects. A purchaser will assume that the possessor has title. But for items of personal property for which ownership is evidenced by a document, such as an automobile certificate of title or a stock certificate, the transferee needs some official recognition of his rights thereto in order to transfer those rights. Statutes in all states permit heirs to avoid probate where the amount of property involved is small, but the states differ as to what kind of, and how much, property can be transferred without a formal administration. Among statutes commonly found are statutes permitting collection of small bank accounts or wage claims, or transfer of an automobile certificate of title to the decedent's heirs, upon affidavit by the heirs. By filling out the appropriate forms and presenting them to the bank, the employer, or the department of motor vehicles, the heir is able to collect the decedent's property or acquire a new certificate of title.

In addition, many states permit close relatives of the decedent to obtain possession of the decedent's personal property by presenting an affidavit to the holder of the property if the estate does not exceed a certain figure. The figure defining a *small estate,* which can be collected upon affidavit, ranges from $5,000 to $100,000. The affidavit procedure authorized by these *collection statutes* does not give title to the recipient of the property, only possession. It merely permits those presumptively entitled to the decedent's property to collect it expeditiously and without a cumbersome estate proceeding. Possession of some types of property is tantamount to ownership.

Finally, statutes in some states permit filing a will for probate solely as a title document, with no formal administration to follow. And in some states title insurance companies will insure real property sold by heirs if a certificate of death and affidavit of heirship is filed; probate proceedings are not required.

A recent study of five states found that the percentage of decedents' estates that underwent probate administration ranged from 20 percent in California to 34 percent in Massachusetts. Robert A. Stein & Ian G. Fierstein, The Demography of Probate Administration, 15 U. Balt. L. Rev. 54 (1985). Thus, by one way or another, the large majority of decedents manage to avoid probate.

PROBLEMS

1. Aaron Green died three weeks ago. His wife has come to your law firm with Green's will in hand: The will devises Green's entire estate "to my wife, Martha, if she survives me; otherwise to my chil-

dren in equal shares." The will names Martha Green as executor. An interview with Mrs. Green reveals that the Green family consists of two adult sons and several grandchildren and that Green owned the following property:

Furniture, furnishings, other items of tangible personal property (estimated value)	$10,000
Savings account in name of Aaron Green	5,000
Joint checking account on which Aaron and Martha Green were both authorized to write checks	1,500
Employer's pension plan, naming Martha Green for survivor's benefits	Life Annuity
Government bonds, payable to "Aaron or Martha Green"	5,000
Ordinary life insurance policy naming Martha Green as primary beneficiary	25,000
Ford car	7,500

Green owned no real property; he and his wife lived in a rented apartment. Green's debts consisted of last month's utility bills ($40) plus the usual consumer charge accounts: Visa card ($300 balance), the local department store ($125), Exxon ($35). There is also a funeral bill ($1,225) and the cost of a cemetery lot ($300). Mrs. Green wants your advice: What should she do with the will? Must it be offered for probate? Must there be an administration of her husband's estate?

2. Same facts as in Problem 1 except that Green died intestate, and the state's statute of descent and distribution provides that where a decedent is survived by a spouse and children, one-half of his real and personal property shall descend to the spouse, and the remaining one-half shall descend to the children.

3. Same facts as in Problem 1 except that Green also owned a house and lot worth $85,000 and another lot worth $8,000. The deeds to both tracts name Aaron Green as grantee. The residential property is subject to a mortgage with a current balance of $42,000; title to the other lot is free of encumbrances. Must (should?) Green's will be probated and his estate formally administered?

4. Let us look at Aaron Green's problem from another perspective. Suppose Green comes to you and tells you that he does not have a will. He describes his family situation and the assets owned by him: the assets listed in Problem 1 but not the real estate described in Problem 3. His question: In view of his family situation and his modest estate, does he really need a will?

d. Universal Succession

The English system of court-supervised administration of estates, which we inherited, was designed to protect creditors and to protect beneficiaries from an untrustworthy executor or heir. On the continent of Europe and in Louisiana, an entirely different system exists, which rarely involves a court at all. It is known as *universal succession*, meaning that the heirs or the residuary devisees succeed to the title of all of the decedent's property; there is no personal representative appointed by a court.

The heirs or the residuary devisees step into the shoes of the decedent at the decedent's death, taking the decedent's title and assuming all the decedent's liabilities and the obligation of paying legacies according to the decedent's will. If, for example, *O* dies intestate, leaving *H* as *O*'s heir, *H* succeeds to ownership of *O*'s property and must pay all of *O*'s creditors and any taxes resulting from *O*'s death. If *O* has three heirs, they hold as tenants in common at *O*'s death, with the ordinary rights of tenants in common. The payment of a commission to a fiduciary is not necessary, and a lawyer need not be employed unless the heirs decide they need legal advice. A system of universal succession can have enormous advantages where the heirs or the residuary devisees are all adults. See European Succession Laws (David Hayton ed. 1998).

The Uniform Probate Code authorizes universal succession as an alternative to probate administration. Under UPC §§3-312 to 3-322, the heirs or the residuary devisees may petition the court for universal succession. If the court ascertains that the necessary parties are included and that the estate is not subject to any current contest or difficulty, it issues a written statement of universal succession. The universal successors then have full power of ownership to deal with the assets of the estate. They assume the liabilities of the decedent to creditors, including tax liability. The successors are personally liable to other heirs omitted from the petition or, in the case of residuary devisees, to other devisees for the amount of property due them. No state has yet adopted these provisions of the UPC. See Eugene F. Scoles, Succession Without Administration: Past and Future, 48 Mo. L. Rev. 371 (1983).

Universal succession is already available to a limited extent in the United States. Under California law, property that passes to the surviving spouse by intestacy or by will is not subject to administration unless the surviving spouse elects to have it administered. If the surviving spouse chooses not to have the property administered, the surviving spouse takes title to the property and assumes personal liability for the decedent's debts chargeable against the property. Cal. Prob. Code §§13500-13650 (1998). This exemption from probate raises an interesting question: If probate is not necessary for property passing to a surviving spouse, why is it necessary for property passing to adult children?

SECTION C.   AN ESTATE PLANNING PROBLEM

1.   *The Client's Letter and Its Enclosures*

January 15, 20 —

Dear _____:

For some time now, Wendy and I have been considering the rewriting of our wills since we now have very simple wills giving our property to each other in case of death and then to our children when the survivor of us dies. However, in this day of air crashes where Wendy and I might die simultaneously, the problems of settling our estate might be complicated.

These, in general, are the assets with which we are concerned:

Residence	cost $125,000	($70,000 mtge.)
Lot, cabin, Lake Murray, ME	cost 20,000	worth more
Chevrolet station wagon	5,000	
Honda	3,000	
Household furniture, etc.	???	
Checking account	2,000 to 4,000	
Savings account	7,000	
Certificate of deposit	20,000	
IRA	30,000	
Stocks	170,000	
Mutual funds	70,000	
My life insurance	125,000	
Wendy's life insurance	100,000	
Mother's house at death	???	
Pension	???	

Wendy and I think our main objectives should be to avoid probate and to eliminate as many inheritance taxes as possible. I am enclosing copies of our present wills. These are some of the questions we would like your help on:

1.   It may be that we do not need wills at all. Can we let our property pass by inheritance or by joint and survivor arrangements? Our bank accounts and some of our stocks are set up to pass by a joint and survivor arrangement.

2.   As a sort of corollary to that first question, we have read in various places that it would be a good idea to set up a living trust to pass our house, cars, etc. With the use of a trust plus the joint and survivor arrangements, could we avoid the need for wills and probate entirely?

3. If you think we should have wills, are our present ones all right?
If not, how should they be changed?

Please let us hear from you at your earliest convenience.

Sincerely yours,

/s/ Howard Brown
Howard Brown

Last Will and Testament of Howard Brown

I, Howard Brown, of the city of Arlington, County of _____,
and State of _____, do hereby make, publish, and declare
this to be my Last Will and Testament, hereby revoking any and all
other wills and codicils thereto, which I have heretofore made.

FIRST: I hereby direct that all of my just debts, funeral expenses,
and expenses of administration of my estate be paid out of my estate
as soon as may be practicable after my death.

SECOND: I name and appoint my wife, Wendy Brown, to be the
executor of this my Last Will and Testament, and I direct that she
not be required to give bond or other security.

THIRD: I give my remainder interest in my mother's house at 423
Elm St., Concord, Delaware, to my sister, Carol Gould.

FOURTH: I give, devise, and bequeath all the rest of my property,
both real and personal, of whatever kind and nature and description,
and wherever located, which I now own or may own at the time of
my death, to my wife, Wendy Brown, should she survive me. Should
she not survive me, I then give, devise, and bequeath all of my property, to my children.

FIFTH: I authorize and empower my Executor, or anyone appointed to administer this my Last Will and Testament, to sell and
convert into cash any and all of my personal property without a court
order and to convey any such real estate by deed without the necessity
of a court order authorizing such conveyance or approving such deed.

SIXTH: In the event that my wife, Wendy Brown, predeceases me,
I name and appoint my wife's sister, Lucy Preston Lipman, of San
Francisco, California, as legal guardian of my children during their
respective minorities.

IN TESTIMONY WHEREOF I have hereunto set my hand and seal
this 27th day of November, 1995.

/s/ Howard Brown
Howard Brown

The above instrument, consisting of two typewritten pages, of which this is the second, with paragraphs FIRST through SIXTH, inclusive, was on the 27th day of November, 1995, signed by Howard Brown, in our presence, and he did then declare this to be his Last Will and Testament, and we at his request and in his presence and in the presence of each other, did sign this instrument as witnesses thereunto and as witnesses to his signature thereto.

WITNESSES:

_____ */s/ Michael Wong* _____

_____ */s/ Patricia Muñoz Garcia* _____

[Wendy Brown's will contains reciprocal provisions, with the exception of the remainder interest in Howard's mother's house. Wendy leaves everything of hers to Howard if he survives and if he does not survive her to her children.]

2. Some Preliminary Questions Raised by Brown's Letter

From time to time, we shall refer back to the Brown estate planning situation in the context of the substantive areas being considered. But before we embark on our studies, it may be profitable to reflect on some of the questions raised in, and by, Brown's letter.

PROBLEMS

1. Examine Howard Brown's present will in the context of the asset and family situation described in his letter. Can you detect any problems that may be raised, or any contingencies that are not provided for, by the will provisions? Here are a few:

Article FIRST: Does the "just debts" clause require the executor to pay off the mortgage on the Browns' home? Would this be desirable? See In re Estate of Miller, 127 F. Supp. 23 (D.D.C. 1955); In re Estate of Keil, 51 Del. 351, 145 A.2d 563 (1958); Annot., 4 A.L.R.3d 1023, §14 (1965). See also discussion of exoneration of liens, infra page 468.

Would death taxes incurred at Howard Brown's death be "just debts," making this a tax apportionment clause requiring payment of all taxes, including those on the remainder interest in his mother's house, out of Howard's residuary estate? See Thompson v. Thompson, 230 S.W.2d 376, 380 (Tex. Civ. App. 1950); Estate of Kyreazis, 701 P.2d 1022 (N.M. App. 1985); Internal Revenue Code of 1986, §§2206, 2207.

Articles SECOND and FIFTH: Has suitable provision been made for appointment of an executor in case Wendy Brown dies before Howard? Does the executor have sufficiently broad powers to enable her to administer the estate effectively?

Article FOURTH: Is the dispositive plan provided by Howard's will a sound one? Should he make an outright distribution of his entire estate to Wendy, or should he consider making some other distribution?

Which of the assets listed in Howard Brown's letter will be governed by his will, and which will pass as nonprobate assets unaffected by the will?

Article SIXTH: If both Howard and Wendy Brown die before all their children attain majority, a guardianship administration will be required. Is this desirable? See infra page 132.

2. In view of the Browns' asset and family situation, do they need wills at all? Will the intestacy laws of their home state provide a satisfactory distributive scheme for their assets at death?

Should the Browns consider alternatives to a will or intestacy, such as joint and survivor arrangements and inter vivos trusts, as a means of transferring their property at death?

Perhaps it has occurred to you by now that we don't really know very much about the Brown family or the assets they own. Without further information, we cannot answer these questions. What further information should we obtain from the clients before we can proceed further?

3.   Additional Data on the Browns' Family and Assets

Following receipt of the letter from Howard Brown asking for a review of the present wills of Howard and Wendy Brown, a conference was held with the clients, and the following additional information was obtained.

a.   Family Data

Members of Immediate Family		Age	Birth Date	Health
Husband	Howard Brown	43	7/12/ —	good
Wife	Wendy Brown	41	6/1/ —	"
Child of Wendy	Michael Walker	20	9/25/ —	"
Child	Sarah Brown	14	11/19/ —	"
Child	Stephanie Brown	11	8/22/ —	"

Michael is Wendy's son by her first husband, Brian Walker, whom Wendy divorced when Michael was three years old. A year later, Wendy and Howard married, and Howard has raised Michael as a member of his family, though never formally adopting him. Brian stopped making child support payments a couple of years after the divorce and moved out of state. He has not been heard from in many years. Michael has left home and is living with (but not married to) an older woman, Candace Robinson, age 33. They have a child, Andy, age 1.

Howard Brown is an industrial design engineer and manager of a department at Tresco Machine Tool Company in Arlington. He has been with this firm for the past eight years and feels that he has a secure and responsible position with the firm. His annual salary is $70,000.

Wendy Brown has a degree in Modern Languages and during the early years of their marriage taught German and French at a secondary school in Arlington. She then worked for several years only in the home. Four years ago Wendy decided to go to law school. Last year she finished law school and received a J.D. degree. (She did *not* take a course in wills and trusts.) Wendy has just accepted a position as an associate of Hanlon and Putz, a medium-size law firm. Her annual salary is $55,000.

Residence

Home address: 2220 Casino Lane, Arlington. 477-5882
Period of residence in this state: all of life since college.
Note: No problems regarding domicile. Also, note that none of present assets acquired while residing in another state. Howard owns out-of-state property — a lot in Maine and a remainder interest in his mother's house in Delaware.

Parents; collateral relatives

Howard's parents. Howard Brown's father, Frank, died of a heart attack at age 60. His mother, Margaret Brown, a widow, is 63 years old, is in good health, and lives in Concord, Delaware. Howard stated that his mother has a modest but comfortable income from property left by her husband and from social security. Howard says his father devised his home to his wife Margaret for life, and on her death to Howard and his sister Carol Gould.

Howard estimated that his mother owns property worth about $240,000, of which $75,000 is represented by her residence. Howard is familiar with the terms of his mother's will; it provides for an equal distribution between himself and Carol Gould. Howard is named as executor under the will.

Howard's collateral relatives. Howard has a younger sister, Carol Gould, who is a police officer with the Concord police department. Carol is divorced and lives with her mother; Carol has no children.

Wendy's parents. Wendy Brown's parents (Robert Preston, age 65, and Zoë Preston, age 62) are both living. Wendy stated that her father is a well-known doctor in Boston and is quite well off. When asked how well off, Wendy said he is probably "worth" around $500,000 (probably a conservative estimate). Wendy may acquire a substantial inheritance upon the death of her parents.

Wendy's collateral relatives. Wendy Brown's siblings: one sister, Lucy Preston Lipman, a writer, lives in San Francisco with her husband, Jonathan Lipman. They have two children. Her brother, Simon Preston, is married to Antonia Preston, has no children, and is a salesman. Her other sister, Ruth Preston, unmarried, is a professor of archeology at Swarthmore.

Wendy Brown also has a maternal aunt, Fanny Fox of Lexington, Kentucky. Aunt Fanny is a rich widow without children and has a large house full of antiques, paintings, silver — things she and her husband collected during their marriage. Wendy will likely inherit some of Aunt Fanny's things and possibly a substantial sum of money.

Special family problems

Michael is a stepchild of Howard. Michael has an out-of-wedlock child, Andy.

b. Assets

The Browns have lived in Arlington since they were married 16 years ago. Since neither brought into the marriage any property of substantial value, there appears to be no problem in establishing their marital rights in the property they now own. All life insurance policies were taken out after the Browns married.

Tangible personal property

Tangible personalty consists of the usual furnishings in a family residence, two automobiles, outboard motor boat, personal effects such as clothing and jewelry, and other miscellaneous items. No items of unusual value. Estimated value: $20,000

Real estate

(1) Family residence. The Browns purchased their home at 2220 Casino Lane, Arlington, 15 years ago. Although the purchase price for the property was $125,000, Howard believes that it is now worth around $160,000, but this is a guesstimate. Present balance on mortgage loan (note held by Arlington Federal Savings & Loan Assn.) is $70,000. The deed shows that title to the property was taken by "Howard Brown and Wendy Brown, as joint tenants with right of survivorship and not as tenants in common." $160,000

(2) Lot and cabin, Lake Murray, Maine. Twelve years ago the Browns purchased a lot and cabin on Lake Murray for $20,000. Title to the land was taken in Howard Brown's name alone. Based on current values, the Browns believe they could sell the property for at least $75,000. No mortgage indebtedness. 75,000

(3) Mother's house. Howard has a remainder interest in 423 Elm St., Concord, Delaware, with his sister. House worth about $75,000. Howard's remainder roughly valued at $20,000. 20,000

Bank accounts

(1) Checking account, Arlington National Bank. The account balance fluctuates from around $2,000 to $4,000 each month. Howard and Wendy Brown are both authorized to draw checks on the account; the balance is payable to the survivor. $ 3,000

(2) Savings account, Arlington Federal Savings & Loan Assn. The account is in the name of Wendy Brown. 7,000

(3) Certificate of deposit, Arlington Federal Savings & Loan Assn. at 6 percent for four years. CD was issued in the name of "Howard Brown and Wendy Brown, as joint tenants with right of survivorship."   20,000

(4) IRA (Individual Retirement Account), Arlington Federal Savings & Loan Assn. Established by Howard Brown in 1990. Income taxes on contributions are deferred until the money is withdrawn or Howard reaches 70½ or sooner dies. Current balance is $30,000. If Howard dies before withdrawal, balance is payable to Wendy Brown.   30,000

Securities

(1) 1,600 shares, General Corporation common stock. Given to Howard under his aunt's will six years ago. Current value: $50 per share. Registered in the name of Howard Brown as owner. $80,000

(2) 1,000 shares, Varoom Mutual Fund. When Howard's father died five years ago, his mother gave each of her children $7,500. Howard used all of this money to purchase 400 shares of the Varoom Fund, which has appreciated in value since his purchase. Howard has reinvested the ordinary income and capital gains dividends paid by the fund and now owns an additional 600 shares. Present value is $30 per share. Registered in the name of Howard Brown as owner.   30,000

(3) 1,000 shares, American Growth Mutual Fund. Over the years the Browns have invested in the American Growth Fund under some form of monthly investment plan. Their objective was to establish an educational fund for their children. The purchase price has fluctuated over the years from $28 to $42 a share. Present price is $40 a share. Howard says that he has kept records on the price of the shares as purchased. Registered in the name of "Howard Brown and Wendy Brown, as joint tenants with right of survivorship and not as tenants in common."   40,000

(4) 1,200 shares, Union National Bank common stock. Was given to Wendy Brown by her parents. Registered in the name of Wendy Brown as owner.   90,000

Life insurance

(1) Mutual of New York policy #624-05-91, ordinary
life, participating, acquired 14 years ago. Annual premium $2,050. Cash surrender value this year $20,500;
CSV is increasing at about $1,600/year. $100,000
    (2) Aetna Life Group policy, group term. Premiums
are paid by Howard Brown's employer.   25,000
    (3) Prudential Life policy, group term. Premiums
are paid by Wendy Brown's employers.   100,000

Policies (1) and (2) name Howard Brown as "insured" and
"owner." The policies name Wendy Brown as primary beneficiary and
the estate of Howard Brown as contingent beneficiary. Policy (3)
names Wendy Brown as "insured" and "owner." The policy names
Howard Brown as beneficiary. It names Wendy's children as secondary
beneficiaries.

Employee benefits of Howard Brown

In addition to the group insurance mentioned above, Howard
Brown's employer provides medical insurance, disability insurance,
and a qualified pension plan. The plan will provide substantial retirement benefits to Howard, under a formula based on his years of
service and his average annual salary. The present projection is that
Howard would be able to retire at age 65 with an annuity of about
$45,000.

The pension plan provides survivor benefits for the surviving
spouse. If Howard survives to retirement age, the pension is payable
as a joint and survivor annuity to Howard and his surviving spouse.

Employee benefits of Wendy Brown

In addition to the group insurance mentioned above, Wendy's law
firm, Hanlon and Putz, provides group medical coverage. There are
no pension benefits for associates, only for partners. Wendy Brown
has been in practice for only a month. It is likely that her income
will substantially exceed Howard's in a few years.

c.   Liabilities

Real estate mortgages: $70,000 mortgage loan, Arlington Federal Sav-
ings & Loan Assn.

Other notes to banks, etc.: None.
Loans on insurance policies: None.
Accounts to others: "Usual" store, etc. accounts.
Other: None.

d.   Assets and Liabilities: Summary

(1) Estate of Howard and Wendy Brown[9]	
Tangible personalty	$20,000
Realty:	
Residence (joint tenancy)	160,000
Lake Murray property (in Howard's name)	75,000
Remainder interest in mother's home (Howard)	20,000*
Bank accounts:	
Checking (joint and survivor)	3,000
Savings (in Wendy's name)	7,000
Certificate of deposit (joint tenancy)	20,000
IRA (Howard's, payable on death to Wendy)	30,000
Securities:	
Varoom Mutual Fund (in Howard's name)	30,000*
General Corp. common (in Howard's name)	80,000*
American Growth Mutual Fund (joint tenancy)	40,000
Union Natl. Bank common (in Wendy's name)	90,000*
Life insurance on Howard	125,000
Life insurance on Wendy	100,000
Tresco pension plan (Howard's contributions)	10,000
	$810,000
(2) Liabilities	
Mortgage loan, Arlington Federal Savings & Loan Assn.	$ 70,000
(3) Other factors:	

Probable inheritance by Howard Brown of about $120,000 from his mother. Probability of substantial inheritance by Wendy Brown from her parents and her Aunt Fanny — but

---

9.   Items marked by asterisk were acquired by gift or inheritance from Howard's and Wendy's respective relatives. All other assets are attributable to Howard Brown's earnings during their marriage. In a community property state, property acquired with a spouse's earnings is community property unless the spouses have changed it into another form of ownership.

no knowledge of whether this would be outright or in some form of trust arrangement.

4.   Professional Responsibility

Simpson v. Calivas
Supreme Court of New Hampshire, 1994
139 N.H. 1, 650 A.2d 318

HORTON, J.   The plaintiff, Robert H. Simpson, Jr., appeals from a directed verdict, grant of summary judgment, and dismissal of his claims against the lawyer who drafted his father's will. The plaintiff's action, sounding in both negligence and breach of contract, alleged that the defendant, Christopher Calivas, failed to draft a will which incorporated the actual intent of Robert H. Simpson, Sr. to leave all his land to the plaintiff in fee simple. Sitting with a jury, the Superior Court (Dickson, J.) directed a verdict for the defendant based on the plaintiff's failure to introduce any evidence on . . . breach of duty. The trial court also granted summary judgment on collateral estoppel grounds based on findings of the Strafford County Probate Court and dismissed the action, ruling that under New Hampshire law an attorney who drafts a will owes no duty to intended beneficiaries. We reverse and remand.

In March 1984, Robert H. Simpson, Sr. (Robert Sr.) executed a will that had been drafted by the defendant. The will left all real estate to the plaintiff except for a life estate in "our homestead located at Piscataqua Road, Dover, New Hampshire," which was left to Robert Sr.'s second wife, Roberta C. Simpson (stepmother). After Robert Sr.'s death in September 1985, the plaintiff and his stepmother filed a joint petition in the Strafford County Probate Court seeking a determination, essentially, of whether the term "homestead" referred to all the decedent's real property on Piscataqua Road (including a house, over one hundred acres of land, and buildings used in the family business), or only to the house (and, perhaps, limited surrounding acreage). The probate court found the term "homestead" ambiguous, and in order to aid construction, admitted some extrinsic evidence of the testator's surrounding circumstances, including evidence showing a close relationship between Robert Sr. and plaintiff's stepmother. The probate court, however, did not admit notes taken by the defendant during consultations with Robert Sr. that read: "House to wife as a life estate remainder to son, Robert H. Simpson, Jr. . . . Remaining land . . . to son Robert A. [sic] Simpson, Jr." The probate court construed the will to provide Roberta with a life estate

in all the real property. After losing the will construction action —
then two years after his father's death — the plaintiff negotiated with
his stepmother to buy out her life estate in all the real property for
$400,000.

The plaintiff then brought this malpractice action, pleading a contract count, based on third-party beneficiary theory, and a negligence
count. . . .

The plaintiff raises . . . [these] issues on appeal: (1) whether the
trial court erred in ruling that under New Hampshire law a drafting
attorney owes no duty to an intended beneficiary; (2) whether the
trial court erred in ruling that the findings of the probate court
on testator intent collaterally estopped the plaintiff from bringing a
malpractice action. . . .

We reverse and remand.

I. DUTY TO INTENDED BENEFICIARIES

In order to recover for negligence, a plaintiff must show that "there
exists a duty, whose breach by the defendant causes the injury for
which the plaintiff seeks to recover." Goodwin v. James, 134 N.H.
579, 583, 595 A.2d 504, 507 (1991). The critical issue, for purposes
of this appeal, is whether an attorney who drafts a testator's will owes
a duty of reasonable care to intended beneficiaries. We hold that
there is such a duty.

As a general principle, "the concept of 'duty' . . . arises out of a
relation between the parties and the protection against reasonably
foreseeable harm." Morvay v. Hanover Insurance Co., 127 N.H. 723,
724, 506 A.2d 333, 334 (1986). The existence of a contract between
parties may constitute a relation sufficient to impose a duty to exercise
reasonable care, but in general, "the scope of such a duty is limited
to those in privity of contract with each other." Robinson v. Cole-
brook Savings Bank, 109 N.H. 382, 385, 254 A.2d 837, 839 (1969).
The privity rule is not ironclad, though, and we have been willing to
recognize exceptions particularly where, as here, the risk to persons
not in privity is apparent. Id. In *Morvay*, for example, we held that
investigators hired by an insurance company to investigate the cause
of a fire owed a duty to the insureds to perform their investigation
with due care despite the absence of privity. Accordingly, the insureds
stated a cause of action by alleging that the investigators negligently
concluded that the fire was set, thereby prompting the insurance
company to deny coverage. *Morvay*, 127 N.H. at 726, 506 A.2d at 335;
see also Spherex, Inc. v. Alexander Grant & Co., 122 N.H. 898, 451
A.2d 1308 (1982) (accountants may be liable in negligence to those
who reasonably rely on their work despite lack of privity); *Robinson*,

109 N.H. at 382, 254 A.2d at 837 (bank owes duty to beneficiary of account with survivorship feature set up by depositor).

Because this issue is one of first impression, we look for guidance to other jurisdictions. The overwhelming majority of courts that have considered this issue have found that a duty runs from an attorney to an intended beneficiary of a will. R. Mallen & J. Smith, Legal Malpractice 3d. §26.4, at 595 (1989 & Supp. 1992); see, e.g., Stowe v. Smith, 184 Conn. 194, 441 A.2d 81 (1981); Needham v. Hamilton, 459 A.2d 1060 (D.C. 1983); Ogle v. Fuiten, 102 Ill. 2d 356, 80 Ill. Dec. 772, 466 N.E.2d 224 (1984); Hale v. Groce, 304 Or. 281, 744 P.2d 1289 (1987). A theme common to these cases, similar to a theme of cases in which we have recognized exceptions to the privity rule, is an emphasis on the foreseeability of injury to the intended beneficiary. As the California Supreme Court explained in reaffirming the duty owed by an attorney to an intended beneficiary:

> When an attorney undertakes to fulfil the testamentary instructions of his client, he realistically and in fact assumes a relationship not only with the client but also with the client's intended beneficiaries. The attorney's actions and omissions will affect the success of the client's testamentary scheme; and thus the possibility of thwarting the testator's wishes immediately becomes foreseeable. Equally foreseeable is the possibility of injury to an intended beneficiary. In some ways, the beneficiary's interests loom greater than those of the client. After the latter's death, a failure in his testamentary scheme works no practical effect except to deprive his intended beneficiaries of the intended bequests.

Heyer v. Flaig, 70 Cal. 2d 223, 74 Cal. Rptr. 225, 228-29, 449 P.2d 161, 164-65 (1969). We agree that although there is no privity between a drafting attorney and an intended beneficiary, the obvious foreseeability of injury to the beneficiary demands an exception to the privity rule.

The defendant in his brief, however, urges that if we are to recognize an exception to the privity rule, we should limit it to those cases where the testator's intent as expressed in the will — not as shown by extrinsic evidence — was frustrated by attorney error. See Kirgan v. Parks, 60 Md. App. 1, 478 A.2d 713, 719 (1984) ("testamentary beneficiary . . . has no cause of action against the testator's attorney for alleged negligence in drafting the will when . . . the will is valid, the testamentary intent as expressed in the will has been carried out, and there is no concession of error by the attorney"), cert. denied, 301 Md. 639, 484 A.2d 274 (1984); see also Ventura Cty. Humane Soc. for P.C.C. & A., Inc. v. Holloway, 40 Cal. App. 3d 897, 115 Cal. Rptr. 464 (1974); Espinosa v. Sparber, Shevin, Shapo, Rosen & Heilbronner, 586 So. 2d 1221, 1223 (Fla. Dist. Ct. App. 1991); Schreiner v. Scoville, 410 N.W.2d 679, 683 (Iowa 1987). Under such a limited exception to the privity rule, a beneficiary whose interest violated the rule against perpetuities would have a cause of action against the drafting attorney, but a beneficiary whose interest was omitted by a drafting error would not. Similarly, application of such a rule to the facts of this case would require dismissal even if the allegations — that the defendant botched Robert Sr.'s instructions to leave all his land to his son — were true. We refuse to adopt a rule that would produce such inconsistent results for equally foreseeable harms, and hold that an intended beneficiary states a cause of action simply by pleading sufficient facts to establish that an attorney has negligently failed to effectuate the testator's intent as expressed to the attorney.

We are not the only court to reject the distinction urged by the defendant. In Ogle v. Fuiten, 102 Ill. 2d at 357, 80 Ill. Dec. at 773, 466 N.E.2d at 225, for example, nephews of the testator sued the testator's attorney for failing to provide in the will for the possibility that the testator's wife might not die in a common disaster, but might nonetheless fail to survive him by thirty days. The testator's wife died in the period not dealt with in the will, and without a provision in the will providing for this situation, the estate devolved by intestacy. On appeal after the dismissal of the nephews' claims, the court flatly rejected the argument that intended beneficiaries do not state a cause of action where the testator's alleged intent does not appear in the will. Id. at 359, 80 Ill. Dec. at 775, at 227; see also Teasdale v. Allen, 520 A.2d 295, 296 (D.C. 1987) (expressly rejecting *Kirgan* and *Ventura*); cf. Stowe v. Smith, 184 Conn. 194, 441 A.2d 81 (1981); Needham v. Hamilton, 459 A.2d 1060 (D.C. 1983); Hale v. Groce, 304 Or. 281, 744 P.2d 1289 (1987).

The plaintiff also argues that the trial court erred in failing to recognize that the writ stated a cause of action in contract. We agree.

The general rule that a nonparty to a contract has no remedy for breach of contract is subject to an exception for third-party beneficiaries. Arlington Trust Co. v. Estate of Wood, 123 N.H. 765, 767, 465 A.2d 917, 918 (1983). Third-party beneficiary status necessary to trigger this exception exists where "the contract is so expressed as to give the promisor reason to know that a benefit to a third party is contemplated by the promisee as one of the motivating causes of his making the contract." Tamposi Associates, Inc. v. Star Market Co., 119 N.H. 630, 633, 406 A.2d 132, 134 (1979). We hold that where, as here, a client has contracted with an attorney to draft a will and the client has identified to whom he wishes his estate to pass, that identified beneficiary may enforce the terms of the contract as a third-party beneficiary. See Stowe v. Smith, 441 A.2d at 84; Ogle v. Fuiten, 102 Ill. 2d at 359, 80 Ill. Dec. at 775, 466 N.E.2d at 227; Hale v. Groce, 744 P.2d at 1292.

Because we hold that a duty runs from a drafting attorney to an intended beneficiary, and that an identified beneficiary has third-party beneficiary status, the trial court erred by dismissing the plaintiff's writ.

II. COLLATERAL ESTOPPEL

The defendant insists, however, that even if a duty runs from a testator's attorney to an intended beneficiary, the superior court properly granted summary judgment on collateral estoppel grounds. We disagree.

The elements of collateral estoppel are well-established: "the issue subject to estoppel must be identical in each action, the first action must have resolved the issue finally on the merits, and the party to be estopped must have appeared in the first action, or have been in privity with someone who did so." Daigle v. City of Portsmouth, 129 N.H. 561, 570, 534 A.2d 689, 693 (1987). Further, the party to be estopped must have had a full and fair opportunity to litigate the issue, id., and the finding must have been essential to the first judgment. Restatement (Second) of Judgments §27 (1980); cf. Ainsworth v. Claremont, 108 N.H. 55, 56, 226 A.2d 867, 869 (1967) (collateral estoppel only applicable to those matters "directly in issue").

The thrust of defendant's collateral estoppel argument is as follows. The probate court found that the will as enforced represented Robert Sr.'s actual intent. Thus, the crux of both the negligence and contract counts — that the will did not reflect Robert Sr.'s actual intent — was already decided in the probate court. In support of this argument, the defendant points out that the probate court considered not only the four corners of the will, but also extrinsic evidence of Robert Sr.'s "circumstances." The defendant further insists that upon proper proffer, the plaintiff even could have introduced the notes of the defendant that recorded Robert Sr.'s direct declarations of intent at their conference. In sum, the defendant argues, the probate court either did consider or could have considered all of the evidence of actual intention that the superior court was entitled to hear.

The primary question is whether the issues before the probate and superior courts were identical. We agree with defendant that comparison of the respective evidence which each court was competent to hear is one factor, but note that an identity of evidence is not dispositive of an identity of issues. Instead, determination of "identity" necessarily requires inquiry into each court's role and the nature of the respective findings.

The principal task of the probate court is to determine the testator's intent, In the Matter of Shirley's Estate, 117 N.H. 922, 923, 379 A.2d 1261, 1262 (1977), limited by the requirement that it determine the "intention of the testator as shown by the language of the whole

will. . . ." Dennett v. Osgood, 108 N.H. 156, 157, 229 A.2d 689, 690
(1967) (emphasis added). In this effort, the probate court is always
permitted to consider the "surrounding circumstances" of the testator, id.; Royce v. Denby's Estate, 117 N.H. 893, 379 A.2d 1256 (1977),
and where the terms of a will are ambiguous, as here, extrinsic evidence may be admitted to the extent that it does not contradict the
express terms of the will. In re Estate of Sayewich, 120 N.H. 237, 242,
413 A.2d 581, 584 (1980). Direct declarations of a testator's intent,
however, are generally inadmissible in all probate proceedings. Id.; 4
Page on the Law of Wills §32.9 (Bowe-Parker ed. 1961). The defendant argues that even though his notes of his meeting with the decedent recorded the decedent's direct declarations of intent, they could
have been admissible as an exception to the general rule had there
been a proper proffer. We need not reach the issue of whether the
defendant's notes fall within an exception to the general rule because
even assuming admissibility and therefore an identity of evidence,
there remain distinct issues. Quite simply, the task of the probate
court is a limited one: to determine the intent of the testator as
expressed in the language of the will. Obviously, the hope is that the
application of rules of construction and consideration of extrinsic
evidence (where authorized) will produce a finding of expressed intent that corresponds to actual intent. Further, the likelihood of such
convergence presumably increases as the probate court considers
more extrinsic evidence; however, even with access to all extrinsic
evidence, there is no requirement or guarantee that the testator's
intent as construed will match the testator's actual intent.

The defendant, however, insists that whether or not required to do
so, the probate court in this case did make an explicit finding of
actual intent when it concluded: "There is nothing to suggest that
[the testator] intended to grant a life estate in anything less than the
whole." We need not reach the issue of whether this language constitutes a finding of actual intent because collateral estoppel will not lie
anyway. Collateral estoppel is only applicable if the finding in the first
proceeding was essential to the judgment of that court. Restatement
(Second) of Judgments §27. Inasmuch as the mandate of the probate
court is simply to determine and give effect to the intent of the
testator as expressed in the language of the will, a finding of actual
intent is not necessary to that judgment. Accordingly, even an explicit
finding of actual intent by a probate court cannot be the basis for
collateral estoppel. . . .

Reversed and remanded.

NOTES

1. The large majority of courts that have considered malpractice
suits against the attorney-drafter has concluded that the suit may be

based on either the tort theory or contract theory or both, as did the New Hampshire court. In a few states, courts have continued to hold that the lack of privity of contract between the drafter and the beneficiaries prevents a malpractice action by the beneficiaries. These include Maryland, Nebraska, New York (lower courts), Ohio, and Texas. The recent Texas case of Barcelo v. Elliott, 923 S.W.2d 575 (Tex. 1996), maintaining the privity bar, contains a count of the states. Accord, Noble v. Bruce, 349 Md. 730, 709 A.2d 1264 (1998).

The argument against the privity defense was stated succinctly by Vice Chancellor Megarry of England in rejecting the privity defense.

> In broad terms, the question is whether solicitors who prepare a will are liable to a beneficiary under it if, through their negligence, the gift to the beneficiary is void. The solicitors are liable, of course, to the testator or his estate for a breach of the duty that they owed to him, though as he has suffered no financial loss it seems that his estate could recover no more than nominal damages. Yet it is said that however careless the solicitors were, they owed no duty to the beneficiary, and so they cannot be liable to her. If this is right, the result is striking. The only person who has a valid claim has suffered no loss, and the only person who has suffered a loss has no valid claim. [Ross v. Caunters, [1980] 1 Ch. 297, 299, 3 All Eng. Rep. 580, 582.]

See Martin D. Begleiter, Attorney Malpractice in Estate Planning — You've Got to Know When to Hold Up, Know When to Fold Up, 38 Kan. L. Rev. 193 (1990); Gerald P. Johnston, Avoiding Malpractice Liability in the Estate Planning Context, 43 Major Tax Plan. ¶1700 (1991); Gerald P. Johnston, Legal Malpractice in Estate Planning — Perilous Times Ahead for the Practitioner, 67 Iowa L. Rev. 629 (1982).

2. In Simpson v. Calivas, the validity and construction of the will were matters for the probate court to decide. The negligence of the lawyer was a matter for a court of general jurisdiction. This is true in most states.

Historically, probate courts were inferior courts, with jurisdiction limited to determining the will's validity and supervising administration of the decedent's estate. Legislatures were often unwilling to provide suitable compensation and clerical assistance, particularly in rural areas, because of the small amount of business. In some states, probate judges may be lay persons, without legal training. Anyone can run for the office. The National Law Journal, Dec. 24, 1984, at 39, reported the election of an 18-year-old man, just six months out of high school, as probate judge for Valencia County, New Mexico. Because of lack of confidence in probate judges, their powers were curtailed. In the twentieth century, in most states probate courts were appropriately staffed and the badges of inferiority removed.

They were authorized to pass on more questions regarding wills, including construction of wills.

Nonetheless, even though probate courts are now authorized to construe wills, most courts, like the New Hampshire Court, reject the claim that conclusions reached by the probate court as to the testator's intent in a construction suit are determinative in a malpractice suit. The issues and the evidentiary rules for proving intent applied in the two proceedings are different. See William M. McGovern, Jr., The Increasing Malpractice Liability of Will Drafters, 133 Tr. & Est., Dec. 1994, at 10.

3. Smith v. Lewis, 13 Cal. 3d 349, 358, 530 P.2d 589, 595, 118 Cal. Rptr. 621, 627 (1975):

> As the jury was correctly instructed, an attorney does not ordinarily guarantee the soundness of his opinions and, accordingly, is not liable for every mistake he may make in his practice. He is expected, however, to possess knowledge of those plain and elementary principles of law which are commonly known by well informed attorneys, and to discover those additional rules of law which, although not commonly known, may readily be found by standard research techniques. If the law on a particular subject is doubtful or debatable, an attorney will not be held responsible for failing to anticipate the manner in which the uncertainty will be resolved. But even with respect to an unsettled area of the law, we believe an attorney assumes an obligation to his client to undertake reasonable research in an effort to ascertain relevant legal principles and to make an informed decision as to a course of conduct based upon an intelligent assessment of the problem.

It is the duty of an attorney who is a general practitioner to refer the client to a specialist if the attorney cannot handle the matter with reasonable skill and care. If the attorney fails to refer to or consult a specialist when a specialist is needed, the attorney may be held to the standard of skill ordinarily possessed by a specialist. See Horne v. Peckham, 97 Cal. App. 3d 404, 158 Cal. Rptr. 714 (1979).

Hotz v. Minyard
Supreme Court of South Carolina, 1991
304 S.C. 225, 403 S.E.2d 634

GREGORY, J. This appeal is from an order granting respondents summary judgment on several causes of action. We reverse in part and affirm in part.

Respondent Minyard (Tommy) and appellant (Judy) are brother and sister. Their father, Mr. Minyard, owns two automobile dealerships, Judson T. Minyard, Inc. (Greenville Dealership), and Minyard-Waidner, Inc. (Anderson Dealership). Tommy has been the dealer in charge of the Greenville Dealership since 1977. Judy worked for her father at the Anderson Dealership beginning in 1983; she was also a vice-president and minority shareholder. In 1985, Mr. Minyard signed a contract with General Motors designating Judy the successor dealer of the Anderson Dealership.

Respondent Dobson is a South Carolina lawyer practicing in Greenville and a member of respondent Dobson & Dobson, P.A. (Law Firm). Dobson is also a certified public accountant, although he no longer practices as one. In 1985, Dobson sold the tax return preparation practice of Law Firm to respondent Dobson, Lewis & Saad, P.A. (Accounting Firm). Although his name is included in Accounting Firm's name, Dobson is merely a shareholder and director and does not receive remuneration as an employee.

Dobson did legal work for the Minyard family and its various businesses for many years. On October 24, 1984, Mr. Minyard came to Law Firm's office to execute a will with his wife, his secretary, and Tommy in attendance. At this meeting he signed a will which left Tommy the Greenville Dealership, gave other family members bequests totalling $250,000.00, and divided the remainder of his estate equally between Tommy and a trust for Judy after his wife's death. All present at the meeting were given copies of this will. Later that afternoon, however, Mr. Minyard returned to Dobson's office and signed a second will containing the same provisions as the first except that it gave the real estate upon which the Greenville Dealership was located to Tommy outright. Mr. Minyard instructed Dobson not to disclose the existence of the second will. He specifically directed that Judy not be told about it.

In January 1985, Judy called Dobson requesting a copy of the will her father had signed at the morning meeting on October 24, 1984. At Mr. Minyard's direction, or at least with his express permission, Dobson showed Judy the first will and discussed it with her in detail.

Judy testified she had the impression from her discussion with Dobson that under her father's will she would receive the Anderson Dealership and would share equally with her brother in her father's estate. According to Dobson, however, he merely explained Mr. Minyard's intent to provide for Judy as he had for Tommy when and if she became capable of handling a dealership. Dobson made a notation to this effect on the copy of the will he discussed with Judy. Judy claimed she was led to believe the handwritten notes were part of her father's will.

In any event, Judy claims Dobson told her the will she was shown was in actuality her father's last will and testament. Although Dobson denies ever making this express statement, he admits he never told her the will he discussed with her had been revoked.

In January 1986, Mr. Minyard was admitted to the hospital for various health problems. In April 1986, he suffered a massive stroke. Although the date of the onset of his mental incompetence is disputed, it is uncontested he is now mentally incompetent.

Judy and Tommy agreed that while their father was ill, Judy would attend to his daily care and Tommy would temporarily run the Anderson Dealership until Judy returned. During this time, Tommy began making changes at the Anderson Dealership. Under his direction, the Anderson Dealership bought out another dealership owned by Mr. Minyard, Judson Lincoln-Mercury, Inc., which was operating at a loss. Tommy also formed a holding company which assumed ownership of Mr. Minyard's real estate leased to the Anderson Dealership. Consequently, rent paid by the dealership was greatly increased.

Judy questioned the wisdom of her brother's financial dealings. When she sought to return to the Anderson Dealership as successor dealer, Tommy refused to relinquish control. Eventually, in August 1986, he terminated Judy from the dealership's payroll.

Judy consulted an Anderson law firm concerning her problems with her brother's operation of the Anderson Dealership. As a result, on November 15, 1986, Mr. Minyard executed a codicil removing Judy and her children as beneficiaries under his will. Judy was immediately advised of this development by letter.

In March 1987, Judy met with Tommy, her mother, and Dobson at Law Firm's office. She was told if she discharged her attorneys and dropped her plans for a lawsuit, she would be restored under her father's will and could work at the Greenville Dealership with significant fringe benefits. Judy testified she understood restoration under the will meant she would inherit the Anderson Dealership and receive half her father's estate, including the real estate, as she understood from her 1985 meeting with Dobson. Judy discharged her attorneys and moved to Greenville. Eventually, however, Tommy terminated her position at the Greenville Dealership.

As a result of the above actions by Tommy and Dobson, Judy commenced this suit alleging various causes of action. The causes of action against Tommy for tortious interference with contract, a shareholder derivative suit for wrongful diversion of corporate profits, and fraud survived summary judgment and are not at issue here. Judy appeals the trial judge's order granting summary judgment on the remaining causes of action against Tommy, Dobson, and the professional associations. We address only the trial judge's ruling on the cause of action against Dobson for breach of fiduciary duty.

ANALYSIS

Judy's complaint alleges Dobson breached his fiduciary duty to her by misrepresenting her father's will in January 1985. As a result, in

March 1987 she believed she would regain the Anderson Dealership if she refrained from pursuing her claim against her brother. This delay gave Tommy additional time in control of the Anderson Dealership during which he depleted its assets. Law Firm and Accounting Firm are charged with vicarious liability for Dobson's acts.

The trial judge granted Dobson, Law Firm, and Accounting Firm summary judgment on the ground Dobson owed Judy no fiduciary duty because he was acting as Mr. Minyard's attorney and not as Judy's attorney in connection with her father's will. We disagree.

We find the evidence indicates a factual issue whether Dobson breached a fiduciary duty to Judy when she went to his office seeking legal advice about the effect of her father's will. Law Firm had prepared Judy's tax returns for approximately twenty years until September 1985 and had prepared a will for her she signed only one week earlier. Judy testified she consulted Dobson personally in 1984 or 1985 about a suspected misappropriation of funds at one of the dealerships and as late as 1986 regarding her problems with her brother. She claimed she trusted Dobson because of her dealings with him over the years as her lawyer and accountant.

A fiduciary relationship exists when one has a special confidence in another so that the latter, in equity and good conscience, is bound to act in good faith. Island Car Wash, Inc. v. Norris, 292 S.C. 595, 599, 358 S.E.2d 150, 152 (Ct. App. 1987). An Attorney/client relationship is by nature a fiduciary one. In re Green, 291 S.C. 523, 354 S.E.2d 557 (1987). Although Dobson represented Mr. Minyard and not Judy regarding her father's will, Dobson did have an ongoing attorney/client relationship with Judy and there is evidence she had "a special confidence" in him. While Dobson had no duty to disclose the existence of the second will against his client's (Mr. Minyard's) wishes, he owed Judy the duty to deal with her in good faith and not actively misrepresent the first will. We find there is a factual issue presented whether Dobson breached a fiduciary duty to Judy. We conclude summary judgment was improperly granted Dobson on this cause of action.

Similarly, we find evidence to present a jury issue whether Law Firm should be held vicariously liable for Dobson's conduct since Dobson was acting in his capacity as a lawyer when he met with Judy to discuss the will in January 1985. There is no evidence, however, that Dobson was acting in his capacity as an accountant on that occasion since he was giving legal advice and not rendering accounting services. We find no basis for vicarious liability against Accounting Firm. Accordingly, we reverse the granting of summary judgment on this cause of action as to Dobson and Law Firm and affirm as to Accounting Firm. . . .

Reversed in part; Affirmed in part.

NOTES

1. Some years ago it was predicted that legal malpractice liability would prove to be a strong force for reform of property law. Jesse Dukeminier, Cleansing the Stables of Property: A River Found at Last, 65 Iowa L. Rev. 151 (1979). And so it is turning out. The fear of malpractice liability is fueling movements to excuse errors in will execution (see infra pages 259-261), correct mistakes by lawyers in drafting instruments to carry out the client's intent (see pages 427-438), cure perpetuities violations by either judicial reformation of the instrument or adoption of the wait-and-see doctrine (see infra pages 830-840), and reform wills and trusts after the decedent's death to obtain tax advantages lost by the lawyer's mistake (see infra page 654).

2. In subsequent chapters, in connection with a number of different aspects of estate planning, we shall raise malpractice questions about attorneys' acts that have led, or might well lead, to malpractice litigation. Forewarned is forearmed. In addition, we shall raise, for discussion, ethical issues the practitioner faces. The estates field is mined with conflicts of interest, which principled and trustworthy lawyers should avoid.

For useful student texts, covering the materials in this book, see Roger W. Andersen, Understanding Trusts and Estates (2d ed. 1999); Paul G. Haskell, Preface to Wills, Trusts, and Administration (2d ed. 1999); Lucy A. Marsh, Wills, Trusts, and Estates: Practical Applications of the Law (1998); and Mark Reutlinger, Wills, Trusts, and Estates, Essential Terms and Concepts (2d ed. 1998).

2

INTESTACY: AN ESTATE PLAN
BY DEFAULT

SECTION A. THE BASIC SCHEME

1. Introduction

Studies indicate that the large majority of people die intestate, forsaking wills and legal advice. The richer and older a person is, the more likely he or she has a will. Why do people of moderate wealth not seek legal advice and make wills? One reason of course is that most people cannot accept and plan for the fact of their own death; insurance salesmen are careful to omit the word "death" from their discussions with clients ("If anything should happen to you . . ." *If,* indeed!). As Freud wrote, "Our own death is indeed unimaginable, and whenever we make the attempt to imagine it we can perceive that we really survive as spectators. Hence . . . at bottom no one believes in his own death, or to put the same thing in another way, in the unconscious every one of us is convinced of his own immortality." Sigmund Freud, Our Attitude Towards Death, *in* 4 Collected Papers 304 (1925).

Another reason why people do not make wills is the cost involved. It seems like a "big deal" to go to a lawyer. And, of course, many people arrange to transfer their property at death by way of joint tenancy, payable-on-death designations on life insurance, pension plans, and such, or revocable trusts created during life, avoiding probate and wills. Whatever the reason, a person who does not make a will or dispose of all his or her property by nonprobate transfers necessarily accepts the intestacy law as his or her estate plan by default.

Distribution of the probate property of a person who dies without a will, or whose will does not make a complete disposition of the estate, is governed by the statute of descent and distribution of the pertinent state. Generally speaking, the law of the state where the decedent was domiciled at death governs the disposition of personal property, and the law of the state where the decedent's real property is located governs the disposition of such real property.

Since it is a safe bet that the law of intestacy is not exactly the same in all details in any two states, it is essential that you become familiar with the intestacy statutes of the state in which you intend to practice. It is quite impossible to answer any specific question as to who succeeds to property without looking at the statutes of a particular state. We reproduce here the intestacy provisions of the Uniform Probate Code and later, throughout the book, the UPC provisions relevant to the particular topic under discussion.

The Uniform Probate Code was originally promulgated in 1969. Subsequently, about one-third of the states adopted laws substantially conforming to major parts of the 1969 Code, and several other states enacted particular sections of the Code. Article VI of the Code, dealing with nonprobate transfers, was substantially revised in 1989. Article II of the Code, dealing with intestacy, wills, and donative transfers, was overhauled in 1990. See John H. Langbein & Lawrence W. Waggoner, Reforming the Law of Gratuitous Transfers: The New Uniform Probate Code, 55 Alb. L. Rev. 871 (1992). Some of the Code sections have been revised further in the 1990s. You should compare the probate code provisions of your own state with the revised Uniform Probate Code and think carefully about whether the UPC solution is better than the one adopted in your state and better than any you can come up with. It is our object to help you develop an independent critical judgment about matters in this field, including the Uniform Probate Code. It is likely that legislatures will be selective in enacting sections of the 1990 revised Code, as they were with the 1969 Code.

Uniform Probate Code (1990)

§2-101.   INTESTATE ESTATE

(a) Any part of a decedent's estate not effectively disposed of by will passes by intestate succession to the decedent's heirs as prescribed in this Code, except as modified by the decedent's will.

(b) A decedent by will may expressly exclude or limit the right of an individual or class to succeed to property of the decedent passing by intestate succession. If that individual or a member of that class survives the decedent, the share of the decedent's intestate estate to which that individual or class would have succeeded passes as if that individual or each member of that class had disclaimed his [or her] intestate share.

§2-102.   SHARE OF SPOUSE[1]

The intestate share of a decedent's surviving spouse is:
(1) the entire intestate estate if:
(i) no descendant or parent of the decedent survives the decedent; or
(ii) all of the decedent's surviving descendants are also descendants of the surviving spouse and there is no other descendant of the surviving spouse who survives the decedent;
(2) the first [$200,000], plus three-fourths of any balance of the intestate estate, if no descendant of the decedent survives the decedent, but a parent of the decedent survives the decedent;
(3) the first [$150,000], plus one-half of any balance of the intestate estate, if all of the decedent's surviving descendants are also descendants of the surviving spouse and the surviving spouse has one or more surviving descendants who are not descendants of the decedent;
(4) the first [$100,000], plus one-half of any balance of the intestate estate, if one or more of the decedent's surviving descendants are not descendants of the surviving spouse.

§2-103.   SHARE OF HEIRS OTHER THAN SURVIVING SPOUSE

Any part of the intestate estate not passing to the decedent's surviving spouse under Section 2-102, or the entire intestate estate if there is no surviving spouse, passes in the following order to the individuals designated below who survive the decedent:
(1) to the decedent's descendants by representation;
(2) if there is no surviving descendant, to the decedent's parents equally if both survive, or to the surviving parent;
(3) if there is no surviving descendant or parent, to the descendants of the decedent's parents or either of them by representation;
(4) if there is no surviving descendant, parent, or descendant of a parent, but the decedent is survived by one or more grandparents or descendants of grandparents, half of the estate passes to the decedent's paternal grandparents equally if both survive, or to the surviv-

1. The Uniform Probate Code's alternate section for community property states (§2-102A) provides for the same distribution of separate property as is provided in §2-102 and further provides that all community property passes to the surviving spouse whether or not the decedent is survived by issue or parents. — Eds.

ing paternal grandparent, or to the descendants of the decedent's paternal grandparents or either of them if both are deceased, the descendants taking by representation; and the other half passes to the decedent's maternal relatives in the same manner; but if there is no surviving grandparent or descendant of a grandparent on either the paternal or the maternal side, the entire estate passes to the decedent's relatives on the other side in the same manner as the half.

§2-105. NO TAKER

If there is no taker under the provisions of this Article, the intestate estate passes to the [state].

QUESTION

Under all intestate succession statutes, parents are not heirs if the decedent leaves a child. Why should this be so if the child is an adult? Why aren't the decedent's assets used to support aging parents rather than an able-bodied child? Why must support of the poor or incapacitated elderly come from public resources rather than from a child's estate? See Joel C. Dobris, Review of an Aging World, Dilemmas and Challenges for Law and Public Policy (John Eekelaar & David Pearl eds. 1989), in 52 Ohio St. L.J. 625, 637-641 (1991).

2. *Share of Surviving Spouse*

What policies are involved in framing an intestacy statute? The primary policy, of course, is to carry out the probable intent of the average intestate decedent. This policy requires that we decide what persons who die intestate would most likely want. In the last 20 years, a number of empirical studies have been made of popular preferences as to intestate succession. Although these studies do not always agree, they unanimously support the conclusion that the spouse's share given by most intestacy statutes is too small. They show that most persons want everything to go to the surviving spouse when there are no children from a prior marriage, thus excluding parents and brothers and sisters. This preference is particularly strong among persons with moderate estates, who believe the surviving spouse will need the entire estate for support. The richer the person, the greater the desire that children or collaterals share with the spouse in the estate. See Mary L. Fellows, Rita J. Simon & William Rau, Public Attitudes About Property Distribution at Death and Intestate Succession Laws in the

United States, 1978 A.B.F. Res. J. 319, 348-364; Comment, A Comparison of Iowans' Dispositive Preferences with Selected Provisions of the Iowa and Uniform Probate Codes, 63 Iowa L. Rev. 1041, 1078-1100 (1978). Earlier studies are cited in these publications. An empirical study by John R. Price, The Transmission of Wealth at Death in a Community Property Jurisdiction, 50 Wash. L. Rev. 277 (1975), supports giving the surviving spouse all of the decedent's interest in community property.

Under current law, the single most common statutory provision is to give the surviving spouse a one-half share if only one child or issue of one child survives, and a one-third share if more than one child or one child and issue of a deceased child survive. But there are variations, such as giving the surviving spouse one-half or one-third regardless of the number of children or descendants or giving the surviving spouse a child's share.

The Uniform Probate Code provision for the surviving spouse (§2-102) is considerably more generous than are the current provisions for the surviving spouse under most state intestacy laws. Observe that, under the UPC, if all the decedent's descendants are also descendants of the surviving spouse, and the surviving spouse has no other descendant, the surviving spouse takes the entire estate to the exclusion of the decedent's descendants. Giving everything to the spouse and nothing to the children, under these circumstances, is a novel statutory solution. The provisions in subsections (3) and (4), giving the surviving spouse less when either spouse has a child by a previous marriage, are also unusual. The theory of this section is discussed in Lawrence M. Waggoner, The Multiple-Marriage Society and Spousal Rights Under the Revised Uniform Probate Code, 76 Iowa L. Rev. 223, 229-235 (1991). See also Martin L. Fried, The Uniform Probate Code: Intestate Succession and Related Matters, 55 Alb. L. Rev. 927, 929-933 (1992).

If there is no descendant, most states provide, as does the Uniform Probate Code, that the spouse share with the decedent's parents, if any. If no parent survives, the spouse usually takes all to the exclusion of collateral kin, as the UPC provides, but in a number of states the spouse shares with brothers and sisters and their descendants.

PROBLEMS AND QUESTION

1.   Intestate succession laws are acts of the states, not of individuals. Under the Fourteenth Amendment to the United States Constitution, states must act so as to provide citizens with due process and equal protection of the laws. This means, among other things, that intestate succession statutes must bear a rational relationship to a permissible

state objective. MacCallum v. Seymour, 165 Vt. 452, 686 A.2d 935 (1996).

Refer back to the estate planning problem of Howard and Wendy Brown on pages 49-59. Howard has two children by Wendy. Wendy has two children by Harold and a child by a previous marriage. If Howard dies before Wendy intestate, what will be Wendy's share under UPC §2-102? If Wendy dies before Howard intestate, what will be Howard's share? Do the different amounts provided under §§2-102(3) and (4) have a rational basis?

If Howard dies intestate, and Wendy does not have a child by a previous marriage, Wendy takes all of Howard's estate under UPC §2-102(1)(ii). But because Wendy has a child by a previous marriage, Wendy's share is cut back to $150,000 plus one-half of the balance. Does this carry out Howard's wishes? Would he want his biological children to take the balance at his death and create a future problem for Wendy who presumably would want all her children to inherit equal wealth? See Note, The Spousal Share in Intestate Succession: Stepparents Are Getting Shortchanged, 74 Minn. L. Rev. 631 (1990), which is highly critical of reducing the surviving spouse's share when the surviving spouse is the parent of all the decedent's children but also has a child by a previous marriage. See also Alberta Law Reform Institute, Reform of the Intestate Succession Act 66-67 (1996) (rejecting UPC reduction of spouse's share in this situation on ground it "can only lead to resentment and encourage bitterness").

One of the virtues of UPC §2-102(1), giving all to the surviving spouse, is that a guardianship of minor children is avoided. But in the Browns' case, because of the existence of a stepchild, guardianship may be necessary for the two minor children if one of the spouses dies intestate. For the disadvantages of guardianship, see infra pages 132-133.

2. *H* and *W* have been married one year. *H* dies, survived by *W* and a brother, but no parent. What is *W*'s share? Compare the elective share provisions of UPC §2-202(a), infra page 483, which give the surviving spouse of a one-year marriage only 3 percent of the decedent's estate if the decedent leaves a will and the spouse elects to take against will. Why does the UPC take into account the length of the marriage in determining the spouse's forced share but not the spouse's intestate share? Is this sound? Should it matter whether *H* and *W* are age 55 or age 25 when they marry?

3. Henry dies intestate. Anne, with whom he has been living, claims a spouse's share. Is Anne entitled to such if she married Henry, but the marriage is bigamous? If she did not marry Henry, but common law marriage is recognized? See William M. McGovern, Jr., Sheldon F. Kurtz & Jan E. Rein, Wills, Trusts and Estates §2.3 (1988). If Anne and Henry did not marry because they perceived, as did the

Princess of Cleves long ago, that there's nothing like marriage to spoil a perfect love, but Henry promised to take care of Anne? See infra pages 319-321, dealing with contracts to make wills. Suppose that Henry and Anne had married, but Henry had moved out and filed for divorce. What result? For Canadian law, see Miron v. Trudel, [1995] 2 S.C.R. 418.

In a few states, statutes disqualify a spouse from inheritance if the spouse abandoned or refused to support the decedent. See, e.g., N.Y. Est., Powers & Trusts Law §5-1.2 (1998); Ky. Rev. Stat. §392.090 (1998); Va. Code §64.1-16.3 (1998). Compare Chinese inheritance law, which punishes bad behavior, infra page 147.

4. How should surviving committed cohabiting partners be treated? The number of opposite-sex and same-sex committed relationships is reported growing at a rapid pace, and in 1994 comprised 7 percent of the nation's couples. Should a committed partner be given an intestate share? What would be the criteria for "commitment"? Should the intestate share be given to same-sex committed partners as well as opposite-sex partners? For a thorough discussion, see Mary L. Fellows, Monica K. Johnson, Amy Chiericozzi, Ann Hale, Christopher Lee, Robin Preble & Michael Voran, Committed Partners and Inheritance: An Empirical Study, 16 Law & Ineq. J. 1 (1998). This study concludes that a substantial majority of committed partners want the surviving partner to take a share of the decedent's estate, and this preference is even greater among same-sex partners.

In Hawaii, persons who are forbidden by law to marry (e.g., same-sex couples) can register with the state as "reciprocal beneficiaries." "Reciprocal beneficiaries" are given many of the benefits of surviving spouses, including the right to inherit under the intestacy statute the same share as a legal spouse receives and the right to an elective share (see infra page 499). Haw. Rev. Stat. Ann. §§560:2-102, 2-201 to 2-214 (1998).

Simultaneous death. A person succeeds to the property of an intestate or testate decedent only if the person survives the decedent for an instant of time. With the development of the automobile and the airplane came an increase of deaths of closely related persons in common disasters. Thus the question arose: When a person dies simultaneously with his heir or devisee, does the heir or devisee succeed to the person's property? The Uniform Simultaneous Death Act (1953), drafted to deal with this problem, provides that where "*there is no sufficient evidence*" of the order of deaths, the beneficiary is deemed to have predeceased the benefactor. The act further provides that if two joint tenants, *A* and *B*, die simultaneously, one-half of the property is distributed as if *A* survived and one-half is distributed as if *B* survived. The same rule is applied to property held in tenancy by the entirety or community property. With respect to life insurance, when the insured and the beneficiary die simultaneously the proceeds are distributed as if the insured survived the beneficiary. The decedent may, of course, provide for a different distribution in a will or insurance contract.

<h1 style="text-align:center">Janus v. Tarasewicz</h1>

Illinois Appellate Court, First District, 1985
135 Ill. App. 3d 936, 482 N.E.2d 418

O'CONNOR, J.   This non-jury declaratory judgment action arose out of the death of a husband and wife, Stanley and Theresa Janus, who died after ingesting Tylenol capsules which had been laced with cyanide by an unknown perpetrator prior to its sale in stores. Stanley Janus was pronounced dead shortly after he was admitted to the hospital. However, Theresa Janus was placed on life support systems for almost two days before being pronounced dead. Claiming that there was no sufficient evidence that Theresa Janus survived her husband, plaintiff Alojza Janus, Stanley's mother, brought this action for the proceeds of Stanley's $100,000 life insurance policy which named Theresa as the primary beneficiary and plaintiff as the contingent beneficiary. Defendant Metropolitan Life Insurance Company paid the proceeds to defendant Jan Tarasewicz, Theresa's father and the administrator of her estate. The trial court found sufficient evidence that Theresa survived Stanley Janus. We affirm.

The facts of this case are particularly poignant and complex. Stanley and Theresa Janus had recently returned from their honeymoon when, on the evening of September 29, 1982, they gathered with other family members to mourn the death of Stanley's brother, Adam Janus, who had died earlier that day from what was later determined to be cyanide-laced Tylenol capsules. While the family was at Adam's home, Stanley and Theresa Janus unknowingly took some of the contaminated Tylenol. Soon afterwards, Stanley collapsed on the kitchen floor.

Theresa was still standing when Diane O'Sullivan, a registered nurse and a neighbor of Adam Janus, was called to the scene. Stanley's pulse was weak so she began cardiopulmonary resuscitation (CPR) on him. Within minutes, Theresa Janus began having seizures. After paramedic teams began arriving, Ms. O'Sullivan went into the living room to assist with Theresa. While she was working on Theresa, Ms. O'Sullivan could hear Stanley's "heavy and labored breathing." She believed that both Stanley and Theresa died before they were taken to the ambulance, but she could not tell who died first.

Ronald Mahon, a paramedic for the Arlington Heights Fire Department, arrived at approximately 5:45 P.M. He saw Theresa faint and go into a seizure. Her pupils did not respond to light but she was breathing on her own during the time that he worked on her. Mahon also assisted with Stanley, giving him drugs to stimulate heart contractions. Mahon later prepared the paramedic's report on Stanley. One entry in the report shows that at 18:00 hours Stanley had "zero blood pressure, zero pulse, and zero respiration." However, Mahon stated that the times in the report were merely approximations. He was able to say that Stanley was in the ambulance en route to the hospital when his vital signs disappeared.

When paramedic Robert Lockhart arrived at 5:55 P.M., both victims were unconscious with non-reactive pupils. Theresa's seizures had ceased but she was in a decerebrate posture in which her arms and legs were rigidly extended and her arms were rotated inward toward her body, thus, indicating severe neurological dysfunction. At that time, she was breathing only four or five times a minute and, shortly thereafter, she stopped breathing on her own altogether. Lockhart intubated them both by placing tubes down their tracheae to keep their air passages open. Prior to being taken to the ambulance, they were put on "ambu-bags" which is a form of artificial respiration whereby the paramedic respirates the patient by squeezing a bag. Neither Stanley nor Theresa showed any signs of being able to breathe on their own while they were being transported to Northwest Community Hospital in Arlington Heights, Illinois. However, Lockhart stated that when Theresa was turned over to the hospital personnel, she had a palpable pulse and blood pressure.

The medical director of the intensive care unit at the hospital, Dr. Thomas Kim, examined them when they arrived in the emergency room at approximately 6:30 P.M. Stanley had no blood pressure or pulse. An electrocardiogram detected electrical activity in Stanley Janus' heart but there was no synchronization between his heart's electrical activity and its pumping activity. A temporary pacemaker was inserted in an unsuccessful attempt to resuscitate him. Because he never developed spontaneous blood pressure, pulse or signs of respiration, Stanley Janus was pronounced dead at 8:15 P.M. on September 29, 1982.

Like Stanley, Theresa Janus showed no visible vital signs when she was admitted to the emergency room. However, hospital personnel were able to get her heart beating on its own again, so they did not insert a pacemaker. They were also able to establish a measurable, though unsatisfactory, blood pressure. Theresa was taken off the "ambu-bag" and put on a mechanical respirator. In Dr. Kim's opinion, Theresa was in a deep coma with "very unstable vital signs" when she was moved to the intensive care unit at 9:30 P.M. on September 29, 1982.

While Theresa was in the intensive care unit, numerous entries in her hospital records indicated that she had fixed and dilated pupils. However, one entry made at 2:32 A.M. on September 30, 1982, indicated that a nurse apparently detected a minimal reaction to light in Theresa's right pupil but not in her left pupil.

On September 30, 1982, various tests were performed in order to assess Theresa's brain function. These tests included an electroencephalogram (EEG) to measure electrical activity in her brain and a cerebral blood flow test to determine whether there was any blood circulating in her brain. In addition, Theresa exhibited no gag or cord reflexes, no response to pain or other external stimuli. As a result of these tests, Theresa Janus was diagnosed as having sustained total brain death, her life support systems then were terminated, and she was pronounced dead at 1:15 P.M. on October 1, 1982.

Death certificates were issued for Stanley and Theresa Janus more than three weeks later by a medical examiner's physician who never examined them. The certificates listed Stanley Janus' date of death as September 29, 1982, and Theresa Janus' date of death as October 1, 1982. Concluding that Theresa survived Stanley, the Metropolitan Life Insurance Company paid the proceeds of Stanley's life insurance policy to the administrator of Theresa's estate.

On January 6, 1983, plaintiff brought the instant declaratory judgment action against the insurance company and the administrators of Stanley and Theresa's estates, claiming the proceeds of the insurance policy as the contingent beneficiary of the policy. Also, the administrator of Stanley's estate filed a counterclaim against Theresa's estate seeking a declaration as to the disposition of the assets of Stanley's estate.

During the trial, the court heard the testimony of Ms. O'Sullivan, the paramedics, and Dr. Kim. There was also testimony that, while Theresa was in the intensive care unit, members of Theresa's family requested that termination of her life support system be delayed until the arrival of her brother who was serving in the military. However, Theresa's family denied making such a request.

In addition, Dr. Kenneth Vatz, a neurologist on the hospital staff, was called as an expert witness by plaintiff. Although he never actually examined Theresa, he had originally read her EEG as part of hospital routine. Without having seen her other hospital records, his initial evaluation of her EEG was that it showed some minimal electrical activity of living brain cells in the frontal portion of Theresa's brain. After reading her records and reviewing the EEG, however, he stated that the electrical activity measured by the EEG was "very likely" the result of interference from surrounding equipment in the intensive care unit. He concluded that Theresa was brain dead at the time of her admission to the hospital but he could not give an opinion as to who died first.

The trial court also heard an evidence deposition of Dr. Joseph George Hanley, a neurosurgeon who testified as an expert witness on behalf of the defendants. Based on his examination of their records, Dr. Hanley concluded that Stanley Janus died on September 29, 1982. He further concluded that Theresa Janus did not die until her vital signs disappeared on October 1, 1982. His conclusion that she did not die prior to that time was based on: (1) the observations by hospital personnel that Theresa Janus had spontaneous pulse and blood pressure which did not have to be artificially maintained; (2) the instance when Theresa Janus' right pupil allegedly reacted to light; and (3) Theresa's EEG which showed some brain function and which, in his opinion, could not have resulted from outside interference. At the conclusion of the trial, the court held that the evidence was sufficient to show that Theresa survived Stanley, but the court was not prepared to say by how long she survived him. Plaintiff and the administrator of Stanley's estate appeal. In essence, their main contention is that there is not sufficient evidence to prove that both victims did not suffer brain death prior to their arrival at the hospital on September 29, 1982.

Dual standards for determining when legal death occurs in Illinois were set forth in the case of In re Haymer (1983), 115 Ill. App. 3d 349, 71 Ill. Dec. 252, 450 N.E.2d 940. There, the court determined that a comatose child attached to a mechanical life support system was legally dead on the date he was medically determined to have sustained total brain death, rather than on the date that his heart stopped functioning. The court stated that in most instances death could be determined in accordance with the common law standard which is based upon the irreversible cessation of circulatory and respiratory functions. . . . If these functions are artificially maintained, a brain death standard of death could be used if a person has sustained irreversible cessation of total brain function. . . . In a footnote, the court stated that widely accepted characteristics of brain death include: (1) unreceptivity and unresponsivity to intensely painful stimuli; (2) no spontaneous movement or breathing for at least one hour; (3) no blinking, no swallowing, and fixed and dilated pupils; (4) flat EEGs taken twice with at least a 24-hour intervening period; and (5) absence of drug intoxication or hyperthermia. . . . However, the court refused to establish criteria for determining brain death because it noted that the advent of new research and technologies would continue to change the tests used for determining cessation of brain function. . . . Instead, the court merely required that the diagnosis of death under either standard must be made in accordance with "the usual and customary standards of medical practice." 115 Ill. App. 3d 349, 355, 71 Ill. Dec. 252, 450 N.E.2d 940.

Even though *Haymer* was decided after the deaths of Stanley and Theresa, we find that the trial court properly applied the *Haymer* standards under the general rule that a civil case is governed by the law as it exists when judgment is rendered, not when the facts underlying the case occur. . . . The application of *Haymer* is not unfair since the treating physicians made brain death diagnoses at the time of the deaths, and the parties presented evidence at trial regarding brain death.

Regardless of which standard of death is applied, survivorship is a fact which must be proven by a preponderance of the evidence by the party whose claim depends on survivorship. (In re Estate of Moran (1979), 77 Ill. 2d 147, 150, 32 Ill. Dec. 349, 395 N.E.2d 579.) The operative provisions of the Illinois version of the Uniform Simultaneous Death Act provides in pertinent part:

> If the title to property or its devolution depends upon the priority of death and there is no sufficient evidence that the persons have died otherwise than simultaneously and there is no other provision in the will, trust agreement, deed, contract of insurance or other governing instrument for distribution of the property different from the provisions of this Section:
>
> (a) The property of each person shall be disposed of as if he had survived. . . .
>
> (d) If the insured and the beneficiary of a policy of life or accident insurance have so died, the proceeds of the policy shall be distributed as if the insured had survived the beneficiary.

Ill. Rev. Stat. 1981, ch. 110 1/2, par. 3-1.

In cases where the question of survivorship is determined by the testimony of lay witnesses, the burden of sufficient evidence may be met by evidence of a positive sign of life in one body and the absence of any such sign in the other. (In re Estate of Lowrance (1978), 66 Ill. App. 3d 159, 162, 22 Ill. Dec. 895, 383 N.E.2d 703; Prudential Insurance Co. v. Spain (1950), 339 Ill. App. 476, 90 N.E.2d 256.) In cases such as the instant case where the death process is monitored by medical professionals, their testimony as to "the usual and customary standards of medical practice" will be highly relevant when considering what constitutes a positive sign of life and what constitutes a criteria for determining death. (See In re Haymer (1983), 115 Ill. App. 3d 349, 71 Ill. Dec. 252, 450 N.E.2d 940.) Although the use of sophisticated medical technology can also make it difficult to determine when death occurs, the context of this case does not require a determination as to the exact moment at which the decedents died.

Rather, the trial court's task was to determine whether or not there was sufficient evidence that Theresa Janus survived her husband. Our task on review of this factually disputed case is to determine whether the trial court's finding was against the manifest weight of the evidence. . . . We hold that it was not.

In the case at bar, both victims arrived at the hospital with artificial respirators and no obvious vital signs. There is no dispute among the treating physicians and expert witnesses that Stanley Janus died in both a cardiopulmonary sense and a brain death sense when his vital signs disappeared en route to the hospital and were never reestablished. He was pronounced dead at 8:15 P.M. on September 29, 1982, only after intensive procedures such as electro-shock, medication, and the insertion of a pacemaker failed to resuscitate him.

In contrast, these intensive procedures were not necessary with Theresa Janus because hospital personnel were able to reestablish a spontaneous blood pressure and pulse which did not have to be artificially maintained by a pacemaker or medication. Once spontaneous circulation was restored in the emergency room, Theresa was put on a mechanical respirator and transferred to the intensive care unit. Clearly, efforts to preserve Theresa Janus' life continued after more intensive efforts on Stanley's behalf had failed.

It is argued that the significance of Theresa Janus' cardiopulmonary functions, as a sign of life, was rendered ambiguous by the use of artificial respiration. In particular, reliance is placed upon expert testimony that a person can be brain dead and still have a spontaneous pulse and blood pressure which is indirectly maintained by artificial respiration. The fact remains, however, that Dr. Kim, an intensive care specialist who treated Theresa, testified that her condition in the emergency room did not warrant a diagnosis of brain death. In his opinion, Theresa Janus did not suffer irreversible brain death until much later, when extensive treatment failed to preserve her brain function and vital signs. This diagnosis was confirmed by a consulting neurologist after a battery of tests were performed to assess her brain function. Dr. Kim denied that these examinations were made merely to see if brain death had already occurred. At trial, only Dr. Vatz disagreed with their finding, but even he admitted that the diagnosis and tests performed on Theresa Janus were in keeping with the usual and customary standards of medical practice.

There was also other evidence presented at trial which indicated that Theresa Janus was not brain dead on September 29, 1982. Theresa's EEG, taken on September 30, 1982, was not flat but rather it showed some delta waves of extremely low amplitude. Dr. Hanley concluded that Theresa's EEG taken on September 30 exhibited brain activity. Dr. Vatz disagreed. Since the trier of fact determines the credibility of expert witnesses and the weight to be given to their testimony . . . , the trial court in this case could have reasonably given greater weight to Dr. Hanley's opinion than to Dr. Vatz'. In addition, there is evidence that Theresa's pupil reacted to light on one occasion. It is argued that this evidence merely represents the subjective impression of a hospital staff member which is not corroborated by any other instance where Theresa's pupils reacted to light. However, this argument goes to the weight of this evidence and not to its admissibility. While these additional pieces of neurological data were by no means conclusive, they were competent evidence which tended to support the trial court's finding, and which also tended to disprove the contention that these tests merely verified that brain death had already taken place.

In support of the contention that Theresa Janus did not survive Stanley Janus, evidence was presented which showed that only Theresa Janus suffered seizures and exhibited a decerebrate posture shortly after ingesting the poisoned Tylenol. However, evidence that persons with these symptoms tend to die very quickly does not prove that Theresa Janus did not in fact survive Stanley Janus. Moreover, the evidence introduced is similar in nature to medical presumptions of survivorship based on decedents' health or physical condition which are considered too speculative to prove or disprove survivorship. (See In re Estate of Moran (1979), 77 Ill. 2d 147, 153, 32 Ill. Dec. 349, 395 N.E.2d 579.) Similarly, we find no support for the allegation that the hospital kept Theresa Janus on a mechanical respirator because her family requested that termination of her life support systems be delayed until the arrival of her brother, particularly since members of Theresa's family denied making such a request.

In conclusion, we believe that the record clearly established that the treating physicians' diagnoses of death with respect to Stanley and Theresa Janus were made in accordance with "the usual and customary standards of medical practice." Stanley Janus was diagnosed as having sustained irreversible cessation of circulatory and respiratory functions on September 29, 1982. These same physicians concluded that Theresa Janus' condition on that date did not warrant a diagnosis of death and, therefore, they continued their efforts to preserve her life. Their conclusion that Theresa Janus did not die until October 1, 1982, was based on various factors including the restoration of certain of her vital signs as well as other neurological evidence. The trial court found that these facts and circumstances constituted sufficient evidence that Theresa Janus survived her husband. It was not necessary to determine the exact moment at which Theresa died or by how long she survived him, and the trial court properly declined to do so. Viewing the record in its entirety, we cannot say that the trial court's finding of sufficient evidence of Theresa's survivorship was against the manifest weight of the evidence.

Because of our disposition of this case, we need not and do not consider whether the date of death listed on the victims' death certificates should be considered "facts" which constitute prima facie evidence of the date of their deaths. See Ill. Rev. Stat. 1981, ch. 111 1/2, par. 73-25; People v. Fiddler (1970), 45 Ill. 2d 181, 184-86, 258 N.E.2d 359.

Accordingly, there being sufficient evidence that Theresa Janus survived Stanley Janus, the judgment of the circuit court of Cook County is affirmed.

Affirmed.

PROBLEMS AND NOTE

1.   Suppose that *H* and *W* both drown in a boating accident. The evidence shows that *W* was a better swimmer and in better health than *H*. In addition, the autopsy shows *W* drowned after a violent death struggle while *H* passively submitted to death. Is there sufficient evidence of *W*'s survival? See In re Estate of Campbell, 56 Or. App. 222, 641 P.2d 610 (1982).

H and *W* are killed in the crash of a private airplane. An autopsy reveals *W*'s brain is intact and there is carbon monoxide in her bloodstream; *H*'s brain is crushed and there is no carbon monoxide in his bloodstream. Is there sufficient evidence of *W*'s survival? See In re Bucci, 57 Misc. 2d 1001, 293 N.Y.S.2d 994 (Sur. Ct. 1968).

If you are interested in whether a severed head retains feeling and consciousness for a few moments after severance and therefore arguably remains alive for that period, the experiments carried on by French doctors after the invention of the guillotine are instructive. The doctors were trying to discover if death by guillotine was really instantaneous and painless, as Dr. Guillotin, the inventor, claimed. See Alister Kershaw, A History of the Guillotine 80-89 (1958) (severed heads had looks of indignation or astonishment or, as agreed in advance of decapitation, winked in response to questions). See also Antonia Fraser, Mary Queen of Scots 539 (1969), reporting that Mary's lips moved for a quarter of an hour after she was beheaded.

2.   To remedy the "no sufficient evidence" problem, Uniform Probate Code §§2-104 and 2-702 (1990) provide that an heir or devisee or life insurance beneficiary who fails to survive by 120 hours (5 days) is deemed to have predeceased the decedent. The Uniform Simultaneous Death Act was amended in 1991 to require survivorship by 120 hours, making it parallel with the Uniform Probate Code.

Under both the amended UPC and USDA, a claimant must establish
survivorship by 120 hours by clear and convincing evidence, not
merely by some "sufficient evidence" as provided in the original UPC
and USDA.

3.   *Shares of Descendants*

In all jurisdictions in this country, after the spouse's share is set aside,
children and issue of deceased children take the remainder of the
property to the exclusion of everyone else. When one of several children has died before the decedent, leaving descendants, all states
provide that the child's descendants shall *represent* the dead child and
divide the child's share among themselves.

The following diagram involves this situation. Assume that the intestate decedent, A, a widow, has three children. One of her three children, C, dies before A, survived by a husband and two children. The
decedent is survived by two children, B and D, and by five grandchildren, E, F, G, H, and I. Thus:

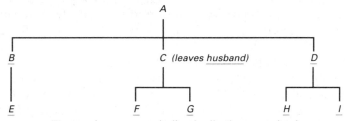

The survivors are underlined; all others are dead.

C's children take C's share by *representation* of their dead parent.
Therefore A's heirs are B ($\frac{1}{3}$), D ($\frac{1}{3}$), F ($\frac{1}{6}$), and G ($\frac{1}{6}$). Observe that
E, H, and I take nothing because their parents are living. (Observe
also that C's spouse (the decedent's son-in-law) takes nothing. Sons-
in-law and daughters-in-law are excluded as intestate successors in
virtually all states. Legislatures have decided that the decedent's property should escheat to the state before allowing a son-in-law or daughter-in-law to inherit.)

In other, more complicated contexts, there are different views
about what taking by representation means. The fundamental issue is
whether the division into shares should begin at the generational level
immediately below the decedent *or* at the closest generational level
with a descendant of the decedent alive. To see this, take this case: A
has two children, B and C. B predeceases A, leaving a child D. C
predeceases A, leaving two children, E and F. A dies intestate leaving
no surviving spouse, and survived by D, E, and F. Thus:

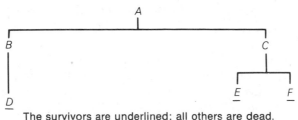

The survivors are underlined; all others are dead.

How is *A*'s estate distributed?

In England, *A*'s property is divided into two shares at the level of *A*'s children, and *D* takes *B*'s one-half by representation and *E* and *F* split *C*'s one-half by representation. The *English distribution per stirpes* ("by the stocks") is to divide the property into as many shares as there are living children of the designated person and deceased children who have descendants living. The children of each descendant represent their deceased parent and are moved into his position beginning at the first generation below the designated person. This system of representation owes much to the English system of primogeniture, in which the son represented the deceased father, and the grandson represented the deceased son. The English system of per stirpes distribution among descendants is followed in about a dozen states. It is sometimes called "strict per stirpes."

The large majority of American states follow a different system of representation. They divide the decedent's estate into shares at the generational level nearest decedent where one or more descendants of the decedent are alive and provide for representation of any deceased descendant on that level by his or her descendants. In the above example, where *B* and *C* are dead, *D, E,* and *F* are all grandchildren, of equal degree of kinship to *A*, and *A*'s estate is divided equally among them. If *F* had predeceased *A*, leaving descendants, *F*'s descendants would represent *F* and take *F*'s one-third. Thus representation is used only to bring the surviving descendants of deceased descendants up to the level where a descendant is alive. This system of representation may be properly called the *modern (American) per stirpes* method, inasmuch as it is followed in a substantial majority of American jurisdictions. Sometimes, particularly among academic writers, it is called *per capita with representation,* but that name has not caught on with judges who continue to refer to the system of representation used in the jurisdiction, be it the English system or the modern system, as a per stirpes distribution.

When a will devises property "to the descendants of *A* per stirpes," the will may or may not be interpreted to call for the same representational system provided by the intestacy laws. The states differ on this. See infra pages 756-759.

PROBLEM

A has two children, *B* and *C*. *B* predeceases *A*, leaving a child *D*. *C* predeceases *A*, leaving two children, *E* and *F*. *E* predeceases *A*, leaving two children, *G* and *H*, who survive *A*. Thus:

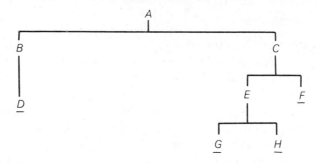

A dies intestate leaving no surviving spouse. How is *A*'s estate distributed under the modern per stirpes system? Under the English per stirpes system? Under the intestacy statute of your state?

Two studies have indicated that an overwhelming majority of people prefer the modern system of per stirpes distribution, dividing the stocks at the level where someone is alive. See Mary L. Fellows, Rita J. Simon, Teal E. Snapp & William D. Snapp, An Empirical Study of the Illinois Statutory Estate Plan, 1976 U. Ill. L.F. 717, 741 (95 percent of the persons interviewed); Comment, A Comparison of Iowans' Dispositive Preferences with Selected Provisions of the Iowa and Uniform Probate Codes, 63 Iowa L. Rev. 1041, 1111 (1978) (87 percent).

The original Uniform Probate Code (1969) defined representation in accordance with the modern per stirpes system. The 1990 UPC changed to a variation on this system known as *per capita at each generation*. The premise of this variation is that those equally related to the decedent should take equal shares: "Equally near, equally dear."

Uniform Probate Code (1990)

SECTION 2-106.   REPRESENTATION

    (a) [Definitions.] [Omitted.]
    (b) [Decedent's Descendants.] If, under Section 2-103(1), a dece-

dent's intestate estate or a part thereof passes "by representation" to the decedent's descendants, the estate or part thereof is divided into as many equal shares as there are (i) surviving descendants in the generation nearest to the decedent which contains one or more surviving descendants and (ii) deceased descendants in the same generation who left surviving descendants, if any. Each surviving descendant in the nearest generation is allocated one share. The remaining shares, if any, are combined and then divided in the same manner among the surviving descendants of the deceased descendants as if the surviving descendants who were allocated a share and their surviving descendants had predeceased the decedent.

Under 1990 UPC §2-106, the initial division of shares is made at the level where one or more descendants are alive (as under modern per stirpes), but the shares of deceased persons on that level are treated as one pot and are dropped down and divided equally among the representatives on the next generational level. Thus in the situation pictured below, *D* takes a one-third share; the two-thirds that would have passed to *B* and *C* had they been living is divided equally among all the children of *B* and *C*. *E, F,* and *G* each take a two-ninth's share.

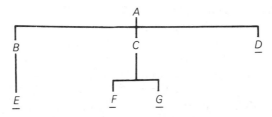

The per capita at each generation system is applied to descendants of parents and grandparents of the decedent, when they are entitled to take, as well as to descendants of the decedent. UPC §2-106(c). UPC §2-106 has been adopted in Alaska, Arizona, Colorado, Hawaii, Michigan, New Mexico, New York, Utah, and West Virginia.

A questionnaire developed by one of the UPC advisors, to which 75 responses from targeted lawyers and their clients were received, revealed that 85 percent of the lawyers responding, perhaps reflecting their law school training in English property law, believed their clients wanted the English per stirpes distribution, but that 71 percent of the clients themselves wanted distribution per capita at each generation. Raymond H. Young, Meaning of "Issue" and "Descendants," 13 Prob. Notes 225 (1988). Although this sampling is small and the methodology flawed, it provides evidence that some lawyers assume what their clients want without explaining the options to the clients. Which of the three systems of representation do you prefer? Which would your parents prefer? Are you sure? Better ask! See Roger W. Andersen, Informed Decisionmaking in Office Practice, 28 B.C.L. Rev. 225 (1987), arguing that a lawyer has a duty to allow a client to make informed decisions on most estate planning issues rather than assuming that the lawyer knows best.

NOTE: NEGATIVE DISINHERITANCE

An old rule of American inheritance law says that disinheritance is not possible by a declaration in a will that "my son John shall receive none of my property." To disinherit John, it is necessary that the entire estate be devised to other persons. If there is a partial intestacy for some reason, John will take an intestate share notwithstanding such a provision in a will. A testator cannot alter the statutory intestate distribution scheme without giving the property to others. See Cook v. Estate of Seeman, 314 Ark. 1, 858 S.W.2d 114 (1993); In re Estate of Cancik, 106 Ill. 2d 11, 476 N.E.2d 738 (1985); Frederic S. Schwartz, Models of the Will and Negative Disinheritance, 48 Mercer L. Rev. 1137 (1997).

Uniform Probate Code §2-101(b), supra page 72, changes this rule and authorizes a negative will. The barred heir is treated as if he disclaimed his intestate share, which means he is treated as having predeceased the intestate. (On disclaimer by heirs, see infra pages 148-151.) Restatement (Third) of Property, Wills and Other Donative Transfers, §2.7 (1999), also authorizes negative wills.

South Dakota, among other states, has adopted UPC §2-101(b). In Estate of Jetter, 570 N.W.2d 26 (S.D. 1997), the decedent left all his property to his brother Martin, a childless bachelor, and specifically disinherited all his other heirs. Martin predeceased the testator. The court, 3 to 2, construed the disinheritance clause to mean the other heirs were disinherited only if Martin survived. The majority avoided escheat, which the dissent thought was the proper result.

4.   Shares of Ancestors and Collaterals

When the intestate is survived by a descendant, the decedent's ancestors and collaterals do not take. When there is no descendant, after deducting the spouse's share, the rest of the intestate's property is usually distributed to the decedent's parents, as under the Uniform Probate Code.

If there is no spouse or parent, the decedent's heirs will be more remote ancestors or collateral kindred. All persons who are related by blood to the decedent but who are not descendants or ancestors are called collateral kindred. Descendants of the decedent's parents, other than the decedent and the decedent's issue, are called first-line collaterals. Descendants of the decedent's grandparents, other than decedent's parents and their issue, are called second-line collaterals. The reason for this terminology can be seen by glancing at the Table of Consanguinity on page 92, which has lines descending from the decedent's ancestors.

If the decedent is not survived by a spouse, descendant, or parent, in all jurisdictions intestate property passes to brothers and sisters and their descendants. The descendants of any deceased brothers and sisters (nephews and nieces) take by representation in the same manner as decedent's descendants, discussed supra at pages 86-90. See, e.g., Uniform Probate Code §2-106(c), which is substantially identical with UPC §2-106(b), supra page 88, and calls for representation per capita at each generation. Hence:

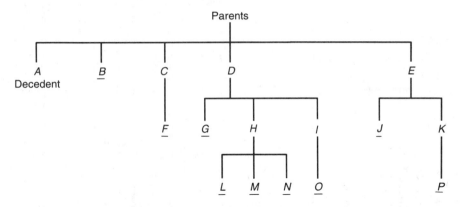

Under the English per stirpes system, division into four shares is made at the level of *A*'s brothers and sisters. So too under the modern per stirpes system, because one sibling, *B*, is alive. Under both these systems, *B* takes ¼; *F* takes ¼; *G* takes ¹⁄₁₂; *L*, *M*, and *N* take ¹⁄₃₆; *O* takes ¹⁄₁₂; *J* takes ⅛; and *P* takes ⅛. Under UPC §2-106(c), *B* takes ¼. The remaining ¾ is divided into six shares of ⅛ each. *F*, *G*, and *J* take ⅛ each. The remaining ⅜ is divided into five shares of ³⁄₄₀. *L*, *M*, *N*, *O*, and *P* take ³⁄₄₀ each.

If there are no first-line collaterals, the states differ as to who is next in the line of succession. Two basic schemes are used: the *parentelic* system and the *degree-of-relationship* system. Under the parentelic system, the intestate estate passes to grandparents and their descendants, and if none to great-grandparents and their descendants, and

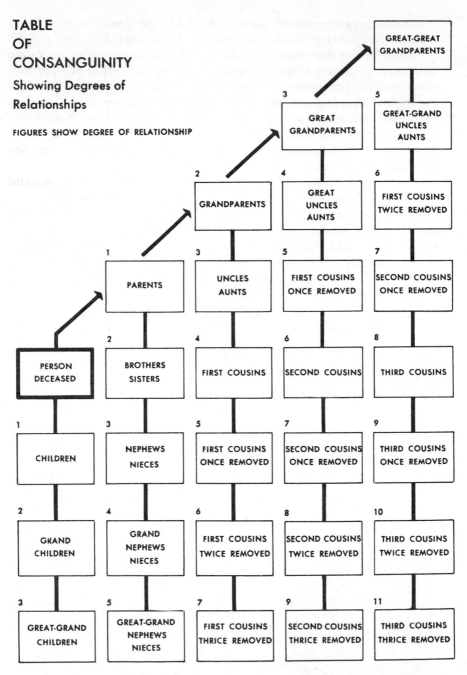

TABLE
OF
CONSANGUINITY

Showing Degrees of Relationships

FIGURES SHOW DEGREE OF RELATIONSHIP

					3	5
					GREAT GRANDPARENTS	**GREAT-GREAT GRANDPARENTS**

GREAT-GREAT GRANDPARENTS (5)

3 — **GREAT GRANDPARENTS**

5 — **GREAT-GRAND UNCLES AUNTS**

2 — **GRANDPARENTS**

4 — **GREAT UNCLES AUNTS**

6 — **FIRST COUSINS TWICE REMOVED**

1 — **PARENTS**

3 — **UNCLES AUNTS**

5 — **FIRST COUSINS ONCE REMOVED**

7 — **SECOND COUSINS ONCE REMOVED**

PERSON DECEASED

2 — **BROTHERS SISTERS**

4 — **FIRST COUSINS**

6 — **SECOND COUSINS**

8 — **THIRD COUSINS**

1 — **CHILDREN**

3 — **NEPHEWS NIECES**

5 — **FIRST COUSINS ONCE REMOVED**

7 — **SECOND COUSINS ONCE REMOVED**

9 — **THIRD COUSINS ONCE REMOVED**

2 — **GRAND CHILDREN**

4 — **GRAND NEPHEWS NIECES**

6 — **FIRST COUSINS TWICE REMOVED**

8 — **SECOND COUSINS TWICE REMOVED**

10 — **THIRD COUSINS TWICE REMOVED**

3 — **GREAT-GRAND CHILDREN**

5 — **GREAT-GRAND NEPHEWS NIECES**

7 — **FIRST COUSINS THRICE REMOVED**

9 — **SECOND COUSINS THRICE REMOVED**

11 — **THIRD COUSINS THRICE REMOVED**

if none to great-great-grandparents and their descendants, and so on down each line (*parentela*) descended from an ancestor until an heir is found. Under the degree-of-relationship system, the intestate estate passes to the closest of kin, counting degrees of kinship. To ascertain the degree of relationship of the decedent to the claimant you count the steps (counting one for each generation) up from the decedent to the nearest common ancestor of the decedent and the claimant, and then you count the steps down to the claimant from the common ancestor. The total number of steps is the degree of relationship. See the Table of Consanguinity on the facing page, where the degree of relationship to the decedent is printed above the upper left-hand corner of the box designating the relationship of the claimant.

There are numerous variations or mixtures of the parentelic and degree-of-relationship systems in force in the various states. Massachusetts, for example, follows a degree-of-relationship system but provides for a "parentelic preference" to break a tie between kin of equal degree.

Massachusetts General Laws Annotated (1998)
ch. 190, §3(6)

If he [the decedent] leaves no issue, and no father, mother, brother or sister, and no issue of any deceased brother or sister, then to his next of kin in equal degree; but if there are two or more collateral kindred in equal degree claiming through different ancestors, those claiming through the nearest ancestor shall be preferred to those claiming through an ancestor more remote.

The number of possible collateral kindred is immense. As Blackstone tells us:

[I]f we only suppose each couple of our ancestors to have left, one with another, two children; and each of those children on an average to have left two more, (and, without such a supposition, the human species must be daily diminishing;) we shall find that all of us have now subsisting near two hundred and seventy millions of kindred in the fifteenth degree; at the same distance from the several common ancestors as ourselves are; besides those that are one or two descents nearer to or farther from the common stock, who may amount to as many more. And if this calculation should appear incompatible with the number of inhabitants on the earth, it is because, by intermarriages among the several descendants from the same ancestor, a hundred or a thousand modes of consanguinity may be consolidated in one person, or he may be related to us a hundred or a thousand different ways. [William Blackstone, Commentaries *205. Blackstone also observes that if you go back 20 generations you have 1,048,576 ancestors (disregarding the possibility of intermarriage among relatives)!]

Should the law permit intestate succession by these remote collaterals, known to lawyers as "laughing heirs" (i.e., persons so distantly related to the decedent as to suffer no sense of bereavement)? This question was brought into sharp focus by three famous cases in the early part of the twentieth century, where hordes of fortune seekers appeared on death. These were the cases of Ella Wendel, Ida Wood, and Henrietta Garrett, all of whom died during the Great Depression.

Ella Wendel, a recluse, died in 1931, leaving a will devising most of her $40,000,000 estate to charity. The only persons who may contest a will are those persons who would take if the will is held invalid. Some 2,303 fortune hunters strove to establish they were her next of kin, so that they might contest her will. Reams of evidence were fabricated, birth and death certificates altered, and tales of bastardy and incest spun. One man was sent to jail for fabricating evidence, and Surrogate Foley referred the activities of six lawyers to the Grievance Committee of the Bar. Ultimately nine persons were established to be her cousins, and they settled out of court with the charities. In re Wendel, 143 Misc. 480, 257 N.Y.S. 87 (Sur. Ct. 1932); 146 Misc. 260, 262 N.Y.S. 41 (Sur. Ct. 1933); 159 Misc. 443, 287 N.Y.S. 893 (Sur. Ct. 1936). The late Justice Harlan's participation in the *Wendel* litigation is traced in Cloyd Laporte, John M. Harlan Saves the Ella Wendel Estate, 59 A.B.A.J. 868 (1973).

Ida Wood, the widow of a United States congressman from New York, died intestate in 1932. For more than 20 years, she and her two sisters (who predeceased her) had barricaded themselves in a New York hotel room, into which no one was permitted to enter. During her life Ida had spun a web of deceit to hide who she really was. The evidence finally accepted by the court showed she had been born Ellen Walsh in Ireland, had moved with her parents to Boston, and had been her husband's mistress for ten years before he legalized her name. Once married and propelled into high society, Ida drew a curtain across her past. She made up vague stories of having been born a Mayfield and brought up in New Orleans. Her mother, and some other members of her family, took the name Mayfield, and Ida carved "Mayfield" on their tombstones. Fearful of a depression, Ida kept $500,000 in cash tied around her waist. When she died, some 1,100 persons claimed to be her next of kin — including a great many persons named Mayfield from Louisiana. Ultimately, the court established as Ida's next of kin some first cousins once removed (none of whom Ida had seen since her marriage to Wood 65 years before).

In re Wood, 164 Misc. 425, 299 N.Y.S. 195 (Sur. Ct. 1937). The whole fascinating story is recounted in Joseph A. Cox, The Recluse of Herald Square (1964).

Henrietta E. Garrett died intestate in Philadelphia in 1930, leaving an estate of over $17,000,000. Nearly 26,000 claims were filed by persons claiming to be her heirs. The testimony covered 390 volumes and over 115,000 pages. Finally, three persons were found to be first cousins of Henrietta. In 1953, after 23 years of litigation, the Supreme Court of Pennsylvania finally ordered the Garrett estate closed. Estate of Garrett, 372 Pa. 438, 94 A.2d 357, cert. denied, 345 U.S. 996 (1953).

With these cases in mind, Professor Cavers predicted that the rules of succession would be revised to abolish laughing heirs. David F. Cavers, Change in the American Family and the "Laughing Heir," 20 Iowa L. Rev. 203, 208 (1935). A substantial minority of jurisdictions has done so. Uniform Probate Code §2-103, supra page 73, is typical. It does not permit inheritance by intestate succession beyond grandparents and their descendants. It eliminates inheritance by more remote relatives traced through great-grandparents and other more remote ancestors. The UPC limitation, incorporated into the Michigan statute of descent, was held to bear a rational relationship to a permissible state objective, and thus to be constitutional, in Estate of Jurek, 170 Mich. App. 778, 428 N.W.2d 774 (1988). For more on laughing heirs, see Note, A Goal-Based Approach to Drafting Intestacy Provisions for Heirs Other than Surviving Spouse, 46 Hastings L.J. 941 (1995); Note, Intestate Succession and the Laughing Heirs: Who Do We Want to Get the Last Laugh?, 12 Quinnipiac Prob. L.J. 153 (1997).

The UPC limitation on inheritance has met with considerable resistance in legislatures. Indeed, some legislatures have moved in the opposite direction — permitting stepchildren and kin of a predeceased spouse to inherit when the decedent leaves no blood relatives. In California, the probate code extends intestate succession not only to stepchildren but also to mothers-in-law, fathers-in-law, brothers-in-law, and sisters-in-law — but not to sons-in-law or daughters-in-law! Cal. Prob. Code §§6402(e), 6402(g) (1998). If *A*'s mother-in-law can inherit from *A*, but *A* cannot inherit from *A*'s mother-in-law, does this have a rational basis?

If the intestate leaves no survivors entitled to take under the intestacy statute, the intestate's property escheats to the state. Escheats of substantial estates are rare. Relatives usually keep tabs on kinfolk of obvious wealth, and thus the larger the estate, the more likely it is that there will be heirs claiming it. Moreover, heir-hunting firms in many jurisdictions seek out unknown heirs and advise an uninformed heir that the firm will disclose the name of an estate to which the person may be an heir in exchange for one-third of the inheritance. See In re Estate of Croake, 218 Ill. App. 3d 124, 578 N.E.2d 567 (1991).

PROBLEMS

1. The decedent is survived by his mother, his sister, and two nephews (children of a deceased brother). How is the decedent's estate distributed under Uniform Probate Code §2-103, supra page 73? Under the intestacy statute of your state?

2. The decedent is survived by one first cousin on his mother's side and by two first cousins on his father's side. How is the decedent's estate distributed under Uniform Probate Code §2-103? Under an intestacy statute of your state? Recall that UPC §2-106, supra page 88, which defines representation, is based upon a goal of providing equal shares to those equally related. Is the UPC treatment of the three first cousins consistent with that goal? Why are three grandchildren or three grandnephews ("equally near, equally dear") treated alike but not three first cousins?

3. The decedent is survived by *A*, the first cousin of the decedent's mother, and by *B*, the granddaughter of the decedent's first cousin. (You can locate these on the Table of Consanguinity, supra page 92.) How is the decedent's estate distributed under Uniform Probate Code §2-103? Under Mass. Gen. Laws ch. 190, §3(6) (1998), supra? Under the intestacy statute of your state?

4. Those interested in genealogy puzzles might like to try the one posed by Charles Lutwidge Dodgson, English writer and mathematician better known as Lewis Carroll, author of Alice's Adventures in Wonderland (1865). The problem: The Governor of Kgovjni wants to give the very smallest dinner party possible and at the same time invite his father's brother-in-law, his brother's father-in-law, his father-in-law's brother, and his brother-in-law's father. To do this, how many guests is it absolutely necessary to invite? The answer: One. If you cannot figure how this is done, using a genealogical tree of only fourteen people, see Lewis Carroll, The Complete Works of Lewis Carroll 1031 (Mod. Lib. ed.).

NOTE: HALF-BLOODS

In England, which put great weight on whole-blood relations, the common law courts wholly excluded relatives of the half-blood from inheriting land through intestate succession. This rule has long been abolished in all the American states. In a large majority of states, a relative of the half-blood (e.g., a half-sister) is treated the same as a relative of the whole-blood. This is the position of Uniform Probate Code §2-107. In a few states a half-blood is given a half share; this was the Scottish rule and was introduced in this country in Virginia. Va. Code §64.1-2 (1998). In a few other states, a half-blood takes only when there are no whole-blood relatives of the same degree. See Miss. Code §91-1-5 (1998). In Oklahoma, half-bloods are excluded when there are whole-blood kindred in the same degree and the inheritance came to the decedent by an ancestor and the half-blood is not a descendant of the ancestor. See Nancy I. Kenderdine, Oklahoma's Archaic Half-Blood Inheritance Statute, 49 Okla. L. Rev. 81 (1996).

PROBLEM

M has one child, *A*, by her first marriage and two children, *B* and *C*, by her second marriage. *M* and her second husband die. Then *C* dies intestate, unmarried, and without descendants. How is *C*'s property distributed under the Uniform Probate Code? Under Va. Code §64.1-2, supra? Under Miss. Code §91-1-5, supra?

SECTION B.   TRANSFERS TO CHILDREN

1.   *Meaning of Children*

a.   Posthumous Children

Where, for purposes of inheritance or of determining property rights, it is to a child's advantage to be treated as in being from the time of conception rather than from the time of birth, the child will be so treated if born alive. The principle is an ancient one. See 1 William Blackstone, Commentaries *130.

Courts have established a rebuttable presumption that the normal period of gestation is 280 days (ten lunar months). If the child claims that conception dated more than 280 days before birth, the burden of proof is usually upon the child. On supposed periods of gestation beyond 280 days, the modern record for a protracted pregnancy apparently belongs to a woman from North Carolina. In Byerly v. Tolbert, 250 N.C. 27, 108 S.E.2d 29 (1959), a child was born to the decedent's widow 322 days after his death. The child (through a guardian ad litem, of course) claimed an intestate share. The trial court held as a matter of law that the infant was not the decedent's child. On appeal, the case was reversed. Although there is a presumption that a child born more than 280 days after death is not the decedent's child, the presumption is not irrebuttable, and the child was entitled to have the issue submitted to a jury.

Uniform Parentage Act §4 presumes that a child born to a woman within 300 (rather than 280) days after the death of her husband is a child of that husband.

b. Adopted Children

Hall v. Vallandingham
Court of Special Appeals of Maryland, 1988
75 Md. App. 187, 540 A.2d 1162

GILBERT, C.J. Adoption did not exist under the common law of England,[2] although it was in use "[a]mong the ancient peoples of Greece, Rome, Egypt and Babylonia." M. Leary and R. Weinberg, Law of Adoption (4th Ed. 1979) 1; Lord Mackenzie, Studies in Roman Law, 130-34 (3rd ed. 1870); American and English Encyclopaedia of Law (1887) 204, n.9. The primary purpose for adoption was, and still is, inheritance rights, particularly in "France, Greece, Spain and most of Latin America." Leary and Weinberg, Law of Adoption, 1. Since adoption was not a part of the common law, it owes its existence in this State, and indeed in this nation, to statutory enactments.

The first two general adoption statutes were passed in Texas and Vermont in 1850. Leary and Weinberg, Law of Adoption, 1. Maryland first enacted an Adoption Statute in Laws 1892, Ch. 244, and that law has continued in existence, in various forms, until the present time. The current statute, Maryland Code, Family Law Article Ann. §5-308 provides, in pertinent part:

> (b) [A]fter a decree of adoption is entered:
>   (1) the individual adopted:
>   (i) is the child of the petitioner for all intents and purposes;[3] and
>   (ii) is entitled to all the rights and privileges of and is subject to all the obligations of a child born to the petitioner in wedlock;

---

2. According to J. W. Madden, Handbook of the Law of Persons and Domestic Relations (Wash. 1931) §106, adoption in the sense of the term as used in this country was not a part of the English law until 1926.

3. Notwithstanding Maryland law, a child who is eligible for social security survivor's benefits through a deceased natural parent under Federal law does not lose eligibility for the continuation of those benefits because of a subsequent adoption. 42 U.S.C., §402(d).

(2) each living natural parent of the individual adopted is:
   (i) relieved of all parental duties and obligations to the individual adopted; and
   (ii) divested of all parental rights as to the individual adopted; and
(3) *all rights of inheritance between the individual adopted and the natural relations shall be governed by the Estates and Trusts Article.* (Emphasis supplied.)

The applicable section of the Md. Estates and Trusts Code Ann. §1-207(a), provides:

An adopted child shall be treated as a natural child of his adopted parent or parents. On adoption, a child no longer shall be considered a child of either natural parent, except that upon adoption by the spouse of a natural parent, the child shall be considered the child of that natural parent.[4]

With that "thumbnail" history of adoption and the current statutes firmly in mind, we turn our attention to the matter sub judice.

Earl J. Vallandingham died in 1956, survived by his widow, Elizabeth, and their four children. Two years later, Elizabeth married Jim Walter Killgore, who adopted the children.

In 1983, twenty-five years after the adoption of Earl's children by Killgore, Earl's brother, William Jr., died childless, unmarried, and intestate. His sole heirs were his surviving brothers and sisters and the children of brothers and sisters who predeceased him.

Joseph W. Vallandingham, the decedent's twin brother, was appointed Personal Representative of the estate. After the Inventory and First Accounting were filed, the four natural children of Earl J. Vallandingham noted exceptions, alleging that they were entitled to the distributive share of their natural uncle's estate that their natural father would have received had he survived William. Est. & Trusts Art. §3-104(b).

The Orphan's Court transmitted the issue to the Circuit Court for St. Mary's County. That tribunal determined that the four natural children of Earl, because of their adoption by their adoptive father, Jim Walter Killgore, were not entitled to inherit from William M. Vallandingham Jr.

Patently unwilling to accept that judgment which effectively disinherited them, the children have journeyed here where they posit to us:

Did the trial court err in construing Maryland's current law regarding natural inheritance by adopted persons so as to deny the Appellants the

---

4. Although the statute speaks in terms of the "adopted child," the person who is adopted need not be a minor child. See Family Law Art. §5-307(a).

right to inherit through their natural paternal uncle, when said Appellants were adopted as minors by their stepfather after the death of their natural father and the remarriage of their natural mother?

When the four natural children of Earl J. Vallandingham were adopted in 1958 by Jim Killgore, then Md. Ann. Code art. 16, §78(b) clearly provided that adopted children retained the right to inherit from their natural parents and relatives.[5] That right of inheritance was removed by the Legislature in 1963 when it declared: "Upon entry of a decree of adoption, the adopted child shall lose all rights of inheritance from its parents and from their natural collateral or lineal relatives." Laws 1963, Ch. 174. Subsequently, the Legislature in 1969 enacted what is the current, above-quoted language of Est. & Trusts Art. §1-207(a). Laws 1969, Ch. 3, §4(c).

The appellants contend that since the explicit language of the 1963 Act proscribing dual inheritance by adoptees was not retained in the present law, Est. & Trusts Art. §1-207(a) implicitly permits adoptees to inherit from natural relatives, as well as the adoptive parents.

The right to receive property by devise or descent is not a natural right but a privilege granted by the State. . . . Every State possesses the power to regulate the manner or term by which property within its dominion may be transmitted by will or inheritance and to prescribe who shall or shall not be capable of receiving that property. A State may deny the privilege altogether or may impose whatever restrictions or conditions upon the grant it deems appropriate. Mager v. Grima, 49 U.S. 490, 8 How. 490, 12 L. Ed. 1168 (1850).[6]

Family Law Art. §5-308(b)(1)(ii) entitles an adopted person to all the rights and privileges of a natural child insofar as the adoptive parents are concerned, but adoption does not confer upon the adopted child *more* rights and privileges than those possessed by a natural child. To construe Est. & Trusts Art. §1-207(a) so as to allow dual inheritance would bestow upon an adopted child a superior status. That status was removed in Laws 1963, Ch. 174 which, as we have said, expressly disallowed the dual inheritance capability of adopted children by providing that "the adopted child shall lose all rights of inheritance from its parents and from their natural collateral or lineal relatives." We think that the current statute, Est. & Trusts Art. §1-207(a), did not alter the substance of the 1963 act which eliminated dual inheritance. Rather, §1-207(a) merely "streamlined" the wording while retaining the meaning.

Family Law Art. §5-308 plainly mandates that adoption be consid-

---

5. "[N]othing in this subtitle shall be construed to prevent the person adopted from inheriting from his natural parents and relatives. . . ."

6. Since the Legislature is elected by the people, it is answerable to the people, and that is the best safeguard against unreasonable laws concerning inheritance.

ered a "rebirth" into a completely different relationship. Once a child is adopted, the rights of both the natural parents and relatives are terminated. L.F.M. v. Department of Social Services, 67 Md. App. 379, 507 A.2d 1151 (1986). Est. & Trusts Art. §1-207(a) and Family Law Art. §5-308 emphasize the clean-cut severance from the natural bloodline. Because an adopted child has no right to inherit *from* the estate of a natural parent who dies intestate, it follows that the same child may not inherit *through* the natural parent by way of representation. What may not be done directly most assuredly may not be done indirectly. The elimination of dual inheritance in 1963 clearly established that policy, and the current language of §1-207(a) simply reflects the continuation of that policy.

We hold that because §1-207(a) eliminates the adopted child's right to inherit from the natural parent it concomitantly abrogated the right to inherit through the natural parent by way of representation.

"The Legislature giveth, and the Legislature taketh away."

Judgment affirmed.

Uniform Probate Code (1990)

§2-113.   INDIVIDUALS RELATED TO DECEDENT THROUGH TWO LINES

An individual who is related to the decedent through two lines of relationship is entitled to only a single share based on the relationship that would entitle the individual to the larger share.

§2-114.   PARENT AND CHILD RELATIONSHIP

(a) Except as provided in subsections (b) and (c), for purposes of intestate succession by, through, or from a person, an individual is the child of his [or her] natural parents, regardless of their marital status. The parent and child relationship may be established under [the Uniform Parentage Act] [applicable state law] [insert appropriate statutory reference].

(b) An adopted individual is the child of his [or her] adopting parent or parents and not of his [or her] natural parents, but adoption of a child by the spouse of either natural parent has no effect on (i) the relationship between the child and that natural parent or (ii) the right of the child or a descendant of the child to inherit from or through the other natural parent.

(c) Inheritance from or through a child by either natural parent or his [or her] kindred is precluded unless that natural parent has openly treated the child as his [or hers], and has not refused to support the child.[7]

NOTES, PROBLEMS, AND QUESTIONS

1. Inheritance rights of an adopted child vary considerably from state to state. In some states, as in Maryland, an adopted child inherits only from adoptive parents and their relatives; in others, for example in Texas, an adopted child inherits from both adoptive parents and natural parents and their relatives; in still others, as provided in the Uniform Probate Code, an adopted child inherits from adoptive relatives and also from natural relatives if the child is adopted by a stepparent. And there are many statutory variations on these three basic schemes.

In view of the diversity and complexities of contemporary family relations created by adoptions, multiple marriages, and single parenthood, it is not easy to discern what the average person (the hypothetical intestate decedent) would want in many of these situations. For analysis of the issues involved in framing a statute dealing with inheritance rights of adopted children, with citations to state laws, see Jan E. Rein, Relatives by Blood, Adoption, and Association: Who Should Get What and Why?, 37 Vand. L. Rev. 711 (1984). For discussion of stepparent adoption, see Margaret M. Mahoney, Stepfamilies in the Law of Intestate Succession and Wills, 22 U.C. Davis L. Rev. 917 (1989); Patricia G. Roberts, Adopted and Nonmarital Children — Exploring the Uniform Probate Code's Intestacy and Class Gift Provisions, 32 Real Prop., Prob. & Tr. J. 539 (1998).

In MacCallum v. Seymour, 165 Vt. 452, 686 A.2d 935 (1996), the court held that denial of an adopted person's right to inherit *through* the adoptive parents from ancestors or collateral kin of the adoptive parents was unconstitutional. The court viewed it as an irrational distinction, denying equal protection of the laws to adopted persons. The court concluded that "presumed intent is not a reasonable consideration of legislative policy. The effect of the presumed intent rationale is to make statutory discrimination lawful as if it were private discrimination. As plaintiff emphasizes, the rationale could as easily

---

7. UPC §2-114(c) is a minority rule, originally applied only to nonmarital fathers. Is it a good idea to extend it to marital as well as nonmarital parents? If so, why not extend it to adoptive parents? Does permitting adoptive parents, but not natural parents, who do not support the child to inherit from the child have a rational basis? See Paula A. Monopoli, "Deadbeat Dads": Should Support and Inheritance Be Linked?, 49 U. Miami L. Rev. 257 (1994); Anne-Marie E. Rhodes, Abandoning Parents Under Intestacy: Where We Are, Where We Need to Go, 27 Ind. L. Rev. 517 (1994). See also the note on Chinese law, infra page 147.

validate racial discrimination in addition to validating discrimination against adopted persons." Id. at 457, 68 A.2d at 938. The court went on to cite United States Supreme Court decisions that rejected the presumed intent argument in invalidating inheritance laws discriminating against illegitimates.

If UPC §2-114(b) had been applicable in Hall v. Vallandingham, Earl's children, adopted by their stepfather, would have inherited from their natural father's brother, William Jr. But observe that William Jr. would not be able to inherit from Earl's children under the UPC. In a stepparent adoption, the children can inherit from their natural relatives, but the natural relatives cannot inherit from them. Is this fair? Does it have a rational basis?

2. *Children born by reproduction technology.* Who is the parent of a child born by surrogate motherhood? Surrogate motherhood can involve (1) an egg of the wife fertilized by the husband's sperm; (2) an egg of the wife fertilized by the sperm of a third party donor; (3) an egg of the surrogate mother fertilized by the husband's sperm; (4) an egg of a third party donor fertilized by the husband's sperm; (5) an egg of a third party donor fertilized by the sperm of a third party donor. As you can see, there may be a genetic connection of both husband and wife to the child, or a genetic connection of only one of them to the child, or no genetic connection between the husband and wife and the child. The law is evolving on who is a parent, and courts are by no means in agreement.

In Johnson v. Calvert, 5 Cal. 4th 84, 851 P.2d 776, cert. denied, 510 U.S. 874 (1993), a husband and wife signed a contract with a woman surrogate providing that an egg of the wife fertilized by the husband's sperm would be implanted in the surrogate woman and, after the child was born, it would be taken into the home of the husband and wife as their child. The surrogate agreed to relinquish all parental rights to the child. The surrogate later changed her mind, claiming parental rights. The court held that parenthood in surrogate mother cases should not be determined by who gave birth or who contributed genetic material, but should turn on the intent of the parties as shown by the surrogacy contract. The court declared the husband and wife the sole parents. The court rejected the argument that the child has two legal mothers.

In many states, surrogacy agreements are prohibited or are enforceable only under certain specified conditions. This complicates matters. See R.R. v. M.H., 426 Mass. 501, 689 N.E.2d 790 (1998) (consent of surrogate mother (A), whose egg was fertilized by sperm of husband of B, void because given for compensation; surrogate mother (A) and husband of B were parents; B cannot adopt child without consent of (A)).

In In re Marriage of Buzzanca, 61 Cal. App. 4th 1410, 72 Cal. Rptr.

2d 280 (1998), husband and wife agreed to have an embryo genetically unrelated to either of them (third party donor's egg fertilized
by third party donor's sperm) implanted in a woman surrogate. Before birth of the child, the husband and wife split up; the husband
petitioned for divorce. The surrogate mother did not claim parenthood. The wife claimed motherhood and claimed also that her erst-
while husband was the father and had to support the child. The
husband claimed that the wife was not the mother and he was not
the father because neither was genetically related to the child. The
court held that both the wife and husband were parents because they
had consented to the artificial insemination that created the child.
Compare Jane Doe v. John Doe, 244 Conn. 403, 710 A.2d 1297 (1998)
(surrogate mother inseminated with sperm of wife's husband surrendered child at birth to husband and wife; upon subsequent divorce,
court held the husband was the father but the wife was not a parent
because she was neither genetically nor gestationally related to the
child; however, wife could be granted custody of the child if in best
interests of child).

Is a determination of who is a parent in custody cases and child
support cases res judicata as to inheritance rights? Are the policies in
the former cases, which are heavily influenced by the best interests of
the child, the same as govern inheritance? See Helene S. Shapo,
Matters of Life and Death: Inheritance Consequences of Reproductive
Technologies, 25 Hofstra L. Rev. 1091 (1997).

In England, the law of parentage of children born to surrogate
mothers appears to be more settled than in this country. In writing
of the law there, Ian Kennedy & Andrew Grubb, Principles of Medical
Law 602-603 (1998), say: "Where a child is born as a result of a
surrogacy arrangement, who are his/her parents? Legally the child's
mother will always be the surrogate; the woman of the commissioning
couple is not the mother even if her eggs were used. Where the
surrogate is married, her husband is the father unless he can prove
that he did not consent to the procedure and the man of the commissioning couple is not the father even if his sperm is used." In order
for the genetic mother to become the legal mother, she must legally
adopt the child.

See generally James E. Bailey, An Analytical Framework for Resolving the Issues Raised by the Interaction Between Reproductive Technology and the Law of Inheritance, 47 DePaul L. Rev. 743 (1998);
Randy Frances Kandel, Which Came First? The Mother or the Egg: A
Kinship Solution to Gestational Surrogacy, 47 Rutgers L. Rev. 165
(1994); Alexa E. King, Solomon Revisited: Assigning Parenthood in
the Context of Collaborative Reproduction, 5 UCLA Women's L.J.
329 (1995); Murray L. Manus, The Proposed Model Surrogate Parenthood Act: A Legislative Response to the Challenges of Reproductive

Technology, 29 U. Mich. J.L. Reform 671 (1996). For inheritance rights of clones, see Ronald Chester, To Be, Be, Be . . . Not Just to Be: Legal and Social Implications of Cloning for Human Reproduction, 49 Fla. L. Rev. 303, 334-336 (1997).

For comprehensive discussion of whether a parent-child relationship exists for inheritance purposes with regard to nonmarital children, adopted children, and children of reproductive technologies, see Ralph C. Brashier, Children and Inheritance in the Nontraditional Family, 1996 Utah L. Rev. 93.

3. *Same-sex parents.* In Adoption of Tammy, 416 Mass. 205, 619 N.E.2d 315 (1993), noted in 107 Harv. L. Rev. 751 (1994), the court approved the adoption of the child, conceived by artificial insemination, of Dr. Susan Love, the eminent breast cancer surgeon, by her lesbian partner, also a surgeon. The court held that both the natural mother and the adoptive mother had postadoptive rights and that the adopted child would inherit from and through both mothers as the child of each. A similar adoption was approved in In re Jacob, 86 N.Y.2d 651, 660 N.E.2d 397, 636 N.Y.S.2d 716 (1995). Suppose that the jurisdiction has enacted Uniform Probate Code §2-114. If the natural mother thereafter dies, survived by the child and the adoptive mother, is the child the natural mother's heir? See Laura M. Padilla, Flesh of My Flesh But Not My Heir: Unintended Disinheritance, 36 J. Fam. L. 219 (1997).

For more on lesbian partners where partner A donated egg for artificial insemination, see West v. Superior Court, 59 Cal. App. 4th 302, 69 Cal. Rptr. 2d 160 (1997) (court denied partner B custody or visitation rights with child when A and B split, even though A and B had jointly agreed to have the child and raise the child together; the contract was not controlling); In re Lynda A.H. v. Diane T.O., 243 App. Div. 2d 24, 673 N.Y.S.2d 989 (1998) (accord); In re Custody of H.S.H.-K., 193 Wis. 2d 649, 533 N.W.2d 419 (1995) (holding B may have visitation rights if B proves a "parent-like relationship with the child"). See also Fred A. Bernstein, This Child Does Have Two Mothers . . . And a Sperm Donor with Visitation, 22 N.Y.U. Rev. L. & Social Change 1 (1996); Nancy D. Polikoff, This Child Does Have Two Mothers: Redefining Parenthood to Meet the Needs of Children in Lesbian-Mother and Other Nontraditional Families, 78 Geo. L.J. 459 (1990).

4. A few cases have arisen where babies have been inadvertently switched at the hospital when born. Here's a story widely reported in the newspapers in 1993. Baby girl Kimberly was switched at birth. Her birth mother was Mrs. Twigg, but Mrs. Twigg took home another baby, believing it to be hers. Mrs. Mays took home Kimberly, mistakenly believing Kimberly was hers. When Kimberly was 14 the mixup was discovered, and scientific evidence showed that Kimberly was the genetic daughter of Mr. and Mrs. Twigg, not Mr. and Mrs. Mays.

"You just wait until your other mother gets home, young man!"

Drawing by M. Stevens
Copyright © The New Yorker Collection 1994.
Reproduced by permission.

Kimberly continued to live with Mr. Mays, Mrs. Mays having died. When Kimberly refused to move into the Twiggs' home, the Twiggs sued for custody of Kimberly. Whose child is Kimberly? See Twigg v. Mays, 1993 WL 330624 (Fla. Cir. 1993) (barring the Twiggs' attempt to prove Kimberly was not Mays's legal child on ground not in best interest of child). Subsequent to the lawsuit, Kimberly changed her mind and moved out of Mays's home and moved in with the Twiggs. Will Kimberly inherit from Mr. and Mrs. Twigg or from Mr. Mays? Consider this statement by the Connecticut court: "We also reject the claim . . . that the child's birth certificate conclusively established that the plaintiff (not genetically or gestationally related to child) is her mother. One does not gain parental status by virtue of false information on a birth certificate." Jane Doe v. John Doe, 244 Conn. 403, at 446, 710 A.2d 1297, at 1319 (1998).

5. If a natural parent refuses to consent to the adoption of the child, the child cannot be adopted by another. To deal with this

situation, when the child has been raised as part of a stepparent's or foster parent's family, Cal. Prob. Code §6408(e) (1998) provides that a foster child or a stepchild inherits from a foster parent or stepparent as a child if "(1) the relationship [of parent and child] began during the person's minority and continued throughout the parties' joint lifetimes and (2) it is established by clear and convincing evidence that the foster parent or stepparent would have adopted the person but for a legal barrier [i.e., but for refusal of a natural parent to consent to adoption]." After the child reaches majority, and the natural parent's veto power ceases, the child cannot inherit under Cal. Prob. Code §6408(e). Estate of Joseph, 17 Cal. 4th 203, 949 P.2d 472, 70 Cal. Rptr. 2d 619 (1998). A formal adoption thereafter is required for inheritance.

6.   *Adult adoption.* Only a few adoption or inheritance statutes draw any distinction between adoption of a minor and adoption of an adult. Occasionally, the adoption of an adult may be useful in preventing a will contest. The only persons who have standing to challenge the validity of a will are those persons who would take if the will were denied probate. If the testator adopts a child, testator's collateral relatives cannot contest the will, since they now can inherit nothing by intestacy. Hence, if a person wishes to leave property to a friend, under some circumstances it might be wise to adopt the friend as a child. In Greene v. Fitzpatrick, 220 Ky. 590, 295 S.W. 896 (1927), a wealthy bachelor adopted a married woman who had been his secretary for many years and with whom, it was alleged, the bachelor had a sexual relationship. In Collamore v. Learned, 171 Mass. 99, 50 N.E. 518 (1898), a 70-year-old man adopted three persons of ages 43, 39, and 25 respectively. In both cases it was held that the adoptions could not be set aside by the persons who would have been the heirs but for the adoptions. In the second case, Holmes, J., remarked that adoption for the purpose of preventing a will contest was "perfectly proper." (Of course the relatives can attack an adoption decree on grounds of mental incapacity or undue influence and, if they succeed in setting aside the adoption, then attack a will leaving property to the adoptee. See In re Adoption of Sewell, 242 Cal. App. 2d 208, 51 Cal. Rptr. 367 (1966) (adoption of woman, 45, by man, 72, attacked); In re Adoption of Russell, 166 Pa. Super. 590, 73 A.2d 794 (1950) (adoption of man, 33, by woman, 71, attacked).)

On the other hand, in New York adoption of an adult *lover* is not possible. In In re Robert Paul P., 63 N.Y.2d 233, 471 N.E.2d 424, 481 N.Y.S.2d 652, 42 A.L.R.4th 765 (1984), the court held that a homosexual male, age 57, could not legally adopt his lover, age 50, although New York statutes permit the adoption of adults. The court thought that a sexual relationship was incompatible with a parent-child relationship. Does this mean that all adult adoptions in New York are vulnerable to attack on the ground that there was a sexual relation between the parties? For a case contrary to the New York view, see In re Adoption of Swanson, 623 A.2d 1095 (Del. 1993), holding a 66-year-old man can adopt a 51-year-old man, his companion for 17 years, to prevent claims against their estates by collateral relatives. The Delaware court expressly rejected the New York holding. See William M. McGovern, Jr., Sheldon F. Kurtz & Jan E. Rein, Wills, Trusts and Estates, §2.2, at 53 (1988), for other restrictions on adult adoptions in a few states.

Should a person adopted when an adult be able to inherit from the adoptive parent's relatives as well as from the adoptive parent? In Greene v. Fitzpatrick, supra, should the adopted woman be able to inherit from the bachelor's sister after the bachelor's death? See Harper v. Martin, 552 S.W.2d 690 (Ky. App. 1977) (holding in the affirmative).

O'Neal v. Wilkes
Supreme Court of Georgia, 1994
263 Ga. 850, 439 S.E.2d 490

FLETCHER, J. In this virtual adoption action, a jury found that appellant Hattie O'Neal had been virtually adopted by the decedent, Roswell Cook. On post-trial motions, the court granted a judgment notwithstanding the verdict to appellee Firmon Wilkes, as administrator of Cook's estate, on the ground that the paternal aunt who allegedly entered into the adoption contract with Cook had no legal authority to do so. We have reviewed the record and conclude that the court correctly determined that there was no valid contract to adopt.

O'Neal was born out of wedlock in 1949 and raised by her mother, Bessie Broughton, until her mother's death in 1957. At no time did O'Neal's biological father recognize O'Neal as his daughter, take any action to legitimize her, or provide support to her or her mother. O'Neal testified that she first met her biological father in 1970.

For four years after her mother's death, O'Neal lived in New York City with her maternal aunt, Ethel Campbell. In 1961, Ms. Campbell brought O'Neal to Savannah, Georgia, and surrendered physical custody of O'Neal to a woman identified only as Louise who was known to want a daughter. Shortly thereafter, Louise determined she could not care for O'Neal and took her to the Savannah home of Estelle Page, the sister of O'Neal's biological father. After a short time with Page, Roswell Cook and his wife came to Savannah from their Riceboro, Georgia home to pick up O'Neal. Page testified that she had heard that the Cooks wanted a daughter and after telling them about O'Neal, they came for her. [Mr. and Mrs. Cook were divorced in the 1970s.]

Although O'Neal was never statutorily adopted by Cook, he raised her and provided for her education and she resided with him until her marriage in 1975. While she never took the last name of Cook, he referred to her as his daughter and, later, identified her children as his grandchildren.

In November 1991, Cook died intestate. The appellee, Firmon Wilkes, was appointed as administrator of Cook's estate and refused to recognize O'Neal's asserted interest in the estate. In December 1991, O'Neal filed a petition in equity asking the court to declare a virtual adoption, thereby entitling her to the estate property she would have inherited if she were Cook's statutorily adopted child.

1. The first essential of a contract for adoption is that it be made between persons competent to contract for the disposition of the child. Winder v. Winder, 218 Ga. 409, 128 S.E.2d 56 (1962); Rucker v. Moore, 186 Ga. 747, 748, 199 S.E. 106 (1938). A successful plaintiff must also prove:

> Some showing of an agreement between the natural and adoptive parents, performance by the natural parents of the child in giving up custody, performance by the child by living in the home of the adoptive parents, partial performance by the foster parents in taking the child into the home and treating [it] as their child, and . . . the intestacy of the foster parent.

Williams v. Murray, 239 Ga. 276, 236 S.E.2d 624 (1977), quoting Habecker v. Young, 474 F.2d 1229, 1230 (5th Cir. 1973). The only issue on this appeal is whether the court correctly determined that Page was without authority to contract for O'Neal's adoption.

2. O'Neal argues that Page, a paternal aunt with physical custody of her, had authority to contract for her adoption and, even if she was without such authority, any person with the legal right to contract for the adoption, be they O'Neal's biological father or maternal aunts or uncles, ratified the adoption contract by failing to object.

As a preliminary matter, we agree with O'Neal that although her biological father was living at the time the adoption contract was allegedly entered into, his consent to the contract was not necessary as he never recognized or legitimized her or provided for her support in any manner. See Williams, 239 Ga. 276, 236 S.E.2d 624 (mother alone may contract for adoption where the father has lost parental control or abandoned the child); OCGA §19-7-25, Code 1933, §74-203 (only mother of child born out of wedlock may exercise parental power over the child unless legitimized by the father); see also OCGA

§19-8-10 (parent not entitled to notice of petition of adoption where parent has abandoned the child). What is less clear are the rights and obligations acquired by Page by virtue of her physical custody of O'Neal after her mother's death.

3. The Georgia Code defines a "legal custodian" as a person to whom legal custody has been given by court order and who has the right to physical custody of the child and to determine the nature of the care and treatment of the child and the duty to provide for the care, protection, training, and education and the physical, mental, and moral welfare of the child. OCGA §15-11-43, Code 1933, §24A-2901. A legal custodian does not have the right to consent to the adoption of a child, as this right is specifically retained by one with greater rights over the child, a child's parent or guardian. OCGA §15-11-43, Code 1933, §24A-2901 (rights of a legal custodian are subject to the remaining rights and duties of the child's parents or guardian); Skipper v. Smith, 239 Ga. 854, 238 S.E.2d 917 (1977) (right to consent to adoption is a residual right retained by a parent notwithstanding the transfer of legal custody of the child to another person); Jackson v. Anglin, 193 Ga. 737, 738, 19 S.E.2d 914 (1942) (parent retains exclusive authority to consent to adoption although child is placed in temporary custody of another); Carey v. Phillips, 137 Ga. App. 619, 624, 224 S.E.2d 870 (1976) (parent's consent is required for adoption of child although child is in physical custody of another).

O'Neal concedes that, after her mother's death, no guardianship petition was filed by her relatives. Nor is there any evidence that any person petitioned to be appointed as her legal custodian. Accordingly, the obligation to care and provide for O'Neal, undertaken first by Campbell, and later by Page, was not a legal obligation but a familial obligation resulting in a custodial relationship properly characterized as something less than that of a legal custodian. Such a relationship carried with it no authority to contract for O'Neal's adoption. See Skipper, 239 Ga. at 856, 238 S.E.2d 917. While we sympathize with O'Neal's plight, we conclude that Page had no authority to enter into the adoption contract with Cook and the contract, therefore, was invalid.

4. Because O'Neal's relatives did not have the legal authority to enter into a contract for her adoption, their alleged ratification of the adoption contract was of no legal effect and the court did not err in granting a judgment notwithstanding the verdict in favor of the appellee. See Foster v. Cheek, 212 Ga. 821, 96 S.E.2d 545 (1957) (adoption contract made between persons not competent to contract for child's adoption specifically enforceable where the parent with parental power over the child acquiesced in and ratified the adoption contract).

Judgment affirmed.

Justice Leah Sears
Appointed to the Georgia Supreme Court in 1992 at age 36.

SEARS, J., dissenting. I disagree with the majority's holding that O'Neal's claim for equitable adoption is defeated by the fact that her paternal aunt was not a person designated by law as one having the authority to consent to O'Neal's adoption.

1. In Crawford v. Wilson, 139 Ga. 654, 658, 78 S.E. 30 (1913), the doctrine of equitable or virtual adoption was recognized for the first time in Georgia. Relying on the equitable principle that "equity considers that done which ought to have been done," id. at 659, 78 S.E. 30; see OCGA §23-1-8, we held that "an agreement to adopt a child, so as to constitute the child an heir at law on the death of the person adopting, performed on the part of the child, is enforceable upon the death of the person adopting the child as to property which is undisposed of by will," id. We held that although the death of the adopting parents precluded a literal enforcement of the contract, equity would "enforce the contract by decreeing that the child is entitled to the fruits of a legal adoption." Id. In *Crawford*, we noted that the full performance of the agreement by the child was sufficient to overcome an objection that the agreement was unenforceable because it violated the statute of frauds. Id. 139 Ga. at 658, 78 S.E. 30. We further held that

> [w]here one takes an infant into his home upon a promise to adopt such as his own child, and the child performs all the duties growing out of the substituted relationship of parent and child, rendering years of service, companionship, and obedience to the foster parent, upon the faith that such foster parent stands in loco parentis, and that upon his death the child will sustain the legal relationship to his estate of a natural child, there is equitable reason that the child may appeal to a court of equity to consummate, so far as it may be possible, the foster parent's omission of duty in the matter of formal adoption. [Id. at 660, 78 S.E. 30.]

Although the majority correctly states the current rule in Georgia that a contract to adopt may not be specifically enforced unless the contract was entered by a person with the legal authority to consent to the adoption of the child, *Crawford* did not expressly establish such a requirement, and I think the cases cited by the majority that have established this requirement are in error.

Instead, I would hold that where a child has fully performed the alleged contract over the course of many years or a lifetime and can sufficiently establish the existence of the contract to adopt, equity should enforce the contract over the objection of the adopting parents' heirs that the contract is unenforceable because the person who consented to the adoption did not have the legal authority to do so. Several reasons support this conclusion.

First, in such cases, the adopting parents and probably their heirs know of the defect in the contract and yet voice no objection to the contract while the child fully performs the contract and the adopting parents reap the benefits thereof. Under these circumstances, to hold that the contract is unenforceable after the child has performed is to permit a virtual fraud upon the child and should not be countenanced in equity. See 2 Corbin on Contracts, §429 (1950). Equity does not permit such action with regard to contracts that are initially unenforceable because they violate the statute of frauds, but instead recognizes that the full performance of the contract negates its initial unenforceability and renders it enforceable in equity. See 2 Corbin, supra, §§420, 421, 429, 432; Harp v. Bacon, 222 Ga. 478, 482-83, 150 S.E.2d 655 (1966).

Moreover, the purpose of requiring consent by a person with the legal authority to consent to an adoption, where such a person exists, is to protect that person, the child, and the adopting parents. See generally Clark, The Law of Domestic Relations, Vol. 2, Section 21.11 (2nd Ed. 1987). However, as equitable adoption cases do not arise until the death of the adopting parents, the interests of the person with the [right to] consent to adopt and of the adopting parents are not in jeopardy. On the other hand, the interests of the child are unfairly and inequitably harmed by insisting upon the requirement that a person with the consent to adopt had to have been a party to the contract. That this legal requirement is held against the child is particularly inequitable because the child, the course of whose life is forever changed by such contracts, was unable to act to insure the validity of the contract when the contract was made.

Furthermore, where there is no person with the legal authority to consent to the adoption, such as in the present case, the only reason to insist that a person be appointed the child's legal guardian before agreeing to the contract to adopt would be for the protection of the child. Yet, by insisting upon this requirement after the adopting parents' deaths, this Court is harming the very person that the requirement would protect.

For all the foregoing reasons, equity ought to intervene on the child's behalf in these types of cases, and require the performance of the contract if it is sufficiently proven. See OCGA §23-1-8. In this case, I would thus not rule against O'Neal's claim for specific performance solely on the ground that her paternal aunt did not have the authority to consent to the adoption.

2. Moreover, basing the doctrine of equitable adoption in contract theory has come under heavy criticism, for numerous reasons. See Clark, supra, at 676-78; Rein, Relatives by Blood, Adoption, and Association: Who Should Get What and Why (The Impact of Adoptions, Adult Adoptions, and Equitable Adoptions on Intestate Succession and Class Gifts), 37 Vand. L. Rev. 710, 770-75, 784-86 (1984). For instance, as we acknowledged in *Wilson,* supra, 139 Ga. at 659, 78 S.E. 30, the contract to adopt is not being specifically enforced as the adopting parents are dead; for equitable reasons we are merely placing the child in a position that he or she would have been in if he or she had been adopted. See Rein at 774. Moreover, it is problematic whether these contracts are capable of being enforced in all respects during the child's infancy. See Rein at 773-74; Clark at 678. Furthermore, because part of the consideration for these contracts is the child's performance thereunder, the child is not merely a third-party beneficiary of a contract between the adults involved but is a party thereto. Yet, a child is usually too young to know of or understand the contract, and it is thus difficult to find a meeting of the minds between the child and the adopting parents and the child's acceptance of the contract. Rein at 772-73, 775. I agree with these criticisms and would abandon the contract basis for equitable adoption in favor of the more flexible and equitable theory advanced by the foregoing authorities. That theory focuses not on the fiction of whether there has been a contract to adopt but on the relationship between the adopting parents and the child and in particular whether the adopting parents have led the child to believe that he or she is a legally adopted member of their family. Rein at 785-87; Clark at 678, 682.

3. Because the majority fails to honor the maxim that "[e]quity considers that done which ought to be done," §23-1-8, and follows a rule that fails to protect a person with superior equities, I dissent. I am authorized to state that Justice Hunstein concurs in the result reached by this dissent.

NOTE, PROBLEM, AND QUESTION

1. Suppose that *H* and *W* take baby *A* into their home and raise *A* as their child but do not formally adopt *A*. Under such circumstances, *A* may be able to inherit from *H* and *W* under the doctrine of *equitable adoption.* Under this doctrine, an oral agreement to adopt

A, between *H* and *W* and *A*'s natural parents, is implied and specifically enforced in equity against *H* and *W.* As against *H* and *W,* equity treats *A* as if the contract had been performed by *H* and *W;* they are estopped to deny a formal adoption took place.

Equitable adoption permits an equitably adopted child to inherit from the foster parents. Lankford v. Wright, 347 N.C. 115, 489 S.E.2d 604 (1997). On the other hand, the foster parents (and their relatives) cannot inherit from the child. Having failed to perform the contract, they have no claim in equity. Estate of Riggs, 109 Misc. 2d 644, 440 N.Y.S.2d 450 (1981). In Board of Education v. Browning, 333 Md. 281, 635 A.2d 373 (1994), the court held that an equitably adopted child could not inherit from her adoptive parent's sister even though the sister's estate thus escheated. The court concluded that the effect of equitable adoption should be limited to inheritance from the parent who is estopped. Compare First National Bank in Fairmont v. Phillips, 344 S.E.2d 201 (W. Va. 1985), holding that an equitably adopted child could inherit from another child of the foster parent. See Note, Equitable Adoption: They Took Him into Their Home and Called Him Fred, 53 Va. L. Rev. 727 (1972).

2. In O'Neal v. Wilkes, suppose that the Juvenile Court had placed Hattie in the custody of Mr. and Mrs. Cook. The Juvenile Court has power to consent to adoption of Hattie by the Cooks. Same result? See Welch v. Welch, 265 Ga. 89, 453 S.E.2d 445 (1995) (holding no equitable adoption, by a 4 to 3 vote).

3. Hattie O'Neal was black, and the country town of Riceboro, Georgia, where she went to live, has a population of 767, of whom 751 are black. There is no lawyer in Riceboro, but there are several lawyers in the county seat, Hinesville, 17 miles away. Does this affect your view of the *O'Neal* case? See Lynda Richardson, Adoptions that Lack Papers, Not Purpose, N.Y. Times, Nov. 25, 1993, at C1, discussing the history and prevalence of informal adoptions in the black community ("of the estimated one million black children in this country who do not live with a biological parent, nearly 800,000 have been informally adopted, usually by a grandparent").

In the *O'Neal* case, the court was divided 5-2. Joining Justice Sears in her dissent was a white woman justice; the majority were all men, including one African-American. Might women look at equitable adoption as less an application of abstract principles and more as a judgment about whether the responsibilities and care involved in a parent-child relationship had been satisfied in a particular case? See the views of Professor Jan Rein, cited in Justice Sears's opinion; Carol Gilligan, In a Different Voice: Psychological Theory and Women's Development (1982).

c. Nonmarital Children

Although innocent of any sin or crime, children of unmarried parents were given harsh, pitiless treatment by the common law.[8] A child born out of wedlock was *filius nullius*, the child of no one, and could inherit from neither father nor mother. Only the child's spouse and descendants could inherit from the child. If the child died intestate and left neither spouse nor descendants, the child's property escheated to the king or other overlord.

All of our states have alleviated this unsympathetic treatment of nonmarital children. All jurisdictions permit inheritance from the mother, but the rules respecting inheritance from the father vary. In Trimble v. Gordon, 430 U.S. 762 (1977), the Supreme Court held unconstitutional, as a denial of equal protection, an Illinois statute denying a nonmarital child inheritance rights from the father. The Court held that state discrimination against nonmarital children, although not a suspect classification subject to the strict scrutiny test, must have a substantial justification as serving an important state interest. The valid state interest recognized by the Court is obtaining reliable proof of paternity. The Court found that total statutory disinheritance from the father was not rationally related to this objective. See also Lalli v. Lalli, 439 U.S. 259 (1978), upholding a New York statute permitting inheritance by a nonmarital child from the father only if the father had married the mother or had been formally adjudicated the father by a court during the father's lifetime.

In the wake of these two cases, most states have amended their intestacy statutes to liberalize inheritance by nonmarital children. Most permit paternity to be established by evidence of the subsequent marriage of the parents, by acknowledgment by the father, by an adjudication during the life of the father, or by clear and convincing proof after his death.

The Uniform Parentage Act (1973), adopted in about one-third of the states, is built upon the concept of a "parent and child relationship," on which the law confers rights and obligations. The parent and child relationship extends to every parent and child, regardless of the marital status of the parents. When the father and mother do not marry or attempt to marry, a parent-child relationship is presumed to exist between a father and a child if (1) while the child is a minor, the father receives the child into his home and openly holds out the child as his natural child, or (2) the father acknowledges his

---

8. For a description of the legal position of the illegitimate child at common law, see 1 William Blackstone, Commentaries *454 ff.; 2 id. *247 ff. In the first book of Blackstone (1 id. *457) you may find out, if you care to, how a child could be "more than ordinarily legitimate."

paternity in a writing filed with an appropriate court or administrative agency. Uniform Parentage Act §4. If a father and child relationship is presumed to exist, an action to determine its existence may be brought at any time; if a child has no presumed father, an action to establish a parent and child relationship must be brought within three years after the child reaches majority. Id. §§6, 7.

Can a father of an illegitimate child inherit from the child? In Estate of Hicks, 174 Ill. 2d 433, 675 N.E.2d 89 (1996), the court held unconstitutional an Illinois statute that allowed only the mother and the mother's descendants to inherit from an illegitimate child, even though the father had acknowledged paternity in court. The court held the statute was not narrowly tailored to effectuate the state's interest in requiring proof of paternity.

QUESTION AND NOTES

1.   Should state courts develop an equitable legitimation doctrine (similar to equitable adoption) so that where a formal adjudication of paternity is required by statute for inheritance, a nonmarital child can inherit from the father if there is clear and convincing evidence of paternity and of the father's intent that the child be treated as an heir? See Prince v. Black, 256 Ga. 79, 344 S.E.2d 411 (1986) (announcing equitable legitimation doctrine) (*Georgia*, did you say? Compare O'Neal v. Wilkes, supra page 108); Note, Davis v. Jones: A Case for Equitable Legitimation, 23 S. Tex. L.J. 250 (1982).

2.   In Alexander v. Alexander, 42 Ohio Misc. 2d 30, 537 N.E.2d 1310 (1988), the plaintiff alleged he was the illegitimate son and sole heir of David Summers, who had been buried. He petitioned the court for an order to disinter Summers so that paternity might be proven by a genetic (DNA) test performed on the remains of Summers. The court granted the petition over the objection of Summers's other relatives. But see In re Estate of Janis, 157 Misc. 2d 999, 600 N.Y.S.2d 416 (1993), refusing to order exhumation for DNA testing.

In Sudwischer v. Estate of Hoffpauir, 589 So. 2d 474 (La. 1991), cert. denied, 504 U.S. 908 (1992), a person claiming to be the illegitimate daughter of the decedent was granted an order requiring the decedent's legitimate daughter to submit to a blood test to obtain the DNA composition of her blood. Accord, Estate of Sandler, N.Y.L.J., May 2, 1994, at 1 (parents of decedent must submit to DNA testing).

3.   In most states, paternity can be proven after the alleged father's death by clear and convincing evidence. California law is more restrictive. Cal. Prob. Code §6453(b) (1998) provides that, unless paternity is presumed to exist under the Uniform Parentage Act, paternity cannot be established after the father's death

unless any of the following conditions exist:

(1) A court order was entered during the father's lifetime declaring paternity.

(2) Paternity is established by clear and convincing evidence that the father has openly held out the child as his own.

(3) It was impossible for the father to hold out the child as his own and paternity is established by clear and convincing evidence.

This statute prevents establishing paternity by DNA testing of the father's body, now permitted in many states, unless it "was impossible for the father to hold out the child as his own." Presumably, this means the father died before the child was born or was unaware of the birth of the child. See Estate of Sanders, 2 Cal. App. 4th 462, 3 Cal. Rptr. 2d 536 (1992), upholding constitutionality of statute.

Hecht v. Superior Court
California Court of Appeal, Second District, 1993
16 Cal. App. 4th 836, 20 Cal. Rptr. 2d 275

LILLIE, P.J. Petitioner, the girlfriend of decedent William E. Kane, seeks a peremptory writ of mandate/prohibition to vacate a January 4, 1993 order directing the personal representative of decedent's estate to destroy all of the decedent's sperm in the custody and control of California Cryobank, Inc. The real parties in interest are the administrator of the decedent's estate (Robert L. Greene), and the decedent's adult son (William E. Kane, Jr.) and adult daughter (Katharine E. Kane). We issued an order to show cause and order staying execution of the January 4, 1993 order.

This proceeding presents several matters of first impression involving the disposition of cryogenically-preserved sperm of a deceased. We conclude that the trial court's order constituted an abuse of discretion in the procedural posture of this case which compels us to set aside such order.

FACTUAL AND PROCEDURAL BACKGROUND

At the age of 48, William E. Kane took his own life on October 30, 1991, in a Las Vegas hotel. For about five years prior to his death, he had been living with petitioner, 38-year-old Deborah Hecht. Kane was survived by two college-aged children of his former wife whom he had divorced in 1976.

In October 1991, decedent deposited 15 vials of his sperm in an account at California Cryobank, Inc., a Los Angeles sperm bank (hereinafter sperm bank). On September 24, 1991, he signed a "Specimen

Storage Agreement" with sperm bank which provided in pertinent part that "In the event of the death of the client [William E. Kane], the client instructs the Cryobank to . . . Continue to store [the specimens] upon request of the executor of the estate [or] release the specimens to the executor of the estate." A provision captioned "Authorization to Release Specimens" states, "I, William Everett Kane, . . . authorize the [sperm bank] to release my semen specimens (vials) to Deborah Ellen Hecht. I am also authorizing specimens to be released to recipient's physician Dr. Kathryn Moyer."[9]

On September 27, 1991, decedent executed a will which was filed with the Los Angeles County Superior Court and admitted to probate. The will named Hecht as executor of the estate, and provides, "I bequeath all right, title, and interest that I may have in any specimens of my sperm stored with any sperm bank or similar facility for storage to Deborah Ellen Hecht." A portion of the will entitled "Statement of Wishes" provided, "It being my intention that samples of my sperm will be stored at a sperm bank for the use of Deborah Ellen Hecht, should she so desire, it is my wish that, should [Hecht] become impregnated with my sperm, before or after my death, she disregard the wishes expressed in Paragraph 3 above [pertaining to disposition of decedent's "diplomas and framed mementoes,"] to the extent that she wishes to preserve any or all of my mementoes and diplomas and the like for our future child or children."

The will also bequeaths a home in Monterey County to Hecht and an adjoining seven-and-one-half acre parcel of unimproved land to William E. Kane, Jr., and Katharine Kane, on condition that they deed and convey .4 acre of unimproved land adjacent to the home to Hecht. The residue of the estate was bequeathed to Hecht, the will stating, "I recognize that my children . . . are financially secure and therefore leave them nothing other than the land included in this bequest, subject to the conditions as set forth above."

An October 21, 1991 letter signed by Kane and addressed to his children stated:

> I address this to my children, because, although I have only two, Everett and Katy, it may be that Deborah will decide — as I hope she will — to have a child by me after my death. I've been assiduously generating frozen sperm samples for that eventuality. If she does, then this letter is for my posthumous offspring, as well, with the thought that I have loved you in

9. On our record, it is unclear whether the "Authorization to Release Specimens" applies to the release of specimens only during Kane's lifetime or includes release of specimens after his death. It is also unclear whether the contract's reference to "executor" means Hecht. In light of the fact that decedent's will names Hecht as executor, decedent may have intended "executor" to refer to Hecht. However, for reasons not clear in our record, Hecht is not the present executor of the estate.

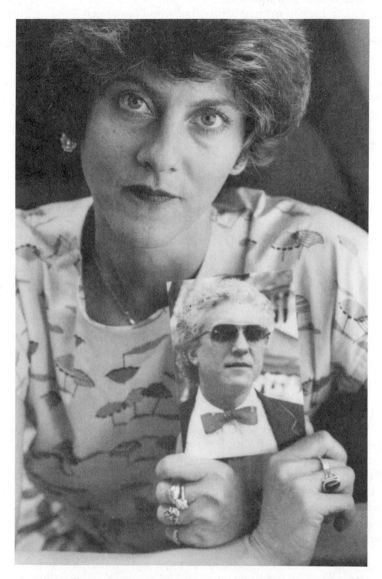

Deborah Hecht holding photo of William Kane

my dreams, even though I never got to see you born. If you are receiving
this letter, it means that I am dead — whether by my own hand or that
of another makes very little difference. I feel that my time has come; and
I wanted to leave you with something more than a dead enigma that was
your father. I am inordinately proud of who I have been — what I made
of me. I'm so proud of that that I would rather take my own life now
than be ground into a mediocre existence by my enemies — who, because
of my mistakes and bravado have gained the power to finish me.

Kane committed suicide on October 30, 1991, in Las Vegas, Nevada.
On November 18, 1991, Robert L. Greene was appointed Special
Administrator of the Estate of William Everett Kane. On December 3,
1991, William Kane, Jr., and Katharine Kane each filed separate will
contests [alleging lack of mental capacity and undue influence by
Hecht]. . . .

On November 5, 1992, Greene, as administrator, filed a "Petition
for Alternative Relief (Instructions to Destroy Decedent's Frozen
Sperm or Order for Preliminary Distribution of Said Sperm and
Order of Determination of Whether Children Conceived from Said
Sperm Shall Be Entitled to Distribution and Instructions Concerning
Administration of Estate Pending Conception and Birth of Said Children)." Greene . . . [stated] in his petition that "decedent's children
have requested that Petitioner Petition this Court for Instructions to
order the sperm destroyed, on public policy grounds. . . . "

Real parties Katharine Kane and William Kane, Jr., filed a Statement
of Interested Parties in which they argued that ordering destruction
of decedent's sperm would "help guard the family unit in two different ways": First, such an order would prevent the birth of children
who will never know their father and "never even have the slightest
hope of being raised in a traditional family." Second, such an order
would "prevent the disruption of existing families by after-born children," and would "prevent additional emotional, psychological and
financial stress on those family members already in existence." They
characterized the desire to father children after one's death as "ego-
tistic and irresponsible," and stated that they "have lost their father
to a tragic death which Hecht could easily have prevented; they do
not wish to suffer any more at her hands. Further, they do not wish
to be troubled for the rest of their lives with worries about the fate
of their half-sibling(s)."[10]

10. On November 12, 1992, decedent's children filed against Hecht a First Amended
Complaint for Wrongful Death and Intentional Infliction of Emotional Distress, wherein
they alleged, inter alia, that their father, who had been unemployed for some time,
became deeply depressed and began to seriously contemplate suicide about September
1, 1991; for six weeks before his death, Hecht was aware of decedent's "disturbed plan"
to end his life; that Hecht convinced him to allow her to have his child after his death
and to leave her a substantial amount of his property to raise and care for this child; in
the week before his death, Hecht encouraged and assisted decedent in transferring
property to her and decedent emptied his personal checking account by issuing a check

Hecht filed a Brief in response to the administrator's petition. She argued that neither the estate nor the children currently hold any property interest in, or right to distribution of, the sperm; it was gifted to her at the time of its deposit into the sperm bank and is either an inter vivos gift or a gift causa mortis. Hecht also maintained that even if the semen is an asset of the estate, the estate should be directed to distribute it to her because . . . the will specifically directs that she is to be the sole beneficiary of the sperm. . . .

At the December 9, 1992, hearing on the petition, the court ordered that the sperm be destroyed. . . . [Upon petition by Hecht, we stayed the trial court order, and granted a hearing.]

. . . [W]e conclude that we cannot uphold the trial court's order. . . .

As we hereinafter explain, the decedent's interest in his frozen sperm vials, even if not governed by the general law of personal property, occupies "an interim category that entitles them to special respect because of their potential for human life" (See Davis v. Davis (Tenn. 1992) 842 S.W.2d 588, 597), and at the time of his death, decedent had an interest, in the nature of ownership, to the extent that he had decision-making authority as to the sperm within the scope of policy set by law. (Ibid.) Thus, decedent had an interest in his sperm which falls within the broad definition of property in Probate Code section 62, as "anything that may be the subject of ownership and includes both real and personal property and any interest therein."

NATURE OF RIGHTS IN SEMEN

Although Davis v. Davis, supra, 842 S.W.2d 588, involved the disposition of frozen preembryos (four to eight-celled entities) of a married couple who had attempted to bear a child through in vitro fertilization but divorced before they could do so, the court's discussion of the legal status of preembryos is informative. For various reasons, not pertinent to our discussion, the Supreme Court of Tennessee concluded that the preembryos could not be considered "persons" under Tennessee law. The court also refused to characterize the interest of the Davises in the preembryos as a property interest under general property law; rather they

> occupy an interim category that entitles them to special respect because of their potential for human life. It follows that any interest that Mary Sue Davis and Junior Davis have in the preembryos in this case is not a true property interest. However, they do have an interest in the nature

---

to Hecht for $80,000; Hecht assisted decedent in purchasing a one-way ticket to Las Vegas and took him to the airport.

of ownership, to the extent that they have decision-making authority concerning disposition of the preembryos, within the scope of policy set by law. (842 S.W.2d at p. 597.)

Sperm which is stored by its provider with the intent that it be used for artificial insemination is thus unlike other human tissue because it is "gametic material" (Davis v. Davis, supra, 842 S.W.2d 588, 597) that can be used for reproduction. Although it has not yet been joined with an egg to form a preembryo, as in *Davis*, the value of sperm lies in its potential to create a child after fertilization, growth, and birth. We conclude that at the time of his death, decedent had an interest, in the nature of ownership, to the extent that he had decision-making authority as to the use of his sperm for reproduction. Such interest is sufficient to constitute "property" within the meaning of Probate Code section 62. Accordingly, the probate court had jurisdiction with respect to the vials of sperm. . . .

We now address the propriety of the trial court's order that the sperm be destroyed. . . .

Real parties attempt to justify the order as premised upon the theory that even if decedent had sufficient right of possession or ownership of the sperm so as to bring it within the jurisdiction of the probate court, his assumed intended use or disposition of the sperm — artificial insemination of Hecht — is invalid on two purported public policy grounds: (1) public policy forbids the artificial insemination of an unmarried woman, and (2) public policy forbids artificial insemination of Hecht with the stored sperm of a deceased man.

ARTIFICIAL INSEMINATION AND UNMARRIED WOMEN

Although artificial insemination in itself is not new, having been performed on animals for centuries, the first recorded successful human artificial insemination was performed in England in 1770. (Shapiro & Sonnenblick, The Widow and the Sperm: The Law of Post-Mortem Insemination (1986) 1 J. Law & Health 229, 234; hereinafter Shapiro & Sonnenblick.) Although the practice was slow to be accepted in the United States until the mid-twentieth century, artificial insemination has now gained widespread acceptance as "medical technology has made it increasingly available and inexpensive to the estimated fifteen percent of all married couples who are infertile." (Ibid.) Artificial insemination was made available to the astronauts in 1961 so they could still father healthy children using stored sperm even if space travel were to harm their reproductive systems.

By 1986, it was estimated that as many as 20,000 women each year were artificially inseminated in the United States; by one estimate,

1,500 of these women were unmarried. (Jhordan C. v. Mary K. (1986) 179 Cal. App. 3d 386, 389, 224 Cal. Rptr. 530, fn. 1.)

In Jhordan C. v. Mary K., supra, 179 Cal. App. 3d 386, the court interpreted Civil Code section 7005, subdivision (b), part of the Uniform Parentage Act (UPA),[11] as affording "unmarried as well as married women a statutory vehicle for obtaining semen for artificial insemination without fear that the donor may claim paternity, and has likewise provided men with a statutory vehicle for donating semen to married and unmarried women alike without fear of liability for child support." (179 Cal. App. 3d at p. 392.)

In Jhordan C., an unmarried woman artificially inseminated herself at home with the semen of a known donor and gave birth to a child, which she wanted to raise jointly with a close woman friend; the donor obtained a paternity judgment from which the mother appealed. In affirming the judgment, the court held that "where impregnation takes place by artificial insemination, and the parties have failed to take advantage of this statutory basis for preclusion of paternity [by providing semen to a licensed physician], the donor of semen can be determined to be the father of the child in a paternity action." (179 Cal. App. 3d 386, 389, 224 Cal. Rptr. 530.)

The court in Jhordan C. was careful to stress

> that our opinion in this case is not intended to express any judicial preference toward traditional notions of family structure or toward providing a father where a single woman has chosen to bear a child. Public policy in these areas is best determined by the legislative branch of government, not the judicial. Our Legislature has already spoken and has afforded to unmarried women a statutory right to bear children by artificial insemination (as well as a right of men to donate semen) without fear of a paternity claim, through provision of the semen to a licensed physician. We simply hold that because Mary omitted to invoke Civil Code section 7005, subdivision (b), by obtaining Jhordan's semen through a licensed physician, and because the parties by all other conduct preserved Jhordan's status as a member of Devin's [the child's] family, the trial court properly declared Jhordan to be Devin's legal father. (179 Cal. App. 3d at pp. 397-398.)

In light of the foregoing, we reject real parties' argument that we are operating in a legal vacuum and are "free to establish policies

11. Civil Code section 7005 provides

(a) If, under the supervision of a licensed physician and with the consent of her husband, a wife is inseminated artificially with semen donated by a man not her husband, the husband is treated in law as if he were the natural father of a child thereby conceived. . . . (b) The donor of semen provided to a licensed physician for use in artificial insemination of a woman other than the donor's wife is treated in law as if he were not the natural father of a child thereby conceived.

with respect to the access of an unmarried woman to a non-coital reproductive technique (artificial insemination)." . . .

We thus conclude that real parties fail to establish with any pertinent authority that the public policy of California prohibits the artificial insemination of Hecht because of her status as an unmarried woman.

POST-MORTEM ARTIFICIAL INSEMINATION

We are aware of only one other court which has addressed the issue of the right of a woman to the sperm of a decedent. In 1984, in Parpalaix v. CECOS, the French Tribunal de Grand Instance ordered CECOS, a government run sperm bank in a Paris suburb, to return stored sperm of a decedent to a doctor chosen by his surviving wife. In light of the discussion in the preceding section pertaining to unmarried women, we find the *Parpalaix* case instructive and pertinent to the issue before us although it dealt with a married couple. We glean the following facts and decision in the *Parpalaix* case from a discussion of it in Shapiro and Sonnenblick, supra, 1 Journal of Law and Health 229, at pages 229-233.

In 1981, Alain Parpalaix, suffering from testicular cancer, made one deposit of sperm at CECOS but left no instructions as to the future use of the sperm. At the time of the deposit, he was living with Corinne, whom he later married on December 23, 1983; as his condition was rapidly deteriorating, Alain died on December 25, 1983 at the age of 26. Corinne requested Alain's sperm deposit from CECOS, which denied the request as other centers had denied the requests of other widows. Corinne, joined by her in-laws, pursued the matter in court, where they contended that as Alain's natural heirs (spouse and parents), they had become the owners of the sperm and CECOS had broken the contract, which was in the nature of a bailment; they also argued they had a moral right to the sperm. . . .

According to Shapiro & Sonnenblick, the French court . . . expressly declined to apply ordinary contract principles raised by both parties, finding "it is impossible to characterize human sperm as movable, inheritable property within the contemplation of the French legislative scheme." (Shapiro & Sonnenblick, supra, 1 J. Law & Health at p. 232.) The court . . . [characterized sperm] as " 'the seed of life . . . tied to the fundamental liberty of a human being to conceive or not to conceive.' This fundamental right must be jealously protected, and is not to be subjected to the rules of contracts. Rather the fate of the sperm must be decided by the person from whom it is drawn. Therefore, the sole issue becomes that of intent." (Ibid.) Property rights and status became irrelevant to that decision. (Id., at p. 233.) The court framed the issues it had to decide as only whether Alain Parpalaix intended his widow to be artificially inseminated with his sperm and whether that intent was "unequivocable." The court found that the testimony of the widow and Alain's parents established his "deep desire" to make his wife "the mother of a common child." (Ibid.) CECOS did not appeal the decision of the court and Corinne was artificially inseminated in November 1984; due to the small quantity and poor quality, she did not become pregnant.

. . . [R]eal parties argue that "this court should adopt a state policy against posthumous conception," because it is "in truth, the creation of orphaned children by artificial means with state authorization," a result which they characterize as "tragic." However, real parties do not cite any authority establishing the propriety of this court, or any court, to make the value judgment as to whether it is better for such a potential child not to be born, assuming that both gamete providers wish to conceive the child. In other words, assuming that both Hecht and decedent desired to conceive a child using decedent's sperm, real parties fail to establish a state interest sufficient to justify interference with that decision. As in Tennessee, we are aware of no statutes in California which contain a "statement of public policy which reveals an interest that could justify infringing on gamete-providers' decisional authority. . . ." (Davis v. Davis, supra, 842 S.W.2d 588, 602.) . . .

Real parties also intimate that the birth of a child by Hecht using decedent's sperm will create psychological burdens on them, decedent's surviving adult children, as well as financial burdens on society and on the estate.

In light of Probate Code sections 6407 and 6408,[12] it is unlikely that the estate would be subject to claims with respect to any such children. . . .

The interest of heirs and courts in the finality of probate rulings was recognized by the Committee which drafted the Uniform Status of Children of Assisted Conception Act, which has been adopted in various forms in North Dakota and Virginia. Section 4 of that Act provides in pertinent part that "(b) An individual who dies before implantation of an embryo, or before a child is conceived other than

---

12. In California, Probate Code section 6407 provides that "Relatives of the decedent conceived before the decedent's death, but born thereafter inherit as if they had been born in the lifetime of the decedent." . . .

[At the time of this case, Cal. Prob. Code §6408 (1993) permitted a nonmarital child to establish paternity after the alleged father's death only if a court order had been entered during the father's life or the father had openly held out the child as his own. Shortly after this case was decided, §6408 was repealed, and §6453, supra page 116, enacted to replace it. Section 6453(b)(3) provides that paternity may be established after the father's death by clear and convincing evidence where it was impossible for the father to hold out the child as his own, which appears to cover the case where the child is conceived after the father's death. — Eds.]

through sexual intercourse, using the individual's egg or sperm, is not a parent of the resulting child."

The Committee Comment states that

> Subsection 4(b) is designed to provide finality for the determination of parenthood of those whose genetic material is utilized in the procreation process after their death. The death of the person whose genetic material is either used in conceiving an embryo or in implanting an already existing embryo into a womb would end the potential parenthood of the deceased. . . . It is designed primarily to avoid the problems of intestate succession which could arise if the posthumous use of a person's genetic material could lead to the deceased being termed a parent. Of course, those who want to explicitly provide for such children in their wills may do so. (9B West's U. Laws Ann. (1987) U. Status of Children of Assisted Conception Act (1988 Act; 1993 Pocket Supp.) Committee Comm. pp. 140-141.)

The result in section 4(b) of the Uniform Status of Children of Assisted Conception Act appears to be consistent with application of Civil Code section 7005 and Probate Code sections 6407 and 6408 to the instant circumstances. (Ante, fn. [12].) . . .[13]

As recently stated by our Supreme Court in a case involving a surrogacy contract: "It is not the role of the judiciary to inhibit the use of reproductive technology when the Legislature has not seen fit to do so; any such effort would raise serious questions in light of the fundamental nature of the rights of procreation and privacy." (Johnson v. Calvert (1993) 5 Cal. 4th 84, 101, 19 Cal. Rptr. 2d 494, 851 P.2d 776.)

For the foregoing reasons we conclude that the trial court abused its discretion in ordering decedent's sperm destroyed.

We emphasize again that we are not adjudicating the issues of the validity of the will, the sperm bank contract, or . . . any other issue not before us.

NOTES AND QUESTIONS

1. After the 1993 decision in the *Hecht* case, the Kane children continued their litigation to deny Hecht the vials of sperm, raising many arguments about legal capacity and undue influence, but chiefly claiming that Hecht had agreed to a settlement under which she received 20 percent of the estate's "residual assets." The children claimed that under this agreement Hecht was to receive only three

---

13. But observe that §6408 was repealed after the case and replaced by a statute that apparently permits paternity to be established where the father dies before conception. See supra footnote 12. — Eds.

of the 15 vials of sperm. After two unsuccessful tries at impregnation by two vials, Hecht, passing the age of 40, sought all the rest of the vials. Finally, in Hecht v. Superior Court, 50 Cal. App. 4th 1289, 59 Cal. Rptr. 2d 222 (1996), the court, expressing exasperation at the children's effort to frustrate their father's will, dismissed all the children's claims and held the property settlement giving Hecht 20 percent of the estate's residual assets did not apply to sperm specifically bequeathed to Hecht. The court ordered all 15 vials of sperm distributed to Deborah Hecht without further delay. The court said, "We do not have before us the many legal questions raised by the possible birth of a child of Hecht through use of Kane's sperm. Thus, we do not decide, for instance, whether that child would be entitled to inherit any property as Kane's heir." From this language, we assume that the court had taken note of the repeal of California Probate Code §6408 and enactment of §6453(b)(3), explained in footnote 12 of the case.

2. The New York Times, March 27, 1999, at A11, carried a story of a woman in Los Angeles giving birth to a girl using the sperm retrieved from her dead husband 30 hours after the man's death. Is the girl the legal child of the father, who did not give his consent? Compare In re Marriage of Witbeck-Wildhagen, 281 Ill. App. 3d 502, 667 N.E.2d 122 (1996) (lack of evidence that husband consented to insemination by a third party donor precludes recognition of a father-child relationship and imposition of a support obligation on the father). Suppose the husband had children by an earlier marriage and had told friends he did not want any more children?

For more on the extraction of sperm from dead or comatose men who do not consent, and the use of such sperm by wives, girlfriends, and parents, see Lori B. Andrews, The Sperminator (a term coined for such a father), N.Y. Times Magazine, Mar. 28, 1999, at 62. The author alleges such practice has now become "common."

3. What are the problems in extending property rights to posthumously conceived children? Do you agree with the Uniform Status of Children of Assisted Conception Act §4(b), providing that the individual who furnishes the egg or sperm for posthumous conception is not a parent of the resulting child? Suppose that the testator devises his property in trust for his children for their lives, remainder to his grandchildren. Should a posthumously conceived child share in the trust, and the children of such a child share in the remainder? See Ronald Chester, Freezing the Heir Apparent: A Dialogue on Postmortem Conception, Parental Responsibility, and Inheritance, 33 Hous. L. Rev. 967 (1996); Kathleen R. Guzman, Property, Progeny, Body Part: Assisted Reproduction and the Transfer of Wealth, 31 U.C. Davis L. Rev. 193 (1997); Anne R. Schiff, Arising From the Dead: Challenges of a Posthumous Procreation, 75 N.C.L. Rev. 901 (1997); Note, Fa-

therhood from the Grave: An Analysis of Postmortem Insemination, 22 Hofstra L. Rev. 521 (1993); Comment, Posthumous Progeny: A Proposed Resolution to the Dilemma of the Posthumously Conceived Child, 41 Loy. L. Rev. 713 (1996); Restatement (Third) of Property, Wills and Other Donative Transfers, §2.5, Reporter's Note 7 (1999).

Under the Social Security Act, state intestate succession law determines rights to social security benefits for a dependent child. A child of the father is eligible for social security dependent benefits due the father's children only if the child inherits from the father under the applicable state law. In 1996, the Social Security Commissioner agreed to pay benefits to a Louisiana child conceived after her father's death, even though under Louisiana law such a child is not an heir. In an earlier case, social security benefits were given an Arizona child conceived after her father's death because Arizona recognizes such a child as the father's heir. The Social Security Commissioner said the case raises significant policy issues not contemplated when the Social Security Act was passed in the 1930s, which was concerned with the treatment of illegitimates, and ruled that it would be inappropriate to deny benefits to the Louisiana child while awarding them to the Arizona child. Changes in the law are now being considered. See Chicago Tribune, March 12, 1996, at N12.

4. California Cryobank, Inc., referred to in *Hecht,* is one of the largest sperm banks in the country. Located near UCLA in Westwood Village, it offers a wide selection of donors from all races and ethnic origins. It recruits as donors college students in California and the Boston area. The donors need to be at least 5'9", between 19 and 34 years old, and not adopted as children. They are extensively screened to eliminate prospective donors with HIV or other sexually transmitted diseases or with certain genetically transmitted diseases. Donors must agree to provide sperm specimens twice a week for a period of one year, preferably two, for which they are paid $35 for each specimen. After a donor's sperm results in ten live births, the donor is retired. Approximately 25 percent of the women requesting artificial insemination are without male partners.

California Cryobank keeps up with its donors and tracks their whereabouts. If, in the future, an adult child born from artificial insemination wishes to find his or her biological father, California Cryobank will furnish the information after securing the father's consent at such future time.

2. Advancements

If any child wishes to share in the intestate distribution of a deceased parent's estate, the child must permit the administrator to include in the determination of the distributive shares the value of any property that the decedent, while living, gave the child by way of an *advancement*. At common law, any lifetime gift to a child was presumed to be an advancement — in effect, a prepayment — of the child's intestate share. To avoid application of the doctrine, the child had the burden of establishing that the lifetime transfer was intended as an absolute gift that was not to be counted against the child's share of the estate. The doctrine is based on the assumption that the parent would want an equal distribution of assets among the children and that true equality can be reached only if lifetime gifts are taken into account in determining the amount of the equal shares. When a parent makes an advancement to the child and the child predeceases the parent, the amount of the advancement is deducted from the shares of such child's descendants if other children of the parent survive.

If a gift is treated as an advancement, the donee must allow its value to be brought into *hotchpot* if the donee wants to share in the decedent's estate. Here is how hotchpot works: Assume decedent leaves no spouse, three children, and an estate worth $50,000. One daughter, *A*, received an advancement of $10,000. To calculate the shares in the estate, the $10,000 gift is added to the $50,000, and the total of $60,000 is divided by three. *A* has already received $10,000 of her share; thus she receives only $10,000 from the estate. Her siblings each take a $20,000 share. If *A* had been given property worth $34,000 as an advancement, *A* would not have to give back a portion of this amount. *A* will stay out of hotchpot, and decedent's $50,000 will be equally divided between the other two children.

PROBLEMS

1. *O* has three children by his first marriage and six children by his second marriage. After his second marriage, *O* gives each of the children by his first marriage a tract of land. *O* subsequently dies intestate. Are these gifts advancements? In re Martinez's Estate, 96 N.M. 619, 633 P.2d 727 (App. 1981).

2. *O* has three children. One daughter, *A*, does not leave home but lives with *O* on *O*'s farm until *O* dies. A few years before death, *O* deeds the farm to *A*. *O* dies intestate. *A* claims the gift is not an advancement but an extra gift for extraordinary services rendered *O*. What result? Thomas v. Thomas, 398 S.W.2d 231 (Ky. 1965).

Suppose that *O* gives his son *B* $20,000. *B* is ill and unable to work and support his family. Is this an advancement?

Suppose that *O*'s daughter *C* is smart, goes to Yale Medical School, and acquires an M.D. degree. *O* pays the tuition ($90,000). Is this an advancement?

Largely because of problems of proof of the donor's intent engendered by the advancements doctrine, many states have reversed the common law presumption of advancement. In these states a lifetime gift is presumed *not* to be an advancement unless it is shown to have been intended as such. In other states, statutes declare that a gift is not an advancement unless it is declared as such in a writing signed by the grantor or grantee. See Carolyn S. Bratt, Kentucky's Doctrine of Advancements: A Time for Reform, 75 Ky. L.J. 341 (1987).

Uniform Probate Code (1990)

§2-109. ADVANCEMENTS

(a) If an individual dies intestate as to all or a portion of his [or her] estate, property the decedent gave during the decedent's lifetime to an individual who, at the decedent's death, is an heir[14] is treated as an advancement against the heir's intestate share only if (i) the decedent declared in a contemporaneous writing or the heir acknowledged in writing that the gift is an advancement or (ii) the decedent's contemporaneous writing or the heir's written acknowledgment otherwise indicates that the gift is to be taken into account in computing the division and distribution of the decedent's intestate estate.

(b) For purposes of subsection (a), property advanced is valued as of the time the heir came into possession or enjoyment of the property or as of the time of the decedent's death, whichever first occurs.

(c) If the recipient of the property fails to survive the decedent, the property is not taken into account in computing the division and distribution of the decedent's intestate estate, unless the decedent's contemporaneous writing provides otherwise.

Observe that UPC §2-109(c) changes the common law if the recipient does not survive the decedent. In that case, the advancement is not taken into account in determining the share of the recipient's issue.

The Uniform Probate Code has been criticized as virtually eliminating the doctrine of advancements from the law of intestate succession. Persons who do not write wills or consult lawyers and die intestate will rarely know that a lifetime gift must be stated in writing to be an

---

14. UPC §2-109 applies to advancements made to spouses and collaterals (such as nephews and nieces) as well as to lineal descendants. In most states, only gifts to lineal descendants are considered advancements. — Eds.

advancement to be charged against the donee's intestate share. See Mary L. Fellows, Concealing Legislative Reform in the Common-Law Tradition: The Advancements Doctrine and the Uniform Probate Code, 37 Vand. L. Rev. 671 (1984), proposing a statute requiring *all* gifts to be treated as advancements absent written evidence of a contrary intent (just the opposite of the UPC).

QUESTION

Which of the following rules do you think is best?

(1) Gifts to children are presumptively advancements.
(2) Gifts to children are presumptively not advancements.
(3) Gifts to children are not advancements unless so stated in writing.
(4) Gifts to children are advancements unless stated not to be in writing.

See Gareth Miller, The Machinery of Succession 282-283 (2d ed. 1996); Restatement (Third) of Property, Wills and Other Donative Transfers, §2.6 (1999) (requiring a writing as in UPC §2-109).

NOTE: TRANSFER OF AN EXPECTANCY

In the eyes of the law no living person has heirs; to use the Latin phrase: *nemo est haeres viventis.* The persons who would be the heirs of *A*, a living person, if *A* died within the next hour, are not the heirs of *A* but the *heirs apparent.* They have a mere *expectancy.* This expectancy can be destroyed by *A*'s deed or will. It is not a legal "interest" at all. Not being an interest, an expectancy cannot be transferred at law. However, a purported transfer of an expectancy, for an adequate consideration, may be enforceable in equity as a contract to transfer if the court views it as fair under all the circumstances. Equity scrutinizes such transactions to protect prospective heirs from unfair bargains.[15] See Ware v. Crowell, 251 Va. 116, 465 S.E.2d 809 (1996). See also Carolyn S. Bratt, A Primer of Kentucky Intestacy Laws, 82 Ky. L.J. 29, 106-113 (1994) (discussing Kentucky's refusal to enforce such

---

15. Undoubtedly, the most famous sale of an expectancy was the sale of Esau's birthright to Jacob for a bowl of pottage. Genesis 25:29-34. Whether this sale was enforceable under Hebrew law has been much debated by Biblical scholars. See David Daube, Studies in Biblical Law 191-200 (1947); Reuben Ahroni, Why Did Esau Spurn the Birthright? 29 Judaism 323 (1980). Under modern American law, was Esau's promise enforceable as a fair bargain?

contracts on the theory they give the transferee an economic incentive to hasten the transferor's death).

3. *Managing a Minor's Property*

Transfers of property to a minor raise special problems. A minor does not have the legal capacity to manage property. It is now time to speak of guardians and of the property management alternatives available to parents of a minor.

A *guardian of the person* has responsibility for the minor child's custody and care. As long as one parent of the child is living and competent, that parent is the natural guardian of the child's person. If both parents die while a child is a minor, and their wills do not designate a guardian, a court will appoint a guardian from among the nearest relatives. This person may not be the person the parents would want to have custody of the child. For a parent with a minor child, one of the principal reasons for having a will is to designate a guardian of the person in case both parents die during the child's minority.

The second principal reason a parent with a minor child needs a will is to deal with management of the child's property. A guardian of the person has no authority to deal with the child's property.

Three alternatives for property management are available: guardianship (or conservatorship), custodianship, and trusteeship. The latter two are available only to persons who create them during lifetime or who die testate, creating these arrangements by will. If a parent dies intestate, leaving property to a minor child, a guardian of the property or a conservator must be appointed by a court.

Guardianship or conservatorship. In feudal times the guardian of a minor ward (usually the overlord) took possession of the ward's lands. The guardian had the duty of supporting the ward, but all income from rents in excess of the amount necessary for support belonged to the guardian personally. Thus guardianships (then known as wardships) were very profitable for the guardian.

After the feudal incidents, including wardship, were abolished in 1660, a new kind of guardianship was recognized, giving the ward the rents from the property and the guardian only a management fee. Nonetheless, the historical odor remained. A guardian of property was looked upon with suspicion and was required to account annually to a court of chancery. To avoid a disagreeable contest later with the ward or chancellor, guardians sought approval for their actions in advance from the chancellor. The product of history is a system wherein the guardian is straitjacketed.

First, the guardian of property, who does not have title to the ward's property, usually cannot change investments without a court order.

The guardian has the duty of preserving the specific property left the minor and delivering it to the ward at age 18, unless the court approves a sale, lease, or mortgage. Second, the guardian ordinarily can use only the income from the property to support the ward; the guardian has no authority to go into principal to support the ward, unless the court approves. Strict court supervision over many of the guardian's acts is burdensome and time-consuming. Each trip to court costs money — for the attorney's fee and court costs. The ward often ends up with less property at the end of a guardianship than at the beginning.

In many states, guardianship laws have been reformed. The guardian of the property has been renamed conservator and given "title as trustee" to the protected person's property, as well as the same investment powers trustees have. Appointment and supervision by a court is still required, but the conservator has far more flexible powers than a guardian, and only one trip to the courthouse annually for an accounting may be necessary. Article V of the Uniform Probate Code is representative of modern conservatorship laws.

In states without modern conservatorship laws, the only effective way to handle guardianship administrations is to avoid them. And, indeed, we conclude that even in states with modern conservatorship laws, the alternative arrangements of custodianship or trusteeship for a minor are preferable, because the court does not become involved unless the minor contests the custodian's or trustee's actions.

Custodianship. A custodian is a person who is given property to hold for the benefit of a minor under the state Uniform Transfers to Minors Act. To provide a convenient procedure for making gifts to minors, who have no legal capacity to manage or sell property, every state has enacted either the Uniform Transfers to Minors Act (1983) or its earlier version, the Uniform Gifts to Minors Act (1956, revised 1966). Under these acts, property may be transferred to a person (including the donor) as *custodian* for the benefit of the minor. A devise or gift may be made to *X* "as custodian for (name of minor) under the (name of state) Uniform Transfers to Minors Act," thereby incorporating the provisions of the state's uniform act and eliminating the necessity of drafting a trust instrument. Hence, creation of a custodianship is quite simple.

Under Uniform Transfers to Minors Act §14(a) the custodian has discretionary power to expend

> for the minor's benefit so much or all the custodial property as the custodian deems advisable for the benefit of the minor, without court order and without regard to (i) the duty or ability of the custodian personally or any other person to support the minor; or (ii) any other income or

property of the minor which may be applicable or available for that purpose. . . .

To the extent that the custodial property is not so expended, the
custodian is required to transfer the property to the minor on his
attaining the age of 21 or, if the minor dies before attaining the age
of 21, to the estate of the minor.

The custodian has the right to manage the property and to reinvest
it. However, the custodian is a fiduciary and is subject to "the standard of care that would be observed by a prudent person dealing with
property of another." §12. The custodian is not under the supervision
of a court — as is a guardian or conservator — and no accounting
to the court annually or at the end of the custodianship is necessary.
The custodian can account directly to the ward when the ward attains
21. A custodianship is useful for modest gifts to a minor, but when a
large amount of property is involved, a trust is usually preferable.

Trust. The third alternative for property management on behalf of
a minor is to establish a trust for a child. A trust is the most flexible
of all property arrangements, and a good part of this book will later
be devoted to it. The testator can tailor the trust specifically to the
family circumstances and the testator's particular desires. Under a
guardianship or conservatorship, the child must receive the property
at 18 and, under a custodianship, at 21, but a trust can postpone
possession until the donor thinks the child is competent to manage
the property. For an examination of guardianship, custodianship, and
trust, concluding the last is preferable in most situations, see William
M. McGovern, Jr., Trusts, Custodianships, and Durable Powers of Attorney, 27 Real Prop., Prob. & Tr. J. 1, 3-17 (1992).

If the testator wants to make a cash bequest to a beneficiary who is
now a minor and does not want to create a custodianship or trust,
the will can provide that any cash bequest to a minor beneficiary can
be distributed to the beneficiary's parents. A bequest to a minor can
be paid to the minor's parents if the will so authorizes. Even if the
will does not expressly authorize payment to the child's parents, many
states have laws permitting the personal representative to pay small
sums from the decedent's estate without requiring the appointment
of a guardian or conservator. See Uniform Probate Code §5-101 (sums
not exceeding $5,000 per year).

PROBLEM

Refer back to the estate planning problem involving Howard and
Wendy Brown (supra pages 49-59). Assume that Howard Brown dies
intestate. After payment of debts, taxes, and expenses of administration, the assets of his estate include:

	Property acquired from H's earnings during marriage[16]	H's property acquired by gift[16]
Tangible personalty:	$ 20,000	
Real estate:		
Residence (title is in "Howard Brown and Wendy Brown, as joint tenants with right of survivorship and not as tenants in common"); subject to mortgage of $70,000	160,000	
Lot and cabin, Lake Murray (title is in Howard alone)	75,000	
Remainder interest in mother's home		$ 20,000
Bank accounts:		
Checking (joint and survivor account with wife)	3,000	
Certificate of deposit ("Howard Brown and Wendy Brown, as joint tenants with right of survivorship")	20,000	
IRA (Howard's, payable on death to Wendy)	30,000	
Securities:		
General Corp. stock (registered in Howard's name)		80,000
Varoom Mutual Fund (registered in Howard's name)		30,000
American Growth Mutual Fund ("Howard Brown and Wendy Brown, as joint tenants with right of survivorship and not as tenants in common")	40,000	
Life insurance:		
(Wendy is named primary beneficiary; Howard's estate is named contingent beneficiary)	125,000	
	$453,000	$130,000

16. The source of the property is irrelevant for intestate distribution in common law property states; how title is held at death is controlling. In community property states, property acquired from a spouse's earnings during marriage is community property and at the spouse's death passes under a different intestate scheme from separate property.

Brown is survived by his wife and two minor children and a stepson. How is Brown's estate distributed under the Uniform Probate Code? Under the intestacy statute of your state? Should Howard have left a will?

AN EXERCISE IN LAWYERING

Wendy Brown writes you:

Dear _____:

We've had some changes in our family since we wrote our wills and our wills need changing.

Two months ago our son, Zachary, was born. A bundle of joy — and sleepless nights! As you know, Howard and I want our property to go absolutely to the survivor, and the main reason for having wills is to provide for the children in case we die in a common disaster or before the survivor can make a will for the children.

You drafted our wills to create a trust for our children if we die and a child is under 25. Do you think we should continue to have a single trust for all the children or should we have separate trusts for each child, permitting each child to receive the principal of the child's trust upon reaching 25? Is a "family trust" or separate trusts fairer to our newborn son? What are the pros and cons of these?

Another problem is my sister Lucy has separated from her husband, Jonathan, and has taken up with a man we don't like at all, Bill Hyde. She says she intends to marry him. Bill is a slick operator with a mysterious source of income. We're sick over this, because we love Lucy and hate for her to get mixed up with this guy. But if she marries Bill, we wouldn't want our children to move into their home if we die in a common disaster. My brother Simon and his wife Antonia don't have children, they both work, and wouldn't want to be in charge of a baby. Ruth is always off on digs in Turkey. Do you have any advice about who should be guardian for our children?

I enclose a copy of Howard's will that you drafted. Mine is the same, with appropriate changes in names, and except for the devise of his mother's house. Please give us your advice about these two matters.

Sincerely,
_____
/s/ *Wendy Brown*

[For more on Wendy and Howard Brown's family, see supra pages 49-59.]

Will of Howard Brown
(With Testamentary Trust)

ARTICLE 1

I, Howard Brown, hereby make my will, and I revoke all other wills and codicils that I have previously made.

ARTICLE 2

I give all my jewelry, clothing, household furniture and furnishings, personal automobiles, books, and other tangible articles of a household or personal nature, or my interest in any such property, not otherwise specifically disposed of by this or in any other manner, together with any insurance on the property, to my wife, Wendy Brown, if she survives me; but if my wife does not survive me, then to my children who survive me, in substantially equal shares as they may select on the basis of valuation. These gifts shall be free of all death taxes.

The executor shall represent any child under age 18 in matters relating to any distribution of tangible personal property, including selecting the assets that shall constitute that child's share. In the executor's absolute discretion, the executor may (1) sell all or part of such child's share which the executor deems unsuitable for the child's use, (2) distribute the proceeds to the Children's Trust or share of such trust for the child's benefit, or (3) deliver the unsold property without bond to the minor if sufficiently mature or to any suitable person with whom the child resides or who has control or care of the child.

ARTICLE 3

I give all my right, title, and interest in my mother's house at 423 Elm St., Concord, Delaware, to my sister Carol Gould.

ARTICLE 4

I give the residue of my estate to my wife, Wendy Brown, if she survives me. If my wife does not survive me and all my children are 25 years of age or older at my death, I give the residue of my estate to my children and to the descendants of any then-deceased child by right of representation. If my wife does not survive me and any of my children is under the age of 25 at my death, I give the residue of my estate to the trustee of the Children's Trust set forth in Article 5.

ARTICLE 5

The trustee of the Children's Trust shall hold, administer, and distribute all property allocated to the Children's Trust for the benefit of my children as follows: The trustee shall pay to or for any child as much of the income as is necessary for the child's health, education, support, or maintenance to maintain the child's accustomed manner of living. The trustee shall add to principal any net income not so distributed.

If the trustee considers the income insufficient, the trustee shall pay to or for a child as much of the principal as the trustee considers reasonably necessary for the child's health, education, support, maintenance, comfort, welfare, or happiness to maintain, at a minimum, the child's accustomed manner of living.

In making distributions, the trustee (1) may consider any other income or resources of the child, including the child's ability to obtain gainful employment and the obligation of others to support the child, known to the trustee and reasonably available for the purposes stated here, (2) may pay more to or apply more for some children than others and may make payments to or applications of benefits for one or more children to the exclusion of others, (3) may consider the value of the trust assets, the relative needs, both present and future, of each child, and the tax consequences to the trust and to any child, and (4) shall charge distributions of income and principal against the entire trust estate and not against the share of the child to whom or for whom the distribution was made.

The trustee, in the trustee's reasonable discretion, may from time to time make preliminary distributions of principal to any of my children who have attained the age of 25, if the trustee finds valid and productive reasons for making the distribution, such as the purchase of a residence or establishment of a business, and if the remaining principal and income will be adequate for the health, support, maintenance, and education of my other children. The trustee shall deduct such preliminary distributions without interest from the share ultimately distributed to such child or to such child's descendants. In the aggregate, the value of any preliminary distributions shall not exceed 50 percent of that child's putative share. The term *putative share* shall mean that portion of the entire trust estate that would be distributable to a particular child, after considering all previous loans and advances, if the entire trust were divided into separate trusts on the date that the distribution to be measured against the putative share is made.

When every child of mine has reached the age of 25 or died before reaching that age, the trustee shall divide the trust into as many equal shares as there are children of mine then living and children of mine then deceased with descendants then living.

On the division of the Children's Trust into shares, the trustee shall distribute each living child's share outright to the child and each deceased child's share to the deceased child's then-living descendants by right of representation.

ARTICLE 6

I nominate as trustee of the Children's Trust Lucy Preston Lipman. If Lucy Preston Lipman fails to qualify or ceases to act, I nominate as successor trustee [the lawyer who drew this will].

The trustee may employ custodians, attorneys, accountants, investment advisers, corporate fiduciaries, or any other agents or advisers to assist the trustee in the administration of this trust, and the trustee may rely on the advice given by these agents. The trustee shall pay reasonable compensation for all services performed by these agents from the trust estate out of either income or principal as the trustee in the trustee's reasonable discretion shall determine. These payments shall not decrease the compensation of the trustee.

No trustee shall be liable to any person interested in this trust for any act or default unless it results from the trustee's bad faith, willful misconduct, or gross negligence.

The trustee shall have the power to continue to hold any property or to abandon any property that the trustee receives or acquires.

The trustee shall have the power to retain, purchase, or otherwise acquire unproductive property.

The trustee shall have the power to manage, control, grant options on, sell (for cash or on deferred payments with or without security), convey, exchange, partition, divide, improve, and repair trust property.

The trustee shall have the power to lease trust property for terms within or beyond the terms of the trust and for any purpose, including exploration for and removal of gas, oil, and other minerals, and to enter into oil leases, pooling, and utilization agreements.

The trustee shall have the power to invest and reinvest the trust estate in every kind of property, real, personal, or mixed, and every kind of investment, specifically including, but not by way of limitation, corporate obligations of every kind, preferred or common stocks, shares in investment trusts, investment companies, mutual funds, money market funds, index funds, and mortgage participations, which persons of prudence, discretion, and intelligence acquire for their own account, and any common trust fund administered by the trustee.

The trustee shall have all the rights, powers, and privileges of an owner of the securities held in trust, including, but not by way of limitation, the power to vote, give proxies, and pay assessments; the power to participate in voting trusts and pooling agreements (whether or not extending beyond the terms of the trust); the power to enter into shareholders' agreements; the power to consent to foreclosure, reorganizations, consolidations, merger liquidations, sales, and leases, and, incident to any such action, to deposit securities with and transfer title to any protective or other committee on such terms as the trustee may deem advisable; and the power to exercise or sell stock subscription or conversion rights.

The trustee shall have the power to hold securities or other property in the trustee's name as trustee under this trust, in the trustee's own name, in the name of a nominee, or in unregistered form so that ownership will pass by delivery.

The trustee shall have the power to carry, at the expense of the trust, insurance of such kinds and in such amounts as the trustee deems advisable to protect the trust estate against any damage or loss and to protect the trustee against liability with respect to third parties.

The trustee shall have the power to loan to any person, including a trust beneficiary or the estate of a trust beneficiary, at interest rates and with or without security as the trustee deems advisable.

Upon termination of the trust, the approval of the accounts of the trustee in an instrument signed by all the adult beneficiaries and guardians of any minor beneficiaries shall be a complete discharge and release of the trustee with respect to the administration of the trust property and shall be binding on all persons.

ARTICLE 7

If my wife, Wendy Brown, does not survive me and if at my death any of my children are minors, I nominate as guardian of the persons and the property of my minor children Lucy Preston Lipman.

ARTICLE 8

The terms *child* and *children* as used in this will refer to my stepson, Michael Walker, and to my children, Sarah Brown and Stephanie Brown, and also to any child or children hereafter born to me.

ARTICLE 9

I nominate as executor of this will my wife, Wendy Brown. If for any reason she fails to qualify or ceases to act I nominate Lucy Preston Lipman to serve as executor.

My executor shall have the same powers granted the trustee under Article 6 to be exercised without court order, as well as any other powers that may be granted by law. I direct that no bond or other security shall be required of any person, including nonresidents named in this will, acting as executor, trustee, or guardian.

———————

I have signed this will, which is typewritten on _____ sheets of paper, on this _____ day of _____, 20 _____, and, for the purposes of identification, I have also written my name on the margin of all pages before this signature page.

———————

Howard Brown

On the _____ day of _____, 20 _____, Howard Brown declared to us, the undersigned, that the foregoing instrument was his last will, and he requested us to act as witnesses to it and to his signature thereon. He then signed the will in our presence, we being present at the same time. We now, at his request, in his presence, and in the presence of each other, hereunto subscribe our names as witnesses, and each of us declares that in his or her opinion this testator is of sound and disposing mind and memory.

Name	Address
Name	Address

SECTION C. BARS TO SUCCESSION

1. Homicide

In re Estate of Mahoney
Supreme Court of Vermont, 1966
126 Vt. 31, 220 A.2d 475

SMITH, J.   The decedent, Howard Mahoney, died intestate on May 6, 1961, of gunshot wounds. His wife, Charlotte Mahoney, the appellant here, was tried for the murder of Howard Mahoney in the Addison County Court and was convicted by jury of the crime of manslaughter in March, 1962. She is presently serving a sentence of not less than 12 nor more than 15 years at the Women's Reformatory in Rutland.

Howard Mahoney left no issue, and was survived by his wife and his father and mother. His father, Mark Mahoney, was appointed administrator of his estate which at the present time amounts to $3,885.89. After due notice and hearing, the Probate Court for the District of Franklin entered a judgment order decreeing the residue of the Estate of Howard Mahoney, in equal shares, to the father and mother of the decedent. An appeal from the judgment order and decree has been taken here by the appellant widow. The question submitted is whether a widow convicted of manslaughter in connection with the death of her husband may inherit from his estate.

The general rules of descent provide that if a decedent is married and leaves no issue, his surviving spouse shall be entitled to the whole of decedent's estate if it does not exceed $8,000. 14 V.S.A. §551(2). Only if the decedent leaves no surviving spouse or issue does the estate descend in equal shares to the surviving father and mother. 14 V.S.A. §551(3). There is no statutory provision in Vermont regulating the descent and distribution of property from the decedent to the slayer. The question presented is one of first impression in this jurisdiction.

In a number of jurisdictions, statutes have been enacted which in certain instances, at least, prevent a person who has killed another from taking by descent or distribution from the person he has killed. . . .

Courts in those states that have no statute preventing a slayer from taking by descent or distribution from the estate of his victim, have followed three separate and different lines of decision.

(1) The legal title passed to the slayer and may be retained by him in spite of his crime. The reasoning for so deciding is that devolution of the property of a decedent is controlled entirely by the statutes of

descent and distribution; further, that denial of the inheritance to the slayer because of his crime would be imposing an additional punishment for his crime not provided by statute, and would violate the constitutional provision against corruption of blood. Carpenter's Estate, 170 Pa. 203, 32 A. 637, 29 L.R.A. 145; Wall v. Pfanschmidt, 265 Ill. 180, 106 N.E. 785, L.R.A. 1915C, 328; Bird v. Plunkett et al., 139 Conn. 491, 95 A.2d 71, 36 A.L.R.2d 951.

(2) The legal title will not pass to the slayer because of the equitable principle that no one should be permitted to profit by his own fraud, or take advantage and profit as a result of his own wrong or crime. Riggs v. Palmer, 115 N.Y. 506, 22 N.E. 188, 5 L.R.A. 340; Price v. Hitaffer, 164 Md. 505, 165 A. 470; Slocum v. Metropolitan Life Ins. Co., 245 Mass. 565, 139 N.E. 816, 27 A.L.R. 1517. Decisions so holding have been criticized as judicially engrafting an exception on the statute of descent and distribution and being "unwarranted judicial legislation." Wall v. Pfanschmidt, supra.

(3) The legal title passes to the slayer but equity holds him to be a constructive trustee for the heirs or next of kin of the decedent. This disposition of the question presented avoids a judicial engrafting on the statutory laws of descent and distribution, for title passes to the slayer. But because of the unconscionable mode by which the property is acquired by the slayer, equity treats him as a constructive trustee and compels him to convey the property to the heirs or next of kin of the deceased.

The reasoning behind the adoption of this doctrine was well expressed by Mr. Justice Cardozo in his lecture on "The Nature of the Judicial Process." "Consistency was preserved, logic received its tribute, by holding that the legal title passed, but it was subject to a constructive trust. A constructive trust is nothing but 'the formula through which the conscience of equity finds expression.' Property is acquired in such circumstances that the holder of legal title may not in good conscience retain the beneficial interest. Equity, to express its disapproval of his conduct, converts him into a trustee." See 4 Scott on Trusts (2d ed. 1956) §402; Bogert, Trusts and Trustees (2d ed. 1960) §478. See Miller v. Belville, 98 Vt. 243, 126 A. 590.

The New Hampshire court was confronted with the same problem of the rights to the benefits of an estate by one who had slain the decedent, in the absence of a statute on the subject. Kelley v. State, 105 N.H. 240, 196 A.2d 68. Speaking for an unanimous court, Chief Justice Kenison said: "But, even in the absence of statute, a court applying common law techniques can reach a sensible solution by charging the spouse, heir or legatee as a constructive trustee of the property where equity and justice demand it." Kelley v. State, supra, pp. 69, 70. We approve of the doctrine so expressed.

However, the principle that one should not profit by his own wrong must not be extended to every case where a killer acquires property from his victim as a result of the killing. One who has killed while insane is not chargeable as a constructive trustee, or if the slayer had a vested interest in the property, it is property to which he would have been entitled if no slaying had occurred. The principle to be applied is that the slayer should not be permitted to improve his position by the killing, but should not be compelled to surrender property to which he would have been entitled if there had been no killing. The doctrine of constructive trust is involved to prevent the slayer from profiting from his crime, but not as an added criminal penalty. Kelley v. State, supra, p.70; Restatement of Restitution, §187(2), Comment a.

The appellant here was, as we have noted, convicted of manslaughter and not of murder. She calls to our attention that while the Restatement of Restitution approves the application of the constructive trust doctrine where a devisee or legatee murders the testator, that such rules are not applicable where the slayer was guilty of manslaughter. Restatement of Restitution, §187, Comment e.

The cases generally have not followed this limitation of the rule but hold that the line should not be drawn between murder and manslaughter, but between voluntary and involuntary manslaughter. Kelley v. State, supra; Chase v. Jennifer, 219 Md. 564, 150 A.2d 251, 254.

We think that this is the proper rule to follow. Voluntary manslaughter is an intentional and unlawful killing, with a real design and purpose to kill, even if such killing be the result of sudden passion or great provocation. Involuntary manslaughter is caused by an unlawful act, but not accompanied with any intention to take life. State v. McDonnell, 32 Vt. 491, 545. It is the intent to kill, which when accomplished, leads to the profit of the slayer that brings into play the constructive trust to prevent the unjust enrichment of the slayer by reason of his intentional killing.

In Vermont, an indictment for murder can result in a jury conviction on either voluntary or involuntary manslaughter. State v. Averill, 85 Vt. 115, 132, 81 A. 461. The legislature has provided the sentences that may be passed upon a person convicted of manslaughter, but provides no definition of that offense, nor any statutory distinction between voluntary and involuntary manslaughter. 13 V.S.A. §2304.

The cause now before us is here on a direct appeal from the probate court. Findings of fact were made below from which it appears that the judgment of the probate court decreeing the estate of Howard Mahoney to his parents, rather than to his widow, was based upon a finding of the felonious killing of her husband by Mrs. Mahoney. However, the appellees here have asked us to affirm the decree below by imposing a constructive trust on the estate in the hands of the widow.

But the Probate Court did not decree the estate to the widow, and then make her a constructive trustee of such estate for the benefit of the parents. The judgment below decreed the estate directly to the parents, which was in direct contravention of the statutes of descent and distribution. The Probate Court was bound to follow the statutes of descent and distribution and its decree was in error and must be reversed.

The Probate Court was without jurisdiction to impose a constructive trust on the estate in the hands of the appellant, even if it had attempted to do so. Probate courts are courts of special and limited jurisdiction given by statute and do not [have powers to establish] . . . purely equitable rights and claims. . . .

However, the jurisdiction of the court of chancery may be invoked in probate matters in aid of the probate court when the powers of that court are inadequate, and it appears that the probate court cannot reasonably and adequately handle the question. The jurisdiction of the chancery court in so acting on probate matters is special and limited only to aiding the probate court. The Probate Court, in making its decree, used the record of the conviction of the appellant for manslaughter for its determination that the appellant had feloniously killed her husband. If the jurisdiction of the court of chancery is invoked by the appellees here it will be for the determination of that court, upon proof, to determine whether the appellant wilfully killed her late husband, as it will upon all other equitable considerations that may be offered in evidence, upon charging the appellant with a constructive trust. "The fact that he is convicted of murder in a criminal case does not dispense with the necessity of proof of the murder in a proceedings in equity to charge him as a constructive trustee." Restatement of Restitution, §187, Comment d.

The jurisdiction over charging the appellant with a constructive trust on the estate of Howard Mahoney lies in the court of chancery, and not in the probate court.

Decree reversed and cause remanded, with directions that the proceedings herein be stayed for sixty days to give the Administrator of the Estate of Howard Mahoney an opportunity to apply to the Franklin County Court of Chancery for relief. If application is so made, proceedings herein shall be stayed pending the final determination thereof. If application is not so made, the Probate Court for the District of Franklin shall assign to Charlotte Mahoney, surviving wife, the right and interest in and to the estate of her deceased husband which the Vermont Statutes confer.[17]

17. In 1972, a statute was enacted in Vermont providing that an heir, devisee, or legatee who "stands convicted in any court . . . of intentionally and unlawfully killing

NOTES AND PROBLEMS

1.   Almost all states have statutes dealing with the rights of a killer in the estate of a victim. These statutes vary in many details and usually fail to deal with one or more aspects of the problem. Among the issues arising under these statutes, the following appear to give rise to the most litigation.

(a) Does the statute apply to nonprobate transfers (joint tenancy, life insurance, pensions, etc.) as well as to wills and intestacy or only to the latter? If only to the latter, will a court apply to nonprobate transfers a common law slayer's rule or a constructive trust to prevent the beneficiary from profiting by killing? Uniform Probate Code §2-803, a well-drafted slayer statute, bars the killer from succeeding to nonprobate as well as probate property. It also provides that a "wrongful acquisition" of property must be treated in accordance with the principle that a killer cannot profit from his wrong.

(b) If the killer is barred from taking, who takes? The usual view is that the killer is treated as having predeceased the victim. The UPC provides that the killer is treated as having disclaimed the property (and under the UPC disclaimer statute, §2-801, the disclaimant is treated as having predeceased the decedent).

If the killer is treated as having predeceased the victim, is a gift in the victim's will to the killer's heirs if the killer does not survive the victim given effect? In Primerica Life Insurance Co. v. Suter, 945 S.W.2d 554 (Mo. App. 1997), the husband named his wife primary beneficiary of his life insurance policy and her father as contingent beneficiary if the wife did not survive the husband. Subsequently, the wife was convicted of complicity in killing her husband and was therefore barred and treated as having predeceased her husband. The court, applying the general rule, gave the life insurance proceeds to the wife's father on the grounds that it would be inappropriate speculation to try to ascertain intent. It was better to have a rule of general application than to try each case seeking the decedent's intent.

The court in In re Estate of Mueller, 275 Ill. App. 3d 128, 655 N.E.2d 1040, review denied, 660 N.E.2d 1269 (1995), differed. There, the decedent by will left 60 percent of his estate to his second wife and if she predeceased him to her children by a prior marriage. The husband was killed by a man solicited by the wife to commit the murder. The wife was barred under Illinois's slayer statute, which provided that the killer should be treated as having predeceased the victim. The court refused to apply the statute literally on the ground that this might result in the killer profiting from her wrong (inherit-

---

the decedent" shall forfeit any share in the decedent's estate. Vt. Stat. Ann. tit. 14, §551(6) (1998). — Eds.

ing from her daughters). The court held the devised property passed
to the decedent's heirs. It opined that a gift over to the killer's heirs
in a will if the killer predeceased the victim would be given effect if
the killer's heirs were also the victim's heirs. The court cited cases
from other states also refusing to apply the statute literally. See also
Bennett v. Allstate Insurance Co. 317 N.J. Super. 324, 722 A.2d 115
(1998).

In Heinzman v. Mason, 694 N.E.2d 1164 (Ind. 1998), there was no
express gift over to the killer's heirs. The husband shot and killed his
wife of 13 years, after she filed for divorce, then he killed himself.
His wife was the stepmother of the husband's four children, whom
she had raised; she had no children of her own. The husband was
named as sole beneficiary of the wife's life insurance policy and of
her bank accounts. The Indiana slayer statute provided that a convicted killer was treated as having predeceased the victim, but it was
inapplicable because the dead husband had not been convicted. The
court, applying principles of equity, held that neither the killer nor
his heirs could benefit from his wrongdoing. Thus his children were
barred from inheriting their stepmother's estate, which went instead
to her aunts and uncles and their issue.

(c) Is a criminal conviction required? UPC §2-803(g) provides that a
criminal conviction of a felonious and intentional killing is conclusive.
Acquittal, however, does not preclude the acquitted individual from
being regarded as the decedent's killer under this statute. In the
absence of a conviction, upon application of an interested person,
the court must determine whether, under the *preponderance of evidence
standard* (not the criminal law standard of beyond a reasonable
doubt), the individual would be found criminally accountable for the
killing. If so found, the individual is barred. The reason for use of a
lower or civil standard of evidence is that probate law is concerned
about a killer not profiting from his wrong, whereas criminal law is
concerned with protection of the accused. Where the killer commits
suicide, the killer may be barred under this section.

The UPC section appears to follow the majority view. See In re
Estate of Cotton, 104 Ohio App. 3d 368, 662 N.E.2d 63 (1995), where
the husband pled guilty to involuntary manslaughter in killing his
wife. The court barred the husband on the ground that even though
he was not convicted of an intentional and felonious killing, the civil
trial court concluded he intentionally and feloniously killed his wife
and therefore the common law barred him from profiting from his
wrong. Thus, a plea of guilty to a lesser crime than specified in the
slayer's statute did not prevent the killer from being barred in a civil
proceeding. See also In re Sengillo, 206 Misc. 75, 134 N.Y.S.2d 800
(Sur. Ct. 1954) (15-year-old boy disqualified from inheritance after

shooting his father, even though his criminal indictment had been dismissed and replaced by adjudication of juvenile delinquency).

2.   For comprehensive discussion of these and other matters, with statutory citations, see Jeffrey G. Sherman, Mercy Killing and the Right to Inherit, 61 U. Cin. L. Rev. 803, 844-874 (1993) (arguing for an exception to permit inheritance by a killer who "proves by clear and convincing evidence that he killed the decedent with the intention of relieving the decedent's suffering attributable to the decedent's affliction"). For earlier studies, see Mary L. Fellows, The Slayer Rule: Not Solely a Matter of Equity, 71 Iowa L. Rev. 489 (1986); William M. McGovern, Jr., Homicide and Succession to Property, 68 Mich. L. Rev. 65 (1969); Annot., 25 A.L.R.4th 787 (1983).

3.   You are a criminal defense lawyer. Lyle and Erik Menendez ask you to represent them. They have just been indicted for murdering their parents, worth $14 million, some 18 months ago. They have collected $600,000 in life insurance, sold the house, and taken possession of most of their parents' assets. They tell you they did kill their parents but claim to have acted in self-defense out of fear their parents would kill them because they threatened to reveal to the public their father's long-time sexual abuse of his sons.

If you represent the Menendez brothers, can you be paid from the assets they will forfeit if convicted of a felonious and intentional killing? Can they use these assets for their defense? Cf. United States v. Monsanto, 491 U.S. 600 (1989), holding, 5 to 4, that assets of defendant frozen by a court, after his indictment for drug trafficking and a court determination that the assets likely would be forfeited, could not be used for his legal defense.

The Chinese system. In the United States, unworthy heirs — whose conduct bars inheritance — are usually limited to killers of the decedent. In a few states, spouses who abandon the decedent or commit adultery are barred (supra page 77), and in a few parents are barred for failure to support a child decedent (supra page 102 footnote 7). Otherwise, inheritance is by a mechanical rule of status (kinship, marriage, adoption).

The People's Republic of China has an entirely different scheme of inheritance, which punishes bad behavior and rewards good behavior. In an illuminating article, Frances H. Foster, Towards a Behavior-Based Model of Inheritance?: The Chinese Experiment, 32 U.C. Davis L. Rev. 77 (1998), Professor Foster examines the Chinese system. The Chinese system encompasses a broad range of misconduct, and it permits courts to reduce or eliminate a wrongdoer's share. It also rewards good behavior, even by worthy nonrelatives at the expense of the decedent's family members who do not support the decedent. It is "highly time-and-labor intensive, requiring courts to evaluate on a case-by-case basis the conduct of all potential claimants and the most appropriate division of each estate. The flexibility that is the hallmark of the behavior-based model today may prove to be its greatest drawback in the future . . . [when] increased social mobility, accumulation of private property, and a rise in the popular use of courts will bring about an increase in the number and complexity of inheritance disputes." Id. at 84-85.

Nonetheless, Professor Foster concludes that the Chinese system has "significant advantages" over the American system which does not penalize unworthy heirs. And it "recognizes the reality of support relationships today. It rewards contributions to the decedent's welfare by individuals outside the nuclear family, including blended and extended family members, nonmarital partners, and other unrelated parties." Id. at 125-126. Professor Foster suggests the Chinese system may provide guidance for reforming the American inheritance system to deal with problems of parental and child neglect and rewarding exemplary conduct by, for instance, personally caring for a disabled person.

California Probate Code (1999)

§259. ABUSE OF AN ELDER OR DEPENDENT ADULT

(a) Any person shall be deemed to have predeceased a decedent . . . where all of the following apply:

(1) It has been proven by clear and convincing evidence that the person is liable for physical abuse, neglect, or fiduciary abuse of the decedent, who was an elder or dependent adult.

(2) The person is found to have acted in bad faith.

(3) The person has been found to have been reckless, oppressive, fraudulent, or malicious in the commission of any of these acts upon the decedent.

(4) The decedent, at the time those acts occurred and thereafter until the time of his or her death, has been found to have been substantially unable to manage his or her financial resources or to resist fraud or undue influence.

2. Disclaimer

Under the common law, when a person dies *intestate*, title to real and personal property passes to the decedent's heirs by operation of law. An intestate successor cannot prevent title from passing to him or her. The original reason for this rule was that there must always be someone seised of the land who was liable for the feudal obligations — a reason once valid but of no importance today. Nonetheless, if the heir refuses to accept (or, more precisely, to keep) the inheritance, the common law treats the heir's renunciation as if title had passed to the heir and then from the heir to the next intestate successor.

On the other hand, if a person dies *testate*, the devisee can refuse to accept the devise, thereby preventing title from passing to the devisee. Any gift, whether inter vivos or by will, requires acceptance by the donee. These different conceptions of how title passes at death formerly produced unexpectedly different tax results. If an heir renounced his inheritance and the common law rule applied, the situation was treated as though the heir had received the intestate share and then made a taxable gift to the persons who took by reason of the renunciation. Hardenburgh v. Commissioner, 198 F.2d 63 (8th Cir.), cert. denied, 344 U.S. 836 (1952). By contrast, if a devisee disclaimed a testamentary gift, there were no gift tax consequences. Brown v. Routzahn, 63 F.2d 914 (6th Cir.), cert. denied, 290 U.S. 641 (1933).

In order to permit people to disclaim property without adverse tax consequences, and to eliminate the difference between disclaiming an intestate share and a devise, almost all states have enacted disclaimer[18] legislation that provides that the disclaimant is treated as having predeceased the decedent. Thus the decedent's property does not pass to the disclaimant, and the disclaimant makes no transfer of it. See Uniform Probate Code §2-801.

The fiction that a disclaimant is treated as having predeceased the decedent can be used to the disclaimant's advantage. Here are some examples.

1. *Saving estate taxes.* Suppose that *O* dies intestate, survived by one sister, *A*. If *A* disclaims, *A* is treated as having predeceased *O*, and *O*'s estate will pass under the intestacy law to *A*'s child, *B*, who is *O*'s niece. In order to pass the property on to *A*'s child without a gift or estate tax being levied on it when it leaves *A*'s hands, *A* may decide to disclaim the inheritance.

Under Internal Revenue Code §2518, only "qualified disclaimers" will avoid gift tax liability by the disclaimant. If a person disclaims, and the disclaimer is not "qualified," gift tax liability results. Section 2518 requires a qualified disclaimer to be made within nine months after the interest is created or after the donee reaches 21, whichever is later. Hence, in the above example, if *A* disclaims a year after *O*'s death, *A* is treated under the tax laws as having accepted the property and having made a taxable gift to *B*.

___

18. By traditional usage, an heir *renounces;* a will beneficiary *disclaims.* Today, the two words are used interchangeably; they are considered synonymous. The term *disclaimer* is the one more commonly used to describe the formal refusal to take by either an heir or a beneficiary.

A disclaimer offers possibilities for post-mortem estate planning, with advantageous tax results, that must be kept in mind by the lawyer handling the estate. A disclaimer can remedy a defective estate plan and correct a drafter's error, saving the estate hundreds of thousands of dollars. In recent years, a rash of cases has arisen charging a lawyer for the estate with malpractice when the lawyer did not advise the beneficiaries of the tax advantages of a disclaimer. See Kinney v. Shinholser, 663 So. 2d 643 (Fla. App. 1995), and infra page 1038.

2. *Avoiding creditors.* Uniform Probate Code §2-801(d)(1), like most disclaimer statutes, provides that a "disclaimer relates back *for all purposes*" to the date of the decedent's death. In the example above, if *A* disclaims, most cases have held that *A*'s creditors cannot reach her share in *O*'s estate because the statute provides that the disclaimer relates back for all purposes to the date of death of the decedent. The disclaimed property is treated as passing directly to others, bypassing the disclaimant. The disclaimer is not a fraudulent transfer. Parks v. Parker, 957 S.W.2d 666 (Tex. Civ. App. 1997). See Adam J. Hirsch, The Problem of the Insolvent Heir, 74 Cornell L. Rev. 587 (1989) (arguing that tort creditors and child support and alimony creditors should be permitted to veto the debtor's disclaimer); S. Alan Medlin, An Examination of Disclaimers under UPC Section 2-801, 55 Alb. L. Rev. 1233, 1262-1268 (1992).

Uncle Sam as a creditor may be treated differently from individual creditors. The state law fiction that the beneficiary is treated as predeceasing the testator may not apply to a federal tax lien. The federal circuit courts are split. United States v. Comparato, 22 F.3d 455 (2d Cir.), cert. denied, 513 U.S. 986 (1994), and Drye Family 1995 Trust v. United States, 152 F.3d (8th Cir. 1998), hold that the government's tax lien attaches to the debtor's interest in an estate even though it is disclaimed. Leggett v. United States, 120 F.3d 592 (5th Cir. 1997), and Mapes v. United States, 15 F.3d (9th Cir. 1994), hold that a disclaimer prevents the taxpayer from acquiring an interest in the disclaimed assets upon which the lien could attach. The Supreme Court has not resolved the conflict.

PROBLEM

O has two children, *A* and *B*. *B* dies, survived by one child, *C*. Then *O*, a widow, dies intestate. *O*'s heirs are *A* and *C*. *A* has four children. *A* disclaims. What distribution is made of *O*'s estate? Uniform Probate Code §2-801(d)(1) provides:

the disclaimed interest devolves as if the disclaimant had predeceased the decedent, but if by law or under the testamentary instrument the descendants of the disclaimant would share in the disclaimed interest by representation or otherwise were the disclaimant to predecease the decedent, then the *disclaimed interest* passes by representation, or passes as directed by the governing instrument, to the descendants of the disclaimant who survive the decedent. [Emphasis added.]

Troy v. Hart
Maryland Court of Special Appeals, 1997
116 Md. App. 468, 697 A.2d 113, cert. denied, 347 Md. 255, 700 A.2d 1215

THIEME, J. This appeal is from an order of the Circuit Court for Washington County (Sharer, J.) denying an attempt by appellant, Richard E. Troy, Personal Representative of the Estate of Paul H. Lettich, to rescind the decedent's renunciation and disclaimer of his inheritance.

. . . The question before us is whether the court erred in holding that the Medicaid recipient could disclaim his inheritance. Our answer to that question is "No," and we shall therefore affirm the judgment of the circuit court.

FACTS

Paul Lettich (Lettich) became a resident of the Cardinal Sheehan Center for the Aging, Stella Maris Hospice (Stella Maris), in April 1992. Prior to his admission, Lettich appointed Richard Troy (Troy) as his attorney in fact and granted him power of attorney, on 4 February 1992.

In conjunction with his duties, Troy applied for medical assistance on behalf of Lettich when Lettich's resources were exhausted. Lettich was ultimately deemed qualified to receive those benefits on or about 1 January 1995. All medical expenses were paid by Medicare and Medicaid from that day forward. On 25 February 1995, Lettich's sister, Alta Mae Lettich (Alta Mae) died intestate, leaving an estate in excess of $300,000. Alta Mae was survived by Lettich and two sisters, Mildred Hart (Hart) and Gladys McGlaughlin (McGlaughlin). To say that personal contact between Lettich and his sisters was sparse is hyperbole. Troy, however, kept family members abreast of Lettich's status, including, specifically, financial and administrative matters such as Troy's legal relationship with Lettich.

On 22 March 1995, Hart was appointed personal representative of Alta Mae's estate with the consent of the surviving siblings. On 28 April 1995, Hart, undeterred by Troy's capacity as Lettich's attorney in fact, visited Lettich and assisted him in executing a disclaimer to his share of his sister's estate. During that visit, Hart overlooked advising Lettich of the ramifications of the disclaimer on his Medicaid status. As a result of dividing Lettich's $100,000 share between themselves,[19] Hart and McGlaughlin each became $50,000 richer. The following month, Troy was notified by Stella Maris's business office that Lettich had renounced his inheritance. Troy promptly retained counsel, on Lettich's behalf, who filed in the orphans' court on 24 June 1995 a petition seeking to rescind the disclaimer and remove Hart as personal representative of Alta Mae's estate.

Hart retained Robert Veil, Jr., Esq., to defend her. On 24 August 1995, one day prior to the deadline for filing Hart's answer to the petition, Veil visited Lettich and requested him to execute a motion to strike the orphans' court petition so as to remove the possible irritation of an attorney, and also to execute a revocation of Troy's power of attorney. A vigilant Stella Maris social worker intervened and suggested that Troy be consulted. When notified, Troy contacted his current counsel, who immediately called Stella Maris and advised Veil that she represented Lettich and that Veil was forbidden to speak to Lettich. For reasons not clear from the record, Veil acquiesced.

Lettich died on 20 September 1995.

Subsequent to the orphans' court's denial of the petition, Troy sought a de novo appeal in the Circuit Court for Washington County. The court granted Hart's motion for judgment with respect to the attempt to have her removed as personal representative of the estate and dismissed the portion of the petition seeking to rescind Lettich's disclaimer. Troy timely filed a notice of appeal.

DISCUSSION . . .

MEDICAID CONSIDERATIONS

Under English Poor Law, "The father and grandfather, mother and grandmother, and children of every poor, old, blind, lame and impotent person, or other person not able to work, being of sufficient ability, shall at their own charges relieve and maintain every other person, in that manner, and according to that rate, as by the justices of that county where such sufficient persons dwell, in their sessions shall be assessed."[20]

Today, however, by 42 U.S.C. §1396a(a)(17)(D), Congress has abrogated the legal duty to support one's parents, and even a cursory perusal of this, or other sections of 42 U.S.C. §1396 (the subsection of the Social Security Act with which we will be attempting to deal),

---

19. . . . [By his will], Lettich's estate was to be distributed among his surviving sisters and his lifelong friend and companion, Hernel Gruber.

20. Poor Relief Act, 1601 (43 Eliz. c.2).

will demonstrate Congress's indifference to the simplicity and clarity of the Elizabethan language.[21]

Medicaid is a "means-tested" program, that is to say, eligibility for Medicaid depends on meeting various income and resource tests. Maryland's Department of Health and Mental Hygiene (DHMH) administers the local aspect of the program and requires, as a condition of eligibility for benefits, that applicants disclose all available assets to the Department of Social Services (DSS). COMAR [Code of Maryland Regulations] 10.09.24.04. An applicant must satisfy asset limits in order to receive coverage.

Once an individual is receiving benefits, it is not inconceivable that his eligibility status might change due to a multitude of financial circumstances. COMAR dictates, as a post-eligibility requirement, that recipients or their representatives shall notify the department "within 10 working days of changes affecting . . . eligibility. . . ." COMAR 10.09.24.12(B)(1). If one fails to disclose such a change, the shadow of fraud surfaces.

Upon his acquisition of an equitable interest in his sister's estate, Lettich — personally, or through his attorney, Hart — had the legal obligation to notify DSS of the inheritance in light of its potential ramifications on Lettich's eligibility. . . .

Lettich's failure to notify DSS constituted a violation of applicable Medicaid law and deprived both state and federal governments of an opportunity to reassess his eligibility.

GENERAL POLICY CONSIDERATIONS

What this Court is more broadly faced with is the propriety of the disclaimer in light of societal interest and overall policy considerations. What is ludicrous, if not repugnant, to public policy is that one who is able to regain the ability to be financially self-sufficient, albeit for a temporary or even brief period of time, may voluntarily relinquish his windfall.[22]

While we are mindful that social agencies are "skewered through

---

21. "The Social Security Act is among the most intricate ever drafted by Congress. Its Byzantine construction, as Judge Friendly has observed, makes the Act 'almost unintelligible to the uninitiated.' " Schweiker, Secretary of Health and Human Services, et al. v. Gray Panthers, 453 U.S. 34, 43, 69 L. Ed. 2d 460, 101 S. Ct. 2633 (1981) (quoting Friedman v. Berger, 547 F.2d 724, 727 n.7 (CA2 1976), cert. denied, 430 U.S. 984, 52 L. Ed. 2d 378, 97 S. Ct. 1681 (1977)). Prior to appellate review of *Friedman* by the Second Circuit Court of Appeals, the District Court in the same case described the Medicaid statute as "an aggravated assault on the English language, resistant to attempts to understand it." 453 U.S. at 43 n.14.

22. Analogously, in divorce cases this Court has refused to award support to a spouse who has voluntarily impoverished himself. See John O. v. Jane O., 90 Md. App. 406, 421, 601 A.2d 149. ("In the context of a divorce proceeding, the term "voluntarily impoverished" means: "freely, or by an act of choice, to reduce oneself to poverty or deprive oneself of resources with the intention of avoiding . . . obligations.")

and through with office pens, and bound hand and foot with red tape,"[23] this acknowledgment does not vitiate a legal obligation to report a recipient's change in financial status. Lettich had a legal obligation to "pay his own way" (by means of the inheritance) until such time as his resources were exhausted. Had the disclaimed funds actually been acquired and exhausted, Lettich most certainly would have been eligible to resume his receipt of Medicaid benefits.

In Molloy v. Bane, 214 A.D.2d 171, 631 N.Y.S.2d 910 (1995), the Supreme Court of New York, Appellate Division, confronted the same issue now before this Court. Molloy, a resident of a nursing home, was a recipient of medical assistance. Upon the death of her daughter, Molloy, pursuant to intestacy law, was entitled to her statutory share of the estate. Prior to disposition of the estate, Molloy renounced her interest in it. Acknowledging that the right to renounce an intestate share is irreconcilable with the principle that public aid is of a limited nature and should only be afforded to those who demonstrate legitimate need, id., 631 N.Y.S.2d at 911, the court found that "[Molloy]'s renunciation of a potentially available asset was the functional equivalent of a transfer of an asset since by refusing to accept it herself, she effectively funneled it to other familial distributees." Id. at 913.

Applying this analysis to the case sub judice, we adopt the reasoning of the New York court. The result of such a transfer prior to application for benefits is that the transferee enjoys a "windfall" for which the applicant/transferor is penalized against the inception of his eligibility. So too should this penalty result in a circumstance in which a Medicaid recipient disclaims or otherwise transfers an inheritance that if accepted would result in a loss of eligibility.

If a recipient renounces an inheritance that would cause him to be financially disqualified from receiving benefits, the renunciation should incur the same penalty of disqualification that acceptance would have brought about, and should render the recipient liable for any payments incorrectly paid by the State in consequence. To permit disclaimed property to pass to transferees free and clear of any obligation would be a violation of public policy. That is precisely the situation before this Court. Lettich's failure to disclose resulted in the improper payment of Medicaid benefits by the State on behalf of Lettich after the expiration of the grace period (during which disclosure was compelled), inasmuch as the inheritance would have caused DHMH/DSS to reassess Lettich's eligibility in light of his changed financial circumstance. COMAR indicates that an applicant/recipient's breach of this particular duty may result in the initiation of criminal or civil action by the State, including the seeking of reimbursement from the recipient. COMAR 10.09.24.12(B)(6). Because

23. Charles Dickens, David Copperfield.

initial eligibility must be established by a lack of financial resources, an action for reimbursement against the recipient or his estate would undoubtedly be futile and similar to attempting to draw blood from a stick. The lack of a mechanism to effectuate the State's interest in reimbursement essentially emasculates the duty to disclose a change in financial status, as there exists no meaningful recourse against individuals who fail to comply.

The effect of Lettich's execution of the disclaimer was to transfer his intestate interest in Alta Mae's estate to his surviving sisters. Accepting the inheritance would have made him financially ineligible for Medicaid. The result of our decision today is that Lettich's disclaimer is valid under Est. & Tr. §9-205. Thus, Mildred Hart and Gladys McGlaughlin will divide the estate of Alta Mae Lettich according to the laws of intestacy. We suggest that this interest should be taken subject to any claim(s) that the State may have against Lettich's estate for any Medicaid benefits improperly paid as a result of Lettich's failure to inform DSS of his acquisition of property while receiving Medicaid benefits.[24]

This Court recently stated that "[a] constructive [trust] is a remedy employed by the courts to convert the holder of legal title to property into a trustee 'for one who in good conscience should reap the benefits of the possession of said property.'" Dulany v. Taylor, 105 Md. App. 619, 634, 660 A.2d 1046 (1995) (Hamilton v. Caplan, 69 Md. App. 566, 583-584, 518 A.2d 1087 (1987), quoting Wimmer v. Wimmer, 287 Md. 663, 668, 414 A.2d 1254 (1980)). "The remedy is applied by operation of law where . . . the circumstances render it inequitable for the party holding the title to retain it." Wimmer, 287 Md. at 668, 414 A.2d 1254 (citations omitted). "The purpose of imposing a constructive trust is to prevent the unjust enrichment of the title holder." Dulany, 105 Md. App. at 634, 660 A.2d 1046 (citing Wimmer, 287 Md. at 668).

In Mass Transit Administration v. Granite Constr. Co., 57 Md. App. 766, 773-774, 471 A.2d 1121 (1984), we explained:

> The doctrine of unjust enrichment applies where " 'the defendant, upon the circumstances of the case, is obliged by the ties of natural justice and equity to refund the money.'" Dobbs, Handbook on the Law of Remedies, §4.2 (1973), quoting Lord Mansfield in Moses v. MacFerlan, 2 Burr. 1005, 97 Eng. Rep. 676 (K.B.1760). This policy against unjust enrichment is the theory behind the restitutionary remedies. Those remedies serve to "deprive the defendant of benefits that in equity and good conscience he ought not to keep, even though he may have received

---

24. At oral argument, Hart's counsel stated that he would be acquiescent to reimbursing the State for any Medicaid benefits erroneously paid for the benefit of her late brother.

those benefits quite honestly in the first instance, and even though the plaintiff may have suffered no demonstrable losses." Dobbs, supra, §4.1.

We think it clear that the State has an equitable and practical interest in both the changed circumstances of a recipient as well as the instrumentality that gives rise to such a change. The "10-day disclosure period" affords the State notice and opportunity to intervene and assert any potential claim(s) against the property or an equitable interest therein. The failure to [disclose] . . . clearly deprives the State of its ability to exercise its rights and may well result in the unjust enrichment of those who surreptitiously dine upon the fruits of inheritance while cloaked by the veil of non-disclosure.

Judgment affirmed.

NOTES AND QUESTIONS

1. The Medicaid program is a cooperative state-federal program intended to provide medical assistance to needy people. The Medicaid program pays for more than 50 percent of all nursing home patients in the United States. The applicant for Medicaid assistance must meet strict income and resource requirements, which vary from state to state. To qualify for Medicaid, the applicant must "spend down" his assets to a few thousand dollars. Giving away property to children before applying for Medicaid may result in disqualification of the applicant for a substantial period of time, depending upon the amount transferred. Certain transfers are exempt, such as home transfers to a spouse and trust transfers for certain disabled persons. In some states, the Medicaid applicant or recipient is required to take steps to get the property back. If a Medicaid recipient dies leaving a probate estate or nonprobate death transfers (such as life insurance), the state may attempt to recover out of these assets benefits paid the Medicaid recipient. See Jan E. Rein, Misinformation and Self-Deception in Recent Long-Term Care Policy Trends, 12 J.L. & Politics 195 (Spring 1996); Note, Long-Term Care Financing Crisis — Recent Federal and State Efforts to Deter Asset Transfers as a Means to Gain Medicaid Eligibility, 74 N. Dak. L. Rev. 383 (1998).

The Kennedy-Kassebaum Health Reform Bill of 1996 made it a federal crime to give away assets or set up trusts with the purpose of qualifying for Medicaid. This provision was repealed in 1997, but the statute was amended to criminalize the behavior of a person who "for a fee knowingly and wilfully counsels or assists an individual to dispose of assets" in order to become eligible for Medicaid "if disposing of the assets results in the imposition of a period of ineligibility." 42 U.S.C. §1320a-7(b)(a)(6).

Would the actions of attorney Robert Veil, Jr., in his visit with Lettich on August 24, 1995, constitute criminal behavior under 42 U.S.C. §1320a-7(b)(a)(6)? If not, were his actions ethical? See American College of Trust and Estate Counsel, Commentaries on the Model Rules of Professional Conduct 151-152 (2d ed. 1995).

2. In Tannler v. State Dept. of Health & Social Services, 211 Wis. 2d 179, 564 N.W.2d 735 (1997), the court upheld the termination of the surviving spouse's eligibility for Medicaid to support her in a nursing home when she did not elect a surviving spouse's forced share (see infra page 490). Although Medicaid law denies eligibility only to those who take "action" to transfer assets to qualify for Medicaid, the court decided that "inaction" (failure to claim a forced share) was a disqualifying "action."

3

WILLS: CAPACITY AND CONTESTS

SECTION A. MENTAL CAPACITY

1. *Why Require Mental Capacity?*

In almost all states, to make a will a person must be age 18 or over. A person must also be of sound mind. But why should this be so? Why is not power of testation extended to all persons regardless of their mental capacity?

In re Strittmater

Court of Errors and Appeals of New Jersey, 1947
140 N.J. Eq. 94, 53 A.2d 205

On appeal from a decree of the Prerogative Court, advised by Vice-Ordinary Bigelow, who filed the following opinion:

"This is an appeal from a decree of the Essex County Orphans Court admitting to probate the will of Louisa F. Strittmater. Appellants challenge the decree on the ground that testatrix was insane.

"The only medical witness was Dr. Sarah D. Smalley, a general practitioner who was Miss Strittmater's physician all her adult life. In her opinion, decedent suffered from paranoia of the Bleuler type of split personality.[1] The factual evidence justifies the conclusion. But I regret not having had the benefit of an analysis of the data by a specialist in diseases of the brain.

"The deceased never married. Born in 1896, she lived with her parents until their death [in] about 1928, and seems to have had a normal childhood. She was devoted to both her parents and they to her. Her admiration and love of her parents persisted after their death to 1934, at least. Yet four years later she wrote: 'My father was a corrupt, vicious, and unintelligent savage, a typical specimen of the majority of his sex. Blast his wormstinking carcass and his whole damn breed.' And in 1943, she inscribed on a photograph of her mother 'That Moronic she-devil that was my mother.'

"Numerous memoranda and comments written by decedent on the margins of books constitute the chief evidence of her mental condition. Most of them are dated in 1935, when she was 40 years old. But there are enough in later years to indicate no change in her condition. The Master who heard the case in the court below, found that the proofs demonstrated 'incontrovertably her morbid aversion to men' and 'feminism to a neurotic extreme.' This characterization seems to me not strong enough. She regarded men as a class with an insane hatred. She looked forward to the day when women would bear children without the aid of men, and all males would be put to death at birth. Decedent's inward life, disclosed by what she wrote, found an occasional outlet such as the incident of the smashing of the clock, the killing of the pet kitten, vile language, etc. On the other hand, — and I suppose this is the split personality, — Miss Strittmater, in her dealings with her lawyer, Mr. Semel, over a period of several years, and with her bank, to cite only two examples, was entirely reasonable and normal.

"Decedent, in 1925, became a member of the New Jersey branch of the National Women's Party. From 1939 to 1941, and perhaps later, she worked as a volunteer one day a week in the New York office, filing papers, etc. During this period, she spoke of leaving her estate to the Party. On October 31, 1944, she executed her last will, carrying this intention into effect. A month later, December 6, she died. Her only relatives were some cousins of whom she saw very little during the last few years of her life.

"The question is whether Miss Strittmater's will is the product of her insanity. Her disease seems to have become well developed by

1. Eugen Bleuler (1857-1930), a Swiss psychiatrist, analyzed and named the condition schizophrenia, dividing it into several types, including paranoid. Bleuler believed that intense ambivalence (e.g., experiencing both love and hate toward an object) was a primary symptom of schizophrenia. He also observed that even normal persons, when preoccupied or distracted, show a number of schizophrenic symptoms, such as peculiar associations, logical blunders, and stereotypes. — Eds.

1936. In August of that year she wrote, 'It remains for feministic organizations like the National Women's Party, to make exposure of women's "protectors" and "lovers" for what their vicious and contemptible selves are.' She had been a member of the Women's Party for eleven years at that time, but the evidence does not show that she had taken great interest in it. I think it was her paranoic condition, especially her insane delusions about the male, that led her to leave her estate to the National Women's Party. The result is that the probate should be set aside."

Per Curiam.

The decree under review will be affirmed, for the reasons stated in the opinion of Vice-Ordinary Bigelow.

———————

The requirement that the testator have mental capacity is an ancient one. It goes back at least as far as the Romans, who invented the will as we know it. Three explanations are usually given for the requirement, all owing something to how persons and property have been viewed in history. The *first* explanation is that a will should be given effect only if it represents the testator's true desires. In ancient times, mad folk were viewed as possessed by an evil spirit or a devil. John tells us of the reaction of the Jews to Jesus' claim to be the good shepherd of the Twenty-third Psalm: "And many of them said, He hath a devil, and is mad; why hear ye him?" John 10:20. Equating madness with possession lasted well into the eighteenth century. In the twentieth century, psychiatrists replaced priests as exorcists, and modern psychiatric concepts and discoveries about mental disorders took over. Psychiatric theory posits that there is a rational self and an irrational self. Freud, for example, held the view that a person might have and act upon unconscious desires of a destructive and irrational kind that overcome the conscious and rational self. Thus modern psychoanalytic theory appears to support denying probate to an "irrational" will that does not represent the testator's rational desires.

The *second* explanation for the mental capacity requirement is that a mentally incompetent man or woman is not defined as a "person." Since the post-renaissance, with its strong emphasis on the individual as the only recognized legal entity (as opposed to the family or clan), philosophers have sought to understand what it means to be a person. As Professor Radin has written, "the concepts of sanity and personhood are intertwined: At some point we question whether the insane person is a person at all." Margaret J. Radin, Property and Personhood, 34 Stan. L. Rev. 957, 969 (1982).

The *third* explanation is that the law requires mental capacity to protect the decedent's family. In primitive societies, property was viewed as tribal property or family property, not owned by individuals. Although individual ownership in time developed, indeed triumphed, the notion persisted that the family was an economic unit with some claim on the parents' property. Giving effect to the expectations of inheritance tends to preserve the family as a unit for mutual support. The institution of inheritance, through the principle of reciprocity, functions as a system for providing care and support for the aged. See Claude Lévi-Strauss, The Principle of Reciprocity, in The Elementary Structures of Kinship 52-97 (rev. ed. 1969); Jeffrey P. Rosenfeld, The Legacy of Aging: Inheritance and Disinheritance in Social Perspective (1979).

Close family members — ordinarily those described as heirs in intestacy statutes — usually render services and give love and comfort to the aging relative. An inheritance is a delayed payment in reciprocity. By giving an economic incentive to heirs apparent, whose expectations cannot be defeated by the testator's insanity, society furthers its objective of caring for the aged in a humane manner. The principle of reciprocity is recognized when the court considers, sometimes *sub silentio*, the fairness of a disposition as a factor in mental capacity cases.

In addition to these three explanations deriving from history, several other possible justifications for the requirement of mental capacity come to mind:

Fourth, to a large extent public acceptance of law rests upon a belief that legal institutions, including inheritance, are legitimate, and legitimacy cannot exist unless decisions are reasoned. Hence, it is important that the succession to property be perceived as a responsible, reasoned act, according the survivors their just deserts.

Fifth, the requirement of mental capacity assures a sane person that the disposition the person desires will be carried out even though the person becomes insane and makes another will. This gives a person of sound mind the advantage of being able, while in a rational mind, to choose what will happen to his or her property in the future and to have confidence that this choice will be carried out.

Sixth, the requirement of mental capacity may protect society at large from irrational acts. This justification is dubious inasmuch as courts can and do strike down particular "anti-social" dispositions as against public policy (see supra pages 24-34). Then too, if society is not protected from a sane person acting irresponsibly, why is it protected against similar acts by a mad person?

Finally, requiring mental capacity may protect a senile or incompetent testator from "exploitation" by cunning persons. Keep in mind, however, that what may look like exploitation to some may give the testator much pleasure. Also, exploitation may be adequately remedied by setting aside transfers on the ground of undue influence.

For discussion of the reasons for, and theoretical underpinning of, the requirement of mental capacity, see Jane B. Baron, Empathy, Subjectivity, and Testamentary Capacity, 24 San Diego L. Rev. 1043 (1987); Alexander M. Meiklejohn, Contractual and Donative Capacity, 39 Case W. Res. L. Rev. 307 (1989); Milton D. Green, Public Policies Underlying the Law of Mental Incompetency, 38 Mich. L. Rev. 1189 (1940).

2.   Test of Mental Capacity

The specific requirements for mental capacity are minimal. The testator only has to have the ability to know (1) the nature and extent of the testator's property, (2) the persons who are the natural objects of the testator's bounty, (3) the disposition the testator is making, and (4) how these elements relate so as to form an orderly plan for the disposition of the testator's property. The testator does not have to have average intelligence as this would incapacitate almost half the people making wills, but the testator must have mind and memory relevant to the four matters mentioned. The testator must understand the significance of the act.

Estate of Wright, 7 Cal. 2d 348, 60 P.2d 434 (1936), nicely illustrates the minimum requirements of mental capacity. The testator had numerous eccentricities and indulged in strange, even bizarre, behavior. Several witnesses expressed the view that the testator was of unsound mind. One witness gave as reasons that he lived in a little shack filled with dirt and junk, that he gave her a fish soaked in kerosene to eat, and that he insisted upon buying her household furniture, which was not for sale. Other witnesses testified that the testator was drunk much of the time, picked up articles from garbage cans and hid them around the house, put paper roses on rose bushes barren of blooms, claimed (falsely) to own a number of houses in Salt Lake City, held his breath and appeared to be dead in order to scare his neighbors, told persons he had sent them Christmas presents but had not done so, failed to speak to his granddaughter in the street, accepted invitations to dinner and then failed to appear or, appearing, left abruptly in the middle of dinner without explanation. The court reversed the order of the trial court denying admission of the will to probate. Said the court:

> Testamentary capacity cannot be destroyed by showing a few isolated acts, foibles, idiosyncrasies, moral or mental irregularities or departures from the normal unless they directly bear upon and have influenced the testamentary act. . . . [The testator] went alone to the scrivener's with a list of beneficiaries prepared by himself, giving his daughter one piece of improved real property and Charlotte Josephine Hindmarch, whom he

"His will reads as follows: 'Being of sound mind and disposition, I blew it all.'"

Drawing by Frank Modell.
Copyright © The New Yorker Collection 1972.
Reproduced by permission.

designated as his friend, the other. To his granddaughter he bequeathed his undivided interest in an estate known as the Brazier Estate, and he named seven others to whom he made nominal bequests. There is no evidence that he did not appreciate his relations and obligations to others, or that he was not mindful of the property which he possessed. The opinions or beliefs of those who testified that he was not of sound mind rest upon testimony of the most trivial character and do not establish testamentary incapacity at the time he executed his will. [Id. at 356-357, 60 P.2d at 438.]

And then the court added, significantly:

It does not appear that his daughter or members of her family were concerned as to his comfort or well-being, as the testimony of some of the witnesses shows that he lived a portion of his time in a condition of squalor and that he was cared for when ill by others. [Id.]

The fact that a person has been declared incompetent and put under a conservator does not necessarily mean the person has no capacity to execute a will thereafter. Capacity to make a will is governed by a different legal test and requires less competency than the power to make a contract or a gift. In the latter situation, the law has the objective of protecting the incompetent contractor or donor from suffering economic loss during lifetime, which might result in impoverishment. Protecting a dead person from economic loss is of course not a consideration. Thus, in Lee v. Lee, 337 So. 2d 713 (Miss. 1976), the testator was placed under a conservatorship in 1968 because of age and physical incapacity. On May 9, 1970, testator executed a *will;* on that same date he executed and delivered a *deed* purporting to convey real property. The Mississippi Supreme Court held that the *deed* was void because one under a conservatorship is without the necessary contractual power to execute a deed but held the *will* valid. The court stated that one whose property is under a conservatorship may write a valid will if the trial court finds, as the trial court did here, that the will was written during a lucid interval. Other cases probating wills executed after the testator has been declared incompetent include In re Estate of Sorenson, 87 Wis. 2d 339, 274 N.W.2d 694 (1979) (testator declared incompetent and confined to Veterans Administration Hospital); In re Estate of Gentry, 32 Or. App. 45, 573 P.2d 322 (1978) (testator, diagnosed as a schizophrenic, institutionalized and declared incompetent).

Legal capacity to make a will requires a greater mental competency than is required for marriage, however. Estate of Park, [1953] 2 All E.R. 408, 411, is authority for the proposition that a person may have insufficient capacity to make a will on the same day as the person has sufficient capacity to marry. Thus, an old man suffering from cerebral arteriosclerosis may be able to marry but not make a will. Marriage alone will give the surviving spouse a share of the senile spouse's estate, even though he has no capacity to devise it to her. See Hoffman v. Kohns, 385 So. 2d 1064 (Fla. App. 1980) (housekeeper marries senile man; will made one day later set aside, but marriage held valid).

To draft a will for an incompetent person is a breach of professional ethics. The lawyer, however, may rely on her own judgment regarding the client's capacity; she does not have to make an investigation of it. Logotheti v. Gordon, 414 Mass. 308, 607 N.E.2d 1015 (1992); Gonsalves v. Superior Court, 19 Cal. App. 4th 1366, 24 Cal. Rptr. 2d 52 (1993). See Jan E. Rein, Ethics and the Questionably Competent Client: What the Model Rules Say and Don't Say, 9 Stan. L. & Policy Rev. 241 (1998).

3.   Insane Delusion

A person may have sufficient mental capacity to execute a will but may be suffering from an insane delusion so as to cause a particular provision in a will — or perhaps the entire will — to fail for lack of testamentary capacity. Only the part of the will caused by the insane delusion fails; if the entire will was caused by the insane delusion, the entire will fails.

An insane delusion is a legal, not a psychiatric, concept. A delusion is a false conception of reality. An example is a belief that all Irishmen have red hair. An insane delusion — which impairs testamentary capacity — is one to which the testator adheres against all evidence and reason to the contrary. Some courts have held that if there is any factual basis at all for the testator's delusion, it is not deemed insane. The majority view, however, is that a delusion is insane even if there is some factual basis for it if a rational person in the testator's situation could not have drawn the conclusion reached by the testator. Insane delusion cases often involve some false belief about a member of the testator's family. See In re Estate of Raney, 247 Kan. 359, 799 P.2d 986 (1990) (a penny-dreadful tale of an angry and mentally disturbed father and his children, who put him under a conservatorship; believing they were plotting against him, for his money, he disinherited them by a will executed while he was in jail under a drunken driving charge; the will was upheld against a claim of insane delusion). See also In re Estate of Zielinski, 208 A.D.2d 275, 623 N.Y.S.2d 653 (1995).

In re Honigman
Court of Appeals of New York, 1960
8 N.Y.2d 244, 168 N.E.2d 676, 203 N.Y.S.2d 859

DYE, J.   Frank Honigman died May 4, 1956, survived by his wife, Florence. By a purported last will and testament, executed April 3, 1956, just one month before his death, he gave $5,000 to each of three named grandnieces, and cut off his wife with a life use of her minimum statutory share plus $2,500, with direction to pay the principal upon her death to his surviving brothers and sisters and to the descendants of any predeceased brother or sister, per stirpes. The remaining one half of his estate was bequeathed in equal shares to his surviving brothers and sisters and to the descendants of any predeceased brother or sister, per stirpes, some of whom resided in Germany.

When the will was offered for probate in Surrogate's Court, Queens County, the widow Florence filed objections. A trial was had on framed issues, only one of which survived for determination by the jury, namely: "At the time of the execution of the paper offered for probate was the said Frank Honigman of sound and disposing mind and memory?" The jury answered in the negative, and the Surrogate then made a decree denying probate to the will.

Upon an appeal to the Appellate Division, Second Department, the Surrogate's decree was reversed upon the law and the facts, and probate was directed. Inconsistent findings of fact were reversed and new findings substituted.

We read this record as containing more than enough competent proof to warrant submitting to the jury the issue of decedent's testamentary capacity. By the same token the proof amply supports the jury findings, implicit in the verdict, that the testator, at the time he made his will, was suffering from an unwarranted and insane delusion that his wife was unfaithful to him, which condition affected the disposition made in the will. The record is replete with testimony, supplied by a large number of disinterested persons, that for quite some time before his death the testator had publicly and repeatedly told friends and strangers alike that he believed his wife was unfaithful, often using obscene and abusive language. Such manifestations of suspicion were quite unaccountable, coming as they did after nearly 40 years of a childless yet, to all outward appearances, a congenial and harmonious marriage, which had begun in 1916. During the intervening time they had worked together in the successful management, operation and ownership of various restaurants, bars and grills and, by their joint efforts of thrift and industry, had accumulated the substantial fortune now at stake.

The decedent and his wife retired from business in 1945 because of decedent's failing health. In the few years that followed he underwent a number of operations, including a prostatectomy in 1951, and an operation for cancer of the large bowel in 1954, when decedent was approximately 70 years of age. From about this time, he began volubly to express his belief that Mrs. Honigman was unfaithful to him. This suspicion became an obsession with him, although all of the witnesses agreed that the deceased was normal and rational in other respects. Seemingly aware of his mental state, he once mentioned that he was "sick in the head" ("Mich krank gelassen in den Kopf"), and that "I know there is something wrong with me" in response to a light reference to his mental condition. In December, 1955 he went to Europe, a trip Mrs. Honigman learned of in a letter sent from Idlewild Airport after he had departed, and while there he visited a doctor. Upon his return he went to a psychiatrist who Mr. Honigman said "could not help" him. Finally, he went to a chiropractor with whom he was extremely satisfied.

On March 21, 1956, shortly after his return from Europe, Mr. Honigman instructed his attorney to prepare the will in question. He never again joined Mrs. Honigman in the marital home.

To offset and contradict this showing of irrational obsession the proponents adduced proof which, it is said, furnished a reasonable basis for decedent's belief, and which, when taken with other factors,

made his testamentary disposition understandable. Briefly, this proof
related to four incidents. One concerned an anniversary card sent by
Mr. Krauss, a mutual acquaintance and friend of many years, bearing
a printed message of congratulation in sweetly sentimental phraseol-
ogy. Because it was addressed to the wife alone and not received on
the anniversary date, Mr. Honigman viewed it as confirmatory of his
suspicion. Then there was the reference to a letter which it is claimed
contained prejudicial matter — but just what it was is not before us,
because the letter was not produced in evidence and its contents were
not established. There was also proof to show that whenever the house
telephone rang Mrs. Honigman would answer it. From this Mr. Honigman drew added support for his suspicion that she was having an
affair with Mr. Krauss. Mr. Honigman became so upset about it that
for the last two years of their marriage he positively forbade her to
answer the telephone. Another allegedly significant happening was an
occasion when Mrs. Honigman asked the decedent as he was leaving
the house what time she might expect him to return. This aroused
his suspicion. He secreted himself at a vantage point in a nearby park
and watched his home. He saw Mr. Krauss enter and, later, when he
confronted his wife with knowledge of this incident, she allegedly
asked him for a divorce. This incident was taken entirely from a
statement made by Mr. Honigman to one of the witnesses. Mrs. Honigman flatly denied all of it. Their verdict shows that the jury evidently
believed the objectant. Under the circumstances, we cannot say that
this was wrong. The jury had the right to disregard the proponents'
proof, or to go so far as to hold that such trivia afforded even additional grounds for decedent's irrational and unwarranted belief. The
issue we must bear in mind is not whether Mrs. Honigman was unfaithful, but whether Mr. Honigman had any reasonable basis for
believing that she was.

In a very early case we defined the applicable test as follows:

> If a person persistently believes supposed facts, which have no real exis-
> tence except in his perverted imagination, and against all evidence and
> probability, and conducts himself, however logically, upon the assump-
> tion of their existence, he is, so far as they are concerned, under a morbid
> delusion; and delusion in that sense is insanity. Such a person is essentially
> mad or insane on those subjects, though on other subjects he may reason,
> act and speak like a sensible man. (American Seamen's Friend Soc. v.
> Hopper, 33 N.Y. 619, 624-625.)

It is true that the burden of proving testamentary incapacity is a
difficult one to carry (Dobie v. Armstrong, 160 N.Y. 584), but when
an objectant has gone forward, as Mrs. Honigman surely has, with
evidence reflecting the operation of the testator's mind, it is the pro-

ponents' duty to provide a basis for the alleged delusion. We cannot conclude that as a matter of law they have performed this duty success- fully. When, in the light of all the circumstances surrounding a long and happy marriage such as this, the husband publicly and repeatedly expresses suspicions of his wife's unfaithfulness; of misbehaving her- self in a most unseemly fashion, by hiding male callers in the cellar of her own home, in various closets, and under the bed; of hauling men from the street up to her second-story bedroom by use of bed sheets; of making contacts over the household telephone; and of pass- ing a clandestine note through the fence on her brother's property — and when he claims to have heard noises which he believed to be men running about his home, but which he had not investigated, and which he could not verify — the courts should have no hesitation in placing the issue of sanity in the jury's hands. To hold to the contrary would be to take from the jury its traditional function of passing on the facts.

. . . Mr. Honigman persisted over a long period of time in telling his suspicions to anyone who would listen to him, friends and strangers alike. That such belief was an obsession with him was clearly established by a preponderance of concededly competent evidence and, prima facie, there was presented a question of fact as to whether it affected the will he made shortly before his death.

The proponents argue that, even if decedent was indeed laboring under a delusion, the existence of other reasons for the disposition he chose is enough to support the validity of the instrument as a will. The other reasons are, first, the size of Mrs. Honigman's independent fortune, and, second, the financial need of his residuary legatees. These reasons, as well as his belief in his wife's infidelity, decedent expressed to his own attorney. We dispelled a similar contention in American Seamen's Friend Soc. v. Hopper (supra . . .) where we held that a will was bad when its "dispository provisions were or *might have been* caused or affected by the delusion" (emphasis supplied). . . .

We turn now to alleged errors committed by the Surrogate when he overruled objections based on section 347 of the Civil Practice Act.[2] Much of Mrs. Honigman's testimony, which should have been

---

2. New York Civil Practice Act §347, now N.Y. Civ. Prac. Law & R. §4519 (1998), is New York's dead man statute. The statute excludes the testimony of a survivor "concerning a personal transaction or communication between the witness and the deceased person." In most states — but not in New York — the dead man's statute is not applicable to proceedings to probate a will on the theory that the testator's will is not a "transaction or communication" between the testator and the legatees. The purpose of the statute is to protect estates of deceased persons from creditors and others making false claims respecting business transactions when testator's lips are sealed, and the statute excludes testimony only in suits upon claims between other persons and the deceased existing prior to his death. See Annot., 11 A.L.R. 1425 (1938). In New York, however, it was early held that the dead man's statute applied to probate of a will. In re Smith, 95 N.Y. 516 (1884).

Dead man statutes are highly unpopular with every evidence scholar and have been

excluded as incompetent since it was evidence "concerning a personal transaction or communication between the witness [an interested party] and the deceased person," was admitted because the Surrogate believed that the proponents, by failing to object to such testimony at the earliest opportunity, irrevocably waived their right to protest on that ground. In de Laurent v. Townsend (243 N.Y. 130) this court was unanimous in holding that the rule as to waiver of objections under section 347 was to be found in that statute "and not elsewhere" (p.133). The statute provides an exception "where the executor, administrator, survivor, committee or person deriving title or interest is examined in his own behalf, or the testimony of the lunatic or deceased person is given in evidence, concerning the same transaction or communication." Since the exception is inapplicable to the circumstances here present, it was error not to exclude Mrs. Honigman's testimony whenever objections based on the prohibition of section 347 were appropriately raised.

Finally, since there is to be a new trial of the issues, the Surrogate's ruling with regard to the clergyman-penitent privilege deserves mention. Father Heitz, a Catholic priest, was called by the objectant, who sought to elicit from him a conversation he had had with the deceased at a time when the latter wanted advice concerning his marital problems. Although Father Heitz was willing, he was not permitted to testify to the conversation, "Specifically on the ground that any conversation with a priest, although not in the confessional, is privileged." There is nothing in the record to indicate the nature of the testimony sought. In this posture it cannot be determined whether such testimony falls within the privilege created by section 351 of the Civil Practice Act.

The order appealed from should be reversed and a new trial granted, with costs to abide the event.

FULD, J. (dissenting). I am willing to assume that the proof demonstrates that the testator's belief that his wife was unfaithful was completely groundless and unjust. However, that is not enough; it does not follow from this fact that the testator suffered from such a delusion as to stamp him mentally defective or as lacking in capacity to make a will. (See, e.g., Matter of Hargrove, 288 N.Y. 604, affg. 262 App. Div. 202; Dobie v. Armstrong, 160 N.Y. 584, 593-594; Matter of White, 121 N.Y. 406, 414; Clapp v. Fullerton, 34 N.Y. 190, 197.) "To sustain the allegation," this court wrote in the *Clapp* case (34 N.Y. 190, 197),

> it is not sufficient to show that his suspicion in this respect was not well founded. It is quite apparent, from the evidence, that his distrust of the

---

abolished in many states. Where they exist, most courts construe them narrowly. See 2 John H. Wigmore, Evidence §578 (James H. Chadbourn rev. 1979). — Eds.

fidelity of his wife was really groundless and unjust; but it does not follow that his doubts evince a condition of lunacy. The right of a testator to dispose of his estate, depends neither on the justice of his prejudices nor the soundness of his reasoning. He may do what he will with his own; and if there be no defect of testamentary capacity, and no undue influence or fraud, the law gives effect to his will, though its provisions are unreasonable and unjust.

As a matter of fact, in the case before us, a goodly portion of the widow's testimony bearing on her husband's alleged delusion should have been excluded, as the court itself notes, by reason of section 347 of the Civil Practice Act. And, of course, if such testimony had not been received in evidence, a number of items of proof upon which the widow relies would not have been available, with the consequence that the record would have contained even less basis for her claim of delusion.

Moreover, I share the Appellate Division's view that other and sound reasons, quite apart from the alleged [delusion], existed for the disposition made by the testator. Indeed, he himself had declared that his wife had enough money and he wanted to take care of his brothers and sisters living in Europe.

In short, the evidence adduced utterly failed to prove that the testator was suffering from an insane delusion or lacked testamentary capacity. The Appellate Division was eminently correct in concluding that there was no issue of fact for the jury's consideration and in directing the entry of a decree admitting the will to probate. Its order should be affirmed.

Chief Judge DESMOND and Judges FROESSEL and BURKE concur with Judge DYE; Judge FULD dissents in an opinion in which Judges VAN VOORHIS and FOSTER concur.

NOTES AND QUESTIONS

1. In The Myth of Testamentary Freedom, 38 Ariz. L. Rev. 235 (1996), Professor Melanie B. Leslie argues that

> many courts do not exalt testamentary freedom above all other principles. Notwithstanding frequent declarations to the contrary, many courts are as committed to insuring that testators devise their estates in accordance with prevailing normative views as they are to effectuating testamentary intent. Those courts impose upon testators a duty to provide for those whom the court views as having a superior moral claim to the testator's assets, usually a financially dependent spouse or persons related by blood to the testator. Wills that fail to provide for those individuals typically are upheld only if the will's proponent can convince the fact-finder that the

testator's deviation from normative values is morally justifiable. This unspoken rule, seeping quietly, but fervently from case law, directly conflicts
with the oft-repeated axiom that testamentary freedom is the polestar of
wills law.

Courts impose and enforce this moral duty to family through the covert
manipulation of doctrine. [Id. at 236.]

Professor Leslie attempts to prove her thesis by examining cases on
undue influence and cases determining whether the testator has met
the technical formal requirements for a will. Would testamentary capacity also be ripe for examination under her microscope?

To this end, consider In re Honigman. Under New York law applicable in 1956, when an intestate was survived by a spouse and brothers
and sisters (as in the *Honigman* case), the spouse took one-half and
the brothers and sisters the other half. Thus, if Mr. Honigman's will
was struck down because of an insane delusion, his estate would go
by intestacy one-half to his wife and one-half to his brothers and
sisters.

New York also gives a surviving spouse a forced or elective share in
the estate of a spouse who dies testate. The surviving spouse can
renounce the will and elect to take this share, which in 1956, in the
case of a testate decedent without issue (as Mr. Honigman was), was
one-half of the decedent's estate. However, New York had a special
provision eliminating this election if the decedent gave his or her
spouse $2,500 outright and put the rest of the surviving spouse's half
in a trust to pay him or her income therefrom for life but giving the
surviving spouse no control of the corpus of the trust at his or her
death. Id. §5-1.1(a).[3] This is what Mr. Honigman's will provided,
which prevented Mrs. Honigman from electing to take 50 percent
outright. The consequence of the decision in *Honigman* (assuming
the wife wins at the new trial) is that Mr. Honigman's will is denied
probate and his wife receives by intestacy one-half of her husband's
property outright rather than an income interest in one-half. What
statements by the majority support Mrs. Honigman's moral claim to
half her husband's fortune outright?

Since the *Honigman* case, New York law has been amended to give
the surviving spouse the entire estate of an intestate if the intestate
leaves no issue. N.Y. Est. Powers & Trusts Law §4-1.1(a)(2) (1998). If
Mr. Honigman died today, and were found to have an insane delusion, Mrs. Honigman would receive everything by intestacy. If he were
not found to have an insane delusion, Mrs. Honigman would have an

---

3. For current New York law on the elective share, see N.Y. Est., Powers & Trusts Law
§5-1.1(c) (1998), giving the surviving spouse one-half of the decedent's estate if there
are no issue. See infra page 512.

elective share of one-half. How do you think the case would come out?

As you read the cases in this book consider the merits of Professor Leslie's hypothesis and how you might modify it.

2. The law draws a distinction between an insane delusion and a mistake. An insane delusion is a belief not susceptible to correction by presenting the testator with evidence indicating the falsity of the belief. A mistake is susceptible to correction if the testator is told the truth. As a general rule, courts do not reform or invalidate wills because of mistake (see infra pages 427-438), whereas they do invalidate wills resulting from an insane delusion. Suppose, for example, that the testator falsely believes that her son has been killed and therefore executes a will leaving all her property to her daughter. In fact the son is alive. The testator is mistaken, not under an insane delusion, and the will is entitled to probate. See Bowerman v. Burris, 138 Tenn. 220, 197 S.W. 490 (1917). Cf. Uniform Probate Code §2-302(c) (1990), giving a child an intestate share where the testator mistakenly believes the child is dead.

3. A study of California cases some years ago indicated that when mental capacity or undue influence was in issue, the jury found for the contestant in 77 percent of the cases, and over half of the verdicts for contestants were reversed by the supreme court upon appeal on grounds of insufficient evidence. Note, Will Contests on Trial, 6 Stan. L. Rev. 91, 92 (1953). See also Estate of Fritschi, 60 Cal. 2d 367, 373, 384 P.2d 656, 659, 33 Cal. Rptr. 264, 267 (1963), complaining that a "legion" of appellate decisions have been necessary to reverse juries who invalidate wills based on nothing more than "their own concepts of how testators should have disposed of their properties." Cf. Note, Undue Influence — Judicial Implementation of Social Policy, 1968 Wis. L. Rev. 569, which finds that in Wisconsin, where the trial judge, not a jury, finds facts in will contests, appellate courts rarely reverse the trial judge's decision in undue influence cases. See also Comment, The Pros and Cons of Jury Trials in Will Contests, 1990 U. Chi. Legal F. 529, proposing abolishing jury trials in will contests over mental capacity or undue influence.

The most recent empirical study is Jeffrey A. Schoenblum, Will Contests — An Empirical Study, 22 Real Prop., Prob. & Tr. J. 607 (1987). Professor Schoenblum studied contested wills over a nine-year period in Davidson County (Nashville), Tennessee. The study confirms what the earlier studies cited above indicate: Juries are considerably more favorable to contestants than are judges.

See also Jeffrey P. Rosenfeld, Will Contests, Legacies of Aging and Social Change, in Inheritance and Wealth in America 173 (Robert K. Miller, Jr. & Stephen J. McNamee eds. 1998) (reporting that divorce and remarriage and the lessening of a cohesive family life have increased estate litigation among stepfamilies and siblings).

4. Statutes in Arkansas, North Dakota, and Ohio permit probate of a will during the testator's life. These statutes authorize a person to institute during life an adversary proceeding to declare the validity of a will and the testamentary capacity and freedom from undue influence of the person executing the will. All beneficiaries named in the will and all testator's heirs apparent must be made parties to the action. Ark. Code Ann. §28-40-202 (1997); N.D. Cent. Code §30.1-08.1-01 (1997); Ohio Rev. Code Ann. §2107.081 (1998). This procedure is known as "living probate" or "ante-mortem probate."

John H. Langbein, Living Probate: The Conservatorship Model
77 Mich. L. Rev. 63, 64-66 (1978)

Discussion of living probate must begin with the problem of the will contest alleging testamentary incapacity. Although we do not have comparative data directly on point, the impression is widespread that such litigation occurs more frequently in the United States than on the Continent or in England. We may point to several factors that bear upon the differential:

(1) In civil law countries, children as well as the spouse have a forced share entitlement in the estate of a parent. The disinherited child, who is the typical plaintiff in American testamentary capacity litigation, is unknown to European law. The European parent can leave his heir disgruntled with the statutory minimum, but that share will often be large enough by comparison with the potential winnings from litigation to deaden the incentive to contest.

(2) Many American jurisdictions permit will contests on the question of capacity to be tried to a jury, which may be more disposed to work equity for the disinherited than to obey the directions of an eccentric decedent who is in any event beyond suffering. Civil jury trial has disappeared from English estate law; it was never known on the Continent.

(3) American law is unique among Western civil procedural systems in failing to charge a losing plaintiff with the attorney fees and other costs incurred by the defendant in the course of resisting the plaintiff's unjustified claim. In testamentary capacity litigation the American rule has the effect of requiring decedents' estates to subsidize the depredations of contestants. Put differently, the American rule diminishes the magnitude of a contestant's potential loss, which diminishes his disincentive to litigate an improbable claim.

(4) Civil law systems provide for the so-called authenticated will, which is executed before a quasi-judicial officer called the notary.

This is not the only means of making a valid will in European countries, and because it is costly it is not widely used. But the notarial procedure does permit a testator who fears a post-mortem contest to generate during his lifetime and have preserved with the will evidence of exceptional quality regarding, *inter alia*, his capacity. The notary before whom the testator executes his will is not a judge; he does not adjudicate capacity. But he is a legally qualified and experienced officer of the state who is obliged to satisfy himself of the testator's capacity as a precondition for receiving or transcribing the testament. The authenticated will is, therefore, extremely difficult for contestants to set aside for want of capacity in post-mortem proceedings. . . .

A major reason that the impact of capacity litigation in America is so difficult to measure is that most of it is directed towards provoking pretrial settlements, typically for a fraction of what the contestants would be entitled to receive if they were to defeat the will. Especially when such tactics succeed, they do not leave traces in the law reports. Thus, the odor of the strike suit hangs heavily over this field. The beneficiaries named in the will are likely to be either charitable organizations whom the testator preferred to his relatives, or else those of his relatives and friends whom he loved most and who are most likely to want to spare his reputation from a capacity suit. They are typically put to the choice of defending a lawsuit in which a skilled plaintiff's lawyer will present evidence to a jury at a public trial touching every eccentricity that might cast doubt upon the testator's condition, or compromising the suit, thereby overriding the disposition desired by the testator and rewarding the contestants for threatening to besmirch his name.

For more on ante-mortem probate, pro and con, see Gregory S. Alexander, The Conservatorship Model: A Modification, 77 Mich. L. Rev. 86 (1978); Gregory S. Alexander & Albert M. Pearson, Alternative Models of Ante-Mortem Probate and Procedural Due Process Limitations on Succession, 78 Mich. L. Rev. 89 (1979); Mary L. Fellows, The Case Against Living Probate, 78 Mich. L. Rev. 1066 (1980); Aloysius A. Leopold & Gerry W. Beyer, Ante-Mortem Probate: A Viable Alternative, 43 Ark. L. Rev. 131 (1990).

SECTION B.   UNDUE INFLUENCE

Undue influence is one of the most bothersome concepts in all the law. It cannot be precisely defined. More than a hundred years ago Lord Hannen gave the classic explanation of what kind of influence is undue in the eyes of the law:

Lord Justice Hannen

We are all familiar with the use of the word "influence"; we say that one person has an unbounded influence over another, and we speak of evil influences and good influences, but it is not because one person has unbounded influence over another that therefore when exercised, even though it may be very bad indeed, it is undue influence in the legal sense of the word. To give you some illustrations of what I mean, a young man may be caught in the toils of a harlot, who makes use of her influence to induce him to make a will in her favour, to the exclusion of his relatives. It is unfortunately quite natural that a man so entangled should yield to that influence and confer large bounties on the person with whom he has been brought into such relation; yet the law does not attempt to guard against those contingencies. A man may be the companion of another, and may encourage him in evil courses, and so obtain what is called an undue influence over him, and the consequence may be a will made in his favour. But that again, shocking as it is, perhaps even worse than the other, will not amount to undue influence.

To be undue influence in the eye of the law there must be — to sum it up in a word — coercion. . . . It is only when the will of the person who becomes a testator is coerced into doing that which he or she does not desire to do, that it is undue influence.

The coercion may of course be of different kinds, it may be in the grossest form, such as actual confinement or violence, or a person in the last days or hours of life may have become so weak and feeble, that a very little pressure will be sufficient to bring about the desired result, and it may even be, that the mere talking to him at that stage of illness and pressing something upon him may so fatigue the brain, that the sick person may be induced, for quietness' sake, to do anything. This would equally be coercion, though not actual violence.

These illustrations will sufficiently bring home to your minds that even very immoral considerations either on the part of the testator, or of some one else offering them, do not amount to undue influence unless the testator is in such a condition, that if he could speak his wishes to the last, he would say, "this is not my wish, but I must do it." [Wingrove v. Wingrove, 11 Prob. Div. 81 (1885).]

Undue influence may occur where there is a confidential relationship between the parties or where there is no such relationship. Proof may be wholly inferential and circumstantial. The influence may be that of a beneficiary or that of a third person imputed to the beneficiary.

In more recent times judges have tried to cabin this unruly concept by saying that, to establish undue influence, it must be proved that the testator was susceptible to undue influence, that the influencer had the disposition and the opportunity to exercise undue influence, and that the disposition is the result of the influence. But this formulation begs the question because it does not tell us what influence is undue. Perhaps the only satisfactory way of acquiring a lawyer's feel about the contours of undue influence is to immerse yourself in the cases.

Lipper v. Weslow
Texas Court of Civil Appeals, 1963
369 S.W.2d 698

McDONALD, C.J.   This is a contest of the will of Mrs. Sophie Block, on the ground of undue influence. Plaintiffs, Julian Weslow, Jr., Julia Weslow Fortson and Alice Weslow Sale, are the 3 grandchildren of Mrs. Block by a deceased son; defendants are Mrs. Block's 2 surviving children, G. Frank Lipper and Irene Lipper Dover (half brother and half sister of plaintiffs' deceased father). (The will left the estate of testatrix to her 2 children, defendants herein; and left nothing to her grandchildren by the deceased son, plaintiffs herein.) Trial was to a jury, which found that Mrs. Block's will, signed by her on January 30, 1956, was procured by undue influence on the part of the proponent, Frank Lipper. The trial court entered judgment on the verdict, setting aside the will.

Defendants appeal, contending there is no evidence, or insufficient evidence, to support the finding that the will was procured by undue influence.

Testatrix was married 3 times. Of her first marriage she had one son, Julian Weslow (who died in 1949), who was father of plaintiffs herein. After the death of her first husband testatrix married a Mr. Lipper. Defendants are the 2 children of their marriage. After Mr. Lipper's death, testatrix married Max Block. There were no children born of this marriage. Max Block died several months after the death of testatrix.

On 30 January, 1956, Sophie Block executed the will in controversy. Such will was prepared by defendant, Frank Lipper, an attorney, one of the beneficiaries of the will, and Independent Executor of the will. The will was witnessed by 2 former business associates of Mr. Block. Pertinent provisions of the will are summarized as follows:

"That I, Mrs. Sophie Block, . . . do make, publish and declare this my last will and testament, hereby revoking all other wills by me heretofore made."

1, 2, 3 AND 4

(Provide for payment of debts; for burial in Beth Israel Cemetery; and for minor bequests to a servant, and to an old folks' home.)

5

(Devises the bulk of testatrix's estate to her 2 children, Mrs. Irene Lipper Dover and Frank Lipper (defendants herein), share and share alike.)

6

(States that $7000. previously advanced to Mrs. Irene Lipper Dover, and $9300. previously advanced to Frank Lipper be taken into consideration in the final settlement of the estate; and cancels such amounts "that I gave or advanced to my deceased son, Julian.")

7

(Appoints G. Frank Lipper Independent Executor of the estate without bond.)

8

(Provides that if any legatee contests testatrix's will or the will of her husband, Max Block, that they forfeit all benefits under the will.)

9

"My son, Julian A. Weslow, died on August 6, 1949, and I want to explain why I have not provided anything under this will for my daughter-in-law, Bernice Weslow, widow of my deceased son, Julian, and her children, Julian A. Weslow, Jr., Alice Weslow Sale, and Julia Weslow Fortson, and I want to go into sufficient detail in explaining my relationship in past years with my said son's widow and his children, before mentioned, and it is my desire to record such relationship so that there will be no question as to my feelings in the matter or any thought or suggestion that my children, Irene Lipper Dover and G. Frank Lipper, or my husband, Max, may have influenced me in any manner in the execution of this will. During the time that my said son, Julian, was living, the attitude of his wife, Bernice, was at times, pleasant and friendly, but the majority of the years when my said son, Julian, was living, her attitude towards me and my husband, Max, was unfriendly and frequently months would pass when she was not in my home and I did not hear from her. When my said son, Julian, was living he was treated the same as I treated my other children; and, my husband, Max, and I gave to each of our children a home and various sums of money from time to time to help in taking care of medical expenses, other unusual expenses, as well as outright gifts. Since my said son Julian's death, his widow, Bernice, and all of her children have shown a most unfriendly and distant attitude towards me, my husband, Max, and my 2 children G. Frank Lipper and Irene Lipper Dover, which attitude I cannot reconcile as I have shown them many kindnesses since they have been members of my family, and their continued unfriendly attitude towards me, my husband, Max, and my said children has hurt me deeply in my declining years, for my life would have been much happier if they had shown a disposition to want to be a part of the family and enter into a normal family relationship that usually exists with a daughter-in-law and grandchildren and great grandchildren. I have not seen my grandson, Julian A. Weslow, Jr. in several years, neither have I heard from him.[4] My granddaughter, Alice Weslow Sale, I have not seen in several years and I have not heard from her, but I heard a report some months ago that she was now living in California and has since married William G. Sale. My granddaughter, Julia Weslow Fortson, wife of Ben Fortson, I have not seen in several years and I was told that she had a child born to her sometime in December 1952, and I have not seen the child or heard from my said granddaughter, Julia, up to this writing, and was informed by a friend that Julia has had another child recently and is now living in Louisiana, having moved from Houston; and needless to say, my said daughter-in-law, Bernice, widow of my deceased son, Julian, I have not seen in several years as she has taken little or no interest in me or my husband, Max, since the death of my son, Julian, with the exception that Christmas a year ago, if I remember correctly, she sent some flowers, which I acknowledged, and I believe she had sent some greeting cards on some occasions prior to that time. My said daughter-in-law, Bernice Weslow, has ex-

---

4. Julian Weslow, Jr., became a professional dog trainer, famed throughout Texas and the Southwest for "snake proofing" hunting dogs. The dog is given a zap of electricity through an electric collar when the dog sniffs a defanged rattlesnake, which strikes at the dog simultaneously. Sometimes the dog leaps two feet straight up, but in any case the dog quickly learns to give snakes a wide berth thereafter. More than 10,000 dogs die each year from snake bite. Weslow is much in demand and has even held "snake proofing" clinics at the Houston Astrodome. See L.A. Times, Sept. 25, 1991, at C6. — Eds.

pressed to me, on several occasions, an intense hatred for my son, G. Frank Lipper, and my daughter, Irene Lipper Dover, which I cannot understand, as my said children have always shown her and her children every consideration when possible, and have expressed a desire to be friendly with her, and them. My said children, G. Frank Lipper, and Irene Lipper Dover, have at all times been attentive to me and my husband, Max, especially during the past few years when we have not been well. I will be 82 years old in June of this year and my husband, Max, will be 80 years of age in October of this year, and we have both been in failing health for the past few years and rarely leave our home, and appreciate any attention that is given us, and my husband, Max, and I cannot understand the unfriendly and distant attitude of Bernice Weslow, widow of my said son, Julian, and his children, before mentioned."

10

(Concerns personal belongings already disposed of.)

"In Testimony Whereof, I have hereunto signed my name. . . .

(S) *Sophie Block*"

(Here follows attestation clause and signature of the 2 witnesses.)

The record reflects that the will in question was executed 22 days before testatrix died at the age of 81 years. By its terms, it disinherits the children of testatrix's son, who died in 1949. Defendant, Frank Lipper, gets a larger share than would have been the case if the plaintiffs were not disinherited. Defendant Lipper is a lawyer, and is admittedly the scrivener of the will. There is evidence that defendant Lipper bore malice against his dead half brother. He lived next door to testatrix, and had a key to her house. The will was not read to testatrix prior to the time she signed same, and she had no discussion with anyone at the time she executed it. There is evidence that the recitations in the will that Bernice Weslow and her children were unfriendly, and never came about testatrix, were untrue. There is also evidence that the Weslows sent testatrix greeting cards and flowers from 1946 through 1954, more times than stated in the will.

Plaintiffs offered no direct evidence pertaining to the making and execution of the will on January 30, 1956, and admittedly rely wholly upon circumstantial evidence of undue influence to support the verdict.

All of the evidence is that testatrix was of sound mind at the time of the execution of the will; that she was a person of strong will; that she was in good physical health for her age; and that she was in fact physically active to the day of her death.

Mrs. Weslow's husband died in 1949; and after 1952 the Weslows came about testatrix less often than before.

The witness Lyda Friberg, who worked at the home of testatrix from 1949 to 1952, testified that in *1952* she had a conversation with Bernice Weslow in which Mrs. Weslow told her if her children didn't get their inheritance she would "sue them through every court in the Union"; that she told testatrix about this conversation, and that testatrix told her "she would have those wills fixed up so there would be no court business," and that she wasn't going to "leave them (the Weslows) a dime." The foregoing was prior to the execution of the will on January 30, 1956.

Subsequent to the execution of the will, testatrix had a conversation with her sister, Mrs. Levy. Mrs. Levy testified:

Q. Who did she say she was leaving her property to?
A. She was leaving it to her son and her daughter.
Q. What else did she say about the rest of her kin, if anything?
A. Well she said that Julian's children had been very ugly to her; that they never showed her any attention whatever; they married and she didn't know they were married; they had children and they didn't let her know. After Julian passed away, she never saw any of the family at all. They never came to see her.
Q. Did she make any statement?
A. Yes she did. When she passed away, she didn't want to leave them anything; that they did nothing for her when she was living.

Shortly before she passed away, testatrix told Mrs. Augusta Roos that she was going to leave her property to her 2 children, and further:

Q. Did she give any reason for it?
A. Yes. She said that Bernice had never been very nice to her and the children never were over.

Again, subsequent to the making of her will, testatrix talked with Effie Landry, her maid. Mrs. Landry testified:

Q. Did Mrs. Block on any occasion ever tell you anything about what was contained in her will?
A. Yes.
Q. What did she tell you about that?
A. She said she wasn't leaving the Weslow children anything.

The only question presented is whether there is any evidence of undue influence. The test of undue influence is whether such control was exercised over the mind of the testatrix as to overcome her free agency and free will and to substitute the will of another so as to cause the testatrix to do what she would not otherwise have done but for such control. Scott v. Townsend, 106 Tex. 322, 166 S.W. 1138; Curry v. Curry, 153 Tex. 421, 270 S.W.2d 208; Boyer v. Pool, 154 Tex. 586, 280 S.W.2d 564.

The evidence here establishes that testatrix was 81 years of age at the time of the execution of her will; that her son, defendant Lipper, who is a lawyer, wrote the will for her upon her instruction; that defendant Lipper bore malice against his deceased half brother (father of plaintiffs); that defendant Lipper lived next door to his mother and had a key to her home; that the will as written gave defendant Lipper a larger share of testatrix's estate than he would otherwise have received; that while testatrix had no discussion with anyone at the time she executed the will, she told the witness Friberg, prior to executing the will, that she was not going to leave anything to the Weslows; and subsequent to the execution of the will she told the witnesses Mrs. Levy, Mrs. Roos, and Mrs. Landry that she had not left the Weslows anything, and the reason why. The will likewise states the reasons for testatrix's action. The testatrix, although 81 years of age, was of sound mind and strong will; and in excellent physical health. There is evidence that the recitation in testatrix's will about the number of times the Weslows sent cards and flowers were incorrect, to the extent that cards and flowers were in fact sent oftener than such will recites.

The contestants established a confidential relationship, the opportunity, and perhaps a motive for undue influence by defendant Lipper. Proof of this type simply sets the stage. Contestants must go forward and prove in some fashion that the will as written resulted from the defendant Lipper substituting his mind and will for that of the testatrix. Here the will and the circumstances might raise suspicion, but it does not supply proof of the vital facts of undue influence — the substitution of a plan of testamentary disposition by another as the will of the testatrix. Boyer v. Pool, supra.

All of the evidence reflected that testatrix, although 81 years of age, was of sound mind; of strong will; and in excellent physical condition. Moreover, subsequent to the execution of the will she told 3 disinterested witnesses what she had done with her property in her will, and the reason therefor. A person of sound mind has the legal right to dispose of his property as he wishes, with the burden on those attacking the disposition to prove that it was the product of undue influence. Long v. Long, 133 Tex. 96, 125 S.W.2d 1034, 1035; Curry v. Curry, 153 Tex. 421, 270 S.W.2d 208.

Testatrix's will did make an unnatural disposition of her property in the sense that it preferred her 2 children over the grandchildren by a deceased son. However, the record contains an explanation from testatrix herself as to why she chose to do such. She had a right to do as she did, whether we think she was justified or not.

Plaintiffs contend that the record supports an inference that testatrix failed to receive the cards and flowers sent to her, or in the alternative that she failed to know she received same, due to conduct of defendant Lipper. Here again, defendant Lipper had the opportunity to prevent testatrix from receiving cards or flowers from the Weslows, but we think there is no evidence of probative force to support the conclusion that he in fact did such. Moreover, the will itself reflected that *some* cards and flowers were in fact received by the testatrix, the dispute in this particular area, going to the number of times that such were sent, rather than to the fact that any were sent. See also: Rothermel v. Duncan et al., Tex. Sup., 369 S.W.2d 917.

We conclude there is no evidence of probative force to support the verdict of the jury. The cause is reversed and rendered for defendants.

QUESTION AND NOTES

1.   Mrs. Block's will included a statement setting forth the reasons why she was not making provision for Julian's children. When the possibility of a will contest is anticipated, is this a desirable practice to follow?

Do you think the failure of Julian's children to pay due attention to their grandmother affected the court's decision? For an extensive examination of the role that reciprocity plays in judicial decisions involving will contests, see Melanie B. Leslie, Enforcing Family Promises: Reliance, Reciprocity, and Relational Contract, 77 N.C. L. Rev. 551 (1999).

2.   The rules about undue influence are complicated in most jurisdictions by nice questions about burdens of proof. A rule often applied is that where (1) a person in a confidential relationship (2) receives the bulk of the testator's property (3) from a testator of weakened intellect, the burden of proof shifts to the person occupying the confidential relation to prove affirmatively the absence of undue influence. In several jurisdictions, however, there must be additional evidence that the beneficiary was active in procuring the execution of the will. See William M. McGovern, Jr., Sheldon F. Kurtz & Jan E. Rein, Wills, Trusts and Estates 279-282 (1988); Ronald R. Volkmer, New Fiduciary Decisions: Handling Cases Involving Undue Influence, Est. Plan. July-Aug. 1995, at 253; Comment, Rethinking Oregon's Law of Undue Influence in Will Contests, 76 Or. L. Rev. 1027 (1997).

3.   If part of a will is the product of undue influence, those portions of the will that are the product of undue influence may be stricken and the remainder of the will allowed to stand if the invalid portions of the will can be separated without defeating the testator's

intent or destroying the testamentary scheme. Williams v. Crickman, 81 Ill. 2d 105, 405 N.E.2d 799 (1980).

NOTE: NO-CONTEST CLAUSES

A no-contest clause provides that a beneficiary who contests the will shall take nothing, or a token amount, in lieu of the provisions made for the beneficiary in the will. A no-contest clause is designed to discourage will contests. In dealing with these clauses, courts have been pulled in several directions by conflicting policies. On the one hand, enforcement of a no-contest clause discourages unmeritorious litigation, family quarrels, and defaming the reputation of the testator. On the other hand, enforcement of a no-contest clause could inhibit a lawsuit proving forgery, fraud, or undue influence and nullify the safeguards built around the testamentary disposition of property.

The majority of courts enforce a no-contest clause unless there is probable cause for the contest. The probable cause rule is adopted by Uniform Probate Code §§2-517 and 3-905 (1990) and by Restatement (Second) of Property, Donative Transfers §9.1 (1983). See Winningham v. Winningham, 966 S.W.2d 48 (Tenn. 1998) (citing cases). In a minority of jurisdictions, courts enforce no-contest clauses unless the contestant alleges forgery or subsequent revocation by a later will or codicil, or the beneficiary is contesting a provision benefitting the drafter of the will or any witness thereto. These jurisdictions believe a probable cause rule encourages litigation and shifts the balance unduly in favor of contestants. See Burch v. George, 7 Cal. 4th 246, 866 P.2d 92, 27 Cal. Rptr. 2d 165 (1994) (California provides a procedure for a declaratory judgment that a particular suit will thwart the intention of the testator and trigger a no-contest clause, which will be strictly enforced). See generally Martin D. Begleiter, Anti-Contest Clauses: When You Care Enough to Send the Final Threat, 26 Ariz. St. L.J. 629 (1994) (arguing in favor of the minority rule). See also Gerry W. Beyer, Rob G. Dickinson & Kenneth L. Wake, The Fine Art of Intimidating Disgruntled Beneficiaries With In Terrorem Clauses, 51 S.M.U. L. Rev. 225 (1998) (pointing out that Texas has never decided whether the probable cause rule is followed, leaving the law unclear).

The lawyer with a client who wishes to contest a will with a no-contest clause must investigate the local law carefully because there are subtle differences from state to state, particularly as to what constitutes a "contest." See Restatement (Second), supra, Statutory Note to §9.1 and Reporter's Note to §9.1.

NOTE: BEQUESTS TO ATTORNEYS

Undue influence. The will in Lipper v. Weslow was drafted by Mrs. Block's son, an attorney and a principal beneficiary under the will. Since the Watergate hearings in the 1970s, which revealed unethical as well as criminal behavior by lawyers, many courts, concerned with the appearance of impropriety, have ruled that a presumption of undue influence arises when an attorney-drafter receives a legacy, except when the attorney is related to the testator. The presumption can be rebutted only by clear and convincing evidence provided by the attorney. See Clarkson v. Whitaker, 657 N.E.2d 139 (Ind. App. 1995); Kirschbaum v. Dillon, 58 Ohio St. 3d 58, 567 N.E.2d 1291 (1991) (citing cases).

In New York, upon probate, the surrogate must investigate any bequest to the attorney who drafted the will. The attorney must submit an affidavit explaining the facts and circumstances of the gift, and if the surrogate is not satisfied with the explanation a hearing is held to determine whether the attorney's bequest was the result of undue influence.

In In re Henderson, 80 N.Y.2d 388, 605 N.E.2d 323, 590 N.Y.S.2d 836 (1992), the court held that a substantial bequest to the testator's long-time attorney, who suggested the client employ another lawyer to draft the will, which she did, was also subject to judicial inquiry since it could be inferred from the facts that the client did not have the full benefit of counselling by an independent lawyer. "Such scrutiny is especially important when attorney-beneficiaries are involved, since the intensely personal nature of the attorney-client relationship, coupled with the specialized training and knowledge that attorneys have, places attorneys in positions that are uniquely suited to exercising a powerful influence over their clients' decision." Id. at 394, 605 N.E.2d at 327, 590 N.Y.S.2d at 840. The court rejected a per se rule that would create a presumption of undue influence whenever a bequest is given an attorney with whom the testator has had a professional relationship in the past. The court thought such a rule could unduly restrict freedom of testators to give property to attorneys who have been kind and helpful, "evok[ing] reciprocal sentiments of gratitude and affection" by the client.

In California, after a Los Angeles Times reporter investigated the practices of a lawyer who opened up an office adjacent to Leisure World, where he acquired 7,000 clients and prepared numerous wills leaving him millions of dollars, the legislature enacted a statute invalidating any bequest to a lawyer who drafts the will unless the lawyer is related by blood or marriage to the testator. Cal. Prob. Code §21350 (1998). There is an exception permitting a bequest to a nonrelated lawyer-drafter if the client consults an independent lawyer who at-

"My goodness! Your dear old uncle seems to have left everything to me."

Drawing by Peter Arno
Copyright © 1942, 1970, 1998, by The New Yorker Magazine, Inc.
Reproduced by permission

taches to the document a "Certificate of Independent Review," which must state that the reviewing lawyer concludes the gift is not due to undue influence, fraud, or duress. Id. §21351(b). For the investigation that brought on this statute, see Davan Maharaj, Lawyer Inherited Millions in Stock, Cash from Clients, L.A. Times, Nov. 22, 1992, at A1.

Unethical conduct. Should an attorney who draws a will containing a bequest to himself or herself be subjected to disciplinary action? See Joseph W. de Furia, Jr., Testamentary Gifts from Client to the Attorney-Draftsman: From Probate Presumption to Ethical Prohibition, 66 Neb. L. Rev. 695 (1987); Gerald P. Johnston, An Ethical Analysis of Common Estate Planning Practices — Is Good Business Bad Ethics?, 45 Ohio St. L.J. 57, 60-86 (1984). See also A.B.A. Model Rules of Professional Conduct, Rule 1.8(c) (1983) (adopted in two-thirds of the states):

CONFLICT OF INTEREST: PROHIBITED TRANSACTIONS

A lawyer shall not prepare an instrument giving the lawyer or a person related to the lawyer as parent, child, sibling, or spouse any substantial gift from a client, including a testamentary gift, except where the client is related to the donee.

The comment to Rule 1.8 further advises:

A lawyer may accept a gift from a client, if the transaction meets general standards of fairness. For example, a simple gift such as a present given at a holiday or as a token of appreciation is permitted. If effectuation of a substantial gift requires preparing a legal instrument such as a will or conveyance, however, the client should have the detached advice that another lawyer can provide. Paragraph (c) recognizes an exception where the client is a relative of the donee or the gift is not substantial.

See Ronald C. Link, Developments Regarding the Professional Responsibility of the Estate Administration Lawyer: The Effect of the Model Rules of Professional Conduct, 26 Real Prop., Prob. & Tr. J. 1 (1991); William M. McGovern, Jr., Undue Influence and Professional Responsibility, 28 Real Prop., Prob. & Tr. J. 643 (1994).

John D. Randall, president of the American Bar Association in 1959-1960, was disbarred by the Iowa Supreme Court in 1979 for naming himself the beneficiary of a client's $4.5 million estate. Committee on Professional Ethics v. Randall, 285 N.W.2d 161 (Iowa 1979), cert. denied, 446 U.S. 946 (1980). In Disciplinary Counsel v. Galinas, 76 Ohio St. 3d 87, 666 N.E.2d 1083 (1996), an attorney was suspended from practice for drafting a will that gave him a share of the estate, even though the will was uncontested.

In re Will of Moses
Supreme Court of Mississippi, 1969
227 So. 2d 829

[Fannie Traylor Moses was thrice married; each of her husbands died. During the second marriage, she struck up a friendship with Clarence Holland, an attorney 15 years her junior. After the death of her third husband, Holland became Mrs. Moses' lover as well as attorney, and this relationship continued for several years until Mrs. Moses died at age 57. During the six or seven years preceding her death, Mrs. Moses suffered from serious heart trouble, had a breast removed because of cancer, and became an alcoholic. Three years before death she made a will devising almost all of her property to Holland. This will was drafted by a lawyer, Dan Shell, who had no connection with Holland, and who did not tell Holland of the will. Mrs. Moses' closest relative was an elder sister. The sister attacked the will on the ground of undue influence. The chancellor found undue influence and denied probate. Holland appealed.]

SMITH, J.   A number of grounds are assigned for reversal. However, appellant's chief argument is addressed to the proposition that even if Holland, as Mrs. Moses' attorney, occupied a continuing fiduciary relationship with respect to her on May 26, 1964, the date of the execution of the document under which he claimed her estate, the presumption of undue influence was overcome because, in making the will, Mrs. Moses had the independent advice and counsel of one entirely devoted to her interests. It is argued that, for this reason, a decree should be entered here reversing the chancellor and admitting the 1964 will to probate. . . .

The evidence supports the chancellor's finding that the confidential or fiduciary relationship which existed between Mrs. Moses and Holland, her attorney, was a subsisting and continuing relationship, having . . . ended only with Mrs. Moses' death. Moreover, its effect was enhanced by the fact that throughout this period, Holland was in almost daily attendance upon Mrs. Moses on terms of the utmost intimacy. There was strong evidence that this aging woman, seriously ill, disfigured by surgery, and hopelessly addicted to alcoholic excesses, was completely bemused by the constant and amorous attentions of Holland, a man 15 years her junior. There was testimony too indicating that she entertained the pathetic hope that he might marry her.[5] Although the evidence was not without conflict and was, in some

___

5. The court perhaps has forgotten the wife of Bath in Chaucer's Canterbury Tales, who had five husbands, the last one 20 years younger than she. She craved another young and healthy husband who could satisfy her hearty sexual appetites, and no reader of Chaucer can doubt she got one. — Eds.

of its aspects, circumstantial, it was sufficient to support the finding that the relationship existed on May 26, 1964, the date of the will tendered for probate by Holland.

The chancellor's factual finding of the existence of this relationship on that date is supported by evidence and is not manifestly wrong. Moreover, he was correct in his conclusion of law that such relationship gave rise to a presumption of undue influence which could be overcome only by evidence that, in making the 1964 will, Mrs. Moses had acted upon the independent advice and counsel of one entirely devoted to her interest.

Appellant takes the position that there was undisputed evidence that Mrs. Moses, in making the 1964 will did, in fact, have such advice and counsel. He relies upon the testimony of the attorney in whose office that document was prepared to support his assertion.

This attorney was and is a reputable and respected member of the bar, who had no prior connection with Holland and no knowledge of Mrs. Moses' relationship with him. He had never seen nor represented Mrs. Moses previously and never represented her afterward. He was acquainted with Holland and was aware that Holland was a lawyer.

A brief summary of his testimony, with respect to the writing of the will, follows:

Mrs. Moses had telephoned him for an appointment and had come alone to his office on March 31, 1964. She was not intoxicated and in his opinion knew what she was doing. He asked her about her property and "marital background." He did this in order, he said, to advise her as to possible renunciation by a husband. She was also asked if she had children in order to determine whether she wished to "pretermit them." As she had neither husband nor children this subject was pursued no further. He asked as to the values of various items of property in order to consider possible tax problems. He told her it would be better if she had more accurate descriptions of the several items of real and personal property comprising her estate. No further "advice or counsel" was given her.

On some later date, Mrs. Moses sent in (the attorney did not think she came personally and in any event he did not see her), some tax receipts for purposes of supplying property descriptions. He prepared the will and mailed a draft to her. Upon receiving it, she telephoned that he had made a mistake in the devise of certain realty, in that he had provided that a relatively low valued property should go to Holland rather than a substantially more valuable property which she said she wanted Holland to have. He rewrote the will, making this change, and mailed it to her, as revised, on May 21, 1964. On the one occasion when he saw Mrs. Moses, there were no questions and no discussion of any kind as to Holland being preferred to the exclusion of her blood relatives. Nor was there any inquiry or discussion as to a possible client-attorney relationship with Holland. The attorney-draftsman wrote the will according to Mrs. Moses' instructions and said that he had "no interest in" how she disposed of her property. He testified "I try to draw the will to suit their purposes and if she (Mrs. Moses) wanted to leave him (Holland) everything she had, that was her business as far as I was concerned. I was trying to represent her in putting on paper in her will her desires, and it didn't matter to me to whom she left it . . . I couldn't have cared less."

When Mrs. Moses returned to the office to execute the will, the attorney was not there and it was witnessed by two secretaries. . . .

The attorney's testimony supports the chancellor's finding that nowhere in the conversations with Mrs. Moses was there touched upon in any way the proposed testamentary disposition whereby preference was to be given a nonrelative to the exclusion of her blood relatives. There was no discussion of her relationship with Holland, nor as to who her legal heirs might be, nor as to their relationship to her, after it was discovered that she had neither a husband nor children.

It is clear from his own testimony that, in writing the will, the attorney-draftsman, did no more than write down, according to the forms of law, what Mrs. Moses told him. There was no meaningful independent advice or counsel touching upon the area in question and it is manifest that the role of the attorney in writing the will, as it relates to the present issue, was little more than that of scrivener. The chancellor was justified in holding that this did not meet the burden nor overcome the presumption.

The sexual morality of the personal relationship is not an issue. However, the intimate nature of this relationship is relevant to the present inquiry to the extent that its existence, under the circumstances, warranted an inference of undue influence, extending and augmenting that which flowed from the attorney-client relationship. Particularly is this true when viewed in the light of evidence indicating its employment for the personal aggrandizement of Holland.

. . . [T]he decree of the chancery court will be affirmed.

ROBERTSON, J. (dissenting). . . . Mrs. Fannie T. Moses was the active manager of commercial property in the heart of Jackson, four apartment buildings containing ten rental units, and a 480-acre farm until the day of her death. All of the witnesses conceded that she was a good businesswoman, maintaining and repairing her properties with promptness and dispatch, and paying her bills promptly so that she would get the cash discount. She was a strong personality and pursued her own course, even though her manner of living did at times embarrass her sisters and estranged her from them.

It was not contended in this case that Holland was in any way actively concerned with the preparation or execution of the will. Appellees rely solely upon the finding of the chancellor that there were suspicious circumstances. However, the suspicious circumstances listed by the chancellor in his opinion had nothing whatsoever to do with the preparation or execution of the will. These were remote antecedent circumstances having to do with the meretricious relationship of the parties, and the fact that at times Mrs. Moses drank to excess and could be termed an alcoholic, but there is no proof in this long record that her use of alcohol affected her will power or her ability to look after her extensive real estate holdings. . . .

The majority was indeed hard put to find fault with . . . [the actions of Dan Shell, the attorney who drew the will,] on behalf of his client. . . . He ascertained that Mrs. Moses was competent to make a will; he satisfied himself that she was acting of her own free will and accord, and that she was disposing of her property exactly as she wished and intended. No more is required.

There is not one iota of testimony in the voluminous record that Clarence Holland even knew of this will, much less that he participated in the preparation or execution of it. The evidence is all to the contrary. The evidence is undisputed that she executed her last will after the fullest deliberation, with full knowledge of what she was doing, and with the independent consent and advice of an experienced and competent attorney whose sole purpose was to advise with her and prepare her will exactly as she wanted it.

In January 1967, about one month before her death and some two years and eight months after she had made her will, she called W.R. Patterson, an experienced, reliable and honorable attorney who was a friend of hers, and asked him to come by her home for a few minutes. Patterson testified:

> She said, "Well, the reason I called you out here is that I've got an envelope here with all of my important papers in it, and *that includes my last will and testament,*" and says, "I would like to leave them with you if you've got a place to lock them up in your desk somewhere there in your office."
> . . . [A]nd she said, "*Now, Dan Shell drew my will for me two or three years ago,*" and she says, "*It's exactly like I want it,*" and says, "*I had to go to his office two or three times to get it the way I wanted it, but this is the way I want it,* and if anything happens to me I want you to take all these papers and give them to Dan," and she says, "He'll know what to do with them." (Emphasis added).

What else could she have done? She met all the tests that this Court and other courts have carefully outlined and delineated. The majority opinion says that this still was not enough, that there were "suspicious circumstances" . . . , but even these were not connected in any shape, form or fashion with the preparation or execution of her will. They had to do with her love life and her drinking habits and propensities. . . .

If full knowledge, deliberate and voluntary action, and independent consent and advice have not been proved in this case, then they just cannot be proved. . . .

I think that the judgment of the lower court should be reversed and the last will and testament of Fannie T. Moses executed on May 26, 1964, admitted to probate in solemn form.

QUESTIONS

1. Why is evidence of a sexual relationship outside of marriage admissible in undue influence cases? In In re Kelly's Estate, 150 Or. 598, 618, 46 P.2d 84, 92 (1935), the court suggested the reason was that a sexual relationship casts a suspicion of deceit and "cautions the court to examine the evidence with unusual care."

Inasmuch as a person ordinarily has a sustained sexual relationship only with a partner for whom there is considerable affection, perhaps even love, why does not evidence of such a relationship indicate that the partner is a natural object of the decedent's bounty? In view of the increase of committed couples living together without marriage, why should sensual pleasures without benefit of clergy continue to be evidence of *undue* influence? See Joseph W. de Furia, Jr., Testamentary Gifts Resulting from Meretricious Relationships: Undue Influence or Natural Beneficence?, 64 Notre Dame L. Rev. 200 (1989); Lawrence A. Frolik, The Biological Roots of the Undue Influence Doctrine: What's Love Got to Do With It?, 57 U. Pitt. L. Rev. 841 (1996).

2. If in In re Will of Moses, Fannie Moses had been a man named Frank, and Clarence had been a woman named Clara, but otherwise the facts were essentially the same, would the result be the same? See In re Launius, 507 So. 2d 27 (Miss. 1987) (sexual relationship between male testator and younger female beneficiary did not give rise to confidential relationship because testator was "strong-willed and emotionally and physically sound at the time the will was executed"); Arlene Derenski & Sally B. Landsberg, The Age Taboo: Older Women-Younger Men Relationships (1981).

Francine du Plessix Gray, The New "Older Woman"
N.Y. Times, §7 (Book Review), Jan. 15, 1978, at 3

Americans' traditional unease with [Older Woman and Younger Man] alliances is not only based on a complex network of puritanical hangups but vastly reinforced by our literature. There is a remarkable dearth of these liaisons in British or American fiction; and novels, for better or for worse, have always fueled our most passionate romantic fantasies and erotic expectations. . . . [The] absence [of the Older Woman and Younger Man theme] from English language fiction since the birth of the novel two and a half centuries ago is most striking compared to its abundant presence on the Continent. The theme is central to . . . classics of European literature, . . . and most particularly the work of Colette. . . .

In any society tainted by Puritanism, I reflect, such a relationship is bound to remain taboo simply because it is too much fun, just as it is bound to flower in that Gallic world of Colette's, divinely un-tainted by any moral strictures that might curb that hedonism of the flesh.

. . . After centuries of calmly approving the myriad 70-year-old Dr. Spocks who take 24-year-old women to their marriage beds, and con-doning vast networks of sugar daddies who heap trinkets on their molls, are we any readier for Colette's radically anti-Calvinist vision of the passive, unemployed younger man who ripens in the shelter of a powerful older woman? In the light of the new egalitarianism, in what sense is it more suspect to be a gigolo, or a man of modest employ-ment living with a successful older woman, than to be a kept woman or a housewife? The taboos still hovering over such relationships may never be lifted until all present notions of traditional "masculinity" and of male dominance are radically demythologized.

IN RE KAUFMANN'S WILL, 20 A.D.2d 464, 247 N.Y.S.2d 664 (1964), aff'd, 15 N.Y.2d 825, 257 N.Y.S.2d 941, 205 N.E.2d 864 (1965). In 1948, at the age of 34, Robert Kaufmann, a multi-millionaire by inheritance, seeking an independent life away from his family, moved from Washington to New York City. There he took up oil painting, engaged a psychoanalyst, the eminent and sought-after Dr. Janet Rioch, and met Walter Weiss, age 39, a man without material assets of conse-quence. Within a year after their meeting, Robert employed Walter as his financial consultant and had all his records moved to New York from the Kaufmann family office in Washington. More or less at the same time Walter moved into Robert's apartment. In 1951 Robert bought an expensive townhouse at 42 East 74th Street. He remodeled the top floor into an office for Walter. The rest of the house was lavishly furnished as a house for Robert and Walter. Walter ran the household, overseeing the cooking, cleaning, and entertaining, answering the mail and the telephone, paying bills from Robert's bank account, recommending doctors for Robert's various complaints. Robert was a talented artist and spent much of his time painting; he opened an art gallery where he exhibited his works and those of other artists. In their social life, Robert and Walter appeared as a couple, entertaining on a grand scale and exhibiting much love, affection, and mutual esteem. (Of course that is not to say that neither had a roving eye. Once, when Robert took a young man off to Paris, Walter followed unannounced a few days later and threw the young man out of the hotel, while Robert stood by silently.) In business matters, Robert gave Walter (who had a law degree but did not practice) his complete confidence and trust. Walter took charge of Robert's bank accounts and investments as if they belonged to the both of them. The two men lived together until 1959, when Robert died unexpectedly.[6]

Beginning in 1951, Robert made wills in successive years, each will increasing Walter's share of his estate. In 1958, Robert executed a will, drafted by a prominent New York law firm, which left substantially all his property to Walter. Accompanying it was a letter addressed to Robert's family signed by Robert in 1951 and passed along with each subsequent will. This letter might be described as a "coming out of the closet at death" letter. It stated that when Robert met Walter, Robert was "terribly unhappy, highly emotional and filled to the brim with a grandly variegated group of fears, guilt and assorted complexes." It stated that Walter encouraged Robert to submit to psychoanalysis and went on to say:

> Walter gave me the courage to start something which slowly but eventually permitted me to supply for myself everything my life had heretofore lacked: an outlet for my long-latent but strong creative ability in painting . . . , a balanced, healthy sex life which before had been spotty, furtive and destructive; an ability to reorientate myself to actual life and to face it calmly and realistically. All of this adds up to Peace of Mind. . . . I am eternally grateful to my dearest friend — best pal, Walter A. Weiss. What could be more wonderful than a fruitful, contented life and who more deserving of gratitude now, in the form of an inheritance, than the person who helped most in securing that life? I cannot believe my family could be anything else but glad and happy for my own comfortable self-determination and contentment and equally grateful to the friend who made it possible.
>
>   Love to you all,
>   *Bob*

6. A rather similar household was The Pines, the celebrated villa occupied by Algernon Charles Swinburne, English poet, novelist, and sage, and Theodore Watts-Dunton, a country solicitor. In 1879, at the age of 42, Swinburne moved in with Watts-Dunton, who had rescued him from delirium tremens and from a house of pleasure in St. John's Wood where a couple of blonde amazons flagellated the customers. Watts-Dunton laid down the rules, managed all of Swinburne's business affairs, ran the household, and doled out the pin money. Swinburne stayed at home and wrote. Watts-Dunton eventually married and his wife moved into The Pines with them. In 1909, Swinburne died, leaving everything to Watts-Dunton. Swinburne's family was hurt and indignant, but no one sued. Mollie Panter-Downes, At The Pines (1971).

In 1952, Robert executed a document granting Walter exclusive power over Robert's corporeal remains and the authority to make all funeral arrangements; in addition, in the event Robert was incapacitated, Walter was granted the power to consent in Robert's behalf to the performance of any operation he deemed necessary after consultation with Robert's physicians. The instrument provided that Walter was to act as "though he were my nearest relative ... and that his instructions and consents shall be controlling, regardless of who may object to them." The document in effect gave Walter the power that a legal spouse would have over these matters.

Robert's family in Washington deeply resented Walter's presence and his interfering business advice about the family-owned Kay Jewelry Stores, in which Robert was a major shareholder. The 1951 letter appeared to confirm the family's suspicion that a homosexual relationship existed between Robert and Walter. Upon Robert's death, his brother Joel sued to have the 1958 will set aside on the ground of undue influence. In his pretrial deposition, Walter denied that a homosexual relationship existed between the two men, but the appellate judges, and probably the jury as well, suspected that this was a lie. Walter did not take the stand at the trial and, therefore, was not subject to cross-examination.

After two jury trials, both finding undue influence, the majority of the appellate division agreed that the evidence was sufficient "to find that the instrument of June 19, 1958, was the end result of an unnatural, insidious influence operating on a weak-willed, trusting, inexperienced Robert whose natural warm family attachment had been attenuated by false accusations against Joel, subtle flattery suggesting an independence he had not realized and which, in fact, Weiss had stultified, and planting in Robert's mind the conviction that Joel and other members of the family were resentful of and obstructing his drive for independence." Although the earlier wills were not directly in issue, the majority thought the undue influence began before 1951 and tainted all the prior wills and gifts to Walter. The letter signed by Robert, mentioned above, was deemed to be "cogent evidence of his complete domination by Weiss," as was Walter's termination of Robert's dalliance in Paris while Robert stood mute.

The court of appeals affirmed, saying:

> Where, as here, the record indicates that testator was pliable and easily taken advantage of, as proponent admitted, that there was a long and detailed history of dominance and subservience between them, that testator relied exclusively upon proponent's knowledge and judgment in the disposition of almost all of the material circumstances affecting the conduct of his life, and proponent is willed virtually the entire estate, we consider that a question of fact was presented concerning whether the

instrument offered for probate was the free, untrammeled and intelligent expression of the wishes and intentions of testator or the product of the dominance of the beneficiary.

QUESTION AND NOTES

1.   If, in In re Kaufmann's Will, Robert had been a woman named Roberta, would the result be the same? What if the cohabitants had been married? See Jeffrey G. Sherman, Undue Influence and the Homosexual Testator, 42 U. Pitt. L. Rev. 225, 239-248 (1981). See also Ray D. Madoff, Unmasking Undue Influence, 81 Minn. L. Rev. 571 (1997), arguing that the undue influence doctrine denies freedom of testation to those testators who deviate from prescribed testamentary norms in failing to provide for their families.

For an analysis of *Kaufmann*, applying psychoanalytic theory and concluding that Walter consciously and wrongfully manipulated the transference to him that gave Robert emotional security, see Thomas L. Shaffer, Death, Property, and Lawyers 243-257 (1970). But compare Theodor Reik, Masochism in Modern Man 159, 164 (1941), pointing out that it takes two to tango and that, contrary to appearances, it is the submissive partner who calls the tune and sets the limits of what the dominant one can do. See also Note, The Caring Influence: Beyond Autonomy as the Foundation of Undue Influence, 71 Ind. L.J. 513 (1996).

2.   For a case upholding a jury finding of no undue influence, on facts similar to those in *Kaufmann*, see Estate of Sarabia, 221 Cal. App. 3d 599, 270 Cal. Rptr. 560 (1990). See also Evans v. May, 923 S.W.2d 712 (Tex. App. 1996), holding no undue influence where one man left all his estate to his male "lifemate," with whom he had lived for 30 years. See also E. Gary Spitko, Gone But Not Conforming: Protecting the Abhorrent Testator from Majoritarian Cultural Norms Through Minority Culture Arbitration, 49 Case W. Res. L. Rev. 275 (1999) (suggesting homosexual testator be permitted to direct in will that any will contest be adjudicated by arbitrator appointed by testator).

3.   The Los Angeles Daily Journal, Aug. 16, 1988, at 1, carried a story entitled Legal Challenges to AIDS Patients' Wills Seen on Rise. The article reported:

> Attorneys in those cities [New York, San Francisco, and Los Angeles] are seeing a growing number of will contests and other fights between blood relatives of AIDS victims and the victims' friends and lovers.

The challenges are usually based on the victims' competency when the will was made out, since loss of mental capacity is a common occurrence in AIDS cases. . . .

San Francisco lawyer Gary J. Wood, who chairs the AIDS referral panel in the city, notes the emotional aspects of such contests. "In large estates, they're fighting over money. But other than that, there's also jealousy about this lover person that's involved in this guy's life, and the family feels that's wrong."

[San Francisco lawyer Clint] Hockenberry says other factors enter into the conflict. "Sometimes it's a contest of cultures or family background. The family might come from the Midwest and, first of all, not know the son was gay; second, that the son had AIDS; and third, that the son had a lover. It's sort of a triple whammy.

"They blame the lover for giving the son AIDS and bringing him out. So there's a lot of anger there — almost all of it misdirected," notes Hockenberry.

. . . "About 60 percent of AIDS victims will have central nervous system involvement by the time they die," according to AIDS expert Dr. Nelson Garcia of the University of California/Irvine Medical Center.

"And about 40 percent, by the time they die, will show some manifestations of AIDS dementia syndrome — intermittent episodes of confusion, forgetfulness or hallucinations," notes Garcia. . . .

[Boston attorney Denise] McWilliams and others also suggest videotaping the signing of the will, if the resources are available. But McWilliams adds, "There are two minds about that. I'm less of a fan of videotaping than others, because of the way a person looks in the advanced stages of the disease — when they've lost a lot of weight, look very gaunt and so forth."

See Stanley M. Johanson & Kathleen F. Bay, Estate Planning for the Client with AIDS, 52 Texas B.J. 217 (1989); Emily Berendt & Laura L. Michaels, Your HIV Client: Easing the Burden on the Family Through Estate Planning, 24 J. Marshall L. Rev. 509 (1991).

AN EXERCISE IN LAWYERING:
SEWARD JOHNSON'S ESTATE

The facts of this exercise are taken from David Margolick's book, Undue Influence: The Epic Battle for the Johnson & Johnson Fortune (1993). The book offers a fascinating glimpse of estates and trusts practice by New York lawyers for the very rich, where lawyers do not send itemized bills but, at year's end, their suggestion of what is a fair charge, in a compelling story of greed and wasted lives of people with too much money. Undue Influence is not only a good read; it also causes a good think.

The story begins in 1968, when Barbara Piasecka, 31, a pretty and shapely immigrant from Poland, secured a job as a cook at the New Jersey estate of J. Seward Johnson, the fabulously rich heir to the Johnson & Johnson Company fortune (baby powder, Band-Aids, etc.). As a cook, Barbara (called Basia — BAH-sha — by her friends) turned out to be a disaster, but Essie Johnson, Seward's wife, took pity on her and made her an upstairs maid, where she caught the eye of Essie's randy septuagenarian husband. Seward, who nearly ran his boat aground when he spotted her sunning in a bikini, hired Basia as his personal art curator (she had studied art history in Poland), made her his scuba partner, took her travelling abroad, and set her up in a fancy apartment on Manhattan's Sutton Place, where he joined her. His batteries recharged by Basia, Seward lavished gifts on her — a $500,000 trust fund, a house on the Mediterranean, art work, furs, and jewels — making her so rich she needed a will, and a lawyer, of her own. Seward did not send her to his own lawyer, one Robert Myers, a Washington lawyer, but turned instead to Shearman & Sterling, one of New York's oldest and most prestigious law firms. There Tom Ford, an estates and trusts partner, assigned the task of drafting Basia's will to a 28-year-old associate, Nina Zagat, a recent graduate of Yale Law School (and perhaps better known as a co-founder of Zagat's Restaurant Survey).

Essie Johnson, not terribly unhappy to be rid of the philandering Seward, agreed to a divorce for $20 million and a couple of houses. Eight days later, in 1971, Seward, age 76, and Basia, age 34, married and began the construction in Princeton of Basia's $25 million dream house, called Jasna Polana, and costing more than any American house since William Randolph Hearst's San Simeon. One thing about Basia, she took immediately to the swank and hauteur of *les grands riches,* and Seward indulged her every whim.

In June 1972, Seward had Myers revise his will to increase Basia's trust to $50 million; the bulk of his estate went to Harbor Branch Foundation, an oceanographic research center he had set up, and presided over, in Fort Pierce, Florida. He left nothing to his six children, for whom he had earlier created trusts of Johnson & Johnson stock that, if still held, would have mushroomed in value to $110 million each. Seward rarely saw his children; they returned his lack of interest; they had been omitted from his wills since the mid-60s. The following January, Seward amended his will again to increase Basia's trust to $100 million. A few days later, another amendment upped Basia's share to one-half of his $370 million fortune — $100

*Seward and Basia frolicking at Children's Bay Cove, the Bahamas,
mid-1970s.*

million in trust, the rest outright. This was, at the time, the maximum
amount he could give Basia tax free.

Not long after Myers made these revisions in Basia's favor, Seward
decided that his interests and Basia's were identical, and, in the late
spring of 1973, Seward returned to Shearman & Sterling, the firm
that had drawn Basia's will, for further estate planning. He had liked
Nina Zagat from the beginning, and made her his lawyer. In the years
following, Nina, who was level-headed, meticulous, and deliberate,
almost the opposite of the mercurial and explosive Basia, became
Basia's best friend. She served the Johnsons and their foundations
(including Harbor Branch) loyally, reliably, and honestly. She trav-
elled with them on vacations, oversaw the legal work generated by
their multifarious activities, and more than once extricated Basia from
hot water into which her impulsive, impetuous nature had flung her.
Nina had a power of attorney over Seward's bank account and paid
the Johnson's bills, including millions for Basia's art and antiques
purchases.

After eight years as an associate in Shearman & Sterling, Nina was
passed over for partnership in 1975. She was given the option of
remaining as a permanent associate, making about $115,000 a year,
with the right to keep all executor's and trustee's fees she earned,

which, as a partner, she would have had to contribute to the firm's kitty. Not long after this snub, in 1976, Seward began fiddling around with his estate plan again. He executed a new will, much like the previous one Myers had drawn, but creating a $20 million trust for Basia's newly born nephew, Seward Piasecka. Knowing that Nina had been denied partnership, he decided that Nina should be a co-executor and trustee and handwrote her name into his will, to serve along with Basia and Seward Junior. "I hope this will be helpful to you," he told her. And it would be helpful indeed: a $375,000 executor's fee at his death plus substantial trustee's fees annually during Basia's life.

When Shearman & Sterling took a close look at the executors' compensation clause in Seward's 1976 will (copied from the will drafted by Myers), they decided it could lead to problems. Myers had kept a tight lid on administrative costs and had limited total executors' commissions and legal fees to 1.5 percent of the estate, requiring the executors to decide how to divvy it up, and perhaps leaving little for the executors after the lawyers got paid. Nina's superiors told her she should suggest to Seward that the compensation formula be changed, so that each executor receive the full statutory percentage provided by New York law in default of a negotiated fee (N.Y. Surr. Ct. Proc. Act §2307 (1986)). And she did.

In 1981 Seward, ailing from some as yet undiagnosed condition, finally got around to following Nina's suggestion. He had Nina prepare a codicil to his will providing that she and his two other executors were each to receive the percentage given by the New York statute — two percent of the estate each. As Seward's estate was then worth $200 million, this would amount to executor's commissions of $4 million for each executor. In addition Nina would collect $500,000 annually in trustee's fees for Basia's life. No record was made as to Seward's motives in vastly increasing Nina's executor's fee.[7] The codicil was witnessed by Nina and Jay Gunther, another senior associate at Shearman & Sterling.

Only a few days after signing this codicil Seward Johnson was diagnosed with cancer.

---

7. After the will contest was over, Margolick reports, Basia told her new advisor, John Fox,

> of a conversation she'd once had with Seward that, for whatever reason, she'd neglected to mention to her lawyers. In it, Seward had told her he'd always considered most lawyers to be self-interested, high-class crooks, and that he'd selected Nina not because she was the best lawyer available but because she was young and impressionable enough to develop loyalties to him. He'd provided for her so handsomely, he continued, because he wanted Nina to protect Basia once he was gone — something she would do properly, he was convinced, only were she totally beyond temptation herself. [Id. at 605.]

Two years later, his health failing, Seward retired to his house in Florida with nurses around the clock and an in-residence doctor. He advised Nina that he wanted to make further changes in his will. The story continues, as told in David Margolick's book Undue Influence:

"Just before heading South himself, Seward had told [Nina] he wanted to leave his Cape Cod property to [Seward] Junior, . . . to give Basia $1 million in mad money, and make some other technical changes in his will. On February 18 she and Gunther flew down to Fort Pierce with a codicil effecting what Seward had requested. . . . Still, Seward was not finished. A week later, when Nina arrived for Basia's birthday, he gave her further instructions. . . . [H]e now wanted to leave Junior $1 million outright in addition to the fees he stood to collect as executor and trustee. Three years earlier, Seward had arranged for Junior to succeed him as the power at Harbor Branch; now, he wanted Nina to draft a letter to Junior, urging him to consult Basia on all important foundation matters. He also wanted to even off the amounts going to Basia and her foundation, on the one hand, and Harbor Branch on the other, which Shearman & Sterling proposed to do by setting up a second trust. This new, so-called QTIP trust,[8] would produce income for Basia, but upon her death, its principal would go to Harbor Branch rather than to whomever she chose.

"By March 10 Nina and Gunther were back in Fort Pierce, with a newly revised will. After lunch . . . Nina went over the latest changes with Seward. Then he signed his latest will. Yet there were still more things on his mind. . . . [H]e raised a more sensitive subject. Would it be possible, he asked Nina, for any of his children to contest the will?

"It was hardly an outlandish thought. Many of the pieces for a will contest were already in place: a fabulous fortune, a much-disliked step-spouse destined to inherit virtually everything, a group of love-starved and financially strapped children who craved more but could easily wage war with what they already had. But what prompted Seward to raise this issue now? Perhaps it was his way of acknowledging that no longer could he play the king in his countinghouse. He knew he would die soon; whatever he wrote now could be for keeps.

"Nina proceeded to recite for Seward something that sounded like *The Golden Book of Will Contests*. A will, she explained, could be challenged on several grounds. One was that it had not been properly executed. Clearly, such a claim could never prevail; she and Jay

---

8. A QTIP trust is a trust giving the surviving spouse all the income for life, but without the right to dispose of the trust property at her death as she sees fit. It qualifies for the federal estate tax marital deduction in the settlor's (Seward's) estate. It was first permitted by the Internal Revenue Code in 1981, which also increased the marital deduction from 50 percent to an unlimited amount. See infra page 1047. — Eds.

Gunther had been through the drill innumerable times. Another was lack of competence; the children could say Seward had not known what he was doing when he'd signed the will. But the mere fact that they were conversing intelligently now took care of that, Nina reassured him; one had almost to be deranged to be considered incompetent. Finally, the children could claim Basia had coerced Seward into doing what he did. But claims of 'undue influence,' like claims of incompetence, rarely held up in court, particularly against a wife. In short, the children wouldn't have a leg to stand on. . . .

"Seward Johnson had already exceeded his biblically allotted life by six years when Nina began working for him. She had spent most of her professional time since then thinking of little but his affairs. And yet, up to this time she had never taken the threat of a will contest seriously, in part because Seward himself hadn't. [On several earlier occasions, Nina had asked Seward whether his children knew they would receive nothing on his death. Always Seward assured her they did, and expected nothing.] Once she'd gotten back to New York, Nina hastily huddled with her Shearman & Sterling colleagues to devise additional ways to safeguard what was by any standard the most important will in the firm's vault. One suggested the inclusion of an '*in terrorem*' clause. Under it, Seward would leave each child a pittance — say, a mere million or two — then threaten to take away even that if they contested things. Nina and Ford rejected that idea because Seward already had; he refused to give them anything, even to buy peace posthumously. Sensing that what they craved still more than money was paternal approval, Nina suggested killing the children with kindness. Up to now, the wills said little about them except, in so many words, that they were being left out of it. Henceforth, they would contain the following words of synthetic solace: 'It was my wish to provide my children with financial independence at an early age, and, accordingly, I created a substantial trust for each of them during my lifetime. It has been a source of pleasure to me to see my children pursue their interests independent of me and in a way that would not have been possible if I had not provided for them in this way.' It was a polite, legalistic way of saying 'You've already gotten yours. Get lost.'[9]

9. Margolick's book contains vignettes of the six Johnson children. Two of them were much in the news.

Seward's eldest son, Seward Johnson, Jr., who was forced out of the management of Johnson & Johnson after a lurid and humiliating divorce had fed the tabloids for months, is a well-known sculptor, who casts super-realistic life-like bronzes of people doing ordinary things (a man sitting on a bench reading a newspaper, for instance). Although scorned by the art elite as kitsch grown-up versions of baby shoes in bronze, the pieces appear to have found favor with the general public.

Seward's eldest daughter, Mary Lea Johnson Ryan D'Arc Richards, whose likeness was immortalized on the Johnson baby powder can, claimed — after her father's death — to be the victim of incest with her father. When her children were young, she fed them

"Nina returned on March 22 with the revised will. To witness it, she brought not only Gunther but James Hoch, another associate in Shearman & Sterling's individual-clients group. It was one of Nina's new precautions; under the law, since she was no longer a witness the children could not question her now unless they formally attacked the will. Ideally, one wouldn't want two associates, one of them quite junior, witnessing a will of such magnitude and portent. But Ford hadn't offered to go himself, and his second-in-command, Henry Ziegler, had vetoed Nina's request to bring along a more senior associate. Seward approved of Nina's new, more disinherited-friendly language, and signed the will, with a pen chosen from the two boxes of his favorite Uni-Balls Nina brought him.

". . . [After an upsetting meeting a week later with his son Seward Junior, who virtually forced Seward to resign as head of Harbor Branch Foundation, so that Seward Junior could succeed him, Seward wanted to change his will again. He told Basia about the meeting.] As she recounted their conversation, he laced into Junior, calling him egotistical, untrustworthy, and ghoulish. Junior, he told Basia, couldn't wait for him to die. And he was going to destroy Harbor Branch; he should have listened to Ed Link, who warned him about his son's incompetence. No longer, he said, did he want the $75 million in the newly established [QTIP] trust to go automatically to the foundation when Basia died; she should have the option of giving it to whomever she wished. Basia later insisted she advised her husband to leave well enough alone, but that Seward was adamant; he wanted to see Nina. . . . Once back in New York Nina spoke to Basia about the change Seward wanted. Rather than calling Seward to discuss the matter with him over the phone, she began preparing a draft and planning a return trip to Florida. . . .

"Back in New York, Nina worked on the next will. At Ziegler's suggestion, the revised version gave Basia the option of bequeathing the money in the new QTIP trust not only to charities of her choice, as Seward had wanted, but to Seward's descendants as well; that way they'd have a $75 million inducement to behave themselves. At Ford's suggestion, Nina and Gunther drafted two additional documents: an

whisky and sleeping pills to keep them quiet. When they grew up, Mary Lea sent them cocaine for Christmas. Mary Lea was a Broadway angel, backing plays, some hits (like Stephen Sondheim's Sweeney Todd and Jerry Herman's La Cage Aux Folles), some turkeys. According to Margolick, she made no bones about her kinky sexual tastes — ménages à trois, sometimes with men, sometimes with women, and a priapic chauffeur whom she shared with her second husband. When she caught the husband and the chauffeur in a plot to murder her, she divorced her husband, and the chauffeur was sent to jail.

Seward's other children stayed out of the news. But from Margolick's account they appear to be a pretty feckless lot. As Seward told a workman at Jasna Polana, only one — a son — was any good. "The others," he said, "aren't worth shit." Id. at 123. — Eds.

affidavit, for [Seward's doctor] Schilling to sign, attesting to the soundness of Seward's mind; and a declaration from Seward that his 1971 prenuptial agreement with Basia [requiring him to leave her $10 million], which had long since been nullified by subsequent wills, had officially been revoked. On the evening of April 13 Nina, Gunther, and Hoch flew to Florida. They retired early, the better to be rested for the events of the next day.

"On Thursday, April 14, 1983, Seward Johnson woke up around seven o'clock. A few minutes later Basia entered his bedroom and, following her daily routine, bade him good morning, kissed him, told him she loved him, heard him say he loved her, and asked whether he wanted his coffee now or later. . . . At 7:40 [Doctor] Wideroff went into Seward's bedroom and began drawing blood. The tests showed a drop in Seward's hemoglobin level; it was time for another transfusion. Having been told nothing about a will signing, Wideroff blithely set one up for the next day. And because she never read the nursing notes — she thought it both intrusive and unnecessary; if Seward had been having problems, surely someone would have told her — Nina knew neither that Seward always ebbed between transfusions or that, as things now stood, he would sign his will at low tide.

"At 8:10 Seward dozed off again. He awoke fifteen minutes later. On duty was a nurse named Patricia Reid. . . . This morning, her fourth, the old man seemed especially off. 'Some what [*sic*] confused for a few minutes,' she wrote. At eight-thirty Basia brought him some honey and water, along with oatmeal and bananas, but ten minutes later, Reid thought Seward was still acting peculiarly. By ten, though, he was looking at his newspaper. . . .

"Around eleven Seward had his back and neck rubbed with Johnson's baby oil, then had some broth and thirty minutes of oxygen. An hour later Nina walked into his bedroom, carrying legal papers and a pad, and closed the door behind her. Seward was sitting up in bed, his favorite robe on his lap. They hugged and kissed one another. . . . Nina reviewed the changes she'd made in his will. Only the provision allowing Basia to bequeath the remainder of the QTIP trust to his descendants bothered him; he agreed to leave it in, but only as long as Basia knew how he felt. Nina then reviewed the forty-eight-page will with Seward, piece by piece but perfunctorily; the document was basically boilerplate, and for the most part was identical to its predecessors. Seward's responses were equally cursory: a 'yes' here, an 'all right' there, a simple nod of the head. Now, Harbor Branch would not get anything unless Basia said so.

"He then told Nina to fetch Basia, who was in the living room. They both signed the revocation of the antenuptial agreement, then Nina explained to her the additional power she would enjoy under the new will. Seward reminded Basia she needn't leave his family anything. Nor, he said, was there any reason to state even informally that he wanted his money to end up with Harbor Branch. 'I want to leave this up to you,' he said. 'Seward, it's your will,' she replied. 'Whatever you want.'

"It was already past lunchtime, and the formal signing was put off until everyone had eaten. . . . [In the early afternoon Basia decided that she did not want the testamentary power of appointment Seward had given her over the QTIP trust, that she felt he really wanted the remainder to go to Harbor Branch. So, after obtaining the approval of her superiors in New York, Nina told Basia to go ahead with her idea of writing Seward a letter to that effect even though, Nina told her, her letter would not be binding. "Dearest Seward," Basia wrote, on her personal stationery, referring to the paragraph in his will giving her the power, "I hereby agree not to exercise said limited testamentary power of appointment in my will so that the property subject to it will go to Harbor Branch Foundation Inc. at the time of my death." After four o'clock, Seward was up from his afternoon nap. Seward was rolled into the living room in his wheelchair.] The time had come once more to execute a will.

"Nina began reviewing the document again. It left Basia almost everything tangible: the artwork, the airplane, the houses, Seward's clothing and personal effects, jewelry, automobiles, boats, silverware, china, livestock, and farm implements. Some $225 million went to the Barbara P. Johnson Trust, from which she could draw the income, plus up to $1 million annually of principal for herself, plus up to $20 million during her lifetime for her relatives (but only, Seward specified, if they no longer lived in a Marxist state). The will authorized Basia's trustees — Basia herself, plus Junior and Nina — to withdraw whatever they deemed appropriate for her welfare. Junior got Seward's house in Chatham plus $1 million; the other children got nothing except the solace of Nina's new more friendly disinheritance language. Anyone who'd worked for the Johnsons between five and ten years collected five thousand dollars; ten-year veterans got twice that. The rest — approximately $75 million — would be in the separate QTIP trust, whose interest went to Basia for life, then, depending on how she felt at the time, either to charity, Harbor Branch, or Seward's kith and kin.

"Once again Seward said 'yes' or 'that's correct' or 'good' or simply nodded as Nina reviewed the will. When she finished, she asked Seward whether it reflected his wishes, and he said it did. She then yielded to Gunther, who turned to its last page. The document had the crisp, grainy, quality-bond feel of a newly minted dollar bill. But whoever cranked it out of Shearman & Sterling's word processor had neglected to change the 'March' left over from the previous will to 'April.' 'Can we all agree that it is April fourteenth?' Gunther asked.

xecutor, shall determine. _____

IN WITNESS WHEREOF, I have hereunto set
1 this 14 day of ~~March~~ April, 1983.

(signature: J.B. Johnson)

EGOING INSTRUMENT consisting
(2) Parts was, on the day
e date thereof, signed,
published and declared by
OHNSON, the Testator therein
as and for his LAST WILL AND

They did. Seward fumbled with the pen Nina had given him, then asked Basia for another, the one with which he sometimes practiced signing his name on the tablet he kept by his bed. Where the blank in 'IN WITNESS WHEREOF, I have hereunto set my hand and seal this day of March, 1983' appeared, Seward wrote '14,' his *1* wavy and perilously close to the preceding *s*. Then, with two strokes of his pen he scratched out 'March' and wrote 'April' on top of it. Had it appeared elsewhere, it would have been barely legible, the *A* broken in two and the *i* endowed with an extra loop; in context, it was the crabbed but comprehensible script of a very old man. Gunther asked Seward to sign the will, and it became clear that all Seward's practicing hadn't helped. He started vigorously with a robust 'JSJ . . .' then trailed off asymptotically over the course of 'ohnson.'

" 'Mr. Johnson, do you declare this to be your will?' Gunther asked.

" 'Yes, this is my will,' Seward replied.

" 'Do you ask the two of us to sign as witnesses?' Gunther continued. 'And do you ask us to do an affidavit saying that we have done all these things?'

" 'Yes,' Seward replied, 'would you be so kind?'

"Gunther and Hoch signed their names and addresses, thereby vouching for the soundness of Seward's mind and the propriety of the procedure. Seward sat back in his wheelchair. 'That will solve a lot of problems,' he said. It was unclear just what he meant by that, and no one pressed him to explain.

206

"Up to now, there'd been no deviations from the usual script. Then Nina told Seward about Basia's surprise letter. 'Basia, you don't have to do that,' Seward said to her.

"'Seward, I want to,' she replied.

"The letter, Nina insisted, would not be binding. 'That doesn't make any difference,' Seward replied. 'That is very sweet of her.'

"[Basia signed the letter, "Love, Basia," Seward signed it too, and Nina and Gunther witnessed it.] . . .

"There was tea and cheesecake for all. There being no further business for them to transact, Gunther and Hoch left to buy some oranges and grapefruit to take back to New York. [They did not, however, prepare any notes about the will-signing ceremony and Seward's mental condition.] Soon the sound of Schilling's helicopter could be heard. The doctor greeted Seward by the poolside, then examined him in the bedroom. He asked the old man the usual questions: how he felt, how his night had been, how his bowels were doing. It was a routine examination, over in twenty or twenty-five minutes. 'Past two days — weaker,' the doctor wrote in his log book. 'Today more active and alert.' When Schilling completed his examination, Nina approached him in the hallway and handed him the form she'd prepared, in which he'd certify that Seward was 'of sound mind and memory and aware of his acts.' Schilling, who had never been asked to do anything like that before, perused it quickly, remarked that Seward's mental condition was 'first-rate,' and signed it. It required no deliberation; sure, there were fancier ways to test a person's mental capacity — having him count backward or to name the president of the United States — but those were used only when one had doubts, and he had none." [Id. at 140-158.]

A couple of weeks after Nina returned to New York, she had an unsettling telephone call from Seward Junior, advising her that two of Seward's daughters might contest the will (which they had not seen). And indeed, all the children might contest it, "if it is a cold fish in the face." Nina, not wanting to alienate Seward Junior, promised to say nothing to Seward or Basia about this conversation. She immediately huddled with Ford and her associates at the law firm. One of them advised that if the will was contested Basia would need cash to live on until the will was probated. Nina then drafted an "anchor to windward" trust (using one of Seward's nautical phrases), putting into it $9 million in bonds Seward kept on hand for emergencies. Nina would be trustee, with income and principal, if necessary, payable to Basia when Seward died. On May 3, Nina flew back to Fort Pierce, telling Seward of the new trust, which would pay Basia income immediately upon his death, without waiting for probate, but she did not tell Seward that a will contest was in the wind. Seward signed the trust agreement with a scrawl, telling Basia, "This may be very helpful to you."

On May 23, 1983, Seward Johnson died, leaving an estate of $402,824,972. The will was filed for probate in New York. On the value of Seward's estate at his death, Nina Zagat now stood to collect $8 million in executor's commissions and $900,000 in trustee's fees annually for Basia's life. On September 30, the six Johnson children and Harbor Branch Foundation filed a will contest, alleging that Seward Johnson lacked the capacity to make a will and that it had been produced by the undue influence of his widow, Basia, acting in concert with her lawyer, Nina Zagat.

The trial began on February 18, 1986, before Surrogate Marie Lambert, who early on called Basia "that tomato," showing where she stood. The children were represented by Milbank, Tweed, Hadley & McCloy, and Harbor Branch by Dewey, Ballantine, Bushby, Palmer & Wood, both top New York law firms. Basia and Nina, the executors, were represented by Sullivan & Cromwell, equally prestigious.

The jury trial went on and on — the nurses, the doctors, the bodyguards and servants in the Johnson homes, guests, and business associates were all heard from. The contestants claimed that Basia dominated Seward with temper tantrums, sometimes berating him and calling him "stupid old man." They further claimed that her scoldings of her servants as well as her husband were relevant because they demonstrated her "tyrannical disposition" and the "coercive and oppressive atmosphere" in which Seward spent his final years. Surrogate Lambert routinely admitted almost all evidence the contestants wanted in, including a tape recording of Basia screaming at a maid she fired (recorded by the maid), which electrified the trial. On the other hand, the surrogate would not admit some of the proponents' most important evidence. She ruled that Basia's lawyers could not tell the jury about the value of the trusts Seward had set up for his children during his life (even the poorest of the siblings had trust assets of about $23 million). Nina was nervous and unappealing as a witness, searching every question for an ambiguity or misstatement and speaking so slowly and deliberately that the surrogate chastised her. She was subjected to a withering cross-examination attacking her credibility, motives, and legal work. Neither she nor her gentlemanly counsel from Sullivan & Cromwell was a match for the tough Milbank attorney with the killer instinct who pictured her as Basia's agent and accomplice, devoted more to Basia's interests and her own than to her client Seward's. Basia said, "It's a pity Kafka isn't here to see this. He would understand the reality of it all."

As the trial wore on, Sullivan & Cromwell despaired of winning the verdict before the egregiously biased judge, and Milbank was frightened of losing the appeal. So, on June 2, after three months in combat, the parties decided to settle. Under the settlement each child got $6 million tax free, and Seward Junior got $7 million to make up for his lost executor's fees (he gave up the executorship when he contested the will). Harbor Branch got $20 million, less $1 million it owed Dewey, Ballantine in fees. The surrogate terminated the trusts for Basia, giving her $340 million outright, thus eliminating Nina's trustee's fees; Nina's executor's commission was slashed to $1.8 million. Milbank, Tweed collected $10 million in lawyer's fees; Sullivan & Cromwell got $7.3 million. After the settlement, Surrogate Lambert attended a celebration by the children and their lawyers. A juror told the judge he wasn't sure how he and his colleagues would have ruled on undue influence. "You wouldn't have had any doubts after I'd finished with my charge!" she replied.

Although she had won $340 million, and flashed a V-for-victory sign for the newspaper reporters, Basia bitterly resented having had to go through a trial, particularly one that cost her $80 million when her counsel had at the beginning advised her she had zero chance of losing. She refused to pay Shearman & Sterling's bill for $4 million and sued the firm and Nina for malpractice. But eventually, after running up more millions in lawyers' fees and tiring of litigation, Basia paid Shearman & Sterling's bill as well as Nina's $1.8 million executor's fee.

After the contest, Basia returned to Poland for a visit, where she impulsively offered to buy the Lenin Shipyard in Gdansk for $100 million and save the workers' jobs. But after worker resistance to her capitalistic reforms, the negotiations collapsed. Instead, she bought herself a Polish castle. According to Forbes Magazine, Oct. 1998, Basia is worth $1.7 billion. (The Johnson children are worth, collectively, $1.8 billion.) A fairy tale ending for the penniless Polish farmer's daughter!

For more on the will contest, particularly the cross-examination of Nina Zagat, see Ellen J. Pollock, The Eight Million Dollar Associate, The American Lawyer, May 1986, at 33.

NOTES AND QUESTIONS

1. If a will contest had been foreseeable, what omissions or mistakes did Shearman & Sterling make in preparing for it?

Consider whether Seward's attorney should have taken these precautions:

(a) The attorney requests the client to write, in the client's handwriting, a letter to the attorney setting forth in detail the disposition the client wishes to make. Upon receipt of the letter, the attorney replies, detailing the consequences of the disposition on the client's heirs and emphasizing the disinheritance of one or more of them, and asks for a letter setting forth the reasons for the disposition. After receipt of this letter, the will is drafted as the client wants. The letters are kept in the attorney's files to show any prospective contestant or to enter into evidence at trial, if necessary. This procedure is recommended by Leon Jaworski, The Will Contest, 10 Baylor L. Rev. 87, 91-93 (1958). Compare the letter written by Robert Kaufmann, at his attorney's request, supra page 194.

(b) The attorney videotapes or records a discussion between the testator and the attorney before witnesses wherein the testator explains why he or she wants to dispose of the property in the manner provided in his or her will. The discussion may include why the testator wants to disinherit an heir (but, remember, any facts stated by the testator as justifying disinheritance may be contradicted by contestants, alleging a mistake). The witnesses execute affidavits reciting why they believe the testator is of sound mind and acting freely. Henry Ford II left a videotape that explained the dispositions in his will when he died in December 1987. See Gerry W. Beyer & William R. Buckley, Videotape and the Probate Process: The Nexus Grows, 42 Okla. L. Rev. 43 (1989); Comment, Videotaped Wills: An Evidentiary Tool or a Written Will Substitute, 77 Iowa L. Rev. 1187 (1992). In In re Estate of Peterson, 232 Neb. 105, 439 N.W.2d 516 (1989), and Hammer v. Powers, 819 S.W.2d 669 (Tex. Civ. App. 1991), videotapes were found to be convincing evidence of mental capacity and no undue influence.

(c) Substantial documentation of Seward's mental capacity is made each time he signs a will after his health begins to fail. If the attorney does not document mental capacity, so as to ward off a foreseeable lawsuit, it may be malpractice. Rathblott v. Levin, 697 F. Supp. 817 (D.N.J. 1988).

(d) The will contains a no-contest clause. The will gives each child one or two million dollars, which is forfeited if they contest the will.

(e) "The best defense against the allegation that Basia and Nina conspired to impose Basia's scheme upon Seward's will should have been a videotape or an affidavit, in which Seward explained not only why he favored Basia and disinherited his children, but also why he chose to lavish millions on avoidable executor fees for Nina. He would have needed to declare that he knew that one executor might suffice where his will ordained three at a price tag in excess of $6 million each, and that lawyers normally serve as lawyers without being named as executors. He should also have been guided to explain that he knew that the New York statutory fee was a default formula, and that he had declined to negotiate a much lower fee. How much of this Seward actually understood is far from clear." John H. Langbein,

Will Contests, 103 Yale L.J. 2039, 2047-2048 (1994) (review of David Margolick, Undue Influence).

2. Were any of the actions of Nina Zagat unethical? Is it unethical for a lawyer to draft or witness a will naming the lawyer executor or trustee? In In re Estate of Weinstock, 40 N.Y.2d 1, 351 N.E.2d 674, 386 N.Y.S.2d 1 (1976), two attorneys (father and son) drafted a will for an 81-year-old man they had just met and named themselves executors. The court held the attorneys were guilty of "impropriety" and "overreaching" that constituted constructive fraud on the testator, precluding their appointment as executors. In State v. Gulbankian, 54 Wis. 2d 605, 196 N.W.2d 733 (1972), the court warned that a routine practice by an attorney to name the attorney as executor was suspicious and decided that it was unethical for the attorney-drafter to suggest, directly or indirectly, that the attorney be named as executor or lawyer for the executor. See Joseph W. de Furia, Jr., A Matter of Ethics Ignored: The Attorney-Draftsman as Testamentary Fiduciary, 36 U. Kan. L. Rev. 275 (1988); Gerald P. Johnston, An Ethical Analysis of Common Estate Planning Practices — Is Good Business Bad Ethics?, 45 Ohio St. L.J. 57, 86-101 (1984); Edward D. Spurgeon & Mary J. Ciccarello, The Lawyer in Other Fiduciary Roles: Policy and Ethical Considerations, 62 Fordham L. Rev. 1357 (1994); Report of the ABA Special Committee on Professional Responsibility, Preparation of Wills and Trusts That Name Drafting Lawyer as Fiduciary, 28 Real Prop. Prob. & Tr. J. 803 (1994).

Was it unethical for Nina to suggest to Seward that the executors' commission be increased to the amount provided by New York's statutory fee schedule? Suppose there had been no compensation clause in the prior will, so that the executors would have taken statutory commissions. Would that change your conclusion?

Why did Nina Zagat not want to be a witness to the May 14 will? If the drafting attorney witnesses the will, and as a witness would testify to mental capacity in a contest, the attorney may be disqualified from representing the personal representative in a will contest because of the conflict of interest. See ABA Model Rules of Professional Conduct 3.7, which provides that a "lawyer shall not act as an advocate at a trial in which the lawyer is likely to be a necessary witness." Rule 3.7 disqualifies the drafting attorney who witnesses a will, but it does not disqualify a member of the drafting attorney's firm from acting as counsel in a lawsuit unless the firm member witnesses the will. In any case, the drafting attorney's credibility as a witness to capacity would be impaired by her personal interest in the outcome of a lawsuit. See Larkin v. Pirthauer, 700 So. 2d 182 (Fla. App. 1997); In re Estate of Giantasio, 661 N.Y.S.2d 935 (Sur. Ct. 1997); Ronald C. Link, Developments Regarding the Professional Responsibility of the Estate Administration Lawyer: The Effect of the Model Rules of Professional Conduct, 26 Real Prop., Prob. & Tr. J. 1, 93-98 (1991).

It is common in some states for the drafting attorney to name himself or herself as attorney for the executor. Is this enforceable? Is it ethical? See Johnston, supra, at 101-114.

3. What conflicts of interest did Shearman & Sterling have in the Johnson family affairs? Observe that Shearman & Sterling were counsel for Seward, his wife Basia, and the Harbor Branch Foundation (Seward's charitable beneficiary, which received less and less while Basia received more and more by successive wills). Should Seward and Basia have had separate lawyers for their estate planning? See American College of Trust and Estate Counsel, Commentaries on the Model Rules of Professional Conduct 85-109 (2d ed. 1995) (Model Rule 1.7); Report of the ABA Special Committee on Professional Responsibility, Comments and Recommendations on the Lawyer's Duties in Representing Husband and Wife, 28 Real Prop., Prob. & Tr. J. 765 (1994).

4. *More on New York Surrogate's Courts.* New York Surrogates hand out millions upon millions of dollars annually to lawyers appointed as guardians ad litem for minors or incompetents. Guardians ad litem are required by New York law if a minor or incompetent person is beneficially interested in the estate. Many of these plums go to the elected surrogate's friends and supporters. Mayor Fiorello H. LaGuardia called the surrogate's court "the most expensive undertaking establishment in the world" when, during his anti-Tammany administration, he found himself unable to cut off this source of patronage to Tammany lawyers.

"What most disturbs critics is that political figures seem to enjoy a preferred position. Often, the patronage can be blatant. In one extreme case 11 years ago, Joseph A. Cox, who was retiring as Surrogate, said he had named as special guardian to a large estate the son of his fellow Manhattan Surrogate, S. Samuel DiFalco. The assignment was a 'wedding present' for the younger DiFalco, Mr. Cox said." Tom Goldstein, Once More, Surrogate Talk, N.Y. Times, Sept. 4, 1977, at E5.

In the late 1980s, the federal government opened an investigation into charges that Surrogate Lambert awarded millions of dollars in fees to a small clique of lawyers in return for possible kickbacks. In her last week in office, Lambert awarded a fee of $345,000 in an estate worth $1.5 million. Several lawyers receiving her patronage were convicted of tax evasion, mail fraud, money laundering, and stealing from their wards' estates. Newsday, April 19, 1994, at A26.

The prestigious New York law firms, counsel for the superrich whose wealth passes through the Manhattan Surrogate's Court, have never evinced much interest in cleaning up the abuses of guardianships. Why do you suppose not? See David Margolick, Undue Influence 313 (1993).

In the Seward Johnson litigation, no guardian ad litem was appointed to represent Seward's minor and unborn descendants, who were among the objects of the special power of appointment Seward gave Basia over $75 million ("that way they'd have a $75 million inducement to behave themselves," supra page 203). No guardian was appointed because possible appointees of a power of appointment do not have a property interest, but only a hope of receiving something. Nonetheless, were the grandchildren of Seward, then in being as well as afterborn, disadvantaged by the settlement terminating the trust? Were their interests overlooked by the surrogate?

5. Should a probate court require the parties to enter into mediation (as in divorce or family disputes) before going to trial? Such a procedure is recommended by Susan N. Gary, Mediation and the Elderly: Using Mediation to Resolve Disputes Over Guardianship and Inheritance, 32 Wake Forest L. Rev. 397 (1997).

SECTION C.   FRAUD

It is fairly easy to state the test for fraud but often difficult to apply it on particular facts. Fraud occurs where the testator is deceived by a misrepresentation and does that which the testator would not have done had the misrepresentation not been made. It is usually said that the misrepresentation must be made with both the *intent* to deceive the testator and the *purpose* of influencing the testamentary disposition. A provision in a will procured by fraud is invalid. The remaining portion of the will stands unless the fraud goes to the entire will or the portions invalidated by fraud are inseparable from the rest of the will.

Where the probate court cannot do justice by refusing probate, the will may be probated and then a court with equity powers can impose a constructive trust on the wrongdoer, compelling the wrongdoer to surrender the property acquired by the wrongful conduct.

If fraud occurs in the testamentary setting, it is usually either fraud in the inducement or fraud in the execution.

Fraud in the inducement occurs when a person misrepresents facts, thereby causing the testator to execute a will, to include particular provisions in the wrongdoer's favor, to refrain from revoking a will, or not to execute a will. Thus:

> *Case 1.* O's heir apparent, *H*, induces O not to execute a will in favor of *A* by promising O that *H* will convey the property to *A*. At the time *H*

makes the promise, *H* has no intent to convey the property to *A*. This is fraud in the inducement. If, on the other hand, at the time of his promise *H* had intended to convey the property to *A*, but *H* had changed his mind after *O*'s death and had refused to convey to *A*, no fraud is involved. However, *A* still may be able to recover from *H* on the theory of a secret trust. See infra page 616.

Questions of whether the legacy is the fruit of the fraud are particularly tricky. A fraudulently procured inheritance or bequest is invalid only if the testator would not have left the inheritance or made the bequest had the testator known the true facts. The interesting question, of course, is: What would the testator have done if the true facts had been known?

Estate of Carson, 184 Cal. 437, 194 P. 5 (1920), is a dramatic illustration of the problem. In this case one J. Gamble Carson went through a marriage ceremony with Alpha O. Carson, which she believed was a real wedding. After living together thereafter happily for a year, Alpha died, devising most of her estate "to my husband J. Gamble Carson." It then came to light that Alpha had been "seduced by a marital adventurer into a marriage with him which was no marriage in the eyes of the law because of the fact, which he concealed from her, that he had already had at least one, if not more, spouses, legal and illegal, who were still living and undivorced." But was the devise the fruit of the fraud? That was the question. Said the court:

Now a case can be imagined where, nothing more appearing, as in this case, than that the testatrix had been deceived into a void marriage and had never been undeceived, it might fairly be said that a conclusion that such deceit had affected a bequest to the supposed husband would not be warranted. If, for example, the parties had lived happily together for 20 years, it would be difficult to say that the wife's bequest to her supposed husband was founded on her supposed legal relation with him, and not primarily on their long and intimate association. It might well be that if undeceived at the end of that time her feeling would be, not one of resentment at the fraud upon her, but of thankfulness that she had been deceived into so many years of happiness. But, on the other hand, a case can easily be imagined where the reverse would be true. If in this case the will had been made immediately after marriage, and the testatrix had then died within a few days, the conclusion would be well-nigh irresistible, in the absence of some peculiar circumstance, that the will was founded on the supposed legal relation into which the testatrix had been deceived into believing she was entering. Between these two extreme cases come those wherein it cannot be said that either one conclusion or the other is wholly unreasonable, and in those cases the determination of the fact is for the jury. Of that sort is the present. [Id. at 443, 194 P. at 8-9.]

Fraud in the execution occurs when a person misrepresents the character or contents of the instrument signed by the testator, which does not in fact carry out the testator's intent. Thus:

> *Case 2. O*, with poor eyesight, asks her heir apparent, *H*, to bring her the document prepared for her as a will so that she can sign it. *H* brings *O* a document that is not *O*'s intended will, knowing it is not the document *O* wants. *O* signs it, believing it to be her will. This is fraud in the execution.

PROBLEM

T's first will devised everything to her favorite niece, Jean, who lived in a distant city. *T*'s second will, executed in the hospital two days before she died, revoked her prior will and devised everything to her friend, Carol. After *T*'s death a nurse in the hospital testifies that the day before the will was executed he heard Carol tell *T* that Jean had died. "In that case," *T* said, "I want you [Carol] to have everything." In fact, as Carol knew, Jean was alive. What result? See 5 Austin W. Scott, Trusts §489.3 (William F. Fratcher 4th ed. 1989).

Latham v. Father Divine
Court of Appeals of New York, 1949
299 N.Y. 22, 85 N.E.2d 168, 11 A.L.R.2d 802

DESMOND, J.   The amended complaint herein has, in response to a motion under rule 106 of the Rules of Civil Practice, been dismissed for insufficiency. Its principal allegations are these: plaintiffs are first cousins, but not distributees [next of kin], of Mary Sheldon Lyon, who died in October, 1946, leaving a will, executed in 1943, which gave almost her whole estate to defendant Father Divine,[10] leader of

---

10. Father Divine, a charismatic religious leader during the Depression who proclaimed his own divinity, attracted thousands of believers, mostly black, but some, like Mary Sheldon Lyon, white. Whatever the merits of his claim, Father Divine was a master of theater. His inspirational sermons at a Harlem church roused his followers to spirited expression; his exuberant and melodious services were standing room only. Father Divine went beyond the spiritual; he preached racial equality and social action against segregation. He established communes ("heavens") and religious cooperatives around the country, often in white neighborhoods, where blacks from the ghetto could move to find work and food. Father Divine taught there was only one race, no "Negro" and "white"; people just had darker or lighter complexions. The press of the time disparaged Father Divine as a con man of the cloth. Yet, in the last decade, scholars searching for the roots of the black churches' commitment to social action have come to reevaluate Father Divine. Many now view him as an influential and serious religious leader who gave his followers a feeling of goodness and worth, who stuck his thumb in the eye of the white establishment (he rode around in a chauffeured Rolls-Royce or, alternatively, a Duesenberg, inhabited the fanciest houses, hosted sumptuous feasts, and claimed for blacks every perquisite of rich whites), and who crystallized the commitment of black churches to the struggle for racial justice. See Jill M. Watts, God, Harlem U.S.A.: The Father Divine Story (1992); Robert Weisbrot, Father Divine and the Struggle for Racial Equality (1983).

The turn in Father Divine's fortunes, which transformed him from a minor religious

a religious cult, and to two corporate defendants in some way connected with that cult, and to an individual defendant (Patience Budd)
said to be one of Father Divine's active followers; that said will has
been, after a contest instituted by distributees, probated under a compromise agreement with the distributees, by the terms of which agreement, to which plaintiffs were not parties, the defendants just above
referred to will receive a large sum from the estate; that after the
making of said will, decedent on several occasions expressed "a desire
and a determination to revoke the said will, and to execute a new will
by which the plaintiffs would receive a substantial portion of the estate," "that shortly prior to the death of the deceased she had certain
attorneys draft a new will in which the plaintiffs were named as legatees for a very substantial amount, totalling approximately $350,000";
that "by reason of the said false representations, the said undue influence and the said physical force" certain of the defendants "prevented the deceased from executing the said new Will"; that, shortly
before decedent's death, decedent again expressed her determination
to execute the proposed new will which favored plaintiffs, and that
defendants "thereupon conspired to kill, and did kill, the deceased
by means of a surgical operation performed by a doctor engaged by
the defendants without the consent or knowledge of any of the relatives of the deceased."

Nothing is better settled than that, on such a motion as this, all the
averments of the attacked pleading are taken as true. For present
purposes, then, we have a case where one possessed of a large property and having already made a will leaving it to certain persons,
expressed an intent to make a new testament to contain legacies to
other persons, attempted to carry out that intention by having a new

---

figure into an adored incarnation of God, came as a result of a brush with the law in
1932. Father Divine had bought a large house in Sayville on the south shore of Long
Island. On Sundays, flocks of the faithful from Harlem gathered there for some joyous
prayer sessions. The white neighbors objected. Father Divine was arrested for disturbing
the peace and conducting a public nuisance. This event was picked up by the national
press. Father Divine was pictured as a martyr to racial prejudice. On trial, the jury found
Father Divine guilty as charged. Some of Father Divine's partisans warned the judge that
if he sent Father Divine to jail something terrible would happen to him. The judge,
unheeding, gave Father Divine the maximum sentence of a year in jail. Three days later,
perhaps by sheer coincidence, the judge keeled over and died. "When the warden and
the guards found out about it in the middle of the night," writes Professor Henry Louis
Gates, Jr., "they raced to Father Divine's cell and woke him up. Father Divine, they said,
your judge just dropped dead of a heart attack. Without missing a beat, Father Divine
lifted his head and told them: 'I *hated* to do it.' " Henry L. Gates, Jr., Whose Canon Is
It Anyway?, N.Y. Times, Feb. 20, 1989, §7 (Book Review), at 1. Although the story has
been questioned, its repetition established Father Divine — among the believers — as
an authentic voice of God.

Father Divine left New York in the 1950s and retired to a 72-acre estate outside Philadelphia. His apparent powers of retribution faded. Judge Desmond, who wrote the opinion
in *Latham*, died in 1987, at the age of 91. — Eds.

Father Divine, calling the faithful to dinner.

217

will drawn which contained a large legacy to those others, but was, by means of misrepresentations, undue influence, force, and indeed, murder, prevented, by the beneficiaries named in the existing will, from signing the new one. Plaintiffs say that those facts, if proven, would entitle them to a judicial declaration, which their prayer for judgment demands, that defendants, taking under the already probated will, hold what they have so taken as constructive trustees for plaintiffs, whom decedent wished to, tried to, and was kept from, benefiting.

We find in New York no decision directly answering the question as to whether or not the allegations above summarized state a case for relief in equity. But reliable texts, and cases elsewhere, see 98 A.L.R. 477 et seq., answer it in the affirmative. Leading writers, 3 Scott on Trusts, pp. 2371-2376; 3 Bogert on Trusts and Trustees, part 1, §§473-474, 498, 499; 1 Perry on Trusts and Trustees [7th ed.], pp. 265, 371, in one form or another, state the law of the subject to be about as it is expressed in Comment i under section 184 of the Restatement of the Law of Restitution: "*Preventing revocation of will and making new will.* Where a devisee or legatee under a will already executed prevents the testator by fraud, duress or undue influence from revoking the will and executing a new will in favor of another or from making a codicil, so that the testator dies leaving the original will in force, the devisee or legatee holds the property thus acquired upon a constructive trust for the intended devisee or legatee."

A frequently-cited case is Ransdel v. Moore, 153 Ind. 393, at pages 407-408, 53 N.E. 767, at page 771, 53 L.R.A. 753, where, with listing of many authorities, the rule is given thus: "when an heir or devisee in a will prevents the testator from providing for one for whom he would have provided but for the interference of the heir or devisee, such heir or devisee will be deemed a trustee, by operation of law, of the property, real or personal, received by him from the testator's estate, to the amount or extent that the defrauded party would have received had not the intention of the deceased been interfered with. This rule applies also when an heir prevents the making of a will or deed in favor of another, and thereby inherits the property that would otherwise have been given such other person." To the same effect, see 4 Page on Wills [3d ed.], p. 961.

While there is no New York case decreeing a constructive trust on the exact facts alleged here, there are several decisions in this court which, we think, suggest such a result and none which forbids it. Matter of O'Hara's Will, 95 N.Y. 403, 47 Am. Rep. 53; Trustees of Amherst College v. Ritch, 151 N.Y. 282, 45 N.E. 876, 37 L.R.A. 305; Edson v. Bartow, 154 N.Y. 199, 48 N.E. 541, and Ahrens v. Jones, 169 N.Y. 555, 62 N.E. 666, 88 Am. St. Rep. 620, which need not be closely analyzed here as to their facts, all announce, in one form or another, the rule that, where a legatee has taken property under a will, after agreeing outside the will, to devote that property to a purpose intended and declared by the testator, equity will enforce a constructive trust to effectuate that purpose, lest there be a fraud on the testator. In Williams v. Fitch, 18 N.Y. 546, a similar result was achieved in a suit for money had and received. In each of those four cases first above cited in this paragraph, the particular fraud consisted of the legatee's failure or refusal to carry out the testator's designs, after tacitly or expressly promising so to do. But we do not think that a breach of such an engagement is the only kind of fraud which will impel equity to action. A constructive trust will be erected whenever necessary to satisfy the demands of justice. Since a constructive trust is merely "the formula through which the conscience of equity finds expression," Beatty v. Guggenheim Exploration Co., 225 N.Y. 380, 386, 122 N.E. 378, 380 . . . , its applicability is limited only by the inventiveness of men who find new ways to enrich themselves unjustly by grasping what should not belong to them. Nothing short of true and complete justice satisfies equity, and always assuming these allegations to be true, there seems no way of achieving total justice except by the procedure used here. . . .

This is not a proceeding to probate or establish the will which plaintiffs say testatrix was prevented from signing. . . . The will Mary Sheldon Lyon did sign has been probated and plaintiffs are not contesting, but proceeding on, that probate, trying to reach property which has effectively passed thereunder. . . .

We do not agree with appellants that Riggs v. Palmer, 115 N.Y. 506, 22 N.E. 188, 5 L.R.A. 340, 12 Am. St. Rep. 819, completely controls our decision here. That was the famous case where a grandson, over-eager to get the remainder interest set up for him in his grandfather's will, murdered his grandsire. After the will had been probated, two daughters of the testator who, under the will, would take if the grandson should predecease testator, sued and got judgment decreeing a constructive trust in their favor. It may be, as respondents assert, that the application of Riggs v. Palmer, supra, here would benefit not plaintiffs, but this testator's distributees. We need not pass on that now. But Riggs v. Palmer, supra, is generally helpful to appellants, since it forbade the grandson profiting by his own wrong in connection with a will; and, despite an already probated will and the Decedent Estate Law, Riggs v. Palmer, supra, used the device or formula of constructive trust to right the attempted wrong, and prevent unjust enrichment. . . .

This suit cannot be defeated by any argument that to give plaintiffs judgment would be to annul those provisions of the Statute of Wills requiring due execution by the testator. Such a contention, if valid, would have required the dismissal in a number of the suits herein cited. The answer is in Ahrens v. Jones, 169 N.Y. 555, 561, 62 N.E. 666, 668, 88 Am. St. Rep. 620, supra:

> The trust does not act directly upon the will by modifying the gift, for the law requires wills to be wholly in writing; but it acts upon the gift itself as it reaches the possession of the legatee, or as soon as he is entitled to receive it. The theory is that the will has full effect by passing an absolute legacy to the legatee, and that then equity, in order to defeat fraud, raises a trust in favor of those intended to be benefited by the testator, and compels the legatee, as a trustee ex maleficio, to turn over the gift to them.

The judgment of the Appellate Division, insofar as it dismissed the complaint herein, should be reversed, and the order of Special Term affirmed, with costs in this court and in the Appellate Division.

NOTES

1. Another view of the contest of Mary Sheldon Lyon's will is presented by a biographer of Father Divine, Sara Harris, Father Divine 278-281 (1953). Harris says that Mary Sheldon Lyon was a devotee of Father Divine from 1938 to 1946, and took the spiritual name of Peace Dove. "She was sweet goodness personified. That was why, when she attended banquets, she was always granted a holy seat at God's own table. That was why the followers made a fuss over her." Harris reports that, after Father Divine lost in the court of appeals and after subsequent lower court rulings adverse to him, a settlement was reached giving Father Divine a small fraction of the amount bequeathed him. Harris suggests that the court rulings were motivated, at least in part, by racial prejudice against Father Divine and a belief that his church (called a "cult" by the court) was not quite a legitimate religious group.

2. A constructive trust is sometimes said to be a "fraud-rectifying" trust. But a constructive trust may be imposed where no fraud is involved but the court thinks that unjust enrichment would result if the person retained the property. As Judge Cardozo, speaking for the Court of Appeals of New York, said: "A constructive trust is the formula through which the conscience of equity finds expression. When property has been acquired in such circumstances that the holder of the legal title may not in good conscience retain the beneficial interest, equity converts him into a trustee." Beatty v. Guggenheim Exploration Co., 225 N.Y. 380, 386, 122 N.E. 378 (1919). On constructive trusts imposed where there is interference with willmaking, see 5 Austin W. Scott, Trusts §§489-489.6 (William F. Fratcher 4th ed. 1989).

3. In Pope v. Garrett, 147 Tex. 18, 211 S.W.2d 559 (1948), some, but not all, of Carrie Simmons's expectant heirs "by physical force or by creating a disturbance" prevented Carrie from executing a will in favor of her friend Claytonia Garrett. Shortly after this incident, Carrie lapsed into a coma and died. The court imposed a constructive trust in favor of Claytonia, not only on the heirs who had participated in the disturbance but also on the innocent heirs. The court reasoned that the innocent heirs would be unjustly enriched if they were permitted to keep the property, since, but for the wrongful acts, they would have inherited nothing. See Scott, supra, §489.5.

4. Observe that if, in *Latham*, a constructive trust were to be imposed on Father Divine's churches, the court would *in effect* be distributing property according to a completely unexecuted will, a will that Mary Lyon might never have signed or, having signed, might later revoke. Keep this in mind as you consider the cases in the next chapter, where courts refuse to give effect to signed wills clearly intended as wills, but defectively executed for some reason. In these cases there is far more certainty than in *Latham* that the testator intended the document to be his or her will.

NOTE: TORTIOUS INTERFERENCE WITH EXPECTANCY

In the *Latham* case the plaintiffs asked for a constructive trust to be imposed upon the defendants to rectify alleged fraud or undue influence. Another theory that can be used is tortious interference with an expectancy. Restatement (Second) of Torts §774B (1979) includes intentional interference with an expected inheritance or gift as a valid cause of action. This theory extends to expected inheritances the protection courts have accorded commercial expectancies, such as the prospect of obtaining employment or customers. Under this theory, the plaintiff must prove that the interference involved conduct tortious in itself, such as fraud, duress, or undue influence. The theory cannot be used when the challenge is based on testator's mental incapacity. See Nemeth v. Banhalmi, 125 Ill. App. 3d 938, 466 N.E.2d 977 (1984); Note, Intentional Interference with Inheritance, 30 Real Prop., Prob. & Tr. J. 325 (1995).

A tort action for tortious interference with an expectancy is not a will contest. It does not challenge the probate or validity of a will but rather seeks to recover tort damages from a third party for tortious interference. The action is not subject to the typically short state statute of limitations on will contests, but the tort statute of limitations starts running on the action at the time the plaintiff discovered or should have discovered the fraud or undue influence. Most courts require the plaintiff to pursue probate remedies first, if they are adequate, and failure to do so may result in barring a tortious interference suit. See Martin v. Martin, 687 So. 2d 903 (Fla. App. 1997) (holding testator's sons did not have an adequate remedy in contesting the testator's will in probate when testator transferred $8 million into an inter vivos trust for second wife and poured over $300,000 into it by will, all through the alleged undue influence of the second wife, and thus could sue second wife in tort). If the plaintiff contests the will, and loses, ordinarily the plaintiff is barred by the principle of res judicata from suing later in tort. See Annot., 18 A.L.R.5th 211 (1994).

Since a suit for tortious interference with an expectancy is not a will contest, a no-contest clause (supra page 184) does not apply to such a suit. Punitive damages may be recovered against the wrongdoer in a suit in tort but not, of course, in a suit seeking to prevent probate of a will on the ground of undue influence or fraud. See Estate of Legeas, 210 Cal. App. 3d 385, 258 Cal. Rptr. 858 (1989) (awarding punitive damages against persons fraudulently interfering with an expectancy).

Massachusetts recently refused to recognize a cause of action for tortious interference with an expectancy. The court believed that plaintiffs had adequate remedies under current law. Labonte v. Giordana, 426 Mass. 319, 687 N.E.2d 1253 (1997).

PROBLEM

The will beneficiary sues the witnesses of a will for tortious interference with an inheritance. The beneficiary contends that the witnesses falsely testified that the testator's signature was not on the will when they witnessed it. What result? See Jurgensen v. Haslinger, 295 Ill. App. 3d 139, 692 N.E.2d 347 (1998). If the beneficiary loses, should her attorney be sanctioned for bringing a lawsuit harassing witnesses?

4

WILLS: FORMALITIES AND FORMS

SECTION A. EXECUTION OF WILLS

1. *Attested Wills*

Ashbel G. Gulliver & Catherine J. Tilson, Classification
of Gratuitous Transfers
51 Yale L.J. 1, 2-5, 9-10 (1941)

One fundamental proposition is that, under a legal system recognizing the individualistic institution of private property and granting to the owner the power to determine his successors in ownership, the general philosophy of the courts should favor giving effect to an intentional exercise of that power. . . .

If this objective is primary, the requirements of execution, which concern only the form of the transfer — what the transferor or others must do to make it legally effective — seem justifiable only as implements for its accomplishment, and should be so interpreted by the courts in these cases. They surely should not be revered as ends in themselves, enthroning formality over frustrated intent. Why do these requirements exist and what functions may they usefully perform? . . .

In the first place, the court needs to be convinced that the statements of the transferor were deliberately intended to effectuate a transfer. People are often careless in conversation and in informal writings. Even if the witnesses are entirely truthful and accurate, what is a court to conclude from testimony showing only that a father once stated that he wanted to give certain bonds to his son John? Does this remark indicate *finality of intention to transfer*, or rambling meditation about some future disposition. . . . Or suppose the evidence shows, without more, that a writing containing dispositive language was found among papers of the deceased at the time of his death? Does this demonstrate a deliberate transfer, or was it merely a tentative draft of some contemplated instrument, or perhaps random scribbling? . . . Dispositive effect should not be given to statements which were not intended to have that effect. The formalities of transfer therefore generally require the performance of some ceremonial for the purpose of impressing the transferor with the significance of his statements and thus justifying the court in reaching the conclusion, if the ceremonial is performed, that they were deliberately intended to be operative. This purpose of the requirements of transfer may conveniently be termed their *ritual function.*

Secondly, the requirements of transfer may increase the reliability of the proof presented to the court. The extent to which the quantity and effect of available evidence should be restricted by qualitative standards is, of course, a controversial matter. Perhaps any and all evidence should be freely admitted in reliance on such safeguards as cross-examination, the oath, the proficiency of handwriting experts, and the discriminating judgment of courts and juries. On the other hand, the inaccuracies of oral testimony owing to lapse of memory, misinterpretation of the statements of others, and the more or less unconscious coloring of recollection in the light of the personal interest of the witness or of those with whom he is friendly, are very prevalent; and the possibilities of perjury and forgery cannot be disregarded. These difficulties are entitled to especially serious consideration in prescribing requirements for gratuitous transfers, because the issue of the validity of the transfer is almost always raised after the alleged transferor is dead, and therefore the main actor is usually unavailable to testify, or to clarify or contradict other evidence concerning his all-important intention. At any rate, whatever the ideal solution may be, it seems quite clear that the existing requirements of transfer emphasize the purpose of supplying satisfactory evidence to the court. This purpose may conveniently be termed their *evidentiary function.*

Thirdly, some of the requirements of the statutes of wills have the stated prophylactic purpose of safeguarding the testator, at the time of the execution of the will, against undue influence or other forms of imposition. . . . It may conveniently be termed the *protective function.* . . . This [protective function] is difficult to justify under modern conditions. . . . The protective provisions first appeared in the Statute of Frauds, from which they have been copied, perhaps sometimes blindly, by American legislatures. While there is little direct evidence, it is a reasonable assumption that, in the period prior to the Statute of Frauds, wills were usually executed on the death bed. A testator in this unfortunate situation may well need special protection against imposition. His powers of normal judgment and of resistance to improper influences may be seriously affected by a decrepit physical condition, a weakened mentality, or a morbid or unbalanced state of mind. Furthermore, in view of the propinquity of death, he would not have as much time or opportunity as would the usual inter vivos transferor to escape from the consequences of undue influence or other forms of imposition. Under modern conditions, however, wills are probably executed by most testators in the prime of life and in the presence of attorneys. [Emphasis added.]

Professor Langbein suggests that in addition to serving the ritual (or cautionary, as he calls it), evidentiary, and protective functions, the formalities requirements of the Wills Act serve a channeling function. They create a safe harbor, which provides the testator with assurance that his wishes will be carried out.

> Compliance with the Wills Act formalities for executing witnessed wills results in considerable uniformity in the organization, language, and content of most wills. Courts are seldom left to puzzle whether the document was meant to be a will. . . .
>
> The standardization of testation achieved under the Wills Act also benefits the testator. He does not have to devise for himself a mode of communicating his testamentary wishes to the court, and to worry whether it will be effective. Instead, he has every inducement to comply with the Wills Act formalities. The court can process his estate routinely, because his testament is conventionally and unmistakably expressed and evidenced. The lowered costs of routinized judicial administration benefit the estate and its ultimate distributees. [John H. Langbein, Substantial Compliance with the Wills Act, 88 Harv. L. Rev. 489, 494 (1975).]

The formal requirements for execution of wills vary considerably in detail from state to state. Some of these variations result from the fact that England had two basic acts governing the execution of wills, the Statute of Frauds (1677) and the Wills Act (1837). Prior to enactment of the Statute of Frauds, personal property was transferable at death by either a written or oral will, perhaps given to the priest as part of the last confession.[1] Land was made devisable "by last will and testament in writing," by the Statute of Wills in 1540, but the statute required no signature or other formalities. The Statute of Frauds, coming 137 years later, required a written will signed by the testator in the presence of three witnesses for testamentary disposition of land. Less stringent formalities, which need not concern us here, applied to testamentary dispositions of personalty. Having different requirements for wills of realty and for wills of personalty proved unsatisfactory, and in 1837 England passed a Wills Act requiring the same formalities for all wills.

The formalities required by the Wills Act of 1837 were stricter than those required by the Statute of Frauds. Under the Statute of Frauds, the three witnesses did not have to be present at the same time; each could attest separately. And the testator did not have to sign at any particular place on the document. The Wills Act reduced the number of necessary witnesses to two, but it provided that the witnesses must both be present when the will is signed or acknowledged; in addition, the will must be signed "at the foot or end" of the will. (The exact language of the Wills Act is set out in the court's opinion in In re Groffman, infra page 231.) These two additional requirements of the Wills Act have given rise to much litigation.

Some states copied the English Statute of Frauds, others copied the Wills Act of 1837. In a few states, the legislature added a requirement that the testator must "publish" the will by declaring before the witnesses that the instrument is his will. The Uniform Probate Code generally adopts the less strict requirements of the Statute of Frauds but reduces the required number of witnesses to two.[2]

Uniform Probate Code (1990)

§2-502. Execution; Witnessed Wills; Holographic Wills

(a) Except as provided in subsection (b) and in Sections 2-503, 2-506, and 2-513, a will must be:

1. A few states permit nuncupative (oral) wills under very limited circumstances. Typically, these wills can be made only during a person's "last sickness" and can be used only to devise personal property of small value (say, up to $1,000); the will must be uttered before three persons, who must reduce the declaration to writing within a specified period. Military personnel and mariners at sea are, in some states, granted the privilege of making an oral will under limited circumstances. Oral wills admitted to probate are extremely rare. See Kay v. Sandler, 718 S.W.2d 872 (Tex. 1986), strictly construing nuncupative will statute. For a list of state nuncupative will statutes, see Restatement (Third) of Property, Wills and Other Donative Transfers, §3.2, Statutory Note (1999).

2. Formerly a number of states required three witnesses. Now, only Vermont requires three witnesses rather than two. Vt. Stat. Ann. tit. 14, §5 (1997). Louisiana requires two witnesses plus a notary. La. Rev. Stat. §9.2442 (1998).

For a list of state witnessing requirements, see Restatement (Second) of Property, supra, §33.1, Statutory Note.

(1) in writing;

(2) signed by the testator or in the testator's name by some other individual in the testator's conscious presence and by the testator's direction; and

(3) signed by at least two individuals, each of whom signed within a reasonable time after he [or she] witnessed either the signing of the will as described in paragraph (2) or the testator's acknowledgment of that signature or acknowledgment of the will.

(b) A will that does not comply with subsection (a) is valid as a holographic will, whether or not witnessed, if the signature and material portions of the document are in the testator's handwriting.

(c) Intent that the document constitute the testator's will can be established by extrinsic evidence, including, for holographic wills, portions of the document that are not in the testator's handwriting.

We are concerned at this point only with UPC §2-502(a), dealing with attested wills. Holographic wills, authorized by §2-502(b), are treated later.

In re Groffman
Probate, Divorce, and Admiralty Division
High Court of Justice, England, 1968
[1969] 1 W.L.R. 733, [1969] 2 All E.R. 108

SIMON, Pres.   In this case the executors of a will dated September 1, 1964, propound it in solemn form of law. The will is of the late Mr. Charles Groffman, who died on April 11, 1967. The first plaintiff, being the first executor named, is the son of the deceased testator. The second plaintiff, Mr. Block, is the second executor named and is the solicitor who prepared the will. The defendant, who claims that the will was not properly executed, is the widow of the deceased; and in the circumstances, the estate being of the region of £8,000 or £9,000 in total, she takes the whole of it in the event of an intestacy. The estate consists partly of what was the matrimonial home (as to just over half the total estate). That house belonged to the deceased. There was also a building society account held by the deceased; the defendant claims that that was held jointly with her, or that at least she has some interest in it.

The defendant was the second wife of the deceased. They married about 1948, the deceased being a widower and the defendant a widow. The marriage was childless; but the deceased had two children, the first plaintiff and a daughter who is in America. The defendant has a daughter by her first marriage, a Miss Berenson.

Most of the relevant events took place in 1964; and I do not think any witness can really be expected to remember the details, even Mr. Block the solicitor who prepared the will. Indeed, I think that many of the witnesses now think that they can remember more than they actually can. But the rough outline of events was this.

Sometime in the summer of 1964, the deceased went to Mr. Block, the solicitor. He was senior partner in the firm of Maxwell and Lawson. The deceased was not a regular client of his, but had been recommended to him by another client. He gave instructions for a will and the instructions were put into a draft, which is exhibit 1 to the plaintiffs' affidavit of scripts. That appointed the executors and trustees; it devises the house to the trustees on trust to allow the defendant to have the use and enjoyment of this during her lifetime. It also bequeaths all chattels to her for use during her life. Then the residue — what was not disposed by the dispositions I have referred to — was disposed of in this way. It was to be divided between the first plaintiff, the daughter in America, and the step-daughter, Miss Berenson. There was in that draft a clause dealing with the advancement of the residuary estate in the interest of the defendant, which subsequently disappeared. That draft was handed by the second plaintiff to the deceased, who took it away to discuss it with his son, the first plaintiff. As a result of that discussion, in which the first plaintiff made no comment as to the dispositions, the draft was brought back to the second plaintiff; some nine corrections were made and the advancement clause to which I have referred was cancelled. The document as amended was then typed out, engrossed ready for execution.

The second plaintiff told the deceased very generally what was the right method of execution; but realising that the deceased was an intelligent man relied in the main on the attestation clause to be a guide to the deceased. That was in the usual form, and it seems to me to have been a perfectly reasonable course for the second plaintiff to have taken.

The deceased and his wife were close family friends of a Mr. and Mrs. David Block and a Mr. and Mrs. Julius Leigh. They spent at least the summer holidays of 1964 together, and it was their custom to meet alternately at their respective houses, generally on a Tuesday night. This was because Mr. Leigh was a taxi driver and the Tuesday was his free evening. On a number of occasions after the engrossed document was handed to the deceased, he mentioned the matter to Mr. David Block, saying that he would like Mr. Block and Mr. Leigh to be witnesses to his will. Mr. Block, in a very usual reaction, said: "There's no hurry about that; there's plenty of time to be thinking about that sort of thing" — or words to that effect. The parties met on a Tuesday evening in September, 1964. That may have been September 1, which is the date that the will bears. They met at the house of Mr. and Mrs. David Block, and the will purports to have been executed that evening in circumstances to which I shall have to refer. It is sufficient to say that, as I have already indicated, the attestation clause is the normal one, and Mr. Block and Mr. Leigh signed as attesting witnesses. The document also bears what is admittedly the signature of the deceased, and the date, September 1, 1964.

I am perfectly satisfied that the document was intended by the deceased to be executed as his will and that its contents represent his testamentary intentions.

After he had obtained the signatures of his friends, he took the will and handed it to his son, the first plaintiff. He appears to have referred to it to Mr. Block on a number of occasions thereafter; but nothing turns on that, since the only question that arises in this suit is as to the execution of the document.

The deceased died, as I have said, on April 11, 1967. The funeral was on April 13, and thereafter the widow and the first plaintiff observed a period of ritual mourning, during which there was no discussion of any testamentary instrument or disposition. At the end of that period, within a matter of a few days, the first plaintiff handed the document to the second plaintiff. At some time towards the end of April, and again within a month or two, there were meetings between the plaintiffs and the defendant; . . . the defendant showed considerable dissatisfaction with the dispositions in the purported will. She used the words, "My Charlie wouldn't have done that to me." . . .

As I have said, the only question that arises for the determination of the court is whether this will was duly executed. That takes me back to the occasion in September, 1964, which may have been September 1 — the episode at the house of Mr. and Mrs. David Block.

Mr. Leigh, the second purported attesting witness, has suffered a disabling ailment; and his evidence has been placed before me only in the form of a statement, dated August 22, 1967, which was obviously taken for the purposes of litigation. It has, therefore, not been cross-examined to. Since I am satisfied that the document propounded represents the deceased's testamentary dispositions and intentions and since the document is in regular form, a very strong presumption arises in its favour. If I merely had the statement of Mr. Leigh and the other witnesses, except for Mr. David Block and his son, Stewart, I should pronounce for the validity of this will. But that is not all I have.

Mr. David Block and his son, Stewart, seem to me to be credible and reliable witnesses. I have it in mind that the evidence they have given contradicts the statement in the attestation clause. I have it in mind that they are friends of the defendant and desire her to succeed in this action. I have it in mind that there is some discrepancy between the evidence that they respectively gave, though no more than I should expect in perfectly honest witnesses trying to recollect what happened over four years ago. I accept the evidence of Mr. David Block, borne out as it is by Stewart, and indeed by what Mr. Leigh says in his proferred statement.

I think that what happened on the evening in question was this. I have already said that the deceased had previously indicated to Mr. David Block that he would like him and Mr. Leigh to witness his will. On the evening in question, which was in all probability a Tuesday and possibly September 1, 1964, the deceased and the defendant, Mr. and Mrs. David Block and Mr. and Mrs. Julius Leigh, were all together in the lounge of the Blocks' house. Mr. Block's son, Stewart, was also in the house, though not in the lounge at the commencement of the transaction to which I refer.

During the course of the evening, when the coffee table, the only available table, was laden with coffee cups and cakes, the deceased said words to this effect, which he addressed to Mr. David Block and Mr. Julius Leigh: "I should like you now to witness my will." I think he may well have gestured towards his coat. The will in question as engrossed was of the usual double foolscap folded in two and then in four, so as to be a convenient size for putting in an inside pocket of a coat. That is where it was on this occasion. However, it was not taken out by the deceased in the lounge. At the most, he gestured towards the pocket where it was. There seems to me to be an overwhelming inference that his signature was on the document at that time. There being no convenient space for the execution in the lounge, Mr. Block led the deceased into the adjacent dining room. That was just across a small hall. There the deceased took the document from his pocket, unfolded it, and asked Mr. Block to sign, giving his occupation and address. The signature, as I have already said, was on the document at the time and was visible to Mr. Block at the time; indeed, he noted this. Mr. Leigh, who seems to have been somewhat cumbrous in his movements, was left behind. He was not there when Mr. Block signed his name. Mr. Block then returned to the lounge, leaving the deceased in the dining room. He said to Mr. Leigh words to this effect: "It is your turn now, don't keep him waiting, it's cold in there." Mr. Leigh then went into the dining room and, according to his statement, and as is indeed borne out by the form of the document that we now have, signed his name beneath that of Mr. David Block. In the meantime Mr. Block had remained in the lounge.

In other words, we are left with this situation — that the signature of the deceased was on the document before he asked either Mr. Block or Mr. Leigh to act as his witnesses; that Mr. Block signed his name in the presence of the deceased but not in the presence of Mr.

Leigh; and that Mr. Leigh signed his name in the presence of the deceased but not in the presence of Mr. Block. The deceased did not sign in the presence of either of them; and the question is whether he acknowledged his signature in the presence of both of them.

As must appear from the fact that I have been satisfied that the document does represent the testamentary intentions of the deceased, I would very gladly find in its favour; but I am bound to apply the statute, which has been enacted by Parliament for good reason. The provision with which I am concerned is section 9 of the Wills Act, 1837. That reads:

> [N]o will shall be valid unless it shall be in writing and executed in manner hereinafter mentioned; (that is to say,) it shall be signed at the foot or end thereof by the testator, or by some other person in his presence and by his direction; and such signature shall be made or acknowledged by the testator in the presence of two or more witnesses present at the same time, and such witnesses shall attest and shall subscribe the will in the presence of the testator, but no form of attestation shall be necessary.

The question, as I have indicated, is whether the testator acknowledged his signature in the presence of Mr. Block and Mr. Leigh, those two witnesses being present at the same time. The matter has been considered by a number of eminent judges, starting with Dr. Lushington, and followed by the members of the Court of Appeal in Blake v. Blake (1882) 7 P.D. 102 and Daintree v. Butcher and Fasulo (1888) 13 P.D. 102. It seems presumptuous to say that I agree with their construction of the statute; but it appears to me to be clear. In any event I am bound by what was decided by the Court of Appeal, even if I were to disagree with it, which I do not. It seems to me that the authorities establish that the signature of the testator must be on the document at the time of acknowledgment (as I think it was), and that the witness saw or had an opportunity of seeing the signature at that time, in other words, at the time of acknowledgment.

In Blake v. Blake, 7 P.D. 102, Sir George Jessel M.R. gave a judgment in which he said, at p.107: "The question, then, arises whether the testatrix acknowledged her signature before the witnesses." That was a case where the testatrix had signed and had asked two attesting witnesses to add their signature, but had covered her own signature with blotting paper, so they could not see it. Sir George Jessel in those circumstances posed the question, at p.107-8: "What is in law a sufficient acknowledgment under the statute?" He answers, "What I take to be the law is correctly laid down in Jarman on Wills, 4th ed. p.108, in the following terms: 'There is no sufficient acknowledgment unless the witnesses either saw or might have seen the signature, not even though the testator should expressly declare that the paper to be attested by them is his will'." ... He quotes Dr. Lushington in Hudson v. Parker (1844) 1 Rob. Eccl. 14, at p.25 "What do the words import but this? 'Here is my name written, I acknowledge that name so written to have been written by me; bear witness'." ...

In deference, however, to the interest and vigour of Mr. Craig's argument, I must deal with various alternative ways in which he puts his case. He says, first, that *Blake* is to be distinguished in that there was a deliberate concealment by the testatrix of her signature, which, he says, is the very negation of acknowledgment. But there is nothing at all in the judgments of Blake v. Blake, 7 P.D. 102, to indicate that that was the ratio decidendi, which was indeed afterwards explained in Daintree v. Butcher and Fasulo, 13 P.D. 102.

Second, he says, there is sufficient acknowledgment if the attesting witnesses had an opportunity to see the will or the signature or both if they had wished to. Opportunity to see, says Mr. Craig, does not mean physical opportunity: it means that they could have seen if they expressed the desire to see. If that were so, it seems to me that Blake v. Blake, 7 P.D. 102, could not have been decided in the way it was. The attesting witnesses could have asked the testatrix to remove the blotting paper, just as in the present case Mr. Block or Mr. Leigh could have asked the testator to remove the paper from his pocket and show it to them, or at least show them his signature.

There is, however, one final argument. Having submitted originally that there was a sufficient acknowledgment to satisfy the statute in what happened in the lounge, when admittedly both attesting witnesses were present, Mr. Craig puts his argument alternatively in this way. He says that what happened was all part of one res gestae — there was no break in the continuity of the transaction. Both attesting witnesses had an opportunity of seeing the signature at the time they signed the will, which was within a matter of seconds of each other and within a matter of seconds of being asked to witness it. On that argument the acknowledgment started in the lounge but ended in the dining room. Now, it seems to me that there is one fatal flaw in that argument; namely, that if the acknowledgment was not completed until the dining room, then there was no completed acknowledgment in the presence of both attesting witnesses being present at the same time.

In the end, therefore, although I would gladly accede to the arguments for the plaintiffs if I could consistently with my judicial duty, in my view there was no acknowledgment or signature by the testator in the presence of two or more witnesses present at the same time; and I am bound to pronounce against this will. . . .

Order accordingly.

NOTES, PROBLEMS, AND QUESTIONS

1.   Specifically, why was Mr. Groffman's will denied probate? What formalities required by the Wills Act were not satisfied?

2.   Were the ritual, evidentiary, and protective policies basing the Wills Act substantially satisfied by the manner in which Groffman's will was executed and attested? If so, should Groffman's will have been denied probate? See Stevens v. Casdorph, 508 S.E. 2d 610 (W.Va. 1998) (in accord with In re Groffman, but with a strong dissent concluding the testator substantially complied with the formalities and dubbing the result "patently absurd").

3.   If Mr. Block, the solicitor who drew the will (to be distinguished from Mr. David Block, the witness), were sued by the beneficiaries named in the will, would he be liable? In Ross v. Caunters, [1980] 1 Ch. 297, a solicitor prepared a will and sent it to the testator with instructions for execution but did not warn the testator that it should not be witnessed by the spouse of a beneficiary. The will was witnessed by the spouse of the beneficiary, who, under English law, was deprived of her legacy. The court held that the solicitor was liable in malpractice to the beneficiary. Many recent cases in the United States have held the lawyer supervising the will execution ceremony liable for faulty execution, though some states still retain the privity barrier. See Auric v. Continental Casualty Co., 111 Wis. 2d 507, 331 N.W.2d 325 (1983) (privity no barrier); Barcelo v. Elliott, 923 S.W.2d 575 (Tex. 1996) (privity still essential); Gerald P. Johnston, Legal Malpractice in Estate Planning, 67 Iowa L. Rev. 629 (1982).

4.   *Presence.* In England and in some American states the requirement that the witnesses sign in the "presence" of the testator is satisfied only if the testator is capable of seeing the witnesses in the act of signing. Under this *line of sight test,* the testator does not actually have to see the witnesses sign but must be able to see them were the testator to look. 1 Thomas Jarman, Wills 138 (8th ed. 1951). An exception is made for a blind person. In other American states, the line of sight rule has been rejected in favor of the *conscious presence test.* Under this test the witness is in the presence of the testator if the testator, through sight, hearing, or general consciousness of events, comprehends that the witness is in the act of signing. Uniform Probate Code §2-502(a), supra page 226, dispenses altogether with the requirement that the witnesses sign in the testator's presence.

Consider these two problems concerning presence:

a. Suppose that *T*'s attorney takes *T*'s will to *T*'s home, where *T* signs the will and the attorney attests as a witness. The attorney returns to her office with the will and has her secretary call *T* on the phone. By telephone, *T* requests the secretary to witness his will; the secretary then signs as an attesting witness. Can the will be probated? See In re Jefferson, 349 So. 2d 1032 (Miss. 1977); In re McGurrin, 113 Idaho 341, 743 P.2d 994 (Ida. App. 1987).

b. Suppose that the president of a bank draws a will for a depositor. The depositor, seriously ill, drives to the bank's drive-in teller window and parks. The president takes the will to the depositor's car, where the depositor signs the will propped on his steering wheel. The bank teller, seated at a teller window overlooking the car, watches the depositor sign. The president signs as a witness in the car, then takes the will inside the teller's office where the teller, sitting in the window, signs as witness and waves to the depositor. The president then takes the will outside and shows it to the depositor who asks the president to keep it. Has the teller signed as witness in the presence of the testator? See In re Weber's Estate, 192 Kan. 258, 387 P.2d 165 (1963), which held, 4 to 3, No, because though the testator could see the teller, the testator could not see the pen and will on the teller's desk as the teller signed. The court thought to apply the conscious presence test on these facts would permit it "to run wild."

5. *Order of signing.* A few days before his death, George Colling, in the hospital, made a will. He started to write his signature in the presence of two witnesses — Jackson, the patient in the bed next to his, and Sister Newman, a nurse. Although they were both present when the testator started to sign, before the testator finished writing "Colling," Sister Newman had to attend to a patient in another part of the ward. In her absence Colling completed his signature, and Jackson witnessed the will in Colling's presence. Sister Newman then returned. Both Colling and Jackson acknowledged their signatures to her, and she then signed as the second witness. May the will be probated? Held: No. The signature is not sufficient because the testator did not complete his signature while both witnesses were present; the later acknowledgment does not suffice because the testator must sign or acknowledge his signature before either of the witnesses attest. In re Colling, [1972] 1 W.L.R. 1440. Accord, In re Estate of Wait, 43 Tenn. App. 217, 306 S.W.2d 345 (1957) (testator, old and feeble, was unable to complete her signature, because her hand was shaking, until after witnesses left; will denied probate).

Compare Wheat v. Wheat, 156 Conn. 575, 244 A.2d 359 (1968), holding that the attestation requirement necessitates that the testator sign first, with Waldrep v. Goodwin, 230 Ga. 1, 195 S.E.2d 432 (1973), upholding a will if the testator and the witnesses all sign while assembled in a room, regardless of the order of signing.

6. *Signature.* A lawyer prepared a will for Patrick Mangeri, who was very ill. Underneath the signature line was typed "Patrick Mangeri." The will was taken to Mangeri in his hospital room. Mangeri signed with an "X" because his hands were too shaky to write his name. The two attesting witnesses then signed. Can the will be probated? See In re Estate of McCabe, 224 Cal. App. 3d 330, 274 Cal. Rptr. 43 (1990).

Suppose that Mangeri had written a shaky "Pat" rather than an "X." Same result? In re Young, 60 Ohio App. 2d 390, 397 N.E.2d 1223 (1978), held that the letter *J* subscribed by Joseph Young was sufficient when Joseph was partially paralyzed from a stroke.

Suppose that, as Mangeri had trouble holding the pen, a witness said, "Here, I'll help you," and assisted Mangeri in signing his name. Can the will be probated? Would it make any difference if Mangeri had asked the witness for help? See In re Estate of DeThorne, 163 Wis. 2d 387, 471 N.W.2d 780 (Wis. App. 1991).

Suppose that Mangeri had a rubber stamp with the name "Patrick Mangeri" on it, and that he had asked one of the attesting witnesses to affix the stamp to the will. The witness did so. Can the will be probated? See Phillips v. Najar, 901 S.W.2d 561 (Tex. App. 1995).

7. *Addition after signature.* Statutes in several states have adopted the Wills Act requirement that the testator sign the will "at the foot or end thereof." Suppose that a typewritten will is found on which is written in testator's handwriting, below the testator's signature and above the witnesses' signatures, the following line: "I give Karen my diamond ring." Is the will entitled to probate? Initially, the answer depends upon whether the line was on the will when it was signed by the testator. If the handwritten line was added *after* the testator signed the will, the will would be admitted to probate, and the line would be ineffective as a subsequent unexecuted codicil. If added *before* the testator signed her name, would the will be admitted? Would it matter if the handwritten addition had not made a disposition of the testator's property but had said: "I appoint Emily executor"? See Clark v. National Bank of Commerce, 304 Ark. 352, 802 S.W.2d 452 (1991); N.Y. Est., Powers & Trusts Law §3-2.1(a)(1) (1998).

8. *Videotape.* Suppose that Robert Reed videotapes his spoken will before two witnesses. Then he puts it in a sealed envelope, on which he writes, "To be played in the event of my death only, Robert Reed," and the two witnesses sign their names. Does this comply with the requirement that the will be a "signed writing"? Is a voice print a writing? See Estate of Reed, 672 P.2d 829 (Wyo. 1983) (held No); Gerry W. Beyer & William R. Buckley, Videotape and the Probate Process: The Nexus Grows, 42 Okla. L. Rev. 43 (1989).

Suppose Reed had prepared the filmed will using animated letters and words. Same result?

9. *Delayed attestation.* Suppose that the witnesses do not get around to signing the will until after the testator dies. Is it too late? Must the witnesses sign while the testator is alive? See In re Estate of Royal, 826 P.2d 1236 (Colo. 1992) (holding witness must attest before the testator's death); In re Estate of Peters, 107 N.J. 263, 526 A.2d 1005 (1987) (holding witnesses must sign within a reasonable period of time after the will is executed, and reasonable period could, under

some circumstances, extend after testator's death; signing 15 months
after execution is unreasonable); Uniform Probate Code §2-502(a),
supra page 226, providing that witnesses must sign within reasonable
time; N.Y. Est. Powers & Trusts Law §3-2.1(a)(4) (1998), requiring
witnesses to sign within 30 days.

10. *Notarization.* Most states require that a deed be notarized to
be recorded in the county recorder's office; witnessing does not suffice. Why must deeds be *notarized* and wills *witnessed*? Would it be a
good idea to permit a will to be either witnessed or notarized?

11.   For an analysis of why the law has relaxed formalities for contracts (basically requiring only one, consideration) while adhering to
strict formalities for wills, see Jane B. Baron, Gifts, Bargains, and
Form, 64 Ind. L.J. 155 (1989). Professor Baron finds that judges readily enforce contracts because market exchanges create wealth, whereas
donative transfers merely redistribute it; hence they are less interested
in effectuating donative transfers. She argues that donative transfers
create reciprocal social and affective benefits for donor and donee
and that society should be as much interested in facilitating them as
it is in market exchanges. See also Melvin A. Eisenberg, The World
of Contract and the World of Gift, 85 Cal. L. Rev. 821 (1997) (examining the same issue).

For a learned and wide-ranging critique of the inconsistencies of
the execution requirements among the states, see Adam J. Hirsch,
Inheritance and Inconsistency, 57 Ohio St. L.J. 1057 (1997).

The Restatement (Third) of Property, Wills and Other Donative
Transfers, §3.1 (1999), contains a useful summary of the wills execution requirements, with citations to statutes and cases.

Estate of Parsons

California Court of Appeal, First District, 1980
103 Cal. App. 3d 384, 163 Cal. Rptr. 70

GRODIN, J.   This case requires us to determine whether a subscribing witness to a will who is named in the will as a beneficiary becomes
"disinterested" within the meaning of Probate Code section 51 by
filing a disclaimer of her interest after the testatrix' death. While our
own policy preferences tempt us to an affirmative answer, we feel
constrained by existing law to hold that a disclaimer is ineffective for
that purpose.

I

Geneve Parsons executed her will on May 3, 1976. Three persons
signed the will as attesting witnesses: Evelyn Nielson, respondent

Marie Gower, and Bob Warda, a notary public. Two of the witnesses, Nielson and Gower, were named in the will as beneficiaries. Nielson was given $100; Gower was given certain real property. Mrs. Parsons died on December 13, 1976, and her will was admitted to probate on the petition of her executors, respondents Gower and Lenice Haymond. On September 12, 1977, Nielson filed a disclaimer of her $100 bequest. Appellants [Mrs. Parsons's heirs] then claimed an interest in the estate on the ground that the devise to Gower was invalid. The trial court rejected their argument, which is now the sole contention on appeal.

Appellants base their claim on Probate Code section 51, which provides that a gift to a subscribing witness is void "unless there are two other and disinterested subscribing witnesses to the will."[3] Although Nielson disclaimed her bequest after subscribing the will, appellants submit that "a subsequent disclaimer is ineffective to transform an interested witness into a disinterested one." Appellants assert that because there was only one disinterested witness at the time of attestation, the devise to Gower is void by operation of law.

Respondents contend that appellants' argument is "purely technical" and "completely disregards the obvious and ascertainable intent" of the testatrix. They urge that the property should go to the person named as devisee rather than to distant relatives who, as the testatrix stated in her will, "have not been overlooked, but have been intentionally omitted." They stress that there has been no suggestion of any fraud or undue influence in this case, and they characterize Nielson's interest as a "token gift" which she relinquished pursuant to the disclaimer statute. (Prob. Code, §190 et seq.) Finally, respondents point to the following language of Probate Code section 190.6: "In every case, the disclaimer shall relate back for all purposes to the date of the creation of the interest." On the basis of that language, respondents conclude that Nielson "effectively became disinterested" by reason of her timely disclaimer. According to respondents, the conditions of Probate Code section 51 have therefore been satisfied, and the devise to Gower should stand.

II

This appears to be a case of first impression in California, and our interpretation of Probate Code section 51 will determine its outcome.

---

3. Probate Code section 51 reads as follows: "All beneficial devises, bequests and legacies to a subscribing witness are void unless there are two other and disinterested subscribing witnesses to the will, except that if such interested witness would be entitled to any share of the estate of the testator in case the will were not established, he shall take such proportion of the devise or bequest made to him in the will as does not exceed the share of the estate which would be distributed to him if the will were not established."

We are required to construe the statute "so as to effectuate the purpose of the law." (Select Base Materials v. Board of Equal. (1959) 51 Cal. 2d 640, 645, 335 P.2d 672.) To ascertain that purpose, we may consider its history.

At common law a party to an action, or one who had a direct interest in its outcome, was not competent to testify in court because it was thought that an interested witness would be tempted to perjure himself in favor of his interest. Centuries ago, this principle concerning the competence of witnesses in litigation was injected into the substantive law of wills. The statute of frauds of 1676 required that devises of land be attested and subscribed "by three or four credible witnesses, or else they shall be utterly void and of none effect." (29 Car. II, ch. 3, §5.) The word "credible" was construed to mean "competent" according to the common law principles then prevailing, and "competent" meant "disinterested" — so that persons having an interest under the will could not be "credible witnesses" within the meaning of the statute. The entire will would therefore fail if any one of the requisite number of attesting witnesses was also a beneficiary. In 1752 Parliament enacted a statute which saved the will by providing that the interest of an attesting witness was void. (25 Geo. II, ch. 6, §I.) Under such legislation, the competence of the witness is restored by invalidating his gift. The majority of American jurisdictions today have similar statutes; and California Probate Code section 51 falls into this category.

The common law disabilities to testify on account of interest have long been abolished. Having become a part of the substantive law of wills, Probate Code section 51, on the other hand, survives. Our task is to ascertain and effectuate its present purpose. When a court seeks to interpret legislation, "the various parts of a statutory enactment must be harmonized by considering the particular clause or section in the context of the statutory framework as a whole." (Moyer v. Workmen's Comp. Appeals Bd. (1973) 10 Cal. 3d 222, 230, 110 Cal. Rptr. 144, 514 P.2d 1224.) We therefore turn to the Probate Code.

In order to establish a will as genuine, it is not always necessary that each and every one of the subscribing witnesses testify in court. Moreover, Probate Code section 51 does not by its terms preclude any witness from testifying; nor does the section void the interest of a subscribing witness when "two other and disinterested" witnesses have also subscribed the will. It is therefore entirely conceivable and perfectly consistent with the statutory scheme that a will might be proved on the sole testimony of a subscribing witness who is named in the will as a beneficiary; and if the will had been attested by "two other and disinterested subscribing witnesses," the interested witness whose sole testimony established the will would also be permitted to take his gift, as provided in the instrument. If Probate Code section

51 serves any purpose under such circumstances, its purpose must necessarily have been accomplished before the will was offered for probate. Otherwise, in its statutory context, the provision would have no effect at all.

The quintessential function of a subscribing witness is performed when the will is executed. We believe that Probate Code section 51 looks in its operation solely to that time. The section operates to ensure that at least two of the subscribing witnesses are disinterested. Although disinterest may be a token of credibility, as at common law, it also connotes an absence of selfish motives. We conclude that the purpose of the statute is to protect the testator from fraud and undue influence at the very moment when he executes his will, by ensuring that at least two persons are present "who would not be financially motivated to join in a scheme to procure the execution of a spurious will by dishonest methods, and who therefore presumably might be led by human impulses of fairness to resist the efforts of others in that direction." (Gulliver & Tilson, Classification of Gratuitous Transfers (1941) 51 Yale L.J. 1, 11.) No other possible construction which has been brought to our attention squares so closely with the statutory framework.

III

Because we hold that Probate Code section 51 looks solely to the time of execution and attestation of the will, it follows that a subsequent disclaimer will be ineffective to transform an interested witness into a "disinterested" one within the meaning of that section. If the execution of a release or the filing of a disclaimer after the will has been attested could effect such a transformation, the purpose of the statute as we have defined it would be undermined.

Respondents' reliance on Probate Code section 190.6[4] is misplaced. That section serves to equalize the tax consequences of disclaimers as between heirs at law and testamentary beneficiaries. Probate Code section 190, subdivision (a) defines "beneficiary" to mean "any person entitled, *but for his disclaimer*, to take an interest" by various means. (Italics added.) Even assuming that an "interest" arises within the meaning of the disclaimer statute from the execution of a will, Evelyn

---

4. Probate Code section 190.6 provides:

Unless otherwise provided in the will, inter vivos trust, exercise of the power of appointment, or other written instrument creating or finally determining an interest, the interest disclaimed and any future interest which is to take effect in possession or enjoyment at or after the termination of the interest disclaimed, shall descend, go, be distributed or continue to be held as if the beneficiary disclaiming had predeceased the person creating the interest. In every case, the disclaimer shall relate back for all purposes to the date of the creation of the interest.

Nielson would *not* have been entitled to take under the will by reason of Probate Code section 51; and she was, therefore, not a "beneficiary" within the meaning of the disclaimer statute. The disclaimer statute therefore has no application here. In this case, when the will was executed and attested, only one of the subscribing witnesses was disinterested. The gifts to the other witnesses were therefore void, by operation of law. (Prob. Code, §51.) Nielson's disclaimer was a nullity, because she had no interest to disclaim.

Respondents' concern for the intentions of the testatrix is likewise misplaced. The construction of the will is not at issue here. We are faced instead with the operation of Probate Code section 51, which makes no reference to the intentions of the testatrix. Legislation voiding the interest of an attesting witness "often upsets genuine expressions of the testator's intent." (Chaffin, Execution, Revocation, and Revalidation of Wills: A Critique of Existing Statutory Formalities (1977) 11 Ga. L. Rev. 297, 317.) But that legislation controls the outcome of this case.

It has been said that statutes such as this are ill suited to guard against fraud and undue influence. "If the potential malefactor does not know of the rules, he will not be deterred. If he does know of them, which is unlikely, he will realize the impossibility of the financial gain supposed to be the motive of the legatee witness, and so will probably escape the operation of the remedy against himself." (Gulliver & Tilson, supra, 51 Yale L.J. at pp. 12-13.) Lord Mansfield observed over 200 years ago, "In all my experience at the Court of Delegates, I never knew a fraudulent will, but what was legally attested; and I have heard the same from many learned civilians." (Wyndham v. Chetwynd (K.B. 1757) 1 Black. W. 95, 100, 96 Eng. Rep. 53.) Yet Probate Code section 51 remains the law in California.

We are mindful that there has been no suggestion of any fraud or other misconduct in the case before us, and it may well be that "the vast majority of testators in modern society do not need the type of 'protection' that is afforded by our statute." (Chaffin, Improving Georgia's Probate Code (1970) 4 Ga. L. Rev. 505, 507.) "[T]he reported decisions give the impression that the remedies are employed more frequently against innocent parties who have accidentally transgressed the requirement than against deliberate wrongdoers, and this further confirms the imaginary character of the difficulty sought to be prevented." (Gulliver & Tilson, supra, 51 Yale L.J. at p.12.) But the Legislature has spoken here, and in matters such as this, "the legislature has a wide discretion in determining the conditions to be imposed." (Estate of Mintaberry (1920) 183 Cal. 566, 568, 191 P. 909.)

Respondents note that a growing number of states have enacted statutes similar to Uniform Probate Code section 2-505, which dispenses with the rule contained in the California statute.[5] Perhaps statutes like California Probate Code section 51 represent a "mediaeval point of view" concerning the proper function of an attesting witness; and perhaps "the question whether he has abused his position should be made one of fact, like any other question having to do with the motives and conduct of parties who take part in the testamentary transaction." (Mechem, Why Not a Modern Wills Act? (1948) 33 Iowa L. Rev. 501, 506-507.) We cannot ignore what the statute commands, however, "merely because we do not agree that the statute as written is wise or beneficial legislation." (Estate of Carter (1935) 9 Cal. App. 2d 714, 718, 50 P.2d 1057.) Any remedial change must come from the Legislature.

That portion of the judgment from which this appeal is taken is therefore reversed.

PROBLEMS: PURGING STATUTES

In 1983 California adopted Uniform Probate Code §2-505, referred to in footnote 5 in the *Parsons* case, which provides that an interested witness does not forfeit a gift under the will. Cal. Prob. Code §6112 (1998).[6] Since UPC §2-505 has been adopted in little more than one-third of the states, however, it is useful to probe further into the operation of purging statutes. California Probate Code §51, referred to in footnote 3 of the *Parsons* case, is substantially similar to purging statutes in many states, which purge the witness only of the benefit the witness receives that exceeds the benefit the witness would have received if the will had not been executed (that is, the "extra benefit"). For a list of state purging statutes, see Restatement (Second) of Property, Donative Transfers §33.1, Statutory Note (1992).

The Massachusetts purging statute, derived from the 1752 English statute referred to in the *Parsons* opinion, is different. It simply voids any devise to an attesting witness, who takes nothing under the will. Thus:

Any person of sufficient understanding shall be deemed to be a competent witness to a will, notwithstanding any common law disqualification for interest or otherwise; but a beneficial devise or legacy to a subscribing witness or to the husband or wife of such witness shall be void unless

5. Uniform Probate Code section 2-505 provides: "(a) Any person generally competent to be a witness may act as a witness to a will. [¶] (b) A will or any provision thereof is not invalid because the will is signed by an interested witness."

6. Cal. Prob. Code §6112 goes on to provide, however, that a devise to a witness creates a presumption that the witness procured the devise by undue influence.

there are two other subscribing witnesses to the will who are not similarly benefited thereunder. [Mass. Ann. Laws ch. 191, §2 (1998).]

Suppose that the real property devised to Marie Gower by Geneve Parsons was worth $50,000 and that under a previous will, not witnessed by Marie, Geneve had bequeathed Marie stock worth $70,000. Suppose also that the May 3, 1976, will contains a clause revoking all prior wills. What result under Cal. Prob. Code §51? Under Mass. Gen. Laws ch. 191, §2? Suppose that the prior will had bequeathed Marie stock worth $30,000. What result?

Suppose that the testator devised a house to the spouse of a witness. Is the devise void? See Dorfman v. Allen, 386 Mass. 136, 434 N.E.2d 1012 (1982) (holding statute purging devise to witness's spouse constitutional, as having a rational purpose, and voiding devise, but implying a substitute gift to the devisee's children).

RECOMMENDED METHOD OF EXECUTING A WILL

In executing a will, a lawyer should not rely on the formalities required by the statute in the client's home state. The client's will may be offered for probate in another state. The client may be domiciled elsewhere at death or may own real property in another state, or the will may exercise a power of appointment governed by the law of another state. Under the usual conflict of laws rules, the law of the decedent's domicile at death determines the validity of the will insofar as it disposes of personal property. The law of the state where real property is located determines the validity of a disposition of real property. If a person domiciled in Illinois executes a will, then moves to New Jersey and dies there, owning Florida real estate, some tangible personal property, and some stocks and bonds, the law of Illinois does not govern the validity of the will at all. New Jersey law determines the validity of the disposition of the tangible and intangible personalty, and Florida law governs the validity of the disposition of the real estate.[7] Most states have statutes recognizing as valid a will executed with the formalities required by (1) the state where the testator was domiciled at death, (2) the state where the will was executed, or (3) the state where the testator was domiciled when the will was executed.

---

7. The Hague Convention of 1989 discards the situs rule for real property and the domicile rule for personal property, replacing them with very different choice of law rules. The Hague Convention has not been ratified by the United States and is sharply criticized by Professor Schoenblum, this country's leading choice-of-law scholar in estate planning matters. See Jeffrey A. Schoenblum, Choice of Law and Succession to Wealth: A Critical Analysis of the Ramifications of the Hague Convention on Succession to Decedents' Estates, 32 Va. J. Intl. L. 83 (1991).

See, e.g., UPC §2-506 (1990). These statutes, where enacted, are not all uniform, however, and sometimes contain ambiguities and internal conflicts. See Jeffrey A. Schoenblum, Multijurisdictional Estates and Article II of the Uniform Probate Code, 55 Alb. L. Rev. 1291 (1992) (criticizing UPC §2-506). A lawyer should draft wills so that there is no need to resort to such an act. Hence, the careful lawyer in our highly mobile society draws a will and has it executed in a manner that satisfies the formal requirements in all states.[8]

If the procedure set forth below[9] is followed, the instrument will be valid in all states, no matter in which state the testator is domiciled at the date of execution or at death or where the property is located.[10] If all these steps are not followed to the letter, in one or more states the will may be either invalid or extremely difficult to prove as a properly executed will.

(1) If the will consists of more than one page, the pages are fastened together securely. The will specifies the exact number of pages of which it consists.

(2) The lawyer should be certain that the testator has read the will and understands its contents.

(3) The lawyer, the testator, two disinterested witnesses and a notary public are brought together in a room from which everyone else is excluded. (If the lawyer is a notary, an additional notary is unnecessary.) The door to the room is closed. No one enters or leaves the room until the ceremony is finished.

(4) The lawyer asks the testator the following three questions:

---

8. If the client owns property in a foreign country or may die domiciled there, the law of the foreign country should be examined and the will executed in compliance with such law. See Jeffrey A. Schoenblum, Multistate and Multinational Estate Planning, §§15.01-15.06 (1982 & Supps.); Donald A. Kozusko & Jeffrey A. Schoenblum, International Estate Planning: Principles and Strategies (1991). See also Uniform International Wills Act, found in Uniform Probate Code §§2-1001 to 2-1010 (1990) and adopted in many states, which sets out the procedure to be followed to comply with the 1973 Washington Convention on Wills. The procedure recommended in the text complies with the International Wills Act, except the self-proving affidavit at the end differs slightly from the affidavit required for an international will. For further discussion of the Washington Convention, ratified by the Senate in 1991, see Recent Development, The Resurgence of the International Will: A Call for Federal Legislation, 26 Vand. JL. Transnatl. L. 417 (1993).

9. This procedure is an up-to-date version of the format recommended by Professor W. Barton Leach in his Cases on Wills 44 (2d ed. 1949) and subsequently refined by Professor A. James Casner in his work, 1 Estate Planning §3.1.1 (6th ed. 1998 with Jeffrey N. Pennell).

10. For Louisiana and Vermont law, see supra page 226, footnote 2. This procedure should satisfy the Vermont requirement of three witnesses because the notary is the third witness, but doubtless careful Vermont lawyers use three witnesses. A notary is required in Louisiana. Both of these states have statutes providing that a will executed out of state is valid if valid either in the state where executed or in the state of the testator's domicile. La. Rev. Stat. §9.2401 (1998); Vt. Stat. Ann. tit. 14, §112 (1998).

(a)   "Is this your will?"[11]
(b)   "Have you read it and do you understand it?"
(c)   "Does it dispose of your property in accordance with your wishes?"

After each question the testator should answer "Yes" in a voice that can be heard by the two witnesses and the notary. It is neither necessary nor customary for the witnesses to know the terms of the will. If, however, the lawyer foresees a possible will contest, added precautions might be taken at this time. See supra pages 209-210.

(5) The lawyer asks the testator the following question. "Do you request _____ and _____ (the two witnesses) to witness the signing of your will?" The testator should answer "Yes" in a voice audible to the witnesses.

(6) The witnesses should be standing or sitting so that all can see the testator sign. The testator signs on the margin of each page of the will. This is done for purposes of identification and to prevent subsequent substitution of pages. The testator then signs his or her name at the end of the will.

(7) One of the witnesses reads aloud the *attestation clause,* which attests that the foregoing things were done. Here is an example: "On the _____ day of _____, 20 ___, Wendy Brown declared to us, the undersigned, that the foregoing instrument was her last Will, and she requested us to act as witnesses to it and to her signature thereon. She then signed the Will in our presence, we being present at the same time. We now, at her request, in her presence, and in the presence of each other, hereunto subscribe our names as witnesses, and each of us declares that in his or her opinion this testator is of sound mind."[12]

11. The testator's declaration that the instrument is his will is called *publication.* The purpose of publication is to assure that the testator is under no misapprehension as to the instrument testator is signing and to impress upon the witnesses the importance of the act and their consequent duties to vouch for the validity of the instrument. Nonetheless, the requirement of publication, a formality mandated in some states, is rarely a bar to probate since the testator may indicate to the witnesses that the instrument is a will by words, signs, or conduct; even the words of another saying it is the testator's will are sufficient. It is only necessary that the evidence show that the testator and the witnesses understand that the instrument is a will. Jackson v. Patton, 952 S.W.2d 404 (Tenn. 1997).

12. No state's statute requires the use of an attestation clause. The requirement of due execution can be satisfied merely by having the witnesses sign below the testator's signature as "witnesses." An attestation clause is very important, however. It makes out a prima facie case that the will was duly executed, and thus the will may be admitted to probate even though the witnesses predecease the testator or cannot recall the events of execution. See Gardner v. Balboni, 218 Conn. 220, 588 A.2d 634 (1991); In re Estate of Collins, 60 N.Y.2d 466, 458 N.E.2d 797, 470 N.Y.S.2d 338 (1983). Moreover, if one of the attesting witnesses testifies that the steps for due execution were not satisfied, the attestation clause gives the will proponent's attorney ammunition for a vigorous cross-examination, and the will can be admitted to probate on the presumption of due execution despite such testimony.

In In re Estate of Koss, 84 Ill. App. 2d 59, 228 N.E.2d 510 (1967), one of the attesting

(8) Each witness then signs and writes his or her address next to the signature.

(9) A *self-proving affidavit,* typed at the end of the will, swearing before a notary public that the will has been duly executed, is then signed by the testator and the witnesses before the notary public, who in turn signs and attaches the required seal. Why attach a self-proving affidavit? Due execution of a will is usually proved after the testator's death by the witnesses testifying in court or executing affidavits. If the witnesses are dead or cannot be located or have moved far away, a self-proving affidavit reciting that all the requirements of due execution have been complied with permits the will to be probated. The will is valid without such an affidavit,[13] but the affidavit makes it easy to probate the will. The affidavit must be executed in front of a notary. Almost all states recognize self-proving affidavits, an invention of the Uniform Probate Code that has proven very popular.

Uniform Probate Code §2-504 (1990) authorizes two kinds of self-proving affidavits. UPC §2-504(a) authorizes a *combined* attestation clause and self-proving affidavit, so that the testator and the witnesses (and the notary) sign their names only once. UPC §2-504(b) authorizes a self-proving affidavit to be affixed to a will already signed and attested, which affidavit must be signed by the testator and witnesses in front of a notary *after* the testator has signed the will and the witnesses have signed the attestation clause. In our recommended procedure, we have followed the two-step process authorized by UPC §2-504(b), which is permitted in more states than is the combined attestation clause and self-proving affidavit.

---

witnesses, a nurse, testified that she did not know that the document was a will, that she was informed by the sole beneficiary that the document was a power of attorney so that the nurses could be paid, that she could not read any portion of the document she signed because her glasses were broken, and that the document she signed consisted of only one page instead of the three pages offered for probate. The court, in admitting the will to probate, said, "Where an attestation clause is in due form and the will bears the genuine signatures of the testatrix and of the witnesses this is prima facie evidence of the due execution of the will, which cannot usually be overcome by the testimony of a witness that there was not compliance with all of the statutory requisites. . . . The testimony of a subscribing witness which seeks to impeach a will is to be viewed with suspicion and received with caution." 84 Ill. App. 2d at 70, 228 N.E.2d at 515-516.

In Young v. Young, 20 Ill. App. 3d 242, 313 N.E.2d 593 (1974), a will executed some 27 years earlier without an attestation clause was denied probate because the witnesses could not remember whether the things necessary to proper execution were done.

13. But see supra page 243, footnote 10, for Louisiana law. Lawyers who do not attach self-proving affidavits may not have kept up with changes in the law and may not be familiar with the advantages of using self-proved wills. Professor Johnston suggests some lawyers may not do so in order to help ensure their retention as attorney for the estate; the executor will have to contact the witnesses in the lawyer's office to prove due execution. Johnston suggests that this is unethical and, to avoid the appearance of unethical conduct, lawyers should always use self-proving affidavits. Gerald P. Johnston, An Ethical Analysis of Common Estate Planning Practices — Is Good Business Bad Ethics?, 45 Ohio St. L.J. 57, 133-140 (1984).

Observe that in In re Will of Ranney, infra page 252, the lawyer included at the end of the will a self-proving affidavit authorized for use in a two-step procedure but failed to include before it an attestation clause for the witnesses to sign. The witnesses signed only the self-proving affidavit. They did not sign an attestation clause as witnesses to the will.

Uniform Probate Code §3-406 provides that, if a will is self-proved, compliance with signature requirements for execution is conclusively presumed. In states adopting the UPC, a self-proved will cannot be attacked on grounds of failure to comply with signature requirements but may, of course, be attacked on other grounds such as undue influence or lack of capacity. In states that permit self-proved wills but have not adopted UPC §3-406, a self-proved will may give rise only to a rebuttable presumption of due execution. See Bruce H. Mann, Self-Proving Affidavits and Formalism in Wills Adjudication, 63 Wash. U. L.Q. 39 (1985).

NOTE: SAFEGUARDING A WILL

What should be done with the client's will after it has been executed? A common practice is to give the will to the client together with instructions that it be kept in a safe place, such as in a safe-deposit box or among valuable papers at the client's home. This may not be the most desirable practice, however. The many reported cases involving notations, interlineations, or other markings on wills indicate that over the years a disturbing number of testators have attempted partial revocations or, perhaps, have used their wills as memo pads on which contemplated modifications have been noted. Also, an occasional testator has taken too seriously the lawyer's advice on safeguarding the will, with the result that the will cannot be located after death.[14] These

14. Consider the case of Oscar P.'s will, a true story told in a letter to one of the editors from Mr. A. J. Robinson, an attorney in Amarillo, Texas. Mr. Robinson was counsel for one group of claimants under the will.

Two men walked into our office in late August and told us that they were Mr. P.'s nephews. They were completely covered with chigger bites from the top of their shoes to their belts. Their legs were swollen and red all over. They told us that their uncle had died in East Texas on a 40-acre farm. They said that he was found dead in his old house that did not have any doors or windows and that the floor was about to fall in, that he kept his eggs in a bucket hanging from a tree limb by wire to keep the snakes from stealing them, that he hung his milk from a tree limb, dangling in a creek, that there was no stove in the house and that he had a wheel barrow with the wheel running at about a 45 degree angle that he pushed to and from town to carry all his supplies. They had been informed that their uncle had left a will, and the entire family had descended on the place over the weekend to hunt for it. They had spent two days digging in every place that they could think of on the entire 40 acres, hunting for the will that they assumed was buried somewhere. When they were about to quit, someone decided to dig up the floor of the chicken house. Underneath the chicken house floor they found a gallon jar, and in the gallon jar was a half-gallon jar, and in the half-gallon was

potential difficulties have prompted some attorneys to follow the practice of retaining the client's will in their files. The client is given an unexecuted Xerox copy of the will, on which the location of the original will is noted. However, keeping client's wills may have the appearance of soliciting business, an unethical practice. In State v. Gulbankian, 54 Wis. 2d 605, 196 N.W.2d 233 (1972), the Wisconsin court discussed the ethics of this practice and said:

> Nor do we approve of attorneys' "safekeeping" wills. In the old days this may have been explained on the ground many people did not have a safe place to keep valuable papers, but there is little justification today because most people do have safekeeping boxes, and if not, sec. 853.09, Stats., provides for the deposit of a will with the register in probate for safekeeping during the lifetime of the testator. The correct practice is that the original will should be delivered to the testator, and should only be kept by the attorney upon specific unsolicited request of the client. [54 Wis. 2d at 611-612, 196 N.W.2d at 736.]

Do you agree with the Wisconsin court? Can you think of a justification for the lawyer keeping the will not mentioned by the Wisconsin court? See Gerald P. Johnston, An Ethical Analysis of Common Estate Planning Practices — Is Good Business Bad Ethics?, 45 Ohio St. L.J. 57, 124-133 (1984); Report, Developments Regarding the Professional Responsibility of the Estate Planning Lawyer: The Effect of the Model Rules of Professional Conduct, 22 Real Prop., Prob. & Trust J. 1, 28 (1987).

Like Wisconsin, many states have statutes permitting deposit of wills with the clerk of the probate court. Uniform Probate Code §2-515 (1990) provides for the deposit of a will in court for safekeeping. Depositing a will with a probate court clerk is a rare practice, however. Most persons do not know such a depository is available, and lawyers usually recommend leaving the will in the lawyer's safe if the client doesn't want to take the will home.

In re Pavlinko's Estate
Supreme Court of Pennsylvania, 1959
394 Pa. 564, 148 A.2d 528

BELL, J. Vasil Pavlinko died February 8, 1957; his wife, Hellen, died October 15, 1951. A testamentary writing dated March 9, 1949,

---

a quart, and in the quart was a pint, and in the pint was a half-pint, and in the half-pint was a key which appeared to fit some safe-deposit box. Upon checking all the banks in the neighboring towns, they finally found a bank that had a safe-deposit box that the key would fit. Upon opening the safe-deposit box they found P.'s holographic will. The first sentence recited that this was Oscar P.'s last will. The second sentence read: "You will find the key to my safety deposit box in a jar under the floor in the chicken house."

Oscar P. left a substantial estate.

which purported to be the will of Hellen Pavlinko, was signed by Vasil Pavlinko, her husband. The residuary legatee named therein, a brother of Hellen, offered the writing for probate as the will of Vasil Pavlinko, but probate was refused. The Orphans' Court, after hearing and argument, affirmed the decision of the Register of Wills.

The facts are unusual and the result very unfortunate. Vasil Pavlinko and Hellen, his wife, retained a lawyer to draw their wills and wished to leave their property to each other. By mistake Hellen signed the will which was prepared for her husband, and Vasil signed the will which was prepared for his wife, each instrument being signed at the end thereof. The lawyer who drew the will and his secretary, Dorothy Zinkham, both signed as witnesses. Miss Zinkham admitted that she was unable to speak the language of Vasil and Hellen, and that no conversation took place between them. The wills were kept by Vasil and Hellen. For some undisclosed reason, Hellen's will was never offered for probate at her death; in this case it was offered merely as an exhibit.

The instrument which was offered for probate was short. It stated: "I, *Hellen* Pavlinko, of . . . , do hereby make, publish and declare this to be *my* Last Will and Testament. . . . "

In the first paragraph she directed her executor to pay her debts and funeral expenses. In the second paragraph she gave her entire residuary estate to "my husband, Vasil Pavlinko . . . absolutely." She then provided:

> Third: If my aforesaid husband, Vasil Pavlinko, should predecease me, then and in that event, I give and bequeath:
> (a) To my brother-in-law, Mike Pavlinko, of McKees Rocks, Pennsylvania, the sum of Two Hundred ($200) Dollars.
> (b) To my sister-in-law, Maria Gerber, (nee Pavlinko), of Pittsburgh, Pennsylvania, the sum of Two Hundred ($200) Dollars.
> (c) The rest, residue and remainder of *my* estate, of whatsoever kind and nature and wheresoever situate, I give, devise and bequeath, absolutely, to *my brother*, Elias Martin, now residing at 520 Aidyl Avenue, Pittsburgh, Pennsylvania.
> I do hereby nominate, constitute and appoint my husband, Vasil Pavlinko, as Executor of this my Last Will and Testament.

It was then mistakenly signed "Vasil Pavlinko [Seal]."

While no attempt was made to probate, as Vasil's will, the writing which purported to be his will but was signed by Hellen, it could not have been probated as Vasil's will, because it was not signed by him at the end thereof.

The Wills Act of 1947 provides in clear, plain and unmistakable language in §2: "Every will, . . . shall be in writing and shall be signed *by the testator* at the end thereof," 20 P.S. §180.2, with certain exceptions not here relevant. The Court below correctly held that the paper which *recited* that it was the will of Hellen Pavlinko and intended and purported to give Hellen's estate to her husband, could not be probated as the will of Vasil and was a nullity.

In order to decide in favor of the residuary legatee, almost the entire will would have to be rewritten. The Court would have to substitute the words "Vasil Pavlinko" for "Hellen Pavlinko" and the words "my wife" wherever the words "my husband" appear in the will, and the relationship of the contingent residuary legatees would likewise have to be changed. To consider this paper — as written — as Vasil's will, it would give his entire residuary estate to "my husband, Vasil Pavlinko, absolutely" and "Third: If my husband, Vasil Pavlinko, should predecease me, then . . . I give and bequeath my residuary estate to my brother, Elias Martin." The language of this writing, which is signed at the end thereof by *Vasil* Pavlinko, is unambiguous, clear and unmistakable, and it is obvious that it is a meaningless nullity. . . .

Once a Court starts to ignore or alter or rewrite or make exceptions to clear, plain and unmistakable provisions of the Wills Act in order to accomplish equity and justice in that particular case, the Wills Act will become a meaningless, although well intentioned, scrap of paper, and the door will be opened wide to countless fraudulent claims which the Act successfully bars.

Decree affirmed. Each party shall pay their respective costs.

MUSMANNO, J. (dissenting).[15] Vasil Pavlinko and his wife, Hellen

---

15. Justice Musmanno was a striking individualist, sometimes injudicious, always colorful. In dissenting from a majority holding that Henry Miller's Rabelaisian Tropic of Cancer was not obscene, Musmanno wrote:

> "Cancer" is not a book. It is a cesspool, an open sewer, a pit of putrefaction, a slimy gathering of all that is rotten in the debris of human depravity. And in the center of all this waste and stench, besmearing himself with its foulest defilement, splashes, leaps, cavorts and wallows a bifurcated specimen that responds to the name of Henry Miller. One wonders how the human species could have produced so lecherous, blasphemous, disgusting and amoral a human being as Henry Miller. One wonders why he is received in polite society. . . . From Pittsburgh to Philadelphia, from Dan to Beersheba, and from the ramparts of the Bible to Samuel Eliot Morison's Oxford History of the American People, I dissent. [Commonwealth v. Robin, 421 Pa. 70, 100, 218 A.2d 546, 561 (1966).]

In his first five years on the Pennsylvania Supreme Court, Musmanno filed more dissenting opinions than all the other members of that court had collectively filed in the preceding 50 years. One dissent got him into a lawsuit. In one case, Chief Justice Stern ordered that Musmanno's dissent not be published in the official state reports because he had not circulated it among the court. Musmanno sought mandamus to compel the state reporter to publish his dissent. The supreme court denied the writ, Musmanno not sitting. Musmanno v. Eldredge, 382 Pa. 167, 114 A.2d 511 (1955). Justice Musmanno then moved his case to the court of last resort, the law reviews. His side of the controversy can be found in Michael A. Musmanno, Dissenting Opinions, 60 Dick. L. Rev. 139 (1956). When asked whether he read Musmanno's dissents, Stern, C.J., replied that he was not "interested in current fiction." The New Republic, Feb. 3, 1968, at 14.

Musmanno's ancestors came from Italy, and he was a leading force in establishing

Pavlinko, being unlettered in English and unlearned in the ways of the law, wisely decided to have an attorney draw up their wills, since they were both approaching the age when reflecting persons must give thought to that voyage from which there is no return. They explained to the attorney, whose services they sought, that he should draw two wills which would state that when either of the partners had sailed away, the one remaining ashore would become the owner of the property of the departing voyager. Vasil Pavlinko knew but little English. However, his lawyer, fortunately, was well versed in his clients' native language, known as Little Russian or Carpathian. The attorney thus discussed the whole matter with his two visitors in their language. He then dictated appropriate wills to his stenographer in English and then, after they had been transcribed, he translated the documents, paragraph by paragraph, to Mr. and Mrs. Pavlinko, who approved of all that he had written. The wills were laid before them and each signed the document purporting to be his or her will. The attorney gave Mrs. Pavlinko the paper she had signed and handed to her husband the paper he had signed. In accordance with customs they had brought with them from the old country, Mrs. Pavlinko turned her paper over to her husband. It did not matter, however, who held the papers since they were complementary of each other. Mrs. Pavlinko left her property to Mr. Pavlinko and Mr. Pavlinko left his property to Mrs. Pavlinko. They also agreed on a common residuary legatee, Elias Martin, the brother of Mrs. Pavlinko. . . .

We have also said time[s] without number that the intent of the testator must be gathered from the four corners of his will. Whether it be from the four corners of the will signed by Vasil Pavlinko or whether from the eight corners of the wills signed by Vasil and Hellen

---

Columbus Day as a special day for Italian-Americans. When Yale accepted the Vinland map as evidence that Norsemen and not an Italian, Christopher Columbus, had discovered America, Musmanno immediately rose to the attack. He dropped all his duties and went to Yale to dispute the archeologists, embarked on a six-month speaking tour attacking the authenticity of the Vinland Map, and wrote a book, Columbus Was First! (1966). (In 1974 the Yale Library pronounced the Vinland Map a fake. In 1995 Yale changed its mind and announced that the Vinland map may be authentic after all.)

Justice Musmanno's last opinion was a freewheeling dissent to a reversal of a rape conviction. The majority held that it was error for the judge to tell the jurors they would have to answer to God for their actions. Commonwealth v. Holton, 432 Pa. 11, 247 A.2d 228 (1968). Wrote Musmanno:

> God is not dead, and judges who criticize the invocation of Divine Assistance had better begin preparing a brief to use when they stand themselves at the Eternal Bar of Justice on Judgment Day. . . . I am perfectly willing to take my chances with [the trial judge] . . . at the gates of Saint Peter and answer on our voir dire that we were always willing to invoke the name of the Lord in seeking counsel. . . . Miserere nobis Omnipotens Deus! [Id. at 41, 43, 247 A.2d at 242-243.]

The next day, Columbus Day, 1968, Justice Musmanno dropped dead and presumably this voir dire took place. — Eds.

Pavlinko, all set out before the court below, the net result is always the same, namely that the residue of the property of the last surviving member of the Pavlinko couple was to go to Elias Martin.

. . . Even if we accept the Majority's conclusion . . . that all provisions in the Pavlinko will, which refer to himself, must be regarded as nullities, . . . it does not follow that the residuary clause must perish. The fact that some of the provisions in the Pavlinko will cannot be executed does not strike down the residuary clause, which is meaningful and stands on its own two feet. We know that one of the very purposes of a residuary clause is to provide a catch-all for undisposed-of or ineffectually disposed-of property. . . . I see no insuperable obstacle to probating the will signed by Vasil Pavlinko. Even though it was originally prepared as the will of his wife, Hellen, he did adopt its testamentary provisions as his own. Some of its provisions are not effective but their ineffectuality in no way bars the legality and validity of the residuary clause which is complete in itself. I would, therefore, probate the paper signed by Vasil Pavlinko. . . .

PROBLEM AND NOTE

1.   Suppose that after Hellen Pavlinko died, the lawyer-drafter discovered the wrong wills had been signed. Vasil was then incompetent. The lawyer photocopied the signature of Vasil on the will prepared for Hellen, superimposed it on the will prepared for Vasil, and photocopied the document. Can the photocopied document be probated? Is this attempt to fix the mistake ethical? See In re Grant, 262 Kan. 269, 936 P.2d 1360 (1997) (lawyer censured).

What would you, as the now-incompetent Vasil's lawyer, do to avoid a malpractice suit against you after Vasil's death?

2.   In re Pavlinko's Estate follows the traditional view that courts do not correct mistakes in wills. But, in recent years, there has been some movement in the direction of correcting mistakes in limited circumstances. See infra pages 427-438.

In one American case the mistake made in *Pavlinko* was corrected. In In re Snide, 52 N.Y.2d 193, 418 N.E.2d 656, 437 N.Y.S.2d 63 (1981), a husband (Harvey) and wife (Rose) mistakenly signed the will intended for the other; the issue was the same as in the *Pavlinko* case. The husband died first. The court of appeals, 4-3, ordered the instrument signed by the husband admitted to probate and reformed by substituting the name "Harvey" wherever the name "Rose" appeared.

Uniform Probate Code §2-503, in what some have called a "revolutionary" change in wills formalities law, gives a court the power to

dispense with formalities if there is clear and convincing evidence
that the decedent intended the document to be his will.

Uniform Probate Code (1990, as amended 1997)

§2-503. HARMLESS ERROR

Although a document or writing added upon a document was not
executed in compliance with Section 2-502, the document or writing
is treated as if it had been executed in compliance with that section
if the proponent of the document or writing establishes by clear and
convincing evidence that the decedent intended the document or
writing to constitute (i) the decedent's will, (ii) a partial or complete
revocation of the will, (iii) an addition to or an alteration of the will,
or (iv) a partial or complete revival of his [or her] formerly revoked
will or of a formerly revoked portion of the will.

In re Will of Ranney
Supreme Court of New Jersey, 1991
124 N.J. 1, 589 A.2d 1339

POLLOCK, J. The sole issue is whether an instrument purporting
to be a last will and testament that includes the signature of two witnesses on an attached self-proving affidavit, but not on the will itself,
should be admitted to probate. At issue is the will of Russell G. Ranney.
The Monmouth County Surrogate ordered probate of the will, but the
Superior Court, Law Division, Probate Part, reversed, ruling that the
will did not contain the signatures of two witnesses as required by
N.J.S.A. 3B:3-2. The Appellate Division found that the self-proving affidavit formed part of the will and, therefore, that the witnesses had
signed the will as required by the statute. 240 N.J. Super. 337, 573 A.2d
467 (1990). It reversed the judgment of the Law Division and remanded
the matter for a plenary hearing on the issue of execution. We granted
the contestant's petition for certification, and now affirm the judgment
of the Appellate Division.

I

The following facts emerge from the uncontested affidavits submitted
in support of probate of the will. On October 26, 1982, Russell and
his wife, Betty (now known as Betty McGregor), visited the law offices
of Kantor, Mandia, and Schuster to execute their wills. Russell's will
consisted of four pages and a fifth page containing a self-proving

affidavit, entitled "ACKNOWLEDGMENT AND AFFIDAVIT RELATING TO EXECUTION OF WILL." The pages of Russell's will were neither numbered nor attached before execution. After Russell and Betty had reviewed their wills, they and their attorney, Robert Kantor, proceeded to a conference room, where they were joined by Kantor's partner John Schuster III and by two secretaries, Laura Stout and Carmella Mattox, who was also a notary.

Consistent with his usual practice, Kantor asked Russell if the instrument represented Russell's will and if Russell wanted Schuster and Stout to act as witnesses. Russell answered both questions affirmatively, and signed the will on the fourth page:

> IN WITNESS WHEREOF, I have hereunto set my hand and seal this 26th day of October, One Thousand Nine Hundred and Eighty Two.

/s/ Russell G. Ranney
_____
Russell G. Ranney

No one else signed the fourth page of the will [because the attestation clause for witnesses had been omitted]. Russell, followed by Schuster and Stout, then signed the self-proving affidavit on the fifth page. Both Schuster and Stout believed that they were signing and attesting the will when they signed the affidavit. Furthermore, both Kantor, who had supervised the similar execution of many wills, and Schuster believed that the witnesses' signatures on the "Acknowledgment and Affidavit" complied with the attestation requirements of N.J.S.A. 3B:3-2. Mattox, whose practice was to notarize a document only if she witnessed the signature, notarized all the signatures.

After execution of the will, Stout stapled its four pages to the self-proving affidavit. The fifth and critical page reads:

Acknowledgment and Affidavit Relating to Execution of Will
STATE OF NEW JERSEY

ss.

COUNTY OF MONMOUTH

RUSSELL G. RANNEY, JOHN SCHUSTER III, and LAURA J. STOUT, the Testator and the witnesses, respectively whose names are signed to the attached instrument, being first duly sworn, do hereby declare to the undersigned authority that the Testator signed and executed the instrument as his Last Will and Testament and that he signed willingly and that he executed it as his free and voluntary act for the purposes therein expressed; and that each witness states that he or she signed the Will as witnesses in the presence and hearing of the Testator and that to the best of his or her knowledge, the Testator was at the time 18 or more years of age, of sound mind and under no constraint or undue influence.

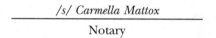

/s/ *Russell G. Ranney*
Russell G. Ranney
/s/ *John Schuster III*

/s/ *Laura J. Stout*

Subscribed, sworn to, and acknowledged before me, by Russell G. Ranney, the Testator, and subscribed and sworn to before me by <u>JOHN SCHUSTER III</u> and <u>LAURA J. STOUT</u>, witnesses, this 26 day of October 1982.

/s/ *Carmella Mattox*
Notary

The acknowledgment and affidavit is almost identical to the language suggested by N.J.S.A. 3B:3-5 for a self-proving affidavit *signed subsequent to the time of execution.* The form for making a will self-proved at the time of execution, as occurred here, is set forth in the preceding section, N.J.S.A. 3B:3-4. Although the subject affidavit was executed simultaneously with the execution of the will, *the affidavit refers to the execution of the will in the past tense and incorrectly states that the witnesses had already signed the will* [emphasis added]. . . .

Russell's will gives Betty a life estate in their apartment in a building at 111 Avenue of Two Rivers in Rumson, the rental income from other apartments in that building, and the tuition and rental income from the Rumson Reading Institute, which was merged into the Ranney School after the execution of Russell's will. The will further directs that on Betty's death, the Avenue of Two Rivers property and the proceeds of the Institute are to be turned over to the trustees of the Ranney School. Additionally, Betty receives all of Russell's personal property except that necessary for the operation of the Institute.

The residue of Russell's estate is to be paid in trust to Betty, Kantor, and Henry Bass, Russell's son-in-law, who were also appointed as executors. Betty and Harland Ranney and Suzanne Bass, Russell's two children, are to receive thirty-two percent each of the trust income, and are to share equally the net income from the operation of Ransco Corporation. Nancy Orlow, Betty's daughter and Russell's step-daughter, is to receive the remaining four percent of the trust income. Russell's will provides further that after Betty's death the income from Ransco Corporation is to be distributed equally between Harland Ranney and Suzanne Bass, and on their deaths is to be distributed to the Ranney School.

Russell died on April 4, 1987, and the Monmouth County Surrogate admitted the will to probate on April 21, 1987. . . . Subsequently, Betty . . . contested the probate of Russell's will. . . . Her sole challenge was that the will failed to comply literally with the formalities of N.J.S.A. 3B:3-2. Suzanne R. Bass, Harland Ranney, Henry Bass, and the Ranney School urged that the will be admitted to probate. . . .

Although the Appellate Division "decline[d] to hold that the placement of the witnesses' signatures is immaterial," 240 N.J. Super. at 344, 573 A.2d 467, it ruled that the self-proving affidavit was part of the will and that the witnesses' signatures on the affidavit constituted signatures on the will, id. at 344-345, 573 A.2d 467. . . .

We disagree with the Appellate Division that signatures on the subsequently-executed self-proving affidavit literally satisfied the requirements of N.J.S.A. 3B:3-2 as signatures on a will. We further hold, however, that the will may be admitted to probate if it substantially complies with these requirements.

II

The first question is whether Russell's will literally complies with the requirements of N.J.S.A. 3B:3-2, which provides:

> [E]very will shall be in writing, signed by the testator or in his name by some other person in his presence and at his direction, and shall be signed by at least two persons each of whom witnessed either the signing or the testator's acknowledgment of the signature or of the will.

In holding that signatures on the self-proving affidavit satisfy N.J.S.A. 3B:3-2, the Appellate Division relied on out-of-state decisions that permitted the probate of wills when the witnesses signed a self-proving affidavit, but not the will. 240 N.J. Super. at 344, 573 A.2d 467. The rationale of those cases is that a self-proving affidavit and an attestation clause are sufficiently similar to justify the conclusion that signatures on a self-proving affidavit, like signatures on the attestation clause, satisfy the requirement that the signatures be on the will. See In re Estate of Charry, 359 So. 2d 544, 545 (Fla. Dist. Ct. App. 1978) (witnesses' signatures on self-proving affidavit on same page as testator's signature satisfied attestation requirements); In re Estate of Petty, 227 Kan. 697, 702-03, 608 P.2d 987, 992-93 (1980) (self-proving affidavit on same page as testator's signature substantially complies with attestation requirements); In re Cutsinger, 445 P.2d 778, 782 (Okla. 1968) (self-proving affidavit executed on same page as testator's signature is an attestation clause in substantial compliance with statutory requirement); see also In re Will of Leitstein, 46 Misc. 2d 656, 657, 260 N.Y.S.2d 406, 407-08 (Sur. 1965) (probating will when witnesses signed affidavit purporting to be attestation clause). The Appellate Division found that the similarity between self-proving affidavits and attestation clauses warrants treating the affidavit attached to Russell's will as the equivalent of an attestation clause. 240 N.J. Super. at 345, 573 A.2d 467. Noting that the absence of an attestation clause does not void a will, but merely requires the proponents to prove due execution, the Appellate Division could find "no reason, either in logic or policy, to deny a similar opportunity to the proponents" of Russell's will. Ibid. . . .

Self-proving affidavits and attestation clauses, although substantially similar in content, serve different functions. Mann, Self-Proving Affidavits and Formalism in Wills Adjudication, 63 Wash. U.L.Q. 39, 41 (1985). Attestation clauses facilitate probate by providing "prima facie evidence" that the testator voluntarily signed the will in the presence of the witnesses. 5 A. Clapp, N.J. Practice: Wills and Administration §133 at 335 (3d ed. 1982). An attestation clause also permits probate of a will when a witness forgets the circumstances of the will's execution or dies before the testator. Id. at 337.

Self-proving affidavits, by comparison, are sworn statements by eyewitnesses that the will has been duly executed. Mann, supra, 63 Wash. U.L.Q. at 40. The affidavit performs virtually all the functions of an attestation clause, and has the further effect of permitting probate without requiring the appearance of either witness. Id. at 41; 8 A. Clapp, supra, §2063 at 9, comment 1. Wills may be made self-proving simultaneously with or after execution. N.J.S.A. 3B:3-4, -5. One difference between an attestation clause and a subsequently-signed, self-proving affidavit is that in an attestation clause, the attestant expresses the present intent to act as a witness, but in the affidavit, the affiant swears that the will has already been witnessed. This difference is more apparent than real when, as here, the affiants, with the intent to act as witnesses, sign the self-proving affidavit immediately after witnessing the testator's execution of the will.

The Legislature first authorized self-proving affidavits in the 1977 amendments to the Probate Code, specifically N.J.S.A. 3A:2A-6. Nothing in the statutory language or history intimates that the Legislature contemplated a subsequently-executed affidavit as a substitute for the attestation clause. Instead, the 1977 amendments indicate that the Legislature envisioned the will, including the attestation clause, as independent from such an affidavit. Hence, the form provided in N.J.S.A. 3B:3-5 for a subsequently-signed affidavit refers to the will as a separate instrument and states that the testator and witnesses have signed the will. Thus, the Legislature indicated its intention that subsequently-executed, self-proving affidavits be used solely in conjunc-

tion with duly-executed wills. Although the execution of Russell's will
and of the self-proving affidavit apparently were contemporaneous,
the affidavit follows the form provided in N.J.S.A. 3B:3-5. Consequently, the signatures of the witnesses on the subject self-proving
affidavit do not literally comply with the statutory requirements.

That finding does not end the analysis. As we stated in In re Estate
of Peters, 107 N.J. 263, 526 A.2d 1005 (1987), in limited circumstances
a will may be probated if it substantially complies with those requirements.

Scholars . . . have supported the doctrine of substantial compliance.
Langbein, Substantial Compliance with the Wills Act, 88 Harv. L. Rev.
489 (1975); Nelson & Starck, Formalities and Formalism: A Critical
Look at the Execution of Wills, 6 Pepperdine L. Rev. 331, 356 (1979).
At the 1990 annual conference, the Commissioners on Uniform State
Laws added a section to the Uniform Probate Code explicitly advocat-
ing the adoption of the doctrine. Uniform Probate Code §2-503 (Na-
tional Conference of Commissioners on Uniform State Laws 1990).
That section, 2-503, provides:

> Although a document . . . was not executed in compliance with §2-502
> [enumerating the wills formalities], the document . . . is treated as if it
> had been executed in compliance with that section if the proponent of
> the document . . . establishes by clear and convincing evidence that the
> decedent intended the document to constitute (i) the decedent's will. . . .

In the 1990 edition of the Restatement (Second) of Property (Donative Transfers) (Restatement), moreover, the American Law Institute
encourages courts to permit probate of wills that substantially comply
with will formalities. §33.1 Comment g (Tentative Draft No. 13) (approved by the American Law Institute at 1990 annual meeting). The
Restatement concludes that in the absence of legislative action, courts
"should apply a rule of excused noncompliance, under which a will
is found validly executed if the proponent establishes by clear and
convincing evidence that the decedent intended the document to
constitute his or her will." Ibid. . . .

III

Substantial compliance is a functional rule designed to cure the ineq-
uity caused by the "harsh and relentless formalism" of the law of
wills. Langbein, supra, 88 Harv. L. Rev. at 489. . . . The underlying
rationale is that the

> finding of a formal defect should lead not to automatic invalidity, but to a
> further inquiry: does the noncomplying document express the decedent's

testamentary intent, and does its form sufficiently approximate Wills Act formality to enable the court to conclude that it serves the purposes of the Wills Act? [Langbein, supra, 88 Harv. L. Rev. at 489.]

Scholars have identified various reasons for formalities in the execution of wills. The primary purpose of those formalities is to ensure that the document reflects the uncoerced intent of the testator. Id. at 492; Mann, supra, 63 Wash. U.L.Q. at 49. Requirements that the will be in writing and signed by the testator also serve an evidentiary function by providing courts with reliable evidence of the terms of the will and of the testamentary intent. Gulliver & Tilson, Classification of Gratuitous Transfers, 51 Yale L.J. 1, 6-7 (1941). Additionally, attestation requirements prevent fraud and undue influence. Id. at 9-10; In re Estate of Peters, supra, 107 N.J. at 276, 526 A.2d 1005. Further, the formalities perform a "channeling function" by requiring a certain degree of uniformity in the organization, language, and content of wills. Langbein, supra, 88 Harv. L. Rev. at 494. Finally, the ceremony serves as a ritual that impresses the testator with the seriousness of the occasion. Gulliver & Tilson, supra, 51 Yale L.J. at 5.

Rigid insistence on literal compliance often frustrates these purposes. Restatement, supra, §33.1 Comment g (strict compliance has in many cases led courts to results that defeated the intent of the testator). To avoid such frustration, some courts, although purporting to require literal compliance, have allowed probate of technically-defective wills. See In re Estate of Bochner, 119 Misc. 2d 937, 938, 464 N.Y.S.2d 958, 959 (Sur. 1983); In re Will of Leitstein, supra, 46 Misc. 2d at 657, 260 N.Y.S.2d at 408. Other courts have refused to probate wills because of technical defects despite evidence that the testator meant the document to be a will. See In re Estate of Sample, 175 Mont. 93, 96-97, 572 P.2d 1232, 1234 (1977) (refusing to probate will signed only on attached self-proving affidavit); Boren v. Boren, 402 S.W.2d 728, 729 (Tex. 1966) (same). Leading authorities have criticized the *Boren* rule, finding no basis in logic or policy for its blind insistence on voiding wills for "the most minute defect[s] in formal compliance . . . no matter how abundant the evidence that the defect [is] inconsequential." Langbein, supra, 88 Harv. L. Rev. at 489; accord In re Estate of Charry, supra, 359 So. 2d at 545 (declining to follow *Boren* rule because it elevated form over substance); Mann, supra, 63 Wash. U.L.Q. at 39-40 (characterizing *Boren* line of cases as "odd and rather perverse"); Nelson & Starck, supra, 6 Pepperdine L. Rev. at 356-57.

We agree with those authorities. Compliance with statutory formalities is important not because of the inherent value that those formalities possess, but because of the purposes they serve. Mann, supra, 63 Wash. U.L.Q. at 60; Nelson & Starck, supra, 6 Pepperdine L. Rev. at

355. It would be ironic to insist on literal compliance with statutory formalities when that insistence would invalidate a will that is the deliberate and voluntary act of the testator. Such a result would frustrate rather than further the purpose of the formalities. Nelson & Starck, supra, 6 Pepperdine L. Rev. at 353-55. . . .

The execution of a last will and testament, however, remains a solemn event. A careful practitioner will still observe the formalities surrounding the execution of wills. When formal defects occur, proponents should prove by clear and convincing evidence that the will substantially complies with statutory requirements. See Uniform Probate Code, supra, §2-503; Restatement, supra, §33.1 Comment g. Our adoption of the doctrine of substantial compliance should not be construed as an invitation either to carelessness or chicanery. The purpose of the doctrine is to remove procedural peccadillos as a bar to probate.

Furthermore, as previously described, a subsequently-signed self-proving affidavit serves a unique function in the probate of wills. We are reluctant to permit the signatures on such an affidavit both to validate the execution of the will and to render the will self-proving. Accordingly, if the witnesses, with the intent to attest, sign a self-proving affidavit, but do not sign the will or an attestation clause, clear and convincing evidence of their intent should be adduced to establish substantial compliance with the statute. For that reason, probate in these circumstances should proceed in solemn form. See N.J.S.A. 3B:3-23; R. 4:84-1. Probate in solemn form, which is an added precaution to assure proof of valid execution, may be initiated on an order to show cause, R. 4:84-1(b), and need not unduly delay probate of a qualified will.

. . . If, after conducting a hearing in solemn form, the trial court is satisfied that the execution of the will substantially complies with the statutory requirements, it may reinstate the judgment of the Surrogate admitting the will to probate.

The judgment of the Appellate Division is affirmed, and the matter is remanded to the Chancery Division, Probate Part.

NOTES, QUESTIONS, AND PROBLEMS

1. The architect of the dispensing power authorized by UPC §2-503 is Professor John Langbein of Yale. Langbein first proposed that courts develop a substantial compliance doctrine in his article, Substantial Compliance With the Wills Act, 88 Harv. L. Rev. 489 (1975). Later in the same year that Langbein wrote, South Australia enacted a statute providing for the probate of a document that was not properly executed if the court "is satisfied that there can be no reasonable doubt that the deceased intended the document to constitute his

will." S. Austl. Wills Act Amendment Act (No. 2) of 1975, §9, amend-
ing Wills Act of 1936, §12(2), 8 S. Austl. Stat. 665. This act excuses
noncompliance with the Wills Act. It gives a court a dispensing
power — the power to validate a document the decedent intended
to be a will even though the formalities are not complied with. In
1981, the neighboring state of Queensland enacted a statute providing
for probate of a will that substantially complies with the will formalities. Queensland Succession Act of 1981, §9(a), 1981 Queensl. Stat.
No. 69.

After observing the South Australian and Queensland experience,
Langbein, in 1987, concluded that the dispensing power was preferable to the substantial compliance doctrine. The reason was that the
"courts read into their substantial compliance doctrine a near-miss
standard, ignoring the central issue of whether the testator's conduct
evidenced testamentary intent." John H. Langbein, Excusing Harmless Errors in the Execution of Wills: A Report on Australia's Tranquil
Revolution in Probate Law, 87 Colum. L. Rev. 1, 53 (1987). From 41
South Australian cases since 1975, Langbein concluded:

> Implicitly, this case law has produced a ranking of the Wills Act formali-
> ties. Of the three main formalities — writing, signature, and attestation —
> writing turns out to be indispensable. Because section 12(2) requires a
> "document," nobody has tried to use the dispensing power to enforce
> an oral will. Failure to give permanence to the terms of your will is not
> harmless. Signature ranks next in importance. If you leave your will un-
> signed, you raise a grievous doubt about the finality and genuineness of
> the instrument. An unsigned will is presumptively only a draft, . . . but
> that presumption is rightly overcome in compelling circumstances such
> as in the switched-wills cases. By contrast, attestation makes a more modest
> contribution, primarily of a protective character, to the Wills Act policies.
> But the truth is that most people do not need protecting, and there is
> usually strong evidence that want of attestation did not result in imposi-
> tion. The South Australian courts have been quick to find such evidence
> and to excuse attestation defects under the dispensing power.
>
> In devaluing attestation while insisting on signature and writing, the
> South Australian legislation and case law has brought the South Australian
> law of wills into a kind of alignment with the American law of will substi-
> tutes, that is, with our nonprobate system, where business practice has
> settled the forms for transfer. In life insurance beneficiary designations;
> in bank transfer arrangements such as pay-on-death accounts, joint ac-
> counts, and Totten trusts; in pension accounts; and in revocable inter
> vivos trusts, writing is the indispensable formality of modern practice,
> and signature is nearly as universal. Attestation, however, is increasingly
> uncommon. . . .
>
> Americans should . . . shudder that we still inflict upon our citizens the
> injustice of the traditional law, and we should join in this movement to
> rid private law of relics so embarrassing. [Id. at 52-54.]

Professor John H. Langbein

Uniform Probate Code §2-503 has been adopted in Colorado, Hawaii, Michigan, Montana, South Dakota, and Utah. Measures similar to UPC §2-503 have been enacted in other Australian states, Manitoba, and Israel. The official comment to the Israeli Succession Law of 5725-1965, §25, adopting a dispensing power, notes: "Jewish Law demands on the one hand strict compliance with certain formulae.... [O]n the other hand it developed the concept of 'a . . . *mitzvah* to carry out the wishes of the deceased.' " Israel Misrad ha-Mishpatim, Hatzaat Hok ha-Yerushah 73 (5712-1952).

Restatement (Third) of Property, Wills and Other Donative Transfers, §3.3 (1999) provides: "A harmless error in executing a will may be excused if the proponent establishes by clear and convincing evidence that the decedent adopted the document as his or her will."

For discussion of the dispensing power and the substantial compliance doctrine, see, in addition to Langbein's articles, Lloyd Bonfield, Reforming the Requirements for Due Execution of Wills: Some Guidance from the Past, 70 Tul. L. Rev. 1893 (1996); Melanie B. Leslie, The Myth of Testamentary Freedom, 38 Ariz. L. Rev. 235, 258-290 (1996); James Lindgren, The Fall of Formalism, 55 Alb. L. Rev. 1009 (1992); Bruce H. Mann, Formalities and Formalism in the Uniform Probate Code, 142 U. Pa. L. Rev. 1033 (1994); C. Douglas Miller, Will Formality, Judicial Formalism, and Legislative Reform: An Examination of the New Uniform Probate Code "Harmless Error" Rule and the Movement toward Amorphism, 43 Fla. L. Rev. 167 (pt. 1), 599 (pt. 2) (1991).

It seems more likely that a court would adopt a substantial compliance doctrine, for which there are many analogies in other areas of the law and which appears to carry out the fundamental intent of the legislature, than adopt a dispensing power, which appears to usurp the legislature's role. See Hickox v. Wilson, 269 Ga. 180, 496 S.E.2d 711 (1998), where the court probated a will not signed by the testator, who signed only the self-proving affidavit before two witnesses and a notary. The court, in a terse opinion, seemingly adopted either a substantial compliance doctrine or a dispensing power.

2.   If attestation defects can be excused by a court, and serve only a modest Wills Act function, as Langbein suggests, why not abolish the attestation requirement entirely? In states permitting holographic wills (see infra page 263), witnesses are not necessary if the will is entirely handwritten by the testator. For an argument that the mini-

mum formalities for a will should be reduced to a writing (typed or handwritten) signed by the testator, see James Lindgren, Abolishing the Attestation Requirement for Wills, 68 N.C. L. Rev. 541 (1990); Lindgren, The Fall of Formalism, supra, at 1024-1033.

3. Suppose that a signed, handwritten, but unwitnessed will is offered for probate. This could not be probated under the substantial compliance doctrine because the testator has not attempted to secure witnesses, but apparently this document could be probated under UPC §2-503. South Australian cases have probated handwritten unwitnessed wills. Would the adoption of UPC §2-503 mean that holographic wills are permitted in jurisdictions having no statute authorizing them? See Langbein, Excusing Harmless Errors, supra, at 18-22.

4. For websites offering interesting wills, see www:courttv.com/legaldocs/newsmakers/wills; www.ca-probate.com/wills.htm.

2. Holographic Wills

The Jolly Testator Who Makes His Own Will[16]

> Ye lawyers who live upon litigants' fees,
> And who need a good many to live at your ease,
> Grave or gay, wise or witty, whate'er your degree,
> Plain stuff or Queen's Counsel, take counsel of me:
> When a festive occasion your spirit unbends,
> You should never forget the profession's best friends;
> So we'll send round the wine, and a light bumper fill
> To the jolly testator who makes his own will.
>
> He premises his wish and his purpose to save
> All dispute among friends when he's laid in the grave;
> Then he straightway proceeds more disputes to create
> Than a long summer's day would give time to relate.
> He writes and erases, he blunders and blots,
> He produces such puzzles and Gordian knots,
> That a lawyer, intending to frame the thing ill,
> Couldn't match the testator who makes his own will.

LORD NEAVES

16. We reproduce only the first two stanzas of Lord Neaves's poem. For the entire poem, see William L. Prosser, The Judicial Humorist 246 (1952). — Eds.

In about half of the states, primarily in the South and West, holographic wills are permitted.[17] A holographic will is a will written by the testator's hand and signed by the testator; attesting witnesses are not required. Holographic wills are of Roman origin and are recognized by the Code Napoleon and civil law countries. They were introduced into this country by a Virginia statute of 1751 and by the reception of the civil law into Louisiana.

Requirements for a valid holographic will vary. Most states allowing holographs have provisions similar to Uniform Probate Code §2-502(b): "A will . . . is valid as a holographic will, whether or not witnessed, if the signature and material portions of the document are in the testator's handwriting." Several states, however, require that a holographic will be "entirely" handwritten, a requirement that may cause problems if typed or printed matter is found on the holographic instrument. For example, in In re Estate of Dobson, 708 P.2d 422 (Wyo. 1985), the testator took her signed handwritten will to her local banker to discuss it with him. To make the will clearer, the banker penciled in certain numbers and parentheses and added to the devise of a tract of land, "including all mineral and oil rights," all with the consent of the testator. The court held the will could not be probated because not entirely in the handwriting of the decedent. See Annot., 37 A.L.R.4th 528 (1985).

A few states require that a holograph be dated, which means a full date of day, month, and year. A date is useful in determining which of two inconsistent testamentary instruments was written later; the last written instrument prevails. But of course the requirement of a date causes an undated instrument to fail even if there is no other inconsistent testamentary instrument.

In almost all states permitting holographs, a holograph may be signed at the end, at the beginning, or anywhere on the will, but if not signed at the end there may be doubt about whether the decedent intended his name to be a signature. See, for example, In re Estate of Fegley, 589 P.2d 80 (Colo. App. 1978), where the court denied probate to a handwritten instrument reading, "I, Henrietta Fegley,

---

17. The states are Alaska, Arizona, Arkansas, California, Colorado, Hawaii, Idaho, Kentucky, Louisiana, Maine, Michigan, Mississippi, Montana, Nebraska, Nevada, New Jersey, North Carolina, North Dakota, Oklahoma, Pennsylvania, South Dakota, Tennessee, Texas, Utah, Virginia, West Virginia, and Wyoming. In Maryland and New York holographic wills are permitted for soldiers and sailors. For a list of state statutes, see Restatement (Third) of Property, Wills and Other Donative Transfers, §3.2, Statutory Note (1999).

Suppose that the testator writes a holographic will in a state recognizing such a will, and then the testator moves to a state that does not recognize holographic wills and dies there. On this matter, states that do not recognize holographs are split. Some permit probate of a holographic will if valid where executed; other states deny probate. See Black v. Seals, 474 So. 2d 696 (Ala. 1985), allowing holographic will of nonresident.

being of sound mind and disposing memory, declare this instrument to be my last will," but not otherwise signed. Compare In re Estate of MacLeod, 206 Cal. App. 3d 1235, 254 Cal. Rptr. 156 (1988), reaching a contrary conclusion on virtually identical facts.

On holographic wills, see Restatement (Third) of Property, Wills and Other Donative Transfers, §3.2 (1999), including the Statutory Note.

ASHBEL G. GULLIVER & CATHERINE J. TILSON, CLASSIFICATION OF GRATUITOUS TRANSFERS, 51 Yale L.J. 1, 13-14 (1941): "The exemption of holographic wills from the usual statutory requirements seems almost exclusively justifiable in terms of the evidentiary function. The requirement that a holographic will be entirely written in the handwriting of the testator furnishes more complete evidence for inspection by handwriting experts than would exist if only the signature were available, and consequently tends to preclude the probate of a forged document. . . . While there is a certain ritual value in writing out the document, casual off-hand statements are frequently made in letters. The relative incompleteness of the performance of the functions of the regular statute of wills, and particularly the absence of any ritual value, may account for the fact that holographic wills are not recognized in the majority of the states, and for some decisions, in states recognizing them, requiring the most precise compliance with specified formalities."

In re Estate of Johnson
Arizona Court of Appeals, 1981
129 Ariz. 307, 630 P.2d 1039

WREN, C.J.   This appeal involves the question of whether the handwritten portions on a printed will form, submitted to the trial court as a holographic will, were sufficient to satisfy the requirements of A.R.S. §14-2503 that the material provisions of such a will must be entirely in the handwriting of the testator.

Arnold H. Johnson, the decedent, died on January 28, 1978 at the age of 79. One of his sons, John Mark Johnson, was appointed personal representative of the estate. In addition to John, the decedent was survived by five other children. Approximately three weeks following appointment of the personal representative, appellants, Barton Lee McLain and Marie Ganssle, petitioned for formal probate of an instrument dated March 22, 1977. The personal representative objected to the petition and filed a motion for summary judgment on the grounds that the instrument was invalid as a will, in that it was not attested by any witnesses as required by A.R.S. §14-2502, and did not qualify as a holographic will under A.R.S. §14-2503, since the material provisions thereof were not in the handwriting of the testator.

Appellants filed a cross-motion for summary judgment, urging that the document did constitute a holographic will. The trial court disagreed with appellants and granted the motion of the personal representative. We affirm.

The document claimed by appellants to be decedent's last will and testament was a printed will form available in various office supply and stationery stores. It bore certain printed provisions followed by blanks where the testator could insert any provisions he might desire. The entire contents of the instrument in question are set forth below, with the portions underscored which are in the decedent's handwriting.

THE LAST WILL AND TESTAMENT

I Arnold H. Johnson a resident of Mesa Arizona of Maricopa County, State of Arizona, being of sound and disposing mind and memory, do make, publish and declare this my last WILL AND TESTAMENT, hereby revoking and making null and void any and all other last Wills and Testaments heretofore by me made.

FIRST — My will is that all my just debts and funeral expenses and any Estate or Inheritance taxes shall be paid out of my Estate, as soon after my decease as shall be found convenient.

SECOND — I give, devise and bequeath to My six living children as follows

To John M. Johnson ⅛ of my Estate	
Helen Marchese	⅛
Sharon Clements	⅛
Mirriam Jennings	⅛
Mary D. Korman	⅛
A. David Johnson	⅛
To W.V. Grant, Souls Harbor Church	
3200 W. Davis Dallas Texas[18]	⅛

18. W. V. Grant is a television evangelist and faith healer, who has been richly successful in raising money from his believers. He lives in a $900,000 home in Dallas (7,000 square feet with nine baths and three bars), drives two Ferraris, and wears $1,500 suits. In 1991 ABC's Diane Sawyer looked into this TV evangelist and his empire, which she essayed into a funny and sad and shocking hour on PrimeTime Live (Nov. 21, 1991).

> One favorite ruse is claiming to have an orphanage in Haiti, and soliciting donations from viewers by showing them photos of starving toddlers. Grant in fact claims to have 64 Haitian orphanages, but Diane Sawyer couldn't find them. . . .
> In some ways, exposing frauds in the televangelical racket is a lost cause. The faithful, who insist on investing hope and money in these tricksters, may not care where the money really does go. [Tom Shales, The Money Changers, Washington Post, Nov. 21, 1991, at D13.]

To Barton Lee McLain   )
and Marie Gansels   )
Address 901 E. Broadway Phoenix   )   ⅛
Az Mesa   )

I nominate and appoint Mirriam Jennings my Daughter of Nashville Tenn. as executress of this my Last Will and Testament Address 1247 Saxon Drive Nashville Tenn.

IN TESTIMONY WHEREOF, I have set my hand to this, My Last Will and Testament, at _____ this 22 day of March, in the year of our Lord, One Thousand Nine Hundred 77.

The foregoing instrument was signed by said Arnold H. Johnson in our presence, and by _____ published and declared as and for _____ Last Will and Testament, and at _____ request, and in _____ presence, and in presence of each other, we hereunto subscribe our Names as Attesting Witnesses, at _____ This 22 day of March, 1977.

My Commission expires   _____
Jan. 16, 1981   Ann C. McGonagill
                                             (Notary public seal)

Initially it is to be noted that Arizona has adopted the Uniform Probate Code, the holographic will provisions being contained in §2-503 [renumbered as §2-502(b) and slightly changed in the 1990 Code], and found in A.R.S. §14-2503:

"A will which does not comply with §14-2502 is valid as a holographic will, whether or not witnessed, if the signature and the material provisions are in the handwriting of the testator."

The statutory requirement that the material provisions be drawn in the testator's own handwriting requires that the handwritten portion clearly express a *testamentary* intent. Estate of Morrison, 55 Ariz. 504, 103 P.2d 669 (1940). Appellants argue that the purported will here should thus be admitted to probate, since all the key dispositive provisions essential to its validity as a will are in the decedent's own handwriting; and further, when all the printed provisions are excised, the requisite intent to make a will is still evidenced. We do not agree. In our opinion, the only words which establish this requisite testamentary intent on the part of the decedent are found in the *printed* portion of the form.

In 1996 W. V. Grant was sent to federal prison for income tax fraud. But now he's back in business. See Steve Blow, TV Preachers Back to Get Rest of Your Money, Dallas Morning News, Aug. 16, 1998, at A37; Twila Decker, Miracles for a Price, St. Petersburg Times, Aug. 9, 1998, at F1.

The official comment to §2-503 of the Uniform Probate Code (ULA) sheds some light upon the situation where, as here, a printed will form is used:

> By requiring only the "material provisions" to be in the testator's handwriting (rather than requiring, as some existing statutes do, that the will be "entirely" in the testator's handwriting) a holograph may be valid even though immaterial parts such as date or introductory wording be printed or stamped. A valid holograph might even be executed on some printed will forms if the printed portion could be eliminated and the handwritten portion could evidence the testator's will. For persons unable to obtain legal assistance, the holographic will may be adequate. . . .

This court, in In re Estate of Mulkins, 17 Ariz. App. 179, 180, 496 P.2d 605, 606 (1972) traced earlier Arizona decisions and determined that the "important thing is that the *testamentary* part of the will be wholly written by the testator and of course signed by him" (citing Estate of Morrison, supra) (emphasis in original). *Mulkins* also found that the printed words of the will, set forth below[19] were not essential to the meaning of the handwritten words and could not be held to defeat the intention of the deceased otherwise clearly expressed.

It is thus clear that, under the terminology of the statute and the comment thereto, an instrument may not be probated as a holographic will where it contains words not in the handwriting of the testator if such words are essential to the testamentary disposition. However, the mere fact that the testator used a blank form, whether of a will or some other document, does not invalidate what would otherwise be a valid will if the printed words may be entirely rejected as surplusage.

In support of their position appellants rely on Estate of Blake v. Benza, 120 Ariz. 552, 587 P.2d 271 (App. 1978). In *Blake* this court upheld the trial court's admission to probate, as a valid holograph the postscript to a personal letter:

---

19. We have omitted the printed will form used in *Mulkins.* The dispositive language handwritten on the printed will form read:

> I hereby make my will to Lettie Smith as Sister now living in Flint Michigan at 2222 on Oklahoma Ave. and Betty Hart Elkins at Rt. 1. Box 267 36 St. Just North of Southern Ave Phoenix, Ariz. about a block. I have 10 acres on Rincon Road. The South 330 feet of the Northwest quarter of the Northeast quarter of Section Twenty six 26 of township eight 8 North range 5 West of the Gila and Salt River base and Meridian Yavapai County of Arizona this 8 day of April 1966.

This makes pretty good sense as a complete disposition. — Eds.

"P.S. You can have my entire estate.

"/x/ Harry J. Blake (SAVE THIS)."

There having been no contention that the letter was not written and signed by the decedent, it was held that the postscript was more than a mere casual statement, and was deemed sufficient to demonstrate a testamentary intent. Analogizing to *Blake* which held that the use of the word "estate" by the decedent inferred that he was making a disposition of his property to take effect upon his death, appellants point to that portion of the document here which states: "TO (the name of the respective person) ⅛ of my estate." as being sufficient to likewise establish the requisite intent. Again, we do not agree.

Blake did not rely solely upon the use of the word "estate" to determine that the testator had a testamentary intent. The opinion focused upon the emphasized words "SAVE THIS" to support the position that the letter was to have a future significance. The fact that the formal signature following the dispositive clause bore the testator's name in full as opposed to simply "Your Uncle Harry," as in previous letters, was also supportive of a testamentary intent. Finally, the dispositive clause itself in *Blake* contained the phrase "you can have," which clearly imported a future connotation.

Contrasting the *Blake* will to the handwritten segments of the purported will before us, we find a marked difference. Though the decedent here used the word "estate," this word alone is insufficient to indicate an animus testandi.

In Webster's New Collegiate Dictionary, G & C Merriam & Company, Springfield, 1975 at 391, one of the definitions of the word, "estate" is, "the assets and liabilities left by a person at death." However, the same word is also defined as: "the degree, quality, nature, and extent of one's interest in land or other property. POSSESSIONS, PROPERTY *esp:* a person's property in land and tenements."

Judgment affirmed.

NOTES AND PROBLEMS

1. In In re Estate of Muder, 159 Ariz. 173, 765 P.2d 997 (1988), the court had before it a will handwritten on a printed will form, signed and notarized but not witnessed. The relevant handwritten dispositive language, inserted in a printed paragraph saying "I give to," read:

> My wife Retha F. Muder, our home and property in Shumway, Navajo County, car — pick up, travel trailer, and all other earthly possessions belonging to me, livestock, cattle, sheep, etc. Tools, savings accounts, checking accounts, retirement benefits, etc.

The court, 3 to 2, upheld the will as a holograph. "Such handwritten provisions may draw testamentary context from both the printed and the handwritten language on the form. We see no need to ignore the preprinted words when the testator clearly did not, and the statute does not require us to do so." The majority opinion cited but did not discuss, approve, or disapprove In re Estate of Johnson. But cf. In re Estate of Foxley, 254 Neb. 204, 575 N.W.2d 150 (1998) (holding that words handwritten on photocopy of will — "her share to be divided between 5 daughters," written next to typewritten name of daughter who predeceased testator, and signed by testator — could not be probated as holograph because handwritten words made no sense as a will without reference to the typed words); In re Estate of Sola, 225 Cal. App. 3d 241, 275 Cal. Rptr. 98 (1990) (handwritten words on formal attested will are meaningless without reference to words of will).

Uniform Probate Code §2-502(c) (1990), supra page 227, provides that testamentary intent can be established for a holographic will by looking at portions of the document that are not in the testator's handwriting. The official comment (rewritten in 1990) says that holographs may be written on a printed will form if the material portions of the document are handwritten. See also Restatement (Third) of Property, Wills and Other Donative Transfers, §3.2, Comment, Illustration 4 (1999).

Correction of harmless error provided in UPC §2-503, supra page 252, applies to holographic wills as well as to attested wills.

2. *Statutory form wills.* Perceiving a public demand for a legally valid do-it-yourself will that can be written on a printed form available at stationery stores, several states have authorized simple statutory "fill-in-the-form wills." These are short wills, with the wording spelled out in a statute. The will provides spaces for the testator to fill in the names of the beneficiaries. A jurisdiction may have several forms of statutory wills — one to leave everything to a spouse; another to leave everything in trust for the spouse for life, remainder to the children; and still another to leave property in trust for children until they reach majority. See, e.g., Cal. Prob. Code §6240 (1998); Mich. Stat. Ann. §27.5123(3) (1997).

Statutory wills must be signed and attested in the same manner as any attested will. A large number of statutory fill-in wills fail in probate because they are improperly completed or executed. See Gerry W. Beyer, Statutory Fill-in Will Forms, 72 Or. L. Rev. 769 (1993); Herbert T. Krimmel, A Criticism of the California Statutory Will, 19 W. State U. L. Rev. 77 (1991). See also Uniform Statutory Will Act (1984).

3. In Estate of Wong, 40 Cal. App. 4th 1198, 47 Cal. Rptr. 2d 707 (1995), the following handwritten document was offered for probate:

All Tai-Kin Wong's → Xi Zhao, my best half

/s/ TKW
_____
12/31/92

Tai-Kin Wong was a 44-year-old bachelor, and Xi Zhao was his girl-friend with whom he had lived for three years. The document was found in a sealed envelope in Wong's office, to which rainbow stickers reading "You're Special" and "Love You" had been added. The court denied probate because the document did not refer to any property of Tai-Kin Wong, and did not contain a word indicating a gift. The arrow was deemed not a word but a symbol of no fixed meaning.

Wong died suddenly late on New Year's Eve, 1992, the day the document was signed. The court made much of the fact that Xi Zhao was that very evening dining at a fancy French restaurant with a man she moved in with two and one-half months later, a rendezvous she had concealed from Wong. Just des(s)ert?

4.   A few months after the death of her husband in March 1984, Esther Smith delivered to Harry Fass, her 84-year-old attorney, a writing that read:

> My entire estate is to be left *jointly* to my step-daughter, Roberta Crowley, and my step-son, David J. Smith.
>
> _/s/ Esther L. Smith_
> _____

According to the attorney's testimony, when Mrs. Smith handed him the writing, which was on a 5 × 7 piece of paper torn from a note-book, she said, "this is my will, this is the way I want my estate to go." The attorney, however, did not treat the paper as a will. He did not put the paper in his safe. He stapled the paper to the probate file of her husband. He wrote on the paper, "Extor-David," meaning David was to be the executor. In September 1984, the attorney wrote Mrs. Smith that he was retiring: "Your file and/or Last Will and Testament in my office is at your disposal if you do not care to retain [the attorney to whom he was transferring his practice]."

Mrs. Smith died in October 1984. Her heirs are her first cousins. Is the paper entitled to probate? In re Will of Smith, 108 N.J. 257, 528 A.2d 918 (1987) (denying probate).

Was Fass's delay in executing Esther Smith's estate plan malpractice? See White v. Jones, [1995] 1 All E.R. 691, 2 W.L.R. 187 (House of Lords) (holding solicitor liable to intended will beneficiaries where solicitor instructed to prepare a new will is negligent in delaying its preparation and securing the client's signature). Compare Krawczyk v. Stingle, 208 Conn. 239, 543 A.2d 733 (1988) (week's delay in preparing a revocable trust not malpractice; "[i]mposition of liability would create an incentive for an attorney to exert pressure on a client to complete and execute estate planning documents summarily."). See also Radovich v. Locke-Paddon, 35 Cal. App. 4th 946, 41 Cal. Rptr. 573 (1995) (holding lawyer had no duty to beneficiaries of will drafted and presented to client, who died two months later of breast cancer without signing it).

Should the document Esther Smith handed to Harry Fass be probated as her will under UPC §2-503?

Kimmel's Estate
Supreme Court of Pennsylvania, 1924
278 Pa. 435, 123 A. 405

SIMPSON, J. One of decedent's heirs at law appeals from a decree of the orphans' court, directing the register of wills to probate the following letter:

Johnstown, Dec. 12.
The Kimmel Bro. and Famly

We are all well as you can espec fore the time of the Year. I received you kind & welcome letter from Geo & Irvin all OK glad you poot your Pork down in Pickle it is the true way to keep meet every piece gets the same, now always poot it down that way & you will not miss it & you will have good pork fore smoking you can keep it from butchern to butchern the hole year round. Boys, I wont agree with you about the open winter I think we are gone to have one of the hardest. Plenty of snow & Verry cold verry cold! I dont want to see it this way but it will come see to the old sow & take her away when the time comes well I cant say if I will come over yet. I will wright in my next letter it may be to ruff we will see in the next letter if I come I have some very valuable papers I want you to keep fore me so if enny thing hapens all the scock money in the 3 Bank liberty lones Post office stamps and my home on Horner St goes to George Darl & Irvin Kepp this letter lock it up it may help you out. Earl sent after his Christmas Tree & Trimmings I sent them he is in the Post office in Phila working.

> Will clost your Truly,
> Father.

This letter was mailed by decedent at Johnstown, Pa., on the morning of its date — Monday, December 12, 1921 — to two of his children, George and Irvin, who were named in it as beneficiaries; the envelope being addressed to them at their residence in Glencoe, Pa. He died suddenly on the afternoon of the same day.

Two questions are raised: First. Is the paper testamentary in character? Second. Is the signature to it a sufficient compliance with our Wills Act? Before answering them directly, there are a few principles, now well settled, which, perhaps, should be preliminarily stated.

While the informal character of a paper is an element in determining whether or not it was intended to be testamentary (Kisecker's Estate, 190 Pa. 476), this becomes a matter of no moment when it appears thereby that the decedent's purpose was to make a posthumous gift. On this point the court below well said: "Deeds, mortgages, letters, powers of attorney, agreements, checks, notes, etc., have all been held to be, in legal effect, wills. Hence, an assignment (Coulter v. Shelmadine, 204 Pa. 120, . . . a deed (Turner v. Scott, 51 Pa. 126), a letter of instructions (Scott's Estate, 147 Pa. 89), a power of attorney (Rose v. Quick, 30 Pa. 225), and an informal letter of requests (Knox's Estate, 131 Pa. 220), were all held as wills."

It is equally clear that where, as here, the words "if enny thing hapens," condition the gift, they strongly support the idea of a testamentary intent; indeed they exactly state what is expressed in or must be implied from every will. True, if the particular contingency stated in a paper, as the condition upon which it shall become effective, has never in fact occurred, it will not be admitted to probate. Morrow's Appeal, 116 Pa. 440; Forquer's Estate, 216 Pa. 331. In the present case, however, it is clear the contingency, "if enny thing hapens," was still existing when testator died suddenly on the same day he wrote and mailed the letter; hence, the facts not being disputed, the question of testamentary intent was one of law for the court. Davis' Estate, 275 Pa. 126.

As is often the case in holographic wills of an informal character, much of that which is written is not dispositive; and the difficulty, in ascertaining the writer's intent, arises largely from the fact that he had little, if any, knowledge of either law, punctuation, or grammar. In the present case this is apparent from the paper itself; and in this light the language now quoted must be construed:

> I think we are gone to have one of the hardest [winters]. Plenty of snow & Verry cold verry cold! I dont want to see it this way but it will come . . . well I cant say if I will come over yet. I will wright in my next letter it may be to ruff we will see in the next letter if I come I have some very valuable papers I want you to keep fore me so if enny thing hapens all . . . [the real and personal property specified] goes to George Darl and Irvin Kepp this letter lock it up it may help you out.

When resolved into plainer English, it is clear to us that all of the quotation, preceding the words "I have some very valuable papers," relate to the predicted bad weather, a doubt as to whether decedent will be able to go to Glencoe because of it, and a possible resolution of it in his next letter; the present one stating "we will see in the next letter if I come." This being so, the clause relating to the valuable papers begins a new subject of thought, and since the clearly dispositive gifts which follow are made dependent on no other contingency than "if enny thing hapens," and death did happen suddenly on the same day, the paper, so far as respects those gifts, must be treated as testamentary.

It is difficult to understand how the decedent, probably expecting an early demise — as appears by the letter itself, and the fact of his sickness and inability to work, during the last three days of the first or second week preceding — could have possibly meant anything else than a testamentary gift, when he said "so if enny thing hapens [the property specified] goes to George Darl and Irvin"; and why, if this was not intended to be effective in and of itself, he should have sent it to two of the distributees named in it, telling them to "Kepp this letter lock it up it may help you out."

The second question to be determined . . . Does the word "Father," when taken in connection with the contents of the paper, show that it was "signed by him?" . . . If the word "Father" was intended as a completed signature to this particular character of paper, it answers all the purposes of the Wills Act. That it was so intended we have no doubt. It was the method employed by decedent in signing all such letters, and was mailed by him as a finished document.

. . . True, a formal will would not be so executed; but this is not a formal will. It is a letter, signed by him in the way he executed all such letters, and, from this circumstance, his "intent to execute is apparent" beyond all question.

Decree affirmed and appeal dismissed, the costs in this court to be paid by the estate of Harry A. Kimmel, deceased.

NOTES

1. In Kimmel's Estate, the will was upon the condition, "if enny thing hapens," meaning "if I die." Suppose the will is written to become operative if death from a stated event occurs, such as death from a surgical operation or death while on a journey. Does the testator want the will to be effective *only* if the event happens *or* to be effective at the testator's death regardless of whether his death is related to the event?

In Eaton v. Brown, 193 U.S. 411 (1904), the testator wrote a holographic will saying: "I am going on a journey and may not return. If I do not, I leave everything to my adopted son." The testator returned from her journey and died some months later. The Supreme Court, per Holmes, J., ordered the will probated. "Obviously the first sen-

Aug 10 1948

NOTICE

Will-of-W.J. Burns-USN-Vetern
Every-thing-I-posses-at-time-of-death
I will-to-my-son-T.E. Burns-615 S. ——————— Ave.
Yakima-Wn.

(s) W.J. Burns [photograph]

Holographic will to testator's son written on bottom of chest of drawers, sawed out and admitted to probate in Los Angeles County.

tence, 'I am going on a journey and may not ever return,' expresses the fact which was on her mind as the occasion and inducement for writing it. . . . She was thinking of the possibility of death or she would not have made a will. But that possibility at that moment took the specific shape of not returning from her journey, and so she wrote 'if I do not return,' before giving her last commands." Id. at 414.

Most of the cases on conditional wills are in accord with Eaton v. Brown. They presume the language of condition does not mean the will is to be probated only if the stated event happens but is, instead, merely a statement of the inducement for execution of the will, which can be probated upon death from any cause. See Succession of Montero, 365 So. 2d 929 (La. 1978) (testator, about to go into surgery for a serious operation, wrote "in the event I do not come out of this OK" my estate is to go to three persons); Mason v. Mason, 268 S.E.2d 67 (W. Va. 1980) ("I am in the hospital for surgery, and in case I do not survive everything belongs to Mervin").

2. Purported holographic wills have taken myriad forms — and

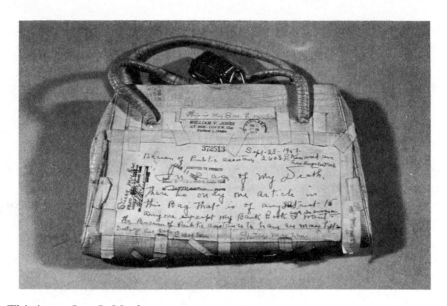

This is my Son S. Meehan
[printed name and address]

Sept-23-1953

Bureau of Public Assistance 2603 S. Kenwood Ave.
Los Angeles 7 Cal.

In case of my Death, there is only one article in this Bag that is of any Interest to anyone except my Bank Book and Insurance. I want the Bureau of Public Assistance to have any money Left. Destroy all papers.

(s) Stella Meehan

Holographic will written on bag, admitted to probate in Los Angeles County.

shapes. Wills have been written on a nurse's petticoat, inscribed on an eggshell, and scratched on a tractor fender. If you are interested in this sort of thing, there is a lot of humor and human interest to be found in Virgil M. Harris, Ancient, Curious and Famous Wills (1911, reprint 1981); Robert S. Menchin, The Last Caprice (1963); Elmer Million, Wills: Witty, Witless, and Wicked, 7 Wayne L. Rev. 335 (1960). We offer a more recent addition to the list, a note to a belly dancer, reported in the Austin (Texas) American-Statesman, October 15, 1968.

Unusual Will Names Dancer

PHILADELPHIA (AP) — A note to a belly dancer scribbled on a bedroom wall was offered Tuesday as a legal last will and testament. An 18-

inch square section of the plaster wall was sawed out under the supervision of Register of Wills John E. Walsh and submitted to Probate Court.

The note, signed by Hermann Schmidt, 49, who died Sept. 15, said in part:

"Genevieve: You take care of all my belongings. This give's you authority. Love, Hermann, 8-14-1968."

Attorney Leio T. Connor said he believes this entitles Genevieve — Genevieve Decker, 42, a belly dancer and Schmidt's fiancee — to Schmidt's $12,000 estate and plans to file it for this purpose.

Would you be as confident as attorney Connor that the piece of plaster is entitled to probate? That Genevieve takes all of Hermann's estate if it is admitted to probate? Compare In re Estate of Gasparovich, 487 P.2d 1148 (Mont. 1971).

SECTION B.   REVOCATION OF WILLS

1.   *Revocation by Writing or Physical Act*

A will is an ambulatory document, which means that it is subject to modification or revocation by the testator during his or her lifetime. All states permit revocation of a will in one of two ways: (1) by a subsequent *writing* executed with testamentary formalities,[20] or (2) by a *physical act* such as destroying, obliterating, or burning the will. On the assumption that oral revocations would open the door wide for fraud, an oral declaration that a will is revoked, without more, is inoperative in all states. *If a duly executed will is not revoked in a manner permitted by statute, the will is admitted to probate.*

The Uniform Probate Code's revocation section is fairly representative of statutes setting forth methods of permissible revocation.

Uniform Probate Code (1990)

§2-507.   REVOCATION BY WRITING OR BY ACT

(a) A will or any part thereof is revoked:

(1) by executing a subsequent will that revokes the previous will or part expressly or by inconsistency; or

---

20. Uniform Probate Code §1-201(56) (1990) defines a *will* to include a codicil and any testamentary instrument that merely appoints an executor or revokes or revises another will.

In states recognizing holographic wills, a holograph can revoke a typewritten, attested will.

(2) by performing a revocatory act on the will, if the testator performed the act with the intent and for the purpose of revoking the will or part or if another individual performed the act in the testator's conscious presence and by the testator's direction. For purposes of this paragraph, "revocatory act on the will" includes burning, tearing, canceling, obliterating, or destroying the will or any part of it. A burning, tearing, or canceling is a "revocatory act on the will," whether or not the burn, tear, or cancellation touched any of the words on the will.

PROBLEM: REVOCATION BY INCONSISTENCY

A subsequent will wholly revokes the previous will by inconsistency if the testator intends the subsequent will to replace rather than supplement the previous will. A subsequent will that does not expressly revoke the prior will but makes a complete disposition of the testator's estate is presumed to replace the prior will and revoke it by inconsistency. If the subsequent will does not make a complete disposition of the testator's estate, it is not presumed to revoke the prior will but is viewed as a codicil. A codicil supplements a will rather than replacing it. See Uniform Probate Code §2-507(b)-(d) (1990); Restatement (Second) of Property, Donative Transfers §34.2, Comment b (1992).

In 1995, *T* executes a will that gives all her property to *A*. In 1997 *T* executes a will that gives her diamond ring to *B* and her car to *C*. It contains no words of revocation. Even though the 1997 will makes no reference to the earlier will, the 1997 will is ordinarily called a codicil.

(a) In 1999 *T* destroys the codicil with the intention of revoking it; *T* dies in 2000. The 1995 will is offered for probate. Should it be admitted? See In re Estate of Hering, 108 Cal. App. 3d 88, 166 Cal. Rptr. 298 (1980).

(b) Suppose, instead, that *T* destroys the 1995 will with the intention of revoking it. After *T*'s death the codicil is offered for probate. Should it be admitted? See Comment, Wills — Revocation by Act to the Document — Effect on Codicil, 60 Mich. L. Rev. 82 (1961).

See Robert Whitman, Revocation and Revival: An Analysis of the 1990 Revision of the Uniform Probate Code and Suggestions for the Future, 55 Alb. L. Rev. 1035 (1992).

Harrison v. Bird
Supreme Court of Alabama, 1993
621 So. 2d 972

HOUSTON, J.   The proponent of a will appeals from a judgment of the Circuit Court of Montgomery County holding that the estate of

Daisy Virginia Speer, deceased, should be administered as an intestate estate and confirming the letters of administration granted by the probate court to Mae S. Bird.

The following pertinent facts are undisputed:

Daisy Virginia Speer executed a will in November 1989, in which she named Katherine Crapps Harrison as the main beneficiary of her estate. The original of the will was retained by Ms. Speer's attorney and a duplicate original was given to Ms. Harrison. On March 4, 1991, Ms. Speer telephoned her attorney and advised him that she wanted to revoke her will. Thereafter, Ms. Speer's attorney or his secretary, in the presence of each other, tore the will into four pieces. The attorney then wrote Ms. Speer a letter, informing her that he had "revoked" her will as she had instructed and that he was enclosing the pieces of the will so that she could verify that he had torn up the original. In the letter, the attorney specifically stated, "As it now stands, you are without a will."

Ms. Speer died on September 3, 1991. Upon her death, the postmarked letter from her attorney was found among her personal effects, but the four pieces of the will were not found. Thereafter, on September 17, 1991, the Probate Court of Montgomery County granted letters of administration on the estate of Ms. Speer, to Mae S. Bird, a cousin of Ms. Speer. On October 11, 1991, Ms. Harrison filed for probate a document purporting to be the last will and testament of Ms. Speer and naming Ms. Harrison as executrix. . . .

Thereafter, the circuit court ruled (1) that Ms. Speer's will was not lawfully revoked when it was destroyed by her attorney at her direction and with her consent, but not in her presence, see Ala. Code 1975, §43-8-136(b); (2) that there could be no ratification of the destruction of Ms. Speer's will, which was not accomplished pursuant to the strict requirements of §43-8-136(b); and (3) that, based on the fact that the pieces of the destroyed will were delivered to Ms. Speer's home but were not found after her death, there arose a presumption that Ms. Speer thereafter revoked the will herself.

. . . [F]inding that the presumption in favor of revocation of Ms. Speer's will had not been rebutted and therefore that the duplicate original will offered for probate by Ms. Harrison was not the last will and testament of Daisy Virginia Speer, the circuit court held that the estate should be administered as an intestate estate and confirmed the letters of administration issued by the probate court to Ms. Bird.

If the evidence establishes that Ms. Speer had possession of the will before her death, but the will is not found among her personal effects after her death, a presumption arises that she destroyed the will. See Barksdale v. Pendergrass, 294 Ala. 526, 319 So. 2d 267 (1975). Furthermore, if she destroys the copy of the will in her possession, a presumption arises that she has revoked her will and all duplicates, even though a duplicate exists that is not in her possession. See Stiles v. Brown, 380 So. 2d 792 (Ala. 1980); see, also, Snider v. Burks, 84 Ala. 53, 4 So. 225 (1887). However, this presumption of revocation is rebuttable and the burden of rebutting the presumption is on the proponent of the will. See *Barksdale,* supra.

Based on the foregoing, we conclude that under the facts of this case there existed a presumption that Ms. Speer destroyed her will and thus revoked it. Therefore, the burden shifted to Ms. Harrison to present sufficient evidence to rebut that presumption — to present sufficient evidence to convince the trier of fact that the absence of the will from Ms. Speer's personal effects after her death was not due to Ms. Speer's destroying and thus revoking the will. See Stiles v. Brown, supra.

From a careful review of the record, we conclude, as did the trial court, that the evidence presented by Ms. Harrison was not sufficient to rebut the presumption that Ms. Speer destroyed her will with the intent to revoke it. We, therefore, affirm the trial court's judgment.

We note Ms. Harrison's argument that under the particular facts of this case, because Ms. Speer's attorney destroyed the will outside of Ms. Speer's presence, "[t]he fact that Ms. Speer may have had possession of the pieces of her will and that such pieces were not found upon her death is not sufficient to invoke the presumption [of revocation] imposed by the trial court." We find that argument to be without merit.

AFFIRMED.

PROBLEMS

1. In Harrison v. Bird, had the torn four pieces of the testator's will been found at her death, would her attorney be liable for malpractice? See Comment, Estate Planning Malpractice: A Guide for the Alabama Practitioner, 45 Ala. L. Rev. 611 (1994).

2. Suppose that the testator's lawyer sends her home with the only executed copy of the testator's will. The will leaves all her property to *A.* After the testator's death, her heir goes in her house looking for her will. The heir reports that she couldn't find a will, and no will is found. What result? See Estate of Travers, 121 Ariz. 282, 589 P.2d 1314 (1978) (opportunity of disinherited heir to destroy will does not rebut presumption of revocation); Lonergan v. Estate of Budahazi, 669 So. 2d 1062 (Fla. App. 1996) (presumption of revocation of lost will disinheriting husband rebutted where husband lived in house with wife and the couple had been fighting before she died); Annots., 70 A.L.R.4th 323 (1989), 84 A.L.R.4th 531 (1991).

NOTE: PROBATE OF LOST WILLS

In the absence of statute, a will that is lost, or is destroyed without the consent of the testator, or is destroyed with the consent of the testator but not in compliance with the revocation statute can be admitted into probate if its contents are proved. A lost will can be proved by a copy in the lawyer-drafter's office or by a secretary who typed the will or by other clear and convincing evidence.

In a few states statutes prohibit the probate of a lost or destroyed will unless the will was "in existence" at the testator's death (and destroyed thereafter) or was "fraudulently destroyed" during the testator's life. Theoretically, under such a statute a will accidentally tossed out by a housekeeper during the testator's life cannot be probated. Thus, on its face, such a statute is in conflict with the state's will revocation statute, since under it a will not legally revoked is nevertheless barred from probate. Courts have chosen to give effect to the will revocation statutes and have gutted the proof statutes by holding *either* that a will not lawfully revoked continues in "legal existence" until the testator's death (and the word "existence" in the statute means "legal existence") *or* that a will destroyed by a method not permitted by the will revocation statute has been "fraudulently destroyed." See Estate of Irvine v. Doyle, 710 P.2d 1366 (Nev. 1985). Compare Sheridan v. Harbison, 101 Ohio App. 3d 206, 655 N.E.2d 256 (1995) (peculiar statute forbidding probate if will lost or destroyed prior to testator's death with the knowledge of the testator).

Thompson v. Royall
Supreme Court of Virginia, 1934
163 Va. 492, 175 S.E. 748

HUDGINS, J.   The only question presented by this record is whether the will of Mrs. M. Lou Bowen Kroll had been revoked shortly before her death.

The uncontroverted facts are as follows: On the 4th day of September, 1932, Mrs. Kroll signed a will, typewritten on the five sheets of legal cap paper; the signature appeared on the last page duly attested by three subscribing witnesses. H. P. Brittain, the executor named in the will, was given possession of the instrument for safe-keeping. A codicil typed on the top third of one sheet of paper dated September 15, 1932, was signed by the testatrix in the presence of two subscribing witnesses. Possession of this instrument was given to Judge S. M. B. Coulling, the attorney who prepared both documents.

On September 19, 1932, at the request of Mrs. Kroll, Judge Coulling and Mr. Brittain took the will and the codicil to her home where she told her attorney, in the presence of Mr. Brittain and another, to destroy both. But, instead of destroying the papers, at the suggestion of Judge Coulling, she decided to retain them as memoranda, to be used as such in the event she decided to execute a new will. Upon the back of the manuscript cover, which was fastened to the five sheets by metal clasps, in the handwriting of Judge Coulling, signed by Mrs. Kroll, there is the following notation:

> This will null and void and to be only held by H.P. Brittain instead of being destroyed as a memorandum for another will if I desire to make same. This 19 Sept. 1932.

> *M. Lou Bowen Kroll*

The same notation was made upon the back of the sheet on which the codicil was written, except that the name S. M. B. Coulling was substituted for H. P. Brittain; this was likewise signed by Mrs. Kroll.

Mrs. Kroll died October 2, 1932, leaving numerous nephews and nieces, some of whom were not mentioned in her will, and an estate valued at approximately $200,000. On motion of some of the beneficiaries, the will and codicil were offered for probate. All the interested parties including the heirs at law were convened, and on the issue devisavit vel non the jury found that the instruments dated September 4 and 15, 1932, were the last will and testament of Mrs. M. Lou Bowen Kroll. From an order sustaining the verdict and probating the will this writ of error was allowed.

For more than 100 years, the means by which a duly executed will may be revoked have been prescribed by statute. These requirements are found in section 5233 of the 1919 Code, the pertinent parts of which read thus:

> No will or codicil, or any part thereof, shall be revoked, unless . . . by a subsequent will or codicil, or by some writing declaring an intention to revoke the same, and executed in the manner in which a will is required to be executed, or by the testator, or some person in his presence and by his direction, cutting, tearing, burning, obliterating, canceling, or destroying the same, or the signature thereto, with the intent to revoke.

The notations, dated September 19, 1932, are not wholly in the handwriting of the testatrix, nor are her signatures thereto attached attested by subscribing witnesses; hence under the statute they are ineffectual as "some writing declaring an intention to revoke." The faces of the two instruments bear no physical evidence of any cutting, tearing, burning, obliterating, canceling, or destroying. The only contention made by appellants is that the notation written in the pres-

ence, and with the approval, of Mrs. Kroll, on the back of the manuscript cover in the one instance, and on the back of the sheet containing the codicil in the other, constitute "canceling" within the
meaning of the statute.

Both parties concede that to effect revocation of a duly executed
will, in any of the methods prescribed by statute, two things are necessary: (1) The doing of one of the acts specified, (2) accompanied by
the intent to revoke — the animo revocandi. Proof of either, without
proof of the other, is insufficient. Malone v. Hobbs, 1 Rob. (40 Va.)
346, 39 Am. Dec. 263; 2 Minor Ins. 925. The proof established the
intention to revoke. The entire controversy is confined to the acts
used in carrying out that purpose. The testatrix adopted the suggestion of her attorney to revoke her will by written memoranda, admittedly ineffectual as revocations by subsequent writings, but appellants
contend the memoranda, in the handwriting of another, and testatrix'
signatures, are sufficient to effect revocation by cancellation. To support this contention, appellants cite a number of authorities which
hold that the modern definition of cancellation includes "any act
which would destroy, revoke, recall, do away with, overrule, render
null and void, the instrument."

Most of the authorities cited that approve the above or a similar
meaning of the word were dealing with cancellation of simple contracts, or other instruments that require little or no formality in execution. However, there is one line of cases which apply this extended
meaning of "canceling" to the revocation of wills. The leading case
so holding is Warner v. Warner's Estate, 37 Vt. 356. In this case proof
of the intent and the act were a notation on the same page with, and
below the signature of, the testator, reading: "This will is hereby
cancelled and annulled. In full this 15th day of March in the year
1859," and written lengthwise on the back of the fourth page of the
foolscap paper, upon which no part of the written will appeared, were
these words, "Cancelled and is null and void. (Signed) I. Warner."
It was held this was sufficient to revoke the will under a statute similar
to the one here under consideration.

In Evans' Appeal, 58 Pa. 238, the Pennsylvania court approved the
reasoning of the Vermont court in Warner v. Warner's Estate, supra,
but the force of the opinion is weakened when the facts are considered. It seems that there were lines drawn through two of the three
signatures of the testator appearing in the Evans will, and the paper
on which material parts of the will were written was torn in four
places. It therefore appeared on the face of the instrument, when
offered for probate, that there was a sufficient defacement to bring it
within the meaning of both obliteration and cancellation. The construction of the statute in Warner v. Warner's Estate, supra, has been
criticized by eminent text-writers on wills, and the courts in the major-

ity of the states in construing similar statutes have refused to follow the reasoning in that case. Jarman on Wills (6th Ed.) 147, note 1; Schouler on Wills (5th Ed.) §391; Redfield on the Law of Wills (4th Ed.) 323-325; 28 R.C.L. 180; 40 Cyc. 1173; Dowling v. Gilliland, 286 Ill. 530, 122 N.E. 70, 3 A.L.R. 839. . . .

The above, and other authorities that might be cited, hold that revocation of a will by cancellation within the meaning of the statute contemplates marks or lines across the written parts of the instrument or a physical defacement, or some mutilation of the writing itself, with the intent to revoke. If written words are used for the purpose, they must be so placed as to physically affect the written portion of the will, not merely on blank parts of the paper on which the will is written. If the writing intended to be the act of canceling does not mutilate, or erase, or deface, or otherwise physically come in contact with, any part of written words of the will, it cannot be given any greater weight than a similar writing on a separate sheet of paper, which identifies the will referred to, just as definitely as does the writing on the back. If a will may be revoked by writing on the back, separable from the will, it may be done by a writing not on the will. This the statute forbids. . . .

The attempted revocation is ineffectual, because testatrix intended to revoke her will by subsequent writings not executed as required by statute, and because it does not in any wise physically obliterate, mutilate, deface, or cancel any written parts of the will.

For the reasons stated, the judgment of the trial court is affirmed.

QUESTIONS AND PROBLEMS

1. If the facts in Thompson v. Royall had occurred in 2001, would Judge Coulling be liable to Mrs. Kroll's heirs for malpractice? Although no one sued for legal malpractice in the 1930s, we have been told by Judge Coulling's grandson that for the rest of his life Judge Coulling suffered greatly from shame and loss of reputation in his community because of the probate of Mrs. Kroll's unrevoked will.

2. What policy is served by the court's decision in the *Thompson* case? Given the clear and uncontroverted evidence of Mrs. Kroll's intention that her will be revoked, how can the court's decision be justified?

Uniform Probate Code §2-507, supra page 276, would change the result in Thompson v. Royall. It provides: "A burning, tearing, or canceling is a 'revocatory act on the will,' whether or not the burn, tear, or cancellation touched any of the words on the will." Words of cancellation must, however, be written on the will, whether or not they touch the words of the will. They cannot be written on another document.

3. Suppose that Mrs. Kroll's will had attached to it a self-proving affidavit and that the notation signed by Mrs. Kroll had been written across the self-proving affidavit. Has the cancellation touched any words of the will? See In re Estate of Dickson, 590 So. 2d 471 (Fla. App. 1991).

4. Suppose that Mrs. Kroll had written, on the left-hand margin of each page of the will, "Cancelled. 19/9/32. M. Kroll." Would this be a valid revocation by physical act? See Kronauge v. Stoecklein, 33 Ohio App. 2d 229, 293 N.E.2d 320 (1972). Would this be a valid revocation in states permitting holographic wills? See McCarthy v. Bank of California, 64 Or. App. 473, 668 P.2d 481 (1983) (valid holographic revocation); but cf. In re Estate of Johnson, supra page 264, dealing with *execution* of holographic will.

5. Suppose that the testator writes "VOID" across the face of an unexecuted Xerox copy of his will. Is this a valid revocation by physical act? In In re Estate of Tolin, 622 So. 2d 988 (Fla. 1993), the testator showed a bluebacked Xerox copy of a codicil to his will to a friend, a retired lawyer, telling the friend he wanted to revoke the codicil. The friend, mistaking the Xerox copy for the original, told him he could revoke the codicil by tearing up the document. The testator did so. After the testator died, the lawyer who drafted his will and codicil produced the original copies. The court held that revocation of a copy is not a valid revocation. However, because of the testator's mistake of fact, believing he was destroying the original, the court imposed a constructive trust on the codicil beneficiary for the benefit of the will beneficiary. Is this an application of the substantial compliance doctrine to the revocation of wills in the guise of a constructive trust to prevent unjust enrichment? Or is it another step toward correcting mistakes in execution and revocation of wills?

Partial Revocation by Physical Act. Although UPC §2-507 and the statutes of many states authorize partial revocation by physical act, in several states a will cannot be revoked in part by an *act* of revocation; it can be revoked in part only by a subsequent instrument. The reasons for prohibiting partial revocation by physical act are two. First, cancelling a gift to one person necessarily results in someone else taking the gift, and this "new gift" — like all bequests — can be made only by an attested writing. Second, permitting partial revocation by physical act offers opportunity for fraud. The person who takes the "new gift" may be the one who made the cancelling marks. If partial revocation by act is not recognized, the will must be admitted to probate in the form in which it was originally executed if the original language can be ascertained.

PROBLEM

T executes a will that devises the residue of her estate to four named relatives. After *T*'s death some years later, her will is found in a stack of papers on her desk. One of the four names in the residuary clause has been lined out with a No. 3 lead pencil. There is no direct evidence that *T* marked out the name.

(a) What result in a state having a statute similar to Uniform Probate Code §2-507? See In re Byrne's Will, 223 Wis. 503, 271 N.W. 48 (1937). Compare In re Estate of Funk, 654 N.E.2d 1174 (Ind. App. 1995).

In In re Estate of Malloy, 134 Wash. 2d 316, 949 P.2d 804 (1997), the court discussed the fundamental inconsistency between allowing partial revocation by physical acts and requiring bequests to be attested, and held that partial revocation by physical act would not be permitted where the intent and effect of the change would result in a substantial enhancement of another bequest. A few cases have held that the testator can revoke a complete devise ("my car to *A*"), but cannot rearrange the shares in a single devise to increase the other devisee's gift. Example: "$10,000 to *A* and *B*, residue to *C*." *T* later lines out *B*'s name. *A*'s gift cannot be increased this way. The $5,000 given to *B* falls into the residuary and goes to *C*.

Restatement (Third) of Property, Wills and Other Donative Transfers, §4.1, Comment i (1999), disapproves of the *Malloy* approach and these other cases limiting partial revocation. "The distinction between revocation of a complete devise and rearranging the shares within a single devise or otherwise to rewrite the terms of the will by deleting selected words is disapproved. It is a classic example of a distinction without a difference. It is not supported by the language of the statutes authorizing partial revocation by act. . . . The legislature not only granted broad approval of deleting words but of the natural consequence of doing so — giving effect to the will as if the deleted words were not present."

(b) What result in a state that does not permit partial revocation by physical act? See Hansel v. Head, 706 So. 2d 1142 (Ala. 1997) (name obliterated with correction fluid); In re Estate of Haurin, 605 P.2d 65 (Colo. App. 1979).

(c) Suppose that *T*'s will is a holographic will in a jurisdiction permitting holographic wills. What result? See La Rue v. Lee, 63 W. Va. 388, 60 S.E. 388 (1908).

2. Dependent Relative Revocation and Revival

Simply put, the doctrine of dependent relative revocation is this: If the testator purports to revoke his will upon a mistaken assumption of law or fact, the revocation is ineffective if the testator would not have revoked his will had he known the truth. The usual case involves a situation where the testator destroys his will under a belief that a new will is valid but for some reason the new will is invalid. If the court finds that the testator would not have destroyed his will had he known the new will was ineffective, the court, applying the doctrine of dependent relative revocation, will cancel the revocation and probate the destroyed will. For example, suppose that *T* duly executes a will devising his property to "Peggy Martin." Thereafter *T* learns that the legal name of the intended devisee is "Margaret Martin," not "Peggy Martin," and *T* decides that this misdescription should be corrected. *T* therefore cancels his old will by writing "VOID" across it and executes a new will devising his property to "Margaret Martin." Unfortunately, Margaret Martin is one of the two witnesses to the new will, and, under the applicable state law, the devise to her is ineffective. Since it is clear that *T* wants Martin to take his property, the doctrine of dependent relative revocation is applied. The revocation of the first will is not given effect; the first will is probated and Margaret Martin (a.k.a. Peggy Martin) takes *T*'s property under that will. The doctrine is applied to carry out the testator's presumed intent. On dependent relative revocation generally, see George E. Palmer, Dependent Relative Revocation and Its Relation to Relief for Mistake, 69 Mich. L. Rev. 989 (1971). See also Kroll v. Nehmer, 348 Md. 616, 705 A.2d 716 (1998).

Carter v. First United Methodist Church of Albany
Supreme Court of Georgia, 1980
246 Ga. 352, 271 S.E.2d 493

NICHOLS, J.   The caveator, Luther Reynolds Carter, appeals from judgment entered in the superior court in behalf of the propounder, First United Methodist Church, admitting to probate, as the will of Mildred C. Tipton, an instrument bearing the date of August 21, 1963.

The 1963 instrument, typed and signed in the form of and purporting to be the last will and testament of Mildred C. Tipton, was found among Mrs. Tipton's other personal papers in her dining room chest after her death on February 14, 1979. It was folded together with a handwritten instrument dated May 22, 1978, captioned as her will but unsigned and unwitnessed, purporting to establish a different scheme of distribution of her property. Pencil marks had been made diagonally through the property disposition provisions of the 1963 document and through the name of one of the co-executors.

The superior court found that from time to time prior to her death, Mrs. Tipton had made it known to her attorney that she needed his services in order to change or revise her will, or to make a new will; that at one time she had written out some proposed changes on tablet paper to be suggested to her lawyer when he prepared a new will for her; and that she did not intend to revoke her will by scratching through some of its provisions and by writing out the proposed changes.

. . . The parties stipulated that the 1963 instrument offered for probate had been found among Mrs. Tipton's records and papers in a drawer of a chest in her dining room, and that the 1963 will was executed by Mrs. Tipton and attested by the witnesses to the will. . . .

The case was submitted to the trial court on stipulated facts, and under stipulation that the depositions of Mrs. Tipton's attorney and one of her friends, relating to her intentions, be admitted in evidence. There is no transcript, and the record is sparse as to facts. Each party seems to have felt that the burden of proof properly was to be placed upon the other party and, accordingly, neither made much effort to develop the facts. The issue resolves itself, however, if certain presumptions are placed into proper perspective with each other.

> As a general rule, the burden is on a person attacking a paper offered for probate as a will to sustain the grounds of his attack. But by express provision of our statute, where a will has been canceled or obliterated in a material part, a presumption of revocation arises, and the burden is on the propounder to show that no revocation was intended . . . Where the paper is found among the testator's effects, there is also a presumption that he made the cancellations or obliterations . . . It having been shown that the paper offered for probate in this case had been in the custody of the deceased up to the time of his death, the propounder was met with both of the presumptions above alluded to. McIntyre v. McIntyre, 120 Ga. 67, 70, 47 S.E. 501 (1904).

The deposition of Mrs. Tipton's attorney, introduced by stipulation in behalf of the propounder, establishes, without contradiction, that Mrs. Tipton had written out some changes in her will on tablet paper and repeatedly had attempted to get her attorney to change or to revise her will, or to make a new will. The parties stipulated that the two writings, the 1963 will and the 1978 manuscript, were found after her death among her personal effects. No evidence appears in the record, and no contention is made, that Mrs. Tipton did not make the marks on the 1963 will or write the 1978 instrument. The presumption that Mrs. Tipton made the pencil marks and wrote the memorandum of her intentions stands unrebutted. Langan v. Cheshire, 208 Ga. 107, 65 S.E.2d 415 (1951); Porch v. Farmer, 158 Ga. 55, 122 S.E. 557 (1924); Howard v. Hunter, 115 Ga. 357, 41 S.E. 638 (1902). The other presumption, that of absolute revocation, is the focal point of our remaining inquiry.

The statute to which McIntyre refers is Code Ann. §113-404, which provides, in part, that an intention to revoke will be presumed from the obliteration or canceling of a material portion of the will. . . . [T]he propounder contends that under the doctrine of dependent relative revocation, or conditional revocation, the facts proven give rise to a presumption in favor of the propounder (which the caveator failed to rebut) that Mrs. Tipton did not intend for her 1963 will to be revoked unless her new dispositions of her property became effective in law. . . .

The doctrine of dependent relative revocation (conditional revocation) has been stated by this court as follows:

> It is a doctrine of presumed intention, and has grown up as a result of an effort which courts always make to arrive at the real intention of the testator. . . . The doctrine, as we understand it and are willing to apply it, is this: The mere fact that the testator intended to make a new will, or made one which failed of effect, will not alone, in every case, prevent a cancellation or obliteration of a will from operating as a revocation. If it is clear that the cancellation and the making of the new will were parts of one scheme, and the revocation of the old will was so related to the making of the new as to be dependent upon it, then if the new will be not made, or if made is invalid, the old will, though canceled, should be given effect, if its contents can be ascertained in any legal way. But if the old will is once revoked, if the act of revocation is completed, as if the will be totally destroyed by burning and the like, or if any other act is done which evidences an unmistakable intention to revoke, though the will be not totally destroyed, the fact that the testator intended to make a new will, or made one which can not take effect, counts for nothing. In other words, evidence that the testator intended to make or did actually make a new will, which was inoperative, may throw light on the question of intention to revoke the old one, but it can never revive a will once completely revoked. McIntyre v. McIntyre, 120 Ga. 67, 71, 47 S.E. 501, 503 supra.

The doctrine has been recognized and applied by the highest courts of many states. Annos. 62 A.L.R. 1401, 115 A.L.R. 721. It has been the subject of considerable discussion by the text writers. 1 Redfearn, Wills and Administration in Georgia (4th Ed.), p. 188, §96; Chaffin, Studies in The Georgia Law of Decedent's Estates and Future Interests, pp. 184, 186.

Professor Chaffin is of the opinion that "*McIntyre* represents a sound approach to the doctrine of dependent relative revocation." He writes that in *McIntyre*, "The doctrine was correctly perceived to be a rule of presumed intention rather than a rule of substantive law. The court refused to set aside the revocation until evidence bearing on testator's intent, including his oral declarations, was examined in an effort to discern what he would have desired if he had been aware of the true facts." He also concludes, correctly, this court believes, that "Most courts have taken the position that dependent relative revocation is judged by a stricter standard in a situation involving revocation by subsequent instrument as opposed to physical act." He is strongly of the opinion that "if the purpose of the doctrine is to effect testator's intent, there is no point in distinguishing between revocation by physical act and by subsequent instrument." Chaffin, supra, pp. 186-187. This court agrees. In Georgia, the doctrine is one of presumed intention. The principle is the same whether the revocation is by physical act or by subsequent instrument. . . .

In the present case, the testatrix wrote the 1978 instrument which the parties have conceded (by the absence of their contentions) cannot be admitted to probate because it lacks some of the requisites of a will. The propounder says, in effect, if not in express words, that the testatrix would have preferred the property disposition clauses of the 1963 will over the only other alternative — intestacy. The caveator contends, in essence, that the testatrix would have preferred intestacy. How stands the record?

The fact that the old will, with pencil lines drawn by Mrs. Tipton through the property disposition provisions, was found among her personal papers folded together with the 1978 writing, that makes a somewhat different disposition of her property, is some evidence tending to establish that "the cancellation and the making of the new will were parts of one scheme, and the revocation of the old will was so related to the making of the new as to be dependent upon it." 120 Ga. at 71. This evidence was sufficient to rebut the statutory presumption of revocation (Code Ann. §113-404) and to give rise to a presumption in favor of the propounder under the doctrine of dependent relative revocation or conditional revocation. *McIntyre,* supra. The stipulation that these two instruments were found together thus shifted the burden of proof to the caveator to prove, in essence, that Mrs. Tipton would have preferred intestacy.

. . . The presumption against intestacy (or in favor of the continued validity of the 1963 will) stands unrebutted in the present case.

Accordingly, the trial court, as finder of the facts, did not err in admitting the will to probate.

Judgment affirmed.

PROBLEMS

1. Clause 5 of *T*'s typewritten will provides: "I bequeath the sum of $1,000 to my nephew, Charles Blake." *T* crosses out the "$1,000" and substitutes therefore "$1,500." *T* then writes her initials and the date in the right-hand margin opposite this entry. After *T*'s death some years later, her will is admitted to probate. Blake contends that he is entitled to $1,500 or, in the alternative, $1,000.

(a) What result in a state that recognizes holographic wills? See Estate of Phifer, 152 Cal. App. 3d 813, 200 Cal. Rptr. 319 (1984); but cf. McCarthy v. Bank of California, supra page 284; In re Estate of Muder, supra page 268.

(b) What result in a state that does not permit partial revocation by physical act?

(c) What result in a state that permits partial revocation by physical act? Should the doctrine of dependent relative revocation be applied? See Carpenter v. Wynn, 252 Ky. 543, 67 S.W.2d 688 (1934).

(d) Suppose that *T* had crossed out "$1,000" and substituted "$500." In a state that permits partial revocation by physical act, should the doctrine of dependent relative revocation be applied? See Ruel v. Hardy, 90 N.H. 240, 6 A.2d 753 (1939).

2. In his typewritten will, which contains a legacy of $5,000 to "John Boone," *T* crosses out "John" and writes in "Nancy." Nancy cannot take because the gift to her is not attested. In a state permitting partial revocation by physical act, should the legacy to John be given effect under the doctrine of dependent relative revocation? See In re Houghten's Estate, 310 Mich. 613, 17 N.W.2d 744 (1945); Estate of Lyles, 615 So. 2d 1186 (Miss. 1993).

In a state that recognizes holographic wills, the change from John to Nancy is not a valid holograph even though *T* signs his name on the margin. Standing alone, the handwritten words are insufficient to constitute a will. Estate of Phifer, supra. On the other hand, if *T*'s will were entirely handwritten and a valid holograph, the change from John to Nancy would be permitted. See Stanley v. Henderson, 139 Tex. 160, 162 S.W.2d 95 (1942); Estate of Archer, 193 Cal. App. 3d 238, 239 Cal. Rptr. 137 (1987).

3. In *Body Heat*, a steamy 1981 *film noir* set in Florida, Matty Walker (Kathleen Turner), a silky sexpot bent on doing away with her rich older husband, entraps a not-so-smart, randy young lawyer, Ned Racine (William Hurt), to do the dirty work. The husband's existing will leaves half his fortune to Matty and half to his 10-year-old niece, Heather. After the husband is done in by Ned, Matty — a sometime legal secretary — produces a second will, written by Matty on stationery stolen from Ned's office, to which she has forged the signatures of her husband and — to his astonishment — Ned as a witness. (The

second witness is — well, it takes too long to explain: You'll have to rent the videocassette.) This second will leaves half to Matty, but it puts Heather's half in a trust that violates the Rule against Perpetuities. At a family conference, the husband's lawyer, oozing unction at every pore, pronounces the second will void. As a result, the lawyer says, the husband died intestate, and under Florida law Matty takes her husband's entire estate. Little Heather and her mother meekly acquiesce and disappear from the movie. Matty ends up on an island paradise with all her husband's money and a new lover; the dupe Ned is left languishing in jail.

Before the movie was made, Florida had adopted wait-and-see for perpetuities violations (see infra page 836). Hence the husband's lawyer was too quick on the trigger; the trust for Heather might not turn out to be void. Apart from this oversight by the screenwriter, what other legal doctrine did the writer overlook that could have saved Heather's share? See In re Estate of Jones, 352 So. 2d 1182 (Fla. App. 1977). Though wills lawyers might grouse, these flaws seem not to have been noticed by the critics. The movie was boffo at the box office.

Courts have set limits on the dependent relative revocation doctrine. With rare exceptions, courts have held that DRR applies only (1) where there is an alternative plan of disposition that fails or (2) where the mistake is recited in the terms of the revoking instrument or, possibly, is established by clear and convincing evidence. The alternative plan of disposition is usually in the form of another will, either duly or defectively executed. By so limiting the doctrine, the kind of extrinsic evidence that can be looked at is narrowed.

NOTE AND PROBLEM

1.   Preparing to make a new will, *T* writes "VOID" across her duly executed will. Several days later she shows the defaced will to her lawyer and instructs the lawyer to prepare a new will. The lawyer prepares a draft of the new will, but when it is shown to *T*, *T* tells the lawyer that it wrongly describes some property and is wrong in some other ways and must be changed. Before the draft can be corrected and executed, *T* dies. The lawyer testifies who the beneficiaries were to be under the new will. Does dependent relative revocation apply so as to cancel the revocation of the earlier will? In In re Estate of Ausley, 818 P.2d 1226 (Okla. 1991), the court refused to apply depen-

dent relative revocation because the lawyer's testimony was insufficient evidence of a definite alternative plan of disposition.

2. *T*'s will bequeaths $5,000 to his old friend, Judy, and the residue of his estate to his brother Mark. *T* later executes a codicil as follows: "I revoke the legacy to Judy, since she is dead." In fact, Judy is still living and survives *T*. Does Judy take $5,000? In Campbell v. French, 3 Ves. Jr. 321, 30 Eng. Rep. 1033 (Ch. 1797), on similar facts, the court held that there was no revocation, "the cause being false."

Suppose that the codicil had read: "I revoke the legacy to Judy, since I have already given her $5,000." In fact, the testator did not give Judy $5,000 during life. What result? See Witt v. Rosen, 765 S.W.2d 956 (Ark. App. 1989).

Suppose that the codicil had read: "I revoke the legacy to Judy." Evidence is offered that shows that three weeks prior to execution of the codicil *T* was told by a friend that Judy had died, believing it to be true. In fact Judy survives *T*. What result? See In re Salmonski's Estate, 38 Cal. 2d 199, 238 P.2d 966 (1951) (holding DRR not applicable because mistake not recited on face of will); Estate of Anderson, 56 Cal. App. 4th 435, 65 Cal. Rptr. 2d 307 (1997) (DRR applicable when mistake inferable from dispositive instruments and supported by lawyer-drafter's testimony).

On dependent relative revocation, see generally Restatement (Third) of Property, Wills and Other Donative Transfers, §4.3 (1999) (renaming it the doctrine of ineffective revocation).

Estate of Alburn

Supreme Court of Wisconsin, 1963
18 Wis. 2d 340, 118 N.W.2d 919

Ottilie L. Alburn, a resident of the city of Fort Atkinson, Jefferson county, died on November 13, 1960, at the age of eighty-five years. On December 5, 1960, Adele Ruedisili, a sister of deceased, filed a petition for appointment of an administrator of the estate, which petition alleged that deceased died intestate. Thereafter, Viola Henkey, a grandniece of the deceased, filed a petition for the probate of a will which deceased executed at Milwaukee, Wisconsin, in 1955 (hereinafter the "Milwaukee will"), in which Viola Henkey was named a legatee and also executrix. After the filing of these two petitions, Lulu Alburn and Doris Alburn filed a petition for the probate of a will which deceased executed at Kankakee, Illinois, in 1959 (hereinafter the "Kankakee will"). Neither of these last-named petitioners is a next-of-kin of the deceased but Lulu Alburn is a sister-in-law of deceased. Objections were filed to both the Milwaukee and Kankakee wills.

The county court held a joint hearing on all three petitions. . . . The court determined that the Kankakee will had been destroyed by deceased under the mistaken belief that by so doing she would revive the Milwaukee will which had been revoked by the revocation clause of the Kankakee will. The court applied the doctrine of dependent relative revocation and held that the Kankakee will was entitled to probate. By a judgment (denominated an "Order") entered December 28, 1961, the Kankakee will was admitted to probate. Adele Ruedisili has appealed this judgment. The proponents of the Milwaukee will have not appealed. Further facts will be stated in the opinion.

CURRIE, J.   This court is committed to the doctrine of dependent relative revocation. Estate of Eberhardt (1957), 1 Wis. 2d 439, 85 N.W.2d 483, and Estate of Callahan (1947), 251 Wis. 247, 29 N.W.2d 352. The usual situation for application of this doctrine arises where a testator executes one will and thereafter attempts to revoke it by making a later testamentary disposition which for some reason proves ineffective. In both the *Eberhardt* and *Callahan* cases, however, the doctrine was applied to the unusual situation in which a testator revokes a later will under the mistaken belief that by so doing he is reinstating a prior will. In this unusual situation, the doctrine of dependent relative revocation is invoked to render the revocation ineffective. The basis of the doctrine is stated in Estate of Callahan, supra, as follows (251 Wis. at p.255, 29 N.W.2d at p.355):

> The doctrine of dependent relative revocation is based upon the testator's inferred intention. It is held that as a matter of law the destruction of the later document is intended to be conditional where it is accompanied by the expressed intent of reinstating a former will and where there is no explanatory evidence. Of course if there is evidence that the testator intended the destruction to be absolute, there is no room for the application of the doctrine of dependent revocation.

The sole question raised by appellant on this appeal is whether the finding of the trial court that deceased revoked the Kankakee will under the mistaken belief that she was thereby reinstating the prior Milwaukee will is against the great weight and clear preponderance of the evidence. This requires that we review the pertinent evidence.

Testatrix was born in Wisconsin. For about thirty years she had resided in San Francisco, California, and later in Cleveland, Ohio. As a widow without children, she came to Milwaukee in the fall of 1954 and lived there with Viola Henkey, her grandniece. While so residing she executed the Milwaukee will on August 12, 1955. The original of this will was left with Attorney George R. Affeldt of Milwaukee, who had drafted it, where it remained until the death of testatrix. Sometime shortly prior to May 22, 1959, testatrix moved to Kankakee, Illinois, and resided there with her brother, Robert Lehmann. On May 22, 1959, she executed the Kankakee will.

On June 28, 1960, testatrix left Kankakee and came to Fort Atkinson, Wisconsin, and lived there with another brother, Edwin Lehmann, until her death in November of 1960. Testatrix was a patient at a hospital in Fort Atkinson during part of October and November of that year. Edwin testified that he had learned of the execution of the Kankakee will prior to the arrival of testatrix on June 28, 1960. On the evening of her arrival, he asked her what she had done with that will, and she replied, "What do you suppose, I got rid of it."[21] The next morning testatrix came downstairs with the torn pieces of the Kankakee will tied up in a handkerchief. Edwin provided her with a paper sack in which she deposited the pieces of the will. Edwin then took the sack with the garbage to the dump. There he opened the sack and let the pieces fly in the wind as testatrix had directed him to do.

Edwin was not questioned about any statement regarding the Milwaukee will which testatrix might have made in his presence at Fort Atkinson. He did testify that after her death he searched through her effects for a will but failed to find one. In view of the following testimony given by Olga Lehmann, his wife, this gives rise to an inference that Edwin was searching for the Milwaukee will.

Olga Lehmann was called as a witness by counsel for proponents of the Kankakee will. . . . Olga Lehmann was then asked the following questions and gave the following answers thereto:

Q. Did the deceased ever discuss in your presence the matter of the Milwaukee will at any other time other than the time we are just now referring to?
A. Yes.
Q. Who was present at that time?
A. Just myself.
Q. What did she tell you concerning the Milwaukee will?
A. That was the one she wanted to stand.
Q. Can you tell me in point of time when this might have been?
A. No, we talked often.

We deem it significant that counsel for appellant did not cross-examine Olga Lehmann with respect to her testimony that testatrix said

---

21. The trial court in its memorandum decision found that the attempted revocation of the Kankakee will took place in Illinois but held that Wisconsin law rather than Illinois law controlled the question of whether the doctrine of dependent relative revocation should be invoked. This ruling is in accord with Restatement, Conflicts, p. 389, §307, which states: "Whether an act claimed to be a revocation of a will is effective to revoke it as a will of movables is determined by the law of the state in which the deceased was domiciled at the time of his death."

she wanted the Milwaukee will to stand. Therefore, Olga Lehmann's testimony was not qualified or limited in any way.

This statement by testatrix clearly occurred after her destruction of the Kankakee will. Appellant now attacks this statement on the ground that it was not made contemporaneously with such destruction. In Estate of Callahan, supra, however, the only evidence regarding the intent of testatrix when she destroyed her 1944 will was her husband's statement in her presence after the destruction and her silence indicating acquiescence. The husband stated that they both had destroyed their 1944 wills because they desired to put their son back in the position he occupied under their 1940 wills. Upon this evidence this court determined the doctrine of dependent relative revocation applied and affirmed the judgment of the county court which had admitted the 1944 will of testatrix to probate.

The plan of testamentary disposition under the two wills was in part as follows: The Milwaukee will contained specific bequests of jewelry and household furnishings to Viola Henkey, the grandniece of testatrix, and directed that any indebtedness owing deceased by Viola Henkey and her husband be deemed satisfied. The residuary clause bequeathed one fourth of the estate to her friend Olga Olson, one fourth to Doris Alburn, one fourth to Lulu Alburn, and one fourth to Viola Henkey. The Kankakee will included a bequest to Olga Olson of 38 shares of stock in the Bank of America National Trust & Savings Association and bequests of jewelry to Lulu and Addie Alburn. The remainder of the estate was bequeathed as follows: four tenths to Lulu Alburn, five tenths to Doris Alburn, and one tenth to Robert Lehmann, brother of testatrix. The Alburns are not related to testatrix but are relatives of her deceased husband. Viola Henkey, although a blood relative of testatrix, is not one of her next-of-kin who would inherit in the event testatrix had died intestate. The next-of-kin consist of four surviving brothers and one sister plus a large number of nieces and nephews of testatrix, the children of four deceased sisters and one deceased brother. Thus under the Milwaukee will, none of the next-of-kin were named as legatees, whereas under the Kankakee will, the only next-of-kin named a legatee was Robert, her brother. His share under the Kankakee will is somewhat less than the one-tenth share of the entire estate which he would receive if testatrix had died intestate. The bulk of the estate under both wills was bequeathed to the Alburns and Olga Olson. This plan of testamentary disposition extended as late as May, 1959.

There is no evidence of any change of circumstances occurring thereafter that would indicate any reason why testatrix should die intestate and nine tenths of her estate go to next-of-kin not named in either will. The one change in circumstance was her leaving the home of her brother Robert and moving in with her brother Edwin.

This move might provide a reason for her desiring to revoke the Kankakee will, but certainly not for her wishing to die intestate. The learned trial judge, in the supplemental memorandum decision of December 26, 1961, stated, "I have a strong conviction that decedent did not want to die intestate." The evidence fully supports this conclusion despite the fact that testatrix took no steps between June 29, 1960, and her death nearly five months later to draft a new will. We deem that a reasonable inference, to be drawn from the competent evidence in this case, for her failure to make a new will is her evident belief that her Milwaukee will was still operative. Testatrix must have known that the original of the Milwaukee will was still in possession of Attorney Affeldt and believed that the only impediment to this will was the revocation clause of the Kankakee will. She also knew that the Kankakee will had been destroyed by tearing it in pieces and scattering the pieces so that they could not be found.[22]

We are constrained to conclude that the statement made to Olga Lehmann that testatrix wished her Milwaukee will to stand, the inference that she did not wish to die intestate, and the fact that she took no steps following the destruction of the Kankakee will to make a new will are sufficient evidence to support the finding that she destroyed the Kankakee will under the mistaken belief that the Milwaukee will would control the disposition of her estate. Furthermore there is no evidence which controverts this finding. Therefore, it is not against the great weight and clear preponderance of the evidence.

Counsel for respondents Alburn request a review by this court of several rulings by the trial court which excluded certain evidence pursuant to objections made by counsel for appellant Ruedisili. This excluded evidence related to further statements made by testatrix, after destruction of the Kankakee will, that she then considered her Milwaukee will to be in effect or desired this result. In view of our conclusion that the trial court's determination may be sustained upon the evidence admitted, we find it unnecessary to review these rulings.

Judgment affirmed.

NOTE: REVIVAL

Under Wisconsin law the will executed by Ottilie Alburn in Milwaukee in 1955 could not be revived after it had been expressly revoked by the 1959 Kankakee will. Why not? The explanation requires a brief discussion of the doctrine of revival.

The question of revival typically arises under the following facts

---

22. The contents of the Kankakee will were proved by a carbon copy in the possession of the lawyer who had drafted it at Kankakee, Illinois.

(which were present in Estate of Alburn): Testator executes will #1. Subsequently testator executes will #2, which revokes will #1 by an express clause or by inconsistency. Later testator revokes will #2. Is will #1 revived?

The states generally fall within one of three groups. A few courts in the United States take the view of the English common law courts that will #1 is not revoked unless will #2 remains in effect until the testator's death. The theory is that, since a will does not operate until the testator's death, will #2 is not legally effective during the testator's life. Therefore will #1 is not "revoked" by will #2. Technically, this theory does not involve "revival" at all, because the first will has never been revoked.

The large majority of jurisdictions assumes that will #2 legally revokes will #1 at the time will #2 is executed. But they divide into two groups. A majority of states holds that upon revocation of will #2, will #1 is revived if the testator so intends. The testator's intent may be shown from the circumstances surrounding revocation of will #2 or from the testator's contemporaneous or subsequent oral declarations that will #1 is to take effect.

A minority of states takes the view that a revoked will cannot be revived unless reexecuted with testamentary formalities or republished by being referred to in a later duly executed testamentary writing. Wisconsin is in this group of states. See In re Eberhardt's Estate, 1 Wis. 2d 439, 85 N.W.2d 483 (1957). See also Restatement (Third) of Property, Wills and Other Donative Transfers, §4.2 (1999).

UPC §2-509, reproduced below, has been adopted in a substantial number of states, either in its 1969 or 1990 version.

Uniform Probate Code (1990)

§2-509.   Revival of Revoked Will

(a) If a subsequent will that wholly revoked a previous will is thereafter revoked by a revocatory act under Section 2-507(a)(2), the previous will remains revoked unless it is revived. The previous will is revived if it is evident from the circumstances of the revocation of the subsequent will or from the testator's contemporary or subsequent declarations that the testator intended the previous will to take effect as executed.

(b) If a subsequent will that partly revoked a previous will is thereafter revoked by a revocatory act under Section 2-507(a)(2), a revoked part of the previous will is revived unless it is evident from the circumstances of the revocation of the subsequent will or from the testator's contemporary or subsequent declarations that the testator did not intend the revoked part to take effect as executed.

(c) If a subsequent will that revoked a previous will in whole or in part is thereafter revoked by another, later, will, the previous will remains revoked in whole or in part, unless it or its revoked part is revived. The previous will or its revoked part is revived to the extent it appears from the terms of the later will that the testator intended the previous will to take effect.

PROBLEMS

1.   Under UPC §2-509(a), if a subsequent will that *wholly* revoked the previous will is itself revoked by physical act, the presumption is that the previous will remains revoked. On the other hand, under UPC §2-509(b), if a subsequent will that *partly* revoked the previous will is itself revoked, the presumption is that the previous will is revived.

Suppose that Ottilie Alburn's Kankakee will, executed in 1959, had not contained an express revocation clause. Under UPC §2-509, would the presumption be that the 1955 will was revived? Does the 1959 will wholly or only partly revoke the 1955 will?

2.   In 2000 *T* dies. *T*'s heir is *H*. *T*'s safe-deposit box contains the following three documents, all duly signed and witnessed according to law:

(1) A will executed in 1995 devising all *T*'s property to *A*.
(2) A will executed in 1996 devising all *T*'s property to *B*.
(3) A document executed in 1999 reading: "I hereby revoke my 1996 will."

Under UPC §2-509(c), who takes *T*'s property?

3.   Revocation by Operation of Law: Change in Family Circumstances

In all but a tiny handful of states, statutes provide that a divorce revokes any provision in the decedent's will for the divorced spouse. In the remaining states, revocation occurs only if divorce is accompanied by a property settlement. These revocation statutes ordinarily apply only to wills, not to life insurance policies, pension plans, or other nonprobate transfers.

Uniform Probate Code §2-804 (1990) applies to nonprobate transfers as well as to wills. The term "governing instrument" in §2-804 is defined in UPC §1-201(19) to mean a deed, will, trust, insurance or annuity policy, account with a P.O.D. designation, pension plan, or similar nonprobate donative transfer.

Uniform Probate Code (1990, as amended in 1997)

§2-804.   REVOCATION OF PROBATE AND NONPROBATE TRANSFERS BY DIVORCE; NO REVOCATION BY OTHER CHANGES OF CIRCUMSTANCES

(a) [Definitions.] [Omitted.]

(b) [Revocation Upon Divorce.] Except as provided by the express terms of a governing instrument, a court order, or a contract relating to the division of the marital estate made between the divorced individuals before or after the marriage, divorce, or annulment, the divorce or annulment of a marriage:

(1) revokes any revocable (i) disposition or appointment of property made by a divorced individual to his [or her] former spouse in a governing instrument and any disposition or appointment created by law or in a governing instrument to a relative of the divorced individual's former spouse, (ii) provision in a governing instrument conferring a general or nongeneral power of appointment on the divorced individual's former spouse or on a relative of the divorced individual's former spouse, and (iii) nomination in a governing instrument, nominating a divorced individual's former spouse or a relative of the divorced individual's former spouse to serve in any fiduciary or representative capacity, including a personal representative, executor, trustee, conservator, agent, or guardian; and

(2) severs the interests of the former spouses in property held by them at the time of the divorce or annulment as joint tenants with the right of survivorship, transforming the interests of the former spouses into equal tenancies in common. . . .

(d) [Effect of Revocation.] Provisions of a governing instrument are given effect as if the former spouse and relatives of the former spouse disclaimed all provisions revoked by this section or, in the case of a revoked nomination in a fiduciary or representative capacity, as if the former spouse and relatives of the former spouse died immediately before the divorce or annulment. . . .

(f) [No Revocation for Other Change of Circumstances.] No change of circumstances other than as described in this section and in Section 2-803 [dealing with homicide] effects a revocation.

PROBLEM AND NOTE

1.   *T* executes a will devising all his property to his wife, and if his wife does not survive him to his wife's son (*T*'s stepson). *T* divorces

his wife and then dies. *T*'s heirs are his children by a prior marriage. A state statute revokes all provisions in a will for a divorced spouse and treats the divorced spouse as having predeceased the testator. Does the stepson take *T*'s property? Bloom v. Selfon, 520 Pa. 519, 555 A.2d 75 (1989); In re Group Life Insurance Proceeds of Mallory, 872 S.W.2d 800 (Tex. App. 1994).

Who takes under UPC §2-804?

2. If the state revocation-by-divorce statute does not apply to life insurance proceeds, the life insurance proceeds will, according to most cases, pass to the divorced spouse unless the divorce property settlement expressly provides that the spouse surrenders all rights to collect insurance proceeds. See Hughes v. Scholl, 900 S.W.2d 606 (Ky. 1995). Compare Vasconi v. Guardian Life Ins. Co., 124 N.J. 338, 590 A.2d 1161 (1991), where the court, saying the old rule was out of date, held that a divorce settlement presumptively revokes designation of a spouse as life insurance beneficiary.

Marriage. If the testator executes his will and subsequently marries, a large majority of states have statutes giving the spouse her intestate share, unless it appears from the will that the omission was intentional or the spouse is provided for in the will or by a will substitute with the intent that the transfer be in lieu of a testamentary provision. See Uniform Probate Code §2-301, infra page 534, which is a typical statute. In effect, this kind of statute revokes the will to the extent of the spouse's intestate share. See Estate of Shannon, 224 Cal. App. 3d 1148, 274 Cal. Rptr. 338 (1990), infra page 530.

Where the spouse omitted from a premarital will does not take an intestate share, because mentioned in the will, the spouse may take a "forced share" of the decedent's estate, which is given to all spouses whether intentionally or unintentionally disinherited. See infra page 480.

Birth of children. A small minority of states, either by statute or judicial decision, follow the common law rule that marriage followed by birth of issue revokes a will executed before marriage, but this rule has not been incorporated in the Uniform Probate Code and is rapidly disappearing. However, almost all states have pretermitted child statutes, giving a child born after execution of the parent's will, and not provided for in the will, a share in the parent's estate. See Uniform Probate Code §2-302 and infra page 546. Sometimes, pretermitted child statutes include children born before the execution of the will as well as children born thereafter. A pretermitted child statute, if applicable to the testator's will, results in a revocation of the will to the extent of the child's share.

SECTION C. COMPONENTS OF A WILL

In Section A of this chapter we considered the formalities with which a will must be executed. We saw that if a state's Wills Act is not complied with in all its particulars, a testamentary instrument may not be entitled to probate, no matter how clearly it reflects the testator's intention that it be a will. Yet despite these formal requirements of transfer, it is possible for documents and acts not executed with testamentary formalities to have the effect of determining *who* takes *what* property belonging to the testator. In this section we are primarily concerned with two doctrines that can have this effect, two doctrines that permit extrinsic evidence to resolve the identity of persons or property. These are (1) the doctrine of incorporation by reference and (2) the doctrine of acts of independent significance. Before we consider these doctrines, we must examine two others that are sometimes confused with them.

1. Integration of Wills

Wills are often written on more than one sheet of paper. Under the doctrine of integration, all papers present at the time of execution, intended to be part of the will, are integrated into the will. Hence, the question may arise: Which sheets of paper, present at the time of execution, comprise the testator's duly executed will? Typically, there is no problem, for the pages of the will are physically connected with a staple or ribbon or, failing this, there is a sufficient connection of language carrying over from page to page to show an internal coherence of the provisions. The attorney can prevent any problem from arising under the integration doctrine by seeing to it that the will is fastened together before the testator signs and by having the testator sign or initial each numbered page of the will for identification. The litigated cases involving integration arise when, for example, the pages are not physically connected and there is no internal coherence, or there is evidence that a staple has been removed, or one page is typed with elite type whereas the rest of the will is in pica.

In re Estate of Beale, 15 Wis. 546, 113 N.W.2d 380 (1962), is illustrative of the integration cases. In that case, the testator, a history professor at the University of Wisconsin, planning to take a trip to Russia, dictated his will to his secretary in Madison. He had three sons, 16, 15, and 10, and his earlier will treated the three sons equally. In this new will, the testator left all his property to his wife and two older sons, disinheriting the youngest son. The will consisted of 14 pages, and the secretary gave the testator three carbon copies plus the original. The testator took all these sheets with him to New York on his way to Moscow. At a festive goodbye party in New York, given by a history professor at Columbia, the testator produced his will and asked three of his friends, all professors at eastern colleges, to witness his will. He laid "a pile" of papers on the table, declaring it was his will, and the testator and witnesses signed the last page. After the testator's death, none of the witnesses could identify any page except the signature page, but all pages of the will had the testator's initials on the margin. On the same day as the party, either before or after the execution ceremony, the testator wrote his secretary from New York asking her to retype pages 12 and 13, and make certain changes, including changing the executor from his wife to a friend. The letter to her enclosed pages 12 and 13. These pages were retyped by the secretary after the testator's death, and, as retyped, they too had the testator's initials on the margin! Noting that "the question is one of inference," the court upheld the trial court's decision to admit the will to probate as the will existed before any changes were made.

An oddball Indiana case, Keener v. Archibald, 533 N.E.2d 1268 (Ind. App. 1989), holds that the doctrine of integration is not the law in Indiana, but such a doctrine would seem to be necessary unless wills are required to be written on one page.

2. Republication by Codicil

Under the doctrine of republication by codicil, a will is treated as reexecuted ("republished") as of the date of the codicil. Updating the original will in this manner can have important consequences. For example, suppose that the testator revokes a first will by a second will and then executes a codicil to the first will. The first will is republished, and thus the second will is revoked by implication ("squeezed out"). See In re Estate of Stormont, 34 Ohio App. 3d 92, 517 N.E.2d 259 (1986).

The doctrine of republication by codicil is not applied automatically, but only where updating the will carries out the testator's intent. Case 1 is illustrative.

> Case 1. The jurisdiction has an interested witness statute purging any gift to an attesting witness. In 1998 T executes a will devising all his property to A. A and B are witnesses to the will. In 1999 T executes a codicil bequeathing $5,000 to C. C and D are witnesses to the codicil. In 2000 T executes a second codicil bequeathing C a diamond ring. D and E are witnesses to the second codicil. Under the doctrine of republication by codicil, the will and first codicil are deemed to be re-executed in 2000 by the second

codicil, which has two disinterested witnesses. *A* and *C* are not purged of their gifts. See King v. Smith, 123 N.J. Super. 179, 302 A.2d 144 (1973).

The fundamental difference between republication by codicil and the doctrine of incorporation by reference, discussed below, is that republication applies only to a prior validly executed will, whereas incorporation by reference applies to incorporate into a will instruments that have never been validly executed. In the few jurisdictions that do not recognize incorporation by reference, courts have sometimes used the republication doctrine to give effect to wills that are invalid for some reason other than faulty execution. In New York, for example, which does not in general permit incorporation of unattested documents into a will, a codicil can republish and thereby give testamentary effect to a will that was invalid because of mental incapacity or undue influence, but a codicil cannot republish an instrument never duly executed with the required formalities.

3. Incorporation by Reference

Uniform Probate Code (1990)

§2-510. INCORPORATION BY REFERENCE

Any writing in existence when a will is executed may be incorporated by reference if the language of the will manifests this intent and describes the writing sufficiently to permit its identification.

Clark v. Greenhalge
Supreme Judicial Court of Massachusetts, 1991
411 Mass. 410, 582 N.E.2d 949

NOLAN, J. We consider in this case whether a probate judge correctly concluded that specific, written bequests of personal property contained in a notebook maintained by a testatrix were incorporated by reference into the terms of the testatrix's will.

We set forth the relevant facts as found by the probate judge. The testatrix, Helen Nesmith, duly executed a will in 1977, which named her cousin, Frederic T. Greenhalge, II, as executor of her estate. The will further identified Greenhalge as the principal beneficiary of the estate, entitling him to receive all of Helen Nesmith's tangible personal property upon her death except those items which she "designate[d] by a memorandum left by [her] and known to [Greenhalge], or in accordance with [her] known wishes," to be given to others living at the time of her death.[23] Among Helen Nesmith's possessions was a large oil painting of a farm scene signed by T. H. Hinckley and dated 1833. The value of the painting, as assessed for estate tax purposes, was $1,800.00.

In 1972, Greenhalge assisted Helen Nesmith in drafting a document entitled "MEMORANDUM" and identified as "a list of items of personal property prepared with Miss Helen Nesmith upon September 5, 1972, for the guidance of myself in the distribution of personal tangible property." This list consisted of forty-nine specific bequests of Ms. Nesmith's tangible personal property. In 1976, Helen Nesmith modified the 1972 list by interlineations, additions and deletions. Neither edition of the list involved a bequest of the farm scene painting.

Ms. Nesmith kept a plastic-covered notebook in the drawer of a desk in her study. She periodically made entries in this notebook, which bore the title "List to be given Helen Nesmith 1979." One such entry read: "Ginny Clark farm picture hanging over fireplace. Ma's room." Imogene Conway and Joan Dragoumanos, Ms. Nesmith's private home care nurses, knew of the existence of the notebook and had observed Helen Nesmith write in it. On several occasions, Helen Nesmith orally expressed to these nurses her intentions regarding the disposition of particular pieces of her property upon her death, including the farm scene painting. Helen Nesmith told Conway and Dragoumanos that the farm scene painting was to be given to Virginia Clark, upon Helen Nesmith's death.

Virginia Clark and Helen Nesmith first became acquainted in or about 1940. The women lived next door to each other for approximately ten years (1945 through 1955), during which time they enjoyed a close friendship. The Nesmith-Clark friendship remained constant through the years. In more recent years, Ms. Clark frequently spent time at Ms. Nesmith's home, often visiting Helen Nesmith while she rested in the room which originally was her mother's bedroom. The farm scene painting hung in this room above the fireplace. Virginia Clark openly admired the picture.

According to Ms. Clark, sometime during either January or February of 1980, Helen Nesmith told Ms. Clark that the farm scene painting would belong to Ms. Clark after Helen Nesmith's death. Helen Nesmith then mentioned to Virginia Clark that she would record this gift in a book she kept for the purpose of memorializing her wishes with respect to the disposition of certain of her belongings.[24] After

23. The value of Ms. Nesmith's estate at the time of her death exceeded $2,000,000.00, including both tangible and nontangible assets.

24. According to Margaret Young, another nurse employed by Ms. Nesmith, Ms. Nesmith asked Ms. Young to "print[ ] in [the] notebook, beneath [her] own handwriting, 'Ginny Clark painting over fireplace in mother's bedroom.' " Ms. Young complied with this request. Ms. Young stated that Ms. Nesmith's express purpose in having Ms. Young

Farm painting by Thomas Hinckley (1813-1896) devised to Virginia Clark

that conversation, Helen Nesmith often alluded to the fact that Ms. Clark someday would own the farm scene painting.

Ms. Nesmith executed two codicils to her 1977 will: one on May 30, 1980, and a second on October 23, 1980. The codicils amended certain bequests and deleted others, while ratifying the will in all other respects.

Greenhalge received Helen Nesmith's notebook on or shortly after January 28, 1986, the date of Ms. Nesmith's death. Thereafter, Greenhalge, as executor, distributed Ms. Nesmith's property in accordance with the will as amended, the 1972 memorandum as amended in 1976, and certain of the provisions contained in the notebook.[25] Greenhalge refused, however, to deliver the farm scene painting to Virginia Clark because the painting interested him and he wanted to keep it. Mr. Greenhalge claimed that he was not bound to give effect

---

record this statement in the notebook was "to insure that [Greenhalge] would know that she wanted Ginny Clark to have that particular painting."

25. Helen Nesmith's will provided that Virginia Clark and her husband, Peter Hayden Clark, receive $20,000.00 upon Helen Nesmith's death. Under the terms of the 1972 memorandum, as amended in 1976, Helen Nesmith also bequeathed to Virginia Clark a portrait of Isabel Nesmith, Helen Nesmith's sister with whom Virginia Clark had been acquainted. Greenhalge honored these bequests and delivered the money and painting to Virginia Clark.

to the expressions of Helen Nesmith's wishes and intentions stated in the notebook, particularly as to the disposition of the farm scene painting. Notwithstanding this opinion, Greenhalge distributed to himself all of the property bequeathed to him in the notebook. Ms. Clark thereafter commenced an action against Mr. Greenhalge seeking to compel him to deliver the farm scene painting to her.

The probate judge found that Helen Nesmith wanted Ms. Clark to have the farm scene painting. The judge concluded that Helen Nesmith's notebook qualified as a "memorandum" of her known wishes with respect to the distribution of her tangible personal property, within the meaning of Article Fifth of Helen Nesmith's will.[26] The judge further found that the notebook was in existence at the time of the execution of the 1980 codicils, which ratified the language of Article Fifth in its entirety. Based on these findings, the judge ruled that the notebook was incorporated by reference into the terms of the will. Newton v. Seaman's Friend Soc'y, 130 Mass. 91, 93 (1881). The judge awarded the painting to Ms. Clark.

. . . We . . . now hold that the probate judge correctly awarded the painting to Ms. Clark.

A properly executed will may incorporate by reference into its provisions any "document or paper not so executed and witnessed, whether the paper referred to be in the form of . . . a mere list or memorandum, . . . if it was in existence at the time of the execution of the will, and is identified by clear and satisfactory proof as the paper referred to therein." Newton v. Seaman's Friend Soc'y, supra at 93. The parties agree that the document entitled "memorandum," dated 1972 and amended in 1976, was in existence as of the date of the execution of Helen Nesmith's will. The parties further agree that this document is a memorandum regarding the distribution of certain items of Helen Nesmith's tangible personal property upon her death, as identified in Article Fifth of her will. There is no dispute, therefore, that the 1972 memorandum was incorporated by reference into the terms of the will. *Newton,* supra.

The parties do not agree, however, as to whether the documentation contained in the notebook, dated 1979, similarly was incorporated into the will through the language of Article Fifth. Greenhalge advances several arguments to support his contention that the purported bequest of the farm scene painting written in the notebook was not incorporated into the will and thus fails as a testamentary devise. The points raised by Greenhalge in this regard are not persua-

26. Article Fifth of Helen Nesmith's will reads, in pertinent part, as follows: "that [Greenhalge] distribute such of the tangible property to and among such persons *as I may designate by a memorandum left by me and known to him, or in accordance with my known wishes,* provided that said persons are living at the time of my decease" (emphasis added).

sive. First, Greenhalge contends that the judge wrongly concluded that the notebook could be considered a "memorandum" within the meaning of Article Fifth, because it is not specifically identified as a "memorandum." Such a literal interpretation of the language and meaning of Article Fifth is not appropriate.

"The 'cardinal rule in the interpretation of wills, to which all other rules must bend, is that the intention of the testator shall prevail, provided it is consistent with the rules of law.' " Boston Safe Deposit & Trust Co. v. Park, 307 Mass. 255, 259, 29 N.E.2d 977 (1940), quoting McCurdy v. McCallum, 186 Mass. 464, 469, 72 N.E. 75 (1904). The intent of the testator is ascertained through consideration of "the language which [the testatrix] has used to express [her] testamentary designs," Taft v. Stearns, 234 Mass. 273, 277, 125 N.E. 570 (1920), as well as the circumstances existing at the time of the execution of the will. The circumstances existing at the time of the execution of a codicil to a will are equally relevant, because the codicil serves to ratify the language in the will which has not been altered or affected by the terms of the codicil.

Applying these principles in the present case, it appears clear that Helen Nesmith intended by the language used in Article Fifth of her will to retain the right to alter and amend the bequests of tangible personal property in her will, without having to amend formally the will. The text of Article Fifth provides a mechanism by which Helen Nesmith could accomplish the result she desired; i.e., by expressing her wishes "in a memorandum." The statements in the notebook unquestionably reflect Helen Nesmith's exercise of her retained right to restructure the distribution of her tangible personal property upon her death. That the notebook is not entitled "memorandum" is of no consequence, since its apparent purpose is consistent with that of a memorandum under Article Fifth: It is a written instrument which is intended to guide Greenhalge in "distribut[ing] such of [Helen Nesmith's] tangible personal property to and among . . . persons [who] are living at the time of her decease." In this connection, the distinction between the notebook and "a memorandum" is illusory.

The appellant acknowledges that the subject documentation in the notebook establishes that Helen Nesmith wanted Virginia Clark to receive the farm scene painting upon Ms. Nesmith's death. The appellant argues, however, that the notebook cannot take effect as a testamentary instrument under Article Fifth, because the language of Article Fifth limits its application to "a" memorandum, or the 1972 memorandum. We reject this strict construction of Article Fifth. The language of Article Fifth does not preclude the existence of more than one memorandum which serves the intended purpose of that article. As previously suggested, the phrase "a memorandum" in Article Fifth appears as an expression of the manner in which Helen

Nesmith could exercise her right to alter her will after its execution, but it does not denote a requirement that she do so within a particular format. To construe narrowly Article Fifth and to exclude the possibility that Helen Nesmith drafted the notebook contents as "a memorandum" under that Article, would undermine our long-standing policy of interpreting wills in a manner which best carries out the known wishes of the testatrix. See *Boston Safe Deposit & Trust Co.,* supra. The evidence supports the conclusion that Helen Nesmith intended that the bequests in her notebook be accorded the same power and effect as those contained in the 1972 memorandum under Article Fifth. We conclude, therefore, that the judge properly accepted the notebook as a memorandum of Helen Nesmith's known wishes as referenced in Article Fifth of her will. . . .

. . . The judge further found that the notebook was in existence on the dates Helen Nesmith executed the codicils to her will [which republished her will], . . . and that it thereby was incorporated into the will pursuant to the language and spirit of Article Fifth. . . .

Lastly, the appellant complains that the notebook fails to meet the specific requirements of a memorandum under Article Fifth of the will, because it was not "known to him" until after Helen Nesmith's death. For this reason, Greenhalge states that the judge improperly ruled that the notebook was incorporated into the will. One of Helen Nesmith's nurses testified, however, that Greenhalge was aware of the notebook and its contents, and that he at no time made an effort to determine the validity of the bequest of the farm scene painting to Virginia Clark as stated therein. There is ample support in the record, therefore, to support the judge's conclusion that the notebook met the criteria set forth in Article Fifth regarding memoranda.

We note, as did the Appeals Court, that "one who seeks equity must do equity and that a court will not permit its equitable powers to be employed to accomplish an injustice." Pitts v. Halifax Country Club, Inc., 19 Mass. App. Ct. 525, 533, 476 N.E.2d 222 (1985). To this point, we remark that Greenhalge's conduct in handling this controversy fell short of the standard imposed by common social norms, not to mention the standard of conduct attending his fiduciary responsibility as executor, particularly with respect to his selective distribution of Helen Nesmith's assets. We can discern no reason in the record as to why this matter had to proceed along the protracted and costly route that it did.[27]

Judgment affirmed.

27. And it had a costly aftermath for Greenhalge, the executor and residuary beneficiary of Helen Nesmith's estate. A letter from Thomas D. Burns, counsel for Virginia Clark, to Jesse Dukeminier dated Sept. 27, 1993, reveals:

While the picture was later appraised at about $35,000, its stated value by the executor Greenhalge in the inventory was only $1500. I was awarded a fee of

SIMON V. GRAYSON, 15 Cal. 2d 531, 102 P.2d 1081 (1940): The testator's will, dated March 25, 1932, left $4,000 to his executors "to be paid by them as shall be directed by me in a letter that will be found in my effects and which will be addressed to my executors and dated March 25, 1932." A codicil to the will was executed November 25, 1933, which made a small change not relevant here and otherwise reaffirmed the will. After the testator's death a letter dated July 3, 1933, addressed to the executors was found in the testator's safe-deposit box. It stated: "In my will I have left you $4,000 to be paid to a person named in a letter. I direct you to pay the $4,000 to Esther Cohn." No letter dated March 25, 1932, was found.

The court held that the letter found in the safe-deposit box was the letter referred to in the will, despite the discrepancy in dates. It was incorporated by reference into the will, becoming an integral part of the will. Since the letter was dated prior to the date of the codicil, which republished the will, it complied with the requirement that an incorporated document be in existence on the date of the republished will. The court directed the executors to give the $4,000 to Esther Cohn's estate (she died seven days after testator).

If the testator intended to make a secret gift to Esther Cohn, he failed. A document incorporated by reference becomes part of the probate files, open to the public.

NOTES AND PROBLEMS

1. In Clark v. Greenhalge, suppose that the entry in the notebook, "Ginny Clark farm picture," had been made after the 1980 codicils. Could it have been given effect? Could it have been given effect under UPC §2-503 or the substantial compliance doctrine? Under UPC §2-513, infra page 311?

2. The testator executed a deed to his farm that named his niece as grantee. The deed was sealed in an envelope and placed by the testator in his safe-deposit box at a local bank, where it remained until his death. Sometime later, the testator executed a will containing

---

$80,000 by the Probate Court, which I settled for $70,000 to avoid an appeal. The executor, who was a very terrible guy, refused to give up the picture and I thought the case would be on a pro bono basis, but the Probate judge who heard the case was so incensed by Greenhalge's conduct, he awarded me my full hourly rate upon application.

— Eds.

the following provision: "Sixth: I have already deeded my farm to my niece, Alta J. Pullman, and for that reason I do not devise my farm to her in this Will." After the testator's death it was held that the deed was not effective to convey title to the niece because it was not delivered by the grantor during his lifetime. The niece contends that the deed was incorporated by reference by the language of clause Sixth of the will. What result? See Estate of Dimmitt, 141 Neb. 413, 3 N.W.2d 752, 144 A.L.R. 704 (1942) (deed incorporated by reference!). Since the court cannot openly correct the mistake by adding words to the will (see infra page 427), the court does so in effect by a generous application of the incorporation doctrine.

3. The doctrine of incorporation by reference is not recognized, as a general rule, in Connecticut,[28] Louisiana, and New York. To fill this lacuna, New York courts have stretched the doctrines of republication by codicil (see supra page 303) and integration to carry out the testator's intent. As for the latter, if, for example, the testator refers in his will to a separate memorandum disposing of his tangible personal property, and if such memorandum is attached to the other pages of his will and was present at execution, such memorandum is entitled to probate under the doctrine of integration. In re Will of Hall, 59 Misc. 2d 881, 300 N.Y.S.2d 813 (Sur. Ct. 1969). Indeed, even if the memorandum is attached after the signature page, it will be deemed

---

28. Hathaway v. Smith, 79 Conn. 506, 65 A. 1058 (1907), established that the doctrine of incorporation by reference does not exist in Connecticut. An earlier, more interesting case suggested that ultimate result. In Bryan's Appeal, 77 Conn. 240, 58 A. 748 (1904), the testator, Philo S. Bennett, was a rich Connecticut friend and political ally of the Great Commoner and scourge of eastern capitalists, William Jennings Bryan, who thrice ran unsuccessfully for the Presidency on the Democratic ticket. ("You shall not press down upon the brow of labor this crown of thorns. You shall not crucify mankind on a cross of gold.") While on a visit to Bryan at Lincoln, Nebraska, Bennett, with Bryan's assistance, prepared his will. The will was duly executed on May 22, 1900. It provided: "I give and bequeath unto my wife, Grace Imogene Bennett, the sum of fifty thousand dollars (50,000), in trust, however for the purposes set forth in a sealed letter which will be found with this will." Found with the will, at testator's death, was a letter dated "5/22/1900" addressed to "My Dear Wife," which referred to the $50,000 bequest in the will and stated that the $50,000 conveyed to her in trust was to be paid to William Jennings Bryan inasmuch "as his political work prevents the application of his time and talents to money making." Largely because Bennett left $20,000 to his mistress, Mrs. Bennett, angered by the will, refused to carry out Bennett's desires. Bryan sued and lost. The court held that even if incorporation by reference were recognized, the reference in the will was so vague as to be incapable of being applied to any particular instrument.

Bryan then sued Mrs. Bennett a second time, alleging that she held the $50,000 in a constructive trust for him (see infra page 616 on semisecret testamentary trusts). The court held that no trust arose because Mrs. Bennett had never been apprised of the terms of the will and had made no promise, an essential ingredient of a semisecret testamentary trust. Bryan v. Bigelow, 77 Conn. 604, 60 A. 266 (1905).

It may be that Bryan's Appeal is an example of the old adage that hard cases make bad law. Bryan, a lawyer, had acted indelicately — perhaps even unethically — in participating in this secret gift to himself, and the court was probably not disposed to rule in his favor.

constructively inserted before the signature page so as to comply with the requirement that a will be signed at the end. In re Will of Powell, 90 Misc. 2d 635, 395 N.Y.S.2d 334 (Sur. Ct. 1977).

Uniform Probate Code (1990)

§2-513.   SEPARATE WRITING IDENTIFYING BEQUEST OF TANGIBLE PROPERTY

Whether or not the provisions relating to holographic wills apply, a will may refer to a written statement or list to dispose of items of tangible personal property not otherwise specifically disposed of by the will, other than money. To be admissible under this section as evidence of the intended disposition, the writing must be signed by the testator and must describe the items and the devisees with reasonable certainty. The writing may be referred to as one to be in existence at the time of the testator's death; it may be prepared before or after the execution of the will; it may be altered by the testator after its preparation; and it may be a writing that has no significance apart from its effect on the dispositions made by the will.

Johnson v. Johnson
Supreme Court of Oklahoma, 1954
279 P.2d 928

PER CURIAM.   This is an appeal from a judgment of the District Court of Oklahoma County affirming the County Court of Oklahoma in denying probate to an instrument purporting to be the last will and testament of Dexter G. Johnson, who was sometimes known as D. G. Johnson.

The instrument in question was on a single sheet of paper and contained three typewritten paragraphs, started out with the words, "I, D. G. Johnson also known as Dexter G. Johnson, of Oklahoma City, Oklahoma County, State of Oklahoma do hereby make, publish and declare this to be my last Will and Testament . . ." and made numerous bequests and devises and concluded with recommending the employment of a certain attorney to probate the will. This typewritten portion was not dated nor did the testator sign his name at the conclusion thereof nor was it attested by two witnesses. At the end of the typewritten portion, at the bottom of [the] sheet of paper, appears the following, admitted to be in the handwriting of the deceased:

To my brother James I give ten dollars only. This will shall be complete
unless hereafter altered, changed or rewritten. Witness my hand this April
6, 1947. Easter Sunday, 2:30 P.M.

D. G. Johnson
Dexter G. Johnson

On trial de novo in the District Court the proponents of this purported will, plaintiffs in error here, introduced evidence over objections (which objections were never ruled on by the court) showing
that Dexter G., or D. G. Johnson for many years was a practicing
attorney in Oklahoma City; that during his practice he prepared many
wills, all in proper form, for various clients; that in October, 1946,
deceased told Jack G. Wiggins, his insurance counselor, that he had
a will but it was out of date and needed changing; that in March,
1947, deceased told this insurance counselor that he was working on
his will, making changes, and expected to complete it right away and
told Mr. Wiggins in general the disposition he intended to make of
his property; that in the latter part of 1946 Lowell M. Wickham,
deceased's rental agent, was shown the instrument here in question
at which time it had only the typewritten portions on it; that at that
time deceased told him that was his will and he wanted Wickham to
witness it, but he and deceased started discussing other business and
neglected to do it at that time; that when Wickham left the paper was
lying on deceased's desk; that some months later Wickham asked
deceased about witnessing the will and deceased replied he had
changed his will by codicil and did not need Wickham to sign it as
witness; an offer by statement of counsel was made to show the intention of the testator in leaving his property to the persons he named
as beneficiaries which was rejected by the court and is not helpful in
deciding the questions raised here.

The above is a summary of all the testimony that appears in the
record. None of the testimony presented to the County Court appears
in the record; defendant below, contestant of the will and defendant
in error here, offered no testimony.

Is this instrument one complete, integrated writing, partly typed
and partly handwritten; or is it an unexecuted nonholographic will to
which is appended a valid holographic codicil? If it be the former it
cannot be admitted to probate because it was not signed in the presence of two subscribing witnesses as required by law.

Defendant in error urges that the instrument shows on its face that
it is but one instrument and that it cannot be divided into two parts,
one, the typewritten part to be called a will and the other, the handwritten part, to be called a codicil. In support of his contention he
says that the typewritten portion standing alone is not a will because,
though admittedly testamentary in character, it is not dated, signed,
nor witnessed; that it takes the handwritten portion to complete the

instrument; that by definition to have a codicil there must first be a will.

There is no question in this case that the typewritten instrument which was not signed, dated, nor attested was prepared by D. G. Johnson and that it is testamentary in character, or that he intended same as his will or that it effectively makes complete disposition of his estate. A will may be so defective, as here, that it is not entitled to probate but if testamentary in character it is a will, nonetheless. . . . Nor is there any question that the handwritten words were wholly in the handwriting of the testator.

The question next arises, do these words meet the requirements of a codicil? By definition a codicil is a supplement to, an addition to or qualification of, an existing will, made by the testator to alter, enlarge, or restrict the provisions of the will, to explain or republish it, or to revoke it, and it must be testamentary in character. In re Whittier's Estate, 26 Wash. 2d 833, 176 P.2d 281. A codicil need not be called a codicil, In re Carr's Estate, 93 Cal. App. 2d 750, 209 P.2d 956; In re Atkinson's Estate, 110 Cal. App. 499, 294 P. 425. The intention to add a codicil is controlling. Allgeier v. Brown, 199 Ky. 672, 251 S.W. 851; Stewart v. Stewart, 177 Mass. 493, 59 N.E. 116. The handwritten words are admittedly testamentary in character. It is clear that they made an addition to the provisions of the will theretofore existing. This codicil is on the same sheet of paper and the terms thereof, the circumstances surrounding it, as shown by the evidence indicate that the testator intended it as an addition to and republication of his will.

If it be a codicil, then, is it a valid one? It is written, dated, and signed by the testator. It meets all the requirements of a valid holographic codicil. The fact that the codicil was written on the same piece of paper as the typewritten will will not invalidate the codicil. In re Atkinson's Estate, supra.

It is admitted that a codicil republishes a previous will as modified by the codicil as of the date of the codicil. Can a valid, holographic codicil republish and validate a will which was theretofore inoperative because not dated, signed, or attested according to law?

The general principle of law is that a codicil validly executed operates as a republication of the will no matter what defects may have existed in the execution of the earlier document, that the instruments are incorporated as one, and that a proper execution of the codicil extends also to the will. Twenty-two states and England so hold. For citation of cases see Annotations 21 A.L.R.2d 823. That a properly executed codicil will give effect to a will which has never been signed has been specifically held in Kentucky, New Jersey, and England. See Beall v. Cunningham, 1843, 3 B. Mon. 390, 42 Ky. 390, in which it appeared that a paper wholly written by testator dated 1825 was denied probate, and thereafter there was offered for probate a typewritten will dated in 1827,[29] which was unsigned and unattested, together with a codicil dated 1832 on the same sheet of paper which was signed and attested; the opinion holds that the properly executed codicil had the effect of giving operation to the whole as one will. See also Hurley v. Blankinship, 1950, 313 Ky. 49, 229 S.W.2d 963, 21 A.L.R.2d 817, in which a holographic will which was not signed was held validated by properly executed holographic codicils; Doe v. Evans, 1832, 1 Cromp. & M. 42, 149 Eng. Reprint 307, in which an unsigned typewritten will was held validated by a properly executed codicil on the same sheet of paper; see also McCurdy v. Neall, 1886, 42 N.J. Eq. 333, 7 A. 466 and Smith v. Runkle, 1916, 86 N.J. Eq. 257, 98 A. 1086, in both of which the signatures to the wills were defective because not placed on the will in the presence of witnesses but it was held that valid codicils thereafter executed gave operation to the entire will and codicils; Rogers v. Agricola, 176 Ark. 287, 3 S.W.2d 26, in which an invalid typewritten will (due to only one witness) was held validated by a subsequent holographic codicil; In re Plumel's Estate, 151 Cal. 77, 90 P. 192, an invalid holographic will because of printing thereon was held validated by a subsequent holographic codicil written on the back of the will. . . .[30]

The only exception is New York which modifies the general rule by holding that a properly executed codicil validates a will originally invalid for want of testamentary capacity, undue influence, or revocation but does not validate a will defectively executed because of improper attestation. It will be noted, however, that Justice Cardozo in Re Fowles, 1918, 222 N.Y. 222, 118 N.E. 611, Ann. Cas. 1918D, 834, stated that the rule was malleable and uncertain and he anticipated that New York would abandon its limitations on the rule. . . .

We therefore hold that the valid holographic codicil incorporated the prior will by reference and republished and validated the prior will as of the date of the codicil, thus giving effect to the intention of the testator.

Reversed with directions to enter the will for probate.

JOHNSON, V.C.J. and WELCH, CORN, ARNOLD and BLACKBIRD, JJ., concur. HALLEY, C.J., WILLIAMS and DAVISON, JJ., dissent.

---

29. Typewritten will in 1827? The first typewriters were placed on the market in 1874. Later in this paragraph the court refers to a typewritten will in Doe v. Evans, decided in 1832. In neither Beall v. Cunningham nor in Doe v. Evans was there mention of any typewriting.

This anachronism was called to our attention by John Cutcher, J.D. Vanderbilt 1987, whose sharp eyes spotted it while a student in Professor Jeffrey Schoenblum's wills course at Vanderbilt. — Eds.

30. Examine carefully the facts of the cases cited in this paragraph. Do you see why the cases cited are properly analyzed as applications of either incorporation by reference or integration and that republication by codicil is not involved? — Eds.

CORN, J. (concurring specially).[31] I concur in the per curiam opinion. In so doing I have in mind the purpose of our law-makers in enacting statutes regulating the making of a Will. They require certain steps to be taken in the execution of a Will solely for the purpose of permitting a person to dispose of his property by Will, to take effect after his death the way he desired, and to prevent someone, through fraud or by other means, from permitting this to be done. It was the purpose of our lawmakers, in passing the Act, to make it impossible for fraud or undue influence to be practiced in the execution of the Will, and in the disposition of the property disposed of by the Will.

31. In 1964 Justices Corn and Welch were convicted of federal income tax evasion and sentenced to prison terms of 18 months and 3 years respectively. N.Y. Times, July 19, 1964, at 44; id., Nov. 14, 1964, at 14. Corn and Welch resigned their judicial positions. Subsequently Corn signed a statement in which Corn said Welch, Johnson, and he had accepted more than $150,000 in bribes for throwing cases. In 1965 Justice Johnson was convicted of corruption in office and removed from the court by the Oklahoma legislature. Id., May 14, 1965, at 40.

The newspaper accounts did not mention any evidence of bribery in the principal case of Johnson v. Johnson. Yet when a judge has been convicted of bribery in one case the public may suspect there was bribery in others. (Indeed, when Corn was asked if he could remember any year, in the 24 he served as Justice, when he did not take money for his votes, he replied: "Well, I don't know." Id., May 11, 1965, at 18.) The votes of Corn, Welch, and Johnson were decisive in Johnson v. Johnson. Although there is no report of bribery in this case, *and none is to be inferred from this note*, does the mere appearance of possible impropriety require that the case now be reheard upon petition of the losing party?

In Johnson v. Johnson, 424 P.2d 414 (Okla. 1967), the executor of the losing party in the original case (who had since died) petitioned to have the 1954 decision vacated in view of Justice Corn's participation in that decision. Five of the supreme court justices who were on the court in 1954 disqualified themselves, and five special justices were appointed in their stead. In a unanimous decision, the court denied the petition since there was no allegation of wrongdoing in the particular case. Among the reasons given were the practical consequences of a contrary decision:

> It is apparent that if our holding were in the affirmative every decision from 1938 to January of 1959 in which Corn cast the deciding vote would have to be set aside. There are more than one thousand such cases. Rights of every kind have been settled by the decisions in such cases. Marriages have been contracted upon the basis of divorces granted, titles have been transferred and judgments paid. To now go back and reopen every such case for a possible new decision requiring new arguments and new hearings would cast intolerable and unjust burdens upon all the parties. Titles and status long thought put at rest would be thrown open to doubt. It would indeed create a "shambles" as Respondent contends. And this would be so in every case in which Corn cast the deciding vote even though no corruption occurred in such case.
>
> To us this result seems unthinkable and contrary to the most elementary principles of justice. We think it more just that those cases in which no corruption can be found should be allowed to stand, at the same time giving full right to any person who believes that any such decision has been corruptly obtained, to petition this Court for a hearing, in which, if corruption can be shown, the decision may be set aside.

Cf. Electric Auto-Lite Co. v. P. & D. Manufacturing Co., 109 F.2d 566 (2d Cir. 1940), where a rehearing was granted "because of the disqualification of one member of the original court [Judge Martin T. Manton, convicted of bribery in 1939], not known at the time." — Eds.

It was not the intent of our law-makers, in enacting these statutes, if substantially complied with, to ever allow a miscarriage of justice by a wrongful disposition of the testator's property contrary to his intent. 84 O.S. 1951 §151 provides: "Intention of testator governs. — A will is to be construed according to the intention of the testator. . . . "

In the instant case, the intent expressed by the testator in the written instrument which he prepared, while of sound mind and disposing memory, is clear and beyond any question of doubt, free from fraud or undue influence of any kind. The only objection raised is that the statutes were not strictly complied with in the execution of the Will. I am of the opinion, when a person dies leaving a written instrument which he intended to be his last Will, and it is free from fraud or undue influence and in harmony with the purpose of our law-makers for enacting statutes regulating the execution of Wills, . . . it would be a miscarriage of justice to not admit the Will to probate, and thereby allow the property to be disposed of contrary to the testator's intent.[32]

To hold otherwise would, in effect, permit a contrary disposition of testator's property against the purpose for which the statutory provisions were aimed.

HALLEY, C.J., dissenting. . . . Counsel for the proponents of the purported will have come up with the ingenious idea that this instrument which is partly in typewriting and partly in handwriting is valid and should be admitted to probate for the fantastic reason that the handwriting is a codicil to the typewriting. It is my position that the typewritten part is not a will and the handwritten part is not a codicil. The handwritten part is only a continuation of the typewritten part and, combined, they constitute a will which was not attested and therefore cannot properly be admitted to probate.

. . . [T]here was nothing in the handwriting which referred to a previous will. It spoke of "this will" and not of a previous will. There is nothing about this handwriting to indicate that the testator intended it to be a codicil. He was completing his will with the handwriting.

I think he intended the typewritten portion to be a part of his will, not the completed will. A will is to be interpreted by what is found in its "four corners" and there is nothing to indicate that the testator intended it to be anything but one instrument. Parol or extrinsic evidence should not be admitted to show the contrary when the signed will is one instrument.

Under no circumstances should this be considered a codicil and I can never subscribe to the proposition that a holographic codicil will

---

32. Is Justice Corn's view in concord with a substantial compliance doctrine or the dispensing power of UPC §2-503, supra page 252?

validate as a will an instrument that is typewritten, unfinished as to content, undated, unsigned and unattested. Not a case has been cited where a holographic codicil validates an instrument as a will which was not dated, signed or attested and no reference made in the purported codicil to the preceding will. . . . Something is attempted to be made of the fact that the testator was a lawyer but that would prove nothing as many eminent lawyers have failed to properly prepare and execute their own wills. The will of Samuel J. Tilden is a notable example.

This will was one complete will unattested and therefore not admissible to probate and to give this will the construction that the majority has placed upon it is wholly unwarranted. Why make a mockery of the plain provision of our statutes? Property may only descend by will when the will is executed in conformity with the statutes.

I dissent.

PROBLEMS AND NOTE

1.   In order to probate a holographic will it is necessary to eliminate typed matter on the face of a holographic will on the ground either that it is immaterial or that there is no intent to incorporate the typed matter. In view of this, can the handwritten part of Dexter G. Johnson's document be admitted as a holographic will, and then the typed part incorporated by reference? See Case Note, 23 U. Chi. L. Rev. 316 (1956).

Would the court have any problem probating Johnson's typed will if the handwritten portion had appeared on the back of the typed sheet rather than on the bottom? Could the handwritten portion incorporate the typed material on the back by reference, or are the front and back of a sheet integrated? See In re Estate of Plumel, 151 Cal. 77, 90 P. 192 (1907), referred to in the *Johnson* opinion at page 314.

2.   In Estate of Nielson, 105 Cal. App. 3d 796, 165 Cal. Rptr. 319 (1980), the testator drew lines through the dispositive provisions of his typewritten will and wrote between the lines: "Bulk of Estate — 1. — Shrine Hospital for Crippled Children — Los Angeles, $10,000 — 2. Society for Prevention of Cruelty to Animals." Near the margin of these cancellations and interlineations were the testator's initials and date. At the top and bottom of the will were the handwritten words, "Revised by Lloyd M. Nielson November 29, 1974." The court held the handwritten words constituted a holographic codicil, because they did not intend to incorporate the attested typed material. The holographic codicil republished the typewritten will, as modified.

But compare In re Estate of Sola, 225 Cal. App. 3d 241, 275 Cal.

Rptr. 98 (1990), and In re Estate of Foxley, 254 Neb. 204, 575 N.W.
2d 150 (1998), supra page 269, holding that handwritten words written across an attested will did not constitute a holographic codicil
because they made no sense apart from the typewritten words. Compare also In re Estate of Johnson, 129 Ariz. 307, 630 P.2d 1039 (1981),
supra page 264.

4. *Acts of Independent Significance*

Now we turn to another doctrine permitting extrinsic evidence to
identify the will beneficiaries or property passing under the will. If
the beneficiary or property designations are identified by acts or
events that have a lifetime motive and significance apart from their
effect on the will, the gift will be upheld under the doctrine of acts of
independent significance (also called the doctrine of nontestamentary
acts). This is true even though the phrasing of the will leaves it in
the testator's power to alter the beneficiaries or the property by a
nontestamentary act.

Case 2 illustrates some common applications of the acts of independent significance doctrine.

> *Case 2.* *T*'s will devises "the automobile that I own at my death" to her
> nephew *N*, and gives $1,000 "to each person who shall be in my employ
> at my death." At the time the will is executed *T* owns an old Toyota.
> Shortly before her death *T* trades the Toyota in on a new Cadillac, with
> the result that *T* dies owning a $30,000 automobile rather than one worth
> $3,000. In the year before her death *T* fires two long-time employees and
> hires three new ones. The gifts are valid. While *T*'s act in buying the
> Cadillac had the practical effect of increasing the value of her gift to *N*,
> it is unlikely that this is what motivated her purchase. It is more probable
> that she bought the car because she wanted to drive a Cadillac. Similarly,
> *T*'s acts in hiring and firing various employees were doubtless prompted
> by business needs rather than a desire to make or unmake legatees under
> the will. Indeed, cases involving this form of devise typically assume the
> validity of the gift without discussion of the acts of independent signifi-
> cance doctrine.

Uniform Probate Code (1990)

§2-512. Events of Independent Significance

A will may dispose of property by reference to acts and events that
have significance apart from their effect upon the dispositions made
by the will, whether they occur before or after the execution of the

will or before or after the testator's death. The execution or revocation of another individual's will is such an event.

PROBLEMS

1.   *T* bequeaths the contents of the right-hand drawer of her desk to *A*. In the drawer at *T*'s death are a savings bank passbook in *T*'s name, a certificate for 100 shares of General Electric common stock, and a diamond ring. Does *A* take these items?

T bequeaths the contents of her safe-deposit box in Security Bank to *B* and the contents of her safe-deposit box in First National Bank to *C*. Do *B* and *C* take the items found in the respective boxes? See Annot., 5 A.L.R.3d 466 (1966).

T's will provides: "I have put in my safe-deposit box in Continental Bank shares of stock in several envelopes. Each envelope has on it the name of the person I desire to receive the stock contained in the envelope." At *T*'s death several envelopes are found in *T*'s safe-deposit box with the name of a person written on the envelope. Inside each is a stock certificate. For example, in one envelope is a certificate for 200 shares of Coca-Cola stock and on the envelope is written "For Ruth Moreno." Do Ruth Moreno and the other persons take the stock in the envelopes bearing their names? See Will of Le Collen, 190 Misc. 272, 72 N.Y.S.2d 467 (Sur. Ct. 1947); Smith v. Weitzel, 47 Tenn. App. 375, 338 S.W.2d 628 (Tenn. 1960).

2.   In 1994 Sarah executes her will devising the residue of her estate to any charitable trust established by the last will and testament of her brother, Barney. In 1996 Barney executes his will, devising his property to the Barney Educational Trust, a charitable trust established by his will. In 1997, Barney dies. In 2000, Sarah dies. Is the Barney Educational Trust entitled to the residue of Sarah's estate? See First National Bank v. Klein, 255 Ala. 505, 234 So. 2d 42 (1970); In re Will of Tipler, 1998 Tenn. App. LEXIS 841. Suppose that Barney had survived Sarah. What result? See Restatement (Second) of Property, Donative Transfers §18.4, Comment f (1986).

SECTION D.   CONTRACTS RELATING TO WILLS

A person may enter into a contract *to make a will* or a contract *not to revoke a will.* Contract law, not the law of wills, applies. The contract beneficiary must sue under the law of contracts and prove a valid contract. If, after a contract becomes binding, a party dies leaving a will not complying with the contract, the will is probated but the contract beneficiary is entitled to enforce the contract by having a constructive trust impressed for his benefit upon the estate or devisees of the defaulting party.

1. Contracts to Make a Will

Questions respecting contracts to make a will may arise in a variety of fact situations, such as a claimed promise to make a will in exchange for an agreement to marry, or to serve as nurse and housekeeper, or not to contest a will. In many states, a contract to make a will must be in writing. In these states, if the promisee is not entitled to sue for specific performance, the promisee is entitled to receive the value to the decedent of services rendered (quantum meruit). The value the decedent put on the services in the oral agreement ("I promise to leave you half of my estate") is evidence of the reasonable value of those services. See Hastoupis v. Gargas, 9 Mass. App. Ct. 27, 398 N.E.2d 745 (1980). In some states, an oral contract to make a will is specifically enforceable provided the terms are proved by clear and convincing evidence, the rendition of the services is wholly referable to the contract, and the services are of such peculiar value to the promisor as not to be estimated or compensable by any pecuniary standard. See Musselman v. Mitchell, 46 Or. App. 299, 611 P.2d 675 (1980). See generally Note, The Statute of Frauds' Lifetime and Testamentary Provisions: Safeguarding Decedents' Estates, 50 Fordham L. Rev. 239 (1981).

PROBLEMS

1. *T* makes a contract with *A* to leave everything to *A* at death if *A* will take care of *T* for life. *T* executes a will leaving her estate to *A*. Subsequently, *A* changes her mind and decides not to care for *T*. *T* rescinds the contract. Upon *T*'s death is *A* entitled to take under *T*'s will? See Trotter v. Trotter, 490 So. 2d 827 (Miss. 1986).

2. *A* dies of AIDS. After *A*'s death, *A*'s roommate, *B*, claims half of *A*'s estate. *B* alleges that *A* promised to leave *B* half his estate if *B* cared for *A* for his life. *B* produces a document typed by *B* and signed by *A* and one witness devising one-half of his estate to *B*. The jurisdiction has enacted UPC §2-514, infra page 322, requiring that the contract be evidenced by a writing signed by the decedent. Is *B* entitled to one-half of *A*'s estate? See Estate of Fritz, 159 Mich. App. 69, 406 N.W.2d 475 (1987).

3. If *W* promises *H* to take care of him for his life in consideration of *H* devising her Blackacre, and *H* dies, devising Blackacre to *A*, is the contract enforceable by *W*? Is consideration given by *W*? See Borelli v. Brusseau, 12 Cal. App. 4th 647, 16 Cal. Rptr. 2d 16 (1993) (unenforceable because no consideration; *W* had legal duty to care for *H*). Compare Byrne v. Laura, 52 Cal. App. 4th 1054, 60 Cal. Rptr. 2d 908 (1997) (promise by man to his live-in lover gives rise to claim for quantum meruit).

". . . And to my faithful valet, Sidney, who I promised to remember in my will—Hi there, Sidney!"

QUESTION

Does Sidney have an enforceable claim against his employer's estate?

2. Contracts Not to Revoke a Will

Questions respecting contracts not to revoke a will typically arise where husband and wife have executed a joint will or mutual wills. A *joint will* is one instrument executed by two or more persons as the will of both. When one testator dies, the instrument is probated as the testator's will; when the other testator dies, the instrument is probated as the other testator's will. *Mutual wills* are the separate wills of two or more persons that contain similar or reciprocal provisions. A *joint and mutual will* is a term commonly used by courts to describe a joint will that devises the property in accordance with a contract. In this context, mutuality refers to the contract and not to reciprocal provisions of separate wills. See Kinkin v. Marchesi, 237 Ill. App. 3d 539, 604 N.E.2d 957 (1992).

There are no legal consequences peculiar to joint or mutual wills unless they are executed pursuant to a contract between the testators not to revoke their wills. The initial problem is proof of the contract. Most courts hold that a contract not to revoke is not enforceable unless it is proved by clear and convincing evidence and that the mere execution of a joint will or of mutual wills does not give rise to a presumption of contract. The difficulty, however, is that the existence of a common dispositive scheme, and, in the case of a joint will, the expression of the scheme in a jointly executed instrument, strongly suggests an understanding or underlying agreement and thus invites a claim of contract, the terms of which can be inferred from the will or wills. See, e.g., Black v. Edwards, 248 Va. 90, 445 S.E.2d 107 (1994) (contract established by testimony of drafting attorney that he told couple reciprocal wills create contract that survivor could not revoke). Considerable litigation results. The danger of a lawsuit can be reduced by inserting in every joint or mutual will a provision declaring that the will was or was not executed pursuant to a contract, but the lawyer who is astute enough to be aware of this problem will doubtless also know that joint wills are notorious litigation-breeders that should not be used at all.

To reduce litigation, Uniform Probate Code §2-514 tightens the methods by which contracts relating to wills can be proved.

Uniform Probate Code (1990)

§2-514. CONTRACTS CONCERNING SUCCESSION

A contract to make a will or devise, or not to revoke a will or devise, or to die intestate, if executed after the effective date of this Article, may be established only by (i) provisions of a will stating material provisions of the contract, (ii) an express reference in a will to a contract and extrinsic evidence proving the terms of the contract, or (iii) a writing signed by the decedent evidencing the contract. The execution of a joint will or mutual wills does not create a presumption of a contract not to revoke the will or wills.

Via v. Putnam
Supreme Court of Florida, 1995
626 So. 2d 460

OVERTON, J.   We have for review Putnam v. Via, 638 So. 2d 981 (Fla. 2d DCA 1994). This case involves a dispute between a decedent's surviving spouse, who claimed a share of the decedent's estate under the pretermitted spouse statute,[33] and the children of the decedent's first marriage, who claimed that the mutual wills executed by their parents, naming them residuary beneficiaries of their parents' estates, gave rise to a creditor's contract claim that had priority against the surviving spouse's claim against the estate. The Second District Court of Appeal held that the surviving spouse's right to receive either an elective share or pretermitted spouse's share of the decedent's estate has priority over the claims of the decedent's children. The district court acknowledged conflict with Johnson v. Girtman, 542 So. 2d 1033 (Fla. 3d DCA 1989). We have jurisdiction. Art. V, §3(b)(3), Fla. Const.

For the reasons expressed in this opinion, we approve the decision of the district court and find that Florida has a strong public policy concerning the protection of the surviving spouse of the marriage in existence at the time of the decedent's death. This policy has been continuously expressed in the law of this state and is controlling. We agree with the district court's reasoning and conclude that the children, as third-party beneficiaries under the mutual wills of their parents, should not be given creditor status under section 733.707, Florida Statutes (1993), when their interests contravene the interests of the surviving spouse under the pretermitted spouse statute.

The record reveals the following facts. On November 15, 1985, Edgar and Joann Putnam executed mutual wills, each of which contained the following provision:

> I acknowledge that this is a mutual will made at the same time as my [spouse's] Will and each of us have executed this Will with the understanding and agreement that the survivor will not change the manner in which the residuary estate is to be distributed and that neither of us as

33. §732.301, Fla. Stat. (1993).

survivors will do anything to defeat the distribution schedule set forth herein, such as disposing of assets prior to death by way of trust bank accounts, trust agreements, or in any other manner.

Each will devised that spouse's entire estate to the survivor and provided that the residuary estate would go to the children upon the survivor's death. Joann Putnam died without having done anything to defeat the terms of her mutual will. Edgar Putnam later remarried and failed to execute a subsequent will to provide for his second wife, Mary Rachel Putnam (Rachel Putnam).

Upon Edgar Putnam's death, his mutual will was admitted to probate. Rachel Putnam filed both a Petition to Determine Share of Pretermitted Spouse and an Election to Take Elective Share. In response, the children filed claims against the estate alleging that, by marrying Rachel Putnam, Edgar had breached his contract not to defeat the distribution schedule set forth in his mutual will by subjecting his assets to the statutes governing homestead property, exempt property, pretermitted share, and family allowance. . . . The trial judge, during the course of these proceedings, made the following findings. First, he found that: (a) the mutual will provision previously quoted "constituted a binding contractual agreement," of which the children are third-party beneficiaries; (b) the children properly filed a claim against the estate based upon the decedent's breach of the mutual will; and (c) the surviving spouse, Rachel Putnam, is the pretermitted spouse of Edgar Putnam. Second, the trial judge entered a summary judgment expressly finding that "Edgar J. Putnam breached his joint and mutual will that he made with Joann Putnam when he married Rachel Putnam without taking appropriate steps to protect the interests of the third-party beneficiaries under said will" and that the claims of the children "are class 7 obligations pursuant to §733.707, Florida Probate Code." The trial judge concluded that "any pretermitted spouse share or elective share that Rachel Putnam may have is subject to the class 7 obligations of this estate."

On appeal, the district court reversed and noted that, if the children's residuary beneficiary status in the mutual wills allowed them to assert creditor status against the estate, the surviving spouse in this instance would "receive nothing except family allowance and any exempt property that may pass to her free from claims of creditors." *Putnam*, 638 So. 2d at 982. The district court's decision relied on the reasoning in Shimp v. Huff, 315 Md. 624, 556 A.2d 252, 263 (1989), in which Maryland's highest court, on facts essentially identical to the facts in this case, found that the public policy surrounding the marriage relationship and the elective share statute required it to rule in favor of protecting the surviving spouse's right to receive an elective share. Likewise, the Second District Court of Appeal stated that "the statutes of Florida pertaining to a surviving spouse's elective share or pretermitted share in cases discussing those rights and their predecessor, dower, suggest a strong public policy in favor of protecting a surviving spouse's right to receive an elective share or a pretermitted share." *Putnam,* 638 So. 2d at 984. The district court recognized that its holding conflicts with the Third District Court's decision in Johnson v. Girtman, 542 So. 2d 1033 (Fla. 3d DCA 1989).

. . . [The elective share statute gives the surviving spouse the right to elect against the decedent's will and take a forced share of the decedent's net estate.] The statute reads as follows:

> The elective share shall consist of an amount equal to 30 percent of the fair market value, on the date of death, of all assets referred to in §732.206, computed after deducting from the total value of the assets:
>
> (1) All valid claims against the estate paid or payable from the estate; and
>
> (2) All mortgages, liens, or security interests on the assets.

§732.207, Fla. Stat. (1993).

. . . [T]he pretermitted spouse statute . . . reads as follows:

> When a person marries after making a will and the spouse survives the testator, the surviving spouse shall receive a share in the estate of the testator equal in value to that which the surviving spouse would have received if the testator had died intestate,[34] unless:
>
> (1) Provision has been made for, or waived by, the spouse by prenuptial or postnuptial agreement;
>
> (2) The spouse is provided for in the will; or
>
> (3) The will discloses an intention not to make provision for the spouse.
>
> The share of the estate that is assigned to the pretermitted spouse shall be obtained in accordance with §733.805.

§732.301, Fla. Stat. (1993).

The children argue that they are third-party beneficiaries of the contract between the decedent and their mother and that they deserve creditor status under section 733.707. As creditors, they would have priority over the share of the pretermitted spouse and would

---

34. Under Fla. Stat. 732, 101(1)(c), the intestate share of a surviving spouse is one-half when the decedent leaves lineal descendants, as in this case. Therefore, in Florida the widow can elect against her husband's will and receive 30% of his estate, or, if his will is executed before their marriage, she can claim half his estate under the pretermitted spouse statute.

If the husband executes a will after marriage, which leaves his wife 10%, 50%, all, or nothing of his estate, she has no claim as a pretermitted spouse. She is entitled only to a 30% share under the elective share statute. — Eds.

receive the entire estate. Under this scheme, the second wife would receive only a family allowance, the exempt property, and a life estate in the homestead. . . . [I]t is our view that the legislature did not intend . . . to allow creditors' claims by third-party beneficiaries of previously executed mutual wills to take priority over the statutory rights of a pretermitted spouse and deny the pretermitted spouse any share in the decedent's estate.

We acknowledge that other jurisdictions and the Third District Court of Appeal in *Johnson* take the view that a surviving spouse's statutory share of an estate can be subordinated to claims of third-party beneficiaries of previously executed mutual wills. See *Johnson;* see also Gregory v. Estate of Gregory, 315 Ark. 187, 866 S.W.2d 379 (1993); In re Estate of Stewart, 69 Cal. 2d 296, 70 Cal. Rptr. 545, 444 P.2d 337 (1968); Keats v. Cates, 100 Ill. App. 2d 177, 241 N.E.2d 645 (1968); Baker v. Syfritt, 147 Iowa 49, 125 N.W. 998 (1910); Lewis v. Lewis, 104 Kan. 269, 178 P. 421 (1919); Rubenstein v. Mueller, 19 N.Y.2d 228, 278 N.Y.S.2d 845, 225 N.E.2d 540 (1967); Robison v. Graham, 799 P.2d 610 (Okla. 1990). These courts have advanced four different rationales for giving priority to the contract beneficiaries: (1) The surviving spouse's marital rights attach only to property legally and equitably owned by the deceased spouse, and the will contract entered into before the marriage deprives the deceased spouse of equitable title and places it in the contract beneficiary. *Lewis.* (2) When the surviving testator accepts benefits under the contractual will, an equitable trust is impressed upon the property in favor of the contract beneficiaries, and the testator is entitled to only a life estate in the property with the remainder going to the beneficiaries upon the testator's death. *Rubenstein; Gregory; Keats; Baker; Robison.* (3) When the surviving testator accepts benefits under the contractual will, the testator becomes estopped from making a different disposition of the property, despite any subsequent marriage. *Stewart.* (4) Finally, as expressed in *Johnson,* when the surviving testator breaches the will contract, the contract beneficiaries are entitled to judgment creditor status, thus giving them priority over the rights of the surviving spouse under the applicable state probate code. It is this last theory that the trial judge adopted in ruling for the children in the instant case. Under these four theories, it makes no difference whether the surviving spouse was married to the decedent for one year or twenty-five years; the surviving spouse would be entitled to no interest in the deceased spouse's probatable estate if the third-party beneficiaries' claim consumed the estate.

The Court of Appeals of Maryland, that state's highest court, recently made a detailed analysis of this issue in an opinion by Chief Judge Murphy. See Shimp v. Huff, 315 Md. 624, 556 A.2d 252 (1989). That court, after reviewing the theories identified above, found that the question of priorities between a surviving spouse and beneficiaries under a contract to make a will should be resolved based upon the public policy which surrounds the marriage relationship and which underlies the elective share statute. . . .

In addition to the public policy underlying these statutes, the public policy surrounding the marriage relationship also suggests that the surviving spouse's claim to an elective share should be afforded priority over the claims of beneficiaries of a contract to make a will. Like the majority of other courts, we have recognized the well settled principle that contracts which discourage or restrain the right to marry are void as against public policy.

556 A.2d at 263. Similar views have been expressed by other courts. See e.g., Patecky v. Friend, 220 Or. 612, 350 P.2d 170 (1960); In re Arland's Estate, 131 Wash. 297, 230 P. 157 (1924). The *Shimp* court concluded that the contract that gave rise to the claim of the third-party beneficiaries included an implied limitation. It stated: "[W]e find that the respondent's rights under the contract were limited by the possibility that the survivor might remarry and that the subsequent spouse might elect against the will." *Shimp*, 556 A.2d at 263.

The district court of appeal in the instant case found the reasoning and analysis in *Shimp* to be persuasive. We agree. . . . We emphasize that the justification for the elective share and pretermitted spouse statutes is to protect the surviving spouse of the marriage in existence at the time of death of his or her spouse. The legislature has made these shares of a deceased spouse's estate a part of the marriage contract.

Florida's pretermitted spouse statute applies only "[w]hen a person marries after making a will and the spouse survives the testator." §732.301, Fla. Stat. (1993). The statute sets forth three specific circumstances when a pretermitted spouse would not be entitled to a share of the decedent's estate: (1) when "[p]rovision has been made for, or waived by, the spouse by prenuptial or postnuptial agreement"; (2) when "[t]he spouse is provided for in the will"; or (3) when "[t]he will discloses an intention not to make provision for the spouse." Id. The trial judge found that none of these exceptions applied and that the surviving spouse in this case was a pretermitted spouse under the statute. To hold as suggested by the children would essentially amend the statutory exceptions to the pretermitted spouse statute and add a fourth exception. The legislature enacted these exceptions based on the public policy of protecting the surviving spouse of the marriage contract in existence at the time of the decedent's death. The legislature has clearly taken into account when this provision should apply and when it should not apply. We conclude that we have no authority to judicially modify the public policy protecting a surviving spouse's interest in the deceased spouse's estate by adopting this creditor-theory approach as an exception to the pretermitted spouse statute.

Accordingly, we approve the decision of the district court of appeal in this case and disapprove the decision of the Third District Court of Appeal in *Johnson* to the extent that it conflicts with this opinion.

It is so ordered.

NOTES AND PROBLEMS

1. Suppose that the majority rule (the third party beneficiaries prevail over the second wife) is followed in this state. After Joann Putnam's death, what are Edgar's rights in the property during his lifetime? How is he restricted in what he can do with his own property and the property received from Joann? See Flohr v. Walker, 520 P.2d 833 (Wyo. 1974) (survivor entitled to "income and reasonable portions of principal for his support and ordinary expenditures, . . . but cannot dissipate the estate or alienate by inter vivos transfers . . . to defeat the contract"); Estate of Chayka, 47 Wis. 2d 102, 176 N.W.2d 561 (1970) (inter vivos gifts by survivor can be set aside if not made in good faith). Suppose that Edgar thinks that a round-the-world cruise will be the perfect wedding present for his new bride. Is that permitted? Suppose he wants to buy Rachel an emerald bracelet from Tiffany's. Okay? See Carolyn L. Dessin, The Troubled Relationship of Will Contracts and Spousal Protection: Time for an Amicable Separation, 45 Cath. U. L. Rev. 435 (1996).

2. Does the contract apply only to Edgar's property owned at Joann's death and to property inherited from her, or does it include property acquired by Edgar thereafter? Suppose that Edgar had inherited property from his brother after Joann died. Does the contract apply to this property? See Estate of Maloney v. Carsten, 178 Ind. App. 191, 381 N.E.2d 1263 (Ind. App. 1978). Does the contract apply to nonprobate property, such as life insurance? See Bergheger v. Boyle, 258 Ill. App. 3d 413, 629 N.E.2d 1168 (1994).

3. In In re Cohen, 83 N.Y.2d 148, 629 N.E.2d 1356, 608 N.Y.S.2d 398 (1994), husband and wife, a childless couple, executed reciprocal wills, pursuant to a contract, devising all their property to the survivor for life, with remainder to go one-half to the husband's collateral relatives and one-half to the wife's collateral relatives. At the husband's death, the wife was unable to locate the husband's will, thus raising the presumption that he revoked it. The wife took all her husband's property by intestacy as his sole heir. The court held that the contract was not enforceable by imposition of a constructive trust on the wife's estate because the wife did not receive any benefit under

her husband's will. Since the husband revoked his will and did not perform the contract, the wife need not perform either.

4.   *H* and *W* have children by prior marriages. They want the survivor to have "everything" and "be comfortable," and they want all their property divided equally among their children upon the death of the survivor. But, knowing that the survivor will have closer ties to his or her own children, they feel uncomfortable leaving the disposition entirely in the survivor's hands. This is the basic dilemma suggested by many contractual wills. When you study trusts later in this course, you will find that *H* and *W*'s desires can be better realized, with fewer problems, by creating a trust rather than by using contractual wills.

5

WILL SUBSTITUTES: NONPROBATE TRANSFERS

In this chapter we treat contracts, trusts, and transfers made during life that have the effect of passing property at death but avoid probate.

SECTION A. CONTRACTS WITH PAYABLE-ON-DEATH PROVISIONS

Wilhoit v. Peoples Life Insurance Co.
United States Court of Appeals, Seventh Circuit, 1955
218 F.2d 887

MAJOR, J. The plaintiff, Robert Wilhoit, instituted this action against the defendants, Peoples Life Insurance Company (sometimes referred to as the company) and Thomas J. Owens, for the recovery of money held by the company. Roley Oscar Wilhoit was the insured and Sarah Louise Wilhoit, his wife, the beneficiary in a life insurance policy in the amount of $5,000, issued by Century Life Insurance Company of Frankfort, Indiana. Mr. Wilhoit died prior to October 22, 1930 (the exact date not disclosed by the record), without having changed the beneficiary designated in the policy, and the proceeds thereof became due to and payable to Mrs. Wilhoit. The amount due was paid to her and the policy surrendered, as is evidenced by the following receipt appearing on the back of the policy:

"$4,749.00

"Indianapolis, Ind.,
Oct. 22-1930.

"Received from Century Life Insurance Company Forty Seven hundred forty nine Dollars in full for all claims under the within policy, terminated by death of Roley O. Wilhoit.

"Sarah Louise Wilhoit"

The main body of the policy contained a provision entitled "The Investment" as follows:

> Upon the maturity of this policy, the amount payable hereunder, or any portion thereof, not less than One Thousand Dollars, may be left on deposit with the Company, and the Company will pay interest annually in advance upon the amount so left on deposit at such rate as the Company may declare on such funds so held by it, but never at a rate less than three percent, so long as the amount shall remain on deposit with the Company. The said deposit may be withdrawn at the end of any interest year; or upon the death of the payee of the amount of said deposit will be paid to the executors, administrators or assigns of the payee.[1]

On November 14, 1930, Mrs. Wilhoit (twenty-three days after she had acknowledged receipt of the amount due her under the policy) from her home in Indiana signed and addressed a letter to the company in the same State, which in material parts reads as follows:

> I hereby acknowledge receipt of settlement in full under Policy No. C172 terminated by the death of Roley O. Wilhoit, the Insured, and I direct that the proceeds of $4,749.00 be held in trust[2] by the Peoples Life Insurance Company under the following conditions:

1. Almost all life insurance policies give the beneficiary several options. The beneficiary may draw down the policy proceeds in a lump sum. Or the beneficiary may leave the proceeds with the company and draw interest. Or the beneficiary may elect an installment option. Installment options may include a life annuity, payments for a fixed period or for life whichever is longer, payments for a fixed period, or some other type of periodic payments. The option to which this footnote is appended is known as an *interest option.* — Eds.

2. Although Mrs. Wilhoit directed that the proceeds be held "in trust" and ordered that "this trust fund" be payable to Robert G. Owens upon her death, and the company accepted the agreement creating "a trust fund," no trust was created. A trust involves a duty to manage specific property. A debt involves merely a personal obligation to pay a sum of money. In this case a debt was created. The parties did not intend for the company to segregate $4,749 from its general assets and keep it as separate trust property; they intended the company to mix the money with its general assets. Moreover, the company was required to pay interest at a fixed rate of $3\frac{1}{2}$ percent, not all the income it earned on $4,749. This shows that the parties intended the company to have the use of the money for its own purposes and to be under a personal liability to repay the sum to Mrs. Wilhoit. The company is thus a debtor, not a trustee. See 1 Austin W. Scott, Trusts §12.2 (William F. Fratcher 4th ed. 1987). — Eds.

(1) Said amount or any part thereof (not less than $100.00) to be subject to withdrawal on demand of the undersigned.

(2) While on deposit, said amount or part thereof shall earn interest at the rate of $3\frac{1}{2}\%$, compounded annually, plus any excess interest authorized by the Board of Directors of the Company. Interest may be withdrawn at the end of each six months period or whenever the principal of the fund is withdrawn or may be allowed to accumulate compounded annually. Interest on this trust fund shall begin as of October 9th, 1930.

(3) In the event of my death, while any part of this trust fund is still in existence, the full amount, plus any accrued interest, shall be immediately payable to Robert G. Owens (Relationship) Brother.

The proposal contained in this letter was, on November 17, 1930, accepted by the company in the following form:

The above agreement creating a trust fund is hereby accepted and we acknowledge receipt of the deposit of $4,749.00 under the above specified conditions.

Robert G. Owens, a brother of Mrs. Wilhoit and the person mentioned in her November 14 letter to the company, died January 23, 1932, and Mrs. Wilhoit died April 12, 1951, each leaving a last will and testament. The will of the former by a general clause devised all his property to Thomas J. Owens, a defendant, and was admitted to probate in Marion County, Indiana. The will of Mrs. Wilhoit was admitted to probate in Edgar County, Illinois, and contained the following provision:

I now have the sum of Four Thousand Seven Hundred Forty Nine Dollars ($4,749.00), or approximately that amount, which is the proceeds of an insurance policy on the life of my deceased husband, Oscar Wilhoit, on deposit with the insurance company, the Peoples Life Insurance Company of Frankfort, Indiana. This I give and bequeath to Robert Wilhoit, now of Seattle, Washington, who is another son of my said stepson, the same to be his property absolutely. . . .

The fund in controversy, deposited with the company by Mrs. Wilhoit on November 17, 1930, remained with the company continuously until the date of her death, April 12, 1951. The company refused to recognize the claim to the fund made by Robert Wilhoit, the legatee named in the will of Mrs. Wilhoit and the plaintiff in the instant action. . . . [The defendant] Thomas J. Owens claimed the fund as the legatee under the will of Robert G. Owens. . . . The District Court, on March 11, 1954, without opinion sustained the motion of the plaintiff for summary judgment. . . . Thereupon, judgment was entered in favor of the plaintiff in the sum of $4,749.00, together with interest and costs. . . .

Defendants . . . advance two theories in support of their argument
for reversal, both of which are firmly grounded upon the premise
that the agreement of November 17, 1930, between Mrs. Wilhoit and
the company, was an insurance contract or a contract supplemental
thereto. Thus premised, they argue (1) that the rights of the parties
must be determined by the law of insurance and not by the statute
of wills, and (2) that Mrs. Wilhoit as a primary beneficiary named
Robert G. Owens as the successor beneficiary irrevocably, without
right to revoke or change and without a "pre-decease of beneficiary"
provision, and that as a result the rights of such successor beneficiary
upon his death prior to the death of the primary beneficiary did
not lapse but passed on to the heirs and assigns of such successor
beneficiary.

On the other hand, plaintiff argues, in support of the judgment,
that the disposition of the fund is not controlled by the law of insurance because the agreement between Mrs. Wilhoit and the company
was not an insurance contract or a supplement thereto but was nothing more than a contract of deposit, and that the provision in the
agreement by which Robert G. Owens was to take the funds in the
event of her death was an invalid testamentary disposition. Further, it
is argued that in any event any interest acquired by Robert G. Owens
was extinguished upon his death, which occurred prior to that of Mrs.
Wilhoit.

Defendants cite many cases from numerous jurisdictions which have
held under a variety of circumstances that the proceeds of a life
insurance policy are to be disposed of in accordance with its provisions, and that a beneficiary, if authorized by the policy, may designate
a successor beneficiary to take on the death of the primary beneficiary. . . .

Other cases are cited, some from Indiana, to the effect that the
beneficiary designated in a life insurance policy acquires a vested
interest therein. However, these cases as well as those cited above are
based upon the premise that the agreement under discussion was
either an insurance contract or a supplemental agreement characterized as such because a successor beneficiary had been designated by
the primary beneficiary under authority contained in the policy.

Obviously, defendants' contention is without merit and the cases
cited in support thereof are without application unless we accept the
premise upon which the contention is made, that is, that the agreement between Mrs. Wilhoit and the company was an insurance contract or an agreement supplemental thereto. While there may be
room for differences of opinion, we have reached the conclusion that
the premise is not sound, that the arrangement between the parties
was the result of a separate and independent agreement, unrelated
to the terms of the policy. . . .

The "investment" provision was an offer by the company by which Mrs. Wilhoit, on maturity of the policy, could have left the proceeds with the company on the terms and conditions therein stated. It is plain, however, that she did not take advantage of this offer. Instead, she accepted the proceeds, surrendered the policy and receipted the company in full "for all claims under the within policy," and presumably the proceeds were paid to her at that time. At any rate, it was not until twenty-three days later that she, by letter, made her own proposal to the company, which differed materially from that contained in the policy. The company proposed to pay interest annually in advance on the amount left on deposit, at a rate of interest not less than 3%. Her proposal provided for interest at the rate of $3\frac{1}{2}\%$, compounded annually, with a right to withdraw interest at the end of any six-month period. The company proposal provided that Mrs. Wilhoit could withdraw the deposit only at the end of any interest year, it made no provision for the withdrawal of any amount less than the total on deposit, while the offer of Mrs. Wilhoit provided for the right to withdraw, on demand, any amount or part thereof (not less than $100). Undoubtedly the company was obligated, upon request by Mrs. Wilhoit, to comply with the terms of the investment provision and, upon refusal, could have been forced by her to do so. On the other hand, it was under no obligation to accept the proposal made by her and, upon its refusal, she would have been without remedy.

. . . [We have] concluded that the agreement between Mrs. Wilhoit and the company was neither an insurance contract nor an agreement supplemental thereto. . . . Mrs. Wilhoit deposited her money with the company, which obligated itself to pay interest and return the principal to her on demand. Only "in the event of her death" was the deposit, if it still remained, payable to Robert G. Owens. If Mrs. Wilhoit had deposited her money with a bank rather than with the insurance company under the same form of agreement, we think it would have constituted an ineffectual disposition because of failure to comply with the Indiana statute of wills.

In conclusion, we think it not immaterial to take into consideration what appears to have been the intention of the parties. . . . As already shown, Robert G. Owens, through whom defendants claim, died in 1932, and in his will made no mention of the funds in controversy. . . . On the other hand, Mrs. Wilhoit in her will specifically devised the fund in controversy to plaintiff, Robert Wilhoit. It thus appears plain that Mrs. Wilhoit did not intend that the fund go to the successors of Robert G. Owens but that after his death she thought she had a right to dispose of the fund as she saw fit, as is evidenced by the specific bequest contained in her will. We recognize that the intention of the parties or the belief which they entertained relative to the fund is not controlling, but under the circumstances presented, we think it is entitled to some consideration.

The judgment of the District Court is affirmed.

NOTE

The court in *Wilhoit* strikes down a payable-on-death (P.O.D.) designation in a contract of deposit because it is a testamentary act not executed with the formalities required by the Wills Act. The *Wilhoit* case applies the traditional rule, still followed in some states, that payable-on-death (P.O.D.) designations in contracts other than life insurance contracts are invalid.

Estate of Hillowitz
Court of Appeals of New York, 1968
22 N.Y.2d 107, 238 N.E.2d 723, 291 N.Y.S.2d 325

FULD, C.J.   This appeal stems from a discovery proceeding brought in the Surrogate's Court by the executors of the estate of Abraham Hillowitz against his widow, the appellant herein. The husband had been a partner in an "investment club" and, after his death, the club, pursuant to a provision of the partnership agreement, paid the widow the sum of $2,800, representing his interest in the partnership. "In the event of the death of any partner," the agreement recited, "his share will be transferred to his wife, with no termination of the partnership." The executors contend in their petition that the above provision was an invalid attempt to make a testamentary disposition of property and that the proceeds should pass under the decedent's will as an asset of his estate. The widow maintains that it was a valid and enforceable contract. Although the Surrogate agreed with her, the Appellate Division held that the agreement was invalid as "an attempted testamentary disposition" (24 A.D.2d 891, 264 N.Y.S.2d 868).

A partnership agreement which provides that, upon the death of one partner, his interest shall pass to the surviving partner or partners, resting as it does in contract, is unquestionably valid and may not be defeated by labeling it a testamentary disposition. . . . We are unable to perceive a difference in principle between an agreement of this character and one, such as that before us, providing for a deceased partner's widow, rather than a surviving partner, to succeed to the decedent's interest in the partnership. . . .

These partnership undertakings are, in effect, nothing more or less than third-party beneficiary contracts, performable at death. Like many similar instruments, contractual in nature, which provide for the disposition of property after death, they need not conform to the requirements of the statute of wills. . . . Examples of such instruments include (1) a contract to make a will . . . ; (2) an inter vivos trust in which the settlor reserves a life estate . . . ; and (3) an insurance policy. . . .

In short, members of a partnership may provide, without fear of running afoul of our statute of wills, that, upon the death of a partner, his widow shall be entitled to his interest in the firm. This type of third-party beneficiary contract is not invalid as an attempted testamentary disposition.

The executors may derive little satisfaction from McCarthy v. Pieret (281 N.Y. 407, 24 N.E.2d 102),[3] upon which they heavily rely. In the first place, it is our considered judgment that the decision should be limited to its facts. And, in the second place, the case is clearly distinguishable from the one now before us in that the court expressly noted that the "facts . . . indicate a mere intention on the part of the mortgagee to make a testamentary disposition of the property and not an intention to convey an immediate interest" and, in addition, that the named beneficiaries "knew nothing of the provisions of the extension agreement" (p. 413, 24 N.E.2d p. 104).

The order of the Appellate Division should be reversed, with costs in this court and in the Appellate Division, and the order of the Surrogate's Court reinstated.

The Uniform Probate Code, in 1969, authorized P.O.D. designations in all contracts, and more than half the states followed suit. The current P.O.D. provision in the Code, rewritten in 1989, follows.

Uniform Probate Code (1990)

§6-101.   NONPROBATE TRANSFERS ON DEATH

(a) A provision for a nonprobate transfer on death in an insurance policy, contract of employment, bond, mortgage, promissory note, certificated or uncertificated security, account agreement, custodial agreement, deposit agreement, compensation plan, pension plan, individual retirement plan, employee benefit plan, trust, conveyance, deed of gift, marital property agreement, or other written instrument

---

3. In McCarthy v. Pieret, a mortgage provided that if any installments remained unpaid at the mortgagee's death they should be paid to A. The provision was held to be testamentary and void. — Eds.

of a similar nature is nontestamentary. This subsection includes a written provision that:

(1) money or other benefits due to, controlled by, or owned by a decedent before death must be paid after the decedent's death to a person whom the decedent designates either in the instrument or in a separate writing, including a will, executed either before or at the same time as the instrument, or later;

(2) money due or to become due under the instrument ceases to be payable in the event of death of the promisee or the promisor before payment or demand; or

(3) any property controlled by or owned by the decedent before death which is the subject of the instrument passes to a person the decedent designates either in the instrument or in a separate writing, including a will, executed either before or at the same time as the instrument, or later.

(b) This section does not limit rights of creditors under other laws of this State.

QUESTIONS

1.   Return to the *Wilhoit* case. How should the *Wilhoit* case be decided in a jurisdiction enacting UPC §6-101? Should the court imply a requirement that Robert Owens survive Mrs. Wilhoit in order to take? Observe that UPC §6-101 is silent on whether a death beneficiary named in a contract must survive the contracting benefactor.

Under the law of wills, a devisee is required to survive the testator in order to take; if the devisee predeceases, the gift "lapses." Should the rule applied to wills — that the beneficiary must survive the testator in order to take — be applied to all will substitutes, including contracts? See John H. Langbein, The Nonprobate Revolution and the Future of the Law of Succession, 97 Harv. L. Rev. 1108, 1136-1137 (1984): "Transferors use will substitutes to avoid probate, not to avoid the subsidiary law of wills. The subsidiary rules are the product of centuries of legal experience in attempting to discern transferors' wishes and suppress litigation. These rules should be treated as presumptively correct for will substitutes as well as for wills."

Although UPC §6-101 does not require survivorship by P.O.D. beneficiaries of contracts, when the beneficiary is a close relative of the benefactor the UPC antilapse statute, which applies to nonprobate transfers as well as to wills, substitutes the issue of the named beneficiary who does not survive the benefactor. UPC §2-706 (1990), discussed infra page 446. In the *Wilhoit* case, the P.O.D. beneficiary was Robert Owens, the decedent's brother. If he was survived by issue — if Thomas J. Owens was his descendant, as seems likely — then Robert

Owens's issue would be substituted for Robert as beneficiaries under the contract by UPC §2-706. They would be entitled to the money on deposit. Is this what Mrs. Wilhoit intended?

2. Should the *Wilhoit* case be decided in favor of Robert Wilhoit on the ground that Mrs. Wilhoit had the power to change a P.O.D. beneficiary by will? Consider the following case.

Cook v. Equitable Life Assurance Society
Indiana Court of Appeals, First District, 1981
428 N.E.2d 110, 25 A.L.R.4th 1153

RATLIFF, J. Margaret A. Cook, Administratrix C.T.A. of the Estate of Douglas D. Cook (Douglas); Margaret A. Cook; and Daniel J. Cook (Margaret and Daniel) appeal from an entry of summary judgment granted by the trial court in favor of Doris J. Cook Combs (Doris) in an interpleader action brought by The Equitable Life Assurance Society of the United States (Equitable). We affirm.

FACTS

Douglas purchased a whole life insurance policy on March 13, 1953, from Equitable, naming his wife at that time, Doris, as the beneficiary. On March 5, 1965, Douglas and Doris were divorced. The divorce decree made no provision regarding the insurance policy, but did state the following: "It is further understood and agreed between the parties hereto that the provisions of this agreement shall be in full satisfaction of all claims by either of said parties against the other, including alimony, support and maintenance money."

After the divorce Douglas ceased paying the premiums on his life insurance policy, and Equitable notified him on July 2, 1965, that because the premium due on March 9, 1965, had not been paid, his whole life policy was automatically converted to a paid-up term policy with an expiration date of June 12, 1986. The policy contained the following provision with respect to beneficiaries:

> BENEFICIARY. The Owner may change the beneficiary from time to time prior to the death of the Insured, by written notice to the Society, but any such change shall be effective only if it is endorsed on this policy by the Society . . .

On December 24, 1965, Douglas married Margaret, and a son Daniel, was born to them. On June 7, 1976, Douglas made a holographic will in which he bequeathed his insurance policy with Equitable Life to his wife and son, Margaret and Daniel:

Last Will & Testimint

I Douglas D. Cook
   Being of sound mind do Hereby leave all my Worldly posessions to my
Wife and son, Margaret A. Cook & Daniel Joseph Cook. being my Bank
Accounts at Irwin Union Bank & trust to their Welfair my Insurance
policys with Common Welth of Ky. and Equitable Life. all my machinecal
tools to be left to my son if He is Interested in Working with them If not
to be sold and money used for their welfair all my Gun Collection Kept
as long as they, my Wife & Son and then sold and money used for their
welfair

> I sighn this
> June 7 — 1976
> at Barth Conty
> Hospital Room
> 1114 Bed 2
> /s/ Douglas D. Cook
> /s/ 6-7-76 Margaret A. Cook wife
> /s/ Chas. W. Winkler
> /s/ Mary A. Winkler

This will was admitted to probate in Bartholomew Superior Court
after Douglas's death on June 9, 1979. On August 24, 1979, Margaret
filed a claim with Equitable for the proceeds of Douglas's policy,
but Equitable deposited the proceeds, along with its complaint in
interpleader, with the Bartholomew Circuit Court on March 14, 1980.
Discovery was made; interrogatories and affidavits were filed; and all
parties moved for summary judgment. The trial court found that there
was no genuine issue as to any material fact respecting Doris's claim
to the proceeds of the policy and entered judgment in her favor as
to the amount of the proceeds plus interest, a total of $3,154.09.
Margaret and Daniel appeal from this award.

ISSUE

Is the trial court's entry of summary judgment in this case contrary
to Indiana law because the court entered judgment in favor of the
named beneficiary of an insurance policy rather than in compliance
with the insured testator's intent as expressed in his will?

DISCUSSION AND DECISION

. . . Margaret and Daniel do not dispute the facts in this case, yet they
contend that the court's entry of summary judgment was erroneous
because Indiana law does not require strict compliance with the terms
of an insurance policy relative to a change of beneficiary in all cases.
They argue, therefore, that strict compliance with policy provisions is

not required for the protection of either the insurer or the insured once the proceeds have been paid by the insurer into court in an action for interpleader and that the court should shape its relief in this case upon the equitable principle "that the insured's express and unambiguous intent should be given effect." . . .

Doris agrees that less than strict compliance with policy change requirements may be adequate to change a beneficiary where circumstances show the insured has done everything within his power to effect the change. Nevertheless, Doris asserts that Indiana adheres to the majority rule finding an attempt to change the beneficiary of a life insurance policy by will, without more, to be ineffectual. We agree with Doris.

Margaret and Daniel are correct in asserting that there are no Indiana cases involving precisely the same set of facts as occur in this case. Nevertheless, there is ample case law in this jurisdiction to support the trial court's determination. Almost one hundred years ago our supreme court in Holland v. Taylor, (1887) 111 Ind. 121, 12 N.E. 116, enunciated the general rule still followed in Indiana: an attempt to change the beneficiary of a life insurance contract by will and in disregard of the methods prescribed under the contract will be unsuccessful. . . .

Indiana courts have recognized exceptions to the general rule that strict compliance with policy requirements is necessary to effect a change of beneficiary. Three exceptions were noted by this court in Modern Brotherhood v. Matkovitch, (1914) 56 Ind. App. 8, 14, 104 N.E. 795, and reiterated in Heinzman v. Whiteman, (1923) 81 Ind. App. 29, 36, 139 N.E. 329, trans. denied:

> 1. If the society has waived a strict compliance with its own rules, and in pursuance of a request of the insured to change the beneficiary, has issued a new certificate to him, the original beneficiary will not be heard to complain that the course indicated by the regulations was not pursued.
> 2. If it be beyond the power of the insured to comply literally with the regulations, a court of equity will treat the change as having been legally made.
> 3. If the insured has pursued the course pointed out by the laws of the association, and has done all in his power to change the beneficiary; but before the new certificate is actually issued, he dies, a court of equity will decree that to be done which ought to be done, and act as though the certificate had been issued.

The public policy considerations undergirding this rule and its limited exceptions involve protection of the rights of all the parties concerned and should not be viewed, as appellants advocate, for the exclusive protection of the insurer. Indiana, in fact, has specifically rejected this position. In Stover v. Stover, (1965) 137 Ind. App. 578, 204 N.E.2d 374, 380, on rehearing 205 N.E.2d 178, trans. denied, the court recognized an insured's right to rely on the provisions of the policy in regard to change of beneficiary:

> We must reject appellant's contention that the provisions set forth in the certificate, as mentioned above, are for the exclusive benefit of the insurance company and may be waived at will. The deceased insured himself is entitled to rely upon such provisions that he may at all times know to whom the proceeds of the insurance shall be payable.

In *Holland* the court also recognized that the beneficiary had a right in the executed contract which was subject to defeat only by a change of beneficiary which had been executed in accord with the terms of the insurance contract: "In that contract Anna Laura, the beneficiary, had such an interest as that she had, and has, the right to insist that in order to cut her out, the change of beneficiary should be made in the manner provided in the contract." 111 Ind. 127, 12 N.E. 116. . . .

Clearly it is in the interest of insurance companies to require and to follow certain specified procedures in the change of beneficiaries of its policies so that they may pay over benefits to persons properly entitled to them without subjection to claims by others of whose rights they had no notice or knowledge. Certainly it is also in the interest of beneficiaries themselves to be entitled to prompt payment of benefits by insurance companies which do not withhold payment until the will has been probated in the fear of later litigation which might result from having paid the wrong party. . . . Finally, society's interest in the conservation of judicial energy and expense will be served where the rule and its limited exceptions are clearly stated and rigorously applied. . . .

Under the law of Indiana, therefore, in order for appellants to have defeated the motion for summary judgment in this case they must have made some showing that the insured had done all within his powers or all that reasonably could have been expected of him to comply with the policy provisions respecting a change of beneficiary, but that through no fault of his own he was unable to achieve his goal. Here there is no such indication or implication. Douglas was divorced in March of 1965 and remarried in December 1965. He was notified in July 1965 of the change in his policy, but took no action. A son was born of his second marriage. Eleven years after his divorce Douglas attempted to change the beneficiary of his insurance policy by a holographic will, but did not notify Equitable. He then lived three years after making that will. There is no indication that Douglas took any action in the fourteen years between his divorce from Doris and his death, other than the making of the will, to change the beneficiary of his life insurance policy from Doris to Margaret and Daniel. Surely, if Douglas had wanted to change the beneficiary he had ample time and opportunity to comply with the policy requirements. Nothing in the record suggests otherwise. . . .

We may be sympathetic to the cause of the decedent's widow and son, and it might seem that a departure from the general rule in an attempt to do equity under these facts would be noble. Nevertheless, such a course is fraught with the dangers of eroding a solidly paved pathway of the law and leaving in its stead only a gaping hole of uncertainty. Public policy requires that the insurer, insured, and beneficiary alike should be able to rely on the certainty that policy provisions pertaining to the naming and changing of beneficiaries will control except in extreme situations. We, therefore, invoke a maxim equally as venerable as the one upon which appellants rely in the determination of this cause: Equity aids the vigilant, not those who slumber on their rights.

Judgment affirmed.

NOTES AND QUESTIONS

1.   UPC §6-101 provides that if the contract permits the owner to change the beneficiary by will, the owner may do so. But if the power to change the beneficiary by will is not retained, §6-101 is silent on whether the beneficiary may be changed by will.

2.   The *Cook* case is followed in a large majority of states. See McCarthy v. Kapcar, 92 N.Y.2d 436, 704 N.E.2d 557 (1998).

The *Cook* case also follows the majority rule with respect to revocation of a life insurance beneficiary designation by divorce. As discussed earlier, at page 300, in most states divorce revokes a will in favor of the spouse but does not revoke the designation of the spouse as life insurance beneficiary. See Pepper v. Peacher, 742 P.2d 21 (Okla. 1987), holding that divorce does not revoke designation of remarried teacher's former husband as beneficiary of the teacher's retirement fund. UPC §2-804 (1990), supra page 299, changes this rule and provides that divorce revokes the designation of the divorced spouse as beneficiary of an insurance policy or pension plan or other contract. In Whirlpool Corp. v. Ritter, 929 F.2d 1318 (8th Cir. 1991), the court held that an Oklahoma statute resembling UPC §2-804, and designed to change the result in Pepper v. Peacher, was unconstitutional as applied to beneficiary designations made before the effective date of the statute. Retroactive application was viewed as disrupting the insured's expectations and impermissibly impairing the insured's rights under the contract. Accord, Aetna Life Ins. Co. v. Schilling, 67 Ohio St. 3d 164, 616 N.E.2d 893 (1993).

3.   Federal law, which trumps state law, has fueled the P.O.D. revolution. The federal government long has permitted a death beneficiary to be put on a U.S. savings bond. Beginning in the early 1960s, Congress has enacted changes in the Internal Revenue Code which give favorable tax treatment to various types of savings plans for retire-

ment. Federal law permits death beneficiaries to be put on these plans, including pension and profit-sharing plans, Keogh plans, 401(k) plans, and individual retirement accounts (IRAs).

In 1969, the Uniform Probate Code authorized P.O.D. designations. In states adopting the UPC or otherwise permitting P.O.D. designations beyond those authorized by federal law, brokerage houses will put payable-on-death designations on customers' stock portfolios held in custodial accounts. Mutual funds — favorite stock market investment devices of the 1980s and 1990s — permit payable-on-death designations. The designation of a death beneficiary on these funds need not comply with the Wills Act because they are governed by contract or trust principles. See E.F. Hutton & Co. v. Wallace, 863 F.2d 472 (6th Cir. 1988).

In 1989, a Uniform Transfer-On-Death Registration Act, permitting securities to be registered in a transfer-on-death (T.O.D.) form, was promulgated. This act has been adopted in a substantial number of states. Individual states have pushed the P.O.D. concept further. Kansas has enacted a statute permitting a death beneficiary to be named in a deed of land; such designation, as is true of other P.O.D.s, is revocable by the owner. Kan. Stat. Ann. §59-3501 (1997).

As a result of these late twentieth-century developments, an enormous amount of property can pass, and is passing, to payable-on-death beneficiaries outside the probate system.

4. *A superwill?* In view of the proliferation of nonprobate transfers, would it be a good idea to permit a *superwill?* A superwill would annul the beneficiaries named in various nonprobate instruments (other than a joint tenancy) and name a new beneficiary. Can you think of situations where a superwill would be useful? What are the drawbacks? There is precedent for the superwill concept. A power to revoke an inter vivos trust created by the decedent can be exercised by will, if the trust so provides. And a power of appointment given the decedent over a trust created by another person can be exercised by the will of the decedent. If the decedent can change the beneficiary of trust assets by will, why not beneficiaries of contracts? See Roberta R. Kwall & Anthony J. Aiello, The Superwill Debate: Opening the Pandora's Box?, 62 Temp. L. Rev. 277 (1989): Note, Should the Dead Hand Tighten Its Grasp? An Analysis of the Superwill, 1988 U. Ill. L. Rev. 1019. See also Wash. Rev. Code §§11.11.003–.901 (1999) (superwill statute).

SECTION B.   MULTIPLE-PARTY BANK ACCOUNTS

Multiple-party bank accounts include a joint and survivor account, a payable-on-death account, an agency account, and a savings account (Totten) trust.

The joint bank account gives rise to a number of difficulties because it is used for a variety of purposes. *A*, a bank depositor, may open a joint account with *B*, intending (1) that either *A* or *B* is to have power to draw on the account and the survivor owns the balance of the account (sometimes known as a "true joint tenancy account"), (2) that *B* is not to have power to withdraw on the account during life but is entitled to the balance upon *A*'s death (a P.O.D. account disguised as a joint account), or (3) that *B* is to have power to draw on the account during *A*'s life but is not entitled to the balance at *A*'s death (an agency account disguised as a joint account). Courts are often left with the problem of discerning which type of account is intended. If an agency account is intended, the survivor is not entitled to the proceeds in the account, which belong to the depositor's estate.

Franklin v. Anna National Bank of Anna

Illinois Appellate Court, Fifth District, 1986
140 Ill. App. 3d 533, 488 N.E.2d 1117

WELCH, J.   Plaintiff, Enola Stevens Franklin, as executor of the estate of Frank A. Whitehead, deceased, commenced this action in the circuit court of Union County against defendant Anna National Bank, alleging that the funds in a joint savings account were the property of the estate. The bank interpleaded Cora Goddard, who asserted her right to the money as the surviving joint owner. After a bench trial, the circuit court entered judgment for Mrs. Goddard. Mrs. Franklin appeals. We reverse.

This is the second time this case has been before the appellate court. In the prior appeal, Mrs. Franklin appealed from summary judgment in favor of Mrs. Goddard. This court reversed and remanded for trial. Franklin v. Anna National Bank (1983), 115 Ill. App. 3d 149, 450 N.E.2d 371.

Decedent died December 22, 1980. His wife Muriel Whitehead died in 1974. Mrs. Goddard was Muriel's sister. Decedent had eye surgery in May of 1978, and according to Mrs. Goddard was losing his eyesight in 1978. In April of 1978 Mrs. Goddard moved to Union County to help decedent and live with him. On April 17, 1978, Mrs. Goddard and decedent went to the bank, according to Mrs. Goddard to have his money put in both their names so she could get money when they needed it, "and he wanted me to have this money if I outlived him."

A bank employee prepared a signature card for savings account No. 3816 and Mrs. Goddard signed it. A copy of this card was in evidence at trial. The signatures of decedent and Mrs. Goddard appear on both sides of the card. It appears that Muriel Whitehead's signature was "whited out" and Mrs. Goddard's signature added. The front of the card states that one signature is required for withdrawals. The back of the card states that all funds deposited are owned by the signatories as joint tenants with right of survivorship.

Mrs. Goddard testified that she did not deposit any of the money in savings account No. 3816. She made no withdrawals, though she once took decedent to the bank so he could make a withdrawal. According to Mrs. Goddard, on the day she signed the signature card decedent "asked me if I needed my money because they had bought cemetery lots from me, and I told him, not at this time, that I didn't need it. He wanted to know if I needed any more money at that time and I said, no, and I said, just leave it in here and I will get it out whenever I need it." According to Mrs. Goddard, decedent promised to pay her $1,000 for the lots; she was never paid. Asked whether she ever had the passbook for savings account No. 3816 in her possession, Mrs. Goddard answered, "Only while I was at Frank's. It was there."

Later in 1978, Mrs. Franklin began to care for decedent. In January 1979, decedent telephoned the bank, then sent Mrs. Franklin to the bank to deliver a letter to Mrs. Kedron Boyer, a bank employee. The handwritten letter, dated January 13, 1979, and signed by decedent, stated: "I Frank Whitehead wish by Bank accounts be changed to Enola Stevens joint intendency [sic]. Nobody go in my lock box but me." According to Mrs. Franklin, Mrs. Boyer told her to tell decedent he would have to specify what type of account he was referring to. Decedent gave Mrs. Franklin a second letter which Mrs. Franklin delivered to Mrs. Carol Williams at the bank (Mrs. Boyer was absent). This handwritten letter, dated January 13, 1979, stated: "I Frank Whitehead want Enola Stevens and me only go in my lock box. Account type Saving and Checking. In case I can't see she is to take care of my bill or sick." According to Mrs. Franklin, Mrs. Williams said she would take care of it and give the letter to Mrs. Boyer. Mrs. Franklin testified that she signed the savings passbook in the presence of decedent and Mrs. Boyer. Mrs. Franklin took her present last name on May 8, 1979.

Mrs. Boyer, Mrs. Williams, and bank president Delano Mowery all testified at trial. These witnesses explained the usual procedures for account changes. None remembered much of the circumstances surrounding the bank's receipt of the January 13, 1979, letters. According to Mr. Mowery, the bank would not remove a signature from a signature card based on a letter; the most recent signature card the bank had for savings account No. 3816 was signed by decedent and Mrs. Goddard.

Mrs. Goddard's attorney's assertion at trial that there were no monthly statements on savings account No. 3816 was uncontradicted.

The trial court found that Mrs. Goddard was the sole owner of the funds in savings account No. 3816 by right of survivorship as surviving joint tenant, and that no part of the funds became part of decedent's estate.

Mrs. Franklin argues that decedent did not intend to make a gift of savings account No. 3816 to Mrs. Goddard.

The instrument creating a joint tenancy account presumably speaks the whole truth. In order to go behind the terms of the agreement, the one claiming adversely thereto has the burden of establishing by clear and convincing evidence that a gift was not intended. Each case involving a joint tenancy account must be evaluated on its own facts and circumstances. The form of the agreement is not conclusive regarding the intention of the depositors between themselves. (In re Estate of Schneider (1955), 6 Ill. 2d 180, 186, 127 N.E.2d 445, 449.) Evidence of lack of donative intent must relate back to the time of creation of the joint tenancy. The decision of the donor, made subsequent to the creation of the joint tenancy, that he did not want the proceeds to pass to the survivor, would not, in itself, be sufficient to sever the tenancy. However, it is proper to consider events occurring after creation of the joint account in determining whether the donor actually intended to transfer his interest in the account at his death to the surviving joint tenant. In re Estate of Guzak (1979), 69 Ill. App. 3d 552, 555, 388 N.E.2d 431, 433.

We examine the instant facts in light of the above principles: There appears no serious doubt that in January of 1979, just nine months after adding Mrs. Goddard's name to savings account No. 3816, decedent attempted to remove Mrs. Goddard's name and substitute Mrs. Franklin's. The second of decedent's handwritten letters to the bank in January of 1979 indicates decedent's concern that he might lose his sight and be unable to transact his own banking business. These facts show that decedent made Mrs. Goddard (and later Mrs. Franklin) a signatory for his own convenience, in case he could not get his money, and not with intent to effect a present gift. (See Dixon National Bank v. Morris (1965), 33 Ill. 2d 156, 159, 210 N.E.2d 505, 506; In re Estate of Guzak (1979), 69 Ill. App. 3d 552, 388 N.E.2d 431.) It does not appear that Mrs. Goddard ever exercised any authority or control over the joint account. While decedent's statement that he wanted Mrs. Goddard to have the money in the account if she outlived him suggests decedent's donative intent, taken literally decedent's statement is inconsistent with intent to donate any interest during decedent's lifetime. (See Lipe v. Farmers State Bank (1970), 131 Ill. App. 2d 1024, 1026, 265 N.E.2d 204, 205.) Mrs. Goddard does not argue that there was a valid testamentary disposition in her favor, nor could we so find on the instant facts.

Of the many cases cited by the parties for comparison with the case at bar, the most persuasive is In re Estate of Schneider (1955), 6 Ill. 2d 180, 127 N.E.2d 445. In In re Estate of Schneider, the decedent's executor filed a petition alleging the funds in joint bank accounts belonged to the estate and not to Ralston, the surviving joint tenant. Ralston testified that all of the money in the account was deposited by the decedent, that the decedent at no time told Ralston he wanted Ralston to have any of the money, and that when Ralston's name was added to the accounts the decedent said, "I want your name on these bank accounts so that in case I am sick you can go and get the money for me." The trial court concluded that the decedent intended to retain actual ownership of the money. Our supreme court agreed. We reach the same conclusion here. In the case at bar, decedent's attempts to change the account show his consistent view of the account as his own. The surrounding circumstances show decedent's concern for his health and his relatively brief use of Mrs. Goddard (and later Mrs. Franklin) to assure his access to his funds. The money in account No. 3816 should have been found to be the property of the estate.

For the foregoing reasons, the judgment of the circuit court of Union County is reversed, and this cause is remanded for entry of judgment in favor of plaintiff.

Reversed.

NOTES AND PROBLEMS

1.   Why did not the bank offer Frank Whitehead his choice of three accounts: a true joint tenancy account, an agency account, or a P.O.D. account? If banks did this, much of the litigation over the depositor's intention would disappear.

A payable-on-death account is invalid in some states for reasons given in the *Wilhoit* case, supra page 331. Professor Wellman lists 30 states permitting P.O.D. bank accounts. Richard V. Wellman, Transfer-on-Death Securities Registration: A New Title Form, 21 Ga. L. Rev. 789, 806 n.50 (1987). Even in states permitting P.O.D. bank accounts, however, banks have resisted offering depositors clear choices. They continue to channel depositors into the joint bank account. Id. at 829 n.108.

To eliminate the extensive litigation over the depositor's intent in creating a joint bank account, several courts in recent years have held that a joint bank account *conclusively* establishes a right of survivorship; evidence to the contrary is not admissible. See Wright v. Bloom, 69 Ohio St. 3d 596, 635 N.E.2d 31 (1994); Robinson v. Delfino, 710 A.2d 154 (R.I. 1998).

2.   Suppose that Frank Whitehead had made Enola Stevens Franklin a joint tenant of his safe-deposit box in order that Enola could enter it. The bank card (designated a "Lease of Safe-Deposit Box") signed by Frank and Enola provides: "The lessees are joint tenants with right of survivorship and all property of every kind at any time

placed in said box is the joint property of both lessees and upon the death of either passes to the survivor." In the box are stock certificates, a diamond ring, and $2,000 in cash, all placed there by Frank before the bank card was signed. Does Enola own all the items in the box at Frank's death? See In re Estate of Wilson, 404 Ill. 207, 88 N.E.2d 662 (1949); Steinhauser v. Repko, 30 Ohio St. 2d 262, 285 N.E.2d 55 (1972); Annots., 40 A.L.R.3d 462 (1971), 14 A.L.R.2d 948 (1950).

3. *The savings account trust (or Totten trust).* One type of multiple-party bank account that functions as a P.O.D. account is the savings account trust (not usually available at banks for checking accounts). In the landmark case of In re Totten, 179 N.Y. 112, 71 N.E. 748 (1904), *O* made deposits in a savings account in the name of "*O* as trustee for *A*." *O* retained the right to revoke the trust by withdrawing the funds at any time during his life. Since *A* is entitled only to the amount on deposit at *O*'s death, in practical effect *A* is merely a payable-on-death beneficiary of a "trust" of a savings account. The court upheld this arrangement as not testamentary, declaring that a "tentative" revocable trust had been created at the time of the deposit. At *O*'s death any funds in the account belong to *A*. Savings account trusts, often known at Totten trusts, have now been accepted in a large majority of jurisdictions. See Restatement (Third) of Trusts §26 (T.D. No. 2, 1999); 1A Austin W. Scott, Trusts §58.3 (William F. Frachter 4th ed. 1987).

The beneficiary designation of a Totten trust may be revoked by will and a new beneficiary named. Id.

4. The Uniform Probate Code provisions for multiple-party bank accounts are found in §§6-201 through 6-227. The UPC authorizes a joint tenancy account with the right of survivorship, an agency account, and a payable-on-death account. Short forms for banks to use in establishing each type of account are provided. The Totten trust is abolished; it is treated as a P.O.D. account. Extrinsic evidence is admissible to show that a joint account was opened solely for the convenience of the depositor. UPC §§6-203, 6-204, 6-212, comment (1991).

Joint accounts belong to the parties during their joint lifetimes "in proportion to the net contribution of each to the sums on deposit, unless there is clear and convincing evidence of a different intent." UPC §6-211(b). The beneficiary of a P.O.D. account has no rights to sums on deposit during the lifetime of the depositor.

A requirement of survivorship is imposed on beneficiaries of P.O.D. bank accounts (§6-212), as well as on beneficiaries of securities in T.O.D. registration (§6-307), but not, as discussed above, on beneficiaries of P.O.D. contracts generally. However, the antilapse statute (UPC §2-706) substitutes in place of a deceased beneficiary of a P.O.D. bank account, the beneficiary's issue if the beneficiary was a close relative of the decedent (see infra page 446).

A P.O.D. beneficiary of a bank account cannot be changed by will. UPC §6-213(b). (Recall that UPC §6-101, authorizing P.O.D. designations on contracts, is silent on the question of whether the beneficiary may be changed by will.)

For careful examination of the nonprobate transfer provisions of the UPC, pointing out unexplained inconsistencies in the treatment of the different kinds of nonprobate transfers, see Grayson M.P. McCouch, Will Substitutes Under the Revised Uniform Probate Code, 58 Brook. L. Rev. 1123 (1993), and William M. McGovern, Jr., Nonprobate Transfers Under the Revised Uniform Probate Code, 55 Alb. L. Rev. 1329 (1992).

SECTION C.   JOINT TENANCIES

A joint tenancy or a tenancy by the entirety in land is a common and popular method of avoiding the cost and delay of probate. Perhaps most family homes in this country are owned by husband and wife either in joint tenancy or tenancy by the entirety. See William N. Hines, Real Property Joint Tenancies, 51 Iowa L. Rev. 582 (1966). Upon the death of one joint tenant or tenant by the entirety, the survivor owns the property absolutely, freed of any participation by the decedent. The common law theory is that the decedent's interest vanishes at death, and therefore no probate is necessary because no interest passes to the survivor at death. Joint tenancies and tenancies by the entireties are ordinarily covered in first-year courses in property. Only three features of joint tenancies need mention here.

First, the creation of a joint tenancy in land gives the joint tenants equal interests upon creation. A person who transfers land into a joint tenancy cannot, during life, revoke the transfer and cancel the interest given the other joint tenant. In contrast, P.O.D. designations can be changed by the owner during life, and, under the UPC, a joint bank account can be revoked by a depositor who furnishes all the funds.

Second, a joint tenant cannot devise his or her share by will. If a joint tenant wants someone other than the co-tenant to take his share at death, he must sever the joint tenancy during life, converting it into a tenancy in common. Why is a will ineffective to change survivorship rights in a joint tenancy? The answer dictated by the vanishing theory of the common law is that since no property passes from the decedent joint tenant at death, there is no interest for the decedent's will to operate upon. But perhaps a more persuasive reason lies in policy. If a joint tenant could devise his share, the property would be subject to litigation to determine the validity of the will and, most importantly, whether the will made a disposition of the joint tenancy property. Does a residuary clause ("all the rest and residue of my property") dispose of joint tenancy property? Is a specific reference required? How specific? If joint tenants could devise their share, the mere existence of the testamentary power would give them less assurance that the survivor would take, unentangled by will construction, probate costs, and claims of third parties, because of the possibilities of inadvertent exercise of the power. The overwhelming number of joint tenants select the tenancy precisely because of the high degree of assurance of no entanglement with probate. To continue this assurance, the right of testamentary disposition must be denied, and the few attempts by ignorant testators to devise their joint tenancy property must fail.

If this reasoning is persuasive, does it apply to other will substitutes?

The third feature of joint tenancy to be noted relates to creditors' rights. A creditor of a joint tenant must seize the joint tenant's interest during life. At death the joint tenant's interest vanishes and there is nothing for the creditor to reach; it is too late. See Citizens Action League v. Kizer, 887 F.2d 1003 (9th Cir. 1989); Rembe v. Stewart, 387 N.W.2d 313 (Iowa 1986) (criticizing but upholding rule).

Apart from the vanishing theory of the common law, is there any reason why creditors of a decedent joint tenant cannot reach joint tenancy property if they can reach other will substitutes?

SECTION D. REVOCABLE TRUSTS

1. Introduction

Revocable inter vivos trusts have come into widespread use, particularly among the moderately and very wealthy. A revocable inter vivos trust is the most flexible of all will substitutes because the donor can draft the dispositive provisions and the administrative provisions precisely to the donor's liking.

Under the typical revocable inter vivos trust involving a *deed of trust,* the trust settlor transfers legal title to property to another person as trustee pursuant to a writing in which the settlor retains the power to revoke, alter, or amend the trust and the right to trust income during lifetime.[4] On the settlor's death, the trust assets are to be distributed to or held in further trust for other beneficiaries. While several early cases held these revocable trusts invalid unless executed with testamentary formalities, all jurisdictions now recognize the validity of a trust where property is transferred to another person as trustee and the settlor reserves the power to revoke the trust during life. The settlor may also reserve an income interest and a testamentary power of appointment.

The second context in which the question of validity arises is where there is a *revocable declaration of trust,* under which the settlor declares himself trustee for the benefit of himself during lifetime, with the remainder to pass to others at his death. Since there is little discernible change in the owner's relation to the property during lifetime, should the courts give effect to this arrangement to the extent that it causes assets to pass to others at the owner's death?

Farkas v. Williams
Supreme Court of Illinois, 1955
5 Ill. 2d 417, 125 N.E.2d 600

HERSHEY, J. . . .   The plaintiffs asked the court to declare their legal rights, as co-administrators, in four stock certificates issued by Investors Mutual Inc. in the name of "Albert B. Farkas, as trustee for Richard J. Williams" and which were issued pursuant to written declarations of trust. The decree of the circuit court found that said declarations were testamentary in character, and not having been executed with the formalities of a will, were invalid, and directed that the stock be awarded to the plaintiffs as an asset of the estate of said Albert B. Farkas. Upon appeal to the Appellate Court, the decree was affirmed. See 3 Ill. App. 2d 248, 121 N.E.2d 344. We allowed defendants' petition for leave to appeal.

Albert B. Farkas died intestate at the age of sixty-seven years, a resident of Chicago, leaving as his only heirs-at-law brothers, sisters, a nephew and a niece. Although retired at the time of his death, he had for many years practiced veterinary medicine and operated a veterinarian establishment in Chicago. During a considerable portion of that time, he employed the defendant Williams, who was not related to him.

On four occasions (December 8, 1948; February 7, 1949; February

4. Revocable deeds of land not in trust are dangerous will substitutes that should never be used. The cases are split as to whether revocable deeds of land are testamentary and therefore void for failure to comply with the Wills Act. Since land can be put in a revocable trust, no knowledgeable lawyer ever uses a revocable deed delivered to the grantee.

14, 1950; and March 1, 1950) Farkas purchased stock of Investors
Mutual, Inc. At the time of each purchase he executed a written
application to Investors Mutual, Inc., instructing them to issue the
stock in his name "as trustee for Richard J. Williams." Investors Mutual, Inc., by its agent, accepted each of these applications in writing
by signature on the face of the application. Coincident with the execution of these applications, Farkas signed separate declarations of trust,
all of which were identical except as to dates. The terms of said trust
instruments are as follows:

> Declaration of Trust — Revocable. I, the undersigned, having pur-
> chased or declared my intention to purchase certain shares of capital
> stock of Investors Mutual, Inc. (the Company), and having directed that
> the certificate for said stock be issued in my name as trustee for Richard
> J. Williams as beneficiary, whose address is 1704 W. North Ave. Chicago,
> Ill., under this Declaration of Trust Do Hereby Declare that the terms
> and conditions upon which I shall hold said stock in trust and any addi-
> tional stock resulting from reinvestments of cash dividends upon such
> original or additional shares are as follows:
>
> (1) During my lifetime all cash dividends are to be paid to me individ-
> ually for my own personal account and use; provided, however, that any
> such additional stock purchased under an authorized reinvestment of
> cash dividends shall become a part of and subject to this trust.
>
> (2) Upon my death the title to any stock subject hereto and the right
> to any subsequent payments or distributions shall be vested absolutely in
> the beneficiary.
>
> (3) During my lifetime I reserve the right, as trustee, to vote, sell, re-
> deem, exchange or otherwise deal in or with the stock subject hereto,
> but upon any sale or redemption of said stock or any part thereof, the
> trust hereby declared shall terminate as to the stock sold or redeemed,
> and I shall be entitled to retain the proceeds of sale or redemption for
> my own personal account and use.
>
> (4) I reserve the right at any time to change the beneficiary or revoke
> this trust, but it is understood that no change of beneficiary and no revoca-
> tion of this trust except by death of the beneficiary, shall be effective as
> to the Company for any purpose unless and until written notice thereof
> in such form as the Company shall prescribe is delivered to the Company
> at Minneapolis, Minnesota. The decease of the beneficiary before my
> death shall operate as a revocation of this trust.
>
> (5) In the event this trust shall be revoked or otherwise terminated,
> said stock and all rights and privileges thereunder shall belong to and
> be exercised by me in my individual capacity.

. . . The applications and declarations of trust were delivered to
Investors Mutual, Inc., and held by the company until Farkas' death.
The stock certificates were issued in the name of Farkas as "trustee
for Richard J. Williams" and were discovered in a safety-deposit box

of Farkas after his death, along with other securities, some of which were in the name of Williams alone. . . .

It is conceded that the instruments were not executed in such a way as to satisfy the requirements of the statute on wills; hence, our inquiry is limited to whether said trust instruments created valid inter vivos trusts effective to give the purported beneficiary, Williams, title to the stock in question after the death of the settlor-trustee, Farkas. To make this determination we must consider: (1) whether upon execution of the so-called trust instruments defendant Williams acquired an interest in the subject matter of the trusts, the stock of defendant Investors Mutual, Inc., (2) whether Farkas, as settlor-trustee, retained such control over the subject matter of the trusts as to render said trust instruments attempted testamentary dispositions.

First, upon execution of these trust instruments did defendant Williams presently acquire an interest in the subject matter of the intended trusts?

If no interest passed to Williams before the death of Farkas, the intended trusts are testamentary and hence invalid for failure to comply with the statute on wills. Oswald v. Caldwell, 225 Ill. 224, 80 N.E. 131; Troup v. Hunter, 300 Ill. 110, 133 N.E. 56; Restatement of the Law of Trusts, section 56. But considering the terms of these instruments we believe Farkas did intend to presently give Williams an interest in the property referred to. For it may be said, at the very least, that upon his executing one of these instruments, he showed an intention to presently part with some of the incidents of ownership in the stock. Immediately after the execution of each of these instruments, he could not deal with the stock therein referred to the same as if he owned the property absolutely, but only in accordance with the terms of the instrument. He purported to set himself up as trustee of the stock for the benefit of Williams, and the stock was registered in his name as trustee for Williams. Thus assuming to act as trustee, he is held to have intended to take on those obligations which are expressly set out in the instrument, as well as those fiduciary obligations implied by law. In addition, he manifested an intention to bind himself to having this property pass upon his death to Williams, unless he changed the beneficiary or revoked the trust, and then such change of beneficiary or revocation was not to be effective as to Investors Mutual, Inc., unless and until written notice thereof in such form as the company prescribed was delivered to them at Minneapolis, Minnesota. An absolute owner can dispose of his property, either in his lifetime or by will, in any way he sees fit without notifying or securing approval from anyone and without being held to the duties of a fiduciary in so doing.

It seems to follow that what incidents of ownership Farkas intended to relinquish, in a sense he intended Williams to acquire. . . . It is difficult to name this interest of Williams, nor is there any reason for so doing so long as it passed to him immediately upon the creation of the trust.[5] As stated in 4 Powell, The Law of Real Property, at page 87: "Interests of beneficiaries of private express trusts run the gamut from valuable substantialities to evanescent hopes. Such a beneficiary may have any one of an almost infinite variety of the possible aggregates of rights, privileges, powers and immunities."

An additional problem is presented here, however, for it is to be noted that the trust instruments provide: "The decease of the beneficiary before my death shall operate as a revocation of this trust." The plaintiffs argue that the presence of this provision removes the only possible distinction which might have been drawn between these instruments and a will. Being thus conditioned on his surviving, it is argued that the "interest" of Williams until the death of Farkas was a mere expectancy. Conversely, they assert, the interest of Farkas in the securities until his death was precisely the same as that of a testator who bequeaths securities by his will, since he had all the rights accruing to an absolute owner.

Admittedly, had this provision been absent the interest of Williams would have been greater, since he would then have had an inheritable interest in the lifetime of Farkas. But to say his interest would have been greater is not to say that he here did not have a beneficial interest, properly so-called, during the lifetime of Farkas. The provision purports to set up but another "contingency" which would serve to terminate the trust. The disposition is not testamentary and the intended trust is valid, even though the interest of the beneficiary is contingent upon the existence of a certain state of facts at the time of the settlor's death. (Restatement of the Law of Trusts, section 56, Comment f.) In an example contained in the previous reference, the authors of the Restatement have referred to the interest of a beneficiary under a trust who must survive the settlor (and where the settlor receives the income for life) as a contingent equitable interest in remainder. . . .

Second, did Farkas retain such control over the subject matter of the trust as to render said trust instruments attempted testamentary dispositions?

In each of these trust instruments, Farkas reserved to himself as

---

5. The idea of an interest smaller than any interest you can name, but nonetheless an interest, brings to mind the mathematical concept of the infinitesimal, developed by Isaac Newton and Gottfried Wilhelm von Leibniz. Although scorned by Bishop Berkeley as "ghosts of departed quantities," infinitesimals proved very useful in differential calculus.

Would it be a good idea for the Illinois legislature to settle the matter by passing a statute providing that, if a settlor retained the powers Farkas retained, the beneficiary would be deemed to receive an infinitesimal interest? Should the legislature give the interest a name, such as a farkas, since the court finds naming so difficult? — Eds.

settlor the following powers: (1) the right to receive during his lifetime all cash dividends; (2) the right at any time to change the beneficiary or revoke the trust; and (3) upon sale or redemption of any
portion of the trust property, the right to retain the proceeds therefrom for his own use.

Additionally, Farkas reserved the right to act as sole trustee, and in
such capacity, he was accorded the right to vote, sell, redeem, exchange or otherwise deal in the stock which formed the subject matter
of the trust.

We shall consider first those enumerated powers which Farkas reserved to himself as settlor.

It is well established that the retention by the settlor of the power
to revoke, even when coupled with the reservation of a life interest
in the trust property, does not render the trust inoperative for want
of execution as a will. . . .

A more difficult problem is posed, however, by the fact that Farkas
is also trustee, and as such, is empowered to vote, sell, redeem, exchange and otherwise deal in and with the subject matter of the
trusts. . . .

In the instant case the plaintiffs contend that Farkas, as settlor-
trustee, retained complete control and dominion over the securities
for his own benefit during his lifetime. It is argued that he had the
power to deal with the property as he liked so long as he lived and
owed no enforceable duties of any kind to Williams as beneficiary. . . .

That the retention of the power by Farkas as trustee to sell or
redeem the stock and keep the proceeds for his own use should not
render these trust instruments testamentary in character becomes
more evident upon analyzing the real import and significance of the
powers to revoke and to amend the trust, the reservation of which
the courts uniformly hold does not invalidate an inter vivos trust.

It is obvious that a settlor with the power to revoke and to amend
the trust at any time is, for all practical purpose, in a position to exert
considerable control over the trustee regarding the administration of
the trust. For anything believed to be inimicable to his best interest
can be thwarted or prevented by simply revoking the trust or amend-
ing it in such a way as to conform to his wishes. Indeed, it seems that
many of those powers which from time to time have been viewed as
"additional powers" are already, in a sense, virtually contained within
the overriding power of revocation or the power to amend the trust.
Consider, for example, the following: (1) the power to consume the
principal; (2) the power to sell or mortgage the trust property and
appropriate the proceeds; (3) the power to appoint or remove trustees; (4) the power to supervise and direct investments; and (5) the
power to otherwise direct and supervise the trustee in the administration of the trust. Actually, any of the above powers could readily be

assumed by a settlor with the reserved power of revocation through the simple expedient of revoking the trust, and then, as absolute owner of the subject matter, doing with the property as he chooses. Even though no actual termination of the trust is effectuated, however, it could hardly be questioned but that the mere existence of this power in the settlor is sufficient to enable his influence to be felt in a practical way in the administration of the trust. . . .

In the case at bar, the power in Farkas to vote, sell, redeem, exchange or otherwise deal in the stock was reserved to him as trustee, and it was only upon sale or redemption that he was entitled to keep the proceeds for his own use. Thus, the control reserved is not as great as in those cases where said power is reserved to the owner as settlor. For as trustee he must so conduct himself in accordance with standards applicable to trustees generally. It is not a valid objection to this to say that Williams would never question Farkas' conduct, inasmuch as Farkas could then revoke the trust and destroy what interest Williams has. Such a possibility exists in any case where the settlor has the power of revocation. Still, Williams has rights the same as any beneficiary, although it may not be feasible for him to exercise them. Moreover, it is entirely possible that he might in certain situations have a right to hold Farkas' estate liable for breaches of trust committed by Farkas during his lifetime. In this regard, consider what would happen if, without having revoked the trust, Farkas as trustee had given the stock away without receiving any consideration therefor, had pledged the stock improperly for his own personal debt and allowed it to be lost by foreclosure or had exchanged the stock for another security or other worthless property in such manner as to constitute gross impropriety and gross negligence. In such instances, it would seem in accordance with the terms of these instruments that Williams would have had an enforceable claim against Farkas' estate for whatever damage had been suffered. Contrast this with the rights of a legatee or devisee under a will. The testator could waste the property or do anything with it he wished during his lifetime without incurring any liability to those designated by the will to inherit the property. . . .

Another factor often considered in determining whether an inter vivos trust is an attempted testamentary disposition is the formality of the transaction. Restatement of the Law of Trusts, section 57, Comment g; Stouse v. First National Bank, Ky., 245 S.W.2d 914, 32 A.L.R.2d 1261; United Building and Loan Association v. Garrett, D.C. 64 F. Supp. 460; In re Sheasley's Trust, 366 Pa. 316, 77 A.2d 448. Historically, the purpose behind the enactment of the statute on wills was the prevention of fraud. The requirement as to witnesses was deemed necessary because a will is ordinarily an expression of the secret wish of the testator, signed out of the presence of all concerned. The possibility of forgery and fraud are ever present in such situations. Here, Farkas executed four separate applications for stock of Investors Mutual, Inc., in which he directed that the stock be issued in his name as trustee for Williams, and he executed four separate declarations of trust in which he declared he was holding said stock in trust for Williams. The stock certificates in question were issued in his name as trustee for Williams. He thus manifested his intention in a solemn and formal manner.

For the reasons stated, we conclude that these trust declarations executed by Farkas constituted valid inter vivos trusts and were not attempted testamentary dispositions. It must be conceded that they have, in the words of Mr. Justice Holmes in Bromley v. Mitchell, 155 Mass. 509, 30 N.E. 83, a "testamentary look." Moreover, it must be admitted that the line should be drawn somewhere, but after a study of this case we do not believe that point has been reached. . . .

Reversed and remanded, with directions.

NOTES AND PROBLEM

1. A trust is a management relation whereby the trustee manages property for the benefit of one or more beneficiaries. The trustee holds legal title to the property and, in the usual trust, can sell the trust property and replace it with property thought more desirable. The trustee owes fiduciary duties to the beneficiaries, including loyalty to them and prudence in investments (see infra Chapter 13). If the trustee breaches one of these duties, the trustee is personally liable to the beneficiaries. We call the beneficiaries' interest in a trust "equitable title" because an equity court enforces their rights against the trustee. Thus a trust creates equitable interests in beneficiaries enforceable against the trustee who has legal title.

The trustee can be one of the beneficiaries of the trust. If, however, the trustee is the *sole* beneficiary, there is no trust, because the trustee owes no duties to anyone except himself. It would be silly for a court to entertain a lawsuit by A, the sole beneficiary, charging A, the trustee, with malfeasance in office, and asking for damages. The law rejects this idea by saying that, where one person is the sole beneficiary and the trustee, the equitable and legal titles *merge*, leaving that one person with absolute legal title. This rarely happens, however, because most trusts have multiple beneficiaries.

The question in a revocable declaration of trust, where the settlor is the trustee, is: Does the settlor owe any fiduciary duties to anyone other than himself? Or, to put it another way, has the settlor created any equitable interest in anyone other than himself? If not, there is no trust. The settlor remains the absolute owner of the property.

In Farkas v. Williams what duties did Farkas as trustee owe Williams as a beneficiary? What equitable interest was created in Williams?

2. In Estate of Brenner, 547 P.2d 938 (Colo. App. 1976), R. Forrest Brenner executed a revocable declaration of trust (captioned ''The R. Forrest Brenner Trust'') of certain real property for the benefit of himself for life, remainder to his children by a prior marriage and a niece. On the date the trust instrument was executed, Brenner did not own the real property in question, but five days later this property was conveyed to ''R. Forrest Brenner, Trustee for R. Forrest Brenner.'' On Brenner's death, the validity of the trust was challenged. The court held the trust valid, stating:

> ... [W]e hold that the conveyance of the real property to Brenner as trustee five days after he executed the trust instrument effectively validated the trust. Where, as here, an individual manifests an intention to create a trust in property to be acquired in the future, and thereafter confirms this intent by taking the steps necessary to transfer the property to the trust, the property so transferred becomes subject to the terms of the trust. For reasons stated hereafter, we do not believe that the foregoing rule is inapplicable merely because Brenner was settlor, trustee, and lifetime beneficiary of the trust. Appellant contends, in effect, that the evidence failed to establish Brenner's intent to establish a trust. In support of this contention, appellant relies upon evidence, inter alia, that Brenner failed to prepare and file the requisite Colorado and federal tax forms relative to a trust, that he failed to keep separate books, records, and bank accounts relative to the trust property, that he reported income and expenses from trust property on an individual income tax form, and that he did not advise either [his wife] Evelyn or his accountant of the existence of the trust. However, other evidence established that Brenner took title to the property described in the ''exhibit'' as trustee, that he acquired additional real estate as trustee, and that he executed a contract as trustee relating to both properties. The evidence and inferences therefrom being in conflict, the trial court's determination that Brenner intended to create a trust and thereby provide for his children and niece, as natural objects of his bounty, may not be disturbed on review.
>
> Appellant next contends that the declaration of trust was invalid by reason of the extensive control retained over the trust property by Brenner through his appointment as trustee, his reservation of all income during his lifetime, the right to revoke, alter, or amend the trust, and the sole power to invest, reinvest, manage, and control the trust property. We disagree. See Farkas v. Williams, 5 Ill. 2d 417, 125 N.E.2d 600.

In Taliaferro v. Taliaferro, 260 Kan. 573, 921 P.2d 803 (1996), the settlor declared in writing that he held in a revocable trust all property listed on Schedule A for himself for life, remainder to his wife on his death. Schedule A listed the settlor's Douglass Bank stock, a life insurance policy on the life of another, the settlor's household goods, and

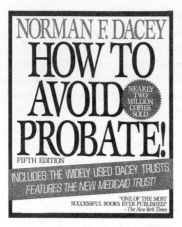

the contents of the settlor's safe deposit box. The settlor never changed legal title to the assets listed on Schedule A to himself as trustee. The court held that a valid trust was created of the items listed on Schedule A.

3. The revocable declaration of trust — sometimes called a *living trust* — is the key feature of Norman F. Dacey's book, How to Avoid Probate!, now in its 5th edition (1993). Upon publication in 1965 the book became a runaway bestseller. In the first edition, Dacey opens his book with a slashing attack on lawyers who profit from the probate system. He charges:

> The probate system, conceived generations ago as a device for protecting heirs, has now become their greatest enemy. Almost universally corrupt, it is essentially a form of private taxation levied by the legal profession upon the rest of the population. All across the land, both large and small estates are being plundered by lawyers specializing in "probate practice." [1st ed. at 15.]

After denouncing the "extortionate legal fees" and delays of probate, Dacey offers a way to avoid probate: Declare yourself trustee of your property by using a revocable declaration of trust, with the trust property to pass to named beneficiaries upon your death. In other words, do what Albert Farkas did in Farkas v. Williams. Dacey's book contains all kinds of do-it-yourself trust and will forms designed for various kinds of assets and different family situations.

The legal profession was not amused by Dacey's book. After publication of the first edition, the New York County Lawyers' Association sought an injunction to ban sale of the book on the ground that Dacey (a nonlawyer) was giving legal advice. The New York Court of Appeals held that Dacey's readers were not his clients because the book was sold to the public at large and no relationship of personal trust and confidence arose. New York County Lawyers' Assn. v. Dacey, 21 N.Y.2d 694, 234 N.E.2d 459, 287 N.Y.S.2d 422 (1967). After this victory, Dacey retaliated by suing the New York County Lawyers' Association for $5,000,000 in damages for interfering with his right to free speech. He lost. Dacey v. New York County Lawyers' Assn., 423 F.2d 188 (2d Cir. 1969). Dacey also unsuccessfully sued the Florida Bar Association for publishing a review of Dacey's book Dacey thought was libelous. Dacey v. Florida Bar, Inc., 427 F.2d 1292 (5th Cir. 1970). Subsequently, in order to avoid income tax on royalties on 2.5 million copies sold, Dacey moved to Ireland, but lawyers had their revenge when the Commissioner of Internal Revenue (a lawyer!) pursued Dacey and forced him to cough up hundreds of thousands of dollars in taxes and penalties because he remained a United States citizen. Dacey v. Commissioner, T.C. Memo 1992-187. In 1988 Dacey renounced his U.S. citizenship and became a citizen of Ireland. Norman Dacey died in London in 1994.

Since Dacey first published his book there has been a groundswell of public demand for a simpler and less costly probate system. Reform has occurred in many states, often in the form of adoption of the Uniform Probate Code. It is fair to suggest that How to Avoid Probate!, and its astonishing reception by the public, served as a catalyst for probate reform. The reforms to date, however, have not deprived the revocable trust of its advantage in bypassing probate. Probate remains costly, time-consuming, and public.

4. For discussion of the revocable trust, and particularly of its evolution and function as an equivalent of a will, see Restatement (Third) of Trusts §25 (T.D. No. 1, 1996).

In re Estate and Trust of Pilafas
Arizona Court of Appeals, 1992
172 Ariz. 207, 836 P.2d 420

McGregor, J.   The remainder beneficiaries (appellants) under an inter vivos trust agreement appeal the trial court's determination that Steve J. Pilafas (decedent) revoked his inter vivos trust and will and died intestate. Appellants raise two issues on appeal. The first is whether appellees presented sufficient evidence that decedent revoked his will. We find the evidence sufficient and affirm that part of the trial court's judgment. The second issue is whether the trial court erred in determining that decedent effectively revoked his inter vivos trust. We hold that the court did err and reverse.

I

On August 30, 1982, decedent executed a trust agreement appointing himself trustee of certain described properties for the benefit of himself and other specified beneficiaries. Decedent immediately funded the trust by executing and recording a deed and an assignment that transferred a Phoenix residence and his interest in a note and deed of trust on a mobile home park to himself as trustee under the trust agreement. The trust corpus also included other real property, an agreement of sale, and, eventually, a promissory note payable to the

trustee and secured by a deed of trust on real property that decedent
acquired on June 2, 1988.

The trust agreement directed the trustee to pay decedent the trust
income and any principal amounts that decedent requested in writing.
The agreement directed that, upon decedent's death, a portion of
the trust estate be distributed to the eight nonprofit organizations
that are appellants in this case. The remaining portion was to be held
in various trusts for decedent's wife, Geraldine P. Pilafas; brother,
appellant Theodore J. Pilafas; sons, Steve J. Pilafas, Jr., and John S.
Pilafas; and granddaughter, appellant Stephanie J. Pilafas. Decedent
explicitly "omitted any provision for his children NICHOLAS S. PILA-
FAS, IRENE PILAFAS PAPPAS, and JAMES S. PILAFAS. . . ."

Article X of the trust agreement, entitled "Revocation," provided:

> The Settlor may at any time or times during the Settlor's lifetime by
> instrument in writing delivered to the Trustee amend or revoke this
> Agreement in whole or in part. . . . This power is personal to the Settlor
> and may not be exercised by the Settlor's Personal Representative or
> others.

In accord with the revocation provision, decedent twice amended
the trust agreement by instrument in writing. On September 16, 1982,
decedent executed a "First Amendment to Trust Agreement" that
substituted a new article VIII regarding trustee succession and added
a new article XI regarding the sale of trust property. On January 19,
1987, after his divorce, decedent executed a "Second Amendment to
Trust Agreement" that revoked article XI and added an amended
article III, thereby deleting his former wife as a trust beneficiary and
increasing the share to be distributed to the eight nonprofit beneficiary organizations.

Decedent simultaneously executed a will and the second trust
amendment. The will explicitly excluded decedent's former wife, disposed of certain personal property, and directed that other personal
property be distributed in accordance with a separate written statement. See A.R.S. §14-2513. The will gave the residue of decedent's
estate to the trust.

After executing the second amendment to his trust agreement and
his new will, decedent apparently improved his relationships with appellees Irene Pappas, James S. Pilafas and Nicholas Pilafas. In commu-
nications with his attorney and his family during the last month of
his life, decedent indicated an intention to revise his estate plan to
include all his children.

Decedent's attorney prepared the trust agreement, the two amendments, and the will, and assisted decedent in executing them. The
attorney did not retain decedent's original documents and, to the

best of his knowledge, gave decedent the signed originals of the trust agreement, the amendments and the will immediately after they were executed.

Decedent died on September 28, 1988. Subsequently, decedent's son, appellee James S. Pilafas, unsuccessfully searched decedent's house and belongings for the original will and trust documents. No information of record indicates their possible whereabouts.

According to appellees James S. Pilafas and Nicholas S. Pilafas, decedent fastidiously saved important records and was unlikely to have lost his original will and trust. At his death, decedent had a room filled with important documents, including photographs, old divorce papers, his selective service card from 1945, and letters from his children. Appellees also testified that decedent was a man of direct action who sometimes acted impulsively, and who had been known to tear or discard papers that offended him.

On December 2, 1988, appellee James S. Pilafas commenced these proceedings by filing a petition for formal appointment of special administrator and special trustee. On March 8, 1989, he filed a petition for adjudication of intestacy, determination of heirs, determination of revocation of trust, and appointment of personal representative. The petition sought a determination that decedent had revoked his trust agreement and will and died intestate, leaving his five adult children as his lawful heirs. The petition asked the court to authorize James S. Pilafas to transfer all the trust assets to decedent's estate.

Appellants objected to the petition, seeking a determination that decedent had revoked neither his will nor his trust agreement, and asking that the will be admitted to probate. Appellees filed a response and motion for summary judgment that the trial court granted by its order of December 18, 1989. The court determined decedent revoked his trust agreement and his will and died intestate, leaving his five adult children as heirs. The court authorized James S. Pilafas, as special trustee, to transfer all trust assets to the decedent's estate. Appellants timely appealed. We have jurisdiction pursuant to A.R.S. §12-2101.J.

II

Appellees claim that decedent revoked his will because that document could not be found in a diligent search of his personal effects and papers after his death. This argument relies on the common law presumption that a testator destroyed his will with the intention of revoking it if the will is last seen in the testator's possession and cannot be found after his death. Cf. Estate of Travers, 121 Ariz. 282, 283, 589 P.2d 1314, 1315 (App. 1978) (testator presumed to have destroyed with intent to revoke a will last seen in his possession that cannot be found after his death); see also A.R.S. §14-2507.2 (testator revokes will by destroying it with the intent to revoke).

In response, appellants contend that the common law presumption never arose in this case because appellees proffered insufficient evidence that the will was last seen in decedent's possession or that it could not be found after decedent's death. We disagree. In support of their motion for summary judgment, appellees submitted affidavits tending to prove that decedent took possession of his original will after he executed it; that he meticulously kept important documents; and that appellee James S. Pilafas diligently searched decedent's home after his death and was unable to find the original will. In response, appellants offered no evidence undermining the factual basis for the common law presumption. In our opinion, the trial court correctly determined that decedent revoked his will and died intestate.

III

Appellees ask us to extend to revocable inter vivos trusts the common law presumption that a will last seen in the testator's possession that cannot be found after his death has been revoked. Appellees' reliance on this common law presumption is misplaced, however, if decedent's trust agreement was not susceptible to revocation by physical destruction.

Unlike the execution of a will, the creation of a trust involves the present transfer of property interests in the trust corpus to the beneficiaries. George G. Bogert and George T. Bogert, Trusts & Trustees §998 (2d ed. rev. 1983). "These interests cannot be taken from [the beneficiaries] except in accordance with a provision of the trust instrument, or by their own acts, or by a decree of a court." Id. Even a revocable trust vests the trust beneficiary with a legal right to enforce the terms of the trust. Continental Bank & Trust Co. v. Country Club Mobile Estates, Ltd., 632 P.2d 869, 872 (Utah 1981). The terms of the trust also limit the powers of the settlor and trustee over the trust corpus, even when the settlor declares himself trustee for the benefit of himself and others. See Estate of Brenner, 37 Colo. App. 271, 547 P.2d 938, 942 (1976).

The terms of decedent's trust agreement governing revocation provide: "The Settlor may at any time or times during the Settlor's lifetime by instrument in writing delivered to the Trustee amend or revoke this Agreement in whole or in part." Appellants argue that under this provision decedent could exercise his power to revoke the trust only through an "instrument in writing delivered to the Trustee. . . ." We agree.

This court, when not bound by previous decisions or legislative enactments, follows the Restatement of the Law. See Barnette v.

McNulty, 21 Ariz. App. 127, 129-31, 516 P.2d 583, 585-87 (1973).
Restatement (Second) of Trusts §330 (1959) provides:

> (1) The settlor has power to revoke the trust if and to the extent that
> by the terms of the trust he reserved such a power.
> (2) Except as stated in §§332 and 333, the settlor cannot revoke the
> trust if by the terms of the trust he did not reserve a power of revocation.

Restatement §330(2) makes it clear that, with two narrow exceptions,[6]
a trust is revocable only if the settlor expressly reserves a power to
revoke, and the terms of the trust strictly define and limit the reserved
power of revocation.

These general principles necessarily entail the more specific rule
that when the settlor reserves a power to revoke his trust in a particu-
lar manner or under particular circumstances, he can revoke it only
in that manner or under those circumstances. Austin W. Scott and
William F. Fratcher, Scott on Trusts §§330, 330.8 (4th ed. 1989)
("Where the settlor reserves a power to revoke the trust in a particular
manner, he can revoke it only in that manner."); Bogert and Bogert,
Trusts & Trustees §1001. Accord Connecticut General Life Ins. Co. v.
First Nat'l Bank of Minneapolis, 262 N.W.2d 403, 405 (Minn. 1977);
Estate of Button, 79 Wash. 2d 849, 490 P.2d 731, 733 (1971); Union
Trust Co. v. Watson, 76 R.I. 223, 68 A.2d 916, 918-19 (1949).

Appellees argue that the language of Comment j to Restatement
§330 indicates that a method of revocation designated in the trust
instrument is exclusive only if the language of the trust instrument
expressly makes it so. Comment j states in pertinent part:

> *Where method of revocation specified.* If the settlor reserves a power to
> revoke the trust only in a particular manner or under particular circum-
> stances, he can revoke the trust only in that manner or under those cir-
> cumstances. . . .
> If the settlor reserves a power to revoke the trust by a transaction inter
> vivos, as, for example, by a notice to the trustee, he cannot revoke the
> trust by his will.
> If the settlor reserves a power to revoke the trust only by will, he cannot
> revoke it by a transaction inter vivos.
> If the settlor reserves a power to revoke the trust only by a notice in
> writing delivered to the trustee, he can revoke it only by delivering such
> a notice to the trustee. . . . [Restatement (Second) of Trusts §330, Com-
> ment j, at 139-40.]

---

6. Restatement §332 allows a settlor to reform the written instrument creating a trust
if he intended to reserve a power of revocation or the power to modify the trust but by
mistake omitted the requisite provisions. Restatement §333 provides that "[a] trust can
be rescinded or reformed upon the same grounds as those upon which a transfer of
property not in trust can be rescinded or reformed." Neither of these provisions applies
to the Pilafas trust.

Appellees urge us to interpret the comment's reference to a settlor's reservation of "a power to revoke the trust only in a particular manner" to mean that decedent was free to revoke his trust in any manner because the instrument does not specify that decedent could revoke only by instrument in writing. We find the more reasonable and natural interpretation of the quoted portion of Comment j is that if a settlor only reserves a power to revoke the trust in a particular manner or under particular circumstances, he can revoke the trust only in that manner or under those circumstances. This interpretation, not the strained construction offered by appellees, explains why Comment j also states, "If the settlor reserves a power to revoke the trust by a transaction inter vivos, as, for example, by a notice to the trustee, he cannot revoke the trust by his will." Furthermore, our interpretation accords with the language of Restatement §330 itself, and is followed generally by the commentators and the case law. See, e.g., Estate of Button, 490 P.2d at 733.

Barnette v. McNulty, 21 Ariz. App. 127, 516 P.2d 583 (1973), on which appellees rely, is plainly distinguishable on its facts. In that case, decedent's written trust instrument first expressly reserved to him the power to revoke the trust without specifying a method for doing so. The instrument then listed three specific acts that would be deemed "conclusive evidence" of revocation, implying that other statements or acts not specifically listed could also constitute evidence of revocation. The court correctly concluded that because the settlor had not specified a mode of revocation, Comment i to Restatement (Second) of Trusts §330 controlled,[7] and the settlor could exercise his power to revoke in any manner that sufficiently manifested his intention to do so.

In this case, decedent reserved the power to amend or revoke the trust agreement "by instrument in writing delivered to the Trustee. . . . " Unlike the provision considered in *Barnette,* this provision specified one method of revocation, i.e., by instrument in writing, and no other language in the trust instrument suggested or implied that this method was nonexclusive. Under the settled law of trusts, decedent lacked power to revoke or amend the trust except in accordance with the provisions of the trust agreement.

Appellees claim to discern a trend in the law toward wholesale application of the law of wills to revocable trusts. This trend is logical

---

7. Comment i states:

> *Where no method of revocation specified.* If the settlor reserves a power to revoke the trust but does not specify any mode of revocation, the power can be exercised in any manner which sufficiently manifests the intention of the settlor to revoke the trust.
>
> Any definitive manifestation by the settlor of his intention that the trust should be forthwith revoked is sufficient. . . . [Restatement §330, Comment i, at 138.]

and justified, appellees argue, because revocable trusts often serve as substitutes for wills and the same rules should apply to both. As evidence of this trend, appellees cite decisions that apply statutory rules affecting lapsed bequests and post-will divorce to provisions in revocable inter vivos trusts. See, e.g., Estate of Button, 490 P.2d at 734; Clymer v. Mayo, 393 Mass. 754, 473 N.E.2d 1084, 1093-94 (1985); Miller v. First Nat'l Bank & Trust Co., 637 P.2d 75, 77-78 (Okla. 1981). These decisions, however, involve trust provisions that as a practical matter operate only after the settlor's death. In contrast, the provisions of decedent's inter vivos trust transferred present remainder interests to the trust beneficiaries, who are entitled to insist on full compliance with the terms of the trust instrument. We see no cogent reason the settled and predictable common law rules governing the revocation of trusts should be generally displaced by the distinct statutory rules for the revocation of wills.[8]

Because appellees presented no evidence showing that decedent complied with the required method of revocation, the inter vivos trust was not revoked and remained valid.

IV

For the foregoing reasons, we affirm the trial court's ruling that decedent revoked his will and died intestate, reverse the court's ruling that decedent revoked his trust agreement and the amendments thereto, and remand for proceedings consistent with this opinion.

PROBLEMS

1.   Suppose that Steve J. Pilafas, the settlor in the preceding case, had executed a will expressly revoking the inter vivos trust. This will is found among Pilafas's papers at death. Does it revoke the trust? Has it been delivered to the settlor-trustee? See In re Estate of Lowry, 93 Ill. App. 3d 1077, 418 N.E.2d 10 (1981). Suppose that a bank were trustee. Same result? See Connecticut Gen. Life Ins. Co. v. First Natl. Bank of Minneapolis, 262 N.W.2d 403 (Minn. 1977).

Uniform Trust Act §602(c)(2) (1999 draft) provides that a revocable trust may be revoked, "unless the terms of the trust expressly

---

8. Because we hold that the decedent's trust agreement could not have been revoked by physical destruction, we need not decide whether the common law presumption that a lost will last seen in the testator's possession was revoked by physical destruction may apply under some circumstances to revocable inter vivos trusts. We also need not decide whether Arizona's Statute of Frauds, A.R.S. §44-101, would have required a written instrument to revoke the decedent's trust.

make the specified method exclusive, by a will or any other method manifesting clear and convincing evidence of the settlor's intent.''

2. Ann, age 76, and Mark, age 32, marry in September 1978. The following January, Ann creates a revocable trust with Florida National Bank as trustee. Under the terms of the trust she reserves the income for life and provides for the principal to pass on her death to others than her husband. Ann and Mark divorce in October 1979. In July 1980, Ann and Mark remarry. Five days later Ann writes a letter to the Florida National Bank, revoking her trust. The Bank refuses to accept it on the ground that Ann is under the undue influence of Mark. Must the Bank accept the revocation order? Florida National Bank of Palm Beach County v. Genova, 460 So. 2d 895 (Fla. 1984), held that the settlor of a revocable trust has an absolute right to revoke if she is competent; undue influence is irrelevant. Why can a trust be revoked while under undue influence but not a will?

State Street Bank & Trust Co. v. Reiser
Massachusetts Appeals Court, 1979
7 Mass. App. Ct. 633, 389 N.E.2d 768

KASS, J. State Street Bank and Trust Company (the bank) seeks to reach the assets of an inter vivos trust in order to pay a debt to the bank owed by the estate of the settlor of the trust. We conclude that the bank can do so.

The probate judge found the material facts, and, although the evidence is reported, we accept his findings if not clearly erroneous. . . . We summarize those findings.

Wilfred A. Dunnebier created an inter vivos trust on September 30, 1971, with power to amend or revoke the trust and the right during his lifetime to direct the disposition of principal and income. He conveyed to the trust the capital stock of five closely held corporations. Immediately following execution of this trust, Dunnebier executed a will under which he left his residuary estate to the trust he had established.

About thirteen months later Dunnebier applied to the bank for a $75,000 working capital loan. A bank officer met with Dunnebier, examined a financial statement furnished by him and visited several single family home subdivisions which Dunnebier, or corporations he controlled, had built or were in the process of building. During their conversations, Dunnebier told the bank officer that he had controlling interests in the corporations which owned the most significant assets appearing on the financial statement. On the basis of what he saw of Dunnebier's work, recommendations from another bank, Dunnebier's borrowing history with the bank, and the general cut of

Dunnebier's jib, the bank officer decided to make an unsecured loan to Dunnebier for the $75,000 he had asked for. To evidence this loan, Dunnebier, on November 1, 1972, signed a personal demand note to the order of the bank. The probate judge found that Dunnebier did not intend to defraud the bank or misrepresent his financial position by failing to call attention to the fact that he had placed the stock of his corporations in the trust.

Approximately four months after he borrowed this money Dunnebier died in an accident. His estate has insufficient assets to pay the entire indebtedness due the bank.

Under Article Fourteen of his inter vivos trust, Dunnebier's trustees "... may in their sole discretion pay from the principal and income of this Trust Estate any and all debts and expenses of administration of the Settlor's estate." The bank urges that, since the inter vivos trust was part of an estate plan in which the simultaneously executed will was an integrated document, the instruction in Dunnebier's will that his executor pay his debts[9] should be read into the trust instrument. This must have been Dunnebier's intent, goes the argument.

Leaving to one side whether the precatory language in the will could be read as mandatory, and whether the language of that separate, albeit related, instrument, constitutes a surrounding circumstance ... which could guide us in interpreting the trust,[10] we find the trust agreement manifests no such intent by Dunnebier. Article Fourteen speaks of the sole discretion of the trustees. Subparagraphs A and B of Article Five, by contrast, direct the trustees unconditionally to pay two $15,000 legacies provided for in Dunnebier's will if his estate has insufficient funds to do so. It is apparent that when Dunnebier wanted his trustees unqualifiedly to discharge his estate's obligations, he knew how to direct them. As to those matters which Dunnebier, as settlor, left to the sole discretion of his trustees, we are not free to substitute our judgment for theirs as to what is wise or most to our taste. The court will substitute its discretion only on those relatively rare occasions when it is necessary to prevent an abuse of discretion. Here, the trustees could have considered preservation of the trust corpus for the benefit of the beneficiaries as most consistent with the trust purpose.

During the lifetime of the settlor, to be sure, the bank would have had access to the assets of the trust. When a person creates for his own benefit a trust for support or a discretionary trust, his creditors can reach the maximum amount which the trustee, under the terms

---

9. "It is my wish that all my just debts be fully paid."

10. As was said in First Natl. Bank v. Shawmut Bank, 378 Mass. 137, 143, 389 N.E.2d 1002, 1006 (1979), "In today's estate planning, it is not reasonable to conclude that a will is always of greater significance than an instrument creating an inter vivos trust."

of the trust, could pay to him or apply for his benefit. Ware v. Gulda, 331 Mass. 68, 70, 117 N.E.2d 137 (1954). Restatement (Second) of Trusts §156(2) (1959). This is so even if the trust contains spendthrift provisions. . . . Under the terms of Dunnebier's trust, all the income and principal were at his disposal while he lived.

We then face the question whether Dunnebier's death broke the vital chain. His powers to amend or revoke the trust, or to direct payments from it, obviously died with him, and the remainder interests of the beneficiaries of the trust became vested. The contingencies which might defeat those remainder interests could no longer occur. . . .

As an estate planning vehicle, the inter vivos trust has become common currency. See Second Bank-State St. Trust Co. v. Pinion, 341 Mass. 366, 371, 170 N.E.2d 350 (1960). Frequently, as Dunnebier did in the instant case, the settlor retains all the substantial incidents of ownership because access to the trust property is necessary or desirable as a matter of sound financial planning. Psychologically, the settlor thinks of the trust property as "his," as Dunnebier did when he took the bank's officer to visit the real estate owned by the corporation whose stock he had put in trust. . . . In other circumstances, persons place property in trust in order to obtain expert management of their assets, while retaining the power to invade principal and to amend and revoke the trust. It is excessive obeisance to the form in which property is held to prevent creditors from reaching property placed in trust under such terms. See Restatement of Property, §328, Comment a (1940).

This view was adopted in United States v. Ritter, 558 F.2d 1165, 1167 (4th Cir. 1977). In a concurring opinion in that case Judge Widener observed that it violates public policy for an individual to have an estate to live on, but not an estate to pay his debts with. Id. at 1168. The Internal Revenue Code institutionalizes the concept that a settlor of a trust who retains administrative powers, power to revoke or power to control beneficial enjoyment "owns" that trust property and provides that it shall be included in the settlor's personal estate. I.R.C. §§2038 and 2041.

We hold, therefore, that where a person places property in trust and reserves the right to amend and revoke, or to direct disposition of principal and income, the settlor's creditors may, following the death of the settlor, reach in satisfaction of the settlor's debts to them, to the extent not satisfied by the settlor's estate, those assets owned by the trust over which the settlor had such control at the time of his death as would have enabled the settlor to use the trust assets for his own benefit. Assets which pour over into such a trust as a consequence of the settlor's death or after the settlor's death, over which the settlor did not have control during his life, are not subject to the reach of creditors since, as to those assets, the equitable principles do not apply which place assets subject to creditors' disposal.[11]

The judgment is reversed, and a new judgment is to enter declaring that the assets owned by the trust (Wilfred A. Dunnebier Trust, I) up to the time of Dunnebier's death can be reached and applied in satisfaction of a judgment entered in favor of the plaintiff against the estate of Dunnebier, to the extent assets of the estate are insufficient to satisfy such a judgment.

So ordered.

NOTES AND PROBLEMS

1.   In accord with the *Reiser* case are In re Estate of Nagel, 580 N.W.2d 810 (Iowa 1998) (tort creditors can reach revocable trust after settlor's death); In re Marriage of Perry, 58 Cal. App. 4th 1104, 68 Cal. Rptr. 2d 445 (1997) (revocable trust held liable, after settlor's death, to claim for child support in divorce decree); Belshe v. Hope, 33 Cal. App. 4th 161, 38 Cal. Rptr. 2d 917 (1995) (subjecting revocable trust to recovery of Medicaid benefits when estate inadequate). See also Uniform Trust Act §505 (1999 draft).

2.   With creditors' rights in revocable trusts, compare creditors' rights in other nonprobate assets. Nonprobate assets are not all treated alike. Life insurance proceeds or retirement benefits are usually exempt from the insured's creditors if payable to a spouse or child. U.S. savings bonds with a payable-on-death beneficiary may be exempt. The creditors of a joint tenant holding a joint tenancy in land cannot reach the land after the joint tenant's death for the deceased joint tenant's interest has vanished.

Uniform Probate Code §6-215 (1990) expressly permits the decedent's creditors to reach P.O.D. bank accounts and joint bank accounts, if the probate estate is insufficient. With respect to liability of other nonprobate assets, see UPC §6-102 (1998 amendment); Wash. Rev. Code §11.18.200 (1999).

2.   Pour-over Wills

Along with the increasing use of the revocable trust as an estate planning arrangement has come the development of the *pour-over will.* In concept it is simple. *O* sets up a revocable inter vivos trust naming *X* as trustee. *O* transfers to *X*, as trustee, his stocks and bonds. *O* then

---

11. Apparently the court has in mind here life insurance proceeds payable to the trustee of the inter vivos trust. — Eds.

executes a will devising the residue of his estate to *X*, as trustee, to hold under the terms of the inter vivos trust. The pour-over by will of probate assets into an inter vivos trust is a useful device where *O* wants to establish an inter vivos trust of some of his assets and wants to merge after his death his testamentary estate, insurance proceeds, and other assets into a single receptacle subject to unified trust administration. As you will recall, the testators in the two preceding cases, *Pilafas* and *Reiser*, executed pour-over wills to transfer their residuary estates to the inter vivos trusts they had created.

Two theories were found useful in validating a pour-over of probate assets into an inter vivos trust when pour-overs first developed more than half a century ago. The first is *incorporation by reference.* A will can incorporate by reference a trust instrument in existence at the time the will is executed, but it cannot incorporate trust amendments made after the will is executed. See supra page 303. Hence, if the trust is amended after the will is executed, the probate assets will either be disposed of in accordance with the terms of the trust instrument as it stood at the time of execution of the will and not as subsequently amended, *or*, if this would not be in accordance with testator's intent, pass by intestacy.

The legal effect of incorporation by reference is to make the incorporated document part of the will. Hence, if the trust instrument is incorporated by reference, the probate assets turned over to the trustee are held in a testamentary trust established by will. Having two trusts — an inter vivos trust for assets transferred to the trust during life and a testamentary trust for assets added at death — can result in extra trustee's fees and complications. A single trust simplifies administration. An inter vivos trust may have advantages over a testamentary trust (see infra pages 390-393).

The second theory for validating pour-overs is the doctrine of *independent significance* (see supra page 318). Under this doctrine, a will may dispose of property by referring to some act that has significance apart from disposing of probate assets — in this context, by reference to an inter vivos trust that disposes of assets transferred to the trust during life. Under this doctrine the trust instrument does not have to be in existence when the will is executed, but the trust must have some assets in it before the time of the testator's death. Note the difference between independent significance and incorporation by reference: Independent significance requires that the inter vivos trust have some *property transferred to it during life*, which the trust disposes of; incorporation by reference requires that the *trust instrument be in existence at the time the will is executed.*

Under the doctrine of independent significance, the assets poured over into the inter vivos trust, like the assets transferred to the trust during life, are subject to the terms of (and are treated as an addition to) the inter vivos trust. The will can pour over assets to the trust as amended after execution of the will.

Because of the limitations and uncertainties of these doctrines, estate planners sought the enactment of legislation permitting a will to pour over probate assets into an inter vivos trust as amended on the date of death. The Uniform Testamentary Additions to Trusts Act, promulgated in 1960, or an equivalent statute has been enacted in all jurisdictions. The uniform act was revised in 1990 and incorporated into the Uniform Probate Code as §2-511. The revised act is reproduced below.

Uniform Testamentary Additions to Trusts Act (UPC §2-511, 1990)

§2-511.   TESTAMENTARY ADDITIONS TO TRUSTS

(a) A will may validly devise property to the trustee of a trust established or to be established (i) during the testator's lifetime by the testator, by the testator and some other person, or by some other person, including a funded or unfunded life insurance trust, although the settlor has reserved any or all rights of ownership of the insurance contracts, or (ii) at the testator's death by the testator's devise to the trustee, if the trust is identified in the testator's will and its terms are set forth in a written instrument, other than a will, executed before, concurrently with, or after the execution of the testator's will or in another individual's will if that other individual has predeceased the testator, regardless of the existence, size, or character of the corpus of the trust. The devise is not invalid because the trust is amendable or revocable, or because the trust was amended after the execution of the will or the testator's death.

(b) Unless the testator's will provides otherwise, property devised to a trust described in subsection (a) is not held under a testamentary trust of the testator, but it becomes a part of the trust to which it is devised, and must be administered and disposed of in accordance with the provisions of the governing instrument setting forth the terms of the trust, including any amendments thereto made before or after the testator's death.[12]

(c) Unless the testator's will provides otherwise, a revocation or termination of the trust before the testator's death causes the devise to lapse.

---

12. Compare N.Y. Est., Powers & Trusts Law §3-3.7 (1998), which requires that the trust and any amendments be executed with the formalities required for recording a deed (i.e., notarized) in order to pour over into a trust as amended. — Eds.

The Uniform Testamentary Additions to Trusts Act, as originally drafted, validates a pour-over of probate assets into an inter vivos trust only if the trust instrument is executed (signed) before or concurrently with the will. In this respect, the uniform act resembles the doctrine of incorporation by reference, which requires that the incorporated document be in existence at the time the will is executed; the uniform act differs slightly in that it requires the document to be in existence and signed when the will is executed. The uniform act does not require that some property be transferred to the inter vivos trust during life, as is required by the doctrine of independent significance. If the trust instrument is executed before or concurrently with the will, the probate assets can be poured over into the inter vivos trust as subsequently amended. The trust established at death by the pour-over is treated as an inter vivos trust — that is, as having come into existence before the testator's death! The purpose of this magical transformation is to give pour-over trusts the advantages of inter vivos trusts (see infra pages 390-393).

The 1990 revision to the uniform pour-over act deleted the requirement in the original act that the trust instrument be executed before or concurrently with the will. The revised act permits the trust instrument to be executed after the will. Thus, a testator's will can pour over the testator's probate assets to "a trust with the First National Bank as trustee, which I will execute," if the testator thereafter executes the trust instrument.

QUESTIONS, PROBLEM, AND NOTE

1. Inasmuch as the 1990 revision to the Uniform Testamentary Additions to Trusts Act permits a pour-over to a trust to be created *after* the will is executed, why does UPC §2-510 (the doctrine of incorporation by reference, supra page 303) continue to require a writing to be in existence when it is incorporated into a will? Is there any reason why a signed letter or other document should be treated differently from a signed trust instrument?

2. Assume the Uniform Testamentary Additions to Trusts Act (1990) is the law in this jurisdiction. Refer back to the Brown family estate planning problem, supra pages 49-58. Wendy Brown's Aunt Fanny, who has a house full of things, executes a trust deed that names Wendy as trustee and provides that Wendy shall distribute the trust property in equal shares to Wendy Brown, Lucy Lipman, Simon Preston, and Ruth Preston. The trust deed provides that the trust can

be revoked or amended at any time by a written or oral communication to Wendy from Aunt Fanny. No property is transferred to the trust during Aunt Fanny's life. Aunt Fanny subsequently makes a will pouring over all her property into this trust. Then, Aunt Fanny invites Wendy for a visit and tells Wendy exactly what item she wants to go to whom. After Wendy returns home, Aunt Fanny writes Wendy a letter saying that she is preparing a memorandum about the family silver and heirlooms that will state who is to get what. Upon Aunt Fanny's death, such a memorandum is found. What disposition is made of Aunt Fanny's estate? See Estate of Kirk, 907 P.2d 794 (Idaho 1995). Is it possible to have an oral will by executing a will pouring over probate assets into an inter vivos trust amendable by oral instructions?

3. A will speaks at death and disposes of property acquired by the testator after the will is executed. Thus a devise of "all of my personal property to A" includes personal property acquired after the will is executed. A revocable trust, however, can dispose only of property transferred to the trust during life, and a settlor cannot transfer to the trust property the settlor does not have. Restatement (Second) of Property, Donative Transfers, §32.4, Comment c (1992). The rule that a trust cannot dispose of property acquired after the trust is executed which is not transferred to the trust can be circumvented by executing a will pouring over after-acquired property into the trust. From this bit of information, you doubtless see why a pour-over will is a good idea when the settlor wants the revocable trust to dispose of all her property at her death.

On the other hand, look at this with an eye to the fundamental principle of the law: carry out the transferor's intent. What policy objection is there to a settlor creating a revocable trust of "property presently transferred in trust and all property which I may own at the time of my death"? Why cannot you do with one piece of paper (trust) what you can do with two (trust & will)? See Brainard v. Commissioner, infra page 586, Speelman v. Pascal, infra page 589, and Notes and Problems following the cases.

Clymer v. Mayo
Supreme Judicial Court of Massachusetts, 1985
393 Mass. 754, 473 N.E.2d 1084

HENNESSEY, C.J. This consolidated appeal arises out of the administration of the estate of Clara A. Mayo (decedent). We summarize the findings of the judge of the Probate and Family Court incorporating the parties' agreed statement of uncontested facts.

At the time of her death in November, 1981, the decedent, then fifty years of age, was employed by Boston University as a professor of psychology. She was married to James P. Mayo, Jr. (Mayo), from 1953 to 1978. The couple had no children. The decedent was an only child and her sole heirs at law are her parents, Joseph A. and Maria Weiss.

In 1963, the decedent executed a will designating Mayo as principal beneficiary. In 1964, she named Mayo as the beneficiary of her group annuity contract with John Hancock Mutual Life Insurance Company; and in 1965, made him the beneficiary of her Boston University retirement annuity contracts with Teachers Insurance and Annuity Association (TIAA) and College Retirement Equities Fund (CREF). As a consequence of a $300,000 gift to the couple from the Weisses in 1971, the decedent and Mayo executed new wills and indentures of trust on February 2, 1973, wherein each spouse was made the other's principal beneficiary. Under the terms of the decedent's will, Mayo was to receive her personal property. The residue of her estate was to "pour over" into the inter vivos trust she created that same day.

The decedent's trust instrument named herself and John P. Hill as trustees. As the donor, the decedent retained the right to amend or revoke the trust at any time by written instrument delivered to the trustees. In the event that Mayo survived the decedent, the trust estate was to be divided into two parts. Trust A, the marital deduction trust, was to be funded with an amount "equal to fifty (50%) percent of the value of the Donor's 'adjusted gross estate,'. . . for the purpose of the United States Tax Law, less an amount equal to the value of all interest in property, if any, allowable as 'marital deductions' for the purposes of such law. . . . " Mayo was the income beneficiary of Trust A and was entitled to reach the principal at his request or in the trustee's discretion. The trust instrument also gave Mayo a general power of appointment over the assets in Trust A.

The balance of the decedent's estate, excluding personal property passing to Mayo by will, or the entire estate if Mayo did not survive her, composed Trust B. Trust B provided for the payment of five initial specific bequests totalling $45,000. After those gifts were satisfied, the remaining trust assets were to be held for the benefit of Mayo for life. Upon Mayo's death, the assets in Trust B were to be held for "the benefit of the nephews and nieces of the Donor" living at the time of her death. The trustee was given discretion to spend so much of the income and principal as necessary for their comfort, support, and education. When all of these nephews and nieces reached the age of thirty, the trust was to terminate and its remaining assets were to be divided equally between Clark University and Boston University to assist in graduate education of women.

On the same day she established her trust, the decedent changed the beneficiary of her Boston University group life insurance policy from Mayo to the trustees. One month later, in March, 1973, she also executed a change in her retirement annuity contracts to designate the trustees as beneficiaries. At the time of its creation in 1973, the trust was not funded. Its future assets were to consist solely of the proceeds of these policies and the property which would pour over under the will's residuary clause. The judge found that the remaining trustee has never received any property or held any funds subsequent to the execution of the trust nor has he paid any trust taxes or filed any trust tax returns.

Mayo moved out of the marital home in 1975. In June, 1977, the decedent changed the designation of beneficiary on her Boston University life insurance policy for a second time, substituting Marianne LaFrance for the trustees.[13] LaFrance had lived with the Mayos since 1972, and shared a close friendship with the decedent up until her death. Mayo filed for divorce on September 9, 1977, in New Hampshire. The divorce was decreed on January 3, 1978, and the court incorporated into the decree a permanent stipulation of the parties' property settlement. Under the terms of that settlement, Mayo waived any "right, title or interest" in the decedent's "securities, savings accounts, savings certificates, and retirement fund," as well as her "furniture, furnishings and art." Mayo remarried on August 28, 1978, and later executed a new will in favor of his new wife. The decedent died on November 21, 1981. Her will was allowed on November 18, 1982, and the court appointed John H. Clymer as administrator with the will annexed.

What is primarily at issue in these actions is the effect of the Mayos' divorce upon dispositions provided in the decedent's will and indenture of trust. . . . [T]he court-appointed administrator of the decedent's estate petitioned for instructions with respect to the impact of the divorce on the estate's administration. Named as defendants were Mayo, the decedent's parents (the Weisses), and the trustee under the indenture of trust (John P. Hill).

1. THE JUDGE'S CONCLUSIONS

On November 1, 1983, the judge issued his rulings of law. . . . The rulings that have been challenged by one or more parties on appeal are as follows: (1) the decedent's inter vivos trust, executed contemporaneously with her will, is valid under G.L. c. 203, §3B, despite the fact that the trust did not receive funding until the decedent's death; (2) Mayo does not take under Trust A because that transfer was intended to qualify for a marital deduction for Federal estate tax purposes and this objective became impossible after the Mayos' divorce; (3) Mayo is entitled to take under Trust B because the purpose

---

13. Upon the decedent's death the benefits under said policy were paid to LaFrance.

of that trust was to create a life interest in him, the decedent failed to revoke the trust provisions benefiting Mayo, and G.L. c. 191, §9, operates to revoke only testamentary dispositions in favor of a former spouse; (4) J. Chamberlain, A. Chamberlain, and Hinman, the decedent's nephews and niece by marriage at the time of the trust's creation, are entitled to take under Trust B as the decedent's intended beneficiaries. . . .

For the reasons to follow we affirm the judge's conclusions that: (1) the decedent established a valid trust under G.L. c. 203, §3B; (2) Mayo's interest in Trust A was terminated as a result of the divorce; (3) the Chamberlains and Hinman are entitled to take as intended beneficiaries under Trust B, with the remainder interest to be divided equally between Clark University and Boston University. . . . However, we reverse the judge's ruling that Mayo is to take under Trust B. . . .

2. VALIDITY OF "POUR-OVER" TRUST

The Weisses claim that the judge erred in ruling that the decedent's trust was validly created despite the fact that it was not funded until her death. They rely on the common law rule that a trust can be created only when a trust res exists. New England Trust Co. v. Sanger, 337 Mass. 342, 348 (1958). Arguing that the trust never came into existence, the Weisses claim they are entitled to the decedent's entire estate as her sole heirs at law.

In upholding the validity of the decedent's pour-over trust, the judge cited the relevant provisions of G.L. c. 203, §3B, inserted by St. 1963, c. 418, §1, the Commonwealth's version of the Uniform Testamentary Additions to Trusts Act.

> A devise or bequest, the validity of which is determinable by the laws of the commonwealth, may be made to the trustee or trustees of a trust established or to be established by the testator . . . including a funded or unfunded life insurance trust, although the trustor has reserved any or all rights of ownership of the insurance contracts, if the trust is identified in the will and the terms of the trust are set forth in a written instrument executed before or concurrently with the execution of the testator's will . . . *regardless of the existence, size or character of the corpus of the trust* (emphasis added).

The decedent's trust instrument, which was executed in Massachusetts and states that it is to be governed by the laws of the Commonwealth, satisfies these statutory conditions. The trust is identified in the residuary clause of her will and the terms of the trust are set out in a written instrument executed contemporaneously with the will. However, the Weisses claim that G.L. c. 203, §3B, was not intended to change the common law with respect to the necessity for a trust corpus despite the clear language validating pour-over trusts, "regardless of the existence, size or character of the corpus." The Weisses make no showing of legislative intent that would contradict the plain meaning of these words. It is well established that "the statutory language is the principal source of insight into legislative purpose." Bronstein v. Prudential Ins. Co. of Am., 390 Mass. 701, 704 (1984). Moreover, the development of the common law of this Commonwealth with regard to pour-over trusts demonstrates that G.L. c. 203, §3B, takes on practical meaning only if the Legislature meant exactly what the statute says concerning the need for a trust corpus.

This court was one of the first courts to validate pour-over devises to a living trust. In Second Bank-State St. Trust Co. v. Pinion, 341 Mass. 366, 371 (1960), decided prior to the adoption of G.L. c. 203, §3B, we upheld a testamentary gift to a revocable and amendable inter vivos trust established by the testator before the execution of his will and which he amended after the will's execution. Recognizing the importance of the pour-over devise in modern estate planning, we explained that such transfers do not violate the statute of wills despite the testator's ability to amend the trust and thereby change the disposition of property at his death without complying with the statute's formalities. "We agree with modern legal thought that a subsequent amendment is effective because of the applicability of the established equitable doctrine that subsequent acts of independent significance do not require attestation under the statute of wills." Id. at 369.

At that time we noted that "[t]he long established recognition in Massachusetts of the doctrine of independent significance makes unnecessary statutory affirmance of its application to pour-over trusts." Id. at 371. It is evident from *Pinion* that there was no need for the Legislature to enact G.L. c. 203, §3B, simply to validate pour-over devises from wills to funded revocable trusts.

However, in *Pinion*, we were not presented with an unfunded pour-over trust. Nor, prior to G.L. c. 203, §3B, did other authority exist in this Commonwealth for recognizing testamentary transfers to unfunded trusts. The doctrine of independent significance, upon which we relied in *Pinion*, assumes that "property was included in the purported inter vivos trust, prior to the testator's death."Restatement (Second) of Trusts §54 Comment f (1959). That is why commentators have recognized that G.L. c. 203, §3B, "[m]akes some . . . modification of the *Pinion* doctrine. The act does not require that the trust res be more than nominal or even existent." E. Slizewski, Legislation: Uniform Testamentary Additions to Trusts Act, 1963 Ann. Survey Mass. Law §2.7, 39. See Osgood, Pour Over Will: Appraisal of Uniform Testamentary Additions to Trusts Act, 104 Trusts 768, 769 (1965) ("The Act . . . eliminates the necessity that there be a trust corpus").

For the foregoing reasons we conclude, in accordance with G.L. c. 203, §3B, that the decedent established a valid inter vivos trust in 1973 and that its trustee may properly receive the residue of her estate. We affirm the judge's ruling on this issue. . . .

4. TERMINATION OF TRUST A

The judge terminated Trust A upon finding that its purpose — to qualify the trust for an estate tax marital deduction — became impossible to achieve after the Mayos' divorce. Mayo appeals this ruling. It is well established that the Probate Courts are empowered to terminate or reform a trust in whole or in part where its purposes have become impossible to achieve and the settlor did not contemplate continuation of the trust under the new circumstances. Gordon v. Gordon, 332 Mass. 193, 197 (1955). Ames v. Hall, 313 Mass. 33, 37 (1943).

The language the decedent employed in her indenture of trust makes it clear that by setting off Trusts A and B she intended to reduce estate tax liability in compliance with then existing provisions of the Internal Revenue Code. Therefore we have no disagreement with the judge's reasoning. See Putnam v. Putnam, 366 Mass. 261, 267 (1974). However, we add that our reasoning below — that by operation of G.L. c. 191, §9, Mayo has no beneficial interest in the trust — clearly disposes of Mayo's claim to Trust A.

5. MAYO'S INTEREST IN TRUST B

The judge's decision to uphold Mayo's beneficial interest in Trust B was appealed by the Weisses, as well as by Boston University and Clark University. The judge reasoned that the decedent intended to create a life interest in Mayo when she established Trust B and failed either to revoke or to amend the trust after the couple's divorce. The appellants argue that we should extend the reach of G.L. c. 191, §9, to revoke all Mayo's interests under the trust. General Laws c. 191, §9, as amended through St. 1977, c. 76, §2, provides in relevant part:

> If, after executing a will, the testator shall be divorced or his marriage shall be annulled, the divorce or annulment shall revoke any disposition or appointment of property made by the will to the former spouse, any provision conferring a general or special power of appointment on the former spouse, and any nomination of the former spouse, as executor, trustee, conservator or guardian, unless the will shall expressly provide otherwise. Property prevented from passing to a former spouse because of a revocation by divorce shall pass as if a former spouse had failed to survive the decedent, and other provisions conferring a power of office on the former spouse shall be interpreted as if the spouse had failed to survive the decedent.

The judge ruled that Mayo's interest in Trust B is unaffected by G.L. c. 191, §9, because his interest in that trust is not derived from a "disposition . . . made by the will" but rather from the execution of an inter vivos trust with independent legal significance. We disagree, but in fairness we add that the judge here confronted a question of first impression in this Commonwealth.

. . . In this case we must determine what effect, if any, G.L. c. 191, §9, has on the former spouse's interest in the testator's pour-over trust.

While, by virtue of G.L. c. 203, §3B, the decedent's trust bore independent significance at the time of its creation in 1973, the trust had no practical significance until her death in 1981. The decedent executed both her will and indenture of trust on February 2, 1973. She transferred no property or funds to the trust at that time. The trust was to receive its funding at the decedent's death, in part through her life insurance policy and retirement benefits, and in part through a pour-over from the will's residuary clause. Mayo, the proposed executor and sole legatee under the will, was also made the primary beneficiary of the trust with power, as to Trust A only, to reach both income and principal.

During her lifetime, the decedent retained power to amend or revoke the trust. Since the trust was unfunded, her cotrustee was subject to no duties or obligations until her death. Similarly, it was only as a result of the decedent's death that Mayo could claim any right to the trust assets. It is evident from the time and manner in which the trust was created and funded, that the decedent's will and trust were integrally related components of a single testamentary scheme. For all practical purposes the trust, like the will, "spoke" only at the decedent's death. For this reason Mayo's interest in the trust was revoked by operation of G.L. c. 191, §9, at the same time his interest under the decedent's will was revoked.

It has reasonably been contended that in enacting G.L. c. 191, §9, the Legislature "intended to bring the law into line with the expectations of most people. . . . Divorce usually represents a stormy parting, where the last thing one of the parties wishes is to have an earlier will carried out giving everything to the former spouse." Young, Probate Reform, 18 B.B.J. 7, 11 (1974). To carry out the testator's implied intent, the law revokes "any disposition or appointment of property made by the will to the former spouse." It is indisputable that if the decedent's trust was either testamentary or incorporated by reference into her will, Mayo's beneficial interest in the trust would be revoked by operation of the statute. However, the judge stopped short of mandating the same result in this case because here the trust had "independent significance" by virtue of c. 203, §3B. While correct, this characterization of the trust does not end our analysis. For example, in Sullivan v. Burkin, 390 Mass. 864, 867 (1984), we ruled prospectively that the assets of a revocable trust will be considered part of the "estate of the decedent" in determining the surviving spouse's statutory share.

Treating the components of the decedent's estate plan separately, and not as parts of an interrelated whole, brings about inconsistent results. Applying c. 191, §9, the judge correctly revoked the will provisions benefiting Mayo. As a result, the decedent's personal property — originally left to Mayo — fell into the will's residuary clause and passed to the trust. The judge then appropriately terminated Trust A for impossibility of purpose thereby denying Mayo his beneficial interest under Trust A. Yet, by upholding Mayo's interest under Trust B, the judge returned to Mayo a life interest in the same assets that composed the corpus of Trust A — both property passing by way of the decedent's will and the proceeds of her TIAA/CREF annuity contracts.

We are aware of only one case concerning the impact of a statute similar to G.L. c. 191, §9, on trust provisions benefiting a former spouse. In Miller v. First Nat'l Bank & Trust Co., 637 P.2d 75 (Okla. 1981), the testator also simultaneously executed an indenture of trust and will naming his spouse as primary beneficiary. As in this case, the trust was to be funded at the testator's death by insurance proceeds and a will pour-over. Subsequently, the testator divorced his wife but failed to change the terms of his will and trust. The District Court revoked the will provisions favoring the testator's former wife by applying a statute similar to G.L. c. 191, §9. Recognizing that "[t]he will without the trust has no meaning or value to the decedent's estate plan," the Oklahoma Supreme Court revoked the trust benefits as well. Id. at 77. However, we do not agree with the court's reasoning. Because the Oklahoma statute, like G.L. c. 191, §9, revokes dispositions of property made by will, the court stretched the doctrine of incorporation by reference to render the decedent's trust testamentary. We do not agree that reference to an existing trust in a will's pour-over clause is sufficient to incorporate that trust by reference without evidence that the testator intended such a result. See Second Bank-State St. Trust Co. v. Pinion, 341 Mass. 366, 367 (1960). However, it is not necessary for us to indulge in such reasoning, because we have concluded that the legislative intent under G.L. c. 191, §9, is that a divorced spouse should not take under a trust executed in these circumstances. In the absence of an expressed contrary intent, that statute implies an intent on the part of a testator to revoke will provisions favoring a former spouse. It is incongruous then to ignore that same intent with regard to a trust funded in part through her will's pour-over at the decedent's death. As one law review commentator has noted, "[t]ransferors use will substitutes to avoid probate, not to avoid the subsidiary law of wills. The subsidiary rules are the product of centuries of legal experience in attempting to discern transferors' wishes and suppress litigation. These rules should be treated as presumptively correct for will substitutes as well as for wills." Langbein, The Nonprobate Revolution and the Future of the Law of Succession, 97 Harv. L. Rev. 1108, 1136-1137 (1984).

Restricting our holding to the particular facts of this case — specifically the existence of a revocable pour-over trust funded entirely at the time of the decedent's death — we conclude that G.L. c. 191, §9, revokes Mayo's interest under Trust B.[14]

6.   NEPHEWS AND NIECES OF DONOR

According to the terms of G.L. c. 191, §9, "[p]roperty prevented from passing to a former spouse because of revocation by divorce shall pass as if a former spouse had failed to survive the decedent. . . ." In this case, the decedent's indenture of trust provides that if Mayo failed to survive her, "the balance of 'Trust B' shall be held . . . for the benefit of the nephews and nieces of the Donor living at the time of the death of the Donor." The trustee is directed to expend as much of the net income and principal as he deems "advisable for [their] reasonable comfort, support and education" until all living nephews and nieces have attained the age of thirty. At that time, the trust is to terminate and Boston University and Clark University are each to receive fifty percent of the trust property to assist women students in their graduate programs.

The decedent had no siblings and therefore no nephews and nieces who were blood relations.[15] However, when she executed her trust in 1973, her husband, James P. Mayo, Jr., had two nephews and one niece — John and Allan Chamberlain and Mira Hinman. Before her divorce, the decedent maintained friendly relations with these young people and, along with her former husband, contributed toward their educational expenses. The three have survived the decedent.

The Weisses, Boston University, and Clark University appeal the decision of the judge upholding the decedent's gift to these three individuals. They argue that at the time the decedent created her trust she had no "nephews and nieces" by blood and that, at her

14. As an alternative ground the appellants argue that the terms of the Mayos' divorce settlement, in which Mayo waived "any right, title or interest" in the assets that later funded the decedent's trust, amount to a disclaimer of his trust interest. We decline to base our holding on such reasoning because a disclaimer of rights "must be clear and unequivocal," Second Bank-State St. Trust Co. v. Yale Univ. Alumni Fund, 338 Mass. 520, 524 (1959), and we find no such disclaimer in the Mayos' divorce agreement.

15. Considering the ages of all concerned, it could not reasonably be argued that the decedent might have contemplated the possibility of siblings to be born after the trust was executed.

death, her marital ties to Mayo's nephews and niece had been severed by divorce. Therefore, they contend that the class gift to the donor's "nephews and nieces" lapses for lack of identifiable beneficiaries.

The judge concluded that the trust language created an ambiguity, and thus he considered extrinsic evidence of the decedent's meaning and intent. Based upon that evidence, he decided that the decedent intended to provide for her nieces and nephews by marriage when she created the trust. Because the decedent never revoked this gift, he found that the Chamberlains and Hinman are entitled to their beneficial interests under the trust. We agree.

The appellants . . . [argue] that the Mayos' divorce left the decedent without *any* nephews and nieces — by blood or marriage — at the time of her death. They argue that even if the decedent had intended to provide for the Chamberlains and Hinman when she executed her indenture of trust, we should rule that the Mayos' divorce somehow "revoked" this gift. According to Boston University, since the beneficiaries are identified by their relationship to the decedent through her marriage and not by name, we should presume that the decedent no longer intended to benefit her former relatives once her marriage ended. General Laws c. 191, §9, does not provide the authority for revoking gifts to the blood relatives of a former spouse. The law implies an intent to revoke testamentary gifts between the divorcing parties because of the profound emotional and financial changes divorce normally engenders. There is no indication in the statutory language that the Legislature presumed to know how these changes affect a testator's relations with more distant family members. We therefore conclude that the Chamberlains and Hinman are entitled to take as the decedent's "nephews and nieces" under Trust B. . . .

In sum, we conclude that the decedent established a valid trust under G.L. c. 203, §3B; Mayo's beneficial interest in Trust A and Trust B is revoked by operation of G.L. c. 191, §9; [and] the Chamberlains and Hinman are entitled to take the interest given to the decedent's "nephews and nieces" under Trust B, leaving the remainder to Clark University and Boston University. . . .

So ordered.

NOTES AND PROBLEM

1.   Where a settlor names the trustee of her inter vivos trust the beneficiary of her life insurance policy, but does not add any other funds or assets to the trust (as happened with Clara Mayo), the inter vivos trust is called an *unfunded life insurance trust.* If the settlor adds other assets to the inter vivos trust, it is called a *funded inter vivos trust.*

An unfunded life insurance trust as well as a funded trust is a valid inter vivos trust.

In the former case, the trust res or property (a necessary ingredient of a valid trust, see infra page 581) is the trustee's contingent right to receive the proceeds of the policy. This right is a valuable property right, for if the insured dies without changing the policy beneficiary the trustee will be entitled to the policy proceeds.

A funded revocable trust has independent significance because the trust instrument disposes of the assets transferred to the trust during life (see supra page 318). Similarly, an unfunded life insurance trust has independent significance since it disposes of nonprobate assets, to wit, the life insurance proceeds.

2. *Revocation by divorce.* Recent statutes in some states provide that divorce revokes any provision in a revocable trust for the spouse, who is deemed to have predeceased the settlor. See, e.g., Ohio Rev. Code §1339.62 (1998); Okla. Stat. Ann. ch. 60, §175 (1998).

Uniform Probate Code §2-804 provides that divorce revokes dispositions in favor of the divorced spouse in revocable inter vivos trusts as well as in other revocable will substitutes such as life insurance, pension plans, P.O.D. contracts, and T.O.D. securities.

UPC §2-804 revokes not only all provisions for the divorced spouse but also any provision for a relative of the divorced spouse. If this act had applied to Clymer v. Mayo, the divorced husband's nieces and nephews would not share in the trust.

3. Pablo executes an unfunded inter vivos trust naming Eduardo as beneficiary. Pablo also executes a will pouring over all his assets into the trust. The will contains a no-contest clause, providing that any person contesting the will shall forfeit any interest given by the will. Subsequently Pablo amends his trust to name Maria as a 50 percent beneficiary of the trust. Upon Pablo's death, Eduardo contests the trust amendment on the ground that Pablo lacked mental capacity when the trust was amended. The court holds there is no probable cause for Eduardo's lawsuit. (On no-contest clauses, see supra page 184.) Does Eduardo forfeit his beneficial interest under the trust instrument? See In re Lindstrom, 191 Cal. App. 3d 375, 236 Cal. Rptr. 376 (1987); Briggs v. Wyoming National Bank, 836 P.2d 263 (Wyo. 1992) (enforcing no-contest clause in the trust); Jo Ann Englehardt, In Terrorem Inter Vivos: Terra Incognita, 26 Real Prop., Prob. & Tr. J. 535 (1991).

4. The unfunded revocable life insurance trust coupled with a will pouring over probate assets into the trust is one means of creating a unified trust of both life insurance proceeds and probate assets. The resulting trust is an inter vivos trust. Another method is to create a trust in the will and designate as beneficiary of the insurance proceeds "the trustee named in my will." The resulting unified trust is a testa-

mentary trust because created by the will, not by an inter vivos instrument. Under the latter method, the insurance proceeds are not payable to the executor of the testator's estate, but to the trustee named in the will. Hence the proceeds do not "go through probate," as do assets under the executor's control.

The insurance proceeds may also be payable to "the estate of the insured." In this event, the proceeds would be payable to the executor, would be treated as probate assets, and would be distributed under the testator's will in the same manner as other property.

3. Use of Revocable Trusts in Estate Planning

a. Introduction

About 1950, Professor A. James Casner of Harvard became interested in exploring ways to avoid the expense, time, publicity, and restrictive rules of probate. Casner recognized that a direct attack on these aspects of probate would meet strong resistance from the bar. He therefore looked for a way to bypass probate altogether. He found it in the revocable trust.

The revocable trust became the centerpiece of Casner's work on Estate Planning, first published in one volume in 1953 and subsequently expanded to six volumes in the fifth edition in 1984 (taken over in the 1990s by Professor Jeffrey Pennell). Casner himself became the great advocate of revocable trusts at innumerable bar meetings and in several law review articles. His advocacy was successful with the Boston bar, of which he was a leading member, but Casner had to overcome substantial resistance in other cities. (Norman Dacey discovered the revocable trust a decade after Casner first began to promote it (see supra page 360); whether Dacey's shrill crusade helped or hindered Casner with lawyers is debatable.) By the end of Casner's career, the revocable trust had become a standard estate planning device in all states. We want here to examine it in closer detail.

A revocable trust can be created by a *declaration of trust*, whereby the settlor becomes the trustee of the trust property. In the trust instrument, the settlor should name a successor trustee to take over the trusteeship upon the settlor's death or incompetency. Where the trust is to end on the settlor's death, and the trust is merely a means of avoiding probate, the death beneficiary should ordinarily be named successor trustee. At the settlor's death, the successor trustee automatically takes over, without a court order, and distributes the property to the trust beneficiaries. A revocable declaration of trust was involved in Farkas v. Williams, supra page 352, and in In re Estate and Trust of Pilafas, supra page 361.

A revocable trust can also be created by a *deed of trust,* naming a third party as trustee. The settlor can be co-trustee, if desired. A revocable trust can be funded, as in State Street Bank & Trust Co. v. Reiser, supra page 368, where the settlor transferred his stock to the trust; or the trust can be unfunded, as in Clymer v. Mayo, supra page 375.

The terms of a revocable trust may call for distribution of the trust assets at the settlor's death. Or the revocable trust may provide the "main vehicle" for the disposition of the settlor's estate, either outright or in further trust after his death; assets in the settlor's probate estate can be poured over into the revocable trust to bring about a uniform disposition of the settlor's assets. In fact, if unified control of assets is desired during life, the settlor can change all the beneficiary designations on the settlor's nonprobate assets to make them payable to the revocable trust and also execute a will pouring over all probate assets to the revocable trust. After doing this, the settlor has consolidated under one document his dispositive plan for all his assets. He can later amend it as he could amend a will. Under this scheme, the revocable trust, with amendments, functions as a will did in the days before the proliferation of will substitutes.

It is rather ironic that a generation after the will began to lose its dominance because of the public's desire to avoid probate, the revocable trust has replaced it as a document with almost all the same attributes of a will, but without probate. Because we were unwilling to abolish probate or make it optional, in giving people what they demanded, we paid a substantial cost in complexity. Perhaps we should think anew about making probate optional, as it is in California for all transfers to a spouse.

Now let us take a closer look at the advantages and disadvantages of revocable trusts (often called living trusts, particularly in the popular literature). While the revocable trust may have advantages for many clients, for some it will be unsuitable.

b.   Consequences During Life of Settlor

(1)   Property management by fiduciary

A third-party trustee may be selected to manage a funded revocable trust. The settlor may want to be relieved of the burdens of financial management. Although a custodianship account for securities or other assets is often used for this purpose, a custodianship is an agency relationship and terminates on the disability or death of the principal. By contrast, a revocable trust continues during the settlor's incapacity and can provide for disposition of the trust assets at the settlor's death. The settlor can evaluate the trustee's performance and name a new trustee if not satisfied — an opportunity not available to the settlor's executor.

On the other hand, when property is put in trust, some inconveniences may arise upon sale or mortgage of the property. Third parties such as banks and transfer agents may want to see copies of the trust instrument to determine whether the trustee has power to engage in the transaction. It is not as easy to conduct some transactions when title to the property is in a trustee as it is when title is in a private individual.

(2) Keeping title clear

A revocable trust is useful in keeping separate and apart property that a husband or wife or both want not to be commingled with their other assets. A husband and wife, for example, may want to establish separate revocable trusts of property each brings to the marriage or acquires by inheritance. This may prevent ambiguities of ownership from developing later, with consequent problems upon divorce or death.

Spouses who move from a community property state to a separate property state may create a revocable trust for their community property in order to avoid a stepped-up income tax basis on all the property when one spouse dies (see infra page 528).

(3) Income and gift taxes

Under the federal income, gift, and estate taxes, assets in a revocable trust are treated as still owned by the settlor. When the revocable trust is created, it is not treated as a completed gift to the beneficiaries under the federal gift tax (see infra page 986). Because of the retained power to revoke, trust income is taxable to the settlor regardless of to whom it is paid. Internal Revenue Code of 1986 §676(a). There are no federal tax advantages in creating a revocable trust.

(4) Dealing with incompetency

Increased longevity has brought with it an increased chance that a person's last days (or perhaps months or years) may be spent in a state of mental or physical disability, requiring some form of fiduciary administration of the person's assets. Many persons are reluctant to have a spouse or parent formally adjudicated an incompetent. Moreover, guardianship or conservatorship proceedings are cumbersome and expensive, and invite unwanted publicity. Even the modern UPC §5-406 stipulates an elaborate court procedure protecting the alleged incompetent. When Groucho Marx was in his 80s, he was declared incompetent by a court, against his wishes. At the time he was living with a woman named Erin Fleming, who said he preferred her as his guardian if he had to have one. After a messy court fight, with the newspapers titillating readers with intimate family details, a relative of Marx was appointed guardian.

A revocable trust can be used in planning for the contingency of incapacity. The settlor may be co-trustee, with the trust instrument providing that either trustee alone may act on behalf of the trust. Or the trust instrument may provide that the other co-trustee shall act as sole trustee if the settlor becomes incompetent. An alternative to a revocable trust is a durable power of attorney, described infra page 396.

QUESTION

In drafting revocable trust provisions dealing with incompetency, what provisions would you make for determining when the settlor is incompetent?

c.   Consequences at Death of Settlor: Avoidance of Probate

(1)   Costs

Assets transferred during life to a revocable trust avoid probate because legal title to the assets passes to the trustee, and there is no need to change the title to the trust assets by probate administration on the settlor's death. Although trustee's fees may be payable if a third-party trustee is named, these fees will be considerably smaller than court costs, attorney's fees, and executor's commissions incurred in probate.

Against the savings in probate fees, certain other costs must be offset. Lawyers charge more to draft a revocable trust than a will, particularly when there are related pour-over documents. These documents are more complicated than a will. In addition, transferring title of assets to the trustee may entail certain costs, for example, stock transfer fees.

(2)   Delays

In an estate administration, the assets may be in the executor's possession and control for a substantial period of time. A typical estate takes 18 months or two years to settle. Under a revocable trust, income and principal can be disbursed to the beneficiaries much more quickly.

In some states, executors (viewed as temporary "caretakers") are restricted to purchasing very safe investments. On the other hand, trustees are viewed as managers governed only by the prudent investor rule. Because rules governing trustees are more liberal than rules applicable to executors, it is usually simpler for a trustee rather than an executor to deal with an ongoing business in the form of a partnership or sole proprietorship, and for a trustee to exercise options, borrow money, and participate in reorganizations.

(3)   Creditors

In probate a short-term statute of limitations is applicable to creditors (see supra page 41). If creditors do not file claims within a short period after the testator's death, the creditors are forever barred. There is no short-term statute of limitations applicable to revocable trusts; the limitations period is the normal one applicable to the particular claim. Where it is important to cut off the rights of creditors — as might be true with professionals such as doctors or lawyers where the statute of limitations on malpractice runs from discovery — probate holds an advantage over the revocable trust. On creditors' rights against revocable trusts, see State Street Bank & Trust Co. v. Reiser, supra page 368.

(4)   Publicity

A will is a public record, open to disappointed heirs, newspaper reporters, and the just plain curious. Any inventory of property and the named beneficiaries are there for all the world to see. An inter vivos trust is not recorded in a public place. The identity and amount of the settlor's property and the names of the beneficiaries need not be disclosed to any public officials except the tax authorities (whose records are private). Hence, revocable trusts are especially attractive to persons desiring secrecy. Such persons include personalities trying to keep out of the tabloids and persons of great wealth who fear kidnapping or other victimization of their beneficiaries or theft of their art collections, jewels, or other property. For example, in In re Estate of Hearst, 67 Cal. App. 3d 777, 136 Cal. Rptr. 821 (1977), William Randolph Hearst had created a testamentary trust to care for his descendants and relatives. After Patty Hearst was kidnapped by the Symbionese Liberation Army, the trustees asked the court to cut off public access to the probate files in Hearst's estate, fearing that radicals would find hitherto unnoticed members of the family and the location of their homes and properties. The court agreed to restrict public access while the Hearst family was in danger of attack. If W. R. Hearst had created a revocable inter vivos trust of his property, the family records would have been kept private.

(5)   Ancillary probate

If the settlor owns real property located outside the domiciliary state, any will passing title to that property must be probated in the state where the land is located. To avoid ancillary probate, which may be cumbersome and expensive, land in another state can be transferred to a revocable inter vivos trust. Through this device, title to the land is changed to the trustee during the owner's life.

(6)   Avoiding restrictions protecting family members

In many states the surviving spouse is given by statute an elective share in the decedent's probate estate only. The elective share does not extend by statute to revocable trusts created by the decedent spouse. Courts in most of these jurisdictions, however, exercising equity powers, have permitted the surviving spouse to reach the assets in a revocable trust created by the decedent spouse. See infra pages 500-513. Nonetheless, a disgruntled spouse might be able to create a funded revocable trust in another state not recognizing the spouse's right to reach the trust and thereby defeat a spouse's elective share.

A funded revocable trust may be used to put assets beyond the reach of an illegitimate child, protected by a pretermission statute, whom the client does not wish to mention in his will. Pretermission statutes apply only to probate property. See infra page 545.

(7)   Avoiding restrictions on testamentary trusts

A testamentary trust is a trust created by a will. It is sometimes called a court trust because it comes into being by an order of the probate court that supervises the administration of the estate, and in many states this court continues to supervise the administration of the testamentary trust after the estate is closed. An inter vivos trust, on the other hand, created by the settlor during lifetime, comes into being without any court order. It is not subject to any court supervision unless the beneficiary or the trustee comes into court to settle some trust matter.

Inasmuch as a testamentary trust is created by a court order, the trustee may have the duty to account to the court. Judicial approval of a trustee's accounts is often a time-consuming and expensive procedure. It may require the appointment of guardians ad litem to represent unborn and unascertained beneficiaries. To avoid this, the will may provide that certain beneficiaries (perhaps all adult, competent beneficiaries) have the power to approve the trustee's accounts without a court proceeding. Although such a provision would be effective in an inter vivos trust, whether it is effective in testamentary trusts varies from jurisdiction to jurisdiction. In some states, the probate court, having brought the testamentary trust into being, may refuse to be deprived of its authority to oversee the trustee's work. To avoid judicial accounting, the settlor may create a revocable inter vivos trust.

In some states, a nondomiciliary bank or a nonresident person cannot serve as testamentary trustee under the will of a testator who was a domiciliary of the state. See Austin W. Scott, Trusts §558 (William F. Fratcher 4th ed. 1989). By contrast, the settlor of an inter vivos trust can name as trustee a bank in, or a resident of, another state. Where the beneficiaries reside in another state, the settlor may wish to appoint a trustee in their state, particularly where the trustee is given discretionary powers that can be soundly exercised only on the basis of personal contact with the beneficiaries.

(8) *Choosing the law of another jurisdiction to govern*

As a general rule, the settlor of an inter vivos trust of personal property may choose the state law that is to govern the trust. (If a trust asset is land, the law of the state where the land is located governs.) The settlor may choose the law of the domicile of the settlor or of the beneficiaries, or the law of the state where the trust is administered. A testator may not have this freedom of choice. Many states apply the law of the settlor's domicile to a testamentary trust, because it was created by a will probated in that state, regardless of the testator's intent that the law of another state apply. Hence, to avoid some local restriction on trusts, the settlor may want to create an inter vivos trust in another state.

The settlor of an inter vivos trust can create a trust in a state that has the most permissive period of perpetuities. Delaware, Illinois, Maine, New Jersey, Rhode Island, South Dakota, and Wisconsin, for example, have abolished the application of the Rule against Perpetuities to trusts, if the trustee has a power to sell the trust assets (see infra page 854). As we shall see (infra page 849), a perpetual dynasty trust for the settlor's descendants, which incurs no federal estate or generation-skipping transfer taxes at the expiration of each generation, can be created in these states. Persons domiciled in other states can take advantage of these permissive laws by creating inter vivos trusts in these states.

Uniform Probate Code §2-703 changes the old law and provides that the testator may select the state law to govern the meaning and legal effect of his will, including trusts created by will, unless that law is contrary to the domiciliary state's law protecting the surviving spouse or any other public policy of the domiciliary state. This provision aligns testamentary choice of law rules with those generally used for inter vivos trusts, and, where adopted, it lessens the need to create an inter vivos trust to achieve some benefit available in some other state. It is not wholly clear, however, when applying foreign law to the will of a domiciliary testator would violate public policy of the domiciliary state.

(9)   Lack of certainty in the law

Where a revocable trust is used as a substitute for a will, the law may be more uncertain in solving a problem that arises than it would be in case of a will. Wills rules developed over the centuries — for dealing with divorce, adoption, lapse, ademption, simultaneous death, apportionment of death taxes, and creditor's rights — may or may not be applicable to revocable trusts. Most of these issues can be solved by appropriate drafting if the drafter is awake to the problems.

(10)   Avoiding will contests

A revocable trust, like a will, can be contested for lack of mental capacity and undue influence. In practice, however, it is more difficult to set aside a funded revocable trust than a will on these grounds. In the first place, the heirs of the decedent are not entitled to see the trust instrument, which is not a public document but a private document available only to the trust beneficiaries.[16] If the heirs bring suit, they will be able to learn the trust terms, but they are thereby forced to commit themselves to legal fees in a lawsuit without a realistic

---

16. The trust beneficiaries are entitled to see the entire trust document so that they can evaluate whether the trustee is discharging her duties properly. Fletcher v. Fletcher, 253 Va. 30, 480 S.E.2d 488 (1997), infra page 937. However, if the trust document expressly limits the beneficiaries' right to inspect the document, such a restriction might be enforced unless such information is reasonably necessary to protect the beneficiaries' rights. Taylor v. NationsBank Corp., 125 N.C. App. 515, 481 S.E.2d 358 (1997).

appraisal of their chances of winning. Secondly, if a trust continues as an ongoing operation for several years, generating monthly or yearly statements, sales of assets and reinvestments, a jury or a court will be most reluctant to set the trust aside. Do you see why? If a will contest is foreseen, creating a revocable trust of the client's assets may be advisable.

(11)   Estate taxation

As mentioned above, there are no federal tax advantages to a revocable trust. The assets of a revocable trust are included in the gross estate of the settlor under §2038 of the Internal Revenue Code of 1986. See infra page 1027.

(12)   Controlling surviving spouse's disposition

When one spouse wants some assurance that the surviving spouse's property will be disposed of in accordance with a mutual estate plan, both spouses can create a revocable trust of their property — to become irrevocable upon the death of one spouse. The trust may provide, for example, that all the income shall be payable to the surviving spouse, with the right of the surviving spouse to dip into principal if necessary to support her, and upon the surviving spouse's death the trust principal shall be divided equally between the husband's son and the wife's daughter by prior marriages. This use of the revocable trust may be especially attractive in second marriages and is much preferable to trying to control the surviving spouse's disposition by contract (see supra pages 322-329).

(13)   Custodial trusts

An alternative to an individually tailored revocable trust, in states that have enacted the Uniform Custodial Trust Act (1987), is a statutory custodial trust. The act provides a statutory trust for the support of the beneficiary. The terms of the trust are spelled out in the statute. Someone other than the beneficiary must be named trustee. Until the beneficiary is incapacitated, the trustee must pay so much or all of the trust property as the beneficiary directs. If the beneficiary becomes incapacitated, the trustee may use the trust property for the support of the beneficiary and for the beneficiary's dependents. Upon the death of the beneficiary, the trust terminates and the trust assets are transferred to the persons designated by the beneficiary in a written document delivered to the trustee. The trust can be created by a transfer of property "to *X* as custodial trustee for *A*, under the (state) Uniform Custodial Trust Act."

The custodial trust is designed for elderly persons of modest means who consult attorneys in general practice, not estate planning specialists, and who want an inter vivos trust for management of assets in the event of incapacity. Because the terms of a custodial trust are fixed by statute, there is little flexibility. Most lawyers will have trust forms of their own and will prefer to draft a trust for the particular client's objectives rather than use an unvariable form. But, where that is impracticable, a custodial trust is better than a guardianship upon a person's incapacity. See Gerry W. Beyer, Simplification of Inter Vivos Trust Instruments — From Incorporation by Reference to the Uniform Custodial Trust Act and Beyond, 32 So. Tex. L. Rev. 203 (1991).

NOTE: MARKETING OF LIVING TRUSTS

Because of the public demand for living (or revocable) trusts, in some states a living trust industry has developed, run by bankers and financial consultants, sometimes in consultation with lawyers. These nonlawyers market living trusts to the public. Lawyers have begun to fight these purveyors of living trusts, alleging unauthorized practice of law. In The Florida Bar v. American Senior Citizens Alliance, Inc., 689 So. 2d 255 (Fla. 1997), the court ruled that a for-profit corporation managed by nonlawyers in the business of selling complex estate planning documents, including wills, living trusts, and durable powers of attorney was engaged in the unauthorized practice of law. The court also thought that lawyer participation in such living trust marketing schemes compromised the lawyer's duty of loyalty to the lawyer's client and independent professional judgment. Accord, Akron Bar Assn. v. Miller, 80 Ohio St. 3d 6, 684 N.E.2d 188 (1997). In 1993, Illinois enacted a statute providing that the assembly, drafting, and execution of a living trust by a nonlawyer or by a corporation not authorized to do trust business is an unlawful business practice. Ill. Comp. Stat. Ann. ch. 815, §505/2BB (1998).

In Committee on Professional Ethics v. Baker, 492 N.W.2d 695 (Iowa 1992), the court reprimanded a lawyer for participating in a living trust marketing scheme with a nonlawyer, who the court thought was engaging in the unauthorized practice of law. However, a lawyer who markets pre-printed or form living trusts is free to do so. In re Pozarny, 677 N.Y.S.2d 714 (Sur. Ct. 1998) (criticizing lawyer for marketing a living trust in the form of loose pages in a three-ring binder).

The rise of a lay industry to meet consumer demand for living trusts to avoid probate contains an obvious lesson: Reform probate and the law of wills so that a will can have all the attributes of a living trust if desired. If this were done, the living trust business would collapse. But until it is done, suppressing nonlawyers who are giving the public what it wants, while lawyers are not, is not likely to be a rousing success.

SECTION E.   PLANNING FOR INCAPACITY

The topics in this section are not usually referred to as nonprobate transfers of property. Indeed, they do not necessarily involve transfers of property at all. Nonetheless, it is convenient to treat the methods of dealing with incapacity here, immediately after revocable trusts, as durable powers of attorney and health care directives as well as revocable trusts are among the tools available to the attorney planning for the possible incapacity of the client.

1. *The Durable Power of Attorney*

The durable power of attorney, like the revocable trust, is useful in planning for incapacity. Unlike an ordinary power of attorney, which terminates on the incapacity of the principal, a durable power continues throughout the incapacity of the principal until the principal dies. A durable power is permitted by Uniform Probate Code §§5-501 to 5-505 (1990) and by statutes in all states. Some specific language is required in the instrument creating the durable power expressing the intent of the principal that the power not terminate upon incapacity. Durable powers are controlled by the law of agency, except the rule that the agent's power terminates on the principal's incapacity does not apply. The principal, if competent, can terminate the agency and durable power at any time. Durable powers must be created by a written instrument, and in some states witnessed or notarized. In some states, durable powers can be created by using a statutory short form, incorporating by reference statutory powers given the agent, or a durable power can be created by an instrument tailored to fit the wishes of a particular client.

The holder of a durable power is somewhat like a trustee, but there are important differences. First, a durable power ceases when the principal dies; the holder of the power can make no transfers after the principal's death. A durable power does not avoid probate. A trust continues after the settlor's death, transferring property without probate. Moreover, the trustee can be given authority to take action after the settlor's death to cure defects in the estate plan that surface for the first time when all the relevant facts are known. An agent cannot act after the death of the principal. Second, if an agent dies, the power terminates unless a successor agent is named by the principal. If a trustee dies, a successor trustee is appointed by a court. Third, a trustee has title to the trust assets and generally has all the powers an owner has. The trustee can sell and reinvest the trust property. The law of trustees' powers and duties is well-developed and well-known. In contrast, an agent does not own the property, and agency law traditionally sparingly implies powers and strictly construes express powers. Third parties readily deal with trustees but are cautious about dealing with agents. Some banks and other financial institutions, uncertain of an agent's authority and unfamiliar with a durable power, may refuse to accept a durable power of appointment. The upshot is that durable powers are useful for persons seeking a way of dealing with incompetency without creating a trust, but trusts are more flexible and satisfactory for most clients. Durable powers of attorney have, nonetheless, become an extremely popular device for dealing with incapacity among persons of modest means.

Franzen v. Norwest Bank Colorado
Supreme Court of Colorado, 1998
955 P.2d 1018

SCOTT, J.   This case arises out of a disagreement over the disposition of assets in a trust created for the benefit of Frances Franzen by her late husband, James Franzen. The court of appeals held that James O'Brien, Mrs. Franzen's brother, was authorized to dissolve the trust by virtue of a power of attorney executed by Mrs. Franzen. . . . We affirm the judgment of the court of appeals. . . .

I.

On February 4, 1992, James Franzen, the settlor, executed an instrument creating a trust designed to provide for himself and his wife, Frances Franzen, in their old age. The corpus of the trust initially consisted of three bank accounts containing a total of $74,251.19, but it did not include certain other assets held by Mr. and Mrs. Franzen as joint tenants, such as the family home. Norwest Bank, then known as United Bank of Denver, was named as the sole trustee in the trust agreement.

James Franzen was terminally ill when he created the trust, and he died four months later. Upon Mr. Franzen's death, a trust officer at the bank sent a letter to Frances Franzen, who was living in a nursing home, notifying her that she had "certain rights regarding the trust." A copy of the trust agreement was enclosed, and the letter referred to Article 5.1, which states:

> At ... [James'] death, if Frances survives ... [him], she may direct ... [the] trustee in writing to deliver the residuary trust estate to her within three months of [James'] death. If she does not so direct, this trust shall continue to be administered as provided in Article 3. If she so directs, the trust shall terminate on the date the trust estate is distributed to her.

The letter asked Mrs. Franzen for a decision in writing by August 1, 1992, "so that we have time to make arrangements for the transfer of assets if necessary." A handwritten note at the bottom of the letter, signed by Mrs. Franzen and dated July 14, 1992, says, "I wish to leave the trust intact for my lifetime."

The bank, concerned about the disposition of the vacant house and other assets not included in the trust, contacted Mrs. Franzen's nephews, who were named as remaindermen of the trust. The two nephews were reluctant to assume responsibility for Mrs. Franzen's affairs, though, and Mrs. Franzen's brother, James O'Brien, intervened. O'Brien moved Mrs. Franzen to a nursing home in Kentucky, where he lived, and asked the bank to turn over Mrs. Franzen's assets to him.

In the course of dealing with the bank, the nephews expressed concerns about O'Brien's motives. The bank declined to comply with O'Brien's request, and filed a Petition for Instruction and Advice in the Denver Probate Court. Before the hearing, O'Brien sent the bank a copy of a power of attorney purporting to authorize him to act in Mrs. Franzen's behalf and a letter attempting to revoke the trust and to remove the bank as trustee, citing Article 6.2 and Article 8 of the trust agreement.

Article 6.2 of the trust provides that after the death of James Franzen, Frances Franzen "may remove any trustee," and that "[a]ny removal under this ... [paragraph] may be made without cause and without notice of any reason and shall become effective immediately upon delivery of ... [written notice] to the trustee" unless Frances Franzen and the trustee agree otherwise.

Article 8 of the trust agreement gives James Franzen "the right to amend or revoke this trust in whole or in part ... by a writing delivered to ... [the] trustee. ... After my death, Frances may exercise these powers with respect to the entire trust estate."

The hearing was continued, and the bank filed a Petition for Appointment of a Conservator, asking the probate court to appoint someone to manage and protect Mrs. Franzen's assets. When the hearing on both petitions was held, the probate court ruled that the power of attorney had created a valid agency but that the trust had not been revoked and continued in existence. The probate court found that Mrs. Franzen needed protection, but a conservator was not available, so the court appointed the bank as "special fiduciary" with responsibility for both trust and non-trust assets pursuant to sections 15-14-408 and 15-14-409, 5 C.R.S. (1997). The probate court ordered the bank to use the assets to make payments for Mrs. Franzen's benefit.

Franzen appealed the probate court rulings. On appeal, the court of appeals reversed, holding that the power of attorney authorized O'Brien to remove the bank as trustee and to revoke the trust. . . .

II.

A power of attorney is an instrument by which a principal confers express authority on an agent to perform certain acts or kinds of acts on the principal's behalf. See Willey v. Mayer, 876 P.2d 1260 (Colo. 1994). In Colorado, the use and interpretation of such instruments is governed by statute. See §§15-14-601 to -610, 5 C.R.S. (1997). Under the power of attorney statute, the scope of an agent's authority to alter a trust is narrowly construed. "An agent may not revoke or amend a trust that is revocable or amendable by the principal without specific authority and specific reference to the trust in the agency instrument." §15-14-608(2), 5 C.R.S. (1997).

Norwest notes that the power of attorney executed by Mrs. Franzen did not refer specifically to the Franzen trust. Thus, Norwest argues, O'Brien was not authorized to remove the trustee or revoke the trust. The statutory specificity requirement, however, did not take effect until January 1, 1995, almost two years after the power of attorney was executed by Mrs. Franzen.

General principles of statutory construction lead us to conclude that the power of attorney statute is inapplicable to any agency instrument executed prior to its effective date. See §2-4-202, 1 C.R.S. (1997) (statutes are presumed prospective); see also People v. Munoz, 857 P.2d 546, 548 (Colo. App. 1993) (applying the statute). In addition, the General Assembly expressly stated that the power of attorney statute does not "in any way invalidate any agency or power of attorney executed . . . prior to January 1, 1995," conclusively demonstrating that no retroactive effect was intended. See §15-14-611, 5 C.R.S. (1997).

Norwest responds that the specificity requirement in section 15-14-608(2) merely restated the common law in effect prior to its adoption, so the same result should be reached even though the statute was not intended to be applied retroactively. The bank asserts that the common law would require the power of attorney to refer to the trust by name.

Unfortunately for Norwest, the cases it cites state no such common law rule. Instead, these cases stand for the unremarkable proposition that a power of attorney giving an agent broad authority to act on behalf of the principal should be construed in light of the surrounding circumstances. Where a broadly worded power of attorney arguably authorizes acts that may be inconsistent with the principal's interests or intent, the instrument should not be interpreted as allowing the agent to undertake such acts in the absence of specific authority.

For example, in Estate of Casey v. Commissioner of Internal Revenue, 948 F.2d 895 (4th Cir. 1991), the Fourth Circuit applied Virginia law to hold that an agent acting under a power of attorney that conferred wide-ranging authority to act on the principal's behalf was not authorized to give away the principal's property. The court said, "[T]he failure to enumerate a specific power, particularly one with the dangerous implications of the power to make unrestricted gifts of the principal's assets, reflects deliberate intention." Id. at 898.

Similarly, in Bryant v. Bryant, 125 Wash. 2d 113, 882 P.2d 169 (1994), the Supreme Court of Washington held that an agent acting under a broadly worded power of attorney was not authorized to make gifts of the principal's assets. The court noted the consensus view that "gift transfers or transfers without substantial consideration inuring to the benefit of the principal violate the scope of authority conferred by a general power of attorney to sell, exchange, transfer, or convey property for the benefit of the principal." Id. 882 P.2d at 172 (citation omitted).

The principle recognized in these cases logically might extend by analogy to situations where a power of attorney gives an agent wide authority to make decisions on behalf of the principal but makes no mention of the power to alter the principal's rights under any trust. We are willing to assume, for the sake of argument, that the scope of the agent's authority under the common law in such circumstances would not extend to revocation of a trust established to benefit the principal.

Even so, we are not persuaded that under the common law, an agency instrument must expressly refer to a particular trust by name in order to confer authority on the agent to revoke it. Under the reasoning of the cases previously cited, the terms of the power of attorney need only evince an intention to authorize the agent to make decisions concerning the principal's interests in trusts generally, not necessarily a particular trust.

Section 1(c) of the power of attorney executed by Mrs. Franzen expressly authorizes O'Brien "to manage . . . and in any manner deal with any real or personal property, tangible or intangible, or any interest therein . . . in my name and for my benefit, upon such terms as . . . [O'Brien] shall deem proper, including the funding, creation, and/or revocation of trusts or other investments."

We have little trouble concluding that the quoted language expressly authorizes O'Brien to revoke the Franzen trust, even though it does not mention the trust specifically by name. . . .

In conclusion, we hold that under the common law, a power of attorney that appears to give the agent sweeping powers to dispose of the principal's property is to be narrowly construed in light of the circumstances surrounding the execution of the agency instrument. However, the principal may confer authority to amend or revoke trusts on an agent without referring to the trusts by name in the power of attorney.

Accordingly, we affirm the judgment of the court of appeals.

PROBLEMS AND NOTES

1. Suppose that O'Brien does not know the contents of Mrs. Franzen's will, which devises her home to him. Exercising his power of appointment *attorney*, O'Brien sells the home and uses the proceeds to pay for Mrs. Franzen's care. Under the common law of ademption, when the devised property is not owned by the testator at death, the devise is adeemed and the devisee takes nothing. See Wasserman v. Cohen, 414 Mass. 172, 606 N.E.2d 901 (1993), infra page 459. (In some states the common law been changed by statute. See infra pages 464-467.) Upon Mrs. Franzen's death, what are O'Brien's rights under the common law? See In re Estate of Hegel, 76 Ohio St. 3d 476, 668 N.E.2d 474 (1996) (holding devise adeemed). Here is a paragraph from the dissent:

> Today's decision gives a dangerous power to all attorneys-in-fact to change a will once their charge becomes incompetent. There is now no protection against the greedy or unscrupulous attorneys-in-fact. At least in Hegel's case, Boettger [the agent] did what she believed was best for her charge, innocently depriving herself of her inheritance and providing an unintended windfall to the other heirs. But now, nothing prevents an attorney-in-fact from altering a will to his or her benefit. For example, a house, the main asset in the estate, may be left to Heir A. Heir B inherits the remaining cash. Heir B is appointed attorney-in-fact. The testator becomes incompetent. Heir B sells the house, claiming the cash is insufficient to pay debts. The bequest is adeemed; Heir B now inherits everything. Heir A is out in the cold. At least in a guardianship, a court can

supervise an estate and prevent such injustice. Under this court's holding, there would be no recourse.

2.   A mother with two daughters has been giving each child $10,000 each year to take advantage of the annual exclusion of $10,000 gifts from the federal gift tax (see infra page 991). Mother grants the younger daughter a durable power of attorney. After mother becomes incompetent the daughter exercising the power of attorney continues to make $10,000 annual gifts to herself and her sister until her mother's death. Must the younger daughter return to mother's estate the $10,000 gifts she made to herself exercising the durable power?

Under the federal estate tax, inter vivos transfers by the decedent over which the decedent retains the power to revoke are included in the decedent's taxable gross estate. In Townsend v. United States, 889 F. Supp. 369 (D. Neb. 1995), it was held that gifts made by an agent under a durable power were includible in the principal's gross estate because the power of attorney did not expressly authorize gifts. Without such authorization, the decedent could revoke the gifts. Accord, Estate of Casey v. Commissioner, 948 F.2d 895 (4th Cir. 1991). Drafting moral: Include in a durable power of attorney the power to make gifts if the donor so desires.

3.   For a comprehensive examination of the durable power of attorney, see Carolyn L. Dessin, Acting as Agent under a Financial Durable Power of Attorney, 75 Neb. L. Rev. 574 (1996). Professor Dessin writes:

> Recently, however, concerns have been voiced that perhaps we have created an instrument of abuse rather than a useful tool. Sometimes the problems are as clear as wrongful misappropriation of the principal's property by the agent. Often, however, problems arise because the standards governing the behavior of agents under durable powers of attorney have never been clearly defined. In many instances, those standards have not even been considered. Legislatures, courts, and commentators have often simply assumed the application of various bodies of law without careful reflection. In light of the popularity of the financial durable power of attorney, it is surprising that there has been no in-depth consideration of the parameters of the agent's duty. There has been only the occasional sentence written, often merely noting the application of general fiduciary principles. . . .
>
> Once a financial durable power of attorney is validly executed, it can be an extremely powerful document, authorizing an agent to perform virtually any act with respect to the principal's property that the principal could perform. This breadth of power coupled with few required execution formalities creates a fear of overreaching by unscrupulous agents. [Id. at 575-576, 582.]

Professor Dessin's fears about the abuse of durable powers can be confirmed by searching under "durable powers of attorney" in Lexis or Westlaw, where a disturbing number of cases litigate misappropriation by the agent — usually a friend or relative of the principal.

4. If a lawyer drafts a durable power of attorney, the lawyer should carefully examine the use of the power in the particular client's estate plan. The power should be tailored to the client's needs and wishes.

If the client does not have a revocable trust, for instance, a durable power may authorize the holder of the power to create a revocable trust for the client upon the client's incompetency. For example, *O* may execute a durable power of attorney authorizing *A*, upon *O's* incompetency, to execute, on behalf of *O*, a trust for *O's* benefit, revocable by *O*, and also authorizing *A* to transfer *O's* assets to the trustee of the trust. The revocable trust may be drafted at the same time the power is executed and attached to the power.

The holder of a durable power may be authorized to amend or revoke an existing trust or a payable-on-death designation, sever joint tenancies, or make lifetime gifts of the incompetent's property (useful for taking advantage of the $10,000 annual exclusion from gift taxes, see infra page 991). It is doubtful, however, whether the holder of the power can be authorized to make, amend, or revoke a will of the principal, as the Wills Act may be construed to require personal knowing action of the testator. Upon close analysis, however, there seems no good reason why a holder of a durable power cannot be authorized by the principal to make, amend, or revoke a will inasmuch as similar authorization can be given a holder of a durable power with respect to a revocable inter vivos trust.

See Restatement (Third) of Trusts §11, Comment f and Reporter's Notes (T.D. No. 1, 1996); William M. McGovern, Jr., Trusts, Custodianships, and Durable Powers of Attorney, 27 Real Prop., Prob. & Tr. J. 1 (1992).

2. Directives Regarding Health Care and Disposition of the Body

a. Living Wills

The Supreme Court has held that each person has a constitutional right to make health-care decisions, including the right to refuse medical treatment. Cruzan v. Director, Missouri Department of Health, 497 U.S. 261 (1990). If state law requirements are met, a person may state his wishes about termination of medical treatment or appoint a surrogate to make the decision for him.

In recent years a document has been created called, rather confusingly it seems to us, a *living will.* It contains directives concerning termination of medical treatment, but it possibly could be viewed as an advance disposition of a person's life when competence is lost. The document provides that the signer's life shall not be artificially prolonged by extraordinary measures when there is no reasonable expectation of recovery from extreme physical or mental disability. Almost all states have living will legislation. These statutes vary in many particulars and often provide forms that must be followed. The lawyer advising a client to execute a living will document should consult local law. See Bretton J. Hortter, A Survey of Living Will and Advanced Health Care Directives, 74 N. Dak. L. Rev. 233 (1998) (examining laws of each state).

In 1991 Congress enacted the Patient Self-Determination Act. Omnibus Budget Reconciliation Act of 1990, Requirements for Advance Directives, Pub. L. No. 101-508, §4751, 104 Stat. 1388, 1388-204 (codified in scattered sections of 42 U.S.C.) (1991). The PSDA requires that every patient admitted to a hospital receiving federal funds must be advised of the right to sign an advance directive indicating a desire to withdraw medical treatment in specified situations. For a study concluding that the PSDA has achieved only limited success in advancing its goals, see Edward J. Larson & Thomas A. Eaton, The Limits of Advance Directives: A History and Assessment of the Patient Self-Determination Act, 32 Wake Forest L. Rev. 249 (1997).

The living will statute of virtually every state contains a pregnancy exception: the provisions of a living will authorizing the discontinuation of heroic measures do not apply when the patient is pregnant. Is this a good idea? See Note, A Matter of Life and Death: Pregnancy Clauses in Living Will Statutes, 70 B.U. L. Rev. 867 (1990).

b. Durable Power of Attorney for Health Care

An alternative to a living will is a durable power of attorney for health care. A person can appoint an agent to make health care decisions in case of the person's incompetency. The power of the agent does not expire with the principal's incompetency (hence it is called "durable"); it expires only with the principal's death. A living will states the patient's wishes under generalized circumstances; a durable power puts decisions in the hands of a third person. The durable power enables the agent to respond flexibly to changing circumstances when the patient's wishes are not known.

The Uniform Health-Care Decisions Act, promulgated in 1993, authorizes a person to give instructions as to future health care (a living will) or to grant to an agent a durable power of attorney to make all health-care decisions. The agent must make decisions in accordance with the patient's wishes. The health-care provider must follow the instructions except where contrary to the provider's conscience or contrary to generally accepted medical practice.

Elder law. A new field of law, called elder law, dealing with legal problems of the elderly, began to develop in the 1990s. Elder law deals primarily with two issues: (1) health care and (2) income and asset preservation. Under the first category come nursing home care, continuing care retirement communities, and Medicaid eligibility. The latter category includes property problems such as pension plans and social security, estate planning, durable powers of attorney, conservatorship, and trusts to preserve assets if the old person is admitted into a state institution (see infra page 469). See Lawrence A. Frolik & Alison P. Barnes, Elder Law (2d ed. 1998); Lawrence A. Frolik & Richard L. Kaplan, Elder Law in a Nutshell (2d ed. 1999); John J. Regan, Rebecca C. Morgan & David M. English, Tax, Estate & Financial Planning for the Elderly (1998); George P. Smith II, Legal and Healthcare Ethics for the Elderly (1996).

c. Disposition of the Body

Historically, a person other than a monarch has had little say about what is done to his body after death. Until this century, burials were regarded as a matter of "sentiment and superstition" and were left to the jurisdiction of the church. With the rise of secularism, courts began to exercise a "benevolent discretion" to carry out the wishes of the deceased person, provided these wishes do not conflict unreasonably with the desires of the living. This power has been exercised in such a way that a person now has something more than a hope, but far less than an assurance, that his or her wishes will be carried out at death if the family objects.[17] In addition, if a person dies by violence or in suspicious circumstances, statutes in all states require an autopsy regardless of the wishes of the deceased person or next of

17. In Holland v. Metalious, 105 N.H. 290, 198 A.2d 654, 7 A.L.R.3d 742 (1964), the will of Grace Metalious, author of the best-selling novel Peyton Place, forbade funeral services; the court refused to enjoin funeral services by the family. See Annot., 54 A.L.R.3d 1037 (1974).

In Meksrus Estate, 24 Pa. Fiduc. 249 (Orph. Ct. 1974), a testamentary direction to inter diamonds, jewelry, and paintings with the decedent's body was held to be against public policy and void. Such a provision, if enforced, the court thought, "is almost certain to tempt some people and invite others to overt action to procure the" buried treasure.

In March 1977, Sandra Ilene West of Beverly Hills died, devising her multimillion dollar estate to her brother-in-law upon the condition that he bury her in her 1964 baby-blue Ferrari dressed in a lace nightgown and with the seat slanted comfortably. Upon the brother-in-law's petition, the court ordered her buried, in the manner directed by her will, beside her husband in a cemetery in San Antonio, Texas. Los Angeles Times, May 20, 1977, pt. 1, at 3.

kin. See Tanya K. Hernandez, The Property of Death, 60 U. Pitt. L. Rev. ____ (1999).

With the advent of cadaver organ transplantation, the first principle of law, medicine, and ethics — saving human life — became a relevant consideration in the disposition of the dead. To increase the quantity of cadaver organs for transplantation, all states have enacted the Uniform Anatomical Gift Act, either verbatim or in some modified version. This act permits a person to give his or her body to any hospital, physician, medical school, or body bank for research or transplantation. It also permits a gift of a body, or parts thereof, to any specified individual for therapy or transplantation needed by the individual. Under the original Uniform Anatomical Gift Act of 1968, the gift can be made by a duly executed will or by a card carried on the person if the card is "signed by the donor in the presence of two witnesses who must sign the document in his presence." Id. §4(a). In 1987, a revised Uniform Anatomical Gift Act was promulgated. The witnessing requirement was eliminated; only a signature on a card is required. In some states, additional legislation has been enacted providing for an organ donation form to be affixed to the back of a driver's license. The Uniform Act provides that a surgeon who relies on the validity of the card or will "in good faith" is not civilly or criminally liable.

The Uniform Anatomical Gift Act has had little effect on easing the shortage of organs. Only a small number of suitable organ donors (the best being healthy young persons who die from accidents) have signed instruments of gift. There are a number of reasons for this: (1) the difficulty of imagining one's death and others' using one's organs; (2) the fear that physicians might hasten a person's death in order to obtain organs; (3) unwillingness to be cut open after death, perhaps because of religious belief; (4) simply not thinking about the matter.

A number of commentators, and some entrepreneurs ready to buy and sell organs, have suggested that a market in human organs be established. A market, after all, is the traditional way of remedying inadequate supply. In 1984, however, Congress forbade the sale of human organs. National Organ Transplant Act, 42 U.S.C.A. §274(e) (1998). The British Parliament outlawed sale of human organs in 1989, after a public outcry over the sale of a kidney to a Londoner for £2,000 by a Turkish peasant flown to London for the operation. N.Y. Times, Aug. 1, 1989, §B, at 5. Suppose that the federal government gave an income tax deduction of $10,000 to the estate of any cadaver organ donor. Should that be prohibited as a sale? Suppose that health insurance companies, as a result of collective bargaining or governmental requirement, offered lower premiums to persons who agreed to donate their organs at death. Would this be a sale?

For an argument in favor of a futures market in cadaver organs, see Gregory S. Crespi, Overcoming the Legal Obstacles to the Creation of a Futures Market in Bodily Organs, 55 Ohio St. L.J. 1 (1994). See also Mark F. Grady, Politicization of Commodities: The Case of Cadaveric Organs, 20 Iowa J. Corp. L. 51 (1994).

Sensing that seeking the decedent's prior consent would not produce the necessary organs, the federal government in 1986 took another tack. Hospitals should put pressure on the next of kin to consent. A government report urged states to adopt statutes requiring hospitals to request from families of prospective donors at the time of death permission to remove organs for transplantation. And a federal regulation of the same year made "routine request" a condition of hospital Medicare eligibility. See U.S. Dept. of Health & Human Services, Report of Task Force on Organ Transplantation (Apr. 1986). Most states have enacted "routine request" statutes. Yet, in view of difficulties families have in facing such requests in time of shock and grief, it is questionable whether the routine request approach will be successful. A study in five states in 1988 and 1989 by the Center for Biomedical Ethics at the University of Minnesota found that less than one-third of families gave their consent to remove an organ from a family member who had died. Glenn Ruffenach, Trying to Cure Shortage of Organ Donors, Wall St. J., Mar. 13, 1991, at B1.

Others have favored establishing a nationwide system whereby every individual must answer the question: Do you give your organs for transplantation upon your death? The question could be required to be answered upon an application for a social security number or a driver's license. This system is called "mandated choice," and is recommended by Sheldon F. Kurtz & Michael J. Saks, The Transplant Paradox: Overwhelming Public Support for Organ Donation vs. Under-Supply of Organs: The Iowa Organ Procurement Study, 21 Iowa J. Corp. L. 767 (1996).

A significant increase in the quantity of cadaver organs available for transplantation might result if usable organs were routinely removed from cadavers unless, before the time of removal, an objection were entered, either by the deceased person during life or by the next-of-kin knowing of the decedent's objection immediately after the decedent's death. This method presumes that the deceased person has consented. Thus, it favors preserving life; the burden of objecting is put upon those who would deny life to another. See Jesse Dukeminier, Supplying Organs for Transplantation, 68 Mich. L. Rev. 811 (1970); Linda C. Fentiman, Organ Donation as National Service: A Proposed Federal Organ Donation Law, 27 Suffolk L. Rev. 1593 (1993).

Presumed consent legislation is in effect in Austria, Belgium, and several other European countries. In Belgium, organ donation increased 119 percent in the first three years after implementation of the law. For a thorough evaluation of the presumed consent approach, see Ian Kennedy & Andrew Grubb, Medical Law 1160-1173 (2d ed. 1994); Committee Report, Ethical and Social Issues in Organ Procurement for Transplantation, 93 N.Y. St. J. Med., No. 1, at 30 (1993).

See generally Symposium, Organ Donation, 20 Iowa J. Corp. L. 1 (1994).

6

CONSTRUCTION OF WILLS

In speaking of the Sergeant of the Lawe, Chaucer, himself trained as a clerk in the Inns of Court, wrote:

> Therto he koude endite and make a thyng,
> Ther koude no wight pynche at his writyng.[1]

Beginning in this chapter, most of the cases in the rest of the book raise an issue that could have been — and should have been — solved by appropriate drafting. One of the objectives of this book is to help you acquire the ability of Chaucer's Sergeant at Law so that no one can fault your drafting. It is a skill that should stand you in good stead in drafting not only wills and trusts, but all kinds of instruments.

SECTION A. ADMISSION OF EXTRINSIC EVIDENCE

1. Interpretation of Wills

In construing wills, a majority of jurisdictions follow (or purport to follow) the plain meaning rule: A plain meaning in a will cannot be

---

1. Geoffrey Chaucer, Prologue to Canterbury Tales (line 325). Done into modern English by Frank E. Hill, The Canterbury Tales 9 (1946):

> And he could write, and pen a deed in law
> So in his writing none could pick a flaw.

disturbed by the introduction of extrinsic evidence that another meaning was intended.

Mahoney v. Grainger
Supreme Judicial Court of Massachusetts, 1933
283 Mass. 189, 186 N.E. 86

RUGG, C.J.   This is an appeal from a decree of a probate court denying a petition for distribution of a legacy under the will of Helen A. Sullivan among her first cousins who are contended to be her heirs at law. The residuary clause was as follows: "All the rest and residue of my estate, both real and personal property, I give, devise and bequeath to my heirs at law living at the time of my decease, absolutely; to be divided among them equally, share and share alike. . . ."

The trial judge made a report of the material facts in substance as follows: The sole heir at law of the testatrix at the time of her death was her maternal aunt, Frances Hawkes Greene, who is still living and who was named in the petition for probate of her will. The will was duly proved and allowed on October 8, 1931, and letters testamentary issued accordingly. The testatrix was a single woman about sixty-four years of age, and had been a school teacher. She always maintained her own home but her relations with her aunt who was her sole heir and with several first cousins were cordial and friendly. In her will she gave general legacies in considerable sums to two of her first cousins. About ten days before her death the testatrix sent for an attorney who found her sick but intelligent about the subjects of their conversation. She told the attorney she wanted to make a will. She gave him instructions as to general pecuniary legacies. In response to the questions "Whom do you want to leave the rest of your property to? Who are your nearest relations?" she replied "I've got about twenty-five first cousins . . . let them share it equally." The attorney then drafted the will and read it to the testatrix and it was executed by her.

The trial judge ruled that statements of the testatrix "were admissible only in so far as they tended to give evidence of the material circumstances surrounding the testatrix at the time of the execution of the will; that the words heirs at law were words in common use, susceptible of application to one or many; that when applied to the special circumstances of this case that the testatrix had but one heir, notwithstanding the added words 'to be divided among them equally, share and share alike,' there was no latent ambiguity or equivocation in the will itself which would permit the introduction of the statements of the testatrix to prove her testamentary intention." Certain first cousins have appealed from the decree dismissing the petition for distribution to them.

There is no doubt as to the meaning of the words "heirs at law living at the time of my decease" as used in the will. Confessedly they refer alone to the aunt of the testatrix and do not include her cousins. Gilman v. Congregational Home Missionary Society, 276 Mass. 580, 177 N.E. 621; Calder v. Bryant (Mass.) 184 N.E. 440.

A will duly executed and allowed by the court must under the statute of wills (G.L. [Ter. Ed.] c. 191, §1 et seq.) be accepted as the final expression of the intent of the person executing it. The fact that it was not in conformity to the instructions given to the draftsman who prepared it or that he made a mistake does not authorize a court to reform or alter it or remould it by amendments. The will must be construed as it came from the hands of the testatrix. Polsey v. Newton, 199 Mass. 450, 85 N.E. 574, 15 Ann. Cas. 139. Mistakes in the drafting of the will may be of significance in some circumstances in a trial as to the due execution and allowance of the alleged testamentary instrument. Richardson v. Richards, 226 Mass. 240, 115 N.E. 307. Proof that the legatee actually designated was not the particular person intended by the one executing the will cannot be received to aid in the interpretation of a will. Tucker v. Seaman's Aid Society, 7 Metc. 188, 210. See National Society for the Prevention of Cruelty to Children v. Scottish National Society for the Prevention of Cruelty to Children, [1915] A.C. 207. When the instrument has been proved and allowed as a will oral testimony as to the meaning and purpose of a testator in using language must be rigidly excluded. Sibley v. Maxwell, 203 Mass. 94, 104, 89 N.E. 232; Saucier v. Saucier, 256 Mass. 107, 110, 152 N.E. 95; Calder v. Bryant (Mass.) 184 N.E. 440.

It is only where testamentary language is not clear in its application to facts that evidence may be introduced as to the circumstances under which the testator used that language in order to throw light upon its meaning. Where no doubt exists as to the property bequeathed or the identity of the beneficiary there is no room for extrinsic evidence; the will must stand as written. Barker v. Comins, 110 Mass. 477, 488; Best v. Berry, 189 Mass. 510, 512, 75 N.E. 743, 109 Am. St. Rep. 651.

In the case at bar there is no doubt as to the heirs at law of the testatrix. The aunt alone falls within that description. The cousins are excluded. The circumstance that the plural word "heirs" was used does not prevent one individual from taking the entire gift. Calder v. Bryant (Mass.) 184 N.E. 440.

Decree affirmed.[2]

---

2. Chief Justice Rugg was not a man plagued by doubts about the law, nor was he much interested in equal rights for women. In Commonwealth v. Welosky, 276 Mass. 398, 177 N.E. 656 (1931), the question was whether, after women acquired the right to

NOTES AND PROBLEM

1.   In Gustafson v. Svenson, 373 Mass. 273, 366 N.E.2d 761 (1977), the Massachusetts court reaffirmed Mahoney v. Grainger. The will devised property to Enoch Anderson or "his heirs per stirpes." Enoch predeceased the testator, leaving a wife but no issue. Under Massachusetts law, Enoch's widow was his heir. The court held that testimony of the drafting attorney that the testator did not intend Enoch's devise to go to his widow was inadmissible since the court was of the opinion that the phrase "heirs per stirpes" was not ambiguous. Hence Enoch's widow took the devise.

2.   In re Estate of Smith, 198 Ill. App. 3d 400, 555 N.E.2d 1111 (1990). In this case the testator left a bequest to "PERRY MANOR, INC., Pinckneyville, Illinois." At the time the will was executed, Perry Manor, Inc., a Nevada corporation, operated a nursing home called Perry Manor in Pinckneyville. Before the testator died, Perry Manor, Inc., sold the nursing home to Lifecare Center of Pinckneyville, Inc. Lifecare continued to operate the nursing home and continued to call it Perry Manor. The court held the bequest went to the Nevada corporation, which alone fit exactly the description of the legatee: "PERRY MANOR, INC." The words, "Pinckneyville, Illinois," which were not capitalized, merely described the location of the named legatee at the time of execution. Hence there was no ambiguity, and extrinsic evidence of the testator's intent was inadmissible. To consider such evidence, the court said, "would have the same effect as rewriting the will."

Suppose that the legatee had been described as PERRY MANOR, without the INC. What result?

The *Smith* case is reminiscent of National Society for the Prevention of Cruelty to Children v. Scottish National Society for the Prevention of Cruelty to Children, [1915] A.C. 207. In this case, a Scotsman, who had always lived in Scotland and was interested in Scottish charities, leaving a number of bequests to them by will, bequeathed £500 to "The National Society for the Prevention of Cruelty to Children,"

---

vote by the Nineteenth Amendment, women could serve on juries, a right conferred on "a person qualified to vote" by a Massachusetts statute enacted prior to the Nineteenth Amendment. In denying women this right, Rugg, C.J., reasoned, "The change in the legal status of women wrought by the Nineteenth Amendment was radical, drastic and unprecedented. While it is to be given full effect in its field, it is not to be extended by implication. It is unthinkable that those who first framed and selected the words for the statute [stating qualifications for jury service] had any design that it should ever include women within its scope." Massachusetts did not change its statute, permitting women to serve as jurors, until 1949. In 1950 Harvard Law School followed suit and admitted women as students.

Is Chief Justice Rugg's application of the plain meaning rule to wills consistent with his interpretation of statutes? — Eds.

which was the charter name of a society in London, of which the testator had never heard. Near his home was a branch office of the *Scottish* National Society for the Prevention of Cruelty to Children, whose activities he knew. Which charity should get the £500? The House of Lords held the remote charity in London should get the money because "he had by name designated it." For criticism of this case, in a classic article on the meaning of words, see Zechariah Chaffee, Jr., The Disorderly Conduct of Words, 41 Colum. L. Rev. 381, 385 (1941).

3. *Personal usage exception.* If the extrinsic evidence shows that the testator always referred to a person in an idiosyncratic manner, the evidence is admissible to show that the testator meant someone other than the person with the legal name of the legatee. Thus in Moseley v. Goodman, 138 Tenn. 1, 195 S.W. 590 (1917), the testator, in a list of bequests, left $20,000 to "Mrs. Moseley." Mrs. Lenore Moseley, the wife of the cigar store owner where the testator traded, but whom the testator had never met, claimed the bequest. The court, however, held that the bequest went to Mrs. Lillian Trimble, whom the testator called Mrs. Moseley. Trimble's husband was a salesman in Moseley's cigar store and was called "Moseley" by the testator, and his wife — dubbed Mrs. Moseley by the testator — managed the apartment house where the testator lived and did kind things for him.

4. The plain meaning rule (sometimes called the "no-extrinsic-evidence" rule) has been criticized as fundamentally misdirected.[3] Wigmore, the great authority on evidence, vigorously attacks the rule, saying, "The fallacy consists in assuming that there is or ever can be *some one real* or absolute meaning. In truth there can be only *some person's* meaning: and that person, whose meaning the law is seeking, is the writer of the document. . . . [T]he 'plain meaning' is simply the meaning of the people who did *not* write the document." 9 John H. Wigmore, Evidence §2462 at 198 (James H. Chadbourn rev. 1981) (emphasis in original). The plain meaning rule reflects a dream, a hope, of

> that lawyer's Paradise, where all words have a fixed, precisely ascertained meaning, and where, if the writer has been careful, a lawyer having a document referred to him may sit in his chair, inspect the text, and answer all questions without raising his eyes. . . . But the fatal necessity of looking outside the text in order to identify persons and things, tends steadily to destroy such illusions and to reveal the essential imperfection of language, whether spoken or written. [James B. Thayer, A Preliminary Treatise on Evidence 428 (1898).]

---

3. Another view of the plain meaning rule was expressed by A.P. Herbert's Lord Mildew: "If Parliament does not mean what it says it must say so." A.P. Herbert, Uncommon Law 313 (2d ed. 1936).

The plain meaning rule is rejected by the Restatement (Third) of Property, Donative Transfers, §12.1, Comment d (T.D. No. 1, 1995).

Compare the view of Justice Holmes, who insisted that the proper standard was not what the writer meant to say but what he meant by what he did say:

> [W]e ask, not what this man meant, but what those words would mean in the mouth of a normal speaker of English, using them in the circumstances in which they were used, and it is to the end of answering this last question that we let in evidence as to what the circumstances were. . . . But the normal speaker of English is merely a special variety, a literary form, so to speak, of our old friend the prudent man. He is external to the particular writer, and a reference to him as the criterion is simply another instance of the externality of the law. [Oliver Wendell Holmes, The Theory of Legal Interpretation, 12 Harv. L. Rev. 417, 417-18 (1899).]

See also Jane B. Baron, Intention, Interpretation, and Stories, 42 Duke L.J. 630 (1992); Mary L. Fellows, In Search of Donative Intent, 73 Iowa L. Rev. 611 (1988).

Fleming v. Morrison
Supreme Judicial Court of Massachusetts, 1904
187 Mass. 120, 72 N.E. 499

APPEAL from a decree of the Probate Court for the county of Essex made on April 27, 1903, allowing a certain instrument as the last will and testament of Francis M. Butterfield, late of Lynn.

The case was heard by Loring, J., who found that the testator was of sound mind, that no undue influence was exercised, and that the will was executed properly. At the request of the contestants, he reported the case for determination by the full court.

The report contained the following findings of the justice referred to in the opinion:

> I find that on or about May 18, 1901, Francis M. Butterfield called up Sidney S. Goodridge and requested him to draw up his will, leaving all his property to the Mary Fleming named in the instrument admitted to probate as the will of said Butterfield. Thereupon said Goodridge drew up the said instrument, said Butterfield signed it, and said Goodridge attested and subscribed said instrument as a witness to the signature of said Butterfield. Before Butterfield and Goodridge parted, Butterfield told Goodridge that this was a "fake" will, made for a purpose.
>
> I find by the evidence in this case that . . . the purpose referred to by him was to induce said Fleming to allow him, said Butterfield, to sleep with her. Afterwards said Butterfield . . . produced the instrument before

the other two attesting witnesses, Bryant and Cheney, told them it was his will, that the signature was his signature, and asked them to attest and subscribe it as witnesses, Goodridge, Bryant and Cheney were all competent witnesses.

I find that the words appointing Mary Fleming as "administratrix" were written on the instrument after it was attested and subscribed by Bryant and Cheney.

The instrument offered as a will was as follows:

Be it remembered that I, Francis M. Butterfield of Lynn, County of Essex of Massachusetts in the Commonwealth of Massachusetts, being of sound mind and memory, but knowing the uncertainty of this life, do make this my last will and testament, this 18th day of May, 1901.

After the payment of my just debts and funeral charges, I bequeath and devise as follows:

To Mary Fleming of Lynn State of Massachusetts all of My Possessions at My death of all Real estate and personal property and all that May Come to Me after My death.

Francis M. Butterfield.

I appoint Mary Fleming my Administratrix.

In testimony whereof I hereunto set my hand and in the presence of three witnesses declare this to be my last will this 18th day of May <u>1901 day of 1901</u> in the year one thousand and Nine hundred and one.

On this 18th day of May <u>day of May</u> A.D. 1901 Lynn State of Massachusetts <u>Massachusetts</u>, signed the foregoing instrument in our presence, declaring it to be his last will: and as witnesses thereof we three do now, at his request, in his presence, and in the presence of each other, hereto subscribe our names.

Sidney S. Goodridge,
Eron J. Bryant,
Zella J. Cheney.

LORING, J. All the rulings asked for at the hearing have been waived, and the only contention now insisted upon by the contestants is that, on the finding made at the hearing, the proponent of the will has failed to prove the necessary animus testandi. We are of the opinion that this contention must prevail.

The finding that, before Butterfield and Goodridge "parted," Butterfield told Goodridge that the instrument which had been signed by Butterfield as and for his last will and testament, and declared by

him to be such in the presence of Goodridge, and attested and subscribed by Goodridge as a witness, "was a 'fake' will, made for a
purpose," is fatal to the proponent's case. This must be taken to
mean that what had been done was a sham. . . . The whole finding,
taken together, amounts to a finding that Butterfield had not intended the transaction which had just taken place to be in fact what
it imported to be, that is to say, a finding that when Butterfield signed
the instrument, and asked Goodridge to attest and subscribe it as his
will, he did not, in fact, then intend it to be his last will and testament,
but intended to have Mary Fleming think that he had made a will in
her favor to induce her to let him sleep with her.

We are of opinion that it is competent to contradict by parol the
solemn statements contained in an instrument that it is a will; that it
has been signed as such by the person named as the testator, and
attested and subscribed by persons signing as witnesses. Lister v.
Smith, 3 Sw. & Tr. 282; Nichols v. Nichols, 2 Phill. 180; In the Goods
of Nosworthy, 11 Jur. (N.S.) 570. For similar cases as to wills, see In
the Goods of Hunt, L.R. 3 P. & D. 250, where it was held that it could
be shown by parol that the instrument executed was executed by
mistake, and Hubbard v. Alexander, 3 Ch. D. 738, where it was held
that one of the two codicils duly executed was intended to be a
duplicate. It was lately held by this court that a written agreement,
duly executed, could be shown to have been delivered on a condition.
Elastic Tip Co. v. Graham, 185 Mass. 597, 71 N.E. 117. And see the
cases there cited. . . .

We cannot accede to the argument of the proponent that a will is
like a deed, where witnesses are required to the signature of the
grantor. There it would be enough that the instrument is complete
when delivered. But there is no delivery of a will. The punctum tem-
poris in case of a will is when it is signed, or, having been previously
signed, when the signature is acknowledged in the presence of three
or more witnesses. And where that is done before each witness separately, as it may be done in this Commonwealth (Chase v. Kittredge,
11 Allen 49, 87 Am. Dec. 687), the animus testandi must exist when
it is signed or acknowledged before, and attested and subscribed by,
each of the necessary three witnesses. If this is not done, the statutory
requirements have not been complied with.

Assuming that the acknowledgment animo testandi of a signature
not originally made with that animus is enough, the will in the case
at bar would have been duly executed had Butterfield subsequently
acknowledged the instrument before three in place of two additional
witnesses. But he did not do so. The instrument, having been acknowledged and attested and subscribed by two witnesses only, is not a valid
will, within Rev. Laws, c. 135, §1. . . .

Decree to be entered reversing decree of probate court, and disallowing the instrument as the will of Butterfield.

QUESTIONS

1.   Assume that, after executing the will litigated in Fleming v. Morrison, Francis M. Butterfield showed Mary Fleming the will, and, relying upon its validity, Mary slept with Francis. Does Mary have any remedy against Francis's estate? Contract to devise? Sexual intercourse (battery) by fraud in the inducement? Civil action for rape? Or was Mary essentially engaging in an act of prostitution?

What do you think of the ethics of the lawyer Sidney Goodridge? Should Goodridge's testimony, which contradicts the attestation clause, be "viewed with suspicion and received with caution"? See footnote 12, supra page 244. Should Goodridge be estopped to testify the will was a sham?

Does Mary have any cause of action against Goodridge? Tortious interference with her expectancy (see supra page 221)? Did Goodridge have a duty to warn Mary under Tarasoff v. Regents of University of California, 17 Cal. 3d 425, 131 Cal. Rptr. 14, 551 P.2d 334 (1976) (psychotherapist has a common law duty "to use reasonable care to protect the intended victim" of a patient who "presents a serious danger of violence")?

2.   If the drafting attorney can introduce evidence to show that a will, which recites that it is the testator's will, is not intended as such, thus contradicting the words of the instrument, why cannot the attorney testify that the "plain meaning" of the words of the will was not the meaning intended by the testator?

Estate of Russell
Supreme Court of California, 1968
69 Cal. 2d 200, 444 P.2d 353, 70 Cal. Rptr. 561

SULLIVAN, J.   Georgia Nan Russell Hembree appeals from a judgment (Prob. Code, §1240[4]) entered in proceedings for the determination of heirship decreeing inter alia that under the terms of the will of Thelma L. Russell, deceased, all of the residue of her estate should be distributed to Chester H. Quinn.

4. Hereafter unless otherwise indicated all section references are to the Probate Code.

Thelma L. Russell died testate on September 8, 1965, leaving a validly executed holographic will written on a small card. The front of the card reads:

> Turn
> the card   March 18-1957
> I leave everything
> I own Real &
> Personal to Chester
> H. Quinn & Roxy Russell
> Thelma L. Russell

The reverse side reads:

> My ($10.) Ten dollar gold
> Piece & diamonds I leave
> to Georgia Nan Russell.
> Alverata, Geogia [sic]

Chester H. Quinn was a close friend and companion of testatrix, who for over 25 years prior to her death had resided in one of the living units on her property and had stood in a relation of personal trust and confidence toward her. Roxy Russell was testatrix' pet dog which was alive on the date of the execution of testatrix' will but predeceased her.[5] Plaintiff is testatrix' niece and her only heir-at-law.

In her petition for determination of heirship plaintiff alleges, inter alia, that "Roxy Russell is an Airedale dog";[6] that section 27 enumerates those entitled to take by will; that "Dogs are not included among those listed in . . . Section 27. Not even Airedale dogs"; that the gift of one-half of the residue of testatrix' estate to Roxy Russell is invalid and void; and that plaintiff was entitled to such one-half as testatrix' sole heir-at-law.

At the hearing on the petition, plaintiff introduced without objection extrinsic evidence establishing that Roxy Russell was testatrix' Airedale dog which died on June 9, 1958. To this end plaintiff, in

5. Actually, the record indicates the existence of two Roxy Russells. The original Roxy was an Airedale dog which testatrix owned at the time she made her will, but which, according to Quinn, died after having had a fox tail removed from its nose, and which, according to the testimony of one Arthur Turner, owner of a pet cemetery, was buried on June 9, 1958. Roxy was replaced with another dog (breed not indicated in the record before us) which, although it answered to the name Roxy, was according to the record, in fact registered with the American Kennel Club as "Russel's [sic] Royal Kick Roxy."

6. In his "Petition for Probate of Holographic Will and for Letters of Administration with the Will Annexed," Quinn included under the names, ages and residences of the devisees and legatees of testatrix the following: "Roxy Russell, A 9 year old Airedale dog, [residing at] 4422 Palm Avenue, La Mesa, Calif." [Is this correct? Since the will was executed when the first Roxy was alive, isn't the second Roxy a pretermitted Airedale? — Eds.]

Thelma Russell's property at 4422 Palm Avenue (1999)

addition to an independent witness, called defendant pursuant to former Code of Civil Procedure section 2055 (now Evid. Code, §776). Upon redirect examination, counsel for Quinn then sought to introduce evidence of the latter's relationship with testatrix "in the event that your Honor feels that there is any necessity for further ascertainment of the intent above and beyond the document." Plaintiff's objections on the ground that it was inadmissible under the statute of wills and the parol evidence rule "because there is no ambiguity" and that it was inadmissible under section 105, were overruled. Over plaintiff's objection, counsel for Quinn also introduced certain documentary evidence consisting of testatrix' address book and a certain quitclaim deed "for the purpose of demonstrating the intention on the part of the deceased that she not die intestate." Of all this extrinsic evidence only the following infinitesimal portion of Quinn's testimony relates to care of the dog: "Q [Counsel for Quinn] Prior to the first Roxy's death did you ever discuss with Miss Russell taking care of Roxy if anything should ever happen to her? A Yes." Plaintiff carefully preserved an objection running to all of the above line of testimony and at the conclusion of the hearing moved to strike such evidence. Her motion was denied.

The trial court found, so far as is here material, that it was the intention of testatrix "that Chester H. Quinn was to receive her entire estate, excepting the gold coin and diamonds bequeathed to" plaintiff and that Quinn "was to care for the dog, Roxy Russell, in the event

419

of Testatrix's death. The language contained in the Will, concerning the dog, Roxy Russell, was precatory in nature only, and merely indicative of the wish, desire and concern of Testatrix that Chester H. Quinn was to care for the dog, Roxy Russell, subsequent to Testatrix's death."[7] The court concluded that testatrix intended to and did make an absolute and outright gift to Mr. Quinn of all the residue of her estate, adding: "There occurred no lapse as to any portion of the residuary gift to Chester H. Quinn by reason of the language contained in the Will concerning the dog, Roxy Russell, such language not having the effect of being an attempted outright gift or gift in trust to the dog. The effect of such language is merely to indicate the intention of Testatrix that Chester H. Quinn was to take the entire residuary estate and to use whatever portion thereof as might be necessary to care for and maintain the dog, Roxy Russell." Judgment was entered accordingly. This appeal followed.

Plaintiff's position before us may be summarized thusly: That the gift of one-half of the residue of the estate to testatrix' dog was clear and unambiguous; that such gift was void and the property subject thereof passed to plaintiff under the laws of intestate succession; and that the court erred in admitting the extrinsic evidence offered by Quinn but that in any event the uncontradicted evidence in the record did not cure the invalidity of the gift. . . .

When the language of a will is ambiguous or uncertain resort may be had to extrinsic evidence in order to ascertain the intention of the testator. We have said that extrinsic evidence is admissible "to explain any ambiguity arising on the face of a will, or to resolve a latent ambiguity which does not so appear." (Estate of Torregano (1960) 54 Cal. 2d 234, 246, 5 Cal. Rptr. 137, 144, 352 P.2d 505, 512, 88 A.L.R.2d 597 citing §105.) A latent ambiguity is one which is not

---

7. The memorandum decision elaborates on this point, stating in part: "The obvious concern of the human who loves her pet is to see that it is properly cared for by someone who may be trusted to honor that concern and through resources the person may make available in the will to carry out this entreaty, desire, wish, recommendation or prayer. This, in other words, is a most logical example of a precatory provision. It is the only logical conclusion one can come to which would not do violence to the apparent intent of Mrs. Russell."

The trial court found further: "Testatrix intended that Georgia Nan Russell Hembree was not to have any other real or personal property belonging to Testatrix, other than the gold coin and diamonds." This finding also was elaborated on in the memorandum decision: "In making the will it is apparent she had Georgia on her mind. While there is other evidence in the case about Thelma Russell's frame of mind concerning her real property and her niece, which was admitted by the Court, over counsel's vigorous objection, because it concerned testatrix' frame of mind, a condition relevant to the material issue of intent, nevertheless this additional evidence was not necessary to this Court in reaching its conclusion." The additional evidence referred to included an address book of testatrix upon which she had written: "Chester, Don't let Augusta and Georgia have one penny of my place if it takes it all to fight it in Court. Thelma."

apparent on the face of the will but is disclosed by some fact collateral to it. . . .

Extrinsic evidence always may be introduced initially in order to show that under the circumstances of a particular case the seemingly clear language of a will describing either the subject of or the object of the gift actually embodies a latent ambiguity for it is only by the introduction of extrinsic evidence that the existence of such an ambiguity can be shown. Once shown, such ambiguity may be resolved by extrinsic evidence. . . .

A patent ambiguity is an uncertainty which appears on the face of the will. . . . "When an uncertainty arises upon the face of a will as to the meaning of any of its provisions, the testator's intent is to be ascertained from the words of the will, but the circumstances of the execution thereof may be taken into consideration, excluding the oral declarations of the testator as to his intentions." (Estate of Salmonski, . . . 38 Cal. 2d 199, 214, 238 P.2d 966, 975.) . . .

In order to determine initially whether the terms of *any written instrument* are clear, definite and free from ambiguity the court must examine the instrument in the light of the circumstances surrounding its execution so as to ascertain what the parties meant by the words used. Only then can it be determined whether the seemingly clear language of the instrument is in fact ambiguous. "Words are used in an endless variety of contexts. Their meaning is not subsequently attached to them by the reader but is formulated by the writer and can only be found by interpretation in the light of all the circumstances that reveal the sense in which the writer used the words. The exclusion of parol evidence regarding such circumstances merely because the words do not appear ambiguous to the reader can easily lead to the attribution to a written instrument of a meaning that was never intended." (Universal Sales Corp. v. Cal., etc., Mfg. Co. (1942) 20 Cal. 2d 751, 776, 128 P.2d 665, 679 (Traynor, J., concurring).) "The court must determine the true meaning of the instrument in the light of the evidence available. It can neither exclude evidence relevant to that determination nor invoke such evidence to write a new or different instrument." (Laux v. Freed (1960) 53 Cal. 2d 512, 527, 2 Cal. Rptr. 265, 273, 348 P.2d 873, 881 (Traynor, J., concurring)); see also Corbin, The Interpretation of Words and the Parol Evidence Rule (1965) 50 Cornell L.Q. 161, 164: "[W]hen a judge refuses to consider relevant extrinsic evidence on the ground that the meaning of written words is to him plain and clear, his decision is formed by and wholly based upon the completely extrinsic evidence of his own personal education and experience." . . .

The foregoing reflects the modern development of rules governing interpretation, for in the words of Wigmore "The history of the law of Interpretation is the history of a progress from a stiff and superstitious formalism to a flexible rationalism." (9 Wigmore, [Evidence (3d ed. 1940)], §2461, p.187.) While "still surviving to us, in many Courts, from the old formalism . . . [is] the rule that you *cannot disturb a plain meaning*" (9 Wigmore, op. cit. supra, p.191, original emphasis), nevertheless decisions and authorities like those cited above bespeak the current tendency to abandon the "stiff formalism of earlier interpretation" and to show the meaning of words even though no ambiguity appears on the face of the document. . . .

Accordingly, we think it is self-evident that in the interpretation of a will, a court cannot determine whether the terms of the will are clear and definite in the first place until it considers the circumstances under which the will was made so that the judge may be placed in the position of the testator whose language he is interpreting. . . . Failure to enter upon such an inquiry is failure to recognize that the "ordinary standard or 'plain meaning,' is simply the meaning of the people who did *not* write the document." (9 Wigmore, op. cit. supra, §2462, p.191.)

. . . [E]xtrinsic evidence of the circumstances under which a will is made (except evidence expressly excluded by statute) may be considered by the court in ascertaining what the testator meant by the words used in the will. If in the light of such extrinsic evidence, the provisions of the will are reasonably susceptible of two or more meanings claimed to have been intended by the testator, "an uncertainty arises upon the face of a will" (§105) and extrinsic evidence relevant to prove any of such meanings is admissible. . . . If, on the other hand, in the light of such extrinsic evidence, the provisions of the will are not reasonably susceptible of two or more meanings, there is no uncertainty arising upon the face of the will . . . and any proffered evidence attempting to show an intention *different* from that expressed by the words therein, giving them the only meaning to which they are reasonably susceptible, is inadmissible. . . .

Examining testatrix' will in the light of the foregoing rules, we arrive at the following conclusions: Extrinsic evidence offered by plaintiff was admitted without objection and indeed would have been properly admitted over objection to raise and resolve the latent ambiguity as to Roxy Russell and ultimately to establish that Roxy Russell was a dog. Extrinsic evidence of the surrounding circumstances was properly considered in order to ascertain what testatrix meant by the words of the will, including the words: "I leave everything I own Real & Personal to Chester H. Quinn & Roxy Russell" or as those words can now be read "to Chester H. Quinn and my dog Roxy Russell."

However, viewing the will in the light of the surrounding circumstances as are disclosed by the record, we conclude that the will cannot reasonably be construed as urged by Quinn and determined by

"And to whom do you wish to leave the bulk of your estate, sir?"

the trial court as providing that testatrix intended to make an absolute and outright gift of the entire residue of her estate to Quinn who was "to use whatever portion thereof as might be necessary to care for and maintain the dog." No words of the will give the entire residuum to Quinn, much less indicate that the provision for the dog is merely precatory in nature. Such an interpretation is not consistent with a disposition which by its language leaves the residuum in equal shares to Quinn and the dog.[8] A disposition in equal shares to two beneficiaries cannot be equated with a disposition of the whole to one of them who may use "whatever portion thereof as might be necessary" on behalf of the other. . . .

Accordingly, since in the light of the extrinsic evidence introduced below, the terms of the will are not reasonably susceptible of the meaning claimed by Quinn to have been intended by testatrix, the extrinsic evidence offered to show such an intention should have been

8. This is slippery work in paraphrasing. Thelma Russell did not write "in equal shares." — Eds.

excluded by the trial court.[9] Upon an independent examination of
the will we conclude that the trial court's interpretation of the terms
thereof was erroneous. Interpreting the provisions relating to testatrix' residuary estate in accordance with the only meaning to which
they are reasonably susceptible, we conclude that testatrix intended
to make a disposition of all of the residue of the estate to Quinn and
the dog in equal shares; therefore, as tenants in common. . . . As a
dog cannot be the beneficiary under a will . . . the attempted gift to
Roxy Russell is void. . . . [10]

There remains only the necessity of determining the effect of the
void gift to the dog upon the disposition of the residuary estate. That
portion of any residuary estate that is the subject of a lapsed gift to
one of the residuary beneficiaries remains undisposed of by the will
and passes to the heirs-at-law. . . . The rule is equally applicable with
respect to a void gift to one of the residuary beneficiaries. . . . Therefore, notwithstanding testatrix' expressed intention to limit the extent
of her gift by will to plaintiff . . . , one-half of the residuary estate
passes to plaintiff as testatrix' only heir-at-law (§225). We conclude
that the residue of testatrix' estate should be distributed in equal
shares to Chester H. Quinn and Georgia Nan Russell Hembree, testatrix' niece.

The judgment is reversed.

NOTES, QUESTIONS, AND PROBLEMS

1.   What common law rule, not attacked by Chester's counsel or
questioned by the court, causes the court to get involved in its elaborate discussion of the admission of extrinsic evidence? See the last
paragraph of the court's opinion. Is such a rule sound? Had the court
discarded that rule, the case would have been easy.

2.   *Patent and latent ambiguities.* A latent ambiguity is an ambiguity
that does not appear on the face of the will but appears when the
terms of the will are applied to the testator's property or designated

9. Having concluded that the extrinsic evidence should have been stricken from the
record, we need not reach plaintiff's second contention that, even considering such
extrinsic evidence, "There is neither jot nor tittle of evidence . . . which would support
a finding that Mrs. Russell intended to leave nothing to her dog." However, it is notewor-
thy that, as we pointed out at the beginning of this opinion, the infinitesimal portion
of the extrinsic evidence actually referring to the care of the dog was devoid of all
probative value.

10. As a consequence, the fact that Roxy Russell predeceased the testatrix is of no
legal import. As appears, we have disposed of the issue raised by plaintiff's frontal attack
on the eligibility of the dog to take a testamentary gift and therefore need not concern
ourselves with the novel question as to whether the death of the dog during the lifetime
of the testatrix resulted in a lapsed gift. (§92.)

beneficiaries. For example, in Ihl v. Oetting, 682 S.W.2d 865 (Mo. App. 1984), the testator devised his home to "Mr. and Mrs. Wendell Richard Hess, or the survivor of them, presently residing at No. 17 Barbara Circle." When the will was executed in 1979, Wendell Hess and his wife Glenda resided at No. 17 Barbara Circle. Soon thereafter Wendell divorced Glenda, they sold No. 17 Barbara Circle, and Wendell married Verna. At the testator's death in 1983, Verna, relying on the rule that a will speaks as of the testator's death, claimed the "Mrs. Hess" share of the devise. She argued that no extrinsic evidence should be admitted since there was no ambiguity in the will — she alone met the description of "Mrs. Wendell Richard Hess." The court, however, found that a latent ambiguity arose from the description of the beneficiaries as "residing at No. 17 Barbara Circle." (Why was not this struck out as a misdescription? See infra page 426.) Verna Hess met the description of Mrs. Wendell Richard Hess at the time of the testator's death but she never resided at No. 17 Barbara Circle. Glenda met the description of the Mrs. Hess residing at No. 17 Barbara Circle when the will was executed but she no longer met that description at the time of the testator's death. The court admitted extrinsic evidence that, the court decided, showed an intent that Glenda — who shared a common interest in antiques with the testator — take.

A patent ambiguity is an ambiguity that appears on the face of the will. In some states, evidence is not admissible to clarify the ambiguity, and the will fails, but courts often have disposed of the problem by simply construing the language of the will without the aid of extrinsic evidence. For example, in Estate of Akeley, 35 Cal. 2d 26, 215 P.2d 921 (1950), the testator, purporting to devise her entire estate, gave 25 percent to each of three charities. The court construed the clause to give one-third shares to each charity on the theory that the testator intended to devise her entire estate.[11] And in Smith v. Burt, 388 Ill. 162, 57 N.E.2d 493, 157 A.L.R. 1118 (1944), the testator, a distinguished judge, devised to *A* 80 acres out of the Station Street Farm and to *B* the remaining 140 acres of the same farm. The patent ambiguity is: Which 80 acres? The court held that *A* had no right of selection, which other courts might have given *A*, but that *A* and *B* were intended to be tenants in common in fractional shares in the

---

11. Devises of fractional shares that total less or more than one remind us of the old brainteaser about a man whose will specified that his 11 horses be divided so that his eldest son would get $\frac{1}{2}$, his middle son would get $\frac{1}{4}$, and his youngest son would get $\frac{1}{6}$. When he died, his executor could not figure out how to carry out these instructions. After all, horses are of little value when sliced into fractional parts. The executor went to a lawyer for advice. The lawyer solved the problem. How? The lawyer lent the executor his horse. The 12 animals were then easily divided according to the formula in the will, the eldest son getting six, the middle son three, and the youngest two. One horse was then left over, which was returned to the lawyer. That's horse sense for you!

farm. See Stephenson v. Rowe, 315 N.C. 330, 338 S.E.2d 301 (1986) (holding devisee has power to select 30 acres out of 164 and discussing other alternative constructions and cases from many states); Annot., 35 A.L.R.4th 788 (1985).

3. Whether an ambiguity is patent or latent may depend upon who the reader is. In Estate of Black, 211 Cal. App. 2d 75, 27 Cal. Rptr. 418 (1962), the testator, a resident of northern California, left her estate "to the University of Southern California known as The U.C.L.A." The trial court ruled there was no ambiguity and construed the gift to be "to the university in Southern California known as The U.C.L.A." The appellate court reversed, holding the devise to be ambiguous. However, the ambiguity was deemed latent not patent, and extrinsic evidence could be admitted to resolve it. Why not a patent ambiguity?

> The provision in question is not, on its face, susceptible to one of two constructions. The language is clear, intelligible and suggests a single meaning. A reader unacquainted with the fact that there are two universities in Southern California, one known as the University of Southern California, and another commonly referred to by the initials U.C.L.A., would readily attribute to said provision the meaning that it refers to an institution named "University of Southern California," which is known by the initials U.C.L.A. [Id. at 85, 27 Cal. Rptr. at 424.]

Suppose the devise had been "to Harvard University known as M.I.T." Or "to New York Law School known as N.Y.U." Patent or latent ambiguity?

4. *Equivocation.* Admission of evidence to clarify a latent ambiguity first began in cases of equivocation, where a description fits two or more external objects equally well (e.g., a devise "to my niece Alicia," when in fact testator has two nieces named Alicia). The courts reasoned that the extrinsic evidence did not add anything to the will, which would be forbidden; the evidence merely made the terms of the will more specific. See Succession of Bacot, 502 So. 2d 1118 (La. App. 1987) (will left "all to Danny"; court chose one of three homosexual lovers, all named Danny, who extrinsic evidence showed had the closest relationship to testator).

Where there is an equivocation, direct expressions of the testator's intent are admissible in evidence. Oral declarations of intent to the *scrivener* are admitted in most jurisdictions in case of latent ambiguity.

5. *Misdescription of property or person.* A well-established principle is that a mere false description does not make the instrument inoperative. A false description of property or of the intended recipient may be stricken. The classic case of false description of property is Patch v. White, 117 U.S. 210 (1886). There the testator devised "lot number

6 in square 403" to his brother. The testator owned no lot so numbered, but owned lot 3 in square 406. The court struck the misdescription and held that the lot owned by the testator passed to his brother.

Illustrative of misdescription of the person is Breckheimer v. Kraft, 133 Ill. App. 2d 410, 273 N.E.2d 468 (1971). There the testator bequeathed her residuary estate equally to her "nephew Raymond Schneikert and Mabel Schneikert his wife." Raymond's wife was named Evelyn. After hearing evidence that the testator intended Evelyn to be the legatee, the court struck the misdescription "Mabel Schneikert," leaving a bequest to "Raymond Schneikert and his wife."

6. *Malpractice.* When a lawyer has drafted an ambiguous will, should the lawyer be liable in malpractice for any costs and loss from litigation of the will? In Ventura County Humane Society v. Holloway, 40 Cal. App. 3d 897, 115 Cal. Rptr. 464 (1974), the court held that although an attorney is liable to testamentary beneficiaries if the beneficiaries clearly designated by the testator lose their legacy as a direct result of the attorney's negligence, the attorney is not liable for drafting an ambiguous document. "[T]he task of proving whether the claimed ambiguity was the result of negligence of the drafting attorney or whether it was the deliberate choice of the testator, would impose an insurmountable burden on the parties.... The duty thus created would amount to a requirement to draft litigation-proof legal documents ... [and would be an] almost intolerable burden on the legal profession."

7. For a thorough discussion of the problem of resolving ambiguities, see Restatement (Third) of Property, Donative Transfers, §§11.1-11.3 (T.D. No. 1, 1995). See also Stan J. Sokol, Mistakes in Wills in Canada (1995).

2. Correcting Mistakes

Erickson v. Erickson
Supreme Court of Connecticut, 1998
246 Conn. 359, 716 A.2d 92

BORDEN, J. The dispositive issue in this appeal is whether, pursuant to General Statutes (Rev. to 1995) §45a-257 (a), the trial court should have admitted extrinsic evidence regarding the decedent's intent that his will would not be revoked automatically by his subsequent marriage.[12] The named plaintiff, Alicia Erickson,[13] who is the daughter

---

12. General Statutes (Rev. to 1995) §45a-257 (a) provides: "If, after the making of a will, the testator marries ... and no provision has been made in such will for such contingency, such marriage ... shall operate as a revocation of such will...."

13. The decedent's other two daughters, Laura Erickson Kusy and Ellen Erickson Cates, did not appeal from the judgment of the trial court. Hereafter, we refer to Alicia Erickson as the plaintiff.

of the decedent, Ronald K. Erickson, appeals from the judgment of the trial court in favor of the defendant, Dorothy Erickson,[14] the executrix of the estate of the decedent, dismissing the plaintiff's appeal from the decree of the Probate Court for the district of Madison. The Probate Court had admitted the will of the decedent to probate. The trial court ruled that the decedent's will, which had been executed shortly before his marriage to the defendant, provided for the contingency of marriage.

The plaintiff claims on her appeal that the trial court improperly concluded that the decedent's will provided for the contingency of marriage. The defendant claims on her cross appeal that the trial court improperly excluded certain extrinsic evidence regarding the decedent's intent. We conclude that the trial court should have permitted the defendant to introduce extrinsic evidence of the decedent's intent. Accordingly, we reverse the judgment of the trial court and order a new trial.

Certain facts in this appeal are undisputed. On September 1, 1988, the decedent executed a will. At that time, he had three daughters and was unmarried. Two days later, on September 3, 1988, he married the defendant. He died on February 22, 1996.

The six articles of his will provide as follows. The first article provides for the payment of funeral expenses and debts by the estate. The second article states that the residue of the estate will pass to the defendant. The third article provides that if the defendant predeceases the decedent, one half of the residuary estate will pass in equal parts to the decedent's three daughters, Laura Erickson Kusy, Ellen Erickson Cates and Alicia Erickson, and one half of the residuary estate will pass in equal parts to Thomas Mehring, Christopher Mehring, Maureen Mehring and Kathleen Mehring, the children of the defendant. The fourth article appoints the defendant as the executrix of the will, with Attorney Robert O'Brien as the contingent executor in the event that the defendant is unable to or refuses to serve as executrix. The fifth article gives the executrix or executor the power to dispose of property of the estate as necessary. The sixth article appoints the defendant as the guardian of any of the decedent's children who have not reached the age of eighteen at the time of his death.

The Probate Court admitted the decedent's will to probate. The plaintiff appealed from the Probate Court's judgment. Prior to trial, the plaintiff filed a motion in limine to exclude extrinsic evidence of the decedent's intent. The plaintiff argued that "[§] 45a-257 makes the Court's inquiry very simple: to determine whether the will

14. The defendant's name before her marriage to the decedent was Dorothy A. Mehring.

was revoked, the Court need examine only [the decedent's] will, his marriage certificate to [the defendant], and his death certificate. Extrinsic evidence regarding [the decedent's] intentions is inadmissible because the language of [the decedent's] will is unambiguous, and therefore under . . . [§] 45a-257 the operation of the marriage to revoke the will is automatic and mandatory.'' The defendant, in opposition to the plaintiff's motion, made a detailed offer of proof to show the contrary intent of the decedent.[15]

15. The defendant's offer of proof provided: "May it please the court, if [O'Brien and the defendant] were permitted to testify they would testify as follows. [O'Brien] would testify that he is an attorney before the Hartford [bar], that he was for many years prior to the marriage in 1988 the attorney for [the decedent].

"In addition to being his attorney on a variety of business and personal matters, he was also a close friend of [the decedent]. He was aware that [the decedent] was courting [the defendant] who became [his wife] and he was invited to their wedding which was scheduled for September 3, 1988.

"About one week prior to that time he received a call from [the decedent] saying he and [the defendant] immediately after the wedding were going to go to New York and then take a Concorde flight to Ireland and they wanted to arrange, as many of us do prior to events like that, for their wills to be drafted prior to the marriage ceremony.

"He gave him instructions that the wills would be identical, that is, that all of his estate was to go to [the defendant]. If [the defendant] should predecease him it should go to, half should go to his children, half to [the defendant's] children. That [the defendant] should be the executrix of the will and that she would be appointed guardian of his children, and that [her] will be exactly the same.

"On Thursday, September 1, two days before the wedding, the two of them went to Hartford and executed the wills. I would offer [the defendant's] will as a piece of evidence. And I represent to the court that it is a mirror image of [the decedent's] will that you have admitted as an exhibit. She, like [the decedent], leaves everything to him. If he should predecease her half of her estate goes to his children, half to her children. He appoints her guardian of his children and appoints [her] executor of his estate.

"During the course of the execution of the wills there was no conversation whatsoever about the fact that the Saturday marriage would revoke the will that had been drafted on Thursday. The wedding to take place two days later would revoke the will that had been drafted on Thursday, although there was considerable discussion about the marriage itself and the festivities and the guests and things like that.

"[O'Brien] would testify that the reason that he did not place in the will any specific mention of the marriage or talk about it at all with [the defendant] or [the decedent] was because in his view when a man executes a will two days before his marriage in which he leaves everything to the woman that he's about to marry, makes her guardian of his children, makes her executrix of the estate, and if she should predecease him, leaves half of his estate to her kids, . . . [it] clearly makes provision in the will for not just a contingency, but the imminent [inevitability] of the marriage that's going to take place two days later. So he didn't think there was any necessity that he had to put in words when it was so clear that it was making —

"He would further testify that in June of 1995 he received word that [the decedent] was seriously sick. . . . Two or three days after [his] operation [O'Brien] visited him in the hospital. He learned from [the decedent] that [he] was dying and had a terminal disease.

"[The decedent] said that [he] wanted to make sure, he wanted to look at his estate situation and make sure that everything was going to be, was going to go to his wife, [the defendant]. The attorney then returned to his office, checked the will out, made sure that the will said it was going to [the defendant] and so informed [the decedent].

"By Thanksgiving [the decedent's] condition had deteriorated to the extent that he was no longer able to continue functioning in everyday life and he was staying at home being cared for by [the defendant].

"On February 8, 1996, [O'Brien] would testify he again visited his dying friend and his client. [The defendant] was present throughout the course of this conversation which lasted more than two hours.

"Now much of this conversation was the kind of conversation that Your Honor would expect of one who is visiting a dying friend. They reminisced. They talked about politics. They talked about everything other than the disease for a while.

"Then they got onto the topic of his estate. The will itself was taken out of the place where it was kept. They reviewed it. The attorney once again assured the dying man that all of his estate was going to [the defendant].

"He then told the attorney that he wanted to make a separate provision for his children. He wanted the attorney to set up a corporation that would be called Sovereign Electric Company. He gave him a specific description of how the shares should be distributed. Thirteen percent of the shares were to go to each daughter. The attorney did set up that corporation. The shares were distributed to the daughters.

"And [the defendant] will testify that she has purchased the shares from the daughters for one hundred thousand dollars each daughter. That is, three hundred thousand dollars for the 39 percent that they received as a result of that. On February 22, [the decedent] died.

"[The defendant], may it please the court, would testify as follows. In 1987 she was a widow. She had four children, T. Kevin, Kathleen, Maureen and Christopher. [The decedent], who would become her husband, had three children, Laura, Ellen and Alicia. They met in the fall of 1987. They courted and they became engaged on February 14, 1988.

"They obtained a marriage license at the Town Clerk's Office on August 22, 1988.

"They married in a church ceremony. . . .

"The invitations for the wedding and all the plans for the wedding were made for September 3, Saturday, September 3. In talking to [the decedent] they decided that before they flew off to Europe they should get their affairs in order. He made arrangements with his old friend, [O'Brien] in order to get wills drafted. The wills were as I've described to Your Honor, mirror wills.

"On two days before the marriage, September 1, Thursday, they went up to [O'Brien's] office. They conversed about the upcoming wedding. Everyone was aware that the wedding was going to take place, [O'Brien], [the decedent] and his spouse and they executed the wills. During the course of the execution of the wills, there was never a word concerning the fact that a marriage on Saturday might act to revoke a will that was executed on Thursday.

"They did marry on September 3. [O'Brien] was a guest at their wedding. They did fly to Ireland the next day for their honeymoon. They lived happily until June of 1995.

"On June 23, 1995, [the decedent] underwent an operation. Following the operation he was told that he had terminal cancer and was going to die. He was fully aware of that.

"She was not present during the first meeting of [O'Brien] with [the decedent] at the hospital. She was present during the second meeting on February 8, 1996. She, like [O'Brien], would testify that much of the conversation that day was the kind of conversation one would expect between a friend and his friend who was dying, but they also made arrangements with respect, made more practical arrangements with respect to [the decedent's] upcoming death. The will was retrieved. It was reviewed. [O'Brien] assured [the decedent] that his entire estate would pass to his widow.

"He then requested, she would testify as [O'Brien] did, that he then requested him to set up a corporation in which the stock would be owned, 13 percent of the stock would be owned by each of his daughters. [O'Brien] did that and distributed the stock to them and as a result, obviously, a corporation in which this kind of proceeding that we're involved in now is in the background, is not going to be successful.

"And so [the defendant] then paid each of the children, each of [the decedent's] daughters one hundred thousand dollars apiece for their stock. [She] would testify that because of certain concerns that [the decedent] had about his daughters that he wanted to set up the corporation in the particular way that he set it up and that this was his specific intention with respect to taking care of his daughters after his death."

The admission of certain evidence was undisputed, namely, the will, the marriage certificate of the decedent and the defendant, and the decedent's death certificate. The trial . . . granted the motion in limine, however, with respect to any other evidence regarding the decedent's intent.

With respect to the other issue at trial, namely, whether the decedent's will provided for the contingency of his marriage to the defendant, the trial court, in a de novo proceeding, concluded that the Probate Court properly had admitted the will to probate because the will provided for the contingency of marriage. The trial court reasoned that "[the decedent's] will bequeathed all of his estate to the woman he was licensed to marry and did marry two days later. In his will, he named her executrix and designated her the guardian of his daughters, whose mother had previously died. The nature of these provisions, coupled with the extreme closeness in time of the marriage constitutes clear and convincing evidence of provision for the contingency of marriage. It would be preposterous to assume that [the decedent] was instead executing a will to make provisions that were to be revoked two days later." Accordingly, the trial court rendered judgment affirming the Probate Court's judgment admitting the will, and denied the plaintiff's appeal. This appeal followed. . . .

We conclude that the will, in and of itself, did not provide for the contingency of the subsequent marriage of the decedent and, therefore, under existing case law, properly would have been revoked by that marriage pursuant to §45a-257 (a). We also conclude, however, that under the circumstances of this case, the trial court improperly excluded evidence of a mistake by the scrivener that, if believed, would permit a finding that the will provided for the contingency of marriage. We therefore reverse the judgment of the trial court and order a new trial in which such evidence may be considered by the trial court.

On the basis of existing case law, the question of whether a will provides for the contingency of a subsequent marriage must be determined: (1) from the language of the will itself; and (2) without resort to extrinsic evidence of the testator's intent. Fulton Trust Co. v. Trowbridge, 126 Conn. 369, 372, 11 A.2d 393 (1940) . . . Applying this standard, we conclude that the trial court should not have admitted the will because, notwithstanding the inferences that the trial court drew from the dates of the marriage license and the will, and from the identity of certain of the named beneficiaries in the will, there was no language in the will providing for the contingency of the subsequent marriage of the decedent. . . .

This conclusion does not, however, end our inquiry in this case. In Connecticut Junior Republic v. Sharon Hospital, 188 Conn. 1, 2, 448

A.2d 190 (1982),[16] this court considered the issue of "whether extrinsic evidence of a mistake by a scrivener of a testamentary instrument is admissible in a proceeding to determine the validity of the testamentary instrument." In a three to two decision, this court held that such evidence is not admissible. Upon further consideration, we now conclude that the reasons given by the dissent in that case are persuasive and apply to the facts of the present case. We, therefore, overrule *Connecticut Junior Republic,* and hold that if a scrivener's error has misled the testator into executing a will on the belief that it will be valid notwithstanding the testator's subsequent marriage, extrinsic evidence of that error is admissible to establish the intent of the testator that his or her will be valid notwithstanding the subsequent marriage. Furthermore, if those two facts, namely, the scrivener's error and its effect on the testator's intent, are established by clear and convincing evidence, they will be sufficient to establish that "provision has been made in such will for such contingency," within the meaning of §45a-257 (a).

In Connecticut Junior Republic v. Sharon Hospital, supra, 188 Conn. 9, this court reasserted the familiar rule that, although extrinsic evidence is not admissible to prove an intention not expressed in the will itself or to prove a devise or bequest not contained in the will, such evidence is admissible to identify a named devisee or legatee, to identify property described in the will, to clarify ambiguous language in the will, and to prove fraud, incapacity or undue influence. In rejecting the claim that extrinsic evidence should also be admissible to prove a scrivener's error, the majority relied principally on our existing case law and on the risk of subverting the policy of the statute of wills. The majority acknowledged, however, that, as with any rule of law, time and experience could persuade to the contrary. "Princi-

---

16. In Connecticut Junior Republic v. Sharon Hospital, the testator, Richard Emerson, executed a will on May 19, 1960, which created trusts for a designated person for life, remainder to seven named charities (the 1960 charities). In 1969, Emerson executed a codicil to his will deleting six of the seven 1960 charities as remaindermen and substituting for the six 11 different charities (the 1969 charities). Soon after the 1969 codicil was executed, the Internal Revenue Code was amended to deny the charitable deduction to bequests of remainders unless they were made in the form of a unitrust or annuity trust (see infra page 1064); the remainders in Emerson's 1969 codicil did not qualify. The executor and trustee of Emerson's will, Sager McDonald, called this point to the attention of Emerson in 1975, and Emerson instructed his attorney, Paul Doherty, to amend the will and codicil in such a manner as to qualify the trusts as charitable bequests under the Tax Reform Act of 1969. The attorney then drafted a second codicil, making the requested changes but also mistakenly reinstating the 1960 charities as remaindermen and deleting the 1969 charities. Emerson, who had never requested or authorized this change, signed the second codicil in 1975. Upon Emerson's death in 1979, the probate court admitted the second codicil to probate, refusing to permit introduction of extrinsic evidence as to the scrivener's mistake. The supreme court affirmed. — Eds.

Justice Ellen A. Peters
Her dissent in Connecticut Junior
Republic becomes law.

ples of law which serve one generation well may, by reason of changing conditions, disserve a later one. . . . Experience can and often does demonstrate that a rule, once believed sound, needs modification to serve justice better." Id., 17-18. We are now persuaded to the contrary.

The dissent in that case by Justice Peters and joined by Justice Shea, concluded that it "would permit extrinsic evidence of a scrivener's error to be introduced in litigation concerned with the admissibility of a disputed will to probate." Id., 22. The dissent gave three principal reasons for its conclusion, each of which we consider to be persuasive and each of which applies to this case.

First, given that extrinsic evidence is admissible to prove that a will was executed by the testator "in reliance on erroneous beliefs induced by fraud, duress, or undue influence," there is no discernible policy difference between that case and a case in which "a will is executed in reliance on erroneous beliefs induced by the innocent error, by the innocent misrepresentation, of the scrivener of a will." Id., 23. In each instance, "the testamentary process is distorted by the interference of a third person who misleads the testator into making a testamentary disposition that would not otherwise have occurred." Id., 22-23. "In each instance, extrinsic evidence is required to demonstrate that a will, despite its formally proper execution, substantially misrepresents the true intent of the testator." Id., 23.

Similarly, in the present case, there is no discernible policy difference between extrinsic evidence offered to show fraud, duress or undue influence, and extrinsic evidence offered to show that a scrivener's error induced the decedent to execute a will that he believed would survive his subsequent marriage. In both instances, the testamentary process was distorted by the interference of a third person who misled the testator into executing a will that would not otherwise have been executed — in the present case, a will that would be revoked upon his marriage because it did not contain language providing for the contingency of marriage. Thus, as in the case of fraud, duress or undue influence, extrinsic evidence is required to demonstrate that the will that the testator executed did not substantially state his true intention.[17]

Second, the dissent recognized that, based on the policy of the statute of wills, the "risk of subversion of the intent of a testator, who cannot personally defend his testamentary bequest, is without doubt a serious concern." Id., 24. The dissent, however, persuasively under-scored the counterbalancing "risk of blindly enforcing a testamentary disposition that substantially misstates the testator's true intent." Id. Again drawing on the analogy to the case of fraud, duress or undue influence, the dissent stated that "had the decedent's lawyer deliber-ately and fraudulently altered the second codicil, the relevant extrinsic evidence would unquestionably have been admitted." Id., 25. The dissent contended that "innocent misrepresentation is treated as gen-erally equivalent to fraud in terms of its legal consequences." Id. Therefore, the dissent asserted, the "statute of wills does not compel enforcement of testamentary dispositions that a testator never in-tended to make." Id.

Similarly, in the present case, had the decedent's attorney deliber-ately and fraudulently, rather than innocently but mistakenly, misrep-resented to the decedent that his will would be valid despite his subsequent marriage, it is at least arguable that the beneficiaries of that fraudulent conduct, namely, the heirs-at-law of the decedent who would inherit in the event of his intestacy, would not be permitted to take advantage of that fraud, and that a court of equity could impress a constructive trust on their inheritance. We conclude that, analo-gously, in this case, the extrinsic evidence should be admissible to establish the decedent's true intent.

Third, the dissent examined and rejected the two main objections to the admission of extrinsic evidence of a scrivener's error. One objection was "that whatever error the scrivener may have made was validated and ratified by the testator's act in signing his will." Id., 26. The dissent responded, correctly in our view, that, although "signing [a] will creates a strong presumption that the will accurately represents the intentions of the testator, that presumption is a rebutta-ble one." Id. Similarly, in the present case, although the fact that the decedent signed the will may create a rebuttable presumption that he did not intend it to survive his subsequent marriage, that presumption should be rebuttable by persuasive extrinsic evidence to the contrary.

17. We acknowledge that permitting extrinsic evidence of a scrivener's error will lead to the introduction of extrinsic evidence of intent, which, as we noted previously, is not permitted. For the reasons discussed herein, this common-law exception is no different, however, from the extrinsic evidence of intent permitted in cases alleging fraud, undue influence and duress.

The other objection was "that allowing extrinsic evidence of mistake will give rise to a proliferation of groundless will contests." Id. The dissent presented a two part response, with which we also agree. First, it noted that, "in the law of contracts, where the parol evidence rule has undergone considerable erosion, this risk has not been found to have been unmanageable. In the law of wills, the risk is limited by the narrowness of the exception that this case would warrant . . . [namely, to] permit the opponent of a will to introduce extrinsic evidence of the error of a scrivener, and [to] require proof of such an extrinsic error to be established by clear and convincing evidence." Id., 26-27.

Similarly, in the present case, the admissibility of such extrinsic evidence, in our view, will not prove to be any less manageable than in cases of parol evidence in contract disputes. Furthermore, we would impose the same elevated burden of proof on the proponent of the will in a case such as this. The proponent would have to establish the scrivener's error by clear and convincing evidence.

We recognize that the dissent's position in *Connecticut Junior Republic* would have resulted in the consideration of extrinsic evidence of a scrivener's error offered for the purpose of preventing admission of a testamentary document to probate, rather than for the purpose of procuring such admission, as in the present case. Regardless of that distinction, however, the mistake doctrine advocated by the dissent in *Connecticut Junior Republic* applies equally to the present case. The dissent in *Connecticut Junior Republic* phrased the issue in that case as follows: "Must the true intent of the testator be thwarted when, because of the mistake of a scrivener, he has formally subscribed to a written bequest that substantially misstates his testamentary intention?" Id., 22. That is precisely the issue in the present case. The dissent in *Connecticut Junior Republic* answered that question in the negative, recognizing that evidence of a scrivener's mistake should be admissible where offered to establish that a written bequest should not be admitted to probate because its execution was the product of a mistake of the scrivener and, therefore, did not embody the disposition intended by the testator. Likewise, in the present case, evidence of a scrivener's mistake should be admissible to establish that a written bequest should be admitted to probate because the disposition provided by the bequest would have obtained, in accordance with the decedent's intent, but for the scrivener's mistake.

Finally, we address one other consideration that was not present in *Connecticut Junior Republic*, which might be perceived to be present in this case. That is the potential for past reliance by testators on our prior case law. We do not believe that this is a persuasive consideration. It is very unlikely that, in reliance on such case law, any testators executed wills and deliberately omitted language providing for the contingency of marriage in order to be sure that their wills would be revoked by a subsequent marriage. Moreover, it is very unlikely that any testators, having married after executing such wills, deliberately did not make new testamentary dispositions in reliance on the proposition that their prior wills had been revoked by that subsequent marriage.

Applying these principles to the facts of the present case, we conclude that the extrinsic evidence offered, if believed, could prove clearly and convincingly that there was a scrivener's error that induced the decedent to execute a will that he intended to be valid despite his subsequent marriage. The offer of proof indicates that the evidence would be susceptible to an inference by the fact finder that there had been an implied assertion by the scrivener that the will would be valid despite the decedent's subsequent marriage. This inference could have been bolstered, moreover, by the evidence of the conversations between the decedent and the scrivener shortly before the decedent's death.

The judgment is reversed and the case is remanded for a new trial.

QUESTION AND NOTES

1. Is it better to remedy lawyers' drafting mistakes by correcting them or by holding the lawyer liable for malpractice? See Joseph W. de Furia, Jr., Mistakes in Wills Resulting from Scrivener's Errors: The Argument for Reformation, 40 Cath. U. L. Rev. 1 (1990); John H. Langbein & Lawrence W. Waggoner, Reformation of Wills on the Ground of Mistake: Change of Direction in American Law?, 30 U. Pa. L. Rev. 521, 588-590 (1982). Langbein and Waggoner note that reformation is routinely applied to correct mistakes in other donative transfers such as deeds, inter vivos trusts, and life insurance contracts, whether the documents are drawn by the donor or the donor's lawyer. They argue that, under a fundamental principle of the law of restitution, mistakes should be corrected in wills to prevent unjust enrichment of the unintended beneficiary. The essential safeguard, they say, is the clear and convincing evidence standard, policed rigorously.

If drafting mistakes in will substitutes, such as revocable trusts, can be corrected after the settlor's death, why not in wills? See In re Estate of Robinson, 720 So. 2d 540 (Fla. App. 1998).

2. The old law that courts cannot correct mistakes in wills is today under sustained attack by commentators and by the groups drafting Uniform Laws and new Restatements. Recall Uniform Probate Code §2-503, supra page 252, correcting harmless errors in execution of wills. See also Restatement (Third) of Property, Donative Transfers, §12.1 (T.D. No. 1, 1995), infra page 438.

Even under the old law, there are exceptions to the rule that the law does not cure mistakes in wills. Although courts say they cannot supply missing language, they can strike out a mistaken description (see supra page 426). Courts may remedy a mistaken belief about a member of the family by calling it an insane delusion (see supra page 165). Courts may also remedy mistake in the revocation of wills under the doctrine of dependent relative revocation (see supra page 286). The Uniform Probate Code remedies mistake in one context. Section 2-302(c), infra page 564, provides that if a testator fails to provide for a living child solely because he mistakenly believes the child to be dead, the child receives an intestate share in the testator's estate.

In some recent cases, courts have remedied mistakes by the scrivener. In In re Estate of Ikuta, 639 P.2d 400 (Haw. 1981), the court substituted the word "youngest" for the word "oldst [oldest]" where extrinsic evidence showed that "oldst" did not make sense and was a scrivener's mistake. Where there has been an accidental omission by the scrivener or typist, courts have sometimes inserted the missing words when convinced from the face of the will and extrinsic evidence what missing words were intended. In Wilson v. First Florida Bank, 498 So. 2d 1289 (Fla. App. 1986), a will disposed of personal items, made pecuniary gifts, then said "To the University of Georgia" for a scholarship fund, but did not say what was given the university. The court admitted extrinsic evidence, including the embarrassed draftsman's testimony, and held that the will gave the residue to the university. But see Farmers & Merchants Bank of Keyser v. Farmers & Merchants Bank of Keyser, 216 S.E.2d 769 (W. Va. 1975) (refusing to admit lawyer's testimony that the testator intended to leave $35,000 to her church when amount accidentally omitted by the typist); Knupp v. District of Columbia, 578 A.2d 702 (D.C. 1990) (refusing to admit lawyer's testimony identifying residuary beneficiary accidentally omitted by lawyer, resulting in escheat). There is also a growing number of cases reforming testamentary trusts in order to gain some federal tax advantage. See infra page 654.

In line with this trend to remedy scrivener's mistakes, perhaps pushed along by attorney liability for malpractice, English Administration of Justice Act 1982, Pt. IV, §20, provides for reformation of a will because of clerical error or failure to understand the testator's instructions.

3. *Gifts by implication.* One of the recurring oversights in drafting is to leave a gap in the dispositive provisions. A particular contingency (which occurs) is not provided for. To fill gaps in wills, New Jersey has developed a *doctrine of probable intent.* If a contingency for which no provision is made in the will occurs, the court studies the family circumstances and the plan of testamentary disposition set forth in the will. Then the court places itself in the position of the testator and decides how the testator probably would have responded to the

contingency had he envisioned its occurrence. Engle v. Siegel, 74 N.J. 287, 377 A.2d 892 (1977). See also In re Bieley, 91 N.Y.2d 520, 695 N.E.2d 1119, 673 N.Y.S.2d 38 (1998) (implying a gift to fill an omission, where testator's dominant purpose and design to distribute her estate completely was apparent from the face of the will; extrinsic evidence of testator's intent not admissible).

Gifts filling a gap in a will may also be implied by the process of construction. For example, in Estate of Kime, 144 Cal. App. 3d 246, 193 Cal. Rptr. 718 (1983), the testator, using a printed form, filled in blanks as italicized here ("I appoint *Betty J. Hyde* as Execut*ris* of this Will"), but she failed to name a beneficiary. The court ordered the admission of evidence, including oral declarations, tending to show that the testator believed the printed word "appoint" designated a beneficiary and the word "executris" meant one to receive her estate. But compare Burnett v. First Commercial Trust Co., 327 Ark. 430, 939 S.W.2d 827 (1997), where the court held that, where the will was unambiguous on its face, extrinsic evidence was inadmissible to fill an omission even though the evidence showed the omission was by clerical error.

Restatement (Third) of Property, Donative Transfers,
§12.1 (T.D. No. 1, 1995)

§12.1   Reforming Donative Documents to Correct Mistakes

A donative document, though unambiguous, may be reformed to conform the text to the donor's intention if the following are established by clear and convincing evidence:

(1) that a mistake of fact or law, whether in expression or inducement, affected specific terms of the document; and

(2) what the donor's intention was.

Direct evidence of intention contradicting the plain meaning of the text as well as other evidence of intention may be considered in determining whether elements (1) and (2) have been established by clear and convincing evidence.

SECTION B.   DEATH OF BENEFICIARY BEFORE DEATH OF TESTATOR

If a devisee does not survive the testator, the devise lapses (i.e., fails). All gifts made by will are subject to a requirement that the devisee survive the testator, unless the testator specifies otherwise. In nearly all states, however, antilapse statutes have been enacted which, under certain specified circumstances, substitute another beneficiary for the predeceased devisee.

Before examining antilapse statutes, it is important to get a firm hold on the common law rules regarding lapsed devises:

(1) *Specific or general devise.* If a specific or general devise lapses, the devise falls into the residue. Thus:

> *Case 1.* *T*'s will bequeaths her watch (a specific bequest) to *A* and $10,000 (a general bequest) to *B*. The residuary devisee is *C*. *A* and *B* predecease *T*. The watch and the $10,000 go to *C*.

(2) *Residuary devise.* If the devise of the entire residue lapses, because the sole residuary devisee or all the residuary devisees predecease the testator, the heirs of the testator take by intestacy. If a share of the residue lapses, such as happens when one of two residuary devisees predeceases the testator, the lapsed residuary share passes by intestacy to the testator's heirs rather than to the remaining residuary devisees. This rule (called the *no-residue-of-a-residue* rule) was followed in Estate of Russell, supra page 417.

> *Case 2.* After making several specific and general devises to a number of persons, *T* devises the residue of her estate one-half to *B* and one-half to *C*. *B* predeceases *T*. *B*'s one-half share goes to *T*'s heirs, not to *C*.

The no-residue-of-a-residue rule, probably laid down by English courts to protect the interests of the primogenitary heir, does not carry out the average testator's intent in this country and has been roundly criticized by courts and commentators alike. In a majority of states, this rule has been overturned by statute (see, e.g., UPC §2-604(b) (1990)) or judicial decision, and is clearly on its way out. It is also disapproved by Restatement (Third) of Property, Wills and Other Donative Transfers, §5.5, Comment o (T.D. No. 2, 1998).

(3) *Class gift.* If the devise is to a class of persons, and one member of the class predeceases the testator, the surviving members of the class divide the gift. Thus:

> *Case 3.* *T* bequeaths $10,000 to the children of *A* (a class gift). One child of *A*, named *B*, predeceases *T*. At *T*'s death *T* is survived by another child of *A*, named *C*. Because this is a class gift, *C* takes *B*'s share, or the entire $10,000.

(4) *Void devise.* Where a devisee is dead at the time the will is executed, the devise is void. The same general rules govern the disposition of void devises as govern lapsed devises.

These common law rules are default rules; they apply only if the will does not provide what happens when a beneficiary predeceases the testator.

Now let us turn to the effect of an antilapse statute upon a lapsed gift. In a sense, antilapse statutes are misnamed. They do not prevent a lapse; they merely substitute other beneficiaries (usually issue) for the dead beneficiary if certain requirements are met. A typical antilapse statute provides that if a devisee is of a specified relationship to the testator and is survived by issue, who survive the testator, the issue are substituted for the predeceased devisee. The statute changes the common law so as to give the predeceased devisee's gift to his or her issue.

An antilapse statute applies to a lapsed devise *only* if the devisee bears the particular relationship to the testator specified in the statute. Some statutes apply only to descendants of the testator. Others are broader, applying to descendants of the testator's grandparents, or to all kindred of the testator, or, even in a few states, to kindred of the testator's spouse. The antilapse statute in the Uniform Probate Code, for example, applies only to devises to a grandparent or a lineal descendant of a grandparent. (In 1990, the statute was amended to include a devise to a stepchild.)

> *Case 4.* T devises her home to her niece, A, and the residue of her estate to B. A predeceases T, leaving a child C who survives T. Under the Uniform Probate Code antilapse statute, C takes T's home because A is a descendant of T's grandparent and hence comes within the required relationship. If the antilapse statute applies only to T's descendants, C does not take T's home. The devise lapses and falls into the residue given to B.

In requiring a close blood relationship to the testator in order to substitute the devisee's children for the dead devisee, experience has shown that the antilapse statutes are too narrowly drawn. To carry out a perceived intent of a testator to substitute issue for the dead devisee when the statute does not apply, courts have sometimes rather ingeniously found a substitute gift to issue in the words of the will or have stretched the concept of a class gift so as to apply to two persons who are in some way related. In *Case 2*, above, for example, if the court decides that the devise to B and C is to a class, and not to B and C individually, C (and not T's heirs) will take the share given the predeceased class member. There appears to be no empirical evidence to support limiting antilapse statutes to close relatives even though the overwhelming majority of legislatures does so. What do you think? Would the average testator want issue to be substituted for a dead devisee in every case? Why substitute issue only? Why not substitute heirs, including a spouse?

The antilapse statute, which supersedes the common law where applicable, is also a default rule. It applies unless the testator indicates that it not apply. If the testator manifests an intent that the antilapse statute not apply, and he does not include an alternative gift when a devisee predeceases the testator, the common law default rules apply.

For penetrating examinations of the merits and demerits of antilapse statutes, see Susan F. French, Antilapse Statutes Are Blunt Instruments: A Blueprint for Reform, 37 Hastings L.J. 335 (1985); Patricia G. Roberts, Lapse Statutes: Recurring Construction Problems, 37 Emory L.J. 323 (1988).

Uniform Probate Code (1969)

§2-605.　Antilapse; Deceased Devisee; Class Gifts

If a devisee who is a grandparent or a lineal descendant of a grandparent of the testator is dead at the time of execution of the will, fails to survive the testator, or is treated as if he predeceased the testator, the issue of the deceased devisee who survive the testator by 120 hours take in place of the deceased devisee and if they are all of the same degree of kinship to the devisee they take equally, but if of unequal degree then those of more remote degree take by representation. One who would have been a devisee under a class gift if he had survived the testator is treated as a devisee for purposes of this section whether his death occurred before or after the execution of the will.

Uniform Probate Code §2-605 (1969) is a typical antilapse statute.

Allen v. Talley
Texas Court of Appeals, Eleventh District, 1997
949 S.W.2d 59

Wright, J.　This is a will construction case. The question presented is whether the decedent's will contains words of survivorship which preclude application of the anti-lapse statute.[18] The trial court held that it did and granted summary judgment accordingly. We affirm.

The facts are not disputed. The controversy results from the will of Mary B. Boase Shoults, deceased, which provides in relevant part:

> I give, devise and bequeath unto my living brothers and sisters: John Allen, Claude Allen, Lewis Allen, Lera Talley, and Juanita Jordan, to share and share alike, all of the property, real, personal and mixed, of which I may die seized and possessed or be entitled to at my death.

At the time she executed her will, Mary had 3 brothers and 2 sisters who were alive. However, by the time that Mary died, all of her brothers and sisters had predeceased her except for her brother, Claude Allen, and her sister, Lera Talley. Each of the siblings who predeceased Mary left surviving children. Lewis Eugene Allen, Jr. is a surviving child of Lewis Allen, Sr. He filed an application to probate Mary's will. He also asked for the issuance of letters of administration and opposed Lera's request that letters of administration be issued to her. The court admitted the will to probate, but the order did not appoint an administrator.

Both Lewis, Jr. and Lera filed petitions for declaratory judgment. Lera argued that Mary intended that her estate pass to her brothers and sisters who were living at the time of her death and that the phrase "I give, devise and bequeath unto my living brothers and sisters: [naming them], to share and share alike" operates as words of survivorship precluding the application of the anti-lapse statute. On the other hand, Lewis, Jr. maintained that those words are not words of survivorship, that they do not create a class gift, and that

---

18. TEX. PROB. CODE ANN. §68 (Vernon Supp. 1997) provides in relevant part:

(a) If a devisee who is a descendant of the testator or a descendant of a testator's parent is deceased at the time of the execution of the will, fails to survive the testator, or is treated as if the devisee predeceased the testator by Section 47 of this code or otherwise, the descendants of the devisee who survived the testator by 120 hours take the devised property in place of the devisee. The property shall be divided into as many shares as there are surviving descendants in the nearest degree of kinship to the devisee and deceased persons in the same degree whose descendants survived the testator. Each surviving descendant in the nearest degree receives one share, and the share of each deceased person in the same degree is divided among his descendants by representation. For purposes of this section, a person who would have been a devisee under a class gift if the person had survived the testator is treated as a devisee unless the person died before the date the will was executed. [Representation is defined here to mean the modern per stirpes system. See supra page 87. — Eds.] . . .

(e) This section applies unless the testator's last will and testament provides otherwise. For example, a devise or bequest in the testator's will such as "to my surviving children" or "to such of my children as shall survive me" prevents the application of Subsection (a) of this section.

the anti-lapse statute applies. If Lera is correct, then she and her brother, Claude, Mary's only living siblings as of the date of Mary's death, will share the entire estate. If Lewis, Jr.'s position is correct, then three-fifths of the estate will be shared by the survivors of Mary's deceased siblings because of the anti-lapse statute. Under Lewis, Jr.'s theory of the case, the remaining two-fifths would be shared equally by Claude and Lera. Both Lewis, Jr. and Lera filed motions for summary judgment. The trial court agreed with the position taken by Lera and granted her motion for summary judgment. In two points of error, Lewis, Jr. argues that the trial court erred in granting Lera's motion for summary judgment and in denying his motion for summary judgment.

The primary concern of the court in the construction of a will is to determine the testator's intent. Henderson v. Parker, 728 S.W.2d 768, 770 (Tex. 1987). The intent of the testator must be ascertained by reviewing the will in its entirety.

Neither party argues that the will is ambiguous, although both parties offer differing constructions of the will based on the same language. In the absence of ambiguity, we must construe the will based on the express language used. Henderson v. Parker, supra. We must determine what Mary meant by what she actually said, and not by what she should have said, giving the words used in the will their common and ordinary meaning absent a contrary expression in the will. White v. Taylor, 155 Tex. 392, 286 S.W.2d 925 (1956). If the court can give a "certain or definite legal meaning or interpretation" to the words of an instrument, the instrument is unambiguous; and the court may construe it as a matter of law. Coker v. Coker, 650 S.W.2d 391, 393 (Tex. 1983). . . .

Here, Mary's will contained one general provision devising her entire estate to her "living brothers and sisters." There were no other specific provisions. Logically, Mary would not have devised any property owned at her death to any brothers or sisters who were deceased at the time the will was executed. Moreover, when the phrase "living brothers and sisters" is construed in light of the entire sentence, it is clear that Mary intended that it was her brothers and sisters who were living at the time of her death who were to participate in the ownership of her estate. Otherwise, the phrase "share and share alike," followed by no specific provisions to the contrary, would add nothing to the meaning of the will. We construe "living brothers and sisters," as used in the entire context of Mary's will, to be words of survivorship. Therefore, neither those who did not survive Mary nor their heirs are entitled to take under Mary's will. As Mary's only surviving siblings, Lera Talley and Claude Allen are entitled to share equally in the entire estate. Appellant's points of error are overruled.

The judgment of the trial court is affirmed.

PROBLEMS AND NOTES

1. Since an antilapse statute is a default rule, applying only when the testator fails to evidence a "contrary intention," in many cases it is necessary to determine whether the language of the will indicates that the testator has a contrary intention and does not want issue of the deceased devisee substituted by the antilapse statute. Suppose that *T*'s will devises Blackacre "to my son Sidney if he survives me" and devises the residue of this estate to his wife Wilma. Sidney dies in his father's lifetime, leaving a daughter Debby. *T* is survived by Wilma and Debby. Who takes Blackacre, Wilma or Debby?

The issue is whether the words "if he survives me" evidence an intention that Sidney's child not be substituted for Sidney. The large majority of cases holds that an express requirement of survivorship states an intent that the antilapse statute not apply and that Debby not be substituted for her father. See Rumberg v. Rumberg, 1998 Ohio App. Lexis 6195; Erlenbach v. Estate of Thompson, 90 Wash. App. 846, 954 P.2d 350 (1998); Restatement (Second) of Property, Donative Transfers §18.6, Comment a (1984). See also Texas Probate Code §68(e) cited in Allen v. Talley, footnote 18.

The 1990 Uniform Probate Code revised the 1969 UPC antilapse statute (§2-605, reproduced above). The revisers reversed the majority rule and provided in the revised antilapse statute that "words of survivorship, such as in a devise to an individual 'if he survives me,' or in a devise to 'my surviving children,' are not, in the absence of additional evidence, a sufficient indication of an intent contrary to the application of this section." UPC §2-603(b)(3) (1990). The official comment suggests the rationale for discarding the rule that words of survivorship establish a contrary intention:

> The argument is that attaching words of survivorship indicates that the testator thought about the matter and intentionally did not provide a substitute gift to the devisee's descendants. At best, this is an inference only, which may or may not accurately reflect the testator's actual intention. An equally plausible inference is that the words of survivorship are in the testator's will merely because the testator's lawyer used a will form with words of survivorship.

This provision of UPC §2-603 (1990) has come under sharp criticism from commentators. Professor Ascher writes:

> . . . Apparently, the revisers believe their own antilapse provisions are likely to reflect any particular testator's intent more faithfully than *the testator's own will*. This conclusion is not only pretentious, it disputes what should be obvious — that most testators expect *their wills* to dispose of

their property *completely* — without interference from a statute of which they have never heard. Instead of allowing "if he survives me" to mean what almost everyone would expect it to mean, the revisers have translated it into, "if he survives me, and, if he does not survive me, to his issue who survive me." For those unfamiliar with estate planning esoterica, therefore, it has become yet more difficult to figure out what the words in a will actually mean. [Mark L. Ascher, The 1990 Uniform Probate Code: Older and Better, or More Like the Internal Revenue Code?, 77 Minn. L. Rev. 639, 652-655 (1993).]

See also Martin D. Begleiter, Article II of the Uniform Probate Code and the Malpractice Revolution, 59 Tenn. L. Rev. 101, 126-130 (1991) (warning of malpractice risks for lawyers using their old forms in states adopting the 1990 UPC antilapse statute).

The revisers defend their work in Edward C. Halbach, Jr., & Lawrence W. Waggoner, The UPC's New Survivorship and Antilapse Provisions, 55 Alb. L. Rev. 1091 (1992); Mary L. Fellows, Traveling the Road of Probate Reform: Finding the Way to Your Will (A Response to Professor Ascher), 77 Minn. L. Rev. 659 (1993).

2.   *Drafting advice.* In any jurisdiction, you should not rely upon presumptions. You should make the client's intent clear by providing what happens if the intended devisee does not survive the testator. If there is a gift over to another devisee, you should provide what happens if the second devisee predeceases the testator. Thus, for example, "to *A* if *A* survives me, but if *A* does not survive me, to *B* if *B* survives me, and if both *A* and *B* do not survive me, to be added to the residue of my estate." See John L. Garvey, Drafting Wills and Trusts: Anticipating the Birth and Death of Possible Beneficiaries, 71 Or. L. Rev. 47, 49-54 (1992).

3.   After reversing the rule that words of survivorship state an intent that the antilapse statute not apply, the 1990 UPC revisers thought it a good idea to go further and replace the straightforward 1969 antilapse statute (see supra page 441), which has been adopted in many jurisdictions, with an intricately complicated antilapse statute, §2-603 of the 1990 Code. The labyrinthine language of UPC §2-603 (1990), occupying two and one-half printed pages of the Code, requires considerable time to penetrate, and inasmuch as §2-603 has been adopted only in Alaska, Colorado, Hawaii, Michigan, Minnesota, Montana, New Mexico, and North Dakota, it is not reproduced here. The 1969 UPC antilapse statute remains the model followed in most states. (You may, if you wish, find Uniform Probate Code §2-603 in the Uniform Laws Annotated database in Westlaw.)

4.   *Nonprobate transfers.* Under the law of wills, a beneficiary is required to survive the testator in order to take. If a beneficiary does not survive, an antilapse statute may be applicable if its terms are met.

Should the survival requirement and the antilapse statute be applied to nonprobate transfers? Case authority on these matters is slim.

(a) *Payable-on-death designations.* Under the law of contracts, third-party beneficiaries of contracts are not required to survive the benefactor or the time of performance and may pass their contract rights to their heirs or devisees. The 1990 UPC does not change this rule, with one exception. Beneficiaries of P.O.D. bank accounts must survive the depositor. UPC §6-212 (1990).

In practice, however, most contracts with death beneficiaries provide that the funds are payable on the contractor's death "to *A* if she is living." By contract, survivorship is required.

Should the antilapse statute apply to payable-on-death beneficiaries who predecease the contractor? Uniform Probate Code §2-706 (1990) provides an antilapse statute for beneficiaries of insurance policies, bank accounts in P.O.D. form, contracts with a P.O.D. beneficiary, pension plans, and the like. The terms of this statute parallel §2-603, and thus a designation of a beneficiary "if she survives me" does not prevent the application of the antilapse statute.

(b) *Revocable trusts.* Inter vivos trusts ordinarily create vested or contingent remainders in the beneficiaries. The law of future interests thus comes into play, and this law is quite different from the law of wills. Traditionally, no requirement of survivorship is implied when a remainder is created. See infra page 728.

Statutes in a few states require the beneficiary of a revocable trust to survive the transferor and apply an antilapse statute if the beneficiary predeceases the transferor. See Cal. Prob. Code §§21109, 21110 (1998); UPC §2-707 (1990), discussed infra pages 742-750.

(c) *Joint tenancies.* A joint tenant who predeceases the other joint tenant loses her interest in the property. Under common law theory, it vanishes. No antilapse statute applies to joint tenancies.

Jackson v. Schultz
Court of Chancery of Delaware, 1959
38 Del. Ch. 332, 151 A.2d 284

MARVEL, V.C.   Plaintiffs, who are children of the late Bessie H. Bullock, have contracted to sell to defendant a house formerly owned by their stepfather the late Leonard S. Bullock, claiming to hold title to such property at 1012 Kirk Avenue in Wilmington under the terms of Mr. Bullock's will. Mr. Bullock, who had no children of his own, married plaintiffs' mother in 1918, caring for and supporting her three children during their minority, and continuing to support Beatrice after his wife's death some five years ago, a fact which is reflected in his income tax returns. He died on September 8, 1958.

Defendant has refused to perform the contract, claiming that plaintiffs' mother having predeceased the testator, plaintiffs took nothing under their stepfather's will of January 13, 1937, the controversial clause of which provides as follows:

"Second: I give, bequeath and devise unto my beloved wife, Bessie H. Bullock, all my property real, personal and mixed wheresoever situate and of whatever nature and kind, to her and her heirs and assigns forever."[19]

Defendant contends that when a devise is made to a named person, "his heirs and assigns forever," the heirs as such normally take nothing by way of substitution if the devisee predeceases the testator, such expression being deemed one of limitation defining the quantity of the estate devised. . . . In the absence of "something further" in the language used in a will the same rule has been applied in cases where the word "and" appears before the clause "heirs and assigns." . . . However, when "or" is used following a primary devise, the subsequent reference to "heirs" or the like has been deemed to designate those who will take by way of substitution in the event the primary devisee predeceased the testator, and a lapse is thereby avoided. . . .

It has also been held that the words "or" and "and" may be substituted for each other in arriving at a proper construction of a will, "and" having been read as "or" for the purpose of carrying out an obvious testamentary purpose in the cases of Kerrigan v. Tabb, N.J. Ch., 39 A. 701, and Huntress v. Place, 137 Mass. 409. . . . According to the uncontroverted facts before me on plaintiffs' motion for summary judgment, the testator's father, a widower, died on January 7, 1936. He was survived by a brother, Harry, a step-son, Frederick, and his own son, Leonard. On January 18, 1936 these three survivors entered into an agreement which was designed to insure, inter alia, that in the event of Leonard's death during the settlement of his father's estate his share of such estate would go to his wife, Bessie, and not to his Uncle Harry, the latter agreeing to such an arrangement. Thus, while the legal theory of the agreement is dubious, it demonstrates Leonard S. Bullock's clear intent that his share of his father's estate should go to his wife and not to his only living blood relative. In his 1937 will, executed following settlement of his father's estate, he ex-

---

19. At the time of this case, Delaware's antilapse statute applied only to devises and bequests to lineal descendants or brothers and sisters of the testator. In 1974, Delaware adopted §2-605 of the 1969 Uniform Probate Code, supra page 441, which applies to devises to the testator's grandparents and lineal descendants of grandparents. Del. Code Ann. tit. 12, §2313 (1997).

Should the antilapse statute be broadened to apply to devises to the testator's spouse? In a handful of states, the antilapse statute applies to spouses. The California antilapse statute (Cal. Prob. Code §21110(c) (1998)) applies to devises to kindred of the testator's spouse but not to devises to the spouse. — Eds.

pressly directed that his entire estate should go to his wife, "to her and her heirs and assigns forever," and named her executrix.

In addition to this evidence of intent that his sole surviving blood relative should not share in his estate (Harry Bullock being the only one who would take in the absence of a will, there being no living brothers or sisters of either John, Harry or Leonard or descendants of any of them) there is the further fact that in 1939 Harry died. His wife having predeceased him and there being no known next of kin of the testator at the time of his death, his will should be read not only so as to carry out his intent but construed, if possible, so as to avoid not merely intestacy but a total escheat.

While the granting of a decree of specific performance is a matter requiring the exercise of judicial discretion, such decree should normally be granted in a land purchase case such as this unless to do so would require a buyer to accept a defective title subject to attack by an adverse interest not before the Court. . . . Here, however, there being no possibility of any adverse claim, according to the record before me, and being satisfied that there is a solid basis in law for sustaining plaintiffs' claim to a fee simple title in the lands here involved in the light of the uncontroverted facts, I am of the opinion that plaintiffs' motion should be granted.

There being a recognized rule of construction permitting "and" to be read as "or" when so to do will carry out the testator's intent in will construction cases such as this, I adopt such rule of construction in the light of the facts in the record before me. The language used by the draftsman of the will namely, ". . . to her and her heirs . . ." adapts readily to the rule which permits such a substitution. . . . [T]his is a case in which the total testamentary background calls for a finding of intent that a substitutionary gift over to the testator's stepchildren be made in the event of his wife's death prior to his own.

Plaintiffs' motion for summary judgment is granted.

NOTE AND PROBLEM

1.   Hofing v. Willis, 31 Ill. 2d 365, 374, 201 N.E.2d 852, 856-857 (1964):

While there is some support for the proposition that the phrase "and to their heirs" could be considered as words of purchase by reading the word "and" as "or," . . . the presence of the words "and assigns" makes such a construction unacceptable. If the word "and" is read "or," the language creates a substitutionary gift in favor of the "heirs and assigns" of George's sisters, who would take as purchasers. That a deceased sister's heirs should take as purchasers by way of substitution would be quite reasonable. But it is hardly reasonable to suppose that the grantor would create a substitutionary gift and at the same time designate the assigns of the named takers to take by way of substitution.

2.   *H* devises ¾ of his estate to *W* and ¼ to charity. *H*'s two children are mentioned but not provided for in *H*'s will. *W* predeceases *H*. Who takes *H*'s estate?

Class gifts. Under the common law of lapse, a class gift is treated differently from a gift to individuals. If a class member predeceases the testator, the surviving members of the class divide the total gift, including the deceased member's share. The crucial question is: What is a class? The test is often said to be whether the testator is "group minded." The testator is thought to be group minded if he uses a class label in describing the beneficiaries, such as "to *A*'s children" or "to my nephews and nieces." But a class label is not necessary for a class gift. Beneficiaries described by their individual names, but forming a natural class, may be deemed a class gift if the court decides, after admitting extrinsic evidence, that the testator would want the survivors to divide the property.

Dawson v. Yucus
Illinois Appellate Court, 1968
97 Ill. App. 2d 101, 239 N.E.2d 305

JONES, J.   In this will construction case plaintiffs seek a decree finding Clause Two of the will of Nelle G. Stewart, deceased, is a devise to a class. Plaintiffs appeal a trial court decree rendered for defendants.

Nelle G. Stewart, of Girard, Illinois, died on May 29, 1965, leaving a duly executed will dated March 3, 1959, and containing ten dispositive clauses. The first clause directed payment of debts and funeral expenses. The second clause, the interpretation of which is the sole issue in this case, provided:

Through the Will of my late husband, Dr. Frank A. Stewart, I received an undivided one-fifth (⅕) interest in two hundred sixty-one and thirty-eight hundredths (261.38) acres of farm lands located in . . . Sangamon County, Illinois, and believing as I do that those farm lands should go back to my late husband's side of the house, I therefore give, devise and bequeath my one-fifth (⅕) interest in said farm lands as follows: One-half (½) of my interest therein to Stewart Wilson, a nephew, now living in Birmingham, Michigan and One-half (½) of my interest to Gene Burtle, a nephew, now living in Mission, Kansas.

Clauses three and four made bequests of personalty to Ina Mae Yucus, Lola Eades, Hazel Degelow and Ella Hickey. Clauses five, six and seven made bequests of cash to charities. Clause eight provided for the payment of reasonable allowance to Ina Mae Yucus or Hazel Degelow should illness make it necessary for the testatrix to live in either of their homes. Clause nine directed the executrix to convert all "the rest, residue and remainder of my property . . . of whatever kind and character and wheresoever situate, including void or lapsed legacies . . . into cash . . . and the proceeds divided equally between Ina Mae Yucus and Hazel Degelow, or to the survivor or survivors of them, should any of said named persons predecease me." Clause ten appoints Ina Mae Yucus executrix and waives bond.

After the will was admitted to probate, Stewart Wilson filed suit to construe the will alleging that the devise in clause two was a class gift, that Gene Burtle, one of the devisees in clause two, died after the date of execution of the will but before the testatrix and that plaintiff, as the survivor of the class, was entitled to the entire one-fifth interest in the farm. After the complaint was filed, Stewart Wilson conveyed the interest he allegedly received as survivor of the class to the two children of the deceased Gene Burtle[20] and they were substituted as plaintiffs. The defendants, the executrix and the beneficiaries named in the residuary clause of the will, filed answer denying that clause two was a gift to a class, asserting that it was a devise to two specific individuals and that upon the death of Gene Burtle prior to that of the testatrix, the gift to him lapsed and passed into the residuary clause of the will.

At the trial the court found that the death of Gene Burtle prior to that of the testatrix created a latent ambiguity and admitted extrinsic evidence relating to testatrix' intentions. There is no serious dispute over the facts shown by the evidence presented by plaintiffs. Nelle G. Stewart was the widow of Dr. Frank A. Stewart and received as a devisee in his will a one-fifth interest in a 261 acre farm in Sangamon County. Nelle G. Stewart and Dr. Frank A. Stewart had no children. At the death of Dr. Stewart his surviving blood relatives were Gene Burtle, Stewart Wilson, William C. Stewart and Robert T. Stewart, his nephews, and Patti S. Lusby, his niece. Nelle G. Stewart knew all of these relatives of Dr. Stewart. Of these relatives of Dr. Stewart, only Gene Burtle and Stewart Wilson had a close personal relationship with the testatrix. Gene Burtle died on May 15, 1963, and the testatrix knew of his death but made no changes in her previously executed will. There was evidence from four witnesses that in conversations had

---

20. The children of Gene Burtle do not take the share devised to their father because the Illinois antilapse statute applies only to devises to descendants of the testator. Ill. Compiled Stat. Ann. ch. 755, §5/4-11 (Smith-Hurd 1998). — Eds.

with testatrix she stated she wanted the one-fifth interest in the farm to go either to her husband's side of the house, or to Gene Burtle and Stewart Wilson because she felt especially close to them and none other of Dr. Stewart's relatives had any contact with her.

The trial court held, we think correctly, that clause two of testatrix' will did not create a class gift and that the gift in that clause to Gene Burtle lapsed and, pursuant to the Illinois Lapse Statute, Chapt. 3, Sec. 49, I.R.S. 1965, passed into the residue of her estate.

The definition of class gifts and pertinent rules of construction as followed by Illinois courts are set forth in the case of Strohm v. McMullen, 404 Ill. 453, 89 N.E.2d 383:

> The definition of a class gift adopted by this court, as laid down by Mr. Jarman in his work on Wills, Vol. 1, p. 534, 5th Am. Ed., is:
>
> "A gift to a class is defined . . . as a gift of an aggregate sum to a body of persons uncertain in number at the time of the gift, to be ascertained at a future time, and who are all to take in equal or in some other definite proportions, the share of each being dependent for its amount upon the ultimate number of persons."
>
> "A class, in its ordinary acceptation, is a number or body of persons with common characteristics or in like circumstances, or having some common attribute, and, as applied to a devise, it is generally understood to mean a number of persons who stand in the same relation to each other or to the testator." Blackstone v. Althouse, 278 Ill. 481, 116 N.E. 154, 157, L.R.A. 1918B, 230. And it has been definitely decided in this State that in determining whether a devise is to a class or to individuals depends upon the language of the will. If from such language it appears that the amounts of their shares are uncertain until the devise or bequest takes effect, the beneficiaries will generally be held to take as a class; but where at the time of making the gifts the number of beneficiaries is certain, and the share each is to receive is also certain, and in no way dependent for its amount upon the number who shall survive, it is not a gift to a class, but to the individuals.
>
> There is an exception to the rule that naming the individual prevents the gift from becoming a class gift, stated in Strauss v. Strauss, 363 Ill. 442, 2 N.E.2d 699, 105 A.L.R. 1386, holding that the mere fact that the testator mentions by name the individuals who make up the class is not conclusive, and that if the intention to give a right of survivorship is collected from the remaining provisions of the will, as applied to the existing facts, such an intention must prevail.

Admittedly the gift in clause two is not made with the usual generic class description such as "children," "brothers," "nephews," "cousins," "issue," "descendants," or "family" but is in fact to two named individuals, conditions which militate against construction of the clause as a class gift. However, plaintiffs argue that because of the death of Gene Burtle prior to that of the testatrix a latent ambiguity exists and extrinsic evidence was properly received to show the true intention of the testatrix in clause two of her will, and that the phrase in clause two, "and believing as I do that these farm lands should go back to my husband's side of the house," together with the extrinsic evidence, clearly requires class gift construction.

Plaintiffs rely largely upon Krog v. Hafka, 413 Ill. 290, 109 N.E.2d 213. In the *Krog* case, which plaintiffs contend is on all fours with this case, one Frieda Studtmann left a will consisting of four paragraphs. The first paragraph directed payment of debts and funeral expenses; the second made a specific legacy to a church; and the third was as follows: "Third, I hereby give, devise and bequeath to Harry E. Hafka and his wife, Ethel May Hafka, of New Lenox, Illinois, all of my estate both real and personal of every kind and nature whatsoever to have and to hold the same to them and their heirs and assigns forever"; the last paragraph appointed Harry E. Hafka executor. Harry E. Hafka died eight months prior to the death of testatrix. Extrinsic evidence showed that testatrix, a spinster, spent the later part of her life residing on her 170 acre farm; that for approximately seven years prior to her death Harry Hafka and his wife Ethel May Hafka lived with her, operated the farm and furnished extensive care for testatrix, who was under the doctor's attention for four or five years with a goitre and heart ailment; that the testatrix did not care for her cousins (her only relatives); their paths crossed infrequently and she entertained resentment toward them. Testatrix told witnesses she was not interested in leaving her estate to her relatives inasmuch as they had more money than she did; that at her request a nonlawyer friend, eighty years of age, prepared her will and she told him and the witnesses that she was living with the Hafkas, she liked them well, that it was her desire that everything should go to them, that they had agreed to take care of her until she died and to give her a decent burial. She also mentioned her relatives and stated she did not owe them anything, "they are not going to get any of my estate." Other evidence was that the testatrix told her personal physician that she wanted everything she had to go to the Hafkas for they had taken good care of her. The Supreme Court made an extensive review of the law of latent ambiguity and class gifts and concluded . . . that Frieda Studtmann intended that all her property was to go to the Hafkas as a class, and that Ethel May Hafka, as the survivor of the class, took the entire residue of the estate. . . .

In this case the testatrix named the individuals, Stewart Wilson and Gene Burtle, and gave them each a one-half portion of her interest in the farm, thus making certain the number of beneficiaries and the share each is to receive. The shares in no way depend upon the number who shall survive the death of the testatrix. There is nothing in the language of the will that indicates the testatrix intended to create a class or survivorship gift. The only other provision of the will, also contained in clause two, that has any bearing on the question is the statement, ". . . believing as I do that those farm lands should go back to my late husband's side of the house. . . . " While it is true that this language recites testatrix' desire that the one-fifth interest in the farm go back to her husband's side of the house, it does not indicate a survivorship gift was intended. Her intention to return the farm to her husband's side of the house was fulfilled when she named Stewart Wilson and Gene Burtle as the donees of the interest. . . .

Further emphasis for the result we have reached is supplied by other factors found in the will and extrinsic evidence. First, the testatrix created a survivorship gift of the residue of her estate in the ninth clause of her will, thus indicating she knew how to manifest an intent to create a class or survivorship gift; hence, the language of clause two, phrased differently, was intended to create a gift to individuals distributively. Restatement of Property, Future Interests, Sec. 280, Comment g., No. 1. Paragraph No. 2 of the same Restatement citation provides, "The specification . . . of an exact proportion in the subject matter of the conveyance, which is to be received by each of the named and described persons, is strongly indicative of an intent to make a gift to individuals distributively whenever the . . . proportions so specified equals the entire subject matter given by the limitation in question." Secondly, the common characteristic of the alleged class described by plaintiffs is that of relation to Dr. Stewart, or, in the words of clause two, the class is of "my late husband's side of the house." However, this characteristic is also shared by three other heirs of Dr. Stewart of the same degree of relationship to him as Stewart Wilson and Gene Burtle. It thus appears that Gene Burtle and Stewart Wilson do not constitute the alleged class but are individuals named from the class.

. . . Nor do we feel that the *Krog* case is "on all fours" with this one. In that case the language found to create a class gift was much different than that used in the instant will, and the testatrix enjoyed a much closer relationship with the Hafkas than that between Mrs. Stewart and Gene Burtle and Stewart Wilson. Extrinsic evidence shows that the "close personal relationship" consisted of friendly visits by the Burtles and Wilsons about every summer when they came from their homes in Michigan and Kansas to visit in Springfield and Girard. In *Krog,* the testatrix received many years of personal services from the Hafkas and stated upon several occasions that she did not want any of her heirs to have any of her property. . . . Here there is a general testamentary scheme favoring the beneficiaries of the residue of Mrs. Stewart's estate; namely, Ina Mae Yucus and Hazel Degelow — persons with whom she was obviously on an intimate and friendly basis as shown by the fact that she left them the residue of her estate and, per clause eight of her will, contemplated living in either of their homes.

The devise in clause two was not to persons who come within the designation of a class but was to individuals distributively. It was not so made or limited to prevent the operation of the Illinois Lapse Statute which must be given its intended effect. The court below correctly held that upon the death of Gene Burtle prior to that of the testatrix the devise to him lapsed and passed under the residuary clause of the will. The Decree will be affirmed.

Affirmed.

NOTE

In Sullivan v. Sullivan, 26 Mass. App. Ct. 502, 529 N.E.2d 890 (1988), the testator devised her property "to my nephews Marshall John McDonough, and David Condon McDonough, and to my niece Martha McDonough Sullivan, in equal shares, that is one-third each." She omitted mention of two nieces from whom she was estranged. One mentioned nephew (Marshall) predeceased the testator without issue. To avoid intestacy, the court held the residuary devise was to a class and that the property was to be divided equally between the survivors David and Martha.

It has been held that a gift "to Bessie and Louise," who happened to be the testator's close friends, is a class gift, where the court admitted extrinsic evidence of the surrounding circumstances and concluded that the testator would not want Bessie's share to pass by intestacy. Iozapavichus v. Fournier, 308 A.2d 573 (Me. 1973).

In re Moss
Court of Appeal, England, 1899
[1899] 2 Ch. 314, aff'd, [1901] A.C. 187 (H.L.)

Walter Moss by his will dated in 1876, after appointing his wife Elizabeth Moss and his niece Elizabeth Jane Fowler his executrixes, and making sundry devises and bequests, gave all his share or interest in the Daily Telegraph newspaper[21] unto the said E. Moss and E. J.

---

21. The Daily Telegraph was organized as a partnership in 1855 by J. M. Levy. The Levy family held all but a one-eighth interest, which was sold to George Moss for £500. Moss (nicknamed "Pubby") is variously reported to have been the superintendent of Levy's printing plant or the owner of a public house nearby where the printers repaired for ale. The newspaper was an immediate success, selling for a penny a copy, featuring brilliant young writers on politics, and factually reporting titillating court proceedings involving divorce, crime, and sex (a practice continuing to this day in most London newspapers). Levy invented the classified ad with a box number return in which persons could advertise for matrimonial or sexual partners. The Daily Telegraph, together with the New York Herald, sent Stanley to the rescue of Livingston. By the end of the 1800s the Daily Telegraph had the largest circulation in the world.

Moss's investment of £500 proved extremely profitable, soon returning £15,500 annu-

The Daily Telegraph

Britain's biggest-selling quality daily

Fowler "upon trust to pay the income thereof to my said wife for her life, and after her decease, upon trust for the said E. J. Fowler and the child or children of my sister Emily Walter who shall attain the age of twenty-one years equally to be divided between them as tenants in common." And he gave the residue of his estate and effects to his wife. . . .

The testator died in 1893, and his will was proved by his widow, Elizabeth Moss, alone. At the date of his will there were living his niece Elizabeth Jane Fowler, who was then slightly under twenty-one, his sister Emily Walter, and five children of Emily Walter.

Elizabeth Jane Fowler died in 1891, in the testator's lifetime, a spinster. Emily Walter and her five children survived the testator.

The testator's widow, Elizabeth Moss, the tenant for life of his Daily Telegraph share and his residuary legatee, died in 1897, having by her will given her residuary estate . . . in trust for William George Kingsbury absolutely. . . .

At her death all the five children of Emily Walter were living and had attained twenty-one.

The question was whether, in consequence of the death of Elizabeth Jane Fowler in the lifetime of her uncle, the testator, the share bequeathed to her in his Daily Telegraph share had lapsed and fallen into his residuary estate, or whether the entirety passed to Emily Walter's five children: in other words, whether the gift by the testator of his Daily Telegraph share was a gift to a class, so that these five children, as the survivors of the class, took the whole.

To have this question decided, an originating summons was taken out by W.G. Kingsbury . . . to have it declared that the bequest of the testator's share in the Daily Telegraph newspaper upon trust, after the death of his wife, for Elizabeth Jane Fowler and the child or children of Emily Walter who should attain twenty-one equally, was not a gift to a class, but that the share bequeathed to Elizabeth Jane Fowler had lapsed by her death in the testator's lifetime and thus fell into the residue of the estate.

The summons was heard on December 14, 1898, by North J., who, after saying the cases upon the point were so irreconcilable that he

---

ally on Moss's capital investment. Walter Moss, the testator in the principal case, was the son of George Moss.

The Daily Telegraph remains today a leading London newspaper. See Edward F. Burnham, Peterborough Court: The Story of the Daily Telegraph 1-3 (1955). — Eds.

should act independently of them, held that, as he could find nothing in the will to show that Elizabeth Jane Fowler was included in the class, the share given to her lapsed by reason of her death in the testator's lifetime, and so passed to the plaintiffs.

The defendants, the five children of Emily Walter, appealed.

LINDLEY, M.R.   It is very difficult to construe this will by the light of the authorities. I entirely agree with North J. that the authorities do not help one much, because they are in inextricable confusion. I do not think there is any case which can be cited by either side which cannot be matched by a case on the other side more or less difficult to distinguish from it. The practical question which we have to decide on this will is, Who are the persons now entitled to the share of the testator in the Daily Telegraph newspaper? There are several rival views. One view is, and that is the one adopted by the learned judge below, that the share which Elizabeth Jane Fowler would have taken if she were alive — that is, one-sixth, as I understand it — has lapsed and has fallen into the residuary estate, so that, according to that view, one-sixth of that share has gone to persons who were certainly never intended to take it. That is obvious. That may be the legal result of the gift, but it is obvious it was never dreamt of by the testator. What he intended was that his share should go amongst the persons he has named and to no one else.

Now the difficulty lies in this. We hear about classes, and gifts to classes, and definitions of classes. You may define a class in a thousand ways: anybody may make any number of things or persons a class by setting out an attribute more or less common to them all and making that the definition of the class. . . . Now what is to be done with the share of this lady who has died? The testator says it is to be equally divided between her and the children of Emily Walter, to be equally divided between them all. If some of them are dead, are the shares of those who are dead to go to those who survive, or are they to go to someone else? That is the practical question; and whether you call the persons a class or "in effect" a class — as Mr. Theobald does in a passage of his work on wills, where he says (4th ed. p.645), "it is clear that a gift to *A*, and the children of *B*, may in effect be a gift to a class, if the testator treats the legatees as a class" — or whether you call them a number of persons who are to be treated as a class, is quite immaterial. The guiding question here is, What is to be done with this Daily Telegraph share which is to be divided amongst these legatees? It seems to me that it is to go to such of them as shall be living. That is the obvious intention. The alternative view takes the share away where it was never intended to go, and upon that ground it appears to me that we ought to differ from the learned judge. I confess, and I say so frankly, that if this case had come before me in the first instance I should have decided it as North J. did, but my brother Romer has convinced me that is not right. . . .

ROMER, L.J. In the absence of any context negativing this view, I think that, when a testator gives property *X* to *A* and a class of persons — say the children of *B* — in equal shares, he intends that the whole of *X* shall pass by his gift if any one of the children of *B* survive him, even although *A* does not. Clearly, if *A* survived and none of the children of *B* survived so as to share, then *A* would take the whole, for *A* would either have to take the whole or nothing, unless indeed it could be said that you are to look at the number of children of *B* living at the date of the will and say there is an intestacy as to the share of each child dying between the date of the will and the testator's death; but that to my mind is clearly an untenable proposition. If then the testator intended that *A* should take the whole if none of the children of *B* survived him to share, I think also he intended the children of *B* to take the whole if *A* did not survive so as to share. There is no satisfactory distinction, to my mind, between those two cases. I think that, in such a gift as I have mentioned, what the testator really means is that the property is to be shared equally by a body constituted of such of the following as should be existing at the date of the testator's death, that is to say, *A* and the children of *B*. . . . In my opinion it is correct to say that a gift by will to a class properly so called and a named individual such as *A* equally, so that the testator contemplates *A* taking the same share that each member of the class will take, is prima facie a gift to a class.[22]

For those reasons, applying those principles to the case before us, I have no hesitation in saying that, in my opinion, the gift here was a gift to a class, and that Elizabeth Jane Fowler was only intended to share as one of a class; and that inasmuch as she did not survive so as to share, the rest of the class takes the whole of the property.

5 AMERICAN LAW OF PROPERTY §22.13 (1952): "The prevailing view seems to be that a gift 'to *A* and the children of *B*' is a gift to an individual and a class in the absence of additional factors. Thus, if *A* dies before the testator, his share lapses and does not pass to the children of *B*. Likewise, if all the children of *B* die, their share lapses. Also the

---

22. Lord Romer was a professor of mathematics before he took up the study of law, and it shows in his argument. A crucial premise of his theory is that the testator intended E. J. Fowler to take a one-sixth share (or a share equal to that of the other nephews and nieces). His theory wouldn't work if E. J. Fowler was intended to take one-half and the children of Emily the other one-half. Some courts, particularly courts following the English classic per stirpes construction calling for distribution down family lines, would construe the bequest to be one-half to E. J. Fowler and one-half to the children of Emily. Even under this latter construction, however, shouldn't this bequest of Daily Telegraph stock be held to be a class gift? — Eds.

revocation of the share of *A* or of the share given the children of *B* should result in a lapse as to the revoked share.

"Such a view appears to be sound. The inferences deducible from a gift to an entity are such that the finding of a gift to an entity should be made only when the beneficiaries are drawn together, either by language or by circumstances, so that the identity of the individuals is submerged. The language of the cases under discussion does not justify the assumption that *A* is to lose his identity in a group composed of himself and the children of another. Thus, the construction preference should be, as it is, for a gift to an individual and a class."

Compare Restatement of Property §284 (1940), which states that the presumption is that the named individual and the group form one class. The authorities are, as Lord Lindley said in In re Moss, "in inextricable confusion."

Application of Antilapse Statutes to Class Gifts. Almost all states apply their antilapse statutes to class gifts. Many statutes expressly so provide. See UPC §2-605 (1969), supra page 441; Tex. Prob. Code §68(a) (1997), supra page 442, footnote 18. In states where the statute is unclear, courts reason that the antilapse statutes are designed to carry out the average testator's intent and that the average testator would prefer for the deceased beneficiary's share to go to the beneficiary's descendants rather than to the surviving members of the class. However, in some states antilapse statutes do not apply to dispositions to class members who die before execution of the will. See, e.g., Tex. Prob. Code §68(a) (1997), supra page 442, footnote 18. In these states it is assumed that the testator did not have the dead class member in mind and did not want him to take. Thus:

> *Case 5. T*, a widow, dies leaving a will devising Blackacre "to my sisters," and devising her residuary estate to her stepson, *S*. When *T* executed the will, *T* had two sisters living, *A* and *B*. One sister, *C*, died before the will was executed, leaving children who survived *T*. *A* died during *T*'s lifetime leaving two children. *T* is survived by *B*, *A*'s children, *C*'s children, and *S*. Who takes Blackacre? Assuming the antilapse statute applies to devises to sisters, in most states *B* takes a one-third share, *A*'s children a one-third share, and *C*'s children a one-third share. In a minority of states *C*'s children do not share, because *C* was dead when the will was executed, and Blackacre goes one-half to *B* and one-half to *A*'s children. If the antilapse statute did not apply to class gifts, *B*, as the sole surviving member of the class, would take Blackacre.

SECTION C.   CHANGES IN PROPERTY AFTER EXECUTION OF WILL: SPECIFIC AND GENERAL DEVISES COMPARED

Specific devises of real and personal property are subject to the doctrine of *ademption by extinction.* Suppose that the testator's will devises Blackacre to her son, John, and the residuary estate to her daughter, Mary. Some years later, the testator sells Blackacre and uses the sale proceeds to purchase Whiteacre, then dies without having changed her will. The gift of Blackacre is adeemed (from the Latin *adimere:* to take away). Since Blackacre is not owned by the testator at her death, the devise fails. John has no claim to Whiteacre, for the will does not devise Whiteacre to him.

Ademption applies only to *specific* devises. Generally speaking, a specific devise is a disposition of a specific item of the testator's property. Gifts of Blackacre or of "my three-carat diamond ring given to me by my Aunt Jane" are examples. Ademption does not apply to *general* or *demonstrative* devises. A devise is general when the testator intends to confer a general benefit and not give a particular asset — for example, a legacy of $10,000 to *A.* If there is not $10,000 in cash in the testator's estate at death, the legacy is not adeemed; other assets must be sold to satisfy *A*'s general legacy. A demonstrative legacy is a hybrid: A general legacy payable from a specific source. Suppose that the testator's will gives *B* "the sum of $10,000 to be paid from the proceeds of sale of my General Motors stock." Most courts would hold this to be a demonstrative legacy. If the testator owns sufficient General Motors stock at death, in raising the $10,000 the executor must comply with the testamentary direction to sell the stock. But if the testator does not own any GM stock at death, the legacy is not adeemed. Other assets must be sold in order to raise the $10,000.

Wasserman v. Cohen
Supreme Judicial Court of Massachusetts, 1993
414 Mass. 172, 606 N.E.2d 901

LYNCH, J.   This appeal raises the question whether the doctrine of ademption by extinction applies to a specific gift of real estate contained in a revocable inter vivos trust. The plaintiff, Elaine Wasserman, brought an action for declaratory judgment in the Middlesex Division of the Probate and Family Court against the defendant, David E. Cohen (trustee), as he is the surviving trustee of a trust established by Frieda M. Drapkin (Drapkin). In her complaint the plaintiff requested that the trustee be ordered to pay her the proceeds of the sale of an apartment building which, under the trust, would have been conveyed to the plaintiff had it not been sold by Drapkin prior to her death. Pursuant to the trustee's motion to dismiss under Mass. R. Civ. P. 12(b)(6), 365 Mass. 754 (1974), the probate judge dismissed the action. The plaintiff appealed. We granted the plaintiff's application for direct appellate review and now affirm.

1. We summarize the relevant facts. Frieda Drapkin created the Joseph and Frieda Drapkin Memorial Trust (trust) in December, 1982, naming herself both settlor and trustee. She funded the trust with "certain property" delivered on the date of execution, and retained the right to add property by inter vivos transfer and by will. Drapkin also reserved the right to receive and to direct the payment of income or principal during her lifetime, to amend or to revoke the trust, and to withdraw property from the trust. On her death, the trustee was directed to distribute the property as set out in the trust. The trustee was ordered to convey to the plaintiff "12-14 Newton Street, Waltham, Massachusetts, Apartment Building, (consisting of approximately 11,296 square feet)."

When she executed the trust, Drapkin held record title to the property at 12-14 Newton Street in Waltham, as trustee of Z.P.Q. Realty Trust. However, she sold the property on September 29, 1988, for $575,000, and had never conveyed her interest in the property to the trust.[23]

Drapkin died on March 28, 1989. Her will, dated December 26, 1982, devised all property in her residuary estate to the trust to be disposed of in accordance with the trust's provisions.

2. The plaintiff first contends that the probate judge erred in failing to consider Drapkin's intent in regard to the gift when she sold the property. We disagree.

We have long adhered to the rule that, when a testator disposes, during his lifetime, of the subject of a specific legacy or devise in his will, that legacy or devise is held to be adeemed, "whatever may have been the intent or motive of the testator in doing so." Walsh v. Gillespie, 338 Mass. 278, 280, 154 N.E.2d 906 (1959), quoting Richards v. Humphreys, 15 Pick. 133, 135 (1833). Baybank Harvard Trust Co. v. Grant, 23 Mass. App. Ct. 653, 655, 504 N.E.2d 1072 (1987). The focus is on the actual existence or nonexistence of the bequeathed property, and not on the intent of the testator with respect to it. Bostwick v. Hurstel, 364 Mass. 282, 295, 304 N.E.2d 186 (1973). To be effective, a specific legacy or devise must be in existence

---

23. Drapkin amended the trust by instruments dated December 16, 1982, and February 8, 1989. The amendments did not reference the gift to the plaintiff.

and owned by the testator at the time of his death. Moffatt v. Heon, 242 Mass. 201, 203-204, 136 N.E. 123 (1922). Baybank Harvard Trust Co. v. Grant, supra.

The plaintiff asks us to abandon the doctrine of ademption. She contends that, because the doctrine ignores the testator's intent, it produces harsh and inequitable results and thus fosters litigation that the rule was intended to preclude. See Note, Ademption and the Testator's Intent, 74 Harv. L. Rev. 741 (1961). This rule has been followed in this Commonwealth for nearly 160 years. See Richards v. Humphreys, supra. Whatever else may be said about it, it is easily understood and applied by draftsmen, testators, and fiduciaries. The doctrine seeks to give effect to a testator's probable intent by presuming he intended to extinguish a specific gift of property when he disposed of that property prior to his death. As with any rule, exceptions have emerged.[24] These limited exceptions do not lead us to the abandonment of the rule. Its so-called harsh results can be easily avoided by careful draftsmanship and its existence must be recognized by any competent practitioner. When we consider the myriad of instruments drafted in reliance on its application, we conclude that stability in the field of trusts and estates requires that we continue the doctrine.

3. The plaintiff also argues that deciding ademption questions based on a determination that a devise is general or specific is overly formalistic and fails to serve the testator's likely intent. She maintains that the court in Bostwick v. Hurstel, supra, moved away from making such classifications. In *Bostwick*, the court held that a gift of stock was not adeemed where the stock had been sold and repurchased prior to the death of the testatrix, and where it had been subject to two stock splits. However, the court confined the holding specifically to its facts.[25] See Bostwick v. Hurstel, supra at 294-295, 304 N.E.2d 186. In addition, the court stated: "Our holding does not indicate that we

24. This court has created two exceptions to the "identity" theory. In Walsh v. Gillespie, 338 Mass. 278, 154 N.E.2d 906 (1959), a conservator appointed for the testatrix five years after her will was executed sold shares of stock that were the subject of a specific legacy. The court held that the sale did not operate as an ademption as to the unexpended balance remaining in the hands of the conservator at the death of the testatrix. Id. at 284, 154 N.E.2d 906. In Bostwick v. Hurstel, 364 Mass. 282, 304 N.E.2d 186 (1973), a conservator had sold, then repurchased, stock that was the subject of a specific legacy and that had been split twice, before the death of the testatrix. The court held that the bequest of stock was not adeemed but emphasized, "we do not violate our rule that 'identity' and not 'intent' governs ademption cases." Id. at 296, 304 N.E.2d 186. See Baybank Harvard Trust Co. v. Grant, 23 Mass. App. Ct. 653, 655, 504 N.E.2d 1072 (1987).

25. "This conclusion is not based upon our present rejection of the general versus specific legacy distinction for resolving questions concerning stock splits; rather, we think that the concept of ademption in and of itself need not and should not be interpreted to include within its scope the circumstances present in this case." Bostwick v. Hurstel, supra 364 Mass. at 294-295, 304 N.E.2d 186.

have abandoned the classification of bequests as general or specific
for all purposes. We have no occasion at this time to express any
opinion on the continuing validity of such distinctions in those cases
where abatement or ademption of the legacy is at issue. . . ." Id. at
292, 304 N.E.2d 186.[26] We now have such an occasion, and we hold
that, at least in regard to the conveyance of real estate at issue here,
the practice of determining whether a devise is general or specific is
the proper first step in deciding questions of ademption.

4. We have held that a trust, particularly when executed as part of
a comprehensive estate plan, should be construed according to the
same rules traditionally applied to wills. See Second Bank-State St.
Trust Co. v. Pinion, 341 Mass. 366, 371, 170 N.E.2d 350 (1960) (doctrine of independent legal significance applied to pour-over trusts);
Clymer v. Mayo, 393 Mass. 754, 473 N.E.2d 1084 (1985) (G.L. c. 191,
§9, which revokes dispositions made in will to former spouses on
divorce or annulment, applied to trust executed along with will as
part of comprehensive estate plan). In Clymer v. Mayo, supra at 766,
473 N.E.2d 1084, we reasoned that "[t]reating the components of the
decedent's estate plan separately, and not as parts of an interrelated
whole, brings about inconsistent results." We also quoted one commentator who wrote, "The subsidiary rules [of wills] are the product
of centuries of legal experience in attempting to discern transferors'
wishes and suppress litigation. These rules should be treated as presumptively correct for will substitutes as well as for wills." Id. at 768,
473 N.E.2d 1084, quoting Langbein, The Nonprobate Revolution and
the Future of the Law of Succession, 97 Harv. L. Rev. 1108, 1136-1137
(1984). We agree with this reasoning. As discussed above, the doctrine
of ademption has a "long established recognition" in Massachusetts.
See Second Bank-State St. Trust Co. v. Pinion, supra, 341 Mass. at
371, 170 N.E.2d 350. Furthermore, Drapkin created the trust along
with her will as part of a comprehensive estate plan. Under the residuary clause of her will, Drapkin gave the majority of her estate to
the trustee, who was then to dispose of the property on her death
according to the terms of the trust. We see no reason to apply a
different rule because she conveyed the property under the terms of
the trust, rather than her will. Thus, we conclude that the doctrine
of ademption, as traditionally applied to wills, should also apply to
the trust in the instant case.

5. Conclusion. Since the plaintiff does not contest that the devise

---

26. We recognize that some courts criticize the process of first classifying legacies
before determining whether they are adeemed. See Note, Ademption and the Testator's
Intent, 74 Harv. L. Rev. 741, 743-745 (1961). See also Baybank Harvard Trust Co. v.
Grant, supra 23 Mass. App. Ct. at 655 n.4, 504 N.E.2d 1072.

of 12-14 Newton Street was a specific devise,[27] it follows that the devise was adeemed by the act of Drapkin.

So ordered.

NOTES AND PROBLEM

1.   In jurisdictions following the identity theory, courts have developed several escape routes to avoid ademption.

(a) *Classify the devise as general or demonstrative rather than specific.* If *T* bequeaths "100 shares of Tigertail Corporation" to *A*, and *T* owns no shares of Tigertail at death, the court will probably declare this to be a general devise if Tigertail Corporation has widely held stock traded on a major exchange. *A* is entitled to the value of 100 shares of Tigertail at *T*'s death. On the other hand, if testator had said "*my* 100 shares of Tigertail," the court will almost surely hold it a specific devise and adeemed to the extent the shares are missing at death. A gift that looks specific might also be declared to be demonstrative and not adeemed. Thus a bequest "of $10,000, more or less, entered on my bank book" has been held demonstrative. Kenaday v. Sinnott, 179 U.S. 606 (1900).

(b) *Classify the inter vivos disposition as a change in form, not substance.* Suppose that after *T* executes her will giving "my 100 shares of Tigertail Corporation" to *A*, Tigertail Corporation merges into Lion Corporation, which issues 85 shares of Lion stock for every 100 shares of Tigertail. Does *A* take the 85 shares of Lion stock? Most courts hold that corporate merger or reorganization is only a change in form, not substance, and *A* takes the Lion stock. Uniform Probate Code §2-605(a)(2) (1990) agrees.

(c) *Construe the meaning of the will as of the time of death rather than as of the time of execution.* By this technique a bequest of "my Lincoln automobile" passed a 1989 Lincoln owned by testator at her death, though at the time the will was executed testator owned a 1984 Lincoln. McIntyre v. Kilbourn, 885 S.W.2d 54 (Mo. App. 1994). But see Estate of Morris, 11 Misc. 2d 457, 169 N.Y.S.2d 881 (Sur. Ct. 1957), where the bequest failed when testator sold a diamond-studded watch referred to in the will and bought another diamond-studded watch worth approximately five times as much.

(d) *Create exceptions.* If the conservator of an incompetent or in-

---

27. "A specific legacy is one which separates and distinguishes the property bequeathed from the other property of the testator, so that it can be identified. It can only be satisfied by the thing bequeathed; if that has no existence, when the bequest would otherwise become operative, the legacy has no effect." Moffatt v. Heon, 242 Mass. 201, 203, 136 N.E. 123 (1922), quoting Tomlinson v. Bury, 145 Mass. 346, 347, 14 N.E. 137 (1887).

sane person transfers the item, most cases have held the legacy not adeemed on the theory that ademption requires a voluntary act of the testator. See Wasserman v. Cohen, supra, footnote 24; Annot., 84 A.L.R.4th 462 (1987). See also the exceptions provided in the Uniform Probate Code, infra Note 4.

2. *T* bequeaths "my bank account in First National Bank" to *A*. After executing her will, *T* closes the account at First National and purchases certificates of deposit to obtain a higher rate of interest. At *T*'s death is *A* entitled to the certificate of deposit? Is the change only a change in form? See Mayberry v. Mayberry, 318 Ark. 588, 886 S.W.2d 627 (1994) (adeemed); Church v. Morgan, 115 Ohio App. 3d 477, 685 N.E.2d 809 (1996) (adeemed).

3. *Stock splits.* Suppose that *T* executes a will devising 100 shares of stock of Tigertail Corporation to *A*. Subsequently Tigertail Corporation splits its stock three-for-one. At *T*'s death, *T* owns 300 shares of Tigertail stock. Does *A* take 100 shares or 300 shares? The old-fashioned approach was to ask whether the bequest was specific or general. If the court found *T* intended to separate out and bequeath particular shares in *T*'s possession, the bequest was termed specific and *A* received the specified shares (100) as well as any accretions in a stock split (200). On the other hand, if the court found *T* did not have in mind particular property of his own but only desired to confer a general benefit, *A* received only 100 shares of stock. See Rosenfeld v. Frank, 208 Conn. 562, 546 A.2d 236 (1988) (holding bequest of 180 shares of stock to be specific). This mechanical approach does not recognize the basic nature of a stock split, which is a change in form, not substance. The shares held after the split represent the same proportional ownership of the corporation as the number of shares held before the split. The market value of the 300 shares of Tigertail after the split should be approximately the same as 100 shares before the split. Therefore, many modern courts have discarded the old approach in the case of stock splits and have held that, absent a contrary showing of intent, a devisee of stock is entitled to additional shares received by the testator as a result of a stock split. See Bostwick v. Hurstel, 364 Mass. 282, 304 N.E.2d 186 (1973); Shriners' Hosp. for Crippled Children v. Coltrane, 465 So. 2d 1073 (Miss. 1985).

Stock dividends are treated differently from stock splits by some courts. They analogize a stock dividend to a cash dividend and conclude that the devisee cannot logically be awarded the former when he is denied the latter. However, this analogy ignores the fact that after a stock dividend, as after a stock split, the testator's percentage of ownership remains the same. See Note, Rights to Stock Accretions Which Occur Prior to Testator's Death, 36 Alb. L. Rev. 182 (1971).

Uniform Probate Code §2-605 (1990) treats stock splits and stock dividends alike.

4.   The 1969 Uniform Probate Code followed the traditional identity theory used in solving ademption problems, but it provided for five exceptions often followed by courts when the specific property is not in the testator's estate. These include giving the specific devisee (1) any remaining balance on the purchase price of the specific property sold, (2) any unpaid amount of condemnation award for the property, (3) any unpaid fire or casualty insurance proceeds after the property has been destroyed, (4) any property owned by the testator as a result of foreclosing a mortgage devised to the specific devisee, and (5) the sale price of specifically devised property sold by a conservator. UPC §2-608(a) & (b) (1969, as amended 1987).

The 1990 UPC abandoned the identity theory and adopted the intent theory, creating what the official comment calls a "mild presumption" against ademption. The party claiming ademption has occurred has the burden of proof. UPC §2-606(a)(6) (1990). However, the 1990 Code continues the application of the exceptions provisions in the 1969 Code to circumstances falling within them. UPC §2-606(a)(1)-(4) & (b). The 1990 UPC also added an additional exception for replacement property in §2-606(a)(5).

Uniform Probate Code (1990, as amended 1997)

§2-606.   NONADEMPTION OF SPECIFIC DEVISES; UNPAID PROCEEDS OF SALE, CONDEMNATION, OR INSURANCE; SALE BY CONSERVATOR OR AGENT

(a) A specific devisee has a right to the specifically devised property in the testator's estate at death and:

(1) any balance of the purchase price, together with any security agreement, owing from a purchaser to the testator at death by reason of sale of the property;

(2) any amount of a condemnation award for the taking of the property unpaid at death;

(3) any proceeds unpaid at death on fire or casualty insurance or on other recovery for injury to the property;

(4) property owned by the testator at death and acquired as a result of foreclosure, or obtained in lieu of foreclosure, of the security interest for a specifically devised obligation;

(5) real or tangible personal property owned by the testator at death which the testator acquired as a replacement for specifically devised real or tangible personal property; and

(6) if not covered by paragraphs (1) through (5), a pecuniary

devise equal to the value as of its date of disposition of other specifically devised property disposed of during the testator's lifetime but only to the extent it is established that ademption would be inconsistent with the testator's manifested plan of distribution or that at the time the will was made, the date of disposition or otherwise, the testator did not intend that the devise adeem.

(b) If specifically devised property is sold or mortgaged by a conservator or by an agent acting within the authority of a durable power of attorney for an incapacitated principal,[28] or if a condemnation award, insurance proceeds, or recovery for injury to the property are paid to a conservator or to an agent acting within the authority of a durable power of attorney for an incapacitated principal, the specific devisee has the right to a general pecuniary devise equal to the net sale price, the amount of the unpaid loan, the condemnation award, the insurance proceeds, or the recovery.

(c) The right of a specific devisee under subsection (b) is reduced by any right the devisee has under subsection (a).

PROBLEMS AND NOTE

1.   Under UPC §2-606(a)(5), dealing with replacement property, if *T* executes a will bequeathing "my Ford car" to *A* and later sells the Ford and buys a Rolls-Royce, is *A* entitled to the Rolls? Suppose *T* sold the Ford and bought two cars, a Honda and a Rolls-Royce. What result? Suppose *T* sold the Ford and bought a motorcycle. What result?

If *T* devises Blackacre to *A* and sells it and buys Whiteacre with the proceeds, is *A* entitled to Whiteacre?

2.   Aunt Fanny Fox has a collection of Chinese snuff bottles. Snuff bottles were first made in China around 1650 when the First Manchu emperor, Kangzi, began to inhale snuff (powdered tobacco) brought by European traders. Sniffing snuff quickly became popular, and thousands upon thousands of small snuff bottles, each with a tiny spoon, were made to carry around in a pocket. Some snuff bottles were carved from jade, agate, and semi-precious stones; others were made of amber, ivory, and glass, sometimes with a scene painted inside.

---

28. UPC §2-606(b) added to a sale by a conservator, which was covered by the 1969 UPC, a sale by an agent acting under a durable power of attorney. Such sales are exempt from ademption. In In re Estate of Hegel, 76 Ohio St. 3d 476, 668 N.E.2d 474 (1996), the court held that a sale under a durable power of attorney adeemed the devise because the Ohio ademption statute, like the 1969 UPC, excepted only sales by conservators, not sale by agents. The case is criticized in Case Comments in 26 Cap. U.L.R. 201 (1997) and 28 U. Tol. L. Rev. 631 (1997). On ademption by conservator or agent sales, see Annot., 84 A.L.R.4th 462 (1991). — Eds.

Three of Aunt Fanny's snuff bottles. Agate, hair crystal, and glass.

Ordinary Chinese snuff bottles of the eighteenth and nineteenth centuries can be found today for $800 or so, very good ones for perhaps $3,000; exceptional bottles may fetch $50,000 or more. Since each bottle is unique, each is individually priced in accordance with its quality of workmanship, rarity, and particular appeal to collectors' tastes.

Aunt Fanny bought her bottles from the 1950s through the 1970s, one at a time, as she ran across one catching her eye. She kept no records as to costs, and the bottles were not insured.

Aunt Fanny's will bequeaths her snuff bottles to Wendy Brown. At Aunt Fanny's death the snuff bottles are not found in her house. No one knows how many bottles there were. Zoë Preston thinks there were 60 or more; Aunt Fanny displayed only part of her collection at any one time. Wendy recalls seeing "about 20" in Aunt Fanny's display cabinet. Aunt Fanny might have given the bottles away, or sold them, or her nurses may have taken them during her long illness. No one knows for sure. No photographs of her bottles exist except of the three shown above.

What are Wendy's rights under the common law identity theory? Under UPC §2-606(a)(6)?

3. UPC §2-606(a)(6) has been criticized for abandoning the identity theory, on the grounds that the intent theory will increase litigation and that the UPC changes the meaning of a bequest of "my diamond ring" to "my diamond ring or its equivalent value," muddying up clear language and inserting a devise the testator did not make. See Mark L. Ascher, The 1990 Uniform Probate Code: Older and Better or More Like the Internal Revenue Code?, 77 Minn. L.

467

Rev. 639 (1993). For contrary arguments, approving UPC §2-606(a)(6), see Gregory S. Alexander, Ademption and the Domain of Formality in Wills Law, 55 Alb. L. Rev. 1067 (1992); Mary L. Fellows, Traveling the Road of Probate Reform: Finding the Way to Your Will (A Response to Professor Ascher), 77 Minn. L. Rev. 659 (1993). See also Mary K. Lundwall, The Case Against the Ademption by Extinction Rule: A Proposal for Reform, 29 Gonz. L. Rev. 105 (1994).

UPC §2-606(a)(6), adopting the intent theory, has been enacted only in Colorado, Michigan, Montana, and Utah.

NOTE: MORE ON SPECIFIC AND GENERAL DEVISES

1. *Abatement.* The problem of abatement, like the problem of ademption, often turns on the classification of a devise as general or specific. The problem of abatement arises when the estate has insufficient assets to pay debts as well as all the devises; some devises must be abated or reduced. In the absence of any indication in the will as to how devises should abate or be reduced, devises ordinarily abate in the following order: (1) residuary devises are reduced first, (2) general devises are reduced second, and (3) specific and demonstrative devises are the last to abate and are reduced pro rata. This plan is believed to follow the testator's intent that specific devises be given effect before general devises, and both be given effect before a residuary devise. But the residuary devisee is often the most important devisee of the testator.

2. *Exoneration of liens.* When a will makes a specific devise of land, on which there is a mortgage, the question may arise whether the land devised passes free and clear of the mortgage. Suppose that *T*'s will devises Blackacre to her daughter *A*. At *T*'s death, Blackacre is subject to a mortgage that secures a note on which *T* was personally liable. Does *A* take Blackacre subject to the mortgage, or is she entitled to have the note paid out of residuary assets so that the title will pass to *A* free of the lien? In some states, *A* takes Blackacre free of the mortgage. These jurisdictions apply the common law doctrine of "exoneration of liens." Under this doctrine, when a will makes a specific disposition of real or personal property that is subject to a mortgage to secure a note on which the testator is personally liable, it is presumed, absent contrary language in the will, that the testator wanted the debt, like other debts, paid out of the residuary estate. See Robert Whitman, Exoneration Clauses in Wills and Trust Instruments, 4 Hofstra Prop. L.J. 123 (1992).

Dissatisfaction with the exoneration doctrine has led to the enactment, in a number of states, of statutes reversing the common law rule. Uniform Probate Code §2-607 (1990) provides: "A specific devise passes subject to any mortgage interest existing at the date of death, without right of exoneration, regardless of a general directive in the will to pay debts.''

3. *Satisfaction of general pecuniary bequests.* The doctrine of *satisfaction* (sometimes known as ademption by satisfaction) applies when the testator makes a transfer to a devisee after executing the will. If the testator is a parent of the beneficiary (or stands in loco parentis) and after execution of the will transfers to the beneficiary property of a similar nature to that given by the will, there is a rebuttable presumption that the gift is in satisfaction of the gift made by the will. Suppose that *T*'s will bequeaths $50,000 to her son, *S*, and her residuary estate to her daughter, *D*. After executing the will, *T* gives *S* $30,000. There is a presumption that the gift was in partial satisfaction of the legacy, so that *S* will take only $20,000 at *T*'s death.

This doctrine, which bears kinship to the doctrine of advancements under intestacy law (see supra page 128), applies to general pecuniary bequests, but not to specific bequests. When specific property is given to the beneficiary during the testator's life there is ademption by extinction, not satisfaction. Satisfaction may also apply to residuary gifts and to demonstrative gifts, but the cases are not uniform in their holdings. In all states satisfaction depends upon the intention of the testator.

Because the intent of the testator is frequently difficult to ascertain, some states have enacted statutes requiring that the intention of a testator to adeem by satisfaction must be shown in writing. Uniform Probate Code §2-609 (1990) so provides, paralleling its rule on advancements (§2-109, supra page 130). Under such a statute, of course, there is no presumption of satisfaction by a gift to a child.

7

RESTRICTIONS ON THE POWER OF DISPOSITION: PROTECTION OF THE SPOUSE AND CHILDREN

SECTION A. RIGHTS OF THE SURVIVING SPOUSE

1. *Introduction to Marital Property Systems*

In the United States, two basic marital property systems exist — the system of separate property, originating in the common law of England, and the system of community property, originating on the continent of Europe and brought to this country by French and Spanish settlers. The fundamental difference between these systems is that under the common law system husband and wife own separately all property each acquires (except those items one spouse has agreed to put into joint ownership with the other), whereas under community property husband and wife own all acquisitions from earnings after marriage in equal undivided shares. There are, to be sure, many variations among the states adhering to one or another of these systems, and community property ideas have made noticeable inroads into the separate property system within the last fifty years. Nonetheless, separate property and community property are quite different ways of thinking about marital property ownership. The former stresses the individual's autonomy over his or her earnings, the latter sharing of earnings between husband and wife.

Community property developed throughout the continent of Europe, allegedly spread by Germanic tribes after the fall of Rome. From these western countries it was taken by European settlers to Central and South America, Mexico, and states along the southern and western borders of the United States. It is odd, then, that in England — separated from the continent by only a 21-mile-wide channel of water — a separate property system, based on the husband's autonomy and effacement of the wife, grew. Why the English resisted so powerful an idea as the sharing principle of community property has intrigued scholars for generations. The most plausible explanations connect the separate property system with the highly centralized English feudal system, dominated by a powerful king, which required succession of power (land) from father to son and fealty between a (male) lord and a (male) tenant. Women were supported by their husbands, but they were denied an ownership share of, or power over, their husbands' acquests. Whatever the reason for its existence, the English separate property system became well entrenched by the fourteenth century and was taken by the English settlers to the eastern seaboard of the United States, whence it spread westward.

Under the separate property system, whatever the worker earns is his — or hers. There is no sharing of earnings. If one spouse is the wage earner while the other spouse works in the home, the wage-earning spouse will own all the property acquired during marriage (other than gifts or inheritances from relatives or gifts by the wage earner to the homemaker). A crucial issue under a separate property system is: What protection against disinheritance should be given the surviving spouse who works in the home or works at a lower-paying job? Almost all of the separate property states answer this question by giving the surviving spouse, by statute, an elective (or forced) share in the estate of the deceased spouse. The elective share is not limited to a share of property acquired with earnings, however. It is enforceable against all property owned by the decedent spouse at death.

In eight states (Arizona, California, Idaho, Louisiana, Nevada, New Mexico, Texas, and Washington) a community property system has long existed. The fundamental principle of community property is that all earnings of the spouses and property acquired from earnings are community property. Each spouse is the owner of an undivided one-half interest in the community property. The death of one spouse dissolves the community. The deceased spouse owns and has testamentary power only over his or her one-half community share.

The difference between the principles underlying the separate property and the community property systems can be seen by a simple illustration.

> *Case 1. H* works outside the home, earning $50,000 a year. *W* works in the home, earning nothing. At the end of 20 years, *H* has through savings of his salary bought a house in his name, a life insurance policy payable to his daughter, and $100,000 worth of stocks in his name. Under a separate property regime, during life *W* owns none of that property. At *H*'s death,

W has an elective share (usually one-third) of the house and the stocks but usually not the insurance policy because it is not in *H*'s probate estate. In a community property state, *W* owns half of *H*'s earnings during life, and thus at *H*'s death *W* owns one-half of the acquisitions from earnings (the house, the insurance proceeds, and the stocks). If *W* dies first, *W* can dispose of her half of the community property by will. In a separate property state, if *W* dies first, she has no property to dispose of.

Community property is based on the idea that husband and wife are a marital partnership, that they decide together how to use the time of each so as to maximize their income, and that they should share their earnings equally. Property acquired before marriage and property acquired during marriage by gift, devise, or descent is the acquiring spouse's separate property.

In the late twentieth century, community property came to be favored by many academics and some legislators. In 1983, the National Conference of Commissioners on Uniform State Laws promulgated a Uniform Marital Property Act. The act adopts community property principles, though the phrase "community property" is avoided and "marital property" used instead. Wisconsin adopted the Uniform Marital Property Act in 1984. Wis. Stat. Ann. §§766.001-766.097 (1998). Hence, Wisconsin must now be reckoned a community property state.

In 1998, Alaska enacted a statute permitting married couples to elect to hold their property as community property. Alaska Stat. §§34.75.010-.160 (1998). This seems a good idea, worthy of consideration in all separate property states. It gives couples choices of marital property systems. It provides a test of which system married couples prefer, which has never been done. In community property states, couples can elect to hold their property separately, but this rarely happens in first marriages.

In examining the surviving spouse's rights, we turn first to rights of the surviving spouse to *support,* which (except for dower) are generally the same in both separate property and community property states. We next turn to the central topic — the right of the surviving spouse to a *share* in the decedent spouse's property or in the marital property. We examine this matter first in the separate property states, then in the community property states. For an examination of the topics covered in this chapter, see Ralph C. Brashier, Disinheritance and the Modern Family, 45 Case West. Res. L. Rev. 83 (1994).

2. Rights of Surviving Spouse to Support

a. Social Security

In the 1930s, Congress established the social security system, under which retirement benefits are paid to a worker and his or her surviv-

"Now read me the part again where I disinherit everybody."
Drawing by Peter Arno
Copyright © 1940, 1968, 1996 by The New Yorker Magazine, Inc.
Reproduced by permission.

474

ing spouse. The social security system thus incorporates the principle of community property that the benefits of earnings should be shared by husband and wife. The worker has no right to shift the survivor's benefit to a person other than the spouse (though benefits may be paid to a deceased retired worker's dependents as well as to the worker's spouse).

Social security benefits are computed by a formula that takes into account the amount of quarters worked (it takes 40 quarters — ten years — to be fully insured), the amount of earnings taxed, and the age of retirement. A large majority of all persons aged 65 or older receive social security benefits. In 1998, the average monthly benefit for surviving spouses was $736. 61 Social Security Bulletin No. 3 (1998), Table 1, B3.

b. Private Pension Plans

Private pension plans funded by employers or jointly funded by employer and employee contributions mushroomed in the twentieth century. Trillions of dollars are now held in private pension funds. Most of these plans are governed by the federal Employee Retirement Income Security Act of 1974 (ERISA), 29 U.S.C. §§1001 et seq. (1998). ERISA, as amended by the Retirement Equity Act in 1984, requires that the spouse of an employee must have survivorship rights if the employee predeceases the spouse. Its purpose is to insure a stream of income to surviving spouses. If the employee spouse survives to retirement age, the pension paid must be paid as a joint and survivor annuity to the employee and his or her spouse, unless the nonemployee spouse consents to some other form of payment of the retirement benefit. If the employee dies before retirement and the pension is vested, the surviving spouse must be entitled to a preretirement survivor annuity. ERISA will substantially increase the amount of income payable to workers' surviving spouses. For a summary of spousal rights in pensions, see John H. Langbein & Bruce A. Wolk, Pension and Employee Benefit Law 545-609 (2d ed. 1995).

ERISA preempts state law relating to the spouse's rights in pension plans. In Boggs v. Boggs, 520 U.S. 833 (1997), a first wife had a community property share in her husband's pension, which, under community property law, she could devise to whom she pleased. She devised this to her husband for life, then to her three sons. The husband married again after his first wife's death. Upon his death, the Supreme Court held that his pension benefits must be used to support his second wife in order to carry out ERISA's object of insuring support for surviving spouses. ERISA preempted state community property law to the extent state law allowed the first wife to make a testamentary transfer of her interest in her husband's pension and make it unavailable to a second wife.

Waiver. A spouse may waive her rights to benefits under the employee's pension plan, but ERISA discourages waivers by strict rules regarding their validity. Premarital agreements cannot waive ERISA-covered pension rights. See Hurwitz v. Sher, 982 F.2d 778 (2d Cir. 1992), cert. denied, 508 U.S. 912 (1993).

PROBLEM

W designates *H* as the death beneficiary of her employer's pension plan. Subsequently *W* divorces *H*. Upon *W*'s death before retirement, is *H* entitled to the death benefits? What would be the result if *W* had remarried? What would be the result if *W* had changed the death beneficiary to her sister *S* after the divorce? See Note 2, supra page 300.

c. Homestead

Nearly all states have homestead laws designed to secure the family home to the surviving spouse and minor children, free of the claims of creditors. Such a homestead is frequently called a *probate homestead.* Although the homestead laws vary in many details, generally the surviving spouse has the right to occupy the family home (or maybe the family farm) for his or her lifetime. In some states, the homestead must be established by the decedent during his life, usually by filing a declaration of homestead in some public office; in other states, the probate court has power to set aside real property as a homestead. The amount of the homestead exemption is ridiculously small in some states and provides little protection to the surviving spouse. UPC §2-402 (1990) recommends $15,000. But in several states the homestead exemption is substantial and may even exempt the family home regardless of its value. The decedent has no power to dispose of a homestead so as to deprive the surviving spouse of statutory rights therein. The right to occupy the homestead is given in addition to any other rights the surviving spouse has in the decedent's estate. See Carolyn S. Bratt, Family Protection Under Kentucky's Inheritance Laws: Is the Family Really Protected?, 76 Ky. L.J. 387 (1988) (criticizing homestead, personal property exemptions, and family allowances as being wholly inadequate to protect a decedent's family from hardship).

d. Personal Property Set-Aside

Related to homestead is the right of the surviving spouse (and sometimes of minor children) to have set aside to her certain tangible personal property of the decedent up to a certain value. UPC §2-403 (1990) sets the limit at $10,000. These items, which are also exempt from creditors' claims, usually include household furniture and clothing, but may also include a car and farm animals. The set-aside is usually subject to several conditions and limitations, but, if these are met, the decedent usually has no power to deprive the surviving spouse of the exempt items.

e. Family Allowance

Every state has a statute authorizing the probate court to award a family allowance for maintenance and support of the surviving spouse (and often of dependent children). The allowance may be limited by the statute to a fixed period (typically one year), or it may continue thereafter while the will is being contested or for the entire period of administration. The allowance, as with the homestead and personal property set-aside, is in addition to whatever other interests pass to the surviving spouse.

In some states, the maximum allowance that can be awarded is fixed by statute. In other states, a reasonable allowance tied to the spouse's standard of living is permitted. UPC §2-404 (1990) allows a reasonable allowance, which cannot continue beyond one year if the estate is inadequate to pay creditors. Maintenance of the decedent's spouse and dependent children is not allowed after the estate is closed.

Can the statutory allowances to a surviving spouse and children be paid out of a revocable trust if probate assets are insufficient to satisfy those claims? See Uniform Trust Act §305(a)(3) (1999 draft), saying yes.

English system. In England, expanding on the feudal idea that wives were to be supported but not to share ownership, the law provides that the decedent's property must continue to be used to support those who were dependent upon the decedent during lifetime. Eligible dependents include the decedent's spouse, former spouse who has not remarried, children, and any other person who was being maintained by the decedent. The decedent's spouse is entitled to a financial provision "as would be reasonable in all the circumstances for a husband or wife to receive, whether or not that provision is required for his or her maintenance." Inheritance (Provision for Family and Dependents) Act 1975, §2(a). Other eligible dependents are entitled to receive such financial provision "as it would be reasonable in all the circumstances of the case for the applicant to receive for his maintenance." Id. §2(b). Australia, New Zealand, and several of the Canadian provinces have similar legislation. In England and other Commonwealth jurisdictions surviving spouses do not have a right to an elective share of their spouse's property, only a right to support for life. For a thorough examination of the English system, comparing it with the Uniform Probate Code elective share and concluding that the UPC needs more flexibility in dealing with the needy surviving spouse, see Helene S. Shapo, "A Tale of Two Systems": Anglo-American Problems in the Modernization of Inheritance Legislation, 60 Tenn. L. Rev. 707 (1993). See also Ralph C. Brashier, Disinheritance and the Modern Family, 45 Case West. Res. L. Rev. 84, 121-133 (1994).

Although an occasional commentator has suggested that the English family maintenance system should be adopted here, the weight of opinion in this country opposes it because of the vast discretion such a system gives to the probate judge. The uncertainty would make estate planning much more difficult. See Mary A. Glendon, Fixed Rules and Discretion in Contemporary Family Law and Succession Law, 60 Tul. L. Rev. 1165 (1986); John H. Langbein & Lawrence W. Waggoner, Redesigning the Spouse's Forced Share, 22 Real Prop., Prob. & Tr. J. 303, 304-314 (1987). A spousal maintenance system also is fundamentally inconsistent with the American idea of giving the surviving spouse (by way of an elective share) an ownership share in the economic gains from a marriage.

f. Dower

At common law, a widow had dower in all *land* of which her deceased husband had been seised during marriage and which was inheritable by the issue of husband and wife. Dower entitles the widow to a life estate in one-third of her husband's qualifying land. Thus:

> *Case 2. H*, married to *W*, buys Blackacre, taking title in himself in fee simple. *H* subsequently dies. *W* is entitled to a life estate in one-third of Blackacre. (If *W* had predeceased *H*, her dower interest would be extinguished.)

In feudal times, when land was the chief form of wealth and provided the power base of the head of the family, dower provided generous support to the widow of a propertied man. But today, when many people rent their homes and by far the greater part of wealth is in the form of intangible personal property (such as stocks and bonds), dower may give the surviving spouse no protection at all.

The right of dower attaches the moment the husband acquires title to land or upon marriage, whichever is later. Dower remains inchoate until the husband's death, when it becomes possessory. Once inchoate dower has attached, the husband cannot sell the land free and clear of the wife's dower interest. In Case 2, if *H*, after buying Blackacre, had conveyed it to *A*, *A* would take title subject to *W*'s dower, and if and when *W* survived *H*, *W* would be entitled to a life estate in one-third of Blackacre (now owned by *A*). No purchaser, bona fide or not, can cut off the wife's dower without her consent. Dower functions today primarily to make the signatures of both spouses a practical requirement to the sale of one spouse's land.

At common law, a husband had a support interest in his wife's lands, called curtesy. It was comparable to dower except (1) the husband did not acquire curtesy unless children were born of the marriage and (2) the husband was given a life estate in the entire parcel, not merely in one-third. Curtesy survives today in one or two states only as a label given to the support interest of the husband, which in fact has been made identical with the wife's common law dower.

Dower has been abolished in the great majority of states. In only five jurisdictions does dower as it was known to the common law exist. Ark. Code Ann. §28-11-301 (1998); D.C. Code §19-102 (1998); Ky. Rev. Stat. §§392.020, 392.080 (1998); Mich. Stat. Ann. §26.221 (1998); Ohio Rev. Code Ann. §2103.02 (1998). In all of these, except Michigan, dower has been extended to the husband as well as the wife. The Michigan statute, providing dower for a wife but not for a husband, is of doubtful constitutionality. Similar statutes were found violative of the Equal Protection Clause in Stokes v. Stokes, 271 Ark. 300, 613 S.W.2d 372 (1981), and Boan v. Watson, 281 S.C. 516, 316 S.E.2d 401 (1984). In Iowa, common law dower has been changed to give the surviving spouse a fractional fee simple interest, rather than a life estate, in the decedent's lands owned during marriage. Iowa Code Ann. §633.212 (1997) (one-half if decedent dies intestate); id. §633.238 (one-third if spouse elects against the will).

In most states retaining dower, the surviving spouse must elect to take dower, or to take a statutory share of the decedent's estate, or to take a share under the decedent's will. As the statutory elective share is almost always greater than dower, dower is rarely elected.

PROBLEMS

1. *H*, married to *W*, buys Blackacre, taking title in "*H* for life, remainder to *H*'s daughter *D*." Subsequently *H* buys Whiteacre, tak-

ing title in "*H* and *D* as joint tenants with right of survivorship." *H* dies. Does *W* have dower in Blackacre or Whiteacre? See Spears v. James, 319 Mich. 341, 29 N.W.2d 829 (1947); Jezo v. Jezo, 23 Wis. 2d 399, 129 N.W.2d 195 (1964). Suppose that *D* had died before *H*. Would *D*'s husband have dower in Blackacre?

2. *W*, a real estate developer, wants to be able to buy land and sell it without the consent or interference of her husband. The jurisdiction has common law dower for husbands and wives. *W* consults you. What do you recommend?

3. Rights of Surviving Spouse to a Share of Decedent's Property

a. The Elective Share and Its Rationale

All but one[1] of the separate property states give the surviving spouse, in addition to any support rights mentioned above, a share in the decedent's property. The proclaimed underlying policy (at least in most states) is that the surviving spouse contributed to the decedent's acquisition of wealth and deserves to have a portion of it. This policy is carried out by statutes giving the surviving spouse an *elective share* (sometimes called a *forced share*) of the decedent's property. These statutes provide the surviving spouse with an election: The spouse can take under the decedent's will or can renounce the will and take a fractional share of the decedent's estate.

Caution. There is no subject in this book on which there is more statutory variation than the surviving spouse's elective share. Even most of the states adopting the 1969 or 1990 Uniform Probate Code provisions, which had the purpose of bringing uniformity, made important substantive changes in the elective share provisions. There

---

1. Georgia is the only separate property state without an elective share statute. Professor Chaffin, a leading authority on Georgia wills law, approves of this on the ground that the vast majority of husbands do support their wives after death and the elective share permits the surviving spouse to wreck a sound estate plan. Verner F. Chaffin, A Reappraisal of the Wealth Transmission Process: The Surviving Spouse, Year's Support and Intestate Succession, 10 Ga. L. Rev. 447, 464-470 (1976). Not all his students are convinced, however. A Note, Preventing Spousal Disinheritance in Georgia, 19 Ga. L. Rev. 427 (1985), argues for equitable distribution of a portion of the decedent's property to the surviving spouse. Observing that the Georgia Supreme Court adopted equitable distribution upon divorce on its own after the Georgia legislature failed to act, the note suggests that the court should atone for a supine legislature by extending equitable distribution to termination of marriage by death.

Other scholars, who assume the purpose of the elective share is spousal support, have questioned the need for an elective share for similar reasons. See Elias Clark, The Recapture of Testamentary Substitutes to Preserve the Spouse's Elective Share: An Appraisal of Recent Statutory Reforms, 2 Conn. L. Rev. 513 (1970); Sheldon J. Plager, The Spouse's Nonbarrable Share: A Solution in Search of a Problem, 33 U. Chi. L. Rev. 681 (1966).

are many reasons for this: different opinions about how much the surviving spouse (read *widow*) deserves under various circumstances, including length of marriage, existence of children, and her own wealth; differences about what property of the decedent should be subject to the elective share; and the inability of legislators to decide definitively what is the purpose of the elective share and to carry this purpose through to its logical ends. (Even the drafters of the Uniform Probate Code, which professes the partnership theory of marriage, sometimes lost their nerve and treated the elective share as a spousal support system.)

In a few states, the elective share is limited to a *life estate* in one-third or one-half of the decedent's estate. See, e.g., Conn. Gen. Stat. §45a-436 (1998); R.I. Gen. Laws §33-25-2 (1998). In South Carolina, the decedent can satisfy the elective share of one-third by transferring one-third of his property in trust in such a way as obtains the federal estate tax marital deduction. S.C. Code Ann. §62-2-207 (1998). Inasmuch as a QTIP trust, giving the surviving spouse only the right to income for life, qualifies for the marital deduction (see infra page 1047), a decedent can satisfy the elective share in South Carolina by creating a trust for his spouse of life income from one-third of his estate. New York once had a similar provision, permitting the decedent to satisfy the elective share by creating a life income trust for the surviving spouse, but in 1992 New York repealed that provision.

Statutes providing that the elective share is satisfied by giving the surviving spouse life income from a trust reflect a view that, when push comes to shove, the law should force the decedent to provide his surviving spouse with lifetime support, but that it goes too far to force him to give her a share of ownership of the fruits of the marriage.

Uniform Probate Code (1990)

ARTICLE II, PART 2
ELECTIVE SHARE OF SURVIVING SPOUSE

GENERAL COMMENT
THE PARTNERSHIP THEORY OF MARRIAGE

The partnership theory of marriage, sometimes also called the marital-sharing theory, is stated in various ways. Sometimes it is thought of "as an expression of the presumed intent of husbands and wives to pool their fortunes on an equal basis, share and share alike." M. Glendon, The Transformation of Family Law 131 (1989). Under this approach, the economic rights of each spouse are seen as deriving from an unspoken marital bargain under which the partners agree that each is to enjoy a half interest in the fruits of the marriage, i.e., in the property nominally acquired by and titled in the sole name of either partner during the marriage (other than in property acquired by gift or inheritance). A decedent who disinherits his or her surviving spouse is seen as having reneged on the bargain. Sometimes the theory is expressed in restitutionary terms, a return-of-contribution notion. Under this approach, the law grants each spouse an entitlement to compensation for non-monetary contributions to the marital enterprise, as "a recognition of the activity of one spouse in the home and to compensate not only for this activity but for opportunities lost." Id.

No matter how the rationale is expressed, it is sometimes thought that the community-property system, including that version of community law promulgated in the Uniform Marital Property Act, recognizes the partnership theory, but that the common-law system denies it. In the ongoing marriage, it is true that the basic principle in the common-law (title-based) states is that marital status does not affect the ownership of property. The regime is one of separate property. Each spouse owns all that he or she earns. By contrast, in the community-property states, each spouse acquires an ownership interest in half the property the other earns during the marriage. By granting each spouse *upon acquisition* an immediate half interest in the earnings of the other, the community-property regimes directly recognize that the couple's enterprise is in essence collaborative.

The common-law states, however, also give effect or purport to give effect to the partnership theory when a marriage is dissolved by divorce. If the marriage ends in divorce, a spouse who sacrificed his or her financial-earning opportunities to contribute so-called domestic services to the marital enterprise (such as child-rearing and homemaking) stands to be recompensed . . . [under] the equitable-distribution system.

The other situation in which spousal property rights figure prominently is disinheritance at death. . . .

Elective-share law in the common-law states, however, has not caught up to the partnership theory of marriage. Under typical American elective-share law, including the elective share provided by the pre-1990 Uniform Probate Code, a surviving spouse may claim a one-third share of the decedent's estate — not the 50 percent share of the couple's combined assets that the partnership theory would imply.

Although the policy underlying the elective share is to reward the spouse's contribution to the economic success of the marriage, in most states the elective share only roughly implements that policy.

The traditional elective share gives the surviving spouse a fixed fractional share of the decedent's estate regardless of the length of marriage. The marriage may have lasted one hour[2] or 50 years; the elective share fraction is the same. The 1990 Uniform Probate Code remedies this defect by giving the surviving spouse a sliding-scale percentage of the elective share amount, based upon the duration of the marriage (3 percent after one year, with 3 percent annual accruals for the next ten years, and 4 percent annual accruals thereafter until 50 percent is reached after 15 years of marriage). UPC §2-202(a) (1990, as amended 1993). The 1990 UPC revisers believe that the accrual system will approximate the results reached in most community property marriages, where the amount of acquisitions from earnings (community property) ordinarily increases with the duration of the marriage. A sliding-scale, or accrual, elective share also deals more equitably with second marriages among the elderly, which are not infrequent nowadays.

In addition, Uniform Probate Code §2-202(b) gives to the surviving spouse a $50,000 supplemental elective-share amount in case the surviving spouse's own assets and other entitlements are below this figure. The theory of the supplemental amount is that the surviving spouse is entitled to some minimum amount for support, regardless of the length of the marriage.[3]

Although the Uniform Probate Code revisers attempted to achieve community-property-like results with the redesigned elective share, there remains a profound difference between community property, which gives a present right to each spouse of a share of the earnings of the couple, and an elective share system, which gives a spouse only a possibility of a share in the other spouse's property. Although we speak of a surviving *spouse's* elective share, in the vast majority of cases it is in actuality a *widow's* share. Men earn more than women and have immensely more property acquired from earnings titled in their name. Women, on average, live seven years longer than men. When legislatures provide an elective share, the prototype situation to which it is applicable is a propertied dead husband and a poorer widow. No

2. Or less. In Estate of Neiderhiser, 2 Pa. D. & C.3d 202, 59 Westmoreland County L.J. 60 (1977), the groom dropped dead during the marriage ceremony, after he and the bride had each said "I will" (equal in other marriage ceremonies to "I do"). The court held that marriage is a contract which becomes binding upon the exchange of vows, and the bride was entitled to an elective share in the groom's estate.

3. The supplemental amount is criticized as too small by Margaret V. Turano, UPC Section 2-201 [renumbered §2-202 in 1993]: Equal Treatment of Spouses?, 55 Alb. L. Rev. 983, 1003-1006 (1992), on the ground that it does not adequately protect a woman who gives up her career to work in the home and whose husband dies within ten years of marriage, when her percentage share of her husband's estate is below 25 percent. See also Charles H. Whitebread, The Uniform Probate Code's Nod to the Partnership Theory of Marriage, 11 Prob. L.J. 125, 138 (1992), criticizing sliding scale for the same reason.

matter how ringing the speeches about treating women equally, or how deep the bowing to the ideal of a marital partnership, the notion persists that a wife's role is that of a dependent.

Under an elective share system, the wife must survive her husband in order to share in the "partnership property." And she must elect to claim a share against her husband's will. In a culture where "husband knows best" has long dominated estate planning (see Note below on the marital deduction), election against the husband's will may be psychologically or socially difficult.

In most states, and under the Uniform Probate Code, the right to an elective share is personal to the surviving spouse. It cannot be exercised after the spouse's death. If a wife survives her husband and dies soon thereafter, before she can elect against her husband's will, her heirs and devisees and creditors will receive none of the so-called partnership property except what the husband has voluntarily left the wife in fee simple. This is consistent with a support rationale for the elective share, but it is hardly consistent with rewarding the wife for her contribution to the economic success of the marriage.

The real test of whether an elective share system implements the partnership theory of marriage, however, comes when the wife predeceases her husband. If the wife dies before her husband, she cannot dispose of any of the "partnership property" titled in her husband's name. Suppose, for example, that *H* owns $500,000 in acquisitions from his earnings and *W* owns $100,000 from her earnings. If *W* dies first, *W* can dispose of only her $100,000 (and *H* may even have an elective share in that). If the couple had community property, *W* would own half of it, or $300,000, and could dispose of her half by will. As you study the elective share system you should look for other features that deny the concept of an equal marital partnership.

For further discussion of the dependency role assigned to women by the elective share, the federal estate tax marital deduction, and estate planning practices, see Mary L. Fellows, Wills and Trusts: "The Kingdom of the Fathers," 10 J.L. & Inequality 137 (1991). See also Mary M. Wenig, The Marital Property Law of Connecticut: Past, Present and Future, 1990 Wis. L. Rev. 807, 877 (criticizing UPC elective share as "a nod in the direction of the contribution rationale for the forced share . . . [while] actually resting their device only on the support or need rationale, tempered by a kind of deservedness based on the length of marriage"); Note, The Revised UPC Elective Share: Missing Essential Partnership Principles, 13 Quinnipiac Prob. L.J. 225 (1998).

NOTE: THE ESTATE TAX MARITAL DEDUCTION AND THE DEPENDENCY OF WOMEN

In the 1940s, with a steep increase in federal income tax rates to finance World War II, the income tax advantages of community property became very clear. The earnings of the husband were taxable one-half to the husband and one-half to the wife (who owned one-half). Because of the graduated step-up in brackets, the total tax on earnings split between husband and wife could be considerably less than the one tax on the husband's earnings in separate property states. Similarly, federal estate taxes in community property states were lower because only the husband's half of the community property was taxable at his death whereas all the husband's earned property was taxable at his death in separate property states.

To reap these federal tax advantages, Michigan, Nebraska, Oklahoma, Oregon, and Pennsylvania adopted community property in the 1940s. Several more states had community property bills in the legislative hoppers. But this revolution in marital property was not to be. In 1948, Congress — a virtually all-male club[4] — intervened. Congress amended the Internal Revenue Code to eliminate the tax advantages of community property. It permitted married couples to split their earned income equally between them by filing a joint return.[5] The five states that had switched to community property repealed or abrogated their statutes. See Carolyn Jones, Split Income and Separate Spheres: Tax Law and Gender Roles in the 1940s, 6 L. & Hist. Rev. 259 (1988).

Our concern here is not the federal income tax, but the federal estate tax, which also offered tax advantages in community property states. In 1948, Congress undertook to eliminate them and equalize the estate tax consequences between couples residing in community property states and couples residing in common law property states. The essential problem was how to put the common law property wife, who had acquired no or little property from her earnings, into an estate tax position comparable with the community property wife, who owns half the acquisitions from her husband's earnings. Congress solved the problem by giving the husband an estate tax marital deduction, up to 50 percent of the value of his estate, for property left to his surviving wife in a form comparable to the outright ownership the community property wife had. The word "comparable" is the rub. To equate the position of the separate property wife exactly with the community property wife, the former must end up with *outright ownership* of one-half her husband's earnings. Yet, for Congress to provide

---

4. In the 80th Congress beginning in January 1948, there were 96 senators (all men) and 435 Representatives (six women).

5. Congress did not eliminate all the income tax advantages of community property, however. Community property still has an income tax advantage in that upon the death of the first spouse to die all of the community property gets a stepped-up basis (eliminating any income tax on past capital gain in the property), even though only one half is included in the decedent spouse's estate tax return. With separate property, only the property included in the decedent spouse's estate receives a stepped-up basis. See infra page 528.

a powerful tax incentive for a husband to devise his widow outright ownership of half of his property was highly objectionable to (mostly male) estate planners and trust companies in New York and other rich separate property states; they thought the husband should have the right to put the widow's share in trust for her without suffering a tax disadvantage. The objection was that a housewife, without business experience, might be incapable of managing her inherited wealth. (Never mind that widows in California, Texas, and other community property states had long been legally entrusted with managing their property after their husbands' deaths, with no noticeable adverse consequences to them.[6]) Congress effected a compromise: If a husband gave his wife a *life estate* (support) with the *power to appoint* the property to anyone she wished at her death (equivalent to complete ownership at her death), this arrangement would be deemed comparable to a fee simple and would qualify for the marital deduction.

In 1982, the federal estate tax marital deduction was changed to incorporate a completely new principle: Interspousal transfers will not be taxed at all, provided the donor spouse gives the donee spouse at least a life estate in the property. A gift of a fee simple or its alleged equivalent (a life estate coupled with a general power of appointment) is no longer required for the marital deduction. The marital deduction is unlimited in amount. Internal Revenue Code of 1986, §2056.

The 1948 version of the marital deduction provided a tax incentive to the donor spouse to give the surviving spouse support and an ownership share of the decedent spouse's property (even though complete control of that share could be postponed until the surviving spouse's death). The current marital deduction requires only that the donor spouse create a trust giving his surviving spouse support for life to avoid transfer taxation (called a QTIP trust). Thus, viewed through the precise eye of the marital deduction provisions only, the housewife (or the spouse with lower earnings) appears further now than before from being treated as well as her counterpart in community property states — as deserving a share of outright ownership in recognition of her contribution to the economic gains of a marriage.

The QTIP trust is fundamentally inconsistent with the partnership theory of marriage. For the rich, who must pay estate taxes, Professor Mary Moers Wenig put it crisply: "With QTIP, the new federal law of dower was born." Mary M. Wenig, "Taxing Marriage," 6 So. Cal. Rev. L. & Women's Stud. 561 (1997). See the debate between Professors Gerzog, Zelenak, and Dodge: Wendy C. Gerzog, The Marital Deduction QTIP Provisions: Illogical and Degrading to Women, 5 UCLA Women's L.J. 301 (1995); Lawrence Zelenak: Taking Critical Tax The-

---

6. But cf. the "widow's election," *infra* page 524.

ory Seriously, 76 N.C. L. Rev. 1521 (1998); Wendy C. Gerzog, The Illogical and Sexist QTIP Provisions: I Just Can't Say It Ain't So, 76 N.C. L. Rev. 1597 (1998); Joseph M. Dodge, A Feminist Perspective on the QTIP Trust and the Unlimited Marital Deduction, 76 N.C. L. Rev. 1729 (1998).

The end result of these changes in the federal estate tax law is that today the following transfers qualify for the marital deduction:

   (a) *H* transfers property outright or in fee simple to *W*;

   (b) *H* creates a trust giving *W* income for life and a power to appoint the trust principal at death to whomever she pleases (a life estate coupled with a general power of appointment);

   (c) *H* creates a trust giving *W* income for life (a QTIP trust). For further discussion of the marital deduction, see infra pages 1042-1049.

NOTE: MUST THE SURVIVING SPOUSE ACCEPT A LIFE ESTATE?

Once the amount of the elective share has been determined, when the surviving spouse elects against the will, she is usually credited (or, in legal language, "charged") with the value of all interests given her by the will. If the amount of the bequests to the surviving spouse does not satisfy the elective share, the difference must be made up either by pro rata contributions from all the other beneficiaries (the majority and UPC rule) or from the residuary estate.

Suppose that the decedent has left the surviving spouse a life estate in a certain amount of property. Must the surviving spouse accept the life estate or its value in partial satisfaction of her elective share? Under the original 1969 Uniform Probate Code and the law of most states, if the surviving spouse renounces the life estate and elects to take her share in fee simple, she is not charged for the value of the life estate. In 1975, the 1969 Uniform Probate Code was amended to provide that a life estate given the spouse by will is charged to the surviving spouse. Under the 1969 UPC, as amended, the surviving spouse who rejects the life estate is charged an amount equal to one half the total value of the property subject to the life estate. Charging the surviving spouse with the value of the life estate was carried over into the 1990 Uniform Probate Code, though the valuation method was left open. The practical effect of so charging the surviving spouse forced the surviving spouse to take the life estate given her by the decedent's will. The object of the UPC revisers was to cause as little distortion in the decedent's estate plan as is possible, but charging the widow with a life estate forces the widow to bend to her husband's will and take only lifetime support rather than a share of outright ownership. Under heavy criticism from commentators, in 1993 the Uniform Probate Code was amended to provide that a life estate renounced by the surviving spouse is not charged against her elective share. UPC §2-209 (1990, amended 1993). See Ira M. Bloom, The Treatment of Trust and Other Partial Interests of the Surviving Spouse Under the Redesigned Elective-Share System: Some Concerns and Suggestions, 55 Alb. L. Rev. 941 (1992); Ronald R. Volkmer, Spousal Rights at Death: Reevaluation of the Common Law Premises in Light of the Proposed Uniform Marital Property Act, 17 Creighton L. Rev. 95, 141-48 (1983).

If the surviving spouse effectively renounces a life estate, what happens to the remainder? Under almost all disclaimer statutes she is treated as having predeceased the testator (see supra page 149), and the remainder will accelerate or not upon that assumption.

In Re Estate of Cross
Supreme Court of Ohio, 1996
75 Ohio St. 3d 530, 664 N.E.2d 905

On August 23, 1992, Carroll R. Cross died testate leaving his entire estate to his son, Ray G. Cross, who was not a child of the surviving spouse. At the time of his death, Beulah Cross, the surviving spouse, was apparently close to eighty years old, was suffering from Alzheimer's disease, and was living in a nursing home paid by Medicaid. Due to Mrs. Cross's incompetency, she was unable to make an election under R.C. 2106.01 as to whether she should take against her husband's will. Therefore, pursuant to R.C. 2106.08, the probate court appointed a commissioner, who investigated the matter and determined that the court elect for Mrs. Cross to take her intestate share under R.C. 2105.06 and against the will. As a result of this election, Mrs. Cross would receive twenty-five thousand dollars in spousal allowance and one-half of the net estate, which was approximately nine thousand dollars. Following a hearing before a referee, Judge John E. Corrigan of the probate court elected for Mrs. Cross to take against decedent's will.

Decedent's son appealed the probate court's decision. While the appeal was pending, Mrs. Cross died. The court of appeals, with one judge dissenting, reversed, finding that the election to take against the will was against Mrs. Cross's best interest and was not necessary to provide her adequate support, since the cost of her nursing home care was already covered by Medicaid. Rosemary D. Durkin, Administrator of the Estate of Beulah Cross, filed a notice of appeal to this court, as did intervenor, Cuyahoga County Board of Commissioners.

SWEENEY, J.   At issue in this case is whether Judge Corrigan abused his discretion in electing for decedent Carroll Cross's surviving spouse, who depended solely upon Medicaid benefits for her support and care, to take against the will and under R.C. 2105.06. For the following reasons, we uphold the election made by Judge Corrigan for Mrs. Cross, and reverse the decision of the court of appeals.

Where a surviving spouse is under a legal disability, the probate court is given the authority under R.C. 2106.08 to appoint a suitable person to ascertain the surviving spouse's adequate support needs and to compare the value of the surviving spouse's rights under the will with the value of her rights under the statute of descent and distribution. R.C. 2106.08 further provides that the court may elect for the surviving spouse to take against the will and under R.C. 2105.06 "only if it finds, after taking into consideration the other available resources and the age, probable life expectancy, physical and mental condition, and present and reasonably anticipated future needs of the surviving spouse, that the election to take under 2105.06 of the Revised Code is necessary to provide adequate support for the surviving spouse during his life expectancy."

Prior to the amendment of former R.C. 2107.45 (now renumbered R.C. 2106.08), effective December 17, 1986, the probate court made its determination of whether to elect to take under the will or against the will based upon which provision was "better for such spouse." In essence, the court based its decision on which provision was more mathematically advantageous to the surviving spouse. See In re Estate of Cook (1969), 19 Ohio St. 2d 121, 126, 249 N.E.2d 799, 802. However, in passing R.C. 2106.08, the General Assembly moved away from a simple mathematical calculation, taking into consideration such factors as other available resources, age, life expectancy, physical and mental condition, and the surviving spouse's present and future needs. In either case, the probate court must ascertain what the surviving spouse would have done for her financial benefit had she been competent to make the decision herself. See In re Estate of Hinklin (1989), 66 Ohio App. 3d 676, 679, 586 N.E.2d 130, 132.

In this case, the court of appeals . . . , in striking down the election made by Judge Corrigan for Mrs. Cross to take against the will, . . . ignored Medicaid eligibility requirements.

. . . [E]ligibility for Medicaid benefits is dependent upon a recipient's income or available resources. Ohio Adm. Code 5101:1-39-05. The term "resources" includes "property owned separately by the person, his share of family property, and property devised to him from a parent or spouse." Ohio Adm. Code 5101:1-39-05(A)(4). This also encompasses "those resources in which an applicant/recipient has a legal interest and the legal ability to use or dispose of. . . ." Ohio Adm. Code 5101:1-39-05(A)(8).

Mrs. Cross clearly had a legal interest in and the ability to use or dispose of her intestate share under her right to take against the will. Thus, she had available to her a potential resource for Medicaid eligibility purposes. This is critical to the facts presented, since the Medicaid rules specifically state that the nonutilization of available income renders a Medicaid applicant or recipient ineligible for benefits. According to Ohio Adm. Code 5101:1-39-08(A)(2), "A basic tenet of public assistance is that all income must be considered in determining the need of an individual for public assistance. Potential income must be explored prior to approving medicaid. An individual who does not avail himself of a potential income is presumed to fail to do so in order to make himself eligible for public assistance. Such nonutilization of income available upon request constitutes ineligibility. . . ."

As applied to this case, in order to maintain Mrs. Cross's Medicaid eligibility and to continue to have her nursing home expenses provided for by public assistance, Judge Corrigan was required to elect for Mrs. Cross to take against the will and to receive her intestate share. Otherwise, if the election was to take under the will, Mrs. Cross would receive no income and would be deemed ineligible for benefits for failing to avail herself of a potential income. Thus, the election to take against the will was necessary for Mrs. Cook's future support and met the requirements of R.C. 2106.08. We find that the probate court, by appointing a commissioner to investigate the matter and by electing for Mrs. Cross to take against the will, was correct in its actions. Through his decision, Judge Corrigan acted in the best interests of this surviving spouse and protected the interests of all litigants coming before him. Consequently, Judge Corrigan did not abuse his discretion in electing for Mrs. Cross to take against the will.

Accordingly, we reverse the judgment of the court of appeals and reinstate the judgment of the probate court.

NOTES AND QUESTIONS

1. In Tannler v. Wisconsin Department of Health & Social Services, 211 Wis. 2d 179, 564 N.W.2d 735 (1997), the wife was in a nursing home, supported by Medicaid. Her husband died, leaving all his assets to his grandson and the grandson's wife. The court held that the wife's failure to elect her elective share was an action disqualifying her from Medicaid. "If Tannler had not rejected her share of her spouse's estate, then those assets would have been available to provide for her maintenance and health care without burdening the taxpayers."

In In re Mattei, 169 Misc. 2d 989, 647 N.Y.S.2d 415 (1996), the court ordered the guardian of an incompetent receiving Medicaid benefits to make an election from her deceased husband's estate for the amount necessary to pay for the period of ineligibility which would result from the spouse's failure to elect.

How do these cases square with the idea that the elective share is personal to the surviving spouse (supra page 484) and that creditors of the surviving spouse cannot force her to elect her elective share (so held in Aragon v. Snyder, 314 N.J. Super. 635, 715 A.2d 1045 (1998))?

2.   If the surviving spouse is incompetent, a guardian of the spouse can elect against the decedent's will if it is in the "best interests" of the spouse, with approval of the probate court. A minority of states hold that the guardian should elect to take against the will if it is to the surviving spouse's economic benefit, calculated mathematically. A majority of states hold, as did the court in In re Estate of Cross in considering the legislative shift from the "mathematical view," that all the surrounding facts and circumstances should be taken into consideration by the probate court. The majority view may take into account the preservation of the decedent's estate plan and whether the surviving spouse probably would have wanted to abide by her dead spouse's will. See In re Estate of Clarkson, 193 Neb. 201, 226 N.W.2d 334 (1975); Foman v. Moss, 681 N.E.2d 1113 (Ind. App. 1997).

The 1969 Uniform Probate Code took another view. Section 2-203 provided that the probate court, acting for an incompetent, could order election against the spouse's will only "after finding that exercise is necessary to provide adequate support for the protected person during his probable life expectancy." This implements the view that the elective share is for the support of the surviving spouse, not a share of economic gains from marriage.

The 1990 UPC continued the view that the elective share is for support when the spouse is incompetent, but it implemented the view in a different way. UPC §2-212 (1990, as amended in 1993) provides that if a conservator or guardian elects the elective share, the portion of the elective share that exceeds what the decedent spouse provided for the survivor must be placed in a *custodial trust* for the benefit of the surviving spouse. The trustee of such a trust, appointed by a court, has the power to expend income and principal for the surviving spouse's support, and upon the spouse's death the trustee must transfer the trust property to the residuary devisees under the will of the predeceased spouse against whom the elective share was taken or to the predeceased spouse's heirs. Thus, the husband can prevent the wife's conservator from upsetting his estate plan. The official comment to UPC §2-212 says the purpose of these changes is "to assure that that part of the elective share is devoted to the personal economic benefit and needs of the surviving spouse, but not to the economic benefit of the surviving spouse's heirs or devisees."

Why does a surviving spouse who happens to be incompetent at the decedent's death deserve, in recognition of her contribution to the marriage, only support and not an ownership share which will pass to her heirs? Why should she lose the fractional share of ownership rights she has acquired in her husband's property (the "partnership property"), should she survive, if she develops Alzheimer's disease? Is this attainder for insanity?

A custodial trust established by a conservator's election under UPC §2-212 does not qualify for the federal estate tax marital deduction because, to qualify for the marital deduction, the surviving spouse must be entitled to *all* the income for life and not merely the amount of income necessary for her support (see infra page 1048, QTIP trust).

3.   In some states the elective share is denied to a spouse who has abandoned or refused to support the other spouse. See, e.g., N.Y. Est., Trusts & Powers Law §5-1.2 (1998). The difficulty of proving abandonment is illustrated by In re Riefberg's Estate, 58 N.Y.2d 134, 446 N.E.2d 424, 459 N.Y.S.2d 739 (1983), where the wife, who had excluded her husband from the marital home and lived separately, was held not to have abandoned her husband.

In most states, the spouse who abandons the other spouse is entitled to an elective share. In In re Shiflett, 200 W. Va. 813, 490 S.E.2d 902 (1997), the court held that a wife who had abandoned her husband nine years prior to his death was entitled to an elective share. The court thought this result unjust, but spousal forfeiture was not provided by the statute, which was controlling.

If the rationale for the elective share is sharing the economic fruits of marriage, should one spouse lose his or her share upon leaving the other? Or should the elective share apply only to property the abandoned spouse owned on the date of abandonment?

How is this matter handled in community property states, where the partnership theory underpins community property? In most community property states, if the couple separates, the earnings of both spouses continue to be community property until divorce. In California, earnings acquired after separation are not community property.

4.   Failure of a lawyer to warn the client about the elective share, which would dismantle the client's estate plan, can be grounds for a malpractice action. Johnson v. Sandler, 958 S.W.2d 42 (Mo. App. 1997).

In re Estate of Cooper
New York Supreme Court,
Appellate Division, Second Department, 1993
187 A.D.2d 128, 592 N.Y.S.2d 797

MANGANO, P.J.   The question to be resolved on this appeal is whether the survivor of a homosexual relationship, alleged to be a "spousal relationship," is entitled to a right of election against the decedent's will, pursuant to EPTL 5-1.1. In our view, the question must be answered in the negative.

I

William Thomas Cooper died on February 19, 1988. The decedent died testate, leaving everything to the petitioner [Ernest Chin] as a specific and residuary legatee, with the exception of certain real estate, allegedly constituting over 80% of the value of the estate, which was left to a former homosexual lover of the decedent.

In support of this proceeding to determine that he is entitled to exercise a right of election against the decedent's will, the petitioner alleged, inter alia, as follows:

> I met William Cooper in 1984. From approximately the middle of 1984 until his sudden death from a congenital heart condition in February 1988, I lived with him in Apartment 1, 183 Wyckoff Street, Brooklyn, New York in a spousal-type situation. Except for the fact that we were of the same sex, our lives were identical to that of a husband and wife. We kept a common home; we shared expenses; our friends recognized us as spouses; we had a physical relationship. Of course, we could not obtain a marriage license because no marriage license clerk in New York will issue such a document to two people of the same sex. . . .
>
> The only reason Mr. Cooper and I were not legally married is because marriage license clerks in New York State will not issue licenses to persons of the same sex. . . .
>
> However unconstitutional the denial of the right to a marriage license to Mr. Cooper and myself may have been, the Court cannot undo that now that Mr. Cooper is deceased. Since the Court, however, also is an instrument of the State . . . it cannot compound this unconstitutionality by saying that because we could not obtain a State-issued marriage license, I cannot be recognized as a spouse by a State Court for the purpose of claiming spousal rights. . . .
>
> I ask this Court simply to declare that if I can establish that Mr. Cooper and I, at the time of his death, were living in a spousal-type relationship, I am entitled to spousal rights, and the State-imposed unconstitutional impediment of making it impossible for two people of the same sex to obtain a marriage license does not alter this.

Upon submission of opposing papers and an application to dismiss the petition by the executrix of Cooper's estate, Acting Surrogate Pizzuto held that a survivor of a homosexual relationship, alleged to be a "spousal relationship," was not entitled to a right of election against the decedent's will pursuant to EPTL 5-1.1, stating, inter alia: "This court holds that persons of the same sex have no constitutional rights to enter into a marriage with each other. Neither due process nor equal protection of law provisions are violated by prohibiting such marriages. Nor does Mr. Chin have any right or standing to elect against decedent's will."

II

The right of election by a "surviving spouse," insofar as is relevant to the facts at bar, is contained in EPTL 5-1.1(c)(1)(B), as follows:

> (c) Election by surviving spouse against wills executed and testamentary provisions made after August thirty-first, nineteen hundred sixty-six . . . :
>
>   (1) Where, after August thirty-first, nineteen hundred sixty-six, a testator executes a will disposing of his entire estate, and is survived by a spouse, a personal right of election is given to the surviving spouse to take a share of the decedent's estate, subject to the following:
>
>   (B) The elective share . . . is one-third of the net estate if the decedent is survived by one or more issue and, in all other cases, one-half of such net estate.

We reject the petitioner's argument that he must be considered a "surviving spouse" within the meaning of the statute. "Generally, in the construction of statutes, the intention of the Legislature is first to be sought from a literal reading of the act itself or of all the statutes relating to the same general subject matter" (McKinney's Cons. Laws of N.Y., Book 1, Statutes §92, at 182). The Legislature has expressly defined a "surviving spouse" in EPTL 5-1.2, as follows: "§5-1.2 Disqualifications as surviving spouse. (a) A husband or wife is a surviving spouse within the meaning, and for the purposes of . . . 5-1.1."

Indeed, even in the absence of any express definition of the term "surviving spouse," an interpretation of the statute to the same effect would be warranted. It is well settled that "the language of a statute is generally construed according to its natural and most obvious sense . . . in accordance with its ordinary and accepted meaning, unless the Legislature by definition or from the rest of the context of the statute provides a special meaning" (McKinney's Cons. Laws of N.Y., Book 1, Statutes §94, at 191-193). An illustration of this latter approach may be ascertained from the reasoning of the Supreme Court of Minnesota in Baker v. Nelson, 291 Minn. 310, 191 N.W.2d 185. In that case, the court rejected an argument that the absence of an express statutory prohibition against same-sex marriages evinced a legislative intent to authorize such marriages. The Supreme Court of Minnesota held in this regard (Baker v. Nelson, supra, 191 N.W.2d at 185-186): "[The statute], which governs 'marriage,' employs that term as one of common usage, meaning the state of union between persons of the opposite sex. It is unrealistic to think that the original drafts-men of our marriage statutes, which date from territorial days, would have used the term in any different sense" (see also, Anonymous v. Anonymous, 67 Misc. 2d 982, 325 N.Y.S.2d 499; Morris v. Morris, 31 Misc. 2d 548, 549, 220 N.Y.S.2d 590).

We reject, as meritless, the contention of both the petitioner and the amicus curiae that, based on the Court of Appeals decision in Braschi v. Stahl Assocs. Co., 74 N.Y.2d 201, 544 N.Y.S.2d 784, 543 N.E.2d 49, the traditional definition of the term "surviving spouse" must be rejected, and replaced with a broader definition which would include the petitioner. In Braschi v. Stahl Assocs. Co., the Court of Appeals held that same-sex partners were "family members" for pur-poses of the rent control regulations at issue therein, prohibiting the eviction of "family members" upon the death of the tenant of record. Specifically, the Court of Appeals stated (Braschi v. Stahl Assocs. Co., supra, at 211, 544 N.Y.S.2d 784, 543 N.E.2d 49). "The intended pro-tection against sudden eviction should not rest on fictitious legal dis-tinctions or genetic history, but instead should find its foundation in the reality of family life. In the context of eviction, a more realistic, and certainly equally valid, view of a family includes two adult lifetime partners whose relationship is long term and characterized by an emotional and financial commitment and interdependence. This view comports both with our society's traditional concept of 'family' and with the expectations of individuals who live in such nuclear units."

However, in Matter of Alison D. v. Virginia M., 155 A.D.2d 11, 552 N.Y.S.2d 321, aff'd, 77 N.Y.2d 651, 569 N.Y.S.2d 586, 572 N.E.2d 27, this court held, in an opinion and order subsequently affirmed by the Court of Appeals, that a lesbian partner was not a "parent" under Domestic Relations Law §70 and rejected, as "totally misplaced," the argument that the holding in Braschi v. Stahl Assocs. Co. compelled a different result.

Accordingly, the term "surviving spouse," as used in EPTL 5-1.1, cannot be interpreted to include homosexual life partners.

III

The petitioner and the amicus curiae argue that such a narrow defini-tion of the term "surviving spouse" is unconstitutional as it violates the equal protection clause of the State Constitution. Specifically, they argue that this unconstitutional definition directly derives from, and compounds, the State's unconstitutional conduct in interpreting the relevant provisions of the Domestic Relations Law as prohibiting mem-bers of the same sex from obtaining marriage licenses (see, e.g., Fran-cis B. v. Mark B., 78 Misc. 2d 112, 355 N.Y.S.2d 712; Anonymous v. Anonymous, 67 Misc. 2d 982, 325 N.Y.S.2d 499, supra).

It is to this argument that we now turn.

It is well settled that there are three standards that may be applied in reviewing equal protection challenges: strict scrutiny, heightened scrutiny, and rational basis review (City of Cleburne, Tex. v. Cleburne Living Center, 473 U.S. 432, 440-441).

We note that Acting Surrogate Pizzuto correctly held that any equal protection analysis in the instant factual scenario is to be measured by the rational basis standard, i.e., the legislation (or government action) "is presumed to be valid and will be sustained if the classification drawn . . . is rationally related to a legitimate state interest" (City of Cleburne, Tex. v. Cleburne Living Center, supra, at 440), and not by the more stringent standards of heightened scrutiny or strict scrutiny.

In Baker v. Nelson, 191 N.W.2d 185, supra, the petitioners, both adult males, made application to the clerk of the County District Court for a marriage license pursuant to the relevant Minnesota statute. The clerk declined to issue the license on the sole ground that the petitioners were of the same sex, "it being undisputed that there were otherwise no statutory impediments to a heterosexual marriage by either petitioner" (Baker v. Nelson, supra, at 185).

The Supreme Court of Minnesota rejected the petitioners' argument that a prohibition on same sex marriages denied them equal protection of the laws, holding (Baker v. Nelson, supra, at 186-187):

> These constitutional challenges have in common the assertion that the right to marry without regard to the sex of the parties is a fundamental right of all persons and that restricting marriage to only couples of the opposite sex is irrational and invidiously discriminatory. We are not independently persuaded by these contentions and do not find support for them in any decisions of the United States Supreme Court.
>
> The institution of marriage as a union of man and woman, uniquely involving the procreation and rearing of children within a family, is as old as the book of Genesis. Skinner v. Oklahoma ex rel. Williamson, 316 U.S. 535, 541, 62 S. Ct. 1110, 1113, 86 L. Ed. 1655, 1660 (1942), which invalidated Oklahoma's Habitual Criminal Sterilization Act on equal protection grounds, stated in part: "Marriage and procreation are fundamental to the very existence and survival of the race." This historic institution manifestly is more deeply founded than the asserted contemporary concept of marriage and societal interests for which petitioners contend. The due process clause of the Fourteenth Amendment is not a charter for restructuring it by judicial legislation. . . .
>
> The equal protection clause of the Fourteenth Amendment, like the due process clause, is not offended by the state's classification of persons authorized to marry. There is no irrational or invidious discrimination. Petitioners note that the state does not impose upon heterosexual married couples a condition that they have a proved capacity or declared willingness to procreate, posing a rhetorical demand that this court must read such condition into the statute if same-sex marriages are to be pro-

hibited. Even assuming that such a condition would be neither unrealistic nor offensive under the *Griswold* rationale, the classification is no more than theoretically imperfect. We are reminded, however, that "abstract symmetry" is not demanded by the Fourteenth Amendment.

The appeal from the Minnesota Supreme Court to the United States Supreme Court was dismissed for want of a substantial Federal question (Baker v. Nelson, 409 U.S. 810), and, as Acting Surrogate Pizzuto accurately noted (Matter of Cooper, 149 Misc. 2d 282, 284, 564 N.Y.S.2d 684): "Such a dismissal is a holding that the constitutional challenge was considered and rejected (Hicks v. Miranda, 422 U.S. 332)."

The rational basis standard has been also applied in other similar instances where equal protection challenges have been raised to classifications based on sexual orientation (see, High Tech Gays v. Defense Industrial Security Clearance Office, 895 F.2d 563 (9th Cir.), in which the court, relying on the Supreme Court's ruling in Bowers v. Hardwick, 478 U.S. 186, that homosexual activity is not a fundamental right, applied the rational basis standard, and rejected an equal protection challenge to a Defense Department policy of conducting expanded investigations into backgrounds of all gay and lesbian applicants for secret and top secret security clearance; see also, Adams v. Howerton, 673 F.2d 1036 (9th Cir.), cert. denied, 458 U.S. 1111, in which the court held that a citizen's "spouse" within the meaning of section 201[b] of the Immigration and Nationality Act of 1952, as amended, 8 U.S.C. §1151[b], must be an individual of the opposite sex and that, in accordance with the rational basis standard, such a bar against an alleged homosexual "spouse" was not unconstitutional).

Based on these authorities, we agree with Acting Surrogate Pizzuto's conclusion that "purported [homosexual] marriages do not give rise to any rights . . . pursuant to . . . EPTL 5-1.1 [and that] [n]o constitutional rights have been abrogated or violated in so holding" (Matter of Cooper, supra, 149 Misc. 2d at 288, 564 N.Y.S.2d 684).

Accordingly, the order and decree is affirmed insofar as appealed from.

ORDERED that the order and decree is affirmed insofar as appealed from, *with costs payable by the appellant personally* (emphasis added).

NOTES

1. The *Cooper* case was appealed, but the appeal was dismissed by the New York Court of Appeals on the ground that no substantial constitutional question was directly involved. In re Cooper, 82 N.Y.2d 801, 624 N.E.2d 696, 604 N.Y.S.2d 558 (1993).

2. In Baehr v. Lewin, 852 P.2d 44 (Haw. 1993), a suit was brought

by three same-sex couples whose requests for marriage licenses had been turned down. They claimed the Hawaii law prohibiting issuance of marriage licenses to a same-sex couple was unconstitutional as a denial of equal protection. The Hawaii Supreme Court held that the plaintiffs stated a cause of action under the Hawaii constitution, which forbids sex discrimination, and that the state must have a compelling state interest to forbid same-sex couples to marry. The court remanded the case for trial to hear evidence of the compelling state interest. On remand, the trial court held the state had not met its burden of proving a compelling state interest. The state appealed.

In the fall of 1998, before the Hawaii Supreme Court issued a final opinion in Baehr v. Lewin, the people of the state voted to amend the state constitution to provide that the state legislature could define marriage to be a relationship between persons of the opposite sex. To date, the legislature has not acted to so limit marriage.

Largely prompted by the Hawaii case, the constitutional issues surrounding same-sex marriages have been given a thorough airing in the legal literature. See, e.g., William N. Eskridge, Jr., The Case for Same-Sex Marriage (1996); Patricia A. Cain, Litigating for Lesbian and Gay Rights: A Legal History, 79 Va. L. Rev. 1551 (1993); Craig W. Christensen, If Not Marriage? On Securing Gay and Lesbian Family Values by a "Simulacrum of Marriage," 66 Fordham L. Rev. 1699 (1998); Cass R. Sunstein, Homosexuality and the Constitution, 70 Ind. L.J. 1 (1994).

Another constitutional challenge to the refusal to permit same-sex marriage has occurred in Vermont in the case of Baker v. State. The case is still pending. See Mary Bonauto, Susan M. Murray & Beth Robinson, The Freedom to Marry for Same-Sex Couples: The Opening Appellate Brief of Plaintiffs in *Baker v. State of Vermont*, 5 Mich. J. Gender & L. 409 (1999).

In May 1999 the Supreme Court of Canada struck down a heterosexual definition of the word "spouse" in Ontario's Family Law. The court ruled that the act offended the Canadian Charter of Rights and Freedoms in denying a lesbian partner the right to apply for alimony or spousal support upon the separation of the lesbian couple. The court held that the differential treatment of heterosexual and homosexual partners withholds a benefit from the claimant because of a stereotypical application of presumed group or personal characteristics, and, in addition, had "the effect of perpetuating or promoting the view that the individual is less capable or worthy of recognition or value as a human being or as a member of Canadian society, equally deserving of concern, respect, and consideration. . . . The exclusion of same-sex partners [from alimony] . . . implies that they are judged to be incapable of forming intimate relationships of economic interdependence as compared to opposite-sex couples, without regard to their actual circumstances. Such exclusion perpetuates the disadvantages suffered by individuals in same-sex relationships and contributes to the erasure of their existence." The Attorney General for Ontario v. M. & H., 1999 Can. Sup. Ct. Lexis 28 (Can. Sup. Ct. 1999). For further elaboration of this view under the United States Constitution, see Kenneth L. Karst, Belonging to America: Equal Citizenship and the Constitution (1989).

The American Law Institute, Principles of the Law of Family Dissolution: Analysis and Recommendations, ch. 6 (Domestic Unions) (C.D. No. 5, 1998), provides that, upon dissolution, partners in a long-term, marriage-like, nonmarital relationship, whether of the same or opposite sex, are entitled to compensatory payments and distribution of property acquired during the relationship (more or less equivalent to alimony). Can you distinguish alimony from the elective share?

3. In Hawaii, as a result of the *Baehr* case, an elective share is given to persons who are forbidden to marry (such as same-sex partners and parent and child) if such persons register with the state as "reciprocal beneficiaries." Haw. Rev. Stat. §560:2-202 (1998).

4. Marriage brings a number of legal and economic consequences, mostly beneficial, to a surviving spouse. A married partner is entitled to social security based on the other partner's earnings, to pension rights from the other partner's job, to an elective share of the other partner's estate, and to the federal estate tax marital deduction (eliminating all estate taxes on property one married partner transfers to the other at death). Unmarried surviving partners have none of these benefits.

In 1996, Congress — reacting to Baehr v. Lewin — enacted the Defense of Marriage Act, 28 U.S.C.A. §1738C & 1 U.S.C.A. §7 (1998). Section 2 of the act provides that no state shall be required under the Full Faith and Credit Clause of the Constitution to give effect to a same-sex marriage contracted in another state. Section 3 provides that for all purposes of federal law "the word 'marriage' means only a legal union between one man and one woman as husband and wife, and the word 'spouse' refers only to a person of the opposite sex who is a husband or a wife." The latter section thus deprives same-sex married couples (if any are ever recognized by a state) of the social security, tax, and welfare benefits of federal law. See Patricia McCain, Tax and Financial Planning for Same-Sex Couples, 8 Law & Sexuality 613 (1998).

5. Under the law of some states, the surviving unmarried partner of a life partnership may have rights against the estate of the decedent under contract law, if a contract to share assets, express or implied, was made by the partners. See Watts v. Watts, 137 Wis. 2d 506, 405 N.W.2d 303 (1987). Or the surviving partner may have a claim for

unjust enrichment, enforceable by imposing a constructive trust. A claim of unjust enrichment is grounded on the moral principle that a person who has received a benefit has a duty to make restitution where retaining such a benefit would be unjust. Id. Or the surviving partner may have a claim for quantum meruit (the value of services rendered).

b. Property Subject to the Elective Share

The original elective share statutes gave the surviving spouse a fractional share of the decedent's estate, which implicitly meant *probate estate*. With the proliferation of nonprobate transfers (see Chapter 5), the question arises whether the elective share should be extended to some or all nonprobate transfers. We shall first treat the judicial responses to this question, then the legislative responses.

(1) Judicial Decisions

Sullivan v. Burkin

Supreme Judicial Court of Massachusetts, 1984
390 Mass. 864, 460 N.E.2d 571

WILKINS, J.[7] Mary A. Sullivan, the widow of Ernest G. Sullivan, has exercised her right, under G.L. c. 191, §15, to take a share of her husband's estate. By this action, she seeks a determination that assets held in an inter vivos trust created by her husband during the marriage should be considered as part of the estate in determining that share. A judge of the Probate Court for the county of Suffolk rejected the widow's claim and entered judgment dismissing the complaint. The widow appealed, and, on July 12, 1983, a panel of the Appeals Court reported the case to this court.

In September, 1973, Ernest G. Sullivan executed a deed of trust under which he transferred real estate to himself as sole trustee. The net income of the trust was payable to him during his life and the

---

7. In recent years the Massachusetts Supreme Judicial Court has reclaimed the eminent position among state courts it occupied during the nineteenth century. The court went into marked intellectual decline during the long tenure of Chief Justice Arthur Rugg, who served in the office from 1911 to 1938. Rugg's opinion in Mahoney v. Grainger, page 410, is an example of his imperious style.

Justice Herbert Wilkins, one of the intellectual leaders of the Massachusetts court, appears to make a specialty of trust cases. He writes the opinions in Sullivan v. Burkin; Dewire v. Haveles, page 750; Beals v. State Street Bank & Trust Co., page 688; and Loring v. Marshall, page 702. In 1996 Justice Wilkins was appointed Chief Justice, a position once held by his father. — Eds.

trustee was instructed to pay to him all or such part of the principal of the trust estate as he might request in writing from time to time. He retained the right to revoke the trust at any time. On his death, the successor trustee is directed to pay the principal and any undistributed income equally to the defendants, George F. Cronin, Sr., and Harold J. Cronin, if they should survive him, which they did. There were no witnesses to the execution of the deed of trust, but the husband acknowledged his signatures before a notary public, separately, as donor and as trustee.

Justice Herbert Wilkins

The husband died on April 27, 1981, while still trustee of the inter vivos trust. He left·a will in which he stated that he "intentionally neglected to make any provision for my wife, Mary A. Sullivan and my grandson, Mark Sullivan." He directed that, after the payment of debts, expenses, and all estate taxes levied by reason of his death, the residue of his estate should be paid over to the trustee of the inter vivos trust. The defendants George F. Cronin, Sr., and Harold J. Cronin were named coexecutors of the will. The defendant Burkin is successor trustee of the inter vivos trust. On October 21, 1981, the wife filed a claim, pursuant to G.L. c. 191, §15, for a portion of the estate.[8]

Although it does not appear in the record, the parties state in their briefs that Ernest G. Sullivan and Mary A. Sullivan had been separated for many years. We do know that in 1962 the wife obtained a court order providing for her temporary support. No final action was taken in that proceeding. The record provides no information about the value of any property owned by the husband at his death or about the value of any assets held in the inter vivos trust. At oral argument, we were advised that the husband owned personal property worth

---

8. As relevant to this case, G.L. c. 191, §15, provides:

> The surviving husband or wife of a deceased person . . . within six months after the probate of the will of such deceased, may file in the registry of probate a writing signed by him or by her . . . claiming such portion of the estate of the deceased as he or she is given the right to claim under this section, and if the deceased left issue, he or she shall thereupon take one third of the personal and one third of the real property . . . except that . . . if he or she would thus take real and personal property to an amount exceeding twenty-five thousand dollars in value, he or she shall receive, in addition to that amount, only the income during his or her life of the excess of his or her share of such estate above that amount, the personal property to be held in trust and the real property vested in him or her for life, from the death of the deceased. . . .

approximately $15,000 at his death and that the only asset in the trust was a house in Boston which was sold after the husband's death for approximately $85,000.

As presented in the complaint, and perhaps as presented to the motion judge, the wife's claim was simply that the inter vivos trust was an invalid testamentary disposition and that the trust assets "constitute assets of the estate" of Ernest G. Sullivan. There is no suggestion that the wife argued initially that, even if the trust were not testamentary, she had a special claim as a widow asserting her rights under G.L. c. 191, §15. If the wife is correct that the trust was an ineffective testamentary disposition, the trust assets would be part of the husband's probate estate. In that event, we would not have to consider any special consequences of the wife's election under G.L. c. 191, §15, or, in the words of the Appeals Court, "the present vitality" of Kerwin v. Donaghy, 317 Mass. 559, 572, 59 N.E.2d 299 (1945).

We conclude, however, that the trust was not testamentary in character and that the husband effectively created a valid inter vivos trust. Thus, whether the issue was initially involved in this case, we are now presented with the question (which the executors will have to resolve ultimately, in any event) whether the assets of the inter vivos trust are to be considered in determining the "portion of the estate of the deceased" (G.L. c. 191, §15) in which Mary A. Sullivan has rights. We conclude that, in this case, we should adhere to the principles expressed in Kerwin v. Donaghy, supra, that deny the surviving spouse any claim against the assets of a valid inter vivos trust created by the deceased spouse, even where the deceased spouse alone retained substantial rights and powers under the trust instrument. For the future, however, as to any inter vivos trust created or amended after the date of this opinion, we announce that the estate of a decedent, for the purposes of G.L. c. 191, §15, shall include the value of assets held in an inter vivos trust created by the deceased spouse as to which the deceased spouse alone retained the power during his or her life to direct the disposition of those trust assets for his or her benefit, as, for example, by the exercise of a power of appointment or by revocation of the trust. Such a power would be a general power of appointment for Federal estate tax purposes (I.R.C. §2041(b)(1) [1983]) and a "general power" as defined in the Restatement (Second) of Property §11.4(1) (Tent. Draft No. 5, 1982).

We consider first whether the inter vivos trust was invalid because it was testamentary. A trust with remainder interests given to others on the settlor's death is not invalid as a testamentary disposition simply because the settlor retained a broad power to modify or revoke the trust, the right to receive income, and the right to invade principal during his life. . . . We believe that the law of the Commonwealth is correctly represented by the statement in Restatement (Second) of Trusts §57, Comment h (1959), that a trust is "not testamentary and invalid for failure to comply with the requirements of the Statute of Wills merely because the settlor-trustee reserves a beneficial life interest and power to revoke and modify the trust. The fact that as trustee he controls the administration of the trust does not invalidate it."[9]

We come then to the question whether, even if the trust was not testamentary on general principles, the widow has special interests which should be recognized. Courts in this country have differed considerably in their reasoning and in their conclusions in passing on this question. See 1 A. Scott, Trusts §57.5 at 509-511 (3d ed. 1967 & 1983 Supp.). . . .

The rule of Kerwin v. Donaghy, supra 317 Mass. at 571, 59 N.E.2d 299, is that

> [t]he right of a wife to waive her husband's will, and take, with certain limitations, "the same portion of the property of the deceased, real and personal, that . . . she would have taken if the deceased had died intestate" (G.L. [Ter. Ed.] c. 191, §15), does not extend to personal property that has been conveyed by the husband in his lifetime and does not form part of his estate at his death. Fiske v. Fiske, 173 Mass. 413, 419, 53 N.E. 916 [1899]. Shelton v. Sears, 187 Mass. 455, 73 N.E. 666 [1905]. In this Commonwealth a husband has an absolute right to dispose of any or all of his personal property in his lifetime, without the knowledge or consent of his wife, with the result that it will not form part of his estate for her to share under the statute of distributions (G.L. [Ter. Ed.] c. 190, §§1, 2), under his will, or by virtue of a waiver of his will. That is true even though his sole purpose was to disinherit her.

In the *Kerwin* case, we applied the rule to deny a surviving spouse the right to reach assets the deceased spouse had placed in an inter vivos trust of which the settlor's daughter by a previous marriage was trustee and over whose assets he had a general power of appointment. The rule of Kerwin v. Donaghy has been adhered to in this Commonwealth for almost forty years and was adumbrated even earlier.[10] The bar has

9. Thus the Massachusetts court, like other courts, agrees with Farkas v. Williams, 5 Ill. 2d 417, 125 N.E.2d 600 (1955), supra page 352, that a revocable trust is valid. — Eds.

10. In early opinions, this court considered an intent to deny inheritance rights to be a ground for invalidating an inter vivos transfer, but in the first part of this century it abandoned that position. . . .

Opinions in this Commonwealth, and generally elsewhere, considering the rights of a surviving spouse to a share in assets transferred by the deceased spouse to an inter vivos trust have analyzed the question on grounds of public policy, as if establishing common law principles. These opinions have not relied in any degree on what the Legislature may have intended by granting a surviving spouse certain rights in the "estate" of a deceased spouse.

been entitled reasonably to rely on that rule in advising clients. In the area of property law, the retroactive invalidation of an established principle is to be undertaken with great caution. We conclude that, whether or not Ernest G. Sullivan established the inter vivos trust in order to defeat his wife's right to take her statutory share in the assets placed in the trust and even though he had a general power of appointment over the trust assets, Mary A. Sullivan obtained no right to share in the assets of that trust when she made her election under G.L. c. 191, §15.

We announce for the future that, as to any inter vivos trust created or amended after the date of this opinion, we shall no longer follow the rule announced in Kerwin v. Donaghy. There have been significant changes since 1945 in public policy considerations bearing on the right of one spouse to treat his or her property as he or she wishes during marriage. The interests of one spouse in the property of the other have been substantially increased upon the dissolution of a marriage by divorce. We believe that, when a marriage is terminated by the death of one spouse, the rights of the surviving spouse should not be so restricted as they are by the rule in Kerwin v. Donaghy. It is neither equitable nor logical to extend to a divorced spouse greater rights in the assets of an inter vivos trust created and controlled by the other spouse than are extended to a spouse who remains married until the death of his or her spouse.

The rule we now favor would treat as part of "the estate of the deceased" for the purposes of G.L. c. 191, §15, assets of an inter vivos trust created during the marriage by the deceased spouse over which he or she alone had a general power of appointment, exercisable by deed or by will. This objective test would involve no consideration of the motive or intention of the spouse in creating the trust. We would not need to engage in a determination of "whether the [spouse] has in good faith divested himself [or herself] of ownership of his [or her] property or has made an illusory transfer" (Newman v. Dore, 275 N.Y. 371, 379, 9 N.E.2d 966 [1937]) or with the factual question whether the spouse "intended to surrender complete dominion over the property" (Staples v. King, 433 A.2d 407, 411 [Me. 1981]). Nor would we have to participate in the rather unsatisfactory process of determining whether the inter vivos trust was, on some standard, "colorable," "fraudulent," or "illusory."

What we have announced as a rule for the future hardly resolves all the problems that may arise. . . .

The question of the rights of a surviving spouse in the estate of a deceased spouse, using the word "estate" in its broad sense, is one that can best be handled by legislation. See Uniform Probate Code, §§2-201, 2-202, 8 U.L.A. 74-75 (1983). See also Uniform Marital Property Act, §18 (1983), which adopts the concept of community property as to "marital property." But, until it is, the answers to these problems will "be determined in the usual way through the decisional process." Tucker v. Badoian, 376 Mass. 907, 918-919, 384 N.E.2d 1195 (1978) (Kaplan, J., concurring).

We affirm the judgment of the Probate Court dismissing the plaintiff's complaint.

So ordered.

NOTES AND PROBLEMS

1. In Sullivan v. Burkin, the court rejects several tests applied in various states to determine what nonprobate transfers are subject to the surviving spouse's election. The first, and most famous, is the *illusory transfer* test laid down by Newman v. Dore, 275 N.Y. 371, 9 N.E.2d 966, 112 A.L.R. 643 (1937) (now superseded by statute in New York). In *Newman*, the court upheld a widow's claim that a revocable inter vivos trust established by her husband during their marriage is "illusory" and invalid.[11] After some years of uncertainty and confusion about the holding in *Newman*, courts following *Newman* held that an "illusory" revocable trust is not totally invalid, but merely counts as part of the decedent's assets subject to the elective share; the trustee may have to contribute some of the trust assets to make up the elective share. The illusory transfer test is the most widely adopted of the judicial tests for subjecting nonprobate property to the elective share. See Pezza v. Pezza, 690 A.2d 345 (R.I. 1997) (adopting illusory transfer test and holding that an irrevocable trust created during marriage by husband, who retained some income interests, was not illusory). The illusory transfer test has been adopted by the South Carolina legislature. S.C. Code Ann. §62-7-112 (1997).

What kind of ownership rights retained by the decedent make a transfer illusory was left unclear in *Newman* and was little clarified in later cases. The key is said to be the amount of control retained by the decedent spouse. But how much is too much? Are any of the following nonprobate transfers illusory? Would it matter if these property arrangements were made before marriage or after marriage?

(a) *H* owns an insurance policy naming his two daughters as benefi-

---

11. The facts of Newman v. Dore are unusual. The husband was 80 and his wife in her thirties when they married. After four years of marriage the wife sued for separation, claiming her husband's perverted sexual habits made it impossible to live with him. The record does not make clear what the octogenarian's alleged perversions were, though he did receive monkey glands by surgical transplant. Indignant over his wife's charges, the husband instructed his lawyer to disinherit her. The separation action was still pending at his death. See Elias Clark, Louis Lusky, Arthur W. Murphy, Mark L. Ascher & Grayson M.P. McCouch, Gratuitous Transfers 128 (4th ed. 1999).

ciaries. *H* has the rights to cash the policy in and to change the beneficiaries.

(b) *H* has an account with a stock brokerage house, which holds all his stocks as custodian. *H* has named his daughters as payable-on-death beneficiaries of the account.

(c) *H* has two bank accounts: one naming his daughters as payable-on-death beneficiaries, and a second a joint account with his daughters.

(d) *H* bought Blackacre and took title with his daughters in joint tenancy.

2. Some states found the illusory transfer test itself illusory and adopted instead an *intent to defraud* test. In determining whether the decedent intended to defraud his surviving spouse of her elective share, some look for subjective intent. Others look for objective evidence of intent: the control retained by the transferor, the amount of time between the transfer and death, the degree to which the surviving spouse is left without an interest in the decedent's property or other means of support. See In re Estate of Froman, 803 S.W.2d 176 (Mo. App. 1991) (subjective intent, codified as Mo. Ann. Stat. §474.150(1) (1998)); Hanke v. Hanke, 123 N.H. 175, 459 A.2d 246 (1983) (objective intent).

Another test, slightly different from the intent-to-defraud test, is whether the decedent had a *present donative intent* to transfer a present interest in the property. This test focuses not on what the transferor retained, but on whether the transferor intended to make a present gift. Factors similar to those weighed in the objective intent-to-defraud test appear to be used in applying this test. See In re Estate of Defilippis, 289 Ill. App. 3d 695, 683 N.E.2d 453, review denied, 174 Ill. 2d 562 (1997). Under all of these tests, which do not spell out the criteria specifically, the cases tend to be resolved by examining closely the circumstances of the particular case. In jurisdictions following one of these tests lawyers must advise clients to exercise extreme caution in making nonprobate transfers without the other spouse's consent that might have the effect of diminishing the other spouse's elective share.

In Massachusetts, under Sullivan v. Burkin, suppose that one week before death a husband transfers all his property in an irrevocable trust, retaining a life estate. Can his widow reach the trust to satisfy her elective share?

3. In some states, revocable trusts and other nonprobate transfers are not subject to the elective share. The surviving spouse's elective share is only in the decedent's probate estate. See Dalia v. Lawrence, 226 Conn. 51, 627 A.2d 392 (1993); Dumas v. Estate of Dumas, 68 Ohio St. 3d 405, 627 N.E.2d 978 (1994). This also is provided by Fla. Stat. Ann. §732.206 (1998).

4. *H* and *W*, both 65 years of age, live in State Red. In State Red,

a surviving spouse can include a revocable inter vivos trust created by the decedent in the decedent's assets subject to her elective share. In State Blue, a revocable inter vivos trust is not reachable by the surviving spouse. *H* takes a trip to State Blue and sets up a revocable inter vivos trust there, naming a State Blue bank as trustee. The trust instrument provides that the law of State Blue shall govern the trust. *H* transfers almost all his assets to the State Blue trustee. *H* dies domiciled in State Red. Can *W* reach the assets in the inter vivos trust in State Blue? Compare National Shawmut Bank v. Cumming, 325 Mass. 457, 91 N.E.2d 337 (1950) (applying law of trustee's domicile to defeat elective share claim of spouse domiciled out of state), with In re Clark, 21 N.Y.2d 478, 236 N.E.2d 152, 288 N.Y.S.2d 993 (1968) (applying law of state where couple were domiciled, deeming it to have paramount interest).

Uniform Probate Code §2-202(d) (1990) provides that the law of the decedent's domicile shall govern the right to take an elective share of property located in another state. But not all states agree. Fla. Stat. Ann. §732.205 (1998) provides that "no elective share . . . in Florida property of a decedent not domiciled in Florida shall exist." And in In re Estate of Pericles, 266 Ill. App. 3d 1096, 641 N.E.2d 10 (1994), the court applied the standard conflict of laws rule that the law of the state where real property is located governs the elective share in such real property.

(2) UNIFORM PROBATE CODE

Dissatisfied with vague tests laid down by courts, legislatures in many states have enacted statutes providing objective criteria for determining what nonprobate transfers are subject to the elective share. We take up first the Uniform Probate Code provisions.

(a) *1969 Uniform Probate Code*

The 1969 Uniform Probate Code introduced the concept of the *augmented estate* (the probate estate augmented with certain nonprobate transfers). 1969 UPC §2-202. The surviving spouse is entitled to an elective share of one-third of the augmented estate. The augmented estate includes the probate estate and the following nonprobate and inter vivos transfers made without consideration in money or money's worth at any time *during the marriage:*

1) any transfer under which the decedent retains the right to possession or income from the property;

2) any transfer which the decedent can revoke or invade or dispose of the principal for his own benefit;

3) any transfer in joint tenancy with someone other than the spouse;

4) any transfer made within two years before death exceeding $3,000 per donee per year ($3,000 was, at the time, the maximum amount exempt from the federal gift tax under the annual exclusion);

5) property given to the surviving spouse during life, including a life estate in a trust, and property received by the spouse at death derived from the decedent, such as life insurance and pensions.

The purpose of augmenting the probate estate with items 1) through 4) above was, in the words of the official comment: "to prevent the owner of wealth from making arrangements which transmit his property to others by means other than probate deliberately to defeat the right of the surviving spouse to a share." The augmented estate expressly excluded life insurance payable to a person other than the surviving spouse "because it is not ordinarily purchased as a way of depleting the probate estate and avoiding the elective share of the spouse."

Observe that the 1969 Uniform Probate Code includes in the augmented estate property given to the surviving spouse by the decedent during life (item 5) listed above). The purpose of this innovation is to prevent a spouse who has been well provided for by lifetime or nonprobate transfers from electing against the will and claiming more than a fair share. Thus:

> *Case 3.* H, married to W, owns the family home in joint tenancy with W (the house is worth $80,000 at H's death). H owns insurance on his own life in the amount of $100,000, payable to W. During life H transfers $200,000 to a trust to pay H the income for life, then to pay W the income for life, then to pay the principal to H's children. H dies, leaving a probate estate of $100,000, which he devises to his children. In a majority of states the elective share system does not take into account the property given W. W can elect to take a fractional share of H's probate estate regardless of how much she has received from H by nonprobate routes.

To be equitable, the 1969 UPC includes gifts to the spouse in the decedent's augmented estate, which gifts are credited against the elective share to which the surviving spouse is entitled. (Compare Bravo v. Sauter, 727 So. 2d 1103 (Fla. App. 1999), holding that a surviving spouse who elects against the will is entitled to her income interest under a revocable inter vivos trust largely funded from a pour-over from the testator's probate estate in addition to her elective share of the probate estate; Florida law does not have the UPC provision.)

The 1969 UPC augmented estate version of the elective share system was adopted and remains in effect in a number of states. In addition, the concept of augmenting the probate estate with transfers *during marriage* which the decedent continued to control influenced other states in revising their elective share systems, even though they did not adopt the UPC.

(b)   1990 Uniform Probate Code

The 1990 UPC completely redesigned the elective share and the augmented estate so that it achieves results closer to those of a community property system, which the revisers took to be the desideratum. The central idea of the 1990 UPC elective share is to add up all the property of both spouses and split it according to a percentage based on the length of the marriage. The revisers believe that this will result in treating spouses in common law property jurisdictions in pretty much the same way they are treated in community property jurisdictions, in situations where the spouses have only community property and each spouse owns half of their community property assets.

The 1990 UPC also changed the policy of the 1969 UPC elective share of including in the augmented estate only transfers made during marriage. The 1990 UPC includes in the augmented estate many transfers made before marriage, as well as transfers during marriage, where the decedent retained substantial control of the property. It also includes property or powers received from others. In this respect, the 1990 UPC resembles the Internal Revenue Code, which subjects to estate taxation property transferred by the decedent during life over which the decedent retained substantial control as well as property subject to a general power of appointment given the decedent by others. The purpose of the augmented estate is no longer to protect against "fraud on the widow's share." It is, according to the official general comment, to implement the partnership theory of the elective share by increasing "the entitlement of a surviving spouse in a long-term marriage in cases in which the marital assets were disproportionately titled in the decedent's name."

The 1990 UPC elective share is exceedingly complex, but we can give a bare-bones outline here to show you the way it works. If you want to look at the exact language of the Uniform Probate Code, you can retrieve it from the Uniform Laws Annotated database on Westlaw.

Uniform Probate Code §2-203 (1990, as amended in 1993) combines into one augmented estate the following:

§2-204 — the value of the decedent's net probate estate;
§2-205(1) — the value of the decedent's nonprobate transfers to other persons than the surviving spouse, including:

(i) property over which the decedent had a general power of appointment or a power of revocation, whether the power was created by the decedent or another;

(ii) the decedent's fractional share of joint tenancy property;

(iii) the decedent's ownership interest in property with a payable-on-death designation; and

(iv) proceeds of insurance on the decedent's life owned by the decedent payable to any person other than the surviving spouse.

§2-205(2) — the value of property transferred in any of the following forms by the decedent during marriage:

(i) any irrevocable transfer in which the decedent retained the right to possession or income from the property for life;

(ii) any transfer in which the decedent created a power over income or property for the benefit of the decedent or his estate.

§2-205(3) — the value of property that passed during marriage and during the two years before the decedent's death, including:

(i) any property that would have been included in the augmented estate under paragraphs (1) or (2) had the transfer not been made; and

(ii) any transfer of property to any person other than the surviving spouse to the extent it exceeds $10,000 to any one donee in either of the two years preceding death.

§2-206 — the value of the decedent's nonprobate transfers to the surviving spouse; and

§2-207 — the value of the surviving spouse's property and the value of the surviving spouse's nonprobate transfers to others that would have been included in her augmented estate had she been the decedent.

The surviving spouse is entitled to a percentage, determined by the accrual method of UPC §2-202, supra page 483, of the total value of the decedent's augmented estate. Hence:

Case 4. H and *W* have been married for 25 years, and *W* is entitled to an elective share of 50 percent. *H*'s augmented estate consists of:

(a)	$100,000	probate estate, devised to *A*
(b)	$150,000	nonprobate transfers to others than *W*
(c)	$ 25,000	life insurance payable to *W*
(d)	$ 50,000	*H*'s half interest in joint tenancy held with *W*
(e)	$ 75,000	*W*'s property
(f)	$ 50,000	*W*'s half interest in the joint tenancy
	$450,000	

W has an elective share of 50 percent of the whole, or $225,000. Since *W* owns $75,000 in her own name, this amount is credited against her elective share, reducing it to $150,000. Also credited against the elective share are $25,000 in life insurance received by *W*, $50,000 for *H*'s half of the joint tenancy, and $50,000 for *W*'s half of the joint tenancy. Thus, the amount of *W*'s elective share payable out of *H*'s probate estate and nonprobate transfers is $25,000.

Observe that the 1990 UPC includes in the augmented estate life insurance owned by the decedent, whereas the 1969 Code did not include life insurance.

Although the revisers wanted the elective share to resemble the results of a community property system, differences remain. In addition to the differences noted earlier, the 1990 UPC augmented estate includes all property of both spouses, and not only property acquired from earnings. Community property, owned equally by the spouses, includes only earnings and acquisitions from earnings. It does not apply to property brought to the marriage or acquired by gift or inheritance, which is the separate property of the acquiring spouse. The decedent spouse can dispose of his separate property any way he likes; the surviving spouse has no claim to it.

The revisers justify including all property of the spouses in the redesigned elective share on the ground that it avoids problems of classifying property as community (earned) or separate, particularly when the couple has mixed their property. On the other hand, by including all property of the spouses in the elective share, the 1990 UPC makes it impossible for one spouse to keep his or her property acquired before marriage or by inheritance free of the elective share of the other spouse without the consent of the other spouse.

PROBLEMS AND NOTE

1. Prior to his second marriage, *H* creates an irrevocable trust, reserving the right to income for life, remainder to his daughter *A*. The trustee, a bank, has the power to dip into principal if necessary for *H*'s support. At *H*'s death thereafter, is his second wife entitled to reach the trust to satisfy her elective share under UPC §2-205? Suppose that *H* had made the transfer after marrying his second wife. What result? See Rena C. Seplowitz, Transfers Prior to Marriage and the Uniform Probate Code's Redesigned Elective Share: Why the Partnership is Not Yet Complete, 26 Ind. L. Rev. 1 (1991) (arguing that premarital transfers under which the decedent retained substantial rights should be included in the augmented estate). A transfer by the decedent before marriage, retaining a life estate, is subject to the elective share in New York (infra page 512).

2. Should life insurance owned by the decedent be subject to the elective share? The 1969 UPC exempted it. The 1990 UPC included

it. The life insurance industry has fought this, just as it has fought allowing the policy beneficiary to be changed by will. What is the reason for the opposition?

In the chapter on federal estate taxation at pages 1013-1014, you will see that the life insurance industry has been successful in obtaining favorable treatment from Congress in taxing life insurance.

3.   For analysis and discussion of the UPC augmented estate, see Patricia G. Roberts, The 1990 Uniform Probate Code's Elective Share Provisions — West Virginia's Enactment Paves the Way, 95 W. Va. L. Rev. 55 (1992); Lawrence W. Waggoner, The Multiple-Marriage Society and Spousal Rights Under the Revised Uniform Probate Code, 76 Iowa L. Rev. 223 (1991); Charles H. Whitebread, The Uniform Probate Code's Nod to the Partnership Theory of Marriage: The 1990 Elective Share Revisions, 11 Prob. L.J. 125 (1992). The 1990 UPC elective share provisions have been adopted in less than a dozen states, mainly in the Great Plains.

(3)   OTHER STATUTES

In 1965, New York replaced the illusory transfer test (see supra page 505) with a statutory scheme for subjecting some nonprobate transfers to the elective share. N.Y. Est., Powers & Trusts Law §5-1.1 (1981). In 1992, New York revised its elective share again, rejecting both the sliding scale fraction of the 1990 UPC and the 1990 UPC's redesigned augmented estate. N.Y. Est., Powers & Trusts Law §5-1.1-A (1998). New York now gives the surviving spouse $50,000 or one-third of the decedent's net estate, whichever is greater. (When combined with New York's generous personal property set-aside for the surviving spouse of $56,000 (see supra page 477), the elective share ensures that a spouse is entitled to the entire estate if its value is in the range of $100,000.) The decedent's estate, subject to the elective share, includes the probate estate and the following will substitutes:

(a)   gifts causa mortis;
(b)   gifts made within one year before death, except gifts not exceeding $10,000 per person;
(c)   savings account (Totten) trusts;
(d)   joint bank accounts, to the extent of the decedent's contribution;
(e)   joint tenancies and tenancies by the entireties, to the extent of the decedent's contribution;
(f)   property payable on death to a person other than the decedent;

(g)   lifetime transfers in which the decedent retained possession or life income or "a power to revoke such disposition or a power to consume, invade or dispose of the principal threof."

(h)   pension plans or the like; and

(i)   any property over which the decedent had a general power of appointment enabling him to appoint the property to whomever he pleases.

The amount of the elective share is reduced by deducting the value of any interest, other than a life estate, which passes from the decedent to the surviving spouse by intestacy, by will, or by will substitute. See N.Y. Est., Powers & Trusts Law §5-1.1-A(a)(4)(A).

Delaware takes a different approach. It defines the property subject to the elective share as all property includible in the decedent's gross estate under the federal estate tax, whether or not the decedent files an estate tax return. If a nonprobate transfer is taxable at death (and a revocable trust is, as are P.O.D. contracts and joint tenancies), the surviving spouse — as well as Uncle Sam — can reach it. Del. Code Ann. tit. 12, §902 (1997). This approach has the advantage of incorporating into elective share law the well-defined standards of federal estate tax law, which have evolved out of long experience in dealing with decedents trying to avoid estate tax by lifetime transfers. For detailed examination and approval of using the federal estate tax laws to govern the elective share, see Susan N. Gary, Marital Partnership Theory and the Elective Share: Federal Estate Tax Law Provides a Solution, 49 U. Miami L. Rev. 567 (1995) (limiting the elective share to the part of the federal gross estate that is marital property acquired during marriage); Sidney Kwestel & Rena C. Seplowitz, Testamentary Substitutes: Retained Interests, Custodial Accounts and Contractual Transactions — A New Approach, 38 Am. U. L. Rev. 1 (1988). For discussion of what nonprobate transfers are subject to federal estate taxation, see infra pages 1009-1032.

In re Reynolds
Court of Appeals of New York, 1996
87 N.Y.2d 633, 664 N.E.2d 1209, 642 N.Y.S.2d 147

BELLACOSA, J.   This appeal raises for this Court's review the question whether an inter vivos trust, in which a deceased spouse retained a limited power of appointment, constitutes a testamentary substitute in violation of the surviving spouse's right of election (EPTL 5-1.1). The Appellate Division, with one Justice dissenting, found the trust was not subject to the right of election and ruled against the surviving spouse. This Court granted leave to appeal. We agree with the Surrogate's Court and the dissenting Justice that the trust was a testamentary substitute under the applicable statute and, thus, we modify the Appellate Division's order in that respect.

Appellant William Reynolds and decedent Dorothy Reynolds were married in 1963 and remained wed until her death in 1989. The decedent had four children from a previous marriage. On May 11, 1989, Dorothy Reynolds, suffering from adverse health, created a trust for the purpose of qualifying for Medicaid benefits in the event that nursing home care was needed. She named two of her children from a previous marriage as trustees and, pursuant to the terms of the trust, transferred the majority of her assets to the trust while designating her children as remainder beneficiaries. As the settlor of the trust, she relinquished all right, title and interest in the property thus transferred, except for retaining the right to appoint remainder beneficiaries at any time prior to the termination of the trust. The limitation on the exercise of the retained power was that the settlor could not appoint to herself, her spouse, her creditors, or her estate and its creditors. The trust agreement fixed a termination date of one day prior to the death of the settlor.

Dorothy Reynolds died on August 29, 1989, leaving her entire estate to her children from a previous marriage. The Surrogate's Court, Onondaga County, admitted her will to probate on May 14, 1991. Appellant, her surviving spouse, filed a notice of election, which was given effect by the Surrogate's Court (EPTL 5-1.1). The election and the decree effectuating it are not at issue here.

Subsequently, however, appellant filed objections to the proposed accounting for the estate. He particularly objected to the exclusion of inter vivos trust assets from the estate accounting for purposes of computing his elective share. The Surrogate sustained the objection and decreed that the assets of the trust were part of decedent's estate.

The Appellate Division disagreed and modified so much of the decree as had included the trust in the estate for purposes of determining appellant's elective share. The Appellate Division held that the trust was not a testamentary substitute under EPTL 5-1.1 because the transfer was irrevocable and the decedent had relinquished the right to appoint herself or her estate as beneficiary. As so modified, the Appellate Division affirmed. The validity of the trust, as such, is also not at issue on this appeal.

The answer to the question of whether the decedent's inter vivos trust constitutes a testamentary substitute depends on the application of EPTL 5-1.1 (b) (1) (E). That statute ordains that a transfer of property during the lifetime of a donor may be deemed a testamentary substitute when the disposition is "in trust or otherwise, to the extent that the decedent at the date of his [or her] death retained, either alone or in conjunction with another person, by the express provisions of the disposing instrument, a power to revoke such disposition or a power to consume, invade or dispose of the principal."[12] In construing and applying this important safeguard, this Court has strongly reinforced the legislative intent and history underlying its enactment (Matter of Riefberg, 58 N.Y.2d 134, 139; Matter of Agioritis, 40 N.Y.2d 646, 649-650).

The context of this dispute is the surviving spouse's right of election, whose roots are found in former Decedent Estate Law §18, which, in turn, abolished the common-law rights of dower and curtesy. In their place, a surviving spouse was given a right to elect to take a percentage share of a deceased spouse's estate, limited to assets passing under a will.

Experience developed under that statute indicated the right of election protection for surviving spouses could be easily evaded by timely use of various inter vivos transfers. Adjudicative efforts to recapture asset transfers, which had as their sole purpose the circumvention of the rights of the surviving spouse, proved inadequate or uneven (compare, Matter of Halpern, 303 N.Y. 33; Matter of Crystal, 39 N.Y.2d 934; with Newman v. Dore, 275 N.Y. 371). Thus, the Legislature initiated a special study for the purpose of proposing legislation which would more effectively protect the survival rights of spouses (3d Report of Temp St Commn on Estates ["Bennett Report"], 1964 N.Y. Legis Doc No. 19, at 11). The Bennett Report concluded that certain inter vivos transfers should be subject to a surviving spouse's right of election against deceased spouse's total testamentary dispositional plan.

The Bennett Report suggested that the Legislature follow the basic approach outlined in the Report of the New York State Bar Association Committee on Trusts and Estates, which declared that "whatever test or approach is used, the following types of transfers might be considered subject to the elective rights of the surviving spouse . . . [including those] where a power of appointment has been retained" (1964 N.Y. Legis Doc No. 19, at 138). That is the only type at issue here. While the precise proposed phrasing did not find its way into the law, the enacted version had the same goal and purpose, as reflected in EPTL 5-1.1. The history and language thus strongly demonstrate that the intent behind the "testamentary substitute" protection for the surviving spouse's right of election was to fold into the estate

---

12. Because Dorothy Reynolds died in 1989, the question of whether her trust is a testamentary substitute must be determined under EPTL 5-1.1. That statute has been replaced by EPTL 5-1.1-A for decedents dying on or after September 1, 1992. [The language describing the power is the same in both EPTL §5-1.1 and §5-1.1-A. — Eds.]

[Dorothy Reynolds also retained the right to the income from the trust. Under N.Y. EPTL §5-1.1, a transfer in irrevocable trust, with the settlor retaining the income, was not subject to the elective share. In 1992 this was changed. Under N.Y. EPTL §5-1.1-A(b)(F), enacted in 1992, the retention of the trust income subjects the trust principal to the elective share. — Eds.]

those assets over which a settlor retains meaningful control in addition to the right to receive the lifetime income.

Applying the reasonable and fair interpretation of the statute's words and purpose to the instant case, we conclude that Dorothy Reynolds' retained power of appointment, though limited, left her with meaningful control over the trust during her lifetime, in contravention of the statute's explicit and intended protection. Because the settlor, despite her general relinquishment of title and ownership of the property, was free to designate any person, charity or entity as a beneficiary of the trust except for herself, her spouse or her estate and creditors, she possessed personal power to execute what were essentially testamentary transfers to any number of other specific beneficiaries of her choosing. This was a functional substitute allowing disposal of the entire trust corpus by way of one or a series of specific bequests that constitute a forbidden reserved "power to consume, invade or dispose" (EPTL 5-1.1 [b] [1] [E]). The power here to designate many beneficiaries or classes is essentially indistinguishable from the power to dispose of the principal of the trust as contemplated by the statute (EPTL 5-1.1 [b] [1] [E]; see, Matter of DeVita, 141 A.D.2d 46, 53).

The respondents' estate representatives nevertheless urge a narrow construction of the statute, relying on this Court's Matter of Crystal (39 N.Y.2d 934, supra) and the Appellate Division's holding in the instant case. We held in *Crystal* that the retention of a power of appointment does not, by itself, cause a transfer to be deemed a testamentary disposition or substitute. Notably, though, the transfer there occurred prior to the effective date of the testamentary substitute statute that governs this case. Thus, *Crystal* does not support or compel the result that respondents urge. Moreover, the restrained reading and reach they would impose on the statutory language would frustrate the Legislature's remedial intent to provide greater protection for surviving spouses, not only against outright disinheritance, but also against attempted lifetime evasions of the plain import of the statutory scheme and its balanced policy.

A brief comment is also necessary to answer respondents' argument that the power of appointment terminated one day prior to the settlor's death and, therefore, was not a testamentary power. This power of appointment is no less testamentary here because it purports to expire the day before the settlor's death, particularly since this limitation is temporally indeterminate. Since the termination date of the power cannot be ascertained with any certainty until after the death of the settlor, it is illusory in this case and effects no cognizable or realistic limitation on the exercise of the meaningful power retained by the settlor during virtually her entire lifetime.

Accordingly, the order of the Appellate Division should be modified, with costs payable out of the estate to all parties appearing separately and filing separate briefs, by reinstating the order of Surrogate's Court, Onondaga County, in accordance with this opinion and, as so modified, affirmed.

PROBLEM AND NOTE

1.   Would the power retained by Dorothy Reynolds in the *Reynolds* case cause the property to be included in the augmented estate of the 1969 Uniform Probate Code? In the augmented estate of the 1990 Uniform Probate Code? Would it be subject to the elective share in Delaware, which has incorporated by reference the taxable estate of the Internal Revenue Code? See Internal Revenue Code §2036(a)(2), §2038 (1988), infra pages 1014, 1027.

2.   If a couple wants to opt out of an elective share system, they may do so by a waiver of rights (discussed below). Or the couple may establish an Alaska Community Property Trust. Couples not domiciled in Alaska can transfer their personal property into an Alaska Community Property Trust and provide in the trust agreement that the property is community property. Alaska Stat. §34.75.060(b) (1998). This trust, appointing as trustee a bank in Alaska (or an Alaskan branch bank of a bank in the lower 48 states), will be governed by Alaska law if the settlors so intend. A major advantage of an Alaska Community Property Trust is that it apparently enables residents of non-community property states to take advantage of Internal Revenue Code §1014(b)(6), which provides that, upon the death of one spouse the entire community property is given a stepped-up basis (the value of the property on the date of the spouse's death). The surviving spouse will thus have to pay no tax on capital gain incurred before the decedent's death if she sells the property. See infra page 528. No ruling by the Internal Revenue Service has yet been made, however, as to whether property in an Alaska Community Property Trust created by nonresidents is community property under IRS §1014(b)(6).

c.   Waiver

Uniform Probate Code (1990, as amended in 1993)

§2-213.   WAIVER OF RIGHT TO ELECT AND OF OTHER RIGHTS

(a) The right of election of a surviving spouse and the rights of the surviving spouse to homestead allowance, exempt property, and family allowance, or any of them, may be waived, wholly or partially, before or after marriage, by a written contract, agreement, or waiver signed by the surviving spouse.

(b) A surviving spouse's waiver is not enforceable if the surviving spouse proves that:

(1) he [or she] did not execute the waiver voluntarily; or

(2) the waiver was unconscionable when it was executed and, before execution of the waiver, he [or she]:

(i) was not provided a fair and reasonable disclosure of the property or financial obligations of the decedent;

(ii) did not voluntarily and expressly waive, in writing, any right to disclosure of the property or financial obligations of the decedent beyond the disclosure provided; and

(iii) did not have, or reasonably could not have had, an adequate knowledge of the property or financial obligations of the decedent.

(c) An issue of unconscionability of a waiver is for decision by the court as a matter of law.

(d) Unless it provides to the contrary, a waiver of "all rights," or equivalent language, in the property or estate of a present or prospective spouse or a complete property settlement entered into after or in anticipation of separation or divorce is a waiver of all rights of elective share, homestead allowance, exempt property, and family allowance by each spouse in the property of the other and a renunciation by each of all benefits that would otherwise pass to him [or her] from the other by intestate succession or by virtue of any will executed before the waiver or property settlement.

UPC §2-213 incorporates the standards by which the validity of a premarital agreement is determined under the Uniform Premarital Agreement Act §6. For discussion, see Gail F. Brod, Premarital Agreements and Gender Justice, 6 Yale J.L. & Feminism 229 (1994); Note, Planning for Love: The Politics of Prenuptial Agreements, 49 Stan. L. Rev. 887 (1997) (arguing that abuse of these agreements is the best handled by requiring both parties to consult independent counsel).

For discussion of when husband and wife need separate lawyers and when it is ethical for one lawyer to represent both, see Am. Bar Assn. Special Committee Report, Husband and Wife, 28 Real Prop., Prob. & Tr. J. 762 (1994); John R. Price, Ethics in Action not Ethics in Inaction, 1995 U. Miami Inst. Est. Plan. ¶700.

In re Estate of Garbade
New York Supreme Court,
Appellate Division, Third Department, 1995
221 A.D.2d 844, 633 N.Y.S.2d 878

MERCURE, J.   Respondent and J. Robert Garbade (hereinafter decedent) were married on February 2, 1990. Each had been previously married and divorced. Decedent was a wealthy executive who owned his own construction company and had interests in other enterprises; respondent was unemployed and brought no assets to the marriage. Prior to the wedding, respondent and decedent executed a prenuptial agreement, under the terms of which each waived any right to, inter alia, maintenance, equitable distribution or community property rights with regard to assets titled in the name of the other or, of primary relevance here, an elective share of the other's estate. However, the agreement required decedent to maintain a $100,000 policy of insurance on his life for respondent's benefit.

In July 1992, decedent died unexpectedly at the age of 52, survived by respondent and petitioners, his two sons. Petitioners thereafter qualified as personal representatives of decedent's estate. Notwithstanding her waiver and the fact that she received assets totaling approximately $340,000 by virtue of decedent's death, respondent filed notice of her election to take her share of decedent's estate pursuant to EPTL 5-1.1. Petitioners thereafter moved for summary judgment setting aside respondent's right of election as barred by the waiver contained in the parties' prenuptial agreement. In defense of the motion, respondent alleged that the waiver of her statutory right to elect against decedent's estate was procured by fraud, misrepresentation, duress, imposition or undue influence. Surrogate's Court granted petitioners' motion and authorized the entry of judgment setting aside respondent's notice of election. Respondent now appeals.

We affirm. Fundamentally, "a duly executed antenuptial agreement is given the same presumption of legality as any other contract, commercial or otherwise. It is presumed to be valid in the absence of fraud" (Matter of Sunshine, 51 A.D.2d 326, 327, 381 N.Y.S.2d 260, affd 40 N.Y.2d 875, 389 N.Y.S.2d 344, 357 N.E.2d 999; see, Panossian v. Panossian, 172 A.D.2d 811, 812, 569 N.Y.S.2d 182; Brassey v. Brassey, 154 A.D.2d 293, 294-295, 546 N.Y.S.2d 370; Matter of Zach, 144 A.D.2d 19, 21, 536 N.Y.S.2d 774). Moreover, the party attacking the validity of the agreement has the burden of coming forward with evidence of fraud, which, in the absence of facts from which concealment may reasonably be inferred, will not be presumed (see, Matter of Phillips, 293 N.Y. 483, 490-491, 58 N.E.2d 504; Matter of Sunshine, supra, at 327-328; see also, Matter of Zach, supra). In light of that standard, even crediting every factual allegation advanced by respondent and drawing the most favorable inferences therefrom, we agree with Surrogate's Court that respondent has raised no legitimate triable issue as to whether the prenuptial agreement and, more to the point, respondent's waiver of her right to elect against decedent's estate was the product of fraud, misrepresentation, duress, imposition or undue influence.

Respondent presented evidence establishing at most that (1) it was decedent, and not she, who first raised the issue of a prenuptial agreement and requested that one be executed prior to the wedding, (2) the agreement was prepared by decedent's attorneys, at his request and in accordance with his direction, (3) the prenuptial agreement was executed only a few hours prior to the parties' wedding, (4) respondent did not seek or obtain independent legal counsel and the agreement was not read by her or to her before she signed it, (5) respondent was not specifically advised that the agreement provided for a waiver of her right to elect against decedent's will, and (6) respondent was not furnished with a copy of the agreement.

At the same time, it is uncontroverted that (1) respondent readily acceded to decedent's request that they enter into a prenuptial agreement and willingly signed the instrument because she did not want any of decedent's money or property, she only wanted to be his wife, (2) respondent was advised to obtain the services of independent counsel, (3) respondent was given an adequate opportunity to read the instrument before she signed it, and (4) prior to executing the prenuptial agreement, respondent was provided with detailed disclosure of decedent's $2.5 million net worth.

In our view, respondent has established nothing more than her own dereliction in failing to acquaint herself with the provisions of the agreement and to obtain the benefit of independent legal counsel. Although this dereliction may have caused her to be ignorant of the precise terms of the agreement, the fact remains that, absent fraud or other misconduct, parties are bound by their signatures (Pommer v. Trustco Bank, 183 A.D.2d 976, 978, 583 N.Y.S.2d 553, lv dismissed, lv denied 81 N.Y.2d 758). Further, the absence of independent counsel will not of itself warrant setting aside the agreement (see, Panossian v. Panossian, supra, at 813). There being no competent evidence of fraud, respondent has merely resorted to reliance upon a number of innocuous circumstances (such as the fact that the wedding date was changed from February 14 to February 2, 1990 to accommodate a Florida trip, that decedent's attorney did not finish drafting the agreement until shortly prior to the wedding and, incredibly, that the parties went out to lunch before going to sign the agreement) to fuel speculation that fraud was practiced upon her (see, Matter of Zach, 144 A.D.2d 19, 21, 536 N.Y.S.2d 774, supra).

Respondent's remaining contentions have been considered and found lacking in merit.

Ordered that the order and judgment are affirmed, with costs.

IN RE GRIEFF, 92 N.Y.2d 341, 703 N.E.2d 752, 680 N.Y.S.2d 894 (1998). In a prenuptial agreement between a man, 77, and a woman, 65, the parties waived the statutory right of election as against the estate of the other. Three months after the marriage, the husband died, leaving a will devising his entire estate to his children from a prior marriage. The wife filed a petition for a statutory elective share. The surrogate invalidated the prenuptial agreement on the ground that the husband "was in a position of great influence and advantage" in his relationship with his wife-to-be. The surrogate found the husband exercised bad faith and overreaching, particularly noting the husband "selected and paid for" the wife's attorney.

The appellate division reversed on the law, simply declaring that the wife had failed to establish that her execution of the prenuptial agreement was procured by her then-fiancé's fraud or overreaching. The court of appeals reversed the appellate division. The court of appeals held that the contestant of a prenuptial agreement must "establish a fact-based, particularized inequality before a proponent of a prenuptial agreement suffers a shift in the burden to disprove fraud or overreaching." Inasmuch as the appellate division did not undertake to determine whether, based on all the relevant evidence, the nature of the relationship at the time the agreement was signed was such as to shift the burden of proof to the husband's children, the court of appeals remanded the case to the appellate division to make that determination.

The court of appeals held that "a particularized and exceptional scrutiny" must be given to prenuptial agreements, inasmuch as the relationship between prospective spouses is "by its nature permeated with trust, confidence, honesty and reliance."

4.   Rights of Surviving Spouse in Community Property

a.   Basic Information

As explained earlier, eight states — containing more than one-fourth of the population of the United States — have a system of community property. These community property states, sweeping around the southwest border of the country from the Mississippi River to Canada, are Louisiana, Texas, New Mexico, Arizona, California, Nevada, Washington, and Idaho. In addition, Wisconsin must now be considered a community property state since it has adopted the Uniform Marital Property Act (providing for community property under the name of "marital property"). And Alaska permits spouses to elect community property rather than separate property, if they so choose.

Community property in the United States is a community of acquests: Husband and wife own the earnings and acquisitions from earnings of both spouses during marriage in undivided equal shares. Whatever is bought with earnings is community property. All property that is not community property is the separate property of one spouse or the other or, in the case of a tenancy in common or joint tenancy, of both. Separate property includes property acquired before marriage and property acquired during marriage by gift or inheritance. In Idaho, Louisiana, and Texas, income from separate property is community property. (This rule is also adopted by the Uniform Marital Property Act.) In the other community property states, income from separate property retains its separate character. Where the characterization of the property is doubtful, there is a strong presumption that the property is community property.

Where property has been commingled by the spouse, or acquired from both separate and community funds, states often have a rule about how to characterize the property in a particular situation. For example, if a husband uses his earnings after marriage to pay premiums on a life insurance policy acquired before marriage, some states, applying the inception-of-title rule, hold the policy remains the husband's separate property and the community is entitled only to a return of premiums paid with interest. Other states apply a pro-rata share rule to insurance policies, dividing the policy proceeds between separate and community property according to the proportion of payments paid.

To avoid tracing problems, couples can make agreements regarding the character of their property. By agreement they may change separate property into community property, or they may change community property into a joint tenancy, a tenancy in common, or sole ownership of one spouse. Texas has a peculiar rule. Spouses can convert community property into separate property, but they cannot convert separate property into community property by agreement.

Couples may agree that all their property is held as community property in order to achieve favorable income tax treatment given community property. Upon the death of one spouse, the entire value of community property receives a stepped-up basis for determining capital gains when the property is sold thereafter. Any appreciation in value between acquisition and the date of the spouse's death is never taxed as capital gain. If the property is owned as separate property by the decedent spouse, either alone, in joint tenancy, or in tenancy in common, only the decedent's interest in the property receives a stepped-up basis. See infra page 528.

Upon the death of one spouse, the deceased spouse can dispose of his or her half of the community assets. The surviving spouse owns the other half, which is not, of course, subject to testamentary disposition by the deceased spouse. The one-half of the community property belonging to the deceased spouse may be devised to whomever the decedent pleases, the same as separate property.

Because community property belongs to both, problems arise as to which spouse can manage the property and deal with third persons respecting the property. These problems may concern sale, leasing, or mortgaging the property or subjecting the property to creditors. Each community property state has statutes on this matter. Although these statutes differ in many details, we can indicate broadly the management roles. In Texas, the wife has sole management power over her earnings kept separate and the husband sole power over his. If the earnings are commingled, they are subject to the joint management of the spouses. In California and the other community property states, either the husband or wife, acting alone, has the power to manage community property. Statutes ordinarily require both spouses to join in transfers or mortgages of community real property, however.

In exercising management power, one spouse may sell community property to a purchaser for a valuable consideration, but a spouse cannot freely give away community property. States give various remedies to the nondonor spouse in case of a gift to a third party. Thus:

> *Case 5. H*, married to *W*, purchases a life insurance policy on his life with his earnings. The policy is community property. *H* names *A* as beneficiary. Upon *H*'s death, what are *W*'s rights in the policy proceeds? In California, *W* is entitled, after *H* dies, to set aside the gift to the extent of one-half. (During *H*'s life, *W* is entitled to set aside an entire gift and reclaim the property for the community, but, after *H* dies, a gift by *H* during life of community property is treated as if it were a devise by *H* of his half share.) In Texas, the manager of community property (*H* in this instance) can make reasonable gifts to others, but excessive gifts are deemed in fraud of the other spouse's rights. If the court finds the gift to have been in fraud of *W*'s rights, *W* is entitled to half the policy proceeds. See Givens v. Girard Life Insurance Co., 480 S.W.2d 421 (Tex. Civ. App. 1972). The other community property states divide between the California and Texas views, sometimes with variations.

Almost all the community property states follow the theory that husband and wife own equal shares in each item of community property at death. They do not own equal undivided shares in the aggregate of community property. Thus, if *H* and *W* own Blackacre (worth $50,000) and Whiteacre (worth $50,000), each owns a half share in each tract. *W*'s will cannot devise Blackacre to *H* and Whiteacre to *D*, her daughter by a previous marriage, even though *H* would end up receiving property equal to the value of his community share. (Divorce is different. In most community property states, the divorce court may award Blackacre to *H* and Whiteacre to *W*; it may award specific items of community property to one spouse or the other, provided each spouse ends up with a share of the aggregate value of community property.)

In jurisdictions applying a reasonable gifts rule to lifetime transfers and an item theory to death transfers, should nonprobate transfers to a person other than the spouse be treated as inter vivos transfers or death transfers? If they are death transfers, the surviving spouse is entitled to one-half of each. If they are inter vivos transfers, the surviving spouse may set aside only those transfers deemed unreasonable.

b.   Putting the Survivor to an Election

An estate planning device, known as the *widow's election*, developed in community property states in the days when the husband was the manager of community property and the wife was seen as a housewife without business experience. Even after statutes gave the wife equal management power, after many wives went into business, and after gender-neutral terms were widely adopted, the name "widow's election" is still used to describe this election plan, which may be applicable to widowers as well as to widows. In explaining the widow's election, we shall assume the husband dies first, which is true in most cases.

A widow's election involves a will executed by the husband devising *all* the community property in trust to pay the income to his wife for life, with remainder to others on the wife's death, and requiring the wife to elect between surrendering her half of the community property and taking under the husband's will. If the widow wants to share in her husband's trust, she must surrender her community property. The object of the widow's election is to create, at the death of the husband, one trust of all the community property — both the husband's half and the wife's half — paying the widow all the income for her life. In order to do this, the widow must consent to the transfer of her share of the community property by electing to take under the will. If the widow so elects, the situation is treated as though the widow transferred her one-half community interest to the trust in exchange for receiving a life estate in her husband's one-half community interest. If, instead, the widow elects against the will, she takes the one-half interest in community property to which she is entitled by law, but she forfeits the life estate in the husband's half of the community property devised to her by her husband's will.

The widow's election may have tax advantages, which flow from the fact that the widow has made an exchange for consideration. Observe what happens to title if the widow elects to take under her husband's will. Two transfers are made, one by the husband and one by the wife. The husband's will makes a testamentary transfer of his community property to his wife for life; by electing to take under her husband's will, the wife makes a transfer of her community property, retaining a life estate in her community share. The wife thus has received a life estate in her husband's half of the community property in exchange for transferring a remainder interest in her half of the community property.

This exchange for consideration has federal gift, estate, and income tax consequences. The estate and gift tax consequences may be moderately favorable, but the possible income tax disadvantage is such that most estate planners do not recommend a forced widow's election plan. See John R. Price, Contemporary Estate Planning §§9.23-9.39 (1992). Apart from the tax consequences, a forced election may leave the widow resentful at having to bend to her husband's will. The forced widow's election plan is now out of favor.

An alternative to a forced widow's election is a plan by husband and wife to transfer all the community property into a revocable trust, paying income to husband and wife for their joint lives and for the life of the survivor, remainder to their children or to others. The revocable trust becomes irrevocable upon the death of one spouse. This has none of the possible estate and gift tax benefits of a forced widow's election, because it is not an exchange of the widow's property for consideration. Nor does it have an income tax disadvantage. The joint revocable trust plan may be attractive to couples who want unified trust management of the community property after the death of one of the spouses and assurances that the trust corpus will pass to their issue upon the death of the surviving spouse.

5.   Migrating Couples and Multistate Property Holdings

The classic conflict-of-laws rules used to determine which state law governs marital property are:

(a)   The law of the situs controls problems related to land.

(b)   The law of the marital domicile at the time personal property is acquired controls the characterization of the property (that is, as separate or community).

(c)   The law of the marital domicile at the death of one spouse controls the survivor's marital rights.

The application of these rules is to be briefly examined in this subsection. For a thorough discussion, see Jeffrey A. Schoenblum, Multistate and Multinational Estate Planning §§10.01-10.14 (1982 & Supp. 1997).

It should be noted that although the state of the situs has the power to control its land, it may choose to apply the law of the marital domicile. Uniform Probate Code §2-202(d), for example, provides that the rights of a spouse to an elective share in land located in the state shall be governed by the law of the decedent's domicile at death.

a. Moving from Separate Property State to Community Property State

If a couple acquires property in a separate property state and moves to a community property state, serious problems of fairness to the surviving spouse may arise. The ownership of movable property is determined by the laws of the state where the couple is domiciled when the property is acquired. Thus, if the husband is the wage earner, all of the property is the husband's in a separate property state. The wife is protected by the elective share scheme. When the couple moves to a community property state, the property remains the husband's and is now characterized as the husband's separate property. If the couple remains domiciled in the community property state until the husband dies, the law of the state of domicile at date of death governs the disposition of movable property. If neither spouse works in the community property state, there may be no community property for the surviving spouse. Hence, as a result of the move, the wife loses protection of the elective share system provided by the state where the movable property was acquired and is not protected by the system of community property (which she would have if the couple had been domiciled in the community property state when the husband was working). See Estate of Hanau v. Hanau, 730 S.W.2d 663 (Tex. 1987); Russell J. Weintraub, Obstacles to Sensible Choice of Law for Determining Marital Property Rights on Divorce or in Probate: *Hanau* and the Situs Rule, 25 Hous. L. Rev. 1113 (1988).

Several community property states give a remedy to the surviving spouse in this situation. These states have a concept of *quasi-community property*. Quasi-community property is property owned by the husband or the wife acquired while domiciled elsewhere, which would have been characterized as community property if the couple had been domiciled in the community property state when the property was acquired.[13] Real property situated outside the state is not treated as quasi-community property, because the spouse retains in it any forced share or dower given by the law of the situs.[14] During the continuance of the marriage, quasi-community property is for most purposes treated as the separate property of the acquiring spouse. However,

---

13. Arizona, New Mexico, and Texas have adopted the quasi-community property concept for purposes of equitable division upon divorce. Quasi-community property is treated the same as community property in that situation. Ariz. Rev. Stat. §25-318 (1998); N.M. Stat. Ann. §40-3-8 (1998); Tex. Fam. Code §7.002 (1998). These states do not apply the quasi-community concept to dissolution of the marriage by death.

14. The surviving spouse of a couple domiciled in a separate property state who buy land in a community property state may have the same elective share in the land as she would have in land in the domiciliary state. See Cal. Prob. Code §120 (1998).

upon the death of the acquiring spouse, one-half of the quasi-community property belongs to the surviving spouse; the other half is subject to testamentary disposition by the decedent. If the nonacquiring spouse dies first, the quasi-community property belongs absolutely to the acquiring spouse; the nonacquiring spouse has no testamentary power over it. Quasi-community property is analogous to an elective share in the deceased spouse's property acquired from earnings while domiciled in another state. Cal. Prob. Code §§66, 101 (1998); Idaho Code §15-2-201 (1998); La. Civ. Code Ann. art. 3526 (1998; Wash. Rev. Code Ann. §26.16.220 (1998).

> *Case 6. H* and *W* are domiciled in Illinois. *H* saves $500,000 from his earnings, which he invests in stocks and bonds. In Illinois this is his separate property. *H* and *W* then move to California. The stocks and bonds become quasi-community property in California. Upon *H*'s death, *W* owns one-half of the stocks and bonds. If *W* dies first, she cannot dispose of any part of this wealth by will; *H* owns it all. If, instead, *H* and *W* had moved to Texas, on *H*'s death *W* would have no interest in the assets brought from Illinois.

To prevent a spouse from attempting to defeat the survivor's quasi-community property rights by inter vivos transfers, the surviving spouse may have the right to reach one-half of any nonprobate transfer of quasi-community property where the decedent retained possession or enjoyment, or the right to income, or the power to revoke or consume, or a right of survivorship. See Cal. Prob. Code §102 (1998). Cf. Idaho Code §15-2-202 (1998). These statutes are analogous to those enacted in separate property states to prevent avoidance of the elective share. See supra pages 507-513.

b. Moving from Community Property State to Separate Property State

Suppose that a husband and wife who have acquired community personal property move to a separate property state. What is the effect of this move on the community property? Generally, a change in domicile from a community property state to a separate property state does not change the preexisting property rights of the husband or wife. Community property continues to be community property when the couple and the property move to a separate property state. The Uniform Disposition of Community Property Rights at Death Act (1983), enacted in many separate property states, provides that community property brought into the state (and all property — including land in the state — traceable to community property) remains community property for purposes of testamentary disposition, unless the spouses have agreed to convert it into separate property. Each spouse has the right to dispose of one-half of the community property by will. Under the Uniform Act, community property brought into the state is not subject to the elective share. See Stanley M. Johanson, The Migrating Client: Estate Planning for the Couple from a Community Property State, 9 U. Miami Inst. Est. Plan. ¶¶800 et seq. (1975).

Any couple moving community property into a separate property state should be careful to preserve its community nature, if such is desirable. If the community property is sold and the proceeds used to purchase other assets, title to the new property should be taken in the name of husband and wife as community property. If resistance from transfer agents, bankers, or title companies — who may know little about community property — is met, the husband and wife should take title in the name of both spouses, at the same time executing a written agreement reciting their intention to retain the asset as community property. Or the spouses may preserve the community property character of their property by creating a revocable trust of the community property and stating in the trust instrument that all property of the trust is community property.

Because lawyers in separate property states sometimes lack understanding of the community property system, lawyers may recommend to couples bringing community property into a separate property state that they change the title to joint tenancy or some other separate property form. If this is done, with the intent of changing community property into a common law concurrent interest, the income tax advantage of community property is lost and the lawyer could be liable for malpractice. An example:

> *Case 7.* *H* and *W*, domiciled in Texas, buy property for $100,000. Since the property is paid for out of *H* and *W*'s earnings, it is community property. At *H*'s death several years later, the property is worth $300,000. Under the federal estate tax law one-half the value of the community property ($150,000) is subject to estate tax at *H*'s death (but it qualifies for the marital deduction if devised to *W*, thus incurring no estate taxation). *Note, however, the income tax consequences.* At the death of one spouse, the *entire* value of community property acquires a stepped-up basis for income tax purposes, i.e., its value at *H*'s death ($300,000). Internal Revenue Code of 1986, §§1014(a) and 1014(b)(6). If *W* sells the property after *H*'s death for $325,000, she will pay income tax only on $25,000 capital gain.
>
> Suppose that before *H* dies, *H* and *W* move to Massachusetts. A Massachusetts lawyer advises them to change the title to the property to *H* and *W* as joint tenants. *H* and *W* do this. Then *H* dies, and the property is worth $300,000. The estate tax consequences of joint tenancy are the same as if the property had remained community property, but the income tax consequences are very different. Only one-half the value of joint tenancy property receives a stepped-up basis at *H*'s death. Rev. Rul. 68-80, 1968-1

C.B. 348. *W*'s new basis is $50,000 (her half of the old basis) plus $150,000 (stepped-up basis on *H*'s half) or $200,000. If *W* sells the property for $325,000, she will pay an income tax on $125,000 capital gain. Income tax on $100,000, which could have been avoided, is the result of advice by a lawyer unknowledgeable about community property.

The Commissioner of Internal Revenue has ruled that under the provisions of the Uniform Marital Property Act, as enacted in Wisconsin, the rights of the spouses are community property rights for purposes of federal income taxation. Rev. Rul. 87-13, 1987-1 Cum. Bull. 20. Hence couples domiciled in Wisconsin are entitled in the stepped-up basis given all community property at death.

A new form of community property has been proposed and adopted in several community property states — community property with a right of survivorship (as in a joint tenancy). Under this form, the decedent spouse cannot dispose of his share of the community property by will; it passes under a right of survivorship to the surviving spouse. This form of community property is now an option in Arizona, Idaho, Nevada, New Mexico, Texas, Washington, and Wisconsin (called survivorship marital property). The purpose of this is to avoid probate costs on the passage of the decedent's half of community property to the surviving spouse — in effect making community property with right of survivorship nonprobate property. California took another route to solve the probate cost problem. Cal. Prob. Code §13500 (1998) provides that when property passes at death to the decedent's spouse, no administration is necessary unless the surviving spouse elects administration. California declined to permit community property with right of survivorship because of the fear that it would be treated by the Internal Revenue Service as joint tenancy property, not qualifying for the stepped-up basis, and because it was called community property would mislead couples into thinking it would so qualify. The Internal Revenue Service has not yet ruled definitively on this matter. See Arthur W. Andrews, Community Property with Right of Survivorship: Uneasy Lies the Head that Wears a Crown of Surviving Spouse for Federal Income Tax Basis Purposes, 17 Va. Tax Rev. 577 (1998).

PROBLEM

H and *W* are domiciled in New York. *H* has assets of $3 million in his name; his tax basis for the assets is $75,000. *W* has assets of $200,000. *W* is diagnosed with terminal cancer. If *W* and *H* are agreeable, would you advise them to move to California and after being domiciled there for a year convert all their assets to community property? If *H* sold the assets after *W*'s death, what would be the income tax consequences?

If *H* and *W* can convert their assets into community property after they move to California, with advantageous tax consequences, why cannot they stay in New York and by agreement convert all their assets to community property? In Stein-Sapir v. Stein-Sapir, 52 A.D. 115, 382 N.Y.S.2d 799 (1976), a New York couple married in Mexico, which requires a couple to elect community property or separate property when the marriage license is issued. The couple elected community property. Upon divorce several years later in New York, the New York court held that the couple's property was community property, and the wife owned one-half of the property acquired with her husband's earnings.

If *H* and *W* do not want to move to California or marry in Mexico, they can establish an Alaska Community Property Trust, which will convert their separate property to community property and likely qualify for the stepped-up basis on all community property on the death of one spouse. See supra pages 528-529; Jonathan C. Blattmacher, Howard M. Zaritsky & Mark L. Ascher, Tax Planning With Consensual Community Property: Alaska's New Community Property Law, 33 Real Prop., Prob. & Tr. J. 615 (1999).

6.   *Spouse Omitted from Premarital Will*

Estate of Shannon

California Court of Appeal, Fourth District, 1990
224 Cal. App. 3d 1148, 274 Cal. Rptr. 338

HUFFMAN, P.J.   Gilbert A. Brown, executor of the will of Lila Demos Shannon (also known as Lila King Demos), appeals on behalf of Lila's estate from an order of the probate court denying her petition for determination of heirship as an omitted spouse under Probate Code[15] section 6560 in the estate of Russell Donovan Shannon. We reverse.

FACTUAL AND PROCEDURAL BACKGROUND

On January 25, 1974, Russell, an unmarried widower, executed his last will and testament, naming his daughter, Beatrice Marie Saleski, executrix and sole beneficiary. The will also provided his grandson, Donald Saleski, would inherit his estate in the event Beatrice did not survive him for "thirty (30) days" and contained a disinheritance clause which provided as follows:

---

15. All statutory references are to the Probate Code unless otherwise specified. When referring to statutory subparts we omit repetition of the word "subdivision."

SEVENTH: I have intentionally omitted all other living persons and relatives. If any devises, legatee, beneficiary under this Will, or any legal heir of mine, person or persons claiming under any of them, or other person or persons shall contest this Will or attack or seek to impair or invalidate any of its provisions or conspire with or voluntarily assist anyone attempting to do any of those things mentioned, in that event, I specifically disinherit such person or persons.

If any Court finds that such person or persons are lawful heirs and entitled to participate in my estate, then in that event I bequeath each of them the sum of one ($1.00) dollar and no more.

On April 27, 1986, Russell married Lila. On February 22, 1988, Russell died. He did not make any changes in his will after his marriage to Lila and before his death. His 1974 will was admitted to probate May 9, 1988, and Beatrice was named executrix of his estate.

On September 27, 1988, Lila filed a petition for family allowance (§6540), to set apart probate homestead (§26520) and for determination of entitlement to estate distribution as an omitted surviving spouse (§§1080, 6560). The court denied the petition for family allowance and Lila withdrew her petition to set apart probate homestead. The remaining issue of Lila's entitlement to share in Russell's estate was heard December 14, 1988, and taken under submission.

On March 24, 1989, the probate court issued its order denying Lila's petition to determine heirship. She timely appealed only from this latter order.

During the pendency of this appeal, Lila died and her son Brown was named executor of her estate and substituted in her place as appellant.[16] He has objected to the distribution of Russell's estate until after this appeal is decided.

DISCUSSION

On appeal, Lila contends she was a pretermitted spouse within the meaning of section 6560 and does not fall under any of the exceptions under section 6561 which would preclude her from sharing in Russell's estate as an omitted spouse. We agree and reverse.

Section 6560 . . . states:

Except as provided in Section 6561, if a testator fails to provide by will for his or her surviving spouse who married the testator after the execution of the will, the omitted spouse shall receive a share in the estate consisting of the following property in the estate:

(a) The one-half of the community property that belongs to the testator. . . .

(b) The one-half of the quasi-community property that belongs to the testator. . . .

16. In this opinion, we refer to Lila's estate as Lila.

(c) A share of the separate property of the testator equal in value to that which the spouse would have received if the testator had died intestate, but in no event is the share to be more than one-half the value of the separate property in the estate.

Section 6561 states:

The spouse does not receive a share of the estate under Section 6560 if any of the following is established:
(a) The testator's failure to provide for the spouse in the will was intentional and that intention appears from the will.
(b) The testator provided for the spouse by transfer outside the will and the intention that the transfer be in lieu of a testamentary provision is shown by statements of the testator or from the amount of the transfer or by other evidence.
(c) The spouse made a valid agreement waiving the right to share in the testator's estate.

It is well established section 6560 reflects a strong statutory presumption of revocation of the will as to the omitted spouse based upon public policy. (Estate of Duke (1953) 41 Cal. 2d 509, 261 P.2d 235.) Such presumption is rebutted only if circumstances are such as to fall within the literal terms of one of the exceptions listed in section 6561. (See Estate of Sheldon (1977) 75 Cal. App. 3d 364, 142 Cal. Rptr. 119.) The burden of proving the presumption is rebutted is on the proponents of the will. (See Estate of Paul (1972) 29 Cal. App. 3d 690, 697, 105 Cal. Rptr. 742.)

Here, Russell failed to provide for Lila in his will. Under the language of section 6560, she is thus an omitted spouse and the crucial inquiry becomes whether Beatrice met the burden of rebutting this presumption. Specifically, the issues are whether the will shows a specific intent to exclude Lila pursuant to section 6561(a) and whether Beatrice presented sufficient evidence to show Russell had intended to otherwise provide for Lila outside of his will in lieu of her taking under it pursuant to section 6561(b), or to show Lila waived her rights to share in his estate under section 6561(c).

The will on its face does not evidence an intent on Russell's part to disinherit Lila. As the presumption under section 6560 is only rebutted by a clear manifestation of such intent on the face of the will, "regardless of what may have been the wishes of the [decedent]" (Estate of Basore (1971) 19 Cal. App. 3d 623, 627-628, 96 Cal. Rptr. 874), the section 6561(a) exception has not been established.

Contrary to Beatrice's reliance on Estate of Kurtz (1922) 190 Cal. 146, 210 P. 959, to argue the language "any legal heir of mine" in the disinheritance clause contained in Russell's will somehow shows his intent to disinherit Lila, whom he married 12 years after executing the will, that case has been effectively overruled by subsequent case law. (See Estate of Axcelrod (1944) 23 Cal. 2d 761, 769-770, 147 P.2d 1 (conc. opn. of Carter, J.).) Estate of Axcelrod, supra, 23 Cal. 2d at pp. 765-769, 147 P.2d 1 distinguished the *Kurtz* case and held a general provision in a will that the testator "intentionally omitted all of my heirs who are not specifically mentioned herein, intending thereby to disinherit them," may not be construed as mentioning a subsequently acquired spouse in such a way as to show an intention not to make provision for the spouse, where the testator at the time the will was executed had no spouse who could become "an heir." (Id. at p. 767, 147 P.2d 1.)

Case law has also held exclusionary clauses in wills which fail to indicate the testator contemplated the possibility of a future marriage are insufficient to avoid the statutory presumption. (Estate of Poisl (1955) 44 Cal. 2d 147, 149-150, 280 P.2d 789; Estate of Paul, supra, 29 Cal. App. 3d 690, 105 Cal. Rptr. 742.) Even testamentary clauses specifically disinheriting a named individual whom the testator planned to marry and a clause stating "any other person not specifically mentioned in this Will, whether related by marriage or not" have been held insufficient to disclose the explicit intention of a testator to omit provision for another woman the testator married after executing the will either as a member of the designated disinherited class or as a contemplated spouse. (Estate of Green (1981) 120 Cal. App. 3d 589, 593, 174 Cal. Rptr. 654.) As there is no mention of Lila or the fact of a future marriage in the disinheritance clause of the will, it does not manifest Russell's intent to specifically disinherit Lila as his surviving spouse.

Nor have the circumstances of section 6561(b) or (c) been established. Beatrice asserts a retired California Highway Patrolmen Widow's and Orphan's Fund from which $2,000 was paid to Lila as Russell's beneficiary, coupled with a declaration of Russell's attorney "[t]hat in the twelve months immediately preceding [Russell's death, he] informed this declarant that he had remarried and that his wife was independently wealthy and that she had more than he had and that he wanted his daughter to have his estate upon his death . . . ," evidence Russell's intent to provide for Lila outside the will in lieu of a testamentary provision and satisfy the requirements of section 6561(b). In support of this argument she cites a New Mexico case, Matter of Taggart (1980) 95 N.M. 117, 619 P.2d 562, which held the omission of an after-acquired spouse in a will can be shown to be intentional by a transfer outside the will such as life insurance or other joint arrangement based on evidence of the testator's statements, the amount of the transaction, or other evidence. She claims Russell's intent she take his entire estate is paramount and the presumption under section 6560 must yield to that intent. (See Estate of Smith (1985) 167 Cal. App. 3d 208, 212, 212 Cal. Rptr. 923.)

... [S]uch [evidence] was insufficient to rebut the presumption of section 6560 because it does not show Russell provided the trust fund benefits for Lila in lieu of sharing in his estate.

Moreover, the facts presented at the probate hearing that Russell and Lila kept their property separate during the course of their marriage is not sufficient to show "a valid agreement waiving the right to share" in each other's estate pursuant to section 6561(c). (See Estate of Butler (1988) 205 Cal. App. 3d 311, 318, 252 Cal. Rptr. 210.)

Beatrice has simply not met her burden of proving Russell's intent to disinherit Lila and rebut the presumption of revocation under section 6560. The probate court therefore erred in denying Lila's petition to determine heirship.

DISPOSITION

The order denying Lila's petition for heirship is reversed and remanded for further proceedings consistent with this opinion.

Uniform Probate Code (1990, as amended in 1993)

§2-301. ENTITLEMENT OF SPOUSE; PREMARITAL WILL

(a) If a testator's surviving spouse married the testator after the testator executed his [or her] will, the surviving spouse is entitled to receive, as an intestate share, no less than the value of the share of the estate he [or she] would have received if the testator had died intestate as to that portion of the testator's estate, if any, that is neither devised to a child of the testator who was born before the testator married the surviving spouse and who is not a child of the surviving spouse nor devised to a descendant of such a child or passes under sections 2-603 or 2-604 to such a child or to a descendant of such a child, unless:

(1) it appears from the will or other evidence that the will was made in contemplation of the testator's marriage to the surviving spouse;

(2) the will expresses the intention that it is to be effective notwithstanding any subsequent marriage; or

(3) the testator provided for the spouse by transfer outside the will and the intent that the transfer be in lieu of a testamentary provision is shown by the testator's statements or is reasonably inferred from the amount of the transfer or other evidence.

(b) In satisfying the share provided by this section, devises made by the will to the testator's surviving spouse, if any, are applied first, and other devises, other than a devise to a child of the testator who was born before the testator married the surviving spouse and who is not a child of the surviving spouse or a devise or substitute gift under sections 2-603 or 2-604 to a descendant of such a child, abate as provided in section 3-902.

QUESTIONS AND NOTES

1.   If *H* marries *W* some years after making his will leaving everything to his daughter by a previous marriage, *W* is not entitled to an intestate share in *H*'s estate under UPC §2-301. She must elect to take against the will, where her share may be less than an intestate share. Mongold v. Mayle, 192 W. Va. 353, 452 S.E.2d 444 (1994) (interpreting UPC). On the other hand, if *H* had left his property by will to his alma mater, *W* would take an intestate share. What is the reason for this?

2.   When a surviving spouse elects against a will, in many states the spouse is entitled to include nonprobate assets as part of the decedent's estate (called the "augmented estate" by the Uniform Probate Code). A spouse omitted from a will made before marriage is not able to reach nonprobate assets; her share is solely of the probate estate. See Estate of Allen, 12 Cal. App. 4th 1762, 16 Cal. Rptr. 2d 352 (1993). Why is this? Why did the UPC revisers treat the situations differently?

If the surviving spouse is richer than the decedent spouse, the surviving spouse has no forced share under the 1990 UPC (see supra page 509). But a richer surviving spouse omitted from a premarital will can take an intestate share. Why are the situations treated differently?

3.   The failure of a lawyer to advise a client to execute a new will if the client wants to disinherit a recently married spouse has given rise to malpractice actions in several cases. In Heyer v. Flaig, 70 Cal. 2d 223, 449 P.2d 161, 74 Cal. Rptr. 225 (1969), the client told her lawyer that she was planning to marry a man named Glen and she wished her estate to pass to her two daughters by a previous marriage. The lawyer drafted a will, which the client executed, leaving her estate to the daughters and not mentioning Glen. Subsequently she married Glen, then she died and Glen claimed his intestate share as an omitted spouse. The daughters sued the lawyer for malpractice, claiming damages in the amount of Glen's intestate share. Upon demurrer, the court held the daughters stated a cause of action. "The intended beneficiary . . . suffers a great and irrevocable loss: he has nowhere to turn but to the attorney for compensation. Indeed, Lucas v. Hamm recognizes that unless the beneficiary can recover from the attorney the beneficiary suffers a wrong without a compensating remedy."

Suppose that when the lawyer draws the will, the client has no plans to marry Glen and does not mention him to the lawyer. Four months after executing the will, the lawyer receives an invitation to the wedding of the client and Glen. Does the lawyer have a duty to advise the client of the effect of the marriage upon the client's will? See Am. Bar Assn., Model Code of Professional Responsibility, Disciplinary Rule 2-104(A)(1) (1981), referring to ABA Opinion 210 (1941): "It is our opinion that where the lawyer has no reason to believe that he has been supplanted by another lawyer, it is not only his right but it might even be his duty to advise his client of any change of fact or law which might defeat the client's testamentary purpose as expressed in the will."

SECTION B. RIGHTS OF ISSUE OMITTED FROM THE WILL

In all states except Louisiana,[17] a child or other descendant has no statutory protection against disinheritance by a parent.[18] There is no requirement that a testator leave any property to a child, not even the proverbial one dollar.[19] Nonetheless, even though a parent has the power to disinherit children, the parent should think twice or, better, three times, before exercising the power. The law does not favor cutting children out of the parent's estate when the testator leaves no spouse. To this end, a number of doctrines have been flexibly used to protect children, with the consequence that disinherit-

17. Louisiana has a forced share for children, called a *legitime*, derived from French law. It protects against disinheritance of children under 23, mentally infirm, or disabled. Prior to a constitutional amendment in 1995, the forced share extended to all children. See Katherine S. Spaht, Forced Heirship Changes: The Regrettable Revolution Completed, 57 La. L. Rev. 55 (1996); Forced Heirship Symposium, 43 Loy. L. Rev. 1 (1997).

18. The legal ability to disinherit children has been disapproved by several commentators. See Deborah A. Batts, I Didn't Ask to Be Born: The American System of Disinheritance and a Proposal for Change in a System of Protected Inheritance, 41 Hastings L.J. 1197 (1990) (recommending forced share legislation); Ralph C. Brashier, Protecting the Child from Disinheritance: Must Louisiana Stand Alone?, 57 La. L. Rev. 1 (1996) (recommending requiring parental support for minor children, which would treat them the same as children of divorced parents who have a support decree enforceable against the decedent's estate); Ronald Chester, Should American Children be Protected Against Disinheritance?, 32 Real Prop., Prob. & Tr. J. 405 (1997) (recommending English and Commonwealth family maintenance system; see supra page 477).

19. At common law a child omitted from his parent's will had no remedy. It may have been thought that it was necessary to leave the heir a shilling to disinherit him effectively, but Blackstone says that this was an error. 2 William Blackstone, Commentaries *502. Blackstone says "cutting the heir off with a shilling" is traceable to a Roman law notion that the testator had lost his memory or mind unless he gave some legacy to each child.

ance is almost always a risky affair. A will disinheriting a child virtually invites a will contest. As we saw in Chapter 3, "lack of testamentary capacity," "undue influence," and "fraud" are subtle and elastic concepts that can be used by judges and juries to rewrite the testator's distributive plan in order to "do justice." In contests by disinherited children, judges and juries are frequently influenced by their sympathies for the children. This is well known to practicing lawyers, who will often advise the devisees to agree to an out-of-court settlement with a disinherited child.

We turn now to pretermission statutes, designed to prevent unintentional disinheritance of descendants. It was such a statute that induced Calvin Coolidge, noted for economy of language, to add an opening phrase to his will — the shortest will of any President of the United States. Coolidge's will read in its entirety:

"The White House"
Washington
Will of Calvin Coolidge of Northampton,
Hampshire County, Massachusetts

Not unmindful of my son John, I give all my estate both real and personal to my wife Grace Coolidge, in fee simple — Home at Washington, District of Columbia this twentieth day December, A.D. nineteen hundred and twenty six.

/s/ Calvin Coolidge

Signed by me on the date above in the presence of the testator and of each other as witnesses to said will and the signature thereof.

/s/ Everett Sanders
/s/ Edward T. Clark
/s/ Erwin C. Geisser

Azcunce v. Estate of Azcunce

Florida Court of Appeal, Third District, 1991
586 So. 2d 1216

HUBBART, J.   The central issue presented by this appeal is whether a child who is born after the execution of her father's will but before the execution of a codicil to the said will is entitled to take a statutory share of her father's estate under Florida's pretermitted child statute — when the will and codicils fail to provide for such child and all the other statutory requirements for pretermitted-child status are otherwise satisfied. We hold that where inter alia the subject codicil expressly republishes the original will, as here, the testator's child who is living at the time the codicil is executed is not a pretermitted child within the meaning of the statute. We, accordingly, affirm the final order under review which denies the child herein a statutory share of her father's estate as a pretermitted child.

I

The facts of this case are entirely undisputed. On May 4, 1983, the testator René R. Azcunce executed a will which established a trust for the benefit of his surviving spouse and his then-born children: Lisette, Natalie, and Gabriel; the will contained no provision for after-born children. On August 8, 1983, and June 25, 1986, the testator executed two codicils which did not alter in any way this testamentary disposition and also made no provision for after-born children.

On March 14, 1984, the testator's daughter Patricia Azcunce was born — after the first codicil was executed, but before the second codicil was executed. The first codicil expressly republished all the terms of the original will; the second codicil expressly republished all the terms of the original will and first codicil.

On December 30, 1986, the testator, who was thirty-eight (38) years old, unexpectedly died of a heart attack — four months after executing the second codicil. After the will and codicils were admitted to probate, Patricia filed a petition seeking a statutory share of her father's estate as a pretermitted child; the trial court denied this petition. Patricia appeals.

II

The statute on which Patricia relies for a share of her father's estate provides:

> When a testator omits to provide in his will for any of his children born or adopted after making the will and the child has not received a part of the testator's property equivalent to a child's part by way of advancement, the child shall receive a share of the estate equal in value to that he would have received if the testator had died intestate, unless:
>
> (1) It appears from the will that the omission was intentional; or
> (2) The testator had one or more children when the will was executed and devised substantially all his estate to the other parent of the pretermitted child. Section 732.302, Florida Statutes (1985).

Without dispute, Patricia was a pretermitted child both at the time
the testator's will and the first codicil thereto were executed, as, in
each instance, the testator "omit[ted] to provide in his will [or codi-
cil] for [Patricia who was] born . . . after . . . the will [or codicil was
executed]"; moreover, Patricia at no time received a part of the testator's property by way of advancement, the will and first codicil do not
expressly disinherit Patricia, and the testator did not substantially devise all of his estate to Patricia's mother. The question in this case is
whether the testator's execution of the second codicil to the will
after Patricia had been born destroyed her prior statutory status as a
pretermitted child.

It is well settled in Florida that, as a general rule, the execution of
a codicil to a will has the effect of republishing the prior will as of
the date of the codicil. Waterbury v. Munn, 159 Fla. 754, 32 So. 2d
603 (1947); In re Campbell's Estate, 288 So. 2d 528 (Fla. 3d DCA),
cert. denied, 300 So. 2d 266 (Fla. 1974). Although this is not an
inflexible rule and must at times give way to a contrary intent of the
testator, . . . it always applies where, as here, the codicil expressly
adopts the terms of the prior will; this is so for the obvious reason
that such a result comports with the express intent of the testator.
See T. Atkinson, Law of Wills ch. 10 §91 (2d ed. 1953); 2 W. Bowe &
D. Parker, Page on Wills §23.18 (1960); Evans, Testamentary Republication, 40 Harv. L. Rev. 71, 100-04 (1926).

III

Turning to the instant case, it is clear that the testator's second codicil
republished the original will and first codicil because the second codicil expressly so states. This being so, Patricia's prior status as a pretermitted child was destroyed inasmuch as Patricia was alive when the
second codicil was executed and was not, as required by Florida's
pretermitted child statute, born after such codicil was made. Presumably, if the testator had wished to provide for Patricia, he would have
done so in the second codicil as she had been born by that time;
because he did not, Patricia was, in effect, disinherited, which the
testator clearly had the power to do. Flagler v. Flagler, 94 So. 2d 592
(Fla. 1957); Hooper v. Stokes, 107 Fla. 607, 145 So. 855 (1933). Indeed, the result we reach herein is in full accord with the results
reached by courts throughout the country based on identical circumstances. Young v. Williams, 253 N.C. 281, 116 S.E.2d 778 (1960); La-
borde v. First State Bank & Trust Co., 101 S.W.2d 389 (Tex. Civ. App.
1936); Gooch v. Gooch, 134 Va. 21, 113 S.E. 873 (1922); Francis v.
Marsh, 54 W. Va. 545, 46 S.E. 573 (1904).

To avoid this inevitable result, Patricia argues that the will and two
codicils are somehow ambiguous and that, accordingly, the court

should have accepted the parol evidence adduced below that the testator intended to provide for Patricia; Patricia also urges that the will should have been voided because the draftsman made a "mistake" in failing to provide for Patricia in the second codicil. These arguments are unavailing. First, there is utterly no ambiguity in the subject will and codicils which would authorize the taking of parol evidence herein, and the trial court was entirely correct in rejecting same. Barnett First Nat'l Bank of Jacksonville v. Cobden, 393 So. 2d 78 (Fla. 5th DCA 1981). Second, the mistake of which Patricia complains amounts, at best, to the draftsman's alleged professional negligence in failing to apprise the testator of the need to expressly provide for Patricia in the second codicil; this is not the type of mistake which voids a will under Section 732.5165, Florida Statutes (1987). In re Mullins' Estate, 128 So. 2d 617 (Fla. 2d DCA 1961).

For the above-stated reasons, the final order under review is, in all respects,

Affirmed.

Restatement (Third) of Property, Wills and Other
Donative Transfers (1999)

§3.4   REPUBLICATION BY CODICIL

A will is treated as if it were executed when its most recent codicil was executed, whether or not the codicil expressly republishes the prior will, unless the effect of so treating it would be inconsistent with the testator's intent.

Espinosa v. Sparber, Shevin, Shapo, Rosen & Heilbronner
Supreme Court of Florida, 1993
612 So. 2d 1378

McDONALD, J. We review Espinosa v. Sparber, Shevin, Shapo, Rosen & Heilbronner, 586 So. 2d 1221 (Fla. 3d DCA 1991), which involves the following question of great public importance certified in an unpublished order dated September 17, 1991: UNDER THE FACTS OF THIS CASE . . . MAY A LAWSUIT ALLEGING PROFESSIONAL MALPRACTICE BE BROUGHT, ON BEHALF OF PATRICIA AZCUNCE, AGAINST THE DRAFTSMAN OF THE SECOND CODICIL? We have jurisdiction pursuant to article V, section 3(b)(4) of the Florida Constitution. We answer the question in the negative and approve the decision of the district court.

Howard Roskin, a member of the Sparber, Shevin law firm, drafted a will for René Azcunce, the testator. At the time he signed his will, René and his wife, Marta, had three children, Lisette, Natalie, and Gabriel. Article Seventeenth of the Will specifically provided that:

> (a) References in this, my Last Will and Testament, to my children, shall be construed to mean my daughters, LISSETE AZCUNCE and NATALIE AZCUNCE, and my son, GABRIEL AZCUNCE. (b) References in this, my Last Will and Testament, to my "issue," shall be construed to mean my children [as defined in Paragraph (a), above] and their legitimate natural born and legally adopted lineal descendants.

Article Fourth of the will established a trust for the benefit of Marta and the three named children and also granted Marta a power of appointment to distribute all or a portion of the trust to the named children and their issue. In addition, the will provided that, upon Marta's death, the trust was to be divided into equal shares for each of the three named children.

Neither the will nor the first codicil to the will, executed on August 8, 1983, made any provisions for after-born children. On March 14, 1984, Patricia Azcunce was born as the fourth child of René and Marta. René contacted Roskin and communicated his desire to include Patricia in his will. In response, Roskin drafted a new will that provided for Patricia and also restructured the trust. However, due to a disagreement between René and Roskin on the amount of available assets, René never signed the second will. Instead, on June 25, 1986, he executed a second codicil drafted by Roskin that changed the identity of the co-trustee and co-personal representative, but did not provide for the after-born child, Patricia. When René died on December 30, 1986, he had never executed any document that provided for Patricia.[20]

Marta brought a malpractice action on behalf of Patricia and the estate against Roskin and his law firm. The trial court dismissed the complaint with prejudice for lack of privity and entered final summary judgment for Roskin and his firm. The Third District Court of Appeal

---

20. Patricia brought suit in probate court to be classified as a pretermitted child, which would have entitled her to a share of René's estate. Her mother and adult sibling consented to Patricia's petition being granted. The probate court judge appointed a guardian ad litem for Patricia's two minor siblings, and the guardian opposed the petition. Subsequently, the court ruled that the second codicil destroyed Patricia's status as a pretermitted child, and the decision was upheld on appeal. Azcunce v. Estate of Azcunce, 586 So. 2d 1216 (Fla. 3d DCA 1991). We are not privy to the factors that the guardian ad litem considered in deciding not to consent to Patricia's classification as a pretermitted child, a decision that deprived Patricia of a share in the estate and ultimately led to costly litigation. We hope, however, that a guardian evaluating the facts of this case would not focus strictly on the financial consequences for the child, but would also consider such important factors as family harmony and stability.

reversed the dismissal with regard to the estate, affirmed it with regard to Patricia, and certified the question of whether Patricia has standing to bring a legal malpractice action under the facts of this case.

An attorney's liability for negligence in the performance of his or her professional duties is limited to clients with whom the attorney shares privity of contract. Angel, Cohen & Rogovin v. Oberon Investments, N.V., 512 So. 2d 192 (Fla. 1987). In a legal context, the term "privity" is a word of art derived from the common law of contracts and used to describe the relationship of persons who are parties to a contract. Baskerville-Donovan Engineers, Inc. v. Pensacola Executive House Condominium Ass'n, Inc., 581 So. 2d 1301 (Fla. 1991). To bring a legal malpractice action, the plaintiff must either be in privity with the attorney, wherein one party has a direct obligation to another, or, alternatively, the plaintiff must be an intended third-party beneficiary. In the instant case, Patricia Azcunce does not fit into either category of proper plaintiffs.

In the area of will drafting, a limited exception to the strict privity requirement has been allowed where it can be demonstrated that the apparent intent of the client in engaging the services of the lawyer was to benefit a third party. Rosenstone v. Satchell, 560 So. 2d 1229 (Fla. 4th DCA 1990); Lorraine v. Grover, Ciment, Weinstein & Stauber, P.A., 467 So. 2d 315 (Fla. 3d DCA 1985). Because the client is no longer alive and is unable to testify, the task of identifying those persons who are intended third-party beneficiaries causes an evidentiary problem closely akin to the problem of determining the client's general testamentary intent. To minimize such evidentiary problems, the will was designed as a legal document that affords people a clear opportunity to express the way in which they desire to have their property distributed upon death. To the greatest extent possible, courts and personal representatives are obligated to honor the testator's intent in conformity with the contents of the will. In re Blocks' Estate, 143 Fla. 163, 196 So. 410 (1940).

If extrinsic evidence is admitted to explain testamentary intent, as recommended by the petitioners, the risk of misinterpreting the testator's intent increases dramatically. Furthermore, admitting extrinsic evidence heightens the tendency to manufacture false evidence that cannot be rebutted due to the unavailability of the testator. For these reasons, we adhere to the rule that standing in legal malpractice actions is limited to those who can show that the testator's intent as expressed in the will is frustrated by the negligence of the testator's attorney. Although René did not express in his will and codicils any intention to exclude Patricia, his will and codicils do not, unfortunately, express any affirmative intent to provide for her. Because Patricia cannot be described as one in privity with the attorney or as an intended third-party beneficiary, a lawsuit alleging professional malpractice cannot be brought on her behalf.

René's estate, however, stands in the shoes of the testator and clearly satisfies the privity requirement. Therefore, we agree with the district court's decision that the estate may maintain a legal malpractice action against Roskin for any acts of professional negligence committed by him during his representation of René.[21] Because the alleged damages to the estate are an element of the liability claim and are not relevant to the standing question in this particular case, we do not address that issue.

For the reasons stated above, we answer the certified question in the negative and approve the decision of the district court.

It is so ordered.

NOTES AND PROBLEMS

1. In the district court of appeal in the *Azcunce* and *Espinosa* cases, Judge Levy concurred in the result, which he felt was compelled by Florida law. Nonetheless, he thought Patricia was done a terrible injustice. In his opinion in the *Espinosa* case, he wrote:

> Clearly, in the instant case, the testator's intent is not "expressed in the will." That is exactly the problem! The very essence of Patricia's complaint, as carried forward in the action filed on her behalf against the draftsman of the second codicil, is that the testator's intent was not reflected in the face of the will and, knowing that, the draftsman of the second codicil, acting as the testator's attorney, allowed the testator to sign the second codicil knowing that it specifically republished the testator's original will and first codicil, thereby eliminating Patricia's chances to be protected as a pretermitted child as provided for in Section 732.302, Florida Statutes (1985).
>
> Accordingly, Patricia is relegated to the never-never land of the ultimate in circuitous reasoning. Namely, Patricia would appear to have a colorable claim against the draftsman of the second codicil for not either advising her father of the legal consequences of signing the second codicil (to-wit: that Patricia would lose her status as a pretermitted child) or providing for

---

21. The district court of appeals had this to say about the estate's malpractice action:

The estate's damages, however, are limited to the attorney's fees paid by the testator to the lawyers for their alleged negligence in drafting the will and codicils — and to the attorney's fees and costs in defending a companion suit brought by Patricia to recover a statutory share of the estate as an alleged pretermitted child. See Azcunce v. Estate of Azcunce, 586 So. 2d 1216 (Fla. 3d DCA 1991). This latter suit was directly generated by the lawyer's alleged negligence in failing to provide for Patricia in the will or codicils; had such provision been made, Patricia's action would have been entirely unnecessary. [Espinosa v. Sparber, Shevin, Shapo, Rosen & Heilbronner, 586 So. 2d 1221, 1224 (1991).] — Eds.

her in the second codicil, or some other such document, so as to give life and vitality to her father's (the testator's) wishes. However, according to Florida law, she cannot sue the draftsman of the second codicil for leaving her name out of the second codicil because, wonder of wonders, her name is not mentioned in the second codicil. . . .

In view of the foregoing, one must wonder as to who will have the unenviable task of trying to convince Patricia that, according to the case law of the State of Florida, the Constitution of this State requires that there be a remedy for every wrong. If there ever was a case where a person was wronged, but allowed to fall through a crack in the legal system, this is the case. However, in this case it was not a crack, but rather, a monumental abyss. [Espinosa v. Sparber, Shevin, Shapo, Rosen & Heilbronner, 586 So. 2d 1221, 1227-1228 (Fla. App. 1991) (Levy J., concurring).]

The Florida Supreme Court in *Espinosa* assumes that the lawyer's client is the father of the family, René. Why is not the client the whole family? See Teresa S. Collett, The Ethics of Intergenerational Representation, 62 Fordham L. Rev. 1453 (1994).

Besides suing for a pretermitted child's share and for malpractice, what other remedy might Patricia have?

Does she have a claim against lawyer Roskin for tortious interference with her expectancy (supra page 221)?

If Patricia sues the executor of René's estate as a pretermitted child, and the executor settles her claim for 75 cents on the dollar, can the executor recover this amount as damages from the lawyer Roskin?

Is Patricia entitled to have a constructive trust imposed on the will devisees to prevent unjust enrichment by the negligent act of the lawyer? In Pope v. Garrett, 147 Tex. 18, 211 S.W.2d 559 (1948), supra page 221, the court imposed a constructive trust on innocent heirs when the testator was forcefully prevented by some wrongdoing heirs from executing a will leaving his property to the plaintiff. Can a constructive trust be imposed on innocent parties who profit by the negligence of a lawyer? Compare In re Estate of Tolin, 622 So. 2d 988 (Fla. 1993), supra page 284, where the court imposed a constructive trust when the testator tore up a xerox copy of his will, believing, on the mistaken advice of a retired lawyer, that the act revoked his will.

Can Patricia recover damages from the guardian ad litem of her two minor siblings, criticized by the court in footnote 20?

Sparber, Shevin, Shapo, Rosen & Heilbronner, a law firm with 55 lawyers, was dissolved in 1988.

2.   In McAbee v. Edwards, 340 So. 2d 1167 (Fla. App. 1976), the court held the lawyer liable for malpractice on the following facts: Testator made a will leaving everything to her daughter, then subsequently she remarried. After remarriage, she consulted a lawyer to make sure that her daughter remained the sole beneficiary of her estate. The lawyer assured the testator that no change in her will was

necessary to effect this intention. Upon the testator's death, her second husband claimed and was awarded an intestate share as an omitted spouse. The court held the lawyer liable to the daughter for malpractice.

Is the *Espinosa* case consistent with McAbee v. Edwards?

Uniform Probate Code (1990, as amended in 1993)

§2-302.   OMITTED CHILDREN

(a) Except as provided in subsection (b), if a testator fails to provide in his [or her] will for any of his [or her] children born or adopted after the execution of the will, the omitted after-born or after-adopted child receives a share in the estate as follows:

(1) If the testator had no child living when he [or she] executed the will, an omitted after-born or after-adopted child receives a share in the estate equal in value to that which the child would have received had the testator died intestate, unless the will devised all or substantially all of the estate to the other parent of the omitted child and that other parent survives the testator and is entitled to take under the will.

(2) If the testator had one or more children living when he [or she] executed the will, and the will devised property or an interest in property to one or more of the then-living children, an omitted after-born or after-adopted child is entitled to share in the testator's estate as follows:

(i) The portion of the testator's estate in which the omitted after-born or after-adopted child is entitled to share is limited to devises made to the testator's then-living children under the will.

(ii) The omitted after-born or after-adopted child is entitled to receive the share of the testator's estate, as limited in subparagraph (i), that the child would have received had the testator included all omitted after-born and after-adopted children with the children to whom devises were made under the will and had given an equal share of the estate to each child.

(iii) To the extent feasible, the interest granted an omitted after-born or after-adopted child under this section must be of the same character, whether equitable or legal, present or future, as that devised to the testator's then-living children under the will.

(iv) In satisfying a share provided by this paragraph, devises to the testator's children who were living when the will was executed abate ratably. In abating the devises of the then-living children, the court shall preserve to the maximum extent possible the character of the testamentary plan adopted by the testator.

(b) Neither subsection (a)(1) nor subsection (a)(2) applies if:

(1) it appears from the will that the omission was intentional; or

(2) the testator provided for the omitted after-born or after-adopted child by transfer outside the will and the intent that the transfer be in lieu of a testamentary provision is shown by the testator's statements or is reasonably inferred from the amount of the transfer or other evidence.

(c) If at the time of execution of the will the testator fails to provide in his [or her] will for a living child solely because he [or she] believes the child to be dead, the child is entitled to share in the estate as if the child were an omitted after-born or after-adopted child.

(d) In satisfying a share provided by subsection (a)(1), devises made by the will abate under Section 3-902.

NOTES, PROBLEMS, AND QUESTIONS

1. Pretermitted child statutes, which have been enacted in almost all states, follow one of two patterns. Some statutes protect only children born (or adopted) after execution of the will. See Uniform Probate Code §2-302, supra. Other statutes operate in favor of children alive when the will was executed as well as afterborns. Under these latter statutes, the failure to name all of the testator's living children in the will invites a challenge under the pretermitted child statute.

Pretermitted heir statutes can also be classified as "Missouri" type or "Massachusetts" type. Under a Missouri-type statute, the statute usually is drawn to benefit children "not named or provided for" in the will. Hence, it must appear from the will itself that omission of the child or other heir was intentional. Extrinsic evidence of intent is not admissible. Under the Massachusetts-type statute, the child takes "unless it appears that such omission was intentional and not occasioned by any mistake." Extrinsic evidence is admitted to show both the presence or absence of intent to disinherit. See Annot., 88 A.L.R.4th 779 (1991).

Uniform Probate Code §2-302 does not permit extrinsic evidence to show that the omission was intentional; such intent must be shown by the will itself. However, if a testator made nonprobate transfers to the omitted child, the testator's intent that these transfers bar the child from claiming a pretermitted share can be shown by the testator's statements or other extrinsic evidence.

2. In Azcune v. Estate of Azcune, if René had not made the second codicil to his will and Patricia had been pretermitted, Patricia

would have taken her intestate share. Under Fla. Stat. Ann. §132.103 (1993), her intestate share would be one-eighth of René's estate. What would be her share under UPC §2-302 (1990)? On the distortions pretermission statutes cause in estate plans, see Jan E. Rein, A More Rational System for the Protection of Family Members Against Disinheritance, 15 Gonz. L. Rev. 11 (1979).

3.   When *T* executes her will, she has two living children, *A* and *B*. Her will devises $7,500 to each child. After *T* executes her will she has another child, *C*. *T* dies. To what amount is *C* entitled under UPC §2-302 (1990)? The official comment says *C* is entitled to $5,000 taken one-half from *A*'s devise (reducing it to $5,000) and one-half from *B*'s. Suppose that *T* had devised $10,000 to *A* and $5,000 to *B*. What would *C* take and where would it come from?

4.   In a jurisdiction where the pretermission statute includes children born before execution of the will, what provision would you recommend including in a will so as to cut out a nonmarital child without mentioning the child by name or suggesting his existence? Courts have been sticklers in requiring the testator to indicate clearly an intention to disinherit a nonmarital child, either by express words or by necessary implication. Consider the following cases.

In Estate of Peterson, 74 Wash. 2d 91, 442 P.2d 980 (1968), the testator stated: "I declare that I have no children, no children of deceased children, and no adopted children." The court held that this did not disinherit a child of testator, whose paternity he denied. "[T]he mistaken denial that he has children seems to us a clear example of a situation in which the statute was intended to operate to protect a forgotten child from being disinherited. There is no indication in the will that the testator remembered the petitioner and intended to disinherit him." Id. at 95, 442 P.2d at 983.

In In re Estate of Padilla, 641 P.2d 539 (N.M. App. 1982), the testator's will declared: "I declare that I have no children whom I have omitted to name or provide for herein." The court held that this was not an intentional omission. "To disinherit Sanchez [the nonmarital child], an affirmative, not negative, indication of intention must appear on the face of the Will." Id. at 544.

See also Estate of Torregano, 54 Cal. 2d 234, 352 P.2d 505, 5 Cal. Rptr. 137, 88 A.L.R.2d 597 (1960), holding a bequest of $1 to any person asserting any claim "by virtue of relationship or otherwise" insufficient to bar an omitted child; Estate of Gardner, 31 Cal. 3d 620, 580 P.2d 684, 147 Cal. Rptr. 184 (1978), holding clause, "I declare that I have intentionally failed to provide for any person not mentioned herein," insufficient to bar an omitted child.

In Michigan, a child born as a result of rape is given an intestate share in the (father) testator's estate, regardless of the testator's intent, if the child is not provided for by will. Mich. Comp. Laws

§700.127(3) (1997). See N.Y. Times, July 10, 1994, at A8, reporting that a 50-year-old woman, conceived half a century earlier as a result of the unreported rape of her mother, had the body of the man accused by her mother exhumed after his death, at age 92, proved paternity by DNA testing, and successfully claimed an intestate share against his will.

Would a person who wants to disinherit a nonmarital child be wise to transfer his assets into a revocable inter vivos trust that does not provide for, or mention, the child?

In re Estate of Laura
Supreme Court of New Hampshire, 1997
141 N.H. 628, 690 A.2d 1011

THAYER, J.   The testator, Edward R. Laura, Sr., died on August 23, 1990. The petitioners, two generations of the testator's heirs who were excluded from his will, appeal a decision of the Rockingham County Probate Court (Maher, J.), approving the order of the Master (Gerald Taube, Esq.), that barred them from inheriting any portion of the testator's estate. On appeal, the petitioners argue that the probate court erred in . . . ruling that the testator's great-grandchildren were not pretermitted heirs under RSA 551:10 (1974). . . . We affirm. . . .

The record reveals the following facts. The testator had three children. Two children, Edward R. Laura, Jr. and Shirley Chicoine, survived him. Shirley and Edward each have three children. The testator's third child, Jo Ann Laura, died in 1974. She was survived by two children, Richard Chicoine and Neil F. Chicoine, Jr. Neil died in 1988 and is survived by two children, Cecilia Chicoine and Neil F. Chicoine, III, the testator's great-grandchildren. Richard, acting on behalf of himself and the testator's great-grandchildren, and Edward are the petitioners here.

Sometime prior to September 17, 1984, the testator hired an attorney to draft his will. The will was executed on September 26, 1984. It provided that the testator's estate would pass to his daughter, Shirley, who was also designated as the executrix of his estate. In addition, the will named the testator's deceased daughter, Jo Ann, and explicitly named his son, Edward, and his grandchildren, Richard and Neil, in a paragraph designed to disinherit them. Paragraph seven of the will provided:

> I have intentionally omitted to provide in this Will for any heirs at law, next of kin, or relatives of mine, by blood, marriage or adoption, specifically but not limited to my son, Edward and my grandchildren, Richard and Neil, except as aforesaid, and such omissions are not occasioned by accident or mistake.

The will did not mention the testator's two great-grandchildren. Cecilia Chicoine was born one day before the will was executed; Neil F. Chicoine, III was not born until two years after the will was executed.

In 1990, the testator attempted to execute a codicil to his will. The codicil would have altered the disposition of his estate, giving three equal shares to Edward, Shirley, and Richard, and equal shares to Shirley's and Edward's respective children. The parties agree, however, that the codicil was not properly witnessed and therefore did not become effective.

Following the testator's death, his 1984 will was presented to the probate court. The will was proved and allowed, and Shirley was appointed executrix on September 30, 1990. In 1991, Richard, on behalf of himself and the testator's great-grandchildren, and Edward petitioned the probate court to reexamine the 1984 will. They challenged the will on [the ground that] . . . the testator's great-grandchildren were entitled to an intestate share of his estate because they qualified as pretermitted heirs under RSA 551:10.

. . . The master . . . ruled that the testator's great-grandchildren were not pretermitted heirs under RSA 551:10. . . . The probate court adopted each of the master's findings. . . .

RSA 551:10 protects a testator's heirs against unintentional omission from the testator's will. It provides:

> Every child born after the decease of the testator, and every child or issue of a child of the deceased not named or referred to in his will, and who is not a devisee or legatee, shall be entitled to the same portion of the estate, real and personal, as he would be if the deceased were intestate.

The statute creates a rule of law that the omission of a child or issue of a child from a will is accidental "unless there is evidence in the will itself that the omission was intentional." In re Estate of MacKay, 121 N.H. 682, 684, 433 A.2d 1289, 1290 (1981). "The statute . . . is not a limitation on the power to make testamentary dispositions but rather is an attempt to effectuate a testator's presumed intent. It prevents forgetfulness, not disinheritance." Royce v. Estate of Denby, 117 N.H. 893, 896, 379 A.2d 1256, 1258 (1977).

Relying on the statute, the petitioners argue that the testator's great-grandchildren were not named or referred to in the testator's will and therefore are entitled to an intestate share of his estate. They contend that the testator's decision to specifically name Neil F. Chicoine, Jr., the father of the petitioning great-grandchildren, in paragraph seven of the will was irrelevant in determining whether they are pretermitted heirs under RSA 551:10. According to the petitioners, testators must name or refer to their children (or in this case, grandchildren) as well as the issue of their children (or in this case, great-grandchildren) in their wills; otherwise any issue not named or referred to is pretermitted. We disagree.

We hold that a testator who specifically names one heir in an effort to disinherit him has "referred to" the issue of that heir for purposes of the statute. Accord Towne v. Cottrell, 236 Ore. 151, 387 P.2d 576, 578 (Or. 1963); see In re Barter's Estate, 86 Cal. 441, 25 P. 15, 16 (Cal. 1890); Matter of Estate of Kane, 828 P.2d 997, 999 (Okla. Ct. App. 1992). If a testator has a predeceased child who is neither named, referred to, nor a devisee or legatee under the testator's will, then the naming of the next degree of issue in the line of descent will successfully preclude issue more removed from the testator from invoking the statute. On the other hand, where an issue of a child is named, referred to, or a devisee or legatee, but the testator's child is neither named, referred to, nor a devisee or legatee, then the testator's child is pretermitted, provided the child has not predeceased the testator. See Gage v. Gage, 29 N.H. 533, 543 (1854). Our holding is supported by our case law, in which we have acknowledged that a testator's reference to an heir "need not be direct" to exclude the heir under RSA 551:10. See In re Estate of Osgood, 122 N.H. 961, 964, 453 A.2d 838, 840 (1982); cf. Gage, 29 N.H. at 543 (naming of an heir's issue is not sufficient reference to the heir to preclude application of RSA 551:10).

Here, the testator specifically named Neil Chicoine, Jr., the father of the great-grandchildren, in paragraph seven of his will. As a result, the testator "referred to" the descendant great-grandchildren for purposes of the pretermitted heir statute.

Furthermore, the testator named his daughter, Jo Ann — the grandmother of petitioners Cecilia and Neil — in his will. When a testator's child has been named, referred to, or is a devisee or legatee under the will, the child's issue cannot invoke the statute even if the issue are neither named, referred to, nor devisees or legatees under the will. Accordingly, the testator's great-grandchildren were not pretermitted heirs under RSA 551:10 and were not entitled to collect an intestate share of his estate.

For the sins of your fathers you, though guiltless, must suffer.

— Horace, *Odes III, 6:1*

NOTE: TESTAMENTARY LIBEL

Would you advise a client who wants to disinherit a child to give the reason in the will? In Brown v. DuFrey, 1 N.Y.2d 190, 134 N.E.2d

469 (1956), the testator's will contained the following paragraph: "Fifth: I am mindful of the fact that I have made no provision for John H. Brown, my husband. I do so intentionally because of the fact that during my lifetime he abandoned me, made no provision for my support, treated me with complete indifference and did not display any affection or regard for me." The testator died in 1951. She had married John H. Brown in 1901, and he had secured a divorce from her in 1917 on grounds of adultery. Brown had remarried in 1924 and was living with his second wife at the time of the testator's death. Brown sued the testator's estate for testamentary libel and recovered as damages a sum approximately equal to one-half the estate.

See Leona M. Hudak, The Sleeping Tort: Testamentary Libel, 27 Mercer L. Rev. 1147 (1976), 12 Cal. W. L. Rev. 491 (1976); Osborne M. Reynolds, Jr., Defamation from the Grave: Testamentary Libel, 7 Cal. W. L. Rev. 91 (1971); Paul T. Whitcomb, Defamation by Will: Theories and Liabilities, 27 J. Marshall L. Rev. 749 (1994).

_____ *8* _____

TRUSTS: CREATION, TYPES, AND
CHARACTERISTICS

Of all the exploits of Equity the largest and
the most important is the invention and
development of the Trust. . . .
This perhaps forms the most distinctive
achievement of English lawyers. It seems to us
almost essential to civilization, and yet there is
nothing quite like it in foreign law.

FREDERICK W. MAITLAND
Equity: A Course of Lectures 23
(John Brunyate 2d ed. 1936)

SECTION A. INTRODUCTION

1. *Background*

A trust is, generally speaking, a device whereby a trustee manages
property for one or more beneficiaries. The trust developed out of
the historical circumstance that England had separate courts of law
and equity. The ancestor of the modern trust is the medieval *use*
(from a corruption of the Latin word *opus*, meaning benefit). Legal
historians have traced the use back to the middle of the thirteenth
century when the Franciscan friars came to England. Inasmuch as the
friars were forbidden to own any sort of property, pious benefactors
conveyed land to suitable persons in the neighborhood to hold to the

553

use of the friars. Thus *O*, owner of Blackacre, would enfeoff *A* and his heirs to hold Blackacre *to the use of* the friars. By this transfer, the legal fee simple passed to the *feoffee to uses, A*, who held it for the benefit of the *cestui que use*, the mendicant order. The cestui que use went into possession of Blackacre, with the legal title being held by *A*.

Although there is some evidence that ecclesiastical courts enforced early uses, in the beginning uses were not enforceable in the civil courts. Since no common law form of action existed whereby the cestui could bring an action against the feoffee, the law courts — paralyzed by the rigidity of their procedures — offered no relief. In time, this state of affairs appeared to be unconscionable to the chancellor, the "keeper of the king's conscience," and early in the fifteenth century the chancellor began to compel feoffees to uses to perform as they had promised. Once the chancellor enforced uses, thus removing the risk of faithless feoffees, uses grew rapidly. Landowners found that all sorts of benefits could be accomplished by putting legal title in a feoffee to uses. For example, prior to the Statute of Wills in 1540, land could not be devised by will; it descended to the eldest son. Landowners seeking relief from forced primogeniture turned to the use and found the desired flexibility there. *O* could enfeoff *A* and his heirs to the use of *O* during *O*'s lifetime and then to the use of such persons as *O* might appoint by will. The chancellor enforced the use in favor of *O*'s devisees. Particularly because of its success in evading feudal death taxes (known as feudal incidents), the use became universally popular. It was the use of the use to avoid taxes that brought on the Statute of Uses.

Searching for a way to restore his feudal incidents and replenish his treasury, Henry VIII determined to abolish the use. Henry interested himself personally in a lawsuit in the courts, which resulted in a decision putting into doubt the legality of the use generally. Fearing that uses might become unenforceable, with drastic consequences for the cestuis, Parliament, on Henry's urging, reluctantly enacted the Statute of Uses in 1535, which became effective in 1536. By this statute, uses were not made illegal. On the contrary, legal title was taken away from the feoffee to uses and given to the cestui que use. In the words of the time, the use was executed, that is, converted into a legal interest. The former cestuis — now clothed with legal title — could breathe easy, but they had to pay the king his due upon death.

Although the purpose of the Statute of Uses was to abolish uses, imaginative lawyers and judges found holes in the statute. Courts held that the statute did not operate if the feoffee to uses (trustee in modern language) was given *active duties* to perform. An active trust — imposing a duty on the trustee to deal with the property in a special manner — was regarded as quite different from the old use, where the feoffee merely held legal title and allowed the cestui que use himself to take the profits from the land. This reading of the statute permitted chancery to reassert its jurisdiction over uses under the name of trust and to develop the modern trust, wherein the trustee has legal title and the responsibilities of management and the beneficiaries have equitable title and the benefits flowing from the trustee's management.[1]

As Professor Scott has noted, the trust is a flexible tool that can be used for purposes "as unlimited as the imagination of lawyers." Austin W. Scott, Trusts 4 (William F. Fratcher 4th ed. 1987). These diverse purposes range from a simple estate plan to provide for a surviving spouse and children in accordance with their respective needs, to the running of vast business empires. The trust is a useful device for managing wealth held for charitable purposes or for pensions. It is also used for managing giant investment funds (e.g., common trust funds) or holding security for a loan (e.g., giving a mortgage in the form of a deed of trust). In the practice of law, you will find many other uses for the trust, particularly in situations where there are many beneficiaries or owners and it is desirable to avoid fragmented management of the property. Our present focus, however, is on the *private express trust* gratuitously created for the benefit of individual beneficiaries.

Private express trusts can be created for many purposes. We introduce you here to some of the most common uses of trusts in estate planning.

> *Case 1. Revocable trust.* O declares herself trustee of property to pay the income to O for life, then on O's death to pay the principal to O's children. O retains the power to revoke the trust. A revocable trust avoids the delays, costs, and publicity of probate. The revocable trust has other advantages discussed supra pages 386-396.

> *Case 2. Marital trust.* The federal estate tax law permits a marital deduction for property given to the surviving spouse. The deduction is allowed for a life estate given to the spouse (see infra pages 1047-1049). To get the deduction, H devises property to X in trust to pay the income to W for her life, and on her death to pay the principal to H's children. This trust qualifies for the marital deduction. No estate taxes are payable at H's death; they are postponed until W's death. This trust may be particularly useful when W needs professional money management or is the stepparent of H's children and might not bequeath the property to them if left to her outright.

---

1. For the history of the development of the trust, see Frederic W. Maitland, Equity: A Course of Lectures (John Brunyate 2d ed. 1936). See also Gregory S. Alexander, The Transformation of Trusts as a Legal Category, 1800-1914, 5 L. & Hist. Rev. 303 (1987).

Case 3. Trust for incompetent person. O's son A is mentally or physically handicapped and is unable to manage his property. O transfers property to X in trust to pay the income to A for life, remainder to A's issue, and if A dies without issue to his sister B.

Case 4. Trust for minor. The federal gift tax allows a tax-free gift of $10,000 per year to a donee. A gift to a minor creates special problems inasmuch as the minor is legally unable to manage her property. To permit annual tax-free gifts of $10,000 to his minor daughter A, O creates a trust to use the income and principal for the benefit of A before she reaches 21, and pay A the principal when she reaches 21. Every year O can make a tax-free gift of $10,000 to the trustee for A (see infra page 992).

When the settlor is not seeking the gift tax exclusion, the settlor can create a trust for a minor postponing distribution of the principal to the beneficiary until she reaches age 25 or 30 or later, when the settlor deems the beneficiary mature enough to look after her property.

Case 5. Dynasty trust. T devises property to X in trust to pay the income to T's children for their lives, then to T's grandchildren for their lives, then to pay the principal to T's great-grandchildren. The purpose of a dynasty trust is to preserve the family capital for future generations and to eliminate or reduce estate and generation-skipping transfer taxes at the death of future generations (see infra pages 849-852). The duration of the dynasty trust is controlled by the Rule against Perpetuities in most states. Perhaps you can spot the perpetuities problem in the example above. In Chapter 11, we will discuss how this perpetuities problem can be solved. A dynasty trust can be created to last for about a hundred years or, in some jurisdictions, forever (see infra page 854).

Case 6. Discretionary trust. T devises property to X in trust. The trust provides that the trustee in its sole and absolute discretion may pay the income or principal to A, or for A's benefit, as the trustee may see fit. Or the trustee may be given discretion to pay income to any one or more of a class of persons, such as A and her issue. Discretionary trusts are useful in lessening the tax burden on family wealth by distributing income to the members of the family in the lowest tax brackets. Discretionary trusts are also useful in preventing creditors of the beneficiary — including ex-spouses with alimony or child support judgments, Uncle Sam with an unpaid tax bill, and Medicaid authorities deciding whether the trust is a resource of the trust beneficiary — from reaching the income or principal of the trust (see infra pages 643-651).

These examples are skeletons, which we will flesh out later in this book. But they serve now to show you how trusts can be used for particular purposes in estate planning.

2.   The Parties to a Trust

To create a trust, a property owner transfers assets to a trustee, with the trust instrument or will setting forth the terms of the trust. A properly drafted trust will set forth both the dispositive provisions fixing the beneficiaries' interests and the administrative provisions specifying the powers and duties of the trustee in managing the trust estate. A trust ordinarily involves at least three parties: The settlor, the trustee, and one or more beneficiaries. But three different persons are not necessary for a trust. One person can wear two, or even all three, hats.

a.   The Settlor

The person who creates a trust is the *settlor* (the word comes from our ancestors, who said the person makes a settlement in trust). Sometimes, the settlor is called the *trustor.* The trust may be created during the settlor's life, in which case it is an *inter vivos* trust. Or it may be created by will, in which case it is a *testamentary* trust. An inter vivos trust may be created either by a *declaration of trust* (in which the settlor declares that he holds certain property in trust) or by a *deed of trust* (in which the settlor transfers property to another person as trustee).

Under a declaration of trust, the settlor is the trustee. To make an outright gift of property, the donor must either deliver the property or execute a deed of gift. However, a declaration of trust of personal property requires neither delivery nor a deed of gift. All that is necessary is that the donor manifest an intention to hold the property in trust. Case 1 illustrates an oral declaration of trust of personal property.

> *Case 7. O* orally declares herself trustee of 100 shares of General Electric stock, with the duty to pay the income therefrom to *A* for life, and upon *A*'s death to deliver the stock to *B.* This is a valid declaration of trust. No delivery of the stock is necessary, and since the property is personal property, no written instrument is necessary. Some states require an oral trust to be proven by clear and convincing evidence.

If the trust property is real property, the Statute of Frauds requires a written instrument for a declaration of trust.

The settlor of the trust may be both trustee and a beneficiary. Thus:

> *Case 8. O* executes a written declaration of trust declaring herself trustee of Whiteacre, to pay the income therefrom to herself for life, and upon her death Whiteacre is to pass to *A.* This is a valid trust. *Note:* If *O* were

Austin Wakeman Scott
Professor, Harvard Law School, 1909-1961

Professor Scott, together with Professor George G. Bogert of the University of Chicago, molded the modern law of trusts in this country. Their influential treatises on the law of trusts, constantly cited by courts, are the starting point for analysis of questions of trust law.

the sole beneficiary and also the sole trustee, the trust would not be valid because no one could hold *O* accountable for performance of the trust duties. In order to have a valid trust, the trustee must owe equitable duties to someone other than herself.

If the settlor is not the trustee of an inter vivos trust, a deed of trust is necessary. In order to bring the trust into being, the deed of trust or the trust property must be delivered to the trustee. Thus, in Case 8, if *O* wanted to make her lawyer, *C*, trustee, *O* would have to deliver a deed of trust to *C*.

If the trust is created by will, the settlor cannot, of course, be the trustee. The trustee will necessarily be someone other than the settlor.

PROBLEM

O executes a revocable trust document declaring that she holds in trust all of her Security Bank stock, an insurance policy she owns on the life of another, the contents of her safe deposit box, and all of her household goods and other tangible personal property. The trust document provides that *O* is the income beneficiary of the trust, and that on *O*'s death the trust property will be distributed to *A*. *O* does not transfer the Security Bank stock to herself as trustee nor does she change the name of the owner of the life insurance policy to herself as trustee. She does not open a bank account in the name of the trust. She pays the insurance premiums from her personal bank account. Several months later, *O* dies. Is this a valid trust, with the trust property now distributable to *A*? Taliaferro v. Taliaferro, 260 Kan. 573, 921 P.2d 803 (1996); Estate of Heggstad, 16 Cal. App. 4th 943, 20 Cal. Rptr. 443 (1993). But cf. N.Y. Est., Powers & Trusts Law §7-1.18 (1998).

b.   The Trustee

There may be one trustee or several trustees. The trustee may be an individual or a corporation. Almost every large bank has a trust department set up to manage trusts and carry out the duties expected and required of a trustee.

The trustee may be the settlor or a third party, or the trustee may be a beneficiary. Thus:

Case 9. By will, *H* devises property to *W* in trust to pay the income to *W* for life, and upon *W*'s death the property is to pass to *H*'s children free of trust. This is a valid trust. Although *W* is both trustee and beneficiary, *W* is not the sole beneficiary. *H*'s children have a remainder interest and can bring an action against *W* to enforce her duties as trustee. This trust arrangement has many advantages over a legal life estate in *W*, remainder in *H*'s children. *W* as trustee must keep the trust property separate from her own property and has broader powers of management, sale, and reinvestment than has a legal life tenant (see infra pages 562-566).

If the settlor intends to create a trust but fails to name a trustee, a court will appoint a trustee to carry out the trust. This rule is sometimes stated: *A trust will not fail for want of a trustee.* Thus:

> *Case 10.* *T* dies leaving a will that devises his residuary estate in trust, to pay the income to *A* for life, and on *A*'s death to distribute the trust property to *B*. However, the will does not name anyone as trustee. Since *T*'s will clearly manifests an intention to create a trust, the court will appoint a suitable person as trustee to carry out *T*'s trust purposes. (If the trust is created by a deed of trust and no trustee is named, the trust may fail for want of a transferee or for want of delivery.)

Similarly, if *T*'s will names someone as trustee but the named person refuses the appointment or dies while serving as trustee, and the will does not make provision for a successor trustee, the court will appoint a successor trustee.[2]

The trustee holds legal title to the trust property; the beneficiaries have equitable interests. In managing the trust property, the trustee is held to a very high standard of conduct. The trustee is under a duty to administer the trust solely in the interest of the beneficiaries; self-dealing (wherein the trustee acts in the same transaction both in its fiduciary capacity and in an individual capacity) is sharply limited and for some transactions is prohibited altogether. The trustee must preserve the property, make it productive, and, where required by the trust instrument, pay the income to the beneficiary. In investment decisions, the trustee owes a duty of fairness to both classes of beneficiaries: the income beneficiaries (who are interested in income and high yields) and the remaindermen (who are concerned about preservation of principal and appreciation in values). Other important duties of a trustee include the duty to keep the trust property separate from the trustee's own property, to keep accurate accounts, to invest

---

2. This rule does not apply if the court finds (or if the trust instrument specifies) that the trust powers were *personal to the named trustee*. If it is determined that the settlor intended the trust to continue only as long as the person designated as trustee continues to serve in that capacity, the trust terminates when the named person ceases to serve as trustee. This exception is rarely involved, however. In the usual case, the court will determine that the primary purpose of the settlor was to have the trust continue for the indicated purposes and not that the particular person, and only that person, serve as trustee. See 2 Scott, supra, §101.1.

prudently, and not to delegate trust powers. If the trustee improperly manages the trust estate, the trustee may be denied compensation, subjected to personal liability, and removed as trustee by a court. In Chapter 13, we give extended consideration to the duties and powers of trustees, to important problems in trust administration, and to the distinctive nature of the fiduciary office.

In order to have a trust, it is necessary for the trustee to have some duties to perform. If the trustee has no duties at all, there is no reason to have, or to recognize, a trust. The trust is then said to be "passive," or "dry," and the trust fails. When a trust fails because the trustee has no active duties, the beneficiaries acquire legal title to the trust property.

Because a trustee has onerous duties and liabilities, the law does not impose upon a person the office of trustee unless the person accepts. Once a person accepts the office of trustee, the person can be released from liability only with consent of the beneficiaries or by a court order.

PROBLEM

In January *O* executes a written instrument creating an irrevocable trust and naming *X* as trustee. The trust instrument provides that the income from the trust is to be paid to *A* for life, and upon *A*'s death the corpus is to be distributed to *B*. Shortly thereafter, *O* delivers a copy of the trust instrument and $100,000 in cash to *X* and tells *X* that this money is to be held by *X* under the trust. *X* immediately puts the money in his safe-deposit box.

O dies the following February. In November next, *X*, saying that he does not want to be trustee, divides the money between *D* and *E*, the residuary legatees of *O*'s estate, paying $50,000 to each. Has a trust been established? See 1 Scott, supra, §35. Is *X* liable for $100,000? 2 id. §102.2. Can *A* and *B* recover the $100,000 from *D* and *E*? See 4 id. §292. See also Restatement (Third) of Trusts §35 (T.D. No. 2, 1999).

c.   The Beneficiaries

The beneficiaries hold equitable interests. Generally speaking, this means that the beneficiaries have interests that originated in chancery and have different characteristics from legal interests. Of special importance are the remedies available to the beneficiaries for breach of trust. The beneficiaries have a personal claim against the trustee for breach of trust. However, this personal claim has no higher priority than the claim of other creditors of the trustee and thus might not protect the beneficiaries if it were their only remedy. Equity gives the beneficiaries additional remedies relating to the trust property itself. Personal creditors of the trustee, other than the trust beneficiaries, cannot reach the trust property. If the trustee wrongfully disposes of the trust property, the beneficiaries can recover the trust property unless it has come into the hands of a bona fide purchaser for value. If the trustee disposes of trust property and acquires other property with the proceeds of sale, the beneficiaries can enforce the trust on the newly acquired property. Largely because of these rights to reach the trust property, we say the beneficiaries have equitable title to the trust property.

Private trusts almost always create successive beneficial interests. Typically, trust income is payable to the beneficiary (or class of beneficiaries) for life, perhaps to be followed by life interests in another class of beneficiaries, with the trustee to distribute the trust corpus to yet another class of beneficiaries upon termination of the trust. Thus the creation of a trust involves the creation of one or more equitable future interests as well as a present interest in the income.

> *Case 11. O* transfers securities worth $100,000 to *X* in trust, to pay the income to *A* for life, then to *B* for life. On the death of the survivor of *A* and *B*, the trustee is to distribute the trust principal to *B*'s issue then living. *X* has legal title to the trust assets, and has a fiduciary duty to manage and invest the assets for the benefit of the indicated beneficiaries. *A* has an equitable life estate. *B* has an equitable remainder for life. *B*'s issue have an equitable contingent remainder in fee simple. *O* has an equitable reversion (often called a resulting trust). If on the death of the survivor of *A* and *B* there are no issue of *B* then living, the trust property will revert to *O* (or to *O*'s successors if *O* has died in the meantime).

Today, most life estates and future interests are equitable rather than legal interests; they are created in trusts. Legal life estates and future interests in tangible or intangible personal property are rare and almost always inadvisable. Legal life estates and future interests in land are sometimes encountered. These too are almost always inadvisable. A trust with equitable interests is a much more flexible and useful means of giving property than a disposition that creates legal interests.

3. *A Trust Compared with a Legal Life Estate*

A person who wants to give another a life estate may give the donee either a legal life estate or create a trust with the donee as life beneficiary. A legal life tenant has possession and control of the property, whereas a trustee has legal title to the trust property. Let us compare a legal life estate ("to *A* for life, remainder to *A*'s children") with an equitable life estate ("to *X* in trust for *A* for life, remainder to *A*'s children"). Is a legal life estate more or less desirable than a trust? This question is best answered by looking at problems that may arise during the legal life tenant's life and how proper drafting might solve them.

(1) *Sale.* The legal life tenant has no power to sell a fee simple unless such a power is granted in the instrument creating the life estate. If the life tenant is not granted a power of sale, it is possible for the tenant to go to court and obtain judicial approval of a sale. However, the law on this point is rather unclear. A lawsuit, even if successful, is expensive, and hence no legal life estate should be created without providing a mechanism for sale of the property should circumstances warrant it. (Exception: There may be no need for a power of sale if testator wants to pass grandfather's portrait, or some other item of family sentiment, from generation to generation.) Who is going to have the power of sale? It could be given to the life tenant, but this may be undesirable for reasons noted below. The power of sale could be given to the life tenant and the adult remaindermen jointly, but it may prove difficult to get all interested parties to agree on sale, and the opportunity for sale may be lost.

(2) *Reinvestment of proceeds of sale.* If the property is sold under a power of sale, what is to be done with the proceeds? If the life tenant is given a power of sale under which the proceeds go to the life tenant, the power of sale is in effect a general power of appointment, which has serious estate tax disadvantages.[3] This may defeat the purpose of the life estate — to avoid death taxes on the life tenant's death. To get around this problem, the instrument could provide that the proceeds are to be held in trust (with the life tenant as trustee), to pay the income to the life tenant for life, then the proceeds to go to the remaindermen. However, the terms of this trust must be spelled out in the will; otherwise, litigation may ensue.

(3) *Borrowing money.* During the life tenant's lifetime, the real estate cannot be mortgaged by the life tenant. No banker is so foolish as to lend money with only a life estate as security. To put up the fee simple as security for a loan, it is necessary that the life tenant and

---

3. A general power of appointment is the power to appoint the property to the donee (holder) of the power, the donee's estate, the creditors of the donee, or the creditors of the donee's estate. Property over which a person holds a general power of appointment is included in the person's taxable gross estate at death, on which a federal estate tax may be payable. See infra page 1032.

Property subject to a nongeneral or special power of appointment is not subject to estate taxation at the death of the holder of the power. See infra page 1033.

all the remaindermen and reversioners sign the mortgage. It may be impossible to procure these signatures if the future takers are unascertained. Someone should be given the power to mortgage real estate. Without such a power the life tenant and remaindermen may be stuck with property that cannot be improved because it cannot be mortgaged. If the life tenant is given this power and can appropriate the loan to herself, the power to mortgage is in effect a general power of appointment that may lead to tax problems in the life tenant's estate.

(4) *Leasing.* If rental property is involved, someone should be given the power to lease the property for a period extending beyond the life tenant's death. Otherwise it may be impossible to rent the premises. If the life tenant is given this power, and can accept a lump-sum payment in advance for the rent, the life tenant has the power to appropriate part of the remainder to herself. To the extent the life tenant can appoint the remainder to herself the life tenant has a general power of appointment.

(5) *Waste.* The life tenant may want to take oil out of the land, cut timber, or take down a still usable building. Each of these actions constitutes waste, and the remaindermen may be entitled to an injunction or damages. If the life tenant is given the power to drill for oil, open mines, or commit waste with impunity, the life tenant may be held to have a general power of appointment for tax purposes.

(6) *Expenses.* If land is involved, someone must pay taxes and maintain the property. The general rule is that the life tenant has the duty to pay taxes and keep the property in repair, but only to the extent the income from the property is adequate to cover those charges. The life tenant also has the duty to pay interest on, but not the principal of, the mortgage. However, the life tenant is under no duty to insure buildings on the land. If the life tenant does insure buildings, and the buildings are destroyed by fire, the life tenant has been held entitled to the whole proceeds and the remaindermen nothing. The instrument of gift may require the life tenant to insure the full value of the property or forfeit the life estate. But if this is done, and if the property is destroyed, what is to be done with the insurance proceeds? Similar problems arise as in the case of a sale; if the proceeds are to be held by the life tenant in trust, the trust must be spelled out in the testator's will. Since the life tenant may wish to use the proceeds to rebuild the premises, such a power should be granted the life tenant.

(7) *Creditors.* If the life tenant gets into debt, the creditor can seize the life estate and sell it. Of course, very little may be realized upon sale. Likely the creditor will buy it on judicial sale for a small amount, and if the life tenant lives a long time the creditor reaps a windfall. A forfeiture restraint against involuntary alienation could be put on

the life estate, but its validity is questionable. If the debtor is a remain-derman, the creditor may be able to seize the remainder and sell it. As with the life estate, the remainder may sell for very little, and the creditor usually will be the purchaser.

(8) *Miscellaneous.* Many other problems may arise. Trespassers may damage the property; the government may exercise eminent domain; a third party may be injured on the premises. The respective rights of the life tenant and the remaindermen must be covered in testator's will unless the law regarding the rights of a legal life tenant is clear and certain and satisfactory, and we can assure you that it isn't. If all these foreseeable problems are not covered in testator's will, they may end up being decided in expensive court proceedings.

When we consider all the problems that may arise in the future, we find that a trust is in most cases preferable to a legal life estate. If an independent trustee is not selected, the life tenant should be made a trustee rather than being given a legal life estate. Most of the above problems are administrative problems, and the law of trust administration is well established and extensive. If the trustee's powers are not spelled out in the trust instrument, the law will supply a charter of administration. Trust administration law is for the most part quite rational; in any case, it is simpler and far more rational than the law respecting legal life estates and remainders. Look at the problems above. (1) Standard administrative provisions from any form book almost always give the trustee a power of sale. The lawyer drafting the trust is unlikely to overlook this matter for it is natural to think of the trustee as a manager, whereas the life tenant may be thought of not as a manager but as a user. If the lawyer overlooks a power of sale, the courts are far more ready to find that a power of sale is conferred upon a trustee than upon a legal life tenant. (2) If the property is sold by a legal life tenant and the proceeds are to be put in trust, a trust must be created for the proceeds. This trust should be spelled out in the will, so the lawyer will not be saving words by creating a legal life estate. Why not have a trust from the beginning? (3, 4, 5, and 6) As powers of sale are routinely put in any trust instrument, so are powers to mortgage, to lease, to give oil leases, and to pay taxes, insurance, and current charges. Where these powers are omitted in the trust instrument, the law often gives the trustee these powers. (7) A major difference between legal estates and equitable estates is that the latter can be put out of the reach of creditors. In most states a spendthrift trust, which disables creditors from reaching a beneficiary's interest, is permissible (see infra page 631).

A trustee is required to keep the trust property separate from the trustee's own property. A life tenant who is also trustee must keep separate books and account to the remaindermen. This requirement, plus the necessity for a separate tax return, tends to keep the bookkeeping accurate and up-to-date and tends to eliminate litigation over the respective rights of the life tenant and the remaindermen. If a trustee mingles trust funds with the trustee's personal funds, the burden is on the trustee to show how much of the mingled fund is the trustee's own property. If the trustee cannot do this, the beneficiary may be entitled to the whole mingled fund.

QUESTION AND NOTE

1.   In view of the disadvantages of a legal life estate, why is not a legal life estate converted into a trust by statute? What purposes are served in having two bodies of law, one applicable to legal life estates and one applicable to life estates in trust?

By the English Law of Property Act of 1925, the legal life estate was abolished. Since that date only two kinds of legal estates can exist in England: the fee simple absolute in possession and the leasehold. Apart from leaseholds, all life estates and future interests of every kind (remainders, executory interests, reversions, possibilities of reverter, rights of entry) are equitable interests. The holder of the fee simple absolute in possession holds the property in trust for the other interested parties. The purpose of this legislation is to make land marketable by ensuring that a fee simple absolute owner is always available to sell the land. The result is to turn all family property settlements into trusts. See C. Dent Bostick, Loosening the Grip of the Dead Hand: Shall We Abolish Legal Future Interests in Land, 32 Vand. L. Rev. 1061 (1979); Ronald H. Maudsley, Escaping the Tyranny of Common Law Estates, 42 Mo. L. Rev. 355 (1977).

2.   In recent years scholars have been exploring the functions of the trust and its relationship to other fields of law. Because he believes trust law is currently more rigid than contract law in some respects, Professor Langbein argues that trust law is, at bottom, part of contract law, and should be as flexible as contract law in enabling settlors to achieve their objectives. "The deal between settlor and trustee," he concludes, "is functionally indistinguishable from the modern third-party-beneficiary contract." John H. Langbein, The Contractarian Basis of the Law of Trusts, 105 Yale L.J. 625, 627 (1995) (Langbein also brilliantly traces the historical development of trust law). Professor Langbein has also explored the use of trusts as commercial arrangements. He notes that trusts have become predominantly commercial in function and that the money in private trusts used for intrafamily wealth transfers, though some billions in amount, is trivial compared to the money in commercial private trusts used in American capital markets. John H. Langbein, The Secret Life of the Trust: The Trust as an Instrument of Commerce, 107 Yale L.J. 165 (1997).

Professors Hansmann and Mattei agree with Langbein that so far as the relationships of the parties to the trust are concerned, trust law is similar to contract law. But they see the benefit of trusts not in ordering relationships between the parties to the trust, for which contract law might serve just as well, but in ordering the relationships of the trust parties with third parties — particularly creditors — with whom the trust parties deal. In an illuminating article Hansmann and Mattei show how more advantageous creditor relationships can be constructed with a trust than can be done by contract, agency, or corporation law. As a result of its usefulness in dealing with creditors in capital markets, the trust — an English invention long thought logically inconsistent with civil law concepts — is now being adopted or adapted in European civil law countries. Henry Hansmann & Ugo Mattei, The Functions of Trust Law: A Comparative Legal and Economic Analysis, 73 N.Y.U. L. Rev. 434 (1998).

SECTION B.   CREATION OF A TRUST

1.   *Intent to Create a Trust*

No particular form of words is necessary to create a trust. The words trust or trustee need not be used. The sole question is whether the grantor manifested an intention to create a trust relationship.

Where the grantor conveys property to a grantee to hold "for the use and benefit" of another, this is a sufficient manifestation of an intention to create a trust. Thus, in Fox v. Faulkner, 222 Ky. 584, 1 S.W.2d 1079 (1927), the grantor conveyed land "to Mary Pursiful for the use and benefit of Moses A. Cottrell, during his natural life — if said Moses A. Cottrell should leave children in lawful wedlock it shall go to them." The court held that a trust was created, saying:

> Though Mary Pursiful was designated as party of the second part in the deed, and the qualifying word "trustee" was not added after her name to indicate that she took merely in that capacity, the language of the granting clause is such as to exclude the conclusion that she took under it in any capacity other than as trustee for Moses A. Cottrell. The case is on a par with the celebrated bear case (Prewitt v. Clayton, 5 T.B. Mon. 5), where it was said: "A bear well painted and drawn to the life is yet a picture of a bear, although the painter may omit to write over it, 'This is the bear.' "

Jimenez v. Lee
Supreme Court of Oregon, 1976
274 Or. 457, 547 P.2d 126

O'CONNELL, C.J. This is a suit brought by plaintiff against her father to compel him to account for assets which she alleges were held by defendant as trustee for her. Plaintiff appeals from a decree dismissing her complaint.

Plaintiff's claim against her father is based upon the theory that a trust arose in her favor when two separate gifts were made for her benefit. The first of these gifts was made in 1945, shortly after plaintiff's birth, when her paternal grandmother purchased a $1,000 face value U.S. Savings Bond which was registered in the names of defendant "and/or" plaintiff "and/or" Dorothy Lee, plaintiff's mother. It is uncontradicted that the bond was purchased to provide funds to be used for plaintiff's educational needs. A second gift in the amount of $500 was made in 1956 by Mrs. Adolph Diercks, one of defendant's clients. At the same time Mrs. Diercks made identical gifts for the benefit of defendant's two other children. The $1,500 was deposited by the donor in a savings account in the names of defendant and his three children.

In 1960 defendant cashed the savings bond and invested the proceeds in common stock of the Commercial Bank of Salem, Oregon. Ownership of the shares was registered as "Jason Lee, Custodian under the Laws of Oregon for Betsy Lee [plaintiff]." At the same time, the joint savings account containing the client's gifts to defendant's children was closed and $1,000 of the proceeds invested in Commercial Bank stock.[4] Defendant also took title to this stock as "custodian" for his children.

The trial court found that defendant did not hold either the savings bond or the savings account in trust for the benefit of plaintiff and that defendant held the shares of the Commercial Bank stock as custodian for plaintiff under the Uniform Gift to Minors Act (O.R.S. 126.805-126.880). Plaintiff contends that the gifts for her educational needs created trusts in each instance and that the trusts survived defendant's investment of the trust assets in the Commercial Bank stock.

It is undisputed that the gifts were made for the educational needs of plaintiff. The respective donors did not expressly direct defendant to hold the subject matter of the gift "in trust" but this is not essential

---

4. The specific disposition of the balance of this account is not revealed in the record. Defendant testified that the portion of the gift not invested in the stock "was used for other unusual needs of the children." Defendant could not recall exactly how the money was used but thought some of it was spent for family vacations to Victoria, British Columbia and to satisfy his children's expensive taste in clothing.

to create a trust relationship. It is enough if the transfer of the property is made with the intent to vest the beneficial ownership in a third person. That was clearly shown in the present case. Even defendant's own testimony establishes such intent. When he was asked whether there was a stated purpose for the gift, he replied: ". . . Mother said that she felt that the children should all be treated equally and that she was going to supply a bond to help with Elizabeth's educational needs and that she was naming me and Dorothy, the ex-wife and mother of Elizabeth, to use the funds as may be most conducive to the educational needs of Elizabeth." Defendant also admitted that the gift from Mrs. Diercks was "for the educational needs of the children." There was nothing about either of the gifts which would suggest that the beneficial ownership of the subject matter of the gift was to vest in defendant to use as he pleased with an obligation only to pay out of his own funds a similar amount for plaintiff's educational needs.

Defendant himself demonstrated that he knew that the savings bond was held by him in trust. In a letter to his mother, the donor, he wrote: "Dave and Bitsie [plaintiff] & Dorothy are aware of the fact that I hold $1,000 each for Dave & Bitsie in trust for them on account of your E-Bond gifts." It is fair to indulge in the presumption that defendant, as a lawyer, used the word "trust" in the ordinary legal sense of that term.

Defendant further contends that even if the respective donors intended to create trusts, the doctrine of merger defeated that intent because plaintiff acquired both legal and equitable title when the savings bond was registered in her name along with her parents' names and when Mrs. Diercks' gift was deposited in the savings account in the name of plaintiff and her father, brother and sister. The answer to this contention is found in II Scott on Trusts §99.4, p. 811 (3d ed 1967):

> A trust may be created in which the trustees are *A* and *B* and the sole beneficiary is *A*. In such a case it might be argued that there is automatically a partial extinguishment of the trust, and that *A* holds an undivided half interest as joint tenant free of trust, although *B* holds a similar interest in trust for *A*. The better view is, however, that there is no such partial merger, and that *A* and *B* will hold the property as joint tenants in trust for *A*. . . .

Having decided that a trust was created for the benefit of plaintiff, it follows that defendant's purchase of the Commercial Bank stock as "custodian" for plaintiff under the Uniform Gift to Minors Act was ineffectual to expand defendant's powers over the trust property from that of trustee to that of custodian.[5]

Defendant's attempt to broaden his powers over the trust estate by investing the trust funds as custodian violated his duty to the beneficiary "to administer the trust solely in the interest of the beneficiary." Restatement (Second) of Trusts §170, p.364 (1959).

The money from the savings bond and savings account are clearly traceable into the bank stock. Therefore, plaintiff was entitled to impose a constructive trust or an equitable lien upon the stock so acquired. Plaintiff is also entitled to be credited for any dividends or increment in the value of that part of the stock representing plaintiff's proportional interest. Whether or not the assets of plaintiff's trust are traceable into a product, defendant is personally liable for that amount which would have accrued to plaintiff had there been no breach of trust. Defendant is, of course, entitled to deduct the amount which he expended out of the trust estate for plaintiff's educational needs. However, before he is entitled to be credited for such expenditures, he has the duty as trustee to identify them specifically and prove that they were made for trust purposes. A trustee's duty to maintain and render accurate accounts is a strict one. This strict standard is described in Bogert on Trusts and Trustees §962, pp. 10-13 (2d ed 1962):

> It is the duty of the trustees to keep full, accurate and orderly records of the statutes of the trust administration and of all acts thereunder. . . . "The general rule of law applicable to a trustee burdens him with the duty of showing that the account which he renders and the expenditures which he claims to have been made were correct, just and necessary. . . . He is bound to keep clear and accurate accounts, and if he does not the presumptions are all against him, obscurities and doubts being resolved adversely to him." [Quoting from White v. Rankin, 46 NYS 228, 18 App Div 293, 294, affirmed without opinion 162 NY 622, 57 NE 1128 (1897).] . . . He has the burden of showing on the accounting how much

---

5. If defendant were "custodian" of the gifts, he would have the power under the Uniform Gift to Minors Act (O.R.S. 126.820) to use the property "as he may deem advisable for the support, maintenance, education and general use and benefit of the minor, in such manner, at such time or times, and to such extent as the custodian in his absolute discretion may deem advisable and proper, without court order or without regard to the duty of any person to support the minor, and without regard to any other funds which may be applicable or available for the purpose." As custodian defendant would not be required to account for his stewardship of the funds unless a petition for accounting were filed in circuit court no later than two years after the end of plaintiff's minority. O.R.S. 126.875. As the trustee of an educational trust, however, defendant has the power to use the trust funds for educational purposes only and has the duty to render clear and accurate accounts showing the funds have been used for trust purposes. See O.R.S. 128.010; Restatement (Second) of Trusts §172 (1959).

[The Uniform Transfers to Minors Act is explained supra at pages 133-134. — Eds.]

George G. Bogert
Chicago's great authority on trust law

principal and income he has received and from whom, how much disbursed and to whom, and what is on hand at the time.

Defendant did not keep separate records of trust income and trust expenditures. He introduced into evidence a summary of various expenditures which he claimed were made for the benefit of plaintiff.

It appears that the summary was prepared for the most part from cancelled checks gathered together for the purpose of defending the present suit. This obviously did not meet the requirement that a trustee "maintain records of his transactions so complete and accurate that he can show by them his faithfulness to his trust."[6]

In an even more general way defendant purported to account for the trust assets in a letter dated February 9, 1966, written to plaintiff shortly after her 21st birthday when she was in Europe where she had been receiving instruction and training in ballet. In that letter defendant revealed to plaintiff, apparently for the first time, that her grandmother had made a gift to her of a savings bond and that the proceeds of the bond had been invested in stock. Without revealing the name of the stock, defendant represented that it had doubled in value of the bond from $750 to $1,500. The letter went on to suggest that plaintiff allocate $1,000 to defray the cost of additional ballet classes and that the remaining $500 be held in reserve to defray expenses in returning to the United States and in getting settled in a college or in a ballet company.

Defendant's letter was in no sense a trust accounting. In the first place, it was incomplete; it made no mention of Mrs. Diercks' gift. Moreover, it was inaccurate since it failed to reveal the true value attributable to the Commercial Bank stock. There was evidence which would put the value of plaintiff's interest in the stock at considerably more than $1,500.[7]

Defendant contends that even if a trust is found to exist and that the value of the trust assets is the amount claimed by plaintiff there is sufficient evidence to prove that the trust estate was exhausted by expenditures for legitimate trust purposes. Considering the character of the evidence presented by defendant, it is difficult to understand how such a result could be reached. As we noted above, the trust was for the educational needs of plaintiff. Some of the expenditures made by defendant would seem to fall clearly within the purposes of the trust. These would include the cost of ballet lessons, the cost of subscribing to a ballet magazine, and other items of expenditure related to plaintiff's education.[8] But many of the items defendant lists as trust

6. Wood v. Honeyman, 178 Or. 484, 555-556, 169 P.2d 131, 162 (1946).

7. It appears that with the accumulation of cash and stock dividends the total value of plaintiff's interest at the time she received defendant's letter would amount to as much as $2,135. This figure is an approximation derived from the incomplete stock price information before us. It is important only to demonstrate that defendant did not render an adequate accounting. Our calculation does not include the value of plaintiff's interest in stock purchased with the proceeds of Mrs. Diercks' gift.

8. Defendant's failure to keep proper records makes it difficult, if not impossible, to determine whether some of these expenditures were made from the trust estate or from defendant's own funds. Moreover, it is unclear in some instances whether the expenditure was for educational purposes or simply for recreation. Thus defendant charges plaintiff with expenses incurred in connection with a European tour taken by plaintiff.

expenditures are either questionable or clearly outside the purpose of an educational trust. For instance, defendant seeks credit against the trust for tickets to ballet performances on three different occasions while plaintiff was in high school. The cost of plaintiff's ticket to a ballet performance might be regarded as a part of plaintiff's educational program in learning the art of ballet, but defendant claims credit for expenditures made to purchase ballet tickets for himself and other members of the family, disbursements clearly beyond the purposes of the trust.

Other expenditures claimed by defendant in his "accounting" are clearly not in furtherance of the purposes of the trust. Included in the cancelled checks introduced into evidence in support of defendant's claimed offset against the trust assets were: (1) checks made by defendant in payment of numerous medical bills dating from the time plaintiff was 15 years old (these were obligations which a parent owes to his minor children); (2) checks containing the notation "Happy Birthday" which plaintiff received from her parents on her 17th, 18th and 22nd birthdays; (3) a 1963 check with a notation "Honor Roll, Congratulations, Mom and Dad"; (4) defendant's check to a clothier which contains the notation "Betsy's Slacks and Sweater, Pat's Sweater, Dot's Sweater" (defendant attempted to charge the entire amount against the trust); (5) defendant's check to a Canadian Rotary Club for a meeting attended when he joined plaintiff in Banff after a summer ballet program; (6) $60 sent to plaintiff to enable her to travel from France, where she was studying ballet, to Austria to help care for her sister's newborn babies. There were also other items improperly claimed as expenditures for plaintiff's educational benefit, either because the purpose of the outlay could not be identified or because defendant claimed a double credit.[9]

It is apparent from the foregoing description of defendant's evidence that the trial court erred in finding that "Plaintiff in these proceedings has received the accounting which she sought and . . . is entitled to no further accounting." The trial court also erred in finding that "Defendant did not hold in trust for the benefit of Plaintiff" the product traceable to the two gifts.

The case must, therefore, be remanded for an accounting to be predicated upon a trustee's duty to account, and the trustee's burden to prove that the expenditures were made for trust purposes. There is a moral obligation and in proper cases a legal obligation for a

---

It is not disclosed as to whether this was to provide an educational experience for plaintiff or for some other purpose.

9. The double counting occurs where defendant claims credit for cashier's checks sent to plaintiff while she was staying in Europe and at the same time also claims credit for his personal checks used to purchase the cashier's checks.

parent to furnish his child with higher education. Where a parent is a trustee of an educational trust, as in the present case, and he makes expenditures out of his own funds, his intent on one hand may be to discharge his moral or legal obligation to educate his child or on the other hand to follow the directions of the trust.[10] It is a question of fact in each case as to which of these two purposes the parent-trustee had in mind at the time of making the expenditures.[11] In determining whether defendant has met this strict burden of proof, the trial court must adhere to the rule that all doubts are resolved against a trustee who maintains an inadequate accounting system.

The decree of the trial court is reversed and the cause is remanded for further proceedings consistent with this opinion.[12]

10. The rule stated by Bogert indicates why defendant's intent is important:

> The trustee is entitled to be credited on the accounting with all sums paid or property transferred by him from trust funds, and with sums advanced by him from his own funds, when such payments or transfers were in the exercise of powers expressly or impliedly granted to him by the trust instrument, or powers given him by statute or court order, or reasonably incidental to the exercise of such powers.

Bogert on Trusts and Trustees §972(1) (2d ed. 1962), pp. 218-220.

If defendant made expenditures out of his own funds intending to discharge his obligation to educate his child, the payments were not "sums advanced by him from his own funds . . . in the exercise of [trust] powers." Such expenditures would be in his capacity as plaintiff's father and not as trustee.

11. There is evidence that defendant considered expenditures made prior to February 9, 1966 (the date of defendant's letter to plaintiff which we previously described) as not being for trust purposes because at that date he regarded the proceeds from the savings bond still intact. The letter read:

> I believe that it would be fair and realistic and I should henceforth offset against this $1500 such further funds as you may need to continue with your ballet instruction, or to travel to New York or elsewhere to commence your ballet career on an independent, self-supporting basis.
>
> The situation is comparable to that of the mother bird that finally nudges the baby out of the nest so that it, too, may learn to fly.

12. Jason Lee, the defendant in Jimenez v. Lee, was elected to the Oregon Court of Appeals in 1974, unseating an incumbent judge. As a result of the bitter campaign, a newspaper reporter sued the state bar under Oregon's open records law to reveal its disciplinary records on Jason Lee. In 1975, Lee filed for the Oregon Supreme Court seat of Chief Justice O'Connell, who was retiring in 1976. The decision in Jimenez v. Lee, written by Chief Justice O'Connell, was handed down on March 18, 1976. The next day, March 19, Jason Lee withdrew from the supreme court race. In June 1976, the supreme court decided the reporter's lawsuit and ordered the Jason Lee disciplinary records opened to the public. Lee's files weighed 15 pounds and revealed many complaints. A public letter of reprimand, for ambulance chasing and for directing his secretary as a notary to execute false acknowledgments, had been issued to Lee in 1965.

Judge Jason Lee did not resign from the court of appeals. Still sitting on that court, Lee died of a heart attack in 1980. Lee's will left all his property to his second wife, Merie. If Merie predeceased him (she didn't), his will devised his property in trust for his grandchildren: "I leave nothing but my love to my children."

The information in this footnote was furnished to the editors by Professor Valerie Vollmar of Willamette University College of Law. — Eds.

NOTES

1. *Precatory language.* In a surprisingly large number of cases, the testator expresses a wish that the property devised should be disposed of by the devisee in some particular manner, but the language does not clearly indicate whether the testator intends to create a trust (with a legal duty so to dispose of the property) or merely a moral obligation unenforceable at law. If the language indicates the latter, it is called *precatory* language. (And sometimes courts speak of *precatory trusts,* meaning unenforceable dispositions of this sort.) Typical language raising this issue is a bequest "to *A* with the hope that *A* will care for *B*" or a devise of land "to *C* and it is my wish and desire that *D* should be able to live on the land during her life." To fathom the testator's intent, each will must be construed in accordance with the language used in each particular case in the light of all the circumstances. The result: much litigation. See 1 Austin W. Scott, Trusts §25.2 (William F. Fratcher 4th ed. 1987); Restatement (Third) of Trusts §13, Comment d and Reporter's Notes (T.D. No. 1, 1996) (discussing cases). The problem can be avoided by clear drafting. If only a moral obligation is desired, say, "I wish, but do not legally require, that *C* permit *D* to live on the land."

2. *Equitable charge.* Another distinction needs mention here: the difference between a trust and an equitable charge. If a testator devises property to a person, subject to the payment of a certain sum of money to another person, the testator creates an equitable charge, not a trust. An equitable charge creates a security interest in the transferred property. There is no fiduciary relationship. See Restatement (Third) of Trusts, supra, §5, Comment h.

The Hebrew University Association v. Nye
Supreme Court of Connecticut, 1961
148 Conn. 223, 169 A.2d 641

KING, J.   The plaintiff obtained a judgment declaring that it is the rightful owner of the library of Abraham S. Yahuda, a distinguished Hebrew scholar who died in 1951. The library included rare books and manuscripts, mostly relating to the Bible, which Professor Yahuda, with the assistance of his wife, Ethel S. Yahuda, had collected during his lifetime. Some of the library was inventoried in Professor Yahuda's estate and was purchased from the estate by his wife. There is no dispute that all of the library had become the property of Ethel before 1953 and was her property when she died on March 6, 1955, unless by her dealings with the plaintiff between January, 1953, and the time of her death she transferred ownership to the plaintiff. While the defendants in this action are the executors under the will of Ethel, the controversy as to ownership of the library is, in effect, a contest between two Hebrew charitable institutions, the plaintiff and a charitable trust or foundation to which Ethel bequeathed the bulk of her estate.

The pertinent facts recited in the finding may be summarized as follows: Before his death, Professor Yahuda forwarded certain of the books in his library to a warehouse in New Haven with instructions that they be packed for overseas shipment. The books remained in his name, no consignee was ever specified, and no shipment was made. Although it is not entirely clear, these books were apparently the ones which Ethel purchased from her husband's estate. Professor Yahuda and his wife had indicated to their friends their interest in creating a scholarship research center in Israel which would serve as a memorial to them. In January, 1953, Ethel went to Israel and had several talks with officers of the plaintiff, a university in Jerusalem. One of the departments of the plaintiff is an Institute of Oriental Studies, of outstanding reputation. The library would be very useful to the plaintiff, especially in connection with the work of this institute. On January 28, 1953, a large luncheon was given by the plaintiff in Ethel's honor and was attended by many notables, including officials of the plaintiff and the president of Israel. At this luncheon, Ethel described the library and announced its gift to the plaintiff. The next day, the plaintiff submitted to Ethel a proposed newspaper release which indicated that she had made a gift of the library to the plaintiff. Ethel signed the release as approved by her. From time to time thereafter she stated orally, and in letters to the plaintiff and friends, that she "had given" the library to the plaintiff. She refused offers of purchase and explained to others that she could not sell the library because it did not belong to her but to the plaintiff. On one occasion, when it was suggested that she give a certain item in the library to a friend, she stated that she could not, since it did not belong to her but to the plaintiff.

Early in 1954, Ethel began the task of arranging and cataloguing the material in the library for crating and shipment to Israel. These activities continued until about the time of her death. She sent some items, which she had finished cataloguing, to a warehouse for crating for overseas shipment. No consignee was named, and they remained in her name until her death. In October, 1954, when she was at the office of the American Friends of the Hebrew University, a fund-raising arm of the plaintiff in New York, she stated that she had crated most of the miscellaneous items, was continuously working on cataloguing the balance, and hoped to have the entire library in Israel before the end of the year. Until almost the time of her death, she corresponded with the plaintiff about making delivery to it of the library. In September, 1954, she wrote the president of the plaintiff that she had decided to ship the library and collection, but that it was not to be unpacked unless she was present, so that her husband's ex libris could be affixed to the books, and that she hoped "to adjust" the matter of her Beth Yahuda and her relations to the plaintiff. A "beth" is a building or portion of a building dedicated to a particular purpose.

The complaint alleged that the plaintiff was the rightful owner of the library and was entitled to possession. It contained no clue, however, to the theory on which ownership was claimed. The prayers for relief sought a declaratory judgment determining which one of the parties owned the library and an injunction restraining the defendants from disposing of it. The answer amounted to a general denial. The only real issues raised in the pleadings were the ownership and the right to possession of the library. As to these issues, the plaintiff had the burden of proof. The judgment found the "issues" for the plaintiff, and further recited that "a trust [in relation to the library] was created by a declaration of trust made by Ethel S. Yahuda, indicating her intention to create such a trust, made public by her." We construe this language, in the light of the finding, as a determination that, at the luncheon in Jerusalem, Ethel orally constituted herself a trustee of the library for future delivery to the plaintiff. The difficulty with the trust theory adopted in the judgment is that the finding contains no facts even intimating that Ethel ever regarded herself as trustee of any trust whatsoever, or as having assumed any enforceable duties with respect to the property. The facts in the finding, in so far as they tend to support the judgment for the plaintiff at all, indicate that Ethel intended to make, and perhaps attempted to make, not a mere promise to give, but an executed, present, legal gift inter vivos of the library to the plaintiff without any delivery whatsoever.

Obviously, if an intended or attempted legal gift inter vivos of personal property fails as such because there was neither actual nor constructive delivery, and the intent to give can nevertheless be carried into effect in equity under the fiction that the donor is presumed to have intended to constitute himself a trustee to make the necessary delivery, then as a practical matter the requirement of delivery is abrogated in any and all cases of intended inter-vivos gifts. Of course this is not the law. A gift which is imperfect for lack of a delivery will not be turned into a declaration of trust for no better reason than that it is imperfect for lack of a delivery. Courts do not supply conveyances where there are none. Cullen v. Chappell, 116 F.2d 1017, 1018 (2d Cir.). This is true, even though the intended donee is a charity. Organized Charities Assn. v. Mansfield, 82 Conn. 504, 510, 74 A. 781. The cases on this point are collected in an annotation in 96 A.L.R.

383, which is supplemented by a later annotation in 123 A.L.R. 1335. The rule is approved in 1 Scott, Trusts §31.

It is true that one can orally constitute himself a trustee of personal property for the benefit of another and thereby create a trust enforceable in equity, even though without consideration and without delivery. 1 Scott, op. cit. §28; §32.2, p. 251. But he must in effect constitute himself a trustee. There must be an express trust, even though oral. It is not sufficient that he declare himself a donor. 1 Scott, op. cit. §31, p. 239; 4 id. §462.1. While he need not use the term "trustee," nor even manifest an understanding of its technical meaning or the technical meaning of the term "trust," he must manifest an intention to impose upon himself enforceable duties of a trust nature. Cullen v. Chappell, supra; Restatement (Second), 1 Trusts §§23, 25; 1 Scott, op. cit., pp. 180, 181. There are no subordinate facts in the finding to indicate that Ethel ever intended to, or did, impose upon herself any enforceable duties of a trust nature with respect to this library. The most that could be said is that the subordinate facts in the finding might perhaps have supported a conclusion that at the luncheon she had the requisite donative intent so that, had she subsequently made a delivery of the property while that intent persisted, there would have been a valid, legal gift inter vivos. . . . The judgment, however, is not based on the theory of a legal gift inter vivos but on that of a declaration of trust. Since the subordinate facts give no support for a judgment on that basis, it cannot stand.

[The court remanded the case for a new trial at which the plaintiff could present its case on other theories than a declaration of trust.]

The Hebrew University Association v. Nye
Superior Court of Connecticut, 1966
26 Conn. Supp. 342, 223 A.2d 397

PARSKEY, J.   Most of the facts in this case are recited in Hebrew University Assn. v. Nye, 148 Conn. 223. Additionally, it should be noted that at the time of the announcement of the gift of the "Yahuda Library" the decedent gave to the plaintiff a memorandum containing a list of most of the contents of the library and of all of the important books, documents and incunabula. . . .

The plaintiff claims a gift inter vivos based on a constructive or symbolic delivery . . . For a constructive delivery, the donor must do that which, under the circumstances, will in reason be equivalent to an actual delivery. It must be as nearly perfect and complete as the nature of the property and the circumstances will permit. The gift may be perfected when the donor places in the hands of the donee the means of obtaining possession of the contemplated gift, accompanied with acts and declarations clearly showing an intention to give and to divert himself of all dominion over the property. Candee v. Connecticut Savings Bank, 81 Conn. 372, 375. It is not necessary that the method adopted be the only possible one. It is sufficient if manual delivery is impractical or inconvenient. Gray v. Watters, 243 Iowa 430, 436. Constructive delivery has been found to exist in a variety of factual situations: delivery of keys to safe deposit box — Lawrence v. Hartford National Bank & Trust Co., 24 Conn. Sup. 419, 429; pointing out hiding places where money is hidden — Waite v. Grubbe, 43 Ore. 406, 410; informal memorandum — Matter of Roosevelt, 190 Misc. 341, 345 (N.Y.).

Examining the present case in the light of the foregoing, the court finds that the delivery of the memorandum coupled with the decedent's acts and declarations, which clearly show an intention to give and to divest herself of any ownership of the library, was sufficient to complete the gift. If the itemized memorandum which the decedent transmitted had been incorporated in a formal document, no one would question the validity of the gift. But formalism is not an end in itself. "Whatever the value of the notion of forms, the only use of the forms is to present their contents." Holmes in Justice Oliver Wendell Holmes — His Book Notices and Uncollected Letters and Papers, p. 167 (Shriver Ed.). This is not to suggest that forms and formalities do not serve a useful and sometimes an essential purpose. But where the purpose of formalities is being served, an excessive regard for formalism should not be allowed to defeat the ends of justice. The circumstances under which this gift was made — a public announcement at a luncheon attended by a head of state, accompanied by a document which identified in itemized form what was being given — are a sufficient substitute for a formal instrument purporting to pass title. . . .

The court recognizes, in arriving at this result, that it is abrogating in some respects the requirement of delivery in a case involving an intended gift inter vivos. Obviously, it would be neither desirable nor wise to abrogate the requirement of delivery in any and all cases of intended inter-vivos gifts, for to do so, even under the guise of enforcing equitable rights, might open the door to fraudulent claims. But neither does it mean that the present delivery requirement must remain inviolate. "Equity is not crippled . . . by an inexorable formula." Marr v. Tumulty, 256 N.Y. 15, 21. If it be argued that hard cases make bad law, the short response is, not while this court sits. . . .

. . . Rules of law must, in the last analysis, serve the ends of justice or they are worthless. For a court of equity to permit the decedent's wishes to be doubly frustrated for no better reason than that the rules so provide makes no sense whatsoever. "The plastic remedies of the chancery are moulded to the needs of justice."

Accordingly, judgment may enter declaring that the plaintiff is the legal and equitable owner of the "Yahuda Library" and has a right to the immediate possession of its contents.

NOTES

1.   Not all courts are so strict as the Connecticut Supreme Court in requiring evidence that the donor considers herself a trustee. "The law will delineate a trust where, in view of a sufficiently manifested purpose or intent, that is the appropriate instrumentality, even though its creator calls it something else, or doesn't call it anything." Elyachar v. Gerel Corp., 583 F. Supp. 907, 922 (S.D.N.Y. 1984) (enforcing oral trust where father noted transfers of stock on his books but kept possession of the stock in order to maintain voting control of small corporations).

Professor Scott disapproved of cases where the intention to make a gift seems plain and the gift fails for lack of delivery but courts "torture" the gift into a declaration of trust in order to save it. 1 Austin W. Scott, Trusts §31 (William F. Fratcher 4th ed. 1987) (intimating no objection to liberalizing the requirement of delivery for gifts). But see Sarajane Love, Imperfect Gifts as Declarations of Trust: An Unapologetic Anomaly, 67 Ky. L.J. 309 (1979), taking the opposite view.

2.   Restatement (Third) of Trusts §16(2) (T.D. No. 1, 1996) provides: "If a property owner intends to make an outright gift inter vivos but fails to make the transfer that is required in order to do so, the gift intention will not be given effect by treating it as a declaration of trust." But Comment d goes on to fuzz up the picture considerably:

> If the manifestations of intention provide reliable, objective evidence of a deceased property owner's intended purpose and there is no indication that this purpose has been abandoned, the conduct and words ordinarily are interpreted as intending a type of transaction that would be effective to accomplish this purpose under the circumstances. That is, the preferred interpretation in marginal cases of this type is not that the property owner was merely expressing an intention to make a gift in the future but rather that the owner intended a declaration of trust. (If tenable under the circumstances, it is also possible that marginal acts that might or might not constitute delivery would be treated as a delivery based on a finding that they were in fact undertaken with the intention of making a present, outright gift.)

3.   In a large majority of states a trust created by a written instrument is irrevocable unless there is an express or implied provision

that the settlor reserves the power to revoke. In a few states, including California and Texas, the opposite presumption holds. A trust is revocable unless declared to be irrevocable. Uniform Trust Act §602 (1999 draft) adopts the minority rule.

2. *Necessity of Trust Property*

The usual definition of a trust includes three elements: a trustee, a beneficiary, and trust property. Since a trust is a method of disposing of, or managing, property, it is said that a trust cannot exist without trust property. When the meaning of property is examined, however, we find that it may refer to something other than a piece of land or a hefty chunk of money, such as $100,000. The trust property may be one dollar or one cent or it may be *any interest* in property that can be transferred. Contingent remainders, leasehold interests, choses in action, royalties, life insurance policies — anything that is called property — may be put in trust. The critical question is whether the particular claim will be called property by a court. When one ventures beyond what are historically conceded to be property interests, the circumstances that lead a court to classify a claim as property require a careful analysis of many variables.

Unthank v. Rippstein
Supreme Court of Texas, 1964
386 S.W.2d 134

STEAKLEY, J. Three days before his death C. P. Craft penned a lengthy personal letter to Mrs. Iva Rippstein. The letter was not written in terms of his anticipated early death; in fact, Craft spoke in the letter of his plans to go to the Mayo Clinic at a later date. The portion of the letter at issue reads as follows:

> Used most of yesterday and day before to "round up" my financial affairs, and to be sure I knew just where I stood before I made the statement that I would send you $200.00 cash the first week of each month for the next 5 years, provided I live that long, also to send you $200.00 cash for Sept. 1960 and thereafter send that amount in cash the first week of the following months of 1960, October, November and December. [opposite which in the margin there was written:]
> I have stricken out the words "provided I live that long" and hereby and herewith bind my estate to make the $200.00 monthly payments provided for on this Page One of this letter of 9-17-60.

Mrs. Rippstein, Respondent here, first sought, unsuccessfully, to probate the writing as a [holographic] codicil to the will of Craft. The
Court of Civil Appeals[13] held that the writing was not a testamentary
instrument which was subject to probate. We refused the application
of Mrs. Rippstein for writ of error with the notation "no reversible
error." See Rule 483, Texas Rules of Civil Procedure.

The present suit was filed by Mrs. Rippstein against the executors
of the estate of Craft, Petitioners here, for judgment in the amount
of the monthly installments which had matured, and for declaratory
judgment adjudicating the liability of the executors to pay future
installments as they mature. The trial court granted the motion of
the executors for summary judgment. The Court of Civil Appeals
reversed and rendered judgment for Mrs. Rippstein, holding that the
writing in question established a voluntary trust under which Craft
bound his property to the extent of the promised payments; and that
upon his death his legal heirs held the legal title for the benefit of
Mrs. Rippstein to that portion of the estate required to make the
promised monthly payments.

In her reply to the application for writ of error Mrs. Rippstein states
that the sole question before us is whether the marginal notation
constitutes "a declaration of trust whereby [Craft] agrees to thence-
forth hold his estate in trust for the explicit purpose of making the
payments." She argues that Craft imposed the obligation for the payment of the monies upon all of his property as if he had said "I
henceforth hold my estate in trust for [such] purpose." She recognizes that under her position Craft became subject to the Texas Trust
Act in the management of his property. Collaterally, however, Mrs.
Rippstein takes the position that it being determinable by mathematical computation that less than ten per cent of the property owned by
Craft at the time he wrote the letter would be required to discharge
the monthly payments, the "remaining ninety per cent remained in
Mr. Craft to do with as he would." Her theory is that that portion of
Craft's property not exhausted in meeting his declared purpose would
revert to him by way of a resulting trust eo instante with the legal and
equitable title to such surplus merging in him.

These arguments in behalf of Mrs. Rippstein are indeed ingenious
and resourceful, but in our opinion there is not sufficient certainty
in the language of the marginal notation upon the basis of which a
court of equity can declare a trust to exist which is subject to enforcement in such manner. The uncertainties with respect to the intention
of Craft and with respect to the subject of the trust are apparent. The
language of the notation cannot be expanded to show an intention
on the part of Craft to place his property in trust with the result that

13. In re Craft Estate, 358 S.W.2d 732 (C.C.A. 1962, writ ref. n.r.e.).

his exercise of further dominion thereover would be wrongful except in a fiduciary capacity as trustee, and under which Craft would be subject to suit for conversion at the hands of Mrs. Rippstein if he spent or disposed of his property in a manner which would defeat his statement in the notation that a monthly payment of $200.00 in cash would be sent her the first week of each month. It is manifest that Craft did not expressly declare that all of his property, or any specific portion of the assets which he owned at such time, would constitute the corpus or res of a trust for the benefit of Mrs. Rippstein; and inferences may not be drawn from the language used sufficient for a holding to such effect to rest in implication. The conclusion is compelled that the most that Craft did was to express an intention to make monthly gifts to Mrs. Rippstein accompanied by an ineffectual attempt to bind his estate in futuro; the writing was no more than a promise to make similar gifts in the future and as such is unenforceable. The promise to give cannot be tortured into a trust declaration under which Craft while living, and as trustee, and his estate after his death, were under a legally enforceable obligation to pay Mrs. Rippstein the sum of $200.00 monthly for the five-year period. . . .

The judgment of the Court of Civil Appeals is reversed and that of the trial court is affirmed.

QUESTION, PROBLEM, AND NOTE

1. What policies are served by refusing to give effect to C. P. Craft's written intent? Where there is a written instrument making a gratuitous promise, which shows clearly that the donor intended to be legally bound, should the court give it effect as a declaration of trust? What would be the trust res? See Jane B. Baron, The Trust Res and Donative Intent, 61 Tul. L. Rev. 45 (1986) (arguing that the trust res requirement, supported by unconvincing rationales, defeats donative intent).

Recall that under the Uniform Testamentary Additions to Trusts Act, no res is required for an inter vivos trust if the settlor executes a pour-over will (supra page 373). If a trust res can be dispensed with by exercising a pour-over will, why cannot it be dispensed with in the *Craft* case?

2. *A* executes a deed of trust and gives checks to fund the trust to the person named as trustee and a beneficiary. Two weeks later, *A* dies. After *A* dies, the trustee presents the checks to the bank for payment, but the bank, with notice of the death of *A*, dishonors the checks. Is the trust valid? Hieber v. Uptown National Bank, 199 Ill. App. 3d 542, 557 N.E.2d 408 (1990).

3. The requirement of an identifiable trust res distinguishes a trust

from a debt. A trust involves a duty to deal with some specific property, kept separate from the trustee's own funds. A debt involves an obligation to pay a sum of money to another. The crucial factor in distinguishing between a trust relationship and an ordinary debt is whether the recipient of the funds is entitled to use them as his own and commingle them with his own monies.

Money deposited in a bank ordinarily creates a debt, for the money is not segregated from the bank's general funds. However, the chose in action against the bank can serve as a res if the depositor transfers it in trust to another. What legal consequences might turn on the characterization of a relationship as a trust rather than a debt? See 1 Austin W. Scott, Trusts §12 (William F. Fratcher 4th ed. 1987); Restatement (Third) of Trusts §5, Comment k (T.D. No. 1, 1996).

NOTE: RESULTING AND CONSTRUCTIVE TRUSTS

In Unthank v. Rippstein, Mrs. Rippstein argued that Craft, after transferring all his property into trust, had a resulting trust in the amount of his property not required to meet the payments to Mrs. Rippstein. What is a resulting trust?

A *resulting trust* is a trust that arises by operation of law in one of two situations: (a) where an express trust fails or makes an incomplete disposition or (b) where one person pays the purchase price for property and causes title to the property to be taken in the name of another person who is not a natural object of the bounty of the purchaser. The relationship created by this latter situation is called a *purchase money resulting trust.* Thus:

> *Case 12. O* owns Blackacre. *A* pays *O* $10,000 for Blackacre; the deed conveying Blackacre names *B* as grantee. If *B* is not a natural object of *A*'s bounty, a presumption arises that *A* did not intend to make a gift of the property to *B* but had some other reason for causing *B* to be named as grantee. Unless the presumption is rebutted, *B* holds title on a resulting trust for *A*. The presumption can be rebutted by evidence, including oral testimony, showing that *A* did intend to make a gift to *B*, or that *A* made a loan to *B* of the purchase price. See 5 Scott, supra, §441.

> *Case 12a.* Same facts as in Case 12, except that *B* is *A*'s daughter. Since *B* would be the likely object of a gift from *A*, a presumption arises that *A* intended to make a gift to *B*. The presumption of gift can be rebutted by evidence showing that *A* intended to retain beneficial enjoyment and had a reason for placing title in *B*'s name. See id. §442.

While some of the rules applicable to express trusts are applicable to resulting trusts, the Statute of Frauds is not. Even though the subject matter is real property, it is usually held that resulting trusts, as well as constructive trusts, arise by operation of law and hence are not subject to the Statute of Frauds. Moreover, a resulting trust does not contemplate an ongoing fiduciary relationship wherein the trustee holds and manages the property for the beneficiary. Once a resulting trust is found, the trustee must reconvey the property to the beneficial owner upon demand. On resulting trusts, see Restatement (Third) of Trusts §§7-9 (T.D. No. 1, 1996).

Another kind of fiduciary relationship, sometimes confused with a resulting trust, is the *constructive trust.* A constructive trust also arises by operation of law and not by the express terms of an instrument. Basically, the term constructive trust is the name given a flexible remedy imposed in a wide variety of situations to prevent unjust enrichment. When property has been acquired in such circumstances that the holder of the legal title may not in good conscience retain the beneficial interest, equity converts him into a trustee. A constructive trustee is under a duty to convey the property to another on the ground that retention of the property would be wrongful. The usual requirements for imposition of a constructive trust are: (1) a confidential or fiduciary relationship; (2) a promise, express or implied, by the transferee; (3) a transfer of property in reliance on the promise; and (4) unjust enrichment of the transferee. But the constructive trust remedy is not limited to these circumstances. We have seen how a constructive trust may be imposed upon a person who procures an inheritance through fraud (supra pages 213-221) or upon the estate of a person who breaches a contract not to revoke a will (supra pages 322-328). Later in this chapter we shall see that a constructive trust may be imposed to enforce an oral trust of land which violates the Statute of Frauds (infra page 608) or a secret testamentary trust (infra page 616). In addition, a constructive trust may be imposed in situations where a confidential relationship or promise is not involved, but the court is moved simply by the desire to prevent unjust enrichment. Imposing a constructive trust upon a killer of the decedent to prevent him from profiting from his act (supra pages 141-147) is an example. On constructive trusts, see 5 Scott, supra, §§461-552.

Austin W. Scott, Trusts
(William F. Fratcher 4th ed. 1987)

§31.4.   CHANGE OF POSITION

We have seen that according to the weight of authority an ineffective gift will not be upheld as an express trust. But if the donee, in reliance upon the gift, so changes his position that it would be inequitable to preclude him from obtaining the property, a court of equity will compel the donor to complete the gift by making an effective conveyance. In such a case the donor holds the property upon a constructive trust for the donee until he makes an effective conveyance of it to the donee. Equity is not converting an imperfect gift into a declaration of trust, but is merely imposing a duty on the donor in order to prevent unjust enrichment.

§31.5. EFFECT OF DEATH OF DONOR

Where the owner of property makes an ineffective conveyance of it as an intended gift, he will not ordinarily be compelled to complete the gift; but if he dies believing that he has made an effective gift, and if the donee was a natural object of his bounty, such as a wife or child, it has been held that the donee can obtain the aid of a court of equity to complete the gift as against the heirs or next of kin of the donor. In such a case the donor is not an express trustee of the property, nor are his heirs or next of kin; but equity imposes a constructive trust upon the property.

Brainard v. Commissioner
United States Court of Appeals, Seventh Circuit, 1937
91 F.2d 880, cert. dismissed, 303 U.S. 665

SPARKS, J. This petition for review involves income taxes for the year 1928. The question presented is whether under the circumstances set forth in the findings of the Board of Tax Appeals, the taxpayer created a valid trust, the income of which was taxable to the beneficiaries under section 162 of the Revenue Act of 1928.

The facts as found by the Board of Tax Appeals are substantially as follows: In December, 1927, the taxpayer, having decided that conditions were favorable, contemplated trading in the stock market during 1928. He consulted a lawyer and was advised that it was possible for him to trade in trust for his children and other members of his family. Taxpayer thereupon discussed the matter with his wife and mother, and stated to them that he declared a trust of his stock trading during 1928 for the benefit of his family upon certain terms and conditions. Taxpayer agreed to assume personally any losses resulting from the venture, and to distribute the profits, if any, in equal shares to his wife, mother, and two minor children after deducting a reasonable compensation for his services. During 1928 taxpayer carried on the trading operations contemplated and at the end of the year determined his compensation at slightly less than $10,000, which he reported in his income tax return for that year. The profits remaining were then divided in approximately equal shares among the members of his family, and the amounts were reported in their respective tax returns for 1928. The amounts allocated to the beneficiaries were credited to them on taxpayer's books, but they did not receive the cash, except taxpayer's mother, to a small extent.

In addition to these findings the record discloses that taxpayer's two children were one and three years of age. Upon these facts the Board held that the income in controversy was taxable to the petitioner as a part of his gross income for 1928, and decided that there was a deficiency. It is here sought to review that decision.

In the determination of the questions here raised it is necessary to consider the nature of the trust, if any, that is said to have been created by the circumstances hereinbefore recited. It is clear that the taxpayer, at the time of his declaration, had no property interest in "profits in stock trading in 1928, if any," because there were none in existence at that time. Indeed it is not disclosed that the declarer at that time owned any stock. It is obvious, therefore, that the taxpayer based his declaration of trust upon an interest which at that time had not come into existence and in which no one had a present interest. In the Restatement of the Law of Trusts, vol. 1, §75, it is said that an interest which has not come into existence or which has ceased to exist can not be held in trust. It is there further said:

> A person can, it is true, make a contract binding himself to create a trust of an interest if he should thereafter acquire it; but such an agreement is not binding as a contract unless the requirements of the law of Contracts are complied with. . . .
>
> Thus, if a person gratuitously declares himself trustee of such shares as he may thereafter acquire in a corporation not yet organized, no trust is created. The result is the same where instead of declaring himself trustee, he purports to transfer to another as trustee such shares as he may thereafter acquire in a corporation not yet organized. In such a case there is at most a gratuitous undertaking to create a trust in the future, and such an undertaking is not binding as a contract for lack of consideration.
>
> . . . If a person purports to declare himself trustee of an interest not in existence, or if he purports to transfer such an interest to another in trust, he is liable as upon a contract to create a trust if, but only if, the requirements of the law of Contracts are complied with.

See, also, Restatement, §30b; Bogert, Trusts and Trustees, vol. 1, §112. In 42 Harvard Law Review 561, it is said: "With logical consistency, the courts have uniformly held that an expectancy cannot be the subject matter of a trust and that an attempted creation, being merely a promise to transfer property in the future, is invalid unless supported by consideration." Citing Lehigh Valley R.R. Co. v. Woodring, 116 Pa. 513, 9 A. 58. Hence, it is obvious under the facts here presented that taxpayer's declaration amounted to nothing more than a promise to create a trust in the future, and its binding force must be determined by the requirements of the law of contracts.

It is elementary that an executory contract, in order to be enforceable, must be based upon a valuable consideration. Here there was none. The declaration was gratuitous. If we assume that it was based on love and affection that would add nothing to its enforceability, for love and affection, though a sufficient consideration for an executed conveyance, is not a sufficient consideration for a promise. . . .

What has been said, however, does not mean that the taxpayer had no right to carry out his declaration after the subject matter had come into existence, even though there were no consideration. This he did and the trust thereby became effective, after which it was enforceable by the beneficiaries.

The questions with which we are concerned are at what times did the respective earnings which constitute the trust fund come into existence, and at what times did the trust attach to them. It is obvious that the respective profits came into existence when and if such stocks were sold at a profit in 1928. Did they come into existence impressed with the trust, or was there any period of time intervening between the time they came into existence and the time the trust attached? If there were such intervening time, then during that time the taxpayer must be considered as the sole owner of the profits and they were properly taxed to him as a part of his income.

It is said in the Restatement of the Law of Trusts, §75c: "If a person purports to declare himself trustee of an interest not in existence or if he purports to transfer such an interest to another in trust, no trust arises even when the interest comes into existence in the absence of a manifestation of intention at that time." This we think is especially applicable where, as here, there was no consideration for the declaration. It is further stated, however, in the Restatement, §26k:

> If a person manifests an intention to become trustee at a subsequent time, his conduct at that subsequent time considered in connection with his original manifestation may be a sufficient manifestation of intention at that subsequent time to create a trust. . . . The act of acquiring the property coupled with the earlier declaration of trust *may be* a sufficient manifestation of an intention to create a trust at the time of the acquisition of the property. (Our italics.)

In subsection 1 it is said ". . . Mere silence, however, ordinarily will not be such a manifestation. Whether silence is or is not such a manifestation is a question of interpretation." . . .

From what has been said we are convinced that appellant's profits in question were not impressed with a trust when they first came into existence. The Board was obviously of the impression that the trust first attached when appellant credited them to the beneficiaries on his books of account. This act, it seems to us, constituted his first subsequent expression of intention to become a trustee of the fund referred to in his original and gratuitous declaration. Prior to that time we think it is clear that the declaration could not have been enforced against him, and that his mere silence with respect thereto should not be considered as an expression of his intention to establish the trust at a time earlier than the credits. . . .

The order of the Board is affirmed.

Speelman v. Pascal

Court of Appeals of New York, 1961
10 N.Y.2d 313, 178 N.E.2d 723, 222 N.Y.S.2d 324

DESMOND, C.J.   Gabriel Pascal, defendant's intestate who died in 1954, had been for many years a theatrical producer. In 1952 an English corporation named Gabriel Pascal Enterprises, Ltd., of whose 100 shares Gabriel Pascal owned 98, made an agreement with the English Public Trustee who represented the estate of George Bernard Shaw. This agreement granted to Gabriel Pascal Enterprises, Ltd., the exclusive world rights to prepare and produce a musical play to be based on Shaw's play "Pygmalion" and a motion picture version of the musical play. The agreement recited, as was the fact, that the licensee owned a film scenario written by Pascal and based on "Pygmalion." In fact Pascal had, some time previously, produced a nonmusical movie version of "Pygmalion" under rights obtained by Pascal from George Bernard Shaw during the latter's lifetime. The 1952 agreement required the licensee corporation to pay the Shaw estate an initial advance and thereafter to pay the Shaw estate 3% of the gross receipts of the musical play and musical movie with a provision that the license was to terminate if within certain fixed periods the licensee did not arrange with Lerner[14] and Loewe or other similarly well-known composers to write the musical play and arrange to produce it. Before Pascal's death in July, 1954, he had made a number

14. Alan Jay Lerner, dying in 1986, left what might be called a delicious bequest:

> Third: I give and bequeath to Benjamin Welles, if he survives me, and Sydney Gruson, if he survives me, the sum of $1,000.00 each. The purpose of this modest remembrance is to defray the cost of one evening's merriment to be devoted to cheerful recollections of their departed friend.

The abstemious Bernard Shaw, vegetarian and teetotaler, who scathingly denounced the "artificial happiness, artificial courage, and artificial gaiety" provided by alcohol, would not have been amused. — Eds.

of unsuccessful efforts to get the musical written and produced and it was not until after his death that arrangements were made, through a New York bank as temporary administrator of his estate, for the writing and production of the highly successful "My Fair Lady." Meanwhile, on February 22, 1954, at a time when the license from the Shaw estate still had two years to run, Gabriel Pascal, who died four and a half months later, wrote, signed and delivered to plaintiff a document as follows:

Dear Miss Kingman

This is to confirm to you our understanding that I give you from my shares of profits of the Pygmalion Musical stage version five per cent (5%) in England, and two per cent (2%) of my shares of profits in the United States. From the film version, five per cent (5%) from my profit shares all over the world.

As soon as the contracts are signed, I will send a copy of this letter to my lawyer, Edwin Davies, in London, and he will confirm to you this arrangement in a legal form.

This participation in my shares of profits is a present to you in recognition for your loyal work for me as my Executive Secretary.[15]

Very sincerely yours,
Gabriel Pascal

The question in this lawsuit is: Did the delivery of this paper constitute a valid, complete, present gift to plaintiff by way of assignment of a share in future royalties when and if collected from the exhibition of the musical stage version and film version of "Pygmalion"? A consideration was, of course, unnecessary (Personal Property Law, §33, subd. 4). . . .

The only real question is as to whether the 1954 letter above quoted operated to transfer to plaintiff an enforcible right to the described percentages of the royalties to accrue to Pascal on the production of a stage or film version of a musical play based on "Pygmalion." We see no reason why this letter does not have that effect. It is true that

15. Pascal's loyal "Executive Secretary" is portrayed somewhat differently by Pascal's widow, Valerie, in her book, The Disciple and His Devil (1970). Marianne Speelman, also known as Zaya Kingman, was half Chinese and half Irish and the exotically beautiful widow of a Dutch banker who had made a fortune in China. She invited Gabriel Pascal to dinner in March of 1953 and that same night began a torrid love affair (id. at 252). As a result of her herb teas and food prepared with "life elixir," Pascal experienced "prodigious sexual powers" and felt as if he were flying. Marianne wrote that anybody who had ever made love to her could never again be satisfied with any other woman (id. at 255). Valerie states that soon after delivering the document in this case (id. at 297), Pascal attempted to break off his volcanic affair and, under the influence of an Indian mystic, renounced his fleshly desires forever (id. at 299). Spent, Pascal died some four months later. — Eds.

Marianne Speelman (Zaya Kingman)

at the time of the delivery of the letter there was no musical stage or film play in existence but Pascal, who owned and was conducting negotiations to realize on the stage and film rights, could grant to another a share of the moneys to accrue from the use of those rights by others. There are many instances of courts enforcing assignments of rights to sums which were expected thereafter to become due to

the assignor. A typical case is Field v. Mayor of New York (6 N.Y. 179).
One Bell, who had done much printing and similar work for the City
of New York but had no present contract to do any more such work,
gave an assignment in the amount of $1,500 of any moneys that might
thereafter become due to Bell for such work. Bell did obtain such
contracts or orders from the city and money became due to him
therefor. This court held that while there was not at the time of the
assignment any presently enforcible or even existing chose in action
but merely a possibility that there would be such a chose of action,
nevertheless there was a possibility of such which the parties expected
to ripen into reality and which did afterwards ripen into reality and
that, therefore, the assignment created an equitable title which the
courts would enforce. A case similar to the present one in general
outline is Central Trust Co. v. West India Improvement Co. (169 N.Y.
314) where the assignor had a right or concession from the Colony
of Jamaica to build a railroad on that island and the courts upheld a
mortgage given by the concession owner on any property that would
be acquired by the concession owner in consideration of building the
railroad if and when the railroad should be built. The Court of Appeals pointed out in *Central Trust Co.*, at page 323, that the property
as to which the mortgage was given had not yet come into existence
at the time of the giving of the mortgage but that there was an
expectation that such property, consisting of securities, would come
into existence and accrue to the concession holder when and if the
latter performed the underlying contract. This court held that the
assignment would be recognized and enforced in equity. The cases
cited by appellant (Young v. Young, 80 N.Y. 422; Vincent v. Rix, 248
N.Y. 76; Farmers' Loan & Trust Co. v. Winthrop, 207 App. Div. 356,
mod. 238 N.Y. 477) are not to the contrary. In each of those instances
the attempted gifts failed because there had not been such a completed and irrevocable delivery of the subject matter of the gift as to
put the gift beyond cancellation by the donor. In every such case the
question must be as to whether there was a completed delivery of a
kind appropriate to the subject property. Ordinarily, if the property
consists of existing stock certificates or corporate bonds, as in the
Young and *Vincent* cases (supra), there must be a completed physical
transfer of the stock certificates or bonds. In Farmers' Loan & Trust
Co. v. Winthrop (supra) the dispute was as to the effect of a power
of attorney but the maker of the power had used language which
could not be construed as effectuating a present gift of the property
which the donor expected to receive in the future from another estate.[16] The *Farmers' Loan & Trust Co.* case does not hold that property

16. In Farmers' Loan & Trust Co. v. Winthrop, the settlor executed an inter vivos trust
with Farmers' Loan as trustee of $5,000 "and all other property hereafter delivered." On
the same day she gave a power of attorney to Farmers' Loan authorizing it to collect
the assets she was entitled to receive from the estate of Jabez Bostwick, "and to transfer

to be the subject of a valid gift must be in present physical existence and in the possession of the donor but it does hold that the language used in the particular document was not sufficient to show an irrevocable present intention to turn over to the donee securities which would come to the donor on the settlement of another estate. At page 485 of 238 New York this court held that all that need be established is "an intention that the title of the donor shall be presently divested and presently transferred" but that in the particular document under scrutiny in the *Farmer's Loan & Trust Co.* case there was lacking any language to show an irrevocable intent of a gift to become operative at once. In our present case there was nothing left for Pascal to do in order to make an irrevocable transfer to plaintiff of part of Pascal's right to receive royalties from the productions. . . .

Judgment affirmed.

NOTES AND PROBLEMS

1.   What doctrinal, factual, or other distinction justifies the different results reached in the *Brainard* case and the *Speelman* case? In terms of ritual and evidentiary policies, are the cases consistent?

2.   In which of the following cases has there been an effective transfer? Compare them with what happened in *Brainard* and *Speelman*.

(a) *O* orally declares to *A*: "I give you 5 percent of the profits of a musical play based upon Shaw's Pygmalion, if I produce it and if there are any profits."

(b) *O* orally declares himself trustee for one year of all stocks he owns, with any profits from stock trading to go to *A*. See Barnette v. McNulty, 21 Ariz. App. 127, 516 P.2d 583 (1973).

(c) In a notarized writing *O* declares himself trustee for the benefit of *A* of any profits *O* makes from stock trading during the next calendar year.

(d) *O* orally declares himself trustee for the benefit of *A* of five percent of the profits, if there are any, of a musical play that *O* is writing, based upon Shaw's Pygmalion. See 1A Austin W. Scott, Trusts §86.2 (William F. Fratcher 4th ed. 1987). Compare Tenn. Code §35-50-121 (1997): "Any trust agreement or declaration of trust may be valid even if no corpus is delivered to the trustee at the time of execution of the instrument if the trustee has the right to receive

---

such securities and property to yourself as trustee." Before the executor of the Bostwick estate delivered the property to Farmers' Loan, the settlor died. The court held that the attempted transfer failed. — Eds.

corpus at a later time or times from the trustor, the trustor's estate or other persons or source.''

3. The prevailing view is that a person can assign future earnings from an existing contract. The theory is that the future yield of an existing property right can be transferred even though property to be acquired in the future cannot be. In the *Speelman* case Pascal had exclusive rights (a license) from the Shaw estate to make a musical version of Pygmalion. But the contract with Lerner and Loewe to write the musical version was not made by Pascal's administrator until nearly a year after his death. Was the license enough to give Pascal an assignable right to profits or did the right to profits arise only after Pascal's death when the contract was signed? Or, did it matter at all to the court that Pascal had a license? Should it matter? See E. Allan Farnsworth, Changing Your Mind 143-147 (1998).

Suppose that Cole Porter, writing a musical based on Shakespeare's Taming of the Shrew, handed over to his loyal executive secretary a paper reading: ''I give you 5 percent of the profits of a musical play based on Taming of the Shrew.'' Is the secretary entitled to 5 percent of the profits from Kiss Me Kate? Porter needed no copyright license from Shakespeare, whose works are in the public domain. Should Porter's gift be unenforceable? If you say Porter's gift is good, does this mean that future earnings from a person's human capital — his productive capacity based on his skill and training — are transferable? If so, shouldn't the taxpayer's transfer of future earnings from human capital in *Brainard* be allowed? How is the line drawn between what you have and can transfer and what you do not have and cannot transfer? Compare Elkus v. Elkus, 169 A.D.2d 134, 572 N.Y.S.2d 901 (1991), holding that the career of the opera singer, Fredericka Von Stade, and its accompanying celebrity status, which produced considerable income, was marital property subject to equitable distribution on divorce.

4. Look back at Clymer v. Mayo, supra page 375, where Clara Mayo executed a trust instrument purporting to create a revocable inter vivos trust. On the same day she changed her life insurance policy and retirement annuity contract so as to designate the trustees of her trust as contract beneficiaries. She transferred no other property to the trust. What was the trust res?

NOTE: TAXATION OF GRANTOR TRUSTS

In Brainard v. Commissioner, supra page 586, the settlor of the trust sought to obtain an income tax advantage by creating a trust of his future profits from stock trading. If a valid trust was created, these profits would be taxable to the trust beneficiaries, at a lower bracket, and not to the settlor. This kind of transfer, avoiding income tax to the settlor on future income, is not available to a taxpayer today.

In Helvering v. Clifford, 309 U.S. 331 (1940), the Supreme Court held that where a taxpayer declared a trust of securities for five years with income payable to another for the five-year term but with the settlor retaining complete control over the principal and reversion of the corpus at the end of five years, the taxpayer could be treated as owner, and taxed on the income, by the federal taxing authorities. Subsequently, the Treasury issued regulations spelling out in detail the circumstances under which the settlor of a trust would be taxable on the trust income on the ground of retained dominion and control (the "Clifford regulations"). These were in turn supplanted by Congressional changes in the Internal Revenue Code itself. Sections 671-677 of the Code now govern the circumstances when the settlor is taxable on trust income because of retained dominion and control. Where the settlor wants to avoid being taxed on the trust income, care must be taken to avoid these sections.

Sections 671-677 define what are called *grantor trusts* — trusts in which the income is taxable to the settlor (grantor) because the settlor has retained substantial control and is deemed by the Code still to be the owner of the trust assets. We have noted earlier, at page 388, that trust income of a revocable trust is taxable to the settlor. A revocable trust is an example of a grantor trust. IRC §676. Now we treat grantor trusts where the settlor retains not a right to revoke the trust but some lesser power.

Under these sections of the Code, there is a spousal attribution rule: A settlor is treated as holding any power or interest that is held by the settlor's spouse if the spouse is living with the settlor at the time the property is transferred into trust.

Where the grantor has a *reversionary interest,* either in the corpus or in the income, and the reversionary interest at the inception of the trust exceeds 5 percent of the value of the corpus or the income, the trust is a grantor trust. The income from the trust is taxable to the settlor. IRC §673. There is one important exception. The settlor is exempt from this rule if he or she creates a trust for a minor lineal descendant, who has the entire present interest, and the settlor retains a reversionary interest that will take effect only upon the death of the lineal descendant under the age of 21. IRC §673(b). The drafting moral here is clear: Except in the one case mentioned, do not leave a reversionary interest of any value in the settlor.

Where the *settlor* or a *nonadverse party* — either as trustee or in any individual capacity — is given discretionary power over income or principal exercisable without the consent of an adverse party, the trust is a grantor trust. The income is taxable to the settlor. Internal Revenue Code §674. Thus:

Case 13. O creates a trust, with herself and the First National Bank as co-trustees, to pay the income to *O*'s two children in such amounts as the trustees shall determine or to accumulate it and, upon the death of *O*'s two children, to distribute the principal to *O*'s grandchildren then living. The trustees earn $70,000 income the first year, which the trustees distribute equally to *O*'s two children. The $70,000 income is taxable to *O*, the settlor of a grantor trust, *and O* has made a gift to each child of $35,000. Each gift qualifies for a $10,000 annual gift tax exclusion, so *O* has made a net taxable gift to each child of $25,000. (On the gift tax exclusion, see infra page 991.) The amount received by *O*'s children is not income to them because it is a gift from *O*.

There are two major exceptions to §674. The first is that a discretionary power to distribute, apportion, or accumulate income or to pay out corpus can be given to an *independent* trustee without adverse tax consequences to the settlor. Id. §674(c). If in Case 13 the First National Bank had been named sole trustee, the income would not be taxable to *O*. It is important to distinguish between an independent trustee and a nonadverse party. An independent trustee is one who is not related or subordinate to the settlor nor subservient to her wishes, whereas a nonadverse party is a person who lacks a substantial beneficial interest that would be adversely affected by the exercise or nonexercise of the power.

The second major exception to §674 permits (a) a power to be given the settlor or any trustee to distribute *corpus* pursuant to a "reasonably definite standard which is set forth in the trust instrument" or (b) a power to be given any trustee other than the settlor or the settlor's spouse to distribute *income* pursuant to a "reasonably definite external standard which is set forth in the trust instrument." Id. §§674(b)(5)(A), 674(d).

Another type of grantor trust is one where certain administrative powers can be exercised for the benefit of the settlor rather than for the beneficiaries of the trust. Generally, the settlor will be taxable on the income if there is a power exercisable by the settlor or a nonadverse party (1) to purchase trust assets for less than an adequate consideration, (2) to borrow trust assets without adequate security, (3) to vote or acquire stock in a corporation in which the settlor has a significant voting interest, or (4) to reacquire the trust corpus. Any of these indicia of dominion and control may be sufficient to tax the settlor on the trust income. See Internal Revenue Code §675.

The category of grantor trusts also includes a trust where the settlor, a nonadverse party, or an independent trustee has the power to distribute trust income to the settlor or the settlor's spouse. Id. §677(a). Under §677, income is not taxable to the settlor merely because the trustee may distribute it for the support of a beneficiary (other than the settlor's spouse) whom the settlor is legally obligated to support. If the trust property is in fact used to discharge the settlor's legal obligation, however, the settlor is taxable on the income to the extent income is actually so used. Id. §677(b). Thus:

> *Case 14.* O transfers property to the First National Bank in trust to pay the income in its discretion for the support of O's children. Even though the trustee has discretion to use the income for the support of O's minor children (thereby discharging O's legal obligation of support), O is taxable on the income only to the extent it is actually so applied. If the income used for the support of O's children is in excess of the amount O is legally obligated to provide, the excess income is not taxable to O.

In Case 14, a provision could be inserted in the trust instrument providing that any distributions by the trustee would not discharge the settlor's legal obligation of support. Such a provision would prevent taxation of the income to the settlor and would not, as a practical matter, interfere with any trust distribution by the trustee.

Any lawyer creating an inter vivos trust should pay close attention to §§671-677 of the Internal Revenue Code and the relevant regulations if the settlor desires to escape taxation on the income. Also, it should be kept in mind that although the income tax and the estate and gift taxes are not exactly parallel, if the settlor is treated as owner and taxable on the income of the trust assets there is a good chance that the trust assets will be subject to estate taxation at the settlor's death. See discussion of §§2036 and 2038 at pages 1014, 1027 infra. For a client who wants to avoid income and estate taxation, the lawyer will want to draft a trust that skirts the reach of both the income and estate tax sections of the Code and leaves the client in a safe harbor.

3. Necessity of Trust Beneficiaries

It is said that a trust must have one or more beneficiaries. There must be someone to whom the trustee owes fiduciary duties, someone who can call the trustee to account.

There are exceptions, however, to this rule. The beneficiaries may be unborn or unascertained when the trust is created. Thus a trust created by O, who is childless, for the benefit of her future children would be a valid trust. The courts would protect the interests of the unborn children from improper acts of the trustee. On the other hand, if at the time the trust becomes effective the beneficiaries are

too indefinite to be ascertained, the attempted trust may fail for want
of ascertainable beneficiaries.

Clark v. Campbell
Supreme Court of New Hampshire, 1926
82 N.H. 281, 133 A. 166

SNOW, J. The ninth clause of the will of deceased reads:

> My estate will comprise so many and such a variety of articles of personal
> property such as books, photographic albums, pictures, statuary, bronzes,
> bric-a-brac, hunting and fishing equipment, antiques, rugs, scrapbooks,
> canes and masonic jewels, that probably I shall not distribute all, and
> perhaps no great part thereof, during my life by gift among my friends.
> Each of my trustees is competent by reason of familiarity with the prop-
> erty, my wishes and friendships, to wisely distribute some portion at least
> of said property. I therefore give and bequeath to my trustees all my
> property embraced within the classification aforesaid in trust to make
> disposal by the way of a memento from myself, of such articles to such
> of my friends as they, my trustees, shall select. All of said property, not
> so disposed of by them, my trustees are directed to sell and the proceeds
> of such sale or sales to become and be disposed of as a part of the residue
> of my estate.

The question here reserved is whether . . . the bequest for the benefit
of the testator's "friends" must fail for the want of certainty of the
beneficiaries.

By the common law there cannot be a valid bequest to an indefinite
person. There must be a beneficiary or a class of beneficiaries indicated in the will capable of coming into court and claiming the benefit of the bequest. Adye v. Smith, 44 Conn. 60. This principle applies
to private but not to public trusts and charities. Harrington v. Pier,
105 Wis. 485; 28 R.C.L. 339, 340; Morice v. Bishop of Durham, 9 Ves.
399, 10 Ves. 521. The basis assigned for this distinction is the difference in the enforceability of the two classes of trusts. In the former
there being no definite cestui que trust to assert his right, there is
no one who can compel performance, with the consequent unjust
enrichment of the trustee; while in the case of the latter, performance
is considered to be sufficiently secured by the authority of the attor-
ney-general to invoke the power of the courts. . . .

That the foregoing is the established doctrine seems to be conceded, but it is contended in argument that it was not the intention
of the testator by the ninth clause to create a trust, at least as respects
the selected articles, but to make an absolute gift thereof to the trustees individually. . . . It is a sufficient answer to this contention that the

language of the ninth clause does not warrant the assumed construction. . . . When the clause is elided of unnecessary verbiage the testator is made to say: "I give to my trustees my property (of the described class) in trust to make disposal of to such of my friends as they shall select." It is difficult to conceive of language more clearly disclosing an intention to create a trust.

It is further sought to sustain the bequest as a power. The distinction apparently relied upon is that a power, unlike a trust (Goodale v. Mooney, 60 N.H. 528, 534), is not imperative and leaves the act to be done at the will of the donee of the power. 21 R.C.L. 773; 26 R.C.L. 1169. But the ninth clause by its terms imposes upon the trustees the imperative duty to dispose of the selected articles among the testator's friends. If, therefore, the authority bestowed by the testator by the use of a loose terminology may be called a power, it is not an optional power but a power coupled with a trust to which the principles incident to a trust so far as here involved clearly apply. . . .

We must, therefore, conclude that this clause presents the case of an attempt to create a private trust. . . .

The question presented, therefore, is whether or not the ninth clause provides for definite and ascertainable beneficiaries so that the bequest therein can be sustained as a private trust. . . .

Like the direct legatees in a will, the beneficiaries under a trust may be designated by class. But in such case the class must be capable of delimitation, as "brothers and sisters," "children," "issue," "nephews and nieces." A bequest giving the executor authority to distribute his property "among his relatives and for benevolent objects in such sums as in their judgment shall be for the best" was sustained upon evidence within the will that by "relatives" the testator intended such of his relatives within the statute of distributions as were needy, and thus brought the bequest within the line of charitable gifts and excluded all others as individuals. Goodale v. Mooney, 60 N.H. 528, 536. See Portsmouth v. Shackford, 46 N.H. 423, 425; Gafney v. Kenison, 64 N.H. 354, 356. Where a testator bequeathed his stocks to be apportioned to his "relations" according to the discretion of the trustee, to be enjoyed by them after his decease, it was held to be a power to appoint amongst his relations who were next of kin under the statute of distribution. . . .

In the case now under consideration the cestuis que trustent are designated as the "friends" of the testator. The word "friends" unlike "relations" has no accepted statutory or other controlling limitations, and in fact has no precise sense at all. Friendship is a word of broad and varied application. It is commonly used to describe the undefinable relationships which exist not only between those connected by ties of kinship or marriage, but as well between strangers in blood, and which vary in degree from the greatest intimacy to an acquain-

tance more or less casual. . . . There is no express evidence that the
word is used in any restricted sense. The only implied limitation of
the class is that fixed by the boundaries of the familiarity of the
testator's trustees with his friendships. If such familiarity could be
held to constitute such a line of demarcation as to define an ascertainable group, it is to be noted that the gift is not to such group as a
class, the members of which are to take in some definite proportion
(1 Jarman, Wills, 534; 1 Schouler, Wills, s. 1011) or according to their
needs, but the disposition is to "such of my friends as they, my trustees, may select." No sufficient criterion is furnished to govern the
selection of the individuals from the class. The assertion of the testator's confidence in the competency of his trustees "to wisely distribute
some portion" of the enumerated articles "by reason of familiarity
with the property, my wishes and friendships," does not furnish such
a criterion. . . . Where an executor was given direction to distribute
in a manner calculated to carry out "wishes which I have expressed
to him or may express to him" and such wishes had been orally
communicated to the executor by the testator, the devise could not
be given effect as against the next of kin. Olliffe v. Wells, 130 Mass.
221, 224, 225. Much less can effect be given to the uncommunicated
wishes of the testator here.

It was the evident purpose of the testator to invest his trustees with
the power after his death to make disposition of the enumerated
articles among an undefined class with practically the same freedom
and irresponsibility that he himself would have exercised if living; that
is, to substitute for the will of the testator the will and discretion of
the trustees. Such a purpose is in contravention of the policy of the
statute which provides that "no will shall be effectual to pass any real
or personal estate . . . unless made by a person . . . in writing, signed
by the testator or by some one in his presence and by his direction,
and attested and subscribed in his presence by three or more credible
witnesses." P.L., c. 297, s. 2.

Where a gift is impressed with a trust ineffectively declared and
incapable of taking effect because of the indefiniteness of the cestui
que trust, the donee will hold the property in trust for the next taker
under the will, or for the next of kin by way of a resulting trust. . . .
The trustees therefore hold title to the property enumerated in the
paragraph under consideration, to be disposed of as a part of the
residue, and the trustees are so advised. . . .

Case discharged.

NOTE AND PROBLEM

1. Professor Scott argued that where there is a transfer in trust
for members of an indefinite class of persons, no enforceable trust is

created, but the transferee has a discretionary power to convey the property to such members of the class as he may select. 2 Austin W. Scott, Trusts §122 (William F. Fratcher 4th ed. 1987). In other words, the transferee has a power of appointment.

A valid power of appointment may have a definite class of beneficiaries (e.g. "my issue") or it may not (e.g., "any one except the donee or her creditors or her estate"). The test of validity is: If the class of beneficiaries is so described that some person might reasonably be said to answer the description, the power is valid. An appointment is invalid, however, if it cannot be determined whether the appointee answers the description.

In trusts today, beneficiaries are often given powers of appointment, powers to choose among a designated class of persons. For example, *T* may devise his residuary estate in trust "for my wife *W* for life, and then to distribute the trust assets to such of my issue as my wife appoints." The power of appointment is discretionary; it is a nonfiduciary power. If *W* fails to exercise the power, the trust property passes to *T*'s heirs upon *W*'s death. Powers of appointment are treated in the next chapter, beginning at page 665 infra.

In Clark v. Campbell the court says it cannot treat the will as creating a power of appointment because it is given to *trustees*. They hold it in a fiduciary capacity (unlike a nonfiduciary power given a beneficiary). It is not an optional power but a "power coupled with a trust." Therefore, trust principles apply. If the power of selection had been given "to my sister Polly and my friend Herbert" and not "to Polly and Herbert, *trustees* (or *executors*)" it would be a valid nonfiduciary power of appointment. (What is the drafting moral here?)

Restatement (Second) of Trusts §122 (1959) and Restatement (Third) of Trusts §46(2) (T.D. No. 2, 1999) adopt Scott's position. Restatement (Second) of Property, Donative Transfers §12.1, Comment e (1986), concurs:

> A provision in a will in relation to specified property may authorize the executors to make decisions as to the persons who will receive the property. . . . Rather than failing altogether, the provision should be construed to give the executors a power of appointment exercisable within a reasonable period of time after the appointment of the executors, with the specified property passing in default of appointment if the power is not exercised. Whether the power is general or non-general depends on the relationships and other circumstances involved.

Leach v. Hyatt, 244 Va. 566, 423 S.E.2d 165 (1992), adopted the Restatement rule, described by the court as the minority rule. See generally George E. Palmer, The Effect of Indefiniteness on the Validity of Trusts and Powers of Appointment, 10 UCLA L. Rev. 241 (1963).

2.   With Clark v. Campbell, compare In re Estate of Reiman, 115 Ill. App. 3d 879, 450 N.E.2d 928 (1983). The latter case voided a bequest to an executor to distribute in accordance with "the verbal guide lines last given by me, and in accord with his best judgment." How does this differ from the bequest in Clark v. Campbell?

In re Searight's Estate
Ohio Court of Appeals, Ninth District, 1950
87 Ohio App. 417, 95 N.E.2d 779

HUNSICKER, J. George P. Searight, a resident of Wayne county, Ohio, died testate on November 27, 1948. Item "third" of his will provided:

> I give and bequeath my dog, Trixie, to Florence Hand of Wooster, Ohio, and I direct my executor to deposit in the Peoples Federal Savings and Loan Association, Wooster, Ohio, the sum of $1000.00 to be used by him to pay Florence Hand at the rate of 75 cents per day for the keep and care of my dog as long as it shall live. If my dog shall die before the said $1000.00 and the interest accruing therefrom shall have been used up, I give and bequeath whatever remains of said $1000.00 to be divided equally among those of the following persons who are living at that time, to wit: Bessie Immler, Florence Hand, Reed Searight, Fern Olson and Willis Horn.

At the time of his death, all of the persons, and his dog, Trixie, named in such item third, were living.

Florence Hand accepted the bequest of Trixie, and the executor paid to her from the $1000 fund, 75 cents a day for the keep and care of the dog. The value of Trixie was agreed to be $5.

The Probate Court [held item third valid]. . . .

The questions presented by this appeal on questions of law are:

1. Is the testamentary bequest for the care of Trixie (a dog) valid in Ohio —

(a) as a proper subject of a so-called "honorary trust"?

(b) as not being in violation of the rule against perpetuities? . . .

1(a). The creation of a trust for the benefit of specific animals has not been the subject of much litigation in the courts, and our research, and that of able counsel in this case, have failed to disclose any reported case on the subject in Ohio. The few reported cases in this country, in England and in Ireland have been the subject of considerable comment by the writers of text books and by the law reviews of leading law schools. . . .

We do not have, in the instant case, the question of a trust established for the care of dogs in general or of an indefinite number of dogs, but we are here considering the validity of a testamentary bequest for the benefit of a specific dog. This is not a charitable trust, nor is it a gift of money to the Ohio Humane Society or a county humane society, which societies are vested with broad statutory authority, Section 10062, General Code, for the care of animals.

Text writers on the subject of trusts and many law professors designate a bequest for the care of a specific animal as an "honorary trust"; that is, one binding the conscience of the trustee, since there is no beneficiary capable of enforcing the trust.

The rule in Ohio, that the absence of a beneficiary having a legal standing in court and capable of demanding an accounting of the trustee is fatal and the trust fails, was first announced in Mannix, Assignee v. Purcell, 46 Ohio St. 102, 19 N.E. 572, 2 L.R.A. 753. . . .

In 1 Scott on the Law of Trusts, Section 124, the author says:

> There are certain classes of cases similar to those discussed in the preceding section in that there is no one who as beneficiary can enforce the purpose of the testator, but different in one respect, namely, that the purpose is definite. Such, for example, are bequests for the erection or maintenance of tombstones or monuments or for the care of graves, and bequests for the support of specific animals. It has been held in a number of cases that such bequests as these do not necessarily fail. It is true that the legatee cannot be compelled to carry out the intended purpose, since there is no one to whom he owes a duty to carry out the purpose.
>
> Even though the legatee cannot be compelled to apply the property to the designated purpose, the courts have very generally held that he can properly do so, and that no resulting trust arises so long as he is ready and willing to carry it out. The legatee will not, however, be permitted to retain the property for his own benefit; and if he refuses or neglects to carry out the purpose, a resulting trust will arise in favor of the testator's residuary legatee or next of kin. . . .

The object and purpose sought to be accomplished by the testator in the instant case is not capricious or illegal. He sought to effect a worthy purpose — the care of his pet dog.

Whether we designate the gift in this case as an "honorary trust" or a gift with a power which is valid when exercised is not important, for we do know that the one to whom the dog was given accepted the gift and indicated her willingness to care for such dog, and the executor proceeded to carry out the wishes of the testator.

> Where the owner of property transfers it upon an intended trust for a specific noncharitable purpose and there is no definite or definitely ascertainable beneficiary designated, no trust is created; but the transferee has power to apply the property to the designated purpose, unless he is authorized by the terms of the intended trust so to apply the property

beyond the period of the rule against perpetuities, or the purpose is capricious. I Restatement of the Law of Trusts, Section 124.

To call this bequest for the care of the dog, Trixie, a trust in the accepted sense in which that term is defined is, we know, an unjustified conclusion. The modern authorities, as shown by the cases cited earlier in this discussion, however, uphold the validity of a gift for the purpose designated in the instant case, where the person to whom the power is given is willing to carry out the testator's wishes. Whether called an "honorary trust" or whatever terminology is used, we conclude that the bequest for the care of the dog, Trixie, is not in and of itself unlawful.

1(b). In Ohio, by statute, Section 10512-8, General Code, the rule against perpetuities is specifically defined, and such statute further says: "It is the intention by the adoption of this section to make effective in Ohio what is generally known as the common law rule against perpetuities."

It is to be noted, in every situation where the so-called "honorary trust" is established for specific animals, that, unless the instrument creating such trust limits the duration of the trust — that is, the time during which the power is to be exercised — to human lives, we will have "honorary trusts" established for animals of great longevity, such as crocodiles, elephants and sea turtles. . . .

Restatement of the Law of Property . . . says, at Section 379:

> A limitation of property on an intended trust is invalid when, under the language and circumstances of such limitation, (a) the conveyee is to administer the property for the accomplishment of a specific noncharitable purpose and there is no definite or definitely ascertainable beneficiary designated; and (b) such administration can continue for longer than the maximum period [allowed by the rule against perpetuities]. . . .

If we then examine item third of testator's will, we discover that, although the bequest for his dog is for "as long as it shall live," the money given for this purpose is $1000 payable at the rate of 75¢ a day. By simple mathematical computation, this sum of money, expended at the rate determined by the testator, will be fully exhausted in three years and $238\frac{1}{3}$ days. If we assume that this $1000 is deposited in a bank so that interest at the high rate of 6% per annum were earned thereon, the time needed to consume both principal and interest thereon (based on semiannual computation of such interest on the average unused balance during such six month period) would be four years, $57\frac{1}{2}$ days.

It is thus very apparent that the testator provided a time limit for the exercise of the power given his executor, and that such time limit is much less than the maximum period allowed under the rule against perpetuities.

We therefore conclude that the bequest in the instant case for the care of the dog, Trixie, does not, by the terms of the creating instrument, violate the rule against perpetuities. . . .

The judgment of the Probate Court is affirmed.

NOTES

1.   In *Searight's Estate* the Department of Taxation of Ohio argued that an inheritance tax was levied on the amount used for the care of Trixie. Ohio General Code §5332 levied a tax on all property passing to a "person, institution or corporation." In an omitted portion of the opinion, the court decided that a dog was none of these, and no inheritance tax was levied on the amount used for Trixie's care. A tax was levied, however, on the contingent amount passing to the five persons on the death of Trixie.

In the probate court proceedings, the Department also argued that a dog is personal property and a thing of value and should have been taxed as an inheritance of Florence Hand. The executor of the estate of George P. Searight testified:

> If the Court please: I am an innocent bystander of this situation and am not personally interested one way or the other except to be right. Let me say this to the Court, — I wrote this provision in the Will, and frankly, the question as to whether the dog was taxable or not was never considered. I had no idea we would have such a problem. When the time came to make the Will George was concerned that when something happened to him that the dog was not to go to the dog pound. In fact he had as much affection for his dog as for his relatives. He lived with the dog and lived down there like a recluse.
>
> So far as the tax matter is concerned, let me take Mr. Annat's last contention, so far as taxing the dog as a thing of value. The dog may have a value of two, three or five dollars. It has no value other than that of a mongrel fox-terrier dog. Frankly I would say it could be argued that the fair market value of the dog was zero. If Florence tried to sell the dog I don't think she could give it away. On the contention of whether or not it is a thing of value I am not disposed to argue. Whether it can be sold, I don't know. I do know this, — George had it and I know there was some question about Florence taking it, and only because he made that instruction in the Will she took it.

The parties settled the matter by agreeing that the dog had a value of $5 and Florence Hand owed a tax on that.

The executor's final accounting reported that $255.75 was distributed to Florence Hand for the care of Trixie, who died on October 30, 1949, after being struck by a car. The balance of the $1,000 was divided among the five legatees.

Why did not the Ohio Court of Appeals, in deciding the perpetuities question, take into account the fact that Trixie had actually died before the court's decision was made?

2. Under the Rule against Perpetuities, an honorary trust to support a pet animal is void if it can last beyond relevant lives in being at the creation of the trust plus twenty-one years. See 2 Austin W. Scott, Trusts §124.1 (William F. Fratcher 4th ed. 1987). Under the wait-and-see doctrine, a court does not declare an interest invalid until the wait-and-see period expires. Hence, if the jurisdiction applies wait-and-see for the common law perpetuities period, as Ohio now does (Ohio Rev. Code Ann. §2131.08(c) (1996)), an honorary trust for the life of a pet would seem to be valid for 21 years. After that the pet has to take its chances. If the jurisdiction has adopted the Uniform Statutory Rule Against Perpetuities, which provides a wait-and-see period of 90 years, an honorary trust would seem to be valid for 90 years. Ninety years is sufficiently long to cover most pets, including parrots, but not necessarily including tortoises, which have lived for over 150 years in captivity. See, however, Adam J. Hirsch, Trusts for Purposes: Policy, Ambiguity, and Anomaly in the Uniform Laws, 26 Fla. St. U. L. Rev. 913 (1999), doubting how wait-and-see will apply to honorary trusts.

Several states have statutes permitting a trust for a pet to endure for a given amount of time. California Prob. Code §15212 (1998) provides that a trust for care of a designated domestic or pet animal may be performed by the trustee for the life of the animal. Uniform Probate Code §2-907 (1990) provides that a trust for the care of a designated domestic or pet animal is valid for 21 years or for the life of the animal, whichever period turns out to be shorter. See also Restatement (Third) of Trusts §47 (T.D. No. 2, 1999) permitting a trust to support a pet to continue for the pet's life and any other trust for a specific noncharitable purpose without an ascertainable beneficiary to continue for 21 years.

3. *The high cost of a dog's life in Beverly Hills.* Sidney Altman did not want his cocker spaniel Samantha (age 15), described as "my loving companion," to suffer a major change in her life at his death in 1998. His will left $350,000 for Samantha's upkeep in his Beverly Hills house, $50,000 to his girlfriend of six years, Marie Dana, to redecorate the house and go "on a massive shopping spree at Polo," $60,000 a year tax-free to Marie to live in the house and care for Samantha, and $150,000 to his business partner to check on Samantha every three months to make sure that Samantha was being treated well.

Marie sued for half of Sidney's $6 million estate, claiming that Sidney had promised to support her for her life, not for a dog's life. "I was shocked and deeply disappointed when I learned that at Samantha's death I would be homeless and without support," Marie told a reporter for the Los Angeles Times. See L.A. Times, Sept. 28, 1998, at B1.

NOTE: SHAW'S ALPHABET TRUSTS

George Bernard Shaw was long interested in reforming the English alphabet so that letters, singly and in combination, would have only one pronunciation. He pointed out that fish could be spelled "ghoti" if the "gh" were pronounced like the "gh" in "enough," "o" like the "o" in "women," and "ti" like "ti" in "notion." (He did not note that Shaw could be spelled "pshaw.") Shaw devised the residue of his estate (fattened by royalties from "My Fair Lady") to his executor, in trust for 21 years, to develop a new alphabet of 40 letters and to propagandize for its adoption. Upon the termination of the alphabet trusts "or if and so far as such trusts shall fail through judicial decision," the principal was to be distributed one-third to the British Museum "in acknowledgment of the incalculable value to me of my daily resort to the reading room of that institution at the beginning of my career," one-third to the National Gallery of Ireland, and one-third to the Royal Academy of Dramatic Art. The court held the alphabet trust was not for the advancement of education nor beneficial to the community, and therefore it was not a charitable trust. The court further held that the devise could not be treated as a private trust because it was not in favor of an ascertainable beneficiary. The court referred to the Restatement of Trusts §124 (quoted in In re Searight's Estate), which approves treating the gift as a power, and stated that it was

> not at liberty to validate this trust by treating it as a power. . . . The result is that the alphabet trusts are, in my judgment, invalid, and must fail. It seems that their begetter suspected as much, hence his jibe about failure by judicial decision. I answer that it is not the fault of the law, but of the testator, who failed almost for the first time in his life to grasp the problem or to make up his mind what he wanted. [In re Shaw, [1957] 1 All E.R. 745, 759 (Ch.).]

Who would have thought that the figure of Nemesis would appear to Shaw in the guise of an alphabet trust?

The case was appealed, but while the appeal was pending a compromise was effected by which a sum was set aside to employ a phonetic expert to develop a phonetic alphabet, transliterate Shaw's play "Androcles and the Lion" into the new alphabet, and publish the transliterated play. How would you have drafted Shaw's will to carry out his desires? See William F. Fratcher, Bequests for Purposes, 56 Iowa L. Rev. 773 (1971).

4. Necessity of a Written Instrument

As we have seen, an inter vivos oral declaration of trust of personal property is enforceable. On the other hand, the Statute of Frauds requires any inter vivos trust of land to be in writing. And, of course, the Statute of Wills requires that a testamentary trust be created by a will. Nonetheless, under certain circumstances a court will enforce an inter vivos oral trust of land or an oral trust arising at death. It is to these circumstances that we now turn.

a. Oral Inter Vivos Trusts of Land

Where O conveys land to X upon an oral trust to pay the income to A for life and upon A's death to convey the land to B, the Statute of Frauds prevents enforcement of the express trust. Is X permitted to keep the land? The cases split between permitting X to retain the land, on the ground that the Statute of Frauds forbids proof of the oral trust, and imposing a constructive trust on X to prevent his unjust enrichment. See discussion and collection of cases in 1 Austin W. Scott, Trusts §45 (William F. Fratcher 4th ed. 1987); Restatement (Third) of Trusts §24, Comments h-j (T.D. No. 1, 1996). Most decisions have permitted X to retain the land, but this view appears to be losing ground. In any event, a constructive trust for the beneficiaries will be imposed where the transfer was wrongfully obtained by fraud or duress, where the transferee, X, was in a confidential relationship with the transferor, or where the transfer was made in anticipation of the transferor's death. And most of the cases involve one of these situations.

More common than an oral trust for a third party is an oral trust for the benefit of the transferor. Indeed, judging by the cases, a surprising number of persons from time to time put title to land in another, relying upon the transferee's oral promise to reconvey. Some of the transferors are attempting to avoid their creditors or spouses or to achieve some tax benefit. Of course, any lawyer knows these transferors are asking for trouble and, human nature being what it is, usually they, like King Lear, get it.

Evicted Couple Leave Pictures of Son Who Threw Them Out
L.A. Times, Dec. 10, 1977, pt. 1, at 24

SEATTLE (UPI) — When Tom Rhodes and his wife were evicted, the only possessions they left behind in their $50,000 house were photographs of their son taped across the fireplace.

It was their son, Police Sgt. T. J. Rhodes, Jr., who had obtained the court order for their eviction.

"Now he is just Sgt. T. J. Rhodes," said Mrs. Rhodes, 58, who wept softly as a neighbor placed a comforting hand on her shoulder.

Tom Rhodes, Sr., 60, who had vowed he would have to be carried out of the house, gave in after a talk with Robert Lindquist, chief of the civil division of the King County Police, and walked out peacefully.

At the bottom of the stairs, Rhodes paused to remove an American flag. "That stands for justice," he said bitterly.

His son has steadfastly refused to answer questions about the eviction. His only public comments are in the cold legal language of court records.

"He has not talked to me in four years," the father said. "He will talk to his mother but not to me."

The couple said they had placed the home in their son's name to protect it when the elder Rhodes experienced financial troubles years ago. Monthly payments and taxes were paid by the father to the son, who forwarded them to the bank, the father said.

King County Superior Judge Robert Elston ruled in September that the younger Rhodes owned the house and was legally entitled to evict tenants, in this case his parents. Elston determined that loan papers and other documents showed that the elder Rhodeses had admitted they were "renting" from their son and that the parties had treated the house as rental property in their federal tax statements.

On the basis of the ruling, the younger Rhodes sent his parents a notice dated Sept. 30. "Please take notice," it began, "that the under-signed landlord, Thomas Rhodes, Jr., hereby gives you notice . . . to terminate your tenancy."

The parents went back to court to fight the eviction notice, but won nothing more than an extra 30 days to live in the house.

"I still think this is my house," the senior Rhodes said as he left it.

Hieble v. Hieble

Supreme Court of Connecticut, 1972
164 Conn. 56, 316 A.2d 777

SHAPIRO, J.   In this action the plaintiff sought a reconveyance of real property in the town of Killingworth which she had transferred to the defendant, claiming that he had agreed to reconvey the same to her, upon request, if she recovered from an illness. The trial court rendered judgment for the plaintiff and the defendant has appealed.

The trial court's finding of facts, which is not attacked, discloses that on May 9, 1959, the plaintiff, without consideration, transferred the title of her real estate by survivorship deed to her son, the defendant, and to her daughter. The plaintiff, who had that year undergone surgery for malignant cancer, feared a recurrence but believed that she would be out of danger if the cancer did not reappear within five years. She and the grantees orally agreed that the transfer would be a temporary arrangement; that she would remain in control of the property and pay all expenses and taxes; that once the danger of recrudescence had passed, the defendant and his sister would reconvey the property to the plaintiff on request. After the transfer, the plaintiff continued to reside on the property with her aged mother, whom she supported, her daughter and the defendant. In 1960, after the plaintiff expressed displeasure over the daughter's marriage, the daughter agreed to relinquish her interest in the property. A deed was prepared and the daughter and son, through a strawman, transferred title to the land to the plaintiff and her son in survivorship. In 1964, five years after the original conveyance, the plaintiff requested that the defendant reconvey his legal title to her, since she considered herself out of risk of a recurrence of cancer.

The plaintiff at that time needed money to make improvements on the land, particularly to install running water and indoor plumbing facilities as a convenience for her aged mother. The defendant procrastinated, feigning concern about the boundaries of an adjacent forty-acre parcel which the plaintiff had given him in 1956. Although the defendant refused to convey his interest in the jointly-owned premises, some friends of the plaintiff ultimately prevailed on him to sign a mortgage for an improvement loan in 1965. Thereafter, the defendant assured the plaintiff that he would never marry but would continue to live with her. These were his reasons for refusing reconveyance until his marriage plans were disclosed. Although the plaintiff proposed that her son could keep the property if he remained single, he did marry in 1967 and moved out of the house. After her attempts to obtain his voluntary reconveyance failed, the plaintiff brought suit in 1969. Throughout the entire period of time material to this litigation, the plaintiff has borne all expenses and costs of improvement to the property.

From these facts the trial court concluded that a constructive trust should be decreed on the basis of the oral agreement, the confidential relationship of the parties and their conduct with respect to the property. The defendant's appeal raises primarily the claim that the elements necessary to establish a confidential relationship, as the basis for a constructive trust, are lacking.

It hardly needs reciting that under our Statute of Frauds, General Statutes §52-550, oral agreements concerning interests in land are unenforceable. See Hanney v. Clark, 124 Conn. 140, 144-145, 198 A. 557. In this jurisdiction, however, the law is established that the Statute of Frauds does not apply to trusts arising by operation of law. Reynolds v. Reynolds, 121 Conn. 153, 158, 183 A. 394; Ward v. Ward, 59 Conn. 188, 196, 22 A. 149.

The case before us presents one of the most vexatious problems facing a court of equity in the area of constructive trusts, namely, whether equity should impose a constructive trust where a donee who by deed has received realty under an oral promise to hold and reconvey to the grantor has refused to perform his promise. See 3 Bogert, Trusts and Trustees (2d Ed.) §495; Costigan, "Trusts Based on Oral Promises," 12 Mich. L. Rev. 423, 515. Our task here, however, is considerably alleviated, since the defendant has not attacked the court's finding that the alleged agreement was in fact made, nor does he contest the receipt of parol evidence as having violated the Statute of Frauds. Although the deed recited that consideration was given for the 1959 transfer, the defendant does not attack the finding that there was no consideration for the conveyance. Indeed, in his brief the defendant abandons the claim that a recital of consideration suffices to rebut an allegation of a trust. . . .

Since the finding of facts is not challenged, the conclusion of the court that the parties stood in a confidential relationship must stand unless it is unreasonably drawn or unless it involves an erroneous application of law. The defendant's attack on this conclusion is without merit. He argues that because the plaintiff initiated the transfer and was a woman of mature years, and because he was an inexperienced young man, a court of equity should not recognize a relationship of confidentiality between them. We grant that the bond between parent and child is not per se a fiduciary one; it does generate, however, a natural inclination to repose great confidence and trust. See Suchy v. Hajicek, 364 Ill. 502, 509, 510, 4 N.E.2d 836; Wood v. Rabe, 96 N.Y. 414, 426. Coupled with the plaintiff's condition of weakness, her recent surgery, her anticipation of terminal illness, and the defendant's implicit reassurances of his faithfulness, this relationship becomes a classic example of the confidentiality to which equity will fasten consequences. See Restatement (Second), 1 Trusts §44, pp.115-16; 3 Bogert, supra, §482. . . .

The defendant's next contention questions the sufficiency of the evidence to justify the imposition of a constructive trust. Since he does not attack the finding that there was an underlying oral agreement, he cannot question the sufficiency of evidence to support that finding.

Brockett v. Jensen, 154 Conn. 328, 331, 225 A.2d 190; Davis v. Margolis, 107 Conn. 417, 422, 140 A. 823. Presumably, the defendant objects to the sufficiency of this 1959 oral agreement, standing by itself, to create a constructive trust. Here, three points are in order. First, the trial court reached its conclusion not only on the basis of that agreement but also on the conduct of the parties and the circumstances surrounding the conveyance, seen as a whole. As we have already noted, the defendant has failed to sustain his attack on the court's conclusion that a confidential relationship existed. Second, where a confidential relationship has been established, there is substantial authority that the burden of proof rests on the party denying the existence of a trust — and then, by clear and convincing evidence to negate such a trust. See Suchy v. Hajicek, supra, 364 Ill. 510, 4 N.E.2d 836; 89 C.J.S. Trusts §155. Our decision in Wilson v. Warner, 84 Conn. 560, 80 A. 718, is not contrary. There, in regard to an alleged resulting trust in a decedent's estate, the court said (pp. 564, 565, 80 A. p.719): "But in all cases where the claimed trust title to land is disputed, the facts from which such trust may be implied should be clearly and satisfactorily established." Third, as this court held in Dowd v. Tucker, 41 Conn. 197, 205, it is unnecessary to find fraudulent intent for the imposition of a constructive trust. Whether there be fraud at the inception or a repudiation afterward, the whole significance of such cases lies in the unjust enrichment of the grantee through his unconscionable retention of the trust res. . . .

The defendant's argument that the reconveyances in 1960 extinguished his obligation has no support in the finding. Rather, the court's finding of facts concerning his conduct subsequent to the 1960 transfers undermines his position. The court found that the defendant countered the plaintiff's request with delay, pretending concern about the boundaries of his adjacent forty-acre parcel; that he gave, as a reason for refusing to reconvey, assurances that he would never marry and that he would continue to reside with his mother. Of more weight to a court of equity, however, is the fact that the 1960 transfers effected no essential legal or equitable change in the defendant's initial undertaking. The finding reveals that his interest remained that of a joint tenant with right of survivorship upon the sister's surrender of her title to the plaintiff. Not only has the defendant failed to substantiate his contention, but his claim that the plaintiff's case must fail for lack of a concomitant renewal of the oral agreement in 1960 misconceives the nature of a constructive trust. See the discussion in Moses v. Moses, 140 N.J. Eq. 575, 580-581, 53 A.2d 805. Indeed, the defendant's assertion could amount to no more than a unilateral attempt to extinguish the original oral agreement. In short, the absence of an express renewal of the defendant's promise does not impair the soundness of the court's conclusion.

Finally, the defendant makes the claim that the plaintiff has unclean hands. There is nothing in the record to suggest that the 1959 transfer was an attempt to defraud creditors or to secrete assets from government agencies. Granted that the plaintiff offered to let her son keep the property in order to dissuade him from taking a wife, it cannot be said, as a matter of law, that her hands are tainted with an attempt to tamper with marriage, especially in view of the defendant's earlier assurances that he would never get married.

In light of the unattacked finding of the court that the defendant in fact had agreed to reconvey the property to the plaintiff upon request and the conclusion of the court, amply supported by the finding of fact, that a confidential relationship existed between the plaintiff and the defendant, the case comes squarely within the provisions of §44 of the Restatement (Second) of Trusts:

> Where the owner of an interest in land transfers it inter vivos to another in trust for the transferor, but no memorandum properly evidencing the intention to create a trust is signed, as required by the Statute of Frauds, and the transferee refuses to perform the trust, the transferee holds the interest upon a constructive trust for the transferor, if . . . (b) the transferee at the time of the transfer was in a confidential relation to the transferor.

There is no error.

NOTES AND QUESTION

1.   The law applied in Hieble v. Hieble is approved in Restatement (Third) of Trusts §24 (T.D. No. 1, 1996).

2.   In Pappas v. Pappas, 164 Conn. 242, 320 A.2d 809 (1973), Andrew Pappas, age 67, married a 23-year-old woman while on a visit to Greece. On their return, marital difficulties arose, and just prior to the wife's suing for divorce, Andrew conveyed certain real estate to his son, George. George agreed to transfer the property back to Andrew once his marital difficulties were over. In the divorce action, Andrew testified that he made the conveyance for consideration in satisfaction of certain financial and other obligations. Immediately after the divorce action was concluded, with a lump-sum alimony award to the wife of $25,000, Andrew demanded a reconveyance from George. George refused. The court held that a constructive trust could not be imposed upon George because Andrew, in misrepresenting the nature of the transfer in the divorce action, had perpetrated a fraud on the court and therefore did not have "clean hands."

Suppose Andrew Pappas, before the divorce suit, had consulted you. Would it be ethical to recommend that he transfer real estate to his son with a secret agreement by the son to convey it back after the divorce? See Jan E. Rein, Clients with Destructive and Socially Harmful Choices — What's an Attorney to Do?: Within and Beyond the Competency Construct, 62 Fordham L. Rev. 1101 (1994).

b. Oral Trusts for Disposition at Death

Olliffe v. Wells
Supreme Judicial Court of Massachusetts, 1881
130 Mass. 221

[Ellen Donovan died in 1877 leaving a will devising her residuary estate to the Rev. Eleazer M. P. Wells "to distribute the same in such manner as in his discretion shall appear best calculated to carry out wishes which I have expressed to him or may express to him." Wells was named executor. Ellen's heirs brought suit, claiming the residue should be distributed to them. In his answer, Wells stated that Ellen Donovan, before and after the execution of the will, had orally expressed to him her wish that her estate be used for charitable purposes, and especially for the poor, aged, infirm, and needy under the care of Saint Stephen's Mission of Boston.[17] Wells further stated that

---

17. Eleazer Mather Porter Wells, born in 1783, entered Brown University at the age of 22 but was dismissed as a result of a practical joke played on a professor by his room-

mates. (O tempora! O mores!) Thereafter he was deeply affected by a profound religious experience, including voices in the night saying, "Go and do my work." At age 40, Wells entered the ministry, becoming an Episcopal priest. In 1843, at age 60, Wells opened St. Stephen's Mission. From here he provided food, nursing care, clothing, and shelter for the poor of the West End of Boston. On one occasion he was able to keep the fire at the mission going by burning 100 old volumes of Voltaire's writings, which had been given to the mission. These proved good kindling, and Wells is quoted as having said, "Well, even the worst of men are put to good uses for the benefit of others." The great Boston fire of 1872 destroyed St. Stephen's

The Rev. Wells   Mission, and for the remaining years of his life Wells worked to revitalize the mission to no avail.

Wells died in 1878 at age 95. A resolution adopted by the clergy of the Episcopal Diocese of Massachusetts paid tribute to Wells as,

> A clergyman of stainless reputation and incorruptible integrity; an enthusiast in his sacred calling, especially in his self-selected mission to the destitute and afflicted, the outcast and the erring. . . . The work of Dr. Wells, continued so long a period at St. Stephen's Mission in Boston, and as the trusted almoner of very many of his fellow citizens, and withal his pure and consistent life as a man of God and of unremitting prayer, furnish a splendid commendation of religion.

Information supplied by Mark J. Duffy, Archivist of the Episcopal Diocese of Massachusetts, in a letter to Jesse Dukeminier dated April 13, 1982.

To what extent, if any, does the court's decision in Olliffe v. Wells turn on the facts that St. Stephen's Mission had been destroyed and the "trusted almoner" had died before the case reached the Supreme Judicial Court?

he desired and intended to distribute the residue for these purposes. The parties agreed that the facts alleged in the answer should be taken as true.]

GRAY, C.J.   Upon the face of this will the residuary bequest to the defendant gives him no beneficial interest. It expressly requires him to distribute all the property bequeathed to him, giving him no discretion upon the question whether he shall or shall not distribute it, or shall or shall not carry out the intentions of the testatrix, but allowing him a discretionary authority as to the manner only in which the property shall be distributed pursuant to her intentions. The will declares a trust too indefinite to be carried out, and the next of kin of the testatrix must take by way of resulting trust, unless the facts agreed show such a trust for the benefit of others as the court can execute. Nichols v. Allen, 130 Mass. 211. . . .

It has been held in England and in other States, although the question has never arisen in this Commonwealth, that, if a person procures an absolute devise or bequest to himself by orally promising the testator that he will convey the property to or hold it for the benefit of third persons, and afterwards refused to perform his promise, a trust arises out of the confidence reposed in him by the testator and of his own fraud, which a court of equity, upon clear and satisfactory proof of the facts, will enforce against him at the suit of such third persons. . . .

Upon like grounds, it has been held in England that, if a testator devises or bequeaths property to his executors upon trusts not defined in the will, but which, as he states in the will, he has communicated to them before its execution, such trusts, if for lawful purposes, may be proved by the admission of the executors, or by oral evidence, and enforced against them. . . . And in two or three comparatively recent cases it has been held that such trusts may be enforced against the heirs or next of kin of the testator, as well as against the devisee. . . . But these cases appear to us to have overlooked or disregarded a fundamental distinction.

Where a trust not declared in the will is established by a court of chancery against the devisee, it is by reason of the obligation resting upon the conscience of the devisee, and not as a valid testamentary disposition by the deceased. Cullen v. Attorney General, L.R. 1 H.L. 190. Where the bequest is outright upon its face, the setting up of a trust, while it diminishes the right of the devisee, does not impair any right of the heirs or next of kin, in any aspect of the case; for if the trust were not set up, the whole property would go to the devisee by force of the devise; if the trust setup is a lawful one, it enures to the benefit of the cestuis que trust; and if the trust setup is unlawful, the heirs or next of kin take by way of resulting trust.

Where the bequest is declared upon its face to be upon such trusts as the testator has otherwise signified to the devisee, it is equally clear that the devisee takes no beneficial interest; and, as between him and the beneficiaries intended, there is as much ground for establishing the trust as if the bequest to him were absolute on its face. But as between the devisee and the heirs or next of kin, the case stands differently. They are not excluded by the will itself. The will upon its face showing that the devisee takes the legal title only and not the beneficial interest, and the trust not being sufficiently defined by the will to take effect, the equitable interest goes, by way of resulting trust, to the heirs or next of kin, as property of the deceased, not disposed of by his will. Sears v. Hardy, 120 Mass. 524, 541, 542. They cannot be deprived of that equitable interest, which accrues to them directly from the deceased, by any conduct of the devisee; nor by any intention of the deceased, unless signified in those forms which the law makes essential to every testamentary disposition. A trust not sufficiently declared on the face of the will cannot therefore be set up by extrinsic evidence to defeat the rights of the heirs at law or next of kin. . . .

Decree for the plaintiffs.

NOTES AND PROBLEMS

1.   Olliffe v. Wells is the origin of the distinction between a secret and a semisecret trust followed in a considerable number of states in this country, although it is rejected in England and several states. The distinction is this: If Ellen Donovan had left a legacy to the Reverend Wells absolute on its face, without anything in the will indicating an intent to create a trust, a promise by the Reverend Wells to Ellen Donovan to use the legacy for St. Stephen's Mission would be enforceable by a constructive trust imposed upon Wells. This is called a secret trust because the will indicates no trust. Courts admit evidence of the promise for the purpose of preventing the Reverend Wells from unjustly enriching himself by pocketing the legacy. Having admitted proof of the promise, they proceed to enforce the promise by imposing a constructive trust on Wells for the benefit of St. Stephen's Mission.

On the other hand, if the will indicates that the Reverend Wells is to hold the legacy in trust but does not identify the beneficiary (as was true in Olliffe v. Wells), a semisecret trust is created. Since the will shows on its face an intent not to benefit Wells personally, it is not necessary to admit evidence of Wells' promise in order to prevent his unjust enrichment. Such evidence is excluded, and the legacy to Wells fails.

1 Restatement (Second) of Trusts §55, Comment h (1959), takes

the view that a constructive trust should be imposed in favor of the intended beneficiary in the semisecret, as well as secret, trust situation. Restatement (Third) of Trusts §18, Comment c (T.D. No. 1, 1996), agrees, but admits that enforcing a semisecret trust by imposing a constructive trust "probably does not reflect the current weight of authority," which follows Olliffe v. Wells.

2. Wendy Brown's brother, Simon Preston, is your client (see supra page 54). Simon has a long-time lover, named Camilla Bones, who lives out of town and whom he sees when he travels. Simon wishes to leave Camilla $10,000 at his death, without advertising the matter. Would you recommend that Simon leave $10,000 in his will to his sister Wendy and obtain a secret promise by Wendy that she will give Camilla the $10,000? Would this accomplish his objective of a secret gift? Would you recommend that Wendy make the promise in a signed writing, which Simon is to keep in his safe-deposit box? See Pfahl v. Pfahl, 10 Ohio Misc. 234, 225 N.E.2d 305 (1967). Would you recommend that Simon leave the money to you and you promise to give it to Camilla?

If Simon and his wife, Antonia, had both come to you for estate planning advice, and out of the presence of his wife Simon had told you of his desire to leave Camilla $10,000, what would you do? See Hotz v. Minyard, 304 S.C. 225, 403 S.E.2d 634 (1991), supra page 66; Burnele V. Powell & Ronald C. Link, The Sense of a Client: Confidentiality Issues in Representing the Elderly, 62 Fordham L. Rev. 1197, 1212 (1994).

Refer back to Wendy Brown's Aunt Fanny Fox, an elderly lady with a house full of things and no descendants (supra page 54). Would a secret trust — an absolute devise by Aunt Fanny to Wendy, with a promise by Wendy to distribute in accordance with a memorandum to be left — be enforceable? See 1A Scott, supra, §55.8 at 88. Suppose that Wendy did not promise Aunt Fanny to hold the property in trust but that Aunt Fanny devised all her household contents to Wendy and attached to the will by a paper clip a memorandum addressed to Wendy telling her how to dispose of the household contents. What result?

SECTION C. DISCRETIONARY TRUSTS

Trusts can be divided into mandatory trusts and discretionary trusts. In a *mandatory* trust, the trustee must distribute all the income. Thus:

Case 15. O transfers property to X in trust to distribute all the income to A. This is a mandatory trust. The trustee has no discretion to choose either the persons who will receive the income or the amount to be distributed.

In a *discretionary* trust, the trustee has discretion over payment of either the income or the principal or both. Discretionary powers of a trustee may be drafted in limitless variety. The following hypothetical case illustrates discretionary powers over income:

> *Case 16.* O transfers property to *X* in trust to distribute all the income to one or more members of a group consisting of *A, A*'s spouse, and *A*'s children in such amounts as the trustee determines. This is a kind of discretionary trust known as a spray trust. The trustee must distribute all the income currently, but has discretion to determine who gets it and in what amount. If desired, the trustee could be given discretionary power to accumulate income and add it to principal.

With respect to the principal of the trust, the trust instrument may specify that the trustee has discretionary power to distribute principal to the income beneficiary. Such a power may be limited by a standard ("such amounts as are necessary to support my wife in the style of living to which she has become accustomed"), or the trustee may be given wide discretion.

Marsman v. Nasca

Massachusetts Appeals Court, 1991
30 Mass. App. Ct. 789, 573 N.E.2d 1025,
review denied, 411 Mass. 1102, 579 N.E.2d 1361

DREBEN, J.   This appeal raises the following questions: Does a trustee, holding a discretionary power to pay principal for the "comfortable support and maintenance" of a beneficiary, have a duty to inquire into the financial resources of that beneficiary so as to recognize his needs? If so, what is the remedy for such failure? A Probate Court judge held that the will involved in this case imposed a duty of inquiry upon the trustee. We agree with this conclusion but disagree with the remedy imposed and accordingly vacate the judgment and remand for further proceedings.

1. *Facts.* We take our facts from the findings of the Probate Court judge, supplemented on occasion by uncontroverted evidence. Except as indicated in note [22], infra, her findings are not clearly erroneous.

Sara Wirt Marsman died in September, 1971, survived by her second husband, T. Frederik Marsman (Cappy), and her daughter by her first marriage, Sally Marsman Marlette. Mr. James F. Farr, her lawyer for many years, drew her will and was the trustee thereunder.[18]

Article IIA of Sara's will provided in relevant part:

> It is my desire that my husband, T. Fred Marsman, be provided with reasonable maintenance, comfort and support after my death. Accordingly, if my said husband is living at the time of my death, I give to my trustees, who shall set the same aside as a separate trust fund, one-third ($\frac{1}{3}$) of the rest, residue and remainder of my estate . . . ; they shall pay the net income therefrom to my said husband at least quarterly during his life;[19] and after having considered the various available sources of support for him, my trustees shall, if they deem it necessary or desirable from time to time, in their sole and uncontrolled discretion, pay over to him, or use, apply and/or expend for his direct or indirect benefit such amount or amounts of the principal thereof as they shall deem advisable for his comfortable support and maintenance.

Article IIB provided: "Whatever remains of said separate trust fund, including any accumulated income thereon on the death of my husband, shall be added to the trust fund established under Article IIC. . . . " Article IIC established a trust for the benefit of Sally and her family. Sally was given the right to withdraw principal and, on her death, the trust was to continue for the benefit of her issue and surviving husband.

The will also contained the following exculpatory clause: "No trustee hereunder shall ever be liable except for his own willful neglect or default."

During their marriage, Sara and Cappy lived well and entertained frequently. Cappy's main interest in life centered around horses. An expert horseman, he was riding director and instructor at the Dana Hall School in Wellesley until he was retired due to age in 1972. Sally, who was also a skilled rider, viewed Cappy as her mentor, and each had great affection for the other. Sara, wealthy from her prior marriage, managed the couple's financial affairs. She treated Cappy as "Lord of the Manor" and gave him money for his personal expenses, including an extensive wardrobe from one of the finest men's stores in Wellesley.

---

18. The will provided for two trustees; however, one resigned in April, 1972, and thereafter Farr acted as sole trustee. [James F. Farr, who died in 1993, was a prominent trusts and estates lawyer in Boston and the author of a leading practitioner's handbook, James F. Farr & Jackson W. Wright, Jr., An Estate Planner's Handbook (4th ed. 1979). He also was the author of the sixth edition of Augustus Peabody Loring's Trustee's Handbook, first published in 1898 and the Bible of Boston trustees for several generations, referred to by the court in footnote 22 of the case. — Eds.]

19. The surviving spouse's forced share in Massachusetts is a life estate in one-third of the decedent's estate (see supra page 501, footnote 8), and this is what Sara left Cappy. — Eds.

In 1956, Sara and Cappy purchased, as tenants by the entirety, the property in Wellesley which is the subject of this litigation. Although title to the property passed to Cappy by operation of law on Sara's death, Sara's will also indicated an intent to convey her interest in the property to Cappy. In the will, Cappy was also given a life estate in the household furnishings with remainder to Sally.

After Sara's death in 1971, Farr met with Cappy and Sally and held what he termed his "usual family conference" going over the provisions of the will. At the time of Sara's death, the Wellesley property was appraised at $29,000, and the principal of Cappy's trust was about $65,600.

Cappy continued to live in the Wellesley house but was forced by Sara's death and his loss of employment in 1972 to reduce his standard of living substantially. He married Margaret in March, 1972, and, shortly before their marriage, asked her to read Sara's will, but they never discussed it. In 1972, Cappy took out a mortgage for $4,000, the proceeds of which were used to pay bills. Farr was aware of the transaction, as he replied to an inquiry of the mortgagee bank concerning the appraised value of the Wellesley property and the income Cappy expected to receive from Sara's trust.

In 1973, Cappy retained Farr in connection with a new will. The latter drew what he described as a simple will which left most of Cappy's property, including the house, to Margaret. The will was executed on November 7, 1973.

In February, 1974, Cappy informed the trustee that business was at a standstill and that he really needed some funds, if possible. Farr replied in a letter in which he set forth the relevant portion of the will and wrote that he thought the language was "broad enough to permit a distribution of principal." Farr enclosed a check of $300. He asked Cappy to explain in writing the need for some support and why the need had arisen. The judge found that Farr, by his actions, discouraged Cappy from making any requests for principal.

Indeed, Cappy did not reduce his request to writing and never again requested principal. Farr made no investigation whatsoever of Cappy's needs or his "available sources of support" from the date of Sara's death until Cappy's admission to a nursing home in 1983 and, other than the $300 payment, made no additional distributions of principal until Cappy entered the nursing home.

By the fall of 1974, Cappy's difficulty in meeting expenses intensified.[20] Several of his checks were returned for insufficient funds, and

20. After Sara's death, Cappy's income was limited, particularly considering the station he had enjoyed while married to Sara. In 1973, including the income from Sara's trust of $2,116, his income was $3,441; in 1974 it was $3,549, including trust income of $2,254; in 1975, $6,624, including trust income of $2,490 and social security income of $2,576. Margaret's income was also minimal; $499 in 1974, $4,084 in 1975, including social security income of $1,686. Cappy's income in 1976 was $8,464; in 1977, $8,955; in 1978,

in October, 1974, in order that he might remain in the house, Sally and he agreed that she would take over the mortgage payments, the real estate taxes, insurance, and major repairs. In return, she would get the house upon Cappy's death.

Cappy and Sally went to Farr to draw up a deed. Farr was the only lawyer involved, and he billed Sally for the work. He wrote to Sally, stating his understanding of the proposed transaction, and asking, among other things, whether Margaret would have a right to live in the house if Cappy should predecease her. The answer was no. No copy of the letter to Sally was sent to Cappy. A deed was executed by Cappy on November 7, 1974, transferring the property to Sally and her husband Richard T. Marlette (Marlette) as tenants by the entirety, reserving a life estate to Cappy. No writing set forth Sally's obligations to Cappy.

The judge found that there was no indication that Cappy did not understand the transaction, although, in response to a request for certain papers by Farr, Cappy sent a collection of irrelevant documents. The judge also found that Cappy clearly understood that he was preserving no rights for Margaret, and that neither Sally nor Richard nor Farr ever made any representation to Margaret that she would be able to stay in the house after Cappy's death.

Although Farr had read Sara's will to Cappy and had written to him that the will was "broad enough to permit a distribution of principal," the judge found that Farr failed to advise Cappy that the principal of his trust could be used for the expenses of the Wellesley home. The parsimonious distribution of $300 and Farr's knowledge that the purpose of the conveyance to Sally was to enable Cappy to remain in the house, provide support for this finding. After executing the deed, Cappy expressed to Farr that he was pleased and most appreciative. Margaret testified that Cappy thought Farr was "great" and that he considered him his lawyer.[21]

Sally and Marlette complied with their obligations under the agreement. Sally died in 1983, and Marlette became the sole owner of the property subject to Cappy's life estate. Although Margaret knew before Cappy's death that she did not have any interest in the Wellesley property, she believed that Sally would have allowed her to live in the house because of their friendship. After Cappy's death in 1987, Marlette inquired as to Margaret's plans, and, subsequently, through Farr,

---

$9,681; in 1979, $10,851; in 1980, $11,261; in 1981, $12,651; in 1982, $13,870; in 1983, $12,711; in 1984, $12,500; in 1985, $12,567; in 1986, $12,558. The largest portion from 1975 on came from social security benefits.

21. The judge noted that Farr, in response to an interrogatory filed by the plaintiff, stated that he rendered legal services to Sara from approximately 1948-1971; to Cappy from approximately 1951-1987; to Sally from 1974 until prior to her death; and to Marlette since 1983.

sent Margaret a notice to vacate the premises. Margaret brought this action in the Probate Court.

After a two-day trial, the judge held that the trustee was in breach of his duty to Cappy when he neglected to inquire as to the latter's finances. She concluded that, had Farr fulfilled his fiduciary duties, Cappy would not have conveyed the residence owned by him to Sally and Marlette. The judge ordered Marlette to convey the house to Margaret and also ordered Farr to reimburse Marlette from the remaining portion of Cappy's trust for the expenses paid by him and Sally for the upkeep of the property. If Cappy's trust proved insufficient to make such payments, Farr was to be personally liable for such expenses. Both Farr and Marlette appealed from the judgment, from the denial of their motions to amend the findings, and from their motions for a new trial. Margaret appealed from the denial of her motion for attorney's fees. As indicated earlier, we agree with the judge that Sara's will imposed a duty of inquiry on the trustee, but we disagree with the remedy and, therefore, remand for further proceedings.

2. *Breach of trust by the trustee.* Contrary to Farr's contention that it was not incumbent upon him to become familiar with Cappy's finances, Article IIA of Sara's will clearly placed such a duty upon him. In his brief, Farr claims that the will gave Cappy the right to request principal "in extraordinary circumstances" and that the trustee, "was charged by Sara to be wary should Cappy request money beyond that which he quarterly received." Nothing in the will or the record supports this narrow construction. To the contrary, the direction to the trustees was to pay Cappy such amounts "as they shall deem advisable for his comfortable support and maintenance." This language has been interpreted to set an ascertainable standard, namely to maintain the life beneficiary "in accordance with the standard of living which was normal for him before he became a beneficiary of the trust." Woodberry v. Bunker, 359 Mass. 239, 243, 268 N.E.2d 841 (1971).

Even where the only direction to the trustee is that he shall "in his discretion" pay such portion of the principal as he shall "deem advisable," the discretion is not absolute. "Prudence and reasonableness, not caprice or careless good nature, much less a desire on the part of the trustee to be relieved from trouble . . . furnish the standard of conduct." Boyden v. Stevens, 285 Mass. 176, 179, 188 N.E. 741 (1934), quoting from Corkery v. Dorsey, 223 Mass. 97, 101, 111 N.E. 795 (1916). Holyoke Natl. Bank v. Wilson, 350 Mass. 223, 227, 214 N.E.2d 42 (1966).

That there is a duty of inquiry into the needs of the beneficiary follows from the requirement that the trustee's power "must be exercised with that soundness of judgment which follows from a due appreciation of trust responsibility." Boyden v. Stevens, 285 Mass. at

179, 188 N.E. 741. In Old Colony Trust Co. v. Rodd, 356 Mass. 584, 586, 254 N.E.2d 886 (1970), the trustee sent a questionnaire to each potential beneficiary to determine which of them required assistance but failed to make further inquiry in cases where the answers were incomplete. The court agreed with the trial judge that the method employed by the trustee in determining the amount of assistance required in each case to attain "comfortable support and maintenance" was inadequate. There, as here, the trustee attempted to argue that it was appropriate to save for the beneficiaries' future medical needs. The court held that the "prospect of illness in old age does not warrant a persistent policy of niggardliness toward individuals for whose comfortable support in life the trust has been established. The payments made to the respondent and several other beneficiaries, viewed in light of their assets and needs, when measured against the assets of the trust show that little consideration has been given to the 'comfortable support' of the beneficiaries." Id. at 589-590, 254 N.E.2d 886. See 3 Scott, Trusts §187.3 (Fratcher 4th ed. 1988) (action of trustee is "arbitrary" where he "is authorized to make payments to a beneficiary if in his judgment he deems it wise and he refuses to inquire into the circumstances of the beneficiary"). See also Kolodney v. Kolodney, 6 Conn. App. 118, 123, 503 A.2d 625 (1986).

Farr, in our view, did not meet his responsibilities either of inquiry or of distribution under the trust. The conclusion of the trial judge that, had he exercised "sound judgment," he would have made such payments to Cappy "as to allow him to continue to live in the home he had occupied for many years with the settlor" was warranted.

3. *Remedy against Marlette.* The judge, concluding that, had Farr not been in breach of trust, "[C]appy would have died owning the house and thus able to devise it to his widow, the plaintiff," ordered Marlette to convey the house to Margaret. This was an inappropriate remedy in view of the judge's findings. She found that, although the relationship between Cappy and Sally was "close and loving," there was "no fiduciary relation between them" and that Sally and Marlette "were not unjustly enriched by the conveyance." She also found that "Sally and Richard Marlette expended significant monies over a long period of time in maintaining their agreement with [C]appy."

Because the conveyance was supported by sufficient consideration (the agreement to pay the house expenses) and because Sally and Marlette had no notice of a breach of trust and were not themselves guilty of a breach of fiduciary duty, they cannot be charged as constructive trustees of the property. Jones v. Jones, 297 Mass. 198, 207, 7 N.E.2d 1015 (1937). That portion of the judgment which orders Marlette to convey the property is vacated.

4. *Remainder of Cappy's trust.* The amounts that should have been

expended for Cappy's benefit are, however, in a different category. More than $80,000 remained in the trust for Cappy at the time of his death. As we have indicated, the trial judge properly concluded that payments of principal should have been made to Cappy from that fund in sufficient amount to enable him to keep the Wellesley property. There is no reason for the beneficiaries of the trust under Article IIC to obtain funds which they would not have received had Farr followed the testatrix's direction. The remedy in such circumstances is to impress a constructive trust on the amounts which should have been distributed to Cappy but were not because of the error of the trustee. Even in cases where beneficiaries have already been paid funds by mistake, the amounts may be collected from them unless the recipients were bona fide purchasers or unless they, without notice of the improper payments, had so changed their position that it would be inequitable to make them repay. 5 Scott, Trusts §465, at 341 (Fratcher 4th ed. 1989). See National Academy of Sciences v. Cambridge Trust Co., 370 Mass. 303, 307, 346 N.E.2d 879 (1976). Here, the remainder of Cappy's trust has not yet been distributed, and there is no reason to depart from the usual rule of impressing a constructive trust in favor of Cappy's estate on the amounts wrongfully withheld. There is also no problem as to the statute of limitations. The period of limitations with respect to those we hold to be constructive trustees (the beneficiaries of the trust under Article IIC) has not run as, at the earliest, their entitlement to funds occurred at Cappy's death in 1987.

That Cappy assented to the accounts is also no bar to recovery by his estate. The judge found that he was in the dark as to his rights to receive principal for the upkeep of the home. An assent may be withdrawn by a judge "if it is deemed improvident or not conducive to justice." Swift v. Hiscock, 344 Mass. 691, 693, 183 N.E.2d 875 (1962). The accounts were not allowed, and we need not consider the effect of G.L. c. 206, §24,[22] which permits the impeachment of an account after a final decree has been entered only for "fraud or manifest error." See Holyoke Natl. Bank v. Wilson, 350 Mass. at 228, 214 N.E.2d 42; National Academy of Sciences v. Cambridge Trust Co., 370 Mass. at 309, 346 N.E.2d 879.

The amounts to be paid to Cappy's estate have not been determined.[23] On remand, the Probate Court judge is to hold such hear-

---

22. The docket shows that the judge was in error in finding that the accounts were allowed. They were assented to but not allowed. In Loring, A Trustee's Handbook §62 (Farr rev. 1962) the author states: "[P]reparing annual accounts, signed by the adult beneficiaries and allowing them to continue without adjudication is an unsafe procedure for the trustee."

23. Marlette's expenses, which may constitute evidence of the amounts which should have been paid to Cappy, were not established at the time of the judge's findings.

ings as are necessary to determine the amounts which should have been paid to Cappy to enable him to retain possession of the house.

5. *Personal liability of the trustee.* Farr raises a number of defenses against the imposition of personal liability, including the statute of limitations, the exculpatory clause in the will, and the fact that Cappy assented to the accounts of the trustee. The judge found that Farr's breach of his fiduciary duty to inquire as to Cappy's needs and his other actions in response to Cappy's request for principal, including the involvement of Sally in distributions of principal despite Sara's provision that Cappy's trust be administered separately, led Cappy to be unaware of his right to receive principal for house expenses. The breach may also be viewed as a continuing one. In these circumstances we do not consider Cappy's assent, see Swift v. Hiscock, 344 Mass. at 693, 183 N.E.2d 875, or the statute of limitations to be a bar. The judge also found that Margaret learned of Cappy's right to principal for house expenses only when she sought other counsel after his death.

The more difficult question is the effect of the exculpatory clause. As indicated in part 3 of this opinion, we consider the order to Marlette to reconvey the property an inappropriate remedy. In view of the judge's finding that, but for the trustee's breach, Cappy would have retained ownership of the house, the liability of the trustee could be considerable.

Although exculpatory clauses are not looked upon with favor and are strictly construed, such "provisions inserted in the trust instrument without any overreaching or abuse by the trustee of any fiduciary or confidential relationship to the settlor are generally held effective except as to breaches of trust 'committed in bad faith or intentionally or with reckless indifference to the interest of the beneficiary.' " New England Trust Co. v. Paine, 317 Mass. 542, 550, 59 N.E.2d 263 (1945). The actions of Farr were not of this ilk and also do not fall within the meaning of the term used in the will, "willful neglect or default."

Farr testified that he discussed the exculpatory clause with Sara and that she wanted it included. Nevertheless, the judge, without finding that there was an overreaching or abuse of Farr's fiduciary relation with Sara, held the clause ineffective. Relying on the fact that Farr was Sara's attorney, she stated: "One cannot know at this point in time whether or not Farr specifically called this provision to Sara's attention. Given the total failure of Farr to use his judgment as to [C]appy's needs, it would be unjust and unreasonable to hold him harmless by reason of the exculpatory provisions he himself drafted and inserted in this instrument."

Assuming that the judge disbelieved Farr's testimony that he and Sara discussed the clause, although such disbelief on her part is by no means clear, the conclusion that it "would be unjust and unreasonable to hold [Farr] harmless" is not sufficient to find the overreaching or abuse of a fiduciary relation which is required to hold the provision ineffective. See Restatement (Second) of Trusts §222, Comment d (1959).[24] We note that the judge found that Sara managed all the finances of the couple, and from all that appears, was competent in financial matters.

There was no evidence about the preparation and execution of Sara's will except for the questions concerning the exculpatory clause addressed to Farr by his own counsel. No claim was made that the clause was the result of an abuse of confidence.

The fact that the trustee drew the instrument and suggested the insertion of the exculpatory clause does not necessarily make the provision ineffective. Restatement (Second) of Trusts §222, Comment d. No rule of law requires that an exculpatory clause drawn by a prospective trustee be held ineffective unless the client is advised independently. Cf. Barnum v. Fay, 320 Mass. 177, 181, 69 N.E.2d 470 (1946).

The judge used an incorrect legal standard in invalidating the clause. While recognizing the sensitivity of such clauses, we hold that, since there was no evidence that the insertion of the clause was an abuse of Farr's fiduciary relationship with Sara at the time of the drawing of her will, the clause is effective.

Except as provided herein, the motions of the defendants for a new trial and amended findings are denied. The plaintiff's claim of error as to legal fees fails to recognize that fees under G.L. c. 215, §45, are a matter within the discretion of the trial judge. We find no abuse of discretion in the denial of fees.

The judgment is vacated, and the matter is remanded to the Probate Court for further proceedings to determine the amounts which, if paid, would have enabled Cappy to retain ownership of the resi-

---

24. The Restatement lists six factors that may be considered in determining whether a provision relieving the trustee from liability is ineffective on the ground that it was inserted in the trust instrument as a result of an abuse of a fiduciary relationship at the time of the trust's creation. The six factors are:

(1) whether the trustee prior to the creation of the trust had been in a fiduciary relationship to the settlor, as where the trustee had been guardian of the settlor;
(2) whether the trust instrument was drawn by the trustee or by a person acting wholly or partially on his behalf;
(3) whether the settlor has taken independent advice as to the provisions of the trust instrument;
(4) whether the settlor is a person of experience and judgment or is a person who is unfamiliar with business affairs or is not a person of much judgment or understanding;
(5) whether the insertion of the provision was due to undue influence or other improper conduct on the part of the trustee;
(6) the extent and reasonableness of the provision.

dence. Such amounts shall be paid to Cappy's estate from the trust for his benefit prior to distributing the balance thereof to the trust under Article IIC of Sara's will.[25]

So ordered.

NOTES, PROBLEMS, AND QUESTIONS

1. Would Margaret's elective share apply to the Wellesley house under Massachusetts law as explicated in Sullivan v. Burkin, supra page 500?

2. Why is the trustee's natural tendency to favor the remaindermen over the life tenant, to be conservative in paying out income or principal?

3. If the trustee has simple discretion unqualified by the adjective "sole" or the like, the courts will not substitute their judgment for that of the trustee as long as the trustee "acts not only in good faith and from proper motives, but also within the bounds of a reasonable judgment." 3 Austin W. Scott, Trusts, §187 (William F. Fratcher 4th ed. 1988). When the instrument purports to free the trustee from some or all of these limitations, problems in construction arise. At one extreme are instruments that purport to give unlimited discretionary power to the trustee. But a discretionary power to be exercised "in the trustee's absolute and uncontrolled discretion" is not in fact absolute. As Judge Learned Hand remarked,

> [N]o language, however strong, will entirely remove any power held in trust from the reach of a court of equity. After allowance has been made for every possible factor which could rationally enter into the trustee's decision, if it appears that he has utterly disregarded the interests of the beneficiary, the Court will intervene. Indeed were that not true, the power would not be held in trust at all; the language would be no more than a precatory admonition. [Stix v. Commissioner, 152 F.2d 562, 563 (2d Cir. 1945).]

What, then, are the limitations on the trustee's freedom when the trustee has "absolute and uncontrolled discretion"? Professor Scott argued for a subjective standard, emphasizing the trustee's "good faith" and proper motives and dispensing with the requirement of reasonableness. He suggested, and the Restatement for which he was the chief reporter adopted, a standard of whether the trustee has

---

25. Since Cappy received the income on the "augmented" principal, interest should not be charged on the sums to be distributed to Cappy's estate for the period prior to his death.

acted "in that state of mind in which it was contemplated by the settlor that he should act." 3 Scott, supra; 1 Restatement (Second) of Trusts §187, Comment j (1959). Some courts, relying on the Restatement good faith standard, declare that the trustee must not act arbitrarily or capriciously, seemingly bringing in a reasonableness test under the guise of other words. Other courts apply a reasonableness test even when the discretion is "absolute." In the final analysis, it appears that the difference between simple discretion and "absolute" discretion is one of degree and that the trustee's action must not only be in good faith but also to some extent reasonable, with more elasticity in the concept of reasonableness the greater the discretion given. See Restatement (Third) of Trusts §50, General Comment and Reporter's Notes (T.D. No. 2, 1999), for an extended discussion of judicial control over a trustee's discretion.

4. A troublesome source of litigation is whether a trustee, in exercising a discretionary power to spend income or principal for the beneficiary's support, may consider the other resources of the beneficiary. In Marsman v. Nasca, this matter was covered by the trust instrument: "after having considered the various available sources of support for him [my husband], my trustees shall. . . . " If the husband had been independently wealthy, the trustees would not have had to support him.

Where not dealt with in the trust instrument, the issue may wind up in court. It is a question of interpretation of the trust instrument, but the presumption appears to be that the settlor intended the beneficiary to receive his support from the trust estate regardless of the beneficiary's other financial resources. See Godfrey v. Chandley, 248 Kan. 975, 811 P.2d 1248 (1991) (surviving wife's personal income should not be considered by trustee); 2 Scott, supra, §128.4. However, this presumption can be rebutted by the special circumstances of the case. See In re Estate of Winston, 201 A.D.2d 922, 613 N.Y.S.2d 461 (1994).

5. *The ethical dilemmas of James F. Farr.* In Marsman v. Nasca, James F. Farr was a lawyer for Sara, Cappy, Sally, and Marlette, all more or less at the same time. See footnote 21. Do you have any problems with this? To whom does Farr owe a duty of loyalty? Is it ethical to represent "the family"? Consider this excerpt from Professor Thomas L. Shaffer, who urges estate planning lawyers to define their relationships with clients as "lawyers of the family."

> [T]he most irresponsible thing a lawyer could do is to send either of these people [a husband and wife] to another lawyer, or both of them to two other lawyers. If that is the command of our professional ethics, or even the easiest available "solution" to the case from our regulatory rules, then our ethics and our rules are corrupting. They corrupt the

family in general, and *this* family in particular. A lawyer following the rules is irresponsible because, in fact, the family is the lawyer's client. The lawyer who sends the family away is not able to respond to his client. He is disabled by a false ethic and, in trying to protect himself, he harms his client. [Thomas L. Shaffer, The Legal Ethics of Radical Individualism, 65 Tex. L. Rev. 963, 982 (1987).]

Shaffer believes that a lawyer for the family should facilitate disclosure of estate planning matters among members of the family so there are no secrets and family members can learn how to deal with each other. For a critical analysis of Shaffer's views, and of other commentators on legal ethics in estate planning, see Teresa S. Collett, And the Two Shall Become as One . . . Until the Lawyers Are Done, 7 Notre Dame J.L. Ethics & Pub. Poly. 101 (1993); Russell G. Pearce, Family Values and Legal Ethics: Competing Approaches to Conflicts in Representing Spouses, 62 Fordham L. Rev. 1253 (1994). See also ACTEC, Commentaries on the Model Rules of Professional Conduct 65-71 (2d ed. 1995).

In Marsman v. Nasca, why was not Margaret, Cappy's second wife, part of the "family"?

In the testamentary trust Farr drafted for Sara Marsman, he included an exculpatory clause, excusing him from liability as a trustee except for "willful" neglect or default. The court holds this clause effective because there was no evidence it was inserted as a result of an abuse of confidence reposed by the client in the lawyer. Do *you* think it is ethical to include an exculpatory clause like this in a will you draft naming yourself trustee? Is this a freely and knowingly bargained agreement between lawyer and client? Who should have the burden of showing this? Uniform Trust Act §1106(b) (1999 draft) provides: "An exculpatory term drafted by or on behalf of the trustee is presumed to have been inserted as a result of an abuse of a fiduciary or confidential relationship unless the trustee proves that the exculpatory term is fair under the circumstances and that its existence and contents were adequately communicated to the settlor."

In New York, by statute, an attempted grant to a testamentary trustee of immunity from liability for failure to exercise reasonable care is deemed contrary to public policy and void. N.Y. Est., Powers & Trusts Law §11-1.7 (1998).

Perhaps one reason the trustee Farr was inattentive to Cappy's needs is that the trustee's fee was very small. Cappy's trust was valued at $65,600 at Sara's death, and an appropriate trustee's fee would be less than $1,000 a year. A bank would not agree to serve as trustee of such a small trust, so an individual had to be found who would serve or another solution reached. Other solutions: Cappy himself could have been given the power to go into principal to support himself in the style of living to which he was accustomed, without any discretionary veto power in the trustee (see infra page 682). Cappy would merely have to show by bills, checks, and other records the difference between his income and what it cost to live. Or Cappy could have been given the power to withdraw $5,000 or 5 percent of the corpus each year in his absolute discretion (see infra page 674). Or Sara could have given Cappy his one-third share outright rather than in trust.

American College of Trust and Estate Counsel
Fees of Testamentary Trustees (1993)

MASSACHUSETTS
TRUSTEE'S FEE

There are no statutory rates.
Annual income fee: 7% of income, although it is not uncommon for fiduciaries to decrease the rate as the value of the trust increases.

Annual fee on principal:
$7.00 per $1,000 of first	$ 500,000
$6.00 per $1,000 of next	500,000
$3.00 per $1,000 of next	$1,000,000
$1.00 per $1,000 of balance	

There are customary minimum charges of $3,000 to $5,000 for separately invested accounts and around $1,200 for accounts wholly invested in common trust funds.

NOTE: NEW FORMS OF TRUSTS

During the 1990s, when the stock market was soaring and huge capital gains were being made, it became apparent that new forms of trusts were desirable to deal with this situation. Under the traditional form of trust — life income to *A*, remainder to *B* — all of the capital gains were allotted to the remainder. But, since it would be unfair to the life tenant for a trustee to invest a large percentage of the trust corpus in growth stocks, paying maybe 2 percent dividends, the trustee of a traditional trust could not take advantage of the proven rule that, over the long term, investment in equities pays the highest return (in the form of capital gain). To remedy this situation, discretionary trusts became more popular than ever. If the trustee can pay some of the principal to the income beneficiary, the trustee can allot some of the capital gains to the income beneficiary. With a discretionary trust, the income beneficiary will have a fair income — say 6 percent of the value of the corpus — and the trustee will be able to invest for the highest return in accordance with modern portfolio theory. (On modern portfolio theory, see infra page 962.)

A second method of dealing with this problem is to create a *unitrust* for the life tenant. In a unitrust, the income beneficiary is entitled not to the actual income earned but to a fixed percentage of the value of the trust corpus, which is revalued each year. For example, a unitrust may give the income beneficiary the right to receive 6 percent of the value of the trust corpus each year. If the trust corpus has a value of $2 million this year, the income beneficiary receives $120,000, which may come from traditional income sources or from sales realizing capital gain. If the corpus increases in value to $2.5 million next year, the income beneficiary is entitled to receive next year $150,000. The trustee is free to pursue the highest total return regardless of the form it takes. (For more on unitrusts and their usefulness in freeing the trustee of traditional investment rules, see infra pages 971-972.)

Discretionary powers in the trustee to pay income or principal to the settlor's descendants, generation after generation forever, are now becoming widely used in *perpetual dynasty trusts*, which are permitted in an increasing number of jurisdictions. See infra pages 849, 854.

SECTION D.   CREDITORS' RIGHTS: SPENDTHRIFT TRUSTS

> The law, in its majestic equality, forbids the rich as
> well as the poor to sleep under bridges, to beg in
> the streets, and to steal bread.
>
> ANATOLE FRANCE
> *Le Lys Rouge, ch. 7 (1894)*

The rich have — at least in Anglo-American history — continually sought ways to secure their property to their children and grandchildren so that it remains in the family safe from the accidents of fortune and bad management. The fee tail and later the strict settlement were the standard devices used in England to keep land in the family. The fee tail was early abolished in this country, and the strict settlement never took hold here. The spendthrift trust, an American invention not recognized in England, is their ideological descendant.

In a spendthrift trust, the beneficiaries cannot voluntarily alienate their interests nor can their creditors reach their interests. It is created by imposing a disabling restraint upon the beneficiaries and their creditors. Thus:

> *Case 17.* *T* devises property to *X* in trust to pay the income to *A* for life and upon *A*'s death to distribute the property to *A*'s children. A clause in the trust provides that *A* may not transfer her life estate, and it may not be reached by *A*'s creditors (see the spendthrift clause, numbered (8), in Shelley v. Shelley, infra, at page 633). By this trust *A* is given a stream of income that *A* cannot alienate and her creditors cannot reach.

The two decisions largely responsible for the spendthrift trust doctrine are Nichols v. Eaton, 91 U.S. 716 (1875), and Broadway National Bank v. Adams, 133 Mass. 170 (1882). In Nichols v. Eaton, Justice Miller inserted an elaborate dictum upholding spendthrift trusts. Justice Miller reasoned: "Why a parent, or one who loves another, and wishes to use his own property in securing the object of his affection, as far as property can do it, from the ills of life, the vicissitudes of fortune, and even his own improvidence, or incapacity for self-protection, should not be permitted to do so, is not readily perceived." 91 U.S. at 727. In Broadway National Bank v. Adams, the Massachusetts court upheld the spendthrift trust.

John Chipman Gray, the great, oracular property teacher at Harvard, was so outraged at the introduction of spendthrift trusts that he was moved to write his Restraints on Alienation, first published in 1883, in refutation of Nichols v. Eaton. He said, "The general introduction of spendthrift trusts would be to form a privileged class, who could indulge in every speculation, could practice every fraud, and, provided they kept on the safe side of the criminal law, could yet roll in wealth." John C. Gray, Restraints on the Alienation of Property 262 (1883). In spite of Gray's strictures, by the time the second edition of his book was published, the battle was lost. "State after State has given in its adhesion to the new doctrine . . . and yet I cannot recant." Id. (2d ed. 1885) at iv-v. The spendthrift trust has today been recognized in almost all jurisdictions.

Ohio, one of the few long-time holdouts against spendthrift trusts, finally capitulated and recognized them in Scott v. Bank One Trust Co., 62 Ohio St. 3d 39, 577 N.E.2d 1077 (1991). In New York by statute all trusts are spendthrift unless the settlor expressly makes the beneficiary's interest transferable. N.Y. Est., Powers & Trusts Law §7.1-5 (1998). In other jurisdictions, trusts are not spendthrift unless the settlor expressly inserts a spendthrift clause.

On the rise of the spendthrift trust in the United States, see Anne S. Emanuel, Spendthrift Trusts: It's Time to Codify the Compromise, 72 Neb. L. Rev. 179 (1993). For an analysis of the issues underlying spendthrift trusts, see Adam Hirsch, Spendthrift Trusts and Public Policy: Economic and Cognitive Perspectives, 73 Wash. U. L.Q. 1 (1995) (arguing that spendthrift trusts do not create serious problems for contract creditors).

Shelley v. Shelley

Supreme Court of Oregon, 1960

223 Or. 328, 354 P.2d 282

O'CONNELL, J.   This is an appeal from a decree of the circuit court for Multnomah county establishing the rights of the parties to the income and corpus of a trust of which the defendant, the United States National Bank of Portland (Oregon) is trustee.

The assignments of error are directed at the trial court's interpretation of the trust. The trust involved in this suit was created by Hugh T. Shelley. The pertinent parts of the trust are as follows:

> NINTH: All of the rest, residue, and remainder of my said estate, . . . I give, devise, and bequeath to the United States National Bank of Portland (Oregon), in trust, . . . upon the following trust: . . .
>
> (2) I direct that all income derived from my trust estate be paid to my wife, Gertrude R. Shelley, as long as she lives, said income to be paid to her at intervals of not less than three (3) months apart; . . .
>
> (4) If my said wife, Gertrude R. Shelley, shall predecease me, and my said son is then alive, or upon my wife's death after my death and my son being alive, it is my desire, and I direct that the United States National Bank of Portland (Oregon), as trustee, shall continue this estate in trust and pay all income derived therefrom to my son, Grant R. Shelley, as long as he lives, said income to be paid to him at intervals not less than three (3) months apart; Provided, Further, That when my son, Grant R. Shelley, arrives at the age of thirty (30) years, my trustee may then, or at any time thereafter, and from time to time, distribute to my son absolutely and as his own all or any part of the principal of said trust fund that it may then or from time to time thereafter deem him capable of successfully investing without the restraints of this trust; Provided, However, That such disbursements of principal of said trust so made to my son after he attains the age of thirty (30) years shall be first approved in writing by either one of my brothers-in-law, that is: Dr. Frank L. Ralston, now of Walla Walla, Washington, or Russell C. Ralston, now of Palo Alto, California, if either of them is then living, but if neither of them is then living, then my trustee is authorized to make said disbursements of principal to my son in the exercise of its sole and absolute judgment and discretion; Provided, Further, That said trust shall continue as to all or any part of the undistributed portion of the principal thereof to and until the death of my said son.
>
> (5) I further direct and authorize my trustee, from time to time (but only upon the written approval of my said wife if she be then living, otherwise in the exercise of my trustee's sole discretion) to make disbursements for the use and benefit of my son, Grant R. Shelley, or his children, in case of any emergency arising whereby unusual and extraordinary expenses are necessary for the proper support and care of my said son, or said children. . . .
>
> (8) Each beneficiary hereunder is hereby restrained from alienating,

anticipating, encumbering, or in any manner assigning his or her interest or estate, either in principal or income, and is without power so to do, nor shall such interest or estate be subject to his or her liabilities or obligations nor to judgment or other legal process, bankruptcy proceedings or claims of creditors or others.

The principal question on appeal is whether the income and corpus of the Shelley trust can be reached by Grant Shelley's former wives and his children.

Grant Shelley was first married to defendant, Patricia C. Shelley. Two children were born of this marriage. Patricia divorced Grant in 1951. The decree required Grant to pay support money for the children; the decree did not call for the payment of alimony. Thereafter, Grant married the plaintiff, Betty Shelley. Two children were born of this marriage. The plaintiff obtained a divorce from Grant in August, 1958. The decree in this latter suit required the payment of both alimony and a designated monthly amount for the support of the children of that marriage.

Some time after his marriage to the plaintiff, Grant disappeared and his whereabouts was not known at the time of this suit. The defendant bank, as trustee, invested the trust assets in securities which are now held by it, together with undisbursed income from the trust estate. The plaintiff obtained an injunction restraining the defendant trustee from disbursing any of the trust assets. Patricia Shelley brought a garnishment proceeding against the trustee, by which she sought to subject the trust to the claim for support money provided for in the 1951 decree of divorce. . . .

The defendant bank finally brought a bill of interpleader tendering to the court for disbursement of all of the funds held in trust, praying for an order establishing the respective rights of the interpleaded parties to the trust assets.

The trial court entered a decree subjecting the accrued income of the trust to the existing claims of the plaintiff and Patricia Shelley; subjecting future income of the trust to the periodic obligations subsequently accruing by the terms of the decrees in the divorce proceedings brought by plaintiff and Patricia Shelley; and further providing that in the event that the trust income was insufficient to satisfy such claims, the corpus of the trust was subject to invasion.

We shall first consider that part of the decree which subjects the income of the trust to the claims of plaintiff and of defendant, Patricia Shelley. The trust places no conditions upon the right of Grant Shelley to receive the trust income during his lifetime. Therefore, plaintiff and Patricia Shelley may reach such income unless the spendthrift provision of the trust precludes them from doing so.

The validity of spendthrift trusts has been established by our former cases. . . . The question on this appeal is whether the spendthrift provision will be given effect to bar the claims of the beneficiary's children for support and the plaintiff's claim for alimony. In Cogswell v. Cogswell, 1946, 178 Or. 417, 167 P.2d 324, 335, we held that the spendthrift provision of a trust is not effective against the claims of the beneficiary's former wife for alimony and for support of the beneficiary's child. In that case the court adopted the rule stated in 1 Restatement, Trusts, §157, which reads in part as follows:

> §157. Particular Classes of Claimants
> Although a trust is a spendthrift trust or trust for support, the interest of the beneficiary can be reached in satisfaction of an enforceable claim against the beneficiary,
> (a) by the wife or child of the beneficiary for support, or by the wife for alimony.

The defendant bank concedes that the *Cogswell* case is controlling in the case at bar, but asks us to overrule it on the ground that it is inconsistent with our own cases recognizing the testator's privilege to dispose of his property as he pleases and, further, that it is inconsistent with various Oregon statutes expressing the same policy of free alienation. If we should accept the premise urged by the defendant bank, that a testator has an inviolable right to dispose of his property as he pleases subject only to legislative restriction, the conclusion is inevitable that the testator may create in a beneficiary an interest free from all claims, including those for support and alimony.

But the premise is not sound. The privilege of disposing of property is not absolute; it is hedged with various restrictions where there are policy considerations warranting the limitation. . . . Not all of these restrictions are imposed by statute. The rule against perpetuities, the rule against restraints on alienation, the refusal to recognize trusts for capricious purposes or for illegal purposes, or for any purpose contrary to public policy, are all instances of judge-made rules limiting the privilege of alienation. Many others could be recited. Griswold, Spendthrift Trusts (2d ed.) §553; Simes, Public Policy and the Dead Hand, passim; Scott, Control of Property by the Dead, 65 U. Pa. L. Rev. 527, 632 (1917). See also Nussbaum, Liberty of Testation, 23 A.B.A.J. 183 (1937); McMurray, Liberty of Testation and Some Modern Limitations Thereon, 14 Ill. L. Rev. 96 (1919); Keeton & Gower, Freedom of Testation in English Law, 20 Iowa L. Rev. 326 (1935). It is within the court's power to impose upon the privilege of disposing of property such restrictions as are consistent with its view of sound public policy, unless, of course, the legislature has expressed a contrary view. Our own statutes do not purport to deal with the specific question before us, that is as to whether there should be limitations on the owner's privilege to create a spendthrift trust. . . .

In holding that a spendthrift trust is subject to claims for alimony and support the court, in Cogswell v. Cogswell, supra, did not disclose the reasoning by which it reached its conclusion. This failure to examine the question of public policy in the area of spendthrift trusts is not unusual, for as Griswold, Spendthrift Trusts (2d ed.), p.634 points out in discussing the validity of spendthrift trusts, "examination [of public policy] has rarely, if ever, been attempted by the courts," which he admits that "it is obviously a matter difficult to approach and one about which dogmatic conclusions cannot be reached." But once having recognized the validity of spendthrift trusts, which we have and which conclusion defendant bank endorses, the more specific question of the validity of the restraint of such a trust as against the claims of children for support and of the beneficiary's former wife for alimony presents a narrower question of policy which, we believe, is easier to answer. The question is whether a person should be entitled to enjoy the benefits of a trust and at the same time refuse to pay the obligations arising out of his marriage.

We have no hesitation in declaring that public policy requires that the interest of the beneficiary of a trust should be subject to the claims for support of his children. . . . Certainly the defendant will accept the societal postulate that parents have the obligation to support their children. If we give effect to the spendthrift provision to bar the claims for support, we have the spectacle of a man enjoying the benefits of a trust immune from claims which are justly due, while the community pays for the support of his children. Wetmore v. Wetmore, 1896, 149 N.Y. 520, 44 N.E. 169, 33 L.R.A. 708. We do not believe that it is sound policy to use the welfare funds of this state in support of the beneficiary's children, while he stands behind the shield of immunity created by a spendthrift trust provision. To endorse such a policy and to permit the spectacle which we have described above would be to invite disrespect for the administration of justice. . . .

The justification for permitting a claim for alimony is, perhaps, not as clear. The adjustment of the economic interests of the parties to a divorce may depend upon a variety of factors, including the respective fault of the parties, the ability of the wife to support herself, the duration of the marriage, and other considerations. Whether alimony is to be granted and its amount are questions which are determined in light of these various interests. It is probably fair to say that the duties created by the marriage relation, at least as they are evaluated upon the termination of the marriage, are conceived of as more qualified than those arising out of the paternal relationship. On the theory that divorce terminates the husband's duty to support his former wife and that she stands in no better position than other creditors, some courts have held that the spendthrift provision insulates the beneficiary's interest in the trust from her claim. Lippincott v. Lippincott, 1944, 349 Pa. 501, 37 A.2d 741. Recognizing the difference in marital and parental duties suggested above, it has been held that a spendthrift trust is subject to the claims for the support of children but free from the claims of the former wife. Eaton v. Eaton, 1926, 82 N.H. 216, 132 A. 10, commented upon in 35 Yale L.J. 1025 (1926). . . . A majority of the cases, however, hold that a spendthrift provision will not bar a claim for alimony. . . .

As we have already mentioned, the case of Cogswell v. Cogswell, supra, is in accord with this latter view. We are of the opinion that the conclusion there reached should be affirmed. The duty of the husband to support his former wife should override the restriction called for by the spendthrift provision. The same reason advanced above for requiring the support of the beneficiary's children will, in many cases, be applicable to the claim of a divorced wife; if the beneficiary's interest cannot be reached, the state may be called upon to support her. . . .

We hold that the beneficiaries' interest in the income of the Shelley Trust is subject to the claims of the plaintiff for alimony and to the claims for the support of Grant Shelley's children as provided for under both decrees for divorce. These claims are not without limit. We adopt the view that such claimants may reach only that much of the income which the trial court deems reasonable under the circumstances, having in mind the respective needs of the husband and wife, the needs of the children, the amount of the trust income, the availability of the corpus for the various needs, and any other factors which are relevant in adjusting equitably the interests of the claimants and the beneficiary. Griswold, Spendthrift Trusts (2d ed.) §339; 2 Scott on Trusts, §157.1; Note, 28 Va. L. Rev. 527 (1942). . . .

The question of the claimants' rights to reach the corpus of the trust involves other considerations. For the reasons heretofore stated, the beneficiary's interest in the corpus is not made immune from these claims. But, by the terms of the trust, the disbursement of the corpus is within the discretion of the trustee (or, in some instances subject to the approval of others), and, therefore, Grant Shelley's right to receive any part of the corpus does not arise until the trustee has exercised his discretion and has decided to invade the corpus. Until that time, the plaintiff and Patricia Shelley cannot reach the corpus of the trust because the beneficiary has no realizable interest in it. . . . In some jurisdictions a creditor of the beneficiary of a discretionary trust may attach the potential interest of the beneficiary. Sand v. Beach, 1936, 270 N.Y. 281, 200 N.E. 821; Hamilton v. Drogo, 1926, 241 N.Y. 401, 150 N.E. 496; 214 App. Div. 819, 210 N.Y.S. 859, commented upon in 26 Colum. L. Rev. 776 (1926). See Griswold, Spendthrift Trusts (2d ed.), §§367, 368, 357, 2 Scott on Trusts, §155.1.

There is no such procedure in Oregon available to the creditor. . . . It follows that the decree of the lower court in making the corpus of the Shelley Trust subject to the plaintiff's claim for alimony was erroneous.

The claims for the support of Grant Shelley's children, provided for in the two divorce decrees, involve a different problem. The trust directed and authorized the trustee, in the exercise of its sole discretion upon the death of the settlor's wife, to make disbursements for the use and benefit not only of Grant Shelley, but also for his children. The disbursements were to be made "in case of any emergency arising whereby unusual and extraordinary expenses are necessary for the proper support and care of my said son, or said children." Here the children are named as beneficiaries of the trust and need not claim derivatively through their father. However, they are entitled to a share of the corpus only if, in the trustee's discretion, it is determined that an emergency exists. The defendant bank contends that the expenses of supporting Grant Shelley's children claimed in this case were for the usual and ordinary costs of support and do not, therefore, constitute "unusual and extraordinary expenses" within the meaning of the trust provision. . . . We disagree with defendant's interpretation. We construe the clause to include the circumstances involved here, i.e., where the children are deserted by their father and are in need of support. We think that the testator intended to provide that in the event that the income from the trust was not sufficient to cover disbursements for the support and care of either the son or his children an "emergency" had arisen and the corpus could then be invaded. The decree of the lower court would permit the corpus to be employed if the "assets in the hands of the Executor [trustee] and the income cash from said trust shall be insufficient to pay the obligations of Defendant Grant R. Shelley." . . . The decree is too broad, . . . because it permits encroachment upon the corpus without reference to whether the trustee has exercised his discretion or whether there has been an emergency as contemplated by the testator.

. . . The decree, therefore, should have permitted an invasion of the corpus only if it was necessary to first reach the income under the circumstances just mentioned and such income was insufficient. And further, the decree should have made such corpus available only in the event of the trustee's exercise of discretion authorizing the disbursement for the support of the children under the emergency circumstances provided for in the trust. After the entry of such a decree, if the trustee should refuse to exercise his discretion, or if it is claimed that he exercised it unreasonably, relief may be sought in a court of equity by the children.

The decree of the lower court is affirmed and the cause remanded with directions to modify the decree in accordance with the views expressed in this opinion.

NOTES AND QUESTIONS

1. The protection of spendthrift trusts from creditors has several exceptions.

a. *Self-settled trusts.* A spendthrift trust cannot be set up by the settlor for the settlor's own benefit. Creditors of the settlor can reach the settlor's interest in income or principal in a mandatory trust. If, for example, the settlor is entitled to the income, the settlor's creditors can require the trustee to pay the income to them. In a discretionary trust, creditors can reach the maximum amount the trustee could, in the trustee's discretion, pay the settlor or apply for the settlor's benefit. See 2A Austin W. Scott, Trusts §156 (William F. Fratcher 4th ed. 1987). Why is protection from creditors available only to recipients of *inherited* wealth and not also to persons who *earn* wealth and create a self-settled trust?

Persons with earned (or inherited) wealth can protect their assets from creditors by creating a self-settled spendthrift trust on an offshore island in the Caribbean or the South Seas, which, applying local law, refuses to permit creditors to reach such a trust. See Lynn M. LoPucki, The Death of Liability, 106 Yale L.J. 1, 32-38 (1996). Alaska and Delaware have now joined these offshore tax havens by enacting legislation extending spendthrift protection to an irrevocable trust of which the settlor is a *discretionary* beneficiary of income or principal, if the trust is not created with the intent to defraud creditors. See Alaska Stat. §34.40.110 (1997); Del. Code ch. 12, §§3570-3574 (1997); John E. Sullivan III, Gutting the Rule Against Self-Settled Trusts: How the New Delaware Trust Law Competes with Offshore Trusts, 23 Del. J. Corp. L. 423 (1998). Such self-settled creditor-proof trusts can be created in these states by residents of other states. These statutes are promoted by banks seeking fees from managing trusts of successful earners of great wealth.

b. *Child support and alimony.* Judgments for child or spousal support can be enforced against the debtor's interest in spendthrift trusts in the majority of states, as in Shelley v. Shelley. See In re Marriage of Chapman, 297 Ill. App. 3d 611, 697 N.E.2d 365 (1998). In a substantial minority, however, a spouse or child cannot reach a spendthrift trust to satisfy judgments for support. In some states statutes permit courts to order child and spousal support payments from spendthrift or discretionary trusts. See Cal. Prob. Code §15305 (1998); Tex. Fam. Code §154.005 (1998). See 2A Scott, supra, §157; Carolyn L. Dessin, Feed a Trust and Starve a Child: The Effectiveness of Trust Protective

Techniques Against Claims for Support and Alimony, 10 Ga. St. U. L. Rev. 691 (1994).

c. *Furnishing necessary support.* A person who has furnished necessary services or support can reach the beneficiary's interest in a spendthrift trust. See 2A Scott, supra, §157.2. Whether a state supporting a beneficiary can claim reimbursement for furnishing necessary support is explored infra at page 649.

d. *Federal tax lien.* The United States or a state can reach the beneficiary's interest to satisfy a tax claim against the beneficiary. Federal tax law trumps state spendthrift trust rules. La Salle National Bank v. United States, 636 F. Supp. 874 (N.D. Ill. 1986); United States v. Riggs National Bank, 636 F. Supp. 172 (D.D.C. 1986) (upholding government levy in spite of a clause providing for forfeiture of the beneficiary's interest in case of any levy of execution).

e. *Excess over amount needed for support.* In several states the beneficiary's creditors can reach that part of spendthrift trust income in excess of the amount needed for the support and education of the beneficiary. See, e.g., N.Y. Est., Powers & Trusts Law §7-3.4 (1992). Several states copied this New York statute. In determining what is necessary for the support of the beneficiary and what is excess (reachable by creditors), courts developed a *station-in-life rule.* Creditors can reach only the amount in excess of what is needed to maintain the beneficiary in his station in life. The station-in-life rule rendered these excess-income statutes relatively useless to creditors. Spendthrift trusts are usually created only by persons of considerable wealth who have raised their children in substantial luxury. The accustomed manner of living of the child-beneficiary is likely to require the full income from the trust.[26]

f. *Percentage levy.* In a few states a creditor is permitted to reach a

---

26. John Chipman Gray was even more scornful of the New York scheme than of spendthrift trusts.

> It may be said that, if the Courts have been wrong in tolerating spendthrift trusts, a remedy is to be found in the legislatures. If the remedy is like that applied in New York, it is, if not worse, more disgusting than the disease. . . . The Statutes of New York, as interpreted by the Courts, provide that the surplus of income given in trust beyond what is necessary for the education and support of the beneficiary shall be liable for his debts. . . . The Court takes into account that the debtor is "a gentleman of high social standing, whose associations are chiefly with men of leisure, and who is connected with a number of clubs," and that his income is not more than sufficient to maintain his position according to his education, habits, and associations.
>
> To say that whatever money is given to a man cannot be taken by his creditors is bad enough; at any rate, however, it is law for rich and poor alike; but to say that from a sum which creditors can reach one man, who has lived simply and plainly, can deduct but a small sum, while a large sum may be deducted by another man because he is "of high social standing" . . . is to descend to a depth of as shameless snobbishness as any into which the justice of a country was ever plunged.
> [John C. Gray, Restraints on the Alienation of Property x-xi (2d ed. 1895).]

certain percentage (usually between 10 and 30 percent) of the income of the spendthrift trust beneficiary in a garnishment proceeding ordinarily applicable to wage earners. See 2A Scott, supra, §152.1. In several states, dollar limits are placed on the amount that can be shielded in a spendthrift trust.

g. *Tort creditors.* Whether a spendthrift clause prevents tort creditors of the trust beneficiary from reaching the trust is not settled. Commentators are solidly opposed to extending the spendthrift trust doctrine to bar tort creditors. In Sligh v. Sligh, 704 So. 2d 1020 (Miss. 1997), the Mississippi court apparently became the first court to hold that a tort creditor could enforce a judgment against the tortfeasor's interest in a spendthrift trust or in a discretionary trust. The very next year the Mississippi legislature enacted the "Family Trust Preservation Act," which reversed *Sligh* and exempted spendthrift trusts from tort creditors. Miss. Code §91-9-503 (1998).

2. *Restraints on remainders.* In a majority of jurisdictions, a spendthrift restraint may be imposed upon a remainder interest as well as upon an income interest in trust. If the restraint is imposed on a remainder interest, the remainderman's creditors cannot reach the principal of the trust until the remainderman is entitled to receive the principal. 2A Scott, supra, §153. See also Knight v. Knight, 182 A.D.2d 342, 589 N.Y.S.2d 195 (1992) (applying California law and voiding gift of a restrained remainder).

In England, which does not permit restraints upon equitable remainders, a lively auction market in remainders and reversions has developed. Persons who would rather have cash now than wait until the life beneficiary dies put up their future interests for sale. See N.Y. Times, Mar. 6, 1978, at D1. No such organized market exists in this country.

3. *Pension trusts.* The federal Employee Retirement Income Security Act (ERISA), 29 U.S.C. §1056(d)(1) (1998), requires that, "Each pension plan [covered by the act] shall provide that benefits provided under the plan may not be assigned or alienated." ERISA also provides that such benefits may be reached for child support, alimony, or marital property rights. Id. §1056(d)(3). The principle underlying ERISA is that the employee's future retirement security should be protected even at the expense of current creditors. See Guidry v. Sheet Metal Workers Natl. Pension Fund, 493 U.S. 365 (1990); John H. Langbein & Bruce A. Wolk, Pension and Employee Benefit Law 545-548 (2d ed. 1995).

Compare the exclusion of a self-settled trust from protection under the spendthrift trust doctrine. Creditors of the settlor can reach the trust. Is this consistent with exemption of pensions under ERISA, inasmuch as in a sense the wage earner is the settlor of a trust for his own benefit? Which rule is wiser: the spendthrift trust rule or the ERISA rule? See id.

Does protection of pension plans from creditors to some extent compensate for limiting spendthrift trusts to inherited wealth?

4. *Bankruptcy.* A beneficial interest in a spendthrift trust cannot be reached by creditors in bankruptcy. The Bankruptcy Code provides that an interest in trust which is not alienable under local law does not pass to the trustee in bankruptcy. 11 U.S.C. §541(c)(2) (1998). The Code also excludes from the bankrupt's estate any interest in a pension trust covered by ERISA, inasmuch as such interests are made nonassignable by ERISA. Patterson v. Shumate, 504 U.S. 753 (1992). See Langbein & Wolk, supra, 605-609 (discussing exemption of IRAs, Keogh plans, and 401(k) and 403(b) plans); Anthony M. Sabino & John P. Clarke, The Last Line of Defense: The New Test for Protecting Retirement Plans from Creditors in Bankruptcy Cases, 48 Ala. L. Rev. 613 (1997).

5. *Support trusts.* A *support trust* is a trust that requires the trustee to make payments of income (or, if so specified, of principal too) to the beneficiary in an amount necessary for the education or support of the beneficiary in accordance with an ascertainable standard. A support trust is a gift of support to the beneficiary — whatever is required to support the beneficiary, no more, no less. The beneficiary of a support trust cannot alienate her interest. Nor can creditors of the beneficiary reach the beneficiary's interest, except suppliers of necessaries may recover through the beneficiary's right to support. Cf. Restatement (Third) of Trusts §§50 & 60 (T.D. No. 2, 1999).

PROBLEM

O transfers property to *X* in trust to pay the income annually during *A*'s lifetime "to *A* personally, to be for *A*'s support," and on *A*'s death, to pay the principal to *B*. One year later *A* gratuitously writes, signs, and delivers to his cousin, *C*, the following memorandum: "I hereby assign to my cousin *C* all my right to receive future income for my lifetime from the trust," identifying the above trust in the memorandum. *X*, who has no notice of the assignment, pays the next annual installment of income, $5,000, to *A*, who, having meanwhile become angry with *C*, refuses to pay this sum over to *C*. Instead *A* uses it to buy stock for himself. The stock is now worth $10,000. Does *C* have any claim against *A*? See 2A Scott, supra, §154.

United States v. O'Shaughnessy
Supreme Court of Minnesota, 1994
517 N.W.2d 574

WAHL, J.   The United States District Court, District of Minnesota, certified to this court, pursuant to Minn. Stat. §480.061 (1992), the following question of state law:

> Under Minnesota law, does the beneficiary of a discretionary trust with the provisions described herein have "property" or any "right to property" in nondistributed trust principal or income before the trustees have exercised their discretionary powers of distribution under the trust agreement?

According to the facts set out in the Order, Lawrence P. O'Shaughnessy is a beneficiary of two separate identical trusts established by his grandparents, I. A. O'Shaughnessy and Lillian G. O'Shaughnessy on December 26, 1951 (the 1951 Trusts) for their 16 (later 17) grandchildren. First Trust National Association (First Trust), Lawrence M. O'Shaughnessy, and Donald E. O'Shaughnessy (Co-Trustees) are the current trustees of the 1951 Trusts.

The 1951 Trust Agreements allow the trustees, in their discretion, to distribute the principal and income of the Trusts to the beneficiaries. Article III provides, in part:

> The Trustees in their discretion may pay to [Lawrence P. O'Shaughnessy], or for his benefit, all or such part of the principal or the annual net income of the trust estate as they shall see fit during his lifetime. . . .
> Net income not paid out shall be accumulated and at the end of each calendar year added to the principal of the trust estate. . . .

Article VIII of the Trust Agreements further provides that:

> If at any time or times in the opinion of the Trustees it is advisable to do so, the Trustees may pay to or expend for any beneficiary such sum from the principal of such beneficiary's share of the trust estate as the Trustees in their sole discretion deem wise, and the discretion so given to the Trustees shall be absolute and binding upon all persons in interest.

Although the trustees have the discretion to distribute or withhold trust assets during Lawrence P. O'Shaughnessy's lifetime, the 1951 Trust Agreements give him a limited power of appointment exercisable only by his last will and testament to a certain class of individuals. If Lawrence P. O'Shaughnessy dies without exercising his power of appointment, Article III dictates the distribution of the principal and undistributed income at his death.

In October 1989, a delegate of the Secretary of the Treasury assessed a $412,921.27 federal income tax deficiency against Lawrence P. O'Shaughnessy for the years 1983 through 1986. On August 1, 1990, First Trust was served with a Notice of Levy upon "property or rights to property" belonging to Lawrence P. O'Shaughnessy and held by First Trust to satisfy the deficiency. No distribution of principal or income from the 1951 Trusts was pending when the levy was served.

The government filed suit in federal court on April 26, 1993 seeking judicial enforcement of the levy. First Trust and the Co-Trustees moved to dismiss the complaint pursuant to Fed. R. Civ. P. 12(b)(6) asserting that at the time the levy was served, they did not hold property or rights to property belonging to Lawrence P. O'Shaughnessy. After a hearing, the federal district court determined that the issue raised by the Motion to Dismiss presented a question of state law appropriate for certification to this court.

The United States has a lien for the amount of any tax deficiency, including interest, upon "all property and rights to property, whether real or personal, belonging to [the delinquent taxpayer]." 26 U.S.C. §6321(1988). Although the federal courts decide whether a federal tax lien can attach to a particular interest, the threshold question of whether a taxpayer possesses "property" or "rights to property" must be resolved by reference to state law. Aquilino v. United States, 363 U.S. 509, 512-13 (1960).

An express trust creates two separate interests in the subject matter of the trust — a legal interest vested in the trustee and an equitable interest vested in the beneficiary. Farmers State Bank of Fosston v. Sig Ellingson & Co., 218 Minn. 411, 16 N.W.2d 319, 322 (1944). Under a discretionary express trust, "a beneficiary is entitled only to so much of the income or principal as the trustee in his uncontrolled discretion shall see fit to [distribute] . . . [The beneficiary] cannot compel the trustee to pay him or to apply for his use any part of the trust property." IIA Austin W. Scott & William F. Fratcher, The Law of Trusts §155 (4th ed. 1987) [hereinafter Scott on Trusts]. Because discretionary trusts give the trustee complete discretion to distribute all, some, or none of the trust assets, the beneficiary has a "mere expectancy" in the nondistributed income and principal until the trustee elects to make a payment. George G. Bogert & George T. Bogert, The Law of Trusts and Trustees §228 (1992). Creditors, who stand in the shoes of the beneficiary, have no remedy against the trustee until the trustee distributes the property. Id.

We are unpersuaded by the government's claim that the 1951 Trusts are not discretionary. The Trust Agreements do not direct the trustees to distribute the trust assets to Lawrence P. O'Shaughnessy. Rather, the agreements state that the trustees "*may pay* . . . all or such part of the principal or the annual net income of the trust estate as they shall see fit during his lifetime." (Emphasis added.) This use of precatory language reveals the settlors' intent to create a discretionary trust. Moreover, even though the trustees do not have express authority to exclude Lawrence P. O'Shaughnessy from receiving any trust income or principal, the "sole discretion" given the trustees is "absolute and binding upon all persons in interest." While the trustees cannot exercise their discretion in a way that defeats the intent of the settlors or the purpose of the 1951 Trusts, this fact does not change the nature of the 1951 Trusts. Even where trustees have absolute, unlimited, or uncontrolled discretion, any attempt to violate the settlor's intent or the trust's purpose is considered an abuse of that discretion. Restatement (Second) on Trusts §187 cmt. j (1959). So long as the trustees act in good faith, from proper motives, and within the bounds of reasonable judgment, the court will not interfere with their decisions. Scott on Trusts §187.

The parties agree that Lawrence P. O'Shaughnessy has an equitable interest in the 1951 Trusts that entitles him to bring suit to compel the trustees to perform their duties, to enjoin the trustees from committing a breach of trust, or to remove the trustees altogether. See Restatement (Second) of Trusts §199; Farmers State Bank, 16 N.W.2d at 322. It is also undisputed that the 1951 Trusts give Lawrence P. O'Shaughnessy a testamentary power of appointment. The parties disagree, however, as to whether these interests rise to the level of property rights.

Property is broadly defined by the Minnesota Probate Code as "real and personal property or any interest therein . . . [or] anything that may be the subject of ownership." Minn. Stat. §524.1-201(29) (1992). This definition, however, is little help in discerning the nature of undistributed discretionary trust assets. More on point is a recent court of appeals decision addressing the nature of undistributed discretionary trust assets in the context of state-funded medical assistance. In re Leona Carlisle Trust, 498 N.W.2d 260 (Minn. App. 1993). In In re Leona Carlisle Trust, the court of appeals held that the assets of a discretionary trust were not available assets for the purpose of determining a person's eligibility for public medical assistance. Id. at 266. The court recognized that support trusts, which direct the trustee to distribute trust income or principal as necessary for the support of the beneficiary, usually are considered available assets while discretionary trusts are not. Id. at 264. The court explained that this was because beneficiaries of support trusts legally can compel the trustee to distribute trust assets while beneficiaries of discretionary trusts cannot. Id. See Restatement (Second) of Trusts §198 cmt. c.

Cases from other states support the holding in In re Leona Carlisle Trust. See, e.g., Chenot v. Bordeleau, 561 A.2d 891 (R.I. 1989) (discretionary trust assets not available because trustees have discretion to withhold payments); First Nat'l Bank of Md. v. Dept. of Health & Mental Hygiene, 284 Md. 720, 399 A.2d 891 (1979) (state could not compel trustees of discretionary trust to pay for beneficiary's stay in state hospital); Town of Randolph v. Roberts, 346 Mass. 578, 195 N.E.2d 72 (1964) (state welfare agency could not recover from discretionary trust for disability payments). Additionally, some states have enacted statutes that preclude creditors from reaching nondistributed discretionary trust proceeds. See Mont. Code Ann. §72-33-304(1) (1993) (creditor cannot compel trustee to exercise discretion); Nev. Rev. Stat. §166.110 (1993) (trustee's discretion "shall never be interfered with for any consideration of the needs, station in life or mode of life of the beneficiary, or for uncertainty, or on any pretext whatever"). Even in California, where the legislature gave courts the authority to order trustees to distribute discretionary trust assets to reimburse the state for public assistance payments, Cal. Prob. Code §15306(a)(2) (West 1991), there is no similar provision for tax obligations. . . .

Under Minnesota law the beneficiary of a discretionary trust with the provisions described in the 1951 Trust Agreements does not have "property" or any "right to property" in nondistributed trust principal or income before the trustees have exercised their discretionary powers of distribution under the trust agreement.

Certified Question answered in the negative.

Although a creditor cannot, by judicial order, compel the trustee of a discretionary trust to pay him, a creditor may, in some states, be entitled to an order directing the trustee to pay the creditor before paying the beneficiary. The trustee need not pay any part of the trust fund to the beneficiary, but if the trustee determines to do so, the trustee must pay the creditors who now stand in the beneficiary's shoes. By this procedure, a creditor can deprive the beneficiary of trust income even though the creditor will not necessarily be paid.

This cutting-off-income procedure was approved in New York in Hamilton v. Drogo, 241 N.Y. 401, 150 N.E. 496 (1926), referred to in Shelley v. Shelley at page 637, noting that Oregon had no such procedure. Hamilton v. Drogo involved a discretionary trust established by the will of the dowager Duchess of Manchester to provide her spendthrift son, the ninth duke,[27] freedom from the travails of penury. Andrews, J., explained how the rule worked:

---

27. William Angus Drogo Montagu, ninth Duke of Manchester, "had been kept so short of cash as a boy, with pocket money of one penny a day, that he grew up with no real sense of its value. On an allowance of £400 a year at Cambridge, he ran up debts totalling £2,000. He spent much time in America, Africa, and India, avoiding creditors, looking for a rich wife, and sponging off his friends." David Cannadine, The Decline and Fall of the British Aristocracy 403 (1990).

We may not interfere with the discretion which the testatrix has vested in the trustee any more than her son may do so. Its judgment is final. But at least annually this judgment must be exercised. And if it is exercised in favor of the duke [the beneficiary], then there is due him the whole or such part of the income as the trustee may allot to him. After such allotment, he may compel its payment. At least for some appreciable time, however brief, the award must precede the delivery of the income he is to receive, and during that time the lien of the execution attaches.

Since the trustee is said to exercise discretion to pay the beneficiary at a moment in time before the property is transferred to the beneficiary, during which period the lien attaches, it is important to know what acts constitute an exercise of discretion. Crediting the beneficiary's account on the trustee's books or an oral or written declaration to the beneficiary may be a sufficient act to indicate the power has been exercised. After such exercise by the trustee, the creditor may seize the property awarded to the beneficiary while it remains in the hands of the trustee. Even this limited amount of protection given creditors, however, can be circumvented by a provision in the trust instrument permitting the trustee in its discretion not to pay the beneficiary directly but to pay third parties for the support of the beneficiary. Observe that in United States v. O'Shaughnessy the trustees could pay Lawrence "*or for his benefit*," which enables the trustees to pay his bills directly, never creating a property interest in him.

QUESTION

Does the idea that the discretionary beneficiary of a trust has no "interest" in the trust for purposes of liability to creditors make sense in other contexts? For example, only a person who has a pecuniary interest in the result can challenge probate of a will. Does the beneficiary of a testamentary discretionary trust have such an interest? In Marbone v. Marbone, 257 Va. 199, 509 S.E.2d 302 (1999), the discretionary beneficiary of a 1991 will challenged the probate of a 1995 will on the grounds of undue influence by the beneficiary of the 1995 will. The court held that a beneficiary of a discretionary trust created by a will does not have a legally ascertainable pecuniary interest and therefore has no standing to challenge the probate of a later will.

It is, of course, fallacious to move the word "interest" from one

---

After the ninth duke's death, the Manchester family fortunes continued in an irreversible decline set in motion by three spendthrift dukes in a row (the seventh, eighth, and ninth). All the family land was sold off to support high living. The tenth duke moved to Kenya seeking a new fortune, but Kenyan independence sank that venture. The eleventh duke became an alligator hunter in Australia, but after a while he moved back to England where he became a business consultant in Bedford.

context to another without regard to the different purposes at work in the different contexts. As that renowned fallacy-hunter, Walter Wheeler Cook, pointed out more than a half century ago, "the tendency to assume that a word which appears in two or more rules, and so in connection with more than one purpose, has and should have precisely the same scope in all of them runs all through legal discussions. It has all the tenacity of original sin and must constantly be guarded against." Walter W. Cook, Logical and Legal Bases of the Conflict of Laws 159 (1942). Did the court in Marbone v. Marbone fall into the fallacy of the transplanted category?

NOTE: TRUSTS FOR THE STATE-SUPPORTED

Qualifying for Medicaid. An individual qualifies for Medicaid and public support benefits only if the individual has financial resources less than a few thousand dollars. The question arises whether trusts benefiting the individual can be counted as resources available for the support of the individual. Federal law draws a distinction between self-settled trusts and trusts created by third parties for the benefit of the individual.

Let us look first at *self-settled trusts.* For Medicaid purposes, a trust is created by the individual applicant "if assets of the individual were used to form all or part of the corpus of the trust" and the trust was established by the individual, by the individual's spouse, or by a person or court with legal authority to act in behalf of, or upon request of, the individual or the individual's spouse. 42 U.S.C. §1396p(d) (1998). If the trust is revocable by the individual, the corpus and all income of the trust are considered resources available to the individual. If the trust is irrevocable, any income or corpus which *under any circumstances* could be paid to or applied for the benefit of the individual are considered resources of the individual. Hence, in case of a discretionary trust, the Medicaid applicant will be deemed to have resources in the maximum amount that could be distributed to him, assuming full exercise of discretion by the trustee in his favor. See Masterson v. Department of Social Services, 969 S.W.2d 746 (Mo. 1998). If the individual transfers assets into a self-settled trust, the period of ineligibility for Medicaid benefits may last up to sixty months. See Note, Long-Term Care Financing Crisis — Recent Federal and State Efforts to Deter Asset Transfers as a Means to Gain Medicaid Eligibility, 74 N. Dak. L. Rev. 383 (1998). Compare Canter v. Commissioner of Public Welfare, 423 Mass. 425, 668 N.E.2d 783 (1996).

There are two important exceptions. First, a discretionary trust created by the *will* of one spouse for the benefit of the surviving spouse is not deemed a resource available to the surviving spouse. 42 U.S.C.

§1396p(d)(2)(A). This makes it possible for one spouse to create a wholly discretionary trust for the benefit of the surviving spouse, who may qualify for Medicaid if the survivor's other resources are below the eligibility amount. Second, if a trust is established for a disabled individual, from the individual's property, by a parent, grandparent, or guardian of the individual or by a court, and the trust provides that the state will receive upon the individual's death all amounts remaining in the trust up to the amount equal to the total medical assistance paid by the state, the trust will not be considered a resource available to the Medicaid recipient. 42 U.S.C. §1396p(d)(4)(A). This makes it possible to settle the proceeds of a tort recovery, after an accident in which an individual is disabled, in a trust to provide supplemental care for the individual above what the state provides, if the trust reimburses the state out of the trust assets at the individual's death.

With respect to trusts *established by a third person* for the benefit of a Medicaid applicant, the rules are different. Medicaid regulations provide that trust income or principal is "considered available both when actually available and when the applicant or recipient has a legal interest in a liquidated sum and has the legal ability to make such sum available for support and maintenance." 45 Code Fed. Reg. §233.20(a)(3)(ii)(D) (1998). Thus, if a mandatory or support trust is created, wherein the beneficiary has the legal right to income, such income is treated as a resource available to the beneficiary. But if a discretionary trust is created, giving the individual no legal right to trust income or principal, the trust is not considered a resource available to the individual in applying for Medicaid unless it was intended to be used for the applicant's support. See generally Medicare & Medicaid Guide (CCH).

Reimbursement for state-supported trust beneficiaries. In most states, persons institutionalized in state hospitals are responsible for the cost of their care. In seeking to reach self-settled trusts, courts have permitted states to recover the maximum amount that could be paid to the settlor (generally the same amount as is deemed an available resource under the Medicaid eligibility rules). The courts follow the common law rule applicable to creditors of settlors of self-settled trusts (see supra page 639, note 1a). See State v. Hawes, 169 A.D.2d 919, 564 N.Y.S.2d 637 (1991).

If a trust has been set up by a third party for the institutionalized beneficiary, the courts have generally applied to the state the common law rules applicable to creditors of beneficiaries of mandatory, support, and discretionary trusts. If the beneficiary has a right to trust income or principal, the state can reach it. A spendthrift clause is unenforceable against the state because the state is furnishing necessaries to the institutionalized beneficiary. Most of the litigation concerns discretionary trusts. Generally, the state cannot reach discretionary trusts. Many trusts are hybrid trusts, however, combining the purpose of support with discretion in the trustee ("to provide for the comfort and support of my daughter in the trustee's sole and absolute discretion"). If a beneficiary of a discretionary trust can, under some conceivable circumstances, obtain a court order requiring payment to the beneficiary, because the trustee has an obligation to exercise discretion consistent with the purpose of the trust, it is possible that the trust assets may be reached by the state. See Estate of Rosenberg v. Department of Public Welfare, 545 Pa. 27, 679 A.2d 767 (1996). On the other hand, if the settlor intended to provide only benefits that the state is unable or unwilling to provide (a "supplemental needs trust"), the state cannot reach the trust assets. See Miller v. Department of Mental Health, 432 Mich. 426, 442 N.W.2d 617 (1989); Minn. Stat. Ann. §501B.89 (1997); N.Y. Est., Powers & Trusts L. §7-1.12 (1998) (permitting creation of supplemental needs trust not reachable by state). See Comment, Supplemental Needs Trusts: A Means to Conserve Family Assets and Provide Increased Quality of Life for the Disabled Family Member, 32 Duq. L. Rev. 555 (1994); Comment, [California] Probate Code Section 15306: Discretionary Trusts as a Financial Solution for the Disabled, 37 UCLA L. Rev. 595 (1990).

Because this is an evolving area of the law involving unsettled questions of public policy at both state and federal levels, increasing pressures on the public purse, and not-very-predictable judicial interpretations of trust language, practitioners must use great caution in advising clients who want to create a trust for a disabled child that the state cannot reach.

PROBLEMS

1. Barbara is a developmentally disabled person. Her mother, Edith, neglected Barbara and failed to provide for her with social security benefits Edith had received on behalf of Barbara. Upon suit by Barbara's aunt, her guardian, a consent decree was entered ordering Edith to fund a trust for the benefit of Barbara with $150,000 Edith had inherited from her sisters. Edith complied by creating a discretionary trust for Barbara with a spendthrift provision. The trust agreement named Edith as settlor. It directed the trustee to terminate the trust immediately should any agency providing support for Barbara attempt to reach it. Can the trust assets be reached by the state to provide for Barbara's care? Hertsberg Trust v. Department of Mental Health, 457 Mich. 430, 578 N.W.2d 289 (1998).

2. Wendy and Howard Brown's elder daughter, Sarah, has been

injured in an automobile accident that left her unable to care for herself or manage her affairs. Sarah has been placed in a nursing home. The cost of the nursing home is $40,000 a year. Sarah received $200,000 in insurance proceeds. Howard, as Sarah's conservator, has applied for Medicaid. (For more on the Brown family, see supra pages 52-58.)

Howard and Wendy want your advice as to (1) what to do with the $200,000 and (2) what provisions they should make in their wills to provide more comfortable support for Sarah than the minimum provided by Medicaid. Advise them.

See Cricchio v. Pennisi, 90 N.Y.2d 296, 683 N.E.2d 301, 660 N.Y.S.2d 679 (1997); Comment, Medicaid Estate Planning: Congress' Ersatz Solution for Long-Term Health Care, 44 Cath. U. L. Rev. 1217 (1995).

SECTION E.   MODIFICATION AND TERMINATION OF TRUSTS

If the *settlor* and *all the beneficiaries* consent, a trust may be modified or terminated. No one else has any beneficial interest in the trust. The trustee has no beneficial interest and cannot object. Such a right exists even if the trust contains a spendthrift clause. See Johnson v. First National Bank of Jackson, 386 So. 2d 1112 (Miss. 1980).

If, however, the settlor is dead or does not consent to the modification or termination of the trust, the question arises whether the beneficiaries can modify or terminate the trust if they all agree. Let us look first at the law in England. In Saunders v. Vautier, 49 Eng. Rep. 282, 4 Beav. 115 (1841), the English court held that a trust can be terminated at any time if all the beneficiaries are adult and sui juris and all consent. In the 1950s, at the behest of trust beneficiaries who urgently sought to modify trusts to escape serious tax disadvantages, Parliament enacted the English Variation of Trusts Act of 1958, 6 & 7 Eliz. 2, ch. 53, §1, which greatly expanded the power of courts to modify or terminate trusts. The act provides that a court may consent to modification or termination of a trust on behalf of incompetent, minor, or unborn beneficiaries whenever the court finds it beneficial to these beneficiaries. See Graham Moffat, Trusts Law 245-259 (2d ed. 1994). Similar statutes have been enacted in Canada and Australia. What has happened in England and some of the Commonwealth countries is that, after the settlor's death, the trust is regarded as the beneficiaries' property, not as the settlor's property — and the dead hand continues to rule only by the sufferance of the beneficiaries.

Variation or termination of trusts in England is strikingly different from the practice in this country, where the settlor's intent cannot be set aside after his death.

In re Trust of Stuchell
Oregon Court of Appeals, 1990
104 Or. App. 332, 801 P.2d 852,
review denied, 311 Or. 166, 806 P.2d 1153

BUTTLER, J. Petitioner appeals from the trial court's dismissal of her petition for approval of an agreement to modify a trust. The stated purpose of the proposed modification is to protect a retarded remainder beneficiary. We affirm.

Petitioner is one of two surviving life-income beneficiaries of a testamentary trust established by her grandfather, J. W. Stuchell, in his 1947 will. The trust will terminate on the death of the last income beneficiary, at which time the remainder is to be distributed equally to petitioner's children or their lineal descendants, per stirpes. One of petitioner's four children, John Harrell (Harrell), is a mentally retarded 25 year old who is unable to live independently without assistance. His condition is not expected to improve, and he will probably require care and supervision for the rest of his life. No guardian or conservator has been appointed for him. The Oregon Mental Health Division currently provides his basic care in the Eastern Oregon Training Center, a residential facility for mentally and physically disabled persons. He receives Medicaid and Social Security benefits, both of which have income and resource limitations for participants.

In December, 1989, petitioner requested the court to approve, on behalf of Harrell, an agreement, which had been approved by the other income beneficiary and remaindermen, to modify the trust. If the trust is not modified, Harrell's remainder will be distributed directly to him if he survives the two life-income beneficiaries. If and when that happens, his ability to qualify for public assistance will be severely limited. The proposed modification provides for the continuation of the trust, if Harrell survives the two life-income beneficiaries, and contains elaborate provisions that are designed to avoid his becoming disqualified, in whole or in part, for any public assistance programs. The stated purpose is to ensure that the trust funds be used only as a secondary source of funds to supplement, rather than to replace, his current income and benefits from public assistance.

Petitioner relies on . . . the common law. She contends that Closset v. Burtchaell, 112 Or. 585, 230 P. 554 (1924), is authority for allowing a court to approve her proposed modification. That case holds that a trust may be terminated, if (1) all of the beneficiaries agree, (2) none of the beneficiaries is under a legal disability and (3) the trust's purposes would not be frustrated by doing so. 112 Or. at 597, 230 P. 554. The court said: "It is a well-established rule that where the purposes for which a trust has been created have been accomplished and all of the beneficiaries are sui juris, a court will, on the application of all of the beneficiaries or of one possessing the entire beneficial interest declare a termination of the trust[.]" Restatement (Second) Trusts §337 (1959) follows that rule. By its terms, that rule applies only to the termination of a trust under very limited circumstances. Petitioner, relying on Restatement (Second) Trusts §167(1) (1959), urges us to extend the rule to permit modification. That section provides:

> The court will direct or permit the trustee to deviate from a term of the trust if owing to circumstances not known to the settlor and not anticipated by him compliance would defeat or substantially impair the accomplishment of the purposes of the trust; and in such case, if necessary to carry out the purposes of the trust, the court may direct or permit the trustee to do acts which are not authorized or are forbidden by the terms of the trust.

Comment b to that section states:

> The court will not permit or direct the trustee to deviate from the terms of the trust merely because such deviation would be more advantageous to the beneficiaries than a compliance with such direction.

See In re Traung's Estate, 207 Cal. App. 2d 818, 833-34, 24 Cal. Rptr. 872 (1962), and Dyer v. Paddock, 70 N.E.2d 49, 395 Ill. 288 (1946), which apply the rule as stated in that comment. Even assuming that the Restatement rule were to be adopted as the law in Oregon, it is clear that the limitation imposed by the comment would preclude permitting the proposed amendment, the only purpose of which is to make the trust more advantageous to the beneficiaries. The most obvious advantage would be to the three remaindermen who have consented to the amendment.

There being no statutory or common law authority for a court to approve the proposed agreement modifying the trust, the trial court did not err in dismissing the petition.[28]

Affirmed.

---

28. We express no opinion as to whether the proposed modification would survive a challenge by state or federal agencies that are providing assistance to Harrell.

NOTES AND QUESTIONS

1. In recent years, courts in several states have reformed or modified a trust so as to obtain income or estate tax advantages. Sometimes the courts have corrected a lawyer's error in drafting the instrument; at other times the courts have modified the trust because of changed circumstances. See Pond v. Pond, 424 Mass. 894, 678 N.E.2d 1321 (1997), infra page 1057 (modifying trust to qualify for marital deduction); In re Estate of Branigan, 129 N.J. 324, 609 A.2d 431 (1992) (modifying trust to take advantage of changes in the tax law); Austin W. Scott, Trusts §167 (William F. Fratcher 4th ed. 1987; Supp. 1998 by Mark L. Ascher at 272) (discussing numerous cases from New York surrogate's courts modifying trusts to minimize taxes). Restatement (Third) of Property, Donative Transfers, §12.2 (T.D. No. 1, 1995) approves: "A donative document may be modified, in a manner that does not violate the donor's probable intention, to achieve the donor's tax objectives." Uniform Trust Act §414 (1999 draft) also provides a court may modify a trust to achieve the settlor's tax objectives.

What would be the result in *Stuchell* if the settlor had died in 1997 rather than 1947 and the settlor had instructed his lawyer to draft a trust that provided John Harrell benefits only supplementing what Harrell received from the government? Should the trust be reformed? Does it matter that the welfare department rather than the Internal Revenue Service suffers the loss through reformation? Compare In re Heller Trust, 161 Misc. 2d 369, 613 N.Y.S.2d 809 (Sur. 1994) (splitting irrevocable trust into two trusts to protect some of the trust assets from potential creditors).

2. *Drafting advice.* When you are drafting a trust that is to last into the unforeseeable future, you should consider giving a beneficiary — either the life tenant or a remainderman — or an independent third party the power to modify or terminate the trust. This power can be in the form of a special power of appointment. A special power is a power to appoint the property to, or modify a trust for the benefit of, anyone except the donee. A special power has no adverse tax consequences to the donee of the power, because under the Internal Revenue Code the donee is not treated as the owner inasmuch as the donee cannot benefit herself.

If the petitioner in *Stuchell*, the life beneficiary, had had a special power to amend the trust, she could have changed Harrell's interest to a discretionary trust to supplement his government support, saving the remainder for other family members. The lawyer who drafted the testator's will some 40 years earlier did not, and could not, foresee the future and did not write into the trust a means of changing the trust when circumstances change. The lawyer left the testator's family in a strait-jacket.

3.   Several modification cases have involved a widow who cannot live comfortably on the income from a trust created by her husband and asks a court to permit invasion of principal for support. Unless all the remainder beneficiaries consent (which usually is not possible because the remainder may ultimately vest in persons now unascertained or unborn), relief is denied unless the trust is construed to contain a power to invade, express or implied. See Estate of Van Deusen, 30 Cal. 2d 285, 182 P.2d 565 (1947); Staley v. Ligon, 239 Md. 61, 210 A.2d 384, 31 A.L.R.3d 299 (1965). There is, however, a good deal of unhappiness with the state of the law.

Uniform Trust Act §411(a) (1999 draft) loosens the general requirements for modification of a trust in this situation. It provides "the court shall modify the administrative or dispositive terms of a trust or terminate the trust if, because of circumstances not anticipated by the settlor, modification or termination will substantially further the settlor's purpose in creating the trust." See also N.Y. Est., Powers & Trusts Law §7-1.6(b) (giving court discretion to make allowance from principal to provide sufficient support for income beneficiary, if court is satisfied that such invasion effectuates the intention of the settlor). See also 2A Scott, supra, §168 at 306-309 (discussing other statutes).

If a trust settlor leaves a beneficiary an annuity of a specified sum per year (for example, $5,000 a year), this amount may decrease drastically in purchasing power with inflation. Unless a court can be convinced that the primary purpose of the annuity was support of the annuitant, which the cases indicate is a hard sell, courts deny any increase in the amount of the annuity. 2A Scott, supra, §168 at 309.

4.   *Deviation in exercising administrative powers.* Courts have been much more liberal in permitting trustees to deviate from administrative directions in the trust, because of change of circumstances, than they have been in permitting modification of distributive provisions. For example, in 1911 Joseph Pulitzer's will created a trust for the benefit of his descendants. Pulitzer bequeathed to the trustees shares of stock in a corporation publishing the World newspapers, and his will provided that the sale of these shares was not authorized under any circumstances. After several years of large and increasing losses from the publication of the World, the trustees in 1931 petitioned the court to approve sale of the shares. The court held that, even though sale was prohibited by Pulitzer, it had power to authorize sale in circumstances where the trust estate was in jeopardy, and it approved the sale. In re Pulitzer, 139 Misc. 575, 249 N.Y.S. 87 (Sur. Ct. 1931). See 2A Scott, supra, §167, at 273.

5.   Richard A. Posner, Economic Analysis of Law 556 (5th ed. 1998): ". . . [S]ince no one can foresee the future, a rational donor knows that his intentions might eventually be thwarted by unpredicta-

ble circumstances and may therefore be presumed to accept implicitly a rule permitting modification of the terms of the bequest in the event that an unforeseen change frustrates his original intention. The presumption is not absolute. Some rational donors, mistrustful of judicial capacity intelligently to alter the terms of the bequests in light of changed conditions, might prefer to assume the risks involved in rigid adherence to the original terms. Should their desire be honored? Notice that doing so would make wills more rigid than constitutions, which can be amended, though with difficulty."

In the United States, the great weight of authority holds that a trust cannot be terminated prior to the time fixed for termination, even though all the beneficiaries consent, *if termination would be contrary to a material purpose of the settlor.* The leading case establishing this rule is Claflin v. Claflin, 149 Mass. 19, 20 N.E. 545 (1889), and the rule is often referred to as the Claflin doctrine. In that case, a trust was established for testator's son, with principal to be paid to the son at age 30. After age 21 the son sued to terminate the trust, pointing out that he was the sole beneficiary. The court refused to permit termination as this would violate the intent of the testator.

> [A] testator has a right to dispose of his own property with such restrictions and limitations, not repugnant to law, as he sees fit, and . . . his intentions ought to be carried out, unless they contravene some positive rule of law, or are against public policy. . . . It cannot be said that these restrictions upon the plaintiff's possession and control of the property are altogether useless, for there is not the same danger that he will spend the property while it is in the hands of the trustees as there would be if it were in his own. [149 Mass. at 23, 20 N.E. at 456.]

Although the Claflin doctrine is easy to state, there is considerable disagreement as to the circumstances under which termination would be contrary to the purpose of the settlor. Generally, a trust cannot be terminated if it is a spendthrift trust, if the beneficiary is not to receive the principal until attaining a specified age, if it is a discretionary trust, or if it is a trust for support of the beneficiary. Such provisions are usually deemed to state a material purpose of the settlor. The cases are collected in George G. Bogert & George T. Bogert, Trusts and Trustees §§1007-1008 (rev. 2d ed. 1983); 4 Scott, supra, §§337-337.8. See Gail B. Bird, Trust Termination: Unborn, Living, and Dead Hands — Too Many Fingers in the Trust Pie, 36 Hast. L.J. 563 (1985).

In re Estate of Brown
Supreme Court of Vermont, 1987
148 Vt. 94, 528 A.2d 752

GIBSON, J.   The trustee of a testamentary trust appeals an order of the Washington Superior Court granting the petition of the lifetime and residual beneficiaries of the trust to terminate it and to distribute the proceeds to the life tenants. We reverse.

The primary issue raised on appeal is whether any material purpose of the trust remains to be accomplished, thus barring its termination. The appellant/trustee also raises the closely related issue of whether all beneficiaries are before the court, i.e., whether the class of beneficiaries has closed.

Andrew J. Brown died in 1977, settling his entire estate in a trust, all of which is held by the trustee under terms and conditions that are the subject of this appeal. The relevant portion of the trust instrument provides:

> (3) The . . . trust . . . shall be used to provide an education, particularly a college education, for the children of my nephew, Woolson S. Brown. My Trustee is hereby directed to use the income from said trust and such part of the principal as may be necessary to accomplish this purpose. Said trust to continue for said purpose until the last child has received his or her education and the Trustee, in its discretion, has determined that the purpose hereof has been accomplished.
>
> At such time as this purpose has been accomplished and the Trustee has so determined, *the income from said trust and such part of the principal as may be necessary shall be used by said Trustee for the care, maintenance and welfare of my nephew, Woolson S. Brown and his wife, Rosemary Brown, so that they may live in the style and manner to which they are accustomed, for and during the remainder of their natural lives.* Upon their demise, any remainder of said trust, together with any accumulation thereon, shall be paid to their then living children in equal shares, share and share alike. (Emphasis added.)

The trustee complied with the terms of the trust by using the proceeds to pay for the education of the children of Woolson and Rosemary Brown. After he determined that the education of these children was completed, the trustee began distribution of trust income to the lifetime beneficiaries, Woolson and Rosemary.

On June 17, 1983, the lifetime beneficiaries petitioned the probate court for termination of the trust, arguing that the sole remaining purpose of the trust was to maintain their lifestyle and that distribution of the remaining assets was necessary to accomplish this purpose. The remaindermen, the children of the lifetime beneficiaries, filed consents to the proposed termination. The probate court denied the petition to terminate, and the petitioners appealed to the Washington Superior Court. The superior court reversed, concluding that continuation of the trust was no longer necessary because the only material purpose, the education of the children, had been accomplished. This appeal by the trustee followed.

Ordinarily, a trial court's conclusions will be upheld where they are supported by its findings. Dartmouth Savings Bank v. F.O.S. Associates, 145 Vt. 62, 66, 486 A.2d 623, 625 (1984). Here, the superior court's conclusion that the trust could be terminated because the material purpose of the trust had been accomplished has an insufficient basis in its findings, and this conclusion cannot stand.

An active trust may not be terminated, even with the consent of all the beneficiaries, if a material purpose of the settlor remains to be accomplished. See, e.g., Ambrose v. First National Bank, 87 Nev. 114, 117, 482 P.2d 828, 829 (1971); Sundquist v. Sundquist, 639 P.2d 181, 187 (Utah 1981); Restatement (Second) of Trusts §337 (1959); 4 A. Scott, Scott on Trusts §337, at 2655 (3d ed. 1967). This Court has invoked a corollary of this rule in a case where partial termination of a trust was at issue. In re Bayley Trust, 127 Vt. 380, 385, 250 A.2d 516, 519 (1969).

As a threshold matter, we reject the trustee's argument that the trust cannot be terminated because it is both a support trust and a spendthrift trust. It is true that, were either of these forms of trust involved, termination could not be compelled by the beneficiaries because a material purpose of the settlor would remain unsatisfied. See Restatement (Second) of Trusts §337.

The trust at issue does not qualify as a support trust. A support trust is created where the trustee is directed to use trust income or principal for the benefit of an individual, but only to the extent necessary to support the individual. 2 A. Scott, Scott on Trusts §154, at 1176; G. Bogert, Trusts and Trustees §229, at 519 (2d ed. rev. 1979). Here, the terms of the trust provide that, when the educational purpose of the trust has been accomplished and the trustee, in his discretion, has so determined, "the income ... and such part of the principal as may be necessary shall be used by said Trustee for the care, maintenance and welfare of ... [Rosemary and Woolson Brown] so that they may live in the style and manner to which they are accustomed. ..." The trustee has, in fact, made the determination that the educational purpose has been accomplished and has begun to transfer the income of the trust to the lifetime beneficiaries. Because the trustee must, at the very least, pay all of the trust income to beneficiaries Rosemary and Woolson Brown, the trust cannot be characterized as a support trust.

Nor is this a spendthrift trust. "A trust in which by the terms of the trust or by statute a *valid restraint on the voluntary and involuntary transfer of the interest* of the beneficiary is imposed is a spendthrift trust." Restatement (Second) of Trusts §152(2). (Emphasis added.) While no specific language is needed to create a spendthrift trust, id. at Comment c, here the terms of the trust instrument do not manifest Andrew J. Brown's intention to create such a trust. See Huestis v. Manley, 110 Vt. 413, 419, 8 A.2d 644, 646 (1939). . . .

Although the issue as to whether a material purpose of the trust remains cannot be answered through resort to the foregoing formal categories traditionally imposed upon trust instruments, we hold that termination cannot be compelled here because a material purpose of the settlor remains unaccomplished. In the interpretation of trusts, the intent of the settlor, as revealed by the language of the instrument, is determinative. In re Jones, 138 Vt. 223, 228, 415 A.2d 202, 205 (1980) (citing Destitute of Bennington County v. Putnam Memorial Hospital, 125 Vt. 289, 293, 215 A.2d 134, 137 (1965)).

We find that the trust instrument at hand has two purposes. First, the trust provides for the education of the children of Woolson and Rosemary Brown. The Washington Superior Court found that Rosemary Brown was incapable of having more children and that the chance of Woolson Brown fathering more children was remote; on this basis, the court concluded that the educational purpose of the trust had been achieved.

The settlor also intended a second purpose, however: the assurance of a life-long income for the beneficiaries through the management and discretion of the trustee. We recognize that, had the trust merely provided for successive beneficiaries, no inference could be drawn that the settlor intended to deprive the beneficiaries of the right to manage the trust property during the period of the trust. Estate of Weeks, 485 Pa. 329, 332, 402 A.2d 657, 658 (1979) (quoting Restatement (Second) of Trusts §337 Comment f). Here, however, the language of the instrument does more than create successive gifts. The settlor provided that the trustee must provide for the "care, maintenance and welfare" of the lifetime beneficiaries "so that they may live in the style and manner to which they are accustomed, *for and during the remainder of their natural lives.*" (Emphasis added.) The trustee must use all of the income and such part of the principal as is necessary for this purpose. We believe that the settlor's intention to assure a life-long income to Woolson and Rosemary Brown would be defeated if termination of the trust were allowed. See 4 Scott, Scott on Trusts §337.1, at 2261-64; see also Will of Hamburger, 185 Wis. 270, 282, 201 N.W. 267, 271 (1924) (court refused to terminate trust since testator desired it to continue during life of his wife).

Because of our holding regarding the second and continuing material purpose of the trust, we do not reach the question of whether the trial court erred in holding that the educational purpose of the trust has been accomplished.

Reversed; judgment for petitioners vacated and judgment for appellant entered.

NOTES

1. A few states have enacted statutes that permit courts to terminate trusts prior to the time specified by the settlor. See Mo. Rev. Stat. §456.590.2 (1997), construed in Hamerstrom v. Commerce Bank of Kansas City, 80 S.W.2d 434 (Mo. App. 1991), as permitting "adult beneficiaries who are not disabled" to modify or terminate a trust regardless of the settlor's purpose if a court agrees that this would benefit disabled, minor, unborn, or unascertained beneficiaries. See also Va. Code Ann. §55-19.4 (1998) (permitting a court to modify or terminate a trust "for good cause"). And see Cal. Prob. Code §15409 (1998) (permitting modification or termination in changed circumstances which would defeat the purposes of the trust); 20 Pa. Cons. Stat. §6102 (1998); Wis. Stat. §701.13 (1998).

2. It may be possible to terminate a testamentary trust by a compromise agreement between the beneficiaries and heirs entered into soon after the testator's death. In most states, courts will approve compromise agreements that deliberately eliminate trusts, even spendthrift trusts. In Budin v. Levy, 343 Mass. 644, 180 N.E.2d 74 (1962), the court decided that a compromise agreement was effective without regard to whether a material purpose of the testator was defeated thereby.

> Such an agreement of compromise as to interests which might be received from an estate is apart from the provisions of the will. Rights under the agreement are wholly contractual and in no sense testamentary. . . . Indeed, the result may be quite contrary to the testator's intent. This means that before the allowance of a will a trust may be changed or even eliminated by a compromise otherwise valid and approved by the court. [Id. at 649, 180 N.E.2d at 77.]

Some courts, however, refuse to approve a will compromise where the compromise destroys a trust that is essential to a material purpose of the settlor. See Adams v. Link, 145 Conn. 634, 145 A.2d 753 (1958). See also Annot., 29 A.L.R.3d 8 (1970).

3. Isn't it odd that Americans permit more extensive dead-hand control through trusts than do the English — a people whose whole history since the Conquest has been marked by inventions of lawyers to assist their rich clients in controlling their descendants' fortunes

after their deaths? The English do not permit a spendthrift trust, though they do give some protection from creditors through a protective trust.[29] If dissatisfied with a trust, English beneficiaries can terminate a trust at will if all are adult. If there are minors or unborn beneficiaries, a court can agree on their behalf to termination if it is in the best interests of the beneficiaries. The desire of a dead settlor to continue a trust is of no importance.

Many unforeseen problems may arise during long-term trusts: changes in the beneficiaries, their needs, and abilities; changes in the tax laws and in different types of investment opportunities; inflation and changes in the purchasing power of the dollar. Modernizing the law regulating modification and termination of trusts will be one of the primary trust issues in the twenty-first century, particularly in view of the increasing number of states that permit perpetual trusts. See infra page 854.

NOTE: CHANGING TRUSTEES

Suppose that the beneficiaries are dissatisfied with the performance of the trustee or are dissatisfied with the fees charged. Can the beneficiaries remove the trustee and have a new trustee appointed? Unless the trustee has been guilty of breach of trust or has shown unfitness, the answer is No. The standard rule is that inasmuch as the settlor reposed special confidence in the designated trustee, the court will not change trustees merely because the beneficiaries want to. Restatement (Second) of Trusts §107 (1959); 2 Austin W. Scott, Trusts §§107-107.3 (William F. Fratcher 4th ed. 1987).

The inability of beneficiaries to change trustees lessens competition among trust companies and contributes to higher trustees' fees. Should this rule be changed?

In answering this question, consider the erosion of personal traditional fiduciary relationships in recent years. In some states, entire inventories of trust accounts are now routinely bought and sold between banks. Beneficiaries may currently be served by a bank or trust company never selected by the settlor. Should the beneficiaries now be offered the opportunity to change trustees if they are disadvantaged by these transactions?

---

29. Under a "protective trust," a trust is created to pay income to *A*, but if *A*'s creditors attach *A*'s interest, *A*'s mandatory income interest ceases, whereupon a discretionary trust automatically arises. The trustee then has discretion to apply the income for *A*'s benefit, and the creditors of *A* cannot demand any part of it. Thus, the discretionary trust can be used in England, as it can be used in this country, to protect the beneficiary from creditors.

Kathy Kristof, An Heir of Confidence
Chicago Tribune, May 21, 1996, at C7

"How do you get a small fortune? Give a bank trust department a large one," goes a popular banking industry saw.

But to Martin Crusky Jr., it's no joke.

Martin, who asked that his name be changed for publication, is one of seven heirs to a $6 million estate. When alive, his father had set up a living trust — stocks and tax-free bonds — and named a local bank as the successor trustee. When the elder Crusky died, the bank got sole control of the assets.

Martin Jr. and the bank have been at odds ever since. Martin says it's because the bank sold all the trust's assets, triggering a whopping tax bill while dramatically reducing the trust's investment performance. He estimates the bank's management cost the trust's heirs $260,000.

The bank argues that Martin's interests don't always coincide with those of other beneficiaries. The bank must treat all heirs equally — even if that hurts a few. The bank's attorney even encouraged Martin to sue, but added that the bank would use assets from the Crusky family trust to defend itself.

Martin's story isn't unique. In fact, it's been played out so many times in so many cities that a support group, called Heirs Inc., has sprung up specifically to advise heirs on how to wrangle with bank trust departments. It's also not an issue that solely affects the rich and famous.

Indeed, the median value of trusts administered by Federal Reserve member banks is just $250,000, says Standish H. Smith, founder of Villanova, Pa.-based Heirs. There are 11 million Americans who are either direct or secondary beneficiaries of these trusts, he says.

"There is a whole host of transgressions that banks commonly indulge in," Smith adds. "There is a lack of disclosure, a lack of accountability. The only way to describe it is nefarious."

Bankers deny that they make poor corporate trustees. Squeaky wheels get all the attention, while the vast majority of satisfied customers never are heard from, notes Jayne Lipe, executive vice president of Overland Bank and Trust in Ft. Worth.

However, some acknowledge that heirs can have trouble with any corporate trustee, if the benefactor — the person who originally set up the trust — wasn't careful about how the document was written.

To be specific, unless there is a co-trustee or a "removal clause," heirs can find it difficult — if not impossible — to remove an unresponsive corporate trustee. The reason boils down to dollars and cents. In most cases, unless all heirs — including secondary heirs who will inherit money only after primary heirs die — are in complete agreement, beneficiaries of a trust must go to court to get a corporate trustee removed. Most trusts allow the corporate trustee to use the trust's assets to fight the removal.

What are the chances of winning? Attorneys maintain that trust laws favor corporate trustees, so the bank's behavior has to be fairly bad to win at all. To win damages, the behavior usually must be shocking.

"There is not a level playing field when it comes to trust litigation," acknowledges Howard Kipnis, partner at Hilding, Kipnis, Lyon & Kelly in San Diego. Kipnis, who represents numerous banks, notes that legal provisions forcing heirs to pay legal fees for both sides deter heirs from suing. But there have been a few cases where heirs have won and banks have been forced to dip into their own pockets to pay damages.

Notably, a few simple moves on the part of the benefactor when setting up the trust can head off most of the complications. Solving problems after the benefactor's death is far more difficult.

For example, Lipe suggests that benefactors consider naming a co-trustee, who would share investment or distribution authority with the bank. If there's no savvy friend or relative available to do the job for free, consider hiring an outside party.

Most contemporary trust agreements also include a removal clause, which allows heirs to change corporate trustees without going to court, Lipe adds.

Smith thinks benefactors might also want to contractually set annual fees, so that banks won't be able to hike their prices after the benefactor dies and the heirs are stuck.

Finally, make sure a friend or relative has a copy of the trust agreement to ensure the bank follows the stipulated rules.

Uniform Trust Act (1999 draft)

§706. REMOVAL OF TRUSTEE

(a) A trustee may be removed by the court on its own initiative or on petition of a settlor, cotrustee, or beneficiary.

(b) The court may remove a trustee if:

(1) the trustee has committed a material breach of trust;

(2) lack of cooperation among cotrustees substantially impairs the administration of the trust;

(3) the investment decisions of the trustee, although not constituting a breach of trust, have resulted in investment performance persistently and substantially below those of comparable trusts;

(4) because of changed circumstances, unfitness, or inability to administer the trust, removal of the trustee would be in the best interests of the beneficiaries.

(c) Pending a final decision on a petition to remove the trustee, or in lieu of or in addition to removing a trustee, the court may order such appropriate relief under Section 1102 as may be necessary to protect the trust property or the interests of the beneficiaries.

PROBLEM

Abraham Rosenberg fled Nazi Germany in 1938, emigrating to the United States, after his store was ruined in Kristallnacht, when Hitler's street brawlers, the Brownshirts, smashed the glass fronts of Jewish-owned stores. Several of his relatives were killed in the gas chambers of Auschwitz. In 1990 Rosenberg died, creating a testamentary trust for his descendants with Bankers Trust Co. of New York as trustee.

In 1999 Bankers Trust was acquired by Deutsche Bank, Germany's biggest bank, which played a key role in the financing of the Nazi war effort. Deutsche Bank lent money that built Auschwitz. Deutsche Bank sold to foreign countries gold extracted from Jews' teeth, wedding bands, and personal jewelry, which provided Hitler's war machine with hard currency. It donated annually a large amount of money to the "Adolph Hitler Fund", which funded the activities of Hitler's Brownshirts and those of SS head Heinrich Himmler. N.Y. Times, Aug. 1, 1998, at A2; N.Y. Times, Feb. 5, 1999, at A9.

Rosenberg's descendants, the beneficiaries of his trust, are incensed, indeed revolted, by the continuation of Bankers Trust, now owned by Deutsche Bank, as trustee. Can they have Bankers Trust removed as trustee?

9

BUILDING FLEXIBILITY INTO TRUSTS: POWERS OF APPOINTMENT

SECTION A.   INTRODUCTION

1.   Types of Powers

We now turn to powers of appointment in trust *beneficiaries*, powers that give the beneficiaries the ability to deal flexibly with changing circumstances in the future — with births, deaths, and marriages in the family; with the ability of children to manage property; with changes in the economy and investment returns; and with changes in the laws. Since no one can foresee the future, there are few trusts where the skillful drafter does not give some thought to whether one or more beneficiaries should have a power of appointment.

In studying the law of powers, the first thing to do is to get the terminology and relationships straight. The person who creates the power of appointment is the *donor* of the power; the person who holds the power is the *donee*. The persons in whose favor the power may be exercised are the *objects* of the power. When a power is exercised in favor of a person, such person becomes an *appointee*. The instrument creating the power may provide for *takers in default of appointment* if the donee fails to exercise the power.

All powers can be divided into general powers and special powers. A *general power* is, in the language of the Internal Revenue Code, "a power which is exercisable in favor of the decedent [donee], his estate, his creditors, or the creditors of his estate."[1] Under the federal

---

1. Int. Rev. Code of 1986, §2041(b) (estate tax). The comparable definition under the federal gift tax is in §2514(c). The Code goes on to exclude from the definition of a general power a power to consume principal "limited by an ascertainable standard

estate and gift tax laws, any power that is not a general power is classified as a special power. Thus, a *special power* is a power not exercisable in favor of the donee, his estate, his creditors, or the creditors of his estate. Prevailing professional usage of these terms is in accord with the definitions contained in the tax laws.[2]

A general power of appointment may permit the donee to do most of the things an owner of the fee simple could do. This is true of a general power presently exercisable. Thus:

> *Case 1. T* devises property to *X* in trust to pay the income to *A* for life or until such time as *A* appoints and to distribute the principal to such person or persons as *A* shall appoint either by deed during *A*'s lifetime or by will; if *A* does not exercise the power of appointment, at *A*'s death *X* is to distribute the principal to *B*. *T* is the donor. *A* is the donee of a general power of appointment exercisable by deed or will. *B* is the taker in default of appointment.

In Case 1, *A* is very close to being absolute owner of the property since the only thing that stands between *A* and absolute ownership is a piece of paper *A* can sign at any time. To acquire title, *A* has merely to write, "I hereby appoint to myself." Even though *A* can acquire absolute ownership at any time, however, *A* does not have ownership until the power is exercised in *A*'s favor. If *A* does not exercise the power, the property will pass to the taker in default, *B*, and not to *A*'s heirs. If the creating instrument does not name a taker in default, the property passes back to the donor or the donor's estate if the power is not exercised.

The objects of a general power of appointment are necessarily broader than the objects of a special power. The most common kind of special power is the power to appoint among the issue of the donee. Thus:

> *Case 2. T* devises property to *X* in trust to pay the income to *A* for life, and on *A*'s death to distribute the principal to such one or more of *A*'s issue as *A* shall appoint by will; if *A* does not exercise the power of appointment, at *A*'s death *X* is to distribute the principal to *A*'s then living issue, such issue to take per stirpes.

There is a profound difference between the general power presently exercisable in Case 1 and the special power in Case 2. In Case 2, *A* occupies a position similar to that of *T*'s agent. *A* can exercise the

---

relating to the health, education, support, or maintenance" of the donee, a power held with an adverse party, and certain powers created prior to 1942. §§2041(b)(1)(A)-2041(b)(1)(C) and §§2514(c)(1)-2514(c)(3). See infra pages 1032-1034.

2. Restatement (Second) of Property, Donative Transfers §11.4 (1984), prefers the term *non-general* to *special*. The special power is sometimes also called a *limited* power.

power to benefit *A*'s issue, but *A* cannot appoint the property in such a way as to benefit *A* or *A*'s estate.[3]

Powers of appointment may be created so as to be exercisable by either deed or will as in Case 1, by deed alone, or by will alone as in Case 2. When exercisable only by will, the power is called a *testamentary* power.

To be absolutely accurate, we should point out that a power of appointment may be created in a trustee, a beneficiary of a trust, a person with a legal interest not held in trust, or in a person who has no other interest in the property. In other words, a power may be created in anyone. Almost all powers of appointment are created in trustees or in beneficiaries of trusts, however. A trustee who has discretion to pay income or principal to a named beneficiary, or discretion to spray income among a group of beneficiaries, has a special power of appointment. Special powers in trustees were treated in the section on Discretionary Trusts in Chapter 8 at pages 617-631. In this chapter, we are primarily concerned with powers of appointment given to beneficiaries of trusts.

2.   Does the Appointive Property Belong to the Donor or the Donee?

Under the common law, property subject to a power of appointment was viewed as owned by the donor, and the power was conceived as merely authority of the donee to do an act for the donor. The donee was thought of as having a power to fill in a blank in the donor's will. This was known as the *relation-back doctrine*. This doctrine pretty much describes how the law treats special powers of appointment, where the donee can reap no personal pecuniary benefit, but it has never been consistently applied to general powers of appointment.

In some situations, the donee of a general power of appointment is treated as owner of the property. The primary example is under the federal tax laws. The donee of a general power is treated as owner of the appointive property for income, estate, and gift tax purposes.

---

3. The existence of the power can, of course, benefit *A* by assuring filial devotion.

It doubtless occurred to the testator that by restraining a disposition of his property except by will, which is in its nature revocable, [his widow] would, to the end of her life, retain the influence over, and secure the respect of, the several objects of his bounty, which he intended her to have — a result less likely to be accomplished if power were given her to dispose of the property by deed or other irrevocable act to take effect in her lifetime. [Hood v. Haden, 82 Va. 588, 591 (1886).]

As someone once said, a special power to appoint a hundred thousand dollars never hurt an old lady — or an old man.

Congress pays no mind to the technicalities of property law here but makes taxation turn upon the fact that the donee, if he chooses, can receive economic benefit by exercising the power.

Irwin Union Bank & Trust Co. v. Long
Indiana Court of Appeals, 1974
160 Ind. App. 509, 312 N.E.2d 908

LOWDERMILK, J.   On February 3, 1957, Victoria Long, appellee herein, obtained a judgment in the amount of $15,000 against Philip W. Long, which judgment emanated from a divorce decree. This action is the result of the filing by appellee of a petition in proceedings supplemental to execution on the prior judgment. Appellee sought satisfaction of that judgment by pursuing funds allegedly owed to Philip W. Long as a result of a trust set up by Laura Long, his mother.

Appellee alleged that the Irwin Union Bank and Trust Company (Union Bank) was indebted to Philip W. Long as the result of its position as trustee of the trust created by Laura Long. On April 24, 1969, the trial court ordered that any income, property, or profits, which were owed to Philip Long and not exempt from execution should be applied to the divorce judgment. Thereafter, on February 13, 1973, the trial court ordered that four percent (4%) of the trust corpus of the trust created by Laura Long which benefited Philip Long was not exempt from execution and could be levied upon by appellee and ordered a writ of execution. . . .

The pertinent portion of the trust created by Laura Long is as follows, to-wit:

ITEM V C

> *Withdrawal of Principal*
> When Philip W. Long, Jr. has attained the age of twenty-one (21) years and is not a full-time student at an educational institution as a candidate for a Bachelor of Arts or Bachelor of Sciences degree, Philip W. Long shall have the right to withdraw from principal once in any calendar year upon thirty (30) days written notice to the Trustee up to four percent (4%) of the market value of the entire trust principal on the date of such notice, which right shall not be cumulative.

The primary issue raised on this appeal is whether the trial court erred in allowing execution on the 4% of the trust corpus.

Appellant contends that Philip Long's right to withdraw 4% of the trust corpus is, in fact, a general power of appointment. Union Bank further contends that since Philip Long has never exercised his right of withdrawal, pursuant to the provisions of the trust instrument, no creditors of Philip Long can reach the trust corpus. Appellant points out that if the power of appointment is unexercised, the creditors cannot force the exercise of said power and cannot reach the trust corpus in this case. . . .

Appellee argues that Philip has absolute control and use of the 4% of the corpus and that the bank does not have control over that portion of the corpus if Philip decides to exercise his right of withdrawal. Appellee argues that the intention of Laura Long was to give Philip not only an income interest in the trust but a fixed amount of corpus which he could use as he saw fit. Thus, Philip Long would have a right to the present enjoyment of 4% of the trust corpus. A summation of appellee's argument, as stated in her brief, is as follows: "So it is with Philip — he can get it if he desires it, so why cannot Victoria get it even if Philip does not desire it?"

We have had no Indiana authority directly in point cited to us by either of the parties and a thorough research of this issue does not reveal any Indiana authority on point. Thus, this issue so far as we can determine is one of first impression in Indiana. . . .

The leading case on this issue is Gilman v. Bell (1881), 99 Ill. 144, 150, 151, wherein the Illinois Supreme Court discussed powers of appointment and vesting as follows:

> No title or interest in the thing vests in the donee of the power until he exercises the power. It is virtually an offer to him of the estate or fund, that he may receive or reject at will, and like any other offer to donate property to a person, no title can vest until he accepts the offer, nor can a court of equity compel him to accept the property or fund against his will, even for the benefit of creditors. If it should, it would be to convert the property of the person offering to make the donation to the payment of the debts of another person. Until accepted, the person to whom the offer is made has not, nor can he have, the slightest interest or title to the property. So the donee of the power only receives the naked power to make the property or fund his own. And when he exercises the power, he thereby consents to receive it, and the title thereby vests in him, although it may pass out of him *eo instanti*, to the appointee.

See, also, 59 A.L.R. 1510. . . .

Contrary to the contention of appellee, it is our opinion that Philip Long has no control over the trust corpus until he exercises his power of appointment and gives notice to the trustee that he wishes to receive his 4% of the trust corpus. Until such an exercise is made, the trustee has the absolute control and benefit of the trust corpus within the terms of the trust instrument.

While not controlling as precedent, we find that the Federal Estate Tax laws are quite analogous to the case at bar. Under §2041, Powers of Appointment, of the Internal Revenue Code, it is clear that the interest given to Philip Long under Item V C would be considered a power of appointment for estate tax purposes. A general power of appointment is defined in §2041(b)(1) as follows:

> (1) General power of appointment. — The term "general power of appointment" means a power which is exercisable in favor of the decedent, his estate, his creditors, or the creditors of his estate; . . .

The regulations pertinent to this issue discuss a power of appointment as it is used for estate tax purposes as follows:

> (b) Definition of "power of appointment" (1) In general. The term "power of appointment" includes all powers which are in substance and effect powers of appointment regardless of the nomenclature used in creating the power and regardless of local property law connotations. For example, if a trust instrument provides that the beneficiary may appropriate or consume the principal of the trust, the power to consume or appropriate is a power of appointment. . . . 20.2041-1(b)(1)

For estate tax purposes even the failure to exercise a power of appointment may lead to tax consequences. Under §2041(b)(2) the lapse of a power of appointment will be considered a release of such power during the calendar year to the extent of the value of the power in question. However, the lapsed power will only be considered a release and includable in the gross estate of a decedent if the value of the lapsed power is greater than $5,000 or 5% of the aggregate value of the assets out of which the lapsed power could have been satisfied.

The trust instrument was obviously carefully drawn with the tax consequences bearing an important place in the overall intent of the testator. The trust as a whole is set up to give the grandchildren of Laura Long the substantial portion of the assets involved. We note with interest that the percentage of corpus which Philip Long may receive is carefully limited to a percentage less than that which would be includable in the gross estate of Philip Long should he die within a year in which he had allowed his power of appointment to lapse.

. . . The trust created in the will of Laura Long, in our opinion, has the legal effect of creating a [general] power of appointment in Philip Long under Item V C of the trust.

Philip Long has never exercised his power of appointment under the trust. Such a situation is discussed in II Scott on Trusts, §147.3 as follows:

> Where the power is a special power, a power to appoint only among a group of persons, the power is not beneficial to the donee and cannot, of course, be reached by his creditors. Where the power is a general

power, that is, a power to appoint to anyone including the donee himself or his estate, the power is beneficial to the donee. If the donee exercises the power by appointing to a volunteer, the property appointed can be reached by his creditors if his other assets are insufficient for the payment of his debts. But where the donee of a general power created by some person other than himself fails to exercise the power, his creditors cannot acquire the power or compel its exercise, nor can they reach the property covered by the power, unless it is otherwise provided by statute.

Indiana has no statute which would authorize a creditor to reach property covered by a power of appointment which is unexercised.

In Gilman v. Bell, supra, the court analyzed the situation where a general power of appointment was unexercised and discussed the position of creditors of the donee of the power as follows:

> But it is insisted, that, conceding it to be a mere naked power of appointment in favor of himself, in favor of creditors he should be compelled by a court of equity to so appoint, or be treated as the owner, and the property subjected to the payment of his debts. The doctrine has been long established in the English courts, that the courts of equity will not aid creditors in case there is a non-execution of the power.

Appellee concedes that if we find that Philip Long had merely an unexercised power of appointment then creditors are in no position to either force the exercise of the power or to reach the trust corpus. Thus, it is clear that the trial court erred. . . .

Reversed and remanded.

NOTES AND QUESTIONS

1. Restatement (Second) of Property, Donative Transfers §13.2 (1986), agrees with the *Long* case. Is this sound? The courts following the rule applied in *Long* start by saying that the power is not the donee's "property"; its exercise is personal to the donee and cannot be exercised by another. As Lord Justice Fry once said: "The power of a person to appoint an estate to himself is, in my judgment, no more his 'property' than the power to write a book or to sing a song." In re Armstrong, 17 Q.B.D. 521, 531 (1886). But, then, if the donee exercises the power by appointing to another, the appointive assets somehow — according to the majority of courts — pass into the donee's hands (or estate) for a scintilla of time and, while in the donee's hands (or estate), equity seizes the assets for the benefit of creditors.

One may reasonably ask why, if the donee of a presently exercisable general power may reach the property simply by asking for it, the donee's creditors cannot reach it? How does the property differ in essence from money in the donee's checking account? In a number of states, statutes enable creditors of a donee of a general power presently exercisable to reach the appointive property, usually with the qualification that the creditors must first exhaust the donee's own assets before resorting to the appointive property. See, e.g., Cal. Prob. Code §682 (1998); Wis. Stat. Ann. §702.17 (1997). Under these statutes, the creditors of the donee of a general testamentary power can also reach the property but only at the donee's death. In New York, creditors of a general power presently exercisable can reach the appointive property, but creditors of a donee of a general testamentary power cannot. N.Y. Est., Powers & Trusts Law §§10-7.2, 10-7.4 (1998).

Under the federal bankruptcy act, a general power presently exercisable passes to the donee's trustee in bankruptcy, but a special power and a general testamentary power do not. 11 U.S.C.A. §541(b)(1) (1998). See Note, Powers of Appointment Under the Bankruptcy Code: A Focus on General Testamentary Powers, 72 Iowa L. Rev. 1041 (1987).

If the donee of a general power is also the donor of the power, creditors may reach the appointive assets. Restatement (Second) of Property, supra, §13.3.

2. *Spouse of the donee.* If the surviving spouse of the donee seeks to reach the appointive property at the donee's death under elective share statutes, the donee of a general power, as well as the donee of a special power, is not, in most states, treated as owning the property. The surviving spouse has a claim against the donee's *probate* estate, and since the appointive assets are not in the donee's probate estate, the spouse may not reach them. See Margaret M. Mahoney, Elective Share Statutes: The Right to Elect Against Property Subject to a General Power of Appointment in the Decedent, 55 Notre Dame Law. 99 (1979). Uniform Probate Code §2-205(1)(i), supra page 509, changes this rule and includes in the augmented estate subject to the elective share any property over which the decedent had a general power of appointment. New York Est., Powers & Trusts Law §5-1.1-A(b)(1)(H) (1998), is to the same effect.

3. *Special powers.* General creditors of a donee of a special power cannot reach the property subject to the power because the donor did not intend that the property be used for the donee's benefit. On the other hand, it has been held that where the life beneficiary of a trust has a special inter vivos power to appoint trust principal to his descendants, children of the donee who have a support order may reach the trust principal even though the trust contains a spendthrift clause. In re Marriage of Chapman, 297 Ill. App. 3d 611, 697 N.E.2d 365 (1998).

Could the donee's children with a support order reach trust principal that is subject to a general inter vivos power in the donee? Compare the ability of children to reach the income interest of their parent in a spendthrift trust, supra page 639.

NOTE: TAX REASONS FOR CREATING POWERS

Powers of appointment are extensively employed in trusts to give the donee considerable control over the trust property while at the same time gaining some tax advantage. The federal tax laws provide that the holder of a general power of appointment over income or principal is treated as owner of the property. The income from the property is taxable to the donee (Internal Revenue Code of 1986, §678). If the donee exercises the power during life, the property transferred by exercise is subject to gift taxation (IRC §2514 and see infra page 1033). If the donee dies holding a general power, the property is included in the donee's federal gross estate and is subject to estate taxation (IRC §2041, discussed infra at pages 1032-1034). On the other hand, *property subject to a special power of appointment is not treated as owned by the donee.* Hence, if your client wants to transfer property and avoid estate taxation at the death of the donee, while giving the donee considerable control over the property, create a special power of appointment and not a general power. Federal estate taxation is imposed on estates exceeding $675,000 in the year 2000, with the tax exemption increasing annually in steps to $1 million in 2006.

Estate tax advantages of special powers. By carefully tailoring the powers given a donee to fit the Internal Revenue Code, a donee can be given power to do almost anything an owner of property can do while not being treated as owner for federal estate and gift tax purposes. Let us see how this can be done. Suppose that *T* wishes to pass property to her daughter, *A*, for *A*'s life and then to *A*'s children. At the same time *T* wishes to give *A* as much power over the property as is possible without causing *A* to be treated as owner for estate tax purposes. Although *T* cannot escape taxation at her death, *T* is looking ahead and wishes to skip estate taxation on *A*'s death. To accomplish *T*'s wishes, *T*'s will can set up a trust along the following lines:

(1)   *T*'s will transfers the legal title to the property to *A* as trustee. *As trustee, A* has the power of management. *A* can decide when to sell and in what to reinvest. If the trustee's powers are broadly drafted, *A* can manage the property almost as if she owned it herself.

(2)   *T*'s will gives to *A, not as trustee but as a beneficiary,* the following rights and powers:

      (a)   the right to receive all the income;

      (b)   a special power of appointment exercisable by deed or will to appoint the trust property to anyone *A* desires except herself, her creditors, her estate, and the creditors of her estate;

      (c)   a power to consume the trust property measured "by an ascertainable standard relating to the health, education, support or maintenance"[4] of *A*; and

      (d)   a power to withdraw each year $5,000 or 5 percent of the corpus, whichever is greater.[5]

  (3) If *T* desires to make sure that *A* will be able to use the entire property if she needs it, *T* can appoint an independent co-trustee and give this co-trustee the power to pay *A* the entire principal or to terminate the trust.

None of the above powers given *A*, individually or collectively, causes *A* to be treated as owner of the trust fund under the federal estate tax. Yet *A* has such broad control over the trust fund that in most instances she can do exactly with the trust funds as she could do if she had been bequeathed the property outright.

Prior to the Tax Reform Act of 1986, federal estate taxes could be avoided over several generations through the creation of successive life estates. To give the desired flexibility to cope with changing events, each successive life tenant could be given special powers of appointment as indicated above. This tax avoidance device has now been curtailed by the imposition of a tax on certain generation-skipping transfers, to which we now turn.

Generation-skipping transfer tax advantages of special powers. In 1986, Congress enacted a generation-skipping transfer tax to deal with estate tax avoidance resulting from exemption of life estates from estate taxation. IRC §§2601-2663, discussed infra at pages 1065-1078. A generation-skipping transfer tax is imposed on the death of a life tenant of a younger generation than the settlor's (on *A*'s death in the above example). It is now Congress's policy to exact a wealth transfer tax at every generation, either an estate tax or a generation-skipping transfer tax.

Nonetheless, special powers of appointment continue to be useful

---

4. Powers to consume measured by an ascertainable standard, limiting the donee's right to go into principal, are not treated as general powers under the Code. See infra pages 1033-1038.

5. Under a "$5,000 or 5 percent" power, $5,000 or 5 percent of the corpus (whichever is greater) will be included in the estate of the donee to the extent the power is not exercised in the year of the donee's death. IRC §2041(b)(2), discussed infra at pages 1033-1034. This is a small price to pay for the flexibility gained thereby. This is the type of power involved in Irwin Union Bank & Trust Co. v. Long, supra.

in securing many tax advantages, both under the estate tax and under the generation-skipping transfer tax. First, the generation-skipping transfer tax does not apply to trusts established before 1986. If the beneficiaries of these pre-1986 trusts have special powers of appointment, as many do, these trusts may be kept going — transfer tax free — for about a hundred years from the date of their creation (which is, roughly speaking, the perpetuities period) by creating new special powers in each succeeding generation. Second, each transferor has a $1 million exemption from GST tax. Each transferor can transfer up to $1 million in a trust, called a dynasty trust, which will be exempt from generation-skipping transfer tax for the duration of the trust. Hence in the above example, *T* could create a trust of $1 million for her daughter *A* and her descendants, giving each generation special powers as outlined above, with the trust to endure until 21 years after the death of all *T*'s living descendants or other named persons living at *T*'s death (the perpetuities period). In some states a dynasty trust for generation after generation can endure in perpetuity (see infra page 854). No generation-skipping transfer tax is payable so long as the trust endures. If *T* is married, she and her husband (using his $1 million exemption) can transfer $2 million in such a GST-tax-exempt dynasty trust. See infra page 1070.

Third, the federal estate tax rates range from 37 percent to 55 percent of the decedent's gross estate; the generation-skipping transfer tax rate is 55 percent of the trust corpus. The decedent has a $675,000 exemption from the estate tax, to be increased to $1 million in 2006; the settlor of a trust has one $1 million exemption from the GST tax, which the settlor can assign to any trust she chooses. If an estate tax is levied on property at the death of a trust beneficiary, a GST tax is not also levied on the property (remember: only one transfer tax once a generation). Because these taxes have different rates and different exemptions, it may be wise to enable the life beneficiary of the trust or a remainderman to choose which tax to pay. Giving a life beneficiary or remainderman a special power of appointment enables the donee to make this choice under Internal Revenue Code §2041(a)(3). The explanation of this is rather technical, involving both the Rule against Perpetuities and the tax code. It can wisely be put aside until a later chapter (see infra pages 827-829). Other uses of special powers of appointment in saving transfer taxes will be dealt with in Chapter 13 on federal wealth transfer taxes.

Although as a rule general powers should not be created if the donor is seeking favorable tax treatment, there is one exception. Property that passes to the surviving spouse in such a manner as to qualify for the *marital deduction* is not taxable under the estate tax. A life estate coupled with a general testamentary power in the surviving spouse qualifies for the marital deduction (IRC §2056(b)(5), discussed infra at page 1046) and is a common estate planning tool. Thus:

> *Case 3.* *H* devises property to *X* in trust to pay the income to *W* and on *W*'s death to distribute the principal to such person or persons as *W* by her will appoints. *H*'s devise qualifies for the marital deduction; no federal estate taxes are payable on the property at *H*'s death. However, since *W* has a general power, the property is subject to estate taxation on *W*'s death. In effect the marital deduction permits taxation to be postponed until the death of the surviving spouse.

Because of adverse tax consequences, general powers are rarely created by the trust settlor in anyone except the surviving spouse.

It has been held that a lawyer who drafts wills and trusts is liable for malpractice if the lawyer does not know the tax consequences of powers of appointment. In Bucquet v. Livingston, 57 Cal. App. 3d 914, 129 Cal. Rptr. 514 (1976), the lawyer failed to recognize that a general power of appointment is the equivalent of ownership for tax purposes. In holding the lawyer liable, the court noted that the creation of general and special powers of appointment is a significant aspect of the law of trusts and estates. The court concluded that a reasonable, diligent, and competent attorney engaged in estate planning should be expected to know the potential tax consequences of creating or holding a general power of appointment.

SECTION B.   CREATION OF A POWER OF APPOINTMENT

1.   *Intent to Create a Power*

To create a power of appointment, the donor must manifest an intent to do so, either expressly or by implication. No particular form of words is necessary. It is not necessary that the words "power of appointment" or "appoint" be used. A power of appointment confers discretion on the donee, who may choose to exercise the power or not, and is to be distinguished from a direct nondiscretionary disposition by the donor. Thus:

> *Case 4.* Aunt Fanny executes a will in 1995 bequeathing her tangible personal property "to my niece Wendy Brown, to dispose of in accordance with a letter addressed to Wendy dated January 4, 1994, which is in my safe-deposit box." Aunt Fanny has incorporated the letter by reference

and the tangible personal property must be distributed in accordance therewith. Wendy does not have a power of appointment.

Words that merely express a wish or desire (*precatory words*) do not create a power of appointment in the absence of other circumstances indicating a contrary intent. If in Case 4 Aunt Fanny had left her tangible personal property to Wendy "with the request that she give some of the property to my other relatives," Wendy would take a fee simple; the precatory words would not create a power of appointment.

PROBLEM

A power of appointment cannot be created in a dead person. In 1996, *T* executes a will devising her residuary estate "to such person or persons as my brother, *B*, shall by his last will appoint." In 1998, *B* dies, leaving a will executed in 1994 that devises "all my property, and all property over which I hold a power of appointment, to *C*." In 2000 *T* dies. *C* claims the residue of *T*'s estate. Is *C* entitled to it (a) as *B*'s appointee, (b) under the theory of incorporation by reference, or (c) under the theory of independent significance? See Curley v. Lynch, 206 Mass. 289, 92 N.E. 429 (1910); Restatement (Second) of Property, Donative Transfers, §18.4 (1986).

2.   Powers to Consume

One of the most frequently litigated problems in regard to creation of powers is whether a power to consume principal has been created and, if so, what standard governs the exercise of the power. Much of this litigation stems from homemade wills, but some litigation, alas, results from inadequate drafting by lawyers.

Sterner v. Nelson
Supreme Court of Nebraska, 1982
210 Neb. 358, 314 N.W.2d 263

KRIVOSHA, C.J.   The instant case involves the construction of the last will and testament of Oscar Wurtele, deceased. The appellants appeal from a summary judgment entered by the District Court for Otoe County, Nebraska, finding that the nature of the devise and bequest made by Oscar Wurtele to his wife, Mary Viola Wurtele, by his last will and testament was a fee simple absolute. We believe the trial court was correct and affirm the judgment.

As noted, the appeal herein arises out of the last will and testament of Oscar Wurtele, executed on August 4, 1939. While the will is simple and to the point, it is not a model for estate planners. It reads in total as follows:

> I, the undersigned, Oscar Wurtele do hereby make, publish and declare the following as and for my Last Will and Testament:
>
> I hereby give, devise and bequeath all of my property of every kind and nature to my wife Mary Viola Wurtele to be her property *absolutely with full power in her to make such disposition of said property as she may desire;* conditioned, however, that if any of said property is remaining upon the death of said Mary Viola Wurtele, or in the event that she predeceases me then and in such event such of said property as remains shall vest in my foster daughter Gladys Pauline Sterner and her children.
>
> I hereby nominate and appoint my said wife, Mary Viola Wurtele, of Nebraska City, Nebraska, as executrix of this My Last Will and Testament.
>
> Dated at Nebraska City, Nebraska, this 4th day of August, 1939. Oscar Wurtele. [Emphasis supplied.]

Following Oscar Wurtele's death in 1955 his will was admitted to probate in the county court of Otoe County, Nebraska, and all of the property which Oscar Wurtele owned at the time of his death was devised and bequeathed to his wife, Mary Viola Wurtele, to be hers absolutely. Certain of the property, including two commercial buildings, a farm, and a residence, were held in joint tenancy and passed to Mary Viola Wurtele by action of law and are not in any manner involved in this case. Two other commercial buildings, however, did pass to Mary Viola Wurtele by reason of the will of her husband, Oscar Wurtele, as well as certain personal property having an estimated value of $19,000. Mary Viola Wurtele thereafter married one Aaron Rose with whom she lived until her death on March 7, 1978. Mary Viola Rose died testate leaving her property to various individuals, including her husband, Aaron, and certain other nieces and nephews, but leaving no property to the appellants herein who are the foster daughter and her children referred to in the last will and testament of Oscar Wurtele. Aaron Rose died on June 24, 1979.

The evidence further discloses that in 1963 Mary Viola Rose sold the four commercial buildings for a total sale price of $70,000. No division of the sale price was made between the joint tenancy property and the property received under the will of her former husband. It is, however, clear from the evidence that none of the original property devised and bequeathed to Mary Viola Wurtele remained at the time of her death, though she did die owning property, some of which may have been purchased from the proceeds of either the personal property or the sale of the real estate. Following a hearing, the trial court found that the will of Oscar Wurtele devised and bequeathed all of his property to his wife, Mary Viola Wurtele, in fee simple absolute, and granted the personal representative's motion for summary judgment. The trial court's opinion provides in part as follows: "The Court is of the opinion that the language in the Oscar Wurtele will is so precise as to create a fee simple title in the wife, Mary Viola Wurtele."

Appellants have raised a number of errors, but the principal issue which needs to be addressed is whether the devise and bequest by Oscar Wurtele to Mary Viola Wurtele was a fee simple absolute or merely a life estate with authority to dispose of so much of the property as she chose during her lifetime. For, obviously, if we conclude, as the trial court did, that the devise and bequest was a fee simple absolute, then Mary Viola Rose was entitled to do whatever she wished with her property, both during her lifetime and upon her death, and Gladys Pauline Sterner and her children would not be entitled to any portions of the property remaining at the death of Mary Viola Rose. . . .

The general and majority rule is as expressed in 28 Am. Jur. 2d Estates §94 at 198-99 (1966), wherein it provides in part:

> It is a well-settled, general rule that where there is a grant, devise, or bequest to one in general terms only, expressing neither fee nor life estate, and there is a subsequent limitation over of what remains at the first taker's death, if there is also given to the first taker an unlimited and unrestricted power of absolute disposal, express or implied, the grant, devise, or bequest to the first taker is construed to pass a fee. The attempted limitation over, following a gift which is in fee with full power of disposition and alienation, is void, . . . the purported gift over merely being an invalid repugnancy.

The American Jurisprudence annotation cited above then goes on to note that the general rule is consistently applied even in cases involving wills of slightly different but substantial tenor, a number of which are similar to the language of the Wurtele will.

One may likewise find cases in Nebraska and other jurisdictions to support the general view expressed in the American Jurisprudence citation. In the case of Moffitt v. Williams, 116 Neb. 785, 788, 219 N.W. 138, 139 (1928), we said: . . . " 'The settled rule of law is that, if a deed or will conveys an absolute title in fee simple, an inconsistent clause in the instrument attempting merely to limit that title or convey to the same person a limited title in the same land will be disregarded.' "

Cases may likewise be found in a majority of the jurisdictions which support the general rule. In the case of Moran v. Moran, 143 Mich. 322, 323, 106 N.W. 206 (1906), the Michigan Supreme Court was presented a will which provided in part as follows: " 'I give and bequeath to my beloved wife . . . all my property real and personal, of every name, nature and description to be hers absolutely, providing however, that if at her death any of the said property be still hers, then the residue still hers shall go to my, not her, nearest heir or heirs.' " The court held that such language created a fee simple absolute in the wife and the provision for the property remaining was void and unenforceable. . . . [Numerous citations from other states omitted.]

In the instant case it is not possible to reconcile the devise given by Oscar Wurtele to his wife, on the one hand, and the expression of desire concerning his foster daughter, on the other.

The grant to Mary Viola Wurtele was clear and unambiguous. She was to have the property to "be her property absolutely with full power in her to make such disposition of said property as she may desire." That intent is clear. By having the property as hers "absolutely" and with "full power" to "dispose" of the property as she may desire, she had not only the right to sell or give away the property during her lifetime but the right to will the property upon her death as well. Anything less would not have granted her the property "absolutely" with "full power in her to make such disposition" as she desired. The authority given was not limited to sale or disposition during her lifetime, but rather was to be *absolute*. . . .

No reason is given to us nor are we able to find any on our own as to why the majority rule following the common law should not be the rule in this jurisdiction. . . . If the testator does not desire for the devisee to have a fee simple, it is easy enough to say so. But having once granted the devise or bequest in language which standing alone constitutes an absolute conveyance, the balance of the limitations should be disregarded, regardless of the intent of the testator, on the basis that the intent is in conflict with the first grant. Either a devisee has received the property absolutely or the devisee has not received the property absolutely. Like honesty, morality, and pregnancy, an absolute devise cannot be qualified. . . .

We, therefore, now adopt the majority rule to the effect that where there is a grant, devise, or bequest to one in general terms only, expressing neither fee nor life estate, and there is a subsequent limitation over of what remains at the first taker's death, if there is also given to the first taker an unlimited and unrestricted power of absolute disposal, express or implied, the grant, devise, or bequest to the first taker is construed to pass a fee. The attempted limitation over, following a gift which is in fee with full power of disposition and alienation, is void.

. . . The judgment of the trial court, therefore, is affirmed.

NOTES AND QUESTIONS

1.   Oscar Wurtele's will appears to have been drafted by a lawyer. Should the lawyer be liable to Gladys for malpractice? See St. Mary's Church of Schuyler v. Tomek, 212 Neb. 728, 325 N.W.2d 164 (1982) (no privity of contract); Jesse Dukeminier, Cleansing the Stables of Property: A River Found at Last, 65 Iowa L. Rev. 151, 169-170 (1979). For discussion of successful ways to make a gift over to Gladys of whatever is left on Mary Viola's death, see William F. Fratcher, Bequests of Orts, 48 Mo. L. Rev. 475 (1983).

2.   In Sterner v. Nelson, the court says, "No reason is given to us nor are we able to find any on our own as to why the majority rule following the common law should not be the rule in this jurisdiction." If counsel and court had dug a bit deeper, they should have unearthed an extended, critical treatment of the rule of repugnancy in Lewis M. Simes & Allan F. Smith, The Law of Future Interests §§1481-1491 (2d ed. 1956), or the summary of criticisms, originating with Professor Gray, in 6 American Law of Property §26.43 (1952). For more criticism of this senseless rule, see the dissenting opinion of Chief Justice Vanderbilt in Fox v. Snow, 6 N.J. 12, 76 A.2d 877 (1950).

The rule of repugnancy is not followed in Caldwell v. Walraven, 268 Ga. 444, 490 S.E.2d 384 (1997) (citing similar cases from other states).

3.   One thing can be said in favor of the rule of repugnancy applied in Sterner v. Nelson. It enables the court to avoid hard questions. If the devise over to Gladys were valid, could Mary Viola use the devised property to support her second husband, to take a round-the-world cruise, to spend the winter in Florida, to build a room on her house? Could she give away the property? Does Mary Viola have to give a bond to protect Gladys' interest in the personal property valued at $19,000? These questions often arise where the life tenant is given a power to consume, and litigation over ambiguous language is extensive. See Annots., 31 A.L.R.3d 6 (1970) (158 pages); id. at 169 (129 pages); id. at 309 (61 pages). Compare the rights of the survivor whose property is bound by a contract not to revoke a will, supra page 328.

A good attorney will never create a *legal* fee simple with the power to consume because of the danger of running afoul of the rule of repugnancy. Nor will a good attorney create a *legal* life estate at all; a trust with a life beneficiary is preferable in almost all situations (see supra page 562 for reasons why). If the life beneficiary of a trust is to have rights to consume the principal, the attorney drafting a will or trust should make it as clear as possible under exactly what circumstances the life tenant can reach the principal.

4. *Taxation of powers to consume.* Property subject to a general power of appointment is in the donee's federal gross estate at death and subject to estate taxation. If a power to consume permits the donee to appoint the property to herself during life, it is a general power of appointment. However, there is an important exception in the tax laws. Internal Revenue Code of 1986, §2041(b)(1)(A) provides that "A power to consume, invade, or appropriate property for the benefit of the decedent which is limited by an ascertainable standard relating to the health, education, support, or maintenance of the decedent shall not be deemed a general power of appointment." Hence, the tax question respecting each power to consume is this: Is the power at hand limited by an ascertainable standard relating to the health, education, support, or maintenance of the decedent? If it is not so limited, the property subject to the power is included in the donee's gross estate. The lawyer drafting a power to consume must choose words very, very carefully and track the words of §2041(b)(1)(A) or the regulations. A power to consume for the donee's "comfort, welfare, or happiness" is not limited by the requisite standard. On the other hand, a power to consume "to maintain the standard of living to which the donee is accustomed" is regarded as limited by the requisite standard. See Estate of Vissering v. Commissioner, 990 F.2d 578 (10th Cir. 1993), infra page 1035, citing numerous cases litigating this question.

The lawyer drafting a trust instrument may decide that rather than give the beneficiary a power to consume, it is safer to give a trustee who is not the beneficiary a discretionary power to use corpus to maintain the beneficiary in the style of living to which she is accustomed.

SECTION C.   RELEASE OF A POWER OF APPOINTMENT

The donor of a life estate coupled with a testamentary power usually intends to protect the donee from an indiscreet or unwise exercise of the power during life. A testamentary power has as one of its purposes keeping the donee free to exercise discretion up until the moment of death. Hence, the donee of a testamentary power of appointment cannot legally contract to make an appointment in the future. Such a contract cannot be specifically enforced, nor can damages be awarded for breach. If the law were otherwise, the donee of a testamentary power could in effect exercise the power during life by contracting to exercise it. Courts will not allow the donor's intent to be defeated in this manner. The promisee of the contract may, however, obtain restitution of the value that the promisee gave the donee.

On the other hand, if the donee promises to exercise a testamentary power in a certain way, and the donee's will exercises the power as promised, the exercise is valid. Benjamin v. Morgan Guaranty Trust Co., 202 A.D.2d 536, 609 N.Y.S.2d 276 (1944).

Although a contract to exercise a testamentary power is not enforceable, a result somewhat close to that which the donee wants to obtain by a contract may sometimes be obtained by releasing the power of appointment. If a power is released, the uncertainty it creates as to the ultimate takers is removed. Thus:

> *Case 5.* *T* devises property in trust for *A* for life, then as *A* by will appoints, and in default of appointment to *A*'s children equally. *A* releases her power of appointment. *A*'s children now have an indefeasibly vested remainder. *A* could not make an enforceable contract to appoint to her children, but she may achieve her objective by a release.

All powers of appointment except powers in trust or imperative powers have been made releasable in all jurisdictions either by judicial decision or by statute. A releasable power may be released with respect to the whole or any part of the appointive property and may also be released in such manner as to reduce or limit the permissible appointees. See Restatement (Second) of Property, Donative Transfers §§14.1, 14.2 (1986), including Statutory Notes and Reporter's Notes.

Seidel v. Werner

New York Supreme Court, Special Term, New York County, 1975
81 Misc. 2d 220, 364 N.Y.S.2d 963,
aff'd on opinion below, 50 A.D.2d 743, 376 N.Y.S.2d 139

SILVERMAN, J.   Plaintiffs, trustees of a trust established in 1919 by Abraham L. Werner, sue for a declaratory judgment to determine who is entitled to one-half of the principal of the trust fund — the share in which Steven L. Werner, decedent (hereinafter "Steven"), was the life beneficiary and over which he had a testamentary power of appointment. The dispute concerns the manner in which Steven exercised his power of appointment and is between Steven's second wife, Harriet G. Werner (hereinafter "Harriet"), along with their children, Anna G. and Frank S. Werner (hereinafter "Anna" and "Frank") and Steven's third wife, Edith Fisch Werner (hereinafter "Edith").

Anna and Frank claim Steven's entire share of the trust remainder on the basis of a Mexican consent judgment of divorce, obtained by Steven against Harriet on December 9, 1963, which incorporated by reference and approved a separation agreement, entered into between Steven and Harriet on December 1, 1963. That agreement included the following provision:

> 10. The Husband shall make, and hereby promises not to revoke, a will in which he shall exercise his testamentary power of appointment over his share in a trust known as "Abraham L. Werner Trust No. 1" by establishing with respect to said share a trust for the benefit of the aforesaid Children, for the same purposes and under the same terms and conditions, as the trust provided for in Paragraph "9" of this Agreement, insofar as said terms and conditions are applicable thereto.

Paragraph 9 in relevant part provides for the wife to receive the income of the trust, upon the death of the husband, for the support and maintenance of the children, until they reach twenty-one years of age, at which time they are to receive the principal in equal shares.

On March 20, 1964, less than four months after entry of the divorce judgment, Steven executed a will in which, instead of exercising his testamentary power of appointment in favor of Anna and Frank, he left everything to his third wife, Edith:

> First, I give, devise and bequeath all of my property . . . including . . . all property over which I have a power of testamentary disposition, to my wife, Edith Fisch Werner.

Steven died in April 1971 and his Will was admitted to probate by the Surrogate's Court of New York County on July 11, 1973.

(1) Paragraph 10 of the Separation Agreement is a contract to exercise a testamentary power of appointment not presently exercisable (EPTL 10-3.3) and as such is invalid under EPTL 10-5.3, which provides as follows:

> (a) The donee of a power of appointment which is not presently exercisable or of a postponed power which has not become exercisable, cannot contract to make an appointment. Such a contract, if made, cannot be the basis of an action for specific performance or damages, but the promisee can obtain restitution of the value given by him for the promise unless the donee has exercised the power pursuant to the contract.

This is a testamentary power of appointment. The original trust instrument provided in relevant part that: ". . . Upon the death of such child [Steven] the principal of such share shall be disposed of as such child shall by its last will direct, and in default of such testamentary disposition then the same shall go to the issue of such child then surviving per stirpes. . . ." It is not disputed that New York law is determinative of the validity of Paragraph 10 of the Separation Agreement; the Separation Agreement itself provides that New York law shall govern.

The reasoning underlying the refusal to enforce a contract to exercise a testamentary power was stated by Justice Cardozo in the case of Farmers' Loan & Trust Co. v. Mortimer, 219 N.Y. 290, 293-4, 114 N.E. 389, 390 (1916):

> The exercise of the power was to represent the final judgment, the last will, of the donee. Up to the last moment of his life he was to have the power to deal with the share as he thought best. . . . To permit him to bargain that right away would be to defeat the purpose of the donor. Her command was that her property should go to her son's issue unless at the end of his life it remained his will that it go elsewhere. It has not remained his will that it go elsewhere; and his earlier contract cannot nullify the expression of his final purpose.

See also, In re Estate of Brown, 33 N.Y.2d 211, 351 N.Y.S.2d 655, 306 N.E.2d 781 (1973).

(2) The question then is whether entry of the Mexican divorce decree, incorporating the Separation Agreement, alters this result; I do not think it does. . . .

[The court held that the Mexican divorce decree was not controlling, because, first, it did not direct Steven to exercise his power of appointment but merely approved the separation agreement as fair and reasonable, and, second, the Mexican court did not pass on or consider rules of New York property law.]

(3) As indicated, the statute makes a promise to exercise a testamentary power in a particular way unenforceable. However, EPTL 10-5.3(b) permits a donee of a power to release the power, and that release, if in conformity with EPTL 10-9.2, prevents the donee from then exercising the power thereafter.

Under the terms of the trust instrument, if Steven fails to exercise his power of appointment, Anna and Frank (along with the children of Steven's first marriage) take the remainder, i.e., the property which is the subject of Steven's power of appointment. Therefore, Harriet, Anna and Frank argue that at a minimum Steven's agreement should be construed as a release of his power of appointment, and that Anna and Frank should be permitted to take as on default of appointment.

There is respectable authority — by no means unanimous authority, and none binding on this Court — to the effect that a promise to appoint a given sum to persons who would take in default of appointment should, *to that extent*, be deemed a release of the power of appointment. See Restatement of Property §336 (1940); Simes & Smith, The Law of Future Interests §1016 (1956).[6]

This argument has the appeal that it seems to be consistent with the exception that the release statute (EPTL 10-5.3(b)) carves out of EPTL 10-5.3(a); and is also consistent with the intentions and reasonable expectation of the parties at the time they entered into the agreement to appoint, here in the separation agreement; and that therefore perhaps in these circumstances the difference between what the parties agreed to and a release of the power of appointment is merely one of form. Whatever may be the possible validity or applicability of this argument to other circumstances and situations, I think it is inapplicable to this situation because:

(a) It is clear that the parties did not intend a release of the power of appointment. Cf. Matter of Haskell, 59 Misc. 2d 797, 300 N.Y.S.2d 711 (N.Y. Co. 1969). Indeed, the agreement — unlike a release of a power of appointment — expressly contemplates that something will be done by the donee of the power in the future, and that that something will be an exercise of the power of appointment. Thus, the agreement, in the very language said to be a release of the power of appointment, says (Par. 10): "the Husband *shall* make . . . a will in which he *shall exercise* his testamentary power of appointment. . . ." (emphasis added).

(b) Nor is the substantial effect of the promised exercise of the power the same as would follow from release of, or failure to exercise, the power.

(i) Under the separation agreement, the power is to be exercised so that the entire appointive property shall be for the benefit of Anna and Frank; under the trust instrument, on default of exercise of the power, the property goes to all of Steven's children (Anna, Frank and two children of Steven's first marriage). Thus the agreement provides for appointment of a greater principal to Anna and Frank than they would get in default of appointment.

(ii) Under the trust instrument, on default of exercise of the power, the property goes to the four children absolutely and in fee. The separation agreement provides that Steven shall create a *trust*, with *income* payable to *Harriet as trustee*, for the support of Anna and Frank until they both reach the age of 21, at which time the principal shall be paid to them or the survivor; and if both fail to attain the age of 21, then the principal shall revert to Steven's estate. Thus, Anna and Frank's interest in the principal would be a defeasible interest if they

---

6. In 1977, two years after this case, the legislature amended EPTL §10-5(3)(b) to provide that a release was valid "except that where the donor designated persons or a class to take in default of the donee's exercise of the power, a release with respect to the appointive property must serve to benefit all those so designated as provided by the donor." — Eds.

did not live to be 21; and indeed at Steven's death they were both still under 21 so that their interest was defeasible.

(iii) Finally, under the separation agreement, as just noted, if Anna and Frank failed to qualify to take the principal, either because they both died before Steven or before reaching the age of twenty-one, then the principal would go to Steven's estate. Under the trust instrument, on the other hand, on default of appointment and an inability of Anna and Frank to take, Steven's share of the principal would not go to Steven's estate, but to his other children, if living, and if not, to the settlor's next of kin.

In these circumstances, I think it is too strained and tortuous to construe the separation agreement provision as the equivalent of a release of the power of appointment. If this is a release then the exception of EPTL 10-5.3(b) has swallowed and destroyed the principal rule of EPTL 10-5.3(a). . . .

Accordingly, I hold that the separation agreement is not the equivalent of a total or partial release of the power of appointment.

(4) Anna and Frank also seek restitution out of the trust fund of the value given by them in exchange for Steven's unfulfilled promise. EPTL 10-5.3(a) provides that although the contract to make an appointment cannot be the basis for an action for specific performance or damages, "the promisee can obtain restitution of the value given by him for the promise unless the donee has exercised the power pursuant to contract."

Anna and Frank's remedy is limited, however, to the claim for restitution that they have (and apparently have asserted) against Steven's estate. They may not seek restitution out of the trust fund, even if their allegation that the estate lacks sufficient assets to meet this claim were factually supported, because the trust fund was not the property of Steven, except to the extent of his life estate, so as to be subject to the equitable remedy of restitution, but was the property of the donor of the power of appointment until it vested in someone else. Farmers' Loan & Trust Co. v. Mortimer, 219 N.Y. 290, 295, 114 N.E. 389, 390 (1916); see Matter of Rosenthal, 283 App. Div. 316, 319, 127 N.Y.S.2d 778, 780 (1st Dept. 1954); see also EPTL §§10-7.1 and 10-7.4.

(5) Finally, Edith moves for summary judgment that she is entitled to receive Steven's share of the trust fund on the ground that Steven exercised his testamentary power in her favor in his will of March 20, 1964, in the provision quoted at the beginning of this decision.

Since there are no factual questions raised as to Steven's exercise of his testamentary power of appointment in Edith's favor in that will provision, and since each of the other defendants' conflicting claims to the share of trust principal has been dismissed, Edith's motion for summary judgment is granted.

(6) Accordingly, on the motions for summary judgment I direct judgment declaring that defendant Edith Fisch Werner is entitled to the one-half share of Steven L. Werner in the principal of the Abraham L. Werner trust; to the extent that the counterclaims and cross-claims asserted by Harriet, Anna and Frank seek relief other than a declaratory judgment, they are dismissed.

QUESTION

Steven Ludwig Werner was a lawyer and, at the time of his death, a professor of labor relations at Cornell. If Steven had known, when he agreed to the divorce settlement, that the contract to appoint the trust fund was unenforceable, was his conduct unethical? If you think so, what would be the remedy?

SECTION D.   EXERCISE OF A POWER OF APPOINTMENT

1.   *Exercise by Residuary Clause in Donee's Will*

Beals v. State Street Bank & Trust Co.
Supreme Judicial Court of Massachusetts, 1975
367 Mass. 318, 326 N.E.2d 896

Wilkins, J.   The trustees under the will of Arthur Hunnewell filed this petition for instructions, seeking a determination of the proper distribution to be made of a portion of the trust created under the residuary clause of his will. A judge of the Probate Court reserved decision and reported the case to the Appeals Court on the pleadings and a stipulation of facts. We transferred the case here.

Arthur Hunnewell died, a resident of Wellesley,[7] in 1904, leaving his wife and four daughters. His will placed the residue of his property in a trust, the income of which was to be paid to his wife during her life. At the death of his wife the trust was to be divided in portions, one for each then surviving daughter and one for the then surviving issue of any deceased daughter. Mrs. Hunnewell died in 1930. One of the four daughters predeceased her mother, leaving no issue. The

_____

7. The town of Wellesley, and the college, are named after Isabella Welles Hunnewell, Arthur's mother. — Eds.

trust was divided, therefore, in three portions at the death of Mrs. Hunnewell. The will directed that the income of each portion held for a surviving daughter should be paid to her during her life and on her death the principal of such portion should "be paid and disposed of as she may direct and appoint by her last Will and Testament duly probated." In default of appointment, the will directed that a daughter's share should be distributed to "the persons who would be entitled to such estate under the laws then governing the distribution of intestate estates."

This petition concerns the distribution of the trust portion held for the testator's daughter Isabella H. Hunnewell, later Isabella H. Dexter (Isabella). Following the death of her mother, Isabella requested the trustees to exercise their discretionary power to make principal payments by transferring substantially all of her trust share "to the Dexter family office in Boston, there to be managed in the first instance by her husband, Mr. Gordon Dexter." This request was granted, and cash and securities were transferred to her account at the Dexter office. The Hunnewell trustees, however, retained in Isabella's share a relatively small cash balance, an undivided one-third interest in a mortgage and undivided one-third interest in various parcels of real estate in the Commonwealth, which Isabella did not want in kind and which the trustees could not sell at a reasonable price at the time. Thereafter, the trustees received payments on the mortgage and proceeds from occasional sales of portions of the real estate. From her one-third share of these receipts, the trustees made further distributions to her of $1,900 in 1937, $22,000 in 1952, and $5,000 in 1953.

In February, 1944, Isabella, who was then a resident of New York, executed and caused to be filed in the Registry of Probate for Norfolk County an instrument which partially released her general power of appointment under the will of her father. See G.L. c. 204, §§27-36, inserted by St. 1943, c. 152. Isabella released her power of appointment "to the extent that such power empowers me to appoint to any one other than one or more of the . . . descendants me surviving of Arthur Hunnewell."

On December 14, 1968, Isabella, who survived her husband, died without issue, still a resident of New York, leaving a will dated May 21, 1965.[8] Her share in the trust under her father's will then consisted

---

8. N.Y. Times, Sept. 28, 1894, at 5:

HARRIMAN — HUNNEWELL

BOSTON, Mass., Sept. 27. — The beautiful country seat of Mr. and Mrs. Arthur Hunnewell, at Wellesley, was a scene of joy and festivity yesterday, when their daughter, Miss Isabella, was married to Herbert M. Harriman of New-York. The ceremony was performed by the Rev. Leighton Parks, pastor of the Emanuel Church. There were no bridesmaids. The groom's brother, Joseph, was best man.

The ushers were Lawrence Kip of New-York, Belmont Tiffany of New-York, Edgar Scott of Philadelphia, Columbus Baldwin of New-York, Gordon Dexter, and

of an interest in a contract to sell real estate, cash, notes and a certificate of deposit, and was valued at approximately $88,000. Isabella did not expressly exercise her power of appointment under her father's will. The residuary clause of her will provided in effect for the distribution of all "the rest, residue and remainder of my property" to the issue per stirpes of her sister Margaret Blake, who had predeceased Isabella.[9] The Blake issue would take one-half of Isabella's trust share, as takers in default of appointment, in all events. If, however, Isabella's will should be treated as effectively exercising her power of appointment under her father's will, the Blake issue would take the entire trust share, and the executors of the will of Isabella's sister Jane (who survived Isabella and has since died) would not receive that one-half of the trust share which would go to Jane in default of appointment.

In support of their argument that Isabella's will did not exercise the power of appointment under her father's will, the executors of Jane's estate contend that (1) Massachusetts substantive law governs all questions relating to the power of appointment, including the interpretation of Isabella's will; (2) the power should be treated as a special power of appointment because of its partial release by Isabella; and (3) because Isabella's will neither expresses nor implies any intention to exercise the power, the applicable rule of construction in this

---

W. S. Patten. Of the bridegroom's kinsfolk there were present: His mother, Mr. and Mrs. Border Harriman, and Mr. and Mrs. Oliver Harriman.

The wedding breakfast was spread beneath the grand old trees which dot the lawn before the mansion. At the expiration of a short wedding trip Mr. and Mrs. Harriman will reside in New-York.

Twelve years later, Isabella Hunnewell and Herbert Harriman were divorced.

N.Y. Times, Dec. 16, 1968, at 47:

MRS. GORDON DEXTER

Mrs. Isabella Hunnewell Dexter, widow of Gordon Dexter, a Boston businessman, clubman and yachtsman, died Saturday in her home at 680 Madison Avenue. Her age was 97.

Mrs. Dexter's previous marriages, to Herbert M. Harriman and J. Searlo Barclay, ended in divorce.

— Eds.

9. The significant portion of the residuary clause reads as follows:

All the rest, residue and remainder of my property of whatever kind and wherever situated (including any property not effectively disposed of by the preceding provisions of this my will and all property over which I have or may have the power of appointment under or by virtue of the last will and testament dated November 27, 1933 and codicils thereto dated January 7, 1935 and January 8, 1935 of my husband, the late Gordon Dexter) . . . I give, devise, bequeath and appoint in equal shares to such of my said nephew George Baty Blake and my said nieces Margaret Cabot and Julia O. Beals as shall survive me and the issue who shall survive me of any of my said nephew or nieces who may predecease me, such issue to take per stirpes.

Commonwealth is that a general residuary clause does not exercise a special power of appointment. The Blake issue, in support of their argument that the power was exercised, contend that (1) Isabella's will manifests an intention to exercise the power and that no rule of construction need be applied; (2) the law of New York should govern the question whether Isabella's will exercised the power and, if it does, by statute New York has adopted a rule that a special power of appointment is exercised by a testamentary disposition of all of the donee's property; and (3) if Massachusetts law does apply, and the will is silent on the subject of the exercise of the power, the principles underlying our rule of construction that a residuary clause exercises a general power of appointment are applicable in these circumstances.

1. We turn first to a consideration of the question whether Isabella's will should be construed according to the law of this Commonwealth or the law of New York.[10] There are strong, logical reasons for turning to the law of the donee's domicil at the time of death to determine whether a donee's will has exercised a testamentary power of appointment over movables. See Restatement 2d: Conflict of Laws, §275, Comment c (1971); Scott, Trusts, §642, p.4065 (3d ed. 1967); Scoles, Goodrich's Conflict of Laws, §§175-177, p.346 (4th ed. 1964). Most courts in this country which have considered the question, however, interpret the donee's will under the law governing the administration of the trust, which is usually the law of the donor's domicil. . . . This has long been the rule in Massachusetts. . . . Fiduciary Trust Co. v. First Natl. Bank, 344 Mass. 1, 2, 181 N.E.2d 6 (1962) (inter vivos trust).[11]

If the question were before us now for the first time, we might well adopt a choice of law rule which would turn to the substantive law of the donee's domicil, for the purpose of determining whether the donee's will exercised a power of appointment. However, in a field where much depends on certainty and consistency as to the applicable

10. The applicable rules of construction where a donee's intention is not clear from his will differ between the two States. In the absence of a requirement by the donor that the donee refer to the power in order to exercise it, New York provides by statute that a residuary clause in a will exercises not only a general power of appointment but also a special power of appointment, unless the will expressly or by necessary implication shows the contrary. 17B McKinney's Consol. Laws of N.Y. Anno., E.P.T.L., c. 17-b, §10-6.1 (1967). See Matter of Hopkins, 46 Misc. 2d 273, 276, 259 N.Y.S.2d 565 (1964). " 'Necessary implication' " exists only where the will permits no other construction. Matter of Deane, 4 N.Y.2d 326, 330, 175 N.Y.S.2d 21, 151 N.E.2d 184 (1958). In Massachusetts, unless the donor has provided that the donee of the power can exercise it only by explicit reference to the power, a general residuary clause in a will exercises a general power of appointment unless there is a clear indication of a contrary intent. . . . However, in Fiduciary Trust Co. v. First Natl. Bank, 344 Mass. 1, 6-10, 181 N.E.2d 6 (1962), we held that a general residuary clause did not exercise a special testamentary power of appointment in the circumstances of that case.

11. Of course, the law of the donee's domicile would be applied if the donor expressed such an intention. . . .

rules of law, we think that we should adhere to our well established rule. Thus, in interpreting the will of a donee to determine whether a power of appointment was exercised, we apply the substantive law of the jurisdiction whose law governs the administration of the trust.

2. Considering the arguments of the parties, we conclude that there is no indication in Isabella's will of an intention to exercise or not to exercise the power of appointment given to her under her father's will. A detailed analysis of the various competing contentions would not add to our jurisprudence.[12] In the absence of an intention disclosed by her will construed in light of circumstances known to her when she executed it, we must adopt some Massachusetts rule of construction to resolve the issue before us. The question is what rule of construction. We are unaware of any decided case which, in this context, has dealt with a testamentary general power, reduced to a special power by action of the donee.

3. We conclude that the residuary clause of Isabella's will should be presumed to have exercised the power of appointment. We reach this result by a consideration of the reasons underlying the canons of construction applicable to general and special testamentary powers of appointment. Considered in this way, we believe that a presumption of exercise is more appropriate in the circumstances of this case than a presumption of nonexercise.

When this court first decided not to extend to a special power of appointment the rule of construction that a general residuary clause executes a general testamentary power (unless a contrary intent is shown by the will), we noted significant distinctions between a general power and a special power. Fiduciary Trust Co. v. First Natl. Bank, 344 Mass. at 6-10, 181 N.E.2d 6. A general power was said to be a close approximation to a property interest, a "virtually unlimited power of disposition," while a special power of appointment lacked this quality. We observed that a layman having a general testamentary power over property might not be expected to distinguish between the appointive property and that which he owns outright, and thus "he can reasonably be presumed to regard this appointive property as his own." On the other hand, the donee of a special power would not reasonably regard such appointive property as his own: "[h]e would more likely consider himself to be, as the donor of the power intended, merely the person chosen by the donor to decide who of the possible ap-

12. Isabella's residuary clause disposed of her "property." Because the trustees had agreed to distribute her trust portion to her and had largely done so and because, in a sense, she had exercised dominion over the trust assets by executing the partial release, a reasonable argument might be made that she regarded the assets in her portion of the trust as her "property." However, a conclusion that she intended by implication to include assets over which she had a special power of appointment within the word "property" is not justifiable because her residuary clause refers expressly to other property over which she had a special power of appointment under the will of her husband.

pointees should share in the property (if the power is exclusive), and the respective shares of the appointees."

Considering the power of appointment given to Isabella and her treatment of that power during her life, the rationale for the canon of construction applicable to general powers of appointment should be applied in this case. This power was a general testamentary power at its inception. During her life, as a result of her request, Isabella had the use and enjoyment of the major portion of the property initially placed in her trust share. Prior use and enjoyment of the appointive property is a factor properly considered as weighing in favor of the exercise of a power of appointment by a will. Fiduciary Trust Co. v. First Natl. Bank, supra, at 10, 181 N.E.2d 6. Isabella voluntarily limited the power by selecting the possible appointees. In thus relinquishing the right to add the trust assets to her estate, she was treating the property as her own. Moreover, the gift under her residuary clause was consistent with the terms of the reduced power which she retained. In these circumstances, the partial release of a general power does not obviate the application of that rule of construction which presumes that a general residuary clause exercises a general power of appointment.

4. A decree shall be entered determining that Isabella H. Dexter did exercise the power of appointment, partially released by an instrument dated February 25, 1944, given to her by art. Fourth of the will of Arthur Hunnewell and directing that the trustees under the will of Arthur Hunnewell pay over the portion of the trust held under art. Fourth of his will for the benefit of Isabella H. Dexter, as follows: one-third each to George Baty Blake and Julia O. Beals; and one-sixth each to Margaret B. Elwell and to the estate of George B. Cabot. The parties shall be allowed their costs and counsel fees in the discretion of the probate court.

So ordered.

NOTES

1. In White v. United States, 680 F.2d 1156 (7th Cir. 1982), the court held that the law of the donee's domicile governs issues concerning the donee's intention to exercise a power of appointment by will. The court said: "We recognize the special need for certainty and consistency in laws affecting trusts [citing *Beals*], but fail to see how that end is promoted by perpetuation of a legal fiction that confuses lawyers and laymen alike."

2. Considerable disagreement exists over whether a residuary clause should presumptively exercise a general or special power of appointment. The large majority of jurisdictions takes the position that a residuary clause does *not* exercise a power of appointment held

by the testator. States adhering to the majority rule differ on whether the search for a contrary intent is limited to the face of the will or may be aided by extrinsic evidence. Restatement (Second) of Property, Donative Transfers §17.3 (1986), presumes that a residuary clause does not exercise a power because "the donee does not own the property subject to the power" but permits use of a wide variety of extrinsic evidence to show a contrary intent.

In a minority of jurisdictions, a residuary clause exercises a general power of appointment unless a contrary intent affirmatively appears. In a few jurisdictions — New York is the leading example — a residuary clause exercises a special power of appointment if the residuary devisees are objects of the power. See Will of Block, 157 Misc. 2d 716, 598 N.Y.S.2d 668 (1993).

At the time of the *Beals* case, Massachusetts adhered to the minority rule, but, in 1978, Massachusetts changed to the majority rule. See Mass. Gen. Laws Ann. ch. 191, §1(A)(4) (1998). A number of other states that formerly adhered to the minority rule have in the recent past enacted statutes adopting the majority rule.

The positions of the various states are analyzed in detail in Susan F. French, Exercise of Powers of Appointment: Should Intent to Exercise Be Inferred from a General Disposition of Property?, 1979 Duke L.J. 749.

3. The lawyer drafting an instrument creating a power should consider whether it is wise to avoid possible conflict of laws problems by specifying in the trust instrument that the law of a particular state governs any question presented in connection with a power of appointment. If the appointive asset is land, the law of the jurisdiction where the land is located governs. But if the appointive assets are personal property, the donor of the power may be able to select the law to govern the trust. If the power is created by an inter vivos trust, the donor may select the law of the domicile of the donor or the donee or of the state where the trust is administered. If the power is created by a testamentary trust, the states are split. Some states permit the donor's intention to control. See, e.g., the *Beals* case, supra, footnote 10. Other states apply the law of the donor's domicile to a testamentary trust and do not permit the donor's intention to control. See, e.g., N.Y. Est., Powers & Trusts Law §3-5.1(g) (1998), providing that a general testamentary power or a special power created by will is to be governed by the law of the donor's domicile.

Uniform Probate Code (1990)

§2-608. EXERCISE OF POWER OF APPOINTMENT

In the absence of a requirement that a power of appointment be exercised by a reference, or by an express or specific reference, to the power, a general residuary clause in a will, or a will making general disposition of all of the testator's property, expresses an intention to exercise a power of appointment held by the testator only if (i) the power is a general power and the creating instrument does not contain a gift if the power is not exercised or (ii) the testator's will manifests an intention to include the property subject to the power.

§2-704. POWER OF APPOINTMENT; MEANING OF SPECIFIC REFERENCE REQUIREMENT

If a governing instrument creating a power of appointment expressly requires that the power be exercised by a reference, an express reference, or a specific reference, to the power or its source, it is presumed that the donor's intention, in requiring that the donee exercise the power by making reference to the particular power or to the creating instrument, was to prevent an inadvertent exercise of the power.

NOTE AND PROBLEM

1. To prevent an unintentional exercise of a power of appointment, the donor may provide that the power can be exercised only by an instrument, executed after the date of the creating instrument, that refers specifically to the power. Courts have been rather strict in requiring a "specific reference" to the creating document. Thus, where a wife was given a power of appointment by her husband's will executed in 1982, and her will specifically exercised a power given her in a similar will executed by her husband in 1966, since revoked, the court held the wife had not exercised the power created by her husband's 1982 will. Estate of Hamilton, 190 A.D.2d 927, 593 N.Y.S.2d 372 (1993).

Blending clauses. Suppose that the donee's residuary clause gives all her property "and all property over which I have a power of appointment" to A. Does this exercise the power under a specific reference requirement?

The official comment to UPC §2-704 says that, under the section, the mere use of a blending clause as in the above example is ineffective to exercise the power because it does not make a specific reference. However, if it could be shown by extrinsic evidence that the donee intended to exercise the power by a blending clause, the power would be exercised.

2. *Lapse: Appointee dies before donee dies.* In the *Beals* case, the court held that the donee, Isabella, exercised her power in favor of the issue of her sister, Margaret Blake, who had predeceased Isabella.

Suppose that Isabella's will had been executed during Margaret's life-time, and Isabella had exercised the power by appointing to Margaret. If Margaret had predeceased Isabella, would Margaret's issue take the appointive property under the antilapse statute? See Thompson v. Pew, 214 Mass. 520, 102 N.E. 122 (1913); Susan F. French, Application of Antilapse Statutes to Appointments Made by Will, 53 Wash. L. Rev. 405, 421-428 (1978).

Suppose that Isabella had a special power to appoint among her nephews and nieces and that she exercised the power by appointing to the issue of a niece who had predeceased her. What result? See id. at 428-431. If Isabella could have appointed to the niece, with the issue of the niece taking the appointive property under the antilapse statute, why not permit Isabella to appoint directly to the issue? See Restatement (Second) of Property, supra, §18.6, providing that takers substituted by an antilapse statute are regarded as objects of the power.

Suppose that Isabella had a general testamentary power created by her husband's will and had appointed to her husband's nephew, who predeceased Isabella, leaving issue. Would the issue of the nephew take under the antilapse statute? See French, supra, at 417-421; Restatement (Second) of Property, supra, §18.6, Comment b.

2. Limitations on Exercise of a Special Power

In almost all jurisdictions, a donee of a *general* power of appointment can appoint outright or in further trust and can create new powers of appointment. Inasmuch as the donee of a general power could first appoint to himself or to his estate and then, by a second instrument or a second clause in his will, appoint in further trust, it makes no sense to forbid the donee to appoint in further trust when he uses only one piece of paper or one clause in his will. With respect to a *special* power of appointment, the donee's authority is more limited.

The donee of a special power may not be able to appoint in further trust unless the creating instrument expressly so permits. In some older cases, courts — influenced by the idea that the donee of a special power was a limited agent of the donor — read the donee's power narrowly. Without authorization, the donee could only select the persons among the designated class and determine the proportion each should take. These cases may still be viable in a few jurisdictions. See Loring v. Karri-Davies, 371 Mass. 346, 357 N.E.2d 11, 94 A.L.R.3d 884 (1976), changing the rule prospectively to allow donees of special powers created after the date of the opinion to appoint in further trust.

In addition to whether the donee of a special power can appoint in further trust, a question may arise about whether the donee can create a new power of appointment. For example, suppose *T* gives *A* a power to appoint among *A*'s issue. Can *A* exercise the power by creating in his daughter *B* a life estate plus a special power to appoint among *B*'s children (who are, of course, objects of the original power)? The answer clearly should be yes; since *A* could appoint outright to *B*, there is no persuasive reason for refusing to permit *A* to appoint to *B* something less than absolute ownership. Yet the older cases are divided on this point. Some of them hold that the creation of a new power is an impermissible delegation of the special power. See 5 American Law of Property §23.49 (1952).

Restatement (Second) of Property, Donative Transfers §19.4 (1986), takes the position that the donee of a special power can create a general power in an object of the special power or create a special power in any person to appoint to an object of the original special power. The latter situation includes an appointment in further trust, giving the trustee discretionary power to appoint to the objects.

A special power may be exclusive or nonexclusive. If it is exclusive, the donee can exclude entirely one or more objects of the power. The donee can appoint all the property to one member of the class of permissible appointees, excluding the rest. If the power is nonexclusive, the donee must appoint some amount to each permissible object. Thus, suppose that *T* bequeaths a fund in trust for *A* for life, remainder as *A* shall appoint by will among his children. *A* has three children, *B*, *C*, and *D*. If the power is exclusive, *A* can appoint all the property to *C*. If the power is nonexclusive, *A* must give some amount each to *B*, *C*, and *D* if *A* exercises the power. You must readily see the great difficulty with nonexclusive powers: How much must the donee give each member of the class? Can *A* appoint $1 each to *B* and *D* and the remainder of the fund to *C*? Apparently, in a few states, the amount cannot be too small because of the "illusory appointment" rule requiring that each permissible appointee receive a "substantial" sum; in most states the illusory appointment rule has been repudiated. See 5 American Law of Property, supra, §23.58.

Whether a power is exclusive or nonexclusive depends upon the intention of the donor as revealed by the creating instrument. A power to appoint to *"any one or more of A's issue* in such amount or amounts and for such estates and interests and upon such conditions and limitations as *A* shall designate" would create an exclusive power. If the creating instrument does not reveal the donor's intent, classification will turn upon the presumption adhered to in the jurisdiction. Restatement (Second) of Property, supra, §21.1, provides that, in the absence of a contrary intent, special powers of appointment are presumptively exclusive. Accord, Ferrell-French v. Ferrell, 691 So. 2d 500

(Fla. App. 1997). The problem, as well as the other possible limitations on the scope of the power mentioned above, can and should
be avoided by proper drafting.

PROBLEM

Appraise the following special power of appointment form: *O* creates a revocable trust to pay the income to *O* for life, then to *O*'s wife
for life, then to *O*'s daughter for life. The trust instrument continues:

> On the death of such daughter, the trustees shall pay the then-remaining
> principal and undistributed income to, or hold the same for the benefit
> of, such one or more of such daughter's issue living at her death or
> born thereafter and such charitable organizations as such daughter shall
> appoint by a will, executed after the death of the survivor of the settlor
> and the settlor's said wife, which refers specifically to this power. The
> exercise of this power by such daughter, however, shall not apply to the
> proceeds of any life insurance on the life of such daughter payable to
> this trust. Subject to the above restrictions in the exercise of this power
> of appointment, the settlor's said daughter may appoint outright or in
> trust; she may select the trustee or trustees if she appoints in trust; she
> may create new powers of appointment in a trustee or trustees or in
> any other appointee; she may, if she appoints in trust, establish such
> administrative powers for the trustee or trustees as she deems appropriate;
> she may create life interests or other limited interests in some of the
> appointees with future interests in favor of other appointees; she may
> impose lawful conditions on an appointment; she may appoint to one or
> more of the objects of this power to the exclusion of other objects and
> she may appoint different types of interests to different objects; she may
> impose lawful spendthrift provisions; and generally she may appoint by
> will in any manner; provided always, however, that no appointment shall
> benefit, either directly or indirectly, one who is not an object of this
> power, and that nothing herein shall be construed as authorizing such
> daughter to appoint to herself, her creditors, her estate, or creditors of
> her estate. [5 A. James Casner, Estate Planning §17.8 at 250 (5th ed.
> 1983).]

Would it be a good idea to include as objects of the power the
spouse of the donee and spouses of issue, including spouses of issue
who predecease the donee? The answer to this question is clearly Yes,
for transfer tax reasons if for no other. If the trust is a generation-
skipping trust, distributing principal to the daughter's children in
default of appointment, the donee can avoid the GST tax at her death
by appointing the trust assets to her spouse. The spouse then could
use up the spouse's estate tax exemption by passing the property to
the couple's issue. The spouse could also create a new generation-

skipping trust of up to $1 million, using the spouse's GST tax exemption, and passing the property to the couple's grandchildren tax-free. Sound tax planning requires that one spouse be able to use the tax exemptions of the other spouse, if the couple desires.

Suppose that the donee desires to appoint a sum to her brother or his children. Should the objects of the power be broadened to include issue of the settlor? Should the power be further broadened to enable the donee to appoint to any person or persons (and charitable organizations) other than the estate of the donee and the creditors of the donee or of the donee's estate? Cf. id. at 244.

Why are the life insurance proceeds excluded from the power of appointment? See infra page 1013.

3.   Fraud on a Special Power

An appointment in favor of a person who is not an object of the power is invalid. An appointment to an object for the purpose of circumventing the limitation on the power is a "fraud on the power" and is void to the extent it is motivated by such purpose. Thus: Elsa Milliken held a special testamentary power to appoint among her "kindred," and in default of appointment the property was to pass to Elsa's descendants or, if none, to the donor's heirs. Elsa, who had no issue, wanted to appoint $100,000 to her husband. She approached her cousin Paul Curtis and told him that she was going to leave him $150,000 and an additional $100,000, which she would like him to give to her husband. Paul said he would be happy to sign a paper to that effect. Elsa's attorney prepared a letter, directed to her and signed by Paul, which read: "I am informed that by your last will and testament you have given me and bequeathed to me the sum of Two Hundred and Fifty Thousand Dollars ($250,000). In the event that you should predecease me and I should receive the bequest before mentioned, I hereby promise and agree, in consideration of the said bequest, that I will pay to your husband, Foster Milliken, Jr., the sum of One Hundred Thousand Dollars ($100,000) out of the said bequest which you have given to me by your said will." Elsa died leaving a will appointing $250,000 to Paul. Is Paul entitled to $250,000, $150,000, or zero? See In re Carroll's Will, 274 N.Y. 288, 8 N.E.2d 864, 115 A.L.R. 923 (1937); Restatement (Second) of Property, Donative Transfers §20.2 (1986).

4.   Ineffective Exercise of a Power

When the donee intends to exercise a power of appointment, but the exercise is ineffective for some reason, it may be possible to carry out the donee's intent through the doctrines of allocation and of capture.

a.   Allocation of Assets

The doctrine of allocation (also known as marshaling) applies when *appointive assets* and *assets owned by the donee* are disposed of under a common dispositive instrument (usually the donee's will). Its purpose is to try to allocate these assets to different provisions under the donee's will to give effect to the donee's intent when the appointive assets cannot go where the donee intended. Typical cases applying allocation involve an ineffective appointment to a nonobject of a power or an appointment that violates the Rule against Perpetuities. It is important to realize that, where assets are allocated by a court, *the donee could have provided for the allocation in specific language and the court is merely doing what the donee would have done but for the ineptness of the donee's lawyer.*

The doctrine of allocation is: If the donee *blends* both the appointive property and the donee's own property in a common disposition, the blended property is allocated to the various interests in such a way as to increase the effectiveness of the disposition. Restatement (Second) of Property, Donative Transfers §§22.1, 22.2 (1986). Thus:

> *Case 6.* A holds a special testamentary power created by her father to appoint trust property among A's issue. The trust assets are worth $100,000. A also owns outright $350,000. A's will provides:
>
>> I give all my property, including any property over which I have a power of appointment, as follows:
>>
>> 1. I give $100,000 to my daughter-in-law, B, widow of my deceased son, S.
>> 2. I give all the rest to my daughter, D.
>
> Since B is not an object of the special power, the trust assets cannot be allocated to her. They will be allocated to D, and $100,000 of A's owned assets will be allocated to B.

If, in Case 6, A had owned assets of only $50,000, B would receive only $50,000 because the trust assets cannot be allocated to B. Hence, to satisfy completely the ineffective appointment, allocation requires that the donee have property of her own sufficient to substitute for the appointive property.

The blending requirement of the doctrine of allocation is met in Case 6 by the introductory clause of A's will. The blending requirement may also be met by a residuary clause disposing of both appointive property and owned property. Suppose that, in Case 6, there had been no introductory clause, and A had bequeathed the appointive property to B and her own property to D. Since A did not blend the property but specifically bequeathed the appointive property to *B*, the appointment would fail, and none of *A*'s owned assets would be allocated to *B*. See Restatement (Second) of Property, supra, §22.1, Comment g.

b. Capture

If the donee of a power makes an ineffective appointment, and the donee's intent cannot be given effect through allocation of assets, to whom does the appointive property pass? The general rule is that the property passes in default of appointment or, if there is no gift in default, to the donor's estate. To this rule is one important exception: the doctrine of capture, which captures the property for the donee's estate.

Capture occurs when the donee of a *general* power "manifests an intent to assume control of the appointive property for all purposes and not merely for the limited purpose of giving effect to the expressed appointment." Restatement (Second) of Property, supra, §23.2. The doctrine of capture rests upon the conception that inasmuch as the donee of a general power could appoint to her estate, the appointive property will pass to her estate if she would prefer that in case of an ineffective appointment. Ineffective appointments raising the issue of whether capture applies usually involve lapse of an appointment to a dead appointee, or a violation of the Rule against Perpetuities, or failure of the donee to comply with some prescribed formality in exercising the power.

The intent of the donee to assume control of the appointive property for all purposes is most commonly manifested by provisions in the donee's will that *blend* the owned property of the donee with the appointive property. As with the doctrine of allocation, the requisite blending can occur in a residuary clause disposing of both the appointive property and the donee's own assets or in an introductory clause stating that the donee intends the appointive property to be treated as her own property. Thus:

Case 7. A is donee of a general power. *A*'s will provides:

> I give all my property and any property over which I have a power of appointment as follows:
>
> 1. $10,000 to my friend *B* [who predeceases *A*, and no antilapse statute applies].
> 2. $15,000 in trust for my dog Trixie [which violates the Rule against Perpetuities].
> 3. All the rest to *C*.

A has captured the appointive property by blending it with her own.
C takes everything, including the appointive property.

Capture applies only to general powers and only when the at-
tempted exercise of the general power is ineffective or incomplete.
See Thomas L. Jones, Consequences of an Ineffective Appointment —
Capture, 18 Ala. L. Rev. 229 (1966); Melanie B. Leslie, The Case
Against Applying the Relation-Back Doctrine to the Exercise of Gen-
eral Powers of Appointment, 14 Cardozo L. Rev. 219 (1992).

SECTION E.   FAILURE TO EXERCISE A POWER OF APPOINTMENT

If the donee of a *general* power fails to exercise it, the appointive
property passes in default of appointment. If there is no gift in default
of appointment, the property reverts to the donor's estate. If the
donee of a *special* power fails to exercise it, and there is no gift in
default of appointment, the appointive property may — if the objects
are a defined limited class — pass to the objects of the power.

Loring v. Marshall
Supreme Judicial Court of Massachusetts, 1985
396 Mass. 166, 484 N.E.2d 1315

WILKINS, J.   This complaint, here on a reservation and report by a
single justice of this court, seeks instructions as to the disposition of
the remainder of a trust created under the will of Marian Hovey. In
Massachusetts Inst. of Technology v. Loring, 327 Mass. 553, 99 N.E.2d
854 (1951), this court held that the President and Fellows of Harvard
College, the Boston Museum of Fine Arts, and Massachusetts Institute
of Technology (the charities) would not be entitled to the remainder
of the trust on its termination. The court, however, did not decide,
as we now must, what ultimate disposition should be made of the
trust principal.

Marian Hovey died in 1898, survived by a brother, Henry S. Hovey,
a sister, Fanny H. Morse, and two nephews, John Torrey Morse, Third,
and Cabot Jackson Morse. By her will, Marian Hovey left the residue
of her estate in trust, the income payable in equal shares to her
brother and sister during their lives. Upon her brother's death in
1900, his share of the income passed to her sister, and, upon her

sister's death in 1922, the income was paid in equal shares to her two nephews. John Torrey Morse, Third, died in 1928, unmarried and without issue. His share of the income then passed to his brother, Cabot Jackson Morse, who remained the sole income beneficiary until his death in 1946.

At that point, the death of the last surviving income beneficiary, Marian Hovey's will provided for the treatment of the trust assets in the following language:

> At the death of the last survivor of my said brother and sister and my two said nephews, or at my death, if none of them be then living, the trustees shall divide the trust fund in their hands into two equal parts, and shall transfer and pay over one of such parts to the use of the wife and issue of each of my said nephews as he may by will have appointed; provided, that if his wife was living at my death he shall appoint to her no larger interest in the property possessed by me than a right to the income during her life, and if she was living at the death of my father, he shall appoint to her no larger interest in the property over which I have a power of disposition under the will of my father than a right to the income during her life; and the same limitations shall apply to the appointment of income as aforesaid. If either of my said nephews shall leave no such appointees then living, the whole of the trust fund shall be paid to the appointees of his said brother as aforesaid. If neither of my said nephews leave such appointees then living the whole trust fund shall be paid over and transferred in equal shares to the Boston Museum of Fine Arts, the Massachusetts Institute of Technology, and the President and Fellows of Harvard College for the benefit of the Medical School; provided, that if the said Medical School shall not then admit women to instruction on an equal footing with men, the said President and Fellows shall not receive any part of the trust property, but it shall be divided equally between the Boston Museum of Fine Arts and the Massachusetts Institute of Technology.[13]

The will thus gave Cabot Jackson Morse, the surviving nephew, a special power to appoint the trust principal to his "wife and issue" with the limitation that only income could be appointed to a widow who was living at Marian Hovey's death.[14] Cabot Jackson Morse was survived by his wife, Anna Braden Morse, who was living at Marian Hovey's death, and by his only child, Cabot Jackson Morse, Jr., a child of an earlier marriage, who died in 1948, two years after his father.

13. The parties have stipulated that at the relevant time the Harvard Medical School admitted women to instruction on an equal footing with men.

14. We are concerned here only with "property possessed" by the testatrix at her death and not property over which she had "a power of disposition under the will of [her] father." That property was given outright to his widow under the residuary clause of the will of Cabot Jackson Morse.

Cabot Jackson Morse left a will which contained the following provisions:

> *Second:* I give to my son, Cabot Jackson Morse, Jr., the sum of one dollar ($1.00), as he is otherwise amply provided for.
>
> *Third:* The power of appointment which I have under the wills of my aunt, Marian Hovey, and my uncle, Henry S. Hovey, both late of Gloucester, Massachusetts, I exercise as follows: I appoint to my wife, Anna Braden Morse, the right to the income during her lifetime of all of the property to which my power of appointment applies under the will of Marian Hovey, and I appoint to my wife the right during her widowhood to the income to which I would be entitled under the will of Henry S. Hovey if I were living.
>
> *Fourth:* All the rest, residue and remainder of my estate, wherever situated, real or personal, in trust or otherwise, I leave outright and in fee simple to my wife, Anna Braden Morse.

In Welch v. Morse, 323 Mass. 233, 81 N.E.2d 361 (1948), we held that the appointment of a life interest to Anna Braden Morse was valid, notwithstanding Cabot Jackson Morse's failure fully to exercise the power by appointing the trust principal. Consequently, the trust income following Cabot Jackson Morse's death was paid to Anna Braden Morse until her death in 1983, when the principal became distributable. The trustees thereupon brought this complaint for instructions.

The complaint alleges that the trustees

> are uncertain as to who is entitled to the remainder of the Marian Hovey Trust now that the trust is distributable and specifically whether the trust principal should be paid in any one of the following manners: (a) to the estate of Cabot Jackson Morse, Jr. as the only permissible appointee of the remainder of the trust living at the death of Cabot Jackson Morse; (b) in equal shares to the estates of Cabot Jackson Morse, Jr. and Anna Braden Morse as the only permissible appointees living at the death of Cabot Jackson Morse; (c) to the estate of Anna Braden Morse as the only actual appointee living at the death of Cabot Jackson Morse; (d) to the intestate takers of Marian Hovey's estate on the basis that Marian Hovey failed to make a complete disposition of her property by her will; (e) to Massachusetts Institute of Technology, Museum of Fine Arts and the President and Fellows of Harvard College in equal shares as remaindermen of the trust; or (f) some other disposition.

Before us each named potential taker claims to be entitled to trust principal.

In our 1951 opinion, Massachusetts Inst. of Technology v. Loring, 327 Mass. at 555-556, 99 N.E.2d 854, we explained why in the circumstances the charities had no interest in the trust:

The rights of the petitioning charities as remaindermen depend upon the proposition that Cabot J. Morse, Senior, did not leave an "appointee" although he appointed his wife Anna Braden Morse to receive the income during her life. The time when, if at all, the "whole trust fund" was to be paid over and transferred to the petitioning charities is the time of the death of Cabot J. Morse, Senior. At that time the whole trust fund could not be paid over and transferred to the petitioning charities, because Anna Braden Morse still retained the income for her life. We think that the phrase no "such appointees then living" is not the equivalent of an express gift in default of appointment, a phrase used by the testatrix in the preceding paragraph.

In Frye v. Loring, 330 Mass. 389, 393, 113 N.E.2d 595 (1953), the court reiterated that the charities had no interest in the trust fund.

It is apparent that Marian Hovey knew how to refer to a disposition in default of appointment from her use of the terms elsewhere in her will. She did not use those words in describing the potential gift to the charities. A fair reading of the will's crucial language may rightly be that the charities were not to take the principal unless no class member who could receive principal was then living (i.e., if no possible appointee of principal was living at the death of the surviving donee). Regardless of how the words "no such appointees then living" are construed, the express circumstances under which the charities were to take did not occur. The question is what disposition should be made of the principal in the absence of any explicit direction in the will.

Although in its 1951 opinion this court disavowed making a determination of the "ultimate destination of the trust fund," the opinion cited the Restatement of Property §367(2) (1940), and 1 A. Scott, Trusts §27.1 (1st ed. 1939) to the effect that, when a special power of appointment is not exercised and absent specific language indicating an express gift in default of appointment, the property not appointed goes in equal shares to the members of the class to whom the property could have been appointed. For more recent authority, see 5 American Law of Property §23.63, at 645 (A. J. Casner ed. 1952 & Supp. 1962) ("The fact that the donee has failed to apportion the property within the class should not defeat the donor's intent to benefit the class"); Restatement (Second) of Property §24.2 (Tent. Draft No. 7, 1984).

Applying this rule of law, we find no specific language in the will which indicates a gift in default of appointment in the event Cabot Jackson Morse should fail to appoint the principal. The charities argue that the will's reference to them suggests that in default of appointment Marian Hovey intended them to take. On the other hand, in Welch v. Morse, 323 Mass. at 238, 81 N.E.2d 361, we commented that Marian Hovey's "will discloses an intent to keep her property in the family." The interests Marian Hovey gave to her sister and brother were life interests, as were the interests given to her nephews. The share of any nephew who died unmarried and without issue, as did one, was added to the share of the other nephew. Each nephew was limited to exercising his power of appointment only in favor of his issue and his widow.[15] We think the apparent intent to keep the assets within the family is sufficiently strong to overcome any claim that Marian Hovey's will "expressly" or "in specific language" provides for a gift to the charities in default of appointment.[16] . . .

[The charities argued that the principle of res judicata was not applicable because the attorney general, the supervisor of public charities, was not a party to Massachusetts Inst. of Technology v. Loring, 327 Mass. 553, 99 N.E.2d 854 (1951). The court rejected this argument and held that "the public interest in protecting the charities' rights was fully accommodated by the Justices of this court in its prior decision."]

What we have said disposes of the claim that the trust principal should pass to Marian Hovey's heirs as intestate property, a result generally disfavored in the interpretation of testamentary dispositions. . . . The claim of the executors of the estate of Anna Braden Morse that her estate should take as the class, or at least as a member of the class, must fail because Marian Hovey's will specifically limits such a widow's potential stake to a life interest.

A judgment shall be entered instructing the trustees under the will of Marian Hovey to distribute the trust principal to the executors of the estate of Cabot Jackson Morse, Jr. The allowance of counsel fees, costs, and expenses from the principal of the trust is to be in the discretion of the single justice.

So ordered.

PROBLEM AND NOTE

1. The theory of the court in Loring v. Marshall was that there was an implied gift in default of appointment to the potential ap-

---

15. The gift to any widow was to be a life interest if she were living at Marian Hovey's death.
16. The nominal distribution made to his son in the donee's will provides no proper guide to the resolution of the issues in this case. We are concerned here with the intention of Marian Hovey, the donor of the special power of appointment. The intentions of the donee of the power of appointment are irrelevant in constructing the donor's intent. Similarly, those who rely on language in Frye v. Loring, 330 Mass. 389, 113 N.E.2d 595 (1953), as instructive in resolving questions in this case miss the point that Cabot Jackson Morse's intention with regard to his exercise of the power of appointment is irrelevant in determining his aunt's intention concerning the consequences of his partial failure to exercise that power.

pointees. This theory is adopted by Restatement (Second) of Property, Donative Transfers §24.2 (1986), referred to in the court's opinion.

Another way of solving the problem in the case is to say that Cabot Jackson Morse had an *imperative* special power of appointment. A special power is imperative when the creating instrument manifests an intent that the permissible appointees be benefited even if the donee fails to exercise the power. If a special power is imperative, the donee must exercise it or the court will divide the assets equally among the potential appointees. The term *imperative power* is used in Cal. Prob. Code §613 (1998) and N.Y. Est., Powers & Trusts Law §10-3.4 (1998).

In most cases it is not likely to make any difference whether a court adopts an implied gift in default theory or an imperative power theory. The same result is ordinarily reached under both because both are based on the inferred intent of the donor. But in a few situations, the theory followed may make a difference. Consider Bridgewater v. Turner, 161 Tenn. 111, 29 S.W.2d 659 (1930). The testator's will provided:

> I bequeath to Eliza V. Seay during her life that portion of the old home tract and household furniture etc., which lies between the Trousdale Ferry turnpike road and the creek of Round Lick and Jennings Fork, and, at her death I desire it to go to one of my nephews and I leave it with her to decide which one it shall be. . . . It is my desire that the above described tract shall remain in the hands of the family as long as possible, for here sleeps my wife, my father and mother.

At the testator's death, he had four nephews, W. S., John C., W. R., and Richard. Richard died before the life tenant, Eliza, leaving as his heirs two children, Elizabeth and Carr. Eliza died without exercising her power of appointment. Who owns the old home tract? Cf. Waterman v. New York Life Insurance & Trust Co., 237 N.Y. 293, 142 N.E. 668 (1923). If Elizabeth and Carr now share in ownership, could Eliza have appointed the old home tract to Elizabeth?

2 In 1982 Evelyn Anderson executed a will that exercised a testamentary power of appointment over a trust created by her deceased husband. In 1993, Evelyn executed a second will that expressly revoked all prior wills and that inadvertently failed to exercise the power of appointment. Extrinsic evidence showed that if the power of appointment were not exercised, Evelyn's estate plan would not be carried out. The court held that the doctrine of dependent relative revocation could be used to probate the 1993 will and the portion of the 1982 will exercising the power of appointment. Estate of Anderson, 56 Cal. App. 4th 235, 65 Cal. Rptr. 2d 307 (1997).

10

CONSTRUCTION OF TRUSTS: FUTURE INTERESTS

SECTION A. INTRODUCTION

Today, future interests ordinarily arise in the context of trust settlements. Whenever a life estate is given, a future interest is also created: Someone is going to take the property upon termination of the life estate. Hence, the attorney drafting trusts must be familiar with the types of future interests that can be employed and with constructional and other problems attendant to their use.

The basic conceptual idea underlying the law of future interests is that future interests are thought of as "things."[1] In your course in property you were introduced to the reification of abstractions, particularly the fee simple. Now, when you think of a fee simple, your mind's eye undoubtedly sees it as a thing, and you probably speak of a fee simple as a *bundle* of rights. Indeed, once you have been introduced to property law, it is hard not to think of a fee simple in any way but as a thing: The owner may transfer *it*, creditors may seize *it*, *it* passes on death, and so forth. Future interests are reified in the same manner.

---

1. Compare the White King speaking to Alice about the two Messengers:

> ". . . And I haven't sent the two Messengers, either. They're both gone to the town. Just look along the road and tell me if you see either of them."
> "I see nobody on the road," said Alice.
> "I only wish *I* had such eyes," the King remarked in a fretful tone. "To be able to see Nobody! And at that distance too! Why, it's as much as *I* can do to see real people, by this light!"

Lewis Carroll, Through the Looking-Glass, ch. 7.

So now we take a look at the law of future interests, for they are the stuff of which the dispositive provisions of trusts are made. We seek to help you gain an understanding of how future interests can be created, precisely tailored to the settlor's intent with respect to future events. You must be able to identify, so that you can avoid, intent-defeating technical rules of future interests law still with us, as well as commonly encountered examples of ambiguous language.

It is written in Psalms 39:6: "Surely every man walketh in a vain shew: . . . he heapeth up riches and knoweth not who shall gather them." When you are admitted to the bar, let not these words of David be said of your clients.

SECTION B.   CLASSIFICATION OF FUTURE INTERESTS

1.   *Types of Future Interests*

Future interests recognized by our legal system are:

1. Interests in the transferor known as:
    a. Reversion
    b. Possibility of reverter
    c. Right of entry (also known as power of termination)
2. Interests in a transferee known as:
    a. Vested remainder
    b. Contingent remainder
    c. Executory interest

These interests are called *future interests* because the person who holds one of them is not entitled to present possession or enjoyment of the property but may or will become entitled to possession in the future. All future interests in property must be placed in one of the above categories.

Future interests are presently existing interests. A person who has a future interest has present rights and liabilities. Take this case: *O* conveys "to *A* for life, then to *B*." *B* has a remainder, which *B* can sell or give away. *B*'s creditors can reach it. *B* can enjoin *A* from committing waste or doing other acts that impair the value of *B*'s right to future possession. If *B* dies before *A*, the value of *B*'s remainder is subject to federal estate taxation. But *B* does not have perhaps the most important right in the bundle — the right to present possession — and it is because of the absence of this right that we call *B*'s interest "future."

Any estate that may be created in possession, such as a fee simple or a life estate, may be created as a future interest. Hence, *O* may convey "to *A* for life, then to *B* for life, then to *C*." *B* has a remainder for life, and *C* has a remainder in fee simple. By saying that *C* has a remainder in fee simple, we mean that when *C*'s remainder becomes possessory it will be a fee simple.

2.   Future Interests in the Transferor

a.   Reversion

There are three types of future interests that may be retained by the transferor: reversion, possibility of reverter, and right of entry for condition broken. By far the most important of these is the reversion. "A reversion is," in the words of Professor Lewis Simes, "the interest remaining in the grantor, or in the successor in interest of a testator, who transfers a vested estate of a lesser quantum than that of the vested estate which he has." 1 American Law of Property §4.16 (1952). A reversion is never created; it is a retained interest that always arises by operation of law because the transferor has conveyed away a lesser estate than the transferor had. If a reversion is retained in an inter vivos conveyance, it is always retained by the grantor. If a reversion is retained by a will, it is retained in the testator's heirs who are substituted by law for the dead transferor.

A reversion cannot be created in a transferee. If by deed or will a future interest is created in a transferee, the future interest must be given one of the labels that we give to future interests in transferees: It is either a remainder or an executory interest.

PROBLEM

T's will devises Blackacre to *A* for life, and the residue of *T*'s property to *B*. What interest does *B* have in Blackacre?

Reversions are thought of as part of the transferor's old estate: what the transferor retained when he conveyed away less than he had. Hence, all reversions are vested interests. The fact that all reversions are vested does not mean, however, that all reversions will become possessory. A reversion following a contingent remainder, for instance, may not become possessory. Thus:

> *Case 1.* O conveys property in trust "for A for life, then to A's children who survive A." A's children have a contingent remainder. O has a *vested reversion*, which will be divested if A leaves surviving children. (*Warning:* Do not call O's interest a "contingent reversion" or a "possibility of reversion" as there are no such interests known to law. If you use the latter term, you may end up confusing a reversion with a possibility of reverter, an entirely different interest. Call the interest by its correct name.)

Case 1 illustrates that the concept of a future interest *vested in interest* — so important in future interests law — has nothing to do with whether the future interest will necessarily become possessory. The reversion in Case 1, vested in interest, may not become possessory. Future interests are deemed vested or not by arbitrary rules of the common law, not by the certainty or uncertainty of future possession.

b. Possibility of Reverter; Right of Entry

A *possibility of reverter* is the future interest that remains in the grantor who conveys a fee simple determinable. For example, O conveys "to School Board so long as used for a school." The School Board has a fee simple determinable; O has a possibility of reverter, which becomes possessory automatically upon expiration of the determinable fee.

A *right of entry* for condition broken is the future interest that is retained by the grantor who conveys a fee simple subject to a condition subsequent. For example, O conveys "to School Board, but if the land ceases to be used for school purposes, O has a right to reenter." The School Board has a fee simple subject to condition subsequent; O has a right of entry, which O has the option to exercise or not.

Possibilities of reverter and rights of entry are almost never encountered in a trust. They are typically retained to control the use of land and are covered in the basic course in Property.

3. *Future Interests in Transferees*

There are three types of future interests in transferees: vested remainders, contingent remainders, and executory interests.

a. Remainders

A remainder is a future interest in a transferee that will become possessory, if at all, upon the expiration of all prior interests simultaneously created. A remainderman waits patiently until the preceding estates expire and then, if the remainder is not contingent, the remainderman is entitled to possession. To be a remainder, it must only be possible, not necessarily certain, that the future interest will become possessory upon the termination of the preceding estates. Thus:

> *Case 2.* O conveys a fund in trust "for A for life, then to B." B has a remainder which will certainly become possessory upon the expiration of A's life estate. Because it is certain to become possessory, we call it an *indefeasibly vested remainder*. If B dies during A's life, B's remainder, like B's other property, passes under B's will or by intestacy to B's heirs. If B leaves neither a will nor heirs, the remainder escheats to the state, and the state is entitled to the property upon A's death.
>
> *Case 3.* O conveys a fund in trust "for A for life, then to B if B survives A." B has a remainder, for it is possible (but not certain) that B will take the property upon A's death. If B is then alive, B will take, and if B is then dead, the property will revert to O. B has a *contingent remainder*.

Remainders are either vested or contingent. A remainder is vested if (1) it is given to a presently ascertained person and (2) it is not subject to a condition precedent (other than the termination of the preceding estates). A remainder is contingent if (1) it is not given to a presently ascertained person or (2) it is subject to a condition precedent. In Case 3, B's remainder is contingent because it is subject to the condition precedent of surviving A.

A remainder given to a class of persons, some but not all of whom are ascertained, and not subject to a condition precedent, is vested in the present members of the class subject to partial divestment by additional persons coming into the class. Thus:

> *Case 4.* O conveys a fund in trust "for A for life, then to A's children." If A has no children at the time of the conveyance, the remainder is contingent because the takers are unascertained. On the other hand, if A has a child (let's call her B), B has a *vested remainder subject to partial divestment* (sometimes called a *vested remainder subject to open* and admit more class members). B's share will be diminished if A has any more children. The amount of B's share will depend on how many children, if any, are subsequently born to A. If A has another child born (let's call her C), B is partially divested, that is, divested of C's share. The class gift will remain subject to partial divestment (or open) until A's death.

A class gift is not vested subject to partial divestment if it is subject to a condition precedent. In Case 4, if the conveyance had been "to A for life, then to *A*'s children who survive *A*," the remainder would be contingent even though *A* had one or more children alive.

Where a remainder is given to a class of persons described as "the heirs of *A* (a living person)," the takers are not ascertained until *A*'s death. A living person has no heirs; heirs cannot be ascertained until the person dies.

PROBLEMS

1. *O* conveys a fund in trust "for *A* for life, and on *A*'s death to *A*'s children in equal shares." At the time of the conveyance *A* has two children, *B* and *C*. Two years later, *D* is born to *A*. A year after that *B* dies intestate, then *A* dies. To whom should the trust assets be distributed? See In re DiBiasio, 705 A.2d 972 (R.I. 1997); Coleman v. Coleman, 256 Va. 64, 500 S.E.2d 507 (1998).

2. In 1995 *O* conveys property in trust "for *A* for life, and on *A*'s death to the heirs of *B*." At the time of the conveyance *A* and *B* are both alive and *B* has two children, *C* and *D*. If *B* were to die intestate immediately after the conveyance, *C* and *D* would be *B*'s heirs. In 1996, *D* dies, leaving a minor son, *E*, and a will devising all his property to his wife, *W*. In 1998, *B* dies, leaving a will that devises *B*'s entire estate to the American Red Cross. *A* dies in 2000; *A* is survived by *C*, *E*, and *W*. To whom should the trust assets be distributed? What would be the result if *B* had died before *D*?

Now we must speak of the difference between a *remainder vested subject to divestment* and a *contingent remainder*. This is a fundamental distinction in the law of future interests and the subject of a good bit of litigation construing ambiguous instruments. A remainder vested subject to divestment is a remainder given to an ascertained person, with a proviso that the remainder will be divested if a *condition subsequent* happens. It is not subject to a condition precedent. Whether a remainder is contingent or vested subject to divestment depends solely upon the language of the instrument. And, with few exceptions, it depends upon *the sequence of words in the instrument.* Interests are classified in sequence as they are written in the instrument. If a condition is incorporated into the gift of the remainder, if it comes — so to speak — between the commas setting apart the remainder, the condition is a condition precedent. But if the remainder is given, and then words of divestment are added, the condition is subsequent. This distinction is best seen by examples.

Case 5. O conveys a fund in trust "for A for life, then to B if B survives A, and if B does not survive A, to C." B has a contingent remainder because the words "if B survives A" are incorporated into B's gift; they come between the commas. (Of course, if the commas were not there, you would have to decide where the court would mentally insert the commas. The essential idea to grasp is that the words "if B survives A" are part of the gift to B.) C has an alternative contingent remainder.

Case 6. O conveys a fund in trust "for A for life, then to B, but if B does not survive A, to C." B has a vested remainder subject to divestment by C's executory interest. Between the commas setting off B's gift there are no words of condition. There is a condition subsequent to B's gift introducing the divesting gift over to C.

As Cases 5 and 6 illustrate, you must look very carefully at the exact language used and classify the interests in sequence. O's intent may be identical in those two cases, but it has been expressed in different ways, resulting in different interests being created. As you can see, much turns on careful drafting.

Let us now return briefly to the subject of reversions, so that you may see how reversions interrelate with vested remainders and contingent remainders. To determine when a transferor has a reversion, you can save yourself much trouble if you will memorize this simple Rule of Reversions: *O, owner of a fee simple, will not have a reversion in fee simple if O transfers a possessory fee simple or a vested remainder in fee simple; in all other cases where O transfers a present possessory interest, O will have a reversion in fee simple.* Hence, whenever O transfers a life estate, not followed by a vested remainder in fee, O has a reversion. If O transfers a life estate followed by 100 contingent remainders in fee, but no vested remainder in fee, O retains a reversion.

You will see why this rule operates if you consider a reversion a shorthand way of saying that when a vested estate of the same duration is not transferred, "there is either a certainty or a possibility that the right to possession will return to the grantor." Thus when the owner of a fee simple carves out a lesser estate and does not add a vested remainder in fee simple, there is a possibility that the property will be his again.

PROBLEMS

1. O conveys Blackacre "to A for life, then to B if B survives A, and if B does not survive A, to C." Does O have a reversion? Yes. But how is it possible for Blackacre to return to O? At common law, the answer was easy: A life estate could terminate prior to the death of the life tenant if the life tenant were convicted of a felony or committed a tortious feoffment. But in the United States forfeiture on these grounds has been abolished. Can you think of any way for Blackacre

to return to *O?* See Jesse Dukeminier, Perpetuities: The Measuring Lives, 85 Colum. L. Rev. 1648, 1690-1692 (1985).

2.   *O* conveys property in trust "for *A* for life, then to *B*, but if *B* dies before *A* without issue surviving *B*, then to *C* at *A*'s death." Does *O* have a reversion? Suppose that *B* dies leaving a surviving child, *D;* *B*'s will devises all her property to her husband, *H*. Then *D* dies. Then *A* dies. To whom should the trust property be distributed?

3.   *O* conveys Blackacre in trust "for *A* for life, then to *B* or her heirs." Subsequently *B* dies, devising her property to *C. B*'s heir is *D*. Upon *A*'s death, who owns Blackacre? See Rowett v. McFarland, 394 N.W.2d 298 (S.D. 1986).

b.   Executory Interests

An executory interest differs from a remainder in that it is a *divesting* interest. A remainder never divests a preceding estate prior to its expiration; that is the job of an executory interest. An executory interest that may divest another transferee if a specified event happens is called a *shifting* executory interest because, if the event happens, the executory interest will shift the property from one transferee to another transferee. In Case 6 above, *C* has a shifting executory interest. An executory interest that may divest the transferor in the future if a specified event happens is called a *springing* executory interest because, if the event happens, the property will spring out from the transferor to the transferee. An old example of a springing executory interest at early common law was a marriage arrangement whereby the father of the bride would convey land "to my daughter *A* when she marries *B*." Springing executory interests are rare today.

Executory interests are future interests that would have been enforced by the court of chancery, but not by the law courts, before the Statute of Uses in 1536. The Statute of Uses converted these interests, previously valid only in equity, into legal interests. For a more extended treatment of the history of executory interests, see Jesse Dukeminier & James E. Krier, Property 266-275 (4th ed. 1998).

Executory interests are almost always created in one of two basic forms. These are illustrated by Cases 7 and 8, below.

Case 7. Executory interest divesting a possessory fee simple upon an uncertain event. O conveys Blackacre "to *A*, but if *A* dies at any time without issue surviving her, to *B*." *A* has a fee simple subject to divestment by *B*'s shifting executory interest. *B*'s executory interest is subject to a condition precedent (*A*'s death without surviving issue) and is not certain to become possessory.

Another example of an executory interest divesting a possessory fee simple is a conveyance by *O* "to *B* if *B* returns from Rome." This gives *B* a springing executory interest divesting the transferor, *O*, rather than a transferee.

More common than Case 7 is Case 8:

> *Case 8. Executory interest divesting a vested remainder. O* conveys a fund in trust "for *A* for life, and on *A*'s death to *B*, but if *B* is not then living, to *C*." *B* has a vested remainder in fee simple subject to divestment by *C*'s shifting executory interest. *C*'s executory interest is subject to a condition precedent (*B* dying before *A* dies) and is not certain to become possessory.

The executory interests in Cases 7 and 8 are analogous to contingent remainders. They are not called contingent remainders because they are divesting interests. However, in almost all situations today, executory interests are treated the same as contingent remainders.

PROBLEMS AND NOTE

1.   (a) *O* conveys a fund in trust "for *A* for life, then to *A*'s children, but if at *A*'s death *A* is not survived by any children, then to *B*." At the time the trust is created, *A* has no children. What interests are created?

(b) Consider the same facts as in Problem 1(a). A few years later, two children, *C* and *D*, are born to *A*. *C* dies, devising his property to his wife, *W*. *A* dies. To whom should the trust assets be distributed?

2.   *O* conveys a fund in trust "for *A* for life, then to such of *A*'s children as survive *A*, but if none of *A*'s children survive *A*, then to *B*." At the time the trust is created, *A* has two children, *C* and *D*. Then *C* dies, devising his property to his wife, *W*. *A* dies. To whom should the trust assets be distributed?

3.   *T* devises Blackacre to *A* for life, then to *A*'s children who survive her. The residuary clause of *T*'s will devises to *B* "all the rest and residue of my property, including any of the foregoing gifts in this will which for any reason fail to take effect." What is the state of the title to Blackacre? See Wythe Holt, The Testator Who Gave Away Less Than All He or She Had: Perversions in the Law of Future Interests, 32 Ala. L. Rev. 69 (1980).

4.   *Remainders in default of appointment.* Exercise of a power of appointment is viewed as operating as a condition subsequent on the remainder in default of appointment. If the donee exercises the power, the remainderman is deprived of his interest. Thus, suppose that *T* devises property in trust "for *A* for life, then to such persons as *A* by will appoints, and in default of appointment to *A*'s children." Because the power is treated as a condition subsequent, this devise is read as if it were "for *A* for life, then to *A*'s children, but if *A* other-

wise appoints by will, to such appointees." Assume *A* has one child, *B*. *B* has a vested remainder subject to partial divestment by the birth of other children and also subject to complete divestment by *A*'s exercise of the power of appointment. If *A* has no children, the remainder is contingent because the takers are not ascertained.

SECTION C.   CONSTRUCTION OF TRUST INSTRUMENTS

You will realize, of course, that the title of this section is a play on words. A court construes an instrument in order to construct an estate plan. In the process, rules of construction are developed. These rules of construction must be heeded by lawyers in constructing their clients' estate plans.

The cases and materials in this section have two purposes. One is to teach the techniques and rules courts have developed in construing instruments. The second, and more important, is to explore the ambiguities lying hidden in common provisions in wills and trusts. The second is more important because only by training in spotting ambiguities, and in foreseeing everything that may happen to the people involved, can you develop the ability to draft an air-tight instrument.

For an analytical examination of construction problems along a lineal time progression, see Raymond C. O'Brien, Analytical Principle: A Guide for Lapse, Survivorship, Death Without Issue, and the Rule, 10 Geo. Mason U. L. Rev. 383 (1988).

1.   *Preference for Vested Interests*

The common law had a strong preference for construing ambiguous instruments as creating a vested rather than a contingent remainder. As Sir Edward Coke said, "the law always delights in vesting of estates, and contingencies are odious in the law, and are the causes of troubles, and vesting and settling of estates, the cause of repose and certainty." Roberts v. Roberts, 2 Bulst. 123, 131, 80 Eng. Rep. 1002, 1009 (K.B. 1613). This preference arose in feudal England at a time when contingent interests were barely recognized as interests, and it continued to modern times because of the allegedly desirable consequences of a vested construction. These consequences were:

(1)   A vested remainder was not subject to the doctrine of *destructibility of contingent remainders* that defeated the grantor's intent. This

doctrine provided that a *legal* contingent remainder in *land* was destroyed if it did not vest at or before the termination of the preceding freehold estate. This doctrine is now obsolete. See Davies v. Radford, 433 N.W.2d 704 (Iowa 1988); Abo Petroleum Corp. v. Amstutz, 93 N.M. 332, 600 P.2d 278 (1979); Jesse Dukeminier, Contingent Remainders and Executory Interests: A Requiem for the Distinction, 43 Minn. L. Rev. 13, 31-41 (1958).

(2)   A vested remainder *accelerated* into possession upon termination of the life estate, solving vexing problems of possession and undisposed income (see below).

(3)   A vested remainder was *transferable inter vivos*, making land more alienable (see infra page 726).

(4)   A vested remainder was not subject to the *Rule against Perpetuities*, a rule that defeats the grantor's intent (see Chapter 11).

In addition to the different consequences at common law attendant upon a vested or contingent classification, a new problem has arisen in modern times. In many states, *upon divorce*, a court makes an equitable distribution of a couple's "property," including inherited property. Is, then, for example, a vested remainder or a contingent remainder in a trust created by the husband's mother the husband's property subject to equitable division? The courts appear to agree that an indefeasibly vested remainder is the husband's property, and can be valued in accordance with life expectancy tables (see infra page 728). On the other hand, a vested remainder subject to divestment if the husband does not survive the life tenant or a remainder contingent upon surviving the life tenant is not the husband's property for purposes of equitable distribution. If the divesting event or contingency is something other than surviving the life tenant, the courts appear to struggle with the vested-contingent dichotomy with varying results. See In re Marriage of Beadle, 268 P.2d 698 (Mont. 1998); King v. King, 1997 Conn. Super. Lexis 613 (1997).

If your client wants to set up a trust with a remainder in a child, you should draft a remainder contingent upon surviving to the time of possession if your client wishes to insulate the remainder from the claims of the child's spouse upon divorce.

a.   Acceleration into Possession

Under the common law, a vested remainder accelerates into possession whenever and however the preceding estate ends. A contingent remainder, on the other hand, does not accelerate because the remaindermen are not entitled to possession until they are all ascertained and any condition precedent has occurred. Thus:

Case 9. *T* devises property in trust for *W* for life, remainder to *T*'s children (who survive *W*). *W* disclaims the life estate. If the language in parentheses is not included in the instrument, the children of *T* have a vested remainder that accelerates into possession. If the language in parentheses is included, the children of *T* have a contingent remainder that will not accelerate into possession. What is then done with the income during *W*'s life?

When a life tenant disclaimed a life estate, the rule that contingent remainders do not accelerate did not always appear to carry out the testator's intent, who might, as in Case 9, have postponed the gift to his children merely to give his spouse life income. If the spouse rejected life income, the testator would not want the trust to continue. Accordingly, courts began to disregard the technical classification of the remainder and decide disclaimer cases on what the testator probably would have intended had he anticipated disclaimer. See Ohio National Bank of Columbus v. Adair, 54 Ohio St. 2d 26, 374 N.E.2d 415, 7 A.L.R.4th 1084 (1978). Because this approach meant that almost every case of disclaimer had to be litigated, legislatures passed disclaimer statutes, such as Uniform Probate Code §2-801, supra page 150. Under these statutes, the disclaimant is treated as having predeceased the testator, and remainders take effect or fail proceeding on this assumption. See Patricia G. Roberts, The Acceleration of Remainders: Manipulating the Identity of the Remaindermen, 42 S.C. L. Rev. 295 (1991).

In Re Estate of Gilbert
New York Surrogate's Court, New York County, 1992
156 Misc. 2d 379, 592 N.Y.S.2d 224

ROTH, S. The executor of the estate of Peter Gilbert asks the court to declare null and void a renunciation by Mr. Gilbert's son, Lester, of his interest in two wholly discretionary trusts under decedent's will.

Mr. Gilbert died on March 26, 1989, leaving an estate of over $40,000,000.[2] He was survived by his wife and four children. Under his will, testator, after making certain pre-residuary legacies, created an elective share trust for the life income benefit of his wife. The amount of decedent's generation-skipping transfer (GST) tax exemption was divided into four discretionary trusts, one for the primary benefit of each of his children. The residue of Mr. Gilbert's estate was similarly divided. Upon the death of the widow, the remainder of

---

2. Peter Gilbert, born in Austria, fled the Nazis with his family at age seven. Gilbert became a pioneer of cable television and the owner of the Colorado Rockies of the National Hockey League, now the New Jersey Devils. — Eds.

Surrogate Renee Roth

her trust is to be added in equal shares to the residuary trusts for decedent's children. The trusts are wholly discretionary. Decedent's son, Lester, is therefore a discretionary income beneficiary of two testamentary trusts, one of which will be augmented at the widow's death. Decedent's issue, including Lester's sisters, nieces and nephews as well as Lester's issue (should he have any), are also discretionary beneficiaries of both of Lester's trusts.

Lester, who has no issue, timely served on the executor a notice of renunciation of his "dispositive share in the estate of Peter Gilbert."

The executor, supported by the guardian ad litem for decedent's minor grandchildren, takes the position that Lester's renunciation should be declared invalid. First, he states that permitting the renunciation would violate the testator's intention to provide for Lester. Second, the executor argues that Lester possesses no current property interest and therefore has nothing to renounce. The executor maintains that Lester's renunciation is premature and may be made only if, and at such time as, the trustees exercise their discretion to distribute income or principal to him.

The executor explains decedent's intention as follows:

> Lester, who is approximately 32 years of age, . . . has left the religion of his birth and has for some time lived in Virginia with a small group of people who share a similar religious doctrine. Some months ago he phoned your petitioner and announced that he planned to renounce whatever bequest was left for him. When asked what he planned to do if he were ever taken seriously ill and needed expensive medical care, he responded "Jesus will provide for me."
>
> The fact that Lester had chosen to alienate himself from his family did not stop the decedent from loving his son or worrying about his future needs. . . . [T]he decedent wanted to know that funds would be available if the Trustees, acting in the manner that they thought the decedent would have acted had he then been living, should ever decide, for example, to pay a medical bill for Lester.

In effect, the executor argues that if the beneficiary of a wholly discretionary trust is permitted to renounce his or her interest, then no trust can ever be created to protect someone who is now disdainful of financial assistance but may in the future be in dire need, or simply have a change of heart.

However, under these circumstances, decedent's intention is not controlling. With respect to every renunciation, the intent to make a transfer is thwarted by the beneficiary who refuses to accept it. But clearly, "the law does not compel a man to accept an estate, either beneficial or in trust, against his will" (Burritt v. Silliman, 13 N.Y. 93, 96; see, also, Matter of Suter, 207 Misc. 1002).

The executor suggests in his memorandum that he might be forced "to inquire into the mental capacity of Lester, since there is no rational reason which explains Lester's conduct." However, the desire to renounce wealth is not necessarily irrational. Presumably, the executor would not argue that a nun who takes a vow of poverty is mentally incompetent. Here, the acceptance of a monetary benefit apparently conflicts with Lester's religious beliefs. It would not be appropriate for the court to determine the validity of those beliefs, even if requested to do so. Furthermore, even if Lester's renunciation were purely whimsical, this would not in itself be sufficient reason either to reject the renunciation (Matter of Suter, supra) or to find him incompetent. In any event, the question of Lester's mental capacity has not been raised. There is no allegation in the petition or in any affidavit that Lester is a person under disability. The court must therefore proceed on the assumption that Lester is competent to make an effective renunciation.

The executor's second argument is that Lester has no current property interest which he can renounce. Rather, the executor maintains that Lester must wait until the trustees exercise their discretion to distribute income or principal to him, at which time, the executor asserts, Lester can renounce the property subject to such exercise of discretion. There appears to be no decision in New York with respect to the renunciation of a discretionary interest.

Renunciations are governed by EPTL 2-1.11. Paragraph (b)(1) of such statute provides that "[a]ny beneficiary of a disposition may renounce all or part of his interest. . . ." EPTL 1-2.4 defines "disposition" as "a transfer of property by a person during his lifetime or by will." "Property" is defined in EPTL 1-2.15 as "anything that may be the subject of ownership. . . ." Therefore, under the statute, a renunciation may be made only with respect to a transfer of something which may be the subject of ownership. The statute, however, does not require that property be transferred to the beneficiary. Instead, the property may be transferred to a trustee for the benefit of a beneficiary (see, e.g., Matter of Chadbourne, 92 Misc. 2d 648, 401 N.Y.S.2d 139). Furthermore, the statute does not require that the beneficiary renounce the disposition itself; rather, he may renounce "all or part of his interest" in the disposition (EPTL 2-1.11[b][1]).

In this case, decedent by his will transferred property to trusts of which Lester is a beneficiary, albeit a discretionary beneficiary. Similarly, the subject of Lester's renunciation is his interest in the trusts, although that interest is discretionary. The renunciation, therefore, appears to satisfy the terms of the statute.

The executor, however, contends that Lester's interest in the trusts does not rise to the level contemplated by the statute. He argues that for a renunciation to be effective, the renounced interest must be in the nature of property. Claiming that Lester's interest is not property, the executor cites Hamilton v. Drogo (241 N.Y. 401), where the Court of Appeals held that a judgment creditor was not entitled to levy on the interest of one of the beneficiaries of a discretionary trust. Holding that the judgment creditor could attach the income if and when the trustee distributed it to the beneficiary, the court observed: "In the present case no income may ever become due to the judgment debtor. We may not interfere with the discretion which the testatrix has vested in the trustee any more than her son may do so. . . . But . . . if it is exercised in favor of the duke then . . . [a]t least for some appreciable time, however brief, the award must precede the delivery of the income he is to receive and during that time the lien of the execution attaches" (at 404).

Similarly, in Matter of Duncan (80 Misc. 2d 32), the court held that a beneficiary of a discretionary trust possesses no property reachable by creditors until distribution is made. The court observed that there was "no absolute right to receive income or principal from the trust and . . . therefore there [was] no property or rights to property belonging to the beneficiaries, specifically Thomas W. Doran, the subject of the levy. If, however, the trustee does at any time elect in his discretion to pay [the beneficiary] . . . the amount of said payment will be subject to the levy" (at 35-36).

But the cases relied upon by the executor are clearly distinguishable from the instant case in that they deal with the rights of creditors and not with those of beneficiaries. More closely analogous are those decisions which determine the rights of beneficiaries to compel distribution by trustees. Although in this case Lester's creditors cannot reach the trusts, Lester may nonetheless have the right to force the trustees to distribute income or principal to him under certain circumstances.

Although our courts cannot ordinarily interfere with the exercise of a trustee's discretion, they can ensure that such discretion is exercised fairly and honestly (Collister v. Fassitt, 163 N.Y. 281; see, also, Ireland v. Ireland, 84 N.Y. 321; Manning v. Sheehan, 75 Misc. 374). In the present case, the trustees' discretion is absolute and not limited by any standard. However, even in such a case, the trustees may be compelled to distribute funds to the beneficiary if they abuse their discretion in refusing to make distribution (see, e.g., Matter of Stillman, 107 Misc. 2d 102).

Thus, Lester may have the right to compel the trustees to distribute trust property to him under certain circumstances. Therefore, even if the court accepts the executor's interpretation of the statute, Lester arguably has a current interest which could be deemed "property" for the purpose of an effective renunciation. . . . [However, as] discussed earlier, a statutory renunciation need not relate to property. Instead, the statute merely requires the disclaimant to renounce his or her interest in a disposition. . . .

Lester's renunciation also applies to his remainder interest in the elective share trust, which is contingent upon his surviving the widow. As discussed above, any interest, whether or not contingent, is within the scope of the statute. Even if the executor's interpretation is correct and a renunciation must relate to an interest in property, a contingent remainder has historically been recognized as a property interest.

Finally, the guardian ad litem argues that if Lester's renunciation is allowed, the remainder interests in his trusts should not be accelerated. The remainder of Lester's trusts would be payable to his issue. As mentioned earlier, Lester has no issue. If the interests are accelerated, Lester's unborn issue would be cut off and decedent's living grandchildren would lose certain present interests in these trusts. It is noted that acceleration of the trust remainders would have no direct tax consequences and any indirect effects would be relatively minor.

The question is whether under EPTL 2-1.11(d) this court has any discretion to suspend acceleration. Such statute, in relevant part, provides that:

> Unless the creator of the disposition has otherwise provided, the filing of a renunciation, as provided in this section, has the same effect with respect to the renounced interest as though the renouncing person had predeceased the creator or the decedent . . . and shall have the effect of accelerating the possession and enjoyment of subsequent interests.

Thus, it appears that under the language of the statute, the remainder interests in Lester's trusts will be accelerated unless the decedent has "otherwise provided." There is no explicit "otherwise provision" in testator's will, but the guardian ad litem argues that the court should infer an "otherwise provision" from the general language of the will and the circumstances surrounding its execution. . . .

When EPTL 2-1.11 was enacted in 1977, the language regarding acceleration was added to resolve the dispute reflected in a number of conflicting decisions. Those cases looked to testator's intent as the appropriate guideline and determined acceleration on a case-by-case basis, with unpredictable results. It is clear the addition of this language was intended to provide uniformity (see, e.g., Memorandum in Support of Amended Bill, New York State Assembly, L. 1977, ch. 861, Governor's Bill Jacket). To engage in the type of analysis suggested by the guardian ad litem would mean a return to the approach rejected by the Legislature.

Based upon the foregoing, it is concluded that Lester's renunciation is valid as to any and all interests in his father's estate. Lester is thus to be treated as if he predeceased his father without issue.

NOTES

1. In In re Estate of Suter, 207 Misc. 1002, 142 N.Y.S.2d 353 (1955), the testator's son, a Yale senior, disclaimed a life estate in trust bequeathed him "for moral and political reasons." The court approved the disclaimer. Income was ordered paid to the holders of the next eventual estate for the son's life. A year or so later, the son changed his mind, alleging he was mentally ill when he disclaimed. With the consent of the other interested parties, the court revoked its prior decree and reinstituted the son as income beneficiary. In re Estate of Suter, 11 Misc. 2d 144, 172 N.Y.S.2d 100 (1958).

2. Under Uniform Probate Code §2-801 and similar uniform disclaimer acts, the donee of a contingent or defeasibly vested interest may wait until nine months after the interest becomes indefeasibly vested to disclaim. This permits the contingent remainderman to decide at the life tenant's death whether to accept the property or not. Thus:

> Case 10. *T* devises property in trust "for my daughter *A* for life, then to my granddaughter *B* (age 21) if *B* survives *A*, and if *B* does not survive *A*, to *B*'s issue." At *A*'s death, *B* can decide whether to disclaim and let the property then pass to *B*'s issue.

Caution: Federal tax law differs from state disclaimer laws. Under federal tax law, a disclaimer is treated as a gift by the disclaimant to the persons who take as a result of the disclaimer, *unless the disclaimer occurs within nine months after the interest is created* or nine months after the donee reaches 21, whichever is later. Internal Revenue Code §2518(b)(2). Thus, if, in Case 10, *B* does not disclaim within nine months after *T* dies, for federal tax purposes *B* is the owner of the remainder, and if *B* disclaims the remainder at *A*'s death, *B* makes a taxable gift to *B*'s issue of the value of the trust assets at *A*'s death.

3. *Disclaimers and the generation-skipping transfer tax.* The federal government imposes a generation-skipping transfer tax upon any transfer to a grandchild or other person two or more generations removed from the transferor. Internal Revenue Code §§2601-2663, infra page 1065. In Case 10, for example, an estate tax is payable at *T*'s death and a generation-skipping transfer tax is payable at *A*'s death, when possession of the property is transferred to *T*'s granddaughter. In Case 10, suppose that *A* disclaims her life estate at *T*'s death. The effect of the disclaimer is that a GST tax is payable at *T*'s death, when *B* (the settlor's grandchild) takes possession, rather than at *A*'s death. The GST tax is in addition to the estate tax levied on *T*'s estate.

This last point is sometimes difficult for students to understand because it looks, at first glance, like double taxation. But remember the tax policy: A transfer tax imposed on each living generation. Therefore, where a transfer is made to a grandchild, an estate tax is imposed on *T*'s transfer of his estate, and, because the first generation below *T* has been skipped over and an estate tax at the death of that generation avoided, a generation-skipping transfer tax is also imposed on the transfer to the second generation below *T*. Were this not so, a person could avoid estate taxes in a child's estate by transferring property directly to a grandchild. Congress has closed this loophole.

The tax effect of *A*'s disclaimer in Case 10 would be that a GST tax becomes payable earlier — at *T*'s death rather than at *A*'s death. You can see why, with the enactment of the generation-skipping transfer tax in 1986, disclaimers became decidedly less popular. For further discussion, see Joan B. Ellsworth, On Disclaimers: Let's Renounce I.R.C. Section 2518, 38 Vill. L. Rev. 693 (1993) (arguing that IRC §2518 should be repealed now that the GST tax has greatly reduced the tax incentives for using disclaimers).

b. Transferability and Taxation

At common law, vested remainders, including defeasibly vested ones, were transferable inter vivos. A contingent remainder or an executory interest, which in early law was thought of not as an interest at all but as a mere chance of ownership, was not transferable. There were a few exceptions to this rule of inalienability. In the United States, over forty states have by statute or judicial decision made contingent interests transferable. In the handful of states remaining, the common law position on alienability is apparently still maintained. See Goodwine State Bank v. Mullins, 253 Ill. App. 3d 980, 625 N.E.2d 1056 (1993) (following common law rule of inalienability of contingent remainder); 2A Richard R. Powell, Real Property ¶275[4] (rev. ed. 1998). Future interests in trust may be made inalienable by a spendthrift clause.

Reversions, remainders, and executory interests are descendible and devisable at death in the same manner as possessory interests. The future interest passes to the heirs or devisees of its owner. Thus:

> *Case 11.* O conveys property in trust "for A for life, then to B." B dies during A's lifetime. B's remainder passes to B's devisees if B leaves a will or to B's heirs if B dies intestate.

A future interest contingent upon surviving to the time of possession is not transferable at death. Thus, if in Case 11 O had conveyed a remainder "to B if B survives A," B could not transmit the remainder to another person if B died during A's lifetime.

The federal government subjects to estate taxation any transfer of a property interest. Internal Revenue Code §2033. A future interest, like a possessory estate, is an interest in property and is subject to federal estate taxation. If, in Case 11, B dies during A's lifetime, the value of B's remainder is subject to estate taxation because it is *transmissible* at death. ("Transmissible" is a term of lawyers' art meaning the interest passes at death by intestacy to the remainderman's heirs or by will to the remainderman's devisees.) Federal estate taxation turns upon whether a future interest is transmissible, not upon whether it is vested or contingent. If it is transmissible, it is subject to taxation.

PROBLEM AND NOTES

1.   *T*'s will devises property in trust "for A for life, then to B, and if B does not survive A to C." If B dies during A's lifetime, is the value of B's remainder includible in B's taxable gross estate under the federal estate tax? If C dies before A and B, is the value of C's future interest includible in C's taxable gross estate?

Caution: As pointed out above, a federal generation-skipping transfer tax is levied upon a transfer from a trust settlor to the settlor's grandchild (see supra page 726). The GST tax is levied at the highest rate of the estate tax, currently 55 percent. If B is T's child and C is B's child, a GST tax will be levied on the trust at A's death if B predeceases A. At that point in time, there will be a transfer from the settlor to the settlor's grandchild. Therefore, avoiding an estate tax at B's death at the cost of paying a GST tax at A's later death is not necessarily a good idea. We shall return later to the taxation of remainders, after taking up a couple of cases on whether a remainderman is required to survive to the time of possession. If you don't quite have a grasp on the estate tax and the GST tax, you will find it easier to understand them in the context of actual family trusts. See infra pages 1065-1069.

2. *Valuation of a future interest.* If a future interest is subject to estate taxation, the value of the future interest depends upon the life tenant's life expectancy and the market rate of interest. The federal government publishes life expectancy tables and valuation tables for future interests that must be used. See Internal Revenue Code §7520. For explanation of how future interests are mathematically valued, see Jesse Dukeminier & James E. Krier, Property 218-219 (4th ed. 1998).

When a future interest cannot be valued by resort to mortality tables, as where, for example, it may be destroyed by the trustee using principal to support the life tenant, the interest is valued with reference to all relevant facts, including the likelihood of the contingent events happening.

3. *Drafting advice.* You can give a remainderman the power to transfer his remainder at death without the remainder being subject to the estate tax. How is this done? Give the remainderman a remainder contingent upon surviving to the time of possession (thereby escaping the estate tax) *and a special power of appointment* (thereby giving the remainderman power to decide who takes the remainder). Property subject to a special power (unlike owned property) is not subject to estate taxation (see supra page 673). Here is an example:

> *Case 12. T* devises his residuary estate in trust "for *A* for life, then to *B* if *B* survives *A*, and if *B* does not survive *A*, then to *B*'s spouse or such one or more of *B*'s issue as *B* appoints by will." *B* has a contingent non-transmissible remainder and a special power of appointment. If *B* dies during *A*'s life, *B*'s remainder disappears, and is not taxable in *B*'s estate. In this event, the property passes on *A*'s death to persons to whom *B* appoints or, if *B* fails to appoint, to *T*'s heirs.

If *A* is the spouse of *T* and *B* is *T*'s child, and *B* dies before *A*, the special power of appointment in *B* also enables *B* to choose to pay an estate tax on the value of the remainder at *B*'s death rather than a GST tax on the value of the trust principal at *A*'s death, when the principal is distributed to *T*'s grandchildren, if the estate tax would be lower than the GST tax (see infra page 827). *Case 12* is an example of skilled estate planning.

c. Requiring Survival to Time of Possession

As a general rule, there is no requirement that a remainderman live to the time of possession. If the remainderman dies before the life tenant, the remainder passes to the remainderman's estate. Of course, the testator may expressly require survival, and in a few situations, hereafter noted, courts will imply a requirement of survival.

If a vested remainder subject to divestment is created, courts ordinarily read the divesting language strictly as written and do not expand it to cause divestment in events other than those stated.

First National Bank of Bar Harbor v. Anthony
Supreme Judicial Court of Maine, 1989
557 A.2d 957

ROBERTS, J.   The children of John M. Anthony, Deborah Alley and Christopher Anthony Perasco, appeal from a summary judgment of the Superior Court, Hancock County (Smith, J.), that denied their claim to a remainder interest in an inter vivos trust created by their now deceased grandfather, J. Franklin Anthony. The court determined that the gift to John M. Anthony, a child of the settlor, of the remainder interest lapsed as a result of John M. Anthony's death prior to the death of the settlor. Because we hold that the remainder interest of John M. Anthony was a present, vested interest at the time of the creation of the inter vivos trust, we vacate the judgment.

FACTS

On May 14, 1975, J. Franklin Anthony, of Bar Harbor, established a revocable inter vivos trust with the First National Bank of Bar Harbor. The income was payable to the settlor for life, then to his widow, Ethel L. Anthony, should she survive him. Upon the death of both J. Franklin and Ethel L. Anthony, the corpus would be divided "in equal shares to [the settlor's] children, John M. Anthony, Peter B. Anthony and Dencie S. Tripp [now Fenno] free and clear of any trust."

Ethel Anthony predeceased her husband on November 22, 1982. On September 9, 1983, John M. Anthony died unmarried, leaving three children: Deborah Alley, Christopher Anthony Perasco and Paul Anthony.

J. Franklin Anthony died on April 2, 1984. On April 10, 1984, his will was admitted to Probate by the Hancock County Probate Court. The will left two-thirds of his estate to Peter B. Anthony and one-third to Dencie S. Fenno; the heirs of John M. Anthony were expressly omitted from the will.

PROCEDURE

The First National Bank of Bar Harbor, in its capacity as trustee, filed a complaint in the Superior Court requesting construction of the

Anthony Trust. The children of John M. Anthony, grandchildren of the settlor, filed a motion for summary judgment. The grandchildren asserted that John M. Anthony's interest in the trust was vested, not contingent, at the time of its creation. John M.'s heirs, therefore, were entitled to his one-third interest in the trust.

The motion was opposed by Dencie S. Fenno and Peter B. Anthony, at that time arguing that the terms of the trust were ambiguous and that extrinsic evidence should be permitted to determine the intent of the settlor. Their memorandum was accompanied by two affidavits stating that affiant's understanding that the deceased settlor wished the children of John M. Anthony to receive nothing from the settlor's estate. In granting summary judgment against the movants, the court (1) declined to consider extrinsic evidence on the ground that the language of the trust was unambiguous, (2) determined that the gift of the remainder to named individuals "in equal shares" was a gift to the individuals and not to a class, (3) held that the gift to John M. Anthony lapsed because his interest did not vest until the death of the survivor of the settlor and his wife, and (4) declined to apply the anti-lapse statute, 18-A M.R.S.A. §2-605 (Supp. 1988), because the statute applies only to testamentary gifts. The court therefore directed the trustee to pay over the lapsed gift to John M. Anthony to the personal representative of the deceased settlor. This appeal followed.

Discussion

Before us all parties now agree that the terms of the trust are unambiguous and that a summary judgment is appropriate. Moreover, all parties agree that the gift of the remainder interest "in equal shares" to the named children of the settlor was a gift to the individuals and not to a class. As a result, we need address only the court's holding that the gift to John M. Anthony lapsed upon his death prior to the death of the settlor.

The parties rely almost exclusively on our prior cases dealing with testamentary dispositions. These cases are of little assistance on the issue before us. Because a will is not operative until the death of the testator, an interest in a testamentary trust cannot vest prior to that event. On the other hand, an inter vivos trust is operative from the date of its creation. We must determine the settlor's intent as expressed in the trust instrument by examining the settlor's overall plan of disposition.

We note the following: (1) the settlor explicitly retained the right to change his beneficiaries if he wanted to alter the trust's disposition; (2) the settlor imposed no restrictions on what his children could do with their respective shares; (3) aside from his power to revoke or amend the trust, the settlor specifically limited his own benefit to income during his lifetime and payment of certain expenses associated with his death; (4) the settlor made survival an explicit condition of any benefit to his wife, but did not include such language in the case of his children. The unexercised right to make a change in beneficiaries, the absence of any control over how the children might dispose of their shares, and the overall assignment of economic benefits lead us to conclude that this plan of disposition effectively eliminated any further interest of the settlor in the trust principal unless he affirmatively chose to intervene. His failure to change the plan coupled with the omission of a survival requirement in the case of the children's shares, suggests a disposition to a predeceased child's estate rather than a reversion to the settlor's estate. As a result of this construction of the instrument, it may be said that the children's interests were vested, subject to defeasance or divestment if the settlor chose to amend or revoke the trust or change his beneficiaries.

We next address the question whether the settlor's reservation of the power of amendment or revocation should alter our conclusion that the children's interests vested. Substantial case law from other jurisdictions persuades us that it should not. A leading case decided by the Ohio Supreme Court holds that an inter vivos trust reserving to the settlor the income for life plus the power to revoke, with a remainder over at the death of the settlor, creates a vested interest in the remainderman subject to defeasance by the exercise of the power of revocation. First National Bank v. Tenney, 165 Ohio St. 513, 138 N.E.2d 15 (1956).

Similarly, an Illinois appellate court, reversing the trial court, held that a delay in enjoyment of possession does not imply a requirement of survival by the remainderman before the remainder is vested. First Galesburg National Bank & Trust Co. v. Robinson, 149 Ill. App. 3d 584, 102 Ill. Dec. 894, 500 N.E.2d 995 (1986). The court concluded that the words "at the death of" do not refer to the time when the remainder vested, but rather to the time when the remainderman was entitled to possession. Id. 102 Ill. Dec. at 895, 500 N.E.2d at 996. The sons of the settlors, therefore, took a present right to the remainder upon execution of the trust instrument, although enjoyment was postponed until the termination of the life estates. Id. at 996-97.

Even when the settlor said "on [the settlor's] death the remainder shall vest," the inter vivos trust has been held to create a present interest subject to divestment by amendment or revocation. Randall v. Bank of America N.T. & S.A., 48 Cal. App. 2d 249, 119 P.2d 754 (1941). An Indiana court has stated that the language of Restatement (Second) of Trusts §112(f) that a person dying prior to the creation of a trust cannot be a beneficiary of that trust is inapplicable to persons living at the time of the creation of an inter vivos trust. Hinds v. McNair, 413 N.E.2d 586 (Ind. App. 1980). See Detroit Bank &

Trust Co. v. Grout, 95 Mich. App. 253, 289 N.W.2d 898 (1980); Matter of Estate of Vondermuhll, 156 N.J. Super. 531, 384 A.2d 185 (1978); In re Trust of Pew, 452 Pa. 509, 307 A.2d 273 (1973). Contra, In re Estate of Button, 79 Wash. 2d 849, 490 P.2d 731 (1971) (applying an anti-lapse statute) (criticized in Annotation, Anti-Lapse Statute as Applicable to Interest of Beneficiary under Inter Vivos Trust who Predeceases Life-Tenant Settlor, 47 A.L.R.3d 358 (1973)). See also Bogert, Trust and Trustees §182, at 394 (1979) ("[if] no requirement of survival is attached to the gift, the beneficiary may take a vested estate").

The trust instrument before us contains no requirement that the remainder beneficiaries survive the life tenants and we see no reason to imply a requirement of survival. Only the settlor's subsequent revocation or substitution would divest the remainder interest. Evidence presented by affidavit of the settlor's desire to revoke the contingent remainder and disinherit his son and son's heirs is simply not relevant. Although the settlor's intention is critical in interpreting the terms of a trust, that intention must be ascertained by analyzing the trust instrument. Mooney v. Northeast Bank & Trust Co., 377 A.2d 120, 122 (Me. 1977). Only when the instrument is ambiguous can a court consider extrinsic evidence. Id. at 122.

Because John M. Anthony's interest vested at the time of the creation of the trust, we do not consider whether Maine's anti-lapse statute, 18-A M.R.S.A. §2-605, could apply to an inter vivos trust.

Judgment vacated.

NOTE

The position of the court in *Anthony* is the orthodox one: a vested remainder in a trust passes to the estate of the remainderman at his death unless the instrument provides expressly that the remainder is divested by his death. An antilapse statute, by its terms, applies only to a devise by *will* where the devisee predeceases the *testator*. Inasmuch as a remainder in a trust may be transmissible at death to the remainderman's estate by the rules of future interests law, there is no need to bring the antilapse statute into the picture in order to pass the remainder on to the remainderman's children. Nonetheless, because a revocable trust is a will substitute, a couple of courts have confused the situation by holding that an antilapse statute applies to a transmissible remainder created in a revocable trust where the remainderman predeceased the settlor. See Dollar Savings & Trust Co. v. Turner, 39 Ohio St. 3d 182, 529 N.E.2d 1261 (1988) (reversed by Ohio Rev. Code Ann. §2107.01 (1998); In re Estate of Button, 79 Wash. 2d 849, 490 P.2d 731 (1971).

In the *Anthony* case, application of the rule that remainders not expressly conditioned on survivorship are transmissible at the remainderman's death and application of the anti-lapse statute would bring the same result. John's remainder would pass to John's children (his heirs) under either theory. But in the following cases the two theories would produce different results:

a. John is survived by a wife and children. Under the transmissible remainder theory, both wife and children share as John's heirs. Under an anti-lapse statute, only John's children take.

b. John leaves a will devising all his property to his wife. Under the transmissible remainder theory, the wife takes the remainder. Under an antilapse statute, only John's children take the remainder.

c. John is not survived by issue and devises his property to his wife (or a friend). Under the transmissible remainder theory, John's wife (or other devisee) takes the remainder. Under the antilapse statute, the result is unclear. There are no issue to substitute for John. Does this mean that the remainder then fails? If so, does applying the antilapse statute result in all remainders in revocable trusts being turned into remainders contingent upon surviving the settlor — just as devises are contingent upon surviving the testator?

As you can see, the transmissible remainder theory gives the remainderman considerably more control over the remainder at death than does an antilapse statute.

Security Trust Co. v. Irvine
Delaware Court of Chancery, 1953
33 Del. Ch. 375, 93 A.2d 528

BRAMHALL, V.C.   In this case this court is asked to determine two issues: (1) whether or not the residuary estate left to brothers and sisters of the testator vested as of the date of his death or at the time of the death of the last life tenant; (2) if it should be decided that the residuary estate vested as of the time of the death of the testator, do the life tenants take as members of the class of brothers and sisters receiving the residuary estate?

Plaintiff is trustee under the last will and testament of James Wilson, deceased, who died on July 29, 1918, leaving a last will and testament dated October 25, 1915. After providing for certain specific bequests, testator gave and devised all his "real and mixed estate" to the Security Trust Company, . . . [in trust for his] two sisters, Martha B. Wilson and Mary E. Wilson, during their joint lives and during the lifetime of the survivor of them. Testator further provided that in the event that his sister, Margaret W. Irvine, should be left a widow, she should share equally with the two sisters above named in the benefits of the trust so provided. As to the remainder, testator provided as follows:

> Upon the death of my two sisters, Martha B. Wilson and Mary E. Wilson, and the survivor of them, then it is my will that all of my real and mixed estate and any proceeds that may have arisen from the sale of any part thereof, together with any unexpended income there may be, shall be equally divided among my brothers and sisters, share and share alike, their heirs and assigns forever, the issue of any deceased brother or sister to take his or her parent's share.

Testator was survived by his five brothers and sisters: Samuel H. Wilson, Margaret W. Irvine, Martha B. Wilson, Mary E. Wilson, and Henry Wilson. At the time of the execution of the will the ages of the brothers and sisters ranged from 39 to 52 years. Martha B. Wilson and Mary E. Wilson, the two life tenants, died respectively on June 9, 1928, and August 18, 1951, unmarried and without issue, the trust therefore terminating on the latter date. The other devisees all predeceased Mary E. Wilson, the surviving life tenant. Samuel H. Wilson died on October 26, 1925, leaving to survive him three children, Frazer Wilson, Jeannette A. Wilson, and Samuel H. Wilson, Jr., and Grace Wilson Gearhart, daughter of a deceased son, Francis Paul Wilson. Samuel H. Wilson, Jr., died in 1924 [1934?], unmarried and without issue.

Samuel Irvine, one of the defendants, is the sole residuary legatee under the will of Margaret W. Irvine, deceased. Martha B. Wilson died testate on June 9, 1928, leaving her residuary estate to her two nieces, Margaret Gregg Wilson, now Margaret W. Hanby, and Mary Hope Wilson, each an undivided one-half interest therein.

Mary E. Wilson died testate on August 18, 1951, leaving her entire residuary estate to Margaret W. Hanby, after providing for the payment of her debts and a legacy to Mary Hope Wilson in the sum of $100.

The estate of Martha B. Wilson has been closed, the final account having been passed on February 9, 1935; the estate of Mary E. Wilson has also been closed, the final account in that estate having been passed on September 15, 1952.

I must first determine whether or not the remainder interest [created by] the testator became vested at the time of his death or at the time of the death of the last life tenant, Mary E. Wilson, on August 18, 1951. In order to resolve this question the intention of the testator at the time of the drafting of the will must first be ascertained. If it should be clear that testator intended this provision of the will to take effect at some future date, then the intention of the testator, so far as it may be legally carried out, will prevail. However, in reaching my

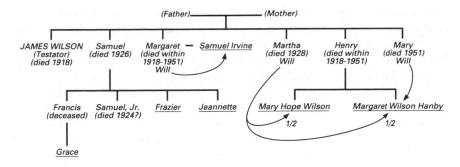

Survivors are underlined.

Do you see that the big fight is between Samuel's descendants and Henry's descendants, and that the latter end up with ⅗ of the trust property and the former with only ⅕?

conclusion, I must accept certain well recognized rules of construction.

The law favors the early vesting of devised estates and will presume that words of survivorship relate to the death of the testator, if fairly capable of that construction. In the absence of a clear and unambiguous indication of an intention to the contrary, the heirs will be determined as of the date of the death of the testator and not at some future date. When the language employed by the testator annexes futurity, clearly indicating his intention to limit his estate to take effect upon a dubious and uncertain event, the vesting is suspended until the time of the occurrence of the event. See Delaware Trust Company v. Delaware Trust Company, 33 Del. Ch. 135, 91 A.2d 44, and cases therein cited.

The assertion that it is indicated in the will that the testator intended the residuary estate to be vested as of the date of the death of the last life tenant is based upon the contentions: (1) the fact that testator left a life estate to two of his sisters and then gave the residuary estate to his brothers and sisters indicates that testator did not intend the two sisters to share in his residuary estate and therefore the residuary estate did not vest until the date of the death of the last life tenant; (2) the use of the words "upon the death of two sisters" and the provision in the will of testator that his estate "should be equally divided among my brothers and sisters" indicates an intention that testator intended a future vesting of his residuary estate.[3]

---

3. The second argument is often called the "divide-and-pay-over" rule. Where the trustee is directed, upon the life tenant's death, "to divide and pay over" the corpus among members of a class, and there is no language of gift to the class members other than the direction to divide and pay over, some courts have held that the class members must survive until the property is divided in order to share. Most jurisdictions find no convincing reasons for this rule and have repudiated it completely. See 5 American Law of Property §21.21 (1952). — Eds.

Whatever may be the law in other states it is well settled in this state that the fact that a life tenant is a member of a class, in the absence of any clear indication in the will to the contrary, does not prevent the life tenant from participating in the remainder of testator's estate as a part of the class. . . .

As to the use of the word "upon," it is equally clear under the decisions in this state and elsewhere, that this word and other words of this nature refer only to the time of payment and not to the substance of the devise. Cann v. Van Sant, 24 Del. Ch. 300, 11 A.2d 388; In re Nelson's Estate, 9 Del. Ch. 1, 74 A. 851. Other Delaware cases are to the same effect. In any event, the use of this word, and the provision for dividing its remainder, under the circumstances of this case would not alone be sufficient to overcome the presumption of immediate vesting.

It is contended on behalf of certain defendants that even though it should be determined that the gift to the brothers and sisters vested as of the date of the death of testator, the life tenants should be excluded from membership in the class of brothers and sisters. They base their contention upon the fact that testator in another item of his will gave them a life interest in his residuary estate.

In endeavoring to ascertain the intention of testator, it is uniformly held that such a provision is not of itself sufficient to prevent the life tenant from participating in the remainder as part of the class. See cases cited in 13 A.L.R. 620. It is not sufficient to show the absence of an intention to include the life tenants; there must be some indication of a clear and unambiguous nature to exclude them. Dillman v. Dillman, 409 Ill. 494, 499, 100 N.E.2d 567; Carver v. Wright, 119 Me. 185, 109 A. 896. I can find no incongruity in the mere fact that testator provided a life estate for his two sisters and later gave the remainder to his brothers and sisters, of which the two sisters were part of the class. They were unmarried. They were no longer young. It seems to be clear from the several provisions in the will of the testator that it was his purpose to provide for them. Such provision does not indicate to me that testator did not intend that they should participate further in his estate. Certainly there is no legal inconsistency in life tenants participating in the remainder. The theory that the testator particularly desired to see that his sisters were provided for is at least as strong as the supposition that he intended to exclude them from participating in the remainder.

I conclude that the life tenants should participate in the remainder devised by testator to his brothers and sisters.

Having determined that the life tenants should participate in the provision for the brothers and sisters, I must next consider the effect of the provision that the "issue of any deceased brothers or sisters to take his or her parent's share."

As to the brothers and sisters who died leaving issue, it was specifically provided that such issue should take the interest of such brother or sister leaving issue. Their interest was thereby divested, their issue being substituted in their place. In such case, the brother or sister dying leaving issue would have no power of disposition of his or her interest in the estate. In re Nelson's Estate, supra.

The will of testator is silent as to any provision relative to any of the brothers and sisters dying without leaving issue. Martha B. Wilson, Mary E. Wilson and Margaret W. Irvine, three sisters of testator, left no issue at the time of their death. Was their interest divested by their death, even though they left no issue, or did their estates receive an absolute interest, free and clear of any conditions subsequent?

Under the will of testator, the death of the life tenants leaving issue caused their interest to be divested. I have determined that the brothers and sisters received an absolute estate, subject to the provision that the interest of any brother or sister dying prior to the death of the life tenant should go by substitution to the issue of such brother or sister. However, this provision of the will does not apply where there is no issue, since there would then be no limitation upon their estate. The decisions in this state are silent as to what would happen under such circumstances. However, the weight of authority in other states is to the effect that in the event of the death of the devisees leaving no issue, the interest of such devisees is not divested by their death. McArthur v. Scott, 113 U.S. 340; Plitt v. Plitt, 167 Md. 252, 173 A. 35, 109 A.L.R. 1; Jacobs v. Whitney, 205 Mass. 477, 91 N.E. 1009; Rutledge v. Fishburne, 66 S.C. 155, 44 S.E. 564; Gardner v. Vanlandingham, 334 Mo. 1054, 69 S.W.2d 947. Since the estates created were absolute except for the condition subsequent, and since the subsequent condition has been removed, the estates of the sisters dying without issue would have an absolute interest unrestricted by any condition.

I believe that such a determination would be in accord with the plain intention of the testator. He apparently desired to provide for his own brothers and sisters and their issue. If he had desired to provide that the interest of any brother or sister dying without issue should go to the surviving brothers or sisters or had intended to make some other similar provision, it would have been easy for him to do so. The fact that he did not, indicates that he had no such intention. I conclude that the interests of Martha B. Wilson, Mary E. Wilson and Margaret W. Irvine, were not divested by their death without issue and that their interests in the estate of the testator under the residuary clause of the will should go to their respective estates.

The estates of Martha B. Wilson and Mary E. Wilson have been closed. In accordance with the opinion of this court in Cooling v. Security Trust Co., 29 Del. Ch. 286, 76 A.2d 1, their shares may be

distributed by the trustee directly to the persons entitled to receive
the same, the trustees first seeing that any taxes which may be due
or any costs which may be incurred by reason thereof are paid.

NOTES

1.   The classification of the future interests in *Irvine* results from
applying standard theory: The court reads the words of the instrument
in sequence, classifying each interest as it goes along, resulting in
remainders vested subject to divestment only if the remainderman is
survived by issue. Almost all courts are in accord.

2.   *Probate of remainders.* A future interest transmissible at death
goes into the probate estate of the remainderman. There it is subject
to probate costs and to creditors. If the remainder is overlooked by
the personal representative and not inventoried in the probate estate,
but is discovered some years later after the estate is closed, as in *Irvine*,
a court may order the property distributed directly to persons entitled
to receive it without reopening the estates. The court in *Irvine* so
ordered. This makes good sense and avoids probate costs.

On the other hand, a transmissible future interest has one considerable advantage: It adds flexibility to the trust where the drafter has
overlooked including a power of appointment (compare the example
of skilled drafting in Case 12, supra page 728). In *Irvine*, the transmissible vested remainders gave each remainderman the equivalent of a
general testamentary power of appointment over his or her share of
the trust assets, if the remainderman left no issue. Margaret devised
her share to her husband. Martha and Mary, the unmarried aunts,
devised their share to Henry's daughters, who doubtless had been
more attentive to them than Samuel's descendants. It is clear that the
primary objects of the settlor's bounty were Martha and Mary, and
the court recognizes that the settlor may well have wanted them to
be able to reward those nieces and nephews who cared for them.
Introducing this sort of flexibility into a trust is desirable because the
settlor cannot foresee the future and determine who is deserving or
needy upon the termination of the trust.

3.   *Taxation of remainders.* A transmissible remainder, like any transferable interest, is subject to federal estate taxation upon the death
of the remainderman (see supra page 727). In the *Irvine* case, the
remainders of Margaret, Martha, and Mary, all of whom died without
issue, are transmissible at their deaths and are subject to federal estate
taxation. Margaret's remainder, which passed by her will to her husband Samuel Irvine, qualifies for the marital deduction and is not
taxable at her death. In the preceding case, First National Bank of
Bar Harbor v. Anthony, John Anthony's remainder in the revocable

trust would be subject to estate taxation at his death, but no taxes would be payable because it could be destroyed unconditionally by the settlor and would have a value of zero. It is accurate to say, then, that a transmissible remainder is subject to estate taxation but that, under the circumstances of a given case, no taxes may be payable.

Before 1986, there was a clear tax advantage in creating remainders contingent upon survival to the time of possession. If the remainderman died before the life tenant, no estate tax was payable on the value of the remainder. This tax advantage was neutralized by the enactment of the generation-skipping transfer tax in 1986 (supra page 674). A generation-skipping transfer tax, levied at the highest estate tax rate, is payable on the life tenant's death if the trust principal is then payable to the settlor's grandchildren or any other person two or more generations below the settlor. If, in the *Anthony* case, John M. Anthony had held a remainder contingent upon his survival to the time of possession, no estate tax would be payable upon his death, but *on the settlor-life tenant's death a 55 percent GST tax would be levied on the value of the property received by John's children* (the settlor's grandchildren).

Since the enactment of the generation-skipping transfer tax, no clear general taxpayer advantage results from creating a remainder contingent upon survival rather than a remainder transferable at death. Tax advantage turns on the individual case — available exemptions from estate and GST taxes, marital deduction for estate tax, stepped-up basis for assets subject to estate tax, the life tenant's life expectancy, etc. As noted earlier (supra page 728), the skilled drafter of a trust with remainders to the settlor's children will create a special power of appointment either in the life tenant or in the remaindermen to let the donee (or donees) determine which tax does the least damage to the family and pay that one.

4.   Although courts do not imply survival requirements in gifts to single-generational classes, such as "children" or "brothers and sisters," they do imply survival requirements in gifts to multi-generational classes, such as "issue" or "descendants." See Edward C. Halbach, Jr., Future Interests: Express and Implied Conditions of Survival, 49 Cal. L. Rev. 297, 314-315 (1961); 5 American Law of Property §21.13 (1952). Thus, suppose that *T*'s will devises property "to *A* for life, then to *A*'s issue." *A* has a son, *B*, and a daughter, *C. B* predeceases *A*, devising all his property to his wife. *B* is also survived by a daughter, *D*. Because a requirement of survival is imposed on *A*'s issue, *B*, who dies during *A*'s life, cannot devise his share to his wife. Instead, *D*, *B*'s child, takes from *T* the share *B* would have taken had *B* survived.

Similarly, where there is a gift to the "heirs" of *A*, a survival requirement to the death of *A* is implied.

5.   When the testator inserts the word "surviving" in a trust instrument, the word is ambiguous unless an additional word or words tell us *at what time* the donee must be surviving. The requirement of survival may relate to surviving the testator, the life tenant, or a preceding remainderman. Take this example: *T* devises property in trust "for *A* for life, then to *B*, but if *B* dies before *A* to *B*'s surviving children." *B* has two children, *C* and *D*. Subsequently *B* dies. Then *D* dies intestate, survived by a child, *E*. *A* dies. Does *E* share? It depends upon whether "surviving" means "surviving *A*," in which case *E* would not share because *D* did not survive *A*, or "surviving *B*," in which case *E* would share because *D* survived *B*. The majority of cases appear to favor the view that "surviving" means surviving to the time of possession, thus excluding *E*. See id. §21.15.

6.   *T* bequeaths a fund in trust "for *A* for life, then to *B*, but if *B* dies without issue surviving her, to *C*." Does *T* intend *C* to take only if *B* dies *before A* without issue? Or does *T* intend *C* to take if *B* dies *at any time* without issue? The majority of courts favors the first construction, which permits the trust to terminate on *A*'s death. Accordingly, if *B* survives *A*, the trust property is distributed to *B* and *C* can never take. See id. §21.53.

Observe also that under orthodox construction there is no requirement that *C* live to the time of possession. If *B* dies before *A*, and then *C* dies during *A*'s life, *C*'s interest passes to *C*'s heirs or devisees. In a couple of states a different rule is followed. If a future interest is contingent upon an event other than survival to the time of possession (such as "if *B* dies without issue"), the future interest is also contingent on surviving to the time of possession. See Rushing v. Mann, 322 Ark. 528, 910 S.W.2d 672 (1995); Lawson v. Lawson, 267 N.C. 643, 148 S.E.2d 546 (1966). The rule may be limited to class gifts. This minority rule has been criticized by all the commentators. See Patricia G. Roberts, Class Gifts in North Carolina — When Do We "Call the Roll?" 21 Wake Forest L. Rev. 1 (1985).

Clobberie's Case
Court of Chancery, England, 1677
2 Vent. 342, 86 Eng. Rep. 476

In one Clobberie's case it was held, that where one bequeathed a sum of money to a woman, at her age of twenty-one years, or day of marriage, to be paid unto her with interest, and she died before either, that the money should go to her executor; and was so decreed by my Lord Chancellor Finch [who was later titled Lord Nottingham and became famous for getting the Rule against Perpetuities started in the Duke of Norfolk's Case, infra page 788].

But he said, if money were bequeathed to one at his age of twenty-one years, if he dies before that age, the money is lost.

On the other side, if money be given to one, to be paid at the age of twenty-one years; there, if the party dies before, it shall go to the executors.

NOTES AND PROBLEM

1. The first and third rules of construction laid down in Clobberie's Case are widely followed today. They apply to immediate gifts as well as to remainders. They apply to a gift to a class as well as to a gift to an individual.

Under the first rule in Clobberie's Case a gift of the *entire income* to a person (or to a class), with principal to be paid at a designated age, indicates survival to the time of possession is not required. The reason for this rule is that all interests in the property — both income and principal — are given to the same person or persons, with only possession of the principal postponed. When the beneficiary dies before reaching the stated age, there is no point in delaying payment of the principal to the beneficiary's estate. See 5 American Law of Property §21.20 (1952). Under the third rule in Clobberie's Case, a gift "payable" at a designated age indicates survival to the time of possession is not required. If the beneficiary dies under that age, the principal will be paid at the beneficiary's death to the beneficiary's estate, unless someone would be harmed by such payment. If the income is payable to another, for example, the principal cannot be paid to the principal beneficiary's estate until the income beneficiary dies. See id. §21.18.

The American cases are split over whether to follow the second rule, which states that a gift "at" a designated age implies a requirement of survivorship to that age. See id. §21.17. The distinction between a legacy "at 21" (survivorship to 21 required) and a legacy "to be paid at 21" (survivorship to 21 is not required) has been criticized by most commentators as a distinction without a difference.

2. *T* bequeaths $10,000 "to *A* when *A* attains 21." *A* is age 15 at *T*'s death. Who is entitled to income from the $10,000 before *A* reaches 21? If *A* dies at age 16, does the legacy fail or is *A*'s administrator entitled to demand payment of $10,000 at *A*'s death or when *A* would have reached 21 had *A* lived? See Edward C. Halbach, Jr., Future Interests: Express and Implied Conditions of Survival, 49 Cal. L. Rev. 297, 299-302 (1961).

3. *T* bequeaths a fund in trust "for *A* for life, then after *A*'s death to *A*'s children, each share payable as each child respectively reaches the age of 30, if he or she has not reached age 30 before *A* dies."

The gift to each child of *A* is vested upon birth, with possession postponed until *A* dies or the child reaches 30, whichever later happens. If a child of *A* dies at age 10 during *A*'s life, the child's administrator can demand payment of the child's share at *A*'s death. There is no requirement that the child survive to the time designated for possession.

4.   Testator bequeathed a fund in trust for the benefit of her child Benjamin "until my child attains age twenty-five (25), at which time the income and principal shall be distributed and paid over to him and the trust shall terminate." The testator's will did not name a trust beneficiary if Benjamin died under 25. Benjamin died at 20 in 1994. Benjamin's heir is his father, who was divorced from Ben's mother in 1983. The court, following the rules in Clobberie's Case, held that the remainder vested in Benjamin upon creation and passed on his death to his father. Summers v. Summers, 121 Ohio App. 3d 263, 699 N.E.2d 958 (1997).

NOTE: UNIFORM PROBATE CODE §2-707 — A NEW SYSTEM OF FUTURE INTERESTS FOR TRUSTS

In 1990, the revisers of the Uniform Probate Code made a revolutionary change in the law of future interests that, if adopted, will change the rules previously studied in this chapter. Under new UPC §2-707, unless the instrument provides otherwise, the following rules apply:

(1)   All future interests in trust are contingent on the beneficiary's surviving to the date of distribution.
(2)   If a remainderman does not survive to the distribution date, UPC §2-707 creates a substitute gift in the remainderman's descendants who survive the date of distribution.
(3)   If a remainderman dies before distribution and leaves no descendants, the remainder fails, and, if there is no alternative remainder that takes effect, the trust property passes to the settlor's residuary devisees or the settlor's heirs.

This sea change in the law of remainders was set in motion by the Code's revisers when they expanded the antilapse idea of the law of wills to include trust remainders. See Jesse Dukeminier, The Uniform Probate Code Upends the Law of Remainders, 94 Mich. L. Rev. 148 (1995).

There may be merit in the idea that antilapse statutes should apply to all revocable will substitutes, including *revocable trusts*, thus requiring the beneficiary to survive the decedent *donor*, and providing a substitute gift to the issue of beneficiaries who do not. It is not worth arguing about, however, because, whether the present vested remainder rule or the UPC rule is followed, the settlor can amend the trust when the remainderman dies during the settlor's life if the settlor doesn't like what happens to the remainder. After the settlor's death, the power to revoke and deal with changed circumstances ceases. Hence, expanding the antilapse idea to a requirement that *all* trust remaindermen must survive to the termination of the trust raises entirely different questions. Irrevocable inter vivos trusts, testamentary trusts, and revocable trusts that continue as irrevocable trusts after the settlor's death are not will substitutes, and the substantive law of wills cannot be applied to them on the theory that they are functionally analogous transfers that can be changed by the settlor if circumstances change. UPC §2-707 can be justified only if it better carries out the settlor's intent than does the common law and better serves subsidiary public policies.

The 1990 UPC revisers do not rest their case on the assumption that §2-707 better carries out the settlors' intent, for there is no empirical evidence of that. The stated rationale for UPC §2-707 is "to prevent cumbersome and costly distributions to and through the estates of deceased beneficiaries of future interests who may have died long before the distribution date." As a matter of policy, it is hard to understand why remainders in trust should be excluded from the remainderman's estate and other nonpossessory interests — such as copyright royalties, an option to purchase, a landlord's reversion, or a legal future interest — excluded. Future interests in trust are certainly no more "cumbersome and costly" to administer — or to value — than other nonpossessory interests.

The Official Comment suggests that if the remainderman's personal representative overlooked the remainder and did not include the remainder as an asset of the remainderman's probate estate, the probate estate will have to be reopened and a new administrator appointed when the life tenant dies in order to pass title to the remainderman's heir or devisees. But this is not necessarily so. In many states, the order for final distribution of a probate estate contains an omnibus clause distributing "hereafter discovered" property to specified persons, in which case no subsequent administration is necessary. Even without an omnibus clause, no good reason appears why the trustee should not be able to distribute the trust principal upon termination of the trust directly to the residuary beneficiaries or heirs if they have been determined in the probate decree. This was done in Security Trust Co. v. Irvine (supra page 733). See also In re Estate of Waller, 559 S.W.2d 312, 317 (Mo. App. 1977).

In any case, probate administration of a remainder seems a small price to pay for the flexibility of the common law, which UPC §2-707 discards. The whole thrust of sound estate planning in the late twentieth century is to create flexibility in trusts, which experience has shown is highly desirable. Indeed, flexibility is of paramount importance in a trust. UPC §2-707 replaces the flexibility of the transmissible remainder rule, which permits the beneficiary to devise the remainder to whomever he pleases, with a rigid substitution of the beneficiary's issue. Thus:

> *Case 13.* *T* devises property in trust "for *A* for life, then to *A*'s daughter *B*." Under present law, if *B* dies during the life of *A*, *B* can devise her remainder to her spouse, to her issue, to charity, or to anyone she pleases, or in further trust, perhaps setting up a discretionary trust for a disabled child. Under UPC §2-707, *B*'s remainder is made contingent upon *B*'s surviving *A*. If *B* dies during *A*'s life leaving issue, *B*'s issue are substituted for *B*. *B* has no power to transfer the remainder to others. If *B* is not survived by issue, the gift fails, and the property reverts to *T*'s residuary devisee or *T*'s heirs on *A*'s death.

In Chapter 9, you studied powers of appointment, which should be considered for every well-drafted trust. Powers of appointment permit beneficiaries to change the beneficiaries of a trust as circumstances may indicate desirable. The transmissible remainder rule gives the remainderman the equivalent of a general testamentary power of appointment over the remainder.

In Security Trust Co. v. Irvine, had UPC §2-707 been the law, Margaret Irvine could not have devised her remainder to her husband. Spouses are likely to be the persons most disadvantaged by UPC §2-707, because only issue, and not spouses, are substituted for the deceased remaindermen; if a remainderman dies without issue, his or her faithful spouse can take nothing. Also, in Security Trust Co. v. Irvine, if UPC §2-707 had been the law, the unmarried sisters, Martha and Mary, would have no power to reward their attentive nieces with an inheritance. The fundamental point is: No statute can pick the substitute takers as well as living persons. This is why English and American law has permitted wills for over 450 years.[4]

4. The two principal drafters of UPC §2-707, Professors Halbach and Waggoner, both have published extensive studies of whether remainders should be construed to be contingent upon survival. Both concluded that they should not be, and that the current transmissible vested remainder construction is preferable to extending antilapse provisions to future interests.

Edward C. Halbach, Jr., Future Interests: Express and Implied Conditions of Survival, 49 Calif. L. Rev. 297, 305 (1961):

> If a testator (or settlor of a living trust) has selected a particular person to receive some interest in his property and has thought no further than that selection, it seems preferable to allow the rights to vest and to let that beneficiary's own desires take effect where the testator's desires are unknown. Since the beneficiary in question is the only person known to have been intended to receive the property, he could at least be given the benefit of deciding who will take in his place. This

Because of the necessity of dealing with two or more alternative future interests, for which substitute gifts are created, and providing for tie-breakers where two groups of substitute takers appear to have equal claims, Uniform Probate Code §2-707 turns out to be devilishly complex, running the Rule against Perpetuities a close second. It invents a whole new vocabulary of future interests. The drafters themselves call the statute "elaborate and intricate" and admit that it will require "a few hours" of intense study. Edward C. Halbach, Jr. & Lawrence W. Waggoner, The UPC's New Survivorship and Antilapse Provisions, 55 Alb. L. Rev. 1091, 1048 (1992).

Uniform Probate Code §2-707 changes many rules that lawyers have relied on for centuries. For example, §2-707 provides that words of survivorship attached to a future interest do *not* state an intent that descendants not be substituted for the deceased remainderman. This rule of construction is likely to trip up the average or the experienced lawyer. Thus:

> *Case 14.* *T* devises a fund in trust "for *A* for life, then to *B* if *B* survives *A*." Under §2-707, the words "if *B* survives *A*" do not indicate that the transferor does not want *B*'s descendants substituted for *B* if *B* predeceases *A*. If *B* predeceases *A*, leaving descendants, the descendants take, in spite of this language.

This rule of construction is taken from the 1990 UPC antilapse statute applicable to wills, §2-603. It has been sharply criticized by commentators as changing the ordinary meaning of words into something unexpected (see supra page 444). It is only one example of how §2-707 will change standard lawyerly language, with settled meaning, to mean something other than intended.

Section 2-707 also abrogates the Rule of Reversions, supra page 715, with respect to inter vivos trusts. Suppose that the settlor creates an irrevocable inter vivos trust for *A* for life, remainder to *B*, similar to Case 13 above. UPC §2-707 converts the remainder to *B* to a remainder "to *B* if *B* survives *A*, and if *B* does not survive *A* to *B*'s issue who survive *A*." If *B* predeceases *A* without issue, at common law the property would revert to the settlor on *A*'s death. Section 2-707 does not permit reversion to the settlor, however, On *A*'s death, even though the settlor is alive, the settlor is treated as dead. On *A*'s death,

---

is what would have happened had he survived to the date the testator seemingly assumed he would.

Lawrence W. Waggoner, Future Interests Legislation: Implied Conditions of Survivorship and Substitutionary Gifts under the New Illinois "Anti-Lapse" Provision, 1969 U. Ill. L.F. 423, 438:

[I]t seems far better for the predeceased legatee, rather than the legislature, to decide how best to provide for his own family.

the property goes to the settlor's heirs ascertained as if the settlor had died the moment before *A*. UPC §2-707(d); UPC §2-711. The settlor's heirs may be remote cousins in whom the settlor has no interest, but the settlor has lost the property to them. Worse, if the settlor survives *A* but has no known heirs at *A*'s death, applying the principle that the settlor is treated as having predeceased *A*, the property escheats to the state.[5] Escheat will surely come as a shocker to the settlor, the lawyer who drafted the trust, and the lawyer's malpractice insurance carrier!

One of the drafters of §2-707, Professor Waggoner, has recanted his earlier views on implied conditions of survival and now advocates the new system of future interests he has written into §2-707. See Lawrence W. Waggoner, The Uniform Probate Code Extends Anti-lapse-Type Protection to Poorly Drafted Trusts, 94 Mich. L. Rev. 2309 (1996). Professor Waggoner's newly minted thesis is that where an instrument is ambiguous and a default rule is required, the default rule should provide a solution that a skilled estate planner would have provided. Few would disagree with that. But then Professor Waggoner asserts that a skilled estate planner would want the remainderman's share distributed to his issue, regardless of age or capabilities, if a remainderman predeceases the life tenant. He asserts that a "capable" estate planner would not give the remainderman a special power of appointment. Id. at 2333.[6] This assertion, as George Orwell might have put it, gives an appearance of solidity to pure wind. An average, unimaginative lawyer in Fargo or Ann Arbor might draw an iron-bound estate plan, using fixed lines of descent, seeking certainty, but an expert knows that flexibility is highly desirable to enable the beneficiaries to deal with unforeseen events. What may seem an appropriate arrangement today may be inappropriate many years from now, when the life tenant dies.

Most expert lawyers will recommend creating one or more special powers of appointment. If the client is not aware of the vicissitudes of life, the legal counselor has a duty of calling them to the client's attention — unexpected deaths, marriages, divorces, remarriages, children with special needs, children with disabilities, changes in the

---

5. The Official Comment says: "Note also that the meaning of the back-stop gift [the "back-stop gift" is what the UPC calls the reversion at common law] is governed by Section 2-711 [reproduced in this book infra at page 775], under which the gift is to the transferor's heirs determined as if the transferor died when *A* died. Thus there will always be a set of substitute takers, even if it turns out to be the State." The settlor is excluded as a substitute taker.

6. Strangely, this assertion is contradicted by UPC §2-707, Example 5: "G created an irrevocable trust, income to A for life, remainder in corpus to B, but if B predeceases A, to the person B appoints by will." Presumably the examples in the UPC are drafted by "capable" estate planners.

tax laws — all of which can best be dealt with by special powers of appointment. The counselor also should explain to the client the tax-saving possibilities of special powers of appointment, including the choice of paying an estate tax rather than a GST tax (supra page 728) and using the donee's spouse's exemptions from the estate tax and GST tax. If the paterfamilias or materfamilias, armed with this information and bearing the future welfare of the family in mind, does not opt for special powers of appointment in a large majority of cases, the lawyer's reputation as a counselor is at risk.

The skilled estate planner may give the life tenant a special power of appointment or, if the life tenant is unsuitable because incompetent or if she has adverse personal relations with the remaindermen (e.g., a stepparent), the expert will make the remainder contingent on surviving the life tenant and give the remaindermen a special power of appointment, exercisable if the remainderman predeceases the life tenant. Even when the life tenant is given a special power of appointment, the expert will give the remainderman who dies before the life tenant a special power exercisable if the life tenant does not exercise her power or cannot exercise her power because of incompetence, which occurs more frequently nowadays as persons live longer. UPC §2-707 provides a rigid default rule, slipping family trusts back to the olden days before powers of appointment came into widespread use, straitjacketing the family.

Giving a contingent remainderman a special power of appointment was first recommended, so far as we can tell, by that master of will drafting, W. Barton Leach, Story Professor of Law at Harvard, in his article, Planning and Drafting a Will, 27 B.U. L. Rev. 157 (1947). This article described his wills course at Harvard, which emphasized intelligent drafting. Implementing his recommendation, Leach created special powers of appointment in remaindermen who predecease the life tenant in Paragraph VII, Clauses (f)(1) & (3) of his model will (id. at 168). Leach later used this model will, with special powers in remaindermen, in his Cases and Text on the Law of Wills 260-264 (2d ed. 1951) (Paragraph VII, Clauses (f)(1) & (3)). Throughout his long and influential career as a brilliant teacher at Harvard, Leach continued to advocate giving remaindermen special powers of appointment when appropriate in the family situation. In his 1961 case-book on estate planning, in discussing a trust created by a testator for his wife for life, remainder to his two sons, Leach asked how the will should be drafted to take care of the situation if one of the sons predeceased the life tenant. His answer: "*Obviously*, provide that if a son predeceases his mother he shall have a special power of appointment over half the principal." W. Barton Leach & James K. Logan, Cases and Text on Future Interests and Estate Planning 329 (1961) (emphasis added). See also Paragraph VII(2)(e)(3) of Leach & Logan's model will creating a special power of appointment in the remainderman (id. at 970-972). Professor Leach was the unmatched teacher of future interests in the mid-twentieth century as well as the tireless advocate of using powers of appointment in estate planning, both in life tenants and remaindermen. There are few skilled estate planners in this country who have not been influenced directly or indirectly by Professor Leach or by his students. (Leach's co-editor, James K. Logan, dean of the University of Kansas law school, was one of the foremost experts on estate planning in the Midwest and also a powerful advocate of powers of appointment. Logan was subsequently appointed to the Tenth Circuit bench. See infra page 1035.)

In a comprehensive examination of the matter some years ago, before the UPC revisers acted, Professor Susan French compared the current rule of transmissible remainders with a proposal to make remainders contingent on survival and impose an antilapse statute on them (UPC §2-707's solution). Susan F. French, Imposing a General Survival Requirement on Beneficiaries of Future Interests: Solving the Problems Caused by the Death of a Beneficiary Before the Time Set for Distribution, 27 Ariz. L. Rev. 801 (1985). Professor French concluded that imposing a requirement of survival on remaindermen was justified only if they were given, by statute, a broad special power of appointment permitting the remainderman maximum flexibility to adapt to changes after the creation of the trust — in other words, providing a default scheme by statute that mirrored what Professor Leach recommended and a skilled estate planner would do.[7] The UPC revisers did not narrow the remainderman's current unlimited power of disposition to a special power as French recommended, thus eliminating tax and probate costs while preserving flexibility. They eliminated the power to deal with changing circumstances altogether. It seems unlikely that any skilled estate planner would draft a trust that resembles what the client of an unskilled lawyer would get under §2-707 — a conclusion also reached in a recent study of §2-707 by Professor David Becker, who suggests that, because it is beset with invisible boomerangs, experienced lawyers will likely block its application by inserting a clause that it is not to apply to instruments they draft.

Professor Becker's study is an extended, in-depth analysis of the complexities of UPC §2-707 and its effect upon the drafting of documents by skilled estate planners, who the proponents of §2-707 allege will not be affected by it. David M. Becker, Uniform Probate Code

---

7. Since the enactment of the generation-skipping transfer tax in 1986, French's sensible proposal has become even more attractive. It gives the remainderman a special power of appointment, which the remainderman can choose to exercise so as to put her remainder in her taxable gross estate, paying an estate tax on the remainder and avoiding a higher generation-skipping transfer tax on the trust principal at the life tenant's death. See supra page 728; infra pages 827-829.

§2-707 and The Experienced Estate Planner: Unexpected Disasters and How to Avoid Them, 47 UCLA L. Rev. _____ (1999 [forthcoming]). Professor Becker notes that the default rule of §2-707 "has a profound effect upon the underlying logic of the system" and argues that it will not suit the experienced estate planner because of its "hidden conflicts and consequences."[8]

> The entire process [of dealing with §2-707] may frighten the very best estate planners. . . . These are the professionals who know that mistakes can be made. Even if they have mastered the statute and retain that mastery, they know that the deviant results yielded by §2-707's overlay are tricky and not readily detected. Mistakes will happen despite their excellent work. And so what is the effect of §2-707? It is a trap. It is a disaster waiting to happen for the very group of lawyers whom proponents of §2-707 said would be unaffected.
>
> This may not, however, be the end of the story. Skilled and conscientious lawyers do have a way to overcome §2-707 and thereby protect themselves and the integrity of the dispositive provisions they design and draft. Because they seek work products that are perfect mosaics — because they include all conditions their clients want and because they account for all eventualities yielded by these conditions — they will in all probability insulate their trusts from outside forces such as the overlay of §2-707. This is their ultimate solution, and they can readily accomplish it with a general provision that totally disclaims the rules of construction embodied by §2-707. And if such a disclaimer becomes boiler-plate for the work products of experienced estate planners, surely it will soon emerge in the trust forms that all lawyers use. Once this happens, the effect of §2-707 is emasculated for all. The bottom line is that §2-707 will either be a disaster waiting to happen for experienced estate planners or in time it will become an exercise in futility. In either case, §2-707 is not a good idea. [Id. at _____.]

Uniform Probate Code §2-707 has been adopted in Alaska, Colorado, Hawaii, Michigan, Montana, New Mexico, and North Dakota. The statutes are not retroactive. In these states the common law of future interests continues to apply to legal future interests in land and personal property, as well as to trusts created prior to the enactment of UPC §2-707. Section 2-707 applies to future interests in trusts created after the statutes were enacted. Thus two systems of future interests are in effect. Section 2-707 has been rejected in a number of jurisdictions that have enacted other sections of the Uniform Probate Code.

Students usually find the common law of future interests tough

---

8. "Preparatory to writing this article, I spent *many* hours studying §2-707 and so did my student research assistants before critiquing my early drafts. We are an intelligent group of people. We think we have mastered §2-707 after many, many hours of collective work. But then again, we are not certain." Becker, supra, at _____.

going. To require them also to learn the different and more complicated UPC system of future interests, unless it has been adopted in their state, seems heartless. Because of the length and complexities of UPC §2-707, it is not reproduced here. You may, if you wish, find §2-707 in the Uniform Laws Annotated database in Westlaw.

For the confused situation in California on the requirement of survival, resulting from some tinkering with the antilapse statute and an unsuccessful attempt to eliminate the preference for vested remainders, see Laura E. Cunningham, The Hazards of Tinkering with the Common Law of Future Interests: The California Experience, 48 Hastings L.J. 667 (1997) (also weighing in against UPC §2-707).

2.   *Gifts to Classes*

a.   **Gifts of Income**

Dewire v. Haveles

Supreme Judicial Court of Massachusetts, 1989
404 Mass. 274, 534 N.E.2d 782

WILKINS, J.   This petition for a declaration of rights seeks answers to questions arising from an artlessly drafted will that, among its many inadequacies, includes a blatant violation of the rule against perpetuities. . . .

Thomas A. Dewire died in January, 1941, survived by his widow, his son Thomas, Jr., and three grandchildren (Thomas, III, Paula, and Deborah, all children of Thomas, Jr.). His will placed substantially all his estate in a residuary trust. The income of the trust was payable to his widow for life and, on her death, the income was payable to his son Thomas, Jr., the widow of Thomas, Jr., and Thomas Jr.'s children.[9]

---

9. The language of the will directing this distribution appears in article third of the will and reads as follows:

> Third: To my wife, Mabel G. Dewire, I give, devise and bequeath all the rest, residue and remainder of all the estate of which I shall die seized, for and during the term of her natural life, and upon her decease to my son, Thomas A. Dewire, Jr., and his heirs and assigns, but in trust nevertheless upon the following trusts and for the following purposes:
>
> A. To hold, direct, manage and conserve the trust estate, so given, for the benefit of himself, his wife and children in the manner following, that is to say:
>
> To expend out of the net income so much as may be necessary for the proper care, maintenance of himself and wife conformable to their station in life, and for the care, maintenance and education of his children born to him in his lifetime, in such manner as in his judgment and discretion shall seem proper, and his judgment and discretion shall be final.

After the testator's death, Thomas, Jr., had three more children by a second wife. Thomas, Jr., died on May 28, 1978, a widower, survived by all six of his children. Thomas, III, who had served as trustee since 1978, died on March 19, 1987, leaving a widow and one child, Jennifer. Among the questions presented, and the most important one for present purposes, is to whom the one-sixth share of the trust income, once payable to Thomas, III, is now payable.

In his will, the testator stated: "It is my will, except as hereinabove provided, that my grandchildren, under guidance and discretion of my Trustee, shall share equally in the net income of my said estate." At another point, he referred to the trust income being "divided equally amongst my grandchildren." The rule against perpetuities violation occurred because the will provided for the trust's termination "twenty-one years after the death of the last surviving child of my said son, Thomas A. Dewire, Jr., when the property of the trust shall be equally divided amongst the lineal descendants of my grandchildren."[10]

There is no explicit provision in the will concerning the distribution of income on the death of a grandchild while the gift of income to grandchildren continues, nor is there any statement as to what the trustee should do with trust income between the death of the last grandchild and the date assigned for termination of the trust twenty-one years later.

Our task is to discern the testator's intention concerning the distribution of a grandchild's share of the trust income on his death. As a practical matter, in cases of this sort, where there is no express intention, we must resort to reasonable inferences in the particular circumstances which on occasion shade into rules of construction that are applied when no intention at all can be inferred on the issue. In this case, the reasonable inference as to the testator's intention is that Jennifer should take her father's share in the income.

Certain points are not in serious controversy and are relatively easy to resolve. The gift of net income to the testator's grandchildren, divided equally or to be shared equally, is a class gift. . . . The class includes all six grandchildren, three of whom were born before and three of whom were born after the testator's death. . . . Because there is a gift over at the end of the class gift, the testator intended the class gift to his grandchildren only to be a gift of a life interest in the income of the trust. . . . The general rule is that, in the absence of a

---

10. As we shall explain, the possibility that Thomas, Jr., would have a child born after the testator's death was sufficient to cause the violation of the rule against perpetuities. The fact that Thomas, Jr., had children born after the testator's death makes possible a violation of the rule in actual fact.

contrary intent expressed in the will or a controlling statute stating otherwise, members of a class are joint tenants with rights of survivorship. Old Colony Trust Co. v. Treadwell, 312 Mass. 214, 218, 43 N.E.2d 777 (1942). Meserve v. Haak, 191 Mass. 220, 223, 77 N.E. 377 (1906). See G.L. c. 191, §22 (1986 ed.) (antilapse statute).

This last stated principle becomes important in deciding whether Jennifer, the child of the deceased grandson, takes her deceased father's share in the trust income or whether the remaining class members, the other five grandchildren, take that income share equally by right of survivorship. Jennifer argues, under the general rule, that the will manifests an intent contrary to a class gift with rights of survivorship. We agree with this conclusion. Thus we need not decide, as Jennifer further argues, whether the rule of construction presuming a right of survivorship in class members should be rejected in the circumstances and replaced by a rule based on principles similar to those expressed in the antilapse statute.[11]

Before we explain why the will expresses an intention that, during the term of the class gift, Jennifer, while living, should take her father's share in the income, we discuss the rule against perpetuities problem.[12] The prospect that interests under this will may vest beyond the permissible limit of the rule against perpetuities is not only theoretically possible, it is actuarially likely. The interests of the grandchildren in the trust income vested at their father's death (if not sooner) and, because he was a life in being at the testator's death, those interests vested within the period of the rule. The gift over at the end

----

11. The Massachusetts antilapse statute applies only to testamentary gifts to a child or other relation of a testator who predeceased the testator leaving issue surviving the testator and to class gifts to children or other relations where one or more class member predeceased the testator (even if the class member had died before the will was executed). G.L. c. 191, §22. The rule of construction of §22 is that the issue of a deceased relation take his share by right of representation "unless a different disposition is made or required by the will."

In this case, no class member predeceased the testator, and, therefore, §22 does not explicitly aid Jennifer. The policy underlying §22 might fairly be seen as supporting, as a rule of construction (absent a contrary intent), the substitution of a class member's surviving issue for a deceased class member if the class is made up of children or other relations of the testator. See Bigelow v. Clap, 166 Mass. 88, 91, 43 N.E. 1037 (1896). It has been suggested that "[t]he policy of [antilapse] statutes [dealing with the death of a class member after the testator's death] commends itself to decisional law." Restatement (Second) of Property, Donative Transfers §27.3 Comment i (Tent. Draft No. 9, 1986). If the antilapse statute protects the interests of the issue of a relation who predeceases a testator, there is a good reason why we should adopt, as a rule of construction, the same principle as to a relation of a testator who survives the testator but dies before an interest comes into possession. In the case of a class gift of income from a trust, the interest could be viewed as coming into possession of each income distribution date.

12. In its classic formulation, the rule against perpetuities declares that: "No interest is good unless it must vest, if at all, not later than twenty-one years after some life in being at the creation of the interest." J. C. Gray, The Rule Against Perpetuities §201, at 191 (4th ed. 1942). See Eastman Marble Co. v. Vermont Marble Co., 236 Mass. 138, 152, 128 N.E. 177 (1920).

of the class gift of income to the grandchildren, however, might not vest seasonably because another grandchild could have been born after the testator's death and could be the surviving grandchild. In this case, in fact, the three youngest grandchildren were born after the death of the testator but they are measuring lives for the term of the class gift. The parties agree that the purported gift of the remainder to the lineal descendants of the testator's grandchildren "twenty-one years after the death of the last surviving" grandchild violates the rule against perpetuities in its traditional form and would be void. See Second Bank-State St. Trust Co. v. Second Bank-State St. Trust Co., 335 Mass. 407, 410-411, 140 N.E.2d 201 (1957). There is no need at this time to decide the question of the proper distribution of trust income or assets at the death of the last grandchild. The question will be acute at the death of the last grandchild, when the class gift of income from the trust will terminate.

The rule against perpetuities problem need not be resolved at this time. It has some bearing, however, on what should be done during the term of the class gift with the one-sixth share of the trust income that is in dispute. We reject the argument that, because of the violation of the rule against perpetuities, the income interests should be treated as being more than life interests. There is no authority for such a proposition. Although the gift over violates the rule against perpetuities in its traditional form and in time may prove to violate it in actual fact, the language providing for such a distribution may properly be considered in determining a testator's intention with respect to other aspects of his will. . . .

We are now in a position to discuss the question whether the class gift of income to grandchildren calls for the payment of income equally to those grandchildren living from time to time (as joint tenants with rights of survivorship) or whether the issue of any deceased grandchild succeeds by right of representation to his income interest. The latter result better conforms with the testator's intentions.

The testator provided that the trust should terminate twenty-one years after the death of his last grandchild. It is unlikely that the testator intended that trust income should be accumulated for twenty-one years, and we would tend to avoid such a construction. See Meserve v. Haak, 191 Mass. 220, 222, 77 N.E. 377 (1906). Certainly, we should not presume that he intended an intestacy as to that twenty-one year period. See Anderson v. Harris, 320 Mass. 101, 104-105, 67 N.E.2d 670 (1946). He must have expected that someone would receive distributions of income during those years. The only logical recipients of that income would be the issue (by right of representation) of deceased grandchildren, the same group of people who would take the trust assets on termination of the trust (assuming no violation of the rule against perpetuities).[13] If these people were intended to receive income during the last twenty-one years of the trust as well as the trust assets on its termination, it is logical that they should also receive income during the term of the class gift if their ancestor (one of the grandchildren) should die. Such a pattern treats each grandchild and his issue equally throughout the intended term of the trust. Where, among other things, every other provision in the will concerning the distribution of trust income and principal (after the death of the testator and his wife) points to equal treatment of the testator's issue per stirpes, there is a sufficient contrary intent shown to overcome the rule of construction that the class gift of income to grandchildren is given to them as joint tenants with the right of survivorship.

Judgment shall be entered declaring that (1) Jennifer Ann Dewire in her lifetime is entitled to one-sixth of the net income of the trust during the period of the class gift of income, that is, until the death of the last grandchild (and a proportionate share of the income of any grandchild who dies leaving no issue), [and] (2) no declaration shall be made at this time concerning the disposition of trust income or principal on the death of the last grandchild of Thomas A. Dewire. . . .

So ordered.

PROBLEM AND NOTE

1.   *T* bequeaths a fund in trust to pay the income "to each of my children Gertrude, Charlotte, and John in equal amounts during their lives, and upon the death of the last survivor, to distribute the principal to their issue per stirpes then living." Gertrude dies. What distribution of income is made? If Charlotte and John receive Gertrude's share, Gertrude's spouse and children are cut off from any benefits they have been receiving from Gertrude's share and the surviving children get richer. Cf. Svenson v. First National Bank of Boston, 5 Mass. App. Ct. 440, 363 N.E.2d 1129 (1977) (devise of income substantially identical except made to testator's servants rather than her children; court held gift of income was a class gift, to be divided by surviving servants); Westervelt v. First Interstate Bank, 551 N.E.2d 1180 (Ind. App. 1990) (holding income goes to surviving child on theory that each child has an implied cross remainder in the other child's share).

13. "[T]he property of the trust shall be equally divided amongst the lineal descendants of my grandchildren." "Equally," referring to a multigenerational class, normally means per stirpes. New England Trust Co. v. McAleer, 344 Mass. 107, 112, 181 N.E.2d 569 (1962).

2. *Drafting advice.* When you give income to a class of persons, do not dispose of the principal upon the death of the survivor, which leaves open the question litigated in *Dewire.* Instead, say "upon the death of each life tenant," and go on to provide what is to be done with the individual life tenant's share. See John L. Garvey, Drafting Wills and Trusts: Anticipating the Birth and Death of Possible Beneficiaries, 71 Or. L. Rev. 47 (1992).

b. Gifts to Children or Issue

(1)   Per stirpes distributions

The law presumes that the word *children* means only the immediate offspring of the parent and does not include grandchildren. Sometimes the testator's probable intent is not carried out by this presumption. Here is a case that happens all too frequently:

> *Case 14. T* bequeaths a fund in trust "for my daughter, *A,* for life, then to *A*'s surviving children." At *T*'s death, *A* has two children, *B* and *C.* Subsequently *C* dies, leaving a child, *D.* Then *A* dies survived by *B* and *D.* If "children" means what it says, *B* takes all the trust fund and *D* does not share. So held in In re Gustafson, 74 N.Y.2d 448, 547 N.E.2d 1152, 548 N.Y.S.2d 625 (1989), denying *A*'s grandchild a share, over a strong dissent.

In cases like Case 14, one has a nagging suspicion that the drafter carelessly chose the word "children" when the word "issue" or "descendants," incorporating the principle of representation so prominent in the law of inheritance, would better have fit the client's intent. This suspicion has given rise to numerous cases, often involving homemade wills, litigating the question of whether the testator (drafter?) meant by "children" persons other than immediate offspring. Sometimes courts have held that other language in the will or extrinsic circumstances indicate that the testator in fact meant descendants. Restatement (Second) of Property, Donative Transfers, §25.1 (1988); Annot., 30 A.L.R.4th 319 (1984); cf. Dewire v. Haveles, supra (gift of income rather than principal).

Where there is a gift "to the issue of *A*," the question arises whether the issue take per capita or per stirpes. If the issue take *per capita,* all issue who are born before the period of distribution take an equal share. Descendants with living parents share equally with their parents. Thus if *A* has three children and one of these children has two children, the property is divided into five shares. If the issue take *per stirpes* or *by right of representation* (the terms are synonymous in most states), the children of a child of the designated ancestor can take nothing if their parent is alive, and if the parent is dead, the children take from the donor by representation. Thus if *A* has three children and one of these three predeceases *A*, leaving two children surviving *A*, the property is divided into three shares and the children of the predeceased child divide that child's one-third share. A devise to the issue of *A* is presumptively distributed per stirpes, even though it is to issue "share and share alike." See First Illini Bank v. Pritchard, 230 Ill. App. 3d 861, 595 N.E.2d 728 (1992).

What does a per stirpes distribution mean? In England the intestacy statute divides the decedent's property into as many shares as there are children of the decedent alive or dead but leaving issue surviving the decedent. The issue of any deceased child succeeds to the child's share. See supra page 87. The English courts interpret the words *per stirpes* in a will to call for a similar distribution. Thus distribution of a bequest to the issue per stirpes of a named person mirrors intestate distribution to the issue of a decedent.

In this country, the first Restatement of Property §303 (1940) took the position — as do the English courts — that the phrases *per stirpes* or *by right of representation,* used in a will, are to be given the same meaning as representation has under the intestacy statutes of the particular jurisdiction. Hence the presumed intent of a testator making a gift to issue is the same as that of an intestate decedent leaving property to issue. The first Restatement's position appears to accord with that taken by a majority of courts. In a large majority of jurisdictions, the intestacy statutes provide for a per stirpes distribution dividing the property into shares at the generational level where a descendant is alive, called the *modern* per stirpes system (see supra page 87). Hence, in most states the words per stirpes in a will, by reference to the intestacy law, call for a modern per stirpes distribution.

The Uniform Probate Code's intestacy law, §2-106, gives an entirely new meaning to representation, defining it to mean per capita at each generation (see supra page 88).

The differences between the English per stirpes system, the modern per stirpes system, and the UPC's system of per capita at each generation, as they apply to a gift to the issue of *A*, are shown by the following case.

> *Case 15.* *T* devises property "to *A* for life, then to *A*'s issue." At *T*'s death, *A* has two children, *B* and *C*, living. Thereafter *B* dies, survived by one child, *D*. Then *C* dies, survived by two children, *E* and *F*. Then *E* dies, survived by two children, *G* and *H*. Then *F* dies, survived by a child, *I*. Then *A* dies. Who takes the property?

Here is a diagram of the family tree in Case 15. Living persons are underlined.

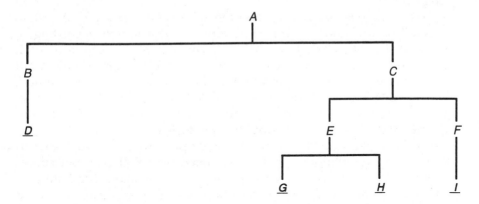

Under the English per stirpes method, the division into shares is made at the level of *A*'s children. *D* takes *B*'s half share by representation. *C*'s half share is divided into quarters. *G* and *H* take *E*'s quarter and *I* takes *F*'s quarter.

Under the modern per stirpes method, the division into shares is made at the level where a descendant is alive, at *D*'s level. *D* takes one-third. *G* and *H* divide *E*'s one-third, taking one-sixth each, and *I* takes *F*'s one-third.

Under the UPC's per capita at each generation system, the division into shares is made at the level where a descendant is alive, at *D*'s level. *D* takes one-third. The two-thirds share of *E* and *F* is divided equally among *G*, *H*, and *I*, each taking two-ninths.

In the last ten years, considerable disagreement has arisen among scholars and law reformers as to how gifts to issue should be divided. As a result, what used to be fairly simple has now become complex. Restatement (Second) of Property, Donative Transfers §28.2 (1988), abandoned the position of the first Restatement. It provides that a gift to "issue" is not to be referred to the intestacy law for meaning. Instead, a gift to "issue" is to be distributed according to the modern per stirpes system, and a gift to "issue per stirpes" is to be distributed according to the English per stirpes system. Uniform Probate Code §§2-708 and 2-709 (1990) draw a distinction between a gift to "issue" and to "issue by representation," on the one hand, and to "issue per stirpes" on the other. A gift to "issue" or to "issue by representation" is to be referred to the intestacy law for meaning, which under UPC §2-106, provides for distribution to issue per capita at each generation (see supra page 89). On the other hand, a gift to "issue per stirpes" is to be distributed according to the English per stirpes method. By giving different meanings to "issue by representation" and "issue per stirpes," which heretofore have been treated as synonymous terms, the Uniform Probate Code may sow considerable confusion and reap litigation.

New York has adopted a variation of the UPC scheme. A gift to "issue" or to "issue by representation" is distributed according to intestacy law, which follows the UPC concept of per capita at each generation. N.Y. Est., Powers & Trusts Law §2-1.2 (Supp. 1998). A gift to "issue per stirpes" is distributed by the modern per stirpes method, not the English per stirpes method as under the UPC. Id. §1-2.14. In California, by statute a gift to "issue" will be distributed according to the intestacy law, which adopts the modern per stirpes system. Cal. Prob. Code §245 (1998). A gift to "issue per stirpes" or to "issue by right of representation" will be distributed by the English per stirpes method. Id. §246. For a case holding a trustee liable for failing to distribute property, given to the settlor's issue per stirpes, in accordance with the meaning of per stirpes followed in the jurisdiction, see Stowers v. Norwest Bank Indiana, 624 N.E.2d 485 (Ind. App. 1993).

In view of the unsettled state of the law, and of legislative solutions going in different directions, sometimes upsetting commonly understood meanings, you may want to define issue or per stirpes in instruments you draft. Here are definitions to choose from:

REFERENCE TO INTESTACY LAW

When a distribution is directed to be made to any person's issue or issue per stirpes, distribution shall be made to such issue in such shares as they would receive under the (state) law of intestate succession if such person had died intestate on the date of the final ascertainment of the membership in the class, owning the subject matter of the gift.

ENGLISH PER STIRPES

When a distribution is directed to be made to any person's issue or issue per stirpes, the property shall be divided into as many equal shares as there are (1) living children of the person, if any, and (2) deceased children who leave issue then living. Each living child of the person shall be allocated one share, and the share of each deceased child who leaves issue then living shall be divided in the same manner.

MODERN PER STIRPES

When a distribution is directed to be made to any person's issue or issue per stirpes, the property shall be divided into as many equal shares as there are (1) living members of the nearest generation of issue then living and (2) deceased members of that generation who leave issue then living. Each living member of the nearest generation of issue then living shall be allocated one share, and the share of each deceased member of that generation who leaves issue then living shall be divided among his or her then living issue in the same manner.

PER CAPITA AT EACH GENERATION

When a distribution is directed to be made to any person's issue or issue per stirpes, the property shall be divided into as many equal shares as there are (1) living members of the nearest generation of issue then living and (2) deceased members of that generation who leave issue then living. Each living member of the nearest generation then living shall be allocated one share, and the remaining shares, if any, shall be combined and then divided among the living issue of the deceased members of that generation as if the issue already allocated a share and their descendants were then dead.

(2) Adopted children

No coast-to-coast statement is possible as to whether a child adopted by *A* is entitled to share in a gift by *T* to the "children," "issue," "descendants," or "heirs" of *A*. Adoption was unknown to the common law and "children" and "issue" necessarily connoted a blood relationship. When adoption laws were enacted in the second half of the nineteenth century, courts were faced with the question of whether an adopted child took under the will of a person who was not the adoptive parent. The early cases were heavily influenced by the inherited reverence for blood relationships; they held an adopted child could not take. These cases gave rise to the stranger-to-the-adoption rule: The adopted child is presumptively barred, whatever generic word is used, except when the donor is the adoptive parent. As adoption became more common and more socially acceptable, courts began to carve exceptions in the stranger-to-the-adoption rule. For example, an adopted child might be permitted to take if adopted before, and not after, the testator's death. Some courts also drew distinctions between a gift to "*A*'s children" and a gift to "*A*'s issue" or the "heirs of *A*'s body." Unlike the latter terms, which were thought to have a biological connotation, a gift to "*A*'s children" presumptively included *A*'s adopted children. Where judicial decisions were found unsatisfactory, legislatures began to intervene in favor of the adopted child. The legislation was seldom retroactive and was sometimes ambiguous. Today, in most states adopted children are presumptively included in gifts by *T* to the "children," "issue," "descendants," and "heirs" of *A*. But the law of many of these states is likely to have been developed by changing judicial decisions and statutes over the twentieth century, and, since the change may not be retroactive, whether the adopted child is included may depend on what the law was at testator's death in, say, 1955. See First Natl. Bank of Chicago v. King, 165 Ill. 2d 533, 651 N.E.2d 127 (1995); In re Estate of Nicolaus, 366 N.W.2d 562 (Iowa 1985); New England Merchants National Bank v. Groswold, 387 Mass. 822, 444 N.E.2d 359 (1983) (setting forth the complicated history of this issue in Massachusetts); Hyman v. Glover, 232 Va. 140, 348 S.E.2d 269 (1986) (overruled by Va. Code §64.1-71.1 (1987)). See Edward C. Halbach, Jr., Issues About Issue: Some Recurrent Class Gift Problems, 48 Mo. L. Rev. 333, 336-340 (1983); Annot., 71 A.L.R.4th 374 (1989).

Uniform Probate Code (1990, as amended in 1991)

§2-705. LASS GIFTS CONSTRUED TO ACCORD WITH INTESTATE SUCCESSION

(a) Adopted individuals and individuals born out of wedlock, and their respective descendants if appropriate to the class, are included in class gifts and other terms of relationship in accordance with the rules for intestate succession. Terms of relationship that do not differentiate relationships by blood from those by affinity, such as "uncles," "aunts," "nieces," or "nephews," are construed to exclude relatives by affinity. Terms of relationship that do not differentiate relationships by the half blood from those by the whole blood, such as "brothers," "sisters," "nieces," or "nephews," are construed to include both types of relationships.

(b) In addition to the requirements of subsection (a), in construing a dispositive provision of a transferor who is not the natural parent, an individual born to the natural parent is not considered the child of that parent unless the individual lived while a minor as a regular member of the household of that natural parent or of that parent's parent, brother, sister, spouse, or surviving spouse.

(c) In addition to the requirements of subsection (a), in construing a dispositive provision of a transferor who is not the adopting parent, an adopted individual is not considered the child of the adopting parent unless the adopted individual lived while a minor, either before or after the adoption, as a regular member of the household of the adopting parent.

Minary v. Citizens Fidelity Bank & Trust Co.
Court of Appeals of Kentucky, 1967
419 S.W.2d 340

OSBORNE, J.   [Amelia S. Minary died in 1932, leaving a will devising her residuary estate in trust, to pay the income to her husband and three sons, James, Thomas, and Alfred, for their respective lives. The trust was to terminate upon the death of the last surviving beneficiary, at which time the corpus was to be distributed as follows:

> After the Trust terminates, the remaining portion of the Trust Fund shall be distributed to my then surviving heirs, according to the laws of descent and distribution then in force in Kentucky, and, if no such heirs, then to the First Christian Church, Louisville, Kentucky.

The husband died, then James died without issue, then Thomas died leaving two children: Thomas Jr. and Amelia Minary Gant. In 1934, Alfred married Myra, and in 1959 he adopted her as his child. The trust terminated upon Alfred's death without natural issue in 1963.]

The question herein presented is, "Did Alfred's adoption of his wife Myra make her eligible to inherit under the provisions of his mother's will?" More specifically, the question is, "Is Myra included in the term 'my then surviving heirs according to the laws of descent and distribution in force in Kentucky'?"

This has revived a lively question in the jurisprudence of this state and presents two rather difficult legal problems. The first being under what conditions, if any, should an adopted child inherit from or through its adoptive parent? We have encountered little difficulty with the problem of inheriting from an adoptive parent but the question of when will an adoptive child inherit through an adoptive parent has given us considerable trouble. As late as 1945 in Copeland v. State Bank and Trust Company, 300 Ky. 432, 188 S.W.2d 1017, we held without hesitation or equivocation that the words "heirs" and "issue" as well as "children" and all other words of similar import as used in a will referred only to the natural blood relations and did not include an adopted child.

In 1950, in Isaacs v. Manning, 312 Ky. 326, 227 S.W.2d 418, we adopted the contrary position and held that an adopted child was included in the phrase "heirs at law" wherein a will devised property to designated children and then upon their death to their heirs at law. In the course of the opinion, we said, "where no language [shows] a contrary intent . . . an adopted daughter clearly falls within the class designated." In this case we distinguish the *Copeland* case, supra.

In 1953, in Major v. Kammer, 258 S.W.2d 506, we again held that an adopted child was included in the term "heirs at law," basing our decision upon the legislative changes made in the adoption laws and overruling Copeland v. State Bank and Trust Company, supra. In Edmands v. Tice, Ky., 324 S.W.2d 491, which was decided in 1959, we held that where testator used the word children, an adopted child could inherit through an adopted parent the same as if heirs at law or issue had been used. . . .

From the foregoing we conclude that when Amelia S. Minary used the phrase, "my then surviving heirs according to the laws of descent and distribution then in force in Kentucky," she included the adoptive children of her sons. This leaves us with the extremely bothersome question of: "Does the fact that Myra Minary was an adult and the wife of Alfred at the time she was adopted affect her status as an 'heir' under the will?" KRS 405.390 provides: "An adult person . . . may be adopted in the same manner as provided by law for the adoption of a child and with the same legal effect. . . ."

KRS 199.520 provides: "From and after the date of the judgment the child shall be deemed the child of petitioners and shall be considered for purposes of inheritance and succession and for all other legal considerations, the natural, legitimate child of the parents adopting it the same as if born of their bodies."

It would appear from examination of the authorities that the adoption of an adult for the purpose of making him an heir has been an accepted practice in our law for many years. However, here it should be pointed out that the practice in its ancient form made the person so adopted the legal heir of the adopting party only. This court has dealt with the problem of adopting adults for the purpose of making them heirs on several occasions. . . .

In 1957, in Bedinger v. Graybill's Executors, Ky., 302 S.W.2d 594, we had before us a case almost identical to the one here under consideration. In that case Mrs. Lulu Graybill, in 1914, set up a trust for her son Robert by will. She then provided after the death of the son that the trust "be paid over and distributed by the Trustee to the heirs at law of my said son according to the laws of descent and distribution in force in Kentucky at the time of his death." There was a devise over to others in the event that Robert died without heirs. Robert having no issue adopted his wife long after his mother's death. We held that the wife should inherit the same as an adopted child, there being no public policy against the adoption of a wife. However, it will be noted that in the course of the opinion it is carefully pointed out that the will directed the estate be paid to the "heirs at law of Robert" and did not provide that the estate should go to "my heirs," "his children" or to "his issue," indicating by this language that if the phrase had been one of the others set out the results might have been different. . . .

This case could properly be distinguished from Bedinger v. Graybill's Executors, supra, on the basis of the difference in language used in the two wills[;] however, no useful purpose could be served by so distinguishing them. The time has come to face again this problem which has persistently perplexed the court when an adult is adopted for the sole purpose of making him or her an heir and claimant to the estate of an ancestor under the terms of a testamentary instrument known and in existence at the time of the adoption. Even though the statute permits such adoption and even though it expressly provides that it shall be "with the same legal effect as the adoption of a child," we, nevertheless, are constrained to view this practice to be an act of subterfuge which in effect thwarts the intent of the ancestor whose property is being distributed and cheats the rightful heirs. We are faced with a situation wherein we must choose between carrying out the intent of deceased testators or giving a strict and rigid construction to a statute which thwarts that intent. In the *Bedinger* case there is no doubt but what the intent of the testatrix, as to the disposition of her property, was circumvented. It is our opinion that by giving a strict and literal construction to the adoption statutes, we thwarted the efforts of the deceased to dispose of her property as she saw fit.

When one rule of law does violence to another it becomes inevitable that one must then give way to the other. It is of paramount importance that a man be permitted to pass on his property at his death to those who represent the natural objects of his bounty. This is an ancient and precious right running from the dawn of civilization in an unbroken line down to the present day. Our adoption statutes are humanitarian in nature and of great importance to the welfare of the public. However, these statutes should not be given a construction that does violence to the above rule and to the extent that they violate the rule and prevent one from passing on his property in accord with his wishes, they must give way. Adoption of an adult for the purpose of bringing that person under the provisions of a preexisting testamentary instrument when he clearly was not intended to be so covered should not be permitted and we do not view this as doing any great violence to the intent and purpose of our adoption laws.

For the foregoing reasons the action of the trial court in declaring Myra Galvin Minary an heir of Amelia S. Minary is reversed.

The judgment is reversed.

NOTES AND PROBLEMS

1.   Adoption may be used for a number of purposes other than creating an ordinary parent-child relationship. *A* may adopt *B* in order to prevent *A*'s parents or more remote relatives from contesting *A*'s will or to qualify *B* as a member of a class given a future interest in a trust, as in the *Minary* case. In the large majority of states, an adult person, married or unmarried, may adopt any other person, minor or adult. The Uniform Adoption Act (1969) provides that "any individual may be adopted." See supra page 107.

The cases are split over whether adult adoptees are included within class gift terminology for purposes of will and trust dispositions. Cases holding they are include Evans v. McCoy, 291 Md. 562, 436 A.2d 436 (1981) (76-year-old woman adopts 21-year-old neighbor and 53-year-old cousin in order to defeat executory interest of her cousins); In re Estate of Fortnoy, 5 Kan. App. 2d 14, 611 P.2d 599 (1980) (90-year-old man adopts 65-year-old nephew of wife); Satterfield v. Bonyhady, 223 Neb. 513, 446 N.W.2d 214 (1989) (stepdaughter, adopted at age 44, included); Solomon v. Central Trust Co., 63 Ohio St. 3d 35, 584 N.E.2d 1185 (1992) (adult adoptee included if parent-child relationship began during adoptee's minority); In re Estate of Joslyn, 38 Cal. App. 4th 1428, 45 Cal. Rptr. 2d 616 (1995) (same as *Solomon*). Cases contra include Cross v. Cross, 177 Ill. App. 3d 588, 532 N.E.2d 486 (1988); Davis v. Neilson, 871 S.W.2d 35 (Mo. App. 1993); Foster v. Foster, 641 S.W.2d 693 (Tex. Civ. App. 1982).

If adult adoptees are included within class gifts in will and trust dispositions, is there any reason for excluding a spouse-adopted-as-a-child from such a gift? See In re Belgard's Trust, 829 P.2d 457 (Colo. App. 1992) (holding adopted adult wife not a proper beneficiary of her mother-in-law's trust despite language in the trust defining a "child" to include "persons legally adopted by my son"; however, adopted wife was entitled to inherit her husband-father's estate through intestacy as his child). Compare adoption of lover, supra page 107.

The use of the adoption procedure for the purpose of creating a child to come within a class gift is in effect using adoption as a special power of appointment. If Amelia Minary had given her sons a power to appoint at least a life estate to their spouses, Alfred's desperate shenanigans would not have been necessary and his wife would not have ended up impoverished. It is hard to believe Alfred's mother would have wanted his widow to live in penury. Likely her lawyer did not suggest a special power of appointment to her because in 1932, when she died, special powers were relatively unknown except among lawyers for the rich in urban states. Speaking of the testator's intent is something of a fiction if her lawyer never brought up the subject of her sons' widows.

2.   *Children "adopted out."* T bequeaths a fund in trust "for my wife for life, then to my issue then living per stirpes." After T's death, his son A dies, leaving a wife and a minor child, B. A's wife remarries, and her second husband adopts B. T's wife then dies. Is B entitled to share in the trust fund? See Newman v. Wells Fargo Bank, 14 Cal. 4th 126, 926 P.2d 969, 59 Cal. Rptr. 2d 2 (1996) (looking at intestacy law as it existed at time of T's death to determine T's intent; B excluded); Lockwood v. Adamson, 409 Mass. 325, 566 N.E.2d 96 (1991) (B shares under T's will even though B would not inherit from T under intestacy law); Note, When Blood Isn't Thicker Than Water: The Inheritance Rights of Adopted-out Children in New York, 53 Brooklyn L.

Rev. 1007 (1988). Restatement (Second) of Property, Donative Transfers §25.5 (1988), provides that a gift to "children" of *A* does not include a child of *A* adopted by another, "if such adoption removes the child from the broader family circle of the designated person."

For an analysis of UPC §2-705's treatment of adopted and nonmarital children, see Patricia G. Roberts, Adopted and Nonmarital Children — Exploring the 1990 Uniform Probate Code's Intestacy and Class Gift Provisions, 32 Real Prop., Prob. & Tr. J. 539 (1998).

3.   Absent expression of a contrary intent by the testator, the term "children" is presumed not to include stepchildren or persons related only by affinity. See Restatement (Second) of Property, supra, §25.6; Margaret M. Mahoney, Stepfamilies in the Law of Intestate Succession and Wills, 22 U.C. Davis L. Rev. 917 (1989).

4.   Adoption, unlike marriage, is not revocable if the relationship turns sour. In 1988 Doris Duke, 75, one of the world's richest women, adopted Chandi Heffner, 35. Chandi had taken her name from the Hindu deity, Chandi, and was a Hare Krishna when Doris met her at a dance class. Doris Duke was the life beneficiary of two trusts created by her father, James Buchanan ("Buck") Duke, in 1917 and 1924. After Doris's death, the income from the trusts was to be payable to Doris's children. Doris had no natural children. Subsequent to the adoption Doris Duke had a big bust-up with her adopted daughter Chandi and tried to exclude her from her father's trust in her will.

Doris Duke died in 1993, a billionaire. She left her fortune to a charitable foundation, over which she put her barely-literate butler, Bernard Lafferty, in charge. After embarking on an extended spending spree, far exceeding the $500,000 a year Doris left him, the butler dropped dead some three years after Doris died. Doris's will provided:

> *TWENTY-ONE*: As indicated in Article SEVEN, it is my intention that Chandi Heffner not be deemed to be my child for purposes of disposing of property under this my Will (or any Codicil thereto). Furthermore, it is not my intention, nor do I believe that it was ever my father's intention, that Chandi Heffner be deemed to be a child or lineal descendant of mine for purposes of disposing of the trust estate of the May 2, 1917 trust which my father established for my benefit or the Doris Duke Trust, dated December 11, 1924, which my father established for the benefit of me, certain other members of the Duke family and ultimately for charity.
>
> I am extremely troubled by the realization that Chandi Heffner may use my 1988 adoption of her (when she was 35 years old) to attempt to benefit financially under the terms of either of the trusts created by my father. After giving the matter prolonged and serious consideration, I am convinced that I should not have adopted Chandi Heffner. I have come to the realization that her primary motive was financial gain. I firmly believe that, like me, my father would not have wanted her to have benefit-

Doris Duke in 1991, with her butler, Bernard Lafferty

ted under the trusts which he created, and similarly, I do not wish her to benefit from my estate.

Her signature was shaky but bold:

IN WITNESS WHEREOF, I have hereunto set my hand and affix my seal to this my Last Will and Testament on this 5ᵗʰ day of April, 1993.

Doris Duke

Upon Doris Duke's death, Chandi Heffner sued the trustees of the Doris Duke Trust created by her father, Buck Duke, demanding that they pay her income as the successive life beneficiary of the Doris Duke Trust, worth $170 million at Doris's death. The trial court ruled against her, on the ground that an adult adoptee was not considered a child of the adopting parent when the trust is created by another. In re Trust of Duke, 305 N.J. Super. 408, 702 A.2d 1008 (1995). Chandi Heffner also sued the trustees of the other trust created by Buck Duke and the executors of Doris Duke, claiming that Doris had promised to support her. While the litigation was proceeding, the parties settled. Chandi Heffner received $60 million from the James Buchanan Duke trusts in settlement of her claim to be a child of Doris and $5 million from the Doris Duke estate. One very expensive adoption!

For more on the Doris Duke litigation, see In re Duke, 87 N.Y.2d 465, 663 N.E.2d 602, 640 N.Y.S.2d 446 (1996); N.Y. Times, May 16, 1996, at B8; N.Y. Times, Nov. 5, 1996, at B8; N.Y. Times, Jan. 24, 1997, at B1 (reporting the feeding frenzy of lawyers).

(3)   Nonmarital children

At common law the word *children* in a will or trust presumptively referred to legitimate children only. With the recent changes in the treatment of nonmarital children in intestacy laws and elsewhere, this presumption has become increasingly unreliable. In a reversal of precedents on the question, In re Hoffman, 53 A.D.2d 55, 385 N.Y.S.2d 49 (1976), held that, absent an express intent to the contrary, the word *issue*, where it appears unqualified in a will, refers to illegitimate as well as legitimate descendants. See also Walton v. Lindsey, 349 So. 2d 41 (Ala. 1977), holding that the existence of a nonmarital child created a latent ambiguity and evidence was admissible to determine whether the testator intended to include the nonmarital child as a member of the class of children to which he was leaving his estate.

In Estate of Dulles, 494 Pa. 180, 431 A.2d 208, 17 A.L.R.4th 1279 (1981), it was held that a statutory canon of construction that nonmarital children not be considered children of their father violated the equal protection clause of the Constitution. In Powers v. Wilkinson, 399 Mass. 650, 506 N.E.2d 842 (1987), the court held — contrary to the *Dulles* case — that the presumption excluding nonmarital children in a gift to issue did not violate the equal protection clause of the Constitution. "Thus we hold that state action is not involved, nor is the equal protection clause of the Fourteenth Amendment implicated, when courts apply rules of construction to wills and trust instruments." However, the Massachusetts court announced it would thereafter presume, as to all instruments executed after the date of the case, that the word *issue* includes nonmarital issue.

Restricting the gift to "lawful issue" in the instrument would, at one time, have excluded illegitimates. But this no longer holds true. Nonmarital children may be considered lawful issue.

Lawyers drafting wills often define words in order to avoid ambiguity. The Sisyphus Prize for Heroic Attempts must go to a prominent Detroit law firm that drafted the will of Clyde H. Giltner, late of Tecumseh, Michigan. The will reads:

(1) The word "descendant" shall mean and include a child, grandchild, great grandchild, great-great grandchild, great-great-great grandchild, and great-great-great-great grandchild, whether by blood, by adoption, or otherwise, of the person whose descendant is referred to, and also any adopted child of any child, grandchild, great grandchild, great-great grandchild or great-great-great grandchild of such person.

(2) The words "child" and "children" shall mean and include, respectively, any child and any children of the person whose child or children is or are referred to by blood, by adoption, or otherwise.

(3) The words "grandchild," "great grandchild," "great-great grandchild," "great-great-great grandchild," or "great-great-great-great grandchild" shall mean and include, respectively, a grandchild, great grandchild, great-great grandchild, great-great-great grandchild, and great-great-great-great grandchild of the person whose grandchild, great grandchild, great-great grandchild, great-great-great grandchild or great-great-great-great grandchild is referred to, whether by blood, by adoption, or otherwise, and also any adopted child of any child, any adopted child of any child of any child, any adopted child of any child of any child of any child and any adopted child of any child of any child of any child of such person.

Can you improve on the Detroit form?

c. Gifts to Heirs

Estate of Woodworth
California Court of Appeal, Fifth District, 1993
18 Cal. App. 4th 936, 22 Cal. Rptr. 2d 676

DiBiaso, J. The Regents of the University of California (Regents) appeal from an order of the probate court which rejected their claim to the remainder of a testamentary trust. We will reverse. We will apply the common law preference for early vesting and hold that, absent evidence of the testator's intent to the contrary, the identity of "heirs" entitled to trust assets must be determined at the date of death of the named ancestor who predeceased the life tenant, not at the date of death of the life tenant.

STATEMENT OF CASE AND FACTS

Harold Evans Woodworth died testate in 1971. His will was thereafter admitted to probate; in 1974 a decree of distribution was entered. According to this decree,[14] a portion of the estate was distributed outright to the testator's surviving spouse, Mamie Barlow Woodworth. The balance of the estate was distributed to Mamie Barlow Woodworth and the Bank of America, to be held, administered and distributed in accord with the terms of a testamentary trust established by the will of Harold Evans Woodworth. The life tenant of the trust was Mamie Barlow Woodworth. Among the trust provisions was the following:

> This trust shall terminate upon the death of MAMIE BARLOW WOODWORTH. Upon the termination of this trust, my trustee shall pay, deliver and convey all of the trust estate then remaining, including all accrued and/or undistributed income thereunto appertaining, to MRS. RAY B. PLASS, also known as Elizabeth Woodworth Plass [Elizabeth Plass], whose present address is 90 Woodland Way, Piedmont, California, if she then survives, and if not then to her heirs at law.

Elizabeth Plass was the testator's sister; he also had two brothers who predeceased him. One died without issue. The other was survived by two children, Elizabeth Woodworth Holden, a natural daughter, and James V. Woodworth, an adopted son.

Elizabeth Plass died in 1980; she was survived by her husband, Raymond Plass. Raymond Plass died testate in 1988. In relevant part, he left the residue of his estate to the Regents for use on the University's Berkeley campus.

Mamie Woodworth, the life tenant, died in 1991. Thereafter, Wells Fargo Bank, as successor trustee of the Woodworth trust, petitioned the probate court pursuant to Probate Code section 17200 to determine those persons entitled to distribution of the trust estate. The petition alleged that "The petitioner [was] uncertain as to whether Elizabeth Plass' 'heirs at law' under [the decree] should be deter-

---

14. The decedent's will was not introduced in the probate court proceedings. A decree of distribution is a conclusive determination of the terms of a testamentary trust and the rights of all parties claiming any interest under it. (Estate of Easter (1944) 24 Cal. 2d 191, 194, 148 P.2d 601.)

mined as of February 14, 1980, the date of her death, or August 13, 1991, the date of Mamie [Barlow] Woodworth's death.''

It is undisputed that (1) as of February 14, 1980, Elizabeth Plass' heirs at law were her husband, Raymond Plass, her niece, Elizabeth Woodworth Holden, and her nephew, James V. Woodworth; and (2) as of August 13, 1991, Elizabeth Plass' heirs at law were Elizabeth Woodworth Holden and James V. Woodworth (the Woodworth heirs).

. . . [T]he probate court concluded that the identity of the heirs entitled to the trust assets must be determined as of the date of death of the life tenant. The probate court therefore ordered the trustee to deliver the remaining trust assets in equal shares to the Woodworth heirs.

Discussion

1. STANDARD OF REVIEW

The decree of distribution constitutes a final and conclusive adjudication of the testamentary disposition which the deceased made of his property. (Estate of Miner (1963) 214 Cal. App. 2d 533, 538, 29 Cal. Rptr. 601.) Thus, the outcome of this appeal turns on the proper construction to be given to the provision in the decree which directs the distribution of the trust assets upon termination. . . .

2. ISSUES

The Regents contend the probate court erroneously failed to apply the general rule of construction which requires that the identity of "heirs" entitled to take a remainder interest be determined as of the date of death of the denominated ancestor, in the absence of any contrary intent expressed by the testator. (See Estate of Stanford (1957) 49 Cal. 2d 120, 124, 315 P.2d 681; Estate of Liddle (1958) 162 Cal. App. 2d 7, 328 P.2d 35; and Estate of Newman (1924) 68 Cal. App. 420, 424, 229 P. 898.) Had the probate court construed the decree in accord with this principle, the Regents would have been entitled to share in the trust assets as a residuary legatee of Raymond Plass, an heir at law of Elizabeth Plass at the time of her death in 1980.

The Woodworth heirs respond by asserting the probate court's decision is consistent with an exception to the general rule which requires that the determination be made at the date of death of the life tenant. (See Wells Fargo Bank v. Title Ins. & Trust Co. (1971) 22 Cal. App. 3d 295, 300, 99 Cal. Rptr. 464; and Estate of McKenzie (1966) 246 Cal. App. 2d 740, 54 Cal. Rptr. 888.) Under this principle, the Regents have no interest in the trust assets, because Raymond Plass predeceased Mamie Barlow Woodworth.[15]

3. THE EARLY VESTING RULE

Estate of Liddle, supra, 162 Cal. App. 2d 7, 328 P.2d 35, reflects the common law preference for vested rather than contingent remainders. Thus, unless a particular instrument disclosed a different intent on the part of the testator, a remainder to a class of persons, such as children, became vested in the class when one or more of its members came into existence and could be ascertained, even though the class was subject to open for future additional members. (Estate of Stanford, supra, 49 Cal. 2d at p. 125, 315 P.2d 681.) Furthermore, the fact that takers of a postponed gift were described by a class designation did not, under the common law rule, give rise to any implied condition of survival.

The circumstances involved in *Liddle* are substantially indistinguishable from those of the present case. In *Liddle*, the remainder of a testamentary trust was to be distributed to the testatrix's attorney or, in the event of his death, the attorney's heirs-at-law. Although the attorney survived the testatrix, he predeceased the life tenant. [His wife was his heir.] The wife's heirs and the administrator of her estate clashed with certain remote cousins of the attorney over the ownership of the trust assets.

The appellate court ruled in favor of the wife's estate. Relying upon statutes, treatises, and case law expressing common law notions, including Estate of Stanford, supra, 49 Cal. 2d 120, 315 P.2d 681, the court construed the phrase "heirs at law" according to its technical meaning, that is, the person or persons who are entitled to succeed to the property of an intestate decedent. The *Liddle* court then held the members of this class must be determined as of the death of the named ancestor. The rule was summarized as follows:

> Normally, when a gift has been made to the "heirs" or "next of kin" of a named individual, the donor has said in effect that he wants the property distributed as the law would distribute it if the named person died intestate. Accordingly, the normal time for applying the statute of descent or distribution is at the death of the named individual. This is, however, merely a rule of construction, and if the testator or grantor manifests an intention that the statute be applied either at an earlier or a later time, such intention will be given effect. (*Liddle*, supra, 162 Cal. App. 2d at p. 19, 328 P.2d 35.)

15. It is undisputed that had the testator in this case died on or after January 1, 1985, the Regents would have no claim to the trust assets. Under Probate Code sections 6150 and 6151 which have been in effect since 1985, a devise of a future interest to a class, such as heirs, includes only those who fit the class description at the time the legacy is to take effect in enjoyment.

The designated ancestor in *Liddle* was the attorney. Because his wife was his intestate heir at the time he died, the court found she was the proper recipient of the trust estate.

4. THE CONTINGENT SUBSTITUTIONAL GIFT EXCEPTION

On the other hand, *Wells Fargo Bank*, supra, 22 Cal. App. 3d 295, 300, 99 Cal. Rptr. 464, reflects the application of an exception to the early vesting principle. In *Wells Fargo Bank*, a woman had conveyed, by a grant deed, a life estate in certain real property to her daughter, with remainders to the grantor's two other children. If the life tenant died without issue and the two other children died without issue before the grantor's death, the instrument provided that the remainder interest in the property would belong to the grantor's "heirs." The trial court determined the heirs should be ascertained as of the date of the grantor's death.

The court of appeal reversed, . . . [relying on] Simes & Smith, The Law of Future Interests (2nd ed.) §735, p. 210. . . . [U]nder consideration at the cited portion of this treatise is the situation where "a testator devises a life estate or defeasible fee to *a person who is one of his heirs*, followed by a remainder or executory interest to the testator's heirs." (Simes & Smith, supra, §735, p. 206; emphasis added.) As Simes and Smith point out, in such circumstances, some courts have rejected the general rule that the members of the class are to be determined at the death of the ancestor (i.e., the testator), and instead have applied an exception which identifies the heirs who will take the remainder as those in being upon the death of the holder of the life estate or defeasible fee. The rationale for these decisions is an assumption the testator did not intend to give both a present and a future interest to the same person. (See Simes & Smith, supra, §735, at pp. 206-210.)

Wells Fargo Bank involved a bequest of the same type as that which is the subject of section 735 of the Simes and Smith treatise. In *Wells Fargo Bank*, the estate of the life tenant would have been entitled to receive a portion of the remainder if the identity of the grantor's heirs was determined at the time of the grantor's death rather than at the date of the life tenant's death. The *Wells Fargo Bank* court essentially adopted the analysis in section 735 of Simes and Smith that: "[I]f the general rule is applied, an incongruous result would be reached by taking the property away from [the holder of the possessory interest] because he died without issue and giving it back to him because of the same reason." (*Wells Fargo Bank*, supra, 22 Cal. App. 3d at p. 300, 99 Cal. Rptr. 464.) . . .

By contrast, in the instant case we do not have a contingent, substituted gift to a class of recipients which includes the deceased interim beneficiary. As in *Liddle*, the class of contingent, substituted heirs does not encompass any prior contingent interim beneficiary. . . .

Thus, we believe the exception to the general rule of early vesting, as implemented in *Wells Fargo Bank*, should not be applied to the remainder interest contained in the decree of distribution here.

5.   OTHER CONSIDERATIONS

For the reasons which follow, we find no other justification for departing from *Liddle*. First, there is nothing in the language of the other provisions of the decree of distribution before us which reveals the testator's intent or desire. Since the record does not include Harold Evans Woodworth's will, we cannot resort to it to attempt to divine his wishes.

Second, the fact that the University, an entity, is not a relative of Elizabeth Plass or one of her heirs at law is not material. Unlike the *Wells Fargo Bank* court, we are unwilling to say that application of the general rule "would result in thwarting the expressed intention of the Grantor by distributing the corpus of the trust to persons or entities other than [Elizabeth Plass'] heirs." (*Wells Fargo Bank*, supra, 22 Cal. App. 3d at p. 301, 99 Cal. Rptr. 464.) Had the instrument in Wells Fargo Bank satisfactorily disclosed the grantor's intentions regarding the distribution of the remainder interest in the property, there would have been no need for the court to have even considered the competing rules of construction in order to decide the case.

It would be pure speculation for us to conclude that Harold Evans Woodworth would not have wanted Raymond Plass to inherit a portion of the trust assets. It appears from the record that Raymond Plass and Elizabeth Plass were married at the time the testator executed his will. It has long been the law in California that a husband is an heir of his deceased wife. Nothing in the decree forecloses the possibility the testator took into account the fact that Elizabeth Plass might predecease, and Raymond Plass might outlive, Mamie Barlow Woodworth, resulting in Raymond Plass' succession to a portion of the trust remainder.

Third, the rule of construction which favors descent according to blood in cases of ambiguity in testamentary dispositions should likewise not determine the result in this case. The general rule favoring early vesting was well-established long before the testator died. We do not think it should be abandoned in order to carry out some purportedly perceived, but entirely speculative, notion about the intent of the testator based upon events which occurred well after the testator's death. (See Estate of McKenzie, supra, 246 Cal. App. 2d at p. 748, 54 Cal. Rptr. 888.) As we noted earlier, it is perfectly conceivable that Harold Evans Woodworth took into account in making his will the possibility that his property would pass to Raymond Plass and there-after be transferred to strangers to the Woodworth line.

. . . In the absence of any firm indication of testamentary intent, the rules of construction must be implemented in order to insure uniformity and predictability in the law, rather than disregarded in order to carry out a court's ad hoc sense of what is, with perfect hindsight, acceptable in a particular set of circumstances. . . .

Last, none of the other exceptions identified in *Wells Fargo Bank* to the early vesting rule apply under the circumstances of this case. This is not a situation where the "life tenant is the sole heir, but the will devises the remainder to the testator's 'heirs.'" (*Wells Fargo Bank*, supra, 22 Cal. App. 3d at p. 300, 99 Cal. Rptr. 464; Estate of Wilson (1920) 184 Cal. 63, 193 P. 581.)

In addition, the language of the decree does not contain any "expression of futurity in the description of the ancestor's heirs" (*Wells Fargo Bank*, supra, 22 Cal. App. 3d at p. 300, 99 Cal. Rptr. 464), such as "my then living heirs-at-law" (Estate of Layton (1933) 217 Cal. 451, 454, 19 P.2d 793). When, as here, "the gift is in terms 'then to the heirs' of a designated person, the word 'then' merely indicates the time of enjoyment and has no significance in relation to the rule [of early vesting]." (Estate of Miner, supra, 214 Cal. App. 2d at p. 542, 29 Cal. Rptr. 601.) . . .

Finally, and contrary to the contention of the Woodworth heirs, we do not find the words "pay to" contained in the instant decree to be equivalent to the word "vest" or otherwise constitute an "expression of futurity" for purposes of determining the identity of the relevant heirs. (*Wells Fargo Bank*, supra, at p. 300, 99 Cal. Rptr. 464.) Rather, the instruction pertains to the time when the recipients of the assets are entitled to have them.

Disposition

Accordingly, we must reverse the probate court's ruling that the Regents have no claim to the assets of the testamentary trust.

The judgment (order) appealed from is reversed.

NOTES

1. The many problems arising from gifts to "heirs" are catalogued in Restatement (Second) of Property, Donative Transfers §§29.1-29.8 (1988).

2. Because a transmissible remainder is subject to the federal estate tax, estate planners in several states have successfully urged legis-

latures to enact a statute providing that where a remainder is given to a person's heirs, the heirs will not be ascertained until the remainder becomes possessory. Under such a statute, no remainderman has a transmissible interest because if he dies before the remainder becomes possessory, he will not be alive when heirs are ascertained and, therefore, cannot be an heir. California Prob. Code §6151, referred to in footnote 15 in the *Woodworth* case and now renumbered §21114, is such a statute. So is Uniform Probate Code §2-711.

Uniform Probate Code (1990, amended in 1993)

§2-711. FUTURE INTERESTS IN "HEIRS" AND LIKE

If an applicable statute or a governing instrument calls for a present or future distribution to or creates a present or future interest in a designated individual's "heirs," "heirs at law," "next of kin," "relatives," or "family," or language of similar import, the property passes to those persons, including the state under Section 2-105, and in such shares as would succeed to the designated individual's intestate estate under the intestate succession law of the designated individual's domicile if the designated individual died when the disposition is to take effect in possession or enjoyment. If the designated individual's surviving spouse is living but is remarried at the time the disposition is to take effect in possession or enjoyment, the surviving spouse is not an heir of the designated individual.

NOTE: THE DOCTRINE OF WORTHIER TITLE

The doctrine of worthier title apparently still exists in some states. Simply put, the doctrine provides that when a settlor transfers property in trust, with a life estate in the settlor or in another, and purports to create a remainder in the *settlor's heirs*, it is presumed that the settlor intended to retain a reversion in himself and not create a remainder in his heirs. Thus the remainder is presumptively not created. The doctrine is a rule of presumed intent, which can be rebutted by evidence that the settlor did intend to create a remainder in his heirs. Thus:

> *Case 16. O* transfers property to *X* in trust "to pay the income to *O* for life, then to distribute the principal to *A* if *A* is living, and if *A* is not living, to distribute the principal to *O*'s heirs." The presumption is that *O* has a reversion and *O*'s heirs do not have a remainder. *O* may convey the reversion by will to whomever *O* chooses.

The doctrine of worthier title was roused from a sleep of several centuries by Judge Cardozo in Doctor v. Hughes, 225 N.Y 305, 122 N.E. 221 (1919), in order to do equity on some particular facts. But the states that followed Cardozo's lead and adopted the doctrine found that it produced a passel of lawsuits involving the most speculative evidence about whether the settlor intended to create a remainder rather than retain a reversion. As a result of this experience, Arkansas, California, Illinois, Massachusetts, Minnesota, Nebraska, New York, North Carolina, Texas, and West Virginia abolished the doctrine of worthier title. The Restatement of Property (Second), Donative Transfers §30.2(1) (1988), says the doctrine exists in states where not specifically abolished, but this is hard to verify with actual cases. Restatement (Third) of Trusts §49, Comment a (T.D. No. 2, 1999), on the other hand, refuses to recognize the doctrine of worthier title, eliminating this antiquated doctrine. Uniform Probate Code §2-710 abolishes the doctrine of worthier title.

Although rejection of the doctrine of worthier title seems sound, it does leave us with the problem of securing consent of the unascertained heirs of a living settlor to modification or termination of a trust. In Case 16, for example, if *O* and *A* want to terminate the trust they must secure the consent of *O*'s unknown heirs. Statutes in some states abolishing worthier title have dealt with this problem by providing that a trust may be revoked by the settlor and other ascertained beneficiaries when the only other interested persons are the settlor's heirs. See, e.g., N.Y. Est., Powers & Trusts Law §7-1.9(b) (1998).

NOTE: THE RULE IN SHELLEY'S CASE

At common law, if land were conveyed to a grantee for life, then to the *grantee's heirs*, the attempted creation of a contingent remainder in the heirs was not recognized. Instead, the grantee took the remainder. The life estate then merged into the remainder, giving the grantee a possessory fee simple absolute.

Here is a simplified statement of the rule: If

(1)   one instrument (deed, will, or trust)
(2)   creates a life estate in land in *A*, and
(3)   purports to create a remainder in *A*'s heirs (or the heirs of *A*'s body), and
(4)   the estates are both legal or both equitable,

the remainder becomes a remainder in fee simple (or fee tail) in *A*. If there is no intervening estate, the life estate merges into the remainder, giving *A* a fee simple (or fee tail). The rule in Shelley's Case is not a rule of construction. It is a rule of law, and it applies regardless of the intent of the transferor. Here is an example:

> *Case 17.* *O* conveys land in trust "for *A* for life, and then to *A*'s heirs." Under the rule in Shelley's Case, *A* (and not *A*'s heirs) has the remainder, which then merges with *A*'s life estate, giving *A* all the equitable interest in the trust. *A* may by will dispose of the land as *A* chooses.

The rule in Shelley's Case has been abolished in practically all states and the District of Columbia, as well as in England. See Restatement (Second) of Property, Donative Transfers §30.1, Statutory Note (1988). In some states, however, the abolition by statute is fairly recent and does not apply retroactively. In these states, cases involving the rule continue to crop up from time to time. Illinois abolished the rule in Shelley's Case in 1953; North Carolina abolished the rule in Shelley's Case in 1987. See John V. Orth, Requiem for the Rule in Shelley's Case, 67 N.C. L. Rev. 681 (1989). Restatement (Third) of Trusts §49, Comment a (T.D. No. 2, 1999), does not recognize the rule in Shelley's Case.

d.   The Class-Closing Rule

(1)   Introduction

A central characteristic of a gift to a class of persons, such as "to the children of *B*," is that if *B* is alive and capable of having more children, the persons to whom the class description applies can increase in number. The problem we now deal with is: How long can the class increase in membership? In a gift "to *B* for life, then to *B*'s children," all of *B*'s children will be alive (or in gestation) when the class is physiologically closed at *B*'s death. No difficulties will be encountered on distributing the property upon *B*'s death among all *B*'s children or their estates. But suppose the disposition is "to *A* for life, then to *B*'s children." Here we may have a different kettle of fish. If *A* dies during *B*'s lifetime, what should be done with the property, inasmuch as *B* may have more children?

There are several alternative solutions possible when the class is not closed physiologically, but one or more members of the class stand ready to take their shares. Distribution could be postponed until all possible class members are on the scene. Or a partial distribution could be made to *B*'s present children and a "reasonable" portion withheld (until *B*'s death) for possible future distribution to later-born children. Or full distribution could be made to the children now at hand, subject to a requirement that they rebate a portion of each share as *B* has more children. Or the class could be "closed" at *A*'s death, with full distribution to the present children and the exclusion of all children later born to *B*.

The practical problems that would be raised by postponing distribution, or by making a partial or defeasible distribution to existing class members, have led the courts to adopt the last alternative. This is called the *class-closing rule* or the *rule of convenience*. It is a rule of construction, giving way to sufficient evidence of the testator's contrary intent, but it is adhered to more closely than any other rule of construction — so closely, in fact, that it has sometimes been referred to erroneously as a rule of law. See Re Wernher's Settlement Trusts, [1961] 1 All E.R. 184.

Under the class-closing rule, *a class will close whenever any member of the class is entitled to possession and enjoyment of his or her share.* The key point in time is when one member is *entitled* to demand payment. The fact that actual payment may be delayed because of administrative problems does not keep the class open; it closes when the right to payment arises.

When a class is open, persons not yet born can come into the class. When a class is closed, no more members can be added to the class. Note well that this is all we mean when we say that a class is closed: *No person born hereafter can share in the property.*[16] The fact that a class is closed does not mean that all members of the class will share in the property. No additional members can come in, but present class members can drop out by failing to meet some condition precedent.

(2) Immediate gifts

The class-closing rule can best be understood by a series of illustrative cases. In all these cases involving gifts to the children of *B*, it is assumed that *B* is alive at the testator's death. Otherwise the class would be physiologically closed.

---

16. More accurately, we would say that no person conceived after this date can share, for here as elsewhere in property law a child is treated as in being from the time of conception if later born alive. We speak of birth, but we mean conception.

Even more accurately, when children are adopted, the time of adoption, not birth, is controlling. In re Silberman's Will, 23 N.Y.2d 98, 243 N.E.2d 736 (1968). The adopted child must be adopted into the class before the class closes. A child in being when the class closes, but subsequently adopted, does not share. Do you see the reason for this? See Samuel M. Fetters, The Determination of Maximum Membership in Class Gifts in Relation to Adopted Children: In Re Silberman's Will Examined, 21 Syracuse L. Rev. 1 (1969).

Where there is an immediate gift to a class, the class closes as soon as any member can demand possession, either at the testator's death or later. Thus:

> *Case 18.* *T* bequeaths $10,000 "to the children of *B.*" *B* is alive and has two children, *C* and *D*. *C* and *D* can demand immediate possession of their shares. The class closes. $5,000 is paid to *C* and $5,000 to *D*. A year later *E* is born to *B*. *E* does not share in the bequest.

There is an exception to this rule if no members of the class have been born before the testator's death. Since the testator must have known there were no class members alive at his death, it is assumed the testator intended all class members, whenever born, to share. Hence, in this case, the class does not close until the death of the designated ancestor of the class. In Case 18, if *B* had no children born before the testator's death, the class would not close until *B*'s death. See Restatement (Second) of Property, Donative Transfers §26.1 (2) (1988).

> *Case 19.* *T* bequeaths $10,000 "to the children of *B* who reach 21." *B* has children alive, but no child is 21 at *T*'s death. The class will close when a child of *B* reaches 21.
> *Case 20.* *T* bequeaths $10,000 "to the children of *B*, to be paid to them in equal shares as they respectively reach 21." *B* has children alive, but all are under 21. The gift is vested with payment postponed. The class will close when the eldest child of *B* reaches 21 or, if the eldest child dies under that age, when the eldest child would have reached 21 had he lived.

PROBLEMS

1.   *T* bequeaths $15,000 "to the children of *B* who reach 21." At *T*'s death, *B* has two children, *C* (age 7) and *D* (age 4). Three years later *E* is born to *B*. Thereafter *C* reaches 21. What distribution is made to *C*? One year thereafter *F* is born to *B*. *D* dies at age 20. Is any distribution made? *E* then reaches 21. Is any distribution made? *F* then reaches 21. Is any distribution made?

2.   A devise of property "to *B* and her children" is obviously ambiguous. Does *B* take a life estate and the children a remainder? Or do *B* and her children take equal shares as tenants in common? Under the rule in Wild's Case, decided in 1599, if *B* has children at the time of the devise, *B* and her children take as tenants in common. Some states continue to follow this rule. Others follow the life estate and remainder construction. See id. §28.3; David M. Becker, De-

bunking the Sanctity of Precedent, 76 Wash. U. L.Q. 853 (1998). If the jurisdiction follows the rule in Wild's Case, what effect does the rule of convenience have on *B*'s children conceived after the testator's death?

(3)   Postponed gifts

If the gift is postponed in possession until a life tenant dies, the class will not close under the class-closing rule until the time for taking possession. Thus a gift to a class of remaindermen will not close until the life tenant is dead, and it will not then close under the rule of convenience unless one remainderman is entitled to possession.

> *Case 21.* *T* bequeaths $10,000 "to *A* for life, then to the children of my daughter *B*." The class will not close in any event, under the rule of convenience, until the death of *A*. Suppose that *B* survives *A*. The class will close at *A*'s death if (a) a child of *B* is then alive, (b) a child of *B* predeceased *T* and the gift did not lapse but went to such child's issue under an antilapse statute, or (c) a child of *B* was alive at *T*'s death or was born after *T*'s death and such child predeceased *A*. In each of those cases, a child or the child's representative can demand payment at *A*'s death.

Suppose that in Case 21, at the death of *A*, *B* has not yet had any children born to her. Will the class be left open until the death of *B*, as in the case of an immediate gift to a class where no one has yet been born at the time of taking possession? Restatement (Second) of Property, supra, §26.2 (2) says yes, but there are few cases on the matter.

The class-closing rule described above applies only to gifts of principal, not to gifts of income. In a trust to pay income to the children of *B*, the class closes for the payment of income periodically as the income is accrued.

PROBLEMS

1.   *T* bequeaths a fund in trust "to pay the income to *A* for life, then to distribute the principal to the children of *B* who reach 21, and in the meantime the children of *B* who are eligible to receive, but have not yet received, a share of the principal are to receive the income." At *A*'s death, *B* is alive and has one child, *C* (age 5). After

A dies, the following events occur: *D* is born to *B*; *C* reaches 21; one year later *E* is born to *B*; *D* and, later, *E* reach 21.

(a)   After *A*'s death, who is entitled to the income?

(b)   When is the first distribution of principal made, to whom, and how much?

(c)   How is the principal ultimately divided?

2.   *T* bequeaths a fund in trust "to divide the fund among the children of *B*, payable to each at age 21, and in the meantime they are to receive the income." At *T*'s death, *B* is alive and has one child, *C* (age 5). One year later, *C* dies. Is *C*'s administrator entitled to demand immediate distribution of *C*'s share? Would your answer be different if *B* *predeceased* *T*?

3.   *T* devises property in trust "for *A* for life, then on *A*'s death to *A*'s children." *A* disclaims. *A* has a child 5 years of age. When does the class close? See Uniform Probate Code §2-801(d)(1); Pate v. Ford, 297 S.C. 294, 376 S.E.2d 775 (1989).

Lux v. Lux

Supreme Court of Rhode Island, 1972
109 R.I. 592, 288 A.2d 701

KELLEHER, J.   The artless efforts of a draftsman have precipitated this suit which seeks the construction of and instructions relating to the will of Philomena Lux who died a resident of Cumberland on August 15, 1968. We hasten to add that the will was drawn by someone other than counsel of record. . . .

Philomena Lux executed her will on May 9, 1966. She left her residuary estate to her husband, Anthony John Lux, and nominated him as the executor. Anthony predeceased his wife. His death triggered the following pertinent provisions of Philomena's will:

Fourth: In the event that my said husband, Anthony John Lux, shall predecease me, then I make the following disposition of my estate:
1. . . .
2. All the rest, residue and remainder of my estate, real and personal, of whatsoever kind and nature, and wherever situated, of which I shall die seized and possessed, or over which I may have power of appointment, or to which I may be in any manner entitled at my death, I give, devise and bequeath to my grandchildren, share and share alike.
3. Any real estate included in said residue shall be maintained for the benefit of said grandchildren and shall not be sold until the youngest of said grandchildren has reached twenty-one years of age.

4. Should it become necessary to sell any of said real estate to pay my debts, costs of administration, or to make distribution of my estate or for any other lawful reason, then, in that event, it is my express desire that said real estate be sold to a member of my family.

Philomena was survived by one son, Anthony John Lux, Jr., and five grandchildren whose ages range from two to eight. All the grandchildren were children of Anthony. The youngest grandchild was born after the execution of the will but before Philomena's death. The son is named in the will as the alternate executor. He informed the trial court that he and his wife plan to have more children. At the time of the hearing, Anthony was 30. The Superior Court appointed a guardian ad litem to represent the interests of the grandchildren. It also designated an attorney to represent the rights of the individuals who may have an interest under the will but who are at this time unknown, unascertained or not in being. . . .

At the time of her death, the testatrix owned real estate valued at approximately $35,000 and tangible and intangible personal property, including bank accounts, that totaled some $7,400. The real estate, which consists of two large tenement houses, is located in Cumberland. The sole dispute is as to the nature of the devise of the real estate. Did Philomena make an absolute gift of it to the grandchildren or did she place it in trust for their benefit? The guardian takes the view that the grandchildren hold the real estate in fee simple. All the other parties take a contrary position.

From the record before us, we believe that Philomena intended that her real estate be held in trust for the benefit of her grandchildren. In reaching this conclusion, we must emphasize that there is no fixed formula as to when a testamentary disposition should be classified as an outright gift or a trust. The result reached depends on the circumstances of each particular case.

We are not unmindful of the formal requirements necessary for the creation of a testamentary trust. It is an elementary proposition of law that a trust is created when legal title to property is held by one person for the benefit of another. . . . However, no particular words are required to create a testamentary trust. The absence of such words as "trust" or "trustee" is immaterial where the requisite intent of the testator can be found. . . . A trust never fails for lack of a trustee. . . .

When the residuary clause in the instant case is viewed in its entirety, it is clear that Philomena did not give her grandchildren a fee simple title to the realty. It appears that she, realizing the nature of this bequest and the age of the beneficiaries, intended that someone would hold and manage the property until they were of sufficient age to do so themselves. The property is income-producing and apparently she felt that the ultimate interest of her grandchildren would be protected if the realty was left intact until the designated time for distribution. The use of the terms "shall be maintained" and "shall not be sold" is a strong indication of Philomena's intent that the property was to be retained and managed by some person for some considerable time in the future for the benefit of her son's children. This is a duty usually associated with a trustee. We therefore hold that Philomena's will does create a trust on her real estate.

Having found the trust, the question of who shall serve as trustee is easily answered. The general rule is that, unless a contrary intention appears in the will or such an appointment is deemed improper or undesirable, the executor would be named to the position of trustee. . . .

The ascertainment of time within which a person who answers a class description such as "children" or "grandchildren" must be born in order to be entitled to share in a testator's bounty is not an easy matter. In seeking a solution, the court must seek to effectuate the testator's intent. . . .

The rationale for permitting a class to increase in size until the time for distribution stems from a judicial recognition that generally, when a testator describes the beneficiaries of his bounty by some group designation, he has in mind all those persons whenever born who come within the definition of the term used to describe the group. Normally, if he had in mind the individual members of the designated group, he would have described them by name. This recognition is tempered by the presumption that testators usually would not intend to keep the class open at the expense of an indefinite delay in the distribution of the estate. Since there is no good reason to exclude any person who is born before the period of distribution, all such persons are, in the absence of a contrary testamentary intent, deemed to be members of the class. Casner, Class Gifts to Others than to "Heirs" or "Next of Kin": Increase in the Class Membership, 51 Harv. L. Rev. 254 (1938); 5 American Law of Property §§22.40, 22.41 (1952); see concurring opinion, Frost and Roberts, JJ., Rhode Island Hospital Trust Co. v. Bateman, 93 R.I. 116, 172 A.2d 84 (1961).

Despite our invocation of the rule requiring the class to remain open until the corpus is distributed, we still must determine what Philomena intended when she said that the corpus has to be preserved until the "youngest grandchild" becomes twenty-one.

There are four possible distribution dates depending on the meaning of "youngest." Distribution might be made when the youngest member of the class in being when the will was executed attains twenty-one; or when the youngest in being when the will takes effect becomes twenty-one; or when the youngest of all living class members in being at any one time attains twenty-one even though it is physically possible for others to be born; or when the youngest whenever it is born attains twenty-one. This last alternative poses a question. Should we delay distribution here and keep the class open until the possibility that Philomena's son can become a father becomes extinct? We think not.

We are conscious of the presumption in the law that a man or a woman is capable of having children so long as life lasts. A construction suit, however, has for its ultimate goal the ascertainment of the average testator's probable intent if he was aware of the problems that lead to this type of litigation. Manufacturers National Bank v. McCoy, 100 R.I. 154, 212 A.2d 53 (1965). It is our belief that the average testator, when faced with the problem presented by the record before us, would endorse the view expressed in 3 Restatement, Property §295, Comment k at 1594 (1940), where in urging the adoption of the rule that calls for the closing of the class when the youngest living member reaches the age when distribution could be made, states:

> When all existent members of the class have attained the stated age, considerations of convenience . . . require that distribution shall then be made and that the property shall not be further kept from full utilization to await the uncertain and often highly improbable conception of further members of the group. The infrequency with which a parent has further children after all of his living children have attained maturity, makes this application of the rule of convenience justifiable and causes it to frustrate the unexpressed desires of a conveyor in few, if any, cases.

We hold, therefore, that distribution of the trust corpus shall be made at any time when the youngest of the then living grandchildren has attained the age of twenty-one. When this milestone is reached, there is no longer any necessity to maintain the trust to await the possible conception of additional members of the class.

Although Philomena declared that the real estate was not to be sold until the youngest grandchildren became twenty-one, her later statements about the necessity of its sale amounted to her awareness that future circumstances might require the liquidation of her real estate sometime prior to the time her youngest grandchild becomes twenty-one. The Superior Court was informed and documentary evidence was introduced which showed such a precipitous drop in the rental income as would warrant a trustee to seek a better investment.

Section 18-4-2(b) provides that, in the absence of any provision to the contrary, every trust shall be deemed to have conferred upon the trustee a discretionary power to sell the trust estate, be it real or personal property. Section 18-4-10 specifically authorizes a trustee, whenever he believes it desirable to sell trust property, to seek the Superior Court's approval for such a transaction.

When the real estate is sold, the proceeds from such sale shall, because of the doctrine of the substitute res, replace the realty as the trust corpus. Industrial National Bank v. Colt, 102 R.I. 672, 233 A.2d 112 (1957); Dresser v. Booker, 76 R.I. 238, 69 A.2d 45 (1949).

The impending sale brings into focus the testatrix's "express *desire* that said real estate be sold to a member of my family" (emphasis added). The words "express desire" are purely precatory. We have said that precatory language will be construed as words of command only if it is clear that the testator intended to impose on the individual concerned a legal obligation to make the desired disposition. Young v. Exum, 94 R.I. 143, 179 A.2d 107 (1962). We think it clear that since Philomena's primary goal was to benefit her grandchildren, we see nothing in the record that would justify a conclusion that she intended that the potential purchasers of her real estate be limited to the members of her family.

Finally, we come to the allocation of income. The will is silent as to this item. Over a half-century ago, we said that if the will shows no intention on the part of the testator that income be accumulated, income is payable to the beneficiary as it accrues. Butler v. Butler, 40 R.I. 425, 101 A. 115 (1917). This rule has been reaffirmed on many occasions. Should Philomena's son's hope for additional progeny become a reality, the quantum of each share of income received by a grandchild would be reduced as each new member of the class joins his brothers and sisters.

The parties may present to this court for approval a form of judgment in accordance with this opinion, which will be entered in the Superior Court.

(4)   Gifts of specific sums

If a specific sum is given to each member of the class, the class closes at the death of the testator regardless of whether any members of the class are then alive. Thus:

> *Case 22.* *T* bequeaths £500 apiece to each child of *A*. *A* has no children living at *T*'s death. The class closes at *T*'s death, and no child of *A* ever takes anything. Rogers v. Mutch, 10 Ch. Div. 25 (1878).

> Life looked rosy to *A* as he sat
> By the crepe-draped casket of *T*.
> Five hundred pounds for each child he begat
> Would soon make him wealthy mused he.
> So he married at once, and began procreating
> At five hundred per, he supposed;
> But you know and I know (what hardly needs stating)
> That the class had already closed.
> Mistakes of this sort are bound to arise
> When a client takes actions like these
> Without seeing his lawyer as soon as *T* dies,
> And paying the usual fees.
>
>   FRANK L. DEWEY[17]

What is the reason for closing the class at the death of the testator when the gift is of a fixed sum to each member of a class?

Gifts of specific sums to each member of a class are sometimes called "per capita" gifts.

17. Reproduced from W. Barton Leach, Langdell Lyrics of 1938 (1938).

11

DURATION OF TRUSTS: THE RULE AGAINST PERPETUITIES

SECTION A.   INTRODUCTION

1.   Development of the Rule

The classic statement of the Rule against Perpetuities, formulated with Delphic simplicity by John Chipman Gray, reads:

> No interest [in real or personal property] is good unless it must vest, if at all, not later than twenty-one years after some life in being at the creation of the interest. [John C. Gray, The Rule Against Perpetuities §201, at 191 (4th ed. 1942).]

By virtue of his erudition, his rigorous logic, his magisterial style, and his position as a celebrated teacher of property law at Harvard, Gray became established in the late nineteenth century as not just a leading authority on the Rule but as *the* authority.[1] Because of the deference paid to Gray's work by the courts, the Rule has sometimes been treated as if it were laid down at one time by this one man. In fact, the Rule had a long and involved evolution over several centuries. The origins of the Rule against Perpetuities are somewhat obscure because of the ambiguous nature of the concept *perpetuity*. The political and social evils attending on perpetual entails, permitted by the

---

1. On the role of Gray, see Stephen A. Siegel, John Chipman Gray, Legal Formalism, and the Transformation of Perpetuities Law, 36 U. Miami L. Rev. 439 (1982).

Statute de Donis (1285), led judges to become jealous of allowing any limitation tying up land in perpetuity.

From the sixteenth until the nineteenth century, judges struggled against perpetuities, without ever defining exactly what a perpetuity was. There were several unrefined notions and ambiguous doctrines that might be called rules against perpetuities. It fell the lot of Lord Chancellor Nottingham[2] to clarify these ancient contradictory decisions and point the way for modern development of the Rule.

The Rule against Perpetuities as we know it began with the Duke of Norfolk's Case, 3 Ch. Cas. 1, 22 Eng. Rep. 931 (Ch. 1682). The Earl of Arundel had eight sons. Thomas, the eldest son and heir apparent, was *non compos mentis,* weak in body, and not expected to have children. Hence, the earl assumed that after his own death and the death of Thomas, the earldom and the estates accompanying it would likely descend to his second son, Henry, and Henry's issue. If Henry did inherit the earldom at Thomas's death, the earl wanted the barony of Grostock, which he planned to give initially to Henry, to shift to his fourth son, Charles. The earl went to an experienced estate planner (known as a conveyancer in those days when land was the chief form of wealth), Sir Orlando Bridgeman. This outstanding member of the bar, who later became Lord Keeper, drew up a set of highly complicated documents. They cannot be easily summarized inasmuch as they require an understanding of some very complex doctrines involving terms of years. It is enough to say that the limitation that brought on the Duke of Norfolk's Case boiled down to this: The barony of Grostock was given to Henry, but a shifting executory limitation was created, providing that if the eldest son, Thomas, should die without issue in the lifetime of Henry, so that Henry inherited the earldom, then the barony would go to Charles.

In 1652, the Earl of Arundel died, and the earldom descended to the mentally defective son, Thomas. Henry then moved into action. He assumed full control of the properties accompanying the title, and he sent Thomas to Padua in Italy where he was incarcerated until his death. Henry also engineered the restoration of the title, "Duke of Norfolk," to the family. In 1572, Queen Elizabeth I had beheaded the fourth duke for intrigues involving Mary, Queen of Scots, and by attainder all his lands and titles were forfeited.[3] In 1660, Parliament,

---

2. Lord Nottingham, born Heneage Finch, was one of the greatest of English Chancellors and called the "Father of Equity" by Justice Story. He was equally devoted to the law and to his family. When he lost his wife, mother of his 14 children, he comforted himself by taking the Great Seal to bed with him. 4 John Lord Campbell, Lives of the Lord Chancellors 273 (1857).

3. The turbulence of the times is reflected in the history of the title of Duke of Norfolk, who is the premier duke, ranking just below the blood royal. The title goes back to the first Earl of Norfolk, one of the Breton followers of William the Conqueror. After several attainders and lapses of the earldom, the dukedom was created anew by Richard II in 1397 and given to his chief supporter Thomas Mowbray, perhaps best remembered for

with the consent of Charles II, restored the dukedom of Norfolk, and the incompetent Thomas became the premier duke of England. When Thomas died without issue in 1677, Henry became the sixth Duke of Norfolk.

After succeeding to the dukedom and its properties, greedy Henry did not want to give up the barony of Grostock. Charles brought a bill in chancery to enforce his interest. Henry resisted, claiming the gift to Charles was in the nature of a perpetuity and hence void. Sympathetic to the rational estate planning of a landowner with an incompetent eldest son, Lord Chancellor Nottingham was of the opinion that Charles's interest would "wear itself out" in a single lifetime (Thomas's) and should not be regarded as a perpetuity. The sole matter of concern, ruled Nottingham, is the time at which a future interest will vest, and if a future interest must vest, if at all, during or at the end of a life in being, it is good. Upon appeal to the House of Lords, after two days of argument in a crowded house with King James II present, the Lords voted almost unanimously to affirm Nottingham's decision.

In the Duke of Norfolk's Case, Lord Nottingham indicated that a rule against perpetuities should be concerned solely with the time of vesting in the future, but he did not attempt a definitive statement of how long dead-hand rule would be allowed. When asked, "Where will you stop?" he replied, "I will tell you where I will stop: I will stop wherever any visible Inconvenience doth appear." From this beginning — judicial acceptance of tying up land for a single life in being — the judges gradually extended the permissible period of

---

his quarrel with Henry Bolingbroke, Duke of Hereford (afterward Henry IV), which forms Act I of Shakespeare's Richard II and which resulted in Mowbray's banishment. After four Mowbray dukes, the title lapsed.

In 1483, after the murder of the princes in the Tower, Richard III conferred the dukedom on Sir John Howard, an heir of the Mowbray estates and the first of the Howard dukes. Two years later, "Jack of Norfolk" died fighting for Richard at Bosworth; the title and the estates were forfeited to the victorious Henry Tudor, who ascended the throne as Henry VII. The first duke's son regained royal favor by commanding, in his 70th year, the army that defeated the Scots at Flodden, and in 1514 Henry VIII restored the title. Two nieces of the third duke, Anne Boleyn and Catherine Howard, were wives of Henry VIII, both beheaded for infidelity. Subsequently, the Howard family fell from grace; the third duke's son was executed on a charge of treason, and the duke himself was arrested, stripped of his title, and ordered to be beheaded. During the night before the morning set for execution, Henry VIII died and the duke was spared. Seven years later, Queen Mary released him from prison and restored the dukedom to him. The third duke was succeeded by his grandson, who in turn was executed by Elizabeth I for plotting with Mary Stuart. His son Philip, through inheritance from Philip's mother, became the Earl of Arundel. His grandson, the third Earl of Arundel, made the disposition at issue in the Duke of Norfolk's Case.

Since the fourteenth century, the Duke of Norfolk has been the hereditary earl marshal of England. The highest ranking Catholic lord of the realm, the duke attends the sovereign upon the opening of Parliament, walking at his or her right hand, and arranges state ceremonies such as coronations, royal marriages, and funerals.

The Sixth Duke of Norfolk
by Gerard Soest, ca. 1677
Tate Gallery, London

Reproduced by permission of the Tate Gallery.

His greed brought on the case that originated the Rule against Perpetuities.

The First Earl of Nottingham, Lord Chancellor
after Godfrey Kneller, 1680
National Portrait Gallery, London

His decision gave the rich the power to secure family wealth for
another generation.

dead-hand rule until, 150 years later, they finally fixed it at lives in being plus 21 years. In Scatterwood v. Edge, 1 Salk. 229, 91 Eng. Rep. 203 (K.B. 1699), it was held that it was sufficient if an interest would vest within a considerable number of lives in being, not merely one or two, "For let the lives be never so many, there must be a survivor, and so it is but the length of that life; for Twisden used to say, the candles were all lighted at once."[4] In Thellusson v. Woodford, 11 Ves. 112, 32 Eng. Rep. 1030 (Ch. 1805), it was held that any number of lives reasonably capable of being traced could be used to measure the applicable perpetuities period. Concurrently with the expansion of lives in being from one or two to a considerable number, the courts were adding, first, a minority period and, subsequently, a period of 21 years in gross. Finally, in Cadell v. Palmer, 1 Cl. & Fin. 372, 6 Eng. Rep. 956 (H.L. 1832, 1833), the period allowed by the Rule was settled: any reasonable number of lives in being plus 21 years thereafter plus any actual periods of gestation.

The classic introduction to the Rule for students is Professor W. Barton Leach's famous article, Perpetuities in a Nutshell, 51 Harv. L. Rev. 638 (1938), updated by Leach in Perpetuities: The Nutshell Revisited, 78 Harv. L. Rev. 973 (1965). This lucid article, written in a lively, piquant style by the modern master of the Rule, for three generations now has introduced students into the magic garden of perpetuities. For a more recent synopsis of the Rule dealing with recent developments such as wait-and-see as well as the traditional Rule, see Jesse Dukeminier, A Modern Guide to Perpetuities, 74 Cal. L. Rev. 1867 (1986). For a more extensive analysis of the methodology for solving perpetuities problems, see David M. Becker, Perpetuities and Estate Planning (1993).

---

4. Justice Twisden's remark was made in Love v. Wyndham, 1 Mod. 50, 54, 86 Eng. Rep. 724, 726 (K.B. 1681).

> *Do You Rule Your Perpetuity?*
> Lives plus one-and-twenty years,
> The learned fathers thought,
> Should be the time for vesting
> Or the gift would come to naught;
>
> As many lives as are ascertained
> Without undue delay,
> For you light the candles all at once,
> As Twisden used to say.
>
> This was to keep the land well oiled
> And free to come and go,
> For a dead man's hand must idle be
> And his mind works awful slow.
>
> *—Anonymous student at Harvard Law School 1932*
> *(Reprinted from W. Barton Leach, Langdell Lyrics of 1938 (1938))*

2.   Summary of the Rule

a.   Introduction

(1)   The rule and its policies

The fundamental policy assumption of the Rule against Perpetuities is that vested interests are not objectionable, but contingent interests are. The Rule therefore limits the time during which property can be made subject to contingent interests to "lives in being plus 21 years."

The assumption that only *contingent* future interests are objectionable is questionable. The Rule has two basic purposes: (1) to keep property marketable and available for productive development in accordance with market demands; and (2) to limit "dead hand" control over the property, which prevents the current owners from using the property to respond to present needs. The second purpose is implemented by curbing trusts, which, after a period of time and change in circumstances, tie up the family in disadvantageous and undesirable arrangements, leaving the beneficiaries unable to meet current newly arising exigencies. In addition, if not limited in their duration, trusts would tend to create a permanent class of rich families, whose wealth would not depend on their abilities. See Restatement (Second) of Property (Donative Transfers), Pt. 1, Introductory Note (1981); Lewis M. Simes, Public Policy and the Dead Hand 36-60 (1955).

Whenever future interests, vested or contingent, exist, these objectives are compromised. These objectives are fully realized only when a person owns an absolute fee simple free of trust. Hence, it is arguable that the Rule against Perpetuities should prohibit all future interests, and not merely contingent interests, that exist beyond the perpetuities period. But history has settled the question differently. The Rule prohibits only those interests that may remain contingent beyond the perpetuities period. Although the Rule is thus not finely tuned for carrying out the policies for which it was designed, it does, by and large, effectively prevent tying up property for an inordinate length of time.

Although the Rule began as a device to curb tying up land for an undue length of time, it was eventually extended to personal property. Today, its primary application is to personal property held in trust.

All legal and equitable contingent future interests created in *transferees* are subject to the Rule against Perpetuities. Hence, all contingent remainders and executory interests come within the ambit of the Rule. Future interests retained by the *transferor* — reversions, possibilities of reverter, and rights of entry — are not subject to the Rule against Perpetuities.

(2)   *Why lives in being are used to measure the period*

At the time of the formulation of the Rule against Perpetuities, heads of families — the fathers — were much concerned about securing the family land, perhaps acquired only a couple of generations earlier, from incompetent sons. In the Duke of Norfolk's Case, Lord Chancellor Nottingham recognized this concern as legitimate, and he and his successor judges developed an appropriate period during which the father's judgment could prevail. The father could realistically and perhaps wisely assess the capabilities of *living* members of his family, and so, with respect to them, the father's informed judgment, solemnly inscribed in an instrument, was given effect. But the head of the family could know nothing of unborn persons. Hence, the father was permitted control only as long as his judgment was informed with an understanding of the capabilities and needs of persons alive when the judgment was made.

Lord Hobhouse put it this way in his lectures on the dead hand:

> A clear, obvious, natural line is drawn for us between those persons and events which the Settlor knows and sees, and those which he cannot know or see. Within the former province we may trust his natural affections and his capacity of judgment to make better dispositions than any external Law is likely to make for him. Within the latter, natural affection does not extend, and the wisest judgment is constantly baffled by the course of events. I submit, then, that the proper limit of Perpetuity is that of lives in being at the time when the settlement takes effect. [Arthur Hobhouse, The Dead Hand 188 (1880).]

Professor Leach observed that the balance struck by the courts permitted "a man of property . . . [to] provide for all of those in his family whom he personally knew and the first generation after them upon attaining majority." 6 American Law of Property §24.16 (1952). To give testators this maneuvering room, it was not necessary that the actual minority period first tacked onto lives in being be converted into a 21-year period in gross, but so it evolved, with questionable justification. In any case, the 21-year period in gross proved fortunate when the rule was extended to business transactions such as options.

(3)   *The rule is a rule of proof*

The essential thing to grasp about the Rule against Perpetuities is that *it is a rule of logical proof.* A contingent future interest is void from the outset, if it is not certain that the interest will either *vest or fail* — that one or the other *must* happen — within 21 years after the death of "some life in being at the creation of the interest." The phrase "some life in being" has always puzzled students. Who is the "life in being? The answer is the life in being can be *any* person if you can prove that the interest will vest or fail within that life or within 21 years after its expiration. In searching for a life by which you can make the necessary proof, it will do you no good to look at all the lives in the telephone directory or at Prince Charles or at the Artist Formerly Known as Prince. *The only lives relevant to your search are persons who can affect vesting of the contingent interest.* These are known as the relevant lives. They may include, depending on the particular disposition involved, (1) the preceding life tenant, (2) the beneficiary, (3) an ancestor of the beneficiary, (4) any person who can affect a condition precedent attached to the gift, or, (5) in the case of a class gift, any person who can affect the size of a class member's share. All other lives are irrelevant to your search for a validating life.

Case 1 shows how to make the necessary proof that an interest will vest or fail within the relevant lives.

> *Case 1. O* transfers a fund in trust "to pay the income to *A* for life, then to *A*'s children for their lives, then to pay the principal to *B*." *A* has no children. *A*'s life estate is vested in possession *upon creation.* The remainder to *A*'s children for their lives will vest in possession or, if there are no children, fail *upon A's death. B*'s remainder is vested in interest *upon creation.* Thus, all interests created by the transfer are valid.

As Case 1 shows, the crucial inquiry under the Rule is: When will the interest vest? An interest that is vested upon creation is not subject to the Rule. A contingent interest satisfies the Rule if it will necessarily vest, if at all, either *in possession* or *in interest* within the relevant lives in being plus 21 years. Observe that in Case 1, *B*'s remainder is valid because it vests in interest upon creation. It is valid despite the fact that it may vest in possession at the death of *A*'s children, which could be well beyond the relevant lives in being plus 21 years if *A* has children born after the transfer.

Observe also that Case 1 contains a trust that may endure for the lives of *A*'s children born after the date of the transfer. The trust thus possibly may last longer than lives in being at the date of the transfer plus 21 years. Nonetheless, the trust is not void. The Rule against Perpetuities does not directly limit trust duration. It is concerned only with the time when interests vest.[5] In Case 1, all interests in the trust

---

5. The Rule against Perpetuities indirectly limits the duration of a trust. By requiring that equitable interests must vest or fail within the perpetuities period, the identity of all persons with a claim to the property will be ascertained within the period. These ascertained beneficiaries can terminate the trust when the perpetuities period expires. The settlor cannot prevent this. See 1A Austin W. Scott, Trusts §62.10 (William F. Fratcher 4th ed. 1987). If they do not terminate the trust, the trust principal will be distributed to the principal beneficiaries when the preceding life estates expire.

either are presently vested or will vest, if at all, within the period allotted by the Rule. Therefore, the trust is valid in its entirety. If an interest in trust violates the Rule, only to that extent is a trust void.

Here are other illustrations of contingent interests that can be proven valid because they will vest, or fail, within the perpetuities period:

> *Case 2.* *T* bequeaths $10,000 "to *A*, when she marries" and $5,000 "to *A*'s first child." *A* is unmarried and without children. The bequest to *A* will vest during *A*'s *life*, if at all; it is valid. The bequest to *A*'s first child also will vest during *A*'s *life*, if at all; it is valid.
>
> *Case 3.* *O*, a teacher, declares a trust of her first edition of Dickens's Bleak House "for the first student in *O*'s current wills class to be sworn in as a judge." The gift will vest or fail within the *lives of the students* in the class. The condition precedent will necessarily be met, if it is ever met, before the last surviving student dies.
>
> *Case 4.* *O* transfers a fund in trust "to pay the income to *A* for life, then to pay the principal to *A*'s children who reach 21." The remainder is valid because it will vest, at the latest, *21 years after A's death*, for all *A*'s children must reach 21 within 21 years after *A* dies (plus a period of gestation).

The period of the Rule includes any actual periods of gestation involved. The Rule follows the general principle of property law that a person is in being from the time of conception, if later born alive. A child *en ventre sa mere* when the perpetuities period begins counts as a life in being, and a child *en ventre sa mere* when the perpetuities period ends can take as a beneficiary.[6]

Because the Rule against Perpetuities is a rule of logical proof, you must look for a life that works in making the proof required. This person, if found, is sometimes known as the *measuring life*, but we prefer the more accurate term, *validating life*.

PROBLEMS AND NOTE

1.   *T* bequeaths a fund in trust "for *A* for life, then to the first child of *A* to be admitted to the bar." Is the latter gift valid? If so, who is the validating life?

2.   Compare the following bequests:

---

6. It has not been decided whether sperm or ova stored in sperm banks can count as lives in being, but Professor Leach thought they should. W. Barton Leach, Perpetuities in the Atomic Age: The Sperm Bank and the Fertile Decedent, 48 A.B.A.J. 942 (1962). Do you see any problems with this proposal?

As for treating a posthumous child born from frozen sperm or ova as an heir of the donor, see supra pages 127-128.

(a) To *A* for life, then to *B* if *B* goes to the planet Saturn.
(b) To *A* for life, then to *B* if any person goes to the planet Saturn.
(c) To *A* for life, then to *B* for life if any person goes to the planet Saturn.

Is *B*'s remainder good in each bequest? Who is the validating life?

3. The validating lives do not have to have any connection with the family involved. The sole issue is whether these lives permit you to prove that the gift will vest or fail within 21 years after their expiration. Professor Leach illustrated the rigorous logic of the Rule in this imaginative and famous passage:

> The settled inclusion of twenty-one years in gross and the admission of extraneous lives bring it about that a testator or settlor, when motivated by vanity, is able to tie up his property, regardless of lives and deaths in his own family, for an unconscionable period — viz., twenty-one years after the deaths of a dozen or so healthy babies chosen from families noted for longevity, a term which, in the ordinary course of events, will add up to about a century. [6 American Law of Property §24.16, at 52 (1952).]

A trust to pay the income to the testator's issue per stirpes, who are living when each income payment is made, until 21 years after the death of the survivor of Amy, Brad, Christopher, Dominique, Esther, Frances, Gabriel, Hilary, Isaac, Joy, Kyle, and Latonya (12 healthy babies born last week in local hospitals), then to distribute the principal to the testator's issue per stirpes then living, is valid.

b. When the Lives in Being Are Ascertained

Although Gray said the life in being must be a person alive *"at the creation of the interest,"* it is more accurate to say that the validating life or lives must be in being *when the perpetuities period starts to run.* Generally, the perpetuities period begins when the instrument takes effect. If an interest is created by *will,* the validating life or lives must be in being at the testator's death. If the interest is created by *deed* or *irrevocable trust,* the validating life or lives must be persons in being when the deed or trust takes effect.

Different rules for determining validating lives govern revocable trusts and interests created by exercise of a power of appointment. If the interest is created by an *inter vivos trust revocable by the settlor alone,* the validating life or lives must be persons in being when the power to revoke terminates. If the power to revoke terminates at the settlor's death, as is usually the case, the validating lives must be persons alive at the settlor's death. The perpetuities period begins when the power to revoke terminates because, so long as one person has the power to revoke the trust and receive absolute title to the trust assets, the property is not tied up.

SECTION B.   THE REQUIREMENT OF NO POSSIBILITY OF REMOTE VESTING

1.   The Fertile Octogenarian

The poet Marianne Moore once wrote of an imaginary garden with real toads in it. Because of the rule that any possibility that an interest might vest too remotely invalidates the interest, the Rule against Perpetuities is much like Marianne Moore's garden. Developed by the active imagination of lawyers, the Rule is the abode of such fantastical characters as the fertile octogenarian, the unborn widow, and other imaginary beings with power to bring the Rule down hard on the head of any trespasser. The first of these characters we meet is the fertile octogenarian.

The fertile octogenarian usually appears in a two-generation trust such as the following.

> *Case 5.* *T* bequeaths a fund in trust for her sister "*A* (age 80) for life, then for *A*'s children for their lives, then to distribute the trust assets to *A*'s issue then living." The law conclusively presumes that *A* is capable of having more children. Because of this assumption, the secondary remainder to *A*'s children for their lives may include an afterborn child of *A*, and the remainder to *A*'s issue might vest on the death of this afterborn child, which is too remote. The remainder to *A*'s issue is void.

The conclusive presumption of fertility was laid down in the old case of Jee v. Audley, 1 Cox 324, 29 Eng. Rep. 1186 (1787). In this case, the Master of the Rolls, Lord Kenyon, said: "I am desired to do in this case something which I do not feel myself at liberty to do, namely, to suppose it impossible for persons in so advanced an age as John and Elizabeth Jee [both septuagenarians] to have children; but if this can be done in one case it may in another, and it is a very dangerous experiment, and introductive of the greatest inconvenience to give a latitude to such sort of conjecture."

Simon de Bruxelles, *Baby Conceived After 60th Birthday Celebration*
The (London) Times, Jan. 16, 1998

The oldest woman to give birth in Britain believes she conceived after celebrating becoming a pensioner, a friend disclosed last night.

Elizabeth Buttle, who will be 61 next month, went into hiding yesterday with her son Joe, now two months old, and boyfriend, Peter Rawstron, as it emerged that she had misled doctors about her age. . . .

Mrs Buttle told the friend she believed she might have conceived on the night of her 60th birthday. Mrs Buttle and Mr Rawstron celebrated the occasion with dinner. The friend said: She's not sure of her exact dates but says it is very likely to have been on her birthday."

The whitewashed cottage two miles outside the town of Lampeter in west Wales, where Mrs Buttle lives with her partner and a herd of goats, was deserted yesterday after the family left with a police escort, spurning offers of riches from tabloid newspapers.

They are believed to have gone to another farm which she owns in the Carmarthenshire countryside. Her eldest grandson, Nick Pleavin, 19, who lives in a caravan behind the house, said: "My gran is amazing. She's just taken this in her stride, although I don't think she is planning any more. She has always been very fit, working on the farm all her life.

"When my mother told me there would be a new baby in the family I thought she meant her not my gran. My mum is in her late thirties and I thought that was a bit late to have another, but for my gran to have one is fantastic." Mr Rawstron's wife, Vera, 56, the mother of his other four children, was less delighted.

She said: "He's been foolish to say the least. I'm very unhappy about the whole situation."

She still sees Mr Rawstron, 58, daily as they run their family agricultural business from home. At night he returns to Mrs Buttle.

Mrs Rawstron says she was upset at what she described at the "scandal" of her husband having a baby by a mistress of 60.

"Most babies are a cause for celebration but this one is not. It is not a happy event. We have four grownup children to consider who have been very upset. This is a small, close-knit community and this trouble could badly affect the family and our business. Peter promised me this would all be kept very hush-hush. Like a lot of wives, I've been left to pick up the pieces."

The Rawstrons' home is at Llangybi, five miles from the village of Cwmann where Mrs Buttle lives. The love affair began while he was delivering food for her goats.

QUESTIONS AND PROBLEMS

1.   If you think the conclusive presumption of fertility is absurd, at what age would you presume women could not bear children? Men? Suppose sperm or ova had been deposited in a fertility bank? See supra pages 117-126 on bequests of sperm deposits, and page 103 on births to postmenopausal women. A person can adopt a child at any age. How does this affect your thinking about the conclusive presumption of fertility?

A few jurisdictions have statutes limiting the presumption of fertility in perpetuities cases to statistically significant child-bearing years (say, between 13 and 65) or permitting the introduction in any case of evidence of capacity to bear children. Ill. Comp. Stat. ch. 765, §305/4(c)(3) (1998); N.Y. Est., Powers & Trusts Law §9-1.3(e) (1998). The Illinois and New York statutes provide that the possibility that a person may adopt a child shall be disregarded.

2.   Could the remainder to A's issue in Case 4 be saved by construing "A's children" to refer to A's children living at T's death? Should the court do this?

3.   Keeping in mind the conclusive presumption of fertility, which of the following bequests would be valid? T devises Blackacre to Mary Hall, but if the Brooklyn Bridge ever falls —

(a)   to the children of Elizabeth Jee now living.
(b)   to the children of Elizabeth Jee then living.
(c)   to the children of Elizabeth Jee now living who are then living.

4.   T bequeaths a fund in trust "for A for life, then to such of A's nephews and nieces as live to attain the age of 21." At the time of T's death, A is living and has a sister, B, and four nephews and nieces (the children of B), all of whom are under age 21. Is the interest given to A's nephews and nieces valid under the Rule against Perpetuities? (A clue: The answer is, "It depends.")

5.   *The Precocious Toddler.* What is the youngest age of procreation presumed by the law? This has never been established. Only one known case has dealt with the issue. In Re Gaite's Will Trusts, [1949] 1 All E.R. 459 (Ch.), the court had before it a bequest that would be void only if it were assumed that a person under the age of five could have a child. The court validated the gift, not on the ground of physical impossibility of a person becoming a parent at an age under five, but on the ground that a child born to so young a person would necessarily be illegitimate and hence excluded as a child. Under modern American law, it is usually presumed, in construing trust instruments, that references to children and other relatives of a person

include illegitimate children. If so, the constructional escape from the Rule used by the court in Re Gaite's Will Trusts is not available.

The youngest mother on record is Lina Medina of Lima, Peru. On May 14, 1939, at the age of five, she was delivered of a 6½-pound boy by Caesarean section.[7] An investigation revealed that she had been raped by a mentally retarded teenage stepbrother. In a story in the New York Times, April 3, 1963, at 70, one of Lina's obstetricians, Dr. Rolando Colareta, recalled that he and his colleagues were astounded to discover that "although Lina had every aspect of a five-year-old infant, her sexual development corresponded to that of a young lady over 15 years old. . . . Surprising though it seems, we confirmed that Lina had menstrual periods since she was one-month old." Dr. Colareta went on to point out that cases of 12- and 13-year-old mothers were common in the Andes, where Lina came from. "As a matter of fact," he said, "I delivered a child to a 9-year-old girl here last week and it didn't even make the newspapers." The New York Times reported that Lina, then 28 and still unmarried, was working as a secretary. Her son Gerardo, then 23, was living with Lina's parents and studying accounting.

For a photograph of the pregnant Lina, age 5, see 8 The Bloodless Phlebotomist, No. 6, p. 2 (1940).

2.   The Unborn Widow

Dickerson v. Union National Bank of Little Rock
Supreme Court of Arkansas, 1980
268 Ark. 292, 595 S.W.2d 677

SMITH, J.   The principal question on this appeal is whether a trust created by the holographic will of Nina Martin Dickerson, who died on June 21, 1967, is void under the rule against perpetuities, because it is possible that the interest of the various beneficiaries may not vest within the period allowed by that rule. Cecil H. Dickerson, Jr., one of

---

7. Occasionally, a questionable story of an even younger mother appears. The National Examiner, Mar. 12, 1985, at 23, reported that a 14-pound baby girl in the Philippines was born pregnant. According to the story, the baby girl had a male fetus growing in her uterus, in the fifth month of its development. A few days after the baby's birth, the fetus was removed by Caesarean section. The newspaper reported that the fetus lived a few hours in an incubator and was baptized Juan according to Catholic rites. The attending doctor said it seemed likely that the developing fetus was really the girl's fraternal twin brother. "Probably the two eggs were fertilized at the same time, but only one became properly implanted in the uterine wall, engulfing the other egg during its faster growth." Id. In medical journals, there have been a few dozen cases of *fetus-in-fetu* reported (as many in boys as in girls!) but no *fetus-in-fetu* has before been alleged to have been born alive. See 82 Am. J. Clinical Pathology 115 (1984).

the testatrix's two sons, attacks the validity of the trust. The chancellor rejected Cecil's attack on two grounds: First, Cecil should have raised the question of the validity of the trust in the probate court in connection with the probate of the will and the administration of the estate. His failure to do so makes the issue res judicata. Second, on the merits, the trust does not violate the rule against perpetuities. We disagree with the chancellor on both grounds.

The facts are not in dispute. The testatrix was survived by her two children. Cecil, 50, was single, and Martin 45, was married. At that time the two sons had a total of seven children, who of course were the testatrix's grandchildren.

The testatrix named the appellee bank as executor and directed that at the close of the administration proceedings the bank transfer to itself as trustee all the assets of the estate. The terms of the trust are quite long, but we may summarize them as follows.

The trust is to continue until the death of both sons and of Martin's widow, *who is not otherwise identified.* The income is to be divided equally between the two sons during their lives, except that Cecil's share is to be used in part to provide for a four-year college education for his two minor children, who are named, and for the support and education of any bodily heirs by a later marriage. When the two named minor children finish college, their share of the income is to revert to Cecil. Upon Martin's death his share of the income is to be paid monthly to his widow and children living in the home, but the share of each child terminates and passes to the widow when that child marries or becomes self-supporting. The trustee is given discretionary power to make advance payments of principal in certain cases of emergency or illness. If either son and his wife and all his bodily heirs die before the final distribution of the trust assets, that son's share in the estate and in the income passes to the other son and then to his bodily heirs.

As far as the rule against perpetuities is concerned, the important part of the will is paragraph VIII, from which we quote:

> VIII. This Trust shall continue until the death of both my sons and my son Martin's widow and until the youngest child of either son has reached the age of twenty-five years, then at that time, the Trust shall terminate and the Union National Bank Trustee shall distribute and pay over the entire balance of the Trust Fund in their hands to the bodily heirs of my son, Cecil H. Dickerson, and the bodily heirs of my son, William Martin Dickerson, in the same manner and in the same proportions as provided for by the general inheritance laws of Arkansas.

Upon the death of the testatrix in 1967, her will was presented to the Faulkner Probate Court by her son Cecil, who lived in Conway,

Arkansas. (The other son, Martin, was living in Indiana.) The probate court entered a routine order reciting that the will had been properly executed, admitting the instrument to probate, and appointing the bank as executor, without bond. On May 31, 1968, the probate court entered another routine order approving the executor's first and final accounting, allowing fees to the executor and its attorneys, discharging the executor, and closing the administration of the estate. That order made no reference to the validity of the trust or to the manner in which the assets of the estate were to be distributed.

In fact, the assets of the estate, except for $18,000 set aside for administration expenses and estate taxes, had already been transferred by the bank to itself as trustee. On August 11, 1967, about a month after the probate of the will, the bank filed in the Faulkner Chancery Court an ex parte "Declaration of Trust," in which the bank expressed its desire to perform the trust and asked the court to find and decree that it held the property in trust for the beneficiaries of the testamentary trust. . . .

Nothing further appears to have taken place in the case until 1977, when Cecil Dickerson filed . . . the present complaint against the bank and its trust officer. The complaint, after reciting the background facts, asserts that the trust is void under the rule against perpetuities. The complaint charges the trust officer with violations of his fiduciary duties in failing to deliver all the assets of the estate to the heirs of the testatrix and in failing to ask the probate court to construe the will with respect to violations of the rule against perpetuities. The complaint charges that the trust officer concealed the trust's defects from the court and from the testatrix's two sons. The prayer is for an order restraining the trustee from making further transfers or distributions of the trust funds, for recovery of Cecil's half interest in the estate, for compensatory and punitive damages, and for other proper relief. The charges of negligence and wrongdoing on the part of the bank were later dismissed without prejudice. The other matters were heard upon stipulated facts, culminating in the decree dismissing Cecil's complaint. . . .

First, there is no merit in the argument that Cecil's failure to challenge the validity of the trust in the probate proceedings precludes him from raising that issue now.

. . . The complications that may be presented by the rule against perpetuities are so numerous and difficult that even experienced lawyers and judges must usually consult the authorities to be certain about its application to a given set of facts. There was not the slightest reason for Cecil or Martin Dickerson to suspect a possible invalidity in their mother's testamentary trust, nor any duty on their part to raise such a question. To deprive them of their property on the basis of res judicata would actually be to deny them their day in court.

Indeed, if there was any duty on anyone to raise the issue, that duty rested on the bank. It was a fiduciary, both as executor and as trustee. It owed a duty of good faith and loyalty to all the beneficiaries of the estate and of the trust and a duty to act impartially as between successive beneficiaries. Restatement of Trusts (2d), §§170 and 232 (1959), and Arkansas Annotations (1939) to those sections. We do not imply any wrongdoing on the part of this appellee, but it is certainly not in a position to ignore the possible invalidity of the trust both in the probate court and in the ex parte chancery court case and then take advantage, to its own pecuniary benefit, of the beneficiaries' similar course of conduct. A contrary rule would compel the beneficiaries of an estate or trust to hire a lawyer to watch the executor or trustee, when the law actually permits them to rely upon the fiduciary.

Second, the trust is void because there is a possibility that the estate will not vest within a period measured by a life or lives in being at the testatrix's death, plus 21 years. A bare possibility is enough. "The interest *must* vest within the time allowed by the rule. If there is any possibility that the contingent event may happen beyond the limits of the rule, the transaction is void." Comstock v. Smith, 255 Ark. 564, 501 S.W.2d 617 (1973).

The terms of this trust present an instance of the "unborn widow," a pitfall that is familiar to every student of the rule against perpetuities. This trust is not to terminate until the deaths of Cecil, Martin, and Martin's widow, but the identity of Martin's widow cannot be known until his death. Martin might marry an 18-year-old woman twenty years after his mother's death, have additional children by her, and then die. Cecil also might die. Martin's young widow, however, might live for another 40 or 50 years, after which the interests would finally vest. But since Cecil and Martin would have been the last measuring lives in being at the death of the testatrix, the trust property would not vest until many years past the maximum time allowed by the rule. The rule was formulated to prevent just such a possibility — uncertainty about the title to real or personal property for an unreasonably long time in the future.

The violation of the rule, except for the interposition of a trust, is actually so clear that the appellee does not argue the point. Instead, it insists that the property would vest in Cecil and Martin's bodily heirs at their deaths, with only the right of possession of the property being deferred until the termination of the trust.

This argument overlooks the fact that the words "bodily heirs" were used in the decisive paragraph VIII of the will not as words of limitation, to specify the duration of an estate granted to Cecil and Martin, but as words of purchase, to specify the persons who would take at the termination of the trust. Obviously the identity of those persons cannot be determined until the death of Martin's widow; so the ownership would not vest until that time. . . .

Here the testatrix directed that at the termination of the trust the property be distributed as provided by the general inheritance laws of Arkansas. At the time of the deaths of Cecil and Martin it would be utterly impossible to say who would take, in the case we have supposed, at the death of Martin's young widow 50 years later. Under our law the surviving descendants would then take per capita if they were related to Cecil and Martin in equal degree, but per stirpes if in unequal degree. Ark. Stat. Ann. §§61-134 and -135 (Repl. 1971). If there were no surviving descendants of one brother, the entire property would go to the surviving descendants of the other. If there were no surviving descendants of either, the property would revert to the testatrix's estate and go to her collateral heirs. Thus it is really too plain for argument that the interest of every descendant (or "bodily heir") of Cecil or Martin would be contingent upon his surviving the death of Martin's widow, at which time — and only at which time — the title would finally vest. . . .

Reversed and remanded for further proceedings.

PROBLEMS AND NOTES

1. Why did not the gift to Cecil's and Martin's bodily heirs vest at their deaths? See Note 4, supra page 739. If the gift had been to Cecil's and Martin's heirs, would the remainder be valid?

2. *T* bequeaths a fund in trust to pay the income "to my son for life, then to my son's widow, if any, for life; then to pay the principal to my son's children, but if no child of my son is alive at the death of the survivor of my son and his widow, then to pay the principal to the American Red Cross." Is any gift invalid? See John H. Morris & W. Barton Leach, The Rule Against Perpetuities 44 (2d ed. 1962).

Any interest that violates the Rule against Perpetuities is struck out and the valid interests are left standing. What is the result of an invalid gift in this trust?

3. New York Est., Powers & Trusts Law §9-1.3(c) (1998) provides: "Where an estate would, except for this paragraph, be invalid because of the possibility that the person to whom it is given or limited may be a person not in being at the time of the creation of the estate, and such person is referred to in the instrument creating such estate as the spouse of another without other identification, it shall be presumed that such reference is to a person in being on the effective date of the instrument." Ill. Comp. Stat. ch. 765, §365/4(c)(1)(C) (1998), is similar.

Why did not the court in *Dickerson* construe the word *widow* to refer to a person in being when the testator died?

4.   *Alternative contingencies.* Under the alternative contingencies doctrine, if the testator makes gifts on alternative contingencies, one of which offends the Rule against Perpetuities and the other of which does not, the gifts are judged separately. The invalid gift fails; the valid gift takes effect if the event happens upon which it is limited. See First Portland National Bank v. Rodrique, 172 A.2d 107 (Me. 1961); 6 American Law of Property §24.54 (1952).

To illustrate this, suppose that *T* bequeaths a fund in trust "to my son *A* for life, then to *A*'s widow for life, then upon the widow's death *or* upon *A*'s death if *A* leaves no widow, to *A*'s issue." *T* has split the contingencies, making a gift on the widow's death and a separate gift on the death of *A* leaving no widow. The gift on the death of the widow is void. The gift to *A*'s issue on *A*'s death is valid if *A* actually leaves no widow. However, the testator must expressly separate the contingencies. The court will not do it for him. Thus, if the words "or upon *A*'s death if *A* leaves no widow" are omitted by the drafter, the gift to *A*'s issue is wholly void, even though this second contingency is implicit in the will as drafted.

3.   *The Slothful Executor*

Another unusual possibility, occasionally overlooked by the drafter, is that a will may not be probated, or an estate distributed, for many years after the testator's death. Although distribution of an estate ordinarily is completed within a few years of the testator's death, in a few cases an estate has been tied up for many years in litigation or the will has been found many years after the testator dies. See, for example, Estate of Garrett, 372 Pa. 438, 94 A.2d 357 (1953), supra page 95 (estate closed after 23 years); Richards v. Tolbert, 232 Ga. 678, 208 S.E.2d 486 (1974) (will found and probated 57 years after the testator's death).

The possibility of remote distribution gives rise to what are known as the slothful executor cases. Thus:

> *Case 6. T* devises property "to *T*'s issue living upon distribution of *T*'s estate." *T*'s purpose is to avoid extra administrative costs and possible taxation in the estates of any of *T*'s issue who die before *T*'s estate is distributed. Yet, because *T*'s estate may not be distributed for many years, perhaps after all *T*'s surviving issue are dead, the gift to *T*'s issue living at distribution may be held void.

There are at least two arguments that can be made to save the gift in Case 6. First, it can be argued that distribution of the estate will not be delayed beyond a reasonable time, which necessarily is less than 21 years. This argument was accepted in Belfield v. Booth, 63 Conn. 299, 27 A. 585 (1893). Second, it can be argued that, inasmuch as the testator did not intend the executor to have the power to select recipients by delaying distribution, the class of issue will close at the time distribution reasonably should be made. See Estate of Taylor, 66 Cal. 2d 855, 428 P.2d 301 (1967).

The administrative contingency involved in Case 6 is a true condition precedent: *T*'s will requires *T*'s issue to survive distribution in order to take. Some administrative contingency cases, however, involve language that ought not to be construed to create a condition precedent to vesting. Examples are "to *A* upon distribution of my estate," "to my issue when my debts are paid," and "to *A* upon probate of this will." Language of this sort, not requiring survival, should be construed as merely postponing possession and not importing a condition precedent. See Deiss v. Deiss, 180 Ill. App. 3d 600, 536 N.E.2d 120 (1989).

The fertile octogenarian, the unborn widow, and the slothful executor cases do not exhaust the extravagant possibilities that can be dreamed up to invalidate gifts. But they should suffice to show that the most remote possibilities can lead to invalidating an interest. It is these cases that have brought the Rule into disrepute.

SECTION C.   APPLICATION OF THE RULE TO CLASS GIFTS

1.   *The Basic Rule: All-or-Nothing*

Under the Rule against Perpetuities, a class gift cannot be partially valid and partially void. It must be valid for all members of the class, or it is valid for none. If the interest of any member possibly can vest too remotely, the entire class gift is bad. This rule was established in Leake v. Robinson, 2 Mer. 363, 35 Eng. Rep. 979 (Ch. 1817).

The all-or-nothing rule requires that (a) the class must close and (b) all conditions precedent for every member of the class must be satisfied, if at all, within the perpetuities period. Case 7 illustrates a common class gift that is void according to these principles.

> *Case 7.* *T* bequeaths property in trust "for *A* for life, then for *A*'s children for life, and then to distribute the property to *A*'s grandchildren." The remainder to *A*'s grandchildren is void because every member of the

class will not be ascertained until the death of *A*'s children, some of whom might not be in being at *T*'s death. If at *T*'s death *A* has a grandchild, *G*, alive, *G*'s gift is vested in interest subject to open up and let in after-born grandchildren, but it is not vested for purposes of the Rule, and it is therefore void. *Repeat: A remainder that is vested subject to open is not vested for purposes of applying the Rule against Perpetuities.* The class must be *closed* before a remainder in a class is vested under the Rule.

Some gifts to a class may be saved through the operation of the *rule of convenience,* which may close the class prior to the time it closes physiologically. Under the rule of convenience, the class will close when any member of the class is entitled to immediate possession and enjoyment. See supra page 778. Thus:

> *Case 8. O* transfers property in an irrevocable trust "for my daughter *A* for life, then to distribute the principal to my grandchildren." At the time of the transfer *O* has one grandchild, *G*, alive. Under the rule of convenience, *G* or her administrator is entitled to demand possession of her share at *A*'s death, closing the class and forcing distribution among the grandchildren then living and the estates of grandchildren then dead.[8] The gift thus is valid. If *O* had no grandchild alive at the date of the transfer, the gift to grandchildren would be void.

QUESTION

If the instrument in Case 8 were a will or a revocable trust rather than an irrevocable trust, the gift to the transferor's grandchildren would be valid regardless of whether a grandchild were alive when the instrument became effective. Do you see why?

It does not necessarily follow from the closing of the class within the perpetuities period that the gift is valid. Every member of the class may be ascertained, but every member may not have satisfied some condition precedent, and this too is required. For a gift of a fee simple to vest, the ultimate number of takers in the class must be fixed so that it neither increases nor decreases. Thus:

8. Suppose that *G* is living in Argentina, doesn't learn of *A*'s death until several years after *A* dies, and therefore doesn't appear at *A*'s death to demand payment. Will the class nevertheless close at *A*'s death? Yes. The class will close whenever a class member has the *right* to demand possession. See supra page 778. Were this not so, the rule of convenience could never save a class gift because it is possible that the qualified class member would not actually demand possession at the time the right to possession arises.

Case 9. T bequeaths property in trust "for *A* for life, then to distribute the property to such of *A*'s children as attain the age of 25." The class will close physiologically at *A*'s death (a life in being), but the exact share each child of *A* will take cannot be determined until all of *A*'s children have passed 25 or have died under that age. Here is what might happen: Suppose, at *T*'s death, *A* has one child, *C*, age 10. After *T*'s death *A* might have another child, *D*. Before *D* reaches age 4, *A* and *C* might die. Since *D* might meet the condition precedent more than 21 years after the expiration of any relevant life in being at *T*'s death, the remainder fails.

QUESTION

Suppose that in Case 9 a child of *A* is age 25 at *T*'s death. Is the gift good? If you say yes, you have not mastered the principle illustrated by this case.

Ward v. Van der Loeff
House of Lords, United Kingdom, 1924
[1924] A.C. 653

[The testator, William John Dalzell Burnyeat, barrister and member of Parliament, died in 1916, survived by his wife Hildegard but no children, by his father and mother, age 67, and by two brothers and two sisters. Each of these brothers and sisters had children living at the testator's death. In 1921, the testator's widow married Mr. Van der Loeff, a Dutch subject. Another nephew of the testator, Philip Ponsonby Burnyeat, was born after the testator's death and after the remarriage of his widow.

The testator left a will executed in 1915, and a codicil executed in 1916. By the will, the testator left his estate in trust for his wife for life, with the remainder to his children. In the event that he had no children (which happened), he gave his wife a power to appoint the trust fund among the children of his brothers and sisters, and in default of appointment the trust fund was to go in equal shares to the children of his brothers and sisters.]

HALDANE, L.C. . . .   About the validity of these trusts no question arises. But it is otherwise with the codicil made by the testator. It was in these terms:

I declare that the life interest given to said wife by my said will shall be terminable on her remarriage unless such remarriage shall be with a

natural born British subject.[9] I revoke the power of appointment among
the children of my brothers and sisters given to my said wife by my said
will. And I declare that after her death my trustees shall stand possessed
of the residuary trust funds in trust for all or any the children or child
of my brothers and sisters who shall be living at the death of my wife or
born at any time afterwards before any one of such children for the time
being in existence attains a vested interest and who being a son or sons
attain the age of twenty-one, or being a daughter or daughters attain that
age or marry if more than one, in equal shares.

On the construction of the will and codicil, two questions arise.
The first is, whether the limitation in favour of children, contained
in the concluding words of the codicil, is valid, having regard to the
rule against perpetuities. The second is whether, if invalid, this new
limitation and the wording of the codicil have been at all events
efficacious as expressing a revocation of his bequest to children contained in the will. If the limitation to children in the codicil be invalid,
and that in the will has not been revoked, then a further question
arises, whether the gift in the will operated in favour of any children
of the brothers and sisters who were not born until after the testator's
death. Philip Ponsonby Burnyeat, who is one of the parties to these
appeals, was a son of the testator's brother, Myles Fleming Burnyeat,
but was not born until after the testator's death and the remarriage
of his widow. It is argued against his claim that the life interest of the
widow was effectively determined by the provision in the codicil and
that the class of children to take was finally ascertained at that date
as the time of distribution. If this be so, Philip Ponsonby Burnyeat is
excluded.

P.O. Lawrence J. was the judge before whom this summons came
in the first instance. He decided that the gift in the codicil in favour
of the children of the testator's brothers and sisters was so framed as
to be void for perpetuity. He held further, that the codicil operated
to revoke the residuary gift in the will only so far as the substituted
provision in the codicil was valid, and that the gift in the will in favour
of these children, therefore, took effect, but merely in favour of such
of the children as were born before the remarriage of the testator's
widow. Philip Ponsonby Burnyeat was thus excluded. . . .

9. The testator's widow, Hildegard Burnyeat (later Van der Loeff), was a Prussian.
During the 1914-1918 war, she was interned on the Isle of Man. We thought this provision
might have been inserted because Van der Loeff was waiting in the wings when Burnyeat
executed his codicil, but Dr. Myles Fredric Burnyeat, the testator's great-nephew, thinks
this provision in the codicil was due to the intensity of anti-German feeling at the time.

Dr. Burnyeat also informed us that Philip Ponsonby Burnyeat, who was closed out of
the class in this case, had the terrible misfortune at the age of three to contract sleeping
sickness, then incurable, and spent his life in an institution. Letter from Dr. Myles Fredric
Burnyeat to Jesse Dukeminier, dated March 25, 1982. — Eds.

My Lords, the principle to be applied in construing instruments for the purpose of ascertaining whether the direction they contain infringes the rule against perpetuity is a well settled one. It was repeated with emphasis in this House in Pearks v. Moseley [5 App. Cas. 714], where it was laid down that in construing the words the effect of the rule must in the first instance be left out of sight, and then, having in this way defined the intention expressed, the Court had to test its validity by applying the rule to the meaning thus ascertained.[10] It is only therefore if, as matter of construction, the words in the codicil, taken in the natural sense in which the testator used them, do not violate the rule that they can be regarded as giving a valid direction. Looking at the language of the testator here, I am wholly unable to read it as not postponing the ascertainment of possible members of the class beyond the period of a life in being and twenty-one years afterwards. No doubt if we were warranted in interpreting the testator as having referred only to the children of those of his brothers and sisters who were alive at his death we might read his language in a way which would satisfy the law. But for so restricting the natural meaning of his words there is no justification in the language used in the context. He speaks of his brothers and sisters generally, and there is no expression which excludes the children of other possible brothers and sisters of the whole or half blood who might in contemplation of law be born. He has nowhere indicated an intention that his words are not to be construed in this, their natural meaning. I think, therefore, that the class to be benefited was not one all the members of which were, as a necessary result of the words used, to be ascertained within the period which the law prescribes, and that the gift in the codicil in favour of children of brothers and sisters is wholly void.

The next question is whether the codicil, although inoperative to this extent, was yet operative to revoke the gift to children of brothers and sisters contained in the will. After consideration, I have come to the conclusion that it was not so operative. There is indeed a revocation expressed in the codicil, but it is confined to the power of appointment given to the wife. It does not extend to what follows. That is, in terms, an attempt at a substantive and independent gift, and,

---

10. Gray expressed this view in stronger language:

> The Rule against Perpetuities is not a rule of construction, but a peremptory command of law. It is not, like a rule of construction, a test, more or less artificial, to determine intention. Its object is to defeat intention. Therefore every provision in a will or settlement is to be construed as if the Rule did not exist, and then to the provision so construed the Rule is to be remorselessly applied. [John C. Gray, The Rule Against Perpetuities §629 (4th ed. 1942).]

— Eds.

as it is wholly void, I think . . . that the provision in the will stands undisturbed. . . .

The only other point is at what period the class of children of brothers and sisters who took under the will is to be ascertained. I think that according to a well-known rule, the period is that of distribution; in other words, taking the valid alteration in the codicil into account, the remarriage of the widow with a foreign subject. Philip Ponsonby Burnyeat is thus excluded.

The result is that the judgment of P.O. Lawrence J. should be [affirmed]. . . .

LORD DUNEDIN. My Lords, the main question in this case seems to me to be determined by what was said in this House by Lord Cairns in the two cases of Hill v. Crook [L.R. 6 H.L. 265] and Dorin v. Dorin [L.R. 7 H.L. 568]. In the former of these cases that noble and learned Lord laid down that when you wish to vary the meaning of a word denoting a class of relations from what the prima facie meaning of that word is — he actually said it of the words legitimate children, but the application is obviously wider — there are two classes of cases only where the primary signification can be departed from. The one is where it is impossible in the circumstances that any person indicated by the prima facie meaning can take under the bequest. That is not the case here because probably in law, though scarcely in fact, the idea of other brothers and sisters to the testator coming into existence could not be excluded, but in any case the half-brother or sister was a real possibility. The second class of cases is where you find something in the will itself, that is, in the expressions used in the will, to exclude the prima facie interpretation. That also seems to be absent. He has used the words "brother and sister" without explanation or glossary, and I am afraid he must take the consequences.[11]

PROBLEMS

1. Do you see why the rule of convenience saves the gift to nephews and nieces in the will and does not save the gift in the codicil?

---

11. *He* must take the consequences?

In construing statutes, Lord Dunedin did not take such a strict, literal approach, but said that a statute should be interpreted to carry out its intent. "I have said before that I think in interpreting a statute a Court must take it that the statute is meant to work, and that it should not allow the statute to be defeated unless the words used are quite inadequate to have the desired effect." Ocean Coal Co. v. Davies, [1927] A.C. 271, 278 (dissenting opinion). Why should statutes be construed to work, but not wills? If the testator must "take the consequences," why not the legislature? The legislature at least has the opportunity of patching up faulty drafting, which the testator does not have. — Eds.

Suppose there had been a nephew 22 years old at the testator's death. Would the gift to the nephews and nieces in the codicil be good?

2.   *T* devises Blackacre "to such of the grandchildren of *A* as shall attain the age of 25." Unless otherwise stated, assume that no grandchild of *A* has reached age 25. Is the gift valid if at *T*'s death:

(a)   *A* is dead?
(b)   *A* and all of *A*'s children are dead?
(c)   *A* is alive and one grandchild of *A* is 25?
(d)   *A* is dead and one grandchild of *A* is 25?
(e)   *A* is dead and one grandchild of *A* is 4?

3.   *T* bequeaths a fund in trust "to pay the income to *A* for life, and then in further trust for the grandchildren of *B*, their shares to be payable at their respective ages of 25." Is the gift valid if *T* is survived by *A* and *B* and,

(a)   the eldest grandchild of *B* is 25 at *T*'s death?
(b)   the eldest grandchild of *B* is 10 at *T*'s death?
(c)   the eldest grandchild of *B* is 2 at *T*'s death?

Suppose that *B* survives *T*, but *A* predeceases *T*, and the eldest grandchild of *B* is 2 at *T*'s death. Is the gift valid?

Suppose that *A* survives *T*, but *B* predeceases *T*, and the eldest grandchild of *B* is 2 at *T*'s death. Is the gift valid?

2.   Exceptions to the Class Gift Rule

We now turn to two exceptions to the all-or-nothing rule of class gifts: (a) gifts to subclasses, and (b) gifts of specific sums to each member of a class. These exceptions are discussed in 6 American Law of Property §§24.29, 24.28 (1952).

a.   Gifts to Subclasses

American Security & Trust Co. v. Cramer
United States District Court, District of Columbia, 1959
175 F. Supp. 367

Youngdahl, J.   Abraham D. Hazen, a resident of the District of Columbia, died in the District on December 4, 1901. His will, executed on October 16, 1900, was admitted to probate on March 11, 1902.

Testator was survived by Hannah E. Duffey, who is referred to in his will as his "adopted daughter." At the time of the testator's death, Hannah had two children: Mary Hazen Duffey [now Cramer], born November 12, 1897, and Hugh Clarence Duffey, born July 11, 1899. After the testator's death, Hannah gave birth to two more children: Depue Hazen Duffey, born October 9, 1903, and Horace Duffey, born July 8, 1908.

The will provided for the payment of debts and certain specific bequests and then provided that the residue of the estate be put in trust for the benefit of testator's wife for life. At her death, one-half of the corpus was to be, and has been, given to testator's sister and brothers; the other half, composed of realty, remained in trust for Hannah for life. At Hannah's death, the income was to go to the children of Hannah "then living or the issue of such of them as may then be dead leaving issue surviving" Hannah, and then "*upon the death of each* the share of the one so dying shall go absolutely to the persons who shall then be her or his heirs at law according to the laws of descent now in force in the said District of Columbia." [Emphasis added.][12]

Testator's widow died on October 31, 1916; Hannah died on May 21, 1915.

On October 5, 1917, the heirs of the testator brought an action in equity to have the provisions of the seventh paragraph of the will stricken as being in violation of the rule against perpetuities. The Supreme Court of the District of Columbia held that the interests of Hannah's children under the will were valid and the Court of Appeals affirmed. Hazen v. American Security & Trust Co., 1920, 49 App. D.C. 297, 265 F. 447. The validity of the remainders over, after the death of each child, was expressly not ruled upon as the life estates were not "so intimately connected with the gift over as to require us now to determine the validity of such gifts."

Hugh, one of the four life tenants after the death of the widow

---

12. The seventh paragraph of testator's will reads [in part]:

> I do direct that Mary Hazen Duffey, the daughter of my adopted daughter and the namesake of my wife and for whom my wife and I have the greatest affection, shall if living at the death of her mother take a share three times as large as the share of each of the other children of my said adopted daughter, which other children shall take in equal shares between and among themselves, and each of the children of said adopted daughter shall take only for and during the terms of their respective lives and upon the death of each the share of the one so dying shall go absolutely to the persons who shall then be her or his heirs at law according to the laws of descent now in force in the said District of Columbia.

Mary took a three-sixths share; each of the other three children took a one-sixth share.

and Hannah, died on December 19, 1928, and shortly thereafter the trustee brought a bill for instructions; this time the validity of the remainder over to Hugh's heirs was in issue. On January 2, 1930, Judge Bailey ruled that "the remainder provided by the will after his [Hugh's] death to the persons who shall then be his heirs at law became vested within the period prescribed by law and is valid."

On December 13, 1954, Depue died and for the fourth time a suit concerning this trust was started in this court. The trustees desired instructions as to the disposition of Depue's one-sixth share. While this action was pending, on December 18, 1957, Horace died. A supplemental bill was then filed, asking for instructions as to the disposition of this one-sixth share as well. The remainder over after the death of the sole living life tenant, Mary, cannot yet take effect; however, due to the request of all the parties concerned, and in order to save both the time of this court and the needless expense it would otherwise cost the estate, the Court will also pass on the validity of this remainder. . . .

The effect of the rule [against perpetuities] is to invalidate ab initio certain future interests that might otherwise remain in existence for a period of time considered inimicable to society's interest in having reasonable limits to dead-hand control and in facilitating the marketability of property. The policy of the law is to permit a person to control the devolution of his property but only for a human lifetime plus twenty-one years and actual periods of gestation. With careful planning, this period could be as long as one hundred years — and this is long enough.

A gift to a class is a gift of an aggregate amount of property to persons who are collectively described and whose individual share will depend upon the number of persons ultimately constituting the class. Evans v. Ockershausen, 1938, 69 App. D.C. 285, 292, 100 F.2d 695, 702, 128 A.L.R. 177. The members of the class must be finally determined within a life or lives in being plus twenty-one years and actual periods of gestation, or the gift will fail. Put another way, the class must close within the period of the rule against perpetuities, if the class gift is to be valid. Unless a contrary intent is indicated by the testator, the class will close when any member of the class is entitled to immediate possession and enjoyment of his share of the class gift. Applying these basic principles to the trust here involved, it is seen that the life estates to Hannah's children had to vest, if at all, at the termination of the preceding life estates of the widow and Hannah. Since Hannah's children had to be born within Hannah's lifetime, and since Hannah was a life in being, the class (Hannah's children) physiologically had to close within the period of the rule. This has already been so held. Hazen v. American Security & Trust Co., supra. . . . Furthermore, the remainder over at Hugh's death has been held valid. The Court now holds that the remainder limited to the heirs of Mary is valid. Both Hugh and Mary were lives in being at the testator's death; the remainders limited to their heirs had to vest, if at all, within the period of the rule. Horace and Depue were born after the testator died; the remainders over at their deaths are invalid.

In applying the rule against perpetuities, it does not help to show that the rule might be complied with or that, the way things turned out, it actually was complied with. After the testator's death, Hannah might have had more children; one of these might have lived more than twenty-one years after the death of all the lives in being at the testator's death. The vesting of the remainder in this after-born's heirs would take place after the expiration of lives in being and twenty-one years, since the heirs could not be ascertained until the after-born's death and an interest cannot be vested until the interest holder is ascertained. Consequently, because of the possibility that this could happen, even though, in fact, it did not,[13] the remainders limited to the heirs of Horace and Depue (both after-borns) are invalid as a violation of the rule against perpetuities.

Counsel have not argued the point of whether the invalidity of the remainders to the heirs of Horace and Depue serves to taint the otherwise valid remainders to the heirs of Mary and Hugh. Of course, the remainder after Hugh's life estate has already been distributed and is not properly in issue. Nevertheless, as shall be demonstrated, it (and the remainder to the heirs of Mary) are not affected by the two invalid remainders, since the four remainders are to subclasses and stand (or fall) separately.

Beginning with Jee v. Audley, 1 Cox Eq. Cas. 324 (1787) and flowering with Leake v. Robinson, 2 Mer. 363, 35 Eng. Rep. 979 (Chancery 1817), there has been the curious anomaly in future interests law that if the interest of any potential member of a class can possibly vest too remotely, the interests of all the members of the class fail. . . . Fortunately, the Court need not apply it in this case because of the limitation put on it by a long line of cases beginning with Cattlin v. Brown, 11 Hare 372, 68 Eng. Rep. 1318 (Chancery, 1853).

In *Cattlin*, the devise was of mortgaged property to *A* for life, then to the children of *A* in equal shares during their lives, and *after the death of any such child*, his share to his children and their heirs. Some of *A*'s children were in being at the time that the testator died; some

---

13. Mary, a life in being at testator's death, is still alive. Therefore, the heirs of Horace and Depue would *actually* be taking within the period of the rule, but in this area of imagination-run-wild, actualities do not count; what could happen is all that matters.

In this case, the above suppositions are not unreasonable since Hannah was in her middle thirties when the testator died. But cf. the cases of "the fertile octogenarian," "the unborn widow," and "the magic gravel pit" in Professor Leach's classic article Perpetuities in a Nutshell, 51 Harv. L.R. 638, 642-645 (1938).

were born after his death. Counsel conceded that the remainders over
to the heirs of those children of *A* born after the testator's death
were invalid. The question was whether those concededly invalid remainders tainted the otherwise valid remainders and rendered them
invalid. The Court held that they did not; the remainders to the heirs
of the children in being at the testator's death were valid. *Leake* was
distinguished on the ground that it concerned remainders to *one* class
(*A*'s children that reach twenty-five) while the remainders involved in
Cattlin were to a group of subclasses (the heirs of each of *A*'s children
was a subclass [with the members to be determined upon the death
of each child of *A*]). In other words, the limitation placed on *Leake*
by *Cattlin* is that if the ultimate takers are not described as a single
class but rather as a group of subclasses, and if the share to which
each separate subclass is entitled will finally be determined within the
period of the rule, the gifts to the different subclasses are separable
for the purpose of the rule.

In the instant case, the language of the will compels the Court to
read it as a devise of remainders to subclasses and within the rule of
Cattlin. The provision in issue reads, in part: ". . . and *each* of the
children of said adopted daughter shall take only for and during the
terms of their *respective* lives and upon the death of *each* the share of
the *one* so dying shall go absolutely to the persons who shall then be
her or his heirs at law . . ." (Emphasis supplied). . . .

When a remainder in fee after a life estate fails, there is no enlarge-
ment or diminution of the life estate; rather there is then a reversion
in the heirs of the testator. . . . The two one-sixth shares held invalid
shall pass to the successors in interest to the heirs of Abraham D.
Hazen. . . .

Counsel will submit an appropriate order.

Estate of Coates, 438 Pa. Super. 195, 652 A.2d 331 (1994), held
that where there is a trust for *A* for life, then to *A*'s children for their
lives, then "to *A*'s grandchildren per stirpes," the subclass doctrine
applies even though possession by the grandchildren was postponed
until the death of all *A*'s children. The shares of the grandchildren
are fixed at the death of each child. Restatement of Property §389,
Comment c (1944), is in accord.

b.   Specific Sum to Each Class Member

In addition to gifts to subclasses, there is another exception to the
all-or-nothing class gift rule where there is a gift of a specific sum to

each member of a class. In Storrs v. Benbow, 3 De Gex, M. & G. 390, 43 Eng. Rep. 153 (Ch. 1853), the testator bequeathed £500 apiece to each grandchild of his brothers, to be paid at age 21. The testator had two brothers living at his death. The court held that, as a matter of construction, applying the ordinary class closing rule applicable to specific sum gifts (see supra page 785), the gift benefited only grandchildren living at the testator's death. The court went on to say, however, in a dictum that has been treated as law ever since, that if the testator meant to include grandchildren born after his death, the bequest would be valid for all children born to the brothers' children living at his death and invalid for all children of the brothers' afterborn children. The amount intended to be received by each member of the class is ascertainable without reference to the number of persons in the class, and hence each gift is tested separately under the Rule. Thus:

> *Case 10.* *T* bequeaths "$1,000 apiece to my nephews and nieces, whether born before or after my death." *T* is survived by his parents, his sister *A*, and *A*'s daughter *B*. After *T*'s death, a child, *C*, is born to *T*'s parents, and *A* has another child, *D*. Twenty years later, *C* marries and has a child, *E*. *B* is entitled to receive $1,000 because her gift vests at *T*'s death. *D* is entitled to receive $1,000 because, viewed at *T*'s death, her gift will necessarily vest during the life of *A*, a person in being at *T*'s death. *E* is not entitled to receive $1,000 because her gift will not necessarily vest during the life of a person in being. The validity of each gift is judged separately since the amount each nephew or niece takes is fixed at $1,000 and cannot increase or decrease by any fluctuation in the number of recipients.

SECTION D.   APPLICATION OF THE RULE TO POWERS OF APPOINTMENT

In applying the Rule against Perpetuities to powers of appointment, it is necessary to separate powers into (a) general powers presently exercisable and (b) general testamentary powers and all special powers. The former are rarely created, except in the form of a power to revoke a trust. Hence, our main concern is with testamentary and special powers.

1.   *General Powers Presently Exercisable*

a.   Validity of Power

General powers presently exercisable are treated as absolute ownership for purposes of the Rule. Nothing stands between the donee and absolute ownership except a piece of paper that can be signed at any time; hence, the property is not tied up. In order to be a valid power, a general inter vivos power must *become exercisable*, or fail, within the perpetuities period. Once the power becomes exercisable, the property becomes marketable, and the policy of the rule is not offended. Hence, if a general inter vivos power will become exercisable, or fail, within lives in being plus 21 years, it is valid. See Restatement (Second) of Property, Donative Transfers §1.2, Comment h (1983). For example, *T* devises property "to *A* for life, then to *A*'s children for their lives, with a general power in each child, exercisable by deed, to appoint a proportionate share of the corpus." Each child's power is valid, because the power in each child will become exercisable at *A*'s death or, if a child is then a minor, within 21 years thereafter.

b. Validity of Exercise

Since the donee of a general power presently exercisable is treated as owner of the property, the validity of an interest created by exercise of the power is determined on the same basis as if the donee owned the property in fee. The perpetuities period begins to run when the power is exercised.

An unconditional power to revoke in one person is treated the same as a general power presently exercisable if the holder can exercise the power to revoke for his or her own exclusive benefit. The perpetuities period does not begin to run until the termination of the power. See Restatement (Second) of Property, supra, §1.2.

PROBLEM

O creates a revocable trust "to pay the income to *O* for life, then to pay the income to *O*'s children for their lives, then to distribute the principal to *O*'s grandchildren." Does the gift to grandchildren violate the Rule against Perpetuities? Would it if the trust were irrevocable?

2. General Testamentary Powers and Special Powers

General testamentary powers and all special powers are treated differently from a general power presently exercisable. A person holding one of these powers does not have an absolute and unlimited present right to alienate the property, and consequently the donee is not treated as owner. The donor is treated as still controlling the property through the exercise of the power. In applying the Rule to these powers, two questions arise: (a) Is the power itself valid? (b) Are the interests created by the exercise of the power valid?

a.　Validity of Power

For a general testamentary power or a special power to be valid, it must not be possible for the power to be exercised beyond the perpetuities period. If it can possibly be exercised beyond the period, it is void ab initio. A testamentary or special power cannot be given to an afterborn person unless its exercise is limited to the perpetuities period.

> *Case 11.* *T* bequeaths a fund in trust "to pay the income to *A* for life, then to *A*'s children for their lives, and, as each child of *A* dies, to pay his or her proportionate part of the principal as such child shall appoint by will." At the time of *T*'s death, *A* has one child, *B*. Another child, *C*, is born a year later. The gift to subclasses doctrine applies to the testamentary powers given *A*'s children, since each child has a power exercisable only over his or her portion of the principal at death. The testamentary power given to *B* is valid, because *B* was in being at *T*'s death. The testamentary power given to *C*, born after *T*'s death, is void.

A discretionary power of distribution in a trustee is the equivalent of a special power of appointment.

> *Case 12.* *T* bequeaths a fund in trust "to pay the income to *A* for life, then in the trustee's *discretion* to pay the income to *A*'s children during their lives or to accumulate the income and add it to principal." *A* has no children at *T*'s death. The discretionary power in the trustee to pay or accumulate income is either partially or totally void (see below).

Gray took the position that a discretionary trust did not create one power that was either entirely valid or entirely void, but a succession of annual powers that were exercisable with respect to each year's income. Thus, a discretionary power in a trustee exercisable during lives not in being, as during the lives of *A*'s children in Case 12, could be exercised for 21 years after *A*'s death but no longer. See John C. Gray, The Rule Against Perpetuities §§410.1 to 410.5 (4th ed. 1942). However, in the few cases in which this issue has been directly before the court, the discretionary power has been held void in its entirety if it is capable of being exercised in favor of persons not in being. See Arrowsmith v. Mercantile-Safe Deposit & Trust Co., 313 Md. 334,

545 A.2d 674 (1988); Bundy v. United States Trust Co., 257 Mass. 72, 153 N.E. 337 (1926).

b.   Validity of Exercise

(1)   Perpetuities period runs from creation of power

General testamentary powers are treated like special powers in determining the validity of the appointment. The donee of a testamentary power or a special power is regarded as an agent of the donor, not as the beneficial owner of the property. The appointments under testamentary and special powers are read back into the instrument creating the power. The perpetuities period applicable to the appointed interests runs from the creation of the power.

Although it is now well settled in most of the states that general testamentary powers are to be treated like special powers under the Rule, in a few states general testamentary powers are treated the same way as general inter vivos powers. The perpetuities period on the appointed interests runs from the exercise of a general testamentary power. See Del. Code Ann. tit. 25, §501 (1998); Mo. Rev. Stat. §442.557 (1997); S.D. Codified Laws Ann. §43-5-5 (1998); Wis. Stat. Ann. §700.16(1)(c) (1998); Industrial National Bank of Rhode Island v. Barrett, 101 R.I. 89, 220 A.2d 517 (1966).

(2)   The second-look doctrine

Any interest created by exercise of a testamentary or special power is void unless it must vest, if at all, *within 21 years after the death of some life in being at the date the power was created.* The exercise of the power is read back into the original instrument — but facts existing on the date of exercise are taken into account. This is known as the *second-look doctrine.* This means we wait and see how the donee actually appoints the property, and then we determine on the basis of facts existing at the date of the appointment whether the appointive interests will vest within the period (computed from the date of creation of the power). Thus:

> *Case 13.* *T* devises property "to *A* for life, remainder to such persons as *A* appoints by will, outright or in further trust." *A* appoints in further trust "to my children for life, remainder to my grandchildren in fee." We now read *A*'s appointment into the will that created the power; the disposition is treated as though *T*'s will read "to *A* for life, then to *A*'s children for life, then to *A*'s grandchildren in fee." However, under the

second-look doctrine we are allowed to take into account facts existing at the time of *A*'s appointment. If, at *A*'s death, all of *A*'s surviving children were born in *T*'s lifetime, the remainder to the grandchildren is valid because it will vest, if at all, at the death of persons in being at *T*'s death. Otherwise the remainder is void.

Second National Bank of New Haven v. Harris Trust & Savings Bank

Connecticut Superior Court, New Haven County, 1971
29 Conn. Supp. 275, 283 A.2d 226

SHEA, J.   In this action the plaintiff trustee seeks a determination of how the portion of a trust fund subject to a power of appointment is to be distributed. . . .

In New Haven on April 21, 1922, Caroline Haven Trowbridge, a resident of that city, created an inter vivos trust with the plaintiff as trustee. The income of the trust was given to the settlor's daughter, Margaret Trowbridge Marsh, and she was also given a general testamentary power of appointment over one-half of the corpus. The remaining one-half, as well as the half subject to the power in default of its exercise, would be distributed to Margaret's surviving children or issue per stirpes or, if there were none, to another daughter of the settlor, Mary Brewster Murray, or her surviving issue per stirpes. During the life of the settlor, a power was reserved to "revoke, modify or alter" the terms of the trust "respecting the payment of income." The settlor, Caroline, died in New Haven on June 26, 1941, without having exercised this power.

Margaret, the life tenant and donee of the testamentary power, a resident of Winnetka, Illinois, died on April 13, 1969, leaving a will purporting to exercise the power by creating another trust, giving the income to her daughter, Mary Marsh Washburne, for a period of thirty years. At that time the trust estate would be distributed to Mary, if living, or, if not, to her surviving children or their descendants per stirpes, with outright distribution at age twenty-one. . . .

Mary, the named beneficiary of the power of appointment as exercised, was born on October 25, 1929. As one of the two surviving children of Margaret, she would share equally with her brother, Charles Allen Marsh, the half of the trust created by Caroline subject to the power, in default of its exercise. If Margaret's exercise of the power under her will is fully effective, the defendant Harris Trust and Savings Bank, as executor and trustee would receive this half of the trust to pay the income to Mary for thirty years following her mother's death, and ultimately to distribute the corpus to Mary. If she did not live that long, upon her death the defendant trustee would make distribution to Mary's surviving children or their surviving descendants.

It appears that all of the living persons having any interest in the trust have been made parties. A guardian ad litem has been appointed to represent any unborn or undetermined persons who may have an interest and also to represent the five children of Mary, all of whom are minors.

The first problem is whether the exercise of the testamentary power of appointment by Margaret's will is invalid because of a claimed violation of the rule against perpetuities.

It is well established that a donee of a power of appointment, in exercising the power, acts as a mere conduit of the donor's bounty. "Whenever such a power is in fact exercised, the validity of the appointment is determined by precisely the same rule as if the original testator, who created the power, had made in his own will the same provision in favor of the same appointee." Bartlett v. Sears, 81 Conn. 34, 42, 70 A. 33, 36. "The appointment is 'read back' into the instrument creating the power, as if the donee were filling in blanks in the donor's instrument." 6 American Law of Property §24.34.

So far as perpetuities are concerned, the period of the rule is reckoned from the date of creation of the power, not from the date of its exercise. Gray, Rule against Perpetuities (4th Ed.) §515, p.499. Where the power has been created by a will, the period is measured from the time of the death of the testator. Gray, op. cit. §520; Simes & Smith, Future Interests (2d Ed.) §1226. Where a deed is the source of the power, the date of delivery would ordinarily start the running of the period. Gray, loc. cit.; Simes & Smith, loc. cit.

In the case of inter vivos instruments, there is an exception for revocable transfers, for the reason that the policy of the rule is not violated where the grantor may at will terminate any future interests by revoking the grant. Where such an unconditional power of revocation is reserved, the period of perpetuities is calculated from the time the power of revocation ceased, usually at the death of the grantor unless the power was released earlier. 6 American Law of Property §24.59; Gray, op. cit. §524.1.

In this case, the defendants who seek to uphold the validity of the exercise of the power by Margaret's will claim that Caroline did retain a power to revoke the trust. The provision upon which they rely is paragraph (i) of the trust instrument, which reads as follows: ". . . as a measure of protection against possible contingencies, I hereby expressly reserve to myself power to revoke, modify or alter the terms hereof respecting the payment of income during my own life, by an instrument in writing, signed, dated and acknowledged, and delivered to the trustee." It seems clear that a power "to revoke, modify or alter the terms . . . respecting the payment of income" would not include a power to revoke the provisions for disposition of the principal of the trust. Such a partial power of revocation could affect only the life tenant, Margaret, during the life of the settlor, Caroline. Such a power would not qualify for the exception applicable to a full and unconditional power of revocation, because the remoteness of the future interests created could not be affected by any exercise of the power. 6 American Law of Property §24.59.

. . . As applied to this case the rule [against perpetuities] would bar any future interest which might not vest within twenty-one years after the life of some person in being on April 21, 1922, the date the trust was established. Since Mary was not born until October 25, 1929, she was not in being at the creation of the trust and her life cannot be taken as a measuring life under the rule against perpetuities. The only relevant life mentioned in the trust is that of Margaret, and, therefore, any valid future interest must vest no later than twenty-one years after her death on April 13, 1969.

In exercising the power of appointment, Margaret in her will used the language of an absolute gift to Mary of the income for thirty years and then a distribution to her of the principal of the trust.[14] The next sentence adds the provision that upon Mary's death within the thirty-year period (or prior to the death of the testatrix, Margaret) the principal of the trust would be distributed to Mary's children or descendants of deceased children surviving her. Such unconditional words of gift would ordinarily be construed as creating a vested interest subject to defeasance upon the occurrence of the condition subsequent contained in the later clause. Howard v. Batchelder, 143 Conn. 328, 336, 122 A.2d 307, 310. "If the conditional element is incorporated into the description of, or into the gift to, the remainderman, then the remainder is contingent; but if, after words giving a vested interest, a clause is added divesting it, the remainder is vested." Gray, op. cit. §108; Howard v. Batchelder, supra, 334, 122 A.2d 307. Such exaltation of verbalism over substance has been criticized, but it is rigidly adhered to in the legalistic sophistry which comprises much of the lore of future interests. As it was once remarked, "I am quite aware that this is all largely [a] matter of words, but so is much of the law of property; and unless we treat such formal distinctions as real, that law will melt away and leave not a rack behind." Commissioner of Internal Revenue v. City Bank Farmers' Trust Co., 2 Cir., 74 F.2d 242, 247.

---

14. Article Three (b) of Margaret's will provided: "At the end of thirty (30) years after the date of my death, said Trustee shall pay over and deliver all of the corpus of the trust estate held under this Article Three to my daughter, Mary Marsh Washburne. In the event of the death of my daughter, Mary Marsh Washburne, prior to my death or prior to the expiration of said thirty (30) year period after my death, said Trustee shall pay over and distribute all of the corpus of the trust estate to" her issue then living per stirpes, with the share of any beneficiary under 21 to be vested in him and payable at age 21. — Eds.

"An interest is 'vested' for purposes of the Rule when the following conditions exist: a. any condition precedent attached to the interest is satisfied, and b. the taker is ascertained, and c. where the interest is included in a gift to a class, the exact amount or fraction to be taken is determined." 6 American Law of Property §24.18. The language creating the gift to Mary imposes no condition precedent, but rather a condition subsequent, i.e. her death within thirty years after Margaret's death. Since the gift is to a named person the identity of the taker is established. The third requirement (c) is not applicable to a gift to an individual.

The construction of the gift of the remainder to Mary as vested rather than contingent is reinforced by the intermediate gift of the income to her. 6 American Law of Property §24.19. A gift in favor of a named individual has historically been treated as vested and not subject to the rule unless it is expressly subject to a condition precedent. Restatement, 4 Property §370, Comment g. The preference of the law for vested rather than contingent interests certainly dictates such a construction in this case, where even the grammatical form of a condition subsequent has been observed by the draftsman. . . .

The gift to Mary's children, following the same verbal formalism, is a contingent remainder,[15] because it is expressly subject to the condition that they survive their mother and that she not live until termination of the thirty-year trust. White v. Smith, 87 Conn. 663, 669-673, 89 A. 272. It is also contingent because, as a gift to a class (surviving children and surviving descendants of deceased children), the fractional interest of each member of the class cannot be ascertained until the contingency (Mary's death) happens. Gray, op. cit. §§369-375.

It is well established that the rule against perpetuities does not affect vested interests, even though enjoyment may be postponed beyond the period of the rule. Connecticut Trust & Safe Deposit Co. v. Hollister, 74 Conn. 228, 232, 50 A. 750; Restatement, 4 Property §386, Comment j. It would not operate therefore, to invalidate either the gift of the income to Mary for life or thirty years or the gift of the remainder after the thirty years. Colonial Trust Co. v. Brown, 105 Conn. 261, 272, 135 A. 555; Bartlett v. Sears, 81 Conn. 34, 44, 70 A. 33. Both of these gifts vested in interest at the death of Margaret within the period of the rule, and the postponement of enjoyment beyond the period of the rule would not invalidate them. Howard v. Batchelder, 143 Conn. 328, 336, 122 A.2d 307.

The permissible duration of a trust is not governed by the rule against perpetuities. Restatement, 4 Property §378; Gray, op. cit. §§232-246. It is no objection, therefore, that Mary's life estate may

---

15. Contingent remainder or executory interest? Does it matter? — Eds.

last beyond the period of the rule. It is also of no significance that her remainder interest may be defeated by her death, which may occur after that time. A vested remainder is exempt from the rule even though it may be subject to complete defeasance. Restatement, 4 Property §370. The rule does bar the contingent remainder to Mary's children because it may vest more than twenty-one years after the death of Margaret, whose life must be taken as the measuring life. This result, abhorrent to the rule, would occur if Mary should die more than twenty-one but less than thirty years after her mother. . . .

"If future interests created by any instrument are avoided by the Rule against Perpetuities, the prior interests become what they would have been had the limitation of the future estate been omitted from the instrument." Gray, op. cit. §247. . . . "Where a divesting interest is void, the interest which would otherwise have been divested becomes absolute." 6 American Law of Property §24.47, p.124. . . .

Under these principles, the gift of the remainder to Mary becomes indefeasibly vested because of the invalidation of the contingent remainder to her children.

In summary, the court has concluded that Mary has a valid income interest, in the half of the trust subject to the power of appointment, for thirty years and is then entitled to receive the principal. If she dies before then, the principal would be distributed to her estate, because her remainder has become indefeasibly vested.

Accordingly, it is ordered that the plaintiff trustee turn over to the defendant Harris Trust and Savings Bank one-half of the trust, to be held by that defendant to pay the income (including accumulated income) to the defendant Mary Marsh Washburne until April 13, 1999, when the principal shall be distributed to her. In the event of her earlier death, the principal shall be distributed to her estate. The court's advice is not sought with respect to any question pertaining to the remaining half of the trust fund. . . .

Judgment may enter accordingly.

QUESTIONS AND NOTE

1. Do you see how, as lawyer for Margaret Trowbridge Marsh, you could have almost certainly carried out her wishes by a further appointment using extraneous persons born before 1922 and living when her will was executed to measure the duration of the trust?

2. Margaret Trowbridge Marsh wanted the trust principal held in trust for her daughter Mary until Mary reached 70 years of age. Is this sound estate planning?

More famous as a controlling mother was the movie actress Joan Crawford. Crawford's will created trusts of $77,500 for her daughters

Cathy and Cynthia, to distribute the principal to them at age 50. The residue of her estate was bequeathed to six charities. Crawford's will also disinherited two children: "TENTH: It is my intention to make no provision herein for my son Christopher or my daughter Christina for reasons which are well known to them." Of course, Christina settled the score in Christina Crawford, Mommie Dearest (1978), which was made into a movie and reaped a profit far exceeding what her mother left her sisters.

3.   If a donee makes an invalid appointment, what are the consequences? The property passes in default of appointment to the takers in default or, if none, to the donor or the donor's estate unless the doctrine of capture applies. On capture, see supra page 701.

NOTE: THE "DELAWARE TAX TRAP" OR HOW THE DONEE CAN CHOOSE BETWEEN PAYING AN ESTATE TAX OR A GENERATION-SKIPPING TRANSFER TAX

In Delaware a statute provides that all interests created by the exercise of *all* powers, *special as well as general*, must vest within 21 years of the death of some life in being at the time the power is *exercised*, not some life in being at the date of creation of the power. Del. Code Ann. tit. 25, §501 (1998). Under the Delaware statute, a new perpetuities period begins each time a special power is exercised. Thus, it is possible to create a private trust that can last forever. *T* can set up a trust giving her child *A* the income for life and a special testamentary power to appoint outright or in further trust among *A*'s descendants. *A* can exercise the power by appointing in further trust for her child *B* for life, giving *B* a special testamentary power in favor of *B*'s descendants. *B* can exercise the power by appointing in further trust for her child — and so on down the generations.

Under the federal estate tax, neither a life estate nor property subject to a special power of appointment is taxable at the death of the life tenant or donee of the power. See supra page 673. Although the property escapes estate taxation at that time, it will become subject to estate taxation within a generation or two thereafter because the standard Rule against Perpetuities ultimately calls a halt to successive life estates. In Delaware, however, life estates can be created in indefinite succession through the exercise of successive special powers of appointment.

Out of concern for estate tax avoidance through the use of Delaware trusts, Congress in 1942 enacted §2041(a)(3) of the Internal Revenue Code. This statute taxes the appointive assets in the donee's estate if the donee exercises a special power "by creating another power of appointment which under the applicable local law can be validly exercised so as to postpone the vesting of any estate or interest in such property, . . . for a period ascertainable without regard to the date of the creation of the first power."

This provision plugs the tax loophole that would otherwise exist for Delaware trusts — but the general language of the statute creates a tax trap for residents of all states. In any jurisdiction, *if a donee by will exercises a special power in such a manner as to create a general inter vivos power, the property subject to the special power will be includible in the donee's gross estate taxable under the estate tax.* Reread the quoted statutory provision, and you will see that this is so.

Although it used to be sound advice never to exercise a special power by creating a general inter vivos power, which would throw the trust assets into the donee's taxable gross estate, such advice is not necessarily sound any longer. In 1986, Congress decided that a wealth transfer tax must be paid by each generation. It enacted the generation-skipping transfer tax, which imposes a GST tax on a transfer to a person two generations below the transferor (see supra page 674). In the trust above, where the transferor's child *A* is given a life estate and a special power of appointment, a GST tax of 55 percent will be levied at *A*'s death if the trust assets pass to the next generation, *unless the trust assets are subject to an estate tax levied on A's estate.* Remember: One wealth transfer tax each generation. By exercising her special power so as to create a general inter vivos power in her child, *B*, *A* can throw the trust assets into her gross estate taxable under the estate tax and avoid a GST tax. Paying an estate tax, which has graduated rates from 37 to 55 percent, may result in a lower tax bill. Hence, the Delaware Tax Trap has turned out to be a device useful in escaping the generation-skipping transfer tax. See Jonathan G. Blattmachr & Jeffrey N. Pennell, Adventures in Generation-Skipping, or How We Learned to Love the "Delaware Tax Trap," 24 Real Prop., Prob. & Tr. J. 75 (1989).

Similarly, giving a remainderman a special power of appointment may permit the remainderman to choose which tax to pay. Take this case:

> *Case 14. T* bequeaths a fund in trust to his wife *W* for life, then to his daughter *A* if *A* survives *W*. If *A* dies before *W*, *A* is given a special power to appoint the distribution of the trust assets at *W*'s death, and in default of appointment to *A*'s children. If *A* dies before *W*, the trust assets will not be included in *A*'s federal gross estate, but a generation-skipping transfer tax on the value of the trust principal will be payable on *W*'s death when the trust principal passes to *T*'s grandchildren. If an estate tax would do less damage to the family, *A* can exercise her power of appointment by creating general inter vivos powers in *A*'s children, thus falling into the Delaware Tax Trap. In that case, an estate tax would be

payable at A's death on the value of the remainder rather than a genera-tion-skipping transfer tax payable at W's death on the value of the trust principal.

SECTION E.　SAVING CLAUSES

Because of the ease with which even experienced attorneys can over-look some remote possibility of untimely vesting, experienced estate planners today always incorporate in trusts they draft a perpetuities saving clause to take care of any possible violation. The perpetuities saving clause[16] is not actually intended to govern the duration of the trust, except in the event some overlooked violation of the Rule unexpectedly extends the trust too long. The perpetuities saving clause's purpose is simply to make sure the Rule is not violated.

　Here is an example of a saving clause:

　Notwithstanding any other provisions in this instrument, this trust shall terminate, if it has not previously terminated, 21 years after the death of the survivor of the beneficiaries of the trust living at the date this instru-ment becomes effective. In case of such termination the then remaining principal and undistributed income of the trust shall be distributed to the then income beneficiaries in the same proportions as they were, at the time of termination, entitled to receive the income. The term "benefi-ciaries" includes persons originally named as beneficiaries in this instru-ment as well as persons, living at the date this instrument becomes effective, subsequently named as beneficiaries by a donee of a power of appointment over the trust assets exercising such power.

Observe that, under this saving clause, the trust terminates 21 years after the death of all beneficiaries, originally or subsequently named as such, who were in being when the trust was created. The principal is then distributed as provided in the saving clause. Because the trust ends within or at the end of the perpetuities period, at which time the trust assets are distributed, no interest in the trust assets can violate the Rule against Perpetuities.

　The last sentence of the saving clause is important. It makes clear that the donee of a power of appointment can change the measuring lives for the trust, provided the donee does not select someone not

---

16. Not saving*s* clause, which is grammatically incorrect. As an adjective, *saving* — without the *s* — has the sense of "rescuing." See William Safire, On Language, N.Y. Times Magazine, April 2, 1995, at 22, explaining that "savings" is the sum of separate acts of saving, as in a savings account.

alive when the trust was created. There may be substantial estate tax or generation-skipping transfer tax advantages in keeping the trust going for the maximum perpetuities period by each generation exercising special powers of appointment prolonging the trust. If the trust is a family dynasty trust and the settlor's issue alive at the creation of the trust have all expired, or are about to expire, the donee of a special power can continue the trust for the lives of twelve healthy persons who were born before the trust was created, plus 21 years, by giving these persons a small beneficial interest in the trust (hence making them beneficiaries). If this is done, the trust can endure for 100 years or so.[17]

For a thorough discussion of a variety of saving clauses, see David M. Becker, Perpetuities and Estate Planning 133-184 (1993).

NOTE: ATTORNEY LIABILITY FOR VIOLATING RULE

In an increasing number of jurisdictions, attorneys are liable to intended beneficiaries of negligently drafted instruments. See supra page 64. Whether it is negligent to draft an instrument that violates the Rule against Perpetuities is not settled. In Lucas v. Hamm, 56 Cal. 2d 583, 364 P.2d 685 (1961), the court held the attorney who violated the Rule was not negligent on the specific facts of the case (involving an administrative contingency). *Lucas,* however, is a shaky precedent. It has been criticized by the Vice-Chancellor of England as an embarrassment to the profession. Robert E. Megarry, Note, 81 L.Q. Rev. 465, 478-481 (1965). A lower California court has warned that *Lucas* is of doubtful validity today, because the legendary traps of the Rule can be easily avoided by the insertion of a perpetuities saving clause. Wright v. Williams, 47 Cal. App. 3d 802, 809 n.2, 121 Cal. Rptr. 194, 199 n.2 (1975). See also Millwright v. Romer, 322 N.W.2d 30 (Iowa 1982), where the court appeared to assume that an attorney who violates the Rule is liable for malpractice but held the suit barred by the statute of limitations.

SECTION F. PERPETUITIES REFORM

In the last half of the twentieth century, extensive debate erupted over whether the Rule against Perpetuities needs reform or should be abolished. The reformers' ideas and judicial and legislative changes

---

17. The English have long used a saving clause in the form of a "royal lives clause." The trust is to continue until 21 years after the death of all the descendants of Queen Victoria (or of George V or of some other British monarch) living at the creation of the trust. The lives thus selected have no connection with the intended beneficiaries, but, because of their prominence, their deaths can usually be ascertained, though sometimes with difficulty, using such sources as Debrett's Peerage and Baronetage (1995) (pub-

in the law can be sorted into three basic kinds: the cy pres doctrine, the wait-and-see doctrine, and abolition of the Rule.

1.   The Cy Pres or Reformation Doctrine

Under the cy pres doctrine, a court reforms a trust that violates the Rule against Perpetuities so as to carry out the testator's intent within the perpetuities period. This doctrine has been adopted in a few states. In exercising the cy pres power (meaning "as near as possible"), a court might insert a saving clause adapted to the particular possibility that causes the gift to be invalid and, in this manner, interfere with the testator's expressed wishes as little as possible. In Case 9, supra page 809, for example, the saving clause might read: "If any child of *A* is under the age of 4 at the death of *A*, the age contingency shall be reduced to the age reached by adding 21 to the age of *A*'s youngest child living at *A*'s death." If no child were under 4 at *A*'s death, no reduction in the age contingency would occur. If the youngest child were age 2 at *A*'s death, the age contingency would be reduced to 23. For illustrations of how a cy pres saving clause works, see Jesse Dukeminier, A Modern Guide to Perpetuities, 74 Cal. L. Rev. 1867, 1898-1901 (1986). See also In re Estate of Anderson, 541 So. 2d 423 (Miss. 1989); Abrams v. Templeton, 320 S.C. 325, 465 S.E.2d 117 (Ct. App. 1995).

Judicial reformation of an invalid interest at the time the instrument becomes effective is authorized by Idaho Code Ann. §55-111 (1998); Mo. Ann. Stat. §442.555 (1997); Okla. Stat. tit. 60, §75 (1998); Tex. Prop. Code Ann. §5.043 (1998).

New York and Illinois have adopted by statute specific cy pres correctives for the most frequent violations of the Rule. Age contingencies in excess of 21 that cause a gift to fail are reduced to 21 as to all persons subject to such contingency. See In re Estate of Kreuzer, 243 A.D.2d 207, 674 N.Y.S.2d 505 (1998). The unborn widow is dealt with by a presumption that a gift to a spouse is a gift to a person in being. Administrative contingencies are presumed to be intended to occur within 21 years. The fertile octogenarian is dealt with by a presumption that a woman is incapable of bearing children after 55 and by the admission of extrinsic evidence of infertility in any case of a living person. It is generally presumed in these states that the transferor intended the interest to be valid, so instruments are construed to avoid the Rule. Ill. Comp. Stat. Ann. ch. 765, §305/4(c) (1998); N.Y. Est., Powers & Trusts Law §§9-1.2 & 9-1.3 (1998).

---

lished every five years). See Re Warren's Will Trusts, 105 Sol. J. 511 (1961). By using all these royal lives, the trust can last well over 100 years, usually about 120.

Professor Bloom recommends adding a general cy pres power to the specific correctives of the New York statutes, to be exercised if these correctives do not apply. Ira M. Bloom, Perpetuities Refinement: There Is an Alternative, 62 Wash. L. Rev. 23 (1987).

As compared to wait-and-see, cy pres has two disadvantages: (1) judicial reformation requires a lawsuit, and (2) the possibility that causes a violation of the Rule will, in most cases, be resolved within a wait-and-see period, resulting in the testator's intent being given complete effect. On the other hand, judicial reformation at the time the future interest is created will avoid problems resulting from the uncertainty under wait-and-see whether the interest will turn out to be valid or void, as well as the uncertainty of how to reform an instrument in the far future if the interest does in fact vest too remotely.

2. The Wait-and-See Doctrine

In 1947, the Pennsylvania legislature decided to eliminate the requirement of the Rule that there be no possibility that an interest might vest too remotely. Pa. Cons. Stat. Ann. tit. 20, §6014 (1998) provides:

> Upon the expiration of the period allowed by the common law rule against perpetuities as measured by actual rather than possible events any interest not then vested and any interest in members of a class the membership of which is then subject to increase shall be void.

In 1952 Professor W. Barton Leach of Harvard began his attack upon the Rule against Perpetuities in its orthodox form. Dubbing the Pennsylvania approach "wait-and-see," Leach strongly approved it in a seminal article, Leach, Perpetuities in Perspective: Ending the Rule's Reign of Terror, 65 Harv. L. Rev. 721 (1952). The essence of the wait-and-see doctrine is that we wait and see what actually happens; we do not invalidate an interest because of what might happen.

Professor Leach, writing with eloquence and wit, and sensing a general unhappiness with the Rule's remote possibilities test, fired up a movement to adopt the wait-and-see doctrine. After Leach first promoted the wait-and-see doctrine, a flood of articles appeared, some in favor of wait-and-see, some against. The primary arguments against wait-and-see were three: (1) inconveniences would arise from not knowing whether an interest was valid or void; (2) wait-and-see was a long step in extending the control of the dead hand; and (3) some critics believed the common law did not provide any measuring lives for a wait-and-see period. Professor Leach replied to his critics in an entertaining article, Perpetuities Legislation, Hail Pennsylvania!, 108 U. Pa. L. Rev. 1124 (1960). For comprehensive lists of articles on wait-and-see, see 5A Richard R. Powell, Real Property ¶¶827A & G (rev.

W. Barton Leach

ed. 1998); Lewis M. Simes & Allan F. Smith, The Law of Future Interests §1230 (2d ed. 1956, with supplements).

When Leach's colleague at Harvard, Professor James Casner, was appointed Reporter for the second Restatement of Property, he wrote wait-and-see into the Restatement. Casner's main argument for wait-and-see was that the what-might-happen test penalizes persons who do not consult skilled lawyers, who avoid the rule by saving clauses or other drafting devices. He wrote this rationalization for wait-and-see: "The adoption of the wait-and-see approach in this Restatement is largely motivated by the equality of treatment that is produced by placing the validity of all nonvested interests on the same plane, whether the interest is created by a skilled draftsman or one not so skilled." Restatement (Second) of Property, Donative Transfers 13 (1983).

QUESTION

The justification offered by the Restatement (Second) of Property for wait-and-see can have far-reaching applications. Think back over the wills and trust cases you have read where the drafter failed to include a special power of appointment (which a skilled drafter almost surely would have included), cut out a child negligently, used ambiguous language, failed to avoid unnecessary taxation. Can the law be changed, in these cases, to give the advantage of skilled drafting to persons who consult the unskilled? How?

The adoption of wait-and-see by the Restatement (Second) provided a renewed stimulus for the wait-and-see movement. Wait-and-see has now been adopted in a majority of states, either by statute or judicial decision. The states divide between states waiting during the common

law perpetuities period and states waiting for 90 years, as provided by
the Uniform Statutory Rule Against Perpetuities.

a.   Wait-and-See for the Common Law Perpetuities Period

Professor Leach believed that the common law provided an inherent wait-and-see period: the lives relevant to vesting of the interest
plus 21 years. The leading English authorities, Vice-Chancellor
Megarry and Professor Wade, saw it the same way:

> . . . [T]he only lives in being which are significant under the rule at
> common law are those which in some way restrict the time within which
> the gift can vest, and which are expressly or impliedly connected with
> the gift by the donor's directions. The available perpetuity period must
> always be ascertained before it can be said whether the gift succeeds
> or fails. The conditions governing the vesting of the gift, and the lives
> implicated in those conditions, necessarily remain the same, whether or
> not the conditions are ultimately satisfied. [Robert Megarry & H. W. R.
> Wade, The Law of Real Property 254 (5th ed. 1984).]

See also in accord J. H. C. Morris & H. W. R. Wade, Perpetuities
Reform at Last, 80 L.Q.R. 486, 497 (1965); David J. Hayton, The Law
of Trusts 79-80 (1989).

Under this view, the lives that can affect vesting fix the common
law perpetuities period applicable to the particular interest. These
lives are sometimes said to be "causally related to vesting." See Jesse
Dukeminier, Perpetuities: The Measuring Lives, 85 Colum. L. Rev.
1648 (1985); Jesse Dukeminier, Wait-and-See: The Causal Relationship
Principle, 102 L.Q. Rev. 250 (1986).

States adopting wait-and-see for the common law perpetuities period measured by the relevant common law lives include Kentucky,
Mississippi, New Hampshire, Ohio, Pennsylvania, Vermont, and Virginia. Iowa waits out a list of lives closely resembling the relevant
common law lives. Maine and Maryland wait out the lives of the preceding life tenants. Illinois and Washington apply wait-and-see to
trusts only and wait out the lives of the trust beneficiaries before
determining the validity of a remainder. Many of these states provide
that, at the end of the waiting period, if an interest has not vested, it
shall be reformed by a court to carry out the intention of the testator
as far as possible within the perpetuities period. (In Illinois and Maine
recent statutes have authorized perpetual trusts, and thus made the
wait-and-see statutes inapplicable to most trusts. See infra page 854.)

Here's how wait-and-see for the common law perpetuities period
works:

Case 15. The Fertile Octogenarian. T bequeaths a fund in trust "for *A* for life, then for *A*'s children for their lives, then to *A*'s issue then living." At common law, the remainder in fee simple is void because *A* is conclusively presumed to be capable of having another child. Under wait-and-see, *the lives relevant to vesting are A and all of A's issue living at T's death. A* and *A*'s children are relevant on two scores: they are preceding life tenants, and they can, by procreating, affect the identity of the remainder beneficiaries. *A*'s grandchildren and great-grandchildren in being at *T*'s death are relevant because they are beneficiaries and also, by procreating or dying, they can affect the identity of the class of issue who take the remainder.

Case 16. Age Contingency. T bequeaths a fund in trust "for *A* for life, then to *A*'s children who reach 25." This is void at common law because *A* can leave, at his death, an afterborn child under the age of 4. The class members will not necessarily take fixed shares within 21 years after *A*'s death. *The wait-and-see lives are A and all of A's children living at T's death. A* qualifies as a measuring life on two counts: *A* is the preceding life tenant, and *A*, by begetting a child who shares in the remainder, can affect the identity of the beneficiaries. The children of *A* in being at *T*'s death who are under 25 can, by dying under 25, affect the identity of the class members. Those children over 25 at *T*'s death are identified beneficiaries in whom the gift vests.

From these examples you should be able to discern the relevant measuring lives for wait-and-see in all cases you can think of, but if you cannot, see Dukeminier, 85 Colum. L. Rev. 1648, supra, where the measuring lives for all of the standard cases arising under the Rule against Perpetuities are set forth. See also Fleet National Bank v. Colt, 529 A.2d 122 (R.I. 1987) (gift to subclasses).

b.   The Uniform Statutory Rule Against Perpetuities

The drafters of the Uniform Statutory Rule Against Perpetuities adopted wait-and-see, but they rejected using causally-related or relevant measuring lives. They took the view that the only relevant lives at common law were those that validated the gift. Therefore, lives that might cause vesting, but did not validate the gift, did not implicitly provide a perpetuities period for the particular interest.[18] Thus, they thought, it was necessary to provide an artificial wait-and-see period. They chose a wait-and-see period of 90 years. Why 90 years? One might surmise that they adopted a 90-year period because it is a fair, if somewhat shorter, approximation of the period produced by using

18. This view has been most forcefully presented in David E. Allen, Perpetuities: Who Are the Lives in Being?, 81 L.Q.R. 106 (1965), and Ronald H. Maudsley, The Modern Law of Perpetuities 94-100 (1979). For a more recent presentation of this view, see Lawrence W. Waggoner, Perpetuities: A Perspective on Wait-and-See, 85 Colum. L. Rev. 1714 (1985).

Professor Leach's "dozen or so healthy babies" plus 21 years (supra page 797), which a skilled lawyer might use as a saving clause. This approach could be justified on the rationale of the Restatement (Second): "placing the validity of all nonvested interests on the same plane, whether the interest is created by a skilled draftsman or one not so skilled" (supra page 833).[19] But Professor Waggoner, the principal drafter, has vigorously, indeed indignantly, denied that the drafters had such a rationale in mind. See Lawrence W. Waggoner, The Uniform Statutory Rule Against Perpetuities: The Rationale of the 90-Year Waiting Period, 73 Cornell L. Rev. 157 (1988). Professor Waggoner says — with nary a winkle of a grin — that the drafters simply assumed that the "average trust" would have a six-year-old beneficiary. A six-year-old has a life expectancy of 69 years, to which 21 years are added, coming up with the nice round figure of 90 years. There is, of course, no empirical evidence whatsoever that the "average trust" (whatever that means) has a six-year-old beneficiary. This Model Moppet is purely a figure of the drafters' imagination. (But never mind: Perpetuities law has long been built on fantasy characters.)

Under USRAP,[20] the common law Rule against Perpetuities is put in abeyance for 90 years. All interests are valid for 90 years after creation. At the end of 90 years, any interest that has not vested is reformed by a court so as to best carry out the intention of the long-dead testator. Although empty of intellectual rationalization, USRAP has been supported by state bar associations. It is easier to tick off the 90-year wait-and-see period than to determine and keep track of the lives causally related to vesting, and a 90-year wait-and-see period effectively eliminates malpractice liability for violating the Rule for a lawyer's entire career at the bar.[21] USRAP has been adopted in Alaska, Arizona, California, Colorado, Connecticut, Florida, Georgia, Hawaii, Indiana, Kansas, Massachusetts, Michigan, Minnesota, Montana, Nebraska, Nevada, New Jersey (repealed in 1999), New Mexico, North Carolina, North Dakota, Oregon, South Carolina, Tennessee and West Virginia.

19. A similar rationale underpins the English Law Commission's recent recommendation of a 125-year period for vesting, with complete abolition of the common law Rule. English Law Commission, The Rules Against Perpetuities and Excessive Accumulations, Report No. 251 (1998), discussed infra page 855. The Commission recommended adopting for wait-and-see a fixed number of years equal to the maximum time a skilled lawyer could obtain using a royal lives clause (see footnote 17, supra page 830).

20. Professor Link finds one aspect of USRAP "puzzling — its pronunciation. Both 'use-rap' and 'us-rap' seem acceptable to its drafter and advocates." Ronald C. Link & Kimberly A. Licata, Perpetuities Reform in North Carolina: Uniform Statutory Rule Against Perpetuities, Nondonative Transfers, and Honorary Trusts, 74 N.C. L. Rev. 1783, 1789 n.28 (1996).

21. *Caution*: When drafting an instrument with the objective of securing exemption from the federal generation-skipping transfer tax, running afoul of Treasury regulations regarding USRAP and the GST tax may result in a hefty malpractice bill. See infra page 846.

Observe that USRAP provides *two* rules against perpetuities: (1) the common law Rule against Perpetuities, and (2) a wait-and-see rule of 90 years. If an interest satisfies the common law Rule *or* actually vests within 90 years after its creation, it is valid. In giving trust settlors the option of ignoring the common law Rule against Perpetuities and creating a 90-year trust, USRAP abandoned the ancient policy of permitting a testator to control property only during lives of persons he knew and whose capacities he can judge. Using a trust enduring for 90 years, a testator can control the fortunes of several generations where no beneficiary was alive at the testator's death. On the other hand, it is arguable that this policy underlying the Rule was abandoned long ago when it was decided that extraneous lives ("12 healthy babies") could measure the perpetuities period.

For analyses and assessments of USRAP, see Ira M. Bloom, Perpetuities Refinement: There Is An Alternative, 62 Wash. L. Rev. 23 (1987); Jesse Dukeminier, The Uniform Statutory Rule Against Perpetuities: Ninety Years in Limbo, 34 UCLA L. Rev. 1023 (1987); Mary L. Fellows, Testing Perpetuity Reforms: A Study of Perpetuity Cases 1984-89, 25 Real Prob., Prob. & Tr. J. 597 (1990); Amy M. Hess, Freeing Property Owners From the RAP Trap: Tennessee Adopts the Uniform Statutory Rule Against Perpetuities, 62 Tenn. L. Rev. 267 (1995); David S. King & Alexander M. Meiklejohn, The Uniform Statutory Rule Against Perpetuities: Wait-and-See for 90 Years, 17 Est. Plan. 24 (1990); Ronald C. Link & Kimberly A. Licata, Perpetuities Reform in North Carolina: The Uniform Statutory Rule Against Perpetuities, Nondonative Transfers, and Honorary Trusts, 74 N.C. L. Rev. 1783 (1996).

Uniform Statutory Rule Against Perpetuities
(1986, as amended in 1990)

§1.   STATUTORY RULE AGAINST PERPETUITIES

(a) *[Validity of Nonvested Property Interest.]* A nonvested property interest is invalid unless:

(1) when the interest is created, it is certain to vest or terminate no later than 21 years after the death of an individual then alive; or

(2) the interest either vests or terminates within 90 years after its creation.

(b) *[Validity of General Power of Appointment Subject to a Condition Precedent.]* A general power of appointment not presently exercisable because of a condition precedent is invalid unless:

(1) when the power is created, the condition precedent is certain

to be satisfied or becomes impossible to satisfy no later than 21 years after the death of an individual then alive; or

(2) the condition precedent either is satisfied or becomes impossible to satisfy within 90 years after its creation.

(c) *[Validity of Nongeneral or Testamentary Power of Appointment.]* A nongeneral power of appointment or a general testamentary power of appointment is invalid unless:

(1) when the power is created, it is certain to be irrevocably exercised or otherwise to terminate no later than 21 years after the death of an individual then alive; or

(2) the power is irrevocably exercised or otherwise terminates within 90 years after its creation.

(d) *[Possibility of Post-death Child Disregarded.]* In determining whether a nonvested property interest or a power of appointment is valid under subsection (a)(1), (b)(1), or (c)(1), the possibility that a child will be born to an individual after the individual's death is disregarded.

(e) *[Effect of Certain "Later-of" Type Language.]* If, in measuring a period from the creation of a trust or other property arrangement, language in a governing instrument (i) seeks to disallow the vesting or termination of any interest or trust beyond, (ii) seeks to postpone the vesting or termination of any interest or trust until, or (iii) seeks to operate in effect in any similar fashion upon, the later of (a) the expiration of a period of time not exceeding 21 years after the death of the survivor of specified lives in being at the creation of the trust or other property arrangement or (b) the expiration of a period of time that exceeds or might exceed 21 years after the death of the survivor of lives in being at the creation of the trust or other property arrangement, that language is inoperative to the extent it produces a period of time that exceeds 21 years after the death of the survivor of the specified lives.

§2. WHEN NONVESTED PROPERTY INTEREST OR POWER OF APPOINTMENT CREATED

(a) Except as provided in subsections (b) and (c) and in Section 5(a), the time of creation of a nonvested property interest or a power of appointment is determined under general principles of property law.

(b) For purposes of this [Act], if there is a person who alone can exercise a power created by a governing instrument to become the unqualified beneficial owner of (i) a nonvested property interest or (ii) a property interest subject to a power of appointment described in Section 1(b) or 1(c), the nonvested property interest or power of appointment is created when the power to become the unqualified beneficial owner terminates. [For purposes of this [Act], a joint power with respect to community property or to marital property under the Uniform Marital Property Act held by individuals married to each other is a power exercisable by one person alone.]

(c) For purposes of this [Act], a nonvested property interest or a power of appointment arising from a transfer of property to a previously funded trust or other existing property arrangement is created when the nonvested property interest or power of appointment in the original contribution was created.

§3. REFORMATION

Upon the petition of an interested person, a court shall reform a disposition in the manner that most closely approximates the transferor's manifested plan of distribution and is within the 90 years allowed by Section 1(a)(2), 1(b)(2), or 1(c)(2) if:

(1) a nonvested property interest or a power of appointment becomes invalid under Section 1 (statutory rule against perpetuities);

(2) a class gift is not but might become invalid under Section 1 (statutory rule against perpetuities) and the time has arrived when the share of any class member is to take effect in possession or enjoyment; or

(3) a nonvested property interest that is not validated by Section 1(a)(1) can vest but not within 90 years after its creation.

§4. EXCLUSIONS FROM STATUTORY RULE AGAINST PERPETUITIES

Section 1 (statutory rule against perpetuities) does not apply to:

(1) a nonvested property interest or a power of appointment arising out of a nondonative transfer.... [Other exclusions omitted.]

§5. PROSPECTIVE APPLICATION

(a) Except as extended by subsection (b), this [Act] applies to a nonvested property interest or a power of appointment that is created on or after the effective date of this [Act]. For purposes of this section, a nonvested property interest or a power of appointment created by the exercise of a power of appointment is created when the power is irrevocably exercised or when a revocable exercise becomes irrevocable.

(b) If a nonvested property interest or a power of appointment was created before the effective date of this [Act] and is determined in a judicial proceeding, commenced on or after the effective date of this [Act], to violate this State's rule against perpetuities as that rule existed before the effective date of this [Act], a court upon the petition of an interested person may reform the disposition in the manner that most closely approximates the transferor's manifested plan of distribution and is within the limits of the rule against perpetuities applicable when the nonvested property interest or power of appointment was created.

In re Trust of Wold

Superior Court of New Jersey, Chancery Division, Middlesex County, 1998
310 N.J. Super. 382, 708 A.2d 787

HAMLIN, P.J.   This written decision amplifies an earlier oral bench opinion rendered on plaintiff's petition for interpretation and direction regarding the application of the "New Jersey Uniform Statutory Rule Against Perpetuities." N.J.S.A. 46.2F-1-8, to a proposed exercise by the beneficiary of her power of appointment under the terms of this 1944 Trust. It is an issue of first impression requiring the court to determine if the ninety year period of N.J.S.A. 46.2F-8 enacted on July 3, 1991, may be invoked by the beneficiary in regard to the exercise of that power of appointment vested in her by the 1944 Trust. The issue arises following inquiry by Elaine Johnson Wold, the life beneficiary of the Trust, to the trustees. More specifically she advised the trustees that she wishes to create a testamentary Trust appointing the proceeds of the 1944 Trust in further trust for the benefit of her spouse and surviving issue. The proposed testamentary trust would create non-vested property interests in one or more issue. By way of illustration the proposed exercise of the power in a new testamentary trust created by Mrs. Wold would permit property held for one of her children, upon the death of that child, to continue in trust for the benefit of that child's own issue. Thus, the trust interest of that child would be considered non-vested since it would pass to the next generation upon the occurrence of a specific event, i.e. the death of the child.

The proposed exercise of Mrs. Wold's power of appointment under the 1944 Trust through the creation of her own testamentary trust would permit such generational structure to continue for the full period permitted under the Rule Against Perpetuities. In delineating the maximum term of the trust she would create for her spouse and issue, Mrs. Wold has expressed to the trustees her intention to rely on the ninety year "wait and see" perpetuities period as codified in the 1991 legislation.

In order to ensure the validity of her long term estate planning and to make certain that the trustees will be permitted to make distributions of the trust estate in accordance with her expressed intentions Mrs. Wold, through the trustees, asks this court to determine the applicability and construction of the New Jersey Rule Against Perpetuities Act as it applies to the exercise of her special power of appointment. In the absence of clear and binding precedent or other authority, neither Mrs. Wold nor the trustees can be assured that the intended disposition will not be later found to violate the applicable rule against perpetuities. Without a present determination, there exists the possibility that the testamentary trust created by Mrs. Wold might, after her death, be voided or reformed in a manner that is inconsistent with her expressed intention. In addition, the trustees seek direction from the court regarding the proposed testamentary exercise of Mrs. Wold's power of appointment under the terms of the 1944 instrument. They assert that they are in doubt as to whether the power granted Mrs. Wold to dispose of the trust res includes the power to appoint the trust assets by a successive testamentary trust. The trustees seek to invoke the traditional equitable power of the Chancery court to resolve their concerns about the exercise of their fiduciary duty as governed by the provision of the original trust which states:

> Upon the death of Elaine Johnson (Wold), the Trustees are directed to divide, transfer and pay over absolutely, outright and forever, the trust property as follows: to the surviving spouse and issue of Elaine Johnson (Wold) or any of them in such shares as she may direct by her Last Will and Testament duly admitted to probate. . . .

All persons having an interest in the issue presented have been served and have chosen not to take a position on the application.

CREATION OF THE 1944 TRUST

J. Seward Johnson (hereinafter Seward) created this trust on October 20, 1944 to benefit his daughter Elaine Johnson Wold.[22] It was one of several trusts he created contemporaneously for each of his children. Each was identical in language with the exception of the named beneficiaries. Subsequently the settlor created at least two additional charitable lead trusts to further benefit his issue. The trust plan was neither haphazard nor one dimensional. The trusts were initially funded by substantial shares of the health care corporate giant, Johnson and Johnson (J&J). Seward and his brother, Robert Wood Johnson were the principal heirs of the controlling stock of J&J, which was

---

22. For more on Seward Johnson and his family, see supra pages 197-209. Elaine Johnson was unmarried and had no children in 1944 when the trust was created. She married Keith Wold in 1949. — Eds.

already a major national corporation at that time. Robert Wood Johnson succeeded to the leadership of the company. Through his efforts and subsequent astute business management, J&J has become a major international diversified business presence. Thus, the original 15,000 shares of J&J stock which initially funded the trust have multiplied in value so that they now constitute one of the most significant family fortunes in America. Since J&J has been headquartered in New Brunswick, New Jersey for over a century and the trusts were created here, the Middlesex County Courts and more specifically the Chancery Division of this venue, have had long interaction with the construction and administration of the various trusts created by Seward. Many accountings have been presented over the years. Specific previous applications by trustees have been the subject of decisions and unpublished opinions. Likewise there has been significant litigation involving the trusts, their creation and purpose, which resulted in published opinions that are helpful to our overall understanding of the trust scheme established by Seward with the assistance of sophisticated estate planning counsel. See Hill v. Estate of Mary Lea Johnson-Richards, 142 N.J. 639, 667 A.2d 695 (1995); Wiedenmayer v. Johnson, 106 N.J. Super. 161, 254 A.2d 534 (App. Div. 1969), aff'd 55 N.J. 81 (1970); Barbara P. Johnson v. Seward Johnson, Jr., 212 N.J. Super. 368, 515 A.2d 255 (Ch. Div. 1986); and Burke v. Director, Division of Taxation, 11 N.J. Tax 29 (1990).

The trust instrument itself is comprehensive and clearly designed to accomplish several salutary ends. Foremost is the provision for support and income to the beneficiary and such of her heirs as she may select. Such income was maximized to the fullest by utilizing tax saving devices permitted by law.

Under the terms of the Trust, the trustees were directed during the lifetime of Elaine Johnson Wold to collect and receive the income and profits from the trust property and, after deducting those expenses of "the trust" which are payable out of the income, to accumulate the net income and add it at the end of each calendar year to the trust property. Once Elaine Johnson Wold attained the age of twenty-one (21) years, the trust agreement authorized the trustees to pay to her so much of the net income in any year as the trustees in their absolute and uncontrolled discretion deemed to be for her best interest. The trust instrument further permits the trustees to transfer and pay over to the life beneficiary ". . . any or all of the Trust property."

Upon the death of Elaine Johnson Wold, the trust agreement directs the trustees to divide, transfer and pay over absolutely, outright and forever, the trust property as follows:

> a. To the surviving spouse and issue of Elaine Johnson (Wold) or any of them in such shares as she may direct by her last Will and Testa-

ment duly admitted to probate, or failing such testamentary direction, then,

b. To her issue in equal shares per stirpes. . . .

DOES THE TRUST PROHIBIT THE PROPOSED EXERCISE?

At the threshold this court notes that the trust instrument, by its very language, vested in the trustees the broadest possible discretion that may be found in any trust instrument. They are to be guided solely by their evaluation of the beneficiary's best interest. Clearly the settlor intended to repose in the trustees maximum flexibility in addressing the needs of the beneficiaries. By way of illustration it is clear that had the trustees distributed the entire income and corpus to Mrs. Wold during her lifetime, leaving nothing to be appointed to subsequent heirs, it would have been permissible absent claim of corruption, intentional misconduct or gross negligence. In regard to the instant matter this court is mindful that the sole inference from the unambiguous language of the trust instrument was the desire of the settlor to create a flexible instrument to meet the developing needs of his children both at the time of the creation of the trust and for unforeseen events that would occur. It is an expansive rather than a restrictive instrument.

The law of trusts lends support to Mrs. Wold's position that she should be able to exercise the special power of appointment created by her father, Seward, in a testamentary trust by her for the benefit of her granddaughters. The Restatement (Second) of Trusts §17 provides that "[a] trust may be created by (d) an appointment of one person having a power of appointment to another person as trustee for the donee of the power or for a third person."

The comments to the section explain that "if a person has a special power of appointment . . . he can effectively appoint interests to trustees for the benefit of objects of the power unless the donor manifested a contrary intent." Restatement (Second) of Trusts, §17 cmt. f. Further, it is clear that one can infer that the donor of a special power intended the donee to have the same discretion in making an appointment that he had in the disposition of his own property, so far as the extent and nature of the interests which he might give to the members of the class are concerned. Id; see also Restatement (Second) of Property §19.3 (1984).

It has long been accepted that a person holding powers of appointment may appoint to the fullest extent of the authority or to such lesser estate or interest as he may see fit in the absence of an express prohibition by the settlor in the trust instrument. Guild v. Mayor and Common Council of City of Newark, 87 N.J. Eq. 38, 99 A. 120 (1916).

The general rule supporting the exercise of a lesser appointment in the absence of a restriction in the trust instrument may be found in other jurisdictions. The commonwealth of Massachusetts has adopted the principal by statute. Mass. Gen. Laws. Ann. Ch. 191-1. New York has reached a similar result in a series of cases. See In Re Hart's Will, 262 A.D. 190, 28 N.Y.S.2d 781 (App. Div. 1941). . . .

While the trust instrument speaks in terms of appointment including distribution of the corpus in fee simple, if the beneficiary saw fit, it should not be construed as a form of limitation. The hallmark of this trust, as the others, is the flexibility of the trustees, and implicitly the donee of the power, to be permitted maximum discretion.

The court is not unmindful of the clear purpose of the settlor to protect the trust from tax burdens to the fullest extent permitted by law. There can be no question that the proposed testamentary trust exercise of the power will effect significant tax savings. As this court observed in a matter involving another long term trust created by Seward, one of the significant purposes of the Trust scheme was ". . . that the Grantor was able to shelter the fund and its appreciation in value from his estate for estate tax purposes and to incorporate then permissible generation skipping features." Such a purpose, as evidenced by the sophisticated estate planning devices used by Seward, are to be given effect in the exercise of the power of appointment rather than restricted. The proposed creation of the testamentary trust as described by Mrs. Wold is well within the contemplation and intent of the trust instrument. The trustees may honor the proposed exercise of the power of appointment at the appropriate time and make a consistent distribution of the trust assets.

THE APPLICATION OF N.J.S.A. 46:2A-1-5

New Jersey adopted the Uniform Statutory Rule Against Perpetuities on July 3, 1991. In so doing it adopted the "wait and see" approach long advocated by reformers of the common law rule against perpetuities so painfully committed to memory by generations of law students. The statute may well sound the death knell for Leach's "Perpetuities In A Nut Shell."

Under the common law approach, if an interest was not certain to vest within the specified period, then the disposition was considered invalid. Under the Act, an interest that would have been invalid at common law is nevertheless valid if it does in fact vest within ninety years of its creation, and becomes invalid only if it remains in existence and does not ultimately vest within that time period. Under the statutory provision, "a non-vested property interest is invalid unless (1) When the interest is created, it is certain to vest or terminate no later than 21 years after the death of an individual then alive, or

(2) the interest either vests or terminates within 90 years after its creation."

The Statute, in a specific and distinguishable fact pattern, was applied prospectively. In Juliano & Sons Enterprises, Inc. v. Chevron U.S.A., Inc., 250 N.J. Super. 148, 593 A.2d 814 (App. Div. 1991), which is the only reported New Jersey decision that has addressed the new statute, the court held that the statutory rule was not retroactive and intended to apply only to property interests created on or after the effective date of the statute. See also U.L.A. Perpetuities 5 (1990). Thus, an interest created under a trust established in 1944 would arguably not fall under the new legislation.

However, while the statute may not apply retroactively as a general matter, for purposes of determining the applicability of the new statutory period the law specifically provides that an interest created pursuant to a power of appointment is deemed to be created upon the exercise of the power. N.J.S.A. 46:2F-5(a). Therefore, even if created under a pre-existing power of appointment, the New Jersey Uniform Statutory Rule Against Perpetuities would apply to an interest created under that power, whether general or specific, if exercised after July 3, 1991.

This interpretation is supported by the clear language of the statute as well as by the comments to the Uniform Laws Annotated. "All provisions of the [Uniform] Act except section 5(b) apply to a non-vested property interest (or power of appointment) created by a donee's exercise of a power of appointment where the donee's exercise, whether revocable or irrevocable, occurs on or after the effective date of [the] Act." (Section 5(b) allows reformation of non-vested interests created before the new law.) The U.L.A. comment also makes clear that the special rule bringing a non-vested interest created under a power of appointment within the scope of the new law "applies to the exercise of all types of powers of appointment — presently exercisable general powers, general testamentary powers, and non-general powers."

Consistent with the language of the statute as well as the persuasive analysis of secondary authority this court concludes that the statutory period applies to the non-vested interest that would be created pursuant to the exercise of the power and measured from the creation of the 1944 Trust.

NOTES AND QUESTIONS

1. In the *Wold* case, the trust created by Seward Johnson in 1944 was grandfathered in and not subject to the generation-skipping transfer tax enacted in 1986, which was not retroactive. Quite naturally,

the donee of the special power of appointment, Elaine Johnson Wold, wanted to prolong this tax-exempt trust as long as possible.

Elaine Johnson Wold wanted to appoint in further trust for 90 years from 1944, benefitting her spouse and descendants. The trust would last until 2034. Why did not the donee want to appoint in further trust using artificial measuring lives (e.g., 12 persons from long-lived families who were infants in 1944) plus 21 years? The statistical probabilities are that this would produce a period longer than one ending in 2034.

Suppose that Elaine Johnson Wold appointed in further trust until 2034 giving her descendants special inter vivos powers of appointment. When the 90-year period is approaching expiration, can the donees exercise the powers, switching the trust duration over to the common law perpetuities period, using lives in being in 1944? USRAP §1(e) does not prohibit switching to the common law perpetuities period at the end of 90 years.

2. In this case it is highly unlikely that the Seward Johnson trust contained a saving clause. Saving clauses came into general use in the 1960s. Suppose, however, that the Seward Johnson trust had contained a saving clause providing that the trust would terminate 21 years after the death of the survivor of Seward's issue living when the trust was created. Could Elaine Johnson Wold change the duration of the trust to 90 years? If not, what does this suggest about the drafting of a perpetuities saving clause (supra page 829)?

3. In 1999 New Jersey repealed the Uniform Statutory Rule Against Perpetuities, replacing it with a rule permitting a perpetual trust if the trustee has power to sell, either expressed or implied, or if there is an unlimited power to terminate the trust in one or more living persons. N.J. A.B. 2804 (1999).

––––––––––––––

USRAP and the Generation-Skipping Transfer Tax. When USRAP was drafted, its drafters ignored the interaction of USRAP with the generation-skipping transfer tax. The generation-skipping transfer tax is, you will recall, payable on a transfer to a person two or more generations removed from the transferor, such as a grandchild (supra page 674). Trusts created before 1986 were grandfathered in. Under Treasury regulations at the time USRAP was drafted, pre-1986 trusts are not subject to the generation-skipping transfer tax unless a special power of appointment over the pre-1986 trust is exercised in a manner that postpones vesting of an interest beyond lives in being at the creation of the trust plus 21 years. The purpose of the regulation is to prevent tax exemption from enduring longer than the perpetuities period beginning at the creation of the trust.

The USRAP drafters paid no attention to the Treasury regulation, and after USRAP was promulgated it was discovered that USRAP contained an unexpected tax trap: In a USRAP jurisdiction, a grandfathered trust loses its GST tax exemption if the donee of a special power of appointment exercises the power so as to violate the common law Rule against Perpetuities, thus bringing into play the 90-year wait-and-see period, which may extend the trust beyond lives in being at the creation of the trust plus 21 years.

When the USRAP tax trap was brought to the attention of the USRAP drafting committee in 1990, the committee negotiated a solution for the problem with the Treasury Department. Treasury accepted the 90-year perpetuities period as the functional equivalent of the common law perpetuities period. Treasury was unwilling, however, to extend a tax exemption to a trust that could continue for either the common law perpetuities period or for 90 years, whichever period turned out to be longer. This could result in an even more substantial extension of the tax exemption as well as give an unfair advantage to longer-of-two-perpetuities-periods trusts available in USRAP states but not in states adhering to the common law. To satisfy Treasury's demand that a clause terminating a trust on the later of the two perpetuities periods be prohibited, USRAP was amended in 1990 by adding section 1(e).

Although section 1(e) may seem impenetrable upon first reading, to put it simply, §1(e) provides that when a gift is made on two alternative contingencies, one of which (A) will necessarily vest, if at all, within the common law perpetuities period, and the second of which (B) might vest beyond that period, section 1(e) renders inoperative the language of (B) to the extent it produces a period in excess of 21 years after the specified lives in being. When a clause terminates a trust at the conclusion of either the common law perpetuities period or a 90-year period, whichever is later, §1(e) gives effect only to the common law perpetuities period termination date.

After USRAP was amended to add §1(e), Treasury issued a regulation stating that if a special power of appointment in a grandfathered trust were "directly or indirectly" exercised in a manner that attempts to obtain the longer of the two perpetuities periods available under USRAP, the GST tax exemption is lost. Treas. Reg. §26.2601-1(b)(1)(v)(B)(2) & (D), Examples 6 and 7 (1997).

Here is how §1(e) works:

Case 17. Seward Johnson creates an irrevocable trust in 1944 to pay the income to his daughter Elaine for life, then as Elaine appoints by will among her spouse and issue and issue of spouses, and in default to her issue per stirpes. Elaine dies in 2000 appointing the income of the trust property to her descendants until the death of the survivor of twelve persons who were infants in 1944 or until 2034, whichever is longer, and then to distribute the principal to her issue per stirpes. This appointment creates two gifts on alternative contingencies, whichever happens last: (A) at the end of lives in being in 1944 plus 21 years or (B) at the end of 90 years from 1944. The appointment is entirely valid under the alternative contingencies doctrine in a USRAP jurisdiction.[23] The gift on event (A) is valid under the common law Rule (USRAP §1(a)(1)); the gift on event (B) is valid under the 90-year wait-and-see period of USRAP §1(a)(2). This appointment would forfeit the GST tax exemption of the trust but for USRAP §1(e). Section 1(e) voids the gift on event (B), leaving only a gift on the death of persons in being in 1944 plus 21 years.

Although the Treasury regulation forbids the exercise of the power in an attempt to obtain the longer of the two USRAP perpetuities periods, it permits the donee to appoint in further trust for 90 years or less. Hence, a grandfathered trust initially governed by the common law perpetuities period may be turned into a 90-year trust by the exercise of a special power of appointment, provided, of course, that the special power may be so exercised under the instrument. This is what Elaine Johnson Wold wanted to do in the *Wold* case, which the court approved.

USRAP §1(e) has not been enacted in some states that adopted USRAP before it was amended in 1990. In these states, when a special power in a grandfathered trust is exercised so as to terminate the trust at the end of the common law perpetuities period or 90 years, whichever is later, such as in Case 17, creating alternative contingencies, the first of which is valid at common law and the second valid under USRAP, the trust may lose its GST tax exemption. See Jesse Dukeminier, The Uniform Statutory Rule Against Perpetuities and the GST Tax: New Perils for Practitioners and New Opportunities, 30 Real Prop., Prob. & Tr. J. 185, 198-199 (1995).

Lawyers in USRAP states who are dealing with grandfathered trusts should take special care not to violate the common law Rule against Perpetuities if they decide not to extend the trust for 90 years. If the common law Rule is violated, bringing into play the 90-year wait-and-see period as an alternative trust termination date, this may result in

---

23. On the alternative contingencies doctrine, see supra page 806. The alternative contingencies doctrine is expressly made a part of USRAP. Uniform Statutory Rule Against Perpetuities, §1, Comment h, 8B Unif. Laws Ann. 352 (1990). The official comment to §1(e), however, overlooks the alternative contingencies doctrine. It asserts that §1(e) is not necessary to prevent a longer-of-two-perpetuities-periods trust even though the Uniform Commissioners adopted it for that very purpose. As a result, in trying to justify §1(e) while denying its reason for being, the official comment has a hollow, hokey character. For the comedy of errors behind the official comment, see Jesse Dukeminier, The Uniform Statutory Rule Against Perpetuities and the GST Tax: New Perils for Practitioners and New Opportunities, 30 Real Prop., Prob. & Tr. J. 185, 187-194 (1995).

the longer of the two perpetuities periods applying and the loss of GST tax exemption. Id. at 199-202.

As you can see, the interaction of USRAP and the GST tax is a complicated matter, which you will have to unravel if you are advising the donee of a special power in a grandfathered trust. USRAP may save the lawyer from malpractice liability for violating the Rule when the GST tax is not involved. But it does not save the lawyer from liability for negligently losing the GST tax exemption.

PROBLEMS AND QUESTIONS

1. Apply the Uniform Statutory Rule Against Perpetuities, as amended by §1(e), to the following devise: "To my issue, two years after the death of my widow or 40 years after my death, whichever is later." Here, we have alternative contingencies, one valid and one void at common law. Under USRAP §1(e), the "language is inoperative to the extent it produces a period of time that exceeds 21 years after the death of" the widow. Why does not the gift get the benefit of the 90-year wait-and-see period, inasmuch as the gift will undoubtedly vest within 90 years? Has the tax tail wagged the dog?

2. Apply the Uniform Statutory Rule Against Perpetuities to the following devise: "In trust to pay income to my descendants from time to time living, per stirpes, for as long as the law allows, then to pay principal to my descendants then living." Is the trust valid for the lives of the testator's descendants living at his death plus 21 years, or for 90 years, or for whichever is longer? Suppose that the jurisdiction has enacted USRAP but has not adopted §1(e). Is the trust valid for whichever of these two periods turns out to be longer? If so construed, would the trust be disqualified for the federal generation-skipping transfer tax exemptions?

3. In states that have adopted wait-and-see, is it still necessary to know and apply the common law Rule? For arguments that it is, see David M. Becker, If You Think You No Longer Need to Know Anything About the Rule Against Perpetuities, Then Read This!, 74 Wash. U. L.Q. 713 (1996).

NOTE: THE DYNASTY TRUST

Each transferor has a $1 million exemption from the generation-skipping transfer tax. The transferor can allocate this exemption to a trust to pay income to his or her descendants in succeeding generations for as long as local law permits the trust to endure. Such a GST-tax-exempt trust is known as a *dynasty trust.*

In a jurisdiction that follows the common law rule against perpetuities, a dynasty trust, free of estate, gift, and GST taxes for its duration, can endure for selected lives in being at the creation of the trust and for a further 21 years after the expiration of these lives. In a jurisdiction that has adopted the Uniform Statutory Rule Against Perpetuities, a dynasty trust can endure for the common law perpetuities period or, alternatively, for 90 years. In states that have abolished the rule against perpetuities (see infra page 854), a dynasty trust can last forever.

A settlor can transfer $1 million to a dynasty trust. The settlor's spouse also has a $1 million GST exemption, which the settlor can use with the spouse's consent. Together, a married couple can create a $2 million dynasty trust.

The $1 million gift can grow into a much larger sum. A settlor who creates a dynasty trust during life can direct the trustee to buy insurance on the settlor's life with the $1 million. Under this arrangement, the trust assets will be considerably larger than $1 million at the settlor's death. For example, if the settlor is age 50 and a standard risk, the trustee can purchase $6.5 million worth of life insurance with a $1 million premium; if the settlor is 60, the trustee can buy a policy paying $4 million. If the settlor's spouse joins in with a $1 million contribution, the policy proceeds (trust principal) could be worth double this amount at the settlor's death. If the spouses are younger, say age 35, the trustee could buy, with a single premium payment of $2 million, a policy paying $62 million on the death of the second-to-die!

The $1 million GST exemption applies to the amount of the settlor's contribution, not to the value of the trust assets upon distribution. If a $1 million dynasty trust is created and grows to much more in time, the trust assets, when distributed, are not subject to GST tax. If the $1 million is invested by the trustee in common stocks, which appreciate in value at the same rate stocks have appreciated over the 20th century, the original trust corpus of $1 million will grow to over $200 million in 100 years (or, adjusted for inflation, to $10 million). If the settlor and spouse have created a life insurance trust, as above, an original $10 million trust capital materializing on the settlor's death may grow to $2 billion upon the termination of the trust (or, adjusted for inflation, to $100 million)!

When the dynasty trust terminates and the trust property is distributed to the settlor's descendants, it will not be subject to any federal transfer tax. Only when these distributees die or give away the property will gift or estate tax be payable, and, depending on the ages of the distributees, this may occur 20, 50, or perhaps 80 years after the termination of the dynasty trust. A dynasty trust thus makes it possible to avoid transfer taxes on a huge amount of wealth for far more than a century.

A dynasty trust, in general outline, may look like this: *O* transfers $1 million to a trust that will pay the income to *O*'s daughter, *A*, for life,

*"I guess people are just going to have to tighten their belts
and fall back on their trust funds for awhile."*

Drawing by William Hamilton
© 1999 William Hamilton from *cartoonbank.com*.
Reproduced by permission.

and then to *A*'s children for their lives, and then in successive life estates down the generations until the perpetuities period expires; at that time, the trust assets will be distributed to *A*'s issue then living. To provide flexibility to deal with changing circumstances, *A* is given a special power to appoint the trust principal during life or by will, outright or in further trust to any one or more of a class of persons consisting of *A*'s spouse, the descendants of *O*, and spouses of such descendants. This power permits *A* to terminate the trust at any time during her life or at death, if it seems wise, by distributing the trust principal among her family.

Each child of *A* is given a similar power of appointment over his or her share, exercisable if *A* does not exercise her power. Similar powers are created in successive generations. Because these powers are not general powers of appointment, the trust principal subject to the power is not treated, for tax purposes, as owned by the donee of the power. No estate tax is imposed at the donee's death.

In a state that has adopted USRAP, a settlor can create a dynasty trust for 90 years or for the common law perpetuities period. Which should the settlor create? The primary advantage of a 90-year dynasty trust is that it locks in wealth transfer tax exemption for 90 years unless the donee of a special power of appointment decides to terminate the trust earlier. In the case of a 90-year trust, the donee must affirmatively opt to forgo continuation of the tax exemption. In contrast, keeping a dynasty trust going for the maximum common law perpetuities period usually requires affirmative action by the donee of a special power who exercises the power to extend the trust for extraneous lives plus 21 years, because the initial measuring lives produce a shorter period.

Relying on a donee of a power to so extend a trust is risky. The donee may not exercise the power because the donee may become incompetent or fail to execute a will exercising the power. The fundamental choice is whether it is better to lock in tax exemption for 90 years or to try for a longer period, taking into account the risk that the trust will endure for less than 90 years because of the donee's failure to extend the trust. The latter course will probably be successful only through careful and continuing supervision by a lawyer for the donee.

For many clients the 90-year dynasty trust — the one size that fits all — will be more satisfactory than the tailor-made suit that requires continuing alteration. The 90-year rule is simple in concept and far easier to explain than the common law perpetuities period and the maneuvers necessary to maximize it. Furthermore, the 90-year trust will probably be easier for the average practitioner to create.

It may be possible for a donee of a special power of appointment to change the duration of the trust from the common law perpetuities period to 90 years (or vice versa) if authorized by the trust instrument or local law. But the Treasury regulations must be carefully examined. See Jesse Dukeminier, Dynasty Trusts: Sheltering Descendants From Transfer Taxes, 23 Est. Plan. 417 (1996).

3.   Abolition of the Rule against Perpetuities

Jesse Dukeminier, The Uniform Statutory Rule Against Perpetuities:
Ninety Years in Limbo
34 UCLA L. Rev. 1023, 1025-1027 (1987)

It is an extraordinary thing to declare a whole body of prohibitory law to be in abeyance for 90 years, with no violation of the law possible for that period of time. . . .

. . . Can the Rule against Perpetuities really survive 90 years in desuetude?

I do not see how it can. If the Rule cannot strike down any interest for 90 years, I predict . . . knowledge of it will be lost to lawyers. . . .

Perpetuities saving clauses in their present form will probably continue to be routinely inserted in trusts for many years, since lawyers are creatures of habit. With the passage of time, however, fewer and fewer will understand why such clauses work. A saving clause may come to be regarded as the seal was in the late nineteenth century, a token of obeisance to the past that must be added without anyone really understanding exactly why.

At the end of 90 years, I cannot believe that anything as complicated as *Gray on Perpetuities* will be brought back to life. If, at the end of 90 years, there are contingent interests more than 90 years old, is it realistic to think that lawyers and judges will dig into the crumbling books of their great-grandparents to see whether these interests have vested under the old common law Rule against Perpetuities, perhaps under some rule about vested with possession postponed, gifts to subclasses, or separate contingencies? Surely the bar will rise (almost in unison, with only the dissent of some antiquarians) and formally abolish the Rule at that point in time.

If the future does shape up this way, the effect of adopting the Uniform Statute is to keep the Rule against Perpetuities formally on the books, but in abeyance, for 90 years, after which we can expect the Rule to be discarded as an obsolete, overcomplicated relic of the Industrial Age, to be wholly replaced by a 90-year limitation on the dead hand. We are assured by the Reporter for the Uniform Statute, Professor Lawrence Waggoner, that the statute is "an evolutionary step in the development and refinement of the wait-and-see doctrine. Far from revolutionary, it is well within the tradition of that doctrine." Well, if setting in motion events that almost inevitably will lead to abolition of the Rule against Perpetuities is not revolutionary, then neither was the Boston Tea Party.

The Rule against Perpetuities no longer commands universal respect or fear. Its storied absurdities seem remnants of a bygone age. The Uniform Statutory Rule Against Perpetuities, abandoning the principle of permitting dead hand control only for the lives of persons known to the donor (plus 21 years) and replacing it with no discernible principle for limiting trust duration other than the life expectancy of a six-year-old imaginary Model Moppet, has seriously, perhaps fatally, weakened the Rule against Perpetuities. There is no longer a consensus on how long the dead hand should be permitted to govern. The question now arises: Should the Rule against Perpetuities be abolished altogether?

South Dakota and Wisconsin abolished the Rule against Perpetuities some years ago. In those states, a trust can endure forever if the trustee has a power to sell the trust assets. S.D. Codified Laws Ann. §§43-5-4; 43-5-8 (1998); Wis. Stat. Ann. §700.16 (1998) In 1999 Rhode Island completely abolished the Rule. R.I. S.B. 869 (1999). Idaho too may have abolished the Rule, but the Idaho statute is very confused. Idaho Code §55-111 (1998).

There is now a movement afoot in other states to abolish the Rule's application to trusts of personal property. This movement is fueled by the federal tax advantages of dynasty trusts, which can endure, free of federal estate and generation-skipping transfer taxes generation after generation, for as long as local law permits. Delaware has repealed the Rule against Perpetuities as applied to trusts. Trusts of real property can last for 110 years. Trusts of personal property can last forever. Del. Code tit. 25, §503(a) (1998). The preamble to the Delaware statute states that its purpose is to keep Delaware competitive in the formation of trust capital "against several innovative jurisdictions that have abolished the rule against perpetuities. Several financial institutions have now organized or acquired trust companies, particularly in South Dakota, at least in part to take advantage of their favorable trust law." The Delaware repeal had the express purpose of attracting perpetual $1 million dynasty trusts into the state.

Illinois, Maine, and New Jersey have followed suit. They now permit a perpetual trust of personal property if the trustee has a power of sale. Ill. Con. Stat. ch. 765, §305/3 (1998); Me. H.B. 371 (1999); N.J. A.B. 2804 (1999). Similar statutes are now being pushed by banking associations in other states, which wish to remain competitive with banks where perpetual trusts are permitted. Remember: The settlor of an inter vivos trust funded with personal property may choose the state law that is to govern the trust. A settlor domiciled in New York can create a perpetual New Jersey trust with a New Jersey bank as trustee.

So, has the role of the Rule against Perpetuities in the course of history about played out? The Rule has two main functions: (1) ensuring that property is freely alienable and (2) curtailing the dead hand, so that property is controlled by the living. As for the first function, property in trust is almost always alienable because the trustee has a power of sale. As for curtailing the dead hand — this is the central issue.

Dead hand control of wealth could be curtailed by giving living trust beneficiaries the power to terminate the trust, whenever it is to the benefit of the beneficiaries, with court approval. In 1983, the Canadian province of Manitoba abolished the Rule against Perpetuities, and at the same time transformed legal future interests into trust interests and gave courts broad power to alter or terminate any trust if this will benefit the beneficiaries. 1982-1983 Man. Rev. Stat. chs. 38, 43. Termination of a trust with court approval requires a lawsuit, however, perhaps a costly one, whereas the Rule against Perpetuities brings about the termination of a trust by force of law, without a lawsuit. For current American law on trust termination, which makes trust termination by the beneficiaries very difficult, see supra pages 651-660.

On the other hand, dead hand control can also be curtailed if the settlor gives one or more living persons powers of appointment enabling the donee or donees to terminate the trust and distribute the trust corpus free of trust. Exercising powers of appointment to terminate a trust avoids the litigation costs of the Manitoba scheme. A statute exempting a trust from the Rule against Perpetuities if it contained such powers of termination would meet the Rule's objective of curtailing the dead hand and would have considerable merit.

In 1998, the English Law Commission completed its several-year study of whether the Rule against Perpetuities should be reformed further or abolished. English Law Commission, The Rules against Perpetuities and Excessive Accumulations, Report No. 251 (1998). The Commission considered arguments pro and con, including arguments that the Rule is unnecessary because curtailing the dead hand may be performed adequately by tax legislation and judicial powers to vary trusts. In addition, some argued, abolition is justified by the simplification of the law that it would bring about, resulting in saving an enormous number of billable hours incurred by lawyers while wrestling with perpetuities problems. And saving law students a lot of grief!

Although a "distinguished minority" of experts consulted urged abolition, the English Commission concluded that some rule was needed to eventually end dead hand control, largely because the Commission felt uneasy about what might happen without such a rule in a country with a long history of ancestral control of property. The Commission rejected a rule directly limiting the duration of trusts. Instead, it recommended abolishing the common law Rule against Perpetuities and replacing it with a rule that any contingent interest that did not actually vest within 125 years would be void. It fixed on 125 years because this is probably the longest period that can be obtained under present law by using a royal lives clause (comparable in this country to a dozen-healthy-babies clause). Note, however, that the recommended rule is a rule against vesting after 125 years, retaining all the obscurities of when an interest is "vested," not a rule requiring trusts to terminate at the end of 125 years. (Do you see the difference?) At the end of 125 years, any then contingent interest would fail and revert to the settlor's estate. (Imagine the tracing problems of determining who has succeeded to the estate of a settlor dead for 125 years!) The Commission rejected giving a court power to reform an invalid interest at the end of 125 years on the ground it would be too uncertain of application and productive of litigation.

For a somewhat similar proposal in this country to abolish the application of the Rule against Perpetuities to trusts and to terminate trusts after 120 years, see Paul G. Haskell, A Proposal for a Simple and Socially Effective Rule Against Perpetuities, 66 N.C. L. Rev. 545 (1988).

What do you think? Is a rule against remote vesting or a rule limiting trust duration better? Is either one needed? Recall the quotation attributed to Tocqueville in the excerpt from Oliver, Shapiro & Press, supra page 14: "What is the most important for democracy is not that great fortunes should not exist, but that great fortune's should not remain in the same hands. In that way there are rich men, but they do not form a class."

SECTION G. THE RULE AGAINST SUSPENSION OF THE POWER OF ALIENATION

Although since the time of Gray it has been settled that the rule against remote vesting is *the* common law Rule against Perpetuities, it was not clear before Gray whether there was also a common law rule against suspension of the power of alienation. Gray insisted there was not, and his view prevailed. However, in 1830 New York enacted statutes forbidding suspension of the power of alienation for more than a specified period. Several other states copied or were influenced by this New York legislation. After Gray's book was published, establishing that the rule against suspension of the power of alienation was not the common law Rule against Perpetuities, these states were left with the problem of determining whether their statutes were declaratory of the common law, as Gray had later interpreted it, or were additions to or replacements of that law.

The rule prohibiting suspension of the power of alienation is clearly distinguishable from the rule against remote vesting. The rule against remote vesting (the common law Rule against Perpetuities) is directed against contingent interests that may remain contingent beyond lives in being plus 21 years. The policy underlying it is that all contingent interests, assignable and nonassignable, impair marketability. The rule against suspension of the power of alienation is directed against interests that make the property inalienable. If there is any possibility that the power of alienation will be suspended longer than lives in being plus 21 years, the interests causing such invalid suspension are void ab initio.

The power of alienation is suspended only when there are not persons in being who can convey an absolute fee. There are two views of when the power of alienation is suspended by the creation of a trust. Under one view, the Wisconsin view, the power of alienation is not suspended if the trustee has a power to sell the trust assets, making them alienable. Wis. Stat. Ann. §700.16 (1998). In Wisconsin, the common law Rule against Perpetuities has been abolished, and a trust can endure forever if the trustee has a power to convey the trust assets. The same view is taken in Idaho, New Jersey, and South Dakota. Idaho Code Ann. §55-111 (1998) (semble; statute confused); N.J. A.B. 2804 (1999); S.D. Codified Laws Ann. §43-5-8 (1998).

The other view, held in New York, is different. In New York, if a transfer is made in trust, the power of alienation is suspended if *either* the legal fee simple to the specific property held in trust cannot be transferred *or* the owners of all the equitable interests cannot convey an equitable fee simple. Even if the trustee is given the power to sell the specific assets, the power of alienation is still suspended unless the beneficiaries of the trust can convey their interests. The policy of alienability is directed both at the specific assets in the trust and at the beneficial interests in the trust.[24]

Since all vested and contingent future interests are assignable or releasable if (1) the holders thereof are ascertainable and (2) there is no express restraint upon alienation, the only interests that suspend the power of alienation, absent an express restraint, are interests given to unborn or unascertained persons. To put it shortly, the rule against remote vesting applies to all contingent interests;[25] the rule against suspension of the power of alienation applies only to interests that are contingent because the taker is unborn or unascertainable (or to interests where the transfer is restrained expressly or by law).

In New York, by statute, an income beneficiary's interest in trust is

---

24. N.Y. Est., Powers & Trusts Law §9-1.1(a) (1998) provides:

> (1) The absolute power of alienation is suspended when there are no persons in being by whom an absolute fee or estate in possession can be conveyed or transferred.
> (2) Every present or future estate shall be void in its creation which shall suspend the absolute power of alienation by any limitation or condition for a longer period than lives in being at the creation of the estate and a term of not more than twenty-one years. . . .

25. The rule against remoteness of vesting is also part of New York law. N.Y. Est., Powers & Trusts Law §9-1.1(b) (1998). Hence, New York has both the common law Rule against Perpetuities and the rule against suspension of the power of alienation.

inalienable, even though the beneficiary is ascertained, unless the settlor of the trust has expressly made it alienable. N.Y. Est., Powers & Trusts Law §7-1.5 (1998). If the income beneficiaries' interests are inalienable, the trust suspends the power of alienation during the income beneficiaries' lives. *Hence, the duration of a spendthrift trust in New York is limited to the perpetuities period.* Such a trust is partially or wholly invalid if it can exceed the perpetuities period in duration. Therein lies the most important difference today between the common law Rule against Perpetuities (which does not directly restrict the duration of trusts) and the New York rule against suspension of the power of alienation. Thus:

> *Case 18. T*, domiciled in New York, dies in 1995. She bequeaths a fund in a spendthrift trust "to pay the income to *A* for life, then to pay the income to *A*'s children for their lives, and then to pay the principal to New York University." The gift does not violate the Rule against Perpetuities. However, the income interests in *A* and *A*'s children are inalienable. Since the power of alienation might be suspended during the lifetime of afterborn persons (*A*'s children born after *T*'s death), the life income interests in *A*'s children are void. The remainder in New York University will be accelerated unless infectious invalidity applies.

If, in Case 18, *T* had by her will expressly provided that *A*'s children could alienate their interests, the trust would be wholly valid. The power of alienation would be suspended only during *A*'s lifetime, a life in being. At *A*'s death all of *A*'s children are in being, and, together with New York University, they can convey a fee simple absolute.

On the suspension rule in New York, and other aspects of New York perpetuities law, see 5A Richard R. Powell, Real Property ¶¶791-807B (rev. ed. 1998).

12

CHARITABLE TRUSTS

SECTION A.   NATURE OF CHARITABLE PURPOSES

Shenandoah Valley National Bank v. Taylor
Supreme Court of Appeals of Virginia, 1951
192 Va. 135, 63 S.E.2d 786

MILLER, J.   Charles B. Henry,[1] a resident of Winchester, Virginia, died testate on the 23rd day of April, 1949. His will dated April 21,

1. The testator, Charles B. Henry, operated a fruit and vegetable stand until shortly before his death. In earlier years in addition to the stand, he hawked fruits and vegetables through the town from a horse-drawn wagon.

A number of years before his death he lost his only child, a very pretty little daughter. This, so I am told, profoundly affected him, causing him to become more and more a recluse and this became even more pronounced after the death of his wife, who predeceased him by some years. Along with this increasing withdrawal from general social intercourse, there seems to have developed an increasing tendency to become miserly. This was indicated by such things as avoidance of use of electric lights except when absolutely necessary and making the produce which was no longer salable a substantial part of his diet.

Nonetheless, perhaps because of memory of his own deceased child, he seems to have maintained a strong affection for children generally. As a fruit vendor, he was widely known among the older generation of local citizens.

He saved and hoarded his money and made some investments, and I recollected being told by someone, possibly an official of the Shenandoah Valley Bank that when the Great Depression struck, he was frantic to the point of unnatural frenzy at the depreciation of his investments.

My firm received the case as a result of the complainant being the babysitter for my partner's sister and brother-in-law and was the second or third cousin to Charlie Henry. For some time she had been helping to look after him and bringing him food, undoubtedly with that expectation so often disappointed that he would

1949, was duly admitted to probate and the Shenandoah Valley National Bank of Winchester, the designated executor and trustee, qualified thereunder.

Subject to two inconsequential provisions not material to this litigation, the testator's entire estate valued at $86,000, was left as follows:

> Second: All the rest, residue and remainder of my estate, real, personal, intangible and mixed, of whatsoever kind and wherever situate, . . ., I give, bequeath and devise to the Shenandoah Valley National Bank of Winchester, Virginia, in trust, to be known as the "Charles B. Henry and Fannie Belle Henry Fund," for the following uses and purposes:
>
> (a) My Trustee shall invest and reinvest my trust estate, shall collect the income therefrom and shall pay the net income as follows:
>
> (1) On the last school day of each calendar year before Easter my Trustee shall divide the net income into as many equal parts as there are children in the first, second and third grades of the John Kerr School of the City of Winchester, and shall pay one of such equal parts to each child in such grades, to be used by such child in the furtherance of his or her obtainment of an education.
>
> (2) On the last school day of each calendar year before Christmas my trustee shall divide the net income into as many equal parts as there are children in the first, second and third grades of the John Kerr School of the City of Winchester, and shall pay one of such equal parts to each child in such grades, to be used by such child in the furtherance of his or her obtainment of an education.

By paragraphs (3) and (4) it is provided that the names of the children in the three grades shall be determined each year from the school records, and payment of the income to them "shall be as nearly equal in amounts as it is practicable" to arrange.

Paragraph (5) provides that if the John Kerr School is ever discontinued for any reason the payments shall be made to the children of the same grades of the school or schools that take its place, and the School Board of Winchester is to determine what school or schools are substituted for it.

Under clause "Third" the trustee is given authority, power, and discretion to retain or from time to time sell and invest and reinvest the estate, or any part thereof, as it shall deem to be the best interest of the trust.

The John Kerr School is a public school used by the local school board for primary grades and had an enrollment of 458 boys and

---

remember her in his will; in fact, I recollect that she claimed that he had flatly promised to do so or by artful insinuation had convinced her that he would. Her disappointment and resulting ire prompted her to seek counsel.

Letter to the editors, dated July 7, 1975, from the Hon. Robert K. Waltz, winning counsel in the *Taylor* case and later circuit court judge in Virginia. — Eds.

girls so there will be that number of pupils or thereabouts who would share in the distribution of the income.

The testator left no children or near relatives. Those who would be his heirs and distributees in case of intestacy were first cousins and others more remotely related. One of these next of kin filed a suit against the executor and trustee, and others challenging the validity of the provisions of the will which undertook to create a charitable trust. . . .

The sole question presented is: does the will create a valid charitable trust?

Construction of the challenged provisions is required and in this undertaking the testator's intent as disclosed by the words used in the will must be ascertained. If his dominant intent as expressed was charitable, the trust should be accorded efficacy and sustained.

But on the other hand, if the testator's intent as expressed is merely benevolent, though the disposition of his property be meritorious and evince traits of generosity, the trust must nevertheless be declared invalid because it violates the rule against perpetuities. . . .

Authoritative definitions of charitable trusts may be found in 4 Pomeroy's Equity Jurisprudence, 5th Ed., sec. 1020, and Restatement of the Law of Trusts, sec. 368, p.1140. The latter gives a comprehensive classification definition. It is:

> Charitable purposes include:
>
> (a) the relief of poverty;
> (b) the advancement of education;
> (c) the advancement of religion;
> (d) the promotion of health;
> (e) governmental or municipal purposes; and
> (f) other purposes the accomplishment of which is beneficial to the community.

In the recent decision of Allaun v. First National Bank, 190 Va. 104, 56 S.E.2d 83, the definition that appears in 3 M.J., Charitable Trust, sec. 2, p.872, was approved and adopted. It reads:

> "A charity," in a legal sense, may be described as a gift to be applied, consistently with existing laws, for the benefit of an indefinite number of persons, either by bringing their hearts under the influence of education or religion, by relieving their bodies from disease, suffering or constraint, by assisting them to establish themselves for life, or by erecting or maintaining public building or works, or otherwise lessening the burdens of government. It is immaterial whether the purpose is called charitable in the gift itself, if it is so described as to show that it is charitable. Generally speaking, any gift not inconsistent with existing laws which is promotive of science or tends to the education, enlightening, benefit

or amelioration of the condition of mankind or the diffusion of useful knowledge, or is for the public convenience is a charity. It is essential that a charity be for the benefit of an indefinite number of persons; for if all the beneficiaries are personally designated, the trust lacks the essential element of indefiniteness, which is one characteristic of a legal charity. (190 Va. p.108.) . . .

In the law of trusts there is a real and fundamental distinction between a charitable trust and one that is devoted to mere benevolence. The former is public in nature and valid; the latter is private and if it offends the rule against perpetuities, it is void. "It is quite clear that trusts which are devoted to mere benevolence or liberality, or generosity, cannot be upheld as charities. Benevolent objects include acts dictated by mere kindness, good will, or a disposition to do good. . . . Charity in a legal sense must be distinguished from acts of liberality or benevolence. To constitute a charity the use must be public in its nature." Zollman on Charities, sec. 398, p.268.

We are, however, reminded that charitable trusts are favored creatures of the law enjoying the especial solicitude of courts of equity and a liberal interpretation is employed to uphold them. Zollman on Charities, sec. 570, p.391; 2 Bogert on Trusts, sec. 369, p.1129. . . .

Appellant contends that the gift . . . not only meets the requirements of a charitable trust as defined in Restatement of the Law of Trusts, supra, but specifically fits two of those classifications, viz.:

> (b) trusts for the advancement of education;
> (f) other purposes the accomplishment of which is beneficial to the community.

We now turn to the language of the will for from its context the testator's intent is to be derived. Sheridan v. Krause, 161 Va. 873, 172 S.E. 508, 91 A.L.R. 1067. Its interpretation must be free from and uninfluenced by the unyielding rule against perpetuities. Yet, when the testator's intent is ascertained, if it is found to be in contravention of the rule, the will, in that particular, must be declared invalid. . . .

In paragraphs (1) and (2), respectively, of clause "Second" in clear and definite language the discretion, power and authority of the trustee in its disposition and application of the income are specified and limited. Yearly on the last school day before Easter and Christmas each youthful beneficiary of the testator's generosity is to be paid an equal share of the income. In mandatory language the duty and the duty alone to make cash payments to each individual child just before Easter and Christmas is enjoined upon the trustee by the certain and explicit words that it "shall divide the net income . . . and shall pay one of such equal shares to each child in such grades."

Without more, that language, and the occasions specified for payment of the funds to the children being when their minds and interests would be far removed from studies or other school activities definitely indicate that no educational purpose was in the testator's mind. It is manifest that there was no intent or belief that the funds would be put to any use other than such as youthful impulse and desire might dictate. But in each instance immediately following the above-quoted language the sentence concludes with the words or phrase "to be used by such child in the furtherance of his or her obtainment of an education." It is significant that by this latter phrase the trustee is given no power, control or discretion over the funds so received by the child. Full and complete execution of the mandate and trust imposed upon the trustee accomplishes no educational purpose. Nothing toward the advancement of education is attained by the ultimate performance by the trustee of its full duty. It merely places the income irretrievably and forever beyond the range of the trust.

Appellant says that the latter phrase, "to be used by such child in furtherance of his or her obtainment of an education," evinces the testator's dominant purpose and intent. Yet it is not denied that the preceding provision "shall divide the net income into as many equal parts ... and shall pay one of each equal parts to such child" is at odds with the phrase it relies upon. The appended qualification, it says, however, discloses a controlling intent that the 450 or more shares are to be used in the furtherance of education, and it was not really intended that a share be paid to each child so that he or she could during the Christmas and Easter holidays, or at any other time, use it "without let or hindrance, encumbrance or care." With that contruction we cannot agree. In our opinion, the words of the will import an intent to have the trustee pay to each child his allotted share. If that be true, — and it is directed to be done in no uncertain language — we know that the admonition to the children would be wholly impotent and of no avail.

In construing wills, we may not forget or disregard the experiences of life and the realities of the occasion. Nor may we assume or indulge in the belief that the testator by his injunction to the donees intended or thought that he could change childhood nature and set at naught childhood impulses and desires.

Appellant asserts that literal performance of the duty imposed upon it — pay to each child his share — would be impracticable and should not be done. Its position in that respect is stated thus: "We do not understand that under the law of Virginia a court would pay money for education into the hands of children who are incapable of handling it." It then says that the funds could be administered by a guardian or under sec. 8-751, Code, 1950 (where the amounts are under $500), a court could direct payment to be made to the recipient's parents.

With these statements, we agree. But because the funds could be administered under applicable statutes has no bearing upon nor may that device be resorted to as an aid to prove or establish the testator's intent. We are of opinion that the testator's dominant intent appears from and is expressed in his unequivocal direction to the trustee to divide the income into as many equal parts as there are children beneficiaries and pay one share to each. This expressed purpose and intent is inconsistent with the appended direction to each child as to the use of his respective share and the latter phrase is thus ineffectual to create an educational trust. The testator's purpose and intent were, we think, to bestow upon the children gifts that would bring to them happiness on the two holidays, but that falls short of an educational trust.

If it be determined that the will fails to create a charitable trust for *educational purposes* (and our conclusion is that it is inoperative to create such a trust), it is earnestly insisted that the trust provided for is nevertheless charitable and valid. In this respect it is claimed that the two yearly payments to be made to the children just before Christmas and Easter produce "a desirable social effect" and are "promotive of public convenience and needs, and happiness and contentment" and thus the fund set up in the will constitutes a charitable trust. 2 Bogert on Trusts, sec. 361, p.1090, and 3 Scott on Trusts, sec. 368, p.1972. . . .

Numerous cases that deal with and construe specific provisions of wills or other instruments are cited by appellant to uphold the contention that the provisions of this will, without reference to and deleting the phrase "to be used by such child in the furtherance of his or her obtainment of an education" meet the requirements of a charitable trust.

Upon examination of these decisions, it will be found that where a gift results in mere financial enrichment, a trust was sustained only when the court found and concluded from the entire context of the will that the ultimate intended recipients were poor or in necessitous circumstances.

A trust from which the income is to be paid at stated intervals to each member of a designated segment of the public, without regard to whether or not the recipients are poor or in need, is not for the relief of poverty, nor is it a social benefit to the community. It is a mere benevolence — a private trust — and may not be upheld as a charitable trust. Restatement of the Law of Trusts, sec. 374, p.1156: ". . . if a large sum of money is given in trust to apply the income each year in paying a certain sum to every inhabitant of a city, whether rich or poor, the trust is not charitable, since although each inhabitant may receive a benefit, the social interest of the community as such is not thereby promoted."

In 2 Bogert on Trusts, sec. 380, we find:

> As previously stated, gifts which are mere exhibitions of liberality and generosity, without regard to their effect upon the donees, are not charitable. There must be an amelioration of the condition of the donees as a result of the gift, and this improvement must be of a mental, physical, or spiritual nature and not merely financial. Thus, trusts to provide gifts to children, regardless of their need, or to make Christmas gifts to members of a certain class, without consideration of need or effect, are not charitable. . . . (p. 1218.)
>
> Gifts which are made out of mere sentiment, and will have no practical result except the satisfying of a whim of the donor, are obviously lacking in the widespread social effect necessary to a charity. (p. 1219.)

Nor do we find any language in this will that permits the trustee to limit the recipients of the donations to the school children in the designated grades who are in necessitous circumstances, and thus bring the trust under the influence of the case styled Appeal of Eliot, 74 Conn. 586, 51 A. 558.

The conclusion there reached was that where a trust is set up and a class is designated as beneficiary which generally contains needy persons, the testator will be presumed to have intended as recipients those members of the class who are in necessitous circumstances.

Payment to the children of their cash bequests on the two occasions specified would bring to them pleasure and happiness and no doubt cause them to remember or think of their benefactor with gratitude and thanksgiving. That was, we think, Charles B. Henry's intent. Laudable, generous and praiseworthy though it may be, it is not for the relief of the poor or needy, nor does it otherwise so benefit or advance the social interest of the community as to justify its continuance in perpetuity as a charitable trust. . . .

No error is found in the decrees appealed from and they are affirmed.

NOTES AND QUESTIONS

1. In general, a charitable trust is exempt from the Rule against Perpetuities and may endure forever. This exemption is not given to a trust for noncharitable purposes. At common law, such a trust is void ab initio if it can last longer than the perpetuities period. This is the rule that the Henry Trust, called the "candy trust" in the newspapers of the day, ran afoul of.

A majority of jurisdictions have modified the common law Rule against Perpetuities by adopting the wait-and-see doctrine. Under this doctrine, the court does not determine the validity of an interest by what might happen, but by what actually happens. In the case of a noncharitable purpose trust, a court might wait to see if the trust does in fact last longer than the perpetuities period. See In re Estate of Keenan, 519 N.W.2d 373 (Iowa 1994). If the jurisdiction waits for the common law perpetuities period to expire before declaring the trust void, a noncharitable purpose trust could endure for 21 years (or, if there are any human lives relevant to vesting, which would be quite unusual, for the relevant lives plus 21 years). Virginia has adopted wait-and-see for the common law perpetuities period. Va. Code Ann. §55-13.3 (1998). Therefore, if the trust for school children in the *Taylor* case had been created today, it probably could last for 21 years.

If the jurisdiction has adopted the Uniform Statutory Rule Against Perpetuities, the wait-and-see period is 90 years. USRAP provides that, at the end of 90 years, a court shall reform the "disposition in the manner that most closely approximates the transferor's manifested plan of distribution and is within the 90 years allowed." Uniform Statutory Rule Against Perpetuities §3. USRAP goes on to provide, however, that a court shall reform a disposition immediately if "a nonvested property interest that [violates the common law Rule against Perpetuities] . . . can vest but not within 90 years after its creation." Id. §3(3), supra page 839. How USRAP would apply in the *Taylor* case is up in the air. The candy trust might be permitted to endure for 90 years, but when would it be reformed to name the ultimate takers? If reformed at the end of 90 years, should the principal of the trust be distributed to the successors of Henry's heirs, or to the John Kerr School if it is in existence, or, if not in existence, to successor public schools of Winchester, or to the children then enrolled as students in the first, second, and third grades of the John Kerr school or its successor? Or should the trust be reformed immediately under §3(3) to specify the ultimate takers? Since the candy trust is intended to be a perpetual trust, in which an equitable fee simple in the principal cannot vest, it appears that the trust cannot be reformed immediately under §3(3). Compare Ball v. Knox, 768 S.W.2d 829 (Tex. App. 1989) (refusing to reform a noncharitable purpose trust under a cy pres statute not providing for wait-and-see, because no equitable interest therein was conveyed to any person; court read statute to authorize reforming only invalid "interests"). For an analysis of how wait-and-see applies to noncharitable purpose trusts, casting doubt on all the solutions suggested above and demonstrating the muddle left by USRAP, see Adam J. Hirsch, Trusts for Purposes: Policy, Ambiguity, and Anomaly in the Uniform Laws, 26 Fla. St. U. L. Rev. 913 (1999).

Uniform Probate Code §2-907(a) provides that a trust for a lawful noncharitable purpose may be performed by the trustee for 21 years but no longer. See also Cal. Prob. Code §15211 (1998); Uniform Trust Act §407 (1999 draft).

For an illuminating examination of the policies underlying the law governing noncharitable purpose trusts, see Adam J. Hirsch, Bequests for Purposes: A Unified Theory, 56 Wash. & Lee L. Rev. 33 (1999). Professor Hirsch points out that the law divides bequests for purposes into three categories — (1) charitable; (2) not charitable but not harmful, and (3) antisocial — and treats each category differently. He argues that apart from a tiny number of bequests for antisocial purposes, bequests for all sorts of purposes, whether deemed charitable or not, merit facilitation because they have social utility.

2.   To be classified as charitable, a trust that is for the benefit of a class of persons and not for the benefit of the community at large must be for the relief of poverty or for the advancement of education, religion, health, or other charitable purpose. A trust is not charitable merely because it is for the benefit of a class of persons. Thus, a trust for the benefit of sick or needy employees is charitable, but a trust for the general benefit of employees is not. Likewise, a trust to pay the salary of a law professor is charitable because it promotes education, but a trust for the general benefit of lawyers is not. 4A Austin W. Scott, Trusts §375 (William F. Fratcher 4th ed. 1989).

A trust may be a valid charitable trust although the persons who directly benefit are limited in number. A trust awarding scholarships or prizes for educational achievement is charitable.

A trust to educate a particular person or named persons is not charitable. So also a trust to educate the descendants of the settlor is not charitable. In re Estate of Keenan, supra. On the other hand, a trust for education of young people has been held charitable even though in selecting beneficiaries the trustee must give preference to the descendants of the settlor's grandparents. 4A Scott, supra, §375.3. And a trust to send a young person through medical school upon her promise that she will return to the testator's hometown to practice has been held charitable. Estate of Carlson, 187 Kan. 543, 358 P.2d 669 (1961).

In In re Gonzalez, 262 N.J. Super. 456, 621 A.2d 94 (1992), the court grappled with what to do with $7,700 given by many donors for medical treatment of Maribel Gonzalez, who died before the money could be spent. The court held the trust was not a charitable trust, refused to apply cy pres to the unconsumed fund, and directed that the money be returned to the donors.

For a comprehensive analysis of charitable gifts, and of the difficulties courts have had in defining "charitable," see Mary Kay Lundwall, Inconsistency and Uncertainty in the Charitable Purposes Doctrine, 41 Wayne L. Rev. 1341 (1995). Professor Lundwall agrees with Professor Scott that what is a charitable gift should be broadly defined, because charitable trusts can be used "to try many experiments to which it would be improper to devote the public funds, or that the public would be unwilling to support until convinced by proof of their success." 4A Scott, supra, §374.7.

3. *Trusts to benefit a political party.* It is against public policy to endow perpetually a political party; hence, a trust to promote the success of a particular political party is not charitable. See Note, Charitable Trusts for Political Purposes, 37 Va. L. Rev. 988 (1951). However, a trust for the improvement of the structure and methods of government, in a manner advocated by a particular political party, is charitable. For example, a trust to advance "the principles of socialism and those causes related to socialism," including supporting candidates for public office espousing socialistic views, has been held charitable. In re Estate of Breeden, 208 Cal. App. 3d 981, 256 Cal. Rptr. 813 (1989).

A trust with the purpose of bringing about a change in the law may be charitable, provided the purpose is not to bring about changes in the law by illegal means, such as revolution or illegal lobbying. See 2 Restatement (Second) of Trusts §374, Comment j (1959).

4. In Estate of Kidd, 106 Ariz. 554, 479 P.2d 697 (1971), James Kidd, a bachelor of frugal nature, wrote a holographic will in 1946 leaving his estate for "reserach [sic] or some scientific proof of a soul of the human body which leaves at death I think in time their [sic] can be a Photograph of soul leaving the human at death." Shortly thereafter, Kidd disappeared without a trace. In 1964, Kidd's will was discovered and offered for probate. His estate amounted to $175,000. More than a hundred claimants stepped forth. Some of the claimants argued that there was no intent to create a charitable trust but an outright bequest to any person who had scientific proof of a soul that leaves the body at death; one of these claimed to have seen her soul leave her body and another claimed that scientific proof included inductive logical arguments based upon the Bible. The court held, however, that a charitable trust was intended. Upon remand, the trial court awarded the bequest to the American Society for Psychical Research in New York City. 110 Tr. & Est. 1058 (1971). In 1975, the society filed a report in the Arizona probate court, stating that it had spent the money from the Kidd estate but had failed to prove the existence of the human soul. N.Y. Times, June 16, 1975, at 30.

5. *Drafting advice.* The lawyer drawing a will making a gift to charity should make sure (a) of the exact legal name of the charity and (b), if the client wants an estate tax charitable deduction, which is usual,

whether the charity is tax-exempt under the Internal Revenue Code. A purpose deemed charitable by a state court may not qualify for a federal estate tax charitable deduction, which denies the deduction to charities that indulge in certain prohibited activities (see infra page 1063). The lawyer drafting a trust giving the trustees discretion to spray the income among charitable organizations should draft the trust so as to restrict the recipient charities to those qualifying as such under the Internal Revenue Code. See Lancaster v. Merchants National Bank, 961 F.2d 713 (1992).

Trusts for "benevolent" or "philanthropic" purposes should be avoided. Some older cases held that these words are broader than "charitable," and, if so, the trust may fail as a charitable trust because the income can be used for noncharitable purposes. Modern American cases tend to construe these words as synonymous with "charitable," but, out of caution, they should be avoided. See Wilson v. Flowers, 58 N.J. 250, 277 A.2d 199 (1971).

6. *Mortmain statutes.* Several states once had statutes permitting spouses and children to set aside death-bed wills making gifts to charity (traceable to the medieval fear of overreaching by priests taking the last confession and will). Except in Georgia, these statutes have all been either repealed or declared unconstitutional as a denial of equal protection of the law.

In Georgia, if a person leaves a spouse or issue, a devise of more than one-third of his estate to charity, excluding the spouse or issue, is void unless the will is executed at least 90 days before death. If the estate exceeds $200,000 in value, this restriction does not apply to the excess over $200,000. Ga. Code §53-2-10 (1998).

SECTION B. MODIFICATION OF CHARITABLE TRUSTS: CY PRES

In England, at common law, there was a royal prerogative power of cy pres as well as a judicial doctrine of cy pres. Under the prerogative power, charitable gifts were expected to comply with public policy as established by the king. Any deviations were corrected by the crown, regardless of the testator's intent. For example, in Da Costa v. De Pas, 1 Amb. 228, 27 Eng. Rep. 150 (Ch. 1754), a Jewish testator left money in trust to form an assembly for the purpose of teaching Jewish law and religion. The trust encouraged a religion other than the state religion and was referred to the king by the chancellor for instructions. Applying prerogative cy pres, the king allotted the money to instruct foundlings in the Christian religion.

Largely as a reaction to the abuse of prerogative cy pres by the crown, disregarding entirely the probable wishes of the testator, courts in this country were reluctant to adopt judicial cy pres. It, too, could be abused. Courts seldom altered an instrument creating a charitable trust until the twentieth century. As the nineteenth century receded into history, however, various changes in circumstances made it difficult or impractical to administer charitable trusts as specifically intended by the donors. A nineteenth-century trust to care for old horses retired from pulling fire wagons and street-cars could not be administered for these purposes in the twentieth century. Hence, American courts finally came to accept a judicial doctrine of cy pres.

In re Neher
Court of Appeals of New York, 1939
279 N.Y. 370, 18 N.E.2d 625

LOUGHRAN, J.   The will of Ella Neher was admitted to probate by the Surrogate's Court of Dutchess County December 22, 1930. Paragraph 7 thereof made these provisions:

> I give, devise and bequeath my home in Red Hook Village, on the east side of South Broadway, consisting of house, barn and lot of ground . . . to the incorporated Village of Red Hook, as a memorial to the memory of my beloved husband, Herbert Neher, with the direction to said Village that said property be used as a hospital to be known as "Herbert Neher Memorial Hospital." The trustees of the Village of Red Hook, consisting of the President and the Trustees, shall constitute the managing board with full power to manage and operate said hospital as they deem wise for the benefit of the people of Red Hook, and each succeeding Board of Trustees shall constitute the Board of Trustees for said hospital, so that any person duly elected and qualified or duly appointed and qualified as a President or Trustee of the said Village of Red Hook shall be a trustee of said hospital during such person's lawful term of office, and shall be succeeded as a trustee on the hospital board by his successor on the Village Board.

All her other estate Mrs. Neher gave to relatives and friends.
    On September 1, 1931, the trustees of Red Hook (hereinafter called the village) resolved to "accept the real property devised and bequeathed by the Will of Ella Neher, deceased, according to the terms of the Will of said Ella Neher."
    In March, 1937, the village presented to the Surrogate's Court its petition asserting that it was without the resources necessary to establish and maintain a hospital on the property devised to it by the testatrix and that a modern hospital theretofore recently established

in the neighboring village of Rhinebeck adequately served the needs of both communities. The prayer of this petition was for a decree "construing and reforming paragraph Seven of the last Will and Testament of said decedent directing and permitting your petitioner to receive said property and to erect and maintain thereon a building for the administration purposes of said Village to be known and designated as the Herbert Neher Memorial Hall, with a suitable tablet placed thereon expressing such memorial."

This petition the Surrogate denied on the single ground "that to read into the will a general intention to devote the property to charitable purposes instead of an intention to limit the use of the property to the operation of a hospital, would do violence to the expressed testamentary design of Mrs. Neher." The Appellate Division has affirmed the Surrogate. The village brings the case here by our leave.

This gift was not a gift to a particular institution. There was to be no singular object of the bounty. This gift was one to a whole community — "to the incorporated Village of Red Hook." The idea initially expressed by the testatrix was that her home should be dedicated to the village in the name of her husband. The only question is whether this first stated design of beneficence at large is necessarily to be denied prime import, because of the words that immediately follow — "with the direction to said Village that said property be used as a hospital to be known as 'Herbert Neher Memorial Hospital.' " This last phrase, it is to be noticed, gave no hint in respect of a predilection for any certain type of the manifold varieties of medical or surgical care. Nor did the will make any suggestion as to management or control, save that the village trustees (as such) were designated as a governing board. So great an absence of particularity is a strong circumstance against the view that the instruction of the testatrix was of the substance of the gift.

When paragraph 7 of the will is taken as a whole, the true construction, we think, is that the paramount intention was "to give the property in the first instance for a general charitable purpose rather than a particular charitable purpose, and to graft on to the general gift a direction as to the desires or intentions of the testator as to the manner in which the general gift is to be carried into effect." Parker, J., in Matter of Wilson, [1913] 1 Ch. 314, 321. Such a grafted direction may be ignored when compliance is altogether impracticable and the gift may be executed cy pres through a scheme to be framed by the court for carrying out the general charitable purpose. See Real Property Law, Consol. Laws, ch. 50, §113, subd. 2; Sherman v. Richmond Hose Co., 230 N.Y. 462, 472, 473, 130 N.E. 613; Matter of Gary's Estate, 248 App. Div. 373, 288 N.Y.S. 382; In re Gary's Will, 272 N.Y. 635, 5 N.E.2d 368; American Law Institute; Restatement of Law of Trusts, §399, comment at page 1211.

The order of the Appellate Division and the decree of the Surrogate's Court should be reversed and the matter remitted to the Surrogate's Court for further proceedings in accordance with this opinion, without costs.

Richard A. Posner, *Economic Analysis of Law*
556 (5th ed. 1998)

A policy of rigid adherence to the letter of the donative instrument is likely to frustrate both the donor's purposes and the efficient use of resources. . . . [Suppose that the settlor] had given the city a tuberculosis sanitarium. . . . As the incidence of tuberculosis declined and advances in medical science rendered the sanitarium method of treating tuberculosis obsolete, the value of the donated facilities in their intended use would have diminished. Eventually it would have become clear that the facilities would be more valuable in another use. . . . [E]nforcement would in all likelihood be contrary to the purposes of the donor, who intended by his gift to contribute to the cure of disease, not to perpetuate useless facilities.

The foregoing discussion may seem tantamount to denying the competence of a donor to balance the value of a perpetual gift against the cost in efficiency that such gifts frequently impose. But since no one can foresee the future, a rational donor knows that his intentions might eventually be thwarted by unpredictable circumstances and may therefore be presumed to accept implicitly a rule permitting modification of the terms of the bequest in the event that an unforeseen change frustrates his original intention. . . .

Where the continued enforcement of conditions in a charitable gift is no longer economically feasible, because of illegality . . . or opportunity costs (in the sanitarium example), the court, rather than declaring the gift void and transferring the property to the residuary legatees (if any can be identified), will authorize the administrators of the charitable trust to apply the assets to a related (cy pres) purpose within the general scope of the donor's intent.

SAN FRANCISCO CHRONICLE: THE BUCK TRUST

In 1975, Beryl Buck, a childless widow, died, a resident of Marin County, California. Marin County, lying across the bay northward from San Francisco, at the north end of the Golden Gate Bridge, is the most affluent of the counties in the Bay Area. Known as the "hot-tub capital of the world," in per capita income Marin is the nation's second-wealthiest county of more than 50,000 residents.

Mrs. Buck's will left the residue of her estate to the San Francisco Foundation, a community trust administering charitable funds in five counties in the San Francisco Bay Area (Alameda, Contra Costa, Marin, San Francisco, and San Mateo). Mrs. Buck's will directed that the residue of her estate, to be known and administered as the Leonard and Beryl Buck Foundation,

> shall always be held and used for exclusively non-profit charitable, religious, or educational purposes in providing care for the needy in Marin County, California, and for other non-profit charitable, religious, or educational purposes in that county.

At the time of Mrs. Buck's death, the largest asset in her estate consisted of a block of stock in Beldridge Oil Company, a privately held company with rich oil reserves in Southern California, founded by her father-in-law. In 1975, this stock was worth about $9 million, but soon thereafter, in 1979, Shell Oil won a bidding war and bought the stock in the Buck Trust for $260 million. This sudden embarrassment of riches, which increased to well over $300 million by 1984, and all of which was directed by Mrs. Buck's will to be spent on 7 percent of the Bay Area's residents in rich Marin County, seemed to threaten the integrity of the San Francisco Foundation in equitably administering charitable dollars in the Bay Area. In 1984, the Foundation brought suit seeking judicial authorization to spend some portion of Buck Trust income in the other four counties of the Bay Area.

The Foundation's petition for cy pres rested upon the following theory: The enormous increase in the value of principal was a posthumous "surprise," a change in circumstances raising substantial doubt whether Mrs. Buck, had she anticipated such an event, would have limited her beneficence to Marin County. This "surprise" warranted inquiry into what Mrs. Buck would have done had she known of this bonanza. The Foundation argued that she would not have limited her beneficence to Marin County because (a) she selected as trustee a foundation administering funds for the benefit of five counties; (b) other philanthropists, as shown by the fifty largest American charitable foundations (with the sole exception of the Buck Trust), reach out beyond their parochial origins as their resources grow and seek to serve a more populous and diverse slice of humanity, following a principle of proportionality; and (c), in the face of such an increase in wealth, the donor would be less interested in a small geographical area and more interested in the efficiency of the charitable dollar. This, the Foundation argued, was the philanthropic standard followed by almost all the great philanthropists of wealth equal to Mrs. Buck's

Beryl H. Buck

posthumous fortune. It was the way other extremely rich philanthropists behave.

The Foundation's action proved to be throwing fat into a fire. Marin County officials were outraged. One called the Foundation "grave-robbing bastards," and characterized the cy pres petition as a "criminal attack upon the sanctity of wills." Marin officials were joined by the Marin Council of Agencies (a consortium of Marin County nonprofit agencies) in opposing the petition. Forty-six individuals and charitable organizations in the other four counties (called

"Objector-Beneficiaries") were allowed to intervene to object to the Marin-only limitation. The Attorney General of California, as supervisor of charitable trusts, also intervened, arguing against cy pres and asking whether the Foundation was in violation of its fiduciary duties for bringing such a suit and ought to be removed as trustee.

The case caused an uproar in San Francisco, with the local newspaper columnists opening all the stops. At first, the commentators were incensed at all that money being spent in rich Marin, but then — on second thought — public opinion began to coalesce behind the idea that Mrs. Buck had the right to do with her property as she wished and the San Francisco Foundation became an object of calumny.

Near the close of the respondent's case, after nearly six months of trial, the Foundation resigned as trustee, and the court dismissed its cy pres petition.

In the course of its opinion refusing to apply cy pres, not officially reported but reprinted in 21 U.S.F. L. Rev. 691 (1987), the trial court said:

> The Restatement (Second) of Trusts, section 399 at 297, describes the cy pres doctrine as follows: "If property is given in trust to be applied to a particular charitable purpose and *it is or becomes impossible or impracticable or illegal to carry out the particular purpose,* and if the settlor manifested a more general intention to devote the property to charitable purposes, the trust will not fail but the court will direct the application of the property to some charitable purpose which falls within the general charitable intention of the settlor. (Emphasis added). . . ."
>
> Ineffective philanthropy, inefficiency and relative inefficiency, that is, inefficiency of trust expenditures in one location given greater relative needs or benefits elsewhere, do not constitute impracticability. . . . Such situation is not the equivalent of impossibility; nor is there any threat that the operation of the trust will fail to fulfill the general charitable intention of the settlor.
>
> To the extent that concepts of effective philanthropy or efficiency relate to achieving the greatest benefit for the cost incurred they should not form the basis for modifying a donor's wishes. No law requires a testator to make a gift which the trustees deem efficient or to constitute effective philanthropy. Moreover, calculating "benefit" involves inherently subjective determinations; thus, what is "effective" or "efficient" will vary, depending on the interests and concerns of the person or persons making the determination. Cy pres does not authorize a court to vary the terms of the bequest merely because the variation will accommodate the desire of the trustee. Connecticut College v. United States (D.C. Cir. 1960) 276 F.2d 491, 493; In re Hawley's Estate (1961) 223 N.Y.S. 803, 805.
>
> To the extent that the term efficiency embraces the concept of relative need, it is not an appropriate basis for modifying the terms of a testamentary trust. If it were otherwise, all charitable gifts, and the fundamental basis of philanthropy would be threatened, as there may always be more

compelling "needs" to fill than the gift chosen by the testator. Gifts to Harvard or Stanford University, for example, could fail simply because institutions elsewhere are more needy. Similarly, needs in the Bay Area cannot be equated with the grueling poverty of India or the soul-wrenching famine in Ethiopia. Moreover, a standard of relative need would interpose governmental regulation on philanthropy because courts would be required to consider questions of comparative equity, social utility, or benefit, perhaps even wisdom, and ultimately substitute their judgments or those of the trustees for those of the donors.

The cy pres doctrine should not be so distorted by the adoption of subjective, relative, and nebulous standards such as "inefficiency" or "ineffective philanthropy" to the extent that it becomes a facile vehicle for charitable trustees to vary the terms of a trust simply because they believe that they can spend the trust income better or more wisely elsewhere, or as in this case, prefer to do so. There is no basis in law for the application of standards such as "efficiency" or "effectiveness" to modify a trust, nor is there any authority that would elevate these standards to the level of impracticability.

No appeal was taken from the superior court decision in *Buck*. The superior court ordered the creation of the Marin Community Foundation, which would replace the San Francisco Foundation in administering the Buck Trust.

The new foundation is governed by seven trustees, two appointed by the Marin County Board of Supervisors, one by the Marin Council of (Nonprofit) Agencies, one by the President of the University of California, one by the Interfaith Council of Marin, one by relatives of Mrs. Buck's husband, and one by the Marin Community Foundation board. The trial judge chose three Marin-based research institutes to divide a substantial portion of the income from the trust: The Buck Center on Aging, The Institute on Alcohol and Other Drug Problems, and The Marin Educational Institute.

Professor Simon is highly critical of the supervisory role assumed by the trial court over the Buck Trust at the end of the trial:

> The extrordinary command role the court reserved for itself over the decision-making process . . . violates the basic concept of private philanthropy and disregards the role assigned to charitable trustees in the nonprofit sector. . . .
>
> [I]t is not obvious that these programs would have been preferred by the donor over distributions to neighboring Bay Area counties served by the [San Francisco] Foundation. . . . [T]he fact that she picked a community foundation focused on the Bay Area as the instrument of her charity cannot be ignored when shaping a cy pres solution [John G. Simon, American Philanthropy and the Buck Trust, 21 U.S.F. L. Rev. 641, 666-668 (1987).]

For other comments on the *Buck* case, see Note, Phantom Selves: The Search for a General Charitable Intent in the Application of the Cy Pres Doctrine, 40 Stan. L. Rev. 973 (1988); Note, Relaxing the Dead Hand's Grip: Charitable Efficiency and the Doctrine of Cy Pres, 74 Va. L. Rev. 635 (1988); Comment, Cy Pres Inexpediency and the Buck Trust, 20 U.S.F. L. Rev. 577 (1986).

The Foundation Directory (1998) reports that the Marin Community Foundation, created out of the Buck Trust, has $695 million in assets. The San Francisco Foundation, without the Buck Trust, has assets of $541 million.

NOTES AND QUESTIONS

1.   Modern academic commentators favor expanding the use of judicial cy pres to change charitable trust provisions to maximize community benefits as required by changing community needs. See Alex M. Johnson, Jr. and Ross D. Taylor, Revolutionizing Judicial Interpretation of Charitable Trusts: Applying Relational Contracts and Dynamic Interpretation to Cy Pres and America's Cup Litigation, 74 Iowa L. Rev. 545 (1989); Ronald Chester, Cy Pres: A Promise Unfulfilled, 54 Ind. L.J. 407 (1979). But cf. Rob Atkinson, Reforming Cy Pres Reform, 44 Hastings L.J. 1112 (1993) (arguing that injecting flexibility into cy pres increases either dead hand control or state involvement); Jonathan R. Macey, Private Trusts for the Provision of Private Goods, 37 Emory L.J. 295 (1988) (arguing that cy pres should be severely limited because the attempt to discern the testator's intent creates increased error costs and transaction costs).

In his thoughtful book, Public Policy and the Dead Hand, Professor Lewis Simes argued that after thirty years courts should have enlarged cy pres power to modify charitable trusts "not only if the original purpose was found impracticable but also if . . . the amount to be expended is out of all proportion to its value to society." Lewis M. Simes, Public Policy and the Dead Hand 139 (1955). Is this a good idea? See also Peter Luxton, Cy-Pres and the Ghost of Things That Might Have Been, 1983 Convey. 107, suggesting giving importance to the testator's intention in the early years of the trust but, at the end of the perpetuities period, treating the property as dedicated to charity.

Uniform Trust Act §408(b) (1999 draft) provides that a court may apply cy pres if a particular charitable purpose becomes "unlawful, impracticable, impossible to fulfill, or *wasteful*" (emphasis added). The comment provides:

> The application of cy pres requires a balancing of the needs of society against an assessment of the settlor's probable intent. In determining the

settlor's probable intent, the court should consider the current and future community needs in the general field of charity for which the trust was created, the settlor's other charitable interests, and the value of the available trust property.

2. Cy pres should be contrasted with *administrative deviation*. A court will permit deviation in the administrative terms of a trust when compliance would defeat or substantially impair the accomplishment of the purposes of the trust. It is not always clear what is an administrative term and what is a central purpose, however, and courts have been known to interpret "administrative" broadly on appealing facts. In Dartmouth College v. City of Quincy, 357 Mass. 521, 258 N.E.2d 745 (1970), for example, the testator in 1870 established a trust to build and support the Woodward School for the education of females born in Quincy, Massachusetts. In 1968, the fund provided only $13,000 toward the school's total $53,000 operating costs, and to generate additional income the trustees proposed to admit non-Quincy-born girls, charging them a higher tuition than Quincy-born girls. The court held that it would permit deviation in the administrative terms of the trust and approved the trustees' plan.

See also Grant Home v. Medlock, 349 S.E.2d 655 (S.C. App. 1986) (permitting trustees operating home for needy white Presbyterians in deteriorating neighborhood to sell home and use proceeds to establish housing subsidy funds for needy Presbyterians of all races residing in Charleston).

3. *Racially or gender restrictive charitable trusts.* Charitable trusts have been created to furnish benefits to one race or one gender. Usually, these trusts benefits are restricted to "whites" or to "men." Such trusts have been the subject of considerable litigation since the 1960s.

If the trustee of a racially restrictive trust is a governmental body (such as a public school granting scholarships to whites), courts have held that the administration of the trust in a racially discriminatory manner is discriminatory state action forbidden by the Equal Protection Clause of the Constitution. Courts have therefore ruled in most cases that the racial restriction is unenforceable. The question then becomes: Would the settlor prefer the trust to continue without the racial restriction or to terminate? Applying cy pres or deviation doctrine, most courts have held that the testator would prefer the charitable trust to continue without the racial restriction.

Where the trustee is a private individual and not a public body, enforcing the racial restriction is not unconstitutional as discriminatory *state* action. But the trust may run afoul of some federal or state statute forbidding racial discrimination. If so, the question arises whether the court should apply cy pres and strike the racial restriction. Most courts have done so.

Restricting the benefits of a private charitable trust to one gender is not unconstitutional, but it may violate a federal or state statute prohibiting gender discrimination in federally or state financed programs. Again, courts in a number of cases have removed the gender restriction under the power of cy pres. See In re Wilson, 59 N.Y.2d 461, 452 N.E.2d 1228, 465 N.Y.S.2d 900 (1983). See generally 4A Austin W. Scott, Trusts, Trusts §399.4A (William F. Fratcher 4th ed. 1989).

A new question is now facing the courts. Is a charitable trust run by a public body giving scholarships exclusively to black persons constitutional? In Podberesky v. Kirwan, 38 F.3d 147 (4th Cir. 1994), cert. denied, 514 U.S. 1120 (1995), the court held that state university scholarships for blacks were invalid under the Equal Protection Clause unless they were justifiable to remedy present effects of past discrimination. The court further held that the University of Maryland had not been able to so justify its scholarships for black students only. See Kirk A. Kennedy, Race-Exclusive Scholarships: Constitutional Vel Non, 30 Wake Forest L. Rev. 759 (1995); Note, Minority Scholarships: A New Battle in the War on Affirmative Action, 77 Iowa L. Rev. 307 (1991).

PHILADELPHIA STORY: THE BARNES FOUNDATION

The Barnes Foundation, in the Philadelphia suburb of Merion, was created by Dr. Albert Barnes, a chemist, who invented Argyrol, which became a leading treatment for colds, prescribed as eyedrops for newborn babies to prevent blindness. Argyrol earned Dr. Barnes a great fortune, which he spent on buying art in the early years of the twentieth century. He descended on Paris, checkbook in hand, and, haunting the garrets and artists' studios in Montparnasse, bought dozens of paintings directly from artists. He amassed a collection of over 180 Renoirs, 100 Cezannes, 60 Matisses, 40 Picassos and dozens of other artists. He hung his 2000 pieces of art five or six atop each other in a gallery he built in Merion.

Dr. Barnes, son of a butcher in South Philadelphia, was high-hatted by Philadelphia Main Line society and by art critics and scholars who panned his art. As a result, he would not permit them in to see the paintings after these artists became celebrated. He barred entry to all except "plain people, that is, men and women who gain their livelihood by daily toil in shops, factories, schools, and stores." Dr. Barnes admitted some scholars and literati on a selective basis. A few others were able to sneak in disguised as chauffeurs, miners, or workmen.

Dr. Barnes had unconventional theories about art education, developed with John Dewey. To further these theories, the Barnes Founda-

ize the gallery). For those who could not see the paintings on the world tour, the trustees produced a CD-ROM, with photographs in color.

The world tour drew record crowds, more in Paris than had ever before lined up to see an art show. But the world tour brought protests from some Philadelphians, who were outraged that Dr. Barnes's intent had been violated in so many ways. The protestors — particularly the neighbors in Merion — were angry that the Barnes Foundation had been transformed from an educational institution serving a few into a museum drawing thousands of people in cars. Dr. Barnes, they said, must be spinning in his grave. But, maybe not. After all, at the end of the tour, the paintings were rehung in the Barnes Gallery exactly as the eccentric Dr. Barnes had hung them — with some of the greatest works placed near the ceiling, difficult to see but hung according to his aesthetic theories. And the tony neighbors were much annoyed.

For a thorough examination of the Barnes Foundation's lawsuits and criticism of the trustees' actions, see Comment, Protecting "Donor Intent" in Charitable Foundations: Wayward Trusteeships and the Barnes Foundation, 145 U. Pa. L. Rev. 665 (1997). See also Note, When It's OK to Sell the Monet: A Trustee-Fiduciary-Duty Framework for Analyzing the Deaccessioning of Art to Meet Museum Operating Expenses, 94 Mich. L. Rev. 1041 (1996). For a portrait of the irascible Dr. Barnes, see Howard Greenfield, The Devil and Dr. Barnes (1987).

Would you, as a judge, have approved the trustees' deviations from Dr. Barnes's bylaws? Recall Professor Simes's views on page 877.

SECTION C.   SUPERVISION OF CHARITABLE TRUSTS

Carl J. Herzog Foundation, Inc. v. University of Bridgeport
Supreme Court of Connecticut, 1997
243 Conn. 1, 699 A.2d 995

NORCOTT, J. The sole issue in this certified appeal is whether the Connecticut Uniform Management of Institutional Funds Act (CUMIFA), General Statutes §§45a-526 through 45a-534, establishes statutory standing for a donor to bring an action to enforce the terms of a completed charitable gift. Because we conclude that the legisla-

Former University of Bridgeport Nursing School

ture did not intend to establish donor standing under the circumstances of this case, we reverse the judgment of the Appellate Court.

The facts and procedural history of this case are aptly set forth in the Appellate Court opinion from which this appeal ensues. "The plaintiff [Carl J. Herzog Foundation, Inc.] commenced an action against the defendant, the University of Bridgeport, seeking injunctive and other relief in connection with a gift made by it to the defendant. The plaintiff [in 1986 made grants to the defendant totaling $250,000] . . . 'to provide need-based merit scholarship aid to disadvantaged students for medical related education.' . . . The grants were used to provide scholarships to students in the defendant's nursing program. On November 21, 1991, however, the plaintiff was informed that the defendant had closed its nursing school on June 20, 1991. . . .[2]

"The plaintiff's alleged injury is that the funds are no longer being

2. The nursing school was closed because the University of Bridgeport ran into severe financial trouble. In 1992, an affiliate of the Rev. Sun Myung Moon's Unification Church bailed out the University and took control of it.

About the same time the law school of the University of Bridgeport pulled up stakes and resettled itself at Quinnipiac College in Hamden, Connecticut. — Eds.

used for their specified purpose. Paragraph fourteen of the revised complaint states: 'The [plaintiff] has been given to understand and believes that the said . . . funds have been co-mingled with the general funds of the [defendant], that said . . . funds are not being used in accordance with the "Gift Instrument" under which said . . . funds were transferred to [the defendant], and that said institutional funds have in fact been spent for general purposes of [the defendant].'

"The plaintiff requested a temporary and permanent injunction, ordering the defendant 'to segregate from its general funds . . . $250,000,' an accounting for the use of the fund from the date of receipt until present, and a reestablishment of the fund in accordance with the purposes outlined in the gift instrument, and, in the event that those purposes could not be fulfilled, to revert the funds and direct them to the Bridgeport Area Foundation, which is prepared to administer the funds in accordance with the original agreement.

"The defendant moved to dismiss the action for lack of subject matter jurisdiction on the ground that the plaintiff lacked standing. The trial court held that the act did not provide a donor with the right to enforce restrictions contained in a gift instrument, and, therefore, the plaintiff lacked standing to bring the action. The trial court noted that the attorney general, pursuant to General Statutes §3-125,[3] could bring an action to enforce the gift, and it dismissed the action." Carl J. Herzog Foundation, Inc. v. University of Bridgeport, 41 Conn. App. 790, 791-93, 677 A.2d 1378 (1996).

The Appellate Court reversed the judgment of the trial court, concluding that General Statutes §45a-533 provides donors with standing to enforce the terms of a completed gift, even though no such right of enforcement was provided for in the gift instrument. . . . We disagree.

"Standing is established by showing that the party claiming it is authorized by statute to bring suit or is classically aggrieved." Steeneck v. University of Bridgeport, 235 Conn. 572, 579, 668 A.2d 688 (1995). The sole basis for standing claimed by the plaintiff is CUMIFA, more particularly, §45a-533 (a). Our task, therefore, devolves into a question of statutory construction. We must determine whether the legislature intended CUMIFA to provide a donor that has made a completed charitable gift to an "institution" as defined by §45a-527 (1) with standing to bring an action to enforce the terms of that gift where, as here, the gift instrument contained no express reservation of control over the disposition of the gift, such as a right of reverter or a right to redirect.

---

3. General Statutes §3-125 provides in relevant part that the attorney general "shall represent the public interest in the protection of any gifts, legacies or devises intended for public or charitable purposes. . . ."

We begin by noting the common law landscape upon which CUMIFA was enacted. . . .

At common law, a donor who has made a completed charitable contribution, whether as an absolute gift or in trust,[4] had no standing to bring an action to enforce the terms of his or her gift or trust unless he or she had expressly reserved the right to do so. "Where property is given to a charitable corporation and it is directed by the terms of the gift to devote the property to a particular one of its purposes, it is under a duty, enforceable at the suit of the attorney general, to devote the property to that purpose." 2 Restatement (Second), Trusts §348, Comment (f), p. 212 (1959); Attorney General v. First United Baptist Church of Lee, 601 A.2d 96, 98 (Me. 1992); see Lefkowitz v. Lebensfeld, 68 A.D.2d 488, 494-95, 417 N.Y.S.2d 715 (1979). "The general rule is that charitable trusts or gifts to charitable corporations for stated purposes are [enforceable] at the instance of the attorney general. . . . It matters not whether the gift is absolute or in trust or whether a technical condition is attached to the gift."[5] Id., 495.

"The theory underlying the power of the attorney general to enforce gifts for a stated purpose is that a donor who attaches conditions to his gift has a right to have his intention enforced." Id., 495-96. The donor's right, however, is enforceable only at the instance of the attorney general; Wier v. Howard Hughes Medical Institute, 407 A.2d 1051, 1057 (Del. 1979) (attorney general "has the exclusive power to bring actions to enforce charitable trusts"); Lopez v. Medford Community Center, Inc., 384 Mass. 163, 167, 424 N.E.2d 229 (1981) (common law rule that "it is the exclusive function of the attorney general to correct abuses in the administration of a public charity by the

---

4. The law governing the enforcement of charitable gifts is derived from the law of charitable trusts. See 4A A. Scott, Trusts (4th Ed. Fratcher 1989) §348.1. "Ordinarily the principles and rules applicable to charitable trusts are applicable to [gifts to] charitable corporations." 2 Restatement (Second), Trusts §348, Comment (f), p. 212 (1959). The plaintiff's gift in the present case is undoubtedly a public gift subject to the enforcement procedures governing charitable trusts. The Appellate Division of the New York Supreme Court has recognized "the never disturbed equitable doctrine that although gifts to a charitable organization do not create a trust in the technical sense, where a purpose is stated a trust will be implied, and the disposition enforced by the attorney general, pursuant to his duty to effectuate the donor's wishes." Lefkowitz v. Lebensfeld, 68 A.D.2d 488, 496, 417 N.Y.S.2d 715 (1979). We rely, therefore, to some extent, upon authorities discussing standing in the context of charitable trusts.

5. Public officials, such as the attorney general, had common law standing to enforce charitable trusts because, by virtue of their positions, they are closely associated with the public nature of charities. A leading treatise on the subject states that "the public benefits arising from the charitable trust justify the selection of some public official for its enforcement. Since the attorney general is the governmental officer whose duties include the protection of the rights of the people of the state in general, it is natural that he has been chosen as the protector, supervisor, and enforcer of charitable trusts, both in England and in the several states . . . ." G. Bogert & G. Bogert, Trusts and Trustees (2d Rev. Ed. 1991) §411, pp. 2-3.

institution of proper proceedings"); and the donor himself has no standing to enforce the terms of his gift when he has not retained a specific right to control the property, such as a right of reverter, after relinquishing physical possession of it. See, e.g., Marin Hospital District v. Dept. of Health, 92 Cal. App. 3d 442, 448, 154 Cal. Rptr. 838 (1979) (fact that charity is bound to use contributions for purposes for which they were given does not confer to donor standing to bring action to enforce terms of gift).[6] . . . [W]e conclude that it is clear that the general rule at common law was that a donor had no standing to enforce the terms of a completed charitable gift unless the donor had expressly reserved a property interest in the gift.[7]

Having concluded that the plaintiff would have had no standing at common law, we now turn to its contention that the common law has been altered by the legislature's adoption of CUMIFA, specifically that portion codified at §45a-533. Subsection (a) of §45a-533 empowers the governing board of an institution to seek a release of an onerous or obsolete restriction without resort to the courts by obtaining the donor's consent. Subsection (b) of §45a-533 empowers the board to apply to the courts for such release in the event of the donor's death, disability or other unavailability. Subsection (c) of §45a-533 precludes the governing board from using a gift unburdened by a restriction for anything other than the "educational, religious, charitable or other eleemosynary purposes" of the institution. Subsection (d) of §45a-533 confirms that the statute was not enacted to supplant but to supplement the doctrines of cy pres and approximation.[8]

---

6. We note that it is well established in the context of charitable trusts that there are others, in addition to the attorney general, who may enforce the terms of a trust. Section 391 of the Restatement (Second) of Trusts provides: "*Who Can Enforce a Charitable Trust.* A suit can be maintained for the enforcement of a charitable trust by the attorney general or other public officer, or by a co-trustee, or by a person who has a special interest in the enforcement of the charitable trust, but not by persons who have no special interest or by the settlor or his heirs, personal representatives or next of kin." . . . Those with no "special interest" have no standing to bring an action to enforce the conditions of the gift. These include persons within the general class of beneficiaries of the charitable trust as well as members of the general public. See Steeneck v. University of Bridgeport, supra, 235 Conn. 588.

7. By expressly reserving a property interest such as a right of reverter, the donor of the gift or the settlor of the trust may bring himself and his heirs within the "special interest" exception to the general rule that beneficiaries of a charitable trust may not bring an action to enforce the trust, but rather are represented exclusively by the attorney general.

8. "The rule of cy-pres is a rule for the construction of instruments in equity, by which the intention of the party is carried out as near as may be, when it would be impossible or illegal to give it literal effect. . . ." Black's Law Dictionary (6th Ed. 1990) p. 387. The doctrine of cy pres may be applied without the consent of the donor. See 2 Restatement (Second), supra, §399, Comment (g).

The fact that the drafters of the Uniform Management of Institutional Funds Act and CUMIFA incorporated reference to the continued validity of the doctrine reflects that the provisions of CUMIFA were meant to supplement and not supplant cy pres.

The plaintiff bases its statutory standing claim primarily on the language of subsection (a) of §45a-533, which provides that "with the written consent of the donor, the governing board may release, in whole or in part, a restriction imposed by the applicable gift instrument on the use or investment of an institutional fund." On the basis of this language, the Appellate Court concluded, and the plaintiff maintains, that "it would be anomalous for a statute to provide for written consent by a donor to change a restriction and then deny that donor access to the courts to complain of a change without such consent." Carl J. Herzog Foundation, Inc. v. University of Bridgeport, supra, 41 Conn. App. 803. We disagree.

The plaintiff concedes, as it must, that nothing in the plain language of §45a-533 (a) or any other portion of CUMIFA expressly provides statutory standing for donors to charitable institutions who have not somehow reserved a property interest in the gift such as a right of reverter. In order to demonstrate that the legislature intended to abrogate the common law, therefore, the plaintiff is left only with the legislative history of CUMIFA and the circumstances surrounding its enactment. The history and background of CUMIFA, however, not only do not support the plaintiff's claim of statutory standing, they directly refute it.

Faced with similar problems of statutory construction of CUMIFA provisions, we have stated that "in the absence of prior authority to aid in the interpretation of §45a-527 (2) (B), we are guided by the meaning ascribed by its drafters to the parallel provision of the Uniform Management of Institutional Funds Act (UMIFA). In 1973, the Connecticut legislature adopted UMIFA. "It is manifest that the legislature in enacting CUMIFA intended to implement the intention, meaning and objectives of the commission that drafted UMIFA." Yale University v. Blumenthal, 225 Conn. 32 at 38, 621 A.2d 1304 (1993). We agree with the defendant that the drafters of UMIFA did not intend to confer donor standing in the matter of the release of gift restrictions, and that our legislature provided no indication when it enacted CUMIFA that it intended any other result.

First, it is unmistakable that the drafters of UMIFA regarded charitable institutions, particularly colleges and universities, as the principal beneficiaries of their efforts.[9] The drafters set forth the explanation of their purpose in the prefatory note to UMIFA. "Over the past several years the governing boards of eleemosynary institutions, particularly colleges and universities, have sought to make more effective use of endowment and other investment funds. They and their counsel have wrestled with questions as to permissible investments, delega-

---

9. The Uniform Management of Institutional Funds Act has been adopted in 42 states. — Eds.

tion of investment authority, and use of the total return concept in investing endowment funds. Studies of the legal authority and responsibility for the management of the funds of an institution have pointed up the uncertain state of the law in most jurisdictions. There is virtually no statutory law regarding trustees or governing boards of eleemosynary institutions, and case law is sparse. . . . One further problem regularly intruded upon the discussion of efforts to free trustees and managers from the alleged limitations on their powers to invest for growth and meet the financial needs of their institutions. Some gifts and grants contained restrictions on use of funds or selection of investments which imperiled the effective management of the fund. An expeditious means to modify obsolete restrictions seemed necessary." UMIFA, prefatory note, 7A U.L.A. 706 (1985).

UMIFA, drafted in the early 1970s, was set against the backdrop of a state of flux for colleges and universities. In a time of dramatic social change that cast new light on many older charitable gift restrictions, these institutions saw their operating costs rise significantly without a similar increase in endowment funds. W. Cary & C. Bright, The Law and Lore of Endowment Funds (1969) p. 1. In the late 1960s, the Ford Foundation commissioned Professors Cary and Bright "to examine the legal restrictions on the powers of trustees and managers of colleges and universities to invest endowment funds to achieve growth, to maintain purchasing power, and to expend a prudent portion of appreciation in endowment funds." UMIFA, prefatory note, 7A U.L.A. 706 (1985). It is evident that the drafters of UMIFA paid heed to the concerns expressed in the Ford Foundation report as their final draft of UMIFA attempted to offer as much relief as possible to charitable institutions, without any mention of concern regarding a donor's ability to bring legal action to enforce a condition on a gift.

The specific area of relief to institutions focused upon by the Appellate Court and the plaintiff is that embodied in §7, of UMIFA, entitled "Release of Restrictions on Use or Investment."[10] The prefatory note to that section provides: "It is established law that the donor may place restrictions on his largesse which the donee institution must honor. Too often, the restrictions on use or investment become outmoded or wasteful or unworkable. There is a need for review of obsolete restrictions and a way of modifying or adjusting them. The Act authorizes the governing board to obtain the acquiescence of the donor to a release of restrictions and, in the absence of the donor, to petition the appropriate court for relief in appropriate cases." Id., 709. In the comment to §7, the drafters of UMIFA expressly provided that the donor of a completed gift would not have standing to enforce

---

10. Section 7 of UMIFA is codified in CUMIFA at §45a-533.

the terms of the gift. "The donor has no right to enforce the restriction, no interest in the fund and no power to change the eleemosynary beneficiary of the fund. He may only acquiesce in a lessening of a restriction already in effect." UMIFA, §7, comment, 7A U.L.A. 724 (1985).

These clear comments regarding the power of a donor to enforce restrictions on a charitable gift arose in the context of debate concerning the creation of potential adverse tax consequences for donors, if UMIFA was interpreted to provide donors with control over their gift property after the completion of the gift. Pursuant to §170 (a) of the Internal Revenue Code and §1.170A-1 (c) of the Treasury Regulations, an income tax deduction for a charitable contribution is disallowed unless the taxpayer has permanently surrendered "dominion and control" over the property or funds in question. Where there is a possibility not "so remote as to be negligible" that the charitable gift subject to a condition might fail, the tax deduction is disallowed. See also I.R.C. §2055; Treas. Reg. §20.2055-2 (b) (similar provisions for estate tax deductions).

The drafters of UMIFA worked closely with an impressive group of professionals, including tax advisers, who were concerned with the federal tax implications of the proposed act. The drafters' principal concern in this regard was that the matter of donor restrictions not affect the donor's charitable contribution deduction for the purposes of federal income taxation. In other words, the concern was that the donor not be so tethered to the charitable gift through the control of restrictions in the gift that the donor would not be entitled to claim a federal charitable contribution exemption for the gift. See I.R.C. §170 (a); Treas. Reg. §1.170A-1 (c).

In resolving these concerns, the drafters of UMIFA clearly stated their position in the commentary. "No federal tax problems for the donor are anticipated by permitting release of a restriction. The donor has no right to enforce the restriction, no interest in the fund and no power to change the eleemosynary beneficiary of the fund. He may only acquiesce in a lessening of a restriction already in effect." UMIFA, §7, comment 7A U.L.A. 724 (1985). The Appellate Court dismissed this language, reasoning that it is limited to "tax implications when a donor does consent in writing to a release of a restriction" and does not answer the question of whether the sole right to speak to the donor's interest in the release of a restriction "lies with the attorney general, to the exclusion of a donor." Carl J. Herzog Foundation, Inc. v. University of Bridgeport, supra, 41 Conn. App. 800. We disagree. Although the comments and the prefatory note to UMIFA do recognize that a donor has an interest in a restriction, as analyzed herein, we find no support in any source for the proposition that the drafters of either UMIFA or CUMIFA intended that a donor or his heirs would supplant the attorney general as the designated enforcer of the terms of completed and absolute charitable gifts.

Indeed, it would have been anomalous for the drafters of UMIFA to strive to assist charitable institutions by creating smoother procedural avenues for the release of restrictions while simultaneously establishing standing for a new class of litigants, donors, who would defeat this very purpose by virtue of the potential of lengthy and complicated litigation.[11]

There similarly is nothing in the history of our legislature's adoption of CUMIFA that contravenes the clear statement of the drafters of UMIFA that a "donor has no right to enforce [a] restriction. . . ." UMIFA, §7, comment, 7A U.L.A. 724 (1985). . . .

On the basis of our careful review of the statute itself, its legislative history, the circumstances surrounding its enactment, the policy it was intended to implement, and similar common law principles governing the same subject matter, we conclude that CUMIFA does not establish a new class of litigants, namely donors, who can enforce an unreserved restriction in a completed charitable gift. Nothing in our review supports the conclusion that the legislature, in enacting CUMIFA, implicitly intended to confer standing on donors.

The judgment of the Appellate Court is reversed and the case is remanded to that court with direction to affirm the judgment of the trial court.

In this opinion BORDEN and PALMER, Js., concurred.

McDONALD, J., with whom BERDON, J., joins, dissenting. I would affirm the thoughtful and well reasoned opinion of the Appellate Court. Carl J. Herzog Foundation, Inc. v. University of Bridgeport, 41 Conn. App. 790, 677 A.2d 1378 (1996).

The majority here holds that the donor itself may not enforce a restriction in a gift to an educational institution when the institution had specifically agreed to that restriction. This decision is simply an approval of a donee, in the words of the donor, "double crossing the donor," and doing it with impunity unless an elected attorney general does something about it.

This decision will not encourage donations to Connecticut colleges and universities. I fail to see why Connecticut, the home of so many respected schools that would honor their promises, should endorse

---

11. The brief of the amici curiae in this appeal, the Connecticut Conference of Independent Colleges, Inc., the Connecticut Association of Independent Schools, Inc., and the National Association of Independent Colleges and Universities persuasively posits that, should the establishment of donor standing become the law, the infinite variety of charitable gift restrictions that affect educational institutions would create the potential for a flood of "time-consuming, fact-sensitive litigation." This "mischief," they argue, would harm the very institutions that the CUMIFA intended to protect. We agree.

such sharp practices and create a climate in this state that will have a chilling effect on gifts to its educational institutions.

Accordingly, I respectfully dissent.

NOTES AND QUESTIONS

1.   Speaking of private express trusts, Professor Scott says the settlor has no standing to enforce the trust. "If the settlor has retained no interest in the trust property, the duties of the trustee are owing not to him but to the beneficiaries of the trust." 3 Austin W. Scott, Trusts §200.1 (William F. Fratcher ed. 1988). Scott also says the settlor cannot maintain an action at law against the trustee for breach of contract. Id. §197.2. Professor Langbein has argued that in a private express trust, "The deal between settlor and trustee is functionally indistinguishable from the modern third-party-beneficiary contract" (see supra page 566). A contractor can sue to enforce a third-party-beneficiary contract. If Langbein is correct, why cannot the settlor sue to enforce a private trust?

With respect to charitable trusts, Uniform Trust Act §408(d) (1999 draft) changes the rule applied in the *Herzog* case and permits a settlor to enforce a charitable trust.

2.   *Beneficiaries with special interests.* As the court notes in the *Herzog* case, a person with a special interest as a beneficiary can enforce a charitable trust. The person must show that he or she is entitled to receive a benefit under the trust that is not available to the public at large or to an average beneficiary. Thus, for example, an elderly, indigent widow living in a charitable home for the aged has been held to have standing to sue the board of trustees who, because of costs of operating an obsolete facility, propose to relocate the residents elsewhere. Hooker v. The Edes Home, 579 A.2d 608 (D.C. 1990). Similarly, a parishioner can sue to enforce a trust for the benefit of his church. Gray v. St. Matthews Cathedral, 544 S.W.2d 488, 94 A.L.R.3d 1197 (Tex. Civ. App. 1976). But compare Fowler v. Bailey, 844 P.2d 141 (Okla. 1992), where members of a church brought suit against the pastor and board of trustees in order to examine the church financial records. They were immediately expelled from the church by other members at a hastily called business meeting after Wednesday night prayer service. The court denied the plaintiffs standing, on the ground that a civil court could not determine the validity of their expulsion, which was an ecclesiastical matter. Accord, Williams v. Board of Trustees of Mt. Jezreel Baptist Church, 589 A.2d 901 (D.C. 1991).

In recent years, the courts have broadened the definition of what constitutes a special interest. A taxpayer has been permitted to sue to prevent the transfer of a library held in trust from Peabody Institute in Baltimore to the Pratt Library in that city. Gordon v. City of Baltimore, 258 Md. 682, 167 A.2d 98 (1970). A citizen has been permitted to sue to enjoin deviation where a gift of land was made to the University of Illinois for a park. Parsons v. Walker, 28 Ill. App. 3d 517, 328 N.E.2d 920 (1975). But taxpayers have no standing to challenge the tax-exempt status of a charitable institution on the grounds that it indulges in impermissible political activity. In re United States Catholic Conference, 885 F.2d 1020 (2d Cir. 1989), cert. denied sub nom. Abortion Rights Mobilization, Inc. v. United States Catholic Conference, 495 U.S. 918 (1990).

Whether students have special standing to sue college trustees is not settled. See Miller v. Aderhold, 228 Ga. 65, 184 S.E.2d 172 (1971) (denying standing); Jones v. Grant, 344 So. 2d 1210 (Ala. 1977) (granting standing); Charles R. Berry & Gerald J. Buchwald, Enforcement of College Trustees' Fiduciary Duties: Students and the Problems of Standing, 9 U.S.F. L. Rev. 1 (1974).

3. The rise of great charitable trusts in the United States came after industrial growth in the late nineteenth century produced enormous fortunes. Capital in charitable trusts has continued to mushroom during the twentieth century, partly, or perhaps principally, because the federal government permits gifts to charity during life to be deducted from the donor's taxable income and gifts to charity at death to be deducted from the donor's taxable estate. Today, charities own property worth billions of dollars. The Foundation Directory ix (1998 ed.) reports that 8,642 charitable foundations, with assets of more than $2 million each, have total assets of $248 billion. In addition, 4,926 foundations with assets between $1 and $2 million have assets totaling $4.8 billion. The Foundation Directory, Part 2, ix (1998 ed.). Twelve foundations have assets exceeding $2 billion each:

	(Figures in $billions)
Ford Foundation	8.1
W.K. Kellogg Foundation	7.6
David & Lucile Packard Foundation	7.4
J. Paul Getty Trust	7.2
Lilly Endowment	6.8
Robert Wood Johnson[12] Foundation	5.6
The Pew Charitable Trusts	4.0
John D. & Catherine T. MacArthur Foundation	3.4
Robert W. Woodruff Foundation	3.0
Rockefeller Foundation	2.7
Andrew F. Mellon Foundation	2.7
The Annenberg Foundation	2.6

12. Robert Wood Johnson was the brother of Seward Johnson, whose fortune did not go to charity. See supra page 197.

This list does not include the William H. Gates Foundation, which in February 1999 was reported to have more than $4 billion in assets transferred after the Foundation Directory was published. N.Y. Times, Feb. 6, 1999, at A12.

The largest charitable foundations in 1997 apportioned their grants as follows:

Education	25%
Human Services	17%
Health	16%
Arts and Culture	12%
Public Benefit	12%
Environment & Animals	5%
Science	4%
Social Science	3%
Religion	2%

Foundation Center, Foundation Grants Index xvii (1998).

The money held by charitable foundations is only part of the story, however. These figures do not include assets of universities, museums, libraries, churches, and other charitable institutions that are not "foundations" and do not make grants. For example, the New York Times, Oct. 21, 1998, at B9, carried an article about how the richest universities (which are not "foundations") keep getting richer. As of 1998, the ten richest universities had the following endowments:

	(Figures in $ Billions)
Harvard	12.8
University of Texas	7.6
Yale	6.6
Princeton	5.6
Emory University	5.0
Stanford	4.7
University of California	3.9
M.I.T.	3.7
Washington University at St. Louis	3.5
Columbia	3.4

Because taxpayers subsidize charities by way of federal tax deductions for charitable gifts, the federal government penalizes inefficiently run private foundations. Internal Revenue Code §4942 imposes substantial tax penalties on private charitable foundations (but not on publicly supported charities) that do not distribute annually income in an amount equal to 5 percent of the value of the endowment. If a foundation has a return of less than 5 percent on its endowment, to avoid taxation it must distribute principal in an amount equal to the difference between the income distributed and 5 percent of the value of the foundation's assets. The purpose of this legislation is to make investing more efficient and to penalize trusts with high expenses and little income.

It is the states, however, that have primary responsibility for assuring the proper administration of charitable trusts. The common law confers power on the attorney general to enforce charitable trusts. But unless newspaper publicity is given to some alleged irregularity, the attorneys general rarely investigate the internal workings of charitable foundations. See Kenneth L. Karst, The Efficiency of the Charitable Dollar: An Unfulfilled State Responsibility, 73 Harv. L. Rev. 433 (1960).

On federal and state regulation of charitable trusts, see generally Evelyn Brody, Institutional Dissonance in the Nonprofit Sector, 41 Vill. L. Rev. 433 (1996). For an extensive examination of the operation of charitable trusts, see Evelyn Brody, The Limits of Charity Fiduciary Law, 57 Md. L. Rev. 1400 (1998).

Richard A. Posner, Economic Analysis of Law
557-558 (5th ed. 1998)

§18.5   THE INCENTIVES OF CHARITABLE FOUNDATIONS

Even where no unforeseen contingencies occur, perpetual charitable gifts raise an economic issue that echoes the concern with the separation of ownership and control in the modern business corporation. A charitable foundation that enjoys a substantial income, in perpetuity, from its original endowment is an institution that does not compete in any product market or in the capital markets and that has no stockholders. Its board of trustees is self-perpetuating and is accountable to no one (except itself) for the performance of the enterprise. (Although state attorneys general have legal authority over the administration of charitable trusts, it is largely formal.) At the same time, neither the trustees nor the staff have the kind of property right in the foundation's assets or income that would generate a strong incentive for them to maximize value. Neither the carrot nor the stick is in play.

The incentives to efficient management of foundation assets could be strengthened by a rule requiring charitable foundations to distribute every gift received, principal and interest, including the original endowment, within a specified period of years. The foundation would not be required to wind up its operations within the period; it could continue indefinitely. But it would have to receive new gifts from time to time in order to avoid exhausting all of its funds. Since donors are unlikely to give money to an enterprise known to be slack, the necessity of returning periodically to the market for charitable donations would give trustees and managers of charitable foundations an incentive they now lack to conduct a tight operation. Foundations — mostly religious and educational — that market their services or depend on continuing charitable support, and are therefore already subject to some competitive constraints, could be exempted from the exhaustion rule.

The objections to the suggested rule are that it is unnecessary — donors are already free to limit the duration of their charitable bequests — and that it might therefore (why therefore?) reduce the incentives to make charitable gifts. A counterargument is that many perpetual foundations were established at a time when the foundation was a novel institution. A person creating one at that time may not have been able to foresee the problem of inefficient and unresponsive management that might plague a perpetual foundation as a result of the peculiar set of constraints (or rather lack of constraints) under which they operate.

HAWAII JOURNAL: THE BISHOP ESTATE

For more than 100 years, the Bishop Estate has been a highly respected, almost untouchable force in Hawaii. The Bishop Estate, one of the world's wealthiest charities, was established in 1884 as a charitable trust under the will of Princess Bernice Pauahi Bishop, the last descendant of King Kamehameha I, Hawaii's first and most powerful king, who unified the islands. The trust assets are estimated at $10 billion, which includes 8 percent of Hawaii's land mass (making it Hawaii's largest landowner) and a 10 percent interest in the New York investment firm of Goldman, Sachs & Co.

The princess's will directed that there be five trustees, appointed by justices of the Supreme Court of Hawaii, which, in those pre-statehood days, also served as the probate court. The trustees were directed to erect two schools, one for boys and one for girls, "giving the preference to Hawaiians of pure or part aboriginal blood," and to expend the annual income of the trust on the maintenance of the schools. Two schools were built shortly after the princess's death, but many decades later they were combined in a single school for boys and girls known today as the Kamehameha Schools. Today, Kamehameha Schools has 3000 students, and competition for admission to the schools is intense, with about 10 applications for each position. Apart from the elite Kamehameha Schools, the Bishop Estate spends little to educate the more disadvantaged native Hawaiians.

The annual income of the Bishop Estate is around $200 million, of which the trustees have spent about $70 million on the schools. Over the last few decades, the rest has been accumulated and added to corpus, even though the princess's will requires spending all annual income currently on education. The trustees have paid themselves handsome fees, averaging $900,000 each in the 1990s.

The trustees, the supreme court, and the Hawaii legislature have had what might charitably be described as a cozy relationship (though others have called it corrupt). To be appointed as a justice on the supreme court, a candidate must be put on an approved list of four to six names by the judicial selection commission, whose nine members are picked by the president of the senate, the speaker of the house, the chief justice, the governor, and the bar. From the approved list, the governor appoints a justice. The Bishop Estate trustees are in turn appointed by the justices. Over the years the board of trustees has come to resemble a who's-who of Hawaii politics. The trustees at the time the scandal broke in 1997 were Richard (Dickie) Wong, former state senate president; Henry Peters, state house speaker when he was chosen; Gerard Jervis, judicial selection commission chairman and aide to the governor; Lokelani Lindsey, chairperson of the governor's re-election committee on Maui; and Oswald Stender, former CEO of the Campbell Trust, Hawaii's second-largest private landowner. Only Stender had any experience in running a major trust or charitable organization.

The trustees' gilt-edged world began to unravel in 1997, when trustee Lokelani Lindsey began to intervene high-handedly in the day-to-day running of the schools. She countermanded decisions of the schools' president, Michael Chun, as well as the principals, and reportedly commanded that nothing in writing leave the campus until it had been personally approved by her. When students protested her attacks on President Chun, the trustee summoned the student body president to her downtown office for a two-hour interrogation, asking him how he would feel if she wrote a letter to Princeton (where he had been offered a scholarship) denouncing him as a rabble-rouser. When trustee Lindsey wanted a particular child admitted to Kamehameha Schools, a red dot would appear in the applicant's file. The alumni, teachers, and students at the school revolted. They marched, 1,000 strong, through downtown Honolulu demanding Lindsey's ouster.

Then came the spark that ignited the firestorm that was soon to engulf the trustees. On August 9, 1997, the Honolulu Star Bulletin published Broken Trust, an article written by four prominent members of the native Hawaiian community (a senior federal district judge; a retired state judge; a former principal of the Kamehameha Schools; and the head trustee of the Queen Liliuokalani Trust) and Professor

Randall Roth of the University of Hawaii Law School, an expert on the law of estates and trusts. This comprehensive article, which discussed the incompetence of the trustees and the many trust abuses, received wide media coverage. It triggered a public outcry for reform of the Bishop Estate. It also prompted the state attorney general, Margery Bronster, to launch an investigation into the trustees' actions.

A few months after the Broken Trust article appeared, a court-appointed special master found many irregularities in accounting and investments, a lack of a coherent professional management system, and a failure to develop any strategic plan for spending the income on education. The master also discovered that the trustees had surreptitiously moved $350 million of accumulated income into corpus without noting it in minutes of trustees meetings or disclosing it in financial statements. He also was troubled that the trustees created conflicts of interest by investing trust money in investments in which they had a personal stake. In 1998, a court-ordered study by the accounting firm of Arthur Anderson found material misstatements in the financial statements of every year under review and a lack of appropriate planning "in virtually all areas of investment and management decision-making." The attorney general found: "The trustees have not only failed to account as required by the will and by the law, but have intentionally concealed the accounts and the true condition of the Estate from the Court and the beneficiaries." The attorney general filed a petition to remove all of the trustees except Stender.

In addition to sloppy investment practices and the trustees' short-changing the schools, many private benefits flowed to the trustees. For example, most of the trustees accepted free golf memberships from country clubs leasing Bishop Estate land. One was alleged to have pocketed substantial director fees from a company in which the estate held a large block of stock. Another used Estate personnel to perform personal services and accepted trips to the Superbowl and Olympics in private jets from persons doing business with the Estate. One trustee "recused" himself as trustee in order to represent an organization that was buying land from the Estate. And a highly-placed employee of the Estate (a former state senator) charged $21,000 to the Estate's credit card in casinos and sex clubs in Honolulu and Las Vegas. (When this was disclosed by newspaper snoops, the trustees gave the employee a retroactive bonus of $21,000 to enable him to repay the Estate.)

Then, as in any good scandal, there was sex. A security guard caught trustee Jervis having sex with an Estate attorney in the toilet cubicle in a hotel men's room. The attorney, a married woman, killed herself the next day. One week later, the trustee took an overdose of sleeping pills, but survived.

Trustee Richard Wong was indicted on charges that he received a

$116,000 kickback in a real estate deal involving the trust and his brother-in-law. Wong's wife was also indicted. Trustee Henry Peters was indicted on a first-degree theft charge of allegedly selling his condominium at an inflated price to a developer who was then given permission to buy a tract of land owned by the Bishop Estate. The trustees fought back. They hired lawyers, allegedly paying them millions in fees from estate funds. They stonewalled. And through their friends in the legislature, some of whom were on the estate payroll, they retaliated against Attorney General Bronster. In April 1999, the state senate refused to confirm her to a second term in office.

Enter the Internal Revenue Service. In 1995, the Internal Revenue Service began to investigate allegations of self-dealing, conflicts of interest, and improper perquisites of the Bishop Estate trustees. The trustees were very uncooperative. The Service announced in 1999 that it would no longer deal with the five trustees on tax issues because of their obvious conflicts of interest. It threatened to take away the trust's tax-exempt status if they were not removed as trustees. The Hawaii probate court appointed five interim trustees to deal with the IRS. In May 1999, the probate court ordered the removal of trustees Peters, Lindsey, Jervis, and Wong, and trustee Stender resigned. See N.Y. Times, May 15, 1999, at 1.

Most observers expect the removed trustees to be hit with millions of dollars in intermediate sanctions (penalty excise taxes) under Internal Revenue Code §4958 for having received "excess benefits." (The trustees paid a former governor, who had appointed all of the current justices, $1 million to lobby against enactment of the federal intermediate sanctions law, which imposes sanctions on the trustees personally rather than punishing the beneficiaries by revoking tax-exempt status, but the law was enacted in 1996.) The trustees may also be liable for millions more for breaches of trust under Hawaii law. If the trustees are unable to pay all such damages, Professor Roth, who was the force behind the Broken Trust article and deserves most of the credit for bringing long overdue scrutiny of the Bishop Estate, notes that the justices who selected the trustees might be sued on a negligent hire theory. Although jurists normally enjoy judicial immunity, the justices were careful to make clear that, in appointing the trustees, they were acting as individuals and not in their official capacities. In 1998, Professor Roth was elected president of the Hawaii State Bar in a record landslide.

When and how the Bishop Trust will be restructured will take years to settle. Bowing to public pressure, four of the five state supreme court justices have announced they will not participate in future trustee selections. The fifth justice contends that he now has authority to make future selections as a majority of one. For the time being, the probate court is in charge of restructuring the trust.

The Bishop Estate debacle raises serious questions about the governance of charitable trusts in all states. Leaving the enforcement of charitable trusts almost exclusively to the attorney general has resulted in sporadic enforcement. Part of the problem is that no one is aware of conduct detrimental to the charitable trust. In the case of inter vivos trusts, no copy is filed with the state; the attorney general may be unaware of the existence of the trust. Even with testamentary trusts, which are created by the probate court, the duty to render periodic accounts is rarely enforced. The attorney general may lack an adequate staff. "Further," as Professor Karst has observed, "and this is by no means an indictment of our attorneys general, any high political official may be expected to approach rather cautiously the investigation of charges that respectable trustees are guilty of wrongdoing or even mismanagement." Kenneth L. Karst, The Efficiency of the Charitable Dollar: An Unfulfilled State Responsibility, 73 Harv. L. Rev. 433, 478-479 (1960). Awareness of the inadequacies of this situation led to the promulgation in 1954 of the Uniform Act for Supervision of Trustees for Charitable Purposes. This act, adopted in many states with large charitable foundations, requires trustees of charitable trusts to register with the attorney general and submit annual financial reports. Nonetheless, unless newspaper publicity is given to some alleged irregularity, the attorneys general rarely investigate the internal workings of charitable foundations. See Symposium, Foundations, Charities and the Law: The Interaction of External Controls and Internal Policies, 13 UCLA L. Rev. 933-1133 (1966).

QUESTIONS

1. In the case of a private corporation, stockholders and creditors can bring suit against the directors. What are the objections to suits by potential beneficiaries to enforce a charitable trust? Should the teachers or students of Kamehameha Schools be able to sue the trustees of the Bishop Estate? A charitable gift deducted from the donor's income tax is in effect a subsidy of the charity by the government. Assuming a taxpayer's suit against the government is allowed under local procedure, should such a suit be allowed against a charity for breach of trust?

2. Most charitable trusts have self-perpetuating boards. The trustees select their successors, who usually look pretty much like their predecessors. In view of the income, estate, and gift tax deduction for charitable gifts, should there be some public input in the selection of

trustees? In the case of the Bishop Estate, what public input procedure would you recommend? After a century, Princess Bernice's trust, with public input through appointment of trustees by justices, became dysfunctional. See David A. Lipton, Significant Private Foundations and the Need for Public Selection of Their Trustees, 64 Va. L. Rev. 779 (1978).

13

TRUST ADMINISTRATION: THE FIDUCIARY OBLIGATION

> For as a trust is an office necessary in the concerns
> between man and man, and which, if faithfully
> discharged, is attended with no small degree of
> trouble, and anxiety, it is an act of great kindness
> in any one to accept it.
>
> LORD CHANCELLOR HARDWICKE
> *in Knight v. Earl of Plymouth,*
> *Dick. 120, 126, 21 Eng. Rep.*
> *214, 216 (1747)*

SECTION A. DUTIES OF THE TRUSTEE

1. *Duty of Loyalty*

The office of trustee, on which the law has fastened many burdensome duties, is onerous. The most fundamental duty is the duty of undivided loyalty to the beneficiaries: The trustee must administer the trust solely in the interest of the beneficiaries.

Hartman v. Hartle
New Jersey Court of Chancery, 1923
95 N.J. Eq. 123, 122 A. 615

FOSTER, V.C. Mrs. Dorothea Geick died testate on April 8, 1921, leaving five children, one of them being the complainant. She named her two sons-in-law executors, and they qualified. Among other matters the will expressly directed her executors to sell her real estate and to divide the proceeds equally among her children.

On February 9, 1922, the executors sold part of the real estate known as the Farm, at public auction, for $3,900 to one of testatrix' sons, Lewis Geick, who actually bought the property for his sister, Josephine Dieker, who is the wife of one of the executors.

On April 11, 1922, Mrs. Dieker sold the property to the defendant Mike Contra (and another, who is not a party to the action) for $5,500, part cash and part on mortgage.

The executors settled their final accounts on April 21, 1922, and at or about that time complainant expressed to the deputy surrogate her dissatisfaction with the price realized from the sale of the farm.

About March 21, 1923, she filed her bill in this cause charging the sale of the farm to have been improperly and fraudulently made by the executors to Mrs. Dieker, and further charging that Mrs. Dieker and the other heirs of the testatrix had agreed at sale, because of slow bidding and inadequate price, to have the farm bid in for the benefit of all the heirs.

At the hearing each and every one of these allegations were shown to be untrue by the great weight of the testimony; and this proof was so conclusive that it left complainant with but one contention to sustain her case, viz. that under the law the sale of the property by the executors and trustee to Mrs. Dieker, the wife of one of them, without previous authority from the court, was illegal and void, and that it should be set aside and the farm resold, or, if that be found impossible because of the sale made by Mrs. Dieker to Contra, an innocent purchaser, then that complainant should have paid to her one-fifth of the $1,600 profits realized by Mrs. Dieker from the sale of the property.

It is the settled law of this state that a trustee cannot purchase from himself at his own sale, and that his wife is subject to the same disability, unless leave so to do has been previously obtained under an order of the court. Scott v. Gamble, 9 N.J. Eq. 218. Bassett v. Shoemaker, 46 N.J. Eq. 538, 20 Atl. 52, 19 Am. St. Rep. 435; Bechtold v. Read, 49 N.J. Eq. 111, 22 Atl. 1085. And under the circumstances of the case complainant cannot be charged with laches under the view expressed in Bechtold v. Read, supra.

In view of the fact that the property is now owned by innocent purchasers, a resale cannot be ordered, but, as an alternative, Mrs. Dieker and the executors will be held to account for complainant's one-fifth share of the profits made on the resale of the property under the authority of Marshall v. Carson, 38 N.J. Eq. 250, 48 Am. Rep. 319, and a decree will be advised to that effect.

NOTES

1. *Self-dealing.* If the trustee engages in self-dealing, good faith and fairness to the beneficiaries are not enough to save the trustee from liability. In case of self-dealing, *no further inquiry* is made; the trustee's

good faith and the reasonableness of the transaction are irrelevant. The beneficiaries can hold the trustee accountable for any profit made on the transaction, or, if the trustee has bought trust property, can compel the trustee to restore the property to the trust, or, if the trustee has sold his own property to the trust, can compel the trustee to repay the purchase price and take back the property. The only defenses the trustee has to self-dealing are that the settlor authorized the self-dealing or that the beneficiaries consented after full disclosure. Even then, the transaction must be fair and reasonable.

The no-further-inquiry rule is based on a general principle of policy and morality formulated by Judge Cardozo in a famous passage in Meinhard v. Salmon, 249 N.Y. 458, 164 N.E. 545 (1928). Cardozo said:

> Many forms of conduct permissible in a work-a-day world for those acting at arms length, are forbidden to those bound by fiduciary ties. A trustee is held to something stricter than the morals of the market place. Not honesty alone, but the punctilio of an honor the most sensitive, is then the standard of behavior. As to this there has developed a tradition that is unbending and inveterate. Uncompromising rigidity has been the attitude of courts of equity when petitioned to undermine the rule of undivided loyalty by the "disintegrating erosion" of particular exceptions. . . . Only thus has the level of conduct for fiduciaries been kept at a level higher than that trodden by the crowd. It will not consciously be lowered by any judgment of this court. [Id. at 464, 164 N.E. at 546.]

In determining what is self-dealing (to which the no-further-inquiry rule applies) and what is a conflict of interest but not self-dealing, courts must assess whether the danger of permitting the trustee to engage in the action is so great as to make the action wholly impermissible or only such as to make the action permissible if justifiable. On what is self-dealing, see 2A Austin W. Scott, Trusts §§170-170.23 (William F. Fratcher 4th ed. 1987). See also Charles B. Baron, Self-Dealing Trustees and the Exoneration Clause: Can Trustees Ever Profit from Transactions Involving Trust Property?, 72 St. John's L. Rev. 43 (1998); Uniform Trust Act §802 (1999 draft).

2. In Robert Cooter and Bradley J. Freedman, The Fiduciary Relationship: Its Economic Character and Legal Consequences, 68 N.Y.U. L. Rev. 1045 (1991), the authors make an economic analysis of the no-further-inquiry rule. They pose the economic question: "How can one party be induced to do what is best for another without specifying exactly what is to be done?" The no-further-inquiry rule, they contend, uses self-interest to compel the trustee to do what is best for the beneficiary. Because appropriation of the trust property is both very profitable for the fiduciary and difficult to detect by the beneficiary, the authors believe the law appropriately infers disloyalty from self-dealing. The fiduciary should have the burden of proving innocence. The authors would increase the sanction for self-dealing to include punitive damages, as yet very rarely awarded against trustees.

3.   *Trust pursuit rule.* One of the remedies afforded in equity for a breach of trust is known as the "trust pursuit rule." If the trustee, in wrongfully disposing of trust property, acquires other property, the beneficiary is entitled to enforce a constructive trust on the property so acquired, treating it as part of the trust assets. Restatement (Second) of Trusts §202 (1959). The trust pursuit rule also is applied where the property ends up in the hands of a third person, unless the third person is a bona fide purchaser for value and without notice of the breach of trust.

The rule is stated in the Restatement, Second, Trusts §284, p.47, as follows:

> (1) If the trustee in breach of trust transfers trust property to, or creates a legal interest in the subject matter of the trust in, a person who takes for value and without notice of the breach of trust, and who is not knowingly taking part in an illegal transaction, the latter holds the interest so transferred or created free of the trust, and is under no liability to the beneficiary.

If the trustee in breach of trust transfers trust property to a person who takes with notice of the breach of trust, the transferee does not hold the property free of the trust, although he paid value for the transfer. (Restatement, Second, Trusts §288.) Likewise if the trustee in breach of trust transfers trust property and no value is given for the transfer, the transferee does not hold the property free of the trust, although he had no notice of the trust. (Restatement, Second, Trusts, §289.) [Kline v. Orebaugh, 214 Kan. 207, 211-12, 519 P.2d 691, 695-96 (1974).]

In re Rothko
Court of Appeals of New York, 1977
43 N.Y.2d 305, 372 N.E.2d 291, 401 N.Y.S.2d 449

Cooke, J.   Mark Rothko, an abstract expressionist painter whose works through the years gained for him an international reputation of greatness, died testate on February 25, 1970. The principal asset of his estate consisted of 798 paintings of tremendous value, and the dispute underlying this appeal involves the conduct of his three executors in their disposition of these works of art. In sum, that conduct as portrayed in the record and sketched in the opinions was manifestly wrongful and indeed shocking.

Rothko's will was admitted to probate on April 27, 1970 and letters testamentary were issued to Bernard J. Reis, Theodoros Stamos and

Mark Rothko
Number 22 (1969)
Collection, The Museum of Modern Art, New York

Morton Levine.[1] Hastily and within a period of only about three weeks and by virtue of two contracts each dated May 21, 1970, the executors dealt with all 798 paintings.

By a contract of sale, the estate executors agreed to sell to Marlborough A.G., a Liechtenstein corporation (hereinafter MAG), 100 Rothko paintings as listed for $1,800,000, $200,000 to be paid on execution of the agreement and the balance of $1,600,000 in 12 equal interest-free installments over a 12-year period. Under the second agreement, the executors consigned to Marlborough Gallery, Inc., a domestic corporation (hereinafter MNY), "approximately 700 paintings listed on a Schedule to be prepared," the consignee to be responsible for costs covering items such as insurance, storage, restoration and promotion. By its provisos, MNY could sell up to 35 paintings a year from each of two groups, pre-1947 and post-1947, for 12 years at the best price obtainable but not less than the appraised estate value, and that it would receive a 50 percent commission on each painting sold, except for a commission of 40 percent on those sold to or through other dealers.

Petitioner Kate Rothko, decedent's daughter and a person entitled to share in his estate by virtue of an election under EPTL §5-3.3,[2]

---

1. The executors were three of Rothko's most intimate companions during his last years. Bernard J. Reis, a certified public accountant who had graduated from law school but had not been licensed to practice law, had acted for years as Rothko's business and professional advisor and confidant. Reis drafted Rothko's will.

Theodoros Stamos was a fellow artist in whose family plot Rothko was buried. Stamos entered into a personal contract with Marlborough Gallery, Inc., on January 1, 1971, whereby Marlborough became Stamos's exclusive art dealer agent for four years at a commission of 50 percent. The Surrogate found "Executor Levine stated, and the court finds, that in a conversation in April, 1970, before the execution of the questioned agreements, executor Stamos related that Marlborough had evidenced interest in his paintings. The conversation led Levine to believe that Stamos was interested in entering into some contractual arrangement with Marlborough which indicated a conflict of interest on the part of Stamos. Levine testified that when he confronted Stamos with the impropriety of such motivation angry exchanges followed." In re Rothko, 84 Misc. 2d 830, 844, 379 N.Y.S.2d 923, 940 (Sur. Ct. 1975).

Morton Levine, professor of anthropology at Fordham University, was chosen by Rothko to act as guardian of his two children. Kate Rothko came of age soon after her father's death and, at her insistence, Levine was removed as guardian of Christopher Rothko. "It is recognized that Levine was neither an art expert nor an experienced fiduciary but he was an educated man who, despite his educational background and his position as a college professor, failed to exercise ordinary prudence in his performance of fiduciary obligations which he assumed. Levine's argument at best is a statement that he undertook a responsibility which he was unqualified to handle. . . ." Id. at 846, 379 N.Y.S.2d at 942.

On the Rothko litigation, see Lee Seldes, The Legacy of Mark Rothko (1979). — Eds.

2. Mark Rothko devised his residuary estate to the Mark Rothko Foundation, a charitable corporation, with Reis, Stamos, and Levine named as directors of the foundation. New York Est., Powers & Trusts Law §5-3.3 (1967) provided that a child of a testator may set aside a testamentary disposition to charity to the extent it exceeds one-half of the testator's estate. Kate Rothko set aside the charitable gift in the amount permitted, with the result that one-half of the residuary gift passed to Rothko's heirs. Kate Rothko — who otherwise was left nothing by Mark Rothko's will — thus obtained an interest in her father's estate and had standing to attack the action of the executors.

instituted this proceeding to remove the executors, to enjoin MNY and MAG from disposing of the paintings, to rescind the aforesaid agreements between the executors and said corporations, for a return of the paintings still in possession of those corporations, and for damages. She was joined by the guardian of her brother Christopher Rothko, likewise interested in the estate, who answered by adopting the allegations of his sister's petition and by demanding the same relief. The Attorney General of the State, as the representative of the ultimate beneficiaries of the Mark Rothko Foundation, Inc., a charitable corporation and the residuary legatee under decedent's will, joined in requesting relief substantially similar to that prayed for by petitioner. . . .

Following a nonjury trial covering 89 days and in a thorough opinion, the Surrogate found: that Reis was a director, secretary and treasurer of MNY, the consignee art gallery, in addition to being a coexecutor of the estate; that the testator had a 1969 inter vivos contract with MNY to sell Rothko's work at a commission of only 10 percent and whether that agreement survived testator's death was a problem that a fiduciary in a dual position could not have impartially faced; that Reis was in a position of serious conflict of interest with respect to the contracts of May 21, 1970 and that his dual role and planned purpose benefited the Marlborough interests to the detriment of the estate; that it was to the advantage of coexecutor Stamos as a "not-too-successful artist, financially," to curry favor with Marlborough and that the contract made by him with MNY within months after signing the estate contracts placed him in a position where his personal interests conflicted with those of the estate, especially leading to lax contract enforcement efforts by Stamos; that Stamos acted negligently and improvidently in view of his own knowledge of the conflict of interest of Reis; that the third coexecutor, Levine, while not acting in self-interest or with bad faith, nonetheless failed to exercise ordinary prudence in the performance of his assumed fiduciary obligations since he was aware of Reis' divided loyalty, believed that Stamos was also seeking personal advantage, possessed personal opinions as to the value of the paintings and yet followed the leadership of his coexecutors without investigation of essential facts or consultation with competent and disinterested appraisers, and that the business transactions of the two Marlborough corporations were admittedly controlled and directed by Francis K. Lloyd. It was concluded that the acts and failures of the three executors were clearly improper to

---

New York Est., Powers & Trusts Law §5-3.3 was repealed in 1981. If Rothko had died after 1981, only the Mark Rothko Foundation and the state attorney general, the overseer of charitable trusts (see supra page 675) would have had standing to sue the executors. — Eds.

such a substantial extent as to mandate their removal under section 711 of the Surrogate's Court Procedure Act as estate fiduciaries. The Surrogate also found that MNY, MAG and Lloyd were guilty of contempt in shipping, disposing of and selling 57 paintings in violation of the temporary restraining order dated June 26, 1972 and of the injunction dated September 26, 1972; that the contracts for sale and consignment of paintings between the executors and MNY and MAG provided inadequate value to the estate, amounting to a lack of mutuality and fairness resulting from conflicts on the part of Reis and Stamos and improvidence on the part of all executors; that said contracts were voidable and were set aside by reason of violation of the duty of loyalty and improvidence of the executors, knowingly participated in and induced by MNY and MAG; that the fact that these agreements were voidable did not revive the 1969 inter vivos agreements since the parties by their conduct evinced an intent to abandon and abrogate these compacts. The Surrogate held that the present value at the time of trial of the paintings sold is the proper measure of damages as to MNY, MAG, Lloyd, Reis and Stamos. . . . It was held that Levine was liable for $6,464,880 in damages, as he was not in a dual position acting for his own interest and was thus liable only for the actual value of paintings sold MNY and MAG as of the dates of sale, and that Reis, Stamos, MNY and MAG, apart from being jointly and severally liable for the same damages as Levine for negligence, were liable for the greater sum of $9,252,000 "as appreciation damages less amounts previously paid to the estate with regard to sales of paintings." . . . The liabilities were held to be congruent so that payment of the highest sum would satisfy all lesser liabilities including the civil fines and the liabilities for damages were to be reduced by payment of the fine levied or by return of any of the 57 paintings disposed of, the new fiduciary to have the option in the first instance to specify which paintings the fiduciary would accept.

The Appellate Division, in an opinion by Justice Lane, modified to the extent of deleting the option given the new fiduciary to specify which paintings he would accept. Except for this modification, the majority affirmed on the opinion of Surrogate Midonick, with additional comments. Among others, it was stated that the entire court agreed that executors Reis and Stamos had a conflict of interest and divided loyalty in view of their nexus to MNY and that a majority were in agreement with the Surrogate's assessment of liability as to executor Levine and his findings of liability against MNY, MAG and Lloyd. The majority agreed with the Surrogate's analysis awarding "appreciation damages" and found further support for his rationale in Menzel v. List (14 N.Y.2d 91). . . . Justices Capozzoli and Nunez, in separate dissenting in part opinions, viewed Menzel v. List as inapplicable and voted to modify and remit to determine the reasonable value of the paintings as of May 1970, when estate contracts with MNY and MAG had their inception in writing.

Since the Surrogate's findings of fact as to the conduct of Reis, Stamos, Levine, MNY, MAG and Lloyd and the value of the paintings at different junctures were affirmed by the Appellate Division, if there was evidence to support these findings they are not subject to question in this Court and the review here is confined to the legal issues raised. . . .

In seeking a reversal, it is urged that an improper legal standard was applied in voiding the estate contracts of May 1970, that the "no further inquiry" rule applies only to self-dealing and that in case of a conflict of interest, absent self-dealing, a challenged transaction must be shown to be unfair. The subject of fairness of the contracts is intertwined with the issue of whether Reis and Stamos were guilty of conflicts of interest.[3] Scott is quoted to the effect that "[a] trustee does not necessarily incur liability merely because he has an individual interest in the transaction. . . . In Bullivant v. First National Bank [246 Mass. 324], it was held that . . . the fact that the bank was also a creditor of the corporation did not make its assent invalid, *if it acted in good faith and the plan was fair . . .*" (emphasis added here) (II Scott on Trusts, §170.24, p.1384), and our attention has been called to the statement in Phelan v. Middle States Oil Corp. (220 F.2d 593, cert. den. sub nom. Cohen v. Glass, 349 U.S. 929) that Judge Learned Hand found "no decisions that have applied [the no further inquiry rule] inflexibly to every occasion in which the fiduciary has been shown to have had a personal interest that might in fact have conflicted with his loyalty" (p.603).

These contentions should be rejected. First, a review of the opinions of the Surrogate and the Appellate Division manifests that they did not rely solely on a "no further inquiry rule," and secondly, there is more than an adequate basis to conclude that the agreements between the Marlborough corporations and the estate were neither fair nor in the best interests of the estate. . . . The opinions under review demonstrate that neither the Surrogate nor the Appellate Division set aside the contracts by merely applying the no further inquiry rule without regard to fairness. Rather they determined, quite properly indeed, that these agreements were neither fair nor in the best interests of the estate.

To be sure, the assertions that there were no conflicts of interest on the part of Reis or Stamos indulge in sheer fantasy. Besides being

---

3. In New York, an executor, as such, takes a qualified legal title to all personalty specifically bequeathed and an unqualified legal title to that not so bequeathed; he holds not in his own right but as a trustee for the benefit of creditors, those entitled to receive under the will and, if all is not bequeathed, those entitled to distribution under the Estates, Powers and Trusts Law. . . .

a director and officer of MNY, for which there was financial remuneration, however slight, Reis, as noted by the Surrogate, had different inducements to favor the Marlborough interests, including his own aggrandizement of status and financial advantage through sales of almost one million dollars for items from his own and his family's extensive private art collection by the Marlborough interests (see 84 Misc. 2d 843-844). Similarly, Stamos benefited as an artist under contract with Marlborough and, interestingly, Marlborough purchased a Stamos painting from a third party for $4,000 during the week in May 1970 when the estate contract negotiations were pending (see 84 Misc. 2d at 845). The conflicts are manifest. Further, as noted in Bogert, Trusts and Trustees (2d ed.), "The duty of loyalty imposed on the fiduciary prevents him from accepting employment from a third party who is entering into a business transaction with the trust" (§543[S], p.573). "While he [a trustee] is administering the trust he must refrain from placing himself in a position where his personal interest or that of a third person does or may conflict with the interest of the beneficiaries" (Bogert, Law of Trusts [Hornbook Series-5th ed.], p.343). Here, Reis was employed and Stamos benefited in a manner contemplated by Bogert (see, also, Meinhard v. Salmon, 249 N.Y. 458, 464, 466-467; Schmidt v. Chambers, 265 Md. 9, 33-38). In short, one must strain the law rather than follow it to reach the result suggested on behalf of Reis and Stamos.

Levine contends that, having acted prudently and upon the advice of counsel, a complete defense was established.[4] Suffice it to say, an executor who knows that his coexecutor is committing breaches of trust and not only fails to exert efforts directed towards prevention but accedes to them is legally accountable even though he was acting on the advice of counsel (Matter of Westerfield, 32 App. Div. 324, 344; III Scott, Trusts [3d ed.], §201, p.1657). When confronted with the question of whether to enter into the Marlborough contracts, Levine was acting in a business capacity, not a legal one, in which he was required as an executor primarily to employ such diligence and

---

4. The three executors sought advice from their legal counsel about entering into the contracts with MAG and MNY. Counsel advised the executors that Reis had a conflict of interest.

By the same letter, this law firm advised the executors that a petition for advance approval of any contracts for liquidation of the estate through Marlborough Galleries would not be entertained by a Surrogate. While it is true, as the law firm advised, that Surrogates do not usually give advance approval concerning matters of business judgment which are within the province of executors, no indication was given that the opposite rule governs when a fiduciary faces a conflict of interest. [In re Rothko, 84 Misc. 2d 830, 840, 379 N.Y.S.2d 923, 936 (Sur. Ct. 1975).]

Is the law firm liable to executor Levine for negligence? See Peter S. Cremer, Should the Fiduciary Trust His Lawyer?, 19 Real Prop., Prob. & Tr. J. 786 (1984). — Eds.

prudence to the care and management of the estate assets and affairs as would prudent persons of discretion and intelligence (King v. Talbot, 40 N.Y. 76, 85-86), accented by "[n]ot honesty alone, but the punctilio of an honor the most sensitive" (Meinhard v. Salmon, 249 N.Y. 458, 464, supra). Alleged good faith on the part of a fiduciary forgetful of his duty is not enough (Wendt v. Fischer, 243 N.Y. 439, 443). He could not close his eyes, remain passive or move with unconcern in the face of the obvious loss to be visited upon the estate by participation in those business arrangements and then shelter himself behind the claimed counsel of an attorney. . . .

Further, there is no merit to the argument that MNY and MAG lacked notice of the breach of trust. The record amply supports the determination that they are chargeable with notice of the executors' breach of duty.

The measure of damages was the issue that divided the Appellate Division (see 56 A.D.2d 500). The contention of Reis, Stamos, MNY and MAG, that the award of appreciation damages was legally erroneous and impermissible, is based on a principle that an executor authorized to sell is not liable for an increase in value if the breach consists only in selling for a figure less than that for which the executor should have sold. For example, Scott states:

> The beneficiaries are not entitled to the value of the property at the time of the decree if it was not the duty of the trustee to retain the property in the trust and the breach of trust consisted *merely* in selling the property for too low a price (emphasis added) (III Scott, Trusts (3d ed.), §208.3, p.1687).
>
> If the trustee is guilty of a breach of trust in selling trust property for an inadequate price, he is liable for the difference between the amount he should have received and the amount which he did receive. He is not liable, however, for any subsequent rise in value of the property sold (Id., §208.6, pp.1689-1690).

A recitation of similar import appears in comment d under Restatement, Trusts, §205:

> d. Sale for less than value. If the trustee is authorized to sell trust property, but in breach of trust he sells it for less than he should receive, he is liable for the value of the property at the time of the sale less the amount which he received. If the breach of trust consists *only* in selling it for too little, he is not chargeable with the amount of any subsequent increase in value of the property under the rule stated in Clause (c), as he would be if he were not authorized to sell the property (see §208) (emphasis added).

However, employment of "merely" and "only" as limiting words suggests that where the breach consists of some misfeasance, other than solely for selling "for too low a price" or "for too little," appreciation damages may be appropriate. Under Scott (§208.3, pp.1686-1687) and the Restatement (§208), the trustee may be held liable for appreciation damages if it was his or her duty to retain the property, the theory being that the beneficiaries are entitled to be placed in the same position they would have been in had the breach not consisted of a sale of property that should have been retained. The same rule should apply where the breach of trust consists of a serious conflict of interest — which is more than merely selling for too little.

The reason for allowing appreciation damages, where there is a duty to retain, and only date of sale damages, where there is authorization to sell, is policy oriented. If a trustee authorized to sell were subjected to a greater measure of damages he might be reluctant to sell (in which event he might run a risk if depreciation ensued). On the other hand, if there is a duty to retain and the trustee sells there is no policy reason to protect the trustee; he has not simply acted imprudently, he has violated an integral condition of the trust.

"If a trustee in breach of trust transfers trust property to a person who takes with notice of the breach of trust, and the transferee has disposed of the property . . . [i]t seems proper to charge him with the value at the time of the decree, since if it had not been for the breach of trust the property would still have been a part of the trust estate" (IV Scott, Trusts [3d ed.], §291.2; see also United States v. Dunn, 268 U.S. 121, 132). This rule of law which applies to the transferees MNY and MAG also supports the imposition of appreciation damages against Reis and Stamos, since if the Marlborough corporations are liable for such damages either as purchasers or consignees with notice, from one in breach of trust, it is only logical to hold that said executors, as sellers and consignors, are liable also pro tanto.

Contrary to assertions of appellants and the dissenters at the Appellate Division, Menzel v. List (24 N.Y.2d 91, supra) is authority for the allowance of appreciation damages. There, the damages involved a breach of warranty of title to a painting which at one time had been stolen from plaintiff and her husband and ultimately sold to defendant. Here, the executors, though authorized to sell, did not merely err in the amount they accepted but sold to one with whom Reis and Stamos had a self-interest. To make the injured party whole, in both instances the quantum of damages should be the same. In other words, since the paintings cannot be returned, the estate is therefore entitled to their value at the time of the decree, i.e., appreciation damages. These are not punitive damages in a true sense, rather they are damages intended to make the estate whole. Of course, as to Reis, Stamos, MNY and MAG, these damages might be considered by some to be exemplary in a sense, in that they serve as a warning to others (see Reynolds v. Pegler, 123 F. Supp. 36, 38, aff'd 223 F.2d 429, cert.

den. 350 U.S. 846), but their true character is ascertained when viewed in the light of overriding policy considerations and in the realization that the sale and consignment were not merely sales below value but inherently wrongful transfers which should allow the owner to be made whole. . . .

The decree of the Surrogate imposed appreciation damages against Reis, Stamos, MNY and MAG in the amount of $7,339,464.72 — computed as $9,252,000 (86 works on canvas at $90,000 each and 54 works on paper at $28,000 each) less the aggregate amounts paid the estate under the two rescinded agreements and interest. Appellants chose not to offer evidence of "present value" and the only proof furnished on the subject was that of the expert Heller whose appraisal as of January 1974 (the month previous to that when trial commenced) on a painting-by-painting basis totaled $15,100,000. There was also testimony as to bona fide sales of other Rothkos between 1971 and 1974. Under the circumstances, it was impossible to appraise the value of the unreturned works of art with an absolute certainty and, so long as the figure arrived at had a reasonable basis of computation and was not merely speculative, possible or imaginary, the Surrogate had the right to resort to reasonable conjectures and probable estimates and to make the best approximation possible through the exercise of good judgment and common sense in arriving at that amount. . . . This is particularly so where the conduct of wrongdoers has rendered it difficult to ascertain the damages suffered with the precision otherwise possible. . . . Significantly, the Surrogate's factual finding as to the present value of these unreturned paintings was affirmed by the Appellate Division and, since that finding had support in the record and was not legally erroneous, it should not now be subjected to our disturbance. . . .

Accordingly, the order of the Appellate Division should be affirmed, with costs to the prevailing parties against appellants, and the question certified answered in the affirmative.

NOTES

1. *Epilogue.* Bernard Reis, Theodoros Stamos, and Morton Levine were removed as executors of Mark Rothko's will, and Kate Rothko was appointed sole administrator c.t.a. of Rothko's estate. Kate Rothko was not agreeable to the bill for legal services presented by her counsel in the amount of $7.5 million and hired another lawyer to resist its collection out of the estate. In view of the fact that her lawyers had successfully recovered paintings then worth $40 million for the estate, the surrogate allowed the firm a fee of $2.6 million, which was

about twice the hourly rate usually charged by the firm. In re Rothko, 98 Misc. 2d 718, 414 N.Y.S.2d 444 (Sur. Ct. 1979).

Marlborough Gallery paid most of the $9.2 million assessed as damages in the principal case, but inasmuch as Reis, Stamos, and Levine were liable for the estate's legal fees and costs, Bernard Reis filed for bankruptcy in 1978. N.Y. Times, Jan. 26, 1978, at C19. Stamos assigned his house to the Rothko estate, which permitted him to retain a life estate in it.

In 1977, Marlborough Gallery owner Frank Lloyd was indicted on charges of tampering with the evidence in the *Rothko* case by altering a gallery stock book containing the purchase and sale prices of Rothko works. Lloyd, a British subject, was outside the country when the indictment was handed up, and upon his return in 1982 he was tried and convicted on the charges. His sentence required him to set up a scholarship fund and art education programs at his gallery. N.Y. Times, Jan. 7, 1983, at 1.

In 1983, a painting by Rothko sold for $1.8 million at an auction at Sotheby's in New York. This price equalled the amount Marlborough A.G. was to pay for 100 paintings under its agreement with Rothko's executors. It was, at the time, the highest price ever paid for a modern work by an American artist. By 1997, Rothko's paintings were selling for $7 million.

For a retrospective view of the litigation, and the subsequent lives of the parties, see A Betrayal the Art World Can't Forget, N.Y. Times, Nov. 2, 1998, at B1.

2. The measure of damages applied in the *Rothko* case is sharply criticized in Richard V. Wellman, Punitive Surcharges Against Disloyal Fiduciaries — Is *Rothko* Right?, 77 Mich. L. Rev. 95 (1978). Professor Wellman would limit recovery against the two disloyal fiduciaries and the gallery to restitution (recovering all amounts received by the gallery for sales and resales of the paintings plus interest from sale dates). Wellman's central point is that appreciation damages (a penalty) may be appropriate where a trustee sells an asset he has no authority to sell but are inappropriate where a trustee has authority to sell (as did Rothko's executors) but is guilty of disloyalty or self-dealing. "[T]he wisdom of assessing any penalty can be questioned when a trustee has, or later may be said to have had, personal interests which conflict with his fiduciary duty. In such instances, it will usually be unclear whether the fiduciary has breached his duty of loyalty: liability is decided by hindsight and may arise in countless unforeseen ways. A penalty exceeding the liability of an insurer against controllable losses is simply an unjust remedy for conduct of only uncertain impropriety. Even in *Rothko*, the wrongfulness of the executors' conduct was not self-evident." Id. at 113.

See also Gustave Harrow, Reflections on Estate of Rothko, 26 Clev.

St. L. Rev. 573 (1977); Note, Trustee Liability for Breach of the Duty of Loyalty, 49 Fordham L. Rev. 1012 (1981).

NOTE: CO-TRUSTEES

If there is more than one trustee, the trustees of a private, noncharitable trust must act as a group and with unanimity, unless the trust instrument provides to the contrary. One of several trustees does not have the power alone to transfer or deal with the property.[5]

One co-trustee may delegate to another co-trustee ministerial functions that do not require the exercise of discretion. A co-trustee may not delegate to another co-trustee discretionary powers, which can be exercised only by the co-trustees together. These powers include the purchase or sale of trust assets, investment of trust funds, allocation of receipts and disbursements between principal and income, and discretionary payments of income or principal to trust beneficiaries. Since co-trustees must act jointly, a co-trustee is liable for the wrongful acts of a co-trustee to which he has consented or which, by his negligence through inactivity or wrongful delegation, he has enabled the co-trustee to commit. It is improper for one trustee to leave to the others the custody and control of the trust property.

In the case of charitable trusts, unanimity of action is not required of the trustees. Action by a majority of the trustees is valid. Uniform Trust Act §703 (1999 draft) rejects the common law rule requiring unanimity among trustees of a private trust. It applies the charitable trust rule to private trusts, permitting a majority to act. Restatement (Third) of Trusts §39 (T.D. No. 2, 1999) permits a majority to act if there are three or more trustees.

PROBLEMS

1.   *A* and *B* are co-trustees. While *A* is on a Caribbean cruise, a $10,000 government bond held in trust comes due. *B* collects the $10,000 and invests the proceeds in common stock of Zany Corpora-

---

5. Statutes in many states provide that a majority of trustees can act if there are three or more trustees. For example, Uniform Trustees' Powers Act §6(a) (1964) provides that:

> Any power vested in 3 or more trustees may be exercised by a majority, but a trustee who has not joined in exercising a power is not liable to the beneficiaries or to others for the consequences of the exercise; and a dissenting trustee is not liable for the consequences of an act in which he joins at the direction of the majority of the trustees, if he expressed his dissent in writing to any of his co-trustees at or before the time of the joinder.

tion, a highly risky venture. Six months later Zany Corporation stock is worthless. The trust beneficiaries sue *A* and *B* for the $10,000 loss. Is *A* liable? Cf. Pank v. Chicago Title & Trust Co., 314 Ill. App. 53, 40 N.E.2d 787 (1942).

2. What would you, as counsel for Levine in the estate of Mark Rothko, have advised him to do when the conflict of interest of Reis became apparent? See 3 Austin W. Scott, Trusts §194 (William F. Fratcher 4th ed. 1988). Could Levine have resigned as executor and trustee? See id., §169.

Restatement (Second) of Trusts (1959)

§258.   CONTRIBUTION OR INDEMNITY FROM CO-TRUSTEE

(1) Except as stated in Subsection (2), where two trustees are liable to the beneficiary for a breach of trust, each of them is entitled to contribution from the other, except that

(a) if one of them is substantially more at fault than the other, he is not entitled to contribution from the other but the other is entitled to indemnity from him; or

(b) if one of them receives a benefit from the breach of trust, the other is entitled to indemnity from him to the extent of the benefit; and for any further liability, if neither is more at fault than the other, each is entitled to contribution.

(2) A trustee who commits a breach of trust in bad faith is not entitled to contribution or indemnity from his co-trustee.

2.   *Duties Relating to Care of the Trust Property*

a.   **Duty to Collect and Protect Trust Property**

A trustee has the duty of obtaining possession of the trust assets without unnecessary delay. What is unreasonable delay depends upon the circumstances. When a testamentary trust is established, the trustee should collect the assets from the executor as promptly as circumstances permit. In addition, a testamentary trustee owes a duty to the beneficiaries to examine the property tendered by the executor to make sure it is what the trustee ought to receive. This means the trustee must look at the acts of the executor and require the executor to redress any breach of duty which diminished the assets intended for the trust. See In re First National Bank of Mansfield, 37 Ohio St. 2d 60, 307 N.E.2d 23, 68 A.L.R.3d 1258 (1974) (trustee is liable to beneficiaries for not objecting to executor's overpayment of inheritance tax); Report, Duties and Responsibilities of a Successor Trustee, 10 Real Prop., Prob. & Tr. J. 310 (1975).

Once having obtained the trust property, a trustee must act as a prudent person in preserving it. If real property is involved, a trustee must keep buildings in repair, guard against theft, pay taxes, and insure against loss by fire.

b.   Duty to Earmark Trust Property

A trustee has a duty to earmark trust property. The reason: If the property is not earmarked, a trustee might later claim that the investments that proved profitable were the trustee's own investments and the investments that lost value were made for the trust. An established exception is that a trustee may invest in bonds payable to bearer instead of registering the bonds in the name of the trustee.

Under the older view, where a trustee commits a breach of trust by failing to earmark a trust investment, a trustee is strictly liable for any loss resulting from the investment. Even though it clearly appears that the loss is not due to the failure to earmark, a trustee is liable for the actual loss sustained by the trust. The more modern view, adopted by the Restatement (Second) of Trusts §179, Comment d (1959), is that a trustee is liable only for such loss as results from the failure to earmark and is not liable for such loss as results from general economic conditions.

PROBLEMS

1.   A trustee deposits money in Security Bank in the trustee's individual name. Security Bank fails. Is the trustee liable for the amount of the deposit? See 2A Austin W. Scott, Trusts §180 (William F. Fratcher 4th ed. 1987). Would it matter if the trustee were an officer or director of the bank and knew the bank was in difficulty? See Epworth Orphanage v. Long, 207 S.C. 384, 36 S.E.2d 37 (1945).

2.   A trustee invests in Baker Company stock, taking title to the certificates in the trustee's individual name. The trustee did this to facilitate later transfer since on subsequent sale the buyer might have to inquire into the terms of the trust if the buyer knew the shares were held in trust. Baker Company stock goes down in value. Is the trustee liable for the loss? Would it make any difference if the trustee had shown on the trustee's records that the stock was purchased for the trust? See White v. Sherman, 168 Ill. 589, 48 N.E. 128 (1897); Miller v. Pender, 93 N.H. 1, 34 A.2d 663, 150 A.L.R. 798 (1943).

Would it make any difference if the trustee took title in the name of a nominee? See Potter v. Union & Peoples National Bank, 105 F.2d 437 (6th Cir. 1939).

c.   Duty Not to Mingle Trust Funds with the Trustee's Own

A trustee is guilty of a breach of trust if the trustee commingles the trust funds with his own, even though the trustee does not use the trust funds for his own purposes. The reason: Commingled trust funds become more difficult to trace and hence subject to the risk that personal creditors of the trustee can reach them. (The prohibition against commingling has been partially abrogated in almost all jurisdictions to permit a corporate fiduciary to hold and invest trust assets in a common trust fund. See 3 Scott, supra, §227.9.)

As with breach of the duty to earmark, there is a divergence of views regarding the extent of a trustee's liability for commingling. The older view is that a trustee is strictly liable, even though the loss would have occurred had there been no commingling. More recent authority holds a trustee liable only to the extent the commingling caused the loss.

PROBLEM

The trustee of a trust under the will of José Martinez places bearer bonds, bought for $10,000, in her individual safe-deposit box, in an envelope marked "Owned by José Martinez Trust." The trustee dies. The market value of the bonds is $9,500. Is the trustee's estate liable for the $500 loss? See Lavarelle's Estate, 13 D. & C. 703 (1930), aff'd, 101 Pa. Super. 448 (1931):

> We freely concede that a trustee may illegally abstract assets from the box maintained in his own name, as trustee, quite as readily as he could by taking the securities from his individual box. On the other hand, either through accident or design, the envelope may become worn, dilapidated, or it may entirely disappear; the markings or writings on the envelope, in time, may fail to remain decipherable; the rubber bands surrounding the envelope may become hard and brittle and disintegrate, or the tape or string with which they are tied may break or disappear. In such event, the securities, unearmarked, may become commingled with those which the trustee may individually own. Should the trustee die under such circumstances, it may become impossible or difficult to segregate the trust securities from those of his own. Or should the trustee become insolvent, a contest with creditors may arise and jeopardize the trust assets. Furthermore, should a trustee keep assets in his individual box, *his* executor, on

his death, may assume custody. Thus, securities come into possession of a stranger to the trust and without bond. Where, however, the box is in the name of the fiduciary as trustee, the appointment of a substituted trustee is requisite before access may be had to the box. This is an added protection to the trust estate. In our opinion, it is quite as reprehensible for a trustee to commingle trust (unregistered) securities with his own as it is to keep the cash of the estate in his own individual bank account.

3. Duty Not to Delegate

Shriners Hospitals for Crippled Children v. Gardiner
Supreme Court of Arizona, 1987
152 Ariz. 527, 733 P.2d 1110

HAYS, J.   Laurabel Gardiner established a trust to provide income to her daughter, Mary Jane Gardiner; her two grandchildren, Charles Gardiner and Robert Gardiner; and a now-deceased daughter-in-law, Jean Gardiner. The remainder of the estate passes to Shriners Hospitals for Crippled Children (Shriners) upon the death of the life income beneficiaries. In re Estate of Gardiner, 5 Ariz. App. 239, 240, 425 P.2d 427, 428 (1967). Laurabel appointed Mary Jane as trustee, Charles as first alternate trustee, and Robert as second alternate trustee. Mary Jane was not an experienced investor, and she placed the trust assets with Dean Witter Reynolds, a brokerage house. Charles, an investment counselor and stockbroker, made all investment decisions concerning the trust assets. At some point in time, Charles embezzled $317,234.36 from the trust. Shriners brought a petition to surcharge Mary Jane for the full $317,234.36. The trial court denied the petition, but a divided court of appeals reversed. Shriners Hospitals for Crippled Children v. Gardiner, 152 Ariz. 519, 733 P.2d 1102 (Ct. App. 1986).

We granted review on three issues:

1) Whether Mary Jane's delegation of investment power to Charles was a breach of Mary Jane's fiduciary duty.

2) Whether Mary Jane's delegation to Charles of investment power was the proximate cause of the loss of $317,234.36.

3) Whether Robert can properly continue to act as successor trustee and as guardian and conservator for the predecessor trustee Mary Jane.

1.   BREACH OF FIDUCIARY DUTY

In Arizona, a trustee has the duty to "observe the standard in dealing with the trust assets that would be observed by a prudent man dealing with the property of another." A.R.S. §14-7302. If the trustee breaches that responsibility, he is personally liable for any resulting loss to the trust assets. Restatement (Second) of Trusts §§201, 205(a). A trustee breaches the prudent man standard when he delegates responsibilities that he reasonably can be expected personally to perform. Restatement (Second) of Trusts §171.

We believe that Mary Jane breached the prudent man standard when she transferred investment power to Charles. Mary Jane argues, and we agree, that a trustee lacking investment experience must seek out expert advice. Although a trustee must seek out expert advice, "he is not ordinarily justified in relying on such advice, but must exercise his own judgment." Restatement (Second) of Trusts §227. In re Will of Newhoff, 107 Misc. 2d 589, 595, 435 N.Y.S.2d 632, 637 (1980) (a trustee must not only obtain information concerning investment possibilities but also is "under a duty to use a reasonable degree of skill in selecting an investment"). Mary Jane, though, did not evaluate Charles' advice and then make her own decisions. Charles managed the trust fund, not Mary Jane. A prudent investor would certainly participate, to some degree, in investment decisions.

Mary Jane's second accounting of the Gardiner trust states:

> From time to time the Trustee made investments ("investments") in the money market and also in the purchase and sale of shares of stock listed on the New York Stock Exchange, the American Stock Exchange and the Over-the-Counter Markets. . . . All of said investments were made on behalf of the Trust Estate by a person qualified in that business, [Charles] who was selected by and in whom the Trustee justifiably had the utmost trust and confidence.

Most damning, however, are the admissions of Mary Jane's own attorney.

> Now, we can show, if the Court pleases, by way of evidence if counsel will not accept my avowal, we can show that Charles Gardiner for the past many years, including several years prior to and since these assets were placed in his hands for investment, was in the business of a consultant and in the business of investing and selecting investments in the stock market, and this he did. And it was only natural that Mary Jane would turn to him to make that selection, to invest those funds and to account in an appropriate proceeding if, as and when required. So the prudent man rule has been adhered to here. She got a man who is capable and fortunately he was a man who was designated as an alternate trustee and for all practical purposes really served as trustee.

Together, the accounting and admissions establish that Charles was functioning as a surrogate trustee. Mary Jane was not exercising any control over the selection of investments. She clearly breached her duties to act prudently and to personally perform her duties as a trustee. In re Kohler's Estate, 348 Pa. 55, 33 A.2d 920 (1943) (fiduciary may not delegate to another the performance of a duty involving discretion and judgment).

Even on appeal, Mary Jane does not argue that she, in fact, exercised any discretionary investment power. Instead, she argues that her lack of investment experience made it prudent for her to delegate her investment power. She relies on the Restatement (Second) of Trusts §171.

> §171. Duty Not To Delegate
> The trustee is under a duty to the beneficiary not to delegate to others the doing of acts which the trustee can reasonably be required personally to perform.

Mary Jane asserts that her lack of investment experience prevented her from personally exercising investment power and consequently permitted delegation of that power. The standard of care required, however, is measured objectively. In re Mild's Estate, 25 N.J. 467, 480-81, 136 A.2d 875, 882 (1957) (the standard of care required of a trustee does not take into account the "differing degrees of education or intellect possessed by a fiduciary"). The trustee must be reasonable in her delegation. A delegation of investment authority is unreasonable and therefore Mary Jane's delegation is a breach of trust. See Estate of Baldwin, 442 A.2d 529 (Me. 1982) (bank trustee liable for losses incurred when it failed to monitor management of grocery store despite bank's lack of expertise in grocery store management).

It is of no import that Charles was named as alternate trustee. A trustee is not permitted to delegate his responsibilities to a co-trustee. Restatement (Second) of Trusts §224(2)(b); see also id., Comment a (improper for co-trustee *A* to direct co-trustee *B* to invest trust funds without consulting *A*). Certainly, then, a trustee is subject to liability when she improperly delegates her investment responsibility to an alternate trustee. Bumbaugh v. Burns, 635 S.W.2d 518, 521 (Tenn. App. 1982) (impermissible for trustee to delegate discretion as to investment of funds to co-trustee).

Mary Jane also argues that broad language in the trust document permitted her to delegate her investment authority to Charles. A trust document may allow a trustee to delegate powers ordinarily nondelegable. The Gardiner Trust permits the trustee "to employ and compensate attorneys, accountants, agents and brokers." This language does not bear on Mary Jane's delegation of investment authority. Mary Jane did not simply employ Charles; she allowed him to serve as surrogate trustee. We view this language as merely an express recognition of the trustee's obligation to obtain expert advice, not as a license to remove herself from her role as a trustee.

2. PROXIMATE CAUSE

Mary Jane next argues that there is no causal connection between her breach and the loss suffered by the trust. The court of appeals rejected this argument in a summary fashion, stating that "the trustee offers no evidence to meet this burden of showing that the loss would have occurred anyway." Shriners Hospitals for Crippled Children, 152 Ariz. at 523, 733 P.2d at 1106. We disagree.

The very nature of the loss indicates that the breach was not causally connected to the loss. The accounting indicates that Charles embezzled the funds. Without the knowledge or consent of the Trustee, said person received from said investments, and diverted to his own use, a total believed by the Trustee to aggregate $317,234.36 ($116,695.55 on January 16, 1981 and $200,537.81 on March 4, 1981). The trustee did not learn of said diversions until long after they occurred. No part of the amount so diverted had been returned or paid to the Trustee or the Trust Estate. . . .

If the trust had suffered because poor investments were made, the delegation of investment authority would unquestionably be the cause of the loss. Otherwise, a causal connection between Charles' diversion of funds and Mary Jane's breach is absent unless the delegation of investment authority gave Charles control and dominion over the trust fund that permitted the defalcation.

A causal connection does not exist simply because "but for" Mary Jane's opening of the account at Dean Witter Reynolds, no loss would have occurred. A trustee is not personally liable for losses not resulting from a breach of trust. Restatement (Second) of Trusts §204; Citizens & Southern Nat'l Bank v. Haskins, 254 Ga. 131, 134, 327 S.E.2d 192, 197 (1985). Mary Jane did not breach her duty by establishing an account at Dean Witter Reynolds, a major brokerage house. Charles was not only the type of person Mary Jane was obliged to seek out for investment advice, but he was a person whom Laurabel Gardiner indicated was trustworthy by naming him as second alternate trustee. Furthermore, the Dean Witter Reynolds account was apparently in Mary Jane's name. If Dean Witter Reynolds wrongfully allowed Charles access to the fund, Mary Jane is not personally liable. Restatement (Second) of Trusts §225 (trustee not generally liable for wrongful acts of agents employed in administration of estate).

Unfortunately, the record does not reveal the nature of the diversion. The relative culpability of Charles, Mary Jane and Dean Witter Reynolds is unclear. The trial court found that Mary Jane was without fault and, therefore, did not consider the causal connection between

Mary Jane's breach and Charles's defalcation. The inadequacy of the record demands a remand for a determination of the relationship between Mary Jane's delegation of investment authority and Charles' diversion of funds.

3. ROBERT GARDINER AS TRUSTEE

If, after remand, the trial court determines that Mary Jane is personally liable for the diversion of funds, Robert must be removed as trustee.[6] A trustee is liable to a beneficiary if he fails to "redress a breach of trust committed by the predecessor [trustee]." Restatement (Second) of Trusts §223(2). Robert would, therefore, have a duty to enforce the surcharge against his aunt and ward, Mary Jane. The conflict between personal responsibilities and trust obligations is obvious and great. Estate of Rothko, 43 N.Y.2d 305, 319, 401 N.Y.S.2d 449, 454, 372 N.E.2d 291, 296 (1977) (while a trustee is administering the trust he must refrain from placing himself in position where his personal interest does or may conflict with interest of beneficiaries). Another trustee, without such conflicts, would have to be appointed.

The decision of the court of appeals is vacated, and the case is remanded for further proceedings consistent with this opinion.

NOTE

The nondelegation rule has been abrogated in the Restatement (Third) of Trusts §171 (1992) and by Uniform Prudent Investor Act §9 (1994). These authorities impose upon the trustee a duty of using care, skill, and caution in selecting an agent, when delegating to obtain the advantage of the agent's specialized investment or other skills. And of course the trustee must review periodically the agent's compliance with the authority granted. See John H. Langbein, Reversing the Nondelegation Rule of Trust-Investment Law, 59 Mo. L. Rev. 105 (1994).

For criticism of the relaxation of the rule against delegation, see Jerome J. Curtis, Jr., The Transmogrification of the American Trust, 31 Real Prop., Prob. & Tr. J. 251 (1996). Professor Curtis argues that the reforms go too far and unnecessarily jeopardize the interests of trust beneficiaries.

---

6. Robert Gardiner is currently serving as trustee because Mary Jane is an invalid and Charles is untrustworthy. Robert is also Mary Jane's guardian-conservator.

Restatement (Third) of Trusts (1992)

§171. DUTY WITH RESPECT TO DELEGATION

A trustee has a duty personally to perform the responsibilities of the trusteeship except as a prudent person might delegate those responsibilities to others. In deciding whether, to whom and in what manner to delegate fiduciary authority in the administration of a trust, and thereafter in supervising agents, the trustee is under a duty to the beneficiaries to exercise fiduciary discretion and to act as a prudent person would act in similar circumstances.

§227. GENERAL STANDARD OF PRUDENT INVESTMENT

COMMENT J:

j. Duty with respect to delegation. In administering the trust's investment activities, the trustee has power, and may sometimes have a duty, to delegate such functions and in such manner as a prudent investor would delegate under the circumstances. See generally §171. On the trustee's duty to select agents with care and to exercise prudence in monitoring or supervising their activities, see *id.*, Comments *a*, *h*, and *k*. . . .

The trustee is not required personally to perform all aspects of the investment function. The trustee must not, however, abdicate the responsibilities of the office and must not delegate unreasonably. Prudent behavior in this matter, as in other aspects of prudent investment management, cannot be reduced to a simple, objective formula.

With professional advice as needed, the trustee personally must define the trust's investment objectives. The trustee must also make the decisions that establish the trust's investment strategies and programs, at least to the extent of approving plans developed by agents or advisers. Beyond these generalizations, expressed in terms that are necessarily imprecise, there is no invariant formula concerning functions that are to be performed by the trustee personally.

Many factors affect the nature and extent of prudent and therefore permissible delegation. These factors include the almost infinite variety that exists in trustees and trusteeships, as well as in investment objectives and techniques and in the types, circumstances, and goals of trusts. For example, it would be impractical for delegation decisions not to take account of the scale of a trust's operations and the nature of the trustee's operating structure. Corporate trustees necessarily act through their employees; between that situation and the individual who acts as a trustee or co-trustee, however, there are many variations of trusteeship, encompassing, for example, institutional governing bodies, law firms, and panels of individuals operating with the support of full-time staff.

The trustee's authority to delegate is not confined to acts that might reasonably be described as "ministerial." Nor is delegation precluded because the act in question calls for the exercise of considerable judgment or discretion. The trustee's decisions with regard to delegation are themselves matters of fiduciary judgment and responsibility falling within the sound discretion of the trustee. . . .

ILLUSTRATIONS:

22. *T* is trustee of a modest-sized testamentary trust for the family of the testator. Under the trust terms, *T* is granted broad discretion over distribution and accumulation of income, as well as power to invade principal. *T* is a close and trusted friend of the testator's family but is not experienced in investment matters. After an initial briefing by a lawyer and consultation with *A*, an investment adviser, *T* decides to invest the bulk of the trust estate in several mutual funds. After a discussion of various types of funds and their characteristics, including the charges associated with each, *T* approves a plan that calls for holding certain types of funds in approximately equal portions. *T* then authorizes *A* to identify suitable mutual funds and to purchase their shares for the trust pursuant to this plan. *A* is then to report the purchases to *T*, who is to review those reports as they are received. All of this is done, as planned, promptly at the outset of trust administration. *T* also authorizes *A* to continue making and reporting additional investments for the trust pursuant to the plan, as unexpended receipts periodically become available and as adjustments become necessary to maintain the portions of the trust estate to be allocated to the various types of funds. Assuming adequate care in selecting the agent and adequate subsequent monitoring and supervision by *T*, this delegation does not constitute a breach of trust.

QUESTIONS

1. John H. Langbein and Richard A. Posner, Market Funds and Trust-Investment Law, Part I, 1976 A.B.F. Res. J. 1 (1976):

There is growing interest within the investment community in what are known as "index" or "market" funds. These are mutual or other investment funds that have abandoned the traditional attempt to "beat the market" by picking and choosing among securities — buying stocks or bonds that they believe to be undervalued and selling those they believe to be overvalued. Instead, they create and hold essentially unchanged a portfolio of securities that is designed to approximate some index of market performance such as the Standard & Poor's 500. The S&P 500 is a hypothetical portfolio consisting of 500 major nonfinancial companies on the New York Stock Exchange weighted by the market value of each company's total outstanding shares. . . .

If a trustee indexes all or part of the trust portfolio by buying the stocks in the Standard & Poor's 500, without investigating the individual securities, has the trustee improperly delegated his duty? Standard & Poor changes the stocks in its index from time to time, substituting one new stock for an old one. If the trustee sells the old stock and buys the new stock without investigating it, is the investment decision being made by someone other than the trustee? See id., 18-24, criticizing nondelegation rule.

2. As expert systems for investing are developed, which may outperform human beings as investors, suppose a trust settlor directs the trustee to invest according to the advice of the expert system (known as AI, for artificial intelligence). Would the trustee violate any duty in following AI? Could AI serve as sole trustee or co-trustee? For a delightful essay exploring these questions, see Lawrence B. Solum, Legal Personhood for Artificial Intelligence, 70 N.C. L. Rev. 1231 (1992).

4. Duty of Impartiality

A trustee has the duty to deal with both the income beneficiary and the remainderman impartially. The trust property must produce a reasonable income while being preserved for the remainderman.

Dennis v. Rhode Island Hospital Trust Co.
United States Court of Appeals, First Circuit, 1984
744 F.2d 893

BREYER, C.J. The plaintiffs are the great-grandchildren of Alice M. Sullivan and beneficiaries of a trust created under her will. They claimed in the district court that the Bank trustee had breached various fiduciary obligations owed them as beneficiaries of that trust. The trust came into existence in 1920. It will cease to exist in 1991 (twenty-one years after the 1970 death of Alice Sullivan's last surviving child). The trust distributes all its income for the benefit of Alice Sullivan's living issue; the principal is to go to her issue surviving in 1991. Evidently, since the death of their mother, the two plaintiffs are the

Judge Stephen Breyer
Appointed to the U.S.
Supreme Court in 1994

sole surviving issue, entitled to the trust's income until 1991, and then, as remaindermen, entitled to the principal.

The controversy arises out of the trustee's handling of the most important trust assets, undivided interests in three multistory commercial buildings in downtown Providence. The buildings (the Jones, Wheaton-Anthony, and Alice Buildings) were all constructed before the beginning of the century, in an area where the value of the property has declined markedly over the last thirty years. During the period that the trust held these interests the buildings were leased to a number of different tenants, including corporations which subsequently subleased the premises. Income distribution from the trust to the life tenants has averaged over $34,000 annually.

At the time of the creation of the trust in 1920, its interests in the three buildings were worth more than $300,000. The trustee was authorized by the will to sell real estate. When the trustee finally sold the buildings in 1945, 1970, and 1979, respectively, it did so at or near the lowest point of their value; the trust received a total of only $185,000 for its interests in them. These losses, in plaintiffs' view, reflect a serious mishandling of assets over the years.

The district court, 571 F. Supp. 623, while rejecting many of plaintiffs' arguments, nonetheless found that the trustee had failed to act impartially, as between the trust's income beneficiaries and the remaindermen; it had favored the former over the latter, and, in doing so, it had reduced the value of the trust assets. To avoid improper favoritism, the trustee should have sold the real estate interests, at least by 1950, and reinvested the proceeds elsewhere. By 1950 the trustee must have, or should have, known that the buildings' value to the remaindermen would be small; the character of downtown commercial Providence was beginning to change; retention of the buildings would work to the disadvantage of the remaindermen. The court ordered a surcharge of $365,000, apparently designed to restore the real value of the trust's principal to its 1950 level.

On appeal, plaintiffs and defendants attack different aspects of the district court's judgment. We have reviewed the record in light of their arguments. We will not overturn a district court's factual determination unless it is "clearly erroneous," Fed. R. Civ. P. 52(a). And, in a diversity case such as this one, involving a technical subject matter primarily of state concern, we are "reluctant to interfere with a reasonable construction of state law made by a district judge, sitting in the state, who is familiar with that state's law and practices." Rose v. Nashua Board of Education, 679 F.2d 279, 281 (1st Cir. 1982). . . . Application of these principles leads us, with one minor exception, to affirm the district court's judgment.

I

a. The trustee first argues that the district court's conclusions rest on "hindsight." It points out that Rhode Island law requires a trustee to be "prudent and vigilant and exercise sound judgment," Rhode Island Hospital Trust Co. v. Copeland, 39 R.I. 193, 98 A. 273, 279 (1916), but "[n]either prophecy nor prescience is expected." Stark v. United States Trust Co. of New York, 445 F. Supp. 670, 678 (S.D.N.Y. 1978). It adds that a trustee can indulge a preference for keeping the trust's "inception assets," those placed in trust by the settlor and commended to the trustee for retention. See Peckham v. Newton, 15 R.I. 321, 4 A. 758, 760 (1886); Rhode Island Hospital Trust Co. v. Copeland, supra. How then, the trustee asks, can the court have found that it should have sold these property interests in 1950?

The trustee's claim might be persuasive had the district court found that it had acted imprudently in 1950, in retaining the buildings. If that were the case, one might note that every 1950 sale involved both a pessimistic seller and an optimistic buyer; and one might ask how the court could expect the trustee to have known then (in 1950) whose prediction would turn out to be correct. The trustee's argument is less plausible, however, where, as here, the district court basically found that in 1950 the trustee had acted not imprudently, but unfairly, between income beneficiaries and remaindermen.

Suppose, for example, that a trustee of farmland over a number of years overplants the land, thereby increasing short run income, but ruining the soil and making the farm worthless in the long run. The trustee's duty to take corrective action would arise from the fact that he knows (or plainly ought to know) that his present course of action will injure the remaindermen; settled law requires him to act impartially, "with due regard" for the "respective interests" of both the life tenant and the remainderman. Restatement (Second) of Trusts §232 (1959). See also A. Scott, The Law of Trusts §183 (1967); G. G.

Downtown Providence, 1947

Bogert & G. T. Bogert, The Law of Trusts and Trustees §612 (1980). The district court here found that a sale in 1950 would have represented one way (perhaps the only practical way) to correct this type of favoritism. It held that instead of correcting the problem, the trustee continued to favor the life tenant to the "very real disadvantage" of the remainder interests, in violation of Rhode Island law. See Industrial Trust Co. v. Parks, 57 R.I. 363, 190 A. 32, 38 (1937); Rhode Island Hospital Trust Co. v. Tucker, 52 R.I. 277, 160 A. 465, 466 (1932).

To be more specific, in the court's view the problem arose out of the trustee's failure to keep up the buildings, to renovate them, to modernize them, or to take other reasonably obvious steps that might have given the remaindermen property roughly capable of continuing to produce a reasonable income. This failure allowed the trustee to make larger income payments during the life of the trust; but the size of those payments reflected the trustee's acquiescence in the gradual deterioration of the property. In a sense, the payments ate away the trust's capital.

The trustee correctly points out that it did take certain steps to keep up the buildings; and events beyond its control made it difficult to do more. In the 1920's, the trustee, with court approval, entered into very longterm leases on the Alice and Wheaton-Anthony buildings. The lessees and the subtenants were supposed to keep the buildings in good repair; some improvements were made. Moreover, the depression made it difficult during the 1930's to find tenants who would pay a high rent and keep up the buildings. After World War II the neighborhood enjoyed a brief renaissance; but, then, with the 1950's flight to the suburbs, it simply deteriorated.

Even if we accept these trustee claims, however, the record provides adequate support for the district court's conclusions. There is considerable evidence indicating that, at least by 1950, the trustee should have been aware of the way in which the buildings' high rents, the upkeep problem, the changing neighborhood, the buildings' age, the failure to modernize, all together were consuming the buildings' value. There is evidence that the trustee did not come to grips with the problem. Indeed, the trustee did not appraise the properties periodically, and it did not keep proper records. It made no formal or informal accounting in 55 years. There is no indication in the record that the trust's officers focused upon the problem or consulted real estate experts about it or made any further rehabilitation efforts. Rather, there is evidence that the trustee did little more than routinely agree to the requests of the trust's income beneficiaries that it manage the trust corpus to produce the largest possible income. The New Jersey courts have pointed out that an impartial trustee must view the overall picture as it is presented from all the facts, and not close its eyes to any relevant facts which might result in excessive burden to the one class in preference to the other. Pennsylvania Co. v. Gillmore, 137 N.J. Eq. 51, 43 A.2d 667, 672 (1945). The record supports a conclusion of failure to satisfy that duty.

The district court also found that the trustee had at least one practical solution available. It might have sold the property in 1950 and reinvested the proceeds in other assets of roughly equivalent total value that did not create a "partiality" problem. The Restatement of Trusts foresees such a solution, for it says that the trustee is under a duty to the beneficiary who is ultimately entitled to the principal not to . . . retain property which is certain or likely to depreciate in value, although the property yields a large income, unless he makes adequate provision for amortizing the depreciation. Restatement (Second) of Trusts §232, Comment b. Rhode Island case law also allows the court considerable discretion, in cases of fiduciary breach, to fashion a remedy, including a remedy based on a hypothetical, earlier sale. In, for example, Industrial Trust Co. v. Parks, 190 A. at 42, the court apportioned payments between income and principal "in the same way as they would have been apportioned if [certain] rights had been sold by the trustees immediately after the death of the testator" for a specified hypothetical value, to which the court added hypothetical interest. In the absence of a showing that such a sale and reinvestment would have been impractical or that some equivalent or better curative steps might have been taken, the district court's use of a 1950 sale as a remedial measure of what the trustee ought to have done is within the scope of its lawful powers.

In reaching this conclusion, we have taken account of the trustee's argument that the buildings' values were especially high in 1950 (though not as high as in the late 1920's). As the trustee argues, this fact would make 1950 an unreasonable remedial choice, other things being equal. But the record indicates that other things were not equal. For one thing, the district court chose 1950, not because of then-existing property values, but because that date marks a reasonable outer bound of the time the trustee could plead ignorance of the serious fairness problem. And, this conclusion, as we have noted, has adequate record support. For another thing, the district court could properly understand plaintiffs' expert witness as stating that the suburban flight that led to mid-1950's downtown decline began before 1950; its causes (increased household income; more cars; more mobility) were apparent before 1950. Thus, the court might reasonably have felt that a brief (1948-52) downtown "renaissance" should not have appeared (to the expert eye) to have been permanent or long-lasting; it did not relieve the trustee of its obligation to do something about the fairness problem, nor did it make simple "building retention" a plausible cure. Finally, another expert testified that the trustee should have asked for power to sell the property "sometime between 1947 and 1952" when institutional investors generally began to diversify portfolios. For these reasons, reading the record, as we must, simply to see if it contains adequate support for the district court's conclusion as to remedy (as to which its powers are broad), we find that its choice of 1950 as a remedial base year is lawful.

Contrary to the trustee's contention, the case law it cites does not give it an absolute right under Rhode Island law to keep the trust's "inception assets" in disregard of the likely effect of retention on classes of trust beneficiaries. Cf. Peckham v. Newton, supra (original holdings should be retained but only so long as there is no doubt as to their safety); Rhode Island Hospital Trust Co. v. Copeland, supra (court not sufficiently informed on safety of holding to order sale or retention). The district court's conclusion that the trustee should have sold the assets if necessary to prevent the trust corpus from being consumed by the income beneficiaries is reasonable and therefore lawful. Cf. Industrial Trust Co. v. Parks, supra (wasting assets); Rhode Island Hospital Trust v. Tucker, supra (similar).

b. . . .

c. The trustee challenges the district court's calculation of the surcharge. The court assumed, for purposes of making the trust principal whole, that the trustee had hypothetically sold the trust's interests in the Wheaton-Anthony and the Alice buildings in 1950, at their 1950 values (about $70,000 and $220,000, respectively). It subtracted, from that sum of about $290,000, the $130,000 the trust actually received when the buildings were in fact sold (about $40,000 for the Wheaton-Anthony interest in 1970 and about $90,000 for the Alice interest in 1979). The court considered the difference of $160,000 to be a loss in the value of the principal, suffered as a result of the trustee's failure to prevent the principal from eroding. The court then assumed that, had the trustee sold the buildings in 1950 and reinvested the proceeds, the trustee would have been able to preserve the real value of the principal. It therefore multiplied the $160,000 by 3.6 percent, the average annual increase in the consumer price index from 1950 to 1982, and multiplied again by 32, the number of full years since 1950. Finally, the court multiplied again by an annual 0.4 percent, designed to reflect an "allowance for appreciation." It added the result ($160,000 × 4 percent × 32), about $205,000, to the $160,000 loss and surcharged the trustee $365,000. . . . [The court approved the district court's calculation except for the additional 0.4 percent, designed to reflect "appreciation." The court found no reason to believe that the trustee would have outperformed inflation. The court therefore recalculated the surcharge, omitting the 0.4 percent, and reduced the surcharge from $365,781.67 to $345,246.56.]

d. The trustee objects to the court's having removed it as trustee.

The removal of a trustee, however, is primarily a matter for the district court. A trustee can be removed even if "the charges of his misconduct" are "not made out." Petition of Slatter, 108 R.I. 326, 275 A.2d 272, 276 (1971). The issue here is whether "ill feeling" might interfere with the administration of the trust. The district court concluded that the course of the litigation in this case itself demonstrated such ill feeling. Nothing in the record shows that the court abused its powers in reaching that conclusion.

II

... [Part II of the opinion omitted.]

The judgment of the district court is modified and as modified affirmed.

NOTE

In the *Dennis* case, the court found the trustee favored the income beneficiaries by investing in property with high income return but depreciating capital value. Suppose it is the other way around: the trustee invests in unproductive assets (say, forest or open land producing no rental income) with high appreciation potential. What remedy is given the income beneficiaries? "When land held in trust appreciates in value to the point it becomes underproductive, and there are conflicting interests between income beneficiaries and remaindermen, the law will imply a duty to sell the land within a reasonable time, even in those instances where the testator authorized the trustee to retain the assets." In re Kuehn, 308 N.W.2d 398 (S.D. 1981). See also Rutanen v. Ballard, 424 Mass. 723, 678 N.E.2d 133 (1997) (awarding damages against the trustees in the amount lost by failure to sell and awarding the income beneficiaries what they would have received had the proceeds of sale been invested in six-month U.S. Treasury bills).

Restatement (Third) of Trusts (1992)

§240.   UNPRODUCTIVE OR UNDERPRODUCTIVE PROPERTY

If a trustee of a trust to pay the income to a beneficiary and thereafter to distribute the principal to others holds property that produces no income or an income substantially less than an appropriate yield on the trust's investments, the trustee is under a duty to the income beneficiary either

(a) to adopt accounting, investment, and other administrative

practices reasonably designed to satisfy the distribution entitle-
ments of the income beneficiary, or

  (b) to sell some or all of that property within a reasonable time.

§241.   ALLOCATION ON DELAYED CONVERSION

(1) If the trustee is under a duty to sell unproductive, underproductive, wasting, or overproductive property that is held in trust to pay
the income to a beneficiary for a designated period and thereafter
to pay the principal to another beneficiary, and if the trustee does
not immediately sell the property, when the sale is made the trustee
must make an appointment of the proceeds as prescribed in Clause
(2) unless the terms of the trust provide otherwise.

(2) The net proceeds received from the sale of the property are
apportioned by ascertaining the sum that, together with simple interest at the current rate of income on trust investments from the time
the duty arose to the time of sale, would equal the net proceeds; the
sum so ascertained is to be treated as principal and the rest of the
net proceeds as income. The net proceeds are determined either by
adding to the net sale price the net income received or by deducting
from the net sale price the net deficit incurred in carrying the property prior to the sale.

NOTES

1.   If you are good in algebra, you will realize that, under the
apportionment formula of the Restatement (Third) of Trusts §241(2),
the amount apportioned to principal is determined by the following
equation:

$$\text{principal} = \frac{\text{net proceeds}}{1 + (\text{period of years}) \,(\text{interest rate})}$$

If algebra is not your forte, perhaps the following illustration will
help.

Testator devises Blackacre, unproductive land, in trust for *A* for life,
remainder to *B*. After one year Blackacre is sold, producing net proceeds of $50,000. If the current rate of interest on trust investments
is 6 percent, the amount allocated to principal is $50,000 divided by
1.06, or $47,170. The amount allocated to income is $2,830. If
Blackacre were sold after 3 years for $70,000, this amount is divided
by 1.18. (Why 1.18? The formula is 1 *plus* the number of years (3)
times the interest rate (.06).) Hence, $59,322 is allocated to principal

and $10,678 to income. Looking at this another way: $59,322 invested at 6 percent will produce $3,559 interest; multiply this sum by 3 (for 3 years) and you get $10,678.

Revised Uniform Principal and Income Act §12 (1962), adopted in most states, provides that, in the case of unproductive property that is sold, a portion of the net proceeds (to be determined by the Restatement formula) shall be allocated to trust income regardless of whether there was a duty to sell the nonproductive property.

2.   Modern portfolio investment theory, which seeks a high total return from the trust principal through wide diversification, raises important questions about how the return can be impartially divided between the income beneficiary and the remaindermen. We take up this matter infra at page 963.

3.   In Re Mulligan, [1998] 1 N.Z.L.R. 481, in 1965 the testator left property in trust for his widow for life, then to his nephews and nieces. The widow and a trust company were named co-trustees. The trustees invested in fixed income securities paying a high rate of interest. The trust company officers tried to persuade the widow to invest in common stock to counter inflation, but she refused. At the widow's death in 1990, the real value of the trust capital was a small proportion of what it was in 1965 because of inflation. The remaindermen sued both the trust company and the widow's estate. The court held that the trustees were liable for not treating the income beneficiary and the remaindermen even-handedly. The trustees were in breach of trust because they recognized the corrosive harm of inflation to trust capital and did nothing to protect against it. The court held the trust company officers had not acted forcefully enough to persuade the widow to invest in common stock nor had they applied to the court for direction when she refused. They should not have deferred to her wishes, particularly in view of her conflict of interest.

5.   *Duty to Inform and Account to the Beneficiaries*

Fletcher v. Fletcher
Supreme Court of Virginia, 1997
253 Va. 30, 480 S.E.2d 488

COMPTON, J.   In this chancery proceeding arising from a dispute over an inter vivos trust, we consider the extent of a trustee's duty to furnish information about the trust instrument and about other documents relating to the trust.

The facts are presented on appeal by a Rule 5:11 agreed statement of facts. During their lifetimes, J. North Fletcher and Elinor Leh

Fletcher, his wife, residents of Fauquier County, accumulated substantial assets.

Following Mr. Fletcher's death in 1984, Mrs. Fletcher executed a revocable, inter vivos "Trust Agreement" in December 1985 in which she placed all her assets. The ten-page document, containing nine articles, named her as both "Grantor" and "Trustee." In August 1993, the Grantor modified the Trust Agreement by executing a "Trust Agreement Amendment." The five-page Amendment replaced Article Six of the Trust Agreement with a new Article Six.

The Trust Agreement as amended (the Trust Agreement) contains, among other things, specific provisions for the establishment of a number of trusts upon the Grantor's death, including three separate trusts for the respective benefit of appellee James N. Fletcher, Jr., an adult child of the Grantor, and his two children, Andrew N. Fletcher, born in 1972, and Emily E. Fletcher, born in 1976 (sometimes collectively, the beneficiaries). The three separate trusts were to be in the amount of $50,000 each. The Trust Agreement appointed appellant Henry L. Fletcher, another adult child of the Grantor, and appellant F & M Bank-Peoples Trust and Asset Management Group, formerly Peoples National Bank of Warrenton, as successor Trustees to act upon the Grantor's death.

Under the Trust Agreement, the Trustees are authorized, in their discretion, to expend for the benefit of James N. Fletcher, Jr., such amounts of the net income and principal of the $50,000 trust as may be necessary to provide him adequate medical insurance and medical care during his lifetime, or until such time as the trust is depleted. In the event the trust is still in existence at Fletcher's death, then the Trustees are required to transfer and pay over to his surviving children his or her proportionate share of the balance of the remaining principal and income.

Under the Trust Agreement, the Trustees also are authorized, in their discretion, to expend for the benefit of Fletcher's children such amounts of the income and principal of each of the $50,000 trusts as they deem advisable.

The Grantor died in June 1994. Upon her death, the Trust Agreement became irrevocable, and the successor Trustees assumed their duties. They established the three $50,000 trusts, and the beneficiaries have benefited from them.

In June 1995, beneficiary James N. Fletcher, Jr., instituted the present proceeding against the Trustees. In a bill of complaint, the plaintiff alleged that the December 1985 instrument recites that the Grantor "transferred, assigned and set over certain cash and securities which were . . . described in a schedule entitled 'A' attached to the trust agreement." The plaintiff further alleged that, upon his mother's death, he was advised that the assets had been transferred to "a new trust" with the defendants as Trustees.

The plaintiff also asserted that he "requested details from the defendants of both the December 3, 1985 trust and the trust created with the assets of that trust upon his mother's death," and that the Trustees have refused to comply with his request. He further asserted that he has been provided with only pages 1, 8 and 9 of the 1985 instrument and "two pages" from the Amendment. The plaintiff also asserted that "without a listing of the precise terms of both trust agreements or a complete listing of the assets of these trusts," he is "unable to determine whether or not the trust estate is being properly protected."

Plaintiff also alleged that Trustee Henry L. Fletcher "has repeatedly made a point of justifying his failure to disclose the requested information . . . by stating that it was his mother's request that the trust terms and dealings be kept confidential, even from the beneficiaries." Further, the plaintiff asserts that Trustee Fletcher "has failed to produce any written direction from [their mother] with respect to the confidentiality." This situation, along with other facts, according to the allegations, has resulted in "an extremely strained relationship between" the brothers.

Concluding, the plaintiff alleged that because he lacks the "relevant information" sought, "he is unable to determine whether or not either trustee is properly performing their duties as a trustee[] according to law." Thus, he asked the court to compel the Trustees "to provide full and complete copies of all trust instruments in their possession that relate to the two trusts referred to herein."

In a demurrer, the Trustees asserted that the bill of complaint failed to state a cause of action. In an answer, the Trustees denied that any "new trust" was created upon the Grantor's death, and asserted that the Trust Agreement remained in effect following the death. The Trustees asserted, however, that upon the death, "separate trusts were created under the express terms of the Trust Agreement," and that the plaintiff has been provided with "all provisions of the Trust Agreement relating to him and his children, along with regular accountings relating to his interest under the Trust Agreement." In sum, the Trustees denied the plaintiff is entitled to the information sought.

In October 1995, pursuant to an agreed order, the Trustees filed the Trust Agreement under seal with the court, to be examined only by the court.

Subsequently, the trial court heard argument on the demurrer and, during the hearing, ruled that the plaintiff was entitled to see all provisions of the Trust Agreement. The court noted that the plaintiff's "interests as a child of" the Grantor and as "a beneficiary of her trust outweighed the arguments advanced" by the Trustees.

Accordingly, in a January 1996 final order, the court said it was of opinion that the plaintiff "has an absolute right to complete copies of the Trust Agreement and all amendments referred to in the pleadings and associated documents." Thus, the court ordered the Trustees to provide the plaintiff with "full and complete copies of the Trust instruments that are referred to in the Bill of Complaint filed in this cause." The Trustees appeal.

The Trustees contend the trial court erred in finding that the plaintiff had an absolute right to review complete copies of the Trust Agreement and in ordering them to provide plaintiff with such copies. Emphasizing that the trust instrument established three separate trusts, the Trustees argue the trial court's order "ignores the fiduciary duty of confidentiality between the Trustees and other beneficiaries under the . . . Trust Agreement." Noting the use of revocable trusts in planning disposition of assets upon death, the Trustees say that following a grantor's death, "the trustees handle the trust assets for the various beneficiaries, in accordance with the grantor's instruction, in a manner appropriate for each beneficiary taking into account the unique circumstances applicable to each beneficiary."

Continuing, the Trustees observe that a grantor, as here, often "directs the trustee to segregate trust assets into separate trusts for the benefit of different beneficiaries." See Code §55-19.3 (trustee may divide a trust into two or more separate trusts). According to the Trustees, "Segregation of a trust into separate trusts for different beneficiaries not only segregates the assets, but also segregates the trustee's duties to the different beneficiaries." The Trustees say that a "trustee has a continuing duty to the grantor to fulfill the trustee's obligations under the trust agreement. The trustee also has a fiduciary duty to the beneficiaries of each trust established under the agreement. The trustee's duties to the beneficiaries of each separate trust do not overlap."

The Trustees point out the plaintiff has not alleged any wrongdoing on their part "nor has he alleged that he has any interest under the . . . Trust Agreement other than his interest in a separate trust established for his benefit." The Trustees state they have provided the plaintiff with copies of the portions of the Trust Agreement that pertain to the establishment and administration of the separate trusts, have submitted a copy of the Trust Agreement to the trial judge so the court may determine whether they have disclosed to the plaintiff all relevant information, and have provided regular accountings to the beneficiaries with respect to their separate trusts. The Trustees argue that the family relationship and the "specter" of disharmony, standing alone do not create a right in the plaintiff to compel disclosure. Finally, the Trustees argue "the trial court's Order compelling disclosure violates the public policy that permits individuals to ensure privacy of their affairs through the use of inter vivos trust agreements in lieu of wills."

We do not agree with the Trustees' contentions. They place too much emphasis upon the duties of trustees while neglecting the rights of beneficiaries.

This is a case of first impression in Virginia. The parties have not referred us to any cases elsewhere that are factually apposite, and we have found none. Nevertheless, text writers and the Restatement articulate settled principles that are applicable.

"The beneficiary is the equitable owner of trust property, in whole or in part. The trustee is a mere representative whose function is to attend to the safety of the trust property and to obtain its avails for the beneficiary in the manner provided by the trust instrument." Bogert, The Law of Trusts and Trustees §961, at 2 (Rev. 2nd ed. 1983). The fact that a grantor has created a trust and thus required the beneficiary to enjoy the property interest indirectly "does not imply that the beneficiary is to be kept in ignorance of the trust, the nature of the trust property and the details of its administration." Bogert, §961, at 2.

Therefore, "the trustee is under a duty to the beneficiary to give him upon his request at reasonable times complete and accurate information as to the nature and amount of the trust property, and to permit him or a person duly authorized by him to inspect the subject matter of the trust and the accounts and vouchers and other documents relating to the trust." Restatement (Second) of Trusts §173 (1959). Accord Bogert, §961, at 3-4; IIA Scott, The Law of Trusts §173, at 462 (4th ed. 1987). Indeed, "where a trust is created for several beneficiaries, each of them is entitled to information as to the trust." Scott, §173, at 464.

And, even though "the terms of the trust may regulate the amount of information which the trustee must give and the frequency with which it must be given, the beneficiary is always entitled to such information as is reasonably necessary to enable him to enforce his rights under the trust or to prevent or redress a breach of trust." Restatement §173 cmt. c. See In Re Estate of Rosenblum, 459 Pa. 201, 328 A.2d 158, 164-65 (Pa. 1974).

Turning to the present facts, we observe that the appellate record fails to establish that the Grantor directed the Trustees not to disclose the terms of the entire Trust Agreement to the beneficiaries. The trust instrument, which we have examined, does not mention the subject. Although the Trustees assert the Grantor orally gave such instructions, the plaintiff questions this fact. And, there was no evidentiary hearing below to decide the matter. Thus, we express no opinion on what effect any directive of secrecy by the Grantor would have on the outcome of this case.

Recognizing the foregoing general principles of the law of trusts, the Trustees nevertheless seek to remove this case from the force of those rules by dwelling on the fact that three separate trusts were created. In essence, the Trustees treat this single integrated Trust Agreement as if there are three distinct trust documents, each entirely independent of the other, a circumstance that simply does not exist.

There is a single cohesive trust instrument based on a unitary corpus. The Trustees seek to avoid the beneficiary's scrutiny of eight pages of the Trust Agreement. They also seek to prevent review of Schedule "A," which lists the cash and securities the Grantor transferred to the trust corpus. This document was not even included in the sealed papers filed with the trial court.

The information not disclosed may have a material bearing on the administration of the Trust Agreement insofar as the beneficiary is concerned. For example, without access to the Trust Agreement (even though there are numerous separate trusts established), the beneficiary has no basis upon which he can intelligently scrutinize the Trustees' investment decisions made with respect to the assets revealed on Schedule "A." The beneficiary is unable to evaluate whether the Trustees are discharging their duty to use "reasonable care and skill to make the trust property productive." Sturgis v. Stinson, 241 Va. 531, 535, 404 S.E.2d 56, 58 (1991) (quoting Restatement (Second) of Trusts §181 (1959)). Also, the beneficiary is entitled to review the trust documents in their entirety in order to assure the Trustees are discharging their "duty to deal impartially" with all the beneficiaries within the restrictions and conditions imposed by the Trust Agreement. Sturgis, 241 Va. at 534-35, 404 S.E.2d at 58.

In sum, we hold that the trial court correctly required the Trustees to disclose the information sought. Thus, the judgment appealed from will be

Affirmed.

QUESTIONS AND NOTE

1.   If the settlor directs the trustee to disclose to a beneficiary only the provisions of the trust relating to that beneficiary, should it be upheld? Should the settlor be able to make, in effect, a secret will by using a revocable trust? See Taylor v. Nationsbank Corp., 125 N.C. App. 515, 481 S.E.2d 358 (1997); Restatement (Second) of Trusts, §173, Comment c (1959).

2.   California Probate Code §16061.5 (1999) provides that when a revocable trust becomes irrevocable because of the death of the set-

tlor, the trustee shall provide a complete copy of the terms of the irrevocable trust to any beneficiary or heir of the settlor who requests it. Why are heirs of the settlor entitled to see a trust document of which they are not beneficiaries? Should this requirement be extended to an irrevocable inter vivos trust?

3.   The trustee has the duty to give beneficiaries advance notice of the proposed sale of trust property "that comprises a significant portion of the value of the trust property unless (i) the fair market value of the property is readily ascertainable, or (ii) such disclosure is forbidden by law or would be seriously detrimental to the interests of the beneficiaries." Uniform Trust Act §813(b)(5) (1999 draft) (codifying holding in Allard v. Pacific National Bank, 99 Wash. 2d 394, 663 P.2d 104 (1983), which surcharged trustee for failing to give beneficiaries advance notice of the proposed sale of real estate that was the sole asset of the trust).

National Academy of Sciences v. Cambridge Trust Co.
Supreme Judicial Court of Massachusetts, 1976
370 Mass. 303, 346 N.E.2d 879

REARDON, J.   This matter is before us for further appellate review, the Appeals Court having promulgated an opinion.

The facts which give rise to the case are essentially as follows. Leonard T. Troland died a resident of Cambridge in 1932 survived by his widow, Florence R. Troland. By his will executed in April, 1931, he left all of his real and personal property to be held in trust by the Cambridge Trust Company (bank) with the net income of the trust, after expenses, "to be paid to, or deposited to the account of [his wife], Florence R. Troland" during her lifetime so long as she remained unmarried. He further provided that

> [k]nowing my wife, Florence's, generosity and unselfishness as I do, I wish to record it as my intention that she should not devote any major portion of her income under the provisions of this will, to the support or for the benefit of people other than herself. It is particularly contrary to my will that any part of the principal or income of my estate should revert to members of my wife's family, other than herself, and I instruct the trustees to bear this point definitely in mind in making decisions under any of the options of this will.

The testator went on to provide in part that on his wife's death or second marriage the bank would transfer the trusteeship to The National Research Council of Washington, D.C., which the petition alleged to be an agency of the National Academy of Sciences (academy), to constitute a trust to be known as the Troland Foundation for Research in Psychophysics. . . .

The will was allowed, the trust was established as provided by the testator, and the bank paid the income thereof to the widow until her death in 1967. During the period from 1932 to 1945 the widow provided eighteen different mailing addresses for income checks to be transmitted to her by the bank. On February 13, 1945, she married Edward D. Flynn in West Palm Beach, Florida, and failed to advise the bank of her remarriage. Following her remarriage she lived in Perth Amboy, New Jersey. Commencing on April 14, 1944, she directed the bank to forward all her monthly checks to her in care of Kenneth D. Custance, her brother-in-law through marriage to her sister. Over the years these checks were forwarded to two Boston addresses and were made payable to "Florence R. Troland." Custance in turn forwarded the checks to Florence R. Flynn who indorsed them in blank "Florence R. Troland" and returned them to Custance who also indorsed them prior to depositing them in bank accounts in his name maintained at the State Street Bank and Trust Company in Boston and the National Bank of Wareham, Massachusetts. After Florence R. Flynn's death on December 25, 1967, the bank for the first time learned of her remarriage.[7] Throughout her second marriage Florence R. Flynn lived with her husband who was able to provide

---

7. A letter from Thomas Quarles, Jr., a lawyer in Manchester, New Hampshire, discloses some interesting information about the parties in this case. Quarles, who came upon this case while a law student using a prior edition of this book, writes:

Leonard Troland

My father, Thomas Quarles, Sr., was the trust officer at the Cambridge Trust Company in charge of the Troland trust at the time of Florence Troland's death in 1967. Leonard Troland, the settlor of the trust, was apparently quite a colorful individual. A professor of psychology at Harvard for many years, he was also one of a group that developed the Technicolor motion picture film process. Proceeds from the sale of this invention formed part of the principal of the Troland trust. Mr. Troland apparently had a flair for the theatrical in his personal life as well. In 1932, he reportedly committed suicide by driving his car off the rim of the Grand Canyon at sunset.

Florence Troland was aware of the limitation in the trust that cut off her interest if she remarried. So was her brother-in-law, Kenneth Custance. Nevertheless, after her remarriage in 1945, he convinced her to keep quiet and to endorse her trust income check over to him. He told her that the money was needed to support a succession of spiritualist churches that he headed in the Onset, Massachusetts area. When Florence died in 1967, Kenneth apparently felt guilty about the years of fraud. At her funeral, he gave Florence's latest trust check to her surviving husband, who contacted the Cambridge Trust Company asking what he should do with it. It was only at that point that the Bank realized that through Mrs. Troland and Mr. Custance's fraud it had paid the wrong beneficiary for 22 years. Fortunately, my father kept his job. He had only been with the Bank for a few years and had only recently taken over the Troland trust.

Letter from Thomas Quarles, Jr., to Jesse Dukeminier, dated Dec. 1, 1986. — Eds.

support for her and who, although aware that she was receiving payments from the trust, was ignorant of the limitation on her rights to receive such payments. . . . The total of all checks collected by Florence R. Flynn following her marriage in 1945 up to the date of her death is $106,013.41. The twelfth through thirty-third accounts of the bank covering that period between her remarriage and October 8, 1966, were presented to the Probate Court for Middlesex County in separate proceedings and allowed. The academy had formal notice prior to the presentation of the twelfth through fourteenth accounts and the eighteenth through thirty-third accounts, and with respect to the fifteenth through seventeenth accounts assented in writing to their allowance. The academy, unaware of the widow's remarriage, did not challenge any of the accounts and they were duly allowed.

The petition brought in the Probate Court by the academy seeks revocation of the seven decrees allowing the twelfth through thirty-third accounts of the bank, the excision from those accounts of "all entries purporting to evidence distributions to or for the benefit of 'Florence R. Troland' . . . subsequent to February 13, 1945," the restoration by the bank to the trust of the amounts of those distributions with interest at the rate of six percent, a final account reflecting the repayments and adjustments, [and] appointment of the academy as trustee. . . .

Following hearing a judge of the Probate Court revoked the seven decrees allowing the twelfth through thirty-third accounts, ordered restoration to the trust of $114,314.18, representing amounts erroneously distributed to Florence R. Flynn plus Massachusetts income taxes paid on those amounts from trust funds, together with interest thereon in the sum of $104,847.17 through March 31, 1973, and interest thereafter at the rate of six percent per annum to the date of restoration in full. . . .

The issues before us have to do with the power of the Probate Court judge to order the revocation of the decrees allowing the twelfth through thirty-third accounts, and the propriety of charging the bank for the amounts erroneously disbursed. . . .

The bank recited in the heading of each of the challenged accounts that the trust was "for the benefit of Florence R. Troland," and stated in schedule E of each account (in the first four accounts specifically as "Distributions to Beneficiary") that monthly payments of $225 or more were made to "Florence R. Troland." The Appeals Court held that these recitals and statements "constituted a continuing representation by the bank to the academy and to the court that the widow remained 'Florence R. Troland' despite her (then unknown) remarriage to Flynn, and that she remained the sole income beneficiary of the trust." . . . The court further held that those representations were technically fraudulent in that "[t]hey were made as of the bank's own knowledge when the bank had no such knowledge and had made absolutely no effort to obtain it." . . . With these views we find ourselves substantially in accord.

The doctrine of constructive or technical fraud in this Commonwealth is of venerable origin. As we pointed out in Powell v. Rasmussen, 355 Mass. 117, 118-119, 243 N.E.2d 167 (1969), the doctrine here was developed in two opinions by Chief Justice Shaw. In Hazard v. Irwin, 18 Pick. 95, 109 (1836), it was defined in the following terms: "[W]here the subject matter is one of fact, in respect to which a person can have precise and accurate knowledge, and . . . he speaks as of his own knowledge, and has no such knowledge, his affirmation is essentially false." This rule was reiterated by Chief Justice Shaw in Page v. Bent, 2 Met. 371, 374 (1841): "The principle is well settled, that if a person make a representation of a fact, as of his own knowledge, in relation to a subject matter susceptible of knowledge, and such representation is not true; if the party to whom it is made relies and acts upon it, as true, and sustains damage by it, it is fraud and deceit, for which the party making it is responsible." In this case the marital status of Mrs. Troland/Flynn was a fact susceptible of precise knowledge, the bank made representations concerning this fact of its own knowledge when it had no such knowledge, and the academy to whom the representations were made relied on them to its detriment. While this standard of fraud in law has been developed primarily in the context of actions seeking rescission of contracts and of tort actions for deceit, we have indicated in past decisions that an analogous standard might be applicable to misrepresentations in the accounts of fiduciaries. See Greene v. Springfield Safe Deposit & Trust Co., 295 Mass. 148, 152, 3 N.E.2d 254 (1936); Welch v. Flory, 294 Mass. 138, 142-143, 200 N.E. 900 (1936); Brigham v. Morgan, 185 Mass. 27, 39-40, 69 N.E. 418 (1904). We hold today that "fraud" as used in G. L. c. 206, §24, contemplates this standard of constructive fraud at least to the extent that the fiduciary has made no reasonable efforts to ascertain the true state of the facts it has misrepresented in the accounts. This rule is not a strict liability standard, nor does it make a trustee an insurer against the active fraud of all parties dealing with the trust. Entries in the accounts honestly made, after reasonable efforts to determine the truth or falsity of the representations therein have failed through no fault of the trustee, will not be deemed fraudulent or provide grounds for reopening otherwise properly allowed accounts. However, in the instant case the probate judge found that the bank, through the twenty-two years covered by the disputed accounts, exerted "no effort at all . . . to ascertain if Florence R. Troland had remarried even to the extent of annually requesting a statement or certificate from her to that effect" and that "in administering the trust acted primarily in a ministerial manner and in disregard of its duties as a trustee to protect the terms of the trust." In these circumstances we have little trouble in concluding that the bank's representations as to the marital status of the testator's widow fully justified the reopening of the accounts.

Cases relied on by the bank in which this court refused to allow previously allowed accounts to be reopened are distinguishable in that either they did not involve representations of fact susceptible of precise knowledge but rather questions of judgment and discretion as to matters fully and frankly disclosed in the accounts ... or that the alleged wrongful acts or mistakes of the trustee were discernible from an examination of the accounts, the trust documents and the law.... We adhere to our decisions that it is the duty of beneficiaries "to study the account presented to the Probate Court by the trustee, and to make their objections at the hearing." Greene v. Springfield Safe Deposit & Trust Co., supra, 295 Mass. at 154, 3 N.E.2d at 257. However, in this case the fact of the widow's remarriage was not discernible from the most scrupulous examination of the accounts, the trust documents and the relevant law, and the bank cannot avoid responsibility here for its misrepresentations by alleging a breach of duty on the part of the academy.

As to the propriety of surcharging the bank for the amounts erroneously disbursed, when a trustee makes payment to a person other than the beneficiary entitled to receive the money, he is liable to the proper beneficiary to make restitution unless the payment was authorized by a proper court.... Since, as we have held the decrees allowing the twelfth through thirty-third accounts were revoked properly, the bank thus became liable to the academy to restore to the trust corpus the payments it made to Mrs. Troland/Flynn when she was not entitled to receive them. In addition to the amounts erroneously disbursed, the bank was also properly charged by the Probate Court judge with simple interest on those payments at the legal rate of six percent per annum....

[T]he decree is affirmed.

NOTE AND QUESTION

1. In order to avoid expensive accountings, provisions are often inserted in a trust instrument providing that judicial accountings should be dispensed with and accounts rendered periodically to the adult income beneficiaries of the trust. In the case of testamentary trusts, a few courts have indicated that a testator will not be permitted to dispense with statutorily required accountings.[8] In the case of inter

---

8. New York courts in particular have had a negative attitude toward "no judicial accounting" provisions. See In re Estates of Brush, 46 Misc. 2d 277, 259 N.Y.S.2d 390 (Sur. Ct. 1965).

vivos trusts, which are not placed under judicial supervision by statute, it would appear that a "no judicial accounting" provision does not contravene public policy. But here again, at least in New York, such a provision may run into trouble. In In re Crane, 34 N.Y.S.2d 9 (Sup. Ct. 1942), aff'd, 266 A.D. 726, 41 N.Y.S.2d 940 (1943), an irrevocable inter vivos trust provided: "The written acceptance of the beneficiary entitled to income of the correctness of any account rendered by the Trustee shall constitute a final and complete discharge to said Trustee in respect of the matters covered by such account." This clause was held not to divest the remaindermen of their right to question the actions of the trustee. The court said:

> It does not seem conscionable to me to hold that the life tenant, who enjoys merely the income and who does not own or directly control the principal, should be permitted to be placed in an immunized position where she might possibly squander, or indirectly control, principal, and thus not only cheat the remaindermen but flagrantly frustrate the settlor's intention. The possibilities for collusion are too obvious and manifold. The opportunities for squeezing every penny of income from the principal so as to shrink the principal — by fair means or foul — to the serious detriment of the vested remaindermen, are so manifest that, unless compelled by mandatory language, the opportunities should not be sanctioned or emboldened. Rather, equity should, I think, barricade the door against the possibilities. [Id. at 14.]

This reasoning is criticized by David Westfall, Nonjudicial Settlement of Trustees' Accounts, 71 Harv. L. Rev. 40, 61 (1957). Professor Westfall argues that if the income beneficiaries can be given a power of appointment that diminishes or destroys the remainder, there is no reason to refuse to give effect to a clause permitting the income beneficiary to absolve the trustee from further accountability. Westfall also contends that public policy does not require the protection of remaindermen when the settlor has implicitly withheld protection.

In Briggs v. Crowley, 352 Mass. 194, 224 N.E.2d 417 (1967), the court held that the clauses in an inter vivos trust instrument purporting to relieve the trustees of the duty to account to anyone were invalid as against public policy insofar as they purported to deprive a court of jurisdiction and the petitioner of standing to require the trustees to show that they had faithfully performed their duties.

2. *O* transfers property to *X* in trust to pay the income to *A* for life, remainder to *A*'s children. *A* is now 42 years old, is not married, and has no issue. To avoid expense, chargeable against the trust assets, *A* seeks to have the trustee account nonjudicially to her, agreeing to indemnify the trustee against any objections to its administration subsequently made by the remaindermen. Should the trustee agree to this?

SECTION B.   POWERS OF THE TRUSTEE

In the absence of legislation, the administrative powers of a trustee are derived exclusively from the instrument creating the trust. There are supposedly no "inherent" powers in a trustee; the task of management differs from that of an executor, who has inherent powers to collect the decedent's property, pay debts, and distribute the property to the beneficiaries. The task of a trustee is to carry out the settlor's intent, which varies from trust to trust.

Although a trustee's administrative powers are to be ascertained initially from the trust instrument, a trustee is not limited to powers expressly conferred. Certain powers may be implied as necessary to accomplish the purposes of the trust. Under proper circumstances, a court of equity can confer powers on a trustee not expressly or impliedly provided in the trust instrument; a deviation from the terms of the trust may be permitted when, because of circumstances not known to the settlor and not anticipated, failure to grant relief would substantially impair the accomplishment of the purposes of the trust.

Having in mind the uncertainty of trustees' powers, legislatures in a large majority of states have enacted legislation to broaden trustees' powers. This legislation has usually taken one of two forms:

(a)   An act permits the settlor to *incorporate by express reference* in the trust instrument all or some enumerated statutory powers similar to those found in Uniform Trustees' Powers Act §3(c) below. This permits a trust drafter to omit a long and detailed list of trustee powers, incorporating the statutory powers instead.

(b)   A broad trustees' powers act *grants to trustees basic powers* set forth in the statute, as exemplified by Uniform Trustees' Powers Act §3(c). Express incorporation of statutory powers in the trust instrument is unnecessary under this type of statute.

Uniform Trustees' Powers Act (1964)

§3.   [POWERS OF TRUSTEES CONFERRED BY THIS ACT]

(a) From time of creation of the trust until final distribution of the assets of the trust, a trustee has the power to perform, without court authorization, every act which a prudent man would perform for the purposes of the trust including but not limited to the powers specified in subsection (c).

(b) . . .

(c) A trustee has the power, subject to subsections (a) and (b):

(1) to collect, hold, and retain trust assets received from a trustor until, in the judgment of the trustee, disposition of the assets should be made; and the assets may be retained even though they include an asset in which the trustee is personally interested;

(2) to receive additions to the assets of the trust;

(3) to continue or participate in the operation of any business or other enterprise, and to effect incorporation, dissolution, or other change in the form of the organization of the business or enterprise;

(4) to acquire an undivided interest in a trust asset in which the trustee, in any trust capacity, holds an undivided interest;

(5) to invest and reinvest trust assets in accordance with the provisions of the trust or as provided by law;

(6) to deposit trust funds in a bank, including a bank operated by the trustee;

(7) to acquire or dispose of an asset, for cash or on credit, at public or private sale; and to manage, develop, improve, exchange, partition, change the character of, or abandon a trust asset or any interest therein; and to encumber, mortgage, or pledge a trust asset for a term within or extending beyond the term of the trust, in connection with the exercise of any power vested in the trustee;

(8) to make ordinary or extraordinary repairs or alterations in buildings or other structures, to demolish any improvements, to raze existing or erect new party walls or buildings;

(9) to subdivide, develop, or dedicate land to public use; or to make or obtain the vacation of plats and adjust boundaries; or to adjust differences in valuation on exchange or partition by giving or receiving consideration; or to dedicate easements to public use without consideration;

(10) to enter for any purpose into a lease as lessor or lessee with or without option to purchase or renew for a term within or extending beyond the term of the trust;

(11) to enter into a lease or arrangement for exploration and removal of minerals or other natural resources or enter into a pooling or unitization agreement;

(12) to grant an option involving disposition of a trust asset, or to take an option for the acquisition of any asset;

(13) to vote a security, in person or by general or limited proxy;

(14) to pay calls, assessments, and any other sums chargeable or accruing against or on account of securities;

(15) to sell or exercise stock subscription or conversion rights; to consent, directly or through a committee or other agent, to the reorganization, consolidation, merger, dissolution, or liquidation of a corporation or other business enterprise;

(16) to hold a security in the name of a nominee or in other

form without disclosure of the trust, so that title to the security may pass by delivery, but the trustee is liable for any act of the nominee in connection with the stock so held;

(17) to insure the assets of the trust against damage or loss, and the trustee against liability with respect to third persons;

(18) to borrow money to be repaid from trust assets or otherwise; to advance money for the protection of the trust, and for all expenses, losses, and liabilities sustained in the administration of the trust or because of the holdings or ownership of any trust assets, for which advances with any interest the trustee has a lien on the trust assets as against the beneficiary;

(19) to pay or contest any claim; to settle a claim by or against the trust by compromise, arbitration, or otherwise; and to release, in whole or in part, any claim belonging to the trust to the extent that the claim is uncollectible;

(20) to pay taxes, assessments, compensation of the trustee, and other expenses incurred in the collection, care, administration, and protection of the trust;

(21) to allocate items of income or expense to either trust income or principal, as provided by law, including creation of reserves out of income for depreciation, obsolescence, or amortization, or for depletion in mineral or timber properties;

(22) to pay any sum distributable to a beneficiary under legal disability, without liability to the trustee, by paying the sum to the beneficiary or by paying the sum for the use of the beneficiary either to a legal representative appointed by the court, or if none, to a relative;

(23) to effect distribution of property and money in divided or undivided interests and to adjust resulting differences in valuation;

(24) to employ persons, including attorneys, auditors, investment advisors, or agents, even if they are associated with the trustee, to advise or assist the trustee in the performance of his administrative duties; to act without independent investigation upon their recommendations; and instead of acting personally, to employ one or more agents to perform any act of administration, whether or not discretionary;

(25) to prosecute or defend actions, claims, or proceedings for the protection of trust assets and of the trustee in the performance of his duties;

(26) to execute and deliver all instruments which will accomplish or facilitate the exercise of the powers vested in the trustee.

NOTES

1. Uniform Trust Act §815 (1999 draft) grants trustees the broadest possible powers appropriate to accomplish the proper manage-

ment, investment, and distribution of the trust property. Section 816 lists specific powers similar to powers listed in §3 of the Uniform Trustees' Powers Act (1964).

2.   A trustee has a duty to investigate the market value of land before offering it for sale. This may require independent appraisal of the property or "testing the market" to determine what a willing buyer would pay. See Allard v. Pacific National Bank, 99 Wash. 2d 394, 663 P.2d 104 (1983) (also holding trustee liable for failing to inform beneficiaries of impending sale, giving them an opportunity to bid on the property); In re Green Charitable Trust, 172 Mich. App. 298, 431 N.W.2d 492 (1988) (surcharging trustees $1.9 million for failing to make adequate efforts to determine the property's value before sale).

Uniform Trustees' Powers Act (1964)

§7.   [THIRD PERSONS PROTECTED IN DEALING WITH TRUSTEE]

With respect to a third person dealing with a trustee or assisting a trustee in the conduct of a transaction, the existence of trust power[s] and their proper exercise by a trustee may be assumed without inquiry. The third person is not bound to inquire whether the trustee has power to act or is properly exercising the power; and a third person, without actual knowledge that the trustee is exceeding his powers or improperly exercising them, is fully protected in dealing with the trustee as if the trustee possessed and properly exercised the powers he purports to exercise. A third person is not bound to assure the proper application of trust assets paid or delivered to the trustee.

Uniform Trustees' Powers Act §7 provides unusually broad protection for third persons who deal with the trustee. A third person is protected unless he has actual knowledge of the trustee's breach. The common law requires third persons dealing with a trustee to inquire into the propriety of the transaction. The third party is charged with knowledge of the information a diligent inquiry would have uncovered. UTPA §7 eliminates the duty of inquiry and good faith with the purpose of facilitating trust administration efficiency in transferring trust property. For eliminating the duty of inquiry, §7 is criticized in Peter T. Wendel, Examining the Mystery Behind the Unusually and Inexplicably Broad Provisions of Section Seven of the Uniform Trustees' Powers Act: A Call for Clarification, 56 Mo. L. Rev. 25 (1991).

See also Uniform Trust Act §1109 (1999 draft), tracking fairly closely UTPA §7.

PROBLEMS

1. *T* devises Blackacre to *X* in trust with power to sell Blackacre if *X* decides that such sale is necessary to raise money for the support of *A*. *X* sells Blackacre to *B*, who has notice of the trust (*T*'s will is recorded) but believes that the sale is necessary for the support of *A*, although in fact it is not necessary. Does *B* take Blackacre free of trust? See 2 Restatement (Second) of Trusts §297, Illustration 4 (1959). Would the result be different if the trust were an inter vivos trust of which *B* had no notice?

2. *X*, as trustee, has no power to invest in nonincome-producing property. *X* buys from *A* desert land, which produces no income. Must *A* refund the purchase price upon demand of the beneficiary? See 4 Austin W. Scott, Trusts §321.1 (William F. Fratcher 4th ed. 1988).

3. *X* is a co-trustee with *Y* of Whiteacre. *X* and *Y* have the power to sell Whiteacre; they sell it to *A*. *A* pays the purchase price to *Y* alone without the consent of *X*, and *Y* misappropriates the money. Can *A* be compelled to pay again? See Coxe v. Kriebel, 323 Pa. 157, 185 A. 770, 106 A.L.R. 102 (1936).

SECTION C.   INVESTMENT OF TRUST FUNDS

John H. Langbein & Richard A. Posner, Market Funds and
Trust Investment Law
1976 Am. B. Found. Res. J. 1, 3-6 (1976)

I.   THE DEVELOPMENT OF THE LAW GOVERNING THE TRUSTEE'S INVESTMENT POWERS

In 1719 the British Parliament authorized trustees to invest in the shares of the South Sea Company. The South Sea "Bubble" burst the next year, share prices fell by 90 percent, and "public confidence in joint stock companies and their securities was destroyed"[9] for the rest of the eighteenth century.

In the period of reaction to the Bubble the standard of prudence

9. Laurence C.B. Gower, The Principles of Modern Company Law 31 (3d ed. London, 1969).

in trust investment acquired three notable characteristics. First, the Court of Chancery developed a "court-list" of presumptively proper investment. The courts "repeatedly decided" that "the trustee would be free from liability if he invested . . . in Government three per cent stock [i.e., bonds]."[10] Some chancellors recognized "well-secured" first mortgages on realty as appropriate, although others questioned them well into the nineteenth century. Statutes extended the categories of presumptively proper investments. Lord St. Leonard's Act added East India stock to the court list and confirmed mortgage investments, "provided that such Investment shall in other respects be reasonable and proper."[11] Successive Parliaments added various local and colonial government issues, and in 1889 certain railway debentures and preferred stocks. Most American jurisdictions maintained similar statutory lists into the 1940s, and a variety survive to this day.

Second, because investments not on the list were improper unless authorized in the trust instrument, England and many American jurisdictions forbade all trust investment in the securities of private enterprises until late in the nineteenth century, and greatly restricted such investments thereafter. Even today, the constitutions of Alabama and Montana forbid their legislatures to authorize trust investment in corporate issues.

Third, trust-investment law developed a preoccupation with the preservation of the corpus (principal) of the trust. In the words of a leading case, "the primary object to be attained by a trustee in the matter of investing the funds confided to his control is their safety."[12] Even in Massachusetts, which had a general "prudent investor" rule rather than court or statutory lists and which permitted investment in corporate securities, it was emphasized that the rule "eschews the exuberance of the speculator."[13]

What emerged, in short, was an emphasis on "safe" investments, a category dominated in the mind of the judges and legislators by long-term fixed-return obligations such as mortgages and bonds. This approach to investment by trustees may have made sense in the eighteenth and nineteenth centuries in light of two facts which are not true today. First, the capital markets were relatively undeveloped and the opportunities to make passive, reasonably liquid investments in common stock were therefore limited. Second, there was relatively little inflation in the eighteenth and nineteenth centuries. Although the interest rate on a fixed-income security will include the anticipated rate of inflation, the investor bears the risk — which in an

---

10. George W. Keeton, The Law of Trusts 248 (9th ed. London, 1968).
11. 22 & 23 Vict., c. 35, sec. 32 (1859).
12. In re Estate of Cook, 20 Del. Ch. 123, 125, 171 A. 730 (1934), cited in 3 Scott, Trusts sec. 227, at 1807.
13. Kimball v. Whitney, 233 Mass. 321, 331, 123 N.E. 665, 666 (1919).

inflationary period is substantial for long-term instruments — that the actual rate of inflation will turn out to be higher than the anticipated rate.

The law of trusts has been adjusting to changing conditions, but slowly. The English still have a statutory list; only in 1961 was it amended to permit half of the trust corpus to be invested in equities. Under pressure from the American Bankers Association, the majority of our states have since 1940 enacted the Model Prudent Man Investment Act, and others have reached a similar position through independent legislation or court decision. The Model Act, which follows Massachusetts law, dispenses with both the statutory list and the prohibition on investment in corporate issues. But it forbids investment "for the purpose of speculation" and directs trustees to consider "the probable income, as well as the probable safety, of their capital." Thus the position of the modern American law is that equities may be prudent investments if they are not "speculative," whatever that means.

England and the various American jurisdictions would not have clung to the traditional standards for such a long time had those standards been mandatory. Because trust settlors can vary the otherwise applicable law, lawyers and corporate fiduciaries have fitted most trust instruments with permissive investment powers. For most of the present century, therefore, the law has imposed the traditional standards largely on the beneficiaries of those trust settlors who failed to hire competent counsel.

Nevertheless, those standards continue to haunt even the most carefully drafted professional trust instruments. The courts have tended to construe grants of investment discretion in trust instruments narrowly. The settlor, it is said, could not have meant to authorize "speculation" with his property when he granted the trustee discretion in the choice of investments.[14] The reviewing court sits in judgment on the trustee with the aid of perfect hindsight,[15] a vantage point from which the temptation to characterize a disappointing investment as "speculative" and to surcharge the trustee may be irresistible. In this way the ancient preoccupation with safety of corpus, designed to protect trust beneficiaries from a recurrence of the South Sea Bubble, continues to supply trust law with its notions of prudence.

---

14. See 3 Scott, Trusts secs. 227.14, 233.5, at 1848-1854, 1933.

15. For an absurd example see In re Chamberlain's Estate, 9 N.J. Misc. 809, 810, 156 A. 42, 43 (1931), where the court, writing in 1931, declared: "It was common knowledge, not only amongst bankers and trust companies, but the general public as well, that the stock market condition at the time . . . [August 1929] was an unhealthy one, that values were very much inflated, and that a crash was almost sure to occur."

Estate of Collins
California Court of Appeal, Second District, 1977
72 Cal. App. 3d 663, 139 Cal. Rptr. 644

KAUS, J. Objectors ("plaintiffs") are beneficiaries under a testamentary trust established in the will of Ralph Collins, deceased. Carl Lamb and C. E. Millikan ("defendants") were, respectively, Collins' business partner and lawyer. They were named in Collins' will as trustees. In 1973 defendants filed a petition for an order approving and settling the first and final account and discharging the trustees. Plaintiffs objected on grounds that defendants had improperly invested $50,000 and requested that defendants be surcharged. After a hearing, the trial court ruled in favor of defendants, and approved the account, terminated the trust, and discharged the trustees. Plaintiff beneficiaries have appealed. . . .

The primary beneficiaries under the testamentary trust were Collins' wife and children; his mother and father were also named as beneficiaries. General support provisions were included; the will also specifically provided that the trustees pay his daughter $4,000 a year for five years for her undergraduate and graduate education.

The will authorized the trustees to purchase "every kind of property, real, personal or mixed, and every kind of investment, specifically including, but not by way of limitation, corporate obligations of every kind, and stocks, preferred or common, irrespective of whether said investments are in accordance with the laws then enforced in the State of California pertaining to the investment of trust funds by corporate trustees."

The will also provided:

> Unless specifically limited, all discretions conferred upon the Trustee shall be absolute, and their exercise conclusive on all persons interest[ed] in this trust. The enumeration of certain powers of the Trustee shall not limit its general powers, the Trustee, subject always to the discharge of its fiduciary obligations, being vested with and having all the rights, powers and privileges which an absolute owner of the same property would have.

Collins died in 1963 and his will was admitted to probate. In June 1965, the court ordered the estate to be distributed. After various other payments and distributions, defendant trustees received about $80,000 as the trust principal. After other distributions, such as the annual $4,000 payment for the education of Collins' daughter, the trustees had about $50,000 available for investment.

Defendant Millikan's clients included two real property developers, Downing and Ward. In March 1965, Millikan filed an action on behalf of Downing and Ward against a lender who refused to honor a commitment to carry certain construction loans. In June 1965, defendants learned that Downing and Ward wanted to borrow $50,000. Millikan knew that the builders wanted the loan because of their difficulties with the lender who had withdrawn its loan commitment.

The loan would be secured by a second trust deed to 9.38 acres of unimproved real property in San Bernardino County near Upland. This property was subject to a $90,000 first trust deed; the note which secured the first trust deed was payable in quarterly installments of interest only, and due in full in three years, that is, in July 1968. The $50,000 loan to be made by defendants would be payable in monthly installments of interest only, at ten percent interest with the full amount due in 30 months, that is, in January 1968.

Defendants knew that the property had been sold two years earlier in 1963 for $107,000. Defendants checked with two real estate brokers in the area, one of whom said that property in that area was selling for $18,000 to $20,000 an acre. They did not have the property appraised, they did not check with the county clerk or recorder in either Los Angeles or San Bernardino County to determine whether there were foreclosures or lawsuits pending against the construction company. In fact, when defendants made the loan in July 1965, there were six notices of default and three lawsuits pending against Downing and Ward.

Defendants obtained and reviewed an unaudited company financial statement. This statement indicated that the Downing and Ward Company had a net worth in excess of $2,000,000.

Downing and Ward told defendants that they were not in default on any of their loans, that they were not defendants in any pending litigation, and that there had never been any liens filed on any of their projects. Defendants phoned the bank with whom Downing and Ward had a line of credit and learned that the bank had a satisfactory relationship with the builders.

Based on this information, on July 23, 1965, defendants lent Downing and Ward $50,000 on the terms described above. In addition to the second trust deed, Downing and Ward pledged 20 percent of the stock in their company as security. However, defendants neither obtained possession of the stock, placed it in escrow, nor placed a legend on the stock certificates. Defendants also obtained the personal guarantees of Downing and Ward and their wives. However, defendants did not obtain financial statements from the guarantors.

When the loan was made in July 1965, construction in the Upland area was, as the trial court said, "enjoying boom times, although the bubble was to burst just a few months later." From July 1965 through September 1966, the builders made the monthly interest payments required by the note. In October 1966, Downing & Ward Construction Corporation was placed in involuntary bankruptcy and thereafter Mr. and Mrs. Ward and Mr. and Mrs. Downing declared personal bankruptcies. Defendants foreclosed their second trust deed in June 1967, and became the owners of the unimproved real property. They spent $10,000 in an unsuccessful effort to salvage the investment by forestalling foreclosure by the holder of the first trust deed. In September 1968, the holder of the first trust deed did foreclose. This extinguished the trustees' interest in the property and the entire investment. In short, about $60,000 of the trust fund was lost.

The trial court made findings of fact and drew conclusions of law. As relevant, the court found that defendant trustees "exercised the judgment and care, under the circumstances then prevailing, which men of prudence, discretion and intelligence exercised in the management of their own affairs, not in regard to speculation, but in regard to the disposition of their funds, considering the probable income, as well as the probable safety of their capital."[16] In making the loan, "the cotrustees used reasonable care, diligence and skill. The cotrustees did not act arbitrarily or in bad faith." . . .

The trial court's finding that defendants exercised the judgment and care "which men of prudence, discretion and intelligence exercised in the management of their own affairs," reflects the standard imposed upon trustees by Civil Code section 2261. (See also, Rest. 2d Trusts, §227 ["Restatement"].)

Plaintiffs contend, and we agree, that contrary to the trial court's findings and conclusions, defendants failed to follow the "prudent investor" standard, first, by investing two-thirds of the trust principal in a single investment, second, by investing in real property secured only by a second deed of trust, and third, by making that investment without adequate investigation of either the borrowers or the collateral.

Although California does not limit the trustee's authority to a list of authorized investments, relying instead on the prudent investor rule (see 7 Witkin, Summary of Cal. Law (8th ed.) Trusts, §63, p.5424), nevertheless, the prudent investor rule encompasses certain guidelines applicable to this case.

First, "the trustee is under a duty to the beneficiary to distribute the risk of loss by reasonable diversification of investments, unless under the circumstances it is prudent not to do so." (Rest., §228. . . .)

Second, ordinarily, "second or other junior mortgages are not proper trust investments," unless taking a second mortgage is a reasonable method of settling a claim or making possible the sale of property. (Rest., §227, p.533.) Stated more emphatically:

16. This language is taken almost verbatim from Harvard College v. Amory, 26 Mass. (9 Pick.) 446, 461 (1830), which laid down the "prudent man" rule, referred to in this case as the "prudent investor" rule. Usually the latter term refers to the newly reformulated investor rule adopted by the Restatement (Third) of Trusts (1992), infra page 967, and by the Uniform Prudent Investor Act (1994), infra page 969, and now widely adopted. — Eds.

While loans secured by second mortgages on land are sometimes allowed, they are almost always disapproved by courts of equity. The trustee should not place the trust funds in a position where they may be endangered by the foreclosure of a prior lien. . . . In rare cases equity will sanction an investment secured by a second mortgage, but only when the security is adequate and unusual circumstances justify the trustee in taking this form of investment. (Bogert, Trusts & Trustees (2d ed.) §675, p.274.)

Third, in "buying a mortgage for trust investment, the trustee should give careful attention to the valuation of the property, in order to make certain that his margin of security is adequate. He must use every reasonable endeavor to provide protection which will cover the risks of depreciation in the property and changes in price levels. And he must investigate the status of the property and of the mortgage, as well as the financial situation of the mortgagor." (Bogert, supra, §674, at p.267.) Similarly, the Restatement rule is that "the trustee cannot properly lend on a mortgage upon real property more than a reasonable proportion of the value of the mortgage property." (Sec. 229.)

We think it apparent that defendants violated every applicable rule. First, they failed totally to diversify the investments in this relatively small trust fund. Second, defendants invested in a junior mortgage on unimproved real property, and left an inadequate margin of security. As noted, the land had most recently sold for $107,000, and was subject to a first trust deed of $90,000. Thus, unless the land was worth more than $140,000, there was no margin of security at all. Defendants did not have the land appraised; the only information they had was the opinion of a real estate broker that property in the area — not that particular parcel — was going for $18,000 to $20,000 an acre. Thus, any assumption that the property was worth about $185,000 — and therefore the $140,000 in loans were well-secured — would have been little more than a guess.

Third, the backup security obtained by defendants was no security at all. The builders pledged 20 percent of their stock, but defendants never obtained possession of the stock, placed it in escrow or even had it legended. They accepted the personal guarantees of the builders and their wives without investigating the financial status of these persons. They accepted at face value the claimed $2,000,000 value of the company shown in an unaudited statement. Defendant Millikan apparently ignored the fact that one lender had, for whatever reasons, reneged on a loan commitment to the builders.

Defendants contend that the evidence sustains the trial court's findings that they exercised the judgment and care under the circumstances then prevailing expected of men of prudence. They rely on the rule that the determination whether an investment was proper must be made in light of the circumstances existing at the time of the investment. (E.g., Witkin, supra, §63, p.5425.) That rule does not help defendants. Nothing that happened after the loan was made can change the fact that defendants invested two-thirds of the principal of the trust in a single second deed of trust on unappraised property, with no knowledge of the borrowers' true financial status, and without any other security. . . .

Defendants alternatively contend that the trust instrument conferred "absolute discretion" on them as trustees, and that the prudent-investor standard did not apply to their conduct. Rather, the only question is whether the trustee avoided arbitrary action and used his best judgment. (Coberly v. Superior Court (1965) 231 Cal. App. 2d 685, 689, 42 Cal. Rptr. 64.)

We leave aside the question whether even a trustee with "absolute discretion" would be permitted to make this kind of investment, consistent with the rule that an absolute discretion does not permit a "trustee to neglect its trust or abdicate its judgment." (Coberly, supra, at p.689, 42 Cal. Rptr. at p.67.) The instrument in this case conferred no such absolute discretion.

Defendants rely particularly on the rule that the prudent investor standard does not apply where the settlor himself specifies that the trustees of his trust are not limited by what the law provides are proper investments. (E.g., Stanton v. Wells Fargo Bank, etc. Co. (1957) 150 Cal. App. 2d 763, 777, 310 P.2d 1010.) Their reliance on that rule is misplaced.

First, the provision in the trust instrument to purchase every kind of property and make every kind of investment "irrespective of whether said investments are in accordance with the laws then enforced in the State of California pertaining to the investment of trust funds by corporate trustees" does not authorize the trustees to make improper investments.

Neither Civil Code section 2261 nor any other authority which we can locate authorizes different types of investments for "corporate trustees" and for amateur trustees. The difference, rather, is that the corporate trustee is held to a greater standard of care based on his presumed expertise. . . . Thus, defendants might have been protected by that clause had they deviated in some respects from the general rules — for example, had they accepted a well-secured second trust deed, or possibly had they accepted a first trust deed without careful investigation. Here, however, defendants did nothing right. Second, the "absolute discretion" in the trust instrument is "specifically limited" by the requirement that the trustee is "subject always to the discharge of its fiduciary obligations. . . ."

In conclusion, the evidence does not support the trial court's conclusion that defendants acted properly in investing $50,000 in the property.

Reversed.

NOTES AND QUESTION

1. *Exculpatory clauses.* Exculpatory (or exoneration) clauses have been strictly construed by the courts. See Hatcher v. United States National Bank of Oregon, 56 Or. App. 643, 643 P.2d 359 (1982); Note, Directory Trusts and the Exculpatory Clause, 65 Colum. L. Rev. 138 (1965). They will not be given effect if the result is to allow a fiduciary to act in bad faith or with reckless indifference to the interests of the beneficiaries. See Rippey v. Denver United States National Bank, 273 F. Supp. 718 (D. Colo. 1967) (holding trustee liable for selling stock to an interested third party without first testing the market).

New York Est., Powers & Trusts Law §11-1.7(a) (1998) provides:

> The attempted grant to an executor or testamentary trustee, or the successor of either, of any of the following enumerated powers or immunities is contrary to public policy:
>
> (1) The exoneration of such fiduciary from liability for failure to exercise reasonable care, diligence and prudence.
>
> (2) The power to make a binding and conclusive fixation of the value of any asset for purposes of distribution, allocation or otherwise.

Note that the New York statute does not apply to inter vivos trusts, in which exoneration provisions may protect a trustee from liability absent recklessness, fraud, or intentional wrongdoing. See Stark v. United States Trust Co. of New York, 445 F. Supp. 670, 683 (S.D.N.Y. 1978).

2. In Witmer v. Blair, 588 S.W.2d 222 (Mo. App. 1979), the testator, dying in 1960, named his niece Jane as trustee for the education of his granddaughter Marguerite, age 7. Jane had no experience as a trustee and for ten years kept $6,000 (about half of the trust assets) in a checking account. She did this, she said, so that she could withdraw the money quickly if Marguerite needed it for college. The court held that failure to invest this sum before Marguerite became of college age was a breach of trust and that Jane was liable for the amount of interest that could have been earned on the money in the checking account. Jane's good faith and inexperience were not a defense.

Was this a safe investment? What risks did the trustee take? How should the trustee diversify assets worth $12,000?

3. For an excellent discussion of how the prudent man rule became a constraint on sound investing, by forbidding various practices, see Jeffrey N. Gordon, The Puzzling Persistence of the Constrained Prudent Man Rule, 62 N.Y.U. L. Rev. 52 (1987). See also Comment, The Prudent Person Rule: A Shield for the Professional Trustee, 45 Baylor L. Rev. 933 (1993).

4. Restatement (Second) of Trusts §228 (1959) requires the trustee to diversify investments, "unless under the circumstances it is prudent not to do so." This duty is continued in Restatement (Third) of Trusts §227 (1992). The purpose of diversification is to minimize risks that one investment will not do well because of factors connected with that investment; diversification leaves a portfolio subject only to the risks of the market falling or rising. See In re Estate of Janes, 90 N.Y.2d 41, 681 N.E.2d 332, 659 N.Y.S.2d 165 (1997) (surcharging trustee for maintaining a stock portfolio received from the settlor in which Eastman Kodak stock represented 71 percent and failing to diversify).

In some states diversification is not required under the prudent man rule. See Malachowski v. Bank One, Indianapolis, 590 N.E.2d 559 (Ind. 1992) (beneficiaries have cause of action against bank trustee, where trust funded solely with Eli Lilly stock, for selling some Lilly stock to diversify when sales resulted in sizeable taxable capital gains and proceeds were invested in bank's common trust funds, increasing bank's fees).

Uniform Prudent Investor Act (1994)

§3.   DIVERSIFICATION

A trustee shall diversify the investments of the trust unless the trustee reasonably determines that, because of special circumstances, the purposes of the trust are better served without diversifying.

COMMENT

Rationale for diversification. "Diversification reduces risk ... [because] stock price movements are not uniform. They are imperfectly correlated. This means that if one holds a well diversified portfolio, the gains in one investment will cancel out the losses in another." Jonathan R. Macey, An Introduction to Modern Financial Theory 20 (American College of Trust and Estate Counsel Foundation, 1991). For example, during the Arab oil embargo of 1973, international oil stocks suffered declines, but the shares of domestic oil producers and coal companies benefitted. Holding a broad enough portfolio allowed the investor to set off, to some extent, the losses associated with the embargo.

Modern portfolio theory divides risk into the categories of "compensated" and "uncompensated" risk. The risk of owning shares in a mature and well-managed company in a settled industry is less than the risk of owning shares in a start-up high-technology venture. The investor requires a higher expected return to induce the investor to bear the greater risk of disappointment associated with the start-up firm. This is compensated risk — the firm pays the investor for bearing the risk. By contrast, nobody pays the investor for owning too few stocks. The investor who owned only international oils in 1973 was running a risk that could have been reduced by having configured the portfolio differently — to include investments in different industries. This is uncompensated risk — nobody pays the investor for owning shares in too few industries and too few companies. Risk that can be eliminated by adding different stocks (or bonds) is uncompensated risk. The object of diversification is to minimize this uncompensated risk of having too few investments. "As long as stock prices do not move exactly together, the risk of a diversified portfolio will be less than the average risk of the separate holdings." R. A. Brealey, An Introduction to Risk and Return from Common Stocks 103 (2d ed. 1983).

There is no automatic rule for identifying how much diversification is enough. The 1992 Restatement says: "Significant diversification advantages can be achieved with a small number of well-selected securities representing different industries. . . . Broader diversification is usually to be preferred in trust investing," and pooled investment vehicles "make thorough diversification practical for most trustees." Restatement of Trusts 3d: Prudent Investor Rule §227, General Note and Comments *e-h*, at 77 (1992). See also Macey, supra, at 23-24, Brealey, supra, at 111-13.

Diversifying by pooling. It is difficult for a small trust fund to diversify thoroughly by constructing its own portfolio of individually selected investments. Transaction costs such as the round-lot (100 share) trading economies make it relatively expensive for a small investor to assemble a broad enough portfolio to minimize uncompensated risk. For this reason, pooled investment vehicles have become the main mechanism for facilitating diversification for the investment needs of smaller trusts.

Most states have legislation authorizing common trust funds; see 3 Austin W. Scott & William F. Fratcher, The Law of Trusts §227.9, at 463-65 n.26 (4th ed. 1988) (collecting citations to state statutes). As of 1992, 35 states and the District of Columbia had enacted the Uniform Common Trust Fund Act (UCTFA) (1938), overcoming the rule against commingling trust assets and expressly enabling banks and trust companies to establish common trust funds. 7 Uniform Laws Ann. 1992 Supp. at 130 (schedule of adopting states). The Prefatory Note to the UCTFA explains: "The purposes of such a common or joint investment fund are to diversify the investment of the several trusts and thus spread the risk of loss, and to make it easy to invest any amount of trust funds quickly and with a small amount of trouble." 7 Uniform Laws Ann. 402 (1985).

Fiduciary investing in mutual funds. Trusts can also achieve diversification by investing in mutual funds. See Restatement of Trusts 3d: Prudent Investor Rule, §227, Comment *m*, at 99-100 (1992) (endorsing trust investment in mutual funds). ERISA §401(b)(1), 29 U.S.C. §1101(b)(1), expressly authorizes pension trusts to invest in mutual funds, identified as securities "issued by an investment company registered under the Investment Company Act of 1940...".

Restatement (Third) of Trusts (1992)

TOPIC 5.   INVESTMENT OF TRUST FUNDS

INTRODUCTION

The foundation of trust investment law in the first and second Restatements has been the so-called "prudent man rule" of Harvard College v. Amory, 9 Pick. (26 Mass.) 446, 461 (1830). The opinion admonishes trustees "to observe how men of prudence, discretion and intelligence manage their own affairs, not in regard to speculation, but in regard to the permanent disposition of their funds, considering the probable income, as well as the probable safety of the capital to be invested." Thus, the rule of the Restatement, Second, of Trusts §227 (1959) directs trustees "to make such investments and only such investments as a prudent man would make of his own property having in view the preservation of the estate and the amount and regularity of the income to be derived." In generally similar language, influenced by the original Restatement, the prudent man rule has been adopted by decision or legislation in most American jurisdictions, often displacing the more restrictive, so-called "legal list" statutes.

Unfortunately, much of the apparent and initially intended generality and adaptability of the prudent man rule was lost as it was further elaborated in the courts and applied case by case. Decisions dealing with essentially factual issues were accompanied by generalizations understandably intended to offer guidance to other courts and trustees in like situations. These cases were subsequently treated as precedents establishing general rules governing trust investments. Specific case results and flexible principles often thereby became crystallized into specific subrules prescribing the types and characteristics of permissible investments for trustees.

Based on some degree of risk that was abstractly perceived as excessive, broad categories of investments and techniques often came to be classified as "speculative" and thus as imprudent per se. Accordingly, the exercise of care, skill, and caution would be no defense if the property acquired or retained by a trustee, or the strategy pursued for a trust, was characterized as impermissible.

Knowledge, practices, and experiences in the modern investment world have demonstrated that arbitrary restrictions on trust investments are unwarranted and often counterproductive. For example, understandable concern has existed that widely accepted theories and practices of investment management cannot properly be pursued by trustees under present judicial and treatise statements of the law. Prohibitions that developed under the traditional prudent man rule have been potential sources of unjustified liability for trustees generally and, more particularly, of inhibitions limiting the exercise of sound judgment by skilled trustees. This is particularly so for trustees whose fiduciary circumstances call for, or at least permit, investment programs that would include some high risk-and-return strategies (such as a venture capital program) or for the use of abstractly high-risk investments or techniques (such as futures or option trading) for the purpose of reducing the risk level of the portfolio as a whole.

These criticisms of the prudent man rule are supported by a large and growing body of literature that is in turn supported by empirical research, well documented and essentially compelling. Much but not all of this criticism is found in writings that have collectively and loosely come to be called modern portfolio theory. The need for modernization or at least clarification of the prudent-man rule is also evidenced by recent legislative trends at both federal and state levels. . . .

With modest reformulation of the *Harvard College* dictum and the basic rule of prior Restatements, the prudent investor rule of this Restatement seeks to modernize trust investment law and to restore the generality and flexibility of the original doctrine. The language of the prudent investor rule and the accompanying Comments in §227 are thus intended to preserve the law's adaptability by confining its mandates to those that seem essential to prudence (based on traditional duties of care, skill, and caution), to the protection of fiduciary goals, and to supplying helpful guidance to courts and trustees. The rule's mandates are limited to principles that are supported by general consensus among various theories and that are adaptable to the differences among various trusts, trustees and their needs and objectives.

Principles of prudence. In addition to the fundamental proposition that no investments or techniques are imprudent per se, there are a few principles of prudence set out in the sections that follow. These principles instruct trustees and courts that: (1) sound diversification is fundamental to risk management and is therefore ordinarily required of trustees; (2) risk and return are so directly related that trustees have a duty to analyze and make conscious decisions concerning the levels of risk appropriate to the purposes, distribution requirements, and other circumstances of the trusts they administer; (3) trustees have a duty to avoid fees, transaction costs and other expenses that are not justified by needs and realistic objectives of the trust's investment program; (4) the fiduciary duty of impartiality requires a balancing of the elements of return between production of current income and the protection of purchasing power; and (5) trustees may have a duty as well as having the authority to delegate as prudent investors would.

(1) The first two of these principles are fundamental to risk management. A duty to diversify was included in §228 of prior Restatements but is so central to modern concepts of prudence that it has been incorporated into the prudent investor rule of §227. This pervasive duty and its vital role in minimizing "uncompensated" risk are emphasized in the commentary, not only as a matter of caution but also as a basic aspect of due care and skill.

(2) Although carrying uncompensated risk is ordinarily undesirable, the same cannot so simply be said of risks that are compensated by expectations of increased return. This so-called *market* risk is unavoidable in investing, and fiduciary decisions are therefore concerned with the appropriate degree of that risk. These decisions are an integral part of investment strategy because of the direct relationship between market risk and portfolio return expectations. Thus, the second of the above principles calls for the trustee to make a deliberate assessment and judgment about a suitable level of risk and reward to be pursued in light of the particular trust's return requirements, risk tolerance, general purposes, specific terms, and other pertinent circumstances.

Case law and prior Restatements have condemned "speculation" and excessive risk without definition, as if such risk could be recognized in the abstract without regard to portfolio context and objectives. The prudent investor rule recognizes that investments and courses of action are properly judged not in isolation but on the basis of the roles they are to play in specific trust portfolios and strategies.

(3) Although trustees are entitled to indemnification for reasonable expenses, the duty to avoid unwarranted costs is given increased emphasis in the prudent investor rule. This is done to reflect the importance of market efficiency concepts and differences in the degrees of efficiency and inefficiency in various markets. In addition, this emphasis reflects the availability and continuing emergence of modern investment products, not only with significantly varied characteristics but also with similar products being offered with significantly differing costs. The duty to be cost conscious requires attention to such matters as the cumulation of fiduciary commissions with agent fees or the purchase and management charges associated with mutual funds and other pooled investment vehicles. In addition, active management

strategies involve investigation expenses and other transaction costs (including capital gains taxation) that must be considered, realistically, in relation to the likelihood of increased return from such strategies.

(4) Modern experience with inflation — so different from experience with the value of money in the formative periods of trust investment law — dictates a greater sensitivity in investment management to the competition between the income and principal interests in a trust, or, more broadly, to reflect the needs of both today and tomorrow. In addition, tax consequences within the trust and the tax positions of the various beneficiaries have come to have considerable importance in the management of trust funds, and the trustee's investment decisions often affect different beneficiaries quite differently in this respect. For these reasons trustees must recognize that the traditional insistence on preservation of principal includes a consideration of the real value of corpus and a need to balance this concern against a life beneficiary's typical interest in the production of trust income, with attention to the after-tax worth of each. The prudent investor rule also recognizes that the life beneficiary's concern over trust accounting income is not the same (or even present) in all trusts, and makes clear in any event that this concern focuses on the portfolio as a whole rather than on each investment. Trust purposes, beneficiary circumstances, and family financial objectives will sometimes allow more than an effort to protect purchasing power and thus may justify a deliberate effort to achieve real growth in some trust estates.

(5) The last of the above-stated principles recognizes that, with proper attention to cost concerns, prudent investing may require or at least benefit from expert assistance in investment matters. Thus, the prudent investor rule views delegation from a positive perspective. Nonetheless, the terms and manner of delegation, the competence of agents, and the supervision or monitoring of agents' activities all remain critical aspects of prudence. The need for delegation may be most readily apparent when complicated or challenging investment strategies are pursued by trustees managing large, diverse portfolios. In quite different ways, however, delegation is also likely to be important to non-expert investors who nevertheless may be well suited and qualified to serve as trustees, as will often be the case with family members or friends. Accordingly, the rule stated in §227 recognizes broad authority to delegate in the prudently exercised discretion of the trustee.

§227. General Standard of Prudent Investment

The trustee is under a duty to the beneficiaries to invest and manage the funds of the trust as a prudent investor would, in light of the purposes, terms, distribution requirements, and other circumstances of the trust.

(a) This standard requires the exercise of reasonable care, skill, and caution, and is to be applied to investments not in isolation but in the context of the trust portfolio and as a part of an overall investment strategy, which should incorporate risk and return objectives reasonably suitable to the trust.

(b) In making and implementing investment decisions, the trustee has a duty to diversify the investments of the trust unless, under the circumstances, it is prudent not to do so.

(c) In addition, the trustee must:

(1) conform to fundamental fiduciary duties of loyalty (§170) and impartiality (§183);

(2) act with prudence in deciding whether and how to delegate authority and in the selection and supervision of agents (§171); and

(3) incur only costs that are reasonable in amount and appropriate to the investment responsibilities of the trusteeship (§188).

(d) The trustee's duties under this Section are subject to the rule of §228, dealing primarily with contrary investment provisions of a trust or statute.

NOTES AND QUESTIONS

1. The Restatement Comment refers to "abstractly high-risk investments or techniques (such as futures or option trading)" as being appropriate investments in some circumstances "for the purpose of reducing the risk level of the portfolio as a whole." Do you see why a "high-risk" investment might reduce the risk level of the portfolio? See George Crawford, A Fiduciary Duty to Use Derivatives?, 1 Stan. J.L. Bus. & Fin. 307 (1995); Paul G. Haskell, The Prudent Person Rule for Trustee Investment and Modern Portfolio Theory, 69 N.C. L. Rev. 87 (1990); Bevis Longstreth, Modern Investment Management and the Prudent Man Rule (1986).

For further explanation of the prudent investor rule of the Restatement (Third), see Edward C. Halbach, Jr., Trust Investment Law in the Third Restatement, 77 Iowa L. Rev. 1151 (1992); Note, Speculating on the Efficacy of "Speculation": An Analysis of the Prudent Person's Slipperiest Term of Art in Light of Modern Portfolio Theory, 48 Stan. L. Rev. 419 (1996); Note, Chasing Down the Devil: Standards of Prudent Investment under the Restatement (Third) of Trusts, 54 Wash. & Lee L. Rev. 335 (1997).

2. Suppose that the settlor directs the trustee to invest only in first

mortgages and government bonds and forbids investment in corporate stock. If the trustee can show that in an inflationary economy
the value of the trust estate will seriously decline by investing in fixed-
value obligations, should the court authorize the trustee to invest in
common stock? See In re Trusteeship Agreement with Mayo, 259
Minn. 91, 105 N.W.2d 900 (1960); Toledo Trust Co. v. Toledo Hospital, 174 Ohio St. 124, 187 N.E.2d 36 (1962).

3.   In 1994, the Commissioners on Uniform State Laws approved
a Uniform Prudent Investor Act. The act is loosely patterned on the
principles of the Restatement (Third) of Trusts §227. The Uniform
Prudent Investor Act has been adopted in a majority of states. The
heart of the Uniform Prudent Investor Act is Section 2.

Uniform Prudent Investor Act (1994)

§2.   STANDARD OF CARE; PORTFOLIO STRATEGY; RISK AND
      RETURN OBJECTIVES

(a) A trustee shall invest and manage trust assets as a prudent
investor would, by considering the purposes, terms, distribution requirements, and other circumstances of the trust. In satisfying this
standard, the trustee shall exercise reasonable care, skill, and caution.

(b) A trustee's investment and management decisions respecting
individual assets must be evaluated not in isolation, but in the context
of the trust portfolio as a whole and as a part of an overall investment
strategy having risk and return objectives reasonably suited to the
trust.

(c) Among circumstances that the trustee shall consider in investing and managing trust assets are such of the following as are relevant
to the trust or its beneficiaries:

(1) general economic conditions;

(2) the possible effect of inflation or deflation;

(3) the expected tax consequences of investment decisions or
strategies;

(4) the role that each investment or course of action plays within
the overall trust portfolio, which may include financial assets, interests in closely held enterprises, tangible and intangible personal
property, and real property;

(5) the expected total return from income and the appreciation
of capital;

(6) other resources of the beneficiaries;

(7) needs for liquidity, regularity of income, and preservation
or appreciation of capital; and

(8) an asset's special relationship or special value, if any, to the
purposes of the trust or to one or more of the beneficiaries.

(d) A trustee shall take reasonable steps to verify facts relevant to the investment and management of trust assets.

(e) A trustee may invest in any kind of property or type of investment consistent with the standards of this [Act].

(f) A trustee who has special skills or expertise, or is named trustee in reliance upon the trustee's representation that the trustee has special skills or expertise, has a duty to use those special skills or expertise.

Income and Principal Allocation. The change to modern portfolio theory in the Uniform Prudent Investor Act necessitates a change in the traditional rules of allocation between income and principal. If the trust principal is invested as a portfolio for total return, the return may include cash dividends, stock dividends, capital gain, insurance policies, mineral royalties, derivatives (hedges, options, futures contracts, and the like) and other receipts. The investments should not favor the income beneficiary (who wants high income) or the remaindermen (who want capital appreciation); the trustee has a duty of impartiality (see supra page 929). Both the 1931 and 1962 Uniform Principal and Income Acts contained explicit rules about what receipts are to be allocated to income and what receipts are to be allocated to principal. The 1962 Act generally allocates receipts in the following manner.

To income:

1. Rent.
2. Interest on loans and bonds.
3. Cash dividends on stock.
4. Net profits from a business or farming operation.
5. Royalties from natural resources, except 27½ percent allocated to principal.
6. Royalties from patents and copyrights (but not in excess of 5 percent per year of inventory value).

To principal, increasing the corpus of the trust:

1. Proceeds from sale of property.
2. Proceeds of insurance on property.
3. Stock splits and stock dividends.
4. Corporate distributions from a merger or acquisition.
5. Payment of bond principal.
6. Royalties from natural resources (27½ percent).

7. Royalties from patents and copyrights in excess of 5 percent of inventory value.

These rules are default rules. The settlor can provide for a different allocation.

The allocation rules are out of date in two respects. First, they do not mention new types of investments now available. Second, the allocation rules may constrain the trustee from making the best investment portfolio for the trust. Studies have shown that over the long run, because of inflation, investment in common stocks will preserve the real value of the principal, whereas investment in bonds will not rise in value with inflation, but lose value. Thus, the trustee may decide that from the longer-run perspective, seeking the highest total return, the best portfolio would include a large percentage (say 60 percent) in common stocks with a high potential for capital appreciation, but paying only 2 percent dividends. If this were done, the income beneficiary, thinking she should receive the usual 6 percent, may suffer from a lack of sufficient income. To be fair and impartial, a trustee operating a total return investment policy must find a way to allocate some of the total return (i.e., capital gain) to the income beneficiary.

In 1997, a new revised Uniform Principal and Income Act was promulgated to take care of the situation where a trust portfolio is invested for the highest total return. Under traditional fiduciary rules respecting allocation to income and principal, the particular form of the return determines the beneficiary's return. For example, cash dividends go to the income beneficiary; stock dividends are added to corpus. These rules, similar to the rules in the earlier Principal and Income Acts, are continued. To free the trustee's hand in choosing investments, however, the 1997 Uniform Principal and Income Act gives the trustee power to reallocate receipts if the trustee concludes that wise investing leads, under the allocation rules, to unfair results. Section 104 of the Act gives the trustee an equitable power to adjust between principal and income to the extent the trustee considers necessary to a fair treatment of the beneficiaries if the trustee invests and manages assets as a prudent investor interested in the total return from the portfolio. This is a default rule, operational only if the settlor does not provide otherwise.

A different solution to the problem of fair allocation is the creation of a unitrust. The unitrust idea (which comes from the charitable remainder unitrust discussed infra, page 1064) is that the settlor of the trust will set in the trust instrument the percentage of the value of the trust principal that must be paid to the income beneficiary each year. The trust principal is revalued each year. Thus if the income beneficiary is entitled to 6 percent of the value of the trust principal and the principal is worth $1 million, the income beneficiary receives $60,000 a year. If the value of the trust principal increases to $1,200,000, the income beneficiary is entitled to $72,000 a year. Both income and principal beneficiaries gain from capital appreciation. The unitrust lets the settlor determine the percentage of the total return that is to be paid to the income beneficiary.

The modern portfolio theory puts pressure on lawyers to discuss with clients the kind of income stream the client wants the income beneficiary to have. A total return trust may be drafted to give the income beneficiary what is traditionally allocated to income, together with a discretionary power in the trustee to distribute principal to the income beneficiary if the trustee deems it needed. Or the trustee may be given discretionary power to allocate both income and principal to the income beneficiary. Or a total return trust may be drafted to allocate to the income beneficiary portions of the total return in accordance with a fixed percentage. There are other trust forms that may satisfy the goal of fairness to the income and principal beneficiaries. For discussion of the new types of trusts that will likely develop as a result of modern portfolio theory, see Joel C. Dobris, New Forms of Private Trusts for the Twenty-First Century — Principal and Income, 31 Real Prop., Prob. & Tr. J. 1 (1996); Jerold L. Horn, Prudent Investor Rule, Modern Portfolio Theory, and Private Trusts: Drafting and Administration Including the "Give-Me-Five" Unitrust, 33 Real Prop., Prob. & Tr. J. 1 (1998); Robert B. Wolf, Defeating the Duty to Disappoint Equally — The Total Return Trust, 32 Real Prop., Prob. & Tr. J. 45 (1997); Robert B. Wolf, Total Return Trusts — Can Your Clients Afford Anything Less, 33 Real Prop., Prob. & Tr. J. 131 (1998) (concluding that the unitrust is best).

For a useful summary of the Prudent Investor Act and its consequences on trust investing, see John H. Langbein, The Uniform Prudent Investor Act and the Future of Trust Investing, 81 Iowa L. Rev. 641 (1996).

NOTE: ERISA

The Employee Retirement Income Security Act of 1974 (ERISA) governs investment of pension funds by the trustees managing the funds. ERISA applies to all pension funds except state and local pension funds exempt under 29 U.S.C. §1003(b). The standard governing investments is the prudent investor rule. The act provides that a fiduciary shall discharge his duties

> with the care, skill, prudence, and diligence under the circumstances then prevailing that a prudent man acting in a like capacity and familiar

with such matters would use in the conduct of an enterprise of a like character and with like aims; by diversifying the investments of the plan so as to minimize the risk of large losses unless under the circumstances it is clearly prudent not to do so. [29 U.S.C. §1104(a) (1982).]

Waiver of these limitations in the trust instrument is forbidden. 29 U.S.C. §1104(a)(1)(D) (1982).

ERISA also provides that the trustee

shall discharge his duties with respect to a plan solely in the interest of the participants and the beneficiaries and . . . for the exclusive purpose of . . . providing benefits to participants and their beneficiaries. [29 U.S.C. §1104(a)(1)(A)(i) (1982).]

This is known as the exclusive benefit rule. The trust law analogue to the exclusive benefit rule is the trustee's duty of loyalty. For a critique of the exclusive benefit rule, see Daniel R. Fischel & John H. Langbein, ERISA's Fundamental Contradiction: The Exclusive Benefit Rule, 55 U. Chi. L. Rev. 1105 (1988).

The management of huge pension and employee benefit funds will undoubtedly bring many changes in the law of trusts dealing with trustees' powers and duties. Common law rules, developed for family trusts, will be reshaped by these giant funds, but only the twenty-first century will tell us exactly how.

QUESTIONS

Can the trustees of a pension fund — or the trustees of a private trust, for that matter — invest the trust assets to accomplish social goals? Can the trustees refuse to invest in the stock of a corporation that pollutes the atmosphere or publishes textbooks that teach the theory of evolution? Or can a labor union pension fund invest in projects that provide jobs to the union members? Do such investments breach the duty of undivided loyalty to the fund beneficiaries? Are they prudent?

See Ian D. Lanoff, The Social Investment of Private Pension Plan Assets: May It Be Done Lawfully under ERISA?, 31 Labor L.J. 387 (1980) (presenting the Department of Labor's conclusion that, under ERISA, the trustee must make investment decisions based on market returns and not in pursuit of a social or political cause). For pension funds not covered by ERISA and for charitable trusts, see John H. Langbein and Richard A. Posner, Social Investing and the Law of Trusts, 79 Mich. L. Rev. 72 (1980) (concluding that social investing is inconsistent with the duty of loyalty).

SECTION D.   LIABILITY OF THE TRUSTEE TO THIRD PARTIES

In caring for the trust property, a trustee may make contracts respecting the property. The traditional rule is that a trustee is personally liable on any contract the trustee makes, in the absence of an express provision in the contract relieving the trustee of liability. This is true regardless of whether the trustee does or does not have power to enter into the contract. The mere fact that the contract is signed by a trustee in a fiduciary capacity (e.g., "*X* as trustee") is not ordinarily sufficient to relieve the trustee of liability.

If the contract is properly made by a trustee, the trustee is entitled to be indemnified out of the trust assets. However, if the trust estate is insufficient to indemnify the trustee, the trustee suffers the loss. A trustee should therefore be very careful to insert in the contract a provision excluding personal liability on the part of the trustee.

A trustee's liability for tort traditionally has followed a similar rule. A trustee is personally liable to the same extent a beneficial owner of the trust property would be liable. A trustee should take out insurance to cover his liability for torts committed by the trustee or an employee of the trustee.

If a trustee is held liable for tort but is not personally at fault, the trustee is entitled to indemnification out of the trust assets. As with contract liability, if the trust assets are insufficient to indemnify the trustee, the trustee suffers the loss.

Contract and tort creditors must sue the trustee personally. After they recover a judgment, they must try to collect the judgment from the trustee's own assets. If these are insufficient, the creditors may proceed to enforce the trustee's right of indemnification against the trust estate. In this proceeding for indemnification, the beneficiaries can assert setoffs against the trustee unrelated to the contract or tort claim. See Cook v. Holland, 575 S.W.2d 468 (Ky. App. 1978); James S. Sligar, Executor and Trustee Liability to a Third Party, 132 Tr. & Est., Apr. 1993, at 30.

The traditional rules have been criticized by many commentators as putting unwarranted burdens on creditors and unfair liability on a trustee where the trustee is not personally at fault and the trust assets are insufficient for indemnification. Many states have enacted statutes reversing the traditional rules and permitting contract and tort creditors to sue a trustee in his representative capacity. Uniform Probate Code §7-306, reproduced below, is typical.

Uniform Probate Code (1990)

§7-306.   [PERSONAL LIABILITY OF TRUSTEE TO THIRD PARTIES]

(a) Unless otherwise provided in the contract, a trustee is not personally liable on contracts properly entered into in his fiduciary capacity in the course of administration of the trust estate unless he fails to reveal his representative capacity and identify the trust estate in the contract.

(b) A trustee is personally liable for obligations arising from ownership or control of property of the trust estate or for torts committed in the course of administration of the trust estate only if he is personally at fault.

(c) Claims based on contracts entered into by a trustee in his fiduciary capacity, on obligations arising from ownership or control of the trust estate, or on torts committed in the course of trust administration may be asserted against the trust estate by proceeding against the trustee in his fiduciary capacity, whether or not the trustee is personally liable therefor.

(d) The question of liability as between the trust estate and the trustee individually may be determined in a proceeding for accounting, surcharge or indemnification or other appropriate proceeding.

For criticism of UPC §7-306, see Jerome J. Curtis, Jr., The Transmogrification of the American Trust, 31 Real Prop., Prob. & Tr. J. 251, 279-297 (1996).

Uniform Trust Act §1108 (1999 draft) contains provisions similar to UPC §7-306, except that subsection (a) of Uniform Trust Act §1108 excuses the trustee from personal liability on a contract if *either* the trustee's representative capacity *or* the identity of the trust is disclosed in the contract. It is assumed that either one of these statements in a contract will put the other party on notice that a trust is involved.

WEALTH TRANSFER TAXATION: TAX PLANNING

SECTION A. INTRODUCTION

1. *A Brief History of Federal Wealth Transfer Taxation*

Death duties have an ancient history and were known to the Greeks, Romans, and even to the Egyptians. In this country until World War I, federal death duties were only levied temporarily during times of urgent need for revenue. When relations with France deteriorated in 1797, Congress imposed stamp taxes on legacies; the taxes disappeared five years later when the revenue crisis had passed. During the Civil War, Congress levied an inheritance tax, which was promptly repealed after the war. Again in the 1890s, seeking revenues to finance our military encounters with Spain, Congress imposed an inheritance tax, which was discarded upon victory. In 1916, with military expenditures mounting, Congress turned again to death duties as an untapped source of revenue and enacted an *estate* tax. (Generally speaking, an estate tax is imposed on the transferor's estate, an inheritance tax on the transferee.)

The 1916 estate tax was not repealed at the end of World War I because the tax had come to be seen as a means of levelling great fortunes as well as a source of revenue. Public hostility toward great wealth began to manifest itself in the late nineteenth century, soon after enormous fortunes had been amassed by John D. Rockefeller, Cornelius Vanderbilt, J. P. Morgan, and others during the "robber baron" era. Inheritance taxes were imposed by several states as a result of populist pressures, and soon after the turn of the century President Theodore Roosevelt proposed a steeply graduated inheritance tax on "swollen fortunes which it is certainly of no benefit to this country to perpetuate."[1] Thereafter the movement for an inheritance tax to break up hereditary accumulations gained many new supporters, even among conservatives. But Congress declined to act until the war required it to find new sources of revenue.

After World War I Congress was subjected to conflicting pressures. Some groups wanted to retain the estate tax to reduce hereditary wealth, others wanted to repeal this "socialistic" tax on capital. Congress responded by leaving the tax in place and reducing rates. In 1931, beset by the need to increase revenues in the Great Depression, Congress again turned to the estate tax. With President Hoover's blessing (Hoover regarded the estate tax as a means of striking at "the evils of inherited economic power"), Congress doubled the rates of the estate tax, pushing the tax on any estate in excess of $10 million to 45 percent. At the same time, Congress imposed a gift tax to prevent avoidance of death taxes by inter vivos gifts.

With the Franklin D. Roosevelt administration, the estate tax entered a new phase. The levelling of great inherited fortunes was formally accepted as an objective of the estate tax. In a message to Congress, President Roosevelt declared:

> The desire to provide security for one's self and one's family is natural and wholesome, but it is adequately served by a reasonable inheritance. Great accumulations of wealth cannot be justified on the basis of personal and family security. In the last analysis such accumulations amount to the perpetuation of great and undesirable concentration of control in a relatively few individuals over the employment and welfare of many, many others. . . . [I]nherited economic power is as inconsistent with the ideals of this generation as inherited political power was inconsistent with the ideals of the generation which established our government. [H.R. Rep. No. 1681, 74th Cong., 1st Sess. 2 (1935), 1939-1 Cum. Bull. (Part 2) 643.]

To level the rich and to raise money to finance World War II, Congress, during the 1930s and 1940s, kept raising the rates every few years. Finally, in the Internal Revenue Code of 1954, the exemption from estate taxes was fixed at $60,000; the rates went up to 77 percent on any estate in excess of $10 million.

Though the rates were high, the loopholes in the 1954 Code were several. The term *loopholes* describes both ways of avoiding estate taxation intentionally provided by Congress and ways subsequently discovered by imaginative lawyers. The gift tax rates were set at 75 percent

---

1. 17 Works of Theodore Roosevelt 434 (Memorial ed. 1925). Our historical summary of the estate tax draws heavily from Louis Eisenstein, The Rise and Decline of the Estate Tax, 11 Tax L. Rev. 223 (1956). This article is well worth reading in its entirety.

of estate tax rates, thus providing an incentive to make gifts before death. Both gift and estate taxes provided an unlimited deduction for transfers to charity. A taxpayer in the 77 percent bracket might well choose to leave huge sums to charity rather than pay 77 percent to the government. The Ford Foundation, for example, was, like many other charitable foundations, established largely to avoid estate taxation. Other ways of avoiding the tax burden, intentionally provided by Congress, included devising property to the taxpayer's spouse (the marital deduction), buying life insurance (life insurance is not included in the gross estate unless the decedent possesses incidents of ownership over it), and creating a trust with successive life beneficiaries (the estate tax, imposed on transferable interests, does not apply on the death of a life tenant, who can transfer nothing).

This last loophole in the 1954 Code, continued from the earliest estate tax days, was the foundation stone of dynastic trusts set up to avoid estate taxes for future generations. A rich person, *O*, could create a trust for *A* for life, then in successive generations for *B* for life, then for *C* for life, and so on until the Rule against Perpetuities calls a halt (approximately 100 years later). Although *O* had to pay either a gift or estate tax upon creating the trust, no estate tax would be levied at the death of *A*, *B*, *C*, or any succeeding life tenant. If *O* created the trust back in, say, 1935, the trust would still be going on today, paying out income to successive life beneficiaries, without an estate tax ever having been levied since the creation of the trust.

The estate and gift tax scheme of the Internal Revenue Code of 1954, described above, lasted about a generation. Beginning in 1976, Congress began tinkering with the Code, first with moderate revisions, later with substantial restructuring that completely changed the life of estate planners. In the Tax Reform Act of 1976, the gift and estate taxes were unified. The same rate schedule was applied to both gifts and estates. The new rate schedule was applied to cumulative gifts and bequests; each taxable gift moved the taxpayer toward a higher bracket, and the estate tax bracket was determined by the sum of cumulative lifetime gifts and the decedent's gross estate at death, in effect making a bequest the final gift. Nonetheless, even though the gift and estate tax rates were unified, tax advantages in lifetime giving still remain (see infra page 984).

The 1976 change was minor. It took a Republican administration to redo completely the federal estate and gift tax system. The Economic Recovery Tax Act of 1981, enacted at the urging of President Reagan, provided considerable tax relief at both the lower and upper ends of the economic scale. The tax exemption (in the form of a credit) was increased to $600,000, thus eliminating estate tax worries of the vast majority of citizens. At the same time the top rate was lowered to 55 percent. An unlimited marital deduction was also introduced into the tax system. A husband or wife can transfer to his or her spouse unlimited amounts of property tax free. Transfer taxes are not levied until the spouses' property is transferred outside the marital unit. With the unlimited marital deduction, and the exemption of estates under $600,000, tax planning became — after 1981 — estate planning for the rich. The middle class — which for more than forty years had skewed its estate plans to avoid taxation on estates exceeding $60,000 — was removed by Congress from the estate taxation system.

A second tax act of the Reagan administration — the Tax Reform Act of 1986 — struck the rich a body blow. It closed the great loophole in the estate tax — the exemption of the life estate from taxation. History may record that this tax act did more damage to dynastic wealth in this country than any previous tax act. The Tax Reform Act of 1986 imposed a *generation-skipping transfer tax*, at the highest rate of the estate tax, upon any generation-skipping transfer (which is, generally speaking, a transfer that skips the estate tax for a generation). Hence, in the trust created by *O* above, a generation-skipping transfer tax is payable at the death of *A*, at the death of *B*, and at the death of *C*. In 1986, Congress decided that a wealth transfer tax must be exacted once every generation from millionaire families. The tax-saving possibilities of the dynastic trust have been severely curtailed.

Federal wealth transfer taxation now consists of three different taxes: (a) gift tax, (b) estate tax, and (c) generation-skipping transfer tax. We shall treat them in that order in this book.

NOTE: ESTATE AND INHERITANCE TAXES DISTINGUISHED

The federal government imposes an estate tax, whereas many of the states impose an inheritance tax. What is the difference? An *estate tax* is a tax upon the privilege of transfer and is levied upon the decedent's "gross estate," a tax term invented to cover the probate estate, nonprobate transfers, and certain other property over which the decedent has powers. The tax is levied on the total amount transferred or, to put it more technically, on the amount of the decedent's gross taxable estate. An *inheritance tax* is a tax imposed upon each beneficiary for the privilege of receiving property from the dead. The amount each beneficiary pays in tax depends upon the size of the bequest received and the relationship of the beneficiary to the decedent (spouses and children pay lower rates than more remote kindred and friends). Under the federal estate tax, if a person dies leaving $2 million to ten children, the amount of tax is the same as if there were only one child. Under an inheritance tax with progressive rates for each beneficiary's share, the total amount of tax would be less for a decedent with ten children than it would be for a decedent with one child.

Whether an estate tax is preferable to an inheritance tax is debatable. An estate tax is generally thought easier to administer since it avoids valuing the share each beneficiary receives (especially where a discretionary trust or contingent future interest is involved). On the other hand, an inheritance tax might seem fairer because it is based upon the amount each beneficiary receives (and not on the size of the donor's estate) and also offers preferential treatment for close relatives.

For proposals to further restructure the wealth transfer taxes, see Mark L. Ascher, Curtailing Inherited Wealth, 89 Mich. L. Rev. 690 (1990); Karen C. Burke and Grayson M. P. McCouch, A Consumption Tax on Gifts and Bequests, 17 Va. Tax Rev. 657 (1998); Michael J. Graetz, To Praise the Estate Tax, Not to Bury It, 93 Yale L.J. 259 (1983); Edward J. McCaffery, The Uneasy Case for Wealth Transfer Taxation, 104 Yale L.J. 283 (1994); Colloquium on Wealth Transfer Taxation, 51 Tax L. Rev. 357 (1996) (articles discussing McCaffery's proposal to abolish the federal estate and gift tax by Anne L. Alstott, Joseph M. Dodge, Douglas Holtz-Eakin, and Eric Rakowski, with commentaries by others).

2. The Unified Federal Estate and Gift Taxes

One of the first things you need to do to understand the unified estate and gift tax system is to see how it works. If you understand the basic principles of the unified system, details and modifications that come later will be easier to understand. In this brief introduction, we want to concentrate on how a cumulative system works and how the unified credit works.

The Tax Reform Act of 1976 unified gift and estate taxes for estates of decedents dying after December 31, 1976, and for gifts made after that date. A single rate schedule applies to both gift and estate taxes. The rates are progressive on the basis of *cumulative* lifetime and death transfers. For lifetime gifts, the amount of the gift tax is determined by applying the rate schedule to cumulative gifts and then subtracting gift taxes payable on gifts made in earlier tax periods. With each substantial gift, the taxpayer steps up into a higher bracket for that gift, until the top bracket is reached. The tentative estate tax is computed by applying the rate schedule to the aggregate of the decedent's taxable estate *plus* taxable gifts made after 1976. From this tentative tax are deducted gift taxes paid on the post-1976 gifts.[2]

2. For a more detailed picture of how the tentative tax is figured, see infra page 1005.

The schedule below sets forth the current transfer tax rates.

Unified Transfer Tax Rate Schedule

(A) Amount subject to tax more than — Amount subject	(B) Amount subject to tax equal or to less than	(C) Tax on amount in column (A)	(D) Rate of tax in excess over amount in column (A) Percent
—	$ 10,000	—	18
$ 10,000	20,000	$ 1,800	20
20,000	40,000	3,800	22
40,000	60,000	8,200	24
60,000	80,000	13,000	26
80,000	100,000	18,200	28
100,000	150,000	23,800	30
150,000	250,000	38,800	32
250,000	500,000	70,800	34
500,000	750,000	155,800	37
750,000	1,000,000	248,300	39
1,000,000	1,250,000	345,800	41
1,250,000	1,500,000	448,300	43
1,500,000	2,000,000	555,800	45
2,000,000	2,500,000	780,800	49
2,500,000	3,000,000	1,025,800	53
3,000,000	—	1,290,800	55

Congress has exempted a certain amount of property from transfer taxation. Prior to 1998, the exemption was $600,000. In 1998, Congress decided to increase the exemption in a series of steps until an exemption of $1 million is reached in 2006. Thus:

In the case of estates of decedents dying, and gifts made, during:	The exemption is:
2000 and 2001	$ 675,000
2002 and 2003	700,000
2004	850,000
2005	950,000
2006 or thereafter	1,000,000

The exemption is given in the form of a tax credit, which is deducted from the tentative estate tax to determine the final estate tax. The amount of the credit is the amount of the tentative tax determined under the rate schedule above which equals the amount of the exemption. If you look at the rate schedule you will see that when the $1 million exemption is fully phased in, the credit against the tentative tax will be $345,800 and the estate tax rate will start at 41 percent. (Yes, talking about credits rather than exemptions makes it extra complicated, but this is what Congress has done.)

After 2007, the $1 million exemption will be indexed for inflation and may increase in multiples of $10,000.

Case 1 illustrates how the tax applies to cumulative gifts and also illustrates the tax credit. To keep it simple, let's assume the gifts are made in 2006 or thereafter, when the $1 million exemption takes effect.

Case 1. In 2006 *W*, a widow, gives Acme stock worth $100,000 to her daughter *D. W* is entitled to make a tax-free gift of up to $10,000 to any donee each year (see infra page 991); hence *W* is entitled to exclude $10,000 of this gift from taxable gifts. *W* makes no gifts of more than $10,000 to any other person in 2006. *W* has not made any taxable gifts in any earlier year. In 2006 *W* files a gift tax return showing:

$100,000	gift to *D* in 2006
− 10,000	annual exclusion
$ 90,000	taxable gift in 2006
+ 0	taxable gifts in earlier years
$ 90,000	cumulative taxable gifts
$ 21,000	tentative gift tax
− 21,000	unified gift tax credit used
$ 0	gift tax due

In 2007 *W* gives Beta stock worth $100,000 to *D. W* makes no gifts in excess of $10,000 to any other person in 2007. In 2007 *W* files a gift tax return showing:

$100,000	gift to *D* in 2007
− 10,000	annual exclusion
$ 90,000	taxable gift in 2007
+ 90,000	taxable gifts in earlier years (Acme stock in 2006)[3]
$180,000	cumulative taxable gifts
48,400	tax on cumulative gifts
− 21,000	tax on preceding gifts (2006)
$ 27,400	tentative gift tax
− 27,400	unified gift tax credit used
$ 0	tax due

In Case 1, observe the effect of a rate schedule based on cumulative

---

3. Taxable gifts in prior years are brought into the computation at their date-of-gift value. If Acme stock were worth $200,000 in 2007, it would still be included in the 2007 return at its previous taxable gift value ($90,000).

gifts. The 2006 gift of Acme stock is taxed at a marginal rate of 28 percent; the 2007 gift of Beta stock of the same value is taxed at a marginal rate of 32 percent. Under the cumulative transfer system, a donor does not start at the bottom rung of the tax rates for taxable gifts in any one year but starts on the rung where prior gifts left the donor. Similarly, a decedent starts on the rung he was on when he made his last inter vivos gift. Observe also that in Case 1 W has used $48,400 of her unified credit of $345,800. If W dies in 2008 or thereafter, without making further gifts, W will have a credit of $297,400 to apply against the estate tax.[4]

QUESTION AND NOTE

1. Apart from taking advantage of the annual exclusion of $10,000 per donee, is there any transfer tax advantage in W's making inter vivos gifts to her daughter, as in Case 1? If W has a choice of giving her daughter a $100,000 corporate bond, paying current market interest rates, due in the year 2020, or $100,000 worth of growth stocks, from the sole point of view of transfer taxes, which should she give?

This bit of information might help you. If W is 40 years old when she makes the gift, and the growth stocks appreciate at the historic rate of return, they will grow to over $5 million after 40 years. If W dies at age 80, she will have gotten this amount out of her estate.

2. One advantage of making a gift, which might not be obvious, results from the fact that the tax base for gifts is the value of the property transferred. If the transfer results in gift tax liability, the gift tax is not included in the gift tax base. On the other hand, the estate tax is levied on the decedent's assets at death, which include the amount that will be transferred to Uncle Sam as estate taxes. To express this difference, sometimes it is said that the gift tax is "tax-exclusive," whereas the estate tax is "tax-inclusive."

To illustrate, assume that O aims to transfer $1,000,000 to her daughter A and that this transfer is subject to a 50 percent rate. For A to receive by gift $1,000,000 subject to a tax of $500,000, O must part with a total of $1,500,000. Hence, the tax rate on the amount parted with is really $33\frac{1}{3}$ percent. In contrast, for O to transfer $1,000,000 to A at death, O must part with $2,000,000 (subject to a 50 percent rate) to get $1,000,000 in the hands of A. The tax preference for lifetime giving can be expressed as a rate reduction. If the

---

4. Actually, it is not technically accurate to say that W will have a credit of only $297,400 to apply against the estate tax. Since the taxable gifts of $180,000 made in 2006 and 2007 must be added to W's gross estate to determine W's estate tax, the entire unified credit of $345,800 is available to W's estate. Our explanation, however, is a simple way of indicating how much credit (and how much exemption) W has left.

maximum estate tax rate is 50 percent, the equivalent gift tax rate is 33⅓ percent. To eliminate the tax preference for lifetime giving, the gift tax itself would have to be included in the gift tax base. As this example shows, the structure of the tax law rewards early transfers.

***

Liability for payment of taxes. The donor has the primary liability for paying the gift tax. If the donor does not pay, the donee is liable for unpaid gift tax. The executor or administrator of a decedent's estate has personal liability for payment of the estate tax but is entitled to reimbursement out of the decedent's estate. If there is no administration of the decedent's estate, persons in possession of the decedent's property are liable for the tax due.

Although the executor or administrator must pay the entire estate tax due, the executor or administrator is entitled to be reimbursed from life insurance beneficiaries for the portion of the tax resulting from the inclusion of life insurance in the decedent's estate. IRC §2206. Similarly, the executor is entitled to proportionate reimbursement from recipients of property over which the decedent had a general power of appointment. Id. §2207. With these two exceptions, the Code does not generally provide for apportionment of estate taxes to the recipients but leaves the matter to state law. A large majority of states follows the rule that federal estate taxes are apportioned and must be borne by each beneficiary pro rata, in the absence of a direction to the contrary in the testator's will. A minority of states follows the opposite rule: Unless the testator's will directs otherwise, the estate tax is paid out of the residuary estate. Uniform Probate Code §3-916 adopts the majority rule.

SECTION B.   THE FEDERAL GIFT TAX

1.   The Nature of a Taxable Gift

Section 2501(a) of the Internal Revenue Code of 1986 imposes a gift tax on "the transfer of property by gift" during each calendar year by an individual. But nowhere in the Code is *gift* defined. The courts have decided that the question is not whether the donor has donative intent, but whether the donor gives up complete dominion and control. If the donor keeps dominion and control, the gift is not complete, and no taxable gift has been made. Creation of a revocable trust does not effect a taxable transfer. The transfer is not complete until the power of revocation ceases. If the power of revocation ceases at the donor's death, no gift tax is due, but the trust property is included in the donor's gross estate under the estate tax.

Holtz's Estate v. Commissioner
United States Tax Court, 1962
38 T.C. 37

DRENNAN, J. . . . The principal issue for decision is whether taxable gifts resulted from transfers to a trust established by [Leon Holtz, the decedent] by deed of trust dated June 12, 1953, wherein Leon was the settlor and Land Title Bank and Trust Company, now Provident Tradesmens Bank and Trust Company, was the sole trustee. The trust instrument provided that the trustee should distribute the net income therefrom and the principal thereof as follows. During the lifetime of settlor the income should be paid to him, and as much of the principal as the trustee "may from time to time think desirable for the welfare, comfort and support of Settlor, or for his hospitalization or other emergency needs," should be paid to him or for his benefit. Upon the death of the settlor, if his wife survived him, the income of the trust was to be paid to her during her lifetime, and a similar provision was made for invasion of principal for her benefit during her lifetime. The trust was to terminate at the death of the survivor of settlor and his wife and the "then-remaining principal" was payable to the estate of the survivor.

On June 12, 1953, Leon transferred property having a value of $384,117 to the trust, and on January 18, 1955, he transferred an additional $50,000 in cash to the trust. Respondent determined that, as a result of these transfers, Leon made taxable gifts in 1953 in the amount of $263,277.63, and in 1955 in the amount of $35,570, computing the value of the taxable gifts by reducing the value of the property transferred in each instance by the actuarial value of Leon's life estate and reversionary interest in each transfer. Petitioner claims the transfers were not completed gifts and that no part of the value thereof was subject to gift tax. . . .

The Internal Revenue Codes of 1939 and 1954 provide no guideposts for determining when a gift becomes complete for gift tax purposes beyond the direction that "the tax shall apply whether the transfer is in trust or otherwise, whether the gift is direct or indirect, and whether the property is real or personal, tangible or intangible." [IRC §2511(a).] It is well settled in cases involving this issue, however, that the question whether a transfer in trust is a completed gift, and thus subject to gift tax, turns on whether the settlor has abandoned sufficient dominion and control over the property transferred to put it beyond recall. Burnet v. Guggenheim, 288 U.S. 280 (1933); Estate of Sanford v. Commissioner, 308 U.S. 39 (1939); Smith v. Shaughnessy, 318 U.S. 176 (1943).

Here we do not have a situation where the settlor either reserved the power in himself alone to modify, alter, or revoke the trust and thus revest the trust property in himself, as in Burnet v. Guggenheim, supra, or reserved the power to alter the disposition of the property or income therefrom in some way not beneficial to himself, as in Estate of Sanford v. Commissioner, supra, or reserved the power in conjunction with someone else to modify, alter, or revoke the trust, as in Camp v. Commissioner, 195 F.2d 999 (C.A. 1, 1952). Leon reserved no rights in himself to change the disposition of the income or principal of the trust as fixed in the trust agreement. However, the trust agreement itself gave the trustee power to pay directly to Leon or for his benefit as much of the principal of the trust as the trustee thought desirable for Leon's welfare, comfort, and support, or for his hospitalization or other emergency needs. The question is whether this discretionary power placed in the trustee by the settlor under the terms of the trust agreement made the gifts of the remainder interests incomplete for gift tax purposes.

A number of cases decided by this and other courts have held that the placing of discretionary power in the trustee to invade corpus makes the gift of corpus incomplete under certain circumstances. The rule of thumb generally accepted seems to be that if the trustee is free to exercise his unfettered discretion and there is nothing to impel or compel him to invade corpus, the settlor retains a mere expectancy which does not make the gift of corpus incomplete. Herzog v. Commissioner, 116 F.2d 591 (C.A. 2, 1941). But if the exercise of the trustee's discretion is governed by some external standard which a court may apply in compelling compliance with the conditions of the trust agreement, and the trustee's power to invade is unlimited, then the gift of corpus is incomplete, Commissioner v. Irving Trust Co., 147 F.2d 946 (C.A. 2, 1945), and this is true even though such words as "absolute" and "uncontrolled" are used in connection with the trustee's discretion, provided the external standards are clearly for the guidance of the trustee in exercising his discretion. Estate of John J. Toeller, 6 T.C. 832 (1946), affd. 165 F.2d 665 (C.A. 7, 1948); Estate of Lelia E. Coulter, 7 T.C. 1280 (1946).

The theory behind this rule seems to be that by placing such standards for guidance of the trustee's discretion in the trust agreement itself, the settlor has not actually lost all dominion and control of the trust corpus or put it completely beyond recall because to ignore the implications and purpose for writing the standards into the invasion clause would be an abuse of discretion on the part of the trustee which the trustee would neither desire to do nor be likely to risk doing under State laws. . . .

The rule of thumb appears to be a reasonable application of the general rule established in the *Guggenheim, Sanford,* and *Shaughnessy* cases because where there is a reasonable possibility that the entire corpus might be repaid to the settlor there can be no assurance that anyone else will receive anything in the form of a gift, and if the corpus should happen to be kept intact until the settlor's death, even though the transfer in trust was not subjected to a gift tax, the corpus of the trust will in all likelihood be subjected to the estate tax in the settlor's estate. See Estate of John J. Toeller, supra; Estate of Lelia E. Coulter, supra.

Applying the above principles to the facts under consideration here, we conclude that no part of or interest in the property transferred to the trust constituted a completed gift for gift tax purposes when transferred to the trust.

The form of the trust agreement indicates that the principal beneficiary of the income, and the principal if it became desirable for his welfare, comfort, support, or emergency needs, was the settlor. The first instructions to the trustee, as shown by the part of the deed of trust quoted in our Findings of Fact, were to distribute net income and principal to the settlor during his lifetime. Only upon the death of the settlor, and if she survived him, was any provision made for payment of either income or principal to the settlor's wife. And only upon the death of the survivor of settlor and his wife was any provision made for distribution of the "then-remaining principal." The trustee had the unfettered power to use all of the corpus for the benefit of settlor, if it thought that it was desirable for the welfare, comfort, or needs of the settlor. The words used were broad enough to cover about anything Leon might want or need. It is reasonable to assume that the trustee would invade corpus and that it would be required to do so by a court if the welfare, comfort, or needs of the settlor made it seem desirable. Otherwise, there would not have been much reason for including the paragraph giving the trustee power to invade principal. It was entirely possible that the entire corpus might be distributed during the settlor's lifetime and no one other than the settlor would receive any portion thereof. As long as that possibility was present, by reason of the language employed by the settlor, the settlor had not abandoned sufficient dominion and control over the property transferred to make the gift consummate. Estate of John J. Toeller, supra.

In addition to the trust agreement itself, the evidence indicates that the settlor, who was 80 years of age when the trust was established, expressed concern over whether he would have available sufficient funds to meet his needs. He asked the trust officer whether he would have enough money to buy an automobile and the trust officer reassured him by telling him that the trust agreement provided for the payment of all income to him and that he could also have money out of the principal, and that the trustee would be liberal in giving him money out of the principal. While the term "liberal" is not defined, the above conversation indicates the understanding of the parties was that the trustee recognized that principal should be distributed at any time the settlor's needs reasonably justified it. . . .

Decision will be entered for the petitioner.

NOTES AND PROBLEMS

1.   *O* transfers property in trust to pay income to her son *A* for life and on *A*'s death to pay the principal to *A*'s daughter *B. O* retains the power to revoke the trust. Because *O* retains the power to revoke the trust, the income from the trust property is taxed to *O* whether the income is paid to *O* or to *A*. See IRC §§676, 677 (income tax). Suppose that the trustee earns $10,000 during the calendar year after the trust is created and the trustee pays the $10,000 to *A*. Who pays income tax on the $10,000? Has a taxable gift been made to *A*?

Suppose that *O* did not reserve the power to revoke the trust but reserved only the power to change the owner of the remainder interest from *B* to *A* at any time during *A*'s life. (At the time of transfer, *O*'s granddaughter *B* was in her teens and was a rather willful, indeed rebellious, young lady experimenting with drugs.) Has *O* made a taxable gift to *A*? To *B*? Suppose that after reaching majority during *A*'s life, *B* irrevocably assigns her interest to a Hindu mystic, under whose influence she has fallen. Has *B* made a taxable gift to the mystic?

If *O* cannot recover the transferred property, why should not *O* be treated as having made a completed gift? Has not *O*'s wealth been irrevocably depleted?

2.   *O* establishes an irrevocable trust that is funded with securities worth $200,000. Trust income is to be paid to *O* for life, "and on her death the trustee shall distribute the trust corpus to such of the Settlor's issue as she shall appoint by will; and in default of such appointment the trustee shall distribute the corpus to the Settlor's issue then living, per stirpes." Has *O* made a taxable gift of a remainder? See Treas. Reg. §25.2511-2(b). Suppose that *O* releases the special power of appointment. Does the release result in a taxable gift of a remainder? If so, how is the remainder valued? See supra page 728.

3.   If the donor can revoke a transfer only with the consent of an adverse party, a taxable gift has been made. Suppose that *O* transfers property in trust to pay the income to *A* for life, and on *A*'s death to distribute the principal to *B. O* retains the power to revoke or amend the trust instrument in whole or in part with the consent of *A*. Has a

taxable gift been made? See Camp v. Commissioner, 195 F.2d 999 (1st Cir. 1952).

4. *Disclaimer.* Suppose that an heir or legatee disclaims his intestate share or the legacy. Has the heir or legatee made a taxable gift to the person who takes the disclaimed property? A disclaimer results in a taxable gift unless §2518 applies. Internal Revenue Code §2518(b) provides that no taxable gift is made if the refusal to take is a "qualified disclaimer." A disclaimer is "qualified" if:

> (a) the disclaimer is in writing, and made either within nine months after the interest is created or within nine months after the disclaimant reaches 21, whichever is later,
> (b) the disclaimant has accepted no interest in the property, and
> (c) the transfer is to persons entitled under local law to disclaimed property and not to persons designated by the disclaimant.

Section 2518 applies only to disclaimers of an interest created by a transfer made after 1976. In the case of interests created earlier, a disclaimer is a gift unless it is made "within a reasonable time after knowledge of the existence of the transfer." Treas. Reg. §25.2511-1(c). See Grayson M. P. McCouch, Timely Disclaimers and Taxable Transfers, 47 U. Miami L. Rev. 1043 (1993).

NOTE: INCOME TAX BASIS

Under the Internal Revenue Code, income tax is levied upon capital gain realized upon the sale of property. The amount of capital gain is the difference between the taxpayer's "basis" and the selling price. Generally speaking, if the taxpayer purchased the property, his basis is the purchase price. If *O* buys land for $50,000, and sells it for $75,000, the capital gain of $25,000 is subject to income taxation.

In the case of property acquired by *gift*, for purpose of computing gain on any subsequent sale by the donee, the donee takes the donor's basis. For the purpose of computing loss, the donee's basis is the value of the property on the date of the gift. IRC §1015. If property is acquired from a *decedent*, the basis of the property for computing both gain and loss is the value of the asset on the decedent's death. Id. §1014. The *stepped-up basis* at death means that any capital gain on property held until death escapes income taxation.

PROBLEM

O purchases 100 shares of IBM common stock for $50 per share. Over the years, the stock's value increases to $150 per share.

(a) If *O* sells the stock for $150 per share, what are the income tax consequences?

(b) If *O* gives the stock to her son *A* and then *A* sells the stock for $150 per share, what are the income tax consequences?

(c) If *O* dies leaving a will that bequeaths the stock to *A* and then *A* sells the stock for $150 per share, what are the income tax consequences?

2.   The Annual Exclusion

Under §2503(b) of the Code, a taxpayer is permitted to exclude from taxable gifts the first $10,000 given to any person during the calendar year. The purpose of the exclusion "is to obviate the necessity of keeping an account of and reporting numerous small gifts, and . . . to fix the amount sufficiently large to cover in most cases wedding and Christmas gifts and occasionally gifts of relatively small amounts." H.R. Rep. No. 708, 72d Cong., 1st Sess. 29 (1932), 1939-1 C.B. (part 2) 457, 478.[5] A donor must file a gift tax return only if gifts (other than marital deduction gifts) to any donee during the year exceed the $10,000 annual exclusion and must report on the return only gifts in excess of $10,000 to any one person. Thus:

> *Case 2. A* gives $12,000 each to *B* and *C* and $5,000 to *D*. *A* must file a tax return reporting the gifts to *B* and *C*, from which two annual exclusions are deducted, leaving $4,000 in taxable gifts. The gift to *D* is not reported on the return because it is covered by the annual exclusion. If *A* had given only $10,000 each to *B* and *C*, no gift tax return need be filed.

In 1997, Congress amended the Code to index the $10,000 exclusion for inflation. It will increase in $1,000 increments if the cost of living rises.

In addition to the annual exclusion of $10,000 per donee, §2503(e) of the Code allows an unlimited exclusion for *tuition payments* and *medical expenses* paid on behalf of any person. With the rising cost of education, the $10,000 annual exclusion might not cover college tuition and educational expenses of children who have reached majority. (A parent generally has no duty to support a child who has reached majority, which in most states is now age 18, and college tuition technically could be considered a gift.) Similarly, some taxpayers incur large medical expenses on behalf of an elderly relative, an adult child, or someone else. Congress has taken the view that such payments

5. The annual exclusion was $5,000 from 1932 to 1939, $4,000 from 1939 to 1942, and $3,000 from 1943 to 1981. Because of inflation, the Economic Recovery Tax Act of 1981 raised the annual exclusion to $10,000, beginning in 1982.

should be exempt from gift taxes without regard to the amounts paid for such purposes or to the relationship between the donor and the donee.

The §2503(e) exclusion applies only to payments made directly to the service provider and does not cover payments to reimburse expenses incurred by the donee. Also, the exclusion for educational expenses covers only "tuition [paid] to an educational institution" and does not include payments for related expenses such as dormitory bills, books, or living expenses.

Gifts of future interests. The annual exclusion is not available for gifts of future interests. The denial of an exclusion for a gift of a future interest rests upon the apprehended difficulty, in many instances, of determining the number of eventual donees and the value of their respective gifts.

> *Case 3.* O gives property worth $100,000 to A for life, remainder to A's issue. Based upon A's life expectancy, A's life estate is worth $65,000; the value of the remainder is worth $35,000. O is entitled to a $10,000 exclusion for the gift to A of a possessory life estate, but O is not entitled to an exclusion for the remainder given to A's issue.
>
> *Case 4.* O creates a trust to pay the income among O's three children in such shares as the trustee in its uncontrolled discretion deems advisable. Even though all the net income must be distributed, since no beneficiary has a right to any ascertainable portion of the income, no beneficiary has a present interest. No exclusions are allowable with respect to the transfers in trust.

The denial of an exclusion for a gift of a future interest creates special problems when property is given to a minor. A child can be given possession of a doll or a toy; the doll or toy is not a future interest. But if the property is income-producing or requires management, ordinarily possession is not given the child. The child takes possession only upon reaching majority. Is, then, any gift of income-producing property to a child a gift of a future interest? The answer is no, with qualifications. If property is given outright to a minor, the gift qualifies for the exclusion. So too does a gift to a guardian of a minor. But guardianship is cumbersome, expensive, and not to the minor's advantage (see supra page 132), and estate planners tend to avoid passing property to guardians. Property can be given in trust for a minor, but care must be taken to draft the trust so as to qualify for the annual exclusion. To permit flexible property management of a minor donee's property, Congress has provided in §2503(c) of the Code a way to avoid having a gift to a minor classified as a future interest.

SEC. 2503(c). TRANSFER FOR THE BENEFIT OF MINOR

> No part of a gift to an individual who has not attained the age of 21 years on the date of such transfer shall be considered a gift of a future interest in property for purposes of subsection (b) if the property and the income therefrom —
>> (1) may be expended by, or for the benefit of, the donee before his attaining the age of 21 years, and
>> (2) will to the extent not so expended —
>>> (A) pass to the donee on his attaining the age of 21 years, and
>>> (B) in the event the donee dies before attaining the age of 21 years, be payable to the estate of the donee or as he may appoint under a general power of appointment as defined in section 2514(c).

To create a §2503(c) trust for a minor qualifying for the annual exclusion, the donor must give the trustee power to expend *all* the income and principal on the donee before the donee reaches 21, and further provide that unexpended income and principal must pass to the donee at 21 or, if the donee dies under 21, to the donee's estate or as the donee appoints under a general power. No person other than the minor can have a beneficial interest in the property.

Section 2503(c) is not limited to transfers in trust. Any transfer that satisfies the statute's requirements qualifies for an exclusion. To provide a convenient form for making gifts to minors, every state has enacted the Uniform Transfers to Minors Act or its equivalent. Under the act, property can be transferred to a person (including the donor) as *custodian* for the benefit of a minor. The custodian's powers over income and principal, set forth in the act (see supra page 133), meet the requirements of §2503(c).

For discussion of gifts that qualify for the annual exclusion, see Jeffrey G. Sherman, 'Tis a Gift to Be Simple: The Need for a New Definition of "Future Interest" for Gift Tax Purposes, 55 U. Cin. L. Rev. 585 (1987); John G. Steinkamp, Common Sense and the Gift Tax Annual Exclusion, 72 Neb. L. Rev. 106 (1993).

PROBLEM

O creates a trust for a minor grandchild *A*. The trustees are directed to use income and principal for *A*'s support and education until *A* reaches 21, when *A* is to receive the principal. The trust also provides that if *A* dies under age 21, the trust assets are to be distributed among such of *O*'s descendants as *A* appoints by will and if *A* fails to exercise the power of appointment, to *A*'s heirs. Is *O* entitled to the annual exclusion? See Ross v. Commissioner, 652 F.2d 1365 (9th Cir. 1981).

*

As you read the next case, keep this in the back of your mind: A person with a general power of appointment (i.e., the power to appoint to himself) is treated under the Internal Revenue Code as owner of the property subject to the general power. IRC §2041, infra page 1032.

Estate of Cristofani v. Commissioner
United States Tax Court, 1991
97 T.C. 74

RUWE, J.   Respondent determined a deficiency in petitioner's Federal estate tax in the amount of $49,486. The sole issue for decision is whether transfers of property to a trust, where the beneficiaries possessed the right to withdraw an amount not in excess of the section 2503(b) exclusion within 15 days of such transfers, constitute gifts of a present interest in property within the meaning of section 2503(b).

FINDINGS OF FACT

Petitioner is the Estate of Maria Cristofani, deceased, Frank Cristofani, executor. Maria Cristofani (decedent) died testate on December 16, 1985. At the time of her death, decedent resided in the State of California. Petitioner's Federal estate tax return (Form 706) was timely filed with the Internal Revenue Service Center in Fresno, California, on September 16, 1986.

Decedent has two children, Frank Cristofani and Lillian Dawson. Decedent's children were both born on July 9, 1948. They were in good health during the years 1984 and 1985.

Decedent has five grandchildren. Two of decedent's five grandchildren are Frank Cristofani's children. They are Anthony Cristofani, born July 16, 1975,[6] and Loris Cristofani, born November 30, 1978.

---

6. In 1999, Anthony Cristofani, 23, and Emma Freeman, 18, students at the University of California in Santa Cruz, were arrested and charged with armed robbery of local shops. Emma Freeman said she did this so she wouldn't have to work while attending school; others said they did it for a thrill. Use of a gun in a robbery in California requires a jail sentence up to 20 years.

"Cristofani is described by friends as a flamboyant fellow, a philosophical merry prankster. He favored bright clothes, often donning orange shoes and silk shirts, and was known to jump atop a table in the cafeteria and dance, or bellow in Italian . . . Several students said . . . [Cristofani and Freeman] were not reluctant to test dorm rules, showering together and pushing the limits of social conduct." L.A. Times, Feb. 12, 1999, at A1.

Like grandmother, like grandson — pushing the limits of the rules? — Eds.

Decedent's three remaining grandchildren are Lillian Dawson's children. They are Justin Dawson, born December 1, 1972, Daniel Dawson, born August 9, 1974, and Luke Dawson, born November 14, 1981. During 1984 and 1985, the parents of decedent's grandchildren were the legal guardians of the person of their respective minor children. There were no independently appointed guardians of decedent's grandchildren's property.

On June 11, 1984, decedent executed a durable power of attorney which named her two children, Frank Cristofani and Lillian Dawson, as her Attorneys in Fact. On that same day, decedent executed her will.

On June 12, 1984, decedent executed an irrevocable trust entitled the Maria Cristofani Children's Trust I (Children's Trust). Frank Cristofani and Lillian Dawson were named the trustees of the Children's Trust.

In general, Frank Cristofani and Lillian Dawson possessed the following rights and interests in the Children's Trust corpus and income. Under Article Twelfth, following a contribution to the Children's Trust, Frank Cristofani and Lillian Dawson could each withdraw an amount not to exceed the amount specified for the gift tax exclusion under section 2503(b). Such withdrawal period would begin on the date of the contribution and end on the 15th day following such contribution. Under Article Third, Frank Cristofani and Lillian Dawson were to receive equally the entire net income of the trust quarter-annually, or at more frequent intervals. After decedent's death, under Article Third, the Trust Estate was to be divided into as many equal shares as there were children of decedent then living or children of decedent then deceased but leaving issue. Both Frank Cristofani and Lillian Dawson survived decedent, and thus the Children's Trust was divided into two equal trusts. Under Article Third, if a child of decedent survived decedent by 120 days, that child's trust would be distributed to the child. Both Frank Cristofani and Lillian Dawson survived decedent by 120 days, and their respective trusts were distributed upon the expiration of the 120-day waiting period. During the waiting period, Frank Cristofani and Lillian Dawson received the entire net income of the separate trusts as provided for in Article Third.

In general, decedent's five grandchildren possessed the following rights and interests in the Children's Trust. Under Article Twelfth, during a 15-day period following a contribution to the Children's Trust, each of the grandchildren possessed the same right of withdrawal as described above regarding the withdrawal rights of Frank Cristofani and Lillian Dawson. Under Article Twelfth, the trustee of the Children's Trust was required to notify the beneficiaries of the trust each time a contribution was received. Under Article Third, had either Frank Cristofani or Lillian Dawson predeceased decedent or failed to survive decedent by 120 days, his or her equal portion of decedent's Children's Trust would have passed in trust to his or her children (decedent's grandchildren).

Under Article Third, the trustees, in their discretion, could apply as much of the principal of the Children's Trust as necessary for the proper support, health, maintenance and education of decedent's children. In exercising their discretion, the trustees were to take into account several factors, including "The Settlor's desire to consider the Settlor's children as primary beneficiaries and the other beneficiaries of secondary importance."

Decedent intended to fund the corpus of the Children's Trust with 100 percent ownership of improved real property, on which a warehouse was located, identified as the 2851 Spring Street, Redwood City, California, property (Spring Street property). Decedent intended that a one-third undivided interest in the Spring Street property be transferred to the Children's Trust during each of the 3 taxable years 1984, 1985, and 1986. The Spring Street property was unencumbered property at all times pertinent to this case.

Consistent with her intent, decedent transferred, on December 17, 1984, an undivided 33-percent interest in the Spring Street property to the Children's Trust by a quitclaim deed. Similarly, in 1985, decedent transferred a second undivided 33-percent interest in the Spring Street property to the Children's Trust by a quitclaim deed which was recorded on November 27, 1985. Decedent intended to transfer her remaining undivided interest in the Spring Street property to the Children's Trust in 1986. However, decedent died prior to making the transfer, and her remaining interest in the Spring Street property remained in her estate.

The value of the 33-percent undivided interest in the Spring Street property that decedent transferred in 1984 was $70,000. The value of the 33-percent undivided interest in the Spring Street property that decedent transferred in 1985 also was $70,000.

Decedent did not report the two $70,000 transfers on Federal gift tax returns. Rather, decedent claimed seven annual exclusions of $10,000 each under section 2503(b) for each year 1984 and 1985. These annual exclusions were claimed with respect to decedent's two children and decedent's five grandchildren.

There was no agreement or understanding between decedent, the trustees, and the beneficiaries that decedent's grandchildren would not exercise their withdrawal rights following a contribution to the Children's Trust. None of decedent's five grandchildren exercised their rights to withdraw under Article Twelfth of the Children's Trust during either 1984 or 1985. None of decedent's five grandchildren received a distribution from the Children's Trust during either 1984 or 1985.

Respondent allowed petitioner to claim the annual exclusions with respect to decedent's two children. However, respondent disallowed the $10,000 annual exclusions claimed with respect to each of decedent's grandchildren claimed for the years 1984 and 1985. Respondent determined that the annual exclusions that decedent claimed with respect to her five grandchildren for the 1984 and 1985 transfers, of the Spring Street property, were not transfers of present interests in property. Accordingly, respondent increased petitioner's adjusted taxable gifts in the amount of $100,000.

OPINION

... Section 2503(b) provides that the first $10,000 of gifts to any person during a calendar year shall not be included in the total amount of gifts made during such year. A trust beneficiary is considered the donee of a gift in trust for purposes of the annual exclusion under section 2503(b). Sec. 25.2503-2(a), Gift Tax Regs.; Helvering v. Hutchings, 312 U.S. 393 (1941). The section 2503(b) exclusion applies to gifts of present interests in property and does not apply to gifts of future interests in property. Sec. 2503(b); sec. 25.2503-3(a), Gift Tax Regs.; United States v. Pelzer, 312 U.S. 399 (1941). The regulations define a future interest to include "reversions, remainders, and other interests or estates, whether vested or contingent, and whether or not supported by a particular interest or estate, which are limited to commence in use, possession or enjoyment at some future date or time." Sec. 25.2503-3(a), Gift Tax Regs.; see Commissioner v. Disston, 325 U.S. 442 (1945); Fondren v. Commissioner, 324 U.S. 18 (1945). The regulations further provide that "An unrestricted right to the immediate use, possession, or enjoyment of property or the income from property (such as a life estate or term certain) is a present interest in property. An exclusion is allowable with respect to a gift of such an interest (but not in excess of the value of the interest)." Sec. 25.2503-3(b), Gift Tax Regs.; see United States v. Pelzer, supra.

In the instant case, petitioner argues that the right of decedent's grandchildren to withdraw an amount equal to the annual exclusion within 15 days after decedent's contribution of property to the Children's Trust constitutes a gift of a present interest in property, thus qualifying for a $10,000 annual exclusion for each grandchild for the years 1984 and 1985. Petitioner relies upon Crummey v. Commissioner, 397 F.2d 82 (9th Cir. 1968), revg. on this issue T.C. Memo. 1966-144.

In Crummey v. Commissioner, T.C. Memo. 1966-144, affd. in part and revd. in part 397 F.2d 82 (9th Cir. 1968), the settlors created an irrevocable living trust for the benefit of their four children, some of whom were minors. The trustee was required to hold the property in equal shares for the beneficiaries. Under the terms of the trust, the trustee, in his discretion, could distribute trust income to each beneficiary until that beneficiary obtained the age of 21. When the beneficiary was age 21 and up until age 35, the trustee was required to distribute trust income to each beneficiary. When the beneficiary was age 35 and over, the trustee was authorized, in his discretion, to distribute trust income to the beneficiary or his or her issue. Upon the death of a beneficiary, his or her trust share was to be distributed to that beneficiary's surviving issue subject to certain age requirements. If a beneficiary died without issue, then his or her trust share was to be distributed equally to the trust shares of the surviving children of the grantors. In addition, each child was given an absolute power to withdraw up to $4,000 in cash of any additions to corpus in the calendar year of the addition, by making a written demand upon the trustee prior to the end of the calendar year.

Relying on these powers, the settlors claimed the section 2503(b) exclusion on transfers of property to the trust for each trust beneficiary.[7] Respondent permitted the settlors to claim the exclusions with respect to the gifts in trust to the beneficiaries who were adults during the years of the additions. However, respondent disallowed exclusions with respect to the gifts in trust to the beneficiaries who were minors during such years. Respondent disallowed the exclusions for the minor beneficiaries on the ground that the minors' powers were not gifts of present interests in property.

In deciding whether the minor beneficiaries received a present interest, the Ninth Circuit specifically rejected any test based upon the likelihood that the minor beneficiaries would actually receive present enjoyment of the property. Instead, the court focused on the legal right of the minor beneficiaries to demand payment from the trustee. The Ninth Circuit, relying on Perkins v. Commissioner, 27 T.C. 601 (1956), and Gilmore v. Commissioner, 213 F.2d 520 (6th Cir. 1954), stated:

> All exclusions should be allowed under the *Perkins* test or the "right to enjoy" test in *Gilmore*. Under *Perkins*, all that is necessary is to find that the demand could not be resisted. We interpret that to mean legally resisted and, going on that basis, we do not think the trustee would have any choice but to have a guardian appointed to take the property demanded. [Crummey v. Commissioner, 397 F.2d at 88.]

The court found that the minor beneficiaries had a legal right to make a demand upon the trustee, and allowed the settlors to claim

---

7. During the years in *Crummey*, 1962 and 1963, the sec. 2503(b) annual exclusion was $3,000.

annual exclusions, under section 2503(b), with respect to the minor trust beneficiaries. . . .

Subsequent to the opinion in *Crummey*, respondent's revenue rulings have recognized that when a trust instrument gives a beneficiary the legal power to demand immediate possession of corpus, that power qualifies as a present interest in property. See Rev. Rul. 85-24, 1985-1 C.B. 329, 330 ("When a trust instrument gives a beneficiary the power to demand immediate possession of corpus, the beneficiary has received a present interest. Crummey v. Commissioner, 397 F.2d 82 (9th Cir. 1968)"); Rev. Rul. 81-7, 1981-1 C.B. 474 ("The courts have recognized that if a trust instrument gives a beneficiary the power to demand immediate possession and enjoyment of corpus or income, the beneficiary has a present interest. Crummey v. Commissioner, 397 F.2d 82 (9th Cir. . . . [1968])."). While we recognize that revenue rulings do not constitute authority for deciding a case in this Court, . . . we mention them to show respondent's recognition that a trust beneficiary's legal right to demand immediate possession and enjoyment of trust corpus or income constitutes a present interest in property for purposes of the annual exclusion under section 2503(b). See Tele-Communications, Inc. v. Commissioner, 95 T.C. 495, 510 (1990). We also note that respondent allowed the annual exclusions with respect to decedent's two children who possessed the same right of withdrawal as decedent's grandchildren.

In the instant case, respondent has not argued that decedent's grandchildren did not possess a legal right to withdraw corpus from the Children's Trust within 15 days following any contribution, or that such demand could have been legally resisted by the trustees. In fact, the parties have stipulated that "following a contribution to the Children's Trust, each of the grandchildren possessed the *same right of withdrawal* as . . . the withdrawal rights of Frank Cristofani and Lillian Dawson." (Emphasis added.) The legal right of decedent's grandchildren to withdraw specified amounts from the trust corpus within 15 days following any contribution of property constitutes a gift of a present interest. Crummey v. Commissioner, supra.

On brief, respondent attempts to distinguish *Crummey* from the instant case. Respondent argues that in *Crummey* the trust beneficiaries not only possessed an immediate right of withdrawal, but also possessed "substantial, future economic benefits" in the trust corpus and income. Respondent emphasizes that the Children's Trust identified decedent's children as "primary beneficiaries," and that decedent's grandchildren were to be considered as "beneficiaries of secondary importance."

Generally, the beneficiaries of the trust in *Crummey* were entitled to distributions of income. Trust corpus was to be distributed to the issue of each beneficiary sometime following the beneficiary's death.

See Crummey v. Commissioner, T.C. Memo. 1966-144. Aside from the discretionary actions of the trustee, the only way any beneficiary in *Crummey* could receive trust corpus was through the demand provision which allowed each beneficiary to demand up to $4,000 in the year in which a transfer to the trust was made. The Ninth Circuit observed:

> In our case . . . if no demand is made in any particular year, the additions are forever removed from the uncontrolled reach of the beneficiary since, with exception of the yearly demand provision, the only way the corpus can ever be tapped by a beneficiary, is through a distribution at the discretion of the trustee. [Crummey v. Commissioner, 397 F.2d at 88.]

In the instant case, the primary beneficiaries of the Children's Trust were decedent's children. Decedent's grandchildren held contingent remainder interests in the Children's Trust. Decedent's grandchildren's interests vested only in the event that their respective parent (decedent's child) predeceased decedent or failed to survive decedent by more than 120 days. We do not believe, however, that *Crummey* requires that the beneficiaries of a trust must have a vested present interest or vested remainder interest in the trust corpus or income, in order to qualify for the section 2503(b) exclusion.

As discussed in *Crummey*, the likelihood that the beneficiary will actually receive present enjoyment of the property is not the test for determining whether a present interest was received. Rather, we must examine the ability of the beneficiaries, in a legal sense, to exercise their right to withdraw trust corpus, and the trustee's right to legally resist a beneficiary's demand for payment. Crummey v. Commissioner, 397 F.2d at 88. Based upon the language of the trust instrument and stipulations of the parties, we believe that each grandchild possessed the legal right to withdraw trust corpus and that the trustees would be unable to legally resist a grandchild's withdrawal demand. We note that there was no agreement or understanding between decedent, the trustees, and the beneficiaries that the grandchildren would not exercise their withdrawal rights following a contribution to the Children's Trust.

Respondent also argues that since the grandchildren possessed only a contingent remainder interest in the Children's Trust, decedent never intended to benefit her grandchildren. Respondent contends that the only reason decedent gave her grandchildren the right to withdraw trust corpus was to obtain the benefit of the annual exclusion.

We disagree. Based upon the provisions of the Children's Trust, we believe that decedent intended to benefit her grandchildren. Their benefits, as remaindermen, were contingent upon a child of decedent's dying before decedent or failing to survive decedent by more than 120 days. We recognize that at the time decedent executed the Children's Trust, decedent's children were in good health, but this does not remove the possibility that decedent's children could have predeceased decedent.

In addition, decedent's grandchildren possessed the power to withdraw up to an amount equal to the amount allowable for the 2503(b) exclusion. Although decedent's grandchildren never exercised their respective withdrawal rights, this does not vitiate the fact that they had the legal right to do so, within 15 days following a contribution to the Children's Trust. Events might have occurred to prompt decedent's children and grandchildren (through their guardians) to exercise their withdrawal rights. For example, either or both of decedent's children and their respective families might have suddenly and unexpectedly been faced with economic hardship; or, in the event of the insolvency of one of decedent's children, the rights of the grandchildren might have been exercised to safeguard their interest in the trust assets from their parents' creditors. In light of the provisions in decedent's trust, we fail to see how respondent can argue that decedent did not intend to benefit her grandchildren.

Finally, the fact that the trust provisions were intended to obtain the benefit of the annual gift tax exclusion does not change the result. As we stated in Perkins v. Commissioner, supra,

> regardless of the petitioners' motives, or why they did what they in fact did, the legal rights in question were created by the trust instruments and could at any time thereafter be exercised. Petitioners having done what they purported to do, their tax-saving motive is irrelevant. [Perkins v. Commissioner, 27 T.C. at 606.]

Based upon the foregoing, we find that the grandchildren's right to withdraw an amount not to exceed the section 2503(b) exclusion, represents a present interest for purposes of section 2503(b). Accordingly, petitioner is entitled to claim annual exclusions with respect to decedent's grandchildren as a result of decedent's transfers of property to the Children's Trust in 1984 and 1985.

Decision will be entered for the petitioner.

NOTES AND PROBLEM

1. The Internal Revenue Service has been not happy with the *Cristofani* decision. It has announced that it will challenge attempts to obtain annual exclusions where the substance of the transfer clearly indicates that the donor's purpose was to obtain the annual exclusion and not to benefit the recipient. If the persons with withdrawal rights

have only discretionary income interests, remote contingent rights to the remainder, or no rights whatsoever in the income or remainder, the Service may challenge the annual exclusions. In these cases, the nonexercise of the withdrawal rights indicates, to the Service, some kind of prearranged understanding with the donor that the rights were not meant to be exercised. Tech. Adv. Mem. 9628004 (July 12, 1996). The Service does not contest gift tax exclusions for Crummey powers held by current income beneficiaries and persons with vested remainders on the theory that it is reasonable for them, with long-term economic interests in the trust, to decide not to exercise the withdrawal powers. See Marc A. Chorney, Transfer Tax Issues Raised by *Crummey* Powers, 33 Real Prop., Prob., & Tr. J. 755 (1999); Comment, A Reluctant Stance by the Internal Revenue Service: The Uncertain Future of the Use of the Section 2508(b) Annual Gift Exclusion Following *Crummey* and *Cristofani*, 38 Santa Clara L. Rev. 589 (1998).

2. Estate planners now have two basic options in drafting trusts for minors: (a) draft a §2503(c) trust, or (b) include a power in the minor, exercisable within a reasonably limited period, to withdraw the amount of the annual exclusion or less. See Richard B. Atkinson, Gifts to Minors: A Roadmap, 42 Ark. L. Rev. 567 (1989).

3. *O* creates a trust to pay the income to her daughter *A* for life, remainder to *A*'s children. *A* is given the power to withdraw $5,000 out of the property *O* gives to the trust in any given year. If *A* does not exercise the power during a particular year, it lapses. *A* is 8 years old. No guardian has been appointed for *A. O* transfers $5,000 to the trust. Does this qualify for the annual exclusion?

As to why we use the figure $5,000 rather than $10,000 (the maximum annual exclusion) here's the explanation: Section 2041(b)(2), infra page 1034, provides that a lapse of a general power of appointment in any calendar year is considered a gift by the donee of the power to the extent that the property over which the power existed exceeded the greater of $5,000 or 5 percent of the value of the assets which could be appointed. If the donee of the power is the life beneficiary of the trust, for example, the lapse of the power may result in a gift to the remaindermen. A gift of a remainder does not qualify for the annual exclusion and may use up a portion of the donee's unified credit. There are two ways of remedying the problem and giving the donee power to withdraw $10,000 a year without running into the limitations of §2041(b)(2). First, give the donee a special power of appointment over the trust assets; if the general power to withdraw $10,000 lapses, the donee makes no gift because he has not given up dominion and control of the property (the donee still has a special power). Second, transfer assets of $200,000 or more into the trust; in this case the lapse of a power over $10,000 will not exceed 5 percent of the value of the trust corpus.

4. Suppose that, in Problem 3, *O* gives the trustee $5,000 each year to pay the premium on a life insurance policy on *O*'s life, which is owned by the trust. *O* gives *A* a right to withdraw $5,000 annually. Does this qualify for the annual exclusion? How much life insurance on the life of a 40-year-old woman (non-smoker) can be purchased with an annual premium of $5,000? It might surprise you to learn it is $3,200,000, which is quite a lot to transfer tax-free to your child.

In his budget message in 1998, President Clinton proposed to eliminate deductions for Crummey powers. This was vigorously opposed by the life insurance industry. This problem should tell you why.

3.   Gifts Between Spouses and from One Spouse to a Third Person

Since 1981, the Code has permitted one spouse to take an *unlimited* marital deduction for gifts to the other spouse (see infra page 1043). Any amount of property (except certain terminable interests) can now be transferred between the spouses, either during life or at death, without payment of a gift or estate tax. The policy is: Husband and wife are permitted to treat their property as assets of a marital unit, transferable between husband and wife without paying any transfer taxes. Only when the assets pass from one of the spouses to a third person is a transfer tax imposed.

The marital deduction is allowed only if a spouse makes transfers to the other spouse that qualify for the marital deduction. The policy of Congress is that if a transfer of property from one spouse to the other is to be exempt from transfer tax, the transfer must be in a form that is subject to taxation when the property is transferred by the donee spouse to a third party. Inasmuch as a terminable interest (e.g., a life estate) is not subject to transfer taxation when it terminates, a *terminable interest* does not qualify for the marital deduction, subject to certain exceptions. The two most important exceptions to the nondeductible terminable interest rule are set forth below as Cases 6 and 7. Inasmuch as we give extended treatment to the marital deduction in connection with the estate tax (see infra page 1042), we only mention the nondeductible terminable interest rule here in passing. It is enough to say — with an explanation to come later — that the following property interests qualify for the marital deduction under the gift tax and the estate tax:

> *Case 5. Fee simple or absolute ownership.* *W* gives *H* $1 million outright. No gift tax is payable by *W*. The $1 million will be included in *H*'s taxable gross estate at death if *H* then owns it. If *H* gives the property to a third person, a gift tax will be payable.

Case 6. Power of appointment trust. W transfers $1 million in trust to pay *H* the income for his life and upon *H*'s death to distribute the principal as *H* appoints by will. *H* has a terminable interest (a life estate), but it qualifies for the marital deduction because *H* has in addition a general power of appointment. No gift tax is payable by *W*. Because *H* has a general power, the value of the trust fund will be included in *H*'s taxable gross estate at death.

Case 7. QTIP (qualified terminable interest property) trust. W transfers $1 million in trust to pay the income to *H* for life and upon *H*'s death to distribute the principal to *W*'s children. *W* may elect under §2523(f) of the Code to take a marital deduction for the terminable interest given *H*; as a result of this election, the value of the trust fund will be included in *H*'s taxable gross estate at death even though *H* has only a life estate.

Observe that in all three transfers above, the gift by the wife qualifies for the marital deduction, but when the property is transferred by the husband to a (noncharitable) third party during life or at death, a gift or estate tax becomes payable. (If you want to know more about the marital deduction and cannot contain your curiosity, skip to page 1042 infra.)

When property is transferred by gift from one spouse to a third person, the transfer is subject to taxation. However, if the other spouse consents, §2513 of the Code permits the gift to be considered as made one half by each spouse. Thus if the wife transfers $200,000 to her daughter, this may be treated — with the husband's consent — as a transfer by the wife of $100,000 and a transfer by the husband of $100,000. One effect of §2513 is to double the available annual exclusions.

PROBLEMS

1. *W* gives property worth $100,000 to *A*, and her husband *H* signifies his consent to splitting the gift by signing at the appropriate point on the gift tax return filed by the donor. Neither *W* nor *H* has made taxable gifts in any earlier year. What is the amount of taxable gift made by *W*? By *H*?

2. *H* and *W* have three children. They want to know (a) what is the maximum amount they can give to each child tax free each year without using any of their unified gift tax credits, and (b) what is the maximum amount they can give the children tax free in one year, using their annual exclusions and their unified gift tax credits. Suppose that *H* dies after making these gifts, leaving all his property to *W*. Is any estate tax payable on *H*'s death?

SECTION C.   THE FEDERAL ESTATE TAX

1.   A Thumbnail Sketch of the Federal Estate Tax

The basic purpose of the federal estate tax is to tax the value of property owned or passing at death plus the value of property given away during lifetime. This is accomplished by imposing a graduated tax rate schedule on the aggregate of the decedent's *taxable estate* plus *adjusted taxable gifts*, against which various *credits* may be applied.

In determining the amount of the taxable estate, the first step is to compute the value of the decedent's *gross estate*. The federal estate tax attempts to subject to taxation all manner of transfers wherein an economic benefit is transferred from the decedent to another person at death. The Internal Revenue Code's definition of the gross estate encompasses three general categories of transfers: (a) transfers by will or intestacy, (b) certain lifetime transfers that, generally speaking, pass economic benefits at the death of the decedent, and (c) certain nonprobate transfers. The details of what transfers are included in the gross estate are spelled out in §§2033-2044 of the Code.

The gross estate includes all property owned at death (§2033). It thus includes all assets in the probate estate as well as assets passing outside of probate by a payable-on-death designation.

The gross estate includes all lifetime transfers wherein the decedent retained a life estate or control of beneficial enjoyment (§2036), revocable transfers such as revocable trusts (§2038), and some gifts made within three years before death (§2035). It includes pension plan benefits passing to survivors (§2039), property held in joint tenancy or tenancy by the entirety (§2040), and life insurance policies over which the decedent had incidents of ownership (§2042). It also includes property over which the decedent had a general power of appointment (§2041).

From the gross estate, certain *deductions* are authorized by the Code. These include deductions for expenses of administration and casualty losses, and — of more importance in estate planning — deductions for transfers to a spouse (the marital deduction) and deductions for transfers to charity.

The gross estate minus deductions equals *taxable estate*. To compute the estate tax, *adjusted taxable gifts* are added to the taxable estate. Adjusted taxable gifts are taxable gifts made after 1976 of property not otherwise includible in the gross estate. If the property was included in the gross estate under §§2033-2044 (such as a remainder in property in which the decedent retained a life estate, includible under §2036), the property is not also includible as an adjusted taxable gift, for that would result in double taxation. Taxable estate plus adjusted taxable gifts equals the *tentative estate tax base*, against which the tax rate schedule is applied to produce a *tentative estate tax*. From the tentative tax as thus computed are deducted gift taxes paid on taxable gifts made after 1976, which may be viewed as an advance payment of estate taxes. Also deducted are various credits to which the estate may be entitled. These include a *credit for state death taxes*, a *credit for gift taxes on pre-1977 gifts* that are included in the gross estate under one of the lifetime transfer sections, a *credit for taxes on prior transfers* that were taxed in the estate of another decedent within the preceding ten years, and a *credit for foreign death taxes*.

The most important credit is the *unified credit against the estate tax*, which is the equivalent of the applicable exemption. For the applicable exemption, see supra page 982.

Here follows an outline of the estate tax provisions of the Internal Revenue Code in table form:

	§2033	Property owned at death
+	§2035	Transfers of life insurance policies and certain other interests within three years of death
+	§2036	Transfers with a retained life estate or with retained controls
+	§2037	Transfers taking effect at death
+	§2038	Revocable transfers
+	§2039	Annuities and employee benefits
+	§2040	Property passing by right of survivorship (joint tenancy)
+	§2041	General powers of appointment
+	§2042	Life insurance
+	§2043	Transfers for a partial consideration
+	§2044	Certain property for which a marital deduction was previously allowed (QTIP property)

= Gross Estate

	§2053	Deduction for administration expenses, debts, funeral expenses
−	§2054	Deduction for casualty losses
−	§2055	Charitable deduction
−	§2056	Marital deduction

= Taxable Estate

<u>+</u>   *Adjusted taxable gifts* (taxable gifts made after 1976, but not including gifts that are includible above in the decedent's gross estate)

= Tentative Estate Tax Base

<u>× §2001</u>   Estate tax rate schedule

= Tentative Estate Tax

− Gift taxes on gifts made after 1976
− §2010   Unified estate tax credit
− §2011   Credit for state death taxes
− §2012   Credit for pre-1977 gift taxes on property included in gross estate
− §2013   Credit for taxes on prior transfers
<u>− §2014   Credit for foreign death taxes</u>

= Federal Estate Tax

2.   *The Gross Estate: Property Passing by Will or Intestacy*

a.   Section 2033: Property Owned at Death

Section 2033 of the Internal Revenue Code provides: "The value of the gross estate shall include the value of property to the extent of the interest therein of the decedent at the time of his death." Section 2033 reaches all property owned at death that passes by will or intestacy. This includes real and tangible personal property; transmissible future interests; intangibles such as securities, patents, and copyrights; interests in an incorporated or unincorporated business; and undivided interests in property (such as the decedent's share of property held in a tenancy in common). In other words, the gross estate includes, under §2033, all items in the decedent's probate estate.[8]

Section 2033 also reaches property owned at death that passes under a payable-on-death provision of a contract (other than life insurance, annuities, or employee death benefits, which are governed by separate sections of the Code).

If the decedent owned a life estate created by another person,[9] nothing is includible in the decedent's gross estate under §2033. Since

---

8. The Taxpayer Relief Act of 1997 added §2033A to the Code, which provides special and favorable exclusion rules for the decedent's interest in a family-owned business.

9. If the decedent made an inter vivos transfer with a retained life estate, the value of the transferred property is includable in the decedent's gross estate under §2036. See infra page 1014.

a life estate terminates at death, the decedent owned no interest that could pass by will or intestacy. This principle is of considerable importance in estate planning. It is possible to transfer property into a trust giving the beneficiary the income from the property for life without causing any *estate* tax to be levied on the life beneficiary's death. It is even possible to give the income beneficiary certain limited powers to invade the corpus of the trust for his or her benefit and a special power to appoint the remainder interest at death, all without estate tax cost (see infra page 1033). However, if the income beneficiary is of a younger generation than the settlor, and the remainder is given to the life tenant's children, a *generation-skipping transfer tax* may be levied at the life tenant's death (see infra pages 1065-1078).

PROBLEM

Decedent is killed while piloting a plane containing several bales of marijuana weighing 662 pounds, which were subsequently confiscated. Is the value of the marijuana includible in the decedent's gross estate? In Pvt. Ltr. Rul. 9207004 (1991), the IRS ruled that the retail street value of the marijuana was includible in the gross estate because the decedent had possession and control over the drugs and was to receive the economic benefit from their disposition. It was not necessary to establish legal ownership. A deduction for its confiscation as a casualty loss was denied because to allow the deduction would violate the public policy against drug trafficking. Suppose that the decedent had survived the plane crash and had died after the marijuana was confiscated. What result?

b. Section 2034: Dower or Curtesy

Property includible under §2033 includes assets passing to the surviving spouse by operation of law and over which the decedent did not have the power of disposition at death. Under §2034, "the value of the gross estate shall include the value of all property to the extent of any interest therein of the surviving spouse, existing at the time of the decedent's death as dower or curtesy, or by virtue of a statute creating an estate in lieu of dower or curtesy." Section 2034 does not apply to community property. In community property states, each spouse is the owner of an undivided one-half interest in community assets and has the power of testamentary disposition over only that one-half share. Only the value of the decedent's community interest is includible as an owned interest under §2033.

3. The Gross Estate: Nonprobate Property

a. Section 2040: Joint Tenancy

The decedent's interest in a joint tenancy is not taxed under §2033 because the decedent's interest terminates at death. A joint tenancy interest is, however, taxed under §2040. In discussing §2040, together with the gift tax rules applicable to the creation of joint tenancies, we must distinguish between (1) a joint tenancy between persons other than spouses and (2) a joint tenancy or tenancy by the entirety between husband and wife.

(1) Joint tenancy between persons other than husband and wife

(a) Gift tax. A joint tenancy is treated differently under the gift tax from the way it is treated under the estate tax. Different principles of taxation are applied by these two taxes. Under the gift tax, a joint tenancy is treated in the same manner as a tenancy in common is treated, on the theory that the donee co-tenant receives the same lifetime rights under both cotenancies. The donee can sever the joint tenancy and turn it into a tenancy in common at any time. Case 8 illustrates the treatment of a tenancy in common created by the donor with the donee.

> *Case 8.* In 2000, *O* pays $40,000 for securities, taking title in the name of *O* and *A* as *tenants in common. O* and *A* each acquire an undivided one-half interest in the securities. *O* has made a gift of one-half the value of the property, or $20,000, to *A*. Deducting the $10,000 annual exclusion, *O* has made a taxable gift of $10,000. (Because of the unified credit against the gift tax, however, no gift tax is actually payable unless *O* has used up her unified credit.)

Since a joint tenant can sever at any time the joint tenancy, destroying the right of survivorship and converting the tenancy into a tenancy in common, the gift tax law assumes the donee joint tenant receives the same economic benefit as does a donee tenant in common. Thus:

> *Case 9.* In 2000, *O* pays $40,000 for securities, taking title in the name of *O* and *A* as *joint tenants with right of survivorship. O* has made a gift to *A* of one-half the value of the property, or $20,000.

A joint and survivor bank account is treated somewhat differently. In such an account, either party can withdraw all funds on deposit, whereas a common law joint tenant can, by partition, only acquire title in severalty to his or her fractional share. Since a depositor in a joint and survivor account can withdraw the amount deposited (in effect, revoking the transfer), no gift occurs until the amount is withdrawn by the nondepositing party. Thus:

> *Case 10.* In 2000, *O* deposits $30,000 in a joint and survivor bank account; money in the account is payable to *O* or *A* or the survivor. Since *O* can withdraw the $30,000, the gift is incomplete (see supra page 985). If *A* withdraws funds from the account, a gift is then made from *O* to *A* of the amount withdrawn. Similarly, if *O* and *A* each deposit $15,000 in a joint account, no gift is made until either *O* or *A* withdraws more than the $15,000 each deposited. Treas. Reg. §25.2511.1(h)(4).

The rules applicable to a joint bank account also apply to a United States government bond registered in the name of "*O* or *A*." Under this "or" form of ownership, either *O* or *A* can present the bond for payment. Thus there is no gift unless *A* cashes in the bond.

(b) Estate tax. The decedent's share of a tenancy in common is included in his gross estate under §2033. If the decedent is one of two tenants in common, one-half the value of the property is included in the decedent's gross estate. Thus:

> *Case 8a.* Refer back to Case 8, involving the creation of a tenancy in common in 2000. *O* dies in 2004. *O* is survived by *A*. On *O*'s death, the securities are worth $60,000. The value of *O*'s one-half interest in the securities, or $30,000, is includible in *O*'s gross estate under §2033 as an interest owned at death. $10,000 is brought into the estate tax computation as an adjusted taxable gift.

A joint tenancy is not treated like a tenancy in common under the federal estate tax. With respect to a joint tenancy, the amount included in the decedent's gross estate is not the value of the decedent's fractional share of ownership. Where spouses are not involved, the portion included is based upon the percentage of the decedent's contribution to the total cost of the property. Section 2040(a) of the Code requires the inclusion of the entire value of the property held in joint tenancy, except such part of the entire value as is attributable to the amount of *consideration furnished* by the other joint tenant or was originally owned by the other joint tenant. This rule applies to property held in joint tenancy, joint bank accounts, and government bonds with survivorship provisions. Thus:

> *Case 9a.* Refer back to Case 9, involving the creation of a joint tenancy in 2000. *O* dies in 2004. At *O*'s death, the securities are worth $60,000. Under §2040, the full value of the securities, or $60,000, is includible in *O*'s gross estate. (There is no adjusted taxable gift inclusion because the

property that was the subject of the gift is included in O's gross estate under §2040.) If O paid a gift tax at the time the joint tenancy was created in 2000, there is no double taxation. Section 2001(b)(2) provides that the tentative estate tax is reduced by the amount of gift taxes paid on gifts made after 1976.

If, in Case 9a, O had contributed three-fourths of the purchase price of the securities ($30,000) and A one-quarter ($10,000), three-fourths of the value of the securities at the date of O's death, or $45,000, would be included in O's gross estate. The burden of showing the amount contributed by the survivor is on the decedent's personal representative. The value of the entire property will be included in the gross estate unless the amount contributed by the survivor is proved. When title is taken in joint tenancy form, it is important to keep records showing the source of the funds with which the property was acquired. Failure to do this may result in needless taxation if the decedent's personal representative cannot satisfactorily establish the amount of the contribution furnished by the survivor. With respect to joint bank owners, the decedent's personal representative must sustain the burden of showing the amount on deposit attributable to the survivor's contributions, or the full amount is included in the decedent's gross estate.

PROBLEM

O purchases Blackacre for $100,000 and takes title in the name of O and A as joint tenants with right of survivorship. O has used up her unified gift tax credit and therefore pays a gift tax on the $40,000 gift to A ($50,000 minus the $10,000 exclusion). A few years later A dies. Is O entitled to a return of the gift tax paid? Is O's executor entitled to credit the gift tax paid against O's estate tax when she dies? Suppose that O sells Blackacre before her death. Is O's executor entitled to credit the gift tax paid against the estate tax?

(2) Joint tenancy and tenancy by the entirety between husband and wife

(a) Gift tax.   Internal Revenue Code §§2056 and 2523 provide for an unlimited marital deduction: Any amount of property may be transferred by one spouse to the other spouse as tenants in common, joint tenants, or tenants by the entirety tax free. Thus, if a wife buys property and takes title in the name of herself and her husband as joint tenants, a gift has been made to the husband of one-half the value of the property, as in Case 9, but the amount of the gift qualifies for the marital deduction and no gift tax is payable.

(b) Estate tax.   The who-furnished-the-consideration test applicable to joint tenancies between nonspouses does not apply to a "qualified joint interest" held between spouses. A qualified joint interest is a tenancy by the entirety or a joint tenancy with right of survivorship where the spouses are the only joint tenants. With respect to both of these forms of property holding, each spouse owns an undivided one-half interest in the property.

Section 2040(b) of the Code provides that with respect to property held by the decedent and the decedent's spouse as joint tenants with right of survivorship or as tenants by the entirety, one-half the value of the property is includible in the decedent's gross estate regardless of which spouse furnished the consideration for the property's acquisition. Hence, for both gift and estate tax purposes a joint tenancy or tenancy by the entirety owned by husband and wife is treated as owned one-half by each. The one-half interest includible in the decedent's gross estate that passes to the surviving spouse qualifies for the unlimited marital deduction. Therefore no estate taxes result from the inclusion of the decedent spouse's one-half interest.

b.   Section 2039: Employee Death Benefits

Section 2039 of the Code provides that employee death benefits receivable by a beneficiary are includible in the gross estate of the decedent if the decedent "possessed the right to receive" any benefits during his lifetime. The type of right that usually causes §2039 to apply is the right of the decedent to an annuity or pension upon retirement. If the decedent has this right, and death benefits — usually in the form of an annuity or a lump sum payment — are payable to a surviving beneficiary, the value of the death benefits is includible in the decedent's gross estate. Individual Retirement Accounts (IRAs) and Keogh plans are included in the decedent's gross estate under §2039.

Section 2039 is inapplicable to "insurance under policies on the life of the decedent," which is governed by §2042.

If the decedent has no power to select the beneficiary of his employee benefits, because the death benefits are payable *by statute* to the decedent's spouse or children, the death benefits are not includable in the decedent's estate. Social Security benefits are excludable, for example.

Employee death benefits included in the decedent's estate and payable to the decedent's spouse ordinarily will qualify for the marital deduction.

Income tax treatment. When employee death benefits are received by a beneficiary after the death of the employee or of the owner of an income-tax-deferred plan (such as IRA or Keogh), the receipts are treated as "income in respect of a decedent" under §691(a) of the Code. Essentially, this means the beneficiary stands in the income tax shoes of the decedent, with no step-up in basis. The beneficiary may deduct from his or her income tax return the estate tax attributable to the benefit. §691(c).

c. Section 2042: Life Insurance

Section 2042 of the Code provides that the gross estate shall include the value of insurance proceeds on the life of the decedent (1) if the decedent possessed at death any of the *incidents of ownership* under the policies, or (2) if the policy proceeds were *payable to the insured's executor or estate.* The incidents of ownership include such policy rights as the right to change the beneficiary, to surrender, cancel, or assign the policy, or to borrow against the cash surrender value in the policy. Where a person takes out a policy on his own life and names some member of the family as beneficiary, the proceeds will be taxed in the insured's estate if he holds any incidents of ownership over the policy. This is true of even a term insurance policy that has no investment features and hence no cash surrender value, for the insured has the right to change the beneficiary designation and also the right to assign or cancel the policy. The retention of only one incident of ownership causes the full value of the insurance proceeds to be taxed under §2042.

At one time, life insurance was included in the decedent's gross estate if the decedent paid the premiums, but the premium-payment test was discarded in 1954.

If an insurance policy owned by a decedent spouse (and therefore includable in the decedent's gross estate) is payable to the surviving spouse in a lump sum, the policy proceeds qualify for the unlimited marital deduction. No taxes result from the inclusion of the policy in the decedent's gross estate.

See generally Robert B. Smith, Reconsidering the Taxation of Life Insurance Proceeds Through the Lens of Current Estate Planning, 15 Va. Tax Rev. 283 (1995).

PROBLEMS

1. *H* is the insured under a $50,000 ordinary life insurance policy that names *W* as the owner of the policy and of all incidents of

ownership therein. The policy was issued in *W*'s name as owner when it was taken out ten years ago, and all policy premiums have been paid out of *W*'s funds. The policy names *W* as primary beneficiary and the couple's daughter, *D*, as contingent beneficiary. *H* dies, and the policy proceeds are paid to *W*. *H* leaves a will that devises his entire estate to *W* and *D* in equal shares. The will names *W* as executor. Are the policy proceeds includable in *H*'s gross estate?

2.　Consider the same facts as in Problem 1 except that *W* predeceases *H*, leaving a will that devises "all my property" to *H*. On the date of *W*'s death, the cash surrender value of the policy is $10,000. *H* dies a year later, and the $50,000 in policy proceeds are paid to the couple's daughter, *D*, as contingent beneficiary. What are the estate tax consequences in *W*'s estate? In *H*'s estate?

3.　If a donee of a special power of appointment can appoint trust property that includes a life insurance policy on the donee's life, the power to appoint is an incident of ownership, and the value of the insurance will be included in the donee's gross estate. In drafting special powers, you should take care to exclude such life insurance from the appointive property. See supra page 698.

4.　*The Gross Estate: Lifetime Transfers*

The gross estate includes certain lifetime transfers made by the decedent. The relevant sections are 2035, 2036, 2037, and 2038. We take them up here in the order that, we think, makes them easiest to understand.

a.　Section 2036: Transfers with Life Estate or Control of Beneficial Rights Retained

Section 2036(a) provides:

> The value of the gross estate shall include the value of all property to the extent of any interest therein of which the decedent has at any time made a transfer (except in case of a bona fide sale for an adequate and full consideration in money or money's worth), by trust or otherwise, under which he has retained for his life or for any period which does not in fact end before his death —
>
> 　　(1) The possession or enjoyment of, or the right to the income from, the property, or
>
> 　　(2) The right, either alone or in conjunction with any person, to designate the persons who shall possess or enjoy the property or the income therefrom.

Note that §2036 includes in the gross estate two types of lifetime transfers. Section 2036(a)(1) applies when the decedent retains a life estate in the transferred property. Although the life estate terminates at death, the transfer is subjected to estate taxation because the decedent retained the most important incident of property ownership: the right to possess and enjoy the property, or the right to its income, for life.

Section 2036(a)(2) reaches transfers in which the decedent retains the right to control beneficial enjoyment of the property, even though the right cannot be exercised in a manner that would benefit the transferor personally. To take an obvious case, when the transferor designates himself as a co-trustee and the trustees have a discretionary power to accumulate trust income or distribute it to the beneficiary, or a power to distribute the income among several beneficiaries in such shares as the trustees shall determine, the transfer is taxed under this section. The transfer is also taxed even though the power is exercisable only with the consent of a person having an interest that could be adversely affected by the exercise of the power.[10]

To a considerable extent, as we shall see, §2036(a)(2) overlaps with §2038, which applies to lifetime transfers where the transferor possesses the power to alter, amend, or revoke.

For a complete discussion of §2036, see Boris I. Bittker, Transfers Subject to Retained Right to Receive the Income or Designate the Income Beneficiary, 34 Rutgers L. Rev. 668 (1982).

PROBLEMS

1.   *O* transfers property to *X* in trust to pay the income to *O* for life and on *O*'s death to distribute the trust assets to *A*. What are the gift and estate tax consequences of this transfer?

---

10. Sections 671-677 of the Internal Revenue Code spell out the circumstances under which the settlor of a trust is taxable on trust *income* on grounds of dominion and control. The income tax provisions are not entirely consistent with the estate tax provisions. A settlor may have succeeded in eliminating the trust income from his gross income but not the principal from his gross estate. For example, if the settlor has the power to control beneficial enjoyment of the income only with the consent of an *adverse party*, the income is not taxable to the settlor. IRC §674(a). But the value of the principal is includable in the settlor's gross estate at death because §§2036 and 2038 do not distinguish between a power held with an adverse party and a power held with a nonadverse party. Or if the settlor as trustee has only a discretionary power to pay income to, or accumulate it for, the life beneficiary, the settlor is not taxable on the income. Id. §674(b)(6). But the value of the trust property will be included in the settlor's gross estate. If your client wishes to create a trust and retain any power over income or principal, both income tax and estate tax sections must be explored if the settlor is to successfully eliminate the income from his gross income and the principal from his gross estate. See supra pages 594-597.

2.   *O* transfers property to *X* in trust. The trustee has unfettered discretion to pay the income to *O* or to accumulate it and to invade the corpus for *O*'s benefit; on *O*'s death, the trustee is to distribute the trust assets to *A*. What are the gift and estate tax consequences?

Estate of Maxwell v. Commissioner
United States Court of Appeals, Second Circuit, 1993
3 F.3d 591

LASKER, J.   This appeal presents challenges to the tax court's interpretation of section 2036(a) of the Internal Revenue Code, relating to "Transfers with retained life estate." The petitioner, the Estate of Lydia G. Maxwell, contends that the tax court erred in holding that the transaction at issue (a) was a transfer with retained life estate within the meaning of 26 U.S.C. §2036 and (b) was not a bona fide sale for adequate and full consideration under that statute.

The decision of the tax court is affirmed.

I

On March 14, 1984, Lydia G. Maxwell (the "decedent") conveyed her personal residence, which she had lived in since 1957, to her son Winslow Maxwell, her only heir, and his wife Margaret Jane Maxwell (the "Maxwells"). Following the transfer, the decedent continued to reside in the house until her death on July 30, 1986. At the time of the transfer, she was eighty-two years old and was suffering from cancer.

The transaction was structured as follows:

1) The residence was sold by the decedent to the Maxwells for $270,000;[11]

2) Simultaneously with the sale, the decedent forgave $20,000 of the purchase price (which was equal in amount to the annual gift tax exclusion to which she was entitled);

3) The Maxwells executed a $250,000 mortgage note in favor of decedent;

4) The Maxwells leased the premises to her for five years at the monthly rental of $1,800; and

5) The Maxwells were obligated to pay and did pay certain expenses associated with the property following the transfer, including property taxes, insurance costs, and unspecified "other expenses."

While the decedent paid the Maxwells rent totalling $16,200 in

---

11. The parties have stipulated that the fair market value of the property on the date of the purported sale was $280,000.

1984, $22,183 in 1985 and $12,600 in 1986, the Maxwells paid the decedent interest on the mortgage totalling $16,875 in 1984, $21,150 in 1985, and $11,475 in 1986. As can be observed, the rent paid by the decedent to the Maxwells came remarkably close to matching the mortgage interest which they paid to her. In 1984, she paid the Maxwells only $675 less than they paid her; in 1985, she paid them only $1,033 more than they paid her, and in 1986 she paid the Maxwells only $1,125 more than they paid her.

Not only did the rent functionally cancel out the interest payments made by the Maxwells, but the Maxwells were at no time called upon to pay any of the principal on the $250,000 mortgage debt; it was forgiven in its entirety. As petitioner's counsel admitted at oral argument, although the Maxwells had executed the mortgage note, "there was an intention by and large that it not be paid." Pursuant to this intention, in each of the following years preceding her death, the decedent forgave $20,000 of the mortgage principal, and, by a provision of her will executed on March 16, 1984 (that is, just two days after the transfer), she forgave the remaining indebtedness.

The decedent reported the sale of her residence on her 1984 federal income tax return but did not pay any tax on the sale because she elected to use the once-in-a-lifetime exclusion on the sale or exchange of a principal residence provided for by 26 U.S.C. §121.

She continued to occupy the house by herself until her death. At no time during her occupancy did the Maxwells attempt to sell the house to anyone else, but, on September 22, 1986, shortly after the decedent's death, they did sell the house for $550,000.

Under I.R.C. §2036(a), where property is disposed of by a decedent during her lifetime but the decedent retains "possession or enjoyment" of it until her death, that property is taxable as part of the decedent's gross estate, unless the transfer was a bona fide sale for an "adequate and full" consideration. 26 U.S.C. §2036.

On the decedent's estate tax return, the Estate reported only the $210,000 remaining on the mortgage debt (following the decedent's forgiveness of $20,000 in the two preceding years). The Commissioner found that the 1984 transaction constituted a transfer with retained life estate — rejecting the petitioners' arguments that the decedent did not retain "possession or enjoyment" of the property, and that the transaction was exempt from section 2036(a) because it was a bona fide sale for full and adequate consideration — , and assessed a deficiency against the Estate to adjust for the difference between the fair market value of the property at the time of decedent's death ($550,000) and the reported $210,000.

The Estate appealed to the tax court, which, after a trial on stipulated facts, affirmed the Commissioner's ruling, holding:

On this record, bearing in mind petitioner's burden of proof, we hold that, notwithstanding its form, the substance of the transaction calls for the conclusion that decedent made a transfer to her son and daughter-in-law with the understanding, at least implied, that she would continue to reside in her home until her death, that the transfer was not a bona fide sale for an adequate and full consideration in money or money's worth, and that the lease represented nothing more than an attempt to add color to the characterization of the transaction as a bona fide sale.

There are two questions before us: Did the decedent retain possession or enjoyment of the property following the transfer? And if she did, was the transfer a bona fide sale for an adequate and full consideration in money or money's worth?

II

Section 2036(a) provides in pertinent part:

> The value of the gross estate shall include the value of all property to the extent of any interest therein of which the decedent has at any time made a transfer (except in case of a bona fide sale for an adequate and full consideration in money or money's worth), by trust or otherwise, under which he has retained for his life or for any period not ascertainable without reference to his death or for any period which does not in fact end before his death — (1) the possession or enjoyment of, or the right to the income from, the property, . . . 26 U.S.C. §2036(a).

In the case of real property, the terms "possession" and "enjoyment" have been interpreted to mean "the lifetime use of the property." United States v. Byrum, 408 U.S. 125, 147, 92 S. Ct. 2382, 2395, 33 L. Ed. 2d 238 (1972).

In numerous cases, the tax court has held, where an aged family member transferred her home to a relative and continued to reside there until her death, that the decedent-transferor had retained "possession or enjoyment" of the property within the meaning of §2036. As stated in Rapelje v. Commissioner, 73 T.C. 82 (1979): "Possession or enjoyment of gifted property is retained [by the transferor] when there is an express or implied understanding to that effect among the parties at the time of transfer." . . . As the *Rapelje* opinion indicates . . . courts have held that §2036(a) requires that the fair market value of such property be included in the decedent's estate if he retained the actual possession or enjoyment thereof, even though he may have had no enforceable right to do so. Estate of Honigman v. Commissioner, 66 T.C. 1080, 1082 (1976); Estate of Linderme v. Commissioner, 52 T.C. 305, 308 (1969). In such cases, the burden is on the decedent's estate to disprove the existence of any adverse implied agreement or understanding and that burden is particularly onerous when intrafamily arrangements are involved. . . .

As indicated above, the tax court found as a fact that the decedent had transferred her home to the Maxwells "with the understanding, at least implied, that she would continue to reside in her home until her death." This finding was based upon the decedent's advanced age, her medical condition, and the overall result of the sale and lease. The lease was, in the tax court's words, "merely window dressing" — it had no substance.

The tax court's findings of fact are reversible only if clearly erroneous. Bausch & Lomb, Inc. v. Commissioner, 933 F.2d 1084, 1088 (2d Cir. 1991). We agree with the tax court's finding that the decedent transferred her home to the Maxwells "with the understanding, at least implied, that she would continue to reside in her home until her death," and certainly do not find it to be clearly erroneous. The decedent did, in fact, live at her residence until she died, and she had sole possession of the residence during the period between the day she sold her home to the Maxwells and the day she died. There is no evidence that the Maxwells ever intended to occupy the house themselves, or to sell or lease it to anyone else during the decedent's lifetime. Moreover, the Maxwells' failure to demand payment by the estate, as they were entitled to do under the lease, of the rent due for the months following decedent's death and preceding their sale of the property, also supports the tax court's finding.

The petitioner argues . . . that the decedent's tenancy alone does not justify inclusion of the residence in her estate, so it argues that the decedent's payment of rent sanctifies the transaction and renders it legitimate. Both arguments ignore the realities of the rent being offset by mortgage interest, the forgiveness of the entire mortgage debt either by gift or testamentary disposition, and the fact that the decedent was eighty-two at the time of the transfer and actually continued to live in the residence until her death which, at the time of the transfer, she had reason to believe would occur soon in view of her poor health.

The Estate relies primarily on Barlow v. Commissioner, 55 T.C. 666 (1971). In that case, the father transferred a farm to his children and simultaneously leased the right to continue to farm the property. The tax court held that the father did not retain "possession or enjoyment," stating that "one of the most valuable incidents of income-producing real estate is the rent which it yields. He who receives the rent in fact enjoys the property." *Barlow*, 55 T.C. at 671 (quoting McNichol's v. Commissioner, 265 F.2d 667, 671 (3d Cir.), cert. denied, 361 U.S. 829, 80 S. Ct. 78, 4 L. Ed. 2d 71 (1959)). However, *Barlow* is clearly distinguishable on its facts: In that case, there was evidence that the rent paid was fair and customary and, equally importantly, the rent paid was not offset by the decedent's receipt of interest from the family lessor.

. . . *Barlow* itself recognized that where a transferor "by agreement" "reserves the right of occupancy as an incident to the transfer," §2036(a) applies. *Barlow*, 55 T.C. at 670. . . .

For the reasons stated above, we conclude that the decedent did retain possession or enjoyment of the property for life and turn to the question of whether the transfer constituted "a bona fide sale for adequate and full consideration in money or money's worth."

III

Section 2036(a) provides that even if possession or enjoyment of transferred property is retained by the decedent until her death, if the transfer was a bona fide sale for adequate and full consideration in money or money's worth, the property is not includible in the estate. Petitioner contends that the Maxwells paid an "adequate and full consideration" for the decedent's residence, $270,000 total, consisting of the $250,000 mortgage note given by the Maxwells to the decedent, and the $20,000 the decedent forgave simultaneously with the conveyance.[12]

The tax court held that neither the Maxwells' mortgage note nor the decedent's $20,000 forgiveness constituted consideration within the meaning of the statute.

$250,000 MORTGAGE NOTE

As to the $250,000 mortgage note, the tax court held that:

Regardless of whether the $250,000 mortgage note might otherwise qualify as "adequate and full consideration in money or money's worth" for a $270,000 or $280,000 house, the mortgage note here had no value at all if there was no intention that it would ever be paid. The conduct of decedent and the Maxwells strongly suggest that neither party intended the Maxwells to pay any part of the principal of either the original note or any successor note.

There is no question that the mortgage note here is a fully secured, legally enforceable obligation on its face. The question is whether it is actually what it purports to be — a bona fide instrument of indebtedness — or whether it is a facade. The petitioner argues not

_____

12. As noted above, the parties have stipulated that the fair market value of the property on the date of the purported sale was $280,000. The Estate contends that $270,000 was full and adequate consideration for the sale, with a broker, for a house appraised at $280,000. We assume this fact to be true for purposes of determining whether the transaction was one for "an adequate and full consideration in money or money's worth."

only that an allegedly unenforceable intention to forgive indebtedness does not deprive the indebtedness of its status as "consideration in money or money's worth" but also that "[t]his is true even if there was an implied agreement exactly as found by the Tax Court."

We agree with the tax court that where, as here, there is an implied agreement between the parties that the grantee would never be called upon to make any payment to the grantor, as, in fact, actually occurred, the note given by the grantee had "no value at all." We emphatically disagree with the petitioner's view of the law as it applies to the facts of this case. As the Supreme Court has remarked, the family relationship often makes it possible for one to shift tax incidence by surface changes of ownership without disturbing in the least his dominion and control over the subject of the gift or the purposes for which the income from the property is used. Commissioner v. Culbertson, 337 U.S. 733, 746, 69 S. Ct. 1210, 1216, 93 L. Ed. 1659 (1949). There can be no doubt that intent is a relevant inquiry in determining whether a transaction is "bona fide." As another panel of this Court held recently, construing a parallel provision of the Internal Revenue Code, in a case involving an intrafamily transfer:

> when the bona fides of promissory notes is at issue, the taxpayer must demonstrate affirmatively that "there existed at the time of the transaction a real expectation of repayment and an intent to enforce the collection of the indebtedness." Estate of Van Anda v. Commissioner, 12 T.C. 1158, 1162 (1949), aff'd per curiam, 192 F.2d 391 (2d Cir. 1951).

In language strikingly apposite to the situation here, the court stated:

> it is appropriate to look beyond the form of the transactions and to determine, as the tax court did here, that the gifts and loans back to decedent were "component parts of single transactions." Id.

The tax court concluded that the evidence "viewed as a whole" left the "unmistakable impression" that regardless of how long decedent lived following the transfer of her house, the entire principal balance of the mortgage note would be forgiven, and the Maxwells would not be required to pay any of such principal.

... [T]he tax court found that, at the time the note was executed, there was "an understanding" between the Maxwells and the decedent that the note would be forgiven. In our judgment, the conduct of decedent and the Maxwells with respect to the principal balance of the note, when viewed in connection with the initial "forgiveness" of $20,000 of the purported purchase price, strongly suggests the existence of an understanding between decedent and the Maxwells that decedent would forgive $20,000 each year thereafter until her death, when the balance would be forgiven by decedent's will.

To conclude, we hold that the conveyance was not a bona fide sale for an adequate and full consideration in money or money's worth.

The decision of the tax court is affirmed.

NOTES

1.   In Wheeler v. United States, 116 F.3d 749 (5th Cir. 1997), the taxpayer, age 60, sold a remainder interest in his ranch to his two sons for the value of a remainder interest set forth in the actuarial tables of the Treasury regulations. The taxpayer reserved a life estate in the ranch and died at age 67. The court held the transfer was for full consideration, and thus the ranch was not part of the transferor's federal gross estate under §2036. Compare Gradow v. United States, 897 F.2d 516 (Fed. Cir. 1990).

2.   Joseph Grace executes a trust instrument providing for payment of income to his wife, Janet, for her life, with payment to her of any part of the principal that a majority of the trustees think advisable. Mrs. Grace is given a special testamentary power of appointment over the trust estate. Named as trustees are Joseph, his nephew, and a third party. Shortly thereafter, Janet Grace, at Joseph's request, executes a virtually identical trust instrument naming Joseph as life beneficiary. Upon Joseph's death is the corpus of either of the trusts includable in Joseph's gross estate? See United States v. Estate of Grace, 395 U.S. 316 (1969).

In the *Grace* case, the court held that, under the reciprocal trust doctrine, the value of the Janet Grace trust must be included in Joseph's estate. "[A]pplication of the reciprocal trust doctrine requires only that the trusts be interrelated, and that the arrangement, to the extent of mutual value, leaves the settlors in approximately the same economic position as they would have been in had they created trusts naming themselves as life beneficiaries."

The reciprocal trust doctrine is rather vague, and, in applying the doctrine, the Internal Revenue Service has won some cases and lost some. It stands as a caution, however, to the lawyer who creates reciprocal trusts. See Estate of Green v. United States, 68 F.3d 151 (6th Cir. 1995); Elena Marty-Nelson, Taxing Reciprocal Trusts: Charting a Doctrine's Fall from Grace, 75 N.C. L. Rev. 1781 (1997).

Old Colony Trust Co. v. United States
United States Court of Appeals, First Circuit, 1970
423 F.2d 601

ALDRICH, J.   The sole question in this case is whether the estate of a settlor of an inter vivos trust, who was a trustee until the date of his death, is to be charged with the value of the principal he contributed by virtue of reserved powers in the trust. The executor paid the tax and sued for its recovery in the district court. All facts were stipulated. The court ruled for the government, 300 F. Supp. 1032, and the executor appeals.

The initial life beneficiary of the trust was the settlor's adult son. Eighty percent of the income was normally to be payable to him, and the balance added to principal. Subsequent beneficiaries were the son's widow and his issue. The powers upon which the government relies to cause the corpus to be includable in the settlor-trustee's estate are contained in two articles. . . .

Article 4 permitted the trustees to increase the percentage of income payable to the son beyond the eighty percent, "in their absolute discretion . . . when in their opinion such increase is needed in case of sickness, or desirable in view of changed circumstances." In addition, under Article 4 the trustees were given the discretion to cease paying income to the son, and add it all to principal, "during such period as the Trustees may decide that the stoppage of such payments is for his best interests."

Article 7 gave broad administrative or management powers to the trustees, with discretion to acquire investments not normally held by trustees, and the right to determine what was to be charged or credited to income or principal, including stock dividends or deductions for amortization. It further provided that all divisions and decisions made by the trustees in good faith should be conclusive on all parties, and in summary, stated that the trustees were empowered, "generally to do all things in relation to the Trust Fund which the Donor could do if living and this Trust had not been executed."

The government claims that each of these two articles meant that the settlor-trustee had "the right . . . to designate the persons who shall possess or enjoy the [trust] property or the income therefrom" within the meaning of section 2036(a)(2) of the Internal Revenue Code of 1954, 26 U.S.C. §2036(a)(2), and that the settlor-trustee at the date of his death possessed a power "to alter, amend, revoke, or terminate" within the meaning of section 2038(a)(1) (26 U.S.C. §2038(a)(1)).

If State Street Trust Co. v. United States, 1 Cir., 1959, 263 F.2d 635, was correctly decided in this aspect, the government must prevail because of the Article 7 powers. There this court, Chief Judge Magruder dissenting, held against the taxpayer because broad powers similar to those in Article 7 meant that the trustees "could very substantially shift the economic benefits of the trusts between the life tenants and the remaindermen," so that the settlor "as long as he lived, in substance and effect and in a very real sense . . . 'retained for his life . . . the right . . . to designate the persons who shall possess or enjoy the property or the income therefrom. . . .' " 263 F.2d at 639-640, quoting 26 U.S.C. §2036(a)(2). We accept the taxpayer's invitation to reconsider this ruling.

It is common ground that a settlor will not find the corpus of the trust included in his estate merely because he named himself a trustee. Jennings v. Smith, 2 Cir., 1947, 161 F.2d 74. He must have reserved a power to himself[13] that is inconsistent with the full termination of ownership. The government's brief defines this as "sufficient dominion and control until his death." Trustee powers given for the administration or management of the trust must be equitably exercised, however, for the benefit of the trust as a whole. Blodget v. Delaney, 1 Cir., 1953, 201 F.2d 589; United States v. Powell, 10 Cir., 1962, 307 F.2d 821; Scott, Trusts §§183, 232 (3d ed. 1967); Rest. 2d, Trusts §§183, 232. The court in *State Street* conceded that the powers at issue were all such powers, but reached the conclusion that, cumulatively, they gave the settlor dominion sufficiently unfettered to be in the nature of ownership. With all respect to the majority of the then court, we find it difficult to see how a power can be subject to control by the probate court, and exercisable only in what the trustee fairly concludes is in the interests of the trust and its beneficiaries as a whole, and at the same time be an ownership power.

The government's position, to be sound, must be that the trustee's powers are beyond the court's control. Under Massachusetts law, however, no amount of administrative discretion prevents judicial supervision of the trustee. Thus in Appeal of Davis, 1903, 183 Mass. 499, 67 N.E. 604, a trustee was given "full power to make purchases, investments and exchanges . . . in such manner as to them shall seem expedient; it being my intention to give my trustees . . . the same dominion and control over said trust property as I now have." In spite of this language, and in spite of their good faith, the court charged the trustees for failing sufficiently to diversify their investment portfolio.

The Massachusetts court has never varied from this broad rule of accountability, and has twice criticized *State Street* for its seeming departure. Boston Safe Deposit & Trust Co. v. Stone, 1965, 348 Mass. 345, 351, n.8, 203 N.E.2d 547; Old Colony Trust Co. v. Silliman, 1967, 352 Mass. 6, 8-9, 223 N.E.2d 504. See also, Estate of McGillicuddy, 54 T.C. No. 27, 2/17/70, CCH Tax Ct. Rep. Dec. 29, 1965. We make it a further observation, which the court in *State Street* failed to note, that the provision in that trust (as in the case at bar) that the trustees could "do all things in relation to the Trust Fund which I, the Donor, could do if . . . the Trust had not been executed," is almost precisely

---

13. The number of other trustees who must join in the exercise of that power, unless the others have antagonistic interest of a substantial nature, is, of course, immaterial. Treas. Reg. §20.2036-1(a)(ii), (b)(3)(i) (1958); §20.2038-1(a) (1958).

the provision which did not protect the trustees from accountability in Appeal of Davis, supra.

We do not believe that trustee powers are to be more broadly construed for tax purposes than the probate court would construe them for administrative purposes. More basically, we agree with Judge Magruder's observation that nothing is "gained by lumping them together." State Street Trust Co. v. United States, supra, 263 F.2d at 642. We hold that no aggregation of purely administrative powers can meet the government's amorphous test of "sufficient dominion and control" so as to be equated with ownership.

This does not resolve taxpayer's difficulties under Article 4. Quite different considerations apply to distribution powers. Under them the trustee can, expressly, prefer one beneficiary over another. Furthermore, his freedom of choice may vary greatly, depending upon the terms of the individual trust. If there is an ascertainable standard, the trustee can be compelled to follow it. If there is not, even though he is a fiduciary, it is not unreasonable to say that his retention of an unmeasurable freedom of choice is equivalent to retaining some of the incidents of ownership. Hence, under the cases, if there is an ascertainable standard the settlor-trustee's estate is not taxed, . . . but if there is not, it is taxed. . . .

The trust provision which is uniformly held to provide an ascertainable standard is one which, though variously expressed, authorizes such distributions as may be needed to continue the beneficiary's accustomed way of life. . . . On the other hand, if the trustee may go further, and has power to provide for the beneficiary's "happiness," Merchants Nat'l Bank v. Com'r of Internal Revenue, 1943, 320 U.S. 256, or "pleasure," Industrial Trust Co. v. Com'r of Internal Revenue, 1 Cir., 1945, 151 F.2d 592, cert. denied 327 U.S. 788, or "use and benefit," Newton Trust Co. v. Com'r of Internal Revenue, 1 Cir., 1947, 160 F.2d 175, or "reasonable requirement[s]," State Street Bank & Trust Co. v. United States, 1 Cir., 1963, 313 F.2d 29, the standard is so loose that the trustee is in effect uncontrolled.

In the case at bar the trustees could increase the life tenant's income "in case of sickness, or [if] desirable in view of changed circumstances." Alternatively, they could reduce it "for his best interests." "Sickness" presents no problem. Conceivably, providing for "changed circumstances" is roughly equivalent to maintaining the son's present standard of living. . . . The unavoidable stumbling block is the trustees' right to accumulate income and add it to capital (which the son would never receive) when it is to the "best interests" of the son to do so. Additional payments to a beneficiary whenever in his "best interests" might seem to be too broad a standard in any event. In addition to the previous cases see Estate of Yawkey, 1949, 12 T.C. 1164, where the court said, at p.1170, "We can not regard the language involved ['best interest'] as limiting the usual scope of a trustee's discretion. It must always be anticipated that trustees will act for the best interests of a trust beneficiary, and an exhortation to act 'in the interests and for the welfare' of the beneficiary does not establish an external standard." Power, however, to decrease or cut off a beneficiary's income when in his "best interests," is even more troublesome. When the beneficiary is the son, and the trustee the father, a particular purpose comes to mind, parental control through holding the purse strings. The father decides what conduct is to the "best interests" of the son, and if the son does not agree, he loses his allowance. Such power has the plain indicia of ownership control. The alternative, that the son, because of other means, might not need this income, and would prefer to have it accumulate for his widow and children after his death, is no better. If the trustee has power to confer "happiness" on the son by generosity to someone else, this seems clearly an unascertainable standard. Cf. Merchants Nat'l Bank v. Com'r of Internal Revenue, supra, 320 U.S. at 261-263.

The case of Hays' Estate v. Com'r of Internal Revenue, 5 Cir., 1950, 181 F.2d 169, is contrary to our decision. The opinion is unsupported by either reasoning or authority, and we will not follow it. With the present settlor-trustee free to determine the standard himself, a finding of ownership control was warranted. To put it another way, the cost of holding onto the strings may prove to be a rope burn. State Street Bank & Trust Co. v. United States, supra.

Affirmed.

NOTE AND QUESTION

1. It might be thought that application of §2036(a)(2) to retained discretionary powers can be avoided by not naming the settlor as trustee or co-trustee. This alone is not enough, however. If the named trustee has these powers, and if the settlor has the power to remove the trustee and appoint himself or a related or subordinate person as successor trustee, the settlor may be deemed to possess the powers, and estate taxation may result. The Internal Revenue Service gives some leeway to trustee removal powers, however. It takes the position that if the decedent possesses the power to remove the trustee and appoint an individual or corporate successor trustee that is not related or subordinate to the decedent, the decedent will not be deemed to retain a trustee's discretionary control over trust income. Rev. Rul. 95-58, 1995-2 CB. 191.

2. Since the entire value of the property will be included in the donor's gross estate under §2036, when the donor retains a life estate, why should the gift of a remainder be taxable as a gift? See Joseph

Isenbergh, Simplifying Retained Interests, Revocable Transfers, and the Marital Deduction, 51 U. Chi. L. Rev. 1 (1984).

b. Section 2038: Revocable Transfers

Section 2038(a) provides that the value of the gross estate shall include the value of all property —

> To the extent of any interest therein of which the decedent has at any time made a transfer (except in case of a bona fide sale for an adequate and full consideration in money or money's worth), by trust or otherwise, where the enjoyment thereof was subject at the date of his death to any change through the exercise of a power (in whatever capacity exercisable) by the decedent alone or by the decedent in conjunction with any other person (without regard to when or from what source the decedent acquired such power), to alter, amend, revoke or terminate, or when any such power is relinquished during the three-year period ending on the date of the decedent's death.

To a considerable extent, §2038 applies to the same transfers caught within §2036(a)(2). However, there are situations covered exclusively by §2038. Section 2036(a)(2) covers only a retained right to designate the *persons* who shall enjoy the property. Section 2038 is applicable if the transferor has the power to effect any change, including the *time* of enjoyment. Hence, §2038 alone applies where the settlor may terminate a trust and accelerate enjoyment by a beneficiary. Note also that §2038, like §2036(a)(2), is applicable even though the power is held in conjunction with an adverse party or is held by the settlor as trustee.

If the power to alter, amend, revoke, or terminate is given to some third person, the transfer is not taxed under §2038 even if the person given the power is a nonadverse party. It is for this reason that a trustee who is not the settlor can be given broad discretionary powers, including the power to distribute a portion or all of the trust corpus (thereby terminating the trust), without adverse tax consequences. This last statement is subject to the same qualification that was made in the discussion of §2036. If a trustee has such a power, and if the transferor has the right to remove the trustee and appoint himself as trustee, the transferor is treated as having the power and §2038 is applicable. Treas. Reg. §20.2038-1(a)(3).

Although §2038 is generally referred to as the provision that includes in the gross estate revocable transfers, it reaches transfers over which the decedent held any one of the enumerated powers, even though the power cannot be exercised in such a way as to benefit the transferor. If *O* creates an irrevocable trust in which *O*, as co-trustee, has a discretionary power to accumulate or distribute trust income, or a discretionary power to distribute corpus to the income beneficiary, the property is included in *O*'s gross estate under §2038; *O*'s discretionary power is a power to alter or amend. (*O*'s reserved power would of course also cause inclusion under §2036(a)(2).)

PROBLEMS

1.   *O* transfers property to the First National Bank in trust to pay the income to *O*'s daughter, *A*, for life, and on *A*'s death to pay the trust principal to *O*'s granddaughter, *B*. The trust is irrevocable. *O* retains the power to invade corpus for the benefit of *B*. On *O*'s death, is any portion of the value of the trust corpus includable in *O*'s gross estate?

2.   What result if, on the facts in Problem 1, *O* has no power to invade corpus but retains the power to direct that all or a portion of trust income be accumulated and added to corpus?

3.   *O* transfers property to the Second National Bank in trust to pay the income to *O*'s daughter, *D*, until she reaches 25, and when *D* reaches 25 or, if *D* dies before reaching 25, when *D* would have reached 25 had she lived, to pay the trust principal to *D* or *D*'s estate. The trust is irrevocable. *O* retains the power to direct that all or a portion of the trust income be accumulated until *D* reaches 25 and also the power to invade corpus for the benefit of *D*. *O* dies; *D* is 19 years old. Is any portion of the value of the trust corpus includable in *O*'s gross estate? See Lober v. United States, 346 U.S. 335 (1953).

4.   Under the Uniform Transfers to Minors Act, supra page 133, if the donor names himself as custodian and dies while serving in that capacity, the value of the custodial property is included in the donor's gross estate for federal estate tax purposes. Because the donor-custodian's discretionary power to distribute the custodial property to the minor is a retained power to alter the time of enjoyment, the value of the custodial property is included in the donor's estate under §2038.

If a parent wants to make a gift of income-producing assets to a minor child and be either the trustee or the custodian, is a trust or a custodianship preferable if estate taxes are a concern?

c.   Section 2037: Transfers with Reversionary Interest Retained

Under §2037 of the Code, the value of property transferred during life is includable in the transferor's gross estate if

(1) possession or enjoyment of the property can ... be obtained only by surviving the decedent, and

(2) the decedent has retained a reversionary interest in the property ..., and the value of such reversionary interest immediately before the death of the decedent exceeds five percent of the value of the property.

Both of the above conditions must be present for §2037 to apply. Thus:

> *Case 11. H* conveys $100,000 to *X* in trust, to pay income to *W* for life, then to distribute the trust principal to *H* if *H* is then living, and if *H* is not then living to his daughter *A* or her issue. Condition (1) above is met. *A* cannot obtain possession or enjoyment without surviving *H*. Therefore if the value of *H*'s reversionary interest exceeded 5 percent of the value of the property, the value of the trust assets, less *W*'s life estate, will be includable in *H*'s gross estate if *H* predeceases *W*. (The value of *H*'s reversionary interest would be measured by the actuarial probability of *H* outliving *W*.)

If no beneficiary's enjoyment of the property depends upon surviving the decedent, §2037 is inapplicable. Thus, in Case 11 if there were no gift over to *A*, §2037 would not apply. Only the value of *H*'s reversionary interest would be included under §2033.

Since instruments are seldom drawn that meet both conditions of §2037, this section is of little concern to the practitioner. For the attorney drafting an irrevocable inter vivos trust, §2037 can be avoided by eliminating any possibility that the trust property will revert to the settlor or the settlor's estate. This can be accomplished by making sure that some person other than the settlor or the settlor's estate will take the property regardless of what contingencies occur. The attorney may include an end-limitation to charity to take effect if all of the designated beneficiaries die before they become entitled to their interests.

d. Section 2035: Transfers Within Three Years of Death

Section 2035 brings into the decedent's gross estate certain inter vivos transfers made within three years prior to death. The purpose of this section is to close some tax avoidance opportunities that would otherwise exist in the few years prior to death. Section 2035 has undergone numerous alterations since 1916, when its predecessor section was first enacted. In 1916, the section taxed transfers "in contemplation of death," with Congress first creating a rebuttable presumption that a transfer within two years of death was in contemplation of death. After ten years, Congress changed the section to create a conclusive presumption, but after another six years, the presumption again became rebuttable. Later, Congress lengthened the presumptive period to three years. Because the question of whether a transfer was in contemplation of death turned on the subjective state of mind of the transferor, much litigation resulted. In 1976, Congress eliminated the contemplation of death language — and the subjective test. It reworded §2035 to require that all gifts made within three years of death be included in the gross estate. Upon reflection, this did not seem necessary inasmuch as the gift and estate taxes were unified in 1976, and any gift made within three years of death would be taxed at the same rate as a bequest. In 1981, the Economic Recovery Tax Act changed §2035 again, this time to eliminate its application to all gifts except those, generally speaking, that have a lower valuation as a gift than they have at death.

Under §2035, any of the following transfers made within three years of death is included in the decedent's gross estate:

> (1) Any gift tax paid by the decedent or his estate on gifts made within three years of death. [The purpose of this subsection is to prevent a person from giving property away immediately prior to death, and removing the amount of gift tax from the gross estate.]
>
> (2) Any transfer or release of an interest in property if, had such interest been retained, the property would have been included in the decedent's gross estate under any of the following sections of the Internal Revenue Code: section 2036 (transfers with retained life estate); section 2037 (transfers taking effect at death); section 2038 (revocable transfers); or section 2042 (life insurance). The gross estate includes the value of any property which would have been included had such transfer or release not been made. [The purpose of this subsection is to prevent persons from avoiding taxes by making gifts soon before death of property that balloons in value at death.]

Unless an inter vivos transfer is referred to above, it is not includable in the decedent's gross estate even though made within three years of death. Hence, if O gives Blackacre to A two months before O's death, a taxable gift is made at the time of transfer, and Blackacre is not included in O's gross estate at death. (The amount of gift tax paid is included in O's gross estate, however.)

It is apparent that Congress' major purpose is to deter taxpayers, in the few years before death, from giving away property that increases greatly in value by reason of the person's death. A gift of a life insurance policy will illustrate this.

Case 12. O owns a life insurance policy on her life with a face value of $100,000. The cash surrender value is $45,000. O gives the policy to her son *A*, paying a gift tax on $35,000 ($45,000 minus the annual exclusion of $10,000). *O* dies one year later, and $100,000 is payable to *A*. If the policy proceeds were not included in *O*'s gross estate, *O* could transfer this asset to *A* at a low gift tax valuation immediately prior to death. Section 2035 requires the inclusion of the policy proceeds in *O*'s gross estate.

But for §2035, the owner of a life insurance policy on the owner's life would have a strong tax incentive to give the policy away prior to death, perhaps on the deathbed. So too would exist a strong tax incentive to release a life estate when death appeared imminent. Thus:

> *Case 13.* In 1994, *O* creates an irrevocable trust of securities worth $300,000, retaining a life estate, with remainder to *O*'s son *A*. This results in a taxable gift to *A* of the value of the remainder in assets worth $300,000. In 2000, the trust assets are worth $500,000, and *O*, ill with cancer, releases her life estate. The release is a taxable gift to *A* of the value of *O*'s life estate in $500,000. *O* dies in 2001. If there were no §2035, *O*'s 2000 release would have eliminated transfer tax on the value of a remainder in $200,000 worth of assets. But §2035 prevents *O* from doing this by requiring the inclusion of the entire $500,000 worth of assets in *O*'s gross estate. (The gift tax paid in 1994 is credited against estate taxes payable at *O*'s death.)

PROBLEMS

1.   Your client, a 72-year-old widow with a $1,200,000 estate, has been diagnosed as having terminal cancer. Her present will leaves her entire estate to her two children in equal shares. The client has a daughter, a son, two in-laws, and five grandchildren. What advice would you give her?

2.   The same client's will includes a bequest of $20,000 to her alma mater. Is there any advantage in the client's making the $20,000 gift to the alma mater during life in lieu of the testamentary gift?

3.   *H*, a widower, is the insured under a paid-up $100,000 life insurance policy that names his daughter *D* as a primary beneficiary. In 1998, *H* irrevocably assigns the policy and all of its incidents of ownership to *D*. At the time of the transfer, the cash surrender value of the property is $40,000. What are the estate tax consequences in *H*'s estate (a) if *H* dies in 2000 and (b) if *H* dies in 2002?

4.   Suppose that *A* wants to purchase a life insurance policy and wants his daughter *B* to be the beneficiary. If *A* purchases the policy, and is named as owner, and thereafter assigns the policy to *B*, *A* has made a gift of insurance proceeds that will be included in *A*'s gross

estate if *A* dies within three years. On the other hand, if *B* is named as owner of the policy as well as beneficiary from the beginning, the proceeds of the policy are not includable in *A*'s gross estate if he dies within three years because *A* never had any incidents of ownership over the policy. It does not matter that *A* pays the premiums. Estate of Headrick v. Commissioner, 918 F.2d 1263 (6th Cir. 1990); Estate of Perry v. Commissioner, 931 F.2d 1044 (5th Cir. 1992).

Suppose that *B* is a minor, age 12. How do you advise *A* to arrange for the purchase of life insurance for which *A* is to pay the premiums?

5.   *A* enters an airport preparing to take a trip on an airplane. At an insurance counter, *A* buys a life insurance policy for the trip payable to *B*. The insurance application asks the applicant to check one of two boxes: ☐ insured is owner, or ☐ beneficiary is owner. Which box should *A* check?

6.   See generally Jon J. Gallo, The Use of Life Insurance in Estate Planning and Drafting — Part I, 33 Real Prop., Prob. & Tr. J. 685 (1999), Part II, 34 supra, at 55.

5.   *The Gross Estate: Powers of Appointment (§2041)*

Sections 2036 and 2038 deal with lifetime transfers by the decedent wherein the decedent retained benefits or controls. By contrast, §2041 deals with powers of appointment given the decedent by another.

Under §2041, the gross estate includes the value of property over which the decedent at the time of his death held a *general power of appointment*. A general power of appointment is defined as a power exercisable in favor of the decedent, his creditors, his estate, or the creditors of his estate. The assets subject to the general power are taxed in the decedent's estate regardless of whether the power was exercisable during lifetime or by will and (if the power was created after October 21, 1942)[14] whether the decedent actually exercised the power.

> *Case 14.* *H*'s will creates a testamentary trust providing for the payment of trust income to *H*'s wife *W* for life and on her death "to pay the trust principal to such person or persons as *W* appoints by her will." On *W*'s subsequent death, the value of the trust corpus is includable in her gross estate regardless of whether *W* exercised the power of appointment by her will. Although *W* was restricted to the income from the trust, and she could not exercise the power of appointment in such a way as to benefit herself or her creditors during her lifetime, she held at death a power

14.   Property subject to a general power created on or before October 21, 1942, is taxed in the estate of the holder of the power only if the power is exercised. IRC §2041(a)(1).

of appointment that was exercisable in favor of her estate or the creditors of her estate.

The donee of a general power of appointment is treated, under the Code, as owner of the property subject to the power. If a donee exercises or releases a general power of appointment, the donee makes a taxable gift. If a donee exercises or releases the power under circumstances that would have resulted in taxability if the property had been the donee's own (such as releasing a general power and reserving a life estate), estate tax liability results. A donee of a general power of appointment is treated as owner under the generation-skipping transfer tax (see infra page 1073).

If the decedent held a special power of appointment, the property subject to the power is not taxed under §2041.[15] A special power of appointment is a power to appoint among a restricted class of persons that does not include the decedent, her creditors, her estate, or the creditors of her estate.

> *Case 15. H*'s will creates a testamentary trust providing for the payment of trust income to *H*'s wife *W* for life and on her death "to pay the trust principal to such one or more of her descendants or spouses of descendants as she shall appoint by her will." On *W*'s subsequent death, the trust corpus is not subject to taxation in her estate. Since *W*'s life estate terminated at her death, nothing is taxed under §2033. Since *W*'s power of appointment was not a general power, nothing is taxed under §2041.

As Case 15 demonstrates, it is possible to give a beneficiary a life income interest in property and also a limited power to control devolution of the property at death without subjecting the property to estate taxation in the beneficiary's estate. It is also possible to give the beneficiary certain limited powers to appoint property to herself during her lifetime without adverse estate tax consequences. Under §2041(b)(1)(A), "[a] power to consume, invade, or appropriate property for the benefit of the decedent which is limited by an ascertainable standard relating to the health, education, support, or maintenance of the decedent shall not be deemed a general power of appointment." Hence a power in the donee to appoint to the donee limited by the quoted standard is not a general power of appointment.

In addition to a power limited by a standard, a donee may be given a "$5,000 or 5 percent" power with little tax cost. Section 2041(b)(2) provides that if the decedent held a power to consume or invade that

---

15. Treas. Reg. §20.2041-1(c)(1) (1958). There is one important, and very useful, exception to this general rule. See the "Delaware Tax Trap," supra page 827.

was limited to the greater of $5,000 or 5 percent of corpus each year, the maximum amount includable in the donee's gross estate is $5,000 or 5 percent of the corpus. If the donee has fully exercised the power in the year of death, withdrawing $5,000 or 5 percent from the trust, nothing is included in the donee's estate.

Under §2041(b)(2), a lapse of a power in any calendar year is considered a release (with resulting gift tax liability) to the extent that the property over which the power existed exceeded the greater of $5,000 or 5 percent of the value of the assets that could be appointed. Thus:

> *Case 16.* In 1998, *T* bequeaths $500,000 in trust to pay income to *A* for life. *A* is given a power to withdraw $5,000 or 5 percent of the corpus of the trust in any given year. The right is noncumulative, so that *A* can never withdraw more than $25,000 in any one year, even though *A* fails to withdraw the full amount in a preceding year. In 1999, *A* does not exercise the power. The power lapses, but no taxable gift results. In 2000, *A* withdraws $25,000. In 2001, *A* dies, after withdrawing $10,000 in that year. The amount still subject to *A*'s power of withdrawal at death — $15,000 — is included in *A*'s gross estate.

Special powers of appointment and limited invasion powers (measured by a standard or "$5,000 or 5 percent"), and also discretionary powers given to a trustee, can be employed to create a flexible estate plan that accommodates the foreseen needs of the grantor's family and yet allows for adjustments if future events should warrant. Contrast such a flexible plan with an old-fashioned settlement of property "to my wife for life, and on her death remainder to my descendants per stirpes." At the time the transfer is made, the income from the property may appear to ensure that the wife's support and other needs will be met. But if the wife (or one of the couple's children) should encounter unusual medical or other expenses, or if inflation erodes the real value of the income interest, the income from the property may be insufficient to meet the wife's needs. If, on the other hand, the trustee is given a discretionary power to distribute corpus to the wife whenever it is needed to supplement the trust's income, and if the wife is given an "ascertainable standard" or "$5,000 or 5 percent" invasion power, the corpus of the trust can be used to satisfy the wife's support and other needs whenever trust income proves insufficient.

Under §2041, all of these powers can be given to the income beneficiary and trustee with little or no estate tax cost. See John G. Steinkamp, Estate and Gift Taxation of Powers of Appointment Limited by Ascertainable Standards, 79 Marq. L. Rev. 195 (1995).

Estate of Vissering v. Commissioner
United States Court of Appeals, Tenth Circuit, 1993
990 F.2d 578

LOGAN, C.J.   The estate of decedent Norman H. Vissering appeals from a judgment of the Tax Court determining that he held at his death a general power of appointment as defined by I.R.C. §2041, and requiring that the assets of a trust of which he was cotrustee be included in his gross estate for federal estate tax purposes. The appeal turns on whether decedent held powers permitting him to invade the principal of the trust for his own benefit unrestrained by an ascertainable standard relating to health, education, support, or maintenance. The trust was created by decedent's mother in Florida and specifies that Florida law controls in the interpretation and administration of its provisions.

The estate argues that decedent was not a trustee at the time of his death because a New Mexico court's adjudication that he was incapacitated two months before his death divested him of those powers. Decedent was not formally removed as trustee; if he ceased to serve it was by operation of Florida law. However, we assume for purposes of this opinion that decedent continued as trustee until his death and that his powers are to be adjudged as if he were fully competent to exercise them at the time of his death.

The trust at issue was created by decedent's mother, and became irrevocable on her death in 1965. Decedent and a bank served as cotrustees. Under the dispositive provisions decedent received all the income from the trust after his mother's death. On decedent's death (his wife, a contingent beneficiary, predeceased him), remaining trust assets were to be divided into equal parts and passed to decedent's two children or were held for their benefit. Decedent developed Alzheimer's disease and entered into a nursing home in 1984, but he tendered no resignation as trustee, nor did his guardian or conservator do so on his behalf after he was found to be incapacitated.

The Tax Court's decision, based entirely upon stipulated facts, resolved only questions of law, and consequently our review is de novo. First Nat'l Bank v. Commissioner, 921 F.2d 1081, 1086 (10th Cir. 1990).

Under I.R.C. §2041 a decedent has a general power of appointment includable in his estate if he possesses at the time of his death a power over assets that permits him to benefit himself, his estate, his creditors, or creditors of his estate. A power vested in a trustee, even with a cotrustee who has no interest adverse to the exercise of the power, to invade principal of the trust for his own benefit is sufficient to find the decedent trustee to have a general power of appointment, unless the power to invade is limited by an ascertainable standard relating to health, education, support, or maintenance. Treas. Reg.

§20.2041-1(c), -3(c)(2). See, e.g., Estate of Sowell v. Commissioner, 708 F.2d 1564, 1568 (10th Cir. 1983) (invasion of trust corpus in case of emergency or illness is an ascertainable standard under §2041(b)(1)(A)); see also Merchants Nat'l Bank v. Commissioner, 320 U.S. 256, 261, 64 S. Ct. 108, 111, 88 L. Ed. 35 (1943) (invasion of trust corpus for "the comfort, support, maintenance and/or happiness of my wife" is not a fixed standard for purposes of charitable deductions); Ithaca Trust Co. v. United States, 279 U.S. 151, 154, 49 S. Ct. 291, 291, 73 L. Ed. 647 (1929) (invasion of trust corpus for any amount "that may be necessary to suitably maintain [decedent's wife] in as much comfort as she now enjoys" is a fixed standard for purposes of charitable deduction).

The relevant provisions of the instant trust agreement are as follows:

> During the term of [this trust], the Trustees shall further be authorized to pay over or to use or expend for the direct or indirect benefit of any of the aforesaid beneficiaries, whatever amount or amounts of the principal of this Trust as may, in the discretion of the Trustees, be required for the continued comfort, support, maintenance, or education of said beneficiary.

The Internal Revenue Service (IRS) and the Tax Court focused on portions of the invasion provision providing that the trust principal could be expended for the "comfort" of decedent, declaring that this statement rendered the power of invasion incapable of limitation by the courts.

We look to state law (here Florida's) to determine the legal interests and rights created by a trust instrument, but federal law determines the tax consequences of those interests and rights. Morgan v. Commissioner, 309 U.S. 78, 80, 60 S. Ct. 424, 425-26, 84 L. Ed. 585 (1940); Maytag v. United States, 493 F.2d 995, 998 (10th Cir. 1974). . . .

Despite the decision in Barritt v. Tomlinson, 129 F. Supp. 642 (S.D. Fla. 1955), which involved a power of invasion broader than the one before us, we believe the Florida Supreme Court would hold that a trust document permitting invasion of principal for "comfort," without further qualifying language, creates a general power of appointment. Treas. Reg. §20.2041-1(c). See First Virginia Bank v. United States, 490 F.2d 532, 533 (4th Cir. 1974) (under Virginia law, right of invasion for beneficiary's "comfort and care as she may see fit" not limited by an ascertainable standard); Lehman v. United States, 448 F.2d 1318, 1320 (5th Cir. 1971) (under Texas law, power to invade corpus for "support, maintenance, comfort, and welfare" not limited by ascertainable standard); Miller v. United States, 387 F.2d 866, 869 (3d Cir. 1968) (under Pennsylvania law, power to make disbursements from principal in amounts "necessary or expedient for [beneficiary's] proper maintenance, support, medical care, hospitalization, or other expenses incidental to her comfort and well-being" not limited by ascertainable standard); Estate of Schlotterer v. United States, 421 F. Supp. 85, 91 (W.D. Pa. 1976) (power of consumption "to the extent deemed by [beneficiary] to be desirable not only for her support and maintenance but also for her comfort and pleasure" not limited by ascertainable standard); Doyle v. United States, 358 F. Supp. 300, 309-10 (E.D. Pa. 1973) (under Pennsylvania law, trustees' "uncontrolled discretion" to pay beneficiary "such part or parts of the principal of said trust fund as may be necessary for her comfort, maintenance and support" not limited by ascertainable standard); Stafford v. United States, 236 F. Supp. 132, 134 (E.D. Wisc. 1964) (under Wisconsin law, trust permitting husband "for his use, benefit and enjoyment during his lifetime," unlimited power of disposition thereof "without permission of any court, and with the right to use and enjoy the principal, as well as the income, if he shall have need thereof for his care, comfort or enjoyment" not limited by ascertainable standard).

However, there is modifying language in the trust before us that we believe would lead the Florida courts to hold that "comfort," in context, does not permit an unlimited power of invasion. The instant language states that invasion of principal is permitted to the extent "required for the continued comfort" of the decedent, and is part of a clause referencing the support, maintenance and education of the beneficiary. Invasion of the corpus is not permitted to the extent "determined" or "desired" for the beneficiary's comfort but only to the extent that it is "required." Furthermore, the invasion must be for the beneficiary's "continued" comfort, implying, we believe, more than the minimum necessary for survival, but nevertheless reasonably necessary to maintain the beneficiary in his accustomed manner of living. These words in context state a standard essentially no different from the examples in the Treasury Regulation, in which phrases such as "support in reasonable comfort," "maintenance in health and reasonable comfort," and "support in his accustomed manner of living" are deemed to be limited by an ascertainable standard. Treas. Reg. §20.2041-1(c)(2). See, e.g., United States v. Powell, 307 F.2d 821, 828 (10th Cir. 1962) (under Kansas law, invasion of the corpus if "it is necessary or advisable . . . for the maintenance, welfare, comfort or happiness" of beneficiaries, and only if the need justifies the reduction in principal, is subject to ascertainable standard); Hunter v. United States, 597 F. Supp. 1293, 1295 (W.D. Pa. 1984) (power to invade for "comfortable support and maintenance" of beneficiaries is subject to ascertainable standard).

We believe that had decedent, during his life, sought to use the assets of the trust to increase significantly his standard of living beyond that which he had previously enjoyed, his cotrustee would have been obligated to refuse to consent, and the remainder beneficiaries of the trust could have successfully petitioned the court to disallow such expenditures as inconsistent with the intent of the trust instrument. The Tax Court erred in ruling that this power was a general power of appointment includable in decedent's estate.

Reversed and remanded.

QUESTION AND NOTE

1. After the death of his mother, Norman Vissering consults you regarding her will (which you did not draw). You spot the drafting error, the use of the word "comfort." To avoid litigation and the possible inclusion of his mother's trust in his federal gross estate, would you recommend that he decline to serve as trustee? That he disclaim the power to go into principal for "comfort"?

Treas. Reg. §25.2518-3(a)(2) takes the position that

> all interests in the corpus of a trust are treated as a single interest [and] in order to have a qualified disclaimer of an interest in corpus the disclaimant must disclaim all such interests, either totally or as to an undivided portion. Thus, if a disclaimant has a testamentary power of appointment over the trust corpus coupled with either an inter vivos power to invade corpus or an interest as discretionary appointee, a disclaimer by that person can constitute a qualified disclaimer only if both such interests are disclaimed.

2. In Kinney v. Shinholser, 663 So. 2d 643 (Fla. App. 1995), the court held a lawyer was liable to the estate of the life tenant who was given a general testamentary power for not explaining the tax consequences of not disclaiming the power of appointment within nine months of the transferor's death. Because the power was not disclaimed, the life tenant's estate was obliged to pay estate taxes of $320,000 on the trust property.

Estate of Kurz v. Commissioner
United States Court of Appeals, Seventh Circuit, 1995
68 F.3d 1027

EASTERBROOK, J.   Between her husband's death, in 1971, and her own, in 1986, Ethel H. Kurz was the beneficiary of two trusts. Kurz received the income from each. She was entitled to as much of the principal of one (which we call the Marital Trust) as she wanted; all she had to do was notify the trustee in writing. She could take only 5 percent of the other (which we call the Family Trust) in any year,

Judge Frank Easterbrook

and then only if the Marital Trust was exhausted. When Kurz died, the Marital Trust contained assets worth some $3.5 million, and the Family Trust was worth about $3.4 million. The estate tax return included in the gross estate the whole value of the Marital Trust and none of the value of the Family Trust. The Tax Court held that Kurz held a general power of appointment over 5 percent of the Family Trust, requiring the inclusion of another $170,000 under 26 U.S.C. §2041(a)(2). 101 T.C. 44 (1993); see also T.C. Memo 1994-221 (computing a tax due of approximately $31,000).

Section 2041(b)(1) defines a general power of appointment as "a power which is exercisable in favor of the decedent, his estate, his creditors, or the creditors of his estate." Kurz had the power to consume or appoint the corpus of the Marital Trust to anyone she pleased whenever she wanted, and the Estate therefore concedes that it belongs in the gross estate. For her part, the Commissioner of Internal Revenue concedes that the 95 percent of the Family Trust that was beyond Kurz's reach even if the Marital Trust had been empty was not subject to a general power of appointment. What of the other 5 percent? None of the Family Trust could be reached while the Marital Trust contained 1¢, and the Estate submits that, until the exhaustion condition was satisfied (which it never was), the power to appoint 5 percent in a given year was not "exercisable," keeping the Family Trust outside the gross estate. To this the Commissioner replies that a power is "exercisable" if a beneficiary has the ability to remove the blocking condition. Suppose, for example, that the Family Trust could not have been touched until Ethel Kurz said "Boo!". Her power to utter the magic word would have been no different from her power, under the Marital Trust, to send written instructions to the trustee.

The Tax Court was troubled by an implication of the Commissioner's argument. Suppose the Family Trust had provided that Kurz could reach 5 percent of the principal if and only if she lost 20 pounds, or achieved a chess rating of 1600, or survived all of her children. She could have gone on a crash diet, or studied the games of Gary Kasparov, or even murdered her children. These are not financial decisions, however, and it would be absurd to have taxes measured by one's ability to lose weight, or lack of moral scruples.

Imagine the trial, five years after a person's death, at which friends and relatives troop to the stand to debate whether the decedent was ruthless enough to kill her children, had enough willpower to lay off chocolates, or was smart enough to succeed at chess. The Tax Court accordingly rejected the Commissioner's principal argument, ruling that raw ability to satisfy a condition is insufficient to make a power of appointment "exercisable."

If not the Commissioner's position, then what? The Estate's position, 180° opposed, is that the condition must be actually satisfied before a power can be deemed "exercisable." The Tax Court came down in the middle, writing that a condition may be disregarded when it is "illusory" and lacks any "significant non-tax consequence independent of the decedent's ability to exercise the power." Of course, illusions are in the eye of the beholder, and we are hesitant to adopt a legal rule that incorporates a standard well suited to stage magicians (though some legal drafters can give prestidigitators a run for their money). No one doubts that the Kurz family had good, non-tax reasons for the structure of the trust funds. The only question we need resolve is whether a sequence of withdrawal rights prevents a power of appointment from being "exercisable." Despite the large number of trusts in the United States, many of them arranged as the Kurz trusts were, this appears to be an unresolved issue. Neither side could find another case dealing with stacked trusts, and we came up empty handed after independent research.

For a question of first principles, this one seems remarkably simple. Section 2041 is designed to include in the taxable estate all assets that the decedent possessed or effectively controlled. If only a lever must be pulled to dispense money, then the power is exercisable. The funds are effectively under the control of the beneficiary, which is enough to put them into the gross estate. Whether the lever is a single-clutch or double-clutch mechanism can't matter. Imagine a trust divided into 1,000 equal funds numbered 1 to 1,000, Fund 1 of which may be invaded at any time, and Fund n of which may be reached if and only if Fund n-1 has been exhausted. Suppose the beneficiary depletes Funds 1 through 9 and dies when $10 remains in Fund 10. Under the Kurz Estate's view, only $10 is included in the gross estate, because Funds 11 through 1,000 could not have been touched until that $10 had been withdrawn. But that would be a ridiculously artificial way of looking at things. Tax often is all about form, see Howell v. United States, 775 F.2d 887 (7th Cir. 1985), but §2041 is an anti-formal rule. It looks through the trust to ask how much wealth the decedent actually controlled at death. The decedent's real wealth in our hypothetical is $10 plus the balance of Funds 11 through 1,000; the decedent could have withdrawn and spent the entire amount in a trice. Whether this series of trusts has spendthrift features (as the Kurz trusts did) or is invested in illiquid instruments (as the Kurz trusts were) would not matter. The Estate does not deny that Kurz had a general power of appointment over the entire Marital Trust, despite these features. If the costs of removing wealth from the trust do not prevent including in the gross estate the entire corpus of the first trust in a sequence (they don't), then the rest of the sequence also is includable.

Wait!, the Estate exclaims. How did first principles get into a tax case? After consulting the statute, a court turns next to the regulations. 26 C.F.R. §20.2041-3(b) provides:

> For purposes of section 2041 (a) (2), a power of appointment is considered to exist on the date of a decedent's death even though the exercise of the power is subject to the precedent giving of notice, or even though the exercise of the power takes effect only on the expiration of a stated period after its exercise, whether or not on or before the decedent's death notice has been given or the power has been exercised. However, a power which by its terms is exercisable only upon the occurrence during the decedent's lifetime of an event or a contingency which did not in fact take place or occur during such time is not a power in existence on the date of the decedent's death. For example, if a decedent was given a general power of appointment exercisable only after he reached a certain age, only if he survived another person, or only if he died without descendants, the power would not be in existence on the date of the decedent's death if the condition precedent to its exercise had not occurred.

The Kurz Estate takes heart from the provision that "a power which by its terms is exercisable only upon the occurrence during the decedent's lifetime of an event or a contingency which did not in fact take place or occur during such time is not a power in existence on the date of the decedent's death." Like the Tax Court, however, we do not find in this language the strict sequencing principle the Estate needs.

This is the Commissioner's language, and the Commissioner thinks that it refers only to conditions that could not have been satisfied. Regulation-writers have substantial leeway in their interpretation, because the delegation of the power to make substantive regulations is the delegation of a law-creation power, and interpretation is a vital part of the law-creation process. See Homemakers North Shore, Inc. v. Bowen, 832 F.2d 408 (7th Cir. 1987). A reading must of course be reasonable — must be an interpretation — else the rulemaker is revising the law without the requisite notice and opportunity for comment. Pettibone Corp. v. United States, 34 F.3d 536, 541-42 (7th Cir. 1994). The Commissioner's understanding of the regulation tracks its third sentence, which is designed to illustrate the second. It says: "For example, if a decedent was given a general power of appointment exercisable only after he reached a certain age, only if he survived another person, or only if he died without descendants, the power would not be in existence on the date of the decedent's death if the condition precedent to its exercise had not occurred." All three examples in the third sentence deal with conditions the decedent could not have controlled, at least not in the short run, or lawfully. The rate of chronological aging is outside anyone's control, whether one person survives another does not present an option that may be exercised lawfully, and whether a person has descendants on the date of death is something that depends on the course of an entire life, rather than a single choice made in the administration of one's wealth.

By contrast, the sequence in which a beneficiary withdraws the principal of a series of trusts barely comes within the common understanding of "event or . . . contingency." No one could say of a single account: "You cannot withdraw the second dollar from this account until you have withdrawn the first." The existence of this sequence is tautological, but a check for $2 removes that sum without satisfying a contingency in ordinary, or legal, parlance. Zeno's paradox does not apply to financial transactions. Breaking one account into two or more does not make the sequence of withdrawal more of a "contingency" — at least not in the sense that §20.2041-3(b) uses that term.

No matter how the second sentence of §20.2041-3(b) should be applied to a contingency like losing 20 pounds or achieving a chess rating of 1600, the regulation does not permit the beneficiary of multiple trusts to exclude all but the first from the estate by the expedient of arranging the trusts in a sequence. No matter how long the sequence, the beneficiary exercises economic dominion over all funds that can be withdrawn at any given moment. The estate tax is a wealth tax, and dominion over property is wealth. Until her death, Ethel Kurz could have withdrawn all of the Marital Trust and 5 percent of the Family Trust by notifying the Trustee of her wish to do so. This case is nicely covered by the first sentence of §20.2041-3(b), the notice provision, and the judgment of the Tax Court is therefore
   AFFIRMED.

6.   *The Marital Deduction*

a.   Introduction

Section 2056 allows a marital deduction for certain dispositions of property to a decedent's spouse. Before 1982, the primary purpose of the marital deduction was to equalize the tax treatment of couples residing in separate property and community property states. The marital deduction enabled spouses to split their gifts and estates for transfer tax purposes, in effect having them taxed the same as community property is taxed. See supra pages 484-485. Generally speaking, if the couple's wills were properly drafted, one-half of the couple's total property would be taxable at the husband's death and one-half at the wife's death.

The marital deduction provisions of the Economic Recovery Tax Act of 1981 were based on an altogether different policy: Interspousal transfers should not be subject to taxation. The act adopted an unlimited marital deduction rule under both the estate tax and the gift tax. Thus, unlimited amounts of property (other than certain "terminable interests") now can be transferred between spouses without the imposition of either a gift tax or an estate tax.

For many couples, the changes made by the 1981 act eliminated any concerns about transfer taxes in the estate of either spouse. Because of the unlimited marital deduction, a husband or wife can leave his or her estate to the other spouse without the imposition of an estate tax. Taxes in the estate of the surviving spouse are not a concern unless the projected value of the survivor's estate is greater than $675,000 in the year 2000 or up to $1 million in the year 2006.

PROBLEM

H has an estate worth about $1,200,000. *H* is married to *W*, and the couple has three adult children. *W* has little property of her own. *H* presently has a will that devises his entire estate outright to *W*, with an alternate gift to the couple's children. What will be the estate taxes (a) in *H*'s estate and (b) in *W*'s estate if *H* dies in 2001 and *W* dies one year later? Assume that deductions for administration expenses, debts, and funeral expenses allowable in *H*'s estate total $50,000, that the value of the property passing from *H* to *W* neither increases nor decreases in value from *H*'s death to *W*'s death, and that deductions for administration expenses, debts, and funeral expenses allowable in *W*'s estate total $30,000.

b.   Interests that Qualify for the Deduction

(1)   The nondeductible terminable interest rule

For an interest to qualify for the marital deduction, five requirements must be met.

(1)   The decedent must have been a citizen or resident of the United States at the time of death.
(2)   The decedent must have been survived by his or her spouse.
(3)   The value of the interest deducted must be includable in the decedent's gross estate.
(4)   The interest must pass from the decedent to the surviving spouse.
(5)   The interest must be a deductible interest. More precisely, it must not be a "nondeductible terminable interest" within the meaning of §2056(b).

The first three of these requirements are straightforward. As for the "passing" requirement, this is defined rather broadly in §2056(c) to include interests passing by will, by inheritance, by trust, by right of survivorship, by dower or elective share, by the exercise or nonexercise of a power of appointment held by the decedent, pursuant to a life insurance beneficiary designation, or by other transfer.

The fifth requirement is the most important and the most productive of litigation. In general, to qualify for the marital deduction the interest passing to the surviving spouse must be such that it is subject to taxation in the spouse's estate (to the extent not consumed or disposed of by the spouse during his or her lifetime). The marital deduction permits deferral of estate taxation until the surviving spouse's death. In effect, Congress has said: "We won't tax your property in your estate, as long as you leave it to your spouse in a form that exposes it to taxation in your spouse's estate on his or her death." The clearest example of an interest that qualifies for the deduction is an outright (or "fee simple") gift of property to the spouse.

From this it does not follow that any interest that will be taxed in the surviving spouse's estate qualifies for the deduction. To qualify, the interest must not run afoul of the *nondeductible terminable interest rule*:

> Where, on the lapse of time, on the occurrence of an event or contingency, or on the failure of an event or contingency to occur, an interest passing to the surviving spouse will terminate or fail, no deduction shall be allowed under this section with respect to such interest —
>
> (A) if an interest in such property passes or has passed (for less than an adequate and full consideration in money or money's worth) from the decedent to any person other than such surviving spouse (or the estate of such spouse); and
>
> (B) if by reason of such passing such person (or his heirs or assigns) may possess or enjoy any part of such property after such termination or failure of such interest so passing to the surviving spouse. [IRC §2056(b)(1).]

Absent special exception, the clearest example of a terminable interest is a life estate given to a surviving spouse, with the remainder to pass to other persons on the spouse's death. On the occurrence of an event or contingency — the spouse's death — the interest will terminate or fail. Upon such termination, an interest in the property — the remainder interest — will pass from the decedent to persons other than the surviving spouse or her estate. By reason of such passing, the remaindermen may possess or enjoy the property on the termination of the spouse's life estate.

PROBLEM

H has a pension plan providing for payments to himself for life and then to his wife *W* for life if *W* survives *H*. On the death of *H* and *W*, all payments will cease. *H* dies, and the value of the annuity (i.e., the discounted value of the remaining annuity payments to which *W* is entitled) is included in *H*'s gross estate under §2039. Does the value of this interest qualify for the marital deduction? See Treas. Reg. §20.2056(b)-1(g), example (3).

(2)   Exceptions to the terminable interest rule

There are four important exceptions to the nondeductible terminable interest rule.

(a) Limited survivorship exception.   In drafting wills, it is a common practice to include a clause requiring that a legatee must survive the testator by a stated period (e.g., 30 or 60 days) in order to take under the will. The purpose of this type of condition is to avoid determining who survived in a common disaster. Section 2056(b)(3) provides that a devise with a limited survival requirement is not a nondeductible terminable interest if (a) the condition of survival is for a period not exceeding six months and (b) the contingency (the spouse's death within the period) does not in fact occur. In short, a requirement of survival for up to six months can be attached to the interest passing to the spouse without disqualifying it for the marital deduction. (If the spouse does not survive for the stated period, no marital deduction will be available since no interest will actually pass from the decedent to the surviving spouse.)

PROBLEM

H devises property to *W* "if she survives distribution of my estate." Does this qualify for the marital deduction? See Estate of Heim v. Commissioner, 914 F.2d 1322 (9th Cir. 1990).

(b) Life estate plus general power of appointment trust exception.   In originally enacting the marital deduction in 1948, Congress permitted one
form of trust disposition to qualify for the marital deduction even
though the surviving spouse is given only a life estate. If the spouse
is given a life estate and also a general power of appointment over
the property, §2056(b)(5) declares that the interest passing to the
spouse qualifies for the marital deduction — provided that four technical requirements imposed by the statute are met:

(1)   The surviving spouse must be entitled to all income for life,
      payable annually or at more frequent intervals.
(2)   The power of appointment must be exercisable in favor of the
      spouse or her estate. In other words, the power must be a gen-
      eral power of appointment. The power may be exercisable dur-
      ing lifetime or by will.
(3)   The power must be exercisable by the spouse "alone and in all
      events." A general testamentary power of appointment satisfies
      the "all events" requirement even though it cannot be exer-
      cised by the spouse during lifetime.
(4)   The spouse's interest must not be subject to a power in anyone
      else to divert the property to someone other than the spouse.
      Thus, the trustee cannot be given a discretionary power to dis-
      tribute trust corpus to, for example, the couple's children.

This important exception to the nondeductible terminable interest
rule led to widespread use of the *life estate plus general power of appointment trust,* commonly referred to in the legal literature and in the
practice as simply the "marital deduction power of appointment
trust."

NOTE

In Estate of Foster v. Commissioner, 725 F.2d 201 (2d Cir. 1984),
the testator, a dairy farmer, left his wife his property for her lifetime
with power to invade principal "for her needs and the needs of my
children as she in her discretion may deem necessary," with remainder over to the children. The court held the bequest did not qualify
for the marital deduction because the wife's power to consume was
not equivalent to a power to appoint "in all events." A power to
consume is limited by a standard of good faith on the part of the
donee of the power.

(c) Estate trust exception.   The *estate trust* exception to the nondeductible terminable interest rule is included within the statement of the

rule (see supra page 1044). An interest is a nondeductible terminable interest only if, on termination of the spouse's interest, the property passes *to someone other than the surviving spouse or the spouse's estate.* Consequently, a disposition of property "to my husband for life, and on his death to his estate," whether in the form of a legal life estate or in a trust settlement, qualifies for the marital deduction.

The estate trust is seldom used as a means of qualifying for the deduction because of its relative inflexibility. Also, an estate trust causes the assets to be subject to creditors' claims and administration expenses in the spouse's estate. However, there is one situation in which an estate trust might be desirable, stemming from the requirement that, under a marital deduction power of appointment trust or a qualified terminable interest property trust (QTIP trust, see below), all trust income must be paid to the surviving spouse for life. If the testator's estate includes *unproductive property,* a marital deduction power of appointment trust or QTIP trust must include a provision authorizing the surviving spouse to compel the trustee to (a) convert the unproductive assets to income-producing property or (b) pay the spouse a reasonable amount out of other trust assets to compensate for lost income. See Treas. Reg. §20.2056(b)-5(f)(5). This could raise a potentially serious problem if, for example, the testator owns closely held stock that does not pay dividends or owns unimproved real estate that is being held for future development. An estate trust might be useful in this situation.

(d) Qualified terminable interest property (QTIP) trust exception. Until 1982, as a practical matter only three forms of transfer could be used to secure the marital deduction for an estate: an outright disposition, a marital deduction power of appointment trust, and an estate trust. All of these forms of transfer had the effect of giving the surviving spouse the unrestricted power of disposition over the property, either during lifetime or at death. When the unlimited marital deduction was enacted in 1981, Congress recognized that, under the existing law,

> the decedent cannot insure that the spouse will subsequently pass the property to his children. Because the maximum marital deduction is limited under present law to one-half of the decedent's adjusted gross estate, a decedent may at least control disposition of one-half of his estate and still maximize current tax benefits. However, unless certain interests that do not grant the spouse total control are eligible for the unlimited marital deduction, a decedent would be forced to choose between surrendering control of his entire estate to avoid imposition of estate tax at his death or reducing his tax benefits at his death to insure inheritance by the children. The committee believes that the tax laws should be neutral and that tax consequences should not control an individual's disposition of property. Accordingly, the committee believes that a deduction should

be permitted for certain terminable interests. [H.R. Rep. No. 4242, 96th Cong., 2d Sess., 161 (1981).]

In 1981 Congress enacted §2056(b)(7), which allows a marital deduction for a *qualified terminable interest*. To qualify for the deduction under this section, two requirements must be met.

(1)   The spouse must be entitled to all income for life, payable annually or at more frequent intervals.
(2)   No person (including the spouse) can have the power to appoint the property during the spouse's lifetime to any person other than the spouse. The spouse may, but need not, be given a special power to appoint the property *by will*.

Since the purpose of the marital deduction is to permit deferral of estate taxes until the death of the surviving spouse, allowance of a marital deduction for a qualified terminable interest property (QTIP) is conditioned on the donor (if a lifetime gift) or the decedent's executor (if a death transfer), making an election to have the property taxed in the surviving spouse's estate. If such an election is made, the value of the property in which the spouse had an income interest is includable in the spouse's gross estate under §2044. To prevent the tax attributable to this interest from increasing the tax burden on the spouse's own heirs, the tax is borne by the persons receiving the qualified terminable interest property on the spouse's death. Thus, if a trust is involved, the tax attributable to the interest (measured by the difference between the estate tax actually paid in the spouse's estate and the tax that would have been due if the property had not been included in the spouse's gross estate) is paid out of the corpus of the trust.

Since the beneficiary of a qualified terminable interest property (QTIP) trust is treated as owner for gift and estate tax purposes, if the surviving spouse makes a lifetime gift of his qualified terminable interest, the value of the entire property (and not just the value of the spouse's income interest) is treated as a taxable gift.

In comparing the QTIP trust with a marital deduction power of appointment trust, observe that both require that all income must be payable to the surviving spouse at least annually *for life*. If the spouse's income interest terminates on remarriage, this disqualifies both a marital deduction power of appointment trust and a QTIP trust. However, there are two important differences. In a power of appointment trust, the spouse must be given the power to appoint the property to any one she wants, including either herself or her estate. In a QTIP trust, the remainder interest on the spouse's death can pass to any beneficiary designated by the settlor or to persons chosen by the spouse exercising a special power of appointment. Second, under a QTIP trust there can be no power in any person *including the spouse* to appoint the property to anyone other than the spouse during her lifetime. Invasions of trust principal by the spouse or by a trustee for the spouse are permitted.

The permissible terms of a qualified terminable interest trust are so attractive that the traditional marital deduction power of appointment trust will probably be far less frequently used in the future. A QTIP trust is particularly useful if the spouses have different natural beneficiaries (e.g., children by a former marriage) or if the testator is concerned about the prospect that his spouse may remarry and then favor the new spouse.

The testator may direct his executor to elect to qualify a terminable interest trust for the marital deduction. Or the testator may direct his executor *not* to so elect. Or the testator may leave the election to the executor's discretion. If the testator leaves it up to the executor, the testator should be careful not to create any conflicts of interest so as to raise difficult questions of fiduciary obligations.

Estate of Rapp v. Commissioner
United States Court of Appeals, Ninth Circuit, 1998
140 F.3d 1211

FLETCHER, J.[16] The executor of Mr. Bert Rapp's estate appeals the tax court's determination that a trust established by Mr. Rapp does not qualify as "qualified terminable interest property" (QTIP), as defined by 26 U.S.C. §2056(b)(7). As such, the value of the trust may not be deducted when determining federal estate taxes owed.

We have jurisdiction, 26 U.S.C. §7482, and we affirm.

I.

The testator, Mr. Bert Rapp, died in February 1988. He was survived by his wife, Laura Rapp, and two children, Richard and David Rapp. Mr. Rapp willed his one-half of the community property to a trust.[17]

---

16. Judge Betty Binns Fletcher is a member of a prominent West Coast family with many connections to the law. Her father and grandfather were lawyers in Washington State. Her husband, Robert Fletcher, is a professor of law emeritus at the University of Washington. Her son William Fletcher, formerly a professor at UC Berkeley, now sits as a judge on the Ninth Circuit Court of Appeals. Her daughter Susan Fletcher French is a professor at UCLA Law School, Reporter for the Restatement of Servitudes, and mother of a young lawyer. Judge Fletcher's brother, nephew, and several of her in-laws also are in the law business.

17. By law of California, Mrs. Rapp received as her one-half of the community property, property valued at five million dollars.

Judge Betty Fletcher

Richard is the executor of the estate under Mr. Rapp's will and trustee of the trust. All relevant parties are citizens of California.

The issue in this case is whether the trust created by Mr. Rapp's will constitutes a QTIP trust, qualifying it for the marital tax deduction. A QTIP is an exception to an exception. Generally, the value of property passed directly from a testator to a surviving spouse is deducted before computing federal estate taxes.[18] 26 U.S.C. §2056(a). However, if the interest passing to the spouse consists only of a life estate or other terminable interest, the value of that interest is not deducted when determining the tax owed. 26 U.S.C. §2056(b). If the terminable interest qualifies as a QTIP, however, the surviving spouse can elect the marital deduction as if the interest passed directly and without restraint to him or her.

The will left by Mr. Rapp did not create a QTIP trust; however, the will as reformed by the California probate court did create a QTIP trust. The primary issue in this case is the effect to be given to the California probate court's reformation.

A.

In 1978, Laurence Clark, Mr. Rapp's attorney, prepared wills for both of the Rapps. Mr. Clark was not an estate attorney, but served as a consultant to Mr. Rapp in his business dealings. The 1978 wills were essentially identical to each other, and provided that household furnishings and other personal effects were to be given to the surviving spouse, and that all other property of the testator was to be held in trust during the life of the surviving spouse. The children were to be given the power as co-trustees to distribute such amounts from the principal and income of the trust as they determined necessary for the surviving spouse's health, education and support.[19] Any decision to do so would be in their "absolute discretion." Upon the death of the surviving spouse, the trust was to cease and the remaining assets were to be distributed to the two children or their living issue.

In 1986, Mr. Clark prepared new wills. These wills revoked the 1978

---

18. The tax deduction is in reality a tax deferral since the property is taxed when (or if) it becomes part of the surviving spouse's estate upon that spouse's death.

19. In this action, Richard is the sole trustee; David relinquished his position as co-trustee.

wills but were substantially similar. Again, Mr. and Mrs. Rapp's wills were nearly identical to each other. The trust was to operate as previously described. Article Fifth (b) of Mr. Rapp's will stated:

> If at any time, in the absolute discretion of the Trustee or co-Trustees, my wife, LAURA B. RAPP, should for any reason be in need of funds for her proper health, education and support, the Trustee may in his absolute discretion pay to or apply for the benefit of my wife, such amounts from the principal and income of the trust estate, up to the whole thereof, as the Trustee from time to time may deem necessary or advisable for her use and benefit.

B.

The 1986 will of Mr. Rapp was admitted to probate on May 5, 1988. Mrs. Rapp asked the probate court to modify her husband's will so that the trust created by the will would qualify for the marital deduction as a QTIP trust. Her petition to the probate court alleged:

> it was decedent's intention that the Trust created . . . for the benefit of Petitioner [i.e., Mrs. Rapp] during her lifetime was intended to qualify for the QTIP election and that decedent believed that the Trustees would pay all of the income from the Trust, at least annually, to or for the benefit of Petitioner during her lifetime.

She claimed that the trust was a "marital deduction gift" as defined by section 21520(b) of the California Probate Code.[20] Her petition relied upon the probate court's power to modify or terminate a trust upon consent of all parties, Cal. Prob. Code §15403, or its power to modify or terminate a trust due to changed circumstances, Cal. Prob. Code §15409(a).[21]

---

20. California defines a "marital deduction gift" as a transfer of property that is intended to qualify for the marital deduction. Cal. Prob. Code §21520(a). A "marital deduction" is defined as that which meets the federal definition of a transfer under section 2056 of the Internal Revenue Code. Id. at §21520(a).

[Cal. Prob. Code §21522 provides:

> If an instrument contains a marital deduction gift:
>   (a) The provisions of the instrument, including any power, duty, or discretionary authority given to a fiduciary, shall be construed to comply with the marital deduction provisions of the Internal Revenue Code.
>   (b) The fiduciary shall not take any action or have any power that impairs the deduction as applied to the marital deduction gift.
>   (c) The marital deduction gift may be satisfied only with property that qualifies for the marital deduction.

— Eds.]

21. Cal. Probate Code §15403 provides:

> [Unless continuance of the trust is necessary to carry out a material purpose of the trust] if all beneficiaries of an irrevocable trust consent, they may compel modification or termination of the trust upon petition to the court.

Oral argument was held before the probate court. A guardian ad litem was appointed to represent Richard Rapp's two minor children. No witnesses were called and no documents were introduced into evidence. Richard Rapp did not contest his mother's petition. He did not ask Mr. Clark, creator of the wills, to testify, and Mr. Clark did not appear.[22] the IRS did not receive notice of the hearing and did not appear. The guardian ad litem did not challenge Mrs. Rapp's petition.

The probate court granted Mrs. Rapp's petition. The court modified Article Fifth (b) to read:

> During the lifetime of my wife, LAURA B. RAPP, the Trustee or co-Trustee shall pay the net income from the corpus of the trust annually or at more frequent intervals to or for the benefit of LAURA B. RAPP, during her lifetime. . . . Any income accrued or held undistributed at the time of my wife's death shall be distributed to her estate.

and added the following provision:

> I authorize my executor to elect to treat the trust created under this Article FIFTH, or any portion thereof, as "qualified terminable interest property" in order to obtain the marital deduction for such property for federal estate tax purposes. Whether or not my executors make such an election, I hereby exonerate my executors from any liability resulting from making or failing to make such an election.

This order was entered October 31, 1988, and became final and unappealable as of April 30, 1989.

C.

Shortly after the probate court's order was entered, the executor filed with the Internal Revenue Service (IRS) an application for extension of time to file a federal estate tax return. The return normally is due 9 months after a testator's death. The executor noted in his application that he intended to make an election under §2056 for

---

Cal. Probate Code §15409 provides that a court may modify or terminate a trust if:

> owing to circumstances not known to the settlor and not anticipated by the settlor, the continuation of the trust under its terms would defeat or substantially impair the accomplishment of the purposes of the trust.

22. Mr. Clark initially was retained as counsel for the estate but was subsequently replaced. Although Mr. Clark did not testify at the reformation hearing, he did testify before the tax court at the behest of the government. He indicated that Mr. Rapp specifically intended to create a trust for his children's benefit, and did not wish to leave outright his money to Mrs. Rapp.

QTIP exemption, but that he could not determine yet which portion of the estate was to be claimed as a QTIP deduction. He also sent a payment of $156,204 as an estimate of the taxes owed on the estate, but offered no explanation as to how he arrived at that figure.

In May 1989, after the probate court's reformation became final, the executor filed the final federal estate tax return. The executor elected to claim a marital QTIP deduction, but only with respect to as much of the estate as would reduce the total estate tax owed to $156,424, the amount that had been previously paid. Thus, the marital deduction claimed on the return totalled $3,683,899.38.

The IRS sent a notice of deficiency to the executor stating that he had failed to substantiate fully the marital deduction claimed. The IRS allowed the deduction only to the extent of the property that passed directly to Mrs. Rapp under Mr. Rapp's will, consisting of the household furnishings and other personal property valued at $435,262.50. The executor appealed the decision and his claim was heard before the tax court.

After hearing argument, the tax court held that the probate court's reformation order was not binding absent an affirmation by the California Supreme Court. In the absence of an affirmation by the California Supreme Court, the tax court considered itself authorized to determine whether the probate court's order was in conformity with California law. After reviewing California law, the tax court concluded that the probate court had erred in reforming Mr. Rapp's will because the will was not ambiguous and there was little or no evidence that Mr. Rapp intended to create a QTIP trust. As such, the tax court held that, for federal estate tax purposes, the trust created by Mr. Rapp was not a QTIP trust, and that the claimed deficiency was correct.

II. . . .

III.

The IRS argues, and the tax court agreed, that the probate court's reformation of Mr. Rapp's will is without binding effect for the purpose of determining federal estate taxes owed, unless California's highest court has affirmed the result. Both rely on Commissioner of Internal Revenue v. Estate of Bosch, 387 U.S. 456 (1967). We agree that *Bosch* is controlling.

A.

In *Bosch*, the respondent, Mrs. Bosch, filed a federal estate tax return in which she claimed a marital deduction. Id. at 458. The IRS denied the deduction. Mr. Bosch's will had created a trust from which Mrs. Bosch was to receive all income and in which Mrs. Bosch had a general power of appointment. If she declined that appointment, however, half of the corpus of the trust was to go to Mr. Bosch's heirs.

The entire trust would qualify as tax exempt only if Mrs. Bosch retained the general power of appointment. Before Mr. Bosch died, Mrs. Bosch executed a release of her general power of appointment. Thus, whether or not the entire value of the trust was to be taxed depended upon the validity of the release. Before the tax court, Mrs. Bosch claimed that the release was invalid. While those proceedings were pending, Mrs. Bosch sought and received a determination from a New York state court that the release was a nullity under state law. The result was that a larger estate was to go to Mrs. Bosch as the surviving spouse, a diminished inheritance was to go to other beneficiaries, and a larger marital deduction could be claimed.

The issue before the Supreme Court was what effect was to be given to the state court's determination regarding the validity of the release. The Court first noted that neither res judicata nor collateral estoppel applied. Id. at 463. The Court then reviewed the legislative history of the marital deduction statute, and concluded that Congress did not intend state court actions to have a determinative effect on federal tax questions. It noted:

> [Congress] said that "proper regard," not finality "should be given to interpretations of the will" by state courts and then only when entered by a court "in a bona fide adversary proceeding." We cannot say that the authors of this directive intended that the decrees of state trial courts were to be conclusive and binding on the computation of the federal estate tax as levied by the Congress. If the Congress had intended state trial court determinations to have that effect on the federal actions, it certainly would have said so — which it did not do.

Id. at 464 (citations omitted). Relying on Erie R.R. Co. v. Tompkins, 304 U.S. 64 (1938), the Court stated:

> when the application of a federal statute is involved, the decision of a state trial court as to an underlying issue of state law should a fortiori not be controlling. . . . If there be no decision by [the State's highest court] then federal authorities must apply what they find to be the state law after giving the "proper regard" to relevant rulings of other courts of the State. In this respect, it may be said to be, in effect, sitting as a state court.

387 U.S. at 465.

This rule remains valid today. . . .

In this case, Mrs. Rapp sought modification in the probate proceeding for the sole purpose of reforming her husband's will so that the trust would qualify as a QTIP trust. As in *Bosch*, the state court proceedings were "brought for the purpose of directly affecting federal estate tax liability," and, as in *Bosch*, the issue before the state court was "determinative of federal estate tax consequences." *Bosch*, 387 U.S. at 462-63. Accordingly, the principle of *Bosch* applies here. The tax court correctly held that it was not bound by the California probate court's reformation of Mr. Rapp's will.

B.

The executor does not argue that the tax court improperly applied California law. In fact, the executor concedes that the probate court's decision to reform Mr. Rapp's will was erroneous. Instead, the executor argues that the tax court was without power to ignore the California probate court decision to reform Mr. Rapp's will, i.e., that *Bosch* is inapplicable to the instant case. He argues that the tax court only needed to determine whether Mrs. Rapp had a QTIP trust as of the proper "measuring date." According to the executor, the proper measuring date is the date on which the executor elected a QTIP deduction, and as of that date, Mrs. Rapp had a QTIP trust because the probate court's order had become final. *Bosch*, he argues, cannot be read to stand for the proposition that a state court order affixing the property rights of a taxpayer may be ignored where the order becomes final and unappealable as of the relevant measuring date for federal tax purposes. . . .

Regardless of the proper measuring date, however, the executor's argument fails because, contrary to the executor's assertion, *Bosch* does stand for the proposition that a probate court decision may be ignored when determining federal tax consequences, even when that order is final, if the decision is contrary to state law.

The executor's argument that *Bosch* is inapplicable is unavailing. The executor argues that *Bosch* does not permit the tax court to ignore the import of a state court decision that has become final and unappealable, i.e., one that cannot be directly challenged. There is no language in *Bosch* or subsequent decisions, however, that would support this position. That the California Supreme Court itself can no longer overrule the probate court's decision is irrelevant. *Bosch* stands only for the proposition that the federal court is not bound by the state court proceedings for determining federal estate taxes; to this end, the tax court decision does nothing to upset the actual outcome of the probate court proceedings. Mrs. Rapp will still enjoy the benefits of the reformation for which she petitioned in probate court. The estate simply will not receive the federal tax benefits of a QTIP.[23]

___

23. To hold that the probate court's order is binding on the federal courts merely because no one appealed would be inconsistent with the underlying policy considerations behind *Bosch*, that is, to prevent collusive state court proceedings brought only to avoid federal estate taxes. See, e.g., Estate of Simpson v. Commissioner of Internal Revenue,

C.

Finally, contrary to the executor's assertion, affirming the tax court would not create a circuit split with the Fifth, Sixth, and Eighth Circuits. As the executor correctly notes, three circuits have held that the correct "measuring date" for determining whether a particular asset is considered part of a QTIP trust is the date of QTIP election, not the date of the testator's death. See Estate of Spencer v. Commissioner of Internal Revenue, 43 F.3d 226 (6th Cir. 1995); Estate of Robertson v. Commissioner of Internal Revenue, 15 F.3d 779 (8th Cir. 1994); Estate of Clayton v. Commissioner of Internal Revenue, 976 F.2d 1486 (5th Cir. 1992).

We need not decide whether these cases are analogous to the case at hand, or whether we agree with their resolutions.[24] We note instead that because the tax court was not bound by the California probate court's reformation of Mr. Rapp's will and because under California law Mr. Rapp's will should not have been reformed, Mrs. Rapp cannot establish for federal estate tax purposes that she had a QTIP trust at any time, either at her husband's death or at the time of QTIP election. Therefore, we need not decide the correct measuring date for QTIP election to resolve this case.

IV.

The tax court properly held that it is not bound by the California probate court's reformation of Mr. Rapp's will as the decision was not affirmed by the California Supreme Court and is contrary to state law.

T.C. Memo 1994-259, 67 T.C.M. (CCH) 3062 (1994) (noting that, "there are a number of aspects to a State court proceeding which can raise questions and cast doubt upon its bona fide, adversary character. . . . Taxpayers can achieve favorable but collusive results from State court proceedings in which the Commissioner has not been made a party or which appear to have been pursued for the purpose of affecting a Federal tax liability.").

24. In each of these cases, the testator's will created a QTIP trust, but left to the executor the decision regarding how much of the testator's property ultimately would be placed into the QTIP trust. The IRS challenged this "wait-and-see" approach, arguing that only property which had been designated as QTIP property as of the date of the testator's death could qualify for the tax deduction. . . .

The court agreed with the executor, holding that "since no property can be QTIP until the election is made, the proper date to determine if property satisfies the requirement of §2056(b)(7) is on the date of the election." Id. at 231. The court explicitly rejected the IRS' suggestion that property "satisfy every requirement for the QTIP counter-exception on the date of decedent's death." Id.

In any event, we note that these cases are distinguishable because they involve the correct measuring date for deciding whether property meets the QTIP definition where the only issue at stake is not whether the trust created was a QTIP trust, but how much of the testator's property could be placed within that trust.

[New proposed Treasury regulations follow these cases. See Prop. Treas. Reg. §§20.2044-1, 20.2056(b)-7, 20.2056(b)-10 (1997). — Eds.]

For federal estate tax purposes, therefore, Mrs. Rapp at no time had a QTIP trust, and the deficiency is correct.

We AFFIRM.

Pond v. Pond

Supreme Judicial Court of Massachusetts, 1997
424 Mass. 894, 678 N.E.2d 1321

LYNCH, J.   The plaintiff, trustee of the Sidney M. Pond Trust 1991, a revocable trust (trust), filed a complaint in the Probate and Family Court seeking reformation of the trust. The plaintiff alleges that, due to scrivener's errors in the form of omissions and ambiguities, the declaration of trust fails to give effect to the settlor's intent. At the request of the parties a Probate Court judge reserved and reported the case to the Appeals Court pursuant to G. L. c. 215, §13, and Mass. R. Civ. P. 64, 365 Mass. 831 (1974). We granted the plaintiff's application for direct appellate review. See Commissioner of Internal Revenue v. Estate of Bosch, 387 U.S. 456, 465 (1967) (Internal Revenue Service need not accept decisions other than those of State's highest court); Simches v. Simches, 423 Mass. 683, 686 n.3, 671 N.E.2d 1226 (1996); Shawmut Bank, N.A. v. Buckley, 422 Mass. 706, 710, 665 N.E.2d 29 (1996).

1.   BACKGROUND

We summarize the undisputed facts as presented by the plaintiff.[25] The settlor, Sidney M. Pond, executed his last will and testament on January 17, 1991. On the same day, the settlor executed a declaration of revocable trust, naming himself and his wife as trustees. Then, they transferred virtually all their assets, except the marital home, into the trust. The settlor died on February 26, 1996.[26]

The trust instrument provided that, during the settlor's lifetime, all of the annual income and such principal as the trustees deemed necessary was to be paid to the settlor and his wife. However, the trust made no provision for income or principal to be paid to his wife if she were to survive the settlor. The trust also provided that, on the death of the settlor and his wife, the trust shall terminate and its assets should be distributed in equal shares to their children. If one of the children predeceased the parents, the trust provided that the deceased child's share shall pass "equally and in equal shares to his/

25. Notice of the proposed reformation was served on the Internal Revenue Service and the Attorney General. Neither the Commonwealth nor the IRS filed an appearance.
26. At the time of the settlor's death, the trust was valued at approximately $650,000.

her issue by right of representation," when the issue reach the age of thirty.

In his will, the settlor bequeathed all his tangible personal property to his wife and the residue of his estate, both real and personal, to the trust. The tax clause in the will authorized his wife, as executrix, "in her sole, exclusive and unrestricted discretion, to determine whether to elect (under Sec. 2056[b][7] of the Internal Revenue Code of 1954, as amended, or any corresponding provision of state law) to qualify all or a specific portion of the SIDNEY M. POND REVOCABLE TRUST dated January 17, 1991 for the federal estate tax marital deduction and any marital deduction available under the law of the state in which I am domiciled at the time of my death." To qualify under §2056, however, the trust must provide the surviving spouse a "qualifying income interest for life." See §2056(b)(7)(B) of the Internal Revenue Code (I.R.C.). Without the marital deduction, the settlor's estate would have to pay $70,000 in otherwise avoidable taxes.

The plaintiff contends that scrivener's errors are apparent when the purposes of the trust are considered. The plaintiff avers that the settlor created the trust to satisfy the requirements for the marital deduction under §2056(b)(7) of the I.R.C. and the corresponding deduction under G. L. c. 65C, §3A. The plaintiff also contends that, pursuant to this estate plan, the settlor intended for the trust's assets to be used to support his surviving spouse. Due to the omission of an income provision for the surviving spouse, both objectives were thwarted because his wife was left with virtually no assets and the trust does not qualify for the marital deduction.

The plaintiff requests that the court reform the trust instrument to give effect to the settlor's intent. First, the plaintiff asks this court to insert a provision which would grant the surviving spouse the right to the trust's annual income, and discretionary principal payments, during her lifetime. Second, the plaintiff also asks this court to incorporate provisions which would correct the ambiguity in the termination provisions. The beneficiaries of the trust, who were named as defendants, assented to the proposed reformation.[27]

2. DISCUSSION

The modification of a trust agreement to conform with a settlor's intent with respect to the marital deduction is a matter of State law which this court may properly decide. See Loeser v. Talbot, 412 Mass. 361, 365, 589 N.E.2d 301 (1992); Berman v. Sandler, 379 Mass. 506,

---

27. The guardians for the minor grandchildren also have assented to the proposed reformation.

509, 399 N.E.2d 17 (1980); Babson v. Babson, 374 Mass. 96, 101-102, 371 N.E.2d 430 (1977); Mazzola v. Myers, 363 Mass. 625, 633, 296 N.E.2d 481 (1973). When a trust instrument fails to embody the settlor's intent because of scrivener's error, it may be reformed on clear and decisive proof of mistake. Loeser v. Talbot, supra. To ascertain the settlor's intent, we look to the trust instrument as a whole and the circumstances known to the settlor on execution. Berman v. Sandler, supra at 510.

The settlor's intent in creating the trust was clearly to qualify for the marital deduction under §2056(b)(7) of the I.R.C. The tax clause in the settlor's will, which was executed on the same day, demonstrates that the settlor thought that the trust qualified for the marital trust deduction.[28] To qualify, the trust must provide the surviving spouse a "qualifying income interest for life." §2056(b)(7)(B). This means the trust must pay income annually or more frequently to the surviving spouse. §2056(b)(7)(B)(ii). Because we read the trust as clearly manifesting an intent that it qualify for a marital deduction, it can only be a scrivener's error that caused a clause to be omitted that would have provided for income to be paid to his wife for life on the death of the settlor.

We are also convinced that the settlor did not intend to deny his wife discretionary use of the principal during her lifetime. The trust was an essential component in the settlor's estate plan. The settlor transferred virtually all his marital assets into this trust. The trust's income and principal were available to the settlor and his wife during his lifetime. The trust, however, omitted any provision for the surviving spouse after the settlor's death. Because we know that the settlor intended to provide income for his wife if he died first and since the trust made principal available for as long as the settlor lived, we conclude that his intent to continue the same arrangement if he should die first is manifest. Babson v. Babson, 374 Mass. at 104-106 (considering will as a whole, testator intended to take maximum advantage of estate tax deductions even though word "maximum" not used). This conclusion is buttressed by the settlor's will bequeathing all his tangible property to his wife and naming her executrix of his estate. There is no indication that the settlor intended to deprive his surviving spouse of the trust's assets during her lifetime.

We conclude that there is clear and decisive proof of mistake due to scrivener's error. The settlor's intent was to minimize estate tax payable by establishing a qualifying terminal interest trust. To qualify

---

28. Under §2056(b)(7) of the I.R.C., qualifying terminal interest property is eligible for a marital deduction in the estate of the settlor if the settlor's executrix so elects. If that election is made and the marital deduction is thus taken in the settlor's estate, the trust property must then be included in the estate of the surviving spouse for Federal estate tax purposes.

under §2056, the trust must distribute income to the surviving spouse. While the discretionary principal payments are not required under §2056, the estate plan demonstrates an intent to treat both spouses equally. Thus, we agree that the trust should be reformed to give effect to the settlor's intent. . . .

The case is remanded to the Probate and Family Court for entry of a judgment of reformation consistent with this opinion.

So ordered.

NOTE AND PROBLEMS

1.   *Post-mortem reformation to save taxes.* In Pond v. Pond, the court reformed a trust, at the request of the family, so as to obtain tax advantages lost, allegedly, by the faulty work of the lawyer. Judicial reformation is a new idea that has been pushed along by the threat of legal malpractice. Massachusetts has led the way in reforming trusts to obtain tax advantages lost through faulty drafting. Note that under the Supreme Court opinion in Commissioner v. Estate of Bosch, 387 U.S. 456 (1967), the Internal Revenue Service is bound only by a construction or reformation approved by the state's highest court. Massachusetts has a special procedure permitting the parties to go directly from the probate court to the Supreme Judicial Court. Most states do not have such a summary appellate procedure. Most require appeal to a middle appellate court and then to the state supreme court, which takes a lot of time and money and may require jumping several procedural hurdles.

2.   *H* by will creates a trust providing *W* with "so much of the net income as she may require to maintain her usual and customary standard of living." Does this qualify for the QTIP deduction? See Estate of Nicholson v. Commissioner, 94 T.C. 666 (1990). Suppose the trust gave the trustee the power to accumulate income in excess of the amount necessary for *W*'s "needs, best interests, and welfare." QTIP deduction? See Estate of Ellingson v. Commissioner, 964 F.2d 959 (1992). Would it matter if the testator's will had stated that his intention was to qualify the trust for the marital deduction? See Wiseley v. United States, 893 F.2d 660 (4th Cir. 1990).

3.   *W* has created a revocable trust for herself to avoid probate. The trust contains a provision that in the event of *W*'s incapacity the trustee may make gifts to members of the family qualifying for the annual $10,000 gift tax exclusion. *H* dies, devising property to *W*'s revocable trust. Does this qualify for the marital deduction?

4.   For criticism of the QTIP deduction as incompatible with the partnership theory of marriage, see supra page 486.

(3)   Noncitizen spouses: qualified domestic trusts

No marital deduction is allowed if the *spouse* of the transferor is not a citizen of the United States, unless the property passes to the spouse in a *qualified domestic trust.* §2056(d)(2). A qualified domestic trust (QDOT) is one where at least one trustee is a citizen of the United States or a domestic corporation. The trust instrument must give the U.S. trustee the right to withhold the deferred estate tax on the QDOT assets. The trust must qualify as a marital deduction power of appointment trust, QTIP trust, or estate trust before it will qualify as a QDOT. If the decedent did not create a QDOT, the noncitizen spouse or the decedent's executor may create a QDOT after the decedent's death. If the decedent's trust does not qualify as a QDOT, it will qualify as a QDOT if reformed by a court to comply with QDOT requirements. §2056(d)(5).

To ensure collection of the deferred estate tax, Treasury has issued regulations requiring a bond of an individual trustee and requiring securities to be kept in the United States. Prop. Reg. §26.2056A-2(d).

c.   Tax Planning

In a compendious treatment of estate taxation such as this, we cannot cover in detail the more complicated tax avoidance devices developed for spouses. However, there is one basic strategy with which you should be familiar. It is to use up the exemptions of both spouses; do not let one exemption go to waste.

Each spouse has an exemption from estate and gift taxation, in the form of a unified credit, which is, let us assume, $1 million. It is possible for a spouse to leave his or her entire estate to the other spouse, deferring all taxation until the death of the surviving spouse. If this is done, however, the first spouse's exemption is lost since *all* of his or her assets will be subject to taxation on the surviving spouse's death. Thus:

> *Case 17.* W owns property worth $1,600,000. *H* owns no property. *H* and *W* have made no taxable gifts. *W* dies, devising all her property to *H*. Because of the unlimited marital deduction, no taxes are paid at *W*'s death. At *H*'s death, *H* leaves an estate of $1,600,000; $1 million is exempt from taxation. An estate tax of $246,000 is payable on the remaining $600,000. (For ease of illustration, we keep the asset values the same in the estates of *W* and *H* and ignore deductions for administration expenses, debts, and funeral expenses, and various credits.)

By devising everything to *H*, *W* in Case 17 did not use her $1 million exemption applicable to property taxable in her estate. To use this exemption, *W* must leave a taxable estate of $1 million, which means that $1 million worth of property should *not* qualify for the marital deduction. Case 18 illustrates how this can be done:

> *Case 18.* Refer back to Case 17. *W* dies, bequeathing $1 million in trust for *H* for life, remainder as *H* appoints by will among *W*'s issue, and in default of appointment to *W*'s issue per stirpes. This bequest would qualify for the marital deduction as a QTIP trust if *W*'s executor so elected, but *W*'s will directs her executor not to elect the marital deduction for this trust. This $1 million is taxable at *W*'s death, but because of *W*'s $1 million exemption in the form of a credit, no taxes are paid (hence this trust is known as a *credit shelter trust* or as a *bypass trust* because no taxes are payable at the spouse's death). The assets in the credit shelter trust are not taxable at *H*'s death because *H* has only a life estate coupled with a special power of appointment.
>
> The remainder of *W*'s assets (worth $600,000) is bequeathed by *W*'s residuary clause outright to *H*. These assets are taxable at *H*'s death, but no taxes are paid because the total is less than $1 million.

By taking advantage of both spouses' exemptions, as is done in Case 18, at total of $2 million can be passed to the couple's children, free of estate taxation. If the spouses desire that the surviving spouse have all the income from the property, this can be arranged as in Case 18. The key to taking advantage of both exemptions is that $1 million worth of property must not qualify for the marital deduction in the estate of the first spouse to die. Putting $1 million in a credit shelter trust will reduce death taxes payable on the surviving spouse's death by an amount equal to at least 41 percent of the value of the trust assets on the surviving spouse's death. (If the value of the assets remains the same at the surviving spouse's death, the tax saving of the estate plan in Case 18, as compared to Case 17, is $246,000.)

The credit shelter trust does not, of course, have to give all the income to the surviving spouse. Case 18 is merely an illustration of a situation where the couple wants all the income to go to the surviving spouse. The credit shelter trust could give discretion to the trustee to spray the income among family members, thus reducing income taxes during the surviving spouse's remaining life. Or the first spouse to die could use his or her $1 million exemption by bequeathing that amount to children or persons other than the surviving spouse.

In discussing Case 17, we have assumed that *W*, the richer of the spouses, will die first. But suppose that *H* dies first. In that case, *H*'s exemption will be lost to the extent of $1 million because *H* owns nothing. At *W*'s death $600,000 ($1,600,000 minus *W*'s $1 million exemption) will be taxable. In order to take advantage of *H*'s exemption, *W* must transfer to *H* during life property worth $600,000. *W* can give *H* property outright or in a trust. The trust can be either a marital deduction power of appointment trust or a QTIP trust, which W elects to be taxable at H's death. No gift tax is payable upon the transfer because any of these transfers qualifies for the gift tax marital deduction. Thus:

> *Case 19.* W creates an inter vivos QTIP trust with all income to be paid to H for his life and upon his death to pay the principal to W's children. W transfers $600,000 to this trust and on her gift tax return elects to take the marital deduction. This results in the trust principal being taxable in H's gross estate, but because of H's exemption, no taxes are payable. W has reduced her taxable estate to $1 million, which is exempt from taxation. (If W wants to have the income on the $600,000 come back to W after H dies, W can create an inter vivos marital deduction power of appointment trust with H as the beneficiary, and H by will can exercise the general power of appointment by appointing the trust funds to W for life, directing his executor not to elect the marital deduction.)

7.   The Charitable Deduction

Section 2055 of the Internal Revenue Code allows an unlimited deduction for transfers for public, charitable, or religious purposes. There is no limitation on the amount that can qualify for a charitable deduction.

A principal question is whether a particular bequest is for uses that qualify for the charitable deduction. The statute and regulations provide guidelines that, while taking care of the clear cases, leave the harder cases for resolution by revenue ruling or case decision. If a bequest is made to a corporation, to qualify as a "charity" the corporation must be

> organized and operated exclusively for religious, charitable, scientific, literary, or educational purposes, including the encouragement of art, or to foster national or international amateur sports competition (but only if no part of its activities involve the provision of athletic facilities or equipment), and the prevention of cruelty to children or animals, no part of the net earnings of which inures to the benefit of any private stockholder or individual, which is not disqualified for tax exemption under §501(c)(3) by reason of attempting to influence legislation, and which does not participate in, or intervene in (including the publishing or distributing of statements), any political campaign on behalf of any candidate for public office.... [IRC §2055(a)(2).]

IRS Publication 76, published biannually, lists the official names of all charitable organizations exempt from taxation under the federal income tax. If the client wants to make a gift to a new charity not on the list, care must be taken to make sure the beneficiary qualifies for the deduction.

If a client wants to make a gift of a *remainder* to charity, special arrangements are required. Except for a remainder in a personal residence or in a farm, not in trust, a charitable deduction for a remainder is disallowed under the federal income, gift, and estate tax laws unless the remainder is in an *annuity trust* or a *unitrust* or unless the gift is to a *pooled income fund.* IRC §§664(d), 2055(e)(2), and 2522(c)(2). A bequest in trust "to pay all the income to *A* for life, remainder to the *Y* charity" does *not* qualify for the charitable deduction because such a trust is not an annuity trust or a unitrust.

A charitable remainder *annuity trust* is one under which a fixed sum, which can be no less than 5 percent of the *original value* of the trust corpus, is paid at least annually to the private beneficiary or beneficiaries. The "income" beneficiary of an annuity trust thus receives a fixed and constant amount each year. A *unitrust* is one under which a fixed percentage, which cannot be less than 5 percent of the trust corpus, *valued annually*, is paid to the beneficiary. The "income" beneficiary of a unitrust thus will receive an annual amount that will fluctuate as the value of the trust changes. A *pooled income fund* is set up by a charitable organization to meet certain specific requirements of the Code. If the trustee or private beneficiary of an annuity trust, a unitrust, or a pooled income fund has a discretionary power to invade principal, the trust does not qualify for a charitable remainder deduction. The objectives of these rules are to reduce the uncertainty involved in valuing the future interest given to charity and to increase the likelihood that an interest will in fact pass to charity on the private beneficiary's death. However, the rules governing the drafting of these trusts are technical and stringent, and must be carefully followed.

We mention only one technicality to illustrate and underscore the need for caution in drafting gifts to charitable remainder trusts. If estate taxes may be paid from a charitable remainder trust, no charitable deduction is allowable. Rev. Rul. 82-128, 1982-27 I.R.S. 7. If taxes are apportioned by state law or by a clause in the decedent's will, a deduction may be denied. The will should provide that the charitable bequest pass free of all taxes.

PROBLEMS

1. *T* was unmarried. *T*'s will bequeaths his property to Princeton University and Johns Hopkins University. A codicil to his will grants *T*'s executors the discretion "to compensate persons who have contributed to my well-being or who have otherwise been helpful to me during my lifetime," providing that no single bequest should exceed

1 percent of the testator's gross estate. The executors determined that only two individuals met the definition of eligible persons and distributed $25,000 to them and the rest to the universities. Is the estate entitled to a charitable deduction? See Estate of Marine v. Commissioner, 990 F.2d 136 (4th Cir. 1993).

2. *W* bequeaths $200,000 in trust to pay the income to *H* for life, remainder to Smith College. The gift to Smith College does not qualify for the charitable deduction in *W*'s estate because the trust is not an annuity trust or a unitrust. *W*'s net estate is worth $1,200,000. *H* elects to take against the will a surviving spouse's elective share, which is one-half of *W*'s estate. *H*'s elective share is $600,000. What effect does *H*'s disclaimer of his life estate have on the charitable deduction? See First National Bank of Fayetteville v. United States, 82-2 U.S. Tax Cas. (CCH) ¶13,478 (W.D. Ark. 1982).

If *H* had not elected to take against the will and *W*'s executor had claimed the marital deduction for the trust as a QTIP trust, would a charitable deduction be allowed in *H*'s estate upon *H*'s death? See IRC §2044.

3. Sometimes statutes or courts reform defective charitable remainder unitrusts to qualify under §2055 as a charitable unitrust, when the intent to obtain the charitable deduction is manifest. Putnam v. Putnam, 425 Mass. 770, 682 N.E.2d 1351 (1997).

4. For discussion of the impact of repeal of estate taxes on the amount of charitable giving, see Eric Rakowski, Estate Tax Reform and Charitable Giving, Tax Notes, Oct. 27, 1997, at 463.

SECTION D.   THE GENERATION-SKIPPING TRANSFER TAX

1.   The Nature of the Tax

Until 1986, it was possible for wealthy persons to make transfers in trust, either during lifetime or by will, in a manner that would insulate the transferred property from estate or gift taxation over several generations. We call this the "dynastic trust." *O* might transfer property worth (say) $5 million to a trust under which the income was payable to *O*'s children for *their lives*, then to the children's children for *their lives*, then to the grandchildren's children for *their lives*, and so on down the generations until the local version of the Rule against Perpetuities, if any, called a halt. Each beneficiary could be given, in addition to a share of the income, a power to consume principal measured by an "ascertainable standard," a "$5,000 or 5 percent" withdrawal power, and a special testamentary power of appointment over his or her share of the trust corpus, all without estate or gift tax cost to the beneficiary. In addition, an independent trustee could be given an unlimited power to distribute trust principal to the beneficiaries with no transfer tax consequences. As each beneficiary died, nothing would be taxed in the beneficiary's estate because the beneficiary held only a life estate and limited powers of appointment. See supra pages 673-676. Through careful drafting to comply with the Rule against Perpetuities, the trust might continue — and be removed from the transfer tax rolls — for several generations. When the assets "resurfaced" on termination of the trust, the new owners could turn around, pay a gift or estate tax on the value of the assets, and make another generation-skipping transfer for another long period of time.

In the Tax Reform Act of 1986, Congress put an end to this tax-avoidance technique by enacting what is titled a "Tax on Generation-Skipping Transfers."[29] Although the rules governing imposition of generation-skipping taxes can become enormously complicated, a general understanding of the generation-skipping transfer tax (GST) is not difficult and is essential for the ordinary estate planner. Our treatment here is designed to give you a basic understanding. The fine details will have to be left to a course in tax planning.

The loophole in the estate and gift taxes that brought on the GST tax is the exemption of the life estate from transfer taxation at the death of the life tenant. The essential idea underlying the GST tax is that a transfer tax (gift, estate, or generation-skipping) should be paid *once a generation*, and that it should not be possible for an owner of property to avoid a generational transfer tax by giving the next generation only a life estate or skipping its members entirely. To implement this idea, the Code imposes a tax on any *generation-skipping transfer*, which is defined in §2611(a) as —

(1)   a *taxable termination,*
(2)   a *taxable distribution,* and
(3)   a *direct skip.*

Generally, a generation-skipping transfer is a transfer to a *skip person* (a new term invented by Congress in imposing this tax). A skip person is a grandchild, great-grandchild, or any other person assigned to a

---

29. The generation-skipping transfer tax provisions, Chapter 13 of the Internal Revenue Code, comprise a separate and distinct tax from the estate tax (Chapter 11) and the gift tax (Chapter 12). The relevant sections are 2601-2663. Another version of the generation-skipping transfer tax was written into the Code by Congress in 1976, but its effective date was annually postponed until 1986, when the earlier generation-skipping transfer tax was retroactively repealed.

generation that is two or more generations below the transferor's generation (§2613(a)). A spouse or a child (or other person in the transferor's generation or the generation just below the transferor's) is a nonskip person. As you will see, it is transfers from a grandparent to a grandchild, either direct or as a future interest, which avoid estate taxation at the death of the donor's children, that are the central concern of the GST tax.

There are three types of generation-skipping transfers. A *taxable termination* is the "termination (by death, lapse of time, release of power, or otherwise) of any interest in property held in a trust unless —

(A) immediately after such termination, a non-skip person has an interest in such property, or

(B) at no time after such termination may a distribution (including distributions on termination) be made from such trust to a skip person" (§2612(a)(1)).

Here is an example:

> *Case 20.* *T* bequeaths $5 million in trust for her son *A* for life, remainder to *A*'s children. At *A*'s death a "taxable termination" takes place. *A*'s life interest terminates and only skip persons (*A*'s children) have an interest in the property. A GST tax must be paid. If the income were payable to *T*'s daughter *B* after *A*'s death, there would be no taxable termination upon *A*'s death; there would, however, be a taxable termination upon *B*'s death, when only skip persons would have an interest in the trust.

The purpose of the exceptions in the definition of a taxable termination ((A) and (B) above) is to limit to *one* the number of taxable terminations, per dollar of property, that can occur in each generation below the transferor's. Where, for example, *T* bequeaths the income from a trust to her children, with principal to be distributed to her grandchildren upon the death of her *last* surviving child, a taxable termination occurs only at the death of the last surviving child. On the other hand, if at the death of one child his or her share is distributed to his or her children, then a taxable termination of a fractional share of the trust principal has occurred (§2612(a)(2)). Each dollar of a generation-skipping transfer is to be taxed once a generation.

A *taxable distribution* takes place whenever any distribution is made from a trust to a skip person (other than a taxable termination or a direct skip). Thus, if in Case 20, *A* had a (special) power to distribute income or corpus to *A*'s children, a taxable distribution would take place when and if such distribution were made. In a discretionary trust, a taxable distribution takes place whenever a distribution is made to a skip person.[30]

It is easy to see, from the explanation of a taxable termination and a taxable distribution, that the old-fashioned dynastic trust, described above in introducing the GST tax, generally will not work any longer in avoiding wealth transfer taxes. At the death of the transferor's children, holding life estates, or upon earlier distribution to the transferor's grandchildren, GST taxes must be paid. It is important to note, however, that the 1986 GST tax does not apply to any irrevocable trust created before the date of the act. All those trusts already established by the Rockefellers, the duPonts, and the Gettys, as well as lesser millionaires — with life estates and special powers of appointment in succeeding generations — will continue untaxed until after the termination of the trust. *Note also that an estate and GST tax free $1 million dynasty trust, which is cut out of the same cloth as the dynastic trusts, can be created using the settlor's $1 million exemption from GST tax.* See supra page 849, infra page 1072.

To prevent the rich from bypassing one generation and making untaxed gifts to grandchildren or more remote descendants, Congress also has imposed a tax on direct skips. A *direct skip* is a transfer of property directly to a skip person. Case 21 illustrates a direct skip:

> *Case 21. T* leaves surviving her son *A* and *A*'s daughter *B. T* bequeaths $3,000,000 to her granddaughter *B*. This is a direct skip. A generation-skipping transfer tax (in addition to the estate tax payable on *T*'s death) is due on *T*'s death. This "double taxation" follows from the principle that a transfer tax must be paid once per generation. Similarly, if *T* had given *B* $3,000,000 during life, a gift tax *and* a generation-skipping transfer tax would be due.

Exceptions. Observe that the principle underlying taxation of a direct skip is that a transfer tax (be it an estate tax, gift tax, or generation-skipping transfer tax) must be paid once a generation, *regardless of whether any person assigned to a particular generation has any present interest or power.* This principle has two important exceptions.

(a) *Multiple skips.* First, skipping over two or more generations is permitted with the payment of only one GST tax. An owner can transfer property to a great-grandchild, paying a GST tax for the direct skip. Although two generations are skipped over, only one tax is paid.

(b) *Predeceased child.* The second exception relates to direct skips to descendants of predeceased children of the transferor. If a child of the transferor is dead at the time of the transfer, the children of that

---

30. An income tax deduction is provided for any GST tax imposed on any income distributions. This deduction prevents the same amount being subject to both income tax and the GST tax. But observe that the GST tax rate is considerably higher than the income tax rate.

child are treated as the children of the transferor. Thus in Case 22 suppose that *A* had predeceased *T*. If this had happened, there would be no direct skip. The child of a predeceased child is treated as the child of the transferor; he or she is moved up a generation (§2651(e)). The children of this child — really *T*'s great-grandchildren — are treated as grandchildren. This makes sense. Since no estate taxes could be levied on this property at *A*'s death, prior to *T*'s death, a GST tax (the functional equivalent of an estate tax) should not be levied upon a gift by *T* to the children of *T*'s dead son.

If the transferor has no lineal descendants, this exception for persons with a predeceased parent applies to transfers to lineal descendants of the parent of the transferor (first line collaterals).

When generation-skipping transfer tax imposed. No doubt you have observed one important difference between a direct skip on the one hand, and a taxable termination or distribution on the other. A direct skip occurs (and is taxable) on the day the transfer is effective; a taxable termination or taxable distribution occurs in the future, sometime after the original transfer in trust. In some cases, it will be certain when the trust is established that the trust will produce a GST tax in the future. In other cases, it will not be. Case 22 is an example.

> *Case 22.* *T*'s will bequeaths property in trust to pay the income to *T*'s child *A* until *A* attains the age of 30, at which time the trustee is to distribute the trust principal to *A*. If *A* dies before reaching age 30, the trustee is to distribute the principal to *A*'s children in equal shares. Whether this trust will produce a generation-skipping transfer will turn on the events that actually occur — and for this purpose we wait to see what happens. If *A* lives to age 30 and receives the trust principal, it will turn out that *T* did not make a generation-skipping transfer. If *A* dies under age 30, and the trust principal is distributed to *A*'s children, a taxable termination will occur.

If a trust turns out to produce a generation-skipping transfer, the tax is payable in the future when such transfer occurs.

PROBLEM

If a person makes a qualified disclaimer (see supra page 725), for purposes of federal gift, estate, and generation-skipping transfer taxes, the disclaimed interest in property is treated as if it had never been transferred to the person making the disclaimer. The disclaimant is *not* treated as having predeceased the transferor, as occurs under many state disclaimer statutes (see UPC §2-801(c), supra page 150). *T* bequeaths $1.2 million to her son *A*. If *A* disclaims, is a GST tax imposed?

2. Rate and Base of Tax

Rate. All generation-skipping transfers are taxed at a flat rate, which is the highest rate applicable under the federal estate tax. The highest estate tax rate currently is 55 percent.

Base. The amount taxed and the person liable for the tax depend upon the type of transfer. Where there is a *direct skip*, the transferor must pay the tax on the amount received by the transferee. In this way, the direct skip resembles the gift tax. The base excludes the amount of tax levied; a direct skip is said to be "tax exclusive" (see supra page 984). Thus, for a transferor to pass $1 million directly to a grandchild, the transferor must part with $1,550,000, in addition to the gift or estate tax imposed. The gift tax is imposed on the amount of the gift and on the amount of the GST tax paid.

Taxable terminations and *taxable distributions* are treated differently. The tax in these events is imposed on a "tax-inclusive" basis (i.e., the taxable amount includes the tax). In this respect, taxable terminations and distributions resemble the estate tax. Upon a taxable termination, the tax base is the entire property with respect to which the termination occurred. The tax is to be paid out of the trust.[31] Upon a taxable distribution, the tax base is the amount received by the beneficiary, who is liable for the tax. Thus, if a generation-skipping trust terminates and the taxable principal is $2 million, the trustee must pay $1.1 million to Uncle Sam and $900,000 is distributed to the beneficiary. Similarly, if a trustee distributes $2 million to a skip person, the donee is liable for $1.1 million in GST tax, leaving a net transfer of $900,000 million.

PROBLEM

O makes a $1 million gift to a grandchild, allocating no exemption to it. Assuming the maximum gift and estate tax rate of 55 percent is applicable, what is the cost of this transfer to *O*? To put the question a different way, how much does *O* have to part with to put $1 million in a grandchild's hands?

What would be the cost to *O* of a $1 million *bequest* to a grandchild?

3. Exemption and Exclusions

Exemption. Section 2631(a) provides an exemption of up to $1 million[32] for each person making generation-skipping transfers. In the

---

31. If the $1 million exemption is allocated to this trust at *T*'s death, no GST tax is payable at *A*'s death, even though the principal has appreciated. See discussion of exemption, infra.

32. In 1997 Congress provided that the $1 million exemption may be increased by annual cost-of-living adjustments by the Treasury in multiples of $10,000.

case of inter vivos transfers by a married person, the transferor and his or her spouse may elect to treat the transfer as made one-half by each spouse (as under §2513 of the gift tax, see supra page 1004). A husband and wife can give away $2 million in generation-skipping transfers without incurring any tax. Thus:

Case 23. During life *W* transfers $2 million to a trustee to pay the income to *W*'s children for their lives, then to distribute the principal to *W*'s grandchildren. *H* consents to treating this transfer as having been made half by him, thus using up his $1 million exemption. A gift tax is payable by *W* at the time of the transfer. At the death of *W*'s children, no GST tax is due.

If, in Case 23, *W* had not made an inter vivos transfer but had bequeathed $2 million in trust, only $1 million would be exempt from GST tax. The split-gift provision applies only to inter vivos gifts. In case of a death transfer, to take advantage of the spouse's GST tax exemption, it is necessary to make the spouse a "transferor" for estate tax purposes. This can be done by bequeathing the spouse outright ownership, or a life estate coupled with a general power of appointment, or a life estate in a QTIP trust. If, in Case 23, the trust had been a testamentary trust and *H* had been bequeathed a life estate in half of $2 million transferred by *W* into trust, *H*'s GST tax exemption of $1 million could be used up too.

If the transferor creates more than one generation-skipping trust, or makes generation-skipping transfers in excess of $1 million, the transferor or his personal representative can allocate the exemption as he sees fit. If not so allocated, §2642 provides some rather complex "default" rules. Generally, under these rules, the exemption is first allocated to direct skips and then to taxable terminations and taxable distributions. The exemption is allocated to the "property" transferred and not, in the case of taxable terminations and taxable distributions, to specific generation-skipping transfers that occur in the future. This means that with respect to trusts that might produce taxable terminations or taxable distributions, the entire exemption or a fraction thereof must be allocated to the trust *at the time of the transfer into trust.*

The allocation, once made, is irrevocable. Therefore, it is important to allocate the exemption so as not to waste it on a trust that is uncertain to produce a generation-skipping transfer, when it could be allocated more effectively elsewhere. It is usually best to allocate the exemption first to direct skips, for this reason and for the additional reason that a tax postponed is better than a tax paid.

Under §2653(b)(1), the exempt fraction of the trust property — determined when the trust is created — remains the same for the duration of the trust. If the trust produces successive skips, the transferor's exemption can eliminate or reduce the GST tax generation after generation. If, for example, a trust provides for payment of income to *T*'s children for their lives, then to *T*'s grandchildren for their lives, and then to distribute the principal to *T*'s great-grandchildren, the transferor's $1 million exemption will shelter the trust, wholly or partially, from GST tax for its entire duration. This tax-shelter trust is known as a *dynasty trust*. For more on dynasty trusts, see supra page 849.

Exclusions. Certain transfers are excluded from the generation-skipping transfer tax. Section 2612(c)(1) excludes any transfer not subject to the gift tax because of the annual exclusion (see supra page 991). Hence transfers of $10,000 or less annually to grandchildren will not produce a GST tax. Section 2611(b)(2) excludes from the term "generation-skipping transfer" any inter vivos transfers excluded under §2503(e) of the gift tax, relating to the direct payment of tuition and medical expenses (see supra page 991). Hence, a grandparent can pay tuition for a grandchild without making a generation-skipping transfer, or a trust can make tuition or medical payments for a skip person without subjecting such distributions to the GST tax.

Section 2611(b)(1) provides that the term "generation-skipping transfer" does not include any transfer from a trust, to the extent such transfer is subject to estate or gift taxes with respect to a person in the first generation below that of the transferor. If property is transferred for the benefit of a child, and the property is subject to estate taxes at the child's death (or gift taxes if the child gives away the property), no GST tax is assessed at the child's death. This exclusion has important estate planning implications. *Each person can avoid the GST tax by transferring property to a child in such a manner as to subject the property to estate tax at the child's death.* The cost of avoiding the GST tax is to involve the child with the gift and estate taxes. In view of the fact that when the $1 million exemption from gift and estate taxes is fully phased in, the effective federal gift and estate tax rates range from 41 percent to 55 percent, whereas the GST tax is 55 percent, it may save tax dollars to give the property to the child in such a way as to cause inclusion of the property in the child's federal gross estate.

PROBLEM

A desirable position for a child to be in is to be able to decide whether to pay an estate tax or to pay a GST tax on his death. This flexibility may give the child the advantage of making use of his and his spouse's exemptions, unified credits, and graduated rates. Can a parent pass property to the child in such a way as to give the child this option, to be elected as future events unfold? Yes. If *O* transfers property in trust for her son *A* for life, then to *A*'s children, and *O* gives *A* a special power to appoint the property to his wife or to one or more of *A*'s descendants, *A* has the choice of which tax to pay. If *A* wants the property in his federal gross estate at death, thereby avoiding GST tax, *A* can by will exercise the special power by creating a *general inter vivos* power in his wife. This exercise causes the property subject to the general power to be includable in *A*'s federal gross estate. See Note: The "Delaware Tax Trap," supra page 827. For discussion, see Jonathan G. Blattmachr & Jeffrey N. Pennell, Adventures in Generation-Skipping, or How We Learned to Love the "Delaware Tax Trap," 24 Real Prop., Prob. & Tr. J. 75 (1989).

4.   Definitions

To round out our picture of how the generation-skipping transfer tax operates, it is necessary to look at some definitions in the Code.

a.   Transferor

Generally, a transferor is a person who is treated as owner (or transferor) under the federal gift and estate taxes. A person transferring a fee simple is a transferor. A person who possesses a general power of appointment is a transferor when the power is exercised or when it lapses or is released. A person possessing a special power of appointment is not treated as a transferor. In case of a QTIP trust, the transferee spouse is the deemed transferor if the transferor spouse (or his executor) so elects. However, by a special provision in §2652(a)(3), the transferor spouse in a QTIP trust can elect to be the transferor for generation-skipping purposes (thus using his GST tax exemption), while at the same time electing to take the estate tax marital deduction. This has come to be called the "reverse QTIP election."

As noted above, gift-splitting by married couples is permitted. Gift-splitting doubles the effect of any exemption or exclusion applicable to inter vivos transfers.

Successive skips. If a trust is created for several generations (for example, for children for their lives, then to grandchildren for their lives, then to great-grandchildren), a taxable termination occurs on the death of the first generation and again on the death of the second generation. This result follows from §2653(a), which provides that in such a trust, *after* a generation-skipping transfer at the death of the children, the "transferor" is dropped down to the children's level for any portion of the trust subject to GST tax. (However, any portion of the trust that has been allocated part of the original settlor's exemption remains exempt for the duration of the trust (see supra page 1071). Thus a dynasty trust of $1 million, allocated the transferor's entire exemption, pays no GST tax for its duration.)

b. Skip Person; Ascertaining Generations

Since a skip person is defined as an individual who is two or more generations below the transferor, it is necessary to define generation. With respect to descendants, the definition is naturally by generations. A grandchild or more remote descendant is a skip person. Similarly, for first and second line collaterals, the generations are natural. Nephews and nieces are treated as of the same generation as children; children of nephews and nieces are skip persons. §2651(b)(1). (See Table of Consanguinity, supra page 92, for a picture of second line collaterals who are on the same generational level as grandchildren.) Descendants and first and second line collaterals of spouses of the transferor are assigned to the same generation they would be assigned to if related to the transferor. §2651(b)(2).

A person who has at any time been married to the transferor is assigned to the transferor's generation. A person who has been married to a descendant (or to a first or second line collateral) of the transferor or the transferor's spouse is assigned to the generation of the individual married. §2651(c).

With respect to a beneficiary who is not a lineal descendant of a grandparent of the transferor or of the transferor's spouse, §2651(d) provides for an assignment of generation based on the beneficiary's age in relation to that of the transferor. A person born not more than $12\frac{1}{2}$ years after the transferor is assigned to the transferor's generation. A person born more than $12\frac{1}{2}$ years but not more than $37\frac{1}{2}$ years after the transferor is assigned to the generation of the transferor's children. Thereafter, generation assignments are made in successive 25-year periods. Hence a gift to someone more than $37\frac{1}{2}$ years younger is treated the same as a gift to a grandchild (a skip person).

PROBLEMS

1. *T*, a bachelor, dies leaving a will that devises his residuary estate in trust, to pay the income to *T*'s sister, *S*, for life, and on *S*'s death

to distribute the trust principal to *S*'s descendants then living per stirpes. Some years later, *S* dies; she is survived by a daughter and by three grandchildren, the children of her deceased son who died after *T* died. Does the generation-skipping transfer tax apply?

2.   *O*, your client, wants some advice. *O* wants to leave $1 million to her sister *S*. Is there any transfer tax advantage in leaving $1 million to *S* for life, remainder to *S*'s son *A*, rather than leaving $1 million to *S* outright?

c.   Interest

We have noted above that a taxable termination occurs when an "interest" in property terminates and certain other conditions are present. A person has an interest if he has "a *right* (other than a future right) to receive income or corpus from the trust" or "is a *permissible current* recipient of income or corpus from the trust." §2652(c). A person who has a future interest, vested or contingent, does not have an interest for purposes of a taxable termination under the generation-skipping tax. When an owner of a future interest dies, no taxable termination takes place. Thus:

> *Case 24.* *T* bequeaths property in trust for her son *A* for life, remainder to *A*'s daughter *B* if *B* is then alive, and if *B* is not then alive to *B*'s children (*T*'s great-grandchildren). Subsequently, *B* dies during the life of *A*. A GST tax is not levied at *B*'s death. Upon the subsequent death of *A*, a GST tax is levied, but a tax at *B*'s generation has been skipped.

A person who is a potential appointee (or object) of a power *currently* exercisable by another has an interest. A discretionary trust will illustrate this type of interest.

> *Case 25.* *T* bequeaths property in trust to pay income to *T*'s son *A* or *A*'s daughter *B* in such amount as the trustee shall determine, or accumulate it, and at the death of *A* and *B* to distribute the principal to *T*'s issue then living, per stirpes. At the death of *A*, a taxable termination occurs and a tax is due. So too at the death of *B*. If the trustee distributes income to *B* during *A*'s life, a taxable distribution occurs.

If the trust in Case 25 had been a discretionary trust for *T*'s issue until the perpetuities period expires, a taxable termination would occur upon the death of the last survivor of each generation. Under §2653(a), once a generation-skipping transfer occurs (at the death of the last survivor of *T*'s children), the transferor of the trust is then considered to be a member of the first generation above any person then having an interest in the trust (see supra page 1073). In other words, the children are then treated as transferors, and the generation-skipping rules start over again.

Although the definitions of taxable termination and taxable distribution refer explicitly to property held in trust, which is the usual arrangement, the GST tax also applies to trust equivalents, such as legal life estates and remainders, estates for years, and insurance and annuity contracts. §2652(b).

5. Tax Strategies

To reduce or avoid the generation-skipping tax, certain strategies are fairly obvious:

(a) Use the annual gift tax exclusion of $10,000 per transferee ($20,000 for a married couple). See supra page 991.

(b) Use the gift tax exclusions for tuition and medical expense payments for grandchildren made directly to the educational institution or medical supplier. See supra page 991.

(c) Use the predeceased child exception, if applicable to the particular family. See supra page 1068.

(d) Use the GST tax exemption of $1 million. See supra page 1070.

(e) Arrange the assets of a married couple so as not to waste the GST tax exemption of either spouse. Where the couple's assets exceed $2 million, each spouse should be made the "transferor" of at least $1 million. To illustrate this, let us assume *H* is very rich and *W* has no assets. *H* should transfer (at least) $1 million in a QTIP trust for *W* for life, then to *H*'s children for their lives, then to *H*'s grandchildren. This qualifies for the marital deduction *and* makes *W* the transferor for GST taxes. An estate tax will be payable at *W*'s death on the amount of property exceeding her unified credit, but no GST tax will be payable when the assets are distributed to the grandchildren.

(f) Create a trust of life insurance for the benefit of skip persons, paying the premiums in an annual amount qualifying for the annual exclusion (perhaps using *Crummey* provisions, see supra page 1002).

(g) Make multiple skips in a direct skip, thus skipping more than one generation (for example, make gifts to great-grandchildren rather than grandchildren). See supra page 1068.

(h) Use the transferor's $1 million exemption ($2 million for a married couple) to establish a dynasty trust for successive generations for as long as the perpetuities period allows, thus avoiding GST tax for the duration of the trust. See supra page 849.

(i) Give children enough property in a form subject to estate taxes in their estates to use up the $1 million exemption from estate tax (unified credit) each child has. Consider giving more property to children outright, subjecting property to estate taxes, rather than GST taxes, at their deaths. This may produce these tax advantages at their deaths: lower graduated estate tax rates, a credit for previously taxed property, and use of $1 million exemptions children have for generation-skipping transfers.

Doubtless tax planners for the very rich will scrutinize the Code intensely, seeking other ways to reduce or eliminate GST taxes. At this point, however, it is doubtful that any terribly large loopholes in the GST tax will be found. Congress adopted a principle of exacting one transfer tax per generation, and, except for the exemptions and exclusions mentioned above, it appears that the estate, gift, and generation-skipping transfer taxes quite effectively implement that principle.

See generally Jon J. Gallo, Estate Planning and the Generation-Skipping Tax, 33 Real Prop., Prob. & Tr. J. 457 (1998). See also Don W. Llewellyn, Gail L. Richmond & Beverly R. Budin, Tax Planning for Lifetime and Testamentary Dispositions — Prototype Plans (1997).

6. Consequences on Estate Planning of Generation-Skipping Transfer Tax

The GST tax is likely to have a profound impact on estate planning, though, as yet, this impact is more or less speculative. Many lawyers may choose not to draft generation-skipping trusts for clients with only a few millions, except to the extent they come within the exemptions from GST tax. They may deem it most desirable to give succeeding generations in the client's family flexibility to deal with transfer taxation. The greatest flexibility usually comes from absolute ownership. The cost of flexibility is a gift or estate tax payable in the next generation. But estate and gift taxes can be lowered by the owner giving away property expected to appreciate greatly in value, or by consuming the property, or by spending capital on education and other enhancers of the next generation's human capital, or, possibly, depleting capital by making income payments from it (taxed at a lower rate) to the next generation. And there may be an income tax advantage available to owners of property. They can decide whether to hold on to the property until death, giving the next generation a stepped-up basis, or give it away now. A generation-skipping trust may deprive the next generation of that flexibility.

The total *amount* of wealth in dynastic trusts may decline as existing dynastic trusts are terminated and rich persons decide that absolute ownership in their children gives them the advantage of flexibility, including the possibility of taking up domicile in some place with no or low wealth transfer taxes. Yet even if the total amount of wealth in dynastic trusts declines, the *number* of such trusts will probably rise. This will likely happen because a $1 million ($2 million per married couple) generation-skipping dynasty trust is exempt from GST tax for its entire duration. With an eye to taxation, each new and old million-aire ought to create a dynasty trust of $1 million for his or her descen-dants. Such a trust will escape GST tax for the perpetuities period and, after the initial transfer, also escape gift and estate taxation for this period. One million dollar dynasty trusts may become common among millionaires.

When the full impact of the GST tax is felt, a generation or so from now, Congress may be hard put to maintain its resolve. But for now, with President Reagan's assent, Congress has given us what Presidents Theodore and Franklin Roosevelt and Herbert Hoover wanted but could never impose — an effective tax to break up swollen fortunes and inherited economic power (see supra page 978). The future of the great fortunes in this country is in some doubt.

SECTION E. STATE WEALTH TRANSFER TAXES

All states except Nevada have death taxes, but less than a dozen impose a gift tax on lifetime transfers.[33] State death taxes fall into one of three general categories. The first category is the *pick-up tax.* This is a tax equal to the maximum credit for state death taxes under the federal estate tax. The maximum credit is fixed by §2011 of the Internal Revenue Code. In the 1920s, when an effort was made to repeal the federal estate tax on the ground that this source of revenue should be reserved to the states, Congress enacted a law allowing a credit against the federal estate tax for death taxes paid a state. Most states responded by enacting death taxes to take full advantage of the

---

33. The death tax laws of all states are compiled in CCH Inheritance, Estate, & Gift Tax Reporter, a multi-volume loose-leaf service.

credit, since it permitted diversion of federal revenues to the state without increasing the tax burden on the state's residents. The amount of the credit in 1928 was 80 percent of the federal tax, but the amount of the credit has been drastically reduced by Congress over the years. The maximum tax credits set out in §2011(b) of the Code range from 1 percent to 16 percent of the federal estate tax due.

In addition to the pick-up tax, about one-half the states have inheritance taxes under which a tax is levied on the amount passing to each legatee, heir, or other beneficiary of decedent's property. The tax rates and exemptions are determined by the beneficiary's relationship to the decedent. While the decedent's personal representative is responsible for filing the tax return and paying the tax to the state taxing authority, absent a contrary will provision the "burden" of the tax is borne by each beneficiary and is deducted from the amount passing to the beneficiary.

Typically, the inheritance tax rates and exemptions turn on whether the beneficiary is a Class *A*, Class *B*, or Class *C* beneficiary. Class *A* beneficiaries might include the spouse and descendants. Class *B* beneficiaries might include parents and descendants of parents. All other persons and organizations are Class *C* beneficiaries, and they pay the highest rates.

Less than a dozen states have an estate tax rather than an inheritance tax. These state estate tax laws do not follow any one pattern, although each incorporates some features of the federal estate tax. New York and Michigan closely pattern their estate tax laws after the federal estate tax, including an unlimited marital deduction for which a QTIP trust qualifies. But other state estate tax laws may not provide for any marital deduction or limit it in some way.

TABLE OF CASES

Principal cases are in italics.

Abo Petroleum Corp. v. Amstutz, 719
Abortion Rights Mobilization v. United States Catholic Conference, 893
Abrams v. Templeton, 831
Adams v. Link, 660
Aetna Life Ins. Co. v. Schilling, 343
Akeley, Estate of, 425
Akron Bar Assn. v. Miller, 395
Alburn, Estate of, 292
Alexander v. Alexander, 116
Allard v. Pacific Natl. Bank, 944, 953
Allen, Estate of, 535
Allen v. Talley, 441
American Heart Assn. v. County of Greenville, 42
American Security & Trust Co. v. Cramer, 813
Anderson, Estate of, 292, 707
Anderson, In re Estate of, 831
Aragon v. Snyder, 491
Archer, Estate of, 290
Armstrong, In re, 671
Armstrong v. United States, 10
Arrowsmith v. Mercantile-Safe Deposit & Trust Co., 820
Attorney Gen. for Ont. v. M. & H., 499
Auric v. Continental Casualty Co., 233
Ausley, In re Estate of, 291
Azcunce v. Estate of Azcunce, 537, 546

Babbitt v. Youpee, 12
Bacot, Succession of, 426
Baehr v. Lewin, 497, 499

Ball v. Knox, 866
Barcelo v. Elliott, 65, 233
Barnette v. McNulty, 593
Beadle, In re Marriage of, 719
Beale, In re Estate of, 301
Beals v. State St. Bank & Trust Co., 500, 688
Beatty v. Guggenheim Exploration Co., 220
Belfield v. Booth, 807
Belgard's Trust, In re, 764
Belshe v. Hope, 371
Benjamin v. Morgan Guaranty Trust Co., 683
Bennett v. Allstate Ins. Co., 146
Bergheger v. Boyle, 328
Black, Estate of, 426
Black v. Edwards, 322
Black v. Seals, 263
Block, Will of, 694
Bloom v. Selfon, 300
Boan v. Watson, 479
Board of Educ. v. Browning, 114
Boggs v. Boggs, 475
Borelli v. Brusseau, 321
Bostwick v. Hurstel, 464
Bowerman v. Burris, 173
Brainard v. Commissioner, 375, 586, 594
Branigan, In re Estate of, 654
Bravo v. Sauter, 508
Breckheimer v. Kraft, 427
Breeden, In re Estate of, 868
Brenner, Estate of, 359

Bridgewater v. Turner, 707
Briggs v. Crowley, 949
Briggs v. Wyoming Natl. Bank, 385
Broadway Natl. Bank v. Adams, 632
Brown, In re Estate of, 657
Brown v. DuFrey, 550
Brown v. Routzahn, 149
Brush, In re Estates of, 948
Bryan v. Bigelow, 310
Bryan's Appeal, 310
Bucci, In re, 85
Bucquet v. Livingston, 676
Budin v. Levy, 660
Bundy v. United States Trust Co., 821
Burch v. George, 184
Burnett v. First Commerical Trust Co.,
  438
Button, In re Estate of, 732
Buzzanca, In re Marriage of, 103
Byerly v. Tolbert, 97
Byrne v. Laura, 321
Byrne's Will, In re, 285

Cadell v. Palmer, 792
Caldwell v. Walraven, 681
Camp v. Commissioner, 990
Campbell, In re Estate of, 85
Campbell v. French, 292
Cancik, In re Estate of, 90
Canter v. Commissioner of Pub. Welfare,
  648
*Carl J. Herzog Found. v. University of
  Bridgeport, 883*
Carlson, Estate of, 867
Carpenter v. Wynn, 290
Carroll's Will, In re, 699
Carson, Estate of, 214
*Carter v. First United Methodist Church of
  Albany, 286*
Casey, Estate of, v. Commissioner, 402
Chapman, In re Marriage of, 639, 672
Chayka, Estate of, 328
Church v. Morgan, 464
Citizens Action League v. Kizer, 351
Claflin v. Claflin, 656
Clark, In re, 507
Clark v. Campbell, 598
Clark v. Greenhalge, 303
Clark v. National Bank of Commerce,
  235
Clarkson, In re Estate of, 491
Clarkson v. Whitaker, 185
Clobberie's Case, 740
Clymer v. Mayo, 375, 387, 594
Coates, Estate of, 817
Cohen, In re, 328
Coleman v. Coleman, 714
Collamore v. Learned, 107
Colling, In re, 234

Collins, Estate of, 957
Collins, In re Estate of, 244
Commissioner v. Estate of Bosch, 1060
Committee on Professional Ethics v.
  Baker, 395
Committee on Professional Ethics v.
  Randall, 187
Commonwealth v. Holton, 250
Commonwealth v. Robin, 249
Commonwealth v. Welosky, 411
Connecticut Gen. Life Ins. Co. v. First
  Natl. Bank of Minneapolis, 367
Cook v. Equitable Life Assurance Socy., 339
Cook v. Estate of Seeman, 90
Cook v. Holland, 975
Cooper, In re, 498
Cooper, In re Estate of, 492
Cotton, In re Estate of, 146
Coxe v. Kriebel, 954
Crane, In re, 949
Cricchio v. Pennisi, 651
Croake, In re Estate of, 96
Cross, In re Estate of, 488
Cross v. Cross, 764
Cruzan v. Director, Missouri Dept. of
  Health, 403
Curley v. Lynch, 677

Dacey v. Commissioner, 361
Dacey v. Florida Bar, 360
Dacey v. New York County Lawyers'
  Assn., 360
Da Costa v. De Pas, 869
Dalia v. Lawrence, 506
Dartmouth College v. City of Quincy,
  878
Davies v. Radford, 719
Davis v. Neilson, 764
Dawson v. Yucus, 449
Defilippis, In re Estate of, 506
Deiss v. Deiss, 807
Dennis v. Rhode Island Hosp. Trust Co., 929
DeThorne, In re Estate of, 235
Dewire v. Haveles, 500, 750
Di Biasio, In re, 714
*Dickerson v. Union Natl. Bank of Little Rock,
  801*
Dickson, In re estate of, 284
Dimmitt, Estate of, 310
Disciplinary Counsel v. Galinas, 187
Dobson, In re Estate of, 263
Doctor v. Hughes, 776
Dollar Savs. & Trust Co. v. Turner, 732
Donner, In re Estate of, 32
Dorfman v. Allen, 242
Drye Family 1995 Trust v. United States,
  150
Duke, In re, 767

Duke, In re Trust of, 767
Duke of Norfolk's Case, 740, 788, 794
Dulles, Estate of, 767
Dumas v. Estate of Dumas, 506

Eaton v. Brown, 273
Eberhardt's Estate, In re, 297
E. F. Hutton & Co. v. Wallace, 344
Electric Auto-Lite Co. v. P. & D. Mfg.
  Co., 315
Elkus v. Elkus, 594
Ellingson, Estate of, v. Commissioner,
  1060
Elyachar v. Gerel Corp., 580
Engle v. Siegel, 438
Epworth Orphanage v. Long, 920
Erickson v. Erickson, 427
Erlenbach v. Estate of Thompson, 444
Espinosa v. Sparber, Shevin, Shapo, Rosen &
  Heilbronner (612 So. 2d 1378), *540*
Espinosa v. Sparber, Shevin, Shapo,
  Rosen & Heilbronner (586 So. 2d
  1221), 543, 544
Estate of _____. *See* decedent's name
Evans v. May, 196
Evans v. McCoy, 764
Eyerman v. Mercantile Trust Co., 33

Farkas v. Williams, 352, 386, 503
Farmers' Loan & Trust Co. v. Winthrop,
  592
Farmers & Merchants Bank of Keyser v.
  Farmers & Merchants Bank of Keyser,
  437
Fegley, In re Estate of, 263
Ferrell-French v. Ferrell, 697
First Illini Bank v. Pritchard, 756
First Natl. Bank v. Klein, 319
First Natl. Bank in Fairmont v. Phillips,
  114
First Natl. Bank of Bar Harbor v. Anthony,
  729, 738
First Natl. Bank of Chicago v. King, 760
First Natl. Bank of Fayetteville v. United
  States, 1065
First Natl. Bank of Mansfield, In re, 919
First Portland Natl. Bank v. Rodrique,
  806
Fleet Natl. Bank v. Colt, 835
Fleming v. Morrison, 414
Fletcher v. Fletcher, 393, 938
Flohr v. Walker, 328
Florida Bar v. American Senior Citizens
  Alliance, 395
Florida Natl. Bank of Palm Beach
  County v. Genova, 368
Foman v. Moss, 491
Fortnoy, In re Estate of, 764

Foster v. Foster, 764
Foster, Estate of, v. Commissioner, 1046
Fowler v. Bailey, 892
Fox v. Faulkner, 567
Fox v. Snow, 681
Foxley, In re Estate of, 269, 318
Franklin v. Anna Natl. Bank of Anna, 345
Franzen v. Norwest Bank Colo., 397
Fritschi, Estate of, 173
Fritz, Estate of, 320
Froman, In re Estate of, 506
Funk, In re Estate of, 285

Gaite's Will Trusts, Re, 800
Garbade, In re Estate of, 518
Gardner, Estate of, 547
Gardner v. Balboni, 244
Garrett, Estate of, 95, 806
Gasparovich, In re Estate of, 276
Gentry, In re Estate of, 165
Giantasio, In re Estate of, 211
Gilbert, In re Estate of, 720
Girard Trust Co. v. Schmitz, 32
Givens v. Girard Life Ins. Co., 523
Godfrey v. Chandley, 628
Gonsalves v. Superior Court, 165
Gonzalez, In re, 867
Goodwine State Bank v. Mullins, 726
Gordon v. City of Baltimore, 893
Gradow v. United States, 1022
Grant, In re, 251
Grant Home v. Medlock, 878
Gray v. St. Matthews Cathedral, 892
Green Charitable Trust, In re, 953
Green, Estate of, v. United States, 1022
Greenberg, In re Estate of, 36
Greene v. Fitzpatrick, 107, 108
Grieff, In re, 520
Groffman, In re, 227
Group Life Ins. Proceeds of Mallory, In
  re, 300
Guidry v. Sheet Metal Workers Natl.
  Pension Fund, 641
Gustafson, In re, 755
Gustafson v. Svenson, 412

Hackett, Estate of, 44
Hall v. Eaton, 32
Hall v. Vallandingham, 98
Hall, In re Will of, 310
Hamerstrom v. Commerce Bank of
  Kansas City, 660
Hamilton, Estate of, 695
Hamilton v. Drogo, 646
Hammer v. Powers, 210
Hanau, Estate of, v. Hanau, 526
Hanke v. Hanke, 506
Hansel v. Head, 285

Hardenburgh v. Commissioner, 149
Harper v. Martin, 108
Harrison v. Bird, 277
Hartman v. Hartle, 903
Harvard College v. Amory, 959
Hastoupis v. Gargas, 320
Hatcher v. United States Natl. Bank of
    Or., 962
Hathaway v. Smith, 310
Haurin, In re Estate of, 285
Headrick, Estate of, v. Commissioner,
    1032
Hearst, In re Estate of, 390
Hebrew Univ. Assn. v. Nye (148 Conn.
    223), *575*
Hebrew Univ. Assn. v. Nye (26 Conn. 342),
    578
Hecht v. Superior Court (50 Cal. App.
    4th 1289), 127
Hecht v. Superior Court (16 Cal. App. 4th
    836), *117*
Hegel, In re Estate of, 401, 466
Heggstad, Estate of, 559
Heim, Estate of, v. Commissioner, 1045
Heinzman v. Mason, 146
Heller Trust, In re, 654
Helvering v. Clifford, 595
Henderson, In re, 185
Hering, In re Estate of, 277
Hersberg Trust v. Department of Mental
    Health, 650
Heyer v. Flaig, 535
Hickox v. Wilson, 261
Hicks, Estate of, 116
Hieber v. Uptown Natl. Bank, 583
Hieble v. Hieble, 609
Hillowitz, Estate of, 336
Hodel v. Irving, 3
Hoffman, In re, 767
Hoffman v. Kohns, 165
Hofing v. Willis, 448
Holland v. Metalious, 405
Holtz's Estate v. Commissioner, 986
Honigman, In re, 166
Hood v. Haden, 667
Hooker v. The Edes Home, 892
Horne v. Peckham, 66
Hotz v. Minyard, 66, 617
Houghten's Estate, In re, 290
H.S.H.-K., In re Custody of, 105
Hughes v. School, 300
Hurwitz v. Sher, 476
Hyman v. Glover, 760

Ihl v. Oetting, 425
Industrial Natl. Bank of R.I. v. Barrett,
    821
In re _____. *See* party's name
Irvine, Estate of, v. Doyle, 280

Irving Trust Co. v. Day, 3
Irwin Union Bank & Trust Co. v. Long,
    668, 674

Jackson v. Patton, 244
Jackson v. Schultz, 446
Jacob, In re, 105
Jane Doe v. John Doe, 104, 106
Janes, In re Estate of, 963
Janis, In re Estate of, 116
Janus v. Tarasewicz, 78
Jee v. Audley, 798
Jefferson, In re, 234
Jetter, Estate of, 90
Jezo v. Jezo, 480
Jimenez v. Lee, 568
Johnson, In re Estate of, 264, 284, 317
Johnson v. Calvert, 103
Johnson v. First Natl. Bank of Jackson,
    651
Johnson v. Johnson (424 P.2d 414), 315
Johnson v. Johnson (279 P.2d 928), *311*
Johnson v. Sandler, 488
Jones, In re Estate of, 291
Jones v. Grant, 893
Joseph, Estate of, 107
Joslyn, In re Estate of, 764
Jurek, Estate of, 95
Jurgensen v. Haslinger, 222

Kaufmann's Will, In re, 193
Kay v. Sandler, 226
Keenan, In re Estate of, 866
Keener v. Archibald, 302
Keil, In re Estate of, 51
Kelly's Estate, In re, 192
Kenaday v. Sinnott, 463
Keuhn, In re, 935
Kidd, Estate of, 868
Kime, Estate of, 438
Kimmel's Estate, 271
King v. King, 719
Kinkin v. Marchesi, 322
Kinney v. Shinholser, 150, 1038
Kirschbaum v. Dillon, 185
Kline v. Orebaugh, 906
Knight v. Earl of Plymouth, 903
Knight v. Knight, 641
Knupp v. District of Columbia, 437
Koss, In re Estate of, 244
Krawczyk v. Stingle, 271
Kreuzer, In re Estate of, 831
Kroll v. Nehmer, 286
Kronauge v. Stoecklein, 284
Kuehn, In re, 936
Kurz, Estate of, v. Commissioner, 1038
Kyreazis, Estate of, 52

Labonte v. Giordana, 222
Lalli v. Lalli, 115
Lancaster v. Merchants Natl. Bank, 869
Laning, In re Estate of, 28
Lankford v. Wright, 114
Larkin v. Pirthauer, 211
Larkin v. Ruffin, 41
La Rue v. Lee, 285
La Salle Natl. Bank v. United States, 640
Latham v. Father Divine, 215
Launius, In re, 192
Laura, In re Estate of, 548
Lavarelle's Estate, 921
Lawson v. Lawson, 740
Leach v. Hyatt, 601
Leake v. Robinson, 807
Le Collen, Will of, 319
Lee v. Lee, 165
Legeas, Estate of, 222
Leggett v. United States, 150
Lindstrom, In re, 385
Lipper v. Weslow, 177, 185
Lober v. United States, 1028
Lockwood v. Adamson, 764
Logotheti v. Gordon, 165
Lonergan v. Estate of Budahazi, 279
Loring v. Karri-Davies, 696
Loring v. Marshall, 500, 702
Love v. Wyndham, 792
Lowry, In re Estate of, 367
Lucas v. Hamm, 830
Lux v. Lux, 781
Lyles, Estate of, 290
Lynda A.J. v. Diane T.O., In re, 105

MacCallum v. Seymour, 76, 102
MacLeod, In re Estate of, 264
Mahoney, In re Estate of, 141
Mahoney v. Grainger, 410, 500
Malachowski v. Bank One, Indianapolis, 963
Malloy, In re Estate of, 285
Maloney, Estate of, v. Carsten, 328
Mapes v. United States, 150
Marbone v. Marbone, 647
Marine, Estate of, v. Commissioner, 1065
Marsman v. Nasca, 618
Martin v. Martin, 222
Martinez's Estate, In re, 129
Mason v. Mason, 274
Masterson v. Department of Sound Services, 648
Mattei, In re, 490
Maxwell, Estate of, v. Commissioner, 1016
Mayberry v. Mayberry, 464
Mayo, In re Trusteeship Agreement with, 970
McAbee v. Edwards, 544
McCabe, In re Estate of, 234

McCarthy v. Bank of Cal., 284, 290
McCarthy v. Kapcar, 343
McGurrin, In re, 234
McIntyre v. Kilbourn, 463
Meinhard v. Salmon, 905
Meksrus Estate, 405
Miller, In re Estate of, 51
Miller v. Aderhold, 893
Miller v. Department of Mental Health, 650
Miller v. Pender, 920
Millwright v. Romer, 830
Minary v. Citizens Fidelity Bank & Trust Co., 760
Miron v. Trudel, 77
Mongold v. Mayle, 535
Montero, Succession of, 274
Morris, Estate of, 463
Moseley v. Goodman, 413
Moses, In re Will of, 188
Moss, In re, 454
Muder, In re Estate of, 268, 290
Mueller, In re Estate of, 145
Mulligan, Re, 938
Musmanno v. Eldredge, 249
Musselman v. Mitchell, 320

Nagel, In re Estate of, 371
National Academy of Sciences v. Cambridge Trust Co., 944
National Shawmut Bank v. Cumming, 507
National Socy. for the Prevention of Cruelty to Children v. Scottish Natl. Socy. for the Prevention of Cruelty to Children, 412
Neher, In re, 870
Neiderhiser, Estate of, 483
Nemeth v. Banhalmi, 221
New England Merchants Natl. Bank v. Groswold, 760
New York County Lawyers' Assn. v. Dacey, 360
Newman v. Dore, 505
Newman v. Wells Fargo Bank, 764
Nichols v. Eaton, 632
Nicholson, Estate of v. Commissioner, 1060
Nicolaus, In re Estate of, 760
Nielson, Estate of, 317
Noble v. Bruce, 65

Ocean Coal Co. v. Davies, 812
Ohio Natl. Bank of Columbus v. Adair, 720
Old Colony Trust Co. v. United States, 1022
Olliffe v. Wells, 614
O'Neal v. Wilkes, 108, 116

Pace, In re Estate of, 33
Padilla, In re Estate of, 547
Pank v. Chicago Title & Trust Co., 919
Pappas v. Pappas, 613
Park, Estate of, 165
Parks v. Parker, 150
Parsons v. Walker, 893
Parsons, Estate of, 236
Patch v. White, 426
Pate v. Ford, 781
Patterson v. Shumate, 642
Pavlinko's Estate, In re, 247
Pepper v. Peacher, 343
Pericles, In re Estate of, 507
Perry, In re Marriage of, 371
Perry, Estate of, v. Commissioner, 1032
Peters, In re Estate of, 235
Peterson, Estate of, 547
Peterson, In re Estate of, 210
Pezza v. Pezza, 505
Pfahl v. Pfahl, 617
Phifer, Estate of, 290
Phillips v. Najar, 235
Pilafas, In re Estate & Trust of, 361, 386
Plumel, In re Estate of, 317
Podberesky v. Kirwan, 879
Pond v. Pond, 654, *1057*
Pope v. Garrett, 221, 544
Potter v. Union & Peoples Natl. Bank, 921
Powell, In re Will of, 311
Powers v. Wilkinson, 767
Pozarny, In re, 395
Primerica Life Ins. Co. v. Suter, 145
Prince v. Black, 116
Pulitzer, In re, 655
Putnam v. Putnam, 1065

Radovich v. Locke-Paddon, 271
Raney, In re Estate of, 166
Ranney, In re Will of, 246, *252*
Rapp, Estate of, v. Commissioner, 1049
Rathblott v. Levin, 210
Re _____. *See* party's name
Reed, Estate of, 235
Reed v. Reed, 38
Reiman, In re Estate of, 602
Rembe v. Stewart, 351
Reynolds, In re, 513
Richards v. Tolbert, 806
Riefberg's Estate, In re, 492
Riggs, Estate of, 114
Rippey v. Denver U.S. Natl. Bank, 962
Robert Paul P., In re, 107
Roberts v. Roberts, 718
Robinson, In re Estate of, 436
Robinson v. Delfino, 348
Rogers v. Mutch, 785
Romero, Estate of, 32

Rosenberg, Estate of, v. Department of
    Public Welfare, 650
Rosenfeld v. Frank, 464
Ross v. Caunters, 65, 233
Ross v. Commissioner, 994
Rothko, In re (43 N.Y.2d 305), *906*
Rothko, In re (98 Misc. 2d 718), 917
Rothko, In re (84 Misc. 2d 830), 909, 913
Rowett v. McFarland, 716
Royal, In re Estate of, 235
R.R. v. M.H., 103
Ruel v. Hardy, 290
Rumberg v. Rumberg, 444
Rushing v. Mann, 740
Russell, Estate of, 417
Russell, In re Adoption of, 107
Rutanen v. Ballard, 936

Salmonski's Estate, In re, 292
Sanders, Estate of, 117
Sandler, Estate of, 116
Sarabia, Estate of, 196
Satterfield v. Bonyhady, 764
Saunders v. Vautier, 651
Scatterwood v. Edge, 792
Scott v. Bank One Trust Co., 632
Searight's Estate, In re, 602
*Second Natl. of New Haven v. Harris
    Trust & Savs. Bank, 822*
Security Trust Co. v. Irvine, 733, 743, 744
Seidel v. Werner, 683
Sengillo, In re, 146
Sewell, In re Adoption of, 1097
Shannon, Estate of, 300, *530*
Shapira v. Union Natl. Bank, 24
Shaw, In re, 607
Shelley v. Shelley, 633, 646
Shelley's Case, 776
*Shenandoah Valley Natl. Bank v. Taylor,
    859*
Sheridan v. Harbison, 280
Shiflett, In re, 492
Shriners' Hosp. for Crippled Children v.
    Coltrane, 464
*Shriners Hosps. for Crippled Children v.
    Gardiner, 922*
Silberman's Will, In re, 778
Simon v. Grayson, 309
Simpson v. Calivas, 59
Sligh v. Sligh, 641
Smith, In re, 169
Smith, In re Estate of, 412
Smith, In re Will of, 270
Smith v. Burt, 425
Smith v. Lewis, 66
Smith v. Weitzel, 319
Snide, In re, 251
Sola, In re Estate of, 269, 317

Solomon v. Central Trust Co., 764
Sorenson, In re Estate of, 165
Spears v. James, 480
Speelman v. Pascal, 375, *589*
Staley v. Ligon, 655
Stanley v. Henderson, 290
Stark v. United States Trust Co. of N.Y., 962
State v. Gulbankian, 211, 247
State v. Hawes, 649
State St. Bank & Trust Co. v. Reiser, 368, 387, 390
Stein-Sapir v. Stein-Sapir, 530
Steinhauser v. Repko, 349
Stephenson v. Rowe, 426
Sterner v. Nelson, 677
Stevens v. Casdorph, 233
Stix v. Commissioner, 627
St. Mary's Church of Schuyler v. Tomek, 681
Stokes v. Stokes, 479
Stormont, In re Estate of, 302
Storrs v. Benbow, 818
Stowers v. Norwest Bank Ind., 758
Strittmater, In re, 159
Stuchell, In re Trust of, 652
Sudwischer v. Estate of Hoffpauir, 116
Sullivan v. Burkin, 500
Sullivan v. Sullivan, 454
Summers v. Summers, 42
Suter, In re Estate of (211 Misc. 2d 144), 725
Suter, In re Estate of (207 Misc. 1002), 7
Svenson v. First Natl. Bank of Boston, 754
Swanson, In re Adoption of, 108

Taliaferro v. Taliaferro, 359, 559
Tammy, Adoption of, 105
Tannler v. Wisconsin Dept. of Health & Soc. Servs., 157, 490
Tarasoff v. Regents of University of Cal., 417
Taylor, Estate of, 807
Taylor v. NationsBank Corp., 393, 943
Thellusson v. Woodford, 792
Thomas v. Thomas, 129
Thompson v. Pew, 696
Thompson v. Thompson, 52
Thompson v. Royall, 280
Tipler, In re Will of, 319
Toledo Trust Co. v. Toledo Hosp., 970
Tolin, In re Estate of, 284, 544
Torregano, Estate of, 547
Totten, In re, 349
Townsend v. United States, 402
Travers, Estate of, 279
Trimble v. Gordon, 115
Trotter v. Trotter, 320

Troy v. Hart, 151
Tulsa Professional Collection Servs. v. Pope, 41
Twigg v. Mays, 106

United States v. Comparato, 150
United States v. Estate of Grace, 1022
United States v. Monsanto, 147
United States v. O'Shaughnessy, 643
United States v. Riggs Natl. Bank, 640
United States Catholic Conference, In re, 893
Unthank v. Rippstein, 581

Van Deusen, Estate of, 655
Vasconi v. Guardian Life Ins. Co., 300
Ventura County Humane Socy. v. Holloway, 427
Via v. Putnam, 323
Vissering, Estate of, v. Commissioner, 682, 1035

Wait, In re Estate of, 234
Waldman, In re Estate of, 44
Waldrep v. Goodwin, 234
Waller, In re Estate of, 743
Walton v. Lindsey, 767
Ward v. Van der Loeff, 809
Ware v. Crowell, 131
Warren's Will Trusts, Re, 831
Wasserman v. Cohen, 401, 459
Waterman v. New York Life Ins. & Trust Co., 707
Watts v. Watts, 499
Weber's Estate, In re, 234
Weinstock, In re Estate of, 211
Welch v. Welch, 114
Wendel, In re, 94
West v. Superior Court, 105
Westervelt v. First Interstate Bank, 754
Wheat v. Wheat, 234
Wheeler v. United States, 1022
Whirlpool Corp. v. Ritter, 343
White v. Jones, 270
White v. Sherman, 920
White v. United States, 693
Wilhoit v. Peoples Life Ins. Co., 331
Will of _____. *See* testator's name
Williams v. Board of Trustees of Mt. Jezreel Baptist Church, 892
Williams v. Crickman, 184
Wilson, In re, 879
Wilson, In re Estate of, 349
Wilson v. First Fla. Bank, 437
Wilson v. Flowers, 869
Winston, In re Estate of, 628
Wiseley v. United States, 1060

Witbeck-Wildhagen, In re Marriage of, 127
Witmer v. Blair, 962
Winningham v. Winningham, 184
Witt v. Rosen, 292
Wold, In re Trust of, 840
Wong, Estate of, 269
Wood, In re, 95
Woodworth, Estate of, 768
Wright, Estate of, 163

Wright v. Bloom, 348
Wright v. Williams, 830

Young, In re, 235
Young v. Young, 245

Zielinski, In re Estate of, 166

AUTHOR INDEX

Ahroni, Reuben, 131
Aiello, Anthony J., 344
Alexander, Gregory S., 175, 467, 555
Allen, David E., 835
Andersen, Roger W., 70, 90
Andrews, Arthur W., 529
Andrews, Lori B, 127
Ascher, Mark L., 16, 445, 467, 505, 530, 654, 981
Atkinson, Richard B., 1002
Atkinson, Rob, 877
Atkinson, T., 539
Averill, Lawrence H., Jr., 43

Bailey, James E., 104
Barnes, Alison P., 405
Baron, Charles B., 905
Baron, Jane B., 163, 236, 414, 583
Batts, Deborah A., 536
Bay, Kathleen F., 197
Becker, David M., 748, 779, 792, 830, 849
Begleiter, Martin D., 65, 184, 445
Bentham, Jeremy, 14, 38
Berendt, Emily, 197
Berkeley, Bishop, 355
Bernstein, Fred A., 105
Berry, Charles R., 893
Beyer, Gerry W., 175, 184, 210, 235, 269, 395
Bird, Gail B., 656
Bishin, William R., 33
Bittker, Boris I., 1015

Blackstone, William, 1, 93, 97, 115, 536
Blattmachr, Jonathan G., 530, 828, 1073
Bleuler, Eugen, 146
Bloom, Ira M., 488, 832
Blow, Steve, 265
Blum, Walter J., 18
Bogert, George G., 364, 644, 656, 865, 933
Bogert, George T., 364, 644, 656, 933
Bonauto, Mary, 498
Bonfield, Lloyd, 261
Bostick, C. Dent, 566
Brashier, Ralph C., 105, 473, 478, 536
Bratt, Carolyn S., 130, 476
Brod, Gail F., 518
Brod, Max, 33
Brody, Evelyn, 895
Brunyate, John, 555
Buchwald, Gerald J., 893
Buckley, William R., 210, 235
Budin, Beverly R., 1077
Burke, Karen C., 981
Burnham, Edward F., 455
Butt, Peter, 28

Cain, Patricia A., 498, 499
Campbell, John Lord, 788
Cannadine, David, 646
Carroll, Lewis, 96, 709
Casner, A. James, 243, 386, 698, 705, 783
Cates, Judith N., 12
Cavers, David F., 95

Chadbourne, James H., 413
Chaffee, Zechariah, Jr., 413
Chaffin, Verner F., 240, 286, 480
Chaucer, Geoffrey, 409
Chester, Ronald, 11, 15, 105, 127, 536, 877
Chiericozzi, Amy, 77
Chorney, Marc A., 1002
Christensen, Craig W., 498
Ciccarello, Mary J., 211
Clark, Elias, 113, 480, 505
Clarke, John P., 642
Clignet, Remi, 15
Collett, Teresa S., 544, 629
Cook, Walter W., 648
Cooter, Robert, 905
Cox, Joseph A., 95
Crawford, Christina, 827
Crawford, George, 969
Cremer, Peter S., 913
Crespi, Gregory S., 407
Cunnigham, Laura E., 750
Curtis, Jerome J., Jr., 926, 976

Dacey, Norman F., 360
Dahlin, Michel, 12
Daube, David, 131
Davis, Adrienne D., 12
De Furia, Joseph W., Jr., 187, 192, 211, 436
Decker, Twila, 266
Derenski, Arlene, 192
Dessin, Carolyn, L., 328, 402, 639
Dewey, Frank L., 786
Dickinson, Rob G., 184
Djalleta, Christine A., 119
Dobris, Joel C., 74, 973
Dodge, Joseph M., 487
Dukeminier, Jesse, 70, 407, 681, 715, 716, 719, 742, 792, 831, 834, 837, 848, 852

Eaton, Thomas A., 404
Eekelaar, John, 74
Eisenberg, Melvin A., 236
Eisenstein, Louis, 978
Ellsworth, Joan B., 726
Emanuel, Anne S., 632
Englehardt, Jo Ann, 385
English, David M., 405
Eskridge, William N., Jr., 498

Farnsworth, E. Allan, 594
Farr, James F., 619
Fellows, Mary L., 74, 77, 88, 131, 147, 175, 414, 445, 467, 484, 837

Fentiman, Linda C., 407
Fetters, Samuel M., 778
Fierstein, Ian G., 44, 46
Fischel, Daniel R., 974
Foster, Frances H., 18, 147
France, Anatole, 631
Fratcher, William F., 215, 220, 365, 575, 585, 608, 644, 681, 905, 920, 964
Fraser, Antonia, 85
Freedman, Bradley J., 905
French, Susan F., 441, 694, 696, 747
Freud, Sigmund, 71
Fried, Martin L., 75
Friedman, Lawrence M., 11
Frolik, Lawrence A., 192, 405

Gale, William G., 15
Gallo, Jon J., 1032, 1077
Garvey, John L., 445, 755
Gary, Susan N., 213, 513
Gates, Henry L., 216
Gerzog, Wendy C., 486
Gilligan, Carol, 114
Glendon, Mary A., 478, 480
Goldstein, Thomas, 212
Gordon, Jeffrey N., 962
Grady, Mark F., 407
Graetz, Michael J., 981
Gray, Francine du Plessix, 192
Gray, John C., 632, 640, 752, 787, 811, 820
Green, Milton D., 163
Greenfield, Howard, 883
Grubb, Andrew, 104, 408
Gulliver, Ashbel G., 223, 239, 258, 264
Guzman, Kathleen R., 127

Hadas, Moses, 33
Halbach, Edward C., Jr., 13, 445, 739, 741, 745, 760, 969
Hale, Ann, 77
Hansmann, Henry, 567
Harris, Sara, 220
Harris, Virgil M., 275
Harrow, Gustave, 917
Haskell, Paul G., 41, 70, 856, 969
Hayton, David J., 48, 834
Herbert, A. P., 413
Hess, Amy M., 837
Hiers, Richard H., 2
Hill, Frank E., 409
Hines, William N., 350
Hirsch, Adam J., 23, 150, 236, 606, 632, 866, 867
Hobhouse, Arthur, 23, 794
Holmes, Oliver Wendell, 414, 579
Holt, Wythe, 717

Horn, Jerold L., 973
Hortter, Bretton J., 404
Hudak, Leona M., 551
Hyman, Meryl, 28

Isenbergh, Joseph, 1027

Jarman, Thomas, 233, 600
Jaworski, Leon, 210
Jefferson, Thomas, 1
Johanson, Stanley M., 197, 528
Johnson, Alex M., Jr., 877
Johnson, Monica K., 77
Johnston, Gerald P., 65, 187, 211, 233, 245, 247
Jones, Thomas L., 702

Kafka, Franz, 33
Kalven, Harry, Jr., 18
Kandel, Randy Frances, 104
Kaplan, Richard L, 405
Karst, Kenneth L., 895, 900
Keeton, George W., 955
Kenderdine, Nancy I., 97
Kennedy, Ian, 104, 408
Kennedy, Kirk A., 879
Kershaw, Alistair, 85
King, Alexa E., 104
King, David S., 837
Kozusko, Donald A., 243
Krier, James E., 716
Krimmel, Herbert T., 269
Kristof, Kathy, 662
Kurtz, Sheldon F., 44, 76, 108, 183, 407
Kwall, Roberta R., 344
Kwestel, Sydney, 513

Landsberg, Sally B., 192
Langbein, John H., 20, 35, 72, 174, 210, 225, 257, 260, 338, 379, 436, 462, 475, 478, 566, 641, 926, 928, 954, 973, 974
Lanoff, Ian D., 974
Laporte, Cloyd, 94
Larson, Edward J., 404
Leach, W. Barton, 243, 747, 792, 796, 832
Leacock, Stephen J., 664
Lee, Christopher, 77
Leibnitz, Gottfried Wilhelm von, 355
Leopold, Aloysius A., 175
Lerner, Alan Jay, 589
Leslie, Melanie B., 171, 183, 261, 702
Lévi-Strauss, Claude, 162
Licata, Kimberly A., 836
Lindgren, James, 261, 262

Link, Ronald C., 187, 211, 617, 836, 837
Lipton, David A., 901
Llewellyn, Don W., 1077
Logan, James K., 747
Longstreth, Bevis, 969
LoPucki, Lynn M., 639
Loring, Augustus Peabody, 619
Love, Sarajane, 41, 580
Lundwall, Mary K., 467, 868
Luria, David, 664
Lusky, Louis, 505
Luxton, Peter, 877

Macey, Jonathan R., 877, 963
Madoff, Ray D., 196
Maharaj, Davan, 187
Mahoney, Margaret M., 102, 672
Maitland, Frederick W., 553, 555
Mann, Bruce H., 246, 256, 261
Manus, Murray L., 104
Margolick, David, 197, 213
Marks, John H., 2
Marsh, Lucy A., 70
Marty-Nelson, Elena, 1022
Mattei, Ugo, 567
Maudsley, Ronald H., 566, 835
McCaffery, Edward J., 981
McCouch, Grayson M. P., 350, 505, 981, 990
McGovern, William M., Jr., 44, 66, 76, 108, 134, 147, 183, 187, 350, 403
McNamee, Stephen J., 11, 15
Medlin, S. Alan, 150
Megarry, Robert E., 830, 834
Meiklejohn, Alexander M., 163, 837
Mellinkoff, David, 37
Menchin, Robert S., 275
Michaels, Laura L., 197
Miller, C. Douglas, 261
Miller, Gareth, 131
Miller, Robert K., Jr., 11, 15
Million, Elmer, 275
Moffat, Graham, 651
Monopoli, Paula A, 102
Moore, Marianne, 798
Morgan, Rebecca C., 405
Morris, J. H. C., 834
Munzer, Stephen R., 23
Murphy, Arthur W., 505
Murray, Susan M., 498
Musmanno, Michael A., 249

Neaves, Lord, 262
Nevins, Francis M., 28
Newton, Isaac, 355

O'Brien, Raymond C., 718
Ogden, C. K., 13
Oliver, Melvin L., 14
Orth, John V., 33, 777

Padilla, Laura M., 105
Palmer, George E., 288, 601
Panter-Downs, Mollie, 194
Pascal, Valerie, 590
Pearce, Russell G., 629
Pearl, David, 74
Pearson, Albert M., 175
Pennell, Jeffrey N., 828, 1073
Plager, Sheldon J., 480
Polikoff, Nancy D., 105
Pollock, Ellen J., 209
Posner, Richard A., 31, 655, 872, 895,
    928, 954, 974
Powell, Burnele V., 617
Powell, Richard R., 727, 832, 858
Preble, Robin, 77
Press, Julie E., 14
Price, John R., 75, 518, 525
Prosser, William L., 262

Radin, Margaret J., 161
Rakowski, Eric, 1065
Rau, William, 74
Regan, John J., 405
Reik, Theodore, 196
Rein, Jan E., 44, 76, 102, 108, 113, 156,
    165, 183, 547, 614
Reutlinger, Mark, 42, 70
Reynolds, Osborne M., Jr., 551
Rhodes, Anne-Marie E., 102
Richmond, Gail L., 1077
Roberts, Patricia G., 102, 441, 512, 720,
    740, 765
Robinson, Beth, 498
Roosevelt, Franklin D., 978
Roosevelt, Theodore, 978
Rosenfeld, Jeffrey P., 162, 173
Ruffenach, Glenn, 407

Sabino, Anthony M., 642
Safire, William, 829
Saks, Michael J., 407
Salmon, Marylynn, 12
Schiff, Anne R., 127
Schoenblum, Jeffrey A., 173, 242, 243,
    525
Scholz, John Karl, 15
Schwartz, Frederic S., 90
Scoles, Eugene F., 48, 691

Scott, Austin W., 215, 220, 332, 349, 365,
    392, 555, 575, 580, 585, 593, 608, 639,
    644, 654, 661, 795, 879, 905, 920, 931,
    964
Seldes, Lee, 909
Seplowitz, Rena C., 511, 513
Shaffer, Thomas L., 196, 628
Shakespeare, William, 38
Shales, Tom, 265
Shammas, Carole, 12
Shapiro, Thomas M., 14
Shapo, Helene S., 104, 478
Shaw, George Bernard, 607
Sherman, Jeffrey G., 34, 147, 196, 993
Siegel, Stephen A., 787
Simes, Lewis M., 635, 681, 793, 833, 877
Simon, John G., 876
Simon, Rita J., 74, 88
Sligar, James S., 975
Smith, Allan F., 681, 833
Smith, David T., 12
Smith, George P. II, 405
Smith, Robert B., 1013
Snapp, Teal E., 88
Snapp, William D., 88
Sokol, Stan J., 427
Solum, Lawrence B., 929
Spaht, Katherine S., 536
Spitko, E. Gary, 196
Spurgeon, Edward D., 211
Stein, Robert A., 44, 46
Steincamp, John G., 993, 1034
Stone, Christopher D., 33
Sullivan, John E. III, 639
Sunstein, Cass R., 498
Sussman, Marvin B., 12
Swanson, Steven R., 664
Swinburne, Algernon Charles, 194

Taylor, Ross D., 877
Thayer, James B., 413
Tilson, Catherine J., 223, 239, 258, 264
Tocqueville, Alexis de, 15
Turano, Margaret V., 483

Volkmer, Ronald R., 183, 488
Von Rad, Gerhard, 2
Voran, Michael, 77

Wade, H. W. R., 834
Waggoner, Lawrence W., 72, 75, 436,
    445, 478, 512, 745, 746, 835, 836
Wake, Kenneth L., 184
Wang, William K. S., 23

Watts, Jill M., 215
Weinberg, R., 98
Weintraub, Russell J., 526
Weisbrot, Robert, 215
Wellman, Richard V., 348, 917
Wendel, Peter T., 953
Wenig, Mary M., 484, 486
Wertheimer, Jack, 28
Westfall, David, 949
Whitcomb, Paul T., 551
Whitebread, Charles H., 483, 512
Whitman, Robert, 277, 468

Wigmore, John H., 170, 413, 422
Wolf, Robert B., 973
Wolff, Edward N., 15
Wolk, Bruce A., 475, 641
Wright, Jackson W., Jr., 619

Young, Raymond H., 89

Zaritsky, Howard M., 530
Zelenak, Lawrence, 486

INDEX

Abatement of legacies, 468
Acceleration of remainders, 488, 720
Accounting
  by personal representative, 43
  by trustee, 392, 944, 948
Acts of independent significance, 318
  pour-over wills, 371
Ademption, 459
Administration of estates. *See* Estate
      administration
Administration of trusts. *See* Trustees
Administrator. *See* Personal
      representative
Adoption, adopted children
  adopted out, 764
  adoption of adult, 107, 763
  adoption of lover, 107
  adoption of spouse, 760
  equitable adoption, 108
  included in gift to children or
      heirs, 759
  inheritance rights, 102
  revocation of adoption, 765
  stranger-to-adoption rule, 759
  to prevent will contest, 107
Advancements, 128
Age contingencies
  reduction of, for Rule against
      Perpetuities, 831
  vested with possession postponed, 741
Alienation. *See* Restraints on alienation;
      Spendthrift trusts;
      Transferability
Alimony
  spendthrift trust, 633
Alphabet trust of George Bernard
      Shaw, 607

Ambiguities. *See also* Mistake
  drafter's liability, 427
  equivocation, 426
  latent, 424
  patent, 424
  plain meaning rule, 409
Anatomical gifts, 405
Ancillary administration, 39
  revocable trust to avoid, 391
Animals
  beneficiaries, 418, 602
  dogs snakeproofed, 179
  honorary trusts, 606
  horse sense, 425
  pretermitted Airedale, 418
Annual exclusion. *See* Federal gift tax
Ante-mortem probate, 174
Antilapse statutes. *See* Lapse
Attestation clause, 244
Attorneys
  bequests to, 185
  designated by will, 211
  ethical conduct
    counselling both husband and
        wife, 212, 518, 628
    named executor, 211
    named trustee, 211
      exculpatory clause, 629
    safekeeping wills, 245, 246
    self-proving affidavits, 245
    will beneficiary, 187
  fees, 44, 210
  malpractice liability, 59, 66
    disclaimer, 150
    drafting ambiguous will, 427
    elective share, 492

Attorneys—*Continued*
    execution of will, 233, 251, 270,
      535, 540
    fueling change in law, 70
    giving advice to trustee, 913
    marriage after execution, 535
    revocation of will, 279, 283
    Rule against Perpetuities, 830
    tax advice, 676
  professional responsibility in will
    preparation, 59
  witness to will, 211
Augmented estate, 507, 509

Bank accounts
  as will substitutes, 344
  federal estate tax, 1010
  joint, 345
  payable-on-death, 345
  safe deposit box, 348
  Totten trust, 349
Barnes Museum, 879
Basis. *See* Capital gain
Beneficiaries
  animals, 418, 602
  as trustee, 559
  changing trustees, 661
  indefinite, in trusts, 600
  modification of trusts, 651
  restrictions on conduct
    interference with family
      relations, 32
    marriage, 24
    religious faith, 24
  rights in discretionary trust, 627, 643,
    647, 648
  termination of trust by, 656, 660
  transferability of interest. *See* Restraints
    on alienation; Spendthrift
    trusts; Transferability
  trust pursuit rule, 906
  witness to will, 236
Bequest. *See also* Testamentary gifts
  defined, 37
  negative, 90
Bible
  Genesis 15:3, Abraham's heir, 2
  Genesis 25:29, Sale of Esau's
    birthright, 131
  John 10:20, Jesus is called mad, 161
  Psalms 39:6, Every man walketh in a
    vain shew, 710
Bishop Estate, 896
Black, Hugo, 33
Body Heat, 290
Body of decedent. *See also* Death
  directions concerning disposition
    of, 405
  exhumation, 116

gift of organs for transplantation, 406
  medical directives, 403
  sale of organs, 406
Bridgeman, Orlando, 788
Brown, Howard & Wendy
  Brown, Howard, 53
    estate plan, 49
    intestacy, 76, 134
    testamentary trust, 137
    will, 50
  Brown kindred, 53
    Brown, Sarah, 52
      disability trust, 650
    Fox, Fanny, 54
      ademption, 466
      incorporation by reference, 676
      revocable trust, 374
      secret trust, 617
      snuff bottles, 467
    Preston, Simon, 54
      secret trust, 617
Bryan, William Jennings, 310
Buck Trust, 872

Capacity. *See* Testamentary capacity
Capital gain
  carryover basis rule, 990
  stepped-up basis, 528, 990
Cartoons. *See* List of Illustrations, xxxiii-
    xxxv
Chancery. *See* Courts; Uses
Charitable foundations. *See also*
      Charitable gifts and trusts
  supervision of, 883
Charitable gifts and trusts
  administrative deviation, 878
  benevolent purposes, 869
  charitable remainder trusts, 1064
  cy pres, 869
  enforcement
    by attorney general, 883
    by donor, 883
    special interests, 892
  federal taxes and deductions, 1063
    annuity trust, 1064
    pooled income fund, 1064
    unitrust, 1064
  gender restrictions, 879
  largest foundations, 893
  modification, 869
  mortmain statutes, 869
  nature of charitable purposes, 859
  racial restrictions, 878
  Rule against Perpetuities, 865
  what qualifies as, 859
Chaucer, Geoffrey, 188, 409
Children. *See also* Gifts to Minors;
      Guardianship
  adopted. *See* Adopted children
  born by reproduction technology, 103

gift to
  including adopted children, 759
  including grandchildren, 755
  including nonmarital children, 767
  inheritance rights, 86
    adopted children, 98
    nonmarital children, 115
    stepchildren, 107, 765
  nonmarital, 115
  posthumous, as heirs, 97, 127
  posthumously conceived, 117
  pretermitted, 536
  same-sex parents, 105
  support rights, 477, 639
  surrogate mothers, 103
  "to *A* and his children," 779
  transfers to minors, 132
  Wild's Case, rule in, 779
China, inheritance law, 18, 147
Choice of law. *See* Conflict of laws
Civil law, 48, 174, 536
Claflin doctrine, 656
Class gifts
  class closing rules, 777
    Rule against Perpetuities, as affected
      by, 808
    specific sum gifts, 785
  death of income beneficiary, 750
  defined, 449
  future interests, 713
  lapse, 439, 454, 458
  Rule against Perpetuities, 807
  rule of convenience, 777
  survival requirement, 728
Codicil
  as partially revoking prior will, 277,
    284
  republication by, 302, 540
Cohabitants, 77, 320, 492, 498
Common trust funds, 928, 964
Community property, 471, 521
  Alaska community property trust, 473,
    517, 530
  by agreement, 522
  elective share compared, 471, 483
  income tax basis, 528
  in separate property states, 527
  quasi-community property, 526
  right of survivorship, 529
  separate property brought to
    community property state, 526
  stepped-up basis, 528
  Uniform Disposition of Community
    Property Rights at Death
    Act, 527
  widow's election wills, 524
Conditional wills, 32, 273
Conditions precedent and subsequent.
    See also Future interests;
    Remainders
  age contingencies, 741

estate tax treatment, 727
  explained, 714
Conflict of laws
  community property brought to
    separate property state, 527
  elective share rights, 507, 525
  execution of wills, 242
  foreign wills, 242
  holographic wills, 263
  intestacy, 72
  marital property, 506, 525
  power of appointment exercise, 688
  revocable trusts, 392
  separate property brought to
    community property state, 526
Conflicts of interest. *See* Trustees
Consanguinity, Table of, 92
Conservator. *See* Guardians;
    Guardianship
Constitution
  due process clause, 41, 75
  equal protection clause, 25, 75, 495
    adoption statute, 102
    dower, 479
    nonmarital children, 115, 767
    same-sex couples, 495
    state action, 25, 878
  takings clause, 3, 10
Construction. *See also* Limitations; Wills
  contract not to revoke will, 328
  future interests, 718. *See also* Future
    interests
  wills, 409
Constructive trusts, 141, 584
  breach of contract, 328
  fraud, 213
  innocent misrepresentation, 434
  killer of decedent, 141
  mistake, 284, 436
  negligence of lawyer, 540
  oral trusts, 609, 614
Consumption, power of. *See* Invasion
    powers
Contests. *See* Will contests
Contingent remainders. *See also* Future
    interests
  acceleration, 719
  age contingencies, 740
  condition precedent explained, 714
  defined, 713
  destructibility doctrine, 718
  estate taxation, 727
  executory interest compared, 717
  gifts to issue or descendants, 755, 760
  survival requirement, 728, 739
  transferability, 726, 738
  Uniform Probate Code §2–707, 742
  vested remainders compared, 713,
    714, 718, 738
  vesting requirement, Rule against
    Perpetuities, 794, 798, 807

Contracts
  effect on elective share statute, 323, 517
  insurance, 339, 343
  liability of trustee for, 975
  marital, 517
  not to revoke will, 322
    construction problems, 328
  payable-on-death, 331
    revocation by will, 337
  to make will, 320
Coolidge, Calvin, 537
Corporate fiduciary. *See* Personal representative; Trustees
Co-trustees. *See* Trustees
Courts
  Chancery, 36, 554, 716
  ecclesiastical, 36
  New York Surrogate's Courts, 212
  probate, 37, 65
  supervision of administration, 39
Crawford, Joan, 826
Creditors. *See also* Spendthrift trusts
  disclaimer, 150
  discretionary trusts, 643
  estate administration, 39
    nonclaim statutes, 41
  exoneration of liens, 468
  joint tenancy, 351
  nonprobate assets, 371
  notice to, 41
  power of appointment, rights against holder, 672
  property exempt from
    family allowance, 477
    homestead, 476
    pensions, 641
  revocable trusts, 368
  self-settled trusts, 639
  support trusts, 642
Curtesy, 479
Custodian. *See* Uniform Transfers to Minors Act
Cy pres
  modification of charitable trusts, 869
  Rule against Perpetuities, 831

Dacey, Norman F., 360
Daily Telegraph, 455
Dead hand, 23, 660, 794, 853
Death. *See also* Body of decedent
  guillotine, 85
  living will, 403
  of beneficiary before testator. *See* Lapse
  simultaneous, 77
  terminating medical treatment, 403
  time of, 85
  Uniform Simultaneous Death Act, 77

Death without issue. *See* Die without issue
Declaration of trust, 352, 557. *See also* Revocable trusts
Deed
  incorporation by reference, 309
  of trust, 557
Delaware tax trap, 675, 827, 1073
Delivery
  as requisite for gift, 578, 580
  as requisite for trust, 559
Demonstrative legacies, 459. *See also* Testamentary gifts
Dependent relative revocation, 286
Descendants. *See also* Issue
  gift to, 755
    per stirpes or per capita, 755
    survival requirement, 739
  inheritance rights, 86
Deutsche Bank, 664
Devise. *See also* Testamentary gifts
  defined, 37
Die without issue
  construction, 740
Disclaimer
  by person with Medicaid, 151
  future interest, 720, 725
  intestate share, 148
  rights of creditors, 150
  tax consequences, 148, 725, 990, 1069
  testamentary gift, 148
  Uniform Probate Code, 150
  witness to will, 236
Discretionary trusts, 617
  creditors' rights in, 643
  duties of trustee, 618
  income taxation of, 595
  Rule against Perpetuities, 820
  standards governing exercise of discretion, 627, 1033, 1035
  state-supported beneficiary, 649
Divorce. *See also* Alimony
  effect on nonprobate transfers
    life insurance, 299
    payable on death designations, 343
    pension plans, 343, 385
    revocable trusts, 385
  effect on will, 298
  equitable division, 480
  remainders, 719
Doctrine of Worthier Title, 775
Dogs. *See* Animals
Dower, 478
  federal estate tax, 1008
Drawings. *See* List of Illustrations, xxxiii-xxxv
Duke, Doris, 765
Duke of Norfolk's Case, 788
Dynasty trust, 675, 849, 854, 1068, 1072

Ecclesiastical courts, 36
Elder law, 405

Elective share statutes, 480
abandonment by spouse, 492
augmented estate, 507, 509
community property compared, 472, 483, 511
conflict of laws, 506
contractual will, 323
dependency role of women, 484
fraud on, 506
guardian of incompetent spouse, election by, 488, 491
illusory transfers, 505
life estate, 481, 487
life insurance, 511
lifetime transfers to defeat, 505
New York statute, 512
powers of appointment, as subject to, 513, 672
premarital transfers, 511
property subject to, 500
revocable trust, 500, 506, 507
same-sex partners, 492, 498
Uniform Probate Code, 481, 483, 507
waiver, 517
Employee benefit plans
estate taxation, 1012, 1045
revocation of beneficiary, 344
spendthrift clause, 641
spousal rights, 475
Employee Retirement Income Security Act, 475, 641, 973
Equitable adoption, 108
Equitable charge, 575
ERISA. *See* Employee Retirement Income Security Act
Escheat, 74, 95
Estate administration, 35. *See also* Personal representative; Probate
ancillary, 39, 391
avoidance of, 44, 331
use of revocable trusts, 389
closing of, 43
cost of, 45
creditors' claims, 41
family allowance, 477
guardian ad litem, 212
independent, 43
informal, 40
judicial supervision of, 43
necessity for, 44
notice requirements, 40
perpetuities violation, 806
revocable trusts to avoid, 389
small estates, 46
universal succession, 48
Estate planning
for married couple with children, 49
introduction, 49
marital deduction, 1042
obtaining data from client, 52

powers of appointment in, 673, 728, 744, 746, 1032
tax planning for spouses, 1061
tax strategies, 1076
trusts in, 555
revocable trusts, 386
Estate tax. *See also* Federal estate tax
state, 1078
Ethics. *See* Attorneys
Ethnic groups
racial restrictions in charitable gifts, 878
restriction on gift tied to marriage within, 24
Evidence. *See also* Ambiguities; Construction; Mistake; Wills
admissibility, 410, 424
dead man's statutes, 169
plain meaning rule, 409
personal usage, 413
pretermitted child statutes, 546
Exculpatory clauses
drafter as trustee, 629
investments by trustee, 962
Execution of attested wills, 225
acknowledgment of signature, 227
age required for, 159
attestation clause, 244
attorney liability, 233
beneficiary as witness, 241
conscious presence test, 233
dispensing power, 259, 316
fraud, 213. *See also* Fraud
harmless error, 252, 261, 269, 309
incorporation by reference, 303
integration, 301
international wills, 243
mental capacity, 159. *See also* Testamentary capacity
mistake, 251. *See also* Mistake
notarization, 236
order of signing, 234
presence of testator, witnesses, 233
proving will in probate, 245
lost will, 280
publication of will, 244
recommended method, 242
republication by codicil, 302
requirements, 225
policies basing, 223
substantial compliance with, 260
self-proved will, 245
signature of testator, 234
substantial compliance with, 260, 284, 309, 316
tortious interference with, 221
undue influence, 175. *See also* Undue influence
videotaping, 210, 235
witnesses, number required, 226. *See also* Witnesses to will
wrong will signed, 247

Executor. *See* Personal representative
Executory interests, 716. *See also* Future
    interests
    transferability, 726
Exoneration
    liens, 468
    trustee liability. *See* Exculpatory clauses
Expectancy
    tortious interference, 221
    transfer, 131

Fallacy of the transplanted category, 648
Family allowance, 477
Family maintenance legislation, 477
Father Divine, 215
Federal estate tax, 1005
    apportionment of, 985
    charitable deduction, 1063
        charitable remainder trusts, 1064
    credit shelter trust, 1062
    credits, 1007, 1078
        unified, 982
    Delaware tax trap, 675, 827, 1073
    disclaimer, 149, 990, 1038
    employee death benefits, 1012
    exemption, 982
    future interests, 727, 738, 1007
    generation-skipping. *See* Federal
            generation-skipping transfer tax
    gifts in contemplation of death, 1029
    gifts within three years of death, 1029
    gross estate, 1007
    history, 977
    inheritance tax distinguished, 980
    invasion powers, 682, 1033, 1035, 1046
    joint tenancy, 1009
        between husband and wife, 1011
        between unmarried persons, 1009
    liability for payment, 985
    life estate, 1007
        retained, 1014
    life insurance, 1013
    lifetime transfers, 1014
    marital deduction. *See* Marital
            deduction
    powers of appointment, 673, 1032
        $5,000 or 5 percent power, 1034
    powers to consume, 682, 1033, 1035
    property owned at death, 1007
    rates, 982
    reciprocal trusts, 1022
    reformation of trusts, 1049, 1057
    remainders, 727, 738
    reversionary interest retained, 1028
    revocable transfers, 1027
    right to remove trustee, 1026
    stepped-up basis, 990
    tax-inclusive, 984
    tenancy by entirety, 1011
    thumbnail sketch, 1005

    transfer with retained control of
        enjoyment, 1022, 1027
    transfer with retained life estate, 1014
    transfer within three years of
        death, 1029
    transmissible interests, 1007
    unified estate and gift tax, 981
    unified estate tax credit, 982
Federal generation-skipping transfer
        tax, 1065
    base of tax, 1070
    definitions, 1073
        interest, 1075
        skip person, 1074
        transferor, 1073
    Delaware tax trap, 675, 827, 1073
    direct skip, 1068
    disclaimer, 726, 1069
    dynasty trust, 1072
    exceptions, 1068
        multiple skips, 1068
        predeceased child, 1068
    exclusions, 1072
    exemption, 1070
    powers of appointment, 674
    rate, 1070
    remainders, 739
    tax strategies, 1076
    taxable distribution, 1067
    taxable termination, 1067
    USRAP tax trap, 846
Federal gift tax, 985
    annual exclusion, 991
    charitable gift, 1063
    completed gift, what constitutes, 986
    Crummey powers, 994, 1002
    disclaimer, 149, 720, 725, 990. *See also*
            Disclaimer
    future interest, 992
    gift defined, 985
    income tax basis, 990
    joint tenancy, 1009, 1011
    lapse of power of appointment, 1002,
            1034
    life insurance premiums, 1003, 1013
    marital deduction, 1003
    minors, gifts to, 992, 1002
    rates, 982
    release of power of appointment, 989,
            1034
    remainder transferred, 989
    renunciation. *See* Disclaimer
    revocable trusts, 388, 989
    spousal gifts, 1003
    tax-exclusive, 984
    tenancy by entirety, 1011
    unified estate and gift tax, 981
    unified gift tax credit, 982
    Uniform Transfers to Minors Act, 993,
            1028. *See also* Uniform Transfers
            to Minors Act

Federal income tax
  basis
    gifts, 990
    inherited property, 990
    stepped-up basis, 528, 990
  charitable foundations, 894
  employee death benefits, 1013
  grantor trusts, 594
  revocable trusts, 388
Fertile octogenarian, 798
Fertility, presumption of, 798
Fiduciary Administration. *See* Estate
    administration; Trust
    administration
Fletcher, Judge Betty, 1049
Forms
  per stirpes definitions, 758
  perpetuities saving clause, 829
  printed will forms, 268
  Will of Howard Brown, 50
  Will of Howard Brown with
    testamentary trust, 137
Fraud, 213
  powers of appointment, 699
Future interests, 709
  acceleration, 498, 719
  class gifts. *See* Class gifts
  classification, 710, 712
    consequences, 718
  construction, 718
  disclaimer, 720, 725
  survival requirement, 728
  taxation, 727
  transferability, 726
  transmissible, 727, 732
  types
    contingent remainder. *See*
      Contingent remainders
    executory interest. *See* Executory
      interests
    possibility of reverter. *See* Possibility
      of reverter
    remainder. *See* Remainders
    reversion. *See* Reversions
    right of entry. *See* Right of entry
  valuation, 728
  vested with possession postponed, 741
  vesting requirement, Rule against
    Perpetuities, 794, 798

Garrett, Henrietta, 95
Gays. *See* Homosexuals
Gender
  discrimination, 38
  same-sex couple, 498
  -trix forms, 38
General legacies. *See also* Testamentary
    gifts
  abatement, 468
  ademption, 459

General power of appointment. *See*
    Powers of appointment
Generation-skipping transfer tax. *See*
    Federal generation-skipping
    transfer tax
Genesis. *See* Bible
Gift tax. *See* Federal gift tax
Gifts. *See also* Federal gift tax
  delivery requirement, 578
  enforceable as trusts, 575
  future royalties, 589
  in contemplation of death, 1029
  to minors. *See* Gifts to minors
  within three years of death, 1029
Gifts to minors, 132, 568, 992, 1002
  section 2053(c) trusts, 993
  Uniform Transfers to Minors Act, 133,
    570
Gilbert, Peter, 720
Grant, W.V., 265
Grantor trusts, 594
Guardian ad litem, 44, 212
Guardians
  guardian of the person, 132
  guardian of the property, 132
Guillotine, 85

Half-blood, inheritance by, 96
Harmless error rule, 252, 261, 269, 309
Health-care directives, 403
Heirs. *See also* Inheritance; Intestacy
  ancestors, 90
  cohabitants, 77
  collaterals, 90
  defined, 38
  descendants, 86
  forced, 11, 480, 536
  future interest
    taxation, 727
    when heirs determined, 713, 768
  heir hunters, 95
  heirs apparent, 131
  laughing, 95
  next-of-kin distinguished, 38
  of grantee. *See* Rule in Shelley's Case
  of grantor. *See* Doctrine of Worthier
    Title
  spouse, 74
    abandonment, 77
Holographic wills, 262
  change in, 284, 317
  incorporation by reference, 317
  letter, 271
  material provisions, 263
  printed will form, 268
  signature, 271
  written on other than paper, 275
Homestead, 476

Homosexuals
  adoption of children, 105
  adoption of lover, 107
  marriage, 492, 498
  spousal elective share, 492, 498
  spousal intestate share, 77
  undue influence, 193
Honorary trusts, 602
  animals, 602. *See also* Animals
  Rule against Perpetuities, 606
Horse sense, 425
Hotchpot, 129
Human capital, 21

Illegitimate children. *See* Nonmarital
    children
Illusory transfer, 505
Illustrations. *See* List of Illustrations,
    xxxiii-xxxv. *See also* Poems;
    Through the Looking Glass
Implication, gifts by, 437, 754
  default of appointment, 706
Income tax. *See* Federal income tax
Incompetency. *See also* Guardians;
    Guardianship; Testamentary
    capacity
  durable power of attorney, 396
  durable power of attorney for health
    care, 404
  forced share election for incompetent
    spouse, 491
  revocable trust, 393
Incompetents
  trust for, 555
Incorporation by reference, 303, 677
  by holographic will, 311
  pour-over will, 371
Indefinite beneficiaries, 600
Independent administration, 43. *See also*
    Estate administration
Independent significance, 318
  pour-over will, 372, 385
Indian land, 3
Inheritance. *See also* Intestacy
  abolition, 11, 16
  arguments pro and con, 13
  constitutional protection, 3
  history, 1, 11
  human capital, 19
Inheritance tax, 980. *See also* State
    succession taxes
Insane delusion, 165
Insurance. *See* Life insurance
Integration of wills, 301
Intestacy, 71. *See also* Adoption;
    Inheritance
  advancements, 128
  ancestors, 90
  bars to succession, 141
    elder abuse, 148

children's share, 86, 97
  adopted children, 98
  nonmarital children, 115
  posthumous children, 97, 117
  stepchildren, 101, 107
collaterals, 90
  degrees of kinship, 93
  half-bloods, 96
  parentelic system, 91
  Table of Consanguinity, 92
descendants, 86
disclaimer, 148
escheat, 95
half-bloods, 96
heirs defined, 38, 72
killer, 141
laughing heirs, 95
next-of-kin defined, 38
per stirpes, 87
representation, 86
simultaneous death, 77
spouse's share, 74
Invasion powers. *See also* Discretionary
    trusts; Powers of appointment
  ascertainable standard relating
    to, 682, 1035
  discretionary power in trustee, 618
  trustee's authority to exercise when
    trust silent, 655
Investments by trustees. *See* Trustees
Issue
  die without, meaning, 740
  gift to, 739, 755
  inheritance rights, 86
  omitted from will, 536
  per stirpes or per capita, 755
  rule in Wild's Case, 779
  survival requirements, 739

Jackson, Shoeless Joe, 42
Johnson, Seward, litigation, 197
Joint bank accounts. *See* Bank accounts
Joint tenancy
  as will substitute, 350
  federal estate and gift tax, 1009
Joint will, 322
Jolly Testator Who Makes His Own
    Will, 262
Judges, dishonest, 315

Kafka, Franz, 33
Killer of decedent, 141

Lambert, Surrogate Marie, 208, 212
Lapse, 438
  antilapse statutes, 440, 445, 732, 742
    class gifts, 449, 458
    nonprobate transfers, 445
    powers of appointment, 695

class gifts, 439, 449, 454
future interests, 732, 742
in residuary clause, 439
nonprobate transfers, 445
powers of appointment, 695
Last will and testament. *See also* Wills
derivation of terminology, 37
Latent ambiguities, 424
Latin gender, 38
Laughing heirs, 95
Lee, Jason, 574
Legacies. *See* Testamentary gifts
Legitime, 536
Lerner, Alan Jay, 589
Lesbians. *See* Homosexuals
Letters
of administration, 39
testamentary, 39
Libel by will, 550
Life estate, 563. *See also* Invasion powers
class member, death of, 750
legal
abolished in England, 566
compared to trust, 562
rights of life tenant, 562
waste, 564
taxation
estate tax, 1007
transfer with life estate
retained, 1014
generation-skipping transfer
tax, 1067
Life insurance
change of beneficiary by will, 339
divorce, effect on beneficiary
designation, 343
federal estate tax, 1013
pour-over trust, 384
testamentary trustee as
beneficiary, 385
transfer within three years of
death, 1029
Limitations
"to *A* and his children," 779
"to *A* and the children of *B*," 457
"to *A* for life, then to *A*'s heirs," 776
"to *A* for life, then to the grantor's
heirs," 775
"to *A* or his heirs," 447
Living probate, 174
Living trust. *See* Revocable trusts; Trusts,
inter vivos
Living will, 403

Malpractice. *See* Attorneys
Manchester, Duke of, 646
Manslaughter. *See* Killer of decedent
Marital deduction, 1042
dependency of women, 484

gift tax, 1003
history, 485
nondeductible terminable interest
rule, 1043
estate trust exception, 1046
life estate plus general power of
appointment exception, 1046
limited survivorship exception, 1045
qualified terminable interest (QTIP)
exception, 1047
qualified domestic trust, 1061
reformation of trusts, 1049, 1057
tax planning, 1061
Marital property systems
community property, 471
separate property, 472
Marriage
bigamous, 76
dependency of women, 484
effect on will, 300, 534
testamentary restriction on
beneficiary's, 24
to senile spouse, 165
unmarried cohabitants, 77, 320, 492
Medicaid
disclaimer of inheritance, 151
elective share liable, 488
trust beneficiary, 648, 654
Medical treatment, 403
Menendez brothers, 147
Mental capacity. *See also* Testamentary
capacity
inter vivos transfers, 165
marriage, 165
revocable trust amendment, 368
Minors. *See also* Guardian ad litem;
Guardians; Guardianship
administration
Crummey trusts, 1002
section 2503(c) trusts, 993
transfers to, by personal
representative, 134
Uniform Transfers to Minors Act, 133
Mistake. *See also* Ambiguities;
Implication, gifts by
by lawyer, 251, 427, 436
description of beneficiaries,
property, 426
harmless error, 252. *See also* Harmless
error rule
in execution of will, 251
in revocation, 284, 286
insane delusion, 166
misdescription, 426
reformation, 436
wrong will signed, 247
Modification of trusts, 651. *See also* Cy
pres
deviation from trust terms, 655, 855
to benefit income beneficiary, 655

Mortmain statutes, 869
Multiple party bank accounts, 344
Murder. *See* Killer of decedent
Musmanno, Justice Michael, 249
Mutual wills, 322

Name change, 32
Negative bequest, 90
Negligence of attorney. *See* Attorneys
Next-of-kin. *See also* Inheritance; Intestacy
  defined, 38
  heirs distinguished, 38
No-contest clauses, 184, 385
Nondeductible terminable interest rule.
    See Marital deduction
Nonmarital children
  DNA test, 116
  gift to children or heirs as
      including, 767
  inheritance rights, 115
  pretermitted child statutes, 547
Nonprobate transfers
  antilapse statutes, 445
  bank accounts, 344
  contracts, 331, 336, 337
  creditors' rights, 371
  declaration of trust, 352
  divorce, 343, 383
  joint interests, 34, 344
  life insurance, 34
  payable-on-death provisions, 35, 331
  revocable trusts, 35, 351
  revocation by will, 344
  securities T.O.D., 344
  survivorship required, 338, 349
  Totten trusts, 349
Nontestamentary acts, 318
Norfolk, Duke of, 790
Nottingham, Lord, 791
Nuncupative wills, 226

Oral trusts, 557, 586, 608, 614
Oral wills, 226
Organ transplantation, 406
Oscar P.'s will, 246

Pascal, Gabriel, 590
Patent ambiguities, 425
Payable-on-death account, 345, 349. *See
    also* Bank accounts; Contracts
Pension plans. *See* Employee benefit
    plans
  divorce, 298, 476
  estate tax, 1012
  spousal rights, 475
Per capita
  gifts to issue as, 755

per capita at each generation, 88, 756
per capita with representation, 87
Perpetuities, Rule against
  abolished in some states, 854
  administrative contingencies, 806
  age contingencies reduced, 831
  alternative contingencies, 806, 848
  attorney malpractice, 830
  charities, 865
  class gifts, 807
    class closing rule, 808
    specific sum, 817
    subclasses, 813
  consequences of violation, 805, 827
  cy pres, 831
  definite purpose trusts, 606, 866
  Delaware tax trap, 827
  discretionary trusts, 820
  duration of trusts, 795
  dynasty trusts, 849, 854
  fertile octogenarian, 798
  fetus-in-fetu, 801
  honorary trusts, 606
  lives in being
    date ascertained, 797
    measuring life, 796
      wait-and-see, 834
    relevant lives, 795
    validating life, 796
    why used, 794
  measuring life, 796
    wait-and sec, 834
  Model Moppet, 836
  New York law, 800, 805, 831, 856
  policies underlying, 793
  powers of appointment, 818
    general powers, 818
      validity of exercise, 819
      validity of power, 818
    testamentary and special
        powers, 819
      application of USRAP, 840
      Delaware tax trap, 827
      second look doctrine, 821
      validity of exercise, 821
      validity of power, 820
  power to revoke, 819
  precocious toddler, 800
  reform, 830
    cy pres, 831
    specific correctives, 831
    wait-and-see, 832
  reformation of void gifts, 831
  relevant lives, 795
  rule of proof, 794
  saving clause, 829
  slothful executor, 806
  split contingencies, 806
  subclasses, 813
  suspension of power of alienation, 856

trust duration, 795
unborn widow, 801
Uniform Statutory Rule against
    Perpetuities, 835
  dynasty trust, 850
  generation-skipping transfer
    tax, 846
validating life, 796
vesting concept, 795, 807
wait-and-see doctrine, 832
  common law period, 834
    measuring lives, 835
  USRAP, 835
Personal property
  disposition of, by unattested
    memorandum, 311
  oral trusts, 557
  oral wills, 226
  set aside to spouse, 477
Personal representative. *See also* Estate
    administration; Probate
  accounting by, 43
  bond requirement, 36
  compensation, 44
  defined, 35
  judicial supervision, 43
  letters of administration, 39
  letters testamentary, 39
  nonresident bank or individual, 36
Per stirpes, 87, 755
Photographs. *See* List of Illustrations,
    xxxiii-xxxv
POD account, 349
Poems
  Do you rule your perpetuity?, 792
  Life looked rosy to *A*, 786
  The Jolly Testator Who Makes His
    Own Will, 262
Possibility of reverter, 712. *See also*
    Future interests
Post-mortem estate planning, 149, 397
Pour-over will, 372. *See also* Revocable
    trusts
  effect of divorce on trust, 385
Power of alienation, suspension of, 856.
    See also Restraints on alienation
Power of attorney, durable, 396
Power of attorney for health care, 404
Powers of appointment. *See also*
    Discretionary trusts; Invasion
    powers
  allocation, 760
  antilapse statutes, 696
  bankruptcy, 672
  capture, 701
  classification, 665
  conflict of laws, 693
  contract to appoint, 683
  creation, 676
  creditors of donee, 668, 671
  Crummey powers, 1002

Delaware tax trap, 675, 827, 1073
donee, 665
donor, 665
elective share statutes, 672
exercise
  by residuary clause, 688
  contract for, 683
  specific reference required, 694
failure to exercise, 699, 702
  implied gift in default, 706
federal estate tax, 673, 1032
fraud on, 699
general
  allocation, 700
  capture, 701
  contract to appoint, 683
  creditors of donee, 668
  defined, 665
  donee treated as owner, 671
  exercise by residuary clause, 688
  Rule against Perpetuities, 818, 819
  taxation, 673, 1032
imperative, 683, 707
ineffective exercise, 699
  allocation, 700
lapse of appointment, 695
marshaling, 700
relation-back doctrine, 667
release, 682
remainders in default, 717
Rule against Perpetuities, 818
special powers, 666
  appointment in further trust, 697
  contract to appoint, 683
  defined, 666
  estate tax, 673
  exclusive, 697
  fraud on, 699
  generation-skipping transfer
    tax, 674
  imperative, 707
  Rule against Perpetuities, 819
  taxation, 1033
takers in default, 665, 717
  implied, 706
tax reasons for creating, 673
unenforceable trusts as, 601
use of powers in estate planning, 673,
    728
Power to consume principal. *See also*
    Invasion powers
  legal fee simple with, 677
  repugnancy rule, 681
  taxation, 682
  trusts
    ascertainable standard relating
      to, 1035
    discretionary power in trustee, 617
Precatory language, 575, 677
Pretermitted child, 536

Principal and income of trusts, 929
  allocation, 971
  discretionary power in trustee
      over, 973
  portfolio theory, 963, 970
  unproductive property, 936
Probate. *See also* Estate administration;
      Personal representative
  ancillary, 39, 391
  avoidance, 44
    revocable trusts, 389
  before death, 174
  closing of, 43
  common form, 40
  cost, 45
  courts, history of, 36
  creditors' claims, 41
  destroyed will, 280
  formal, 40
  informal, 40
  lost wills, 280
  necessity for, 44
  proof of will, 244
    lost wills, 280
  reform, 48
  solemn form, 40
  Uniform Probate Code, 43
  without administration, 43, 48
Professional responsibility. *See* Attorneys
Profit-sharing plans. *See* Employee
      benefit plans
Promise
  as trust, 583

QTIP trust, 486, 1048
Quasi-community property, 526

Race. *See* Ethnic groups
Release
  power of appointment, 682, 1033
Religion. *See also* Ethnic groups
  restriction tied to, in testamentary
      gifts, 24
Remainders, 713. *See also* Contingent
      remainders; Future interests
  acceleration, 488, 719
  age contingencies, 741, 813, 831
  charitable remainder trusts, 1064
  class closing rules, 777
  classification, 710, 712
  contingent. *See* Contingent remainders
  defined, 712
  destructibility, 718
  disclaimer, 720, 725
  implied, 706, 854
  in default of appointment, 717
  survival. *See* Survival, requirement of

transfer
  estate tax, 727, 738
  generation-skipping transfer tax, 739
  transferability, 726
  transmissible, 727, 732, 738
  Uniform Probate Code §2-707, 742
  valuation, 728
  vested indefeasibly, 713
    divorce, 719
    preference for, 718
  vested subject to divestment, 714
  vested subject to open, 713
  vested subject to partial
      divestment, 713
  vested with possession postponed, 741
  vesting requirement, Rule against
      Perpetuities, 795, 807
Renunciation. *See* Disclaimer
Representation. *See also* Per stirpes
  meaning of, 86, 756
Republication by codicil, 302, 540
Res of trust, 581
  future profits, 586
Residuary clause. *See also* Testamentary
      gifts
  exercise of power of appointment
      by, 693
  lapse in, 439
Restraints on alienation. *See also*
      Spendthrift trusts
  suspension of power of alienation, rule
      against, 856
Restraints on marriage, 32
Resulting trusts, 584
Reversions, 711. *See also* Future interests
  estate taxation, 1028
  income taxation, 595
  rule of reversions, 715, 745
Revival of revoked will, 296
Revocable trusts, 351, 386
  antilapse statute, 732
  avoidance of probate, 351, 389
  choice of law, 392
  creditors, 368
  declaration of trust, 352, 386
  divorce, effect of, 385
  elective share, use to avoid, 391, 505
  federal estate tax, 1027
  federal gift tax, 986
  federal income tax, 595, 989
  life insurance trusts, 384
  marketing, 395
  pour-over bequest to, 372
    ademption, 459
    incorporation by reference, 372
    independent significance, 372, 385
    no-contest clause, effect on
        trust, 385
  presumption, 580
  revocation by will, 367

Rule against Perpetuities, 819
secrecy, 390
settlor as trustee, 386
undue influence, 368
Uniform Testamentary Additions to
Trusts Act, 373
use in estate planning, 386
will contests, avoiding, 393
Revocation of wills, 276
by birth of child, 300, 536
by divorce, 298
by holograph, 284, 285, 290
by inconsistent later will, 277
by marriage, 300, 530
by mistake, 284
by person other than testator, 280
by physical act, 276, 283
by writing, 276
cancelling on back of will, 283
codicil, 277
contracts not to revoke, 322
dependent relative revocation, 286
duplicate wills, 277
harmless error, 252, 284, 300
holographs, 284, 285, 290
partial revocation, 284
presumption, 277
revival of revoked will, 296
substantial compliance, 284
Revocation of will substitutes, 344
revocable trust, 361
Right of entry, 712. *See also* Future
interests
Romer, Lord Justice, 457
Rothko, Mark, 907
Rugg, Chief Justice Arthur, 411, 500
Rule against Perpetuities. *See*
Perpetuities, Rule against
Rule in Shelley's Case, 776
Rule in Wild's Case, 779
Rule of convenience, 778

Safeguarding a will, 246
Same-sex couple. *See* Homosexuals
Satisfaction of legacies, 468
Saving clause, 829
Savings account trust. *See* Totten trusts
Secret trusts, 616
Securities. *See also* Stock, bequests of
T.O.D. registration, 344
Self-dealing. *See* Trustees
Self-proved wills, 245
Semisecret trusts, 616
Sex discrimination. *See* Gender;
Homosexuals
Shaw, George Bernard
alphabet trusts, 607
Shelley's Case, Rule in, 776
Simultaneous death, 77
effect on marital deduction, 1045
Sisyphus prize for heroic attempts, 768

Slayer of decedent, 141
Small estates, administration of, 46
Snuff bottles, 467
Social security, 473
Soviet Union, 18
Special power of appointment. *See*
Powers of appointment
Specific.devises and bequests. *See also*
Testamentary gifts
abatement, 468
ademption, 459
Spendthrift trusts, 631
bankruptcy, 642
creditors' rights, 639
exceptions, 639
alimony, 639
child support, 639
New York statutory, 632
suspension of power of alienation,
rule against, 857
pension trusts, 641
self-settled trust, 639
state-supported beneficiary, 649
station-in-life rule, 640
termination, 656
tort creditors, 641
Sperm bank, 128
Spouse, surviving, 471
cohabitant, 77, 492
inheritance rights, 74
omitted from will, 530
protection of
community property. *See* Community
property
contract not to revoke will, 322
dower, 478
elective share. *See* Elective share
family allowance, 477
family maintenance legislation, 477
homestead, 476
marital deduction. *See* Marital
deduction
nonprobate property, 505, 507
omitted from will, 323, 530
pension plans, 475
personal property set-aside, 477
social security, 473
tax planning for, 1061
State succession taxes, 1078
Statute of Frauds
contract to devise, 320
trusts, application to, 557
Statute of Uses, 554
Stepchildren
included in gift to children, 765
inheritance rights, 101
Stock, bequests of. *See also* Securities;
Testamentary gifts; Trustees
stock splits, 464
Superwill, 344

Support trusts, 642. *See also* Discretionary
    trusts
Survival, requirement of, 728
  age contingencies, 741
  class gifts, 732, 739
  contingent remainders, 740
  contracts, 338
  divesting limitation, 738
  gifts to issue or descendants, 755
  lapse compared, 732
  multi-generational classes, 739
  nonprobate transfers, 338
  possession postponed, 741
  tax consequences of, 727
  Uniform Probate Code §2–707, 742
Suspension of power of alienation, rule
    against, 856
  spendthrift trusts, 857
Swinburne, Algernon Charles, 194

Table of Consanguinity, 92
Taxes. *See* Federal estate tax; Federal
    generation-skipping transfer tax;
    Federal gift tax; Federal income
    tax; State succession taxes
Televangelists, 265
Termination of trusts, 651, 855
  by beneficiaries, 656
  Claflin doctrine, 656
  spendthrift trusts, 656
  will compromise, 660
Terminology, 35
Testament, 37
Testamentary capacity, 159. *See also* Will
    contests
  age requirement, 159
  defined, 163
  insane delusion, 165
  jury findings, 173
  person with AIDS, 196
  reasons for requiring, 161
Testamentary gifts
  abatement, 468
  ademption, 459
  bequest defined, 37
  demonstrative legacies, 459
  devise defined, 37
  exoneration of liens, 468
  general legacy, 457, 468
  Indian lands, 3
  lapse, 438
  pour-over, 371
  public policy, gifts void as against
    destruction of property, 32
    interference with family
      relations, 32
    restrictions on marriage of
      beneficiaries, 24
  residuary clause
    lapse, 439

satisfaction of legacies, 468
securities
  ademption, 459
  stock splits, 464
  specific legacy, 459, 468
Testamentary libel, 550
Through the Looking Glass, 709
Title
  passage at death, 148
  passing during life to avoid
    probate, 34
"To *A* and his children," 779. *See also*
    Limitations
Torts
  liability of trustee for, 975
  libel by will, 550
  tortious interference with
    inheritance, 221
Totten trusts, 349
Transferability. *See also* Restraints on
    Alienation; Spendthrift trusts
  of future interests, 726, 738
Troland, Leonard, 945
Trust administration. *See* Trustees
Trustees. *See also* Trusts
  acceptance of trust, 561
  accountings, 392
  changing, 661
  conflicts of interest, 903
  co-trustees, 918
  custodian distinguished, 570
  duties
    accounting, 944, 948
    collect and protect trust assets, 919
    delegation of, 922, 927
    discretionary trusts, 617
    earmark trust property, 920
    impartiality, 929. *See also* Principal
      and income
    invest. *See* investments, below
    loyalty, 903. *See also* self-dealing,
      below
    measure of damage, 917
    not to commingle, 921
    to disclose information, 938
  ERISA, 973
  exculpatory clauses, exoneration, 962
    drafter as trustee, 629
    investments, 962
    judicial accountings, 949
  fees, 630
  investments, 954, 963
    deviation from trust terms, 655, 969
    diversification, 963
    index funds, 928
    market funds, 928
    portfolio performance, 965
    prudent investor rule, 963
    speculation, 967
    unproductive property, 936

liability
   contracts, 975
   torts, 975
portfolio theory, 963
powers
   managerial powers, 950
   of appointment, 665
   powers of sale, 951
   Uniform Trustees' Powers Act, 950,
      953
principal and income. *See* Principal
      and income
removal of trustee, 661, 1026
self-dealing, 904. *See also* duties,
      loyalty, above
settlor as, 557
social investing, 974
testamentary
   beneficiary of insurance
      proceeds, 385
third person dealing with, 953
trust pursuit rule, 906
Trusts. *See also* Trustees
   acceptance by trustee, 561
   beneficiaries, 561, 597, 601
      animals, 606
      state supported, 648
   charitable trust. *See* Charitable gifts
      and trusts
   constructive trust. *See* Constructive
      trusts
   contract law compared, 566
   court trust, 392
   creation, 567
      Statute of Frauds, 557
   custodial, 394, 491
   custodianship distinguished, 570
   debt distinguished, 332, 584
   declaration of, 557, 559
   deed of trust, 557
   discretionary trust. *See* Discretionary
      trusts
   dry trust, 561
   duration, 795, 854
   dynasty trust, 675, 849, 854
   estate planning, use in, 555
      revocable trusts, 351
   gift treated as, 575
   grantor trust, 594
   gratuitous promise distinguished, 581
   history, 553
   honorary trust, 602
   income. *See* Principal and income
   income taxation of, 594
   indefinite beneficiaries, 601
   inter vivos, 557
   legal life estate compared, 562
   modification. *See* Cy Pres; Modification
      of trusts
   oral trust, 557, 586, 608, 614

perpetual trusts, 954
Perpetuities, Rule against, 795, 854
pour-over, 371
   effect of divorce, 385
precatory language, 575
principal. *See* Principal and income
purchase money resulting trust, 584
pursuit into product, 906
reformation, 654
res, requirement of, 581, 583
   future profits, 586, 593
   life insurance proceeds, 594
resulting trust, 584
revocable trust. *See* Revocable trusts
secret trust, 616
semisecret trust, 616
spendthrift trust. *See* Spendthrift trusts
support trust. *See* Support trusts
termination. *See* Termination of trusts
testamentary, 137, 557
Totten trust. *See* Totten trusts
unenforceable trusts, as powers, 601

Unborn widow, 801
Undue influence, 175. *See also* Will
         contests
   AIDS patients' wills, 196
   attorneys, bequests to, 185
   burden of proof, 183
   homosexual relationship, 193
   inter vivos transactions, 386, 393
   Johnson, Seward, will contest, 197
   older woman & younger man, 192
   revocation of trust, 386
   sexual relationship, 192
Uniform Adoption Act, 763
Uniform Anatomical Gift Act, 406
Uniform Custodial Trust Act, 394
Uniform Disposition of Community
      Property Rights at Death
      Act, 527
Uniform Gifts to Minors Act. *See*
      Uniform Transfers to Minors
      Act
Uniform Health-Care Decisions Act, 404
Uniform Marital Property Act, 473, 521,
      529
Uniform Parentage Act, 98, 115
Uniform Principal and Income
      Acts, 938, 971, 972
Uniform Probate Code
   ademption, 465
   administration
      supervised, 43
      unsupervised, 43
   advancements, 130
   animals, trusts for, 606
   antilapse, 338, 439, 441, 444, 445, 458,
      742

Uniform Probate Code—*Continued*
  bank accounts, 349, 371, 446
  child
    meaning of, 101, 760
    mistaken as dead, 173, 546
    pretermitted, 300, 545
  choice of law, 393, 507, 525
  class gifts, 458, 760
  codicil to will, 277
  contracts payable-on-death, 337
  contracts relating to wills, 322
  disclaimer, 150, 720
  durable power of attorney, 396
  elective share, 76, 481, 483, 487, 507,
      509, 525, 672
    choice of law, 507, 525
    incompetent spouse, 491
    waiver, 517
  execution of will, 226, 233, 236
    choice of law, 243
    dispensing power, 252, 262
    harmless error, 252, 269, 271, 309,
      436
    self-proved will, 245
    tangible personal property, 311
    witnesses, 241
  exoneration of liens, 468
  family allowance, 477
  future interests
    antilapse, 742
    class gifts, 760
    disclaimer, 720
    heirs, 775
    issue, 757
    survivorship required, 742
  half-bloods, 97
  harmless error, 252, 269, 271, 309,
      316
  heirs, 73, 775
  holographic will, 226, 269
  homestead, 476
  homicide, 145
  incorporation by reference, 303
  independent significance, 318
  intestacy provisions, 72, 88, 91, 95, 97,
      130, 145
  issue defined, 88, 757
  killer of decedent, 145
  lapse. *See* antilapse
  minors, payment to, 134
  mistake, 437, 564. *See also* harmless
      error
  multiple party accounts, 349
  negative disinheritance, 90
  no-contest clause, 184
  nonprobate transfers, 337, 343
    antilapse, 446
    bank accounts, 349, 371
    creditors, 371

  P.O.D. designations, 337, 344, 350
    antilapse, 446
    revocation by divorce, 299, 343, 385
    T.O.D. securities, 344
  120-hour provision, 85
  payable-on-death contracts, 337
  personal property set aside, 477
  pour-over, 373
  power of appointment, exercise
      of, 694
  premarital will, 535
  pretermitted child, 300, 546
  probate
    closing, 43
    formal, 40
    informal, 40
    nonclaim of creditors, 41
  representation, 88, 756
  republication by codicil, 540
  revival of will, 297
  revocation of will, 276
    divorce, 299
    inconsistency, 277
    partial revocation by act, 284
    revival, 297
    writing or act, 276, 283
  satisfaction, 469
  self-proved will, 245
  simultaneous death, 85
  spouse. *See also* Elective share
    intestate share, 73
    omitted from will, 300, 534
  stock splits, 464
  tangible personal property, 311
  trustee liability
    contracts and torts, 975
  universal succession, 48
  will contest, 184
  will defined, 276
  worthier title, 776
Uniform Prudent Investor Act, 926, 963,
      970
Uniform Simultaneous Death Act, 77, 85
Uniform Status of Children of Assisted
      Conception Act, 127
Uniform Statutory Rule against
      Perpetuities, 835, 837
  dynasty trust, 852
  generation-skipping transfer tax, 846
  honorary trust, 606
  Model Moppet, 836
  powers of appointment, 841
  trust for noncharitable purpose, 866
Uniform Statutory Will Act, 269
Uniform Testamentary Additions to
      Trusts Act, 373
Uniform Transfer-on-Death Registration
      Act, 344
Uniform Transfers to Minors Act, 133,
      570, 993

donor as custodian, 1028
  estate tax consequences, 1028
  federal gift tax, 993
Uniform Trust Act, 371, 477, 581, 629,
      654, 655, 877, 892, 918, 944,
      952
Uniform Trustees' Powers Act, 918, 950,
      953
Unitrusts, 631, 972, 1064
Universal succession, 48
Unjust enrichment. *See* Constructive
      trusts
Unsound mind. *See* Testamentary
      capacity
Uses, 554
  Statute of, 554, 716

Valuation
  future interest, 728
Vest. *See* Future interests; Perpetuities,
      Rule against; Remainders
Vested remainders. *See* Future interests;
      Remainders
Videotapes, 210, 235
Virgil, 33
Virtual adoption, 108

Wait-and-see. *See* Perpetuities, Rule
      against
Wells, Eleazer, 614
Wendel, Ella, 94
Widow's election wills, 524
Wild's Case, Rule in, 779
Wilkins, Justice Herbert, 500
Will contests, 159. *See also* Testamentary
      capacity; Undue influence; Wills
  jury findings in, 173
  no-contest clauses, 184, 385
    tortious interference, 221
  special precautions, 209
  standing to contest will, 647
Will substitutes. *See* Nonprobate transfers
Wills. *See also* Execution of attested wills;
      Revocation of wills
  choice of law, 242
  components of, 301
  conditional, 273
  construction, 409
  contest, standing, 647
  defined, 37, 276
  deposit of, with court, 247

destruction of property, 33
duplicate, 277
fake, 414
history, 1, 36
holographic, 262, 311
incorporation by reference, 303, 311
independent significance, 318
Indian lands, 3
integration, 301
international, 243
interpretation, 409
  false description, 426
  implied gifts, 437
  latent ambiguities, 424
  patent ambiguities, 425
  plain meaning rule, 413
  probable intent, 437
joint, 322
living, 403
lost, 280
mistake, 427
nuncupative, 226
oral, 226
premarital, 530
reciprocal, 322
republication by codicil, 302
revival, 296
safeguarding, 246
self-proved, 245
sham, 414
signature, 234, 273
stationer's forms, 268
statutory, 269
superwill, 344
terminology, history, 35
typewritten wills, earliest, 314
videotaped, 210, 235
widow's election, 524
Witnesses to will. *See also* Execution of
      attested wills
  attestation clause, 244
  beneficiary, 241
  conscious presence test, 233
  interested, 236
  number required, 226, 243
  proving will in probate, 245
    lost will, 280
  purging statutes, 241
  signing after testator's death, 235
  signing in testator's presence, 233
Wood, Ida, 94
Worthier Title, Doctrine of, 775